D0148072

About the Cover Image

Detail from *Dama de Blanco* (White Lady), 1928

A detail from a 1928 portrait of the artist's sister, this striking oil painting by the Mexican artist Frida Kahlo (1907–1954), captures the young woman's intensity. Kahlo had planned to be a doctor, but a horrific near-fatal bus accident confined her to bed for months of recovery, and she began painting, mostly self-portraits and those of family members. These early paintings and her later work explore issues of personal, ethnic, and national identity, especially for women. Despite lifelong health problems and multiple surgeries, she was an active figure in left-wing political and peace movements in Mexico. Kahlo's work was exhibited during her lifetime in the United States and Europe as well as Mexico, and within the last several decades both she and her work have gained widespread acclaim. Mexico declared her paintings national cultural heritage; her self-portraits can be found on posters, T-shirts, and coffee mugs; and her story has been told in ballets, operas, plays, and movies.

Dama de Blanco (White Lady), 1928 (oil on panel), Frida Kahlo (1907–1954)/CHRISTIES IMAGES/Private Collection/Bridgeman Images. © 2017 Banco de México Diego Rivera Frida Kahlo Museums Trust, Mexico, D.F./Artists Rights Society (ARS), New York

A History of
World Societies

ELEVENTH EDITION

Volume 2: Since 1450

MERRY E. WIESNER-HANKS

University of Wisconsin–Milwaukee

PATRICIA BUCKLEY EBREY

University of Washington

ROGER B. BECK

Eastern Illinois University

JERRY DÁVILA

University of Illinois at Urbana-Champaign

CLARE HARU CROWSTON

University of Illinois at Urbana-Champaign

JOHN P. McKAY

University of Illinois at Urbana-Champaign

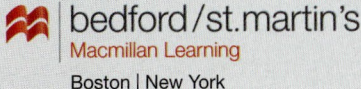

bedford/st.martin's
Macmillan Learning

Boston | New York

FOR BEDFORD/ST. MARTIN'S

Vice President, Editorial, Macmillan Learning Humanities: Edwin Hill

Program Director for History: Michael Rosenberg

Senior Program Manager for History: William J. Lombardo

History Marketing Manager: Melissa Rodriguez

Director of Content Development: Jane Knetzger

Senior Developmental Editor: Heidi L. Hood

Senior Content Project Manager: Christina M. Horn

Senior Workflow Manager: Jennifer Wetzel

Production Assistant: Brianna Lester

Senior Media Project Manager: Michelle Camisa

Media Editor: Tess Fletcher

Associate Editor: Mary Posman Starowicz

Copy Editor: Jennifer Brett Greenstein

Indexer: Leoni Z. McVey

Composition: Jouve

Cartographer: Mapping Specialists, Ltd.

Photo Editor: Christine Buese

Photo Researcher: Bruce Carson

Permissions Editor: Eve Lehmann

Senior Art Director: Anna Palchik

Text Design: Boynton Hue Studio

Cover Design: William Boardman

Cover Art: Dama de Blanco (White Lady), 1928 (oil on panel), Frida Kahlo (1907–1954)/CHRISTIES IMAGES/Private Collection/Bridgeman Images. © 2017 Banco de México Diego Rivera Frida Kahlo Museums Trust, Mexico, D.F./ Artists Rights Society (ARS), New York

Printing and Binding: LSC Communications

Copyright © 2018, 2015, 2012, 2009 by Bedford/St. Martin's

All rights reserved. No part of this book may be reproduced, stored in a retrieval system, or transmitted in any form or by any means, electronic, mechanical, photocopying, recording, or otherwise, except as may be expressly permitted by the applicable copyright statutes or in writing by the Publisher.

Manufactured in the United States of America.

2 1 0 9 8 7
f   e   d   c   b   a

For information, write: Bedford/St. Martin's, 75 Arlington Street, Boston, MA 02116

ISBN 978-1-319-05895-1 (Combined Edition)
ISBN 978-1-319-05931-6 (Volume 1)
ISBN 978-1-319-05933-0 (Volume 2)

ACKNOWLEDGMENTS

Acknowledgments and copyrights appear on the same page as the text and art selections they cover; these acknowledgments and copyrights constitute an extension of the copyright page.

Why This Book This Way

The world is becoming ever more interconnected, and the eleventh edition of *A History of World Societies* responds to this reality. To the social and cultural focus, comprehensive regional organization, and global perspective that have long been its hallmarks, we have added features that emphasize connections and parallel developments. Each of the authors on our collaborative team is a regional expert with deep experience in teaching world history, who brings insights into the text from the classroom, as well as from new secondary works and his or her own research in archives and libraries. In response to the growing emphasis on historical thinking skills in the teaching of history at all levels, as well as to requests from our colleagues and current adopters, we have significantly expanded the book's primary source program to offer a wide variety of sources, both written and visual, presented in several ways. Every chapter now includes Thinking Like a Historian, which groups approximately five sources around a central question; Global Viewpoints, which presents two sources from different parts of the world on the same issue; and Analyzing the Evidence, which features an individual text or visual source. We now have more primary sources than ever before and innovative tools — both print and digital — designed to help students think historically and master the material.

The Story of *A History of World Societies*

In this age of global connections, with their influence on the economy, migration patterns, popular culture, and climate change, among other aspects of life, the study of world history is more vital and urgent than ever before. An understanding of the broad sweep of the human past helps us comprehend today's dramatic changes and enduring continuities. People now migrate enormous distances and establish new lives far from their places of birth, yet migration has been a constant in history since the first humans walked out of Africa. Satellites and cell phones now link nearly every inch of the planet, yet the expansion of communication networks is a process that is thousands of years old. Children who speak different languages at home now sit side by side in schools and learn from one another, yet intercultural encounters have long been a source of innovation, transformation, and at times, unfortunately, conflict.

This book is designed for twenty-first-century students who will spend their lives on this small interconnected planet and for whom an understanding of only local or national history will no longer be sufficient. We believe that the study of world history in a broad and comparative context is

an exciting, important, and highly practical pursuit. It is our conviction, based on considerable experience in introducing large numbers of students to world history, that a book reflecting current trends in scholarship can excite readers and inspire an enduring interest in the long human experience.

Our strategy has been twofold. First, we have made social and cultural history the core elements of our narrative. We know that engaging students' interest in the past is often a challenge, but we also know that the emphasis on individual experience in its social and cultural dimensions connects with students and makes the past vivid and accessible. We seek to re-create the lives of ordinary people in appealing human terms and also to highlight the interplay between men's and women's lived experiences and the ways they reflect on these to create meaning. Thus, in addition to foundational works of philosophy and literature, we include popular songs and stories. We present objects along with texts as important sources for studying history, and this has allowed us to incorporate the growing emphasis on material culture in the work of many historians. At the same time, we have been mindful of the need to give great economic, political, and intellectual developments the attention they deserve. We want to give individual students and instructors an integrated perspective so that they can pursue — on their own or in the classroom — the themes and questions that they find particularly exciting and significant.

Second, we have made every effort to strike an effective global and regional balance. The whole world interacts today, and to understand the interactions and what they mean for today's citizens, we must study the whole world's history. Thus we have adopted a comprehensive regional organization with a global perspective that is clear and manageable for students. For example, Chapter 7 introduces students in depth to East Asia, and at the same time the chapter highlights the cultural connections that occurred via the Silk Road and the spread of Buddhism. We study all geographical areas, conscious of the separate histories of many parts of the world, particularly in the earliest millennia of human development. We also stress the links among cultures, political units, and economic systems, for these connections have made the world what it is today. We make comparisons and connections across time as well as space, for understanding the unfolding of the human story in time is the central task of history. We further students' understanding of these connections with the addition of new timelines in each chapter that put regional developments into a global context.

Primary Sources for Historical Thinking

A History of World Societies offers an extensive program of primary source assignments to help students master a number of key learning outcomes, among them **critical thinking**, **historical thinking**, **analytical thinking**, and **argumentation**, as well as learning about the **diversity of world cultures**. For this eleventh edition, we have added a new feature, **Thinking Like a Historian** (one in each chapter), which typically groups five or six textual or visual sources around a central question, with additional questions to guide students' analysis of the evidence and a "Putting It All Together" assignment that asks them to synthesize the sources with what they have learned in class and use the evidence to create an argument. Topics include "Slavery in Roman and Germanic Society" (Chapter 8), "When and Why Did Foot Binding Begin?" (Chapter 13), "Forced Relocation of Armenians to Persia" (Chapter 17), "The Rights of Which Men?" (Chapter 22), and "The Relationships Between Mosquitoes, People, and Epidemics" (Chapter 33).

To encourage comparisons across chapters and across cultures, we have sharpened the focus of the **Global Viewpoints** feature, which provides students with perspectives from two cultures on a key issue. This feature offers a pair of primary documents on a topic that illuminates the human experience, allowing us to provide more concrete examples of differences in the ways people thought. Anyone teaching world history has to emphasize larger trends and developments, but students sometimes get the wrong impression that everyone in a society thought alike. We hope that teachers can use these passages to get students thinking about diversity within and across societies. The 33 Global Viewpoints assignments—one in each chapter—introduce students to working with sources, encourage critical analysis, and extend the narrative while giving voice to the people of the past. Each includes a brief introduction and questions for analysis. Carefully chosen for accessibility, each pair of documents presents views on a diverse range of topics such as "Roman and Chinese Officials in Times of Disaster" (Chapter 6), "Early Descriptions of Africa from Egypt" (Chapter 10), "Aztec and Spanish Views on Christian Conversion in New Spain" (Chapter 16), "Declarations of Independence: The United States and Venezuela" (Chapter 22), and "Gandhi and Mao on Revolutionary Means" (Chapter 29).

A third type of original source feature, **Analyzing the Evidence** (two in each chapter), features an individual visual or written source, longer and more substantial than those in other features, chosen to extend and illuminate a major historical issue considered in each chapter, with headnotes and questions that help students understand the source and connect it to the information in the rest of the chapter. Selected for their interest and carefully integrated into their historical context, these in-depth looks at sources provide students with firsthand encounters with people of the past and should, we believe, help students "hear" and "see" the past. Topics include "The Teachings of Confucius" (Chapter 4),

"Orthodox Icon of Jesus" (Chapter 8), "Abu Hamid al-Ghazali on the Etiquette of Marriage" (Chapter 9), "Courtly Love Poetry" (Chapter 14), "Lamu Old Town, Lamu Island, Kenya" (Chapter 20), "*Rain, Steam, and Speed—the Great Western Railway*" (Chapter 23), "Reyita Castillo Bueno on Slavery and Freedom in Cuba" (Chapter 27), "C. L. R. James on Pan African Liberation" (Chapter 31), "A Member of China's Red Guards on Democratic Reform" (Chapter 32), and "A Brazilian Band on Globalization" (Chapter 33).

Taken together, the primary source features in this book offer the tools for building historical skills, including **chronological reasoning**, **explaining causation**, **evaluating context**, and **assessing perspective**. The suggestions for essays based on the primary sources encourage students to further expand their skills as they use their knowledge to develop historical arguments and write historical analyses. In LaunchPad these features are each accompanied by autograded questions that test students on their basic understanding of the sources so instructors can ensure students read the sources, quickly identify and help students who may be struggling, and focus more class time on thoughtful discussion and instruction.

In addition, our **primary source documents collection**, *Sources of World Societies*, includes written and visual sources that closely align the readings with the chapter topics and themes of this edition. The documents are available in a fully assignable and assessable electronic format within each chapter in LaunchPad, and the multiple-choice questions—now accompanying each source—measure comprehension and hold students accountable for their reading.

Finally, our new **Bedford Document Collections** modules in LaunchPad, which are also available for customizing the print text, provide a flexible repository of discovery-oriented primary source projects ready to assign. Each curated project—written by a historian about a favorite topic—poses a historical question and guides students through analysis of the sources. Examples include "The Silk Road: Travel and Trade in Premodern Inner Asia"; "The Spread of Christianity in the Sixteenth and Early Seventeenth Centuries"; "The Singapore Mutiny of 1915: Understanding World War I from a Global Perspective"; and "Living Through Perestroika: The Soviet Union in Upheaval, 1985–1991."

Student Engagement with Biography

In our years of teaching world history, we have often noted that students come alive when they encounter stories about real people in the past. To give students a chance to see the past through ordinary people's lives, each chapter includes one of the popular **Individuals in Society** biographical essays, each of which offers a brief study of an individual or group, informing students about the societies in which the individuals lived. This feature grew out of our long-standing focus on people's lives and the varieties of historical experience, and we believe that readers will empathize with these human beings who themselves were seeking to define their own identities. The spotlighting of individuals, both famous and obscure, perpetuates the book's continued attention to cultural and intellectual developments, highlights human agency, and reflects changing interests within the historical profession as well as the development of "microhistory." **NEW** features include essays on Catarina de San Juan, an Indian woman who was enslaved by Portuguese traders and transported to Mexico (Chapter 16); Rebecca Protten, a former slave from Antigua who was part of a mixed-race marriage with a German Moravian missionary (Chapter 19); and Samuel Crompton, inventor of the spinning mule (Chapter 23).

Geographic Literacy

We recognize students' difficulties with geography, and the new edition retains our **Mapping the Past map activities**. Included in each chapter, these activities ask students to analyze a map and make connections to the larger processes discussed in the narrative, giving them valuable practice in reading and interpreting maps. In LaunchPad, these maps come with new assignable activities. Throughout the textbook and online in LaunchPad, nearly **100 full-size maps** illustrate major developments in the chapters. In addition, **75 spot maps** are embedded in the narrative to show specific areas under discussion.

Chronological Literacy in a Global Context

The increased attention to global connections and comparisons that marks this edition can also be seen in new timelines at the end of each chapter. Along with graphically displaying major events and developments from the chapter, they also include key developments in other regions with cross-references to the chapters in which they are discussed. These comparisons situate events in the global story and help students identify similarities and differences among regions and societies.

Helping Students Understand the Narrative

We know firsthand and take seriously the challenges students face in understanding, retaining, and mastering so much material that is often unfamiliar. With the goal of making this the most student-centered edition yet, we continued to enhance the book's pedagogy on many fronts. To focus students' reading, each chapter opens with a chapter preview with focus questions keyed to the main chapter headings. These questions are repeated within the chapter and again in the "Review and Explore" section at the end of each chapter that provides helpful guidance for reviewing key topics. "Review and Explore" also includes "Make

Comparisons and Connections" questions that prompt students to assess larger developments across chapters, thus allowing them to develop skills in evaluating change and continuity, making comparisons, and analyzing context and causation.

Within the narrative, a chapter summary reinforces key chapter events and ideas for students. This is followed by the chapter-closing **Connections** feature, which synthesizes main developments and makes connections and comparisons between countries and regions to explain how events relate to larger global processes, such as the influence of the Silk Road, the effects of the transatlantic slave trade, and the ramifications of colonialism. This also serves as a bridge to the subsequent chapters.

Key terms are bolded in the text, defined in the margin, and listed in the "Review and Explore" section to promote clarity and comprehension, and **phonetic spellings**—increased in this edition—are located directly after terms that readers are likely to find hard to pronounce.

The chapter ends with **Suggested Resources**, which includes up-to-date readings on the vast amount of new work being done in many fields, as well as recommended documentaries, feature films, television, and websites.

The high-quality art and map program has been thoroughly revised and features **hundreds of contemporaneous illustrations**. To make the past tangible, and as an extension of our attention to cultural history, we include numerous artifacts—from weapons and armor to dishes, furnishings, and figurines. As in earlier editions, all illustrations have been carefully selected to complement the text, and all include captions that inform students while encouraging them to read the text more deeply. **Numerous high-quality full-size maps** illustrate major developments in the narrative, and helpful spot maps are embedded in the narrative to locate areas under discussion.

In addition, whenever an instructor assigns the **Launch-Pad e-Book** (which can be bundled for free with the print book), students get full access to **LearningCurve**, an online adaptive learning tool that promotes mastery of the book's content and diagnoses students' trouble spots. With this adaptive quizzing, students accumulate points toward a target score as they go, giving the interaction a game-like feel. Feedback for incorrect responses explains why the answer is incorrect and directs students back to the text to review before they attempt to answer the question again. The end result is a better understanding of the key elements of the text. Instructors who actively assign LearningCurve report their students come to class prepared for discussion and their students enjoy using it. In addition, LearningCurve's reporting feature allows instructors to quickly diagnose which concepts students in their classes are struggling with so they can adjust lectures and activities accordingly. The LaunchPad e-Book with LearningCurve is thus an invaluable asset for instructors who need to support students in all settings, from traditional lectures to hybrid, online, and newer "flipped" classrooms. In LaunchPad, instructors can also assign the **Guided Reading Exercise** for each chapter, which prompts students to read actively to collect information that answers a broad analytic question central to the chapter as a whole. Through these tools and more, Launch-Pad can make the textbook even easier for students to understand and use. To learn more about the benefits of LearningCurve and LaunchPad's other features, see the "Versions and Supplements" section on page x.

All our changes to the book, large and small, are intended to give students and instructors an integrated perspective so that they can pursue—on their own or in the classroom—the historical questions that they find particularly exciting and significant.

Textual Changes

This edition is enhanced by the incorporation of new scholarship and subject areas that immerse students in the dynamic and ongoing work of history. Updates to the eleventh edition include more about Byzantium, Hungary, the Balkans, and the Ottomans (Chapters 14–15); more about technology acquisition and the role of technology in European exploration and more comparisons of Portuguese and Spanish colonization (Chapter 16); more global context for the "little ice age" and more information on the economic and social crises and the popular revolts that occurred in Europe and Asia partly as a result of the climate change (Chapter 18); new coverage on the religious repression of Huguenots under Louis XIII and Cardinal Richelieu (Chapter 18); new material on differences among English, Spanish, and French interactions with indigenous people in the Americas as well as more about the Indians who allied with the French (Chapter 18); reorganized and expanded coverage of the Enlightenment with two new sections covering major thinkers, currents of Enlightenment thought, key debates, global aspects of Enlightenment thought, and the role of women (Chapter 19); new coverage of how colonial contact forged European national identities (Spanish, French, English) as well as "Indian" and "African" identities (Chapter 19); revised coverage of Latin American revolutions with more on the background to the revolutions, the emergence and spread of liberal political ideas, the abolition of slavery, and the events of the revolutions in different parts of Latin America (Chapter 22); new material on the Congress of Vienna and the new "neutral" states of some territories, the neglect of small states, subject peoples, and the question of the future of the European territories of the Ottoman Empire (Chapter 24); revised and expanded coverage of social and economic conflicts that helped spark the 1848 revolutions (Chapter 24); revised discussion of export-led growth in the Americas, giving added focus to social movements (Chapter 27); a sharpened focus on the Cold War as a global phenomenon, enhanced discussion of U.S. intervention in Guatemala and of the Cuban Revolution, enhanced discussion of the Vietnam War as a conflict with global ramifications, and revised treatment of the postwar

reconstruction of Japan (Chapter 31); updated discussion of the European Union in the context of the Greek economic crisis, the refugee crisis, and Britain's vote to exit the European Union (Chapter 32); expanded discussion of China's emergence as a global economic power and updated treatment of the Arab Spring (Chapter 32); updated and expanded discussion of nuclear proliferation, global health in the context of the Zika outbreak, the role of the Islamic State (ISIS) in the contemporary Middle East, the refugee crisis in Europe, and smartphone use in the developing world (Chapter 33).

Helping Instructors Teach with Digital Resources

As noted, *A History of World Societies* is offered in Macmillan's premier learning platform, **LaunchPad**, an intuitive and interactive e-Book and course space. Free when packaged with the print book or available at a low price when used on its own, LaunchPad grants students and teachers access to a wealth of online tools and resources built specifically for this text to enhance reading comprehension and promote in-depth study. LaunchPad's course space and interactive e-Book are ready to use as is (or can be edited and customized with your own material) and can be assigned right away.

Developed with extensive feedback from history instructors and students, **LaunchPad for *A History of World Societies*** includes the complete narrative of the print book; the companion reader, *Sources of World Societies*; and **LearningCurve**, an adaptive learning tool designed to get students to read before they come to class. With **an expanded set of source-based questions in the test bank and in Learning-Curve**, instructors now have more ways to test students on their understanding of sources and narrative in the book. The addition of the **new Bedford Document Collections modules in LaunchPad** means instructors have a flexible repository of discovery-oriented primary source projects to assign and to extend the text, making LaunchPad for *A History of World Societies* a one-stop shop for working with sources and thinking critically in a multitude of modes.

LaunchPad also offers several other distinctly useful assignment options to help students get the most from their reading, including **Guided Reading Exercises** that prompt students to be active readers of the chapter narrative and autograded **primary source quizzes** to test comprehension of written and visual sources in the book, the companion reader, and the Bedford Document Collections modules. These features, plus **additional primary source documents**, **video sources and tools for making video assignments**, **map activities**, **flashcards**, and **customizable test banks**, make Launchpad a great asset for any instructor who wants to enliven world history for students.

With training and support just a click away, LaunchPad can help you take your teaching into a new era. To learn more about the benefits of LearningCurve and LaunchPad, see "Versions and Supplements" on page x.

Acknowledgments

It is a pleasure to thank the many instructors who critiqued the book in preparation for this revision: Gene Barnett, Calhoun Community College; Amanda Carr-Wilcoxson, Pellissippi State Community College; Ted Cohen, Lindenwood University; Fiona Foster, Tidewater Community College; Paul J. Fox, Kennesaw State University; Duane Galloway, Rowan-Cabarrus Community College; Margaret Genvert, Salisbury University; Richard Bach Jensen, Northwestern State University; Kelly Kennington, Auburn University; Alex Pavuk, Morgan State University; Franklin Rausch, Lander University; Ryan L. Ruckel, Pearl River Community College; Dr. Anthony R. Santoro, Christopher Newport University; Chuck Smith, University of the Cumberlands; Molly E. Swords, University of Idaho; Scott N. West, University of Dayton; Dr. Kari Zimmerman, University of St. Thomas; and Michael Andrew Žmolek, University of Iowa.

It is also a pleasure to thank the many editors who have assisted us over the years, first at Houghton Mifflin and now at Bedford/St. Martin's (Macmillan Learning). At Bedford/St. Martin's, these include senior development editor Heidi Hood, associate editor Mary Posman Starowicz, program manager Laura Arcari, director of development Jane Knetzger, senior program director Michael Rosenberg, photo researcher Bruce Carson, text permissions editor Eve Lehmann, and senior content project manager Christina Horn, with the guidance of senior managing editor Michael Granger. Other key contributors were designer Cia Boynton, copy editor Jennifer Brett Greenstein, proofreaders Angela Morrison and Susan Zorn, indexer Leoni McVey, and cover designer William Boardman.

Many of our colleagues at the University of Illinois, the University of Washington, the University of Wisconsin–Milwaukee, and Eastern Illinois University continue to provide information and stimulation, often without even knowing it. We thank them for it. The authors recognize John P. McKay, Bennett D. Hill, and John Buckler, the founding authors of this textbook, whose vision set a new standard for world history textbooks. The authors also thank the many students over the years with whom we have used earlier editions of this book. Their reactions and opinions helped shape our revisions to this edition, and we hope it remains worthy of the ultimate praise they bestowed, that it is "not boring like most textbooks." Merry Wiesner-Hanks would, as always, like to thank her husband, Neil, without whom work on this project would not be possible. Patricia Ebrey thanks her husband, Tom. Clare Haru Crowston thanks her husband, Ali, and her children, Lili, Reza, and Kian, who are a joyous reminder of the vitality of life that we try to showcase in this book. Roger Beck thanks Ann for supporting him through five editions now, and for sharing his love of history. He is also grateful to the World History Association for all past, present, and future contributions to his understanding of world history. Jerry Dávila thanks Liv, Ellen, and Alex, who are reminders of why history matters.

Each of us has benefited from the criticism of his or her coauthors, although each of us assumes responsibility for what he or she has written. Merry Wiesner-Hanks has written and revised Chapters 1, 2, 5, 6, 8, 14, and 15; Patricia Buckley Ebrey has written and revised Chapters 3, 4, 7, 9, 12, 13, 17, 21, and 26; Roger B. Beck has written and revised Chapters 10, 20, 25, and 28–30; Clare Haru Crowston has written and revised Chapters 16, 18, 19, and 22–24; and Jerry Dávila has written and revised Chapters 11, 27, and 31–33.

MERRY E. WIESNER-HANKS
PATRICIA BUCKLEY EBREY
ROGER B. BECK
JERRY DÁVILA
CLARE HARU CROWSTON

VERSIONS AND SUPPLEMENTS

Adopters of *A History of World Societies* and their students have access to abundant print and digital resources and tools, the acclaimed *Bedford Series in History and Culture* volumes, and much more. The LaunchPad course space for *A History of World Societies* provides access to the narrative as well as a wealth of primary sources and other features, along with assignment and assessment opportunities at the ready. See below for more information, visit the book's catalog site at **macmillanlearning.com**, or contact your local Bedford/St. Martin's sales representative.

Get the Right Version for Your Class

To accommodate different course lengths and course budgets, *A History of World Societies* is available in several different versions and formats to best suit your course needs. The comprehensive *A History of World Societies* includes a full-color art program and a robust set of features. Offered now for the first time, *A History of World Societies*, Concise Edition, also provides the full narrative, with a streamlined art and feature program, at a lower price. *A History of World Societies*, Value Edition, offers a trade-sized two-color option with the full narrative and selected art and maps at a steeper discount. The Value Edition is also offered at the lowest price point in loose-leaf, and all versions are available as e-Books. For the best value of all, package a new print book with LaunchPad at no additional charge to get the best each format offers—a print version for easy portability with a LaunchPad interactive e-Book and course space with LearningCurve and loads of additional assignment and assessment options.

- **Combined Volume** (Chapters 1–33): available in paperback, Concise, Value, loose-leaf, and e-Book formats and in LaunchPad
- **Volume 1: To 1600** (Chapters 1–16): available in paperback, Concise, Value, loose-leaf, and e-Book formats and in LaunchPad
- **Volume 2: Since 1450** (Chapters 16–33): available in paperback, Concise, Value, loose-leaf, and e-Book formats and in LaunchPad

As noted below, any of these volumes can be packaged with additional titles for a discount. To get ISBNs for discount packages, visit **macmillanlearning.com** or contact your Bedford/St. Martin's representative.

Assign LaunchPad — an Assessment-Ready Interactive e-Book and Course Space

Available for discount purchase on its own or for packaging with new books at no additional charge, LaunchPad is a breakthrough solution for history courses. Intuitive and easy to use for students and instructors alike, LaunchPad is ready to use as is, and can be edited, customized with your own material, and assigned quickly. LaunchPad for *A History of World Societies* includes Bedford/St. Martin's high-quality content all in one place, including the full interactive e-Book and the companion reader *Sources of World Societies*, plus LearningCurve formative quizzing, guided reading activities designed to help students read actively for key concepts, autograded quizzes for each primary source, and chapter summative quizzes. Through a wealth of formative and summative assessments, including the adaptive learning program of LearningCurve (see the full description ahead), students gain confidence and get into their reading before class. Through the Bedford Document Collections for World History (see full description ahead), embedded within LaunchPad, instructors get a flexible repository of discovery-oriented primary source projects ready to assign. These features, plus additional primary source documents, video sources and tools for making video assignments, map activities, flashcards, and customizable test banks, make LaunchPad an invaluable asset for any instructor.

LaunchPad easily integrates with course management systems, and with fast ways to build assignments, rearrange chapters, and add new pages, sections, or links, it lets teachers build the courses they want to teach and hold students accountable. For more information, visit **launchpadworks.com** or to arrange a demo, contact us at **history@macmillan.com**.

Assign LearningCurve So Your Students Come to Class Prepared

Students using LaunchPad receive access to LearningCurve for *A History of World Societies*. Assigning LearningCurve in place of reading quizzes is easy for instructors, and the reporting features help instructors track overall class trends and spot topics that are giving students trouble so they can adjust their lectures and class activities. This online learning tool is popular with students because it was designed to help them rehearse content at their own pace in a nonthreatening, game-like environment. The feedback for wrong answers provides instructional coaching and sends students back to the book for review. Students answer as many questions as necessary to reach a target score, with repeated chances to revisit material they haven't mastered. When LearningCurve is assigned, students come to class better prepared.

iClicker, Active Learning Simplified

iClicker offers simple, flexible tools to help you give students a voice and facilitate active learning in the classroom. Students can participate with the devices they already bring to class using our iClicker Reef mobile apps (which work with smartphones, tablets, or laptops) or iClicker remotes. We've now integrated iClicker with Macmillan's LaunchPad to make it easier than ever to synchronize grades and promote engagement — both in and out of class. iClicker Reef access cards can also be packaged with LaunchPad or your textbook at a significant savings for your students. To learn more, talk to your Macmillan Learning representative or visit us at **www.iclicker.com**.

Take Advantage of Instructor Resources

Bedford/St. Martin's has developed a rich array of teaching resources for this book and for this course. They range from lecture and presentation materials and assessment tools to course management options. Most can be found in LaunchPad or can be downloaded or ordered at **macmillanlearning.com**.

Bedford Coursepack for Blackboard, Canvas, Brightspace by D2L, or Moodle. We can help you integrate our rich content into your course management system. Registered instructors can download coursepacks that include our popular free resources and book-specific content for *A History of World Societies*. Visit **macmillanlearning.com** to find your version or download your coursepack.

Instructor's Resource Manual. The instructor's manual offers both experienced and first-time instructors tools for presenting textbook material in engaging ways. It includes content learning objectives, annotated chapter outlines, and strategies for teaching with the textbook, plus suggestions on how to get the most out of LearningCurve and a survival guide for first-time teaching assistants.

Guide to Changing Editions. Designed to facilitate an instructor's transition from the previous edition of *A History of World Societies* to this new edition, this guide presents an overview of major changes as well as of changes in each chapter.

Online Test Bank. The test bank includes a mix of fresh, carefully crafted multiple-choice, matching, short-answer, and essay questions for each chapter. Many of the multiple-choice questions feature a map, an image, or a primary source excerpt as the prompt. All questions appear in Microsoft Word format and in easy-to-use test bank software that allows instructors to add, edit, resequence, filter by question type or learning objective, and print questions and answers. Instructors can also export questions into a variety of course management systems.

The Bedford Lecture Kit: Lecture Outlines, Maps, and Images. Look good and save time with *The Bedford Lecture Kit*. These presentation materials include fully customizable multimedia presentations built around chapter outlines that are embedded with maps, figures, and images from the textbook and are supplemented by more detailed instructor notes on key points and concepts.

Print, Digital, and Custom Options for More Choice and Value

For information on free packages and discounts up to 50%, visit **macmillanlearning.com**, or contact your local Bedford/St. Martin's sales representative.

NEW *Sources of World Societies*, Third Edition. Designed to accompany *A History of World Societies*, each chapter of this primary source collection contains approximately five written and visual sources that present history from the perspectives of well-known figures and ordinary individuals alike. *Sources of World Societies* provides a broad selection of 165 primary source documents and images as well as editorial apparatuses to help students understand the sources. Each chapter also includes a selection of sources dedicated to varied viewpoints on a specific topic. This companion reader is an exceptional value for students and offers plenty of assignment options for instructors. Available free when packaged with the print text and included in the LaunchPad e-Book with autograded quizzes for each source. Also available on its own as a downloadable e-Book.

NEW The Bedford Document Collections for World History. Found in the LaunchPad for *A History of World Societies* and available to customize the print text, this collection provides a flexible repository of discovery-oriented primary source projects ready to assign. Each curated project — written by a historian about a favorite topic — poses a historical question and guides students through analysis of the sources. Examples include "The Silk Road: Travel and Trade in Premodern Inner Asia"; "The Spread of Christianity in the Sixteenth and Early Seventeenth Centuries"; "The Singapore Mutiny of 1915: Understanding World War I from a Global Perspective"; and "Living Through Perestroika: The Soviet Union in Upheaval, 1985–1991." For more information, visit **macmillanlearning.com**.

NEW The Bedford Document Collections for World History Custom Print Modules. Choose one or two document projects from the collection (see above) and add them in print to a Bedford/St. Martin's title, or select several to be bound together in a custom reader created specifically for your course. Either way, the modules are affordably priced. For more information, contact your Bedford/St. Martin's representative.

NEW Bedford Tutorials for History. Designed to customize textbooks with resources relevant to individual courses, this collection of brief units, each 16 pages long and loaded with examples, guides students through basic skills such as using historical evidence effectively, working with primary sources, taking effective notes, avoiding plagiarism and citing sources, and more. Up to two tutorials can be added to a Bedford/St. Martin's history survey title at no additional charge, freeing you to spend your class time focusing on content and interpretation. For more information, visit **macmillanlearning.com/historytutorials**.

The Bedford Series in History and Culture. More than 100 titles in this highly praised series combine first-rate scholarship, historical narrative, and important primary documents for undergraduate courses. Each book is brief, inexpensive, and focused on a specific topic or period. New titles in the series include *Apartheid in South Africa: A Brief History with Documents* by David M. Gordon; *Politics and Society in Japan's Meiji Restoration: A Brief History with Documents* by Anne Walthall and M. William Steele; and *The Congo Free State and the New Imperialism: A Brief History with Documents* by Kevin Grant. For a complete list of titles, visit **macmillanlearning.com**. Package discounts are available.

Rand McNally Atlas of World History. This collection of almost 70 full-color maps illustrates the eras and civilizations in world history from the emergence of human societies to the present. Free when packaged.

The Bedford Glossary for World History. This handy supplement for the survey course gives students historically contextualized definitions for hundreds of terms—from *abolitionism* to *Zoroastrianism*—that they will encounter in lectures, reading, and exams. Free when packaged.

Trade Books. Titles published by sister companies Hill and Wang; Farrar, Straus and Giroux; Henry Holt and Company; St. Martin's Press; Picador; and Palgrave Macmillan are available at a 50% discount when packaged with Bedford/St. Martin's textbooks. For more information, visit **macmillanlearning.com/tradeup**.

A Pocket Guide to Writing in History. Updated to reflect changes made in the 2017 *Chicago Manual of Style* revision, this portable and affordable reference tool by Mary Lynn Rampolla provides reading, writing, and research advice useful to students in all history courses. Concise yet comprehensive advice on approaching typical history assignments, developing critical reading skills, writing effective history papers, conducting research, using and documenting sources, and avoiding plagiarism—enhanced with practical tips and examples throughout—has made this slim reference a bestseller. Package discounts are available.

A Student's Guide to History. This complete guide to success in any history course provides the practical help students need to be successful. In addition to introducing students to the nature of the discipline, author Jules Benjamin teaches a wide range of skills from preparing for exams to approaching common writing assignments, and explains the research and documentation process with plentiful examples. Package discounts are available.

BRIEF CONTENTS

CONTENTS

16 The Acceleration of Global Contact
1450–1600   436

photo: From *Codex Ixtlilxochitl*, 1582, pigment on European paper/Bibliothèque Nationale, Paris, France/De Agostini Picture Library/akg-images

17 The Islamic World Powers
1300–1800   468

18 European Power and Expansion
1500–1750   498

photo: *Peace Treaty of Nijmegen*, 1678/Museum of Fine Arts, Budapest, Hungary/Erich Lessing/Art Resource, NY

photo: Chehel Sotoun, or *The 40 Columns*, Isfahan, Iran/Bridgeman Images

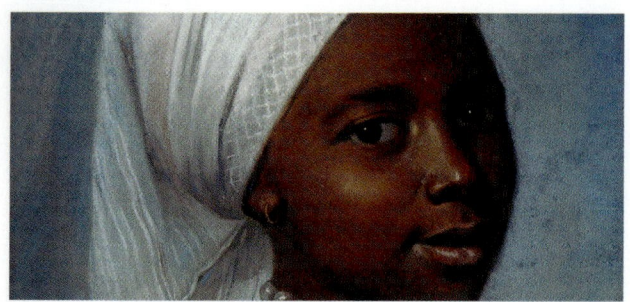

19 New Worldviews and Ways of Life
1540–1790   532

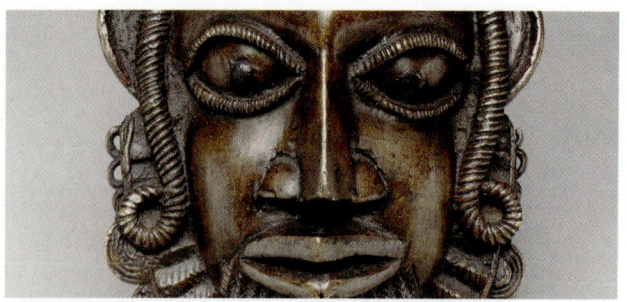

20 Africa and the World
1400–1800   564

photo: *Portrait of a Young Woman*, by an unknown artist, previously attributed to Jean-Etienne Liotard (1702–1789) (pastel on paper)/Saint Louis Art Museum/Bridgeman Images

photo: Hip Ornament: Portuguese Face, 16th–19th century. Brass, iron. Gift of Mr. and Mrs. Klaus G. Perls, 1991 (1991.162.9)/The Metropolitan Museum of Art, New York/ Image copyright © The Metropolitan Museum of Art/Image source: Art Resource, NY

21 Continuity and Change in East Asia
1400–1800 594

photo: Detail, *Portrait of the Imperial Bodyguard Zhanyinbao*, China, 18th century, Qing Dynasty (1644–1911). Hanging scroll; ink and color on silk. Purchase, The Dillon Fund Gift, 1986 (1986.206)/The Metropolitan Museum of Art, New York/Image copyright © The Metropolitan Museum of Art/Image source: Art Resource, NY

22 Revolutions in the Atlantic World
1775–1825 624

photo: *Jean-Baptiste Belley (1747–1805), Deputy of Santo Domingo at the French Convention*, 1797, by Anne-Louis Girodet de Roussy-Trioson (1767–1824) (oil on canvas). Inv. MV4616. Photo: Gerard Blot/Château de Versailles, France/© RMN–Grand Palais/Art Resource, NY

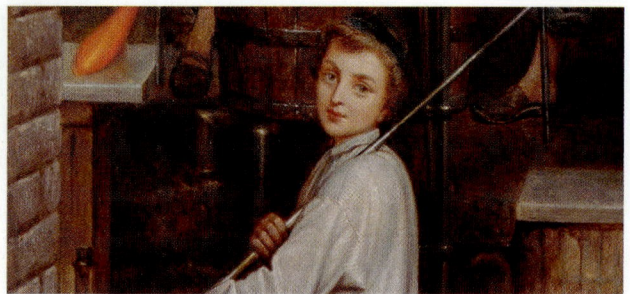

23 The Revolution in Energy and Industry
1760–1850   660

24 Ideologies of Change in Europe
1815–1914   690

photo: *Interior of a Furnace*, 1865 (oil on canvas) (detail) by Charles Housez (1822–1888)/BOURNE GALLERY ARCHIVE/© Bourne Gallery, Reigate, Surrey, UK/Bridgeman Images

photo: © Maurice Branger/Roger-Viollet/The Image Works

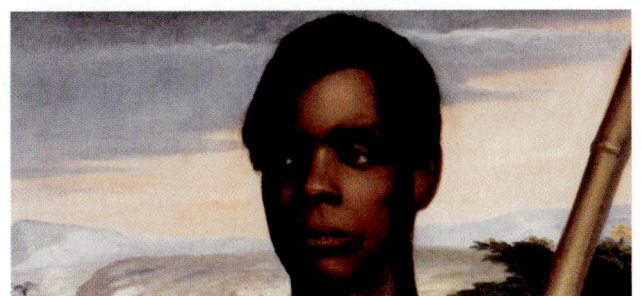

25 Africa, the Ottoman Empire, and the New Imperialism
1800–1914   728

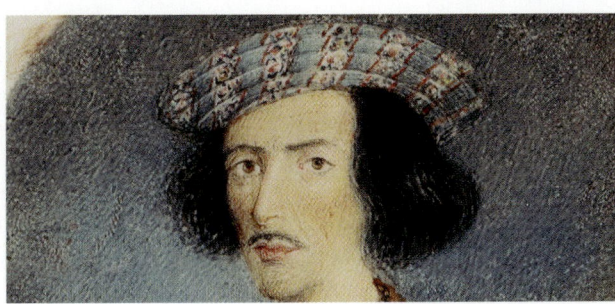

26 Asia and the Pacific in the Era of Imperialism
1800–1914   758

photo: Portrait, 1839, by Nathaniel Jocelyn (1796–1881) (oil on canvas)/Granger, NY— All rights reserved

photo: Victoria and Albert Museum, London, UK/V&A Images/Art Resource, NY

27 The Americas in the Age of Liberalism

1810–1917   788

28 World War and Revolution

1914–1929   818

photo: Edward S. Curtis Collection/Library of Congress, Prints and Photographs Division, Washington, D.C./LC-USZ62-1044492

photo: Private Collection/Archives Charmet/Bridgeman Images

photo: © Dinodia Photo Library/The Image Works

photo: United States Holocaust Memorial Museum, courtesy of Israel Lichtenstein photo: Pictures from History/Bridgeman Images

photo: Thalia Watmough/aliki image library/Alamy Stock Photo

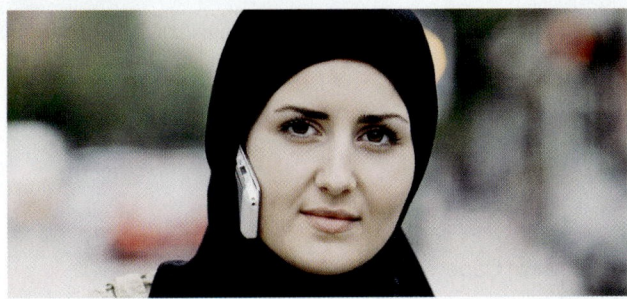

33 The Contemporary World in Historical Perspective   988

photo: Masterfile/Royalty-Free

MAPS, FIGURES, AND TABLES

Maps

Figures and Tables

THINKING LIKE A HISTORIAN

GLOBAL VIEWPOINTS

ANALYZING THE EVIDENCE

INDIVIDUALS IN SOCIETY

MAPPING THE PAST

The Origins of Modern World Societies

The origins of modern societies lie deep in the past. World historians increasingly begin their exploration of the human past millions of years ago, when humans evolved from a primate ancestor in eastern Africa. Humans migrated out of Africa in several waves, walking along coasts and over land, eventually spreading across much of the earth. Their tools were initially multipurpose sharpened stones and sticks, but gradually they invented more specialized tools that enabled them to obtain food more easily, make clothing, build shelters, and decorate their surroundings. Environmental changes, such as the advance and retreat of the glaciers, shaped life dramatically.

The Earliest Human Societies, to 2500 B.C.E.

Studying the physical remains of the past, scholars constructed a model of time and gave labels to eras according to the primary materials out of which tools that survived were made. (Constructing models of time is called "periodization.") Thus the earliest human era became the Stone Age, the next era the Bronze Age, and the next the Iron Age. They further divided the *Stone* Age into the Old Stone Age, or Paleolithic, during which people used stone, bone, and other natural products to make tools and obtained food largely by foraging, that is, by gathering plant products, trapping or catching small animals and birds, and hunting larger prey. This was followed by the New Stone Age, or Neolithic, which saw the beginning of agricultural and animal domestication. People around the world adopted agriculture at various times, and some never did, but the transition between the Paleolithic and the Neolithic is usually set at about 9000 B.C.E., the point at which agriculture was first developed.

In the Paleolithic period, people lived in small groups of related individuals, moving through the landscape in the search for food. Most had few material possessions, and social and gender hierarchies were probably much less pronounced than they would become later. Beginning around 50,000 B.C.E. people in many parts of the world began to decorate their surroundings and the objects they made, often with vivid representations of animals and people, and sometimes with symbols. These, and careful burials of the dead, suggest that people had developed ideas about supernatural or spiritual forces beyond the visible material world.

Beginning about 9000 B.C.E. people living in the Near East, and then elsewhere, began to plant seeds as well as gather wild crops, raise certain animals instead of hunt them, and selectively breed both plants and animals to make them more useful to humans. This domestication of plants and animals, called the Agricultural Revolution, was the most important change in human history. Crop raising began as horticulture, in which people—often women—used hand tools to plant and harvest. Animal domestication began with sheep and goats, which were often herded from place to place so that they could eat the available vegetation, an economic system called pastoralism. The domestication of large animals such as cattle and water buffalo led to plow agriculture, through which humans could raise much more food. Agriculture required more labor than did foraging, but it allowed the human population to grow far more quickly.

The division of labor that plow agriculture required led to growing social hierarchies between those who could afford the new tools and products and those who could not. These were reinforced over generations as children inherited goods and status from their parents, and as social norms and laws were developed that led members of the elite to marry one another. Plow agriculture also strengthened differentiation based on gender; men became more associated with the world beyond the household and women with the domestic realm. Neolithic agricultural communities developed technologies to meet their needs, including pottery, cloth-weaving, and wheeled vehicles, and they often traded with one another for products that they could not obtain locally. In some parts of the world, production and trade included copper and bronze, although most tools continued to be made of stone, bone, and wood. Religious ideas came to reflect the new agricultural society, with fertility as the most important goal and the gods, like humans, arranged in a hierarchy.

Although today's complex world seems very different from that of the earliest human societies, some aspects of life in the Neolithic, and even the Paleolithic, were very slow to change. Foraging, horticulture, pastoralism, and agriculture have been the primary economic activities of most people throughout the entire history of the world. Though today there are only a few foraging groups in very isolated areas, there are significant numbers of horticulturalists and pastoralists, and their numbers were much greater just a century ago. At that point the vast majority of the world's people still made their living directly through agriculture. The social patterns set in early agricultural societies—with most of the population farming the land, and a small number of elite who lived off their labor—lasted for millennia.

The Ancient World, 3500 B.C.E.–500 C.E.

Ten thousand years ago, humans were living in most parts of the planet. They had designed technologies to meet the challenges presented by deep forests and jungles, steep mountains, and blistering deserts. As the climate changed, they adapted, building boats to cross channels created by melting glaciers, and finding new sources of food when old sources were no longer plentiful. In some places the new sources included domesticated plants and animals, which allowed people to live much more closely to one another than they had as foragers.

That proximity created opportunities, as larger groups of people pooled their knowledge to deal with life's challenges, but it also created problems. Human history from that point on can be seen as a response to these opportunities, challenges, and conflicts. As small villages grew into cities, people continued to develop technologies and systems to handle new issues. They created structures of governance based on something beyond the kin group to control their more complex societies, along with military forces and taxation systems to support the structures of governance. In some places they invented writing to record taxes, inventories, and payments, and they later put writing to other uses, including the preservation of stories, traditions, and history.

Writing, first developed around 3000 B.C.E., was perhaps the most important of the new technologies. Written sources provide a wider range of information about past societies than is available from physical evidence alone, which means that we know much more about the societies that left written records than about those that did not. Writing was developed to meet the needs of the more complex urban societies that are often referred to as civilizations, and particularly to meet the needs of the state, a new structure of governance distinct from tribes and kinship groups. In states, a small share of the population is able to coerce resources out of everyone else, and leaders gain and maintain power through organized violence, bureaucracies, systems of taxation, and written laws. These laws generally created more elaborate social and gender hierarchies.

Mesopotamia and Egypt

States first developed in Mesopotamia, the land between the Euphrates and Tigris Rivers. Starting in the southern part of Mesopotamia known as Sumeria, sustained agriculture reliant on irrigation resulted in larger populations, a division of labor, and the growth of cities. Priests and rulers invented ways to control and organize these complex societies, including armies, taxation systems, and cuneiform writing.

Egyptian Home Life This grave painting depicts an intimate moment in the life of an aristocratic family, with the father and mother in the center and their children around them. (Deir el-Medina, Thebes, Egypt/Bridgeman Images)

Conquerors from the north unified Mesopotamian city-states into larger empires and spread Mesopotamian culture over a large area. The most significant of these was the Babylonian empire, which under King Hammurabi in 1790 B.C.E. developed a written code of law and expanded trade connections.

During the third millennium B.C.E., a period known as the Old Kingdom, Egypt grew into a cohesive state under a single ruler in the valley of the Nile, which provided rich farmland and an avenue of communication. The Egyptians developed powerful beliefs in life after death, and the focal point of religious and political life was the pharaoh, a god-king who commanded the wealth, resources, and people of Egypt. For long stretches of history Egypt was prosperous and secure in the fertile Nile Valley, although at times various groups migrated in seeking better lives or invaded and conquered. Often the newcomers adopted aspects of Egyptian religion, art, and politics, and the Egyptians adopted aspects of the newcomers' cultures, such as the Hyksos's techniques for making and casting bronze. During the period known as the New Kingdom (ca. 1550–1070 B.C.E.), warrior-pharaohs expanded their power beyond the Nile Valley and created the first Egyptian empire, during which they first fought and then allied with the iron-using Hittites. After the collapse of the New Kingdom, the Nubian rulers of Kush conquered Egypt, and another group, the Phoenicians, came to dominate trade in the Mediterranean, spreading a letter alphabet.

For several centuries after the collapse of New Kingdom Egypt, a Semitic people known as the Hebrews or the Israelites controlled a small state on the western end of the Fertile Crescent. Their most important legacy was not political, but rather a new form of religious belief, Judaism, based on the worship of a single all-powerful god, Yahweh. The Hebrews wrote down their religious ideas, traditions, laws, advice literature, prayers, hymns, history, and prophecies in a series of books, which came to define the Hebrews as a people. This group of books, the Hebrew Bible, describes the Covenant between Yahweh and the Hebrew people and sets out laws and traditions that structured Hebrew society and family life. Reverence for these written texts was passed from Judaism to the other Western monotheistic religions that grew from it, Christianity and Islam.

In the ninth century B.C.E. the Assyrians began a rise to power from northern Mesopotamia, creating an empire by means of often brutal military conquest. Assyria's success was also due to sophisticated, farsighted, and effective military tactics, technical skills, and organization. From a base in what is now southern Iran, the Persians established an even larger empire, developing effective institutions of government and building roads. Though conquerors, the Persians, unlike the Assyrians, usually respected their subjects and allowed them to practice their native customs, traditions, and religions. Around 600 B.C.E. a new religion based on the teachings of the prophet Zoroaster grew in Persia. This religion emphasized the individual's responsibility to choose between good and evil.

The Greeks

The people of ancient Greece developed a culture that fundamentally shaped the civilization of the western part of Eurasia. The Greeks were the first in the Mediterranean and neighboring areas to explore most of the philosophical questions that still concern thinkers today. Going beyond mythmaking, the Greeks strove to understand the world in logical, rational terms. The result was the birth of philosophy and science, subjects as important to many Greeks as religion. Drawing on their day-by-day experiences, the Greeks also developed the concept of politics, and their contributions to literature still fertilize intellectual life today.

The history of the Greeks is divided into two broad periods: the Hellenic, roughly the time between the founding of the first complex societies in the area that is now the Greek islands and mainland, about 3500 B.C.E., and the rise of the kingdom of Macedonia in the north of Greece in 338 B.C.E.; and the Hellenistic, the years from the reign of Alexander the Great (336–323 B.C.E.) through the spread of Greek culture from Spain to India (ca. 100 B.C.E.). During the Hellenic period Greeks developed a distinctive form of city-state known as the polis and made lasting cultural and intellectual achievements. During the Hellenistic period Macedonian and Greek armies defeated the Persian Empire and built new cities and kingdoms. During their conquests they blended their ideas and traditions with those of the societies they encountered, creating a vibrant culture.

In its earliest history, Greece's mountainous terrain and lack of navigable rivers led to political fragmentation. The Greeks developed the independent city-state, known as the polis, in which individuals governed themselves without elaborate political machinery. The two most important poleis were Sparta and Athens, which formed new social and political structures. Sparta created a military state in which men remained in the army most of their lives and women concentrated on raising healthy soldiers. After much social conflict, Athens created a democracy in which male citizens both voted for their leaders and had a direct voice in an assembly. As was the case in all democracies in ancient Greece, women, slaves, and outsiders could not be citizens.

In the classical period, between 500 and 336 B.C.E., Greek civilization reached its highest peak in politics, thought, and art, even as it engaged in violent conflicts. The Greeks successfully defended themselves from Persian invasions but nearly destroyed themselves in the Peloponnesian War, which pitted Sparta and its allies against Athens and its allies. In the last half of the fifth century B.C.E. the brilliant Athenian leader Pericles turned Athens into the showplace of Greece by sponsoring the construction of temples and other buildings. In other artistic developments, wealthy Athenians paid for theater performances in which dramatists used their art in attempts to portray, understand, and resolve life's basic conflicts. This period also saw the rise of philosophy, and Socrates, Plato, and Aristotle began a broad examination of the universe and the place of humans in it.

Woman at Home In this painting from the side of a vase made in the fifth century B.C.E., a well-to-do young woman sits on an elegant chair inside a house, spinning and weaving. The bed piled high with coverlets on the left was a symbol of marriage in Greek art. (Musée du Louvre, Paris/Erich Lessing/Art Resource, NY)

In the middle of the fourth century B.C.E. the Greek city-states were conquered by King Philip II and his son Alexander, rulers of Macedonia to the north of Greece. A brilliant military leader, Alexander conquered the entire Persian Empire, along with many territories to the east of Persia. He also founded new cities in which Greek and local populations mixed. His successors continued to build cities and colonies, which became powerful instruments in the spread of Greek culture and in the blending of Greek traditions and ideas with those of other peoples. The mixing of peoples in the Hellenistic era influenced religion, philosophy, and science. In the scholarly realm, advances were made in mathematics, astronomy, and mechanical design.

The Greek world was largely conquered by the Romans, and the various Hellenistic monarchies became part of the Roman Empire. In cultural terms the lines of conquest were reversed: The Romans derived their alphabet from the Greek alphabet, though they changed the letters somewhat. Roman statuary was modeled on Greek and was often made by Greek sculptors, who found ready customers among wealthy Romans. The major Roman gods and goddesses were largely the same as the Greek ones, though they had different names.

The influence of the ancient Greeks was not limited to the Romans. Art and thought in northern India was shaped by the blending of Greek and Buddhist traditions. European thinkers and writers made conscious attempts to return to classical ideals in art, literature, and philosophy during the Renaissance. In America political leaders from the Revolutionary era on decided that important government buildings should be modeled on the Parthenon and other temples, complete with marble statuary of their own heroes.

The Romans

Like the Persians and the Macedonians, the Romans conquered vast territories. Their singular achievement lay in their ability to incorporate conquered peoples into the Roman system. Roman history is usually divided into two periods. The first is the republic (509–27 B.C.E.), the age in which Rome grew from a small group of cities in the middle of the Italian peninsula to a state that ruled much of the Mediterranean. The second period is the empire (27 B.C.E.–476 C.E.), when the republican constitution gave way to rule by a single individual.

In its earliest development, Roman culture was influenced by the Etruscans, people who established permanent settlements in northern and central Italy. The Etruscans introduced the Romans to urbanism, industry, trade, and the alphabet. In 509 B.C.E. the Romans won independence from Etruscan rule and continued to expand their territories. They also established a republic, which functioned through a shared government of the people directed by the Senate, summarized by the expression SPQR—*senatus populusque Romanus*, meaning "the Roman senate and people." In the resolution to a social conflict known as the Struggle of the Orders, nobles and ordinary people created a state administered by magistrates elected from the entire population and established a uniform law code.

In a series of wars the Romans conquered the Mediterranean, creating an overseas empire that brought them enormous power and wealth. Yet social unrest came in the wake of the war, opening unprecedented opportunities for ambitious generals who wanted to rule Rome like an empire. Civil war ensued, and it appeared as if the great politician and general Julius Caesar would emerge victorious, but he was assassinated by a group of senators. After his assassination and another period of civil war, his grandnephew Augustus finally restored peace and order to Rome, and assumed control as a single individual.

Augustus's success in creating solid political institutions was tested by the ineptness of some leaders who followed him, but later in the first century C.E. Rome entered a period of political stability, prosperity, and relative peace that lasted until the end of the second century C.E. During this period, later dubbed the *pax Romana*, the city of Rome became the magnificent capital of the empire. The Roman provinces and frontiers also saw extensive prosperity in the second century through the growth of agriculture, trade, and industry, among other factors. As the Roman Empire expanded eastward from Europe, it met opposition, yet even during the fighting, commerce among the Romans and peoples who lived in central and southern Asia thrived along a series of trade routes.

One of the most significant developments during the time of Augustus was the beginning of Christianity. Christianity was a religion created by the followers of Jesus of Nazareth (ca. 3 B.C.E.–29 C.E.), a Jewish man who taught that belief in his divinity led to eternal life. His followers spread their belief across the Roman Empire, transforming Christianity from a Jewish sect into a new religion. Christian groups were informal at first, but by the second century they began to develop hierarchical institutions modeled on those of Rome. At first many pagans in the Roman Empire misunderstood Christian practices and rites, and as a result Christians suffered sporadic persecution under certain Roman emperors. Gradually, however, tensions between pagans and Christians lessened, particularly as Christianity modified its teachings to make them more acceptable to wealthy and educated Romans.

In terms of politics and economics, the prosperity of the Roman Empire in the second century C.E. gave way to a period of civil war, barbarian invasions, and conflict with foreign armies in the third century. These disrupted agriculture, trade, and production and damaged the flow of taxes and troops. At the close of the third century the emperor Diocletian ended the period of chaos, in part because he recognized that the empire had become too great for one man to handle. He therefore divided it into a western and

Ara Pacis In the middle years of Augustus's reign, the Roman Senate ordered a huge altar, the Ara Pacis, built to honor him and the peace he had brought to the empire. This was decorated with life-size reliefs of Augustus and members of his family, prominent Romans, and other people and deities. One side, shown here, depicts a goddess figure, most likely the goddess Peace herself, with twin babies on her lap, flanked by nymphs representing land and sea, and surrounded by plants and animals. (De Agostini Picture Library/Gianni Dagli Orti/Bridgeman Images)

an eastern half. Diocletian and his successor, Constantine, also took rigid control of the struggling economy, but their efforts were not successful. Free tenant farmers lost control of their lands, exchanging them for security that landlords offered against barbarians and other threats. Meanwhile, tolerance of Christianity grew, and Constantine legalized the practice of the religion throughout the empire. The symbol of all the changes in the empire became the establishment of its new capital, Constantinople, the New Rome.

From the third century onward the Western Roman Empire slowly disintegrated. The last Roman emperor in the West, Romulus Augustus, was deposed by the Ostrogothic chieftain Odoacer (OH-duh-way-suhr) in 476, but much of the empire had come under the rule of various barbarian tribes long before this. Thus despite the efforts of emperors and other leaders, by the fifth century the Western Roman Empire no longer existed, a development that scholars who focus on Europe have long seen as one of the great turning points in history.

India

The vast subcontinent of India, protected from outsiders by the towering Himalayan Mountains to the north and by oceans on its other borders, witnessed the development of several early civilizations, primarily in the richly cultivated valley of the Indus River, which flows about 1,980 miles before reaching the ocean. Only in the northwest—the area between modern Afghanistan and Pakistan—was India accessible to invasion. The northwest was also the area of the earliest civilization in India, the Harappan, which built large cities mostly of brick. After the decline of this civilization, the Aryans, a nomadic Indo-European people, entered India by way of the Khyber Pass around 1500 B.C.E. They were able to establish dominance over large areas, including the eastern regions of the Ganges River. By 500 B.C.E. the Aryans ruled a number of large kingdoms in which cities were the centers of culture. The period of Aryan rule saw the evolution of a caste system designed to denote birth or descent and to distinguish Aryan from non-Aryan and rulers from the ruled. The four groups, or castes, that emerged—the *Brahmin* (priests), the *Kshatriya* (warriors), the *Vaishya* (peasants), and the *Shudra* (serfs)—became the dominant features of Indian society. Persons without a place in the hierarchical strata or who lost their caste status because of some violation of ritual were *outcastes*.

Through the Khyber Pass in 513 B.C.E. the Persian king Darius I entered India and conquered the Indus Valley. The Persians introduced political administration and coin-minting techniques, and they brought India into commercial and cultural contact with the sophisticated ancient Middle East. From the Persians the Indians adopted the Aramaic language and script, which they adapted to their needs and languages. In 326 B.C.E. the Macedonian king Alexander the Great invaded the Indus Valley, but his conquests had no lasting effect. Under Ashoka (r. 269–232

Meditating Monk This monk, wearing the traditional patchwork robe, sits in the crossed-legged meditation position. His small niche is to the left of the main image of the Buddha in cave 285 at Dunhuang, a cave completed in 539 C.E. under the patronage of a prince of the Northern Wei imperial house who was then the local governor. (Photo: Lois Conner. Courtesy, Dunhuang Academy)

B.C.E.), ancient India's greatest ruler, India enjoyed peace and stability, but from 180 B.C.E. to 200 C.E. the region suffered repeated foreign invasions. There was no dominant unifying state, and regional cultures flourished. In the northwest rulers such as the Shakas and Kushans came from outside India.

Ancient India's most enduring legacies are the three great religions that flowered in the sixth and fifth centuries B.C.E.: Hinduism, Jainism, and Buddhism. One of the modern world's largest religions, Hinduism holds that the Vedas—hymns in praise of the Aryan gods—are sacred revelations and that these revelations prescribe the caste system. Religiously and philosophically diverse, Hinduism assures believers that there are many legitimate ways to worship Brahman, the supreme principle of life. India's best-loved hymn, the *Bhagavad Gita*, guides Hindus in a pattern of life in the world and of release from it.

Jainism derives from the teachings of the great thinker Vardhamana Mahavira (ca. 540–468 B.C.E.), who held that only an ascetic life leads to bliss and that all life is too sacred to be destroyed. Nonviolence is a cardinal principle of Jainism. Thus a Jain who wishes to do the least violence to life turns to vegetarianism.

Mahavira's contemporary, Siddhartha Gautama (ca. 563–483 B.C.E.), better known as the Buddha, was so deeply distressed by human suffering that he abandoned his Hindu beliefs in a search for ultimate enlightenment. Meditation alone, he maintained, brought total enlightenment in which everything is understood. Buddha developed the "Eightfold Path," a series of steps of meditation that could lead to *nirvana*, a state of happiness attained by the extinction of self and human desires. Buddha opposed all religious dogmatism and insisted that anyone, regardless of sex or class, could achieve enlightenment. He attracted many followers, and although Buddhism split into several branches after his death, Buddhist teachings spread throughout India to China, Japan, Korea, and Vietnam. Buddhism remains one of the great Asian religions and in recent times has attracted adherents in the West.

China

Chinese civilization, which developed initially along the Huang He (Yellow) River, was much farther away from the ancient Middle East than India and had much less in the way of contact with other early civilizations. Still, the Shang Dynasty (ca. 1200 B.C.E.) shared features of other early civilizations, such as bronze technology, cities, and writing. The writing system China developed, with separate symbols for each word, had no connection to the writing systems of other parts of Eurasia and became a key feature of Chinese culture.

The Chinese always looked back on the Zhou period (ca. 1000–256 B.C.E.) as their classical age, when social and political ideas were perfected. After a few centuries, political unity was lost, and China consisted of many states, large and small, that made alliances with each other but also frequently fought each other. Political disorder seems to have stimulated philosophy, and this became the period when "one hundred schools of thought contended." Compared to Indian religious speculation, Chinese thinkers were more secular than religious in outlook. Interested primarily in social and economic problems, they sought universal rules of human conduct from the level of the family up to that of the state. Ancient China witnessed the development of Confucianism, Daoism, and Legalism, philosophies that profoundly influenced subsequent Chinese society and culture.

Confucius (551–479 B.C.E.) was interested in orderly and stable human relationships, and he focused on the proper duties and behavior of the individual. Confucius considered the family the basic unit in society. Within the family, male was superior to female and age to youth. If order was to exist in society, he taught, it must start at the level of the family. Those who help the king govern should be gentlemen, by which he meant men who exhibited the virtues of loyalty, sincerity, deference, generosity, and commitment. Only gentlemanly conduct, which involved a virtuous and ethical life, would lead to well-run government and peaceful conditions in society at large. Self-discipline, courtesy to others, punctiliousness in service to the state, and justice to the people are the obligations and behaviors expected of Confucian gentlemen. Confucius minimized the importance of class distinctions and taught that men of humble birth could achieve a high level of conduct and become gentlemen through education and self-discipline. The fundamental ingredient in the evolution of the Chinese civil service, Confucianism continued to shape Chinese government up to the twentieth century.

Daoism treated the problems of government very differently. In its two surviving books, *Laozi* and *Zhuangzi*, each named after a Daoist master, earnest efforts to perfect society were ridiculed. Daoism maintained that people would be happier only if they abandoned the world and reverted to simpler ways. Daoists insisted that the best government is the least active government. Public works and government services require higher taxes, which lead to unhappiness and popular resistance. According to the Daoists, the people should be kept materially satisfied and uneducated. A philosophy of consolation, Daoism was especially popular among those who were frustrated by the political system.

Legalism is the name given to a number of related political theories originating in the third century B.C.E. The founders of Legalism proposed pragmatic solutions to the problems of government, exalted the power of the state, and favored an authoritarian ruler who would root out dissent. They argued that laws should be made known, the penalties for infractions should be clear and harsh, and the laws and penalties should apply to everyone in society, even the close relatives of the ruler. Though Legalism seemed too harsh to many, it did contribute to the Chinese system of centralized bureaucratic rule.

In the third century B.C.E. the state of Qin adopted Legalism and then set out to defeat all the other states, thus unifying China. The Qin government attempted to achieve uniformity at many levels, standardizing weights and measures, writing systems, and laws. It even tried to do away with ideas it disapproved of by collecting and burning books. The new dynasty was called *Qin*, from which the Western term "China" derives. Under the Qin Dynasty and its successor, the Han, China achieved political and social stability and economic prosperity. On its northern border, however, Qin and Han faced tough military opponents in the Xiongnu, pastoralists who excelled at horsemanship.

The period of the Han Dynasty (206 B.C.E.–220 C.E.) witnessed notable intellectual achievements. First, many of the books that had been burned by the Qin were reconstructed from memory or hidden copies. These texts came to be known as the *Confucian Classics*. Scholars piously studied the books and worked to make them widely accessible as standards of moral behavior. Second, historical writing developed. The historian Sima Qian (145–ca. 85 B.C.E.) produced the *Records of the Grand Historian*, a massive and comprehensive survey of earlier Chinese civilization. These two sets of writings left a permanent mark on Chinese thought and peoples.

The Islamic World, 600–1400

One of the most important developments in world history—whose consequences redound to our own day—was the rise and remarkable expansion of Islam in the early Middle Ages. Muhammad (ca. 570–632), a devout merchant of Mecca in present-day Saudi Arabia, called on his followers to return to God. Even before Muhammad's death his teachings spread through Arabia, uniting the tribes there. Within two centuries his followers controlled Syria, Palestine, Egypt, Iraq, Iran, northern India, Spain, and southern France, and his beliefs were carried eastward across Central Asia to the borders of China. In the ninth, tenth, and eleventh centuries the Muslims created a brilliant civilization centered at Baghdad in Iraq and Córdoba in Spain.

Muhammad believed that God sent him messages or revelations. These were later collected and published as the Qur'an, from an Arabic word meaning "reading" or "recitation." On the basis of God's revelations to him, Muhammad preached a strictly monotheistic faith based on the principle of the absolute unity and omnipotence of God. Since God is all-powerful, believers must submit to him. *Islam* means "submission to God," and the community of Muslims consists of those who have submitted to God by accepting the final revelation of his message as set forth by Muhammad. (Earlier revelations of God, held by Muslims to be the same God worshipped by Jews and Christians, had come from the prophets Abraham, Moses, and Jesus, whose work Muslims believe Muhammad completed.)

The Arabs carried their religion to the east and west by military conquest. Their rapid expansion was made possible by their own economic needs, the political weaknesses of their enemies, a strong military organization, and the practice of establishing army camps in newly conquered territories. In time, many of those in the conquered lands converted to Islam.

The assassination of one of the caliphs, or successors of Muhammad, led to a division within the Islamic community. When the caliph Ali (r. 656–661) was murdered, his followers claimed that, because he was related by blood to Muhammad and because Muhammad had designated him leader of the community prayer, he had been Muhammad's prescribed successor. These supporters of Ali were called *Shi'ites*, or *Shi'a*, partisans of Ali; they claimed to possess special divine knowledge that Muhammad had given his heirs. Other Muslims adhered to traditional beliefs and practices of the community based on precedents set by Muhammad. They were called *Sunnis*, a term derived from the Arabic *Sunna*, a collection of Muhammad's sayings and conduct in particular situations. This schism within Islam continues today. Sufism, an ascetic movement within Islam that sought a direct and mystical union with God, drew many followers from all classes.

Long-distance trade and commerce, which permitted further expansion of the Muslim faith, played a prominent role in the Islamic world, in contrast to the limited position it held in the heavily agricultural medieval West. The Black and Caspian Seas, the Volga River giving access deep into Russia, the Arabian Sea and the Indian Ocean, and to a lesser extent the Mediterranean Sea were the great commercial waterways of the Islamic world. Goods circulated freely over them. Muslim commercial tools such as the bill of exchange, the check, and the joint stock company were borrowed by Westerners. Many economic practices basic to

Playing Chess This page from a thirteenth-century book on chess and other games depicts a Moor and a Christian playing chess together. (Biblioteca Monasterio del Escorial, Madrid, Spain/Index/Bridgeman Images)

capitalism were used by Muslim merchants and business-men long before they became common in the West.

Long-distance trade brought the wealth that supported a gracious and sophisticated culture in the cities of the Muslim world. Baghdad in Iraq and Córdoba in Spain, whose streets were thronged with a kaleidoscope of races, creeds, customs, and cultures and whose many shops offered goods from all over the world, stand out as superb examples of cosmopolitan Muslim civilization. Baghdad and Córdoba were also great intellectual centers where Muslim scholars made advances in mathematics, medicine, and philosophy. The Arabs translated many ancient Greek texts by writers such as Plato and Aristotle. When, beginning in the ninth century, those texts were translated from Arabic into Latin, they came to play an important part in the formation of medieval European scientific, medical, and philosophical thought. Modern scholars consider Muslim civilization in the period from about 900 to 1200 among the most brilliant in the world's history.

Asia, 300–1400

Between about 300 and 1400 the various societies of Asia continued to evolve their own distinct social, political, and religious institutions. Also in these years momentous changes swept across Asia. Buddhism spread from India to Central Asia, China, Korea, Japan, Southeast Asia, and Tibet. Arab conquerors and their Muslim faith reached the Indian subcontinent. The Turks, moving west from the Chinese border, converted to Islam. China, under the Tang and Song Dynasties, experienced a golden age. Japan emerged into the light of written history. The Mongols formed a confederation of the tribes of the steppes of Inner Asia that had extraordinary success in conquering cities from Korea and China to Persia, Baghdad, and Russia. These centuries witnessed cultural developments that have molded and influenced later Asian societies.

India

Under the Gupta kings, who ruled from around 320 to 500, India enjoyed a great cultural flowering. Interest in Sanskrit literature—the literature of the Aryans—led to the preservation of much Sanskrit poetry. A distinctly Indian drama appeared, and India's greatest poet, Kalidasa (ca. 380–450), like Shakespeare, blended poetry and drama. Mathematicians arrived at the concept of zero, essential for higher mathematics, and scientific thinkers wrestled with the concept of gravitation.

The Gupta kings succeeded in uniting much of the subcontinent. They also succeeded in repulsing an invasion by the Huns, but the effort exhausted the dynasty. After 600 India reverted to the pattern of strong local kingdoms in frequent conflict. Between 600 and 1400, India suffered repeated invasion as waves of Arabs, Turks, and Mongols swept down through the northwest corridor. The most successful were Turks from the area of modern Afghanistan, who held power in Delhi for three centuries and managed to turn back the Mongols. By around 1400 India was as politically splintered as it had been before Gupta rule. Under the Turks Islam became dominant in the Indus Valley (modern Pakistan). Elsewhere Hinduism resisted Islam.

One other development had a lasting effect on Indian society: the proliferation and hardening of the caste system. Early Indian society had been divided into four major groups. After the fall of the Guptas, further subdivisions arose, reflecting differences of profession, trade, tribal or racial affiliation, religious belief, and even place of residence. By 800 India had more than three thousand castes, each with its own rules and governing body. As India was politically divided, the castes served to fragment it socially.

China

Scholars consider the period between 580 and 1200, which saw the rule of Tang and Song Dynasties, as China's golden age. In religion, political administration, agricultural productivity, and art, Chinese society attained a remarkable level of achievement. This era was followed by the rise of the Mongols, who in time engulfed China.

Merchants and travelers from India introduced Buddhism to China from the first century C.E. on. Scholars, rulers, the middle classes, and the poor all found appealing concepts in Buddhist teachings, and the new faith won many adherents. China distilled Buddhism to meet its own needs, and Buddhism gained a place next to Confucianism and Daoism in Chinese life.

The Tang Dynasty, which some historians consider the greatest in Chinese history, built a state bureaucracy, the political sophistication of which was unequaled until recent times. Tang emperors subdivided the imperial administration into departments of military organization, maintenance and supply of the army, foreign affairs, justice, education, finance, building, and transportation. To staff this vast administration, an imperial civil service developed in which education, talent, and merit could lead to high office, wealth, and prestige. So effective was the Tang civil service and so deeply rooted did it become in Chinese society that it lasted until the twentieth century.

Under the Song Dynasty (960–1279), greatly expanded agricultural productivity, combined with advances in the technology of coal and iron and efficient water transport, supported a population of 100 million. (By contrast, Europe did not reach this figure until the late eighteenth century.) Greater urbanization followed in China. Political stability and economic growth fostered technological innovation, the greatest being the invention of printing. Tang craftsmen invented the art of carving words and pictures into wooden blocks, inking the blocks, and then pressing them onto paper. The invention of movable type followed in the eleventh century. As would happen in Europe in the fifteenth century, the invention of printing lowered the price and increased the availability of books and contributed to the spread of literacy. Printing led to the use of paper money, replacing bulky copper coinage, and to developments in banking. The highly creative Tang and Song periods also witnessed the invention of gunpowder, originally used for fireworks, and the abacus, which permitted the quick computation of complicated sums. In the creation of a large collection of fine poetry and prose, and in the manufacture of porcelain of superb quality and delicate balance, the Tang and Song periods revealed an extraordinary literary and artistic flowering.

Shipbuilding advanced, and large ships were used both for war and for trade. Trade expanded as Japan and Korea eagerly imported Chinese silks and porcelains. The Muslims shipped Chinese goods across the Indian Ocean to East African and Middle Eastern markets. Southern China participated in a commercial network that stretched from Japan to the Mediterranean.

The thirteenth century witnessed the violent and amazingly fast creation of the Mongol Empire, the largest continuous land empire in world history. The Mongols were a steppe nomadic people in north-central Asia who had fought largely among themselves until about 1200. Their extraordinary expansion was the result of a shortage of pasture land for their sheep, goats, and cattle, and the rise of a great warrior-leader, Chinggis Khan (1162–1227), who united the steppe peoples and led them to conquer and absorb one neighbor after another. Building a vast army of loyal followers to whom he displayed great generosity, and using a policy of terror as a weapon of war, Chinggis swept across Central Asia into northern China. In 1215, he burned Beijing, and many Chinese governors quickly submitted. Chinggis then turned westward and destroyed the Persian Empire, massacring hundreds of thousands of people. Under Chinggis's sons, the Mongols won control of Kievan Russia and Moscow, looted cities in Poland and Hungary, and established the Khanate of the Golden Horde. Chinggis's grandson Khubilai (r. 1260–1294) completed the conquest of China and overran Korea. The Mongols viewed China as their most important conquest; Mongol rule extended over most of East Asia, which they called the Great Khanate. They even invaded, but did not conquer, Japan. The Chinese called the period of Mongol rule the Yuan Dynasty. In 1368 Hungwu, the first emperor of the Ming Dynasty, restored Chinese rule.

Japan

The chain of islands that constitutes Japan entered written history only in sporadic references in Chinese writings, the most reliable set down in 297 C.E. Because the land of Japan is rugged, lacking navigable waterways, and because perhaps only 20 percent of it is arable, political unification by land proved difficult until modern times. The Inland Sea served both as the readiest means of communication and as a rich source of food; the Japanese have traditionally been fishermen and mariners.

Early Japan was divided into numerous political units, each under the control of a particular clan, a large group of families claiming descent from a common ancestor and worshipping a common deity. In the third century C.E. the Yamato clan gained control of the fertile area south of modern Kyoto near Osaka Bay and subordinated many other clans. The Yamato chieftain proclaimed himself emperor and assigned specific duties and functions to subordinate chieftains. The Yamato established their chief shrine in the eastern part (where the sun-goddess could catch the first rays of the rising sun) of Honshu, the largest of Japan's four main islands. Around this shrine local clan cults sprang up, giving rise to a native religion that the Japanese called Shinto, the "Way of the Gods." Shinto became a unifying force and protector of the nation.

Through Korea two significant Chinese influences entered Japan and profoundly influenced Japanese culture: the Chinese system of writing and record keeping, and Buddhism. Under Prince Shotoku (574–622), talented young Japanese were sent to Tang China to learn Chinese methods of administration and Chinese Buddhism. They returned to Japan to share and enforce what they had learned. The Nara era of Japanese history (710–794), so called after Japan's first capital city, north of modern Osaka, was characterized by the steady importation of Chinese ideas and methods. Buddhist monasteries became both religious and political centers, supporting Yamato rule.

Perhaps because Buddhist temples had too much power in Nara, in 794 the imperial family removed the capital to Heian (modern Kyoto), where it remained until 1867. A strong reaction against Buddhism and Chinese influences followed, symbolized by the severance of relations with China in 838. The eclipse of Chinese influences liberated Japanese artistic and cultural forces, and a new Japanese style of art and architecture appeared. In writing, Japanese scholars produced two syllabaries, sets of phonetic signs that stand for syllables instead of whole words or letters. Unshackled from Chinese forms, Japanese writers created their own literary styles and modes of expression. The writing of history and poetry flowered, and the Japanese produced their first novel, *The Tale of Genji*, a classic of court life by the court lady Lady Murasaki written over several years (ca. 1000–1010).

The later Heian period witnessed the breakdown of central authority as aristocrats struggled to free themselves from imperial control. In 1156 civil war among the leaders of the great clans erupted. By 1192 the Minamato clan had defeated all opposition. Its leader Yoritomo (1147–1199) became *shogun*, or general-in-chief. Thus began the Kamakura Shogunate, which lasted from 1185 until 1333.

In addition to the powerful shogun, a dominant figure in the new society was the *samurai*, the warrior who by the twelfth century exercised civil, judicial, and military power over the peasants who worked the land. The samurai held his land in exchange for his promise to fight for a stronger lord. In a violent society strikingly similar to that of western

Europe in the early Middle Ages, the Japanese samurai, like the French knight, constituted the ruling class at the local level. Civil war among the emperor, the leading families, and the samurai erupted again in 1331. In 1338 one of the most important military leaders, Ashikaga Takauji, defeated the emperor and established the Ashikaga Shogunate, which lasted until 1573. Meanwhile, the samurai remained the significant social figure.

By 1400 the continents of Africa, Asia, and Europe experienced considerable cultural contact with one another. Chinese silks passed across the Great Silk Road to southwestern Asia and Europe. The religious ideals of Buddhism spread from India to China and Korea. The expansion of Islam across northern Africa and into the Iberian Peninsula, down the east coast of Africa, across Central Asia and into northern India, and through the Malay Archipelago led to rich commercial contacts. Religious and philosophical ideas, artistic and architectural models, and scientific and medical learning flowed across these international trade routes. The centuries that witnessed the European religious-military-imperialistic expeditions to the Middle East known as the Crusades (ca. 1100–1300) led to the slow filtering of Muslim (and ancient Greek) medical and architectural knowledge to Europe. By way of Islam, features of Chinese technology, such as paper manufacture, and nautical information, such as the compass and the astrolabe, reached Europe.

African Societies and Kingdoms, 1000 B.C.E.–1500 C.E.

Africa is a huge continent with many different climatic zones and diverse geography. The peoples of Africa are as diverse as the topography. Groups relying on herd animals developed in the drier, disease-free steppe regions well suited to domesticated animals, while agricultural settlements developed in the wetter savanna regions. In the tropical forests of central Africa and arid zones of southern Africa, hunter-gatherers dominated. Along the coasts and by lakes and rivers grew maritime communities whose inhabitants relied on fishing and trade for their livelihood.

Because the peoples south of the Sahara are generally described as "black" Africans, the inappropriate concept of race has engendered fierce debate over just who is African. For example, since the days of ancient Greece, historians have debated whether Egypt, because of its proximity to the Mediterranean, should be identified as part of Africa or as part of the Mediterranean world. Race as a concept for determining one's "Africanness" has today generally been discredited as extremist.

Agriculture began very early in Africa. Knowledge of plant cultivation arrived in the Nile Delta in Egypt about the fifth millennium B.C.E. Settled agriculture then traveled down the Nile Valley and moved west across the Sahel to the central and western Sudan. Early societies across the western Sudan were profoundly affected as they switched from

Nok Woman
Hundreds of terracotta sculptures such as the figure of this woman survive from the Nok culture, which originated in the central plateau of northern Nigeria in the first millennium B.C.E.
(Private Collection/Photo © Heini Schneebeli/Bridgeman Images)

hunting and gathering in small bands to form settled farming communities. Populations increased significantly in this rich savanna zone that was ideally suited for grain production. Blood kinship brought together families in communities governed by chiefs or local councils. Animistic religions that recognized ancestral and nature spirits developed. The nature spirits were thought to dwell in nearby streams, forests, mountains, or caves.

Settled agriculture developed independently in West Africa. From there it spread to the equatorial forests. The spread of agriculture was related to the expansion of Bantu-speaking peoples, who originated in the Benue region, the borderlands of modern Cameroon and Nigeria. In the second millennium B.C.E. they began to spread south and east into the forest zone of equatorial Africa, eventually spreading across all of central and southern Africa. Possessing iron tools and weapons, domesticated livestock, and a knowledge of settled agriculture, these Bantu-speakers assimilated, killed, or drove away all the previous inhabitants of these regions.

Lines of trade and communication linked many parts of Africa with each other and with other parts of the world. The peoples of North Africa were closely connected with the Middle Eastern and European civilizations of the Mediterranean basin. Similarly, the peoples of the Swahili coast of East Africa participated in trade with Arabia, the Persian Gulf, India, China, and the Malay Archipelago.

Between 700 and 900, a network of caravan routes running south from the Mediterranean coast across the Sahara to the Sudan developed. Arab-Berber merchants exchanged manufactured goods for African gold, ivory, gum, and slaves from the West African savanna. The most essential component in the trans-Saharan trade was the camel. The camel made it possible for great loads to be hauled across vast stretches of hot, dry desert. The Berbers of North Africa endured these long treks south and then north again across the Sahara. To control this trade they fashioned camel saddles that gave them great political and military advantage. The primary items of trade were salt from the north and gold from the south, although textiles, fruit, ivory, kola nuts, gum, beads, and other goods were also prized by one side or the other. Enslaved West Africans, males and females, were also traded north to slave markets in Morocco, Algiers, Tripoli, and Cairo.

The trans-Saharan trade had three important effects on West African society. First, it stimulated gold mining. Second, it increased the demand for West Africa's second most important commodity, slaves. Third, the trans-Saharan trade stimulated the development of large urban centers in West Africa, such as Gao, Timbuktu, Koumbi Saleh, Sijilmasa, and Jenne. In the period after 700 it had a fourth major effect, introducing Islam to West African society. Conversion led to the involvement of Muslims in African governments, bringing efficient techniques of statecraft and advanced scientific knowledge and engineering skills. Between the ninth and fifteenth centuries, Islam greatly accelerated the development of the African kingdoms. Through the trans-Saharan trade, Africans living in the Sahel zone of West Africa became part of the larger world of Islam.

The period from 800 to 1450 witnessed the flowering of several powerful African states. In the western Sudan, the large empires of Ghana (ca. 900–1100) and Mali (ca. 1200–1450) arose. Each had an elaborate royal court, a massive state bureaucracy, a sizable army, a sophisticated judicial system, and a strong gold industry. The fame of Ghana rested on gold, and when the fabulously rich Mali king Mansa Musa (r. ca. 1312–1337), a devout Muslim, made a pilgrimage to Mecca, his entourage included one hundred elephants, each carrying one hundred pounds of gold.

Mali's strength resulted from two fundamental assets. First, its strong agricultural and commercial base provided for a large population and enormous wealth. Second, Mali

had two rulers, Sundiata and Mansa Musa, who combined military success with exceptionally creative personalities. The city of Timbuktu developed into a great center of scholarship and learning. Architects, astronomers, poets, lawyers, mathematicians, and theologians flocked there. Intermarriage between Arab and North African Muslim intellectuals and traders and local women brought into being a group of racially mixed people. The necessity of living together harmoniously, the traditional awareness of diverse cultures, and the cosmopolitan atmosphere of Timbuktu all contributed to a rare degree of racial toleration and understanding.

Meanwhile, the East African coast gave rise to powerful city-states such as Kilwa, Mombasa, and Mogadishu, which maintained a rich maritime trade with India, China, and the Muslim cities of the Middle East. Like the western Sudan, the East African cities were much affected by Muslim influences. Like East Africa, South Africa was made up of city-states, chief among them Great Zimbabwe, which flourished between the eleventh and fifteenth centuries. Located at the southernmost reach of the Indian Ocean trade network, these city-states exchanged their gold for the riches of Arabia and Asia. Somewhat more isolated, the kingdom of Aksum in Ethiopia utilized its access to the Red Sea to trade north to the Mediterranean and south to the Indian Ocean.

The East African city-states and the kingdoms of the western Sudan were part of the world of Islam. Arabian merchants brought Islam with them as they settled along the East African coast, and Berber traders brought Islam to West Africa. Differing from its neighbors, Ethiopia was a unique enclave of Christianity in the midst of Islamic societies. The Bantu-speaking peoples of Great Zimbabwe were neither Islamic nor Christian, but practiced indigenous forms of worship such as animism.

The Americas, 2500 B.C.E.–1500 C.E.

The first humans settled in the Americas between 40,000 and 15,000 B.C.E., after emigrating from Asia. The melting of glaciers 13,000 to 11,000 years ago separated the Americas from Afroeurasia, and the Eastern and Western Hemispheres developed in isolation from one another. There were many parallels, however: In both hemispheres people initially gathered and hunted their food, and then some groups began to plant crops, adapting plants that were native to the areas they settled. Techniques of plant domestication spread, allowing for population growth. In certain parts of both hemispheres, efficient production and transportation of food supplies led to the growth of cities and to larger political entities such as states and empires.

In the Americas, all the highly varied environments, from polar tundra to tropical rain forests, came to support human settlement. About 8000 B.C.E. people in some parts of the Americas began raising crops as well as gathering wild produce. Maize became the most important crop, with knowledge about its cultivation spreading from

Chinampa Farming This illustration shows farmers in the Aztec Empire building chinampa farming plots by reclaiming land from Lake Texcoco. Farmers created the plots by packing them with vegetation and mud from the lake, supporting their boundaries by planting willow trees. (Museo de la Ciudad de Mexico, Mexico City/De Agostini Picture Library/Gianni Dagli Orti/Bridgeman Images)

Mesoamerica—present-day Mexico and Central America—into North and South America.

Agricultural advancement led to an increase in population, which allowed for greater concentrations of people and the creation of the first urban societies. Towns dependent on agriculture flourished in certain parts of North and South America. Some groups in North America began to build large earthwork mounds; others in Mesoamerica and South America practiced irrigation. The Olmecs created the first society with cities in Mesoamerica, with large ceremonial buildings, an elaborate calendar, and a symbolic writing.

The urban culture of the Olmecs and other Mesoamerican peoples influenced subsequent societies. Especially in what became known as the classical era (300–900 C.E.), various groups developed large states centered on cities, with high levels of technological and intellectual achievement. Of these, the Maya were the longest-lasting, creating a complex written language, multiple-crop milpas (fields) and raised beds for agriculture, roads connecting population centers, trading practices that built unity among Maya communities as well as wealth, and striking art. Peoples living in North America built communities that were smaller than those in Mesoamerica, but many also used irrigation techniques to enhance agricultural production and continued to build earthwork mounds for religious purposes.

In Mesoamerica, the Aztecs, also known as the Mexica, built a unified culture based on the heritage of earlier societies and distinguished by achievements in engineering, sculpture, and architecture, including the streets, canals, public squares, and aqueduct of Tenochtitlan, the most spectacular and one of the largest cities in the world in 1500. In Mexica society, religion was the dynamic factor that transformed other aspects of the culture: economic security, social mobility, education, and especially war. War was an article of religious faith, providing riches and land, sacrificial victims for ceremonies honoring the Aztec gods, warriors for imperial expansion, and laborers. Aztec society was hierarchical, with nobles and priests having special privileges.

In the Andes, Inca achievements built on those of cultures that preceded theirs, including the Moche and Chavín civilizations. Moche, Chavín, and Inca cultures made their home in the valleys along the Peruvian coast and in the Andean highlands, cultivating food crops and cotton. The Incas, who began as a small militaristic group, eventually created the largest empire in South America in the fifteenth century and conquered surrounding groups. Their far-flung empire stretched along the Andes and was kept together by a system of roads, along which moved armies and administrators. The Incas achieved imperial unification by imposing their gods on conquered peoples, forcing local chieftains to participate in the central bureaucracy, and pursuing a policy of colonization. The imperial expansion that increased the Incas' strength also caused stress. Andean society was dominated by clan groups, and Inca measures to disrupt these groups and move people great distances created resentment.

Europe, 500–1500

In the fifteenth century, scholars in Europe began the practice of dividing European history into different periods. They called the time of Greece and Rome the ancient or classical era, and the thousand-year period between the fall of the Western Roman Empire and their own day the Middle Ages. This three-part division—ancient, medieval, and modern—has been very influential, even in areas beyond Europe.

The Middle Ages

The transition from ancient to medieval was a slow process, not a single event. The primary agents in this process of change were the barbarian tribes whose migrations broke the Roman Empire apart. The barbarians brought different social, political, and economic structures with them. Although Greco-Roman art and architecture still adorned the land and people continued to travel on Roman roads, the roads were rarely maintained, and travel itself was much less secure than during the empire. Merchants no longer traded over long distances, so people's access to goods produced outside their local area plummeted. There was intermarriage and cultural assimilation among Romans and barbarians, but there was also violence and great physical destruction.

The Eastern Roman Empire, called the Byzantine Empire, did not fall to barbarian invasions. During the sixth and seventh centuries the Byzantine Empire survived waves of attacks, owing to effective military leadership and to fortifications around Constantinople. From this strong position Byzantine emperors organized and preserved Roman institutions, and the Byzantine Empire lasted until 1453, nearly a millennium longer than the Roman Empire in the West. In particular, the emperor Justinian oversaw creation of the *Code*, which distilled the legal genius of the Romans into a coherent whole, eliminated outmoded laws and contradictions, and clarified the law itself. Just as they valued the law, the Byzantines prized education, and because of them many masterpieces of ancient Greek literature survived to influence the intellectual life of the modern world. In mathematics and science, the Byzantines passed Greco-Roman learning on to the Arabs.

Along with Byzantium, the Christian Church was an important agent of continuity in the transition from ancient to medieval in Europe. Christianity gained the support of the fourth-century emperors and gradually adopted the Roman system of hierarchical organization. The church possessed able administrators and leaders whose skills were tested in the chaotic environment of the end of the Roman Empire in the West. Bishops expanded their activities, and in the fifth century the bishops of Rome, taking the title "pope," began to stress their supremacy over other Christian communities. Monasteries offered opportunities for individuals to develop deeper spiritual devotion and also provided a model of Christian living, methods that advanced agricultural development, and places for education and learning. Missionaries and church officials spread Christianity within and far beyond the borders of what had been the Roman Empire, transforming a small sect into the most important and wealthiest institution in Europe, North Africa, and the eastern Mediterranean.

Christian thinkers reinterpreted the classics in a Christian sense, incorporating elements of Greek and Roman philosophy and of various pagan religious groups into Christian teachings. Missionaries and priests got pagan and illiterate peoples to understand and become more accepting of Christianity by preaching the basic teachings of the religion, stressing similarities between pagan customs and beliefs and those of Christianity, and introducing the ritual of penance and the veneration of saints.

Classical and Christian traditions modified those of barbarian society, although barbarian political systems were very different from those of Rome. Barbarians generally had no notion of the state as we use the term today; they thought in social, not political, terms. The basic social unit was the tribe, made up of kin groups formed by families. Family groups lived in small agriculture-based villages, where there were great differences in wealth and status. Most barbarian kingdoms were weak and short-lived, though the kingdom of the Franks was relatively more unified and powerful. Rulers first in the Merovingian dynasty of the fifth century, and then in the Carolingian of the eighth century, used military victories, strategic marriage alliances, and the help of the church to enhance their authority.

The Frankish kingdom broke down in the late ninth century, and continental Europe was fractured politically. No European political power was strong enough to put up effective resistance to external attack, which came from many directions. Vikings from Scandinavia carried out raids for plunder along the coasts and rivers of Europe and traveled as far as Iceland, Greenland, North America, and Russia. In many places they set up permanent states, as did the Magyars, who came into central Europe from the east. From the south came Muslims, who conquered Sicily and drove northward into Italy. All these invasions as well as civil wars weakened the power of kings, and local nobles became the strongest powers against external threats. They established a new form of decentralized government, later known as feudalism, similar to that of Japan in the era of the samurai. Common people turned to nobles for protection, paying with their land, labor, and freedom.

Beginning in the last half of the tenth century, the invasions that had contributed to European fragmentation gradually ended, and domestic disorder slowly subsided. Feudal rulers began to develop new institutions of law and government that enabled them to assert their power over lesser lords and the general population. Centralized states slowly crystallized, first in western Europe in the eleventh century, and then in eastern and northern Europe. An era of relative

Agricultural Work In this scene from a German manuscript written about 1190, men and women of different ages are sowing seeds and harvesting grain. All residents of a village, including children, engaged in agricultural tasks. (Rheinisches Landesmuseum, Bonn, Germany/Bridgeman Images)

stability and prosperity followed, generally known as the "High Middle Ages," which lasted until climate change and disease brought calamity in the fourteenth century.

At the same time that rulers expanded their authority, energetic popes built their power within the Western Christian Church. They asserted their superiority over kings and emperors, though these moves were sometimes challenged by those secular rulers. Monasteries continued to be important places of learning and devotion, and new religious orders were founded. Meanwhile, Christianity expanded into Europe's northern and eastern regions, and Christian rulers expanded their holdings in Muslim Spain. On a more personal scale, religion structured people's daily lives and the yearly calendar.

A papal call to retake the holy city of Jerusalem from the Muslims led to nearly two centuries of warfare between Christians and Muslims. Christian warriors, clergy, and settlers moved in all directions from western and central Europe, so that through conquest and colonization border regions were gradually incorporated into a more uniform European culture. The enormous popular response to the pope's call reveals the influence of the papacy and the new sense that war against the church's enemies was a duty of nobles. The Crusades were initially successful, and small Christian states were established in the Middle East. They did not last very long, however, and other effects of the Crusades were disastrous: Jewish communities in Europe were regularly attacked; relations between the Western and Eastern Christian Churches were poisoned by the Crusaders' attack on Constantinople; and Christian-Muslim relations became more uniformly hostile than they had been earlier.

For most people, the High Middle Ages did not bring dramatic change. The vast majority of medieval Europeans were rural peasants who lived in small villages and worked their own and their lords' land. Peasants led hard lives, and most were bound to the land, although there were some opportunities for social mobility. Nobles were a tiny fraction of the total population, but they exerted great power over all aspects of life. Aristocratic values and attitudes, often called chivalry, shaded all aspects of medieval culture. Medieval towns and cities grew initially as trading centers and recruited people from the countryside with the promise of greater freedom and new possibilities. They also became centers of production, and merchants and artisans formed guilds to protect their livelihoods. Not everyone in medieval towns and cities shared in the prosperity, however; many residents lived hand-to-mouth on low wages.

The towns that became centers of trade and production in the High Middle Ages also developed into cultural and intellectual centers. Trade brought in new ideas as well as merchandise, and in many cities a new type of educational institution—the university—emerged from cathedral and municipal schools. Universities developed theological, legal, and medical courses of study based on classical models and provided trained officials for the new government and church bureaucracies. People also wanted permanent visible representations of their piety, and church and city leaders supported the building of churches and cathedrals as symbols of their Christian faith and their civic pride. Cathedrals grew larger and more sumptuous, with high towers, soaring arches, and exquisite stained-glass windows in a style known as Gothic. New types of vernacular literature arose in which poems, songs, and stories were written down in local dialects.

In the fourteenth century the prosperity of the High Middle Ages ended. Bad weather brought poor harvests, which contributed to an international economic depression and fostered disease. The Black Death caused enormous population losses and had social, psychological, and economic consequences. Additional difficulties included the Hundred Years' War between England and France, which devastated much of the French countryside and bankrupted England; a schism among rival popes that weakened the Western Christian Church; and peasant and worker frustrations that exploded in uprisings. These revolts were usually crushed, though noble landlords were not always successful in reasserting their rights to labor services instead of cash rents.

The Renaissance

While Europe suffered greatly in the fourteenth century, a new culture was beginning to emerge in southern Europe. First in Italy and then elsewhere scholars, writers, and artists thought that they were living in a new golden age, later termed the Renaissance, French for "rebirth." The word *renaissance* was used initially to describe art that seemed to recapture, or perhaps even surpass, the glories of the classical past, and then came to be used for many aspects of life of the period. The new attitude diffused slowly out of Italy, with the result that the Renaissance "happened" at different times in different parts of Europe.

The Renaissance was characterized by self-conscious awareness among fourteenth- and fifteenth-century Italians, particularly scholars and writers known as humanists, that they were living in a new era. Key to this attitude was a serious interest in the Latin classics, a belief in individual potential, and a more secular attitude toward life. Humanists opened schools to train boys and young men for active lives of public service, but they had doubts about whether humanist education was appropriate for women. As humanism spread to northern Europe, religious concerns became more pronounced, and Christian humanists set out plans for the reform of church and society. Their ideas were spread to a much wider audience than those of early humanists as a result of the development of the printing press with movable metal type, which revolutionized communication.

Interest in the classical past and in the individual shaped Renaissance art in terms of style and subject matter. Also important to Renaissance art were the wealthy patrons who helped fund it.

Social hierarchies in the Renaissance developed new features that contributed to the modern social hierarchies of race, class, and gender. The distinction between free people and slaves was one such hierarchy. Although slavery in Europe was not limited to Africans during the Renaissance, increasing numbers of black Africans entered Europe as slaves to supplement the labor force, and black skin color was increasingly viewed as a mark of inferiority. In terms of class, the medieval hierarchy of orders based on function in society intermingled with a new hierarchy that created a new social elite whose status was based on wealth. In regard to gender, the Renaissance debate about women led many to discuss women's nature and proper role in society, a discussion sharpened by the presence of a number of ruling queens in this era. Nevertheless, women continued to lag behind men in social status and earnings.

During the Renaissance the feudal monarchies of medieval Europe gradually evolved into nation-states. Beginning in the fifteenth century rulers in western Europe used aggressive methods to build up their governments, reducing violence, curbing unruly nobles, and establishing domestic order. They emphasized royal majesty and royal sovereignty and insisted on the respect and loyalty of all subjects. War and diplomacy were important ways that states increased their power, and so was marriage. Because almost all of Europe was ruled by hereditary dynasties, claiming and holding resources involved shrewd marital alliances.

The Renaissance is often seen as a radical change, but it contained many elements of continuity as well. Artists and humanists looked back to the classical era for inspiration, and political leaders played important roles in cultural developments, just as they had for centuries in Europe and other parts of the world. The Renaissance was also closely connected with European exploration and colonization, which you will study in depth in Chapter 16 of this text. Renaissance monarchs paid for the expeditions' ships, crews, and supplies, expecting a large share of any profits gained and increasingly viewing overseas territory as essential to a strong state. The desire for fame, wealth, and power that was central to the Renaissance was thus key to the European voyages and to colonial ventures as well.

A History of
World Societies

ELEVENTH EDITION

16

The Acceleration of Global Contact

1450–1600

Before 1500 Europeans were relatively marginal players in a centuries-old trading system that linked Africa, Asia, and Europe. The Indian Ocean was the locus of a vibrant cosmopolitan Afroeurasian trade world in which Arab, Persian, Turkish, Indian, African, Chinese, and European merchants and adventurers competed for trade in spices, silks, and other goods. Elites everywhere prized Chinese porcelains and silks, while wealthy members of the Celestial Kingdom, as China called itself, wanted gold, ivory, and rhinoceros horn from Africa and exotic goods and peacocks from India. African people wanted textiles from India and cowrie shells from the Maldives in the Indian Ocean. Europeans craved Asian silks and spices, but they had few desirable goods to offer their trading partners.

By 1550 the European search for better access to Asian trade goods had led to a new overseas empire in the Indian Ocean and the accidental discovery of the Western Hemisphere. With this discovery South and North America were drawn into an international network of trade centers and political empires, which Europeans came to dominate. The era of globalization had begun, creating new political systems and forms of economic exchange as well as cultural assimilation, conversion, and resistance.

Nezahualpilli

At the time of the arrival of Europeans, Nezahualpilli was ruler of the city-state of Texcoco, the second-most-important city in the Aztec Empire after Tenochtitlan.

From *Codex Ixtlilxochitl*, 1582, pigment on European paper/Bibliothèque Nationale, Paris, France/De Agostini Picture Library/akg-images

CHAPTER PREVIEW

THE AFROEURASIAN TRADE WORLD
What was the Afroeurasian trade world prior to the era of European exploration?

THE EUROPEAN VOYAGES OF DISCOVERY
How and why did Europeans undertake ambitious voyages of expansion?

CONQUEST AND SETTLEMENT
What was the impact of Iberian conquest and settlement on the peoples and ecologies of the Americas?

THE ERA OF GLOBAL CONTACT
How was the era of global contact shaped by new commodities, commercial empires, and forced migrations?

CHANGING ATTITUDES AND BELIEFS
How did new encounters shape cultural attitudes and beliefs in Europe and the rest of the world?

The Afroeurasian Trade World

What was the Afroeurasian trade world prior to the era of European exploration?

The Afroeurasian trade world linked the products and people of Europe, Asia, and Africa in the fifteenth century. The West was a marginal player in this trading system. Nevertheless, wealthy Europeans were eager consumers of luxury goods from the East, which they received through Italian middlemen.

The Trade World of the Indian Ocean

The Indian Ocean was the center of the Afroeurasian trade world, serving as a crossroads for commercial and cultural exchanges between China, India, the Middle East, Africa, and Europe (Map 16.1). From the seventh through the fourteenth centuries, the volume of this trade steadily increased, declining only during the years of the Black Death.

Merchants congregated in a series of multicultural, cosmopolitan port cities strung around the Indian Ocean. Most of these cities had some form of autonomous self-government, and mutual self-interest largely limited violence and prevented attempts to monopolize trade. The most developed area of this commercial web was made up of the ports surrounding the South China Sea. In the fifteenth century the port of Malacca became a great commercial entrepôt (AHN-truh-poh), a trading center to which goods were shipped for storage while awaiting redistribution. To Malacca came porcelains, silks, and camphor (used in the manufacture of many medications) from China; pepper, cloves, nutmeg, and raw materials such as sandalwood from the Moluccas; sugar from the Philippines; and textiles, copper weapons, incense, dyes, and opium from India.

The Mongol emperors opened the doors of China to the West, encouraging Europeans like the Venetian trader and explorer Marco Polo to do business there. Marco Polo's tales of his travels from 1271 to 1295 and his encounter with the Great Khan fueled Western fantasies about the Orient. After the Mongols fell to the Ming Dynasty in 1368, China entered a period of agricultural and commercial expansion, population growth, and urbanization (see "Ming China" in Chapter 21). Historians agree that China had the most advanced economy in the world until at least the beginning of the eighteenth century.

China also took the lead in exploration, sending Admiral Zheng He's fleet as far west as Egypt. Each of his seven expeditions from 1405 to 1433 involved hundreds of ships and tens of thousands of men. The purpose of the voyages was primarily diplomatic, to enhance China's prestige and seek tribute-paying alliances. The high expense of the voyages in a period of renewed Mongol encroachment led to the abandonment of the maritime expeditions after the deaths of Zheng He and the emperor. China's turning away from external trade opened new opportunities for European states to expand their role in Asian trade.

Another center of Indian Ocean trade was India, the crucial link between the Persian Gulf and the Southeast Asian and East Asian trade networks. The subcontinent had ancient links with its neighbors to the northwest. Trade among ports bordering the Indian Ocean was revived in the Middle Ages by Arab merchants who circumnavigated India on their way to trade in the South China Sea. The inhabitants of India's Coromandel coast traditionally looked to Southeast Asia, where they had ancient trading and cultural ties. Hinduism and Buddhism arrived in Southeast Asia from India during late antiquity, and a brisk trade between Southeast Asian and Coromandel port cities persisted from that time until the arrival of the Portuguese in the sixteenth century. India itself was an important contributor of goods to the world trading system. Most of the world's pepper was grown in India, and Indian cotton and silk textiles were also highly prized.

Peoples and Cultures of the Indian Ocean

Indian Ocean trade connected peoples from the Malay Peninsula (the southern extremity of the Asian continent), India, China, and East Africa, among whom there was an enormous variety of languages, cultures, and religions. In spite of this diversity, certain sociocultural similarities linked these peoples, especially in Southeast Asia.

In comparison to India, China, or even Europe after the Black Death, Southeast Asia was sparsely populated. People were concentrated in port cities and in areas of intense rice cultivation. Another difference between Southeast Asia and India, China, and Europe was the higher status of women — their primary role in planting and harvesting rice gave them authority and economic power. At marriage, which typically occurred around age twenty, the groom paid the bride (or sometimes her family) a sum of money called **bride wealth**, which remained under her control. This practice was in sharp contrast to the Chinese, Indian, and European dowry, which came under the husband's control. Property was administered jointly, in contrast to the

---

bride wealth In early modern Southeast Asia, a sum of money the groom paid the bride or her family at the time of marriage. This practice contrasted with the dowry in China, India, and Europe, which the husband controlled.

MAP 16.1 The Fifteenth-Century Afroeurasian Trading World After a period of decline following the Black Death and the Mongol invasions, trade revived in the fifteenth century. Muslim merchants dominated trade, linking ports in East Africa and the Red Sea with those in India and the Malay Archipelago. The Chinese admiral Zheng He followed the most important Indian Ocean trade routes on his voyages (1405–1433), hoping to impose Ming dominance of trade and tribute.

Chinese principle and Indian practice that wives had no say in the disposal of family property. All children, regardless of gender, inherited equally.

Respect for women carried over to the commercial sphere. Women participated in business as partners and independent entrepreneurs. When Portuguese and Dutch men settled in the region and married local women, their wives continued to play important roles in trade and commerce.

In contrast to most parts of the world other than Africa, Southeast Asian peoples had an accepting attitude toward premarital sexual activity and placed no premium on virginity at marriage. Divorce carried no social stigma and was easily attainable if a pair proved incompatible. Either the woman or the man could initiate a divorce.

Trade with Africa and the Middle East

On the east coast of Africa, Swahili-speaking city-states engaged in the Indian Ocean trade, exchanging ivory, rhinoceros horn, tortoise shells, copra (dried coconut), and slaves for textiles, spices, cowrie shells, porcelain, and other goods. The most important cities were Mogadishu, Mombasa, and Kilwa, which had converted to Islam by the eleventh century.

West Africa also played an important role in world trade. In the fifteenth century most of the gold that reached Europe came from the Sudan region in West Africa. Transported across the Sahara by Arab and African traders on camels, the gold was sold in the ports of North Africa. Other trading routes led to the Egyptian cities of Alexandria and Cairo.

QVILOA

Island of Kilwa The small island of Kilwa, off the coast of modern-day Tanzania, was a vital center of Indian Ocean trade from the thirteenth to the fifteenth centuries. During this period, the sultanate of Kilwa controlled trade among the Swahili-speaking cities of the east coast of Africa; its merchants dealt in gold, silver, pearls, and porcelain. The arrival of the Portuguese in 1498 led to the loss of Kilwa's autonomy.
(Pictures from History/Bridgeman Images)

Inland nations that sat astride the north-south caravan routes grew wealthy from this trade. In the mid-thirteenth century the kingdom of Mali emerged as an important player on the overland trade route. In later centuries, however, the diversion of gold away from the trans-Sahara routes would weaken the inland states of Africa politically and economically.

Gold was one important object of trade; slaves were another. Long before the arrival of Europeans, Arab and African merchants took West African slaves to the Mediterranean to be sold in European, Egyptian, and Middle Eastern markets and also brought eastern Europeans to West Africa as slaves. In addition, Indian and Arab merchants traded slaves in the coastal regions of East Africa.

The Middle East served as an intermediary for trade between Europe, Africa, and Asia and was also an important supplier of goods for foreign exchange. Two great rival empires, the Persian Safavids and the Turkish Ottomans, dominated the region, competing for control over western trade routes to the East. By the mid-sixteenth century the Ottomans had established control over eastern Mediterranean sea routes to trading centers in Syria, Palestine, Egypt, and the rest of North Africa (see "The Expansion of the Ottoman Empire" in Chapter 17). Their power extended into Europe as far west as Vienna.

Mansa Musa This detail from the Catalan Atlas of 1375, a world map created for the Catalan king, depicts a king of Mali, Mansa Musa, who was legendary for his wealth in gold. European desires for direct access to the trade in sub-Saharan gold helped inspire Portuguese exploration of the west coast of Africa in the fifteenth century. (Bibliothèque Nationale, Paris, France/Bridgeman Images)

Genoese and Venetian Middlemen

Europe constituted a minor outpost in the world trading system, for European craftsmen produced few products to rival those of Asia. However, Europeans desired luxury goods from the East, and in the late Middle Ages such trade was controlled by the Italian city-states of Venice and Genoa. Venice had opened the gateway to Asian trade in 1304, when it established formal relations with the sultan of Mamluk Egypt and started operations in Cairo. Because demand for European goods was low, Venetians funded their purchases through shipping and trade in firearms and slaves.

Venice's ancient trading rival was Genoa. By 1270 Genoa dominated the northern route to Asia through the Black Sea. From then until the fourteenth century the Genoese expanded their trade routes as far as Persia and the Far East.

In the fifteenth century, with Venice claiming victory in the spice trade, the Genoese shifted focus from trade to finance and from the Black Sea to the western

Mediterranean. When Spanish and Portuguese voyages began to explore the western Atlantic (see "The European Voyages of Discovery"), Genoese merchants, navigators, and financiers provided their skills and capital to the Iberian monarchs.

A major element of Italian trade was slavery. Merchants purchased slaves in the Balkans of southeastern Europe. After the loss of the Black Sea trade routes—and thus the source of slaves—to the Ottomans, the Genoese sought new supplies of slaves in the West, eventually seizing or buying and selling the Guanches (indigenous peoples from the Canary Islands), Muslim prisoners and Jewish refugees from Spain, and, by the early 1500s, both black and Berber Africans. With the growth of Spanish colonies in the New World, Genoese and Venetian merchants became important players in the Atlantic slave trade.

The European Voyages of Discovery

How and why did Europeans undertake ambitious voyages of expansion?

As Europe recovered after the Black Death, new European players entered the scene with novel technology, eager to spread Christianity and to undo Italian and Ottoman domination of trade with the East. A century after the plague, Iberian explorers began overseas voyages that helped create the modern world, with immense consequences for their own continent and the rest of the planet.

Causes of European Expansion

European expansion had multiple causes. The first was economic. By the middle of the fifteenth century Europe was experiencing a revival of population and economic activity after the lows of the Black Death. This revival created renewed demand for luxuries, especially spices, from the East. Introduced into western Europe by the Crusaders in the twelfth century, spices such as pepper, nutmeg, cinnamon, and cloves added flavor and variety to the monotonous European diet. They were also used in anointing oil and as incense for religious rituals, and as perfumes, medicines, and dyes in daily life. The fall of Constantinople and the subsequent Ottoman control of trade routes created obstacles to fulfilling demands for these precious and prestigious goods. Europeans eager for the profits of trade thus needed to find new sources of precious metal to exchange with the Ottomans or trade routes that bypassed the Ottomans.

Religious fervor and the crusading spirit were the second important catalyst for expansion. Just seven months separated Isabella and Ferdinand's conquest of the emirate of Granada, the last remaining Muslim state on the Iberian Peninsula, and Columbus's departure across the Atlantic. Overseas exploration thus transferred the militaristic religious fervor of the reconquista (reconquest) to new non-Christian territories. As they conquered indigenous empires, Iberians brought the attitudes and administrative practices developed during the reconquista to the Americas.

A third motivation was the dynamic spirit of the Renaissance. Like other men of the Renaissance era, explorers sought to win glory for their exploits and demonstrated a genuine interest in learning more about unknown waters. The detailed journals kept by European voyagers attest to their fascination with the new peoples and places they visited.

The people who stayed at home had a powerful impact on the voyages of discovery. Merchants provided the capital for many early voyages and had a strong say in their course. To gain authorization and financial support for their expeditions, they sought official sponsorship from the Crown. Competition among European monarchs for the prestige and profit of overseas exploration thus constituted another crucial factor in encouraging the steady stream of expeditions that began in the late fifteenth century.

The small number of Europeans who could read provided a rapt audience for tales of fantastic places and unknown peoples. Cosmography, natural history, and geography aroused enormous interest among educated people in the fifteenth and sixteenth centuries. One of the most popular books of the time was the fourteenth-century text *The Travels of Sir John Mandeville*, which purported to be a firsthand account of the author's travels in the Middle East, India, and China.

Technology and the Rise of Exploration

The Iberian powers sought technological improvements in shipbuilding, weaponry, and navigation in order to undertake ambitious voyages of exploration and trade. Medieval European seagoing vessels consisted of open galleys propelled by oars, common in Mediterranean trade, or single-masted sailing ships. Though adequate for short journeys that hugged the shoreline, such vessels were incapable of long-distance journeys or high-volume trade. In the fifteenth century the Portuguese

developed the **caravel**, a three-masted sailing ship. Its multiple sails and sternpost rudder made the caravel a more maneuverable vessel that required fewer crewmen to operate. It could carry more cargo than a galley, which meant it could sail farther without stopping for supplies and return with a larger cache of profitable goods. When fitted with cannon, it could dominate larger vessels and bombard port cities.

This period also saw great strides in cartography and navigational aids. Around 1410 a Latin translation reintroduced western Europeans to **Ptolemy's Geography**. Written in the second century, the work synthesized the geographical knowledge of the classical world. It represented a major improvement over medieval cartography by depicting the world as round and introducing latitude and longitude markings, but it also contained significant errors. Unaware of the Americas, Ptolemy showed the world as much smaller than it is, so that Asia appeared not very far to the west of Europe.

Originating in China, the magnetic compass was brought to the West in the late Middle Ages. By using the compass to determine their direction and estimating their speed of travel over a set length of time, mariners could determine the course of a ship's voyage. The astrolabe, an instrument invented by the ancient Greeks and perfected by Muslim navigators, was used to determine the altitude of the sun and other celestial bodies. It allowed mariners to plot their latitude, that is, their precise position north or south of the equator.

Much of the new technology that Europeans used on their voyages was borrowed from the East. Gunpowder, the compass, and the sternpost rudder were Chinese inventions. The triangular lateen sail, which allowed caravels to tack against the wind, was a product of the Indian Ocean trade world. Advances in cartography and navigation also drew on the rich tradition of Judeo-Arabic mathematical and astronomical learning in Iberia. In exploring new territories, European sailors thus called on techniques and knowledge developed over centuries in China, the Muslim world, and trading centers along the Indian Ocean.

The Portuguese in Africa and Asia

For centuries Portugal was a small and poor nation on the margins of European life whose principal activities were fishing and subsistence farming. Yet Portugal had a long history of seafaring and navigation. Nature favored the Portuguese: winds blowing along their coast offered passage to Africa, its Atlantic islands, and, ultimately, Brazil. Once they had mastered the secret to sailing against the wind to return to Europe (by sailing farther west to catch winds from the southwest), they were poised to lead Atlantic exploration. The objectives

---

caravel A small, maneuverable, three-masted sailing ship developed by the Portuguese in the fifteenth century that gave the Portuguese a distinct advantage in exploration and trade.

Ptolemy's Geography A second-century work translated into Latin around 1410 that synthesized the classical knowledge of geography and introduced latitude and longitude markings.

of Portuguese exploration included achieving military glory; converting Muslims; and finding gold, slaves, and an overseas route to Asian spice markets.

In the early phases of Portuguese exploration, Prince Henry (1394–1460), a younger son of the king, played a leading role. A nineteenth-century scholar dubbed Henry "the Navigator" because of his support for Portuguese voyages of discovery. Henry participated in Portugal's conquest of Ceuta (sa-OO-tah), an Arab city in northern Morocco, in 1415, an event that marked the beginning of European overseas expansion. In the 1420s, under Henry's direction, the Portuguese began to settle the Atlantic islands of Madeira (ca. 1420) and the Azores (1427). In 1443 they founded their first Afri-

can commercial settlement at Arguin in North Africa. By the time of Henry's death in 1460, his support for exploration had resulted in thriving sugar plantations on the Atlantic islands, the first arrival of enslaved Africans in Portugal, and new access to African gold.

The Portuguese next established fortified trading posts, called factories, on the gold-rich Guinea coast and penetrated into the African continent all the way to Timbuktu (Map 16.2). By 1500 Portugal controlled the flow of African gold to Europe. In contrast to the Spanish who conquered the Americas (see "Spanish Conquest of the Aztec and Inca Empires"), the Portuguese did not establish large settlements in West Africa or seek to control the political or cultural lives of those

The Portuguese Fleet Embarked for the Indies This image shows a Portuguese trading fleet in the late fifteenth century bound for the riches of the Indies. Between 1500 and 1635 over nine hundred ships sailed from Portugal to ports on the Indian Ocean in annual fleets composed of five to ten ships. Portuguese sailors used astrolabes, such as the one pictured here, to accurately plot their position. (fleet: Erich Lessing/Art Resource, NY; astrolabe: © The Trustees of the British Museum/Art Resource, NY)

MAPPING THE PAST

MAP 16.2 Overseas Exploration and Conquest in the Fifteenth and Sixteenth Centuries The voyages of discovery marked a dramatic new phase in the centuries-old migrations of European peoples. This map depicts the voyages of the most significant European explorers of the period.

ANALYZING THE MAP Consider the routes and dates of the voyages shown. How might the successes of the earlier voyages have contributed to the later expeditions? Which voyage had the most impact, and why?

CONNECTIONS Do you think the importance of these voyages was primarily economic, political, or cultural? Why?

with whom they traded. Instead they sought to profit by inserting themselves into existing trading systems. For the first century of their relations, African rulers were equal partners with the Portuguese, benefiting from their experienced armies and European vulnerability to tropical diseases.

In 1487 Bartholomew Diaz (ca. 1451–1500) rounded the Cape of Good Hope at the southern tip of Africa (see Map 16.2), but poor conditions forced him to turn back. A decade later Vasco da Gama (ca. 1469–1524) succeeded in rounding the Cape while commanding a fleet in search of a sea route to India. With the help of an Indian guide, da Gama reached the port of Calicut in India. He returned to Lisbon with spices and samples of Indian cloth, having proved the possibility of lucrative trade with the East via the Cape route. Thereafter, a Portuguese convoy set out for passage around the Cape every March.

Lisbon became the entrance port for Asian goods into Europe, but this was not accomplished without a fight. Muslim-controlled port city-states had long controlled the rich trade of the Indian Ocean, and they did not surrender it willingly. From 1500 to 1515 the Portuguese used a combination of bombardment and diplomatic treaties to establish trading factories at Goa, Malacca, Calicut, and Hormuz, thereby laying the foundation for a Portuguese trading empire. The acquisition of port cities and their trade routes brought riches to Portugal, but, as in Africa, the Portuguese

had limited impact on the lives and religious faith of peoples beyond Portuguese coastal holdings.

Inspired by the Portuguese, the Spanish had also begun the quest for empire. Theirs was to be a second, entirely different mode of colonization, leading to the conquest of existing empires, large-scale settlement, and the forced assimilation of huge indigenous populations.

Spain's Voyages to the Americas

Christopher Columbus was not the first to cross the Atlantic. Ninth-century Vikings established short-lived settlements in Newfoundland, and it is probable that others made the voyage, either on purpose or accidentally, carried by westward currents off the coast of Africa. In the late fifteenth century the achievements of Portugal's decades of exploration made the moment

Ptolemy's *Geography* The recovery of Ptolemy's *Geography* in the early fifteenth century gave Europeans new access to ancient geographical knowledge. This 1486 world map is a great advance over medieval maps but contains errors with significant consequences for future exploration. It shows a single continent watered by a single ocean, with land covering three-quarters of the world's surface. Africa and Asia are joined with Europe, making the Indian Ocean a landlocked sea and rendering the circumnavigation of Africa impossible. Australia and the Americas are nonexistent, and the continent of Asia is stretched far to the east, greatly shortening the distance from Europe to Asia via the Atlantic. (Bibliothèque Nationale, Paris, France/Bridgeman Images)

Columbus Describes His First Voyage

On his return voyage to Spain in February 1493, Christopher Columbus composed a letter intended for wide circulation and had copies of it sent ahead to Isabella, Ferdinand, and others when his ship docked at Lisbon. Because the letter sums up Columbus's understanding of his achievements, it is considered the most important document of his first voyage.

■ Since I know that you will be pleased at the great success with which the Lord has crowned my voyage, I write to inform you how in thirty-three days I crossed from the Canary Islands to the Indies, with the fleet which our most illustrious sovereigns gave me. I found very many islands with large populations and took possession of them all for their Highnesses; this I did by proclamation and unfurled the royal standard. No opposition was offered.

I named the first island that I found "San Salvador," in honour of our Lord and Saviour who has granted me this miracle. . . . When I reached Cuba, I followed its north coast westwards, and found it so extensive that I thought this must be the mainland, the province of Cathay.* . . . From there I saw another island eighteen leagues eastwards which I then named "Hispaniola."† . . .

Hispaniola is a wonder. The mountains and hills, the plains and meadow lands are both fertile and beautiful. They are most suitable for planting crops and for raising cattle of all kinds, and there are good sites for building towns and villages. The harbours are incredibly fine and there are many great rivers with broad channels and the majority contain gold.‡ The trees, fruits and plants are very different from those of Cuba. In Hispaniola there are many spices and large mines of gold and other metals.§ . . .

The inhabitants of this island, and all the rest that I discovered or heard of, go naked, as their mothers bore them, men and women alike. A few of the women, however, cover a single place with a leaf of a plant or piece of cotton which they weave for the purpose. They have no iron or steel or arms and are not capable of using them, not because they are not strong and well built but because they are amazingly timid. All the weapons they have are canes cut at seeding time, at the end of which they fix a sharpened stick, but they have not the courage to make use of these, for very often when I have sent two or three men to a village to have conversation with them a great number of them have come out. But as soon as they saw my men all fled immediately, a father not even waiting for his son. And this is not because we have harmed any of them; on the contrary, wherever I have gone and been able to have conversation with them, I have given them some of the various things I had, a cloth and other articles, and received nothing in exchange. But they have still remained incurably timid. True, when they have been reassured and lost their fear, they are so ingenuous and so liberal with all their possessions that no one who has not seen them would believe it. If one asks for anything they have they never say no. On the contrary, they offer a share to anyone with demonstrations of heartfelt affection, and they are immediately content with any small thing, valuable or valueless, that is given them. I forbade the men to give them bits of broken crockery, fragments of glass or tags of laces, though if they could get them they fancied them the finest jewels in the world.

I hoped to win them to the love and service of their Highnesses and of the whole Spanish nation and to persuade them to collect and give us of the things which they possessed in abundance and which we needed. They have no religion and are not idolaters; but all believe that power and goodness dwell in the sky and they are firmly convinced that I have come from the sky with these ships and people. In this belief

right for Christopher Columbus's attempt to find a westward route across the Atlantic to Asia.

Christopher Columbus, a native of Genoa, was an experienced seaman and navigator. He had worked as a mapmaker in Lisbon and had spent time on Madeira. He was familiar with such fifteenth-century Portuguese navigational aids as *portolans*—written descriptions of the courses along which ships sailed—and the use of the compass as a navigational instrument.

Columbus was also a deeply religious man. He had witnessed the Spanish conquest of Granada and shared fully in the religious fervor surrounding that event. Like the Spanish rulers and most Europeans of his age, Columbus understood Christianity as a missionary religion that should be carried to all places of the earth.

Rejected for funding by the Portuguese in 1483 and by Ferdinand and Isabella in 1486, Columbus finally won the support of the Spanish monarchy in 1492. Buoyed by the success of the reconquista and eager to earn profits from trade, the Spanish crown agreed to make him viceroy over any territory he might discover and to give him one-tenth of the material rewards of the journey.

Columbus and his small fleet left Spain on August 3, 1492. Columbus dreamed of reaching the court of they gave me a good reception everywhere, once they had overcome their fear; and this is not because they are stupid—far from it, they are men of great intelligence, for they navigate all those seas, and give a marvellously good account of everything—but because they have never before seen men clothed or ships like these. . . .

In all these islands the men are seemingly content with one woman, but their chief or king is allowed more than twenty. The women appear to work more than the men and I have not been able to find out if they have private property. As far as I could see whatever a man had was shared among all the rest and this particularly applies to food. . . . In another island, which I am told is larger than Hispaniola, the people have no hair. Here there is a vast quantity of gold, and from here and the other islands I bring Indians as evidence.

In conclusion, to speak only of the results of this very hasty voyage, their Highnesses can see that I will give them as much gold as they require, if they will render me some very slight assistance; also I will give them all the spices and cotton they want. . . . I will also bring them as much aloes as they ask and as many slaves, who will be taken from the idolaters. I believe also that I have found rhubarb and cinnamon and there will be countless other things in addition. . . .

So all Christendom will be delighted that our Redeemer has given victory to our most illustrious King and Queen and their renowned kingdoms, in this great matter. They should hold great celebrations and render solemn thanks to the Holy Trinity with many solemn prayers, for the great triumph which they will have, by the conversion of so many peoples to our holy faith and for the temporal benefits which will follow, for not only Spain, but all Christendom will receive encouragement and profit.

This is a brief account of the facts.

Written in the caravel off the Canary Islands.**

15 February 1493

At your orders
THE ADMIRAL

QUESTIONS FOR ANALYSIS

1. How did Columbus explain the success of his voyage?
2. What was Columbus's view of the Native Americans he met?
3. Evaluate Columbus's statements that the Caribbean islands possessed gold, cotton, and spices.
4. Why did Columbus cling to the idea that he had reached Asia?

Source: J. M. Cohen, ed. and trans., *The Four Voyages of Christopher Columbus* (Penguin Classics, 1969), pp. 115–123. Copyright © J. M. Cohen, 1969, London. Used by permission of Penguin Books Ltd.

*Cathay is the old name for China. In the logbook and later in this letter Columbus accepts the natives' story that Cuba is an island that they can circumnavigate in something more than twenty-one days, yet he insists here and during the second voyage that it is in fact part of the Asiatic mainland.

†Hispaniola is the second-largest island of the West Indies; Haiti occupies the western third of the island, the Dominican Republic the rest.

‡This did not prove to be true.

§These statements are also inaccurate.

**Actually, Columbus was off Santa Maria in the Azores.

the Mongol emperor, the Great Khan, not realizing that the Ming Dynasty had overthrown the Mongols in 1368. Based on Ptolemy's *Geography* and other texts, he expected to pass the islands of Japan and then land on the east coast of China.

On October 12 Columbus landed in the Bahamas, which he christened San Salvador and claimed for the Spanish crown. In a letter he wrote to Ferdinand and Isabella on his return to Spain, Columbus described the natives as handsome, peaceful, and primitive. Believing he was somewhere off the east coast of Japan, in what he considered the Indies, he called them "Indi-ans," a name that was later applied to all inhabitants of the Americas. Columbus concluded that they would make good slaves and could quickly be converted to Christianity. (See "Analyzing the Evidence: Columbus Describes His First Voyage," above.)

Scholars have identified the inhabitants of the islands as the Taino (TIGH-noh) people. From San Salvador, Columbus sailed southwest, landing on Cuba on October 28. Deciding that he must be on the mainland of China near the coastal city of Quinsay (now Hangzhou), he sent a small embassy inland with letters from Ferdinand and Isabella and instructions to

Columbus's First Voyage to the New World, 1492–1493

locate the city. Although they found no large settlement, the sight of Taino people wearing gold ornaments on Hispaniola suggested that gold was available in the region. In January, confident that its source would soon be found, he headed back to Spain to report on his discovery.

On his second voyage, Columbus took control of the island of Hispaniola and enslaved its indigenous peoples. On this and subsequent voyages, he brought with him settlers for the new Spanish territories, along with agricultural seed and livestock. Columbus himself, however, had limited skills in governing. Revolt soon broke out against him and his brother on Hispaniola. A royal expedition sent to investigate returned the brothers to Spain in chains, and a royal governor assumed control of the colony.

Spain "Discovers" the Pacific

Columbus never realized the scope of his achievement: that he had found a vast continent unknown to Europeans, except for the fleeting Viking presence centuries earlier. The Florentine navigator Amerigo Vespucci (veh-SPOO-chee) (1454–1512) realized what Columbus had not. Writing about his discoveries on the coast of modern-day Venezuela, Vespucci stated: "Those new regions which we found and explored with the fleet . . . we may rightly call a New World." This letter was the first document to describe America as a continent separate from Asia. In recognition of Amerigo's bold claim, the continent was named for him.

To settle competing claims to the Atlantic discoveries, Spain and Portugal turned to Pope Alexander VI. The resulting **Treaty of Tordesillas** (tawr-duh-SEE-yuhs) in 1494 gave Spain everything to the west of an imaginary line drawn down the Atlantic and Portugal everything to the east.

The search for profits determined the direction of Spanish exploration. Because its profits from Hispaniola and other Caribbean islands were insignificant compared to Portugal's enormous riches from the Asian spice trade, Spain renewed the search for a western passage to Asia. In 1519 Charles I of Spain (who was also Holy Roman emperor Charles V) commissioned

Ferdinand Magellan (1480–1521) to find a direct sea route to Asia. Magellan sailed southwest across the Atlantic to Brazil, and after a long search along the coast he located the strait off the southern tip of South America that now bears his name (see Map 16.2). After passing through the strait into the Pacific Ocean in 1520, his fleet sailed north up the west coast of South America and then headed west into the Pacific.

Terrible storms, disease, starvation, and violence devastated the expedition. Magellan himself was killed in a skirmish in the Malay Archipelago, and only one of the five ships that began the expedition made it back to Spain. This ship returned home in 1522 with only eighteen men aboard, having traveled from the east by way of the Indian Ocean, the Cape of Good Hope, and the Atlantic. The voyage—the first to circumnavigate the globe—had taken close to three years.

Despite the losses, this voyage revolutionized Europeans' understanding of the world by demonstrating the vastness of the Pacific. The earth was clearly much larger than Ptolemy's map had shown. Magellan's expedition also forced Spain's rulers to rethink their plans for overseas commerce and territorial expansion. The westward passage to the Indies was too long and dangerous for commercial purposes. Thus Spain soon abandoned the attempt to oust Portugal from the Eastern spice trade and concentrated on exploiting its New World territories.

Early Exploration by Northern European Powers

Spain's northern European rivals also set sail across the Atlantic during the early days of exploration, searching for a northwest passage to the Indies. In 1497 John Cabot (ca. 1450–1499), a Genoese merchant living in London, landed on Newfoundland. The next year he returned and explored the New England coast. These forays proved futile, and at that time the English established no permanent colonies in the territories they explored.

News of the riches of Mexico and Peru later inspired the English to renew their efforts, this time in the extreme north. Between 1576 and 1578 Martin Frobisher (ca. 1535–1594) made three voyages in and around the Canadian bay that now bears his name. Frobisher brought a quantity of ore back to England, but it proved to be worthless.

Early French exploration of the Atlantic was equally frustrating. Between 1534 and 1541 Frenchman Jacques Cartier (1491–1557) made several voyages and explored the St. Lawrence River of Canada, searching for a passage to the wealth of Asia. When this hope proved vain, the French turned to a new source of profit within Canada itself: trade in beavers and other furs.

Treaty of Tordesillas The 1494 agreement giving Spain everything west of an imaginary line drawn down the Atlantic and giving Portugal everything to the east.

As had the Portuguese in Asia, French traders bartered with local peoples whom they largely treated as autonomous and equal partners. French fishermen also competed with the Spanish and English for the schools of cod they found in the Atlantic waters around Newfoundland.

Conquest and Settlement

What was the impact of Iberian conquest and settlement on the peoples and ecologies of the Americas?

Before Columbus's arrival, the Americas were inhabited by thousands of groups of indigenous peoples with distinct languages and cultures. These groups ranged from hunter-gatherer tribes organized into tribal confederations to settled agriculturalists to large-scale empires containing bustling cities and towns. The best estimate is that the peoples of the Americas numbered between 50 and 60 million in 1492. These numbers were decimated, and the lives of survivors radically altered, by the arrival of Europeans.

Spanish Conquest of the Aztec and Inca Empires

The first two decades after Columbus's arrival in the New World saw Spanish settlement of Hispaniola, Cuba, Puerto Rico, and other Caribbean islands. Based on rumors of a wealthy mainland civilization, the Spanish governor in Cuba sponsored expeditions to the

The Aztec Capital of Tenochtitlan This woodcut map was published in 1524 along with Cortés's letters describing the conquest of the Aztecs. As it shows, Tenochtitlan occupied an island and was laid out in concentric circles. The administrative and religious buildings were at the heart of the city, which was surrounded by residential quarters. Cortés himself marveled at the city in his letters: "The city is as large as Seville or Cordoba. . . . There are bridges, very large, strong, and well constructed, so that, over many, ten horsemen can ride abreast. . . . The city has many squares where markets are held. . . . There is one square . . . where there are daily more than sixty thousand souls, buying and selling. In the service and manners of its people, their fashion of living was almost the same as in Spain, with just as much harmony and order." (Newberry Library, Chicago/Bridgeman Images)

Yucatán coast of the Gulf of Mexico, including one in 1519 under the command of the **conquistador** (kahn-KEES-tuh-dawr) Hernán Cortés (1485–1547). *Conquistador* was Spanish for "conqueror," a Spanish soldier-explorer who sought to conquer the New World for the Spanish crown. Alarmed by Cortés's ambition, the governor withdrew his support, but Cortés quickly set sail before being removed from command. Cortés and his party landed on the Mexican coast on April 21, 1519. His camp soon received visits by delegations of Aztec leaders bearing gifts and news of their great emperor.

The **Aztec Empire**, an alliance between the Mexica people and their conquered allies, had risen rapidly in size and power over the fifteenth century. At the time of the Spanish arrival, the empire was ruled by Moctezuma II (r. 1502–1520), from his capital at Tenochtitlan (tay-nawch-TEET-lahn), now Mexico City. The Aztecs were a sophisticated society and culture, with advanced mathematics, astronomy, and engineering. As in European nations at the time, a hereditary nobility dominated the army, the priesthood, and the state bureaucracy and reaped the gains from the agricultural labor of the common people.

Within weeks of his arrival, Cortés acquired translators who provided vital information on the empire and its weaknesses. (See "Thinking Like a Historian: Who Was Doña Marina?" page 452.) Through his interpreters, Cortés learned of strong local resentment against the Aztec Empire. The Aztec state practiced brutal warfare against neighboring peoples to secure captives for religious sacrifices and laborers for agricultural and building projects. Once conquered, subject tribes paid continual tribute to the empire through their local chiefs. Realizing that he could exploit dissensions within the empire to his own advantage, Cortés forged an alliance with Tlaxcala (tlah-SKAH-lah), a subject kingdom of the Aztecs. In

October a combined Spanish-Tlaxcalan force occupied the Aztec city of Cholula, the second largest in the empire, and massacred thousands of inhabitants. Strengthened by this victory, Cortés formed alliances with other native kingdoms. In November 1519, with a few hundred Spanish men and some six thousand indigenous warriors, he marched on Tenochtitlan.

Unlike other native leaders, Moctezuma refrained from attacking the Spaniards and instead welcomed Cortés and his men into Tenochtitlan. Moctezuma was apparently deeply impressed by Spanish victories and believed the Spanish were invincible. When Cortés took Moctezuma hostage, the emperor's influence crumbled. During the ensuing attacks and counterattacks, Moctezuma was killed. The Spaniards and their allies escaped from the city suffering heavy losses. Cortés quickly began gathering forces and making new alliances against the Aztecs. In May 1521 he led a second assault on Tenochtitlan, leading an army of approximately one thousand Spanish and seventy-five thousand native warriors.[1]

The Spanish victory in late summer 1521 was hard-won and was greatly aided by the effects of smallpox, which had devastated the besieged population of the city. After establishing a new capital in the ruins of Tenochtitlan, Cortés and other conquistadors began the systematic conquest of Mexico, a decades-long and brutal process.

More remarkable than the defeat of the Aztecs was the fall of the remote **Inca Empire** in Peru. Living in a settlement perched more than 9,800 feet above sea level, the Incas were isolated from the Mesoamerican civilization of the Aztecs. Like the Mexica, the Incas had created a polity that rivaled that of the Europeans in population and complexity and that had reached its height in the fifteenth century. The Incas' strength lay largely in their bureaucratic efficiency. Ruled from the capital city of Cuzco, the empire was divided into four major regions, each region into provinces, and each province into districts. Officials at each level used the extensive network of roads to transmit information and orders. While the Aztecs used a system of glyphs for writing, the Incas had devised a complex system of colored and knotted cords, called khipus, for administrative bookkeeping.

By the time of the Spanish invasion, however, the Inca Empire had been weakened by a civil war over succession and an epidemic of disease, probably smallpox, spread through trade with groups in contact with Europeans. The Spanish conquistador Francisco Pizarro (ca. 1475–1541) landed on the northern coast

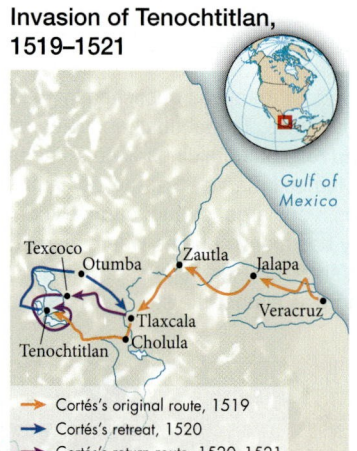

Invasion of Tenochtitlan, 1519–1521

Texcoco
Otumba
Zautla
Jalapa
Veracruz
Gulf of Mexico
Tlaxcala
Cholula
Tenochtitlan

→ Cortés's original route, 1519
→ Cortés's retreat, 1520
→ Cortés's return route, 1520–1521

conquistador Spanish for "conqueror"; a Spanish soldier-explorer, such as Hernán Cortés or Francisco Pizarro, who sought to conquer the New World for the Spanish crown.

Aztec Empire An alliance between the Mexica people and their conquered allies, with its capital in Tenochtitlan (now Mexico City), that rose in size and power in the fifteenth century and possessed a sophisticated society and culture, with advanced mathematics, astronomy, and engineering.

Inca Empire The vast and sophisticated Peruvian empire centered at the capital city of Cuzco that was at its peak in the fifteenth century but weakened by civil war at the time of the Spanish arrival.

of Peru on May 13, 1532, the very day the Inca leader Atahualpa (ah-tuh-WAHL-puh) won control of the empire. As Pizarro advanced across the Andes toward Cuzco (KOOS-ko), the capital of the Inca Empire, Atahualpa was also heading there for his coronation.

Like Moctezuma in Mexico, Atahualpa sent envoys to greet the Spanish. Motivated by curiosity about the Spanish, he intended to meet with them to learn more about them and their intentions. Instead the Spaniards ambushed and captured him, extorted an enormous ransom in gold, and then executed him on trumped-up charges in 1533. The Spanish then marched on to Cuzco, profiting, as with the Aztecs, from internal conflicts and forming alliances with local peoples. When Cuzco fell in 1533, the Spanish plundered immense riches in gold and silver.

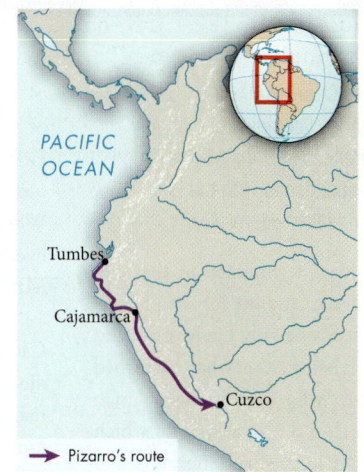

The Conquest of Peru, 1532–1533

How was it possible for several hundred Spanish conquistadors to defeat powerful empires commanding large armies, vast wealth, and millions of inhabitants? Historians seeking answers to this question have emphasized a combination of factors: the military superiority provided by Spanish gunpowder, steel swords, and horses; divisions within the Aztec and Inca Empires, which produced many native allies and interpreters for the Spanish; and, most important, the devastating impact of contagious diseases among the indigenous population. Ironically, the well-organized, urban-based Aztec and Inca Empires were more vulnerable to wholesale takeover than were more decentralized and fragmented groups like the Maya in the Yucatán peninsula, whose independence was not wholly crushed until the end of the seventeenth century.

Portuguese Brazil

Unlike Mesoamerica or the Andes, the territory of Brazil contained no urban empires but instead had roughly 2.5 million nomadic and settled people divided into small tribes and many different language groups. In 1500 the Portuguese crown named Pedro Álvares Cabral commander of a fleet headed for the spice trade of the Indies. En route, the fleet sailed far to the west, claiming the coast where they accidentally landed for Portugal under the terms of the Treaty of Tordesillas. The Portuguese soon undertook a profitable trade with local people in brazilwood, a valued source of red dye, which inspired the name of the new colony.

In the 1520s Portuguese settlers brought sugarcane production to Brazil. They initially used enslaved indigenous laborers on sugar plantations, but the rapid decline in the indigenous population soon led to the use of forcibly transported Africans. In Brazil the Portuguese thus created a new form of colonization in the Americas: large plantations worked by enslaved people. This model of slave-worked sugar plantations would spread throughout the Caribbean in the seventeenth century.

Colonial Administration

By the end of the sixteenth century the Spanish and Portuguese had successfully overcome most indigenous groups and expanded their territory throughout modern-day Mexico, the southwestern United States, and Central and South America. In Mesoamerica and

Inca Women Milking Cows This illustration of Inca women milking cows is from a collection of illustrations by a Spanish bishop that offers a valuable view of life in Peru in the 1780s. (Palacio Real, Madrid, Spain/Photo: Albers Foundation/ Art Resource, NY)

Who Was Doña Marina?

In April 1519 Doña Marina was among twenty women given to the Spanish as slaves. Fluent in Nahuatl and Yucatec Maya (spoken by a Spanish priest accompanying Cortés), she acted as an interpreter and diplomatic guide for the Spanish. She had a close relationship with Cortés and bore his son, Don Martín Cortés, in 1522. Although no writings by Doña Marina survive, she figures prominently in both Spanish and indigenous sources on the conquest.

1 Cortés's letter to Charles I, 1522. This letter to Charles I contains one of only two written references to Doña Marina found in Cortés's correspondence with the king. He describes her as his "interpreter."

■ During the three days I remained in that city they fed us worse each day, and the lords and principal persons of the city came only rarely to see and speak with me. And being somewhat disturbed by this, my interpreter, who is an Indian woman from Putunchan, which is the great river of which I spoke to Your Majesty in the first letter, was told by another Indian woman and a native of this city that very close by many of Mutezuma's men were gathered, and that the people of the city had sent away their women and children and all their belongings, and were about to fall on us and kill us all; and that if she wished to escape she should go with her and she would shelter her. All this she told to Gerónimo de Aguilar, an interpreter whom I acquired in Yucatán, of whom I have also written to Your Highness; and he informed me.

2 Díaz's account of the conquest of the Aztecs. Bernal Díaz del Castillo participated in the conquest of the Aztecs alongside Cortés. His historical account of the conquest, written much later in life, provides the lengthiest descriptions of Doña Marina.

■ Early the next morning many Caciques and chiefs of Tabasco and the neighbouring towns arrived and paid great respect to us all, and they brought a present of gold,...and some other things of little value....This present, however, was worth nothing in comparison with the twenty women that were given us, among them one very excellent woman called Doña Marina, for so she was named when she became a Christian.

...Cortés allotted one of the women to each of his captains and Doña Marina, as she was good looking and intelligent and without embarrassment, he gave to Alonzo Hernández Puertocarrero. When Puertocarrero went to Spain, Doña Marina lived with Cortés, and bore him a son named Don Martin Cortés.

...Her father and mother were chiefs and Caciques of a town called Paynala....Her father died while she was still a little child, and her mother married another Cacique, a young man, and bore him a son. It seems that the father and mother had a great affection for this son and it was agreed between them that he should succeed to their honours when their days were done. So that there should be no impediment to this, they gave the little girl, Doña Marina, to some Indians from Xicalango, and this they did by night so as to escape observation, and they then spread the report that she had died, and as it happened at this time that a child of one of their Indian slaves died they gave out that it was their daughter and the heiress who was dead.

The Indians of Xicalango gave the child to the people of Tabasco and the Tabasco people gave her to Cortés.

...As Doña Marina proved herself such an excellent woman and good interpreter throughout the wars in New Spain, Tlaxcala and Mexico (as I shall show later on) Cortés always took her with him, and during that expedition she was married to a gentleman named Juan Jaramillo at the town of Orizaba.

Doña Marina was a person of the greatest importance and was obeyed without question by the Indians throughout New Spain.

Marina...said that God had been very gracious to her in freeing her from the worship of idols and making her a Christian, and letting her bear a son to her lord and master Cortés and in marrying

ANALYZING THE EVIDENCE

1. How would you compare the attitudes toward Doña Marina displayed in Cortés's letter to the Spanish crown (Source 1) and Díaz's account of the conquest (Source 2)? Why would Cortés downplay his reliance on Doña Marina in correspondence with the Spanish king?
2. What skills and experience enabled Doña Marina to act as an intermediary between the Spanish and the Aztecs? Based on the evidence, what role did she play in interactions between the Spanish and the Aztecs?
3. According to Díaz (Source 2), how did Doña Marina feel about her relationship with Cortés and the Spanish? How do you interpret this passage? Is there any evidence in the other sources that supports or undermines the sentiments he attributed to her?
4. Based on the evidence of these sources, what role did indigenous women play in relations between Spanish and Aztec men? How exceptional was Doña Marina?

(Granger, NYC—All rights reserved)

3 **Doña Marina translating for Hernán Cortés during his meeting with Moctezuma.** This image was created by Tlaxcalan artists shortly after the conquest of Mexico and represents one indigenous perspective on the events.

her to such a gentleman as Juan Jaramillo, who was now her husband. That she would rather serve her husband and Cortés than anything else in the world, and would not exchange her place to be Cacica of all the provinces in New Spain.

Doña Marina knew the language of Coatzacoalcos, which is that common to Mexico, and she knew the language of Tabasco, as did also Jerónimo de Aguilar, who spoke the language of Yucatan and Tabasco, which is one and the same. So that these two could understand one another clearly, and Aguilar translated into Castilian for Cortés.

This was the great beginning of our conquests and thus, thanks be to God, things prospered with us. I have made a point of explaining this matter, because without the help of Doña Marina we could not have understood the language of New Spain and Mexico.

4 **The *Florentine Codex*.** In the decades following the conquest, a Franciscan monk, Bernardino de Sahagún, worked with indigenous partners to compile a history of Aztec society. Known today as the *Florentine Codex*, it contains images and text written in both Nahuatl and Spanish. The following excerpt describes the entry of the victorious Spanish into Tenochtitlan.

■ Next they went to Motecuhzoma's storehouse, in the place called Totocalco, where his personal treasures were kept. The Spaniards grinned like little beasts and patted each other with delight.

When they entered the hall of treasures, it was as if they had arrived in Paradise. They searched everywhere and coveted everything; they were slaves to their own greed. . . .

They seized these treasures as they were their own, as if this plunder were merely a stroke of good luck. And when they had taken all the gold, they heaped up everything else in the middle of the patio.

La Malinche [Doña Marina] called all the nobles together. She climbed up to the palace roof and cried: "Mexicanos, come forward! The Spaniards need your help! Bring them food and pure water. They are tired and hungry; they are almost fainting from exhaustion! Why do you not come forward? Are you angry with them?"

The Mexicas were too frightened to approach. They were crushed by terror and would not risk coming forward. They shied away as if the Spaniards were wild beasts, as if the hour were midnight on the blackest night of the year. Yet they did not abandon the Spaniards to hunger and thirst. They brought them whatever they needed, but shook with fear as they did so. They delivered the supplies to the Spaniards with trembling hands, then turned and hurried away.

PUTTING IT ALL TOGETHER

Using the sources above, along with what you have learned in class and in this chapter, imagine the events and experiences described in these sources from Doña Marina's point of view. Reflect on the various aspects of Doña Marina described in the sources — betrayed daughter, slave, concubine, mother, wife, interpreter, and commander — and write an essay that uses her experience to explore the interaction among Spanish, Aztec, and other indigenous groups during the conquest period.

Sources: (1) Hernán Cortés to Emperor Carlos V, 1522, in *Hernán Cortés: Letters from Mexico*, trans. and ed. Anthony Pagden (New Haven: Yale University Press, 1986), pp. 72–74; (2) Bernal Díaz del Castillo, *The Discovery and Conquest of Mexico, 1517–1521*, trans. A. P. Maudslay (New York: Noonday Press, 1965), pp. 62–63, 64, 66–67; (4) Miguel León-Portilla, ed., *The Broken Spears: The Aztec Account of the Conquest of Mexico*, pp. 68–69. Copyright © 1962, 1990 by Miguel León-Portilla. Expanded and Updated Edition © 1992 by Miguel León-Portilla. Reprinted by permission of Beacon Press, Boston.

the Andes, the Spanish had taken over the cities and tribute systems of the Aztecs and the Incas, basing their control on the prior existence of well-established polities with organized tribute systems.

While early conquest and settlement were conducted largely by private initiatives, the Spanish and Portuguese governments soon assumed more direct control. In 1503 the Spanish granted the port of Seville a monopoly over all traffic to the New World and established the House of Trade to oversee economic matters. In 1523 Spain created the Royal and Supreme Council of the Indies, with authority over all colonial affairs subject to approval by the king. Spanish territories themselves were divided initially into two **viceroyalties**, or administrative divisions: New Spain, created in 1535; and Peru, created in 1542. In the eighteenth century two new viceroyalties, New Granada and La Plata, were created (see Map 16.2).

Within each territory, the viceroy, or imperial governor, exercised broad military and civil authority. The viceroy presided over the *audiencia* (ow-dee-EHN-see-ah), a board of judges that served as his advisory council and the highest judicial body. As in Spain, settlement in the Americas was centered on cities and towns. In each city, the municipal council, or *cabildo*, exercised local authority. Women were denied participation in public life, a familiar pattern from both Spain and precolonial indigenous society.

Portugal adopted similar patterns of rule, with India House in Lisbon functioning much like the Spanish House of Trade and royal representatives overseeing Portuguese possessions in West Africa and Asia. To secure the vast expanse of Brazil, in the 1530s the Portuguese implemented a distinctive system of rule, called **captaincies**, hereditary grants of land given to nobles and loyal officials who bore the costs of settling and administering their territories. Over time, the Crown secured greater power over the captaincies, appointing royal governors to act as administrators. The captaincy of Bahia was the site of the capital, Salvador, home to the governor general and other royal officials.

The Catholic Church played an integral role in Iberian rule. The papacy allowed Portuguese and Spanish officials greater control over the church than was the case at home, allowing them to appoint clerics and collect tithes. This control allowed colonial powers to use the church as an instrument to indoctrinate indigenous people (see "Religious Conversion").

Indigenous Population Loss and Economic Exploitation

From the time of Christopher Columbus in Hispaniola, the Spanish made use of the **encomienda system** to profit from the peoples and territories they encountered in the Americas. This system was a legacy of the methods used to reward military leaders in the time of the reconquista. First in the Caribbean and then on the mainland, conquistadors granted their followers the right to forcibly employ groups of indigenous people as laborers and to demand tribute payments from them in exchange for providing food, shelter, and instruction in the Christian faith. This system was first used in Hispaniola to work gold fields and then in Mexico for agricultural labor and, when silver was discovered in the 1540s, for silver mining.

A 1512 Spanish law authorizing the use of the encomienda (en-ko-me-EN-duh) called for indigenous people to be treated fairly, but in practice the system led to terrible abuses. Spanish missionaries publicized these abuses, leading to debates in Spain about the nature and proper treatment of indigenous people (see "European Debates About Indigenous Peoples"). King Charles I responded to such complaints in 1542 with the New Laws, which set limits on the authority of encomienda holders.

The New Laws provoked a revolt among elites in Peru and were little enforced throughout Spanish territories. Nonetheless, the Crown gradually gained control over encomiendas in central areas of the empire and required indigenous people to pay tributes in cash, rather than in labor. To respond to a shortage of indigenous workers, royal officials established a new government-run system of forced labor, called *repartimiento* in New Spain and *mita* in Peru. Administrators assigned a certain percentage of the inhabitants of native communities to labor for a set period each year in public works, mining, agriculture, and other tasks.

Spanish systems for exploiting the labor of indigenous peoples were both a cause of and a response to the disastrous decline in their numbers that began soon after the arrival of Europeans. Some indigenous people died as a direct result of the violence of conquest and the disruption of agriculture and trade caused by warfare. The most important cause of death, however, was infectious disease. Having little or no resistance to dis-

---

viceroyalties The name for the four administrative units of Spanish possessions in the Americas: New Spain, Peru, New Granada, and La Plata.

captaincies A system established by the Portuguese in Brazil in the 1530s, whereby hereditary grants of land were given to nobles and loyal officials who bore the costs of settling and administering their territories.

encomienda system A system whereby the Spanish crown granted the conquerors the right to forcibly employ groups of indigenous people as laborers and to demand tribute payments from them in exchange for providing food, shelter, and instruction in the Christian faith.

Spanish Exploitation of Indigenous Labor This image depicts Spanish conquistadors supervising indigenous laborers as they carry arms along the steep road from Veracruz to Tlaxcala in 1520. It was part of a larger painting, produced in the postconquest era and known as the *Lienzo de Tlaxcala*, that tells the story of the alliance between the Tlaxcala kingdom and the Spanish and their defeat of the Aztec Empire.
(Sarin Images/Granger, NYC — All rights reserved.)

eases brought from the Old World, the inhabitants of the New World fell victim to smallpox, typhus, influenza, and other illnesses.

The pattern of devastating disease and population loss established in the Spanish colonies was repeated everywhere Europeans settled. Overall, population declined by as much as 90 percent or more but with important regional variations. In general, densely populated urban centers were worse hit than rural areas, and tropical, low-lying regions suffered more than cooler, higher-altitude ones.

Colonial administrators responded to native population decline by forcibly combining dwindling indigenous communities into new settlements and imposing the rigors of the encomienda and the repartimiento. By the end of the sixteenth century the search for fresh sources of labor had given birth to the new tragedy of the Atlantic slave trade (see "Sugar and Early Transatlantic Slavery").

Patterns of Settlement

The century after the discovery of silver in 1545 marked the high point of Iberian immigration to the Americas. Although the first migrants were men, soon whole families began to cross the Atlantic, and the European population began to increase through natural reproduction. By 1600 American-born Europeans, called *Creoles*, outnumbered immigrants.

Iberian settlement was predominantly urban in nature. Spaniards settled into the cities and towns of the former Aztec and Inca Empires as the native population dwindled through death and flight. They also established new cities in which settlers were quick to develop urban institutions familiar to them from home: city squares, churches, schools, and universities.

Despite the growing number of Europeans and the rapid decline of the native population, Europeans remained a small minority of the total inhabitants of the Americas. Iberians had sexual relationships with native women, leading to the growth of a substantial population of mixed Iberian and Indian descent known as *mestizos* (meh-STEE-zohz). The large-scale arrival of enslaved Africans, starting in Brazil in the mid-sixteenth century, added new ethnic and racial dimensions to the population.

The Era of Global Contact

How was the era of global contact shaped by new commodities, commercial empires, and forced migrations?

The centuries-old Afroeurasian trade world was forever changed by the European voyages of discovery and their aftermath. For the first time, a truly global economy emerged in the sixteenth and seventeenth centuries, and it forged new links among far-flung peoples, cultures, and societies. The ancient civilizations of Europe, Africa, the Americas, and Asia confronted each other in new and rapidly evolving ways. Those confrontations often led to conquest, forced migration, and brutal exploitation, but they also contributed to cultural exchange and new patterns of life.

The Columbian Exchange

The travel of people and goods between the Old and New Worlds led to an exchange of animals, plants, and diseases, a complex process known as the **Columbian exchange**. As we have seen, the introduction of new diseases to the Americas had devastating consequences. But other results of the exchange brought benefits not only to the Europeans but also to native peoples.

Everywhere they settled, the Spanish and Portuguese brought and raised wheat. Grapes and olives brought over from Spain did well in parts of Peru and Chile. Perhaps the most significant introduction to the diet of Native Americans came via the meat and milk of the livestock that the early conquistadors brought with them, including cattle, sheep, and goats. The horse enabled both the Spanish conquerors and native populations to travel faster and farther and to transport heavy loads more easily.

In turn, Europeans returned home with many food crops that became central elements of their diet. Crops originating in the Americas included tomatoes, squash, pumpkins, peppers, and many varieties of beans, as well as tobacco. One of the most important of such crops was maize (corn). By the late seventeenth century maize had become a staple in Spain, Portugal, southern France, and Italy, and in the eighteenth century it

became one of the chief foods of southeastern Europe and southern China. Even more valuable was the nutritious white potato, which slowly spread from west to east, contributing everywhere to a rise in population.

While the exchange of foods was a great benefit to cultures across the world, the introduction of European pathogens to the New World had a disastrous impact on the native population. In Europe infectious diseases like smallpox, measles, and influenza—originally spread through contact with domestic animals—killed many people each year. Over centuries of dealing with these diseases, the European population had had time to adapt. Prior to contact with Europeans, indigenous peoples of the New World suffered from insect-borne diseases and some infectious ones, but their lack of domestic livestock spared them the host of highly infectious diseases known in the Old World. The arrival of Europeans spread these microbes among a totally unprepared population, and they fell victim in vast numbers (see "Indigenous Population Loss and Economic Exploitation"). The world after Columbus was thus unified by disease as well as by trade and colonization.

Sugar and Early Transatlantic Slavery

Two crucial and interrelated elements of the Columbian exchange were the transatlantic trade in sugar and slaves. Throughout the Middle Ages, slavery was deeply entrenched in the Mediterranean, but it was not based on race. How, then, did black African slavery enter the European picture and take root in South and then North America? In 1453 the Ottoman capture of Constantinople halted the flow of European slaves from the eastern Mediterranean. Additionally, the successes of the Christian reconquest of the Iberian Peninsula drastically diminished the supply of Muslim captives. Cut off from its traditional sources of slaves, Mediterranean Europe turned to sub-Saharan Africa, which had a long history of slave trading.

As Portuguese explorers began their voyages along the western coast of Africa in the 1440s, one of the first commodities they sought was slaves. While the first slaves were simply seized by small raiding parties, Portuguese merchants soon found that it was easier and more profitable to trade with African leaders, who were accustomed to dealing in enslaved people captured through warfare with neighboring powers. In 1483 the Portuguese established an alliance with the kingdom of Kongo. The royal family eventually converted to Christianity, and Portuguese merchants intermarried with Kongolese women, creating a permanent Afro-Portuguese community. From 1490 to 1530 Portuguese traders brought between three hundred and two thousand enslaved Africans to Lisbon each year.

Columbian exchange The exchange of animals, plants, and diseases between the Old and the New Worlds.

Indians Working in a Spanish Sugar Mill Belgian engraver Theodore de Bry published many images of the European exploration and settlement of the New World. De Bry never crossed the Atlantic himself, instead basing his images on travel accounts and other firsthand sources. This image depicts the exploitation of indigenous people in a Spanish sugar mill. (Album/Art Resource, NY)

In this stage of European expansion, the history of slavery became intertwined with the history of sugar. In the Middle Ages, sugarcane—native to the South Pacific—was brought to Mediterranean islands. Population increases and greater prosperity in the fifteenth century led to increasing demand for sugar. The establishment of sugar plantations on the Canary and Madeira Islands in the fifteenth century after Iberian colonization testifies to this demand.

Sugar was a particularly difficult crop to produce for profit, requiring constant, backbreaking labor. The invention of roller mills to crush the cane more efficiently meant that yields could be significantly augmented, but only if a sufficient labor force was found to supply the mills. Plantation owners solved the labor problem by forcing first native islanders and then transported Africans to perform the backbreaking work.

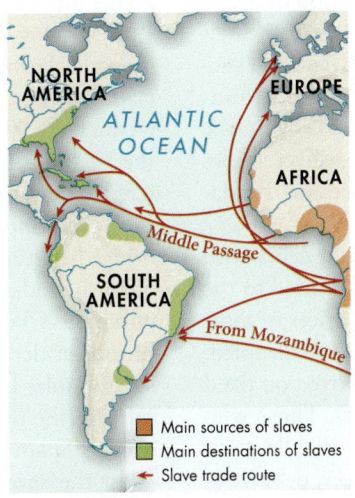

The Transatlantic Slave Trade

The transatlantic slave trade that would ultimately result in the forced transport of over 12 million individuals began in 1518, when Spanish king Charles I authorized traders to bring enslaved Africans to New World colonies. The Portuguese brought the first slaves to Brazil around 1550. After its founding in 1621, the Dutch West India Company transported thousands of Africans to Brazil and the Caribbean, mostly to work on sugar plantations. In the late seventeenth century, with the chartering of the Royal African Company, the English began to bring slaves to Barbados and other English colonies in the Caribbean and mainland North America.

Before 1700, when slavers decided it was better business to improve conditions, some 20 percent of slaves died on the voyage from Africa to the Americas.[2] The most common cause of death was dysentery induced by poor-quality food and water, lack of sanitation, and intense crowding. On sugar plantations, death rates among enslaved people from illness and exhaustion were extremely high. Driven by rising demands for plantation crops, the tragic transatlantic slave trade reached its height in the eighteenth century.

Spanish Silver and Its Economic Effects

The sixteenth century has often been called Spain's golden century, but silver mined in the Americas was the true source of Spain's wealth. In 1545, at an altitude of fifteen thousand feet, the Spanish discovered an extraordinary source of silver at Potosí (poh-toh-SEE) (in present-day Bolivia) in unsettled territory captured from the Inca Empire. By 1550 Potosí yielded perhaps 60 percent of all the silver mined in the world. From Potosí and the mines at Zacatecas (za-kuh-TAY-kuhs) and Guanajuato (gwah-nah-HWAH-toh) in Mexico, huge quantities of precious metals poured forth.

Mining became the most important industry in the colonies. Millions of indigenous laborers suffered brutal conditions and death in the silver mines. Demand for new sources of labor for the mines also contributed to the intensification of the African slave trade. Profits for the Spanish crown were immense. The Crown claimed the quinto, one-fifth of all precious metals mined in South America, which represented 25 percent of its total income. Between 1503 and 1650, 35 million pounds of silver and over 600,000 pounds of gold entered Seville's port.

Spain's immense profits from silver paid for the tremendous expansion of its empire and for the large armies that defended it. However, the easy flow of money also dampened economic innovation. It exacerbated the rising inflation Spain was already experiencing in the mid-sixteenth century, a period of growing population and stagnant production. Several times between 1557 and 1647, King Philip II and his successors wrote off the state debt, thereby undermining confidence in the government and destroying the economy. When the profitability of the silver mines diminished in the 1640s, Spain's power was fundamentally undercut.

As Philip II paid his armies and foreign debts with silver bullion, Spanish inflation was transmitted to the rest of Europe. Between 1560 and 1600 prices in most parts of Europe doubled and in some cases quadrupled. Because money bought less, people who lived on fixed incomes, such as nobles, were badly hurt. Those who owed fixed sums of money, such as the middle class, prospered because in a time of rising prices, debts lessened in value each year. Food costs rose most sharply, and the poor fared worst of all.

In many ways, though, it was not Spain but China that controlled the world trade in silver. The Chinese demanded silver for their products and for the payment of imperial taxes. China was thus the main buyer of world silver, absorbing half the world's production. The silver market drove world trade, with New Spain and Japan acting as major sources of the supply of silver and China dominating demand. The world trade in silver is one of the best examples of the new global economy that emerged in this period.

The Birth of the Global Economy

With Europeans' discovery of the Americas and their exploration of the Pacific, the entire world was linked for the first time in history by seaborne trade. The opening of that trade brought into being three successive commercial empires: the Portuguese, the Spanish, and the Dutch.

In the sixteenth century the Portuguese controlled the sea route to India (Map 16.3). From their bases at Goa on the Arabian Sea and at Malacca on the Malay Peninsula, ships carried goods to the Portuguese settlement at Macao. From Macao Portuguese ships loaded with Chinese silks and porcelains sailed to Japan and the Philippines, where Chinese goods were exchanged for Spanish silver from New Spain. Throughout Asia the Portuguese traded in slaves, some of whom were brought all the way across the Pacific to Mexico. (See "Individuals in Society: Catarina de San Juan," page 460.) They also exported horses from Mesopotamia and copper from Arabia to India; from India they exported hawks and peacocks for the Chinese and Japanese markets. Back to Portugal they brought Asian spices that had been purchased with textiles produced in India and with gold and ivory from East Africa. From their colony in Brazil they also shipped back sugar, produced by African slaves whom they had transported across the Atlantic.

Becoming an imperial power a few decades later than the Portuguese, the Spanish were determined to claim their place in world trade. The Spanish Empire in the New World was basically land based, but across the Pacific the Spaniards built a seaborne empire centered at Manila in the Philippines. Established in 1571, the city of Manila served as the transpacific bridge between Spanish America and China. In Manila Spanish traders used silver from American mines to purchase Chinese silk for European markets. The European demand for silk was so huge that in 1597, for example, 12 million pesos of silver, almost the total value of the transatlantic trade, moved from Acapulco in New Spain to Manila.

In the seventeenth century the Dutch challenged the Spanish and Portuguese Empires. The Dutch East India Company was founded in 1602 with the stated intention of capturing the spice trade from the Portuguese. Drawing on their commercial wealth and long

MAP 16.3 Seaborne Trading Empires in the Sixteenth and Seventeenth Centuries By the mid-seventeenth century trade linked all parts of the world except for Australia. Notice that trade in slaves was not confined to the Atlantic but involved almost all parts of the world.

experience in European trade, the Dutch emerged by the end of the century as the most powerful worldwide seaborne trading power (see "The Dutch Trading Empire" in Chapter 18).

Changing Attitudes and Beliefs

How did new encounters shape cultural attitudes and beliefs in Europe and the rest of the world?

The age of overseas expansion heightened Europeans' contacts with the rest of the world. These contacts gave

birth to new ideas about the inherent superiority or inferiority of different races. Religion became another means of cultural contact, as European missionaries aimed to spread Christianity in both the New World and East Asia. The East-West contacts also led to exchanges of influential cultural and scientific ideas.

Religious Conversion

Converting indigenous people to Christianity was one of the most important justifications for European expansion. The first missionaries to the New World accompanied Columbus on his second voyage, and more than 2,500 Franciscans, Dominicans, Jesuits, and other friars crossed the Atlantic in the following

Catarina de San Juan

A LONG JOURNEY LED CATARINA DE SAN JUAN FROM enslavement in South Asia to adulation as a popular saint in Mexico. Her journey began on the west coast of India around 1610 when Portuguese traders captured a group of children, including the small girl who would become Catarina. Their ship continued around the southern tip of India, across the Bay of Bengal, through the Strait of Malacca, and across the South China Sea. It docked at Manila, a Spanish city in the Philippines, where the girl was sold at a slave auction. In 1619 Catarina boarded a ship that was part of the Manila Galleon, the annual convoy of Spanish ships that crossed the Pacific between Manila and the Mexican port of Acapulco. After a six-month voyage, Catarina arrived in Acapulco; she then walked to Mexico City and continued on to the city of Puebla.

In Puebla, Catarina became the property of a Portuguese merchant and worked as a domestic servant. She was one of thousands of *chinos*, a term for natives of the East Indies who were brought via the Philippines to Spanish America. Many were slaves, transported as part of a transoceanic slave trade that reached from the Indian Ocean to the South China Sea and across the Pacific to the Atlantic world. They constituted a small but significant portion of people forcibly transported by Europeans to the Americas in the late sixteenth and early seventeenth centuries to replace dwindling numbers of indigenous laborers. Chinos were considered particularly apt for domestic labor, and many wealthy Spanish Americans bought them in Manila.

Before crossing the Pacific, Catarina converted to Catholicism and chose her Christian name. In Puebla her master encouraged Catarina's faith and allowed her to attend mass every day. He also drafted a will emancipating her after his death, which occurred in 1619. With no money of her own, Catarina became the servant of a local priest. On his advice, Catarina reluctantly gave up her dream of becoming a lay sister and married a fellow chino named Domingo. The marriage was unhappy; Catarina reportedly refused to enter sexual relations with her husband and suffered from his debts, infidelity, and hostility to her faith. She found solace in renewed religious devotion, winning the admiration of priests and neighbors who flocked to her for spiritual comfort and to hear about her ecstatic visions. After fourteen years of marriage, Catarina became a widow and lived out her life in the home of wealthy supporters.

Catarina's funeral in 1688 drew large crowds. Her followers revered her as an unofficial saint, and soon the leaders of Puebla began a campaign to have Catarina beatified (officially recognized by the Catholic church as a saint). Her former confessors published accounts of her life emphasizing her piety, beauty, and exotic Asian origins and marveling at the miraculous preservation of her virginity through the perils of enslavement, long journeys at sea, and marriage. Much of what we know about Catarina derives from these sources and must be viewed as idealized, rather than as strictly historically accurate.

Women of Puebla, Mexico, in traditional clothing. (De Agostini Picture Library/ Gianni Dagli Orti/Bridgeman Images)

The Spanish Inquisition, which oversaw the process of beatification, rejected Catarina's candidacy and, fearing that popular adulation might detract from the authority of the church, forbade the circulation of images of and texts about her. Despite this ban, popular reverence for Catarina de San Juan continued, and continues to this day in Mexico.

QUESTIONS FOR ANALYSIS

1. Why would the Inquisition react so negatively to popular devotion to Catarina? What dangers did she pose to the Catholic Church in New Spain?
2. What does Catarina's story reveal about the global nature of the Spanish Empire and the slave trade in this period? What does it reveal about divisions within the Catholic Church?

Sources: Tatiana Seijas, *Asian Slaves in Colonial Mexico: From Chinos to Indians* (New York: Cambridge University Press, 2014), pp. 8–26; Ronald J. Morgan, *Spanish American Saints and the Rhetoric of Identity, 1600–1810* (Tucson: University of Arizona Press, 2002), pp. 119–142.

century. Jesuit missionaries were also active in Japan and China in the sixteenth and seventeenth centuries, until authorities banned their teachings.

Catholic friars were among the first Europeans to seek an understanding of native cultures and languages as part of their effort to render Christianity comprehensible to indigenous people. They were also the most vociferous opponents of abuses committed by Spanish settlers.

Religion had been a central element of pre-Columbian societies, and many, if not all, indigenous people were receptive to the new religion that accompanied the victorious Iberians. (See "Global Viewpoints: Aztec and Spanish Views on Christian Conversion in New Spain," page 462.) In addition to spreading Christianity, missionaries taught indigenous peoples European methods of agriculture and instilled obedience to colonial masters. Despite the success of initial conversion efforts, authorities could not prevent the melding together of Catholic teachings with elements of pagan beliefs and practices.

European Debates About Indigenous Peoples

Iberian exploitation of the native population of the Americas began from the moment of Columbus's arrival in 1492. Denunciations of this abuse by Catholic missionaries, however, quickly followed, inspiring vociferous debates in both Europe and the colonies about the nature of indigenous peoples and how they should be treated. Bartolomé de Las Casas (1474–1566), a Dominican friar and former encomienda holder, was one of the earliest and most outspoken critics of the brutal treatment inflicted on indigenous peoples.

Mounting criticism in Spain led King Charles I to assemble a group of churchmen and lawyers to debate the issue in 1550 in the city of Valladolid. One side of the **Valladolid debate**, led by Juan Ginés de Sepúlveda, argued that conquest and forcible conversion were both necessary and justified to save indigenous people from the horrors of human sacrifice, cannibalism, and idolatry. To counter these arguments, Las Casas and his supporters depicted indigenous people as rational and innocent children, who deserved protection and tutelage from more advanced civilizations.

Elsewhere in Europe, audiences also debated these questions. Eagerly reading denunciations of Spanish abuses by critics like Las Casas, they derived the **Black Legend** of Spanish colonialism, the notion that the Spanish were uniquely brutal and cruel in their conquest and settlement of the Americas. This legend helped other European powers overlook their own record of colonial violence and exploitation.

New Ideas About Race

At the beginning of the transatlantic slave trade, most Europeans grouped Africans into the despised categories of pagan heathens or Muslim infidels. As Europeans turned to Africa for new sources of slaves, they drew on myths about Africans' primitiveness and barbarity to defend slavery. (See "Analyzing the Evidence: Mixed Races," page 463.)

Over time, the institution of slavery fostered a new level of racial inequality. Africans gradually became seen as utterly distinct from and wholly inferior to Europeans. In a transition from rather vague assumptions about Africans' non-Christian religious beliefs and general lack of civilization, Europeans developed increasingly rigid ideas of racial superiority and inferiority to safeguard the growing profits gained from plantation slavery. Black skin became equated with slavery itself as Europeans at home and in the colonies convinced themselves that blacks were destined by God to serve them as slaves in perpetuity.

Support for this belief went back to the Greek philosopher Aristotle's argument that some people are naturally destined for slavery and to biblical associations between darkness and sin, derived from the biblical story of Noah's curse upon the descendants of his disobedient son Ham to be the "servant[s] of servants." Biblical genealogies listing Ham's sons as those who peopled North Africa and Cush (which includes parts of modern Egypt and Sudan) were read to mean that all inhabitants of those regions bore Noah's curse.

Chapter Summary

Prior to Columbus's voyages, well-developed trade routes linked the peoples and products of Africa, Asia, and Europe. Overall, Europe played a minor role in the Afroeurasian trade world. As the economy and population recovered from the Black Death, Europeans began to seek more direct and profitable access to the Afroeurasian trade world. Technological innovations, many borrowed from the East, enabled explorers to undertake ever more ambitious voyages.

In the aftermath of their conquests of Caribbean islands and the Aztec and Inca Empires, the Spanish established new forms of governance to dominate indigenous peoples and exploit their labor. The arrival of Europeans brought enormous population losses to

---

Valladolid debate A debate organized by Spanish king Charles I in 1550 in the city of Valladolid that pitted defenders of Spanish conquest and forcible conversion against critics of these practices.

Black Legend The notion that the Spanish were uniquely brutal and cruel in their conquest and settlement of the Americas, an idea propagated by rival European powers.

Aztec and Spanish Views on Christian Conversion in New Spain

In justifying their violent conquest of the Aztec and Inca civilizations, Spanish conquistadors emphasized the need to bring Christianity to heathen peoples. For the conquered, the imposition of Christianity and the repression of their pre-existing religions were often experienced as yet another form of loss. The first document describes the response of the recently vanquished Aztec leaders of Tenochtitlan to Franciscan missionaries. Despite resistance, missionaries eventually succeeded in converting much of the indigenous population to Catholicism. In the second document, a firsthand account of the Spanish conquest written a few decades after the fall of Tenochtitlan, Bernal Díaz del Castillo expresses great satisfaction at the Catholic piety of some indigenous communities.

Aztec Response to the Franciscans' Explanation of Their 1524 Mission

■ You have told us that we do not know the One who gives us life and being, who is Lord of the heavens and of the earth. You also say that those we worship are not gods. This way of speaking is entirely new to us, and very scandalous. We are frightened by this way of speaking because our forebears who engendered and governed us never said anything like this. On the contrary, they left us this our custom of worshiping our gods, in which they believed and which they worshiped all the time that they lived here on earth. They taught us how to honor them. And they taught us all the ceremonies and sacrifices that we make. They told us that through them [our gods] we live and are, and that we were beholden to them, to be theirs and to serve countless centuries before the sun began to shine and before there was daytime. They said that these gods that we worship give us everything we need for our physical existence: maize, beans, chia seeds, etc. . . . .

All of us together feel that it is enough to have lost, enough that the power and royal jurisdiction have been taken from us. As for our gods, we will die before giving up serving and worshiping them.

Bernal Díaz del Castillo, from *The True History of the Conquest of New Spain, 1521*

■ It is a thing to be grateful for to God, and for profound consideration, to see how the natives assist in celebrating a holy Mass. . . . There is another good thing they do [namely] that both men, women and children, who are of the age to learn them, know all the holy prayers in their own languages and are obliged to know them. They have other good customs about their holy Christianity, that when they pass near a sacred altar or Cross they bow their heads with humility, bend their knees, and say the prayer "Our Father," which we Conquistadores have taught them, and they place lighted wax candles before the holy altars and crosses, for formerly they did not know how to use wax in making candles. In addition to what I have said, we taught them to show great reverence and obedience to all the monks and priests, and, when these went to their pueblos, to sally forth to receive them with lighted wax candles and to ring the bells, and to feed them very well. . . . Beside the good customs reported by me they have others both holy and good, for when the day of Corpus Christi comes, or that of Our Lady, or other solemn festivals when among us we form processions, most of the pueblos in the neighbourhood of this city of Guatemala come out in procession with their crosses and lighted wax tapers, and carry on their shoulders, on a litter, the image of the saint who is the patron of the pueblo.

QUESTIONS FOR ANALYSIS

1. What reasons do the leaders of Tenochtitlan offer for rejecting the teachings of Franciscan missionaries? What importance do they accord their own religious traditions?

2. What evidence does Díaz provide for the conversion of the indigenous people in the city of Guatemala?

3. How and why do you think the attitudes of indigenous peoples might have evolved from those expressed in the first document to those described in the second? Do you think the second document tells the whole story of religious attitudes under Spanish rule?

Sources: "The Lords and Holy Men of Tenochtitlan Reply to the Franciscans: Bernardino de Sahagún, Coloquios y doctrina Cristiana," ed. Miguel León-Portilla, in *Colonial Spanish America: A Documentary History*, ed. Kenneth Mills and William B. Taylor, pp. 20–21. Reproduced with permission of ROWMAN & LITTLEFIELD PUBLISHERS, INCORPORATED, in the format Republish in a book via Copyright Clearance Center; Bernal Díaz, *The True History of the Conquest of New Spain*, in Stuart B. Schwartz, *Victors and Vanquished: Spanish and Nahua Views of the Conquest of Mexico* (Boston: Bedford/St. Martin's, 2000), pp. 218–219.

Mixed Races

When Spanish settlers came to the Americas, they brought with them the religious and racial prejudices of the old country. One of the most important of these was the doctrine of *limpieza de sangre*, or purity of blood. This principle was originally adopted during the reconquista to distinguish Spaniards whose ancestors had always been Christian and who were therefore not tainted (in Christians' eyes) by the blood of Jewish or Muslim converts. After the conquest, the Spanish applied this notion in the Americas; because indigenous peoples had never been exposed to Christianity — the Spanish reasoned — they could not be considered impure like Jews and Muslims. Africans, however, fell into the same heretical category as Jews and Muslims. These distinctions help explain why the Spanish decided indigenous people could not be enslaved, while Africans and those of African descent could.

Despite these obsessions with racial purity, Spanish America from its first years was characterized by a high degree of racial mixing, which began as male conquistadors formed unions with women of high-ranking indigenous families. With the arrival of some thirty-five thousand enslaved Africans in Mexico during the sixteenth century, the mixing of peoples increased. Many of these unions were forced, with Spanish men seeking concubines among indigenous women and enslaved women of African descent. The fact that children inherited their legal status from their mothers encouraged enslaved men to seek wives among indigenous and *mestiza* (mixed) women. Defying neat boundaries that were supposed to exist between racial categories, the children born of these unions were viewed with suspicion by state and religious officials, and they suffered from a range of discriminatory laws.

An elaborate terminology emerged to describe the many possible combinations of indigenous, African, and European blood, which were known collectively as *castas*. *Mestizos* referred to people of mixed Spanish and Indian descent, whereas *mulattos* were those of Spanish and African origin. This painting belongs to a genre, known as casta paintings, that emerged in the late seventeenth century in Mexico and depicted couples composed of individuals of different ethnic origin and the children produced of their unions. This genre reflects the ambivalent fascination inspired by the unprecedented mixing of peoples in Spanish America.

QUESTIONS FOR ANALYSIS

1. What do these images suggest about the racial composition of the population of Spanish America and the interaction of people with different racial and ethnic backgrounds?
2. Who do you think the audience might have been for these images, and why would viewers be fascinated by them?
3. What elements of this chapter might suggest that these are romanticized or idealized depictions of relations among different racial and ethnic groups?

(Schalkwijk/Art Resource, NY)

native communities, primarily through the spread of infectious diseases. Disease was one element of the Columbian exchange, a complex transfer of germs, plants, and animals between the Old and New Worlds. These exchanges contributed to the creation of the first truly global economy. Tragically, a major component of global trade was the transatlantic slave trade, in which Europeans transported Africans to labor in the sugar plantations and silver mines of the New World. European nations vied for supremacy in global trade, with early Portuguese success in India and Asia being challenged first by the Spanish and then by the Dutch.

Increased contact with the outside world led Europeans to develop new ideas about cultural and racial differences. Debates occurred in Spain and its colonies over the nature of the indigenous peoples of the Americas and how they should be treated. Europeans had long held negative attitudes about Africans; as the slave trade grew, they began to express more rigid notions of racial inequality and to claim that Africans were inherently suited for slavery. Religion became another means of cultural contact, as European missionaries aimed to spread Christianity in the New World.

NOTES

1. Thomas Benjamin, *The Atlantic World: Europeans, Africans, Indians and Their Shared History, 1400–1900* (Cambridge: Cambridge University Press, 2009), p. 141.
2. Herbert S. Klein, "Profits and the Causes of Mortality," in *The Atlantic Slave Trade*, ed. David Northrup (Lexington, Mass.: D. C. Heath, 1994), p. 116.

CONNECTIONS

Just two years separated Martin Luther's attack on the Catholic Church in 1517 and Ferdinand Magellan's discovery of the Pacific Ocean in 1520. Within a few short years western Europeans' religious unity and notions of terrestrial geography were shattered. In the ensuing decades Europeans struggled to come to terms with religious differences among Protestants and Catholics at home and with the multitudes of new peoples and places they encountered abroad. Like Muslim forces in the first centuries of Islam, Christian Europeans brought their religion with them and sought to convert conquered peoples to their faith. While some Europeans were fascinated and inspired by this new diversity, too often the result was suffering and violence. Europeans endured decades of religious civil war, and indigenous peoples overseas underwent massive population losses as a result of European warfare, disease, and exploitation. Both Catholic and Protestant religious leaders condoned the trade in slaves that ultimately brought suffering and death to millions of Africans.

Even as the voyages of discovery contributed to the fragmentation of European culture, they also played a role in state centralization and consolidation in the longer term. Henceforth, competition to gain overseas colonies became an integral part of European politics. While Spain's enormous profits from conquest ultimately led to a weakening of its power, over time the Netherlands, England, and France used profits from colonial trade to help build modernized, centralized states.

Two crucial consequences emerged from this era of expansion. The first was the creation of enduring contacts among five of the seven continents of the globe — Europe, Asia, Africa, North America, and South America. From the sixteenth century onward, the peoples of the world were increasingly entwined in divergent forms of economic, social, and cultural exchange. The second was the growth of European power. Europeans controlled the Americas and gradually assumed control over existing trade networks in Asia and Africa. Although China remained the world's most powerful economy until at least 1800, the era of European dominance was born.

CHAPTER 16 Review and Explore

Identify Key Terms

Identify and explain the significance of each item below.

bride wealth (p. 438)

caravel (p. 442)

Ptolemy's *Geography* (p. 442)

Treaty of Tordesillas (p. 448)

conquistador (p. 450)

Aztec Empire (p. 450)

Inca Empire (p. 450)

viceroyalties (p. 454)

captaincies (p. 454)

encomienda system (p. 454)

Columbian exchange (p. 456)

Valladolid debate (p. 461)

Black Legend (p. 461)

Review the Main Ideas

Answer the focus questions from each section of the chapter.

1. What was the Afroeurasian trade world prior to the era of European exploration? (p. 438)

2. How and why did Europeans undertake ambitious voyages of expansion? (p. 441)

3. What was the impact of Iberian conquest and settlement on the peoples and ecologies of the Americas? (p. 449)

4. How was the era of global contact shaped by new commodities, commercial empires, and forced migrations? (p. 456)

5. How did new encounters shape cultural attitudes and beliefs in Europe and the rest of the world? (p. 459)

Make Comparisons and Connections

Analyze the larger developments and continuities within and across chapters.

1. If Europe was at the periphery of the global trading system prior to 1492, where was it situated by the middle of the sixteenth century? What had changed? What had not?

2. How does the spread of Christianity in the aftermath of European conquest in the New World compare with the earlier spread of Christianity under the Roman Empire (Chapter 6) and the spread of Buddhism (Chapter 7) and Islam (Chapters 9, 10, 12)?

3. How did European expansion in the period covered in this chapter draw on earlier patterns of trade and migration in Africa (Chapter 10) and Asia (Chapters 12, 13)?

4. To what extent did the European voyages of expansion and conquest inaugurate an era of global history? Did this era represent the birth of "globalization"? Why or why not?

TIMELINE

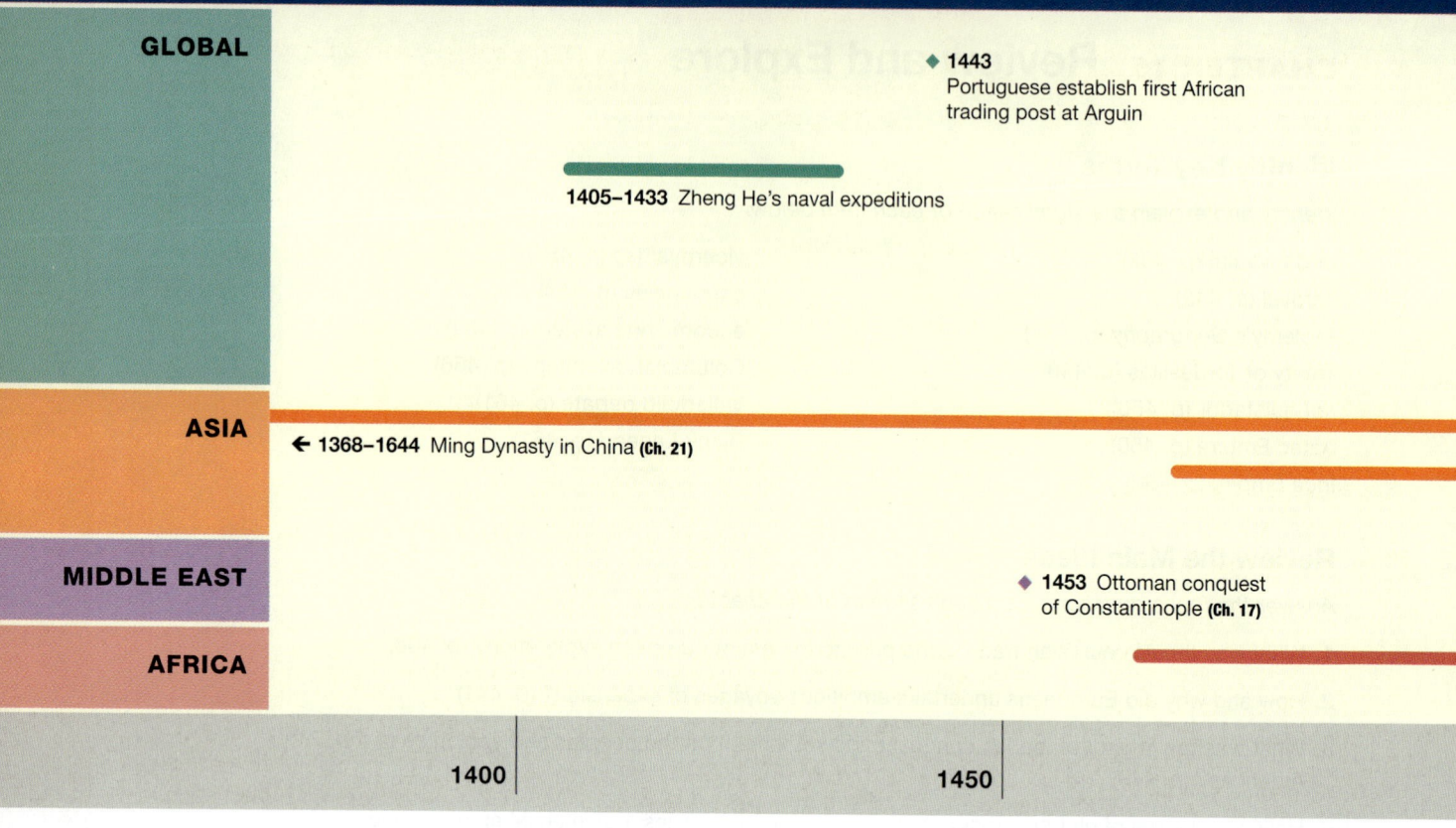

GLOBAL

◆ **1443**
Portuguese establish first African
trading post at Arguin

1405–1433 Zheng He's naval expeditions

ASIA

← **1368–1644** Ming Dynasty in China **(Ch. 21)**

MIDDLE EAST

◆ **1453** Ottoman conquest
of Constantinople **(Ch. 17)**

AFRICA

1400   1450

Suggested Resources

BOOKS

Crosby, Alfred W. *The Columbian Exchange: Biological and Cultural Consequences of 1492,* 30th anniversary ed. 2003. A lively and highly influential account of the environmental impact of the transatlantic movement of animals, plants, and microbes inaugurated by Columbus.

Elliot, J. H. *Empires of the Atlantic World: Britain and Spain in America, 1492–1830.* 2006. A masterful comparative study of the British and Spanish Empires in the Americas.

Fernández-Armesto, Felipe. *Columbus.* 1992. An excellent biography of Christopher Columbus.

Mann, Charles C. *1491: New Revelations on the Americas Before Columbus,* 2d ed. 2011. A highly readable explanation of the peoples and societies of the Americas before the arrival of Europeans.

Menard, Russell R. *Sweet Negotiations: Sugar, Slavery, and Plantation Agriculture in Early Barbados.* 2006. Explores the intertwined history of sugar plantations and slavery in seventeenth-century Barbados.

Parker, Charles H. *Global Interactions in the Early Modern Age, 1400–1800.* 2010. An examination of the rise of global connections in the early modern period, which situates the European experience in relation to the world's other empires and peoples.

Pomeranz, Kenneth, and Steven Topik. *The World That Trade Created: Society, Culture, and the World Economy, 1400 to the Present.* 1999. The creation of a world market presented through rich and vivid stories of merchants, miners, slaves, and farmers.

Restall, Matthew. *Seven Myths of Spanish Conquest.* 2003. A re-examination of common misconceptions about why and how the Spanish conquered native civilizations in the New World.

Subrahmanyam, Sanjay. *The Portuguese Empire in Asia, 1500–1700: A Political and Economic History,* 2d ed. 2012. A masterful study of the Portuguese overseas empire in Asia that draws on both European and Asian sources.

DOCUMENTARIES

America Before Columbus (National Geographic, 2010). Explores the complex societies and cultures of North America before contact with Europeans and the impact of the Columbian exchange.

Conquistadors (PBS, 2000). Traveling in the footsteps of the Spanish conquistadors, the narrator tells their story while following the paths and rivers they used. Includes discussion of the perspectives and participation of native peoples.

1492 Columbus lands on San Salvador

1571 Spanish establish port of Manila in the Philippines

1494 Treaty of Tordesillas ratified

1533 Pizarro conquers Inca Empire

1518 Atlantic slave trade begins

1602 Dutch East India Company founded

1521 Cortés conquers Aztec Empire

1519–1522 Magellan's expedition circumnavigates the world

1467–1600 Period of civil war in Japan (Ch. 21)

1556–1605 Reign of Akbar in Mughal Empire (Ch. 17)

ca. 1464–1591 Songhai kingdom dominates the western Sudan (Ch. 20)

| 1500 | 1550 | 1600 |

1421: The Year China Discovered America? (PBS, 2004). Investigates the voyages of legendary Chinese admiral Zheng He, exploring the possibility that he and his fleet reached the Americas decades before Columbus.

FEATURE FILMS AND TELEVISION DRAMAS

Black Robe (Bruce Beresford, 1991). A classic film about French Jesuit missionaries among Algonquin and Huron Indians in New France in the seventeenth century.

Marco Polo (Hallmark Channel, 2007). A made-for-television film that follows Italian merchant Marco Polo as he travels to China to establish trade ties with Mongol emperor Khubilai Khan.

The Other Conquest (Salvador Carrasco, 1998). A Mexican film depicting the brutality of the Spanish conquest and its social and religious impact, seen from the perspective of a young Aztec man.

WEBSITES

Discovery and Exploration Collection. A Library of Congress digital collection of maps and manuscripts related to exploration and discovery, many of which relate to the period covered in this chapter. **https://www.loc.gov/collections/discovery-and -exploration/**

Explore Mesolore. A website featuring resources on Mesoamerica, including indigenous documents from the sixteenth century, with helpful explanations of the origins and meaning of the documents. **www.mesolore.org**

The Globalization of Food and Plants. Hosted by the Yale University Center for the Study of Globalization, this website provides information on how various foods and plants — such as spices, coffee, and tomatoes — traveled the world in the Columbian exchange. **yaleglobal.yale.edu/about/food.jsp**

17

The Islamic World Powers

1300–1800

After the decline of the Mongol Empire in the mid-fourteenth century, powerful new Islamic states emerged in south and west Eurasia. By the sixteenth century the Ottoman Empire, centered in Anatolia; the Safavid (SAH-fah-vid) Empire in Persia; and the Mughal (MOO-guhl) Empire in India controlled vast territories from West Africa to Central Asia, from the Balkans to the Bay of Bengal.

Lasting more than six centuries (1299–1922), the Ottoman Empire was one of the largest, best-organized, and most enduring political entities in world history. In Persia (now Iran) the Safavid Dynasty created a Shi'a state and presided over a brilliant culture. In India the Mughal leader Babur and his successors gained control of much of the Indian subcontinent. Mughal rule inaugurated a period of radical administrative reorganization in India and the flowering of intellectual and architectural creativity. Although these three states were often at war with each other, they shared important characteristics and challenges. Their ruling houses all emerged from Turkish tribal organizations, and they all had to adapt their armies to the introduction of firearms. Over time, they became strongly linked culturally, as merchants, poets, philosophers, artists, and military advisers moved relatively easily across their political boundaries. Before the end of this period, Europeans were also active in trade in these empires, especially in India.

Chehel Sotoun, or *The 40 Columns*, Isfahan, Iran/Bridgeman Images

Persian Princess

The ruling houses of the Islamic empires were great patrons of art and architecture. This depiction of a princess in a garden is from an early-seventeenth-century palace built by Shah Abbas of the Safavid Dynasty in Persia.

CHAPTER PREVIEW

THE TURKISH RULING HOUSES: THE OTTOMANS, SAFAVIDS, AND MUGHALS
How were the three Islamic empires established, and what sorts of governments did they set up?

CULTURAL FLOWERING
What cultural advances occurred under the rule of the Ottoman, Safavid, and Mughal Empires?

NON-MUSLIMS UNDER MUSLIM RULE
How did Christians, Jews, Hindus, and other non-Muslims fare under these Islamic states?

SHIFTING TRADE ROUTES AND EUROPEAN PENETRATION
How were the Islamic empires affected by the gradual shift toward trade routes that bypassed their lands?

POLITICAL DECLINE
What common factors led to the decline of central power in the Islamic empires in the seventeenth and eighteenth centuries?

The Turkish Ruling Houses: The Ottomans, Safavids, and Mughals

How were the three Islamic empires established, and what sorts of governments did they set up?

Before the Mongols arrived in Central Asia and Persia, another nomadic people from the region of modern Mongolia, the Turks, had moved west, gained control over key territories from Anatolia to Delhi in north India, and contributed to the decline of the Abbasid caliphate in the thirteenth century. As Mongol strength in Persia and Central Asia deteriorated in the late thirteenth to mid-fourteenth centuries, the Turks resumed their expansion. In the late fourteenth century the Turkish leader Timur (1336–1405), also called Tamerlane, built a Central Asian empire from his base in Samarkand that reached into India and through Persia to the Black Sea. After his death, his sons and grandson fought each other for succession, and by 1450 his empire was in rapid decline. Meanwhile, Sufi orders (groups of Islamic mystics) thrived, and Islam became the most important force integrating the region. It was from the many small Turkish chiefs that the founders of the three main empires emerged.

The Expansion of the Ottoman Empire

The **Ottomans** took their name from Osman (r. 1299–1326), the chief of a band of seminomadic Turks that had migrated into western Anatolia while the Mongols still held Persia. The Ottomans gradually expanded at the expense of other small Turkish states and the Byzantine Empire (Map 17.1). Although temporarily slowed by defeat at the hands of Timur in 1402, the Ottomans quickly reasserted themselves after Timur's death in 1405.

Sultan Mehmet II Mehmet was called "the Conqueror" because at age twenty-one he captured Constantinople and ended the Byzantine Empire, but he is also known for his patronage of the arts and appreciation of beauty. (Topkapi Palace Museum, Istanbul, Turkey/Bridgeman Images)

Osman's campaigns were intended to subdue, not to destroy. The Ottomans built their empire by absorbing the Muslims of Anatolia and by becoming the protector of the Orthodox Church and of the millions of Greek Christians in Anatolia and the Balkans. A series of victories between 1326 and 1352 made the Ottomans masters of the Balkans. After these victories, the Ottomans made slaves of many captives and trained them as soldiers. These troops were outfitted with guns and artillery and trained to use them effectively.

In 1453, during the reign of Sultan Mehmet II (r. 1451–1481), the Ottomans conquered Constantinople, capital of the Byzantine Empire, which had lasted a thousand years. Once Constantinople was theirs, the Ottoman **sultans** (supreme political and military rulers) considered themselves successors to both the Byzantine and Seljuk Turk emperors, and they quickly absorbed the rest of the Byzantine Empire. In the sixteenth century they continued to expand through the Middle East and into North Africa.

Empire of Timur, ca. 1405

MAPPING THE PAST

MAP 17.1 The Ottoman Empire at Its Height, 1566 The Ottomans, like their great rivals the Habsburgs, rose to rule a vast dynastic empire encompassing many different peoples and ethnic groups. The army and the bureaucracy served to unite the disparate territories into a single state.

ANALYZING THE MAP Trace the coastlines of the Ottoman Empire. What were the major port cities of the empire? Which regions were encompassed within the empire at its height?

CONNECTIONS If the Ottoman Empire is compared to Europe of the same period (see Map 18.2), which had more of its territory near the sea? How did proximity to the Mediterranean shape the politics of Ottoman-European relations in this period?

To begin the transformation of Constantinople (renamed Istanbul) into an imperial Ottoman capital, Mehmet ordered wealthy residents to build mosques, markets, fountains, baths, and other public facilities. To make up for the loss of population through war, Mehmet transplanted inhabitants of other territories to the city, granting them tax remissions and possession of empty houses. He wanted them to start businesses, make Istanbul prosperous, and transform it into a microcosm of the empire.

Gunpowder, which was invented by the Chinese and adapted to artillery use by the Europeans, played an influential role in the expansion of the Ottoman

state. Mastering this technology, the Ottomans used it to gain control of shipping in the eastern Mediterranean and eliminate the Portuguese from the Red Sea and the Persian Gulf. In 1514, under the superb military leadership of Selim (r. 1512–1520), the Ottomans turned the Safavids back from Anatolia. When the Ottomans acquired Syria and Palestine (1516) and Egypt (1517), they gained control of the holy cities of Islam. Before long the Ottomans had extended their

Ottomans Ruling house of the Turkish empire that lasted from 1299 to 1922.

sultan An Arabic word used by the Ottomans to describe a supreme political and military ruler.

The Interior of an Ottoman Tent Made of leather, linen, cotton, silk, and wool, this magnificent tent would have been used by the Ottoman emperor on campaigns. Nearly 60 feet long, it was acquired by the ruler of Saxony (in Germany) in 1729 and used by him for official events, including royal weddings and military parades. (bpk Bildagentur/Ruestkammer, Staatliche Kunstsammlungen, Dresden, Germany/photo by Elke Estel/Hans-Peter Kuhl/Art Resource, NY)

rule across North Africa to Tunisia and Algeria. For the next four centuries a majority of Arabs lived under Ottoman rule.

Suleiman I (r. 1520–1566) extended Ottoman dominion to its widest geographical extent (see Map 17.1). Suleiman's army crushed the Hungarians at Mohács in 1526, killing the king and thousands of his nobles. Three years later the Turks unsuccessfully besieged the Habsburg capital of Vienna. From the late fourteenth to the early seventeenth centuries, the Ottoman Empire was a key player in European politics. In 1525 Francis I of France and Suleiman struck an alliance; both believed that only their collaboration could prevent Habsburg domination of Europe. The Habsburg emperor Charles V retaliated by seeking an alliance with Safavid Persia. Suleiman renewed the French agreement with Francis's son, Henry II (r. 1547–1559), and this accord became the cornerstone of Ottoman policy in western Europe. Ottoman pressure contributed to the official recognition of Lutheran

Protestants at the Peace of Augsburg in 1555 and the consolidation of the national monarchy in France.

Though usually victorious on land, the Ottomans did not enjoy complete dominion on the seas. Competition with the Habsburgs and pirates for control of the Mediterranean led the Ottomans to conquer Cyprus in 1570 and settle thousands of Turks from Anatolia there. In response, Pope Pius V organized a Holy League against the Turks, which won a victory in 1571 at Lepanto off the west coast of Greece with a squadron of more than two hundred Spanish, Venetian, and papal galleys. Still, the Turks remained supreme on land and quickly rebuilt their entire fleet.

To the east, war with Safavid Persia occupied the sultans' attention throughout the sixteenth and well into the seventeenth century. Several issues lay at the root of the long and exhausting conflict: religious antagonism between the Sunni Ottomans and the Shi'a Persians, competition to expand at each other's expense in Mesopotamia, desire to control trade routes, and European alliances. (For more on the Shi'a faith, see "The Safavid Empire in Persia.") Finally, in 1638 the Ottomans captured Baghdad, and the treaty of Kasr-I-Shirim established a permanent border between the two powers.

The Ottoman political system reached its classic form under Suleiman I. All authority flowed from the sultan to his public servants: provincial governors, police officers, military generals, heads of treasuries, and **viziers** (chief assistants to caliphs). Suleiman ordered Lütfi Paşa (d. 1562), a poet and juridical scholar of slave origin, to draw up a new general code of laws that prescribed penalties for routine criminal acts such as robbery, adultery, and murder. It also sought to reform bureaucratic and financial corruption, such as foreign merchants' payment of bribes to avoid customs duties, imprisonment without trial, and promotion in the provincial administration because of favoritism rather than ability. The legal code also introduced the idea of balanced government budgets. The head of the religious establishment was given the task of reconciling sultanic law with Islamic law.

The Ottomans ruled their more distant lands, such as those in North Africa, relatively lightly. Governors of distant provinces collected taxes and maintained trade routes, but their control did not penetrate deeply into the countryside.

The Ottoman Empire's Use of Slaves

The power of the Ottoman central government was sustained through the training of slaves. Slaves were captured in battle; purchased from Spain, North Africa, and Venice; or drafted through the system known as **devshirme**, by which the sultan's agents compelled Christian families in the Balkans to sell their boys. The slave boys were converted to Islam and trained for the imperial civil service and the standing army. The brightest 10 percent entered the palace school, where they learned to read and write Arabic, Ottoman Turkish, and Persian in preparation for administrative jobs. Other boys were sent to Turkish farms, where they acquired physical toughness in preparation for military service. Known as **janissaries** (Turkish for "recruits"), they formed the elite army corps. Thoroughly indoctrinated and absolutely loyal to the sultan, the janissary corps adapted easily to the use of firearms. The devshirme system enabled the Ottomans to apply merit-based recruitment to military and administrative offices at little cost and provided a means of assimilating Christians living in Ottoman lands.

The Ottoman ruling class included people of varied ethnic origins who rose through the bureaucratic and military ranks, many beginning as the sultan's slaves. In return for their services to the sultan, they held landed estates for the duration of their lives. Because all property belonged to the sultan and reverted to him on the holder's death, Turkish nobles, unlike their European counterparts, did not have a local base independent of the ruler. The absence of a hereditary nobility and of private ownership of agricultural land differentiates the Ottoman system from European feudalism.

Another distinctive characteristic of the Ottomans was the sultan's failure to marry. From about 1500 on, the sultans did not contract legal marriages but perpetuated the ruling house through concubinage. A slave **concubine** (a woman who is a recognized spouse but of lower status than a wife) could not expect to exert power the way a local or foreign noblewoman could. (For a notable exception, see "Individuals in Society: Hürrem," page 474.) When one of the sultan's concubines delivered a boy, she raised him until the age of ten or eleven. Then the child was given a province to govern under his mother's supervision. Because succession to the throne was open to all the sultan's sons, fratricide often resulted upon his death, and the losers were blinded or executed.

Slave concubinage paralleled the Ottoman development of slave soldiers and slave viziers. All held positions entirely at the sultan's pleasure, owed loyalty solely to him, and were thus more reliable than a hereditary nobility. Great social prestige, as well as the opportunity to acquire power and wealth, was attached to being a slave of the imperial household.

The Safavid Empire in Persia

With the decline of Timur's empire after 1450, Persia was controlled by Turkish lords, with no single one dominant until 1501, when fourteen-year-old Isma'il (1487–1524) led a Turkish army to capture Tabriz and declared himself **shah** (Persian word for "king").

The strength of the early **Safavid** state rested on three crucial features. First, the Safavid state utilized the skills of urban bureaucrats and made them an essential part of the civil machinery of government. Second, it secured the loyalty and military support of

---

viziers Chief assistants to caliphs.

devshirme A process whereby the sultan's agents swept the provinces for Christian youths to be trained as soldiers or civil servants.

janissaries Turkish for "recruits"; they formed the elite army corps.

concubine A woman who is a recognized spouse but of lower status than a wife.

shah Persian word for "king."

Safavid The dynasty that ruled all of Persia and other regions from 1501 to 1722; its state religion was Shi'ism.

Hürrem

HÜRREM (1505?–1558) WAS BORN IN THE WESTERN Ukraine (then part of Poland), the daughter of a Ruthenian priest, and was given the Polish name Aleksandra Lisowska. When Tartars raided, they captured and enslaved her. In 1520 she was given as a gift to Suleiman on the occasion of his accession to the throne. The Venetian ambassador (probably relying on secondhand or thirdhand information) described her as "young, graceful, petite, but not beautiful." She was given the Turkish name Hürrem, meaning "joyful."

Hürrem apparently brought joy to Suleiman. Their first child was born in 1521. By 1525 they had four sons and a daughter; sources note that by that year Suleiman visited no other woman. But he waited eight or nine years before breaking Ottoman dynastic tradition by making Hürrem his legal wife, the first slave concubine so honored. For the rest of her life, Hürrem played a highly influential role in the political, diplomatic, and philanthropic life of the Ottoman state. First, great power flowed from her position as mother of the prince, the future sultan Selim II (r. 1566–1574). Then, as the intimate and most trusted adviser of the sultan, she was Suleiman's closest confidant. During his frequent trips to the far-flung corners of his multiethnic empire, Hürrem wrote him long letters filled with her love and longing for him and her prayers for his safety in battle. She also shared political information about affairs in Istanbul, the activities of the grand vizier, and the attitudes of the janissaries. At a time when some people believed that the sultan's absence from the capital endangered his hold on the throne, Hürrem acted as his eyes and ears for potential threats.

Hürrem was the sultan's contact with her native Poland, which sent more embassies to Istanbul than any other power. Through her correspondence with King Sigismund I, peace between Poland and the Ottomans was maintained. When Sigismund II succeeded his father in 1548, Hürrem sent congratulations on his accession, along with two pairs of pajamas (originally a Hindu garment but commonly worn in southwestern Asia) and six handkerchiefs. Also, she sent the shah of Persia gold-embroidered sheets and shirts that she had sewn herself, seeking to display the wealth of the sultanate and to keep peace between the Ottomans and the Safavids.

The enormous stipend that Suleiman gave Hürrem permitted her to participate in his vast building program. In Jerusalem (in the Ottoman province of Palestine) she founded a hospice for fifty-five pilgrims that included a soup kitchen that fed four hundred pilgrims a day. In Istanbul Suleiman built and Hürrem endowed the Haseki (meaning "royal favorite concubine") mosque complex and a public bath for women near the Women's Market.

Hürrem depicted by a contemporary European artist.
(*Rosa, Consort of Suleiman, Emperor of the Turks,* ca. 1600–1670 [oil on canvas], French School/Royal Collections Trust © Her Majesty Queen Elizabeth II, 2017/Bridgeman Images)

Perhaps Hürrem tried to fulfill two functions hitherto distinct in Ottoman political theory: those of the sultan's favorite and of mother of the prince. She also performed the conflicting roles of slave concubine and imperial wife. Many Turks resented Hürrem's interference at court. They believed she was behind the execution of Suleiman's popular son Mustafa on a charge of treason to make way for her own son to succeed as sultan.

QUESTIONS FOR ANALYSIS

1. How does Hürrem compare to powerful women in other places, such as Empress Wu in China, Isabella of Castile, Catherine de' Medici of France, Elizabeth I of England, or any other you know about?
2. What was Hürrem's "nationality"? What role did it play in her life?

Source: Leslie P. Peirce, *The Imperial Harem: Women and Sovereignty in the Ottoman Empire* (New York: Oxford University Press, 1993).

MAP 17.2 The Safavid Empire, 1587–1629 In the late sixteenth century the power of the Safavid kingdom of Persia rested on its strong military force, its Shi'a Muslim faith, and its extraordinarily rich trade in rugs and pottery. Many of the cities on the map, such as Tabriz, Qum, and Shiraz, were great rug-weaving centers.

nomadic Turkish Sufis known as **Qizilbash** (KIH-zihl-bahsh) (a Turkish word meaning "redheads" that was applied to these people because of the red hats they wore). In return for the vast grazing lands granted to them, the Qizilbash supplied the shah with troops.

The third source of Safavid strength was the Shi'a faith, which became the compulsory religion of the empire. The Shi'a believed that leadership among Muslims rightfully belonged to the Prophet Muhammad's descendants. Because Isma'il claimed descent from a line of twelve infallible imams (leaders) beginning with Ali (Muhammad's cousin and son-in-law), he was officially regarded as their representative on earth. Isma'il recruited Shi'a scholars to instruct and guide his people, and he persecuted and exiled Sunni **ulama** (religious scholars who interpret the Qur'an and the Sunna, the deeds and sayings of Muhammad). To this day, Iran remains the only Muslim state in which Shi'ism is the official religion.

Safavid power reached its height under Shah Abbas (r. 1587–1629), who moved the capital from Qazvin to Isfahan. His military achievements, support for trade and commerce, and endowment of the arts earned him the epithet "the Great." In the military realm he

adopted the Ottoman practice of building an army of slaves, primarily captives from the Caucasus, and used them as a counterweight to the Qizilbash, who had come to be considered a threat. He also increased the use of gunpowder weapons and made alliances with European powers against the Ottomans and Portuguese. In his campaigns against the Ottomans, Shah Abbas captured Baghdad, Mosul, and Diarbakr in Mesopotamia (Map 17.2).

Conflict between the Ottomans and the Safavids was not an even match. The Safavids did not have as many people or as much wealth as the Ottomans and continually had to defend against encroachments on their western border. Still, they were able to attract some of the Turks in Ottoman lands who felt that their government had shifted too far from its nomadic roots. After Shah Abbas, Safavid power was sapped by civil war between tribal factions vying for control of the court.

Qizilbash Nomadic Turkish Sufis who supplied the early Safavid state with military troops in exchange for grazing rights.

ulama Religious scholars who interpret the Qur'an and the Sunna, the deeds and sayings of Muhammad.

The Mughal Empire in India

Of the three great Islamic empires of the early modern world, the **Mughal** Empire of India was the largest, wealthiest, and most populous. Extending over 1.2 million square miles at the end of the seventeenth century, with a population between 100 and 150 million, and with fabulous wealth and resources, the Mughal Empire surpassed the other two by a wide margin. In the sixteenth century only the Ming Dynasty in China could compare.

In 1504 Babur (r. 1483–1530), a Turkish ruler forced out of a small territory in Central Asia, captured Kabul and established a kingdom in Afghanistan. An adventurer who claimed descent from Chinggis Khan and Timur, Babur moved southward in search of resources to restore his fortunes. In 1526, with a force of only twelve thousand men equipped with firearms, Babur defeated the sultan of Delhi at Panipat. Babur's capture of the cities of Agra and Delhi, key fortresses of the north, paved the way for further conquests in northern India. Although many of his soldiers wished to return north with their spoils, Babur decided to stay in India.

A gifted writer, Babur wrote an autobiography in Turkish that recounts his military campaigns, describes places and people he encountered, reports his difficulties giving up wine, and shows his wide-ranging interests in everything from fruit and swimming to a Turkish general who excelled at leapfrog. He was not particularly impressed by India, as can be inferred from this description in his memoirs:

> Hindustan is a country which has few pleasures to recommend it. The people are not handsome. They have no idea of the charms of friendly society, of frankly mixing together, or familiar discourse. They have no genius, no comprehension of mind, no politeness of manner, no kindness or fellow-feeling, no ingenuity or mechanical invention in planning or executing their handicraft works, no skill or knowledge in design or architecture; they have no horses, no good flesh, no grapes or muskmelons, no good fruits, no ice or cold water, no good food or bread in their bazaars, no baths or colleges, no candles, no torches, not a candlestick.[1]

During the reign of Babur's son Humayun (r. 1530–1540 and 1555–1556), the Mughals lost most of their territories in Afghanistan. Humayun went into temporary exile in Persia, where he developed a deep appreciation for Persian art and literature. The reign of Humayun's son Akbar (r. 1556–1605) may well have been the greatest in the history of India. A boy of thirteen when he succeeded to the throne, Akbar pursued expansionist policies. Under his dynamic leadership, the Mughal state took definitive form and encompassed most of the subcontinent north of the Godavari River. No kingdom or coalition of kingdoms could long resist Akbar's armies. The once-independent states of northern India were forced into a centralized political system under the sole authority of the Mughal emperor.

Akbar replaced Turkish with Persian as the official language of the Mughal Empire, and Persian remained the official language until the British replaced it with English in 1835. To govern this vast region, Akbar developed an administrative bureaucracy centered on four co-equal ministers: finance; the army and intelligence; the judiciary and religious patronage; and the imperial household, whose jurisdiction included roads, bridges, and infrastructure throughout the empire. Under Akbar's Hindu finance minister, Raja Todar Mal, a uniform system of taxes was put in place. In the provinces imperial governors were appointed by and responsible solely to the emperor. Whereas the Ottoman sultans and Safavid shahs made extensive use of slaves acquired from non-Muslim lands for military and administrative positions, Akbar used the services of royal princes, nobles, and warrior-aristocrats. Initially these men were Muslims from Central Asia, but to reduce their influence, Akbar vigorously recruited Persians and Hindus. No single ethnic or religious faction could challenge the emperor.

Akbar's descendants extended the Mughal Empire further. His son Jahangir (r. 1605–1628) consolidated Mughal rule in Bengal. (See "Global Viewpoints: Mughal and French Views on Priorities for Monarchs," at right.) Jahangir's son Shah Jahan (r. 1628–1658) launched fresh territorial expansion. Faced with dangerous revolts by the Muslims in Ahmadnagar and the resistance of the newly arrived Portuguese in Bengal, Shah Jahan not only crushed this opposition but also strengthened his northwestern frontier. Shah Jahan's son Aurangzeb (r. 1658–1707), unwilling to wait for

The Mughal Empire, 1526–1857

Mughal territory
- In 1525
- Added, by 1539
- Added, by 1605
- Added, by 1707
- Lost, by 1707

HIMALAYA MTS.

Panipat
Delhi • Agra

Arabian Sea

Bay of Bengal

Mughal A term used to refer to the Muslim empire of India, which was the largest, wealthiest, and most populous of the Islamic empires of the early modern world.

Mughal and French Views on Priorities for Monarchs

Jahangir, the fourth Mughal emperor, was as much a patron of the arts as a military commander. Like his great-grandfather Babur, he wrote a memoir. Jahangir's representation of himself and his actions in the memoir can be compared to that of the French king Louis XIV, less than a century later, whose advice to his heir has been preserved.

Jahangir's *Memoirs*

■ At that period when I took my departure from Lahore for Agra, on the occasion recently described, it happily occurred to me to direct that the different landholders on that route should plant at every town and village, and every stage and halting place, all the way from Lahore to Agra, mulberry and other large and lofty trees affording shade, but particularly those with broad leaves and wide-spreading branches, in order that to all time to come the way-worn and weary traveler might find under their shadow repose and shelter from the scorching rays of the sun during the summer heats. . . . And, lastly, at the passage of every river, whether large or small, convenient bridges were erected, so that the industrious traveler might be able to pursue his objects without obstruction or delay. . . .

With regard to the maxims which should govern the policy of sovereign princes, it has been said, that to resolve without the concurrence of men of experience is the most fallacious of proceedings; but I contend, nevertheless, that there is no safety in council, unless founded in rectitude of mind. I maintain, that if we entrust the concerns of the state to the opinions of another, we give to the Almighty an associate in the secrets of the heart. . . . He that conducts the destinies of his country by the judgment of another, must not forget that he will nevertheless be himself responsible, at the awful day of account, for all the exactions, the tyranny, the unjust decisions, violence, and oppression to which the people may have been exposed, through such imprudent delegation. It is from the reigning sovereign that the awful reckoning will be required, not from those who have been his advisers.

Louis XIV's *Memoirs*

■ The cleverest private individuals take advice from other clever people about their little concerns. What should be the rule for kings who have in their hands the public weal, and whose resolutions harm or benefit the whole earth? Decisions of such importance should never be formed, if possible, without calling upon all the most enlightened, reasonable and wise among our subjects. . . . Besides, our lofty position in some way separates us from our people to whom our ministers are closer, and are consequently able to see a thousand things of which we know nothing, but on which nevertheless we must make up our minds and take measures. Add to this their age, experience, deliberations, and their greater liberty to obtain information and suggestions from their inferiors, who in their turn gather them from others, step by step down to the lowest.

But when on important occasions they have reported to us all the aspects and all the opposing reasons, all that is done elsewhere in similar cases, all that has been done formerly, and all that might be done today, it is incumbent upon us, my son, to choose what must be actually done. And in regard to that choice I will make bold to tell you that if we do not lack good sense or courage there is no other who can make a better one than us.

QUESTIONS FOR ANALYSIS

1. Are you more impressed by the similarities between these two monarchs' comments on consultation with advisers or by the differences? What might account for the similarities and the differences?
2. What can you infer about the personalities of these two monarchs from their remarks?
3. Jahangir describes in great detail the improvements to the roads in his empire. Why would a ruler take pride in the improvement of roads?

Sources: David Price, trans., *Memoirs of the Emperor Jahangueir* (London: The Oriental Translation Committee, 1929), pp. 90–91, slightly modified; Herbert Wilson, trans., *A King's Lessons in Statecraft: Louis XIV: Letters to His Heirs* (New York: Albert and Charles Boni, 1925), pp. 63–64.

his father to die, deposed him and confined him for years in a small cell. A puritanically devout and strictly orthodox Muslim, as well as a skillful general and a clever diplomat, Aurangzeb ruled more of India than did any previous Mughal emperor, having extended the realm deeper into south India. His reign, however, also marked the beginning of the empire's decline. His non-Muslim subjects were not pleased with his religious zealotry, and his military campaigns were costly. In the south resistance to Mughal rule led to major uprisings. (For more on Aurangzeb's rule, see "Non-Muslims Under Muslim Rule.")

Cultural Flowering

What cultural advances occurred under the rule of the Ottoman, Safavid, and Mughal Empires?

All three Islamic empires presided over extraordinary artistic and intellectual flowering in everything from carpetmaking to architecture and gardening, from geography and astronomy to medicine. At the same time, new religious practices (and conflicts) emerged, and people found new outlets for socializing and exchanging ideas. Artistic and intellectual advances spread from culture to culture, probably because of the common Persian influence on the Turks since the tenth century. This exchange was also aided by shared languages, especially Arabic, Turkish, and Persian. Persian was used as the administrative language by the Mughals in India, and Arabic was a lingua franca of the entire region because of its centrality in Islam. In Ottoman lands both Persian and Arabic were literary languages, but Turkish slowly became the lingua franca of the realm.

The Arts

One of the arts all three empires shared was carpet-making. Carpet designs and weaving techniques demonstrate both cultural integration and local distinctiveness. Turkic migrants carried their weaving traditions with them as they moved but also readily adopted new motifs, especially from Persia. In Safavid Persia, Shah Abbas was determined to improve his country's export trade and built the small cottage business of carpet weaving into a national industry. In the capital city of Isfahan alone, factories employed more than twenty-five thousand weavers who produced woolen carpets, brocades, and silks of brilliant color, design, and quality. Women and children were often employed as weavers, especially of the most expensive rugs, because their smaller hands could tie tinier knots.

Another art that spread from Persia to both Ottoman and Mughal lands was miniature painting, especially for book illustration. There was an interplay between carpets and miniature painting. Naturalistic depictions of lotus blossoms, peonies, chrysanthemums,

Music in a Garden
This illustration of a courtly romance depicts several women in a garden intently listening to a musician, with cups of a beverage in their hands. (Granger, NYC— All rights reserved.)

Turkish Rug This small carpet (approximately 5½ by 4 feet) was made in seventeenth-century Turkey. Like most other rugs of the region, it is made of hand-knotted wool and features symmetrical geometric designs.

(Lotto type carpet, Ottoman Turkey, 17th-century c.e. Wool [warp, weft and pile]. The James F. Ballard Collection, Gift of James F. Ballard, 1922 [22.100.112]/The Metropolitan Museum of Art, New York, New York, USA/Image copyright © The Metropolitan Museum of Art/Image source: Art Resource, NY)

tulips, carnations, birds, and even dragons appear in both book illustrations and carpets.

In Mughal India, as throughout the Muslim world, books were regarded as precious objects. Time, talent, and expensive materials went into their production, and they were highly coveted because they reflected wealth, learning, and power. Akbar reportedly possessed twenty-four thousand books when he died. The historian Abu'l-Fazl described Akbar's library and love of books:

> His Majesty's library is divided into several parts. . . . Prose works, poetical works, Hindi, Persian, Greek, Kashmirian, Arabic, are all separately placed. In this order they are also inspected. Experienced people bring them daily and read them before His Majesty, who hears every book from beginning to end . . . and rewards the readers with presents of cash either in gold or silver, according to the number of leaves read out by them. . . . There are no historical facts of

past ages, or curiosities of science, or interesting points of philosophy, with which His Majesty, a leader of impartial sages, is unacquainted.[2]

City and Palace Building

In all three empires strong rulers built capital cities and imperial palaces as visible expressions of dynastic majesty. Suleiman "the Magnificent" used his fabulous wealth and thousands of servants to adorn Istanbul with palaces, mosques, schools, and libraries. The building of hospitals, roads, and bridges and the reconstruction of the water systems of the great pilgrimage sites at Mecca and Jerusalem benefited his subjects. Safavid Persia and Mughal India produced rulers with similar ambitions.

The greatest builder under the Ottomans was Mimar Sinan (1491–1588), a Greek-born devshirme recruit who rose to become imperial architect under Suleiman. A contemporary of Michelangelo, Sinan designed 312 public buildings, including mosques, schools, hospitals, public baths, palaces, and burial chapels. His masterpieces, the Shehzade and Suleimaniye Mosques in Istanbul, were designed to maximize the space under the dome.

Shah Abbas made his capital, Isfahan, the jewel of the Safavid Empire. He had his architects place a polo ground in the center and surrounded it with palaces, mosques, and bazaars. In the bazaar one could find splendid rugs, pottery and fine china, metalwork of exceptionally high quality, and silks and velvets of stunning weave and design. A city of perhaps 750,000 people, Isfahan also contained 162 mosques, 48 schools where future members of the ulama learned the sacred Muslim sciences, 273 public baths, and the vast imperial palace. Mosques were richly decorated with blue tile. Private houses had their own garden courts, and public gardens, pools, and parks adorned the wide streets.

Among the Mughal emperors, Shah Jahan had the most sophisticated interest in architecture. Because his capital at Agra was cramped, in 1639 he decided to found a new capital city at Delhi. In the design and layout of the buildings, Persian ideas predominated. The walled palace-fortress alone extended over 125 acres. Built partly of red sandstone, partly of marble, it included private chambers for the emperor; mansions for the wives, widows, and concubines of the imperial household; huge audience rooms for the conduct of public business; baths; and vast gardens filled with flowers, trees, and thirty silver fountains spraying water. In 1650, with living quarters for guards, military officials, merchants, dancing girls, scholars, and hordes of cooks and servants, the palace-fortress housed fifty-seven thousand people. It also boasted a covered public bazaar.

Two Masterpieces of Islamic Architecture
Istanbul's Suleimaniye Mosque, designed by Sinan and commissioned by Suleiman I, was finished in 1557. Its interior (below left) is especially spacious. The Taj Mahal (left), built about a century later in Agra in northern India, is perhaps the finest example of Mughal architecture. Its white marble exterior is decorated with Arabic inscriptions and floral designs. (Taj Mahal: Dinodia/Bridgeman Images; mosque: Murat Tander/Lithium Collection/age-fotostock)

For his palace, Shah Jahan ordered the construction of the Peacock Throne. This famous piece, encrusted with emeralds, diamonds, pearls, and rubies, took seven years to fashion and cost the equivalent of $5 million. It served as the imperial throne of India until 1739, when the Persian warrior Nadir Shah seized it as plunder and carried it to Persia.

Shah Jahan's most enduring monument is the Taj Mahal. Between 1631 and 1648 twenty thousand workers toiled over the construction of this memorial in Agra to Shah Jahan's favorite wife, who died giving birth to their fifteenth child. One of the most beautiful structures in the world, the Taj Mahal is both an expression of love and a superb architectural blending of Islamic and Indian culture.

Gardens

Many of the architectural masterpieces of this age had splendid gardens attached to them. Gardens represent a distinctive and highly developed feature of Persian culture. They commonly were walled, with a pool in the center and geometrically laid-out flowering plants, especially roses. Identified with paradise in Arab tradition, gardens served not only as centers of prayer and meditation but also as places of leisure and revelry. After the incorporation of Persia into the caliphate in the seventh century, formal gardening spread west and east through the Islamic world, as illustrated by the magnificent gardens of Muslim Spain, southern Italy, and, later, south-

Polo Two teams of four on horseback ride back and forth on a field measuring 200 by 400 yards, trying to hit a 4½-ounce wooden ball with a 4-foot mallet through the opponent's goal. Because a typical match involves many high-speed collisions among the horses, each player has to maintain a string of expensive ponies in order to change mounts several times during the game. Students of the history of sports believe the game originated in Persia, as shown in this sixteenth-century miniature, and then spread to India, China, and Japan. Brought from India to England, where it became very popular among the aristocracy in the nineteenth century, polo is a fine example of cross-cultural influences. (Photo by Roland and Sabrina Michaud/ akg-images)

eastern Europe. When Babur established the Mughal Dynasty in India, he adapted the Persian garden to the warmer southern climate. Gardens were laid out near palaces, mosques, shrines, and mausoleums, including the Taj Mahal, which had four water channels symbolizing the four rivers of paradise.

Gardens, of course, are seasonal. To remind themselves of paradise during the cold winter months, rulers, city people, and nomads ordered Persian carpets, most of which feature floral patterns and have formal garden designs.

Intellectual Advances and Religious Trends

Between 1400 and 1800 the culture of the Islamic empires developed in many directions. Particularly notable were new movements within Islam as well as advances in mathematics, geography, astronomy, and medicine. Building on the knowledge of earlier Islamic writers and stimulated by Ottoman naval power, the geographer and cartographer Piri Reis created the *Book of the Sea* (1521), which contained 129 chapters, each with a map incorporating all Islamic (and Western) knowledge of the seas and navigation and describing harbors, tides, dangerous rocks and shores, and storm areas. In the field of astronomy, Takiyuddin Mehmet (1521–1585) built an observatory at Istanbul. His *Instruments of the Observatory* catalogued astronomical instruments and described an astronomical clock that fixed the location of heavenly bodies with greater precision than ever before.

There were also advances in medicine. Under Suleiman the imperial palace itself became a center of medical science, and the large number of hospitals established in Istanbul and throughout the empire testifies to his support for medical research and his concern for the sick. Abi Ahmet Celebi (1436–1523), the chief physician of the empire, produced a study on kidney and bladder stones. Recurrent outbreaks of the plague

Illustrated Medical Manual
The Turkish physician Serafeddin Sabuncuoglu (1385–1470) wrote a treatise of surgery in Turkish, with illustrations, in 1465. This page shows a physician cauterizing leprosy lesions.
(Bibliothèque Nationale, Paris, France/ Archives Charmet/Bridgeman Images)

posed a challenge for physicians in Muslim lands. Muhammad had once said not to go to a country where an epidemic existed but also not to leave a place because an epidemic broke out. As a consequence, when European cities began enforcing quarantines to control the spread of the plague, early Muslim rulers dismissed such efforts. By the sixteenth century, however, a better understanding of contagion led to a redefinition of the proper response to a plague epidemic and allowed for leaving the city in search of clean air.

In the realm of religion, the rulers of all three empires drew legitimacy from their support for Islam. The Sunni-Shi'a split between the Ottomans and Safavids led to efforts to define and enforce religious orthodoxy on both sides. For the Safavids this entailed suppressing Sufi movements and Sunnis, even marginalizing—sometimes massacring—the original Qizilbash warriors, who had come to be seen as politically disruptive. Sectarian conflicts within Islam were not as pronounced in Mughal lands, perhaps because Muslims were greatly outnumbered by non-Muslims, mostly Hindus.

Sufi fraternities thrived throughout the Muslim world in this era, even when the states tried to limit them. In India Sufi orders also influenced non-Muslims. The mystical Bhakti movement among Hindus involved dances, poems, and songs reminiscent of Sufi practice. The development of the new religion of the Sikhs (SEEKS) was also influenced by Sufis. The Sikhs traced themselves back to a teacher in the sixteenth century who argued that God did not distinguish between Muslims and Hindus but saw everyone as his children. Sikhs rejected the caste system (division of society into hereditary groups) and forbade alcohol and tobacco, and men did not cut their hair, covering it instead with a turban. The Sikh movement was most successful in northwest India, where Sikh men armed themselves to defend their communities.

Despite all the signs of cultural vitality in the three Islamic empires, none of them adopted the printing press or went through the sorts of cultural expansion associated with it in China and Europe. Until 1729 the Ottoman authorities prohibited printing books in Turkish or Arabic (Jews, Armenians, and Greeks could establish presses and print in their own languages). Printing was not banned in Mughal India, but neither did the technology spread, even after Jesuit missionaries printed Bibles in Indian languages beginning in the 1550s. The copying of manuscripts was a well-established practice, and those who made their living this way sometimes organized to keep competition at bay. It also needs to be noted that by the end of this period, scientific knowledge was not keeping up with advances made in Europe (see "The Scientific Revolution" in Chapter 19).

Coffeehouses and Their Social Impact

In the mid-fifteenth century a new social convention spread throughout the Islamic world—drinking coffee. Arab writers trace the origins of coffee drinking to

Coffee Drinking

Coffee beans are native to east Africa and were first grown in Ethiopia. They were brought to Yemen by Sufis in the fifteenth century. There the red beans were boiled in water to produce a hot beverage, which was appreciated for its ability to help participants stay awake during long rituals. By the sixteenth century coffee drinking had spread to other Islamic lands. By then people had learned to roast the beans and grind them finely before adding hot water.

In 1511 some conservative imams in Mecca ruled that coffee should be banned because of its stimulating effects, but the Ottoman sultan Suleiman I overturned their ruling in 1524, helping spread the custom of coffee drinking. As a caffeinated drink, coffee was much like tea. Both proved very popular even though they provided no calories. Because alcohol was forbidden to Muslims, coffee in some ways took its place, providing occasions for socializing either in coffeehouses or in homes or palaces.

This painting by an unknown Ottoman artist is in the Persian miniature style, which is noted for its bright colors and finely drawn details. Part of an album of painting and calligraphy on vellum (fine parchment), the image depicts a banquet where coffee drinking is part of the entertainment. The guests of honor are sitting in a recessed alcove, entertained by three musicians. An attendant in the upper right has a set of cups, and elsewhere in the picture men are shown sipping from cups.

QUESTIONS FOR ANALYSIS

1. How many individuals are shown sipping coffee? What other activities are depicted?
2. How does the artist convey differences in the ages of those drinking coffee?
3. Are there any women in the picture, or are the figures all men? How do you know?
4. Does this picture suggest any reasons why coffee became a popular drink?

(© The Trustees of the Chester Beatty Library, Dublin, Ireland/Bridgeman Images)

Yemen Sufis, who sought a trancelike concentration on God to the exclusion of everything else and found that coffee helped them stay awake. Before long, coffee was being used as a business lubricant—an extension of hospitality to a potential buyer in a shop. Merchants carried the Yemenite practice to Mecca in about 1490. From Mecca, where pilgrims were introduced to it, coffee drinking spread to Egypt and Syria. In 1555 two Syrians opened a coffeehouse in Istanbul. (See "Analyzing the Evidence: Coffee Drinking," above.)

Coffeehouses provided a place for conversation and male sociability; there a man could entertain his friends cheaply and more informally than at home. But coffeehouses encountered religious and governmental opposition: some people argued that coffee was intoxicating, making it analogous to wine, which was prohibited

Katib Chelebi on Tobacco

Katib Chelebi (1609–1657) was an Ottoman civil servant who spent much of his time as an accountant for the Turkish army, accompanying it on several important campaigns. Over time, he became passionate about learning and pursued not only Islamic law but also ancient Greek philosophy, geography, and modern European sciences. He wrote several important books, including a bibliographical encyclopedia. The book of essays from which the following extract comes also discusses such contemporary issues as coffee, singing, opium, shaking hands, bowing, and bribery.

■ Sometime in the latter half of the ninth century of the Hijra [in the fifteen century], after some Spanish ships had discovered the New World, the Portuguese and English were exploring its shores to find a passage from the Eastern to the Western Ocean. They came to an island* close to the mainland, called in the Atlas "Gineya." Due to the negative impact of the humidity of the sea air on his nature, a doctor from the crew of the ship suffered from what appeared to be a lymphatic disorder. While he was looking for a cure, employing hot and dry things in accordance with the dictum "Cure is in the opposite," his ship arrived at the aforementioned island, and he saw that some sort of a leaf was burning. Smelling its scent, he understood that it was a hot scent, and he started sucking the smoke through a pipe-like instrument. As he benefited from this, he collected a large quantity of that leaf and used it while he stayed there. The people on the ship, saying "This is a beneficial cure" and following his example, collected a lot of the leaf. They start smoking this way one after another. After the ship arrived in England, smoking spread to France and other places; without knowing about its origin and thinking that it can be used leisurely, people started smoking tobacco. Most of them became addicted and considered it a stimulating drug. As it became a common

phenomena in the East and the West, it remained unhindered by prohibition.

It appeared around 1010 A.H. [1601 C.E.]. Since then various preachers mentioned it, and many learned men wrote treatises; some argued that it is religiously prohibited, and others disapproved. Those who were addicted, on the other hand, replied to these with their own treatises. After a while, in the court of the sultan [that is, in Istanbul], Şeyhi Ibrahim Efendi, the surgeon of the Palace, showed extreme care for the topic and talked about it at length and preached in the public seminar of Sultan Mehemmed Mosque and hung on the wall copies of the counsel and religious opinion [*fatwa*] in vain. As he talked about it, people smoked more and became more obstinate. Seeing it doesn't help, he gave in.

Later, towards the end of his reign, Sultan Murad IV [1612–1640] banned coffee houses in order to close down the door of evil acts and tobacco because it caused some fires [in the city]. When people disregarded the prohibition, the power of the Sultan necessitated reprimanding those who by smoking performed the sin of acting against the imperial order. Occasionally, [due to] the sultan's ruthlessness in suppression and in accordance with the dictum "Mankind craves what is forbidden," people's desire and craving to smoke equally increased. Many men were sent to the realm of nothingness due to this crime. At the encampments on the way to the Baghdad campaign, while fifteen to twenty leading soldiers were being executed in the presence of the sultan with extreme torment with the accusation of smoking tobacco, they still carried little pipes, some under their shirts, and some in their pockets and smoked at every opportunity. In Istanbul, there was no end to those who smoked in the barracks and public latrines. Even under such harsh suppression, those who smoked were more than those who didn't. After he [Sultan Murad IV] passed away, at times it was prohibited, and at times it was permitted, and finally, during the

to Muslims, and others asserted that political discussion in coffeehouses could lead to sedition. On the other hand, the coffee trade was a major source of profit that local notables sought to control.

Although debate over the morality of coffeehouses continued through the sixteenth century, their eventual acceptance represented a revolution in Islamic life: socializing was no longer confined to the home. In the seventeenth century coffee and coffeehouses spread to Europe. (For reaction to another new product that spread quickly despite opposition, see "Analyzing the Evidence: Katib Chelebi on Tobacco," above.)

Non-Muslims Under Muslim Rule

How did Christians, Jews, Hindus, and other non-Muslims fare under these Islamic states?

Drawing on Qur'anic teachings, Muslims had long practiced a religious tolerance unknown in Christian Europe. Muslim rulers for the most part guaranteed the lives and property of Christians and Jews in exchange for their promise of obedience and the payment of a time of the late grand mufti Bahai Effendi issued a fatwa ruling that tobacco was permissible; among the people smoking became prevalent and popular once more. Yet, thanks to the fact that the high imperial order chastised the addicts from time to time, some quit. However, in all of the fourth of the world that is inhabited it was being smoked. Such is the story of tobacco. Now, let's consider the contexts for and characteristics of smoking in the form of a few arguments:

The first argument is that people can be prevented through prohibition and can quit tobacco. Since habit is second nature, we need to push aside this possibility. Addicts cannot be made to quit this way. . . .

The second discussion concerns the question of whether tobacco is good or bad with respect to reason. We can neglect the approval of it by addicts, and the intelligent accepted it as bad; either the judgment of good or bad have to be determined by both reason and religious law. . . .

The third argument is about its benefits and harmful effects. There is no doubt that it is financially harmful. However, since it becomes one of the most essential items for the addict, he doesn't mind its financial harm. Its harm on the body is well attested. Since tobacco pollutes the essence of air breathed by people, it is physically harmful.

The fourth argument is whether or not it is an innovation according to religion. It is an innovation according to the religious law, since it appeared in recent times. Moreover, it cannot be argued that it is an acceptable innovation. It is also rationally an innovation, because smoking hasn't been seen or heard of by the intelligent since the time of Adam. . . .

The fifth argument concerns if it is religiously abominable or not. There is no way to deny that it is abominable in reason and in religion; everyone has accepted this argument. Since the scent of tobacco smoke and the scent of its leaves are not abominable in themselves, for it to be accepted as abominable, its excessive use is a condition.† . . .

The sixth argument is about its being unlawful or not. To produce a judgment on a topic through independent reasoning is accepted as a method in books of religious law.

There are sufficient conditions collected to proscribe tobacco through an analysis of available proof. Yet it is preferable not to proclaim it forbidden. It is recommended to accept it as religiously permissible in order to protect people from insisting on sin by doing forbidden acts through the application of a legal principle.

The seventh argument is whether or not it is religiously permissible. Since tobacco appeared in recent times, it is not clearly considered and mentioned in books of religious law. Consequently, following the dictum, "In things permissibility is inherent," smoking is considered as permissible and legitimate.

QUESTIONS FOR ANALYSIS

1. What do you learn about social life in the Ottoman Empire from this essay?
2. What can you infer about the sorts of arguments that were made by Islamic jurists in Katib Chelebi's day?
3. How open-minded was Katib Chelebi? What evidence from the text led you to your conclusion?

Source: *Mecmu'a-i Ulum* [Journal of Sciences] 1.2 (November 30, 1879): 79–125, trans. Selim S. Kuru.

*Some learned people argue that since the name of the island meant "sheet [*tabaka*]," a sheet of tobacco is named after that. However, this claim couldn't be verified.

†For example, as long as one doesn't drink boza [a slightly intoxicating drink made from millet] to the level that he gets drunk it is not religiously prohibited.

---

poll tax. In the case of the Ottomans, this tolerance was extended not only to the Christians and Jews who had been living under Muslim rule for centuries but also to the Serbs, Bosnians, Croats, and other Orthodox Christians in the newly conquered Balkans. In 1454 Rabbi Isaac Sarfati sent a letter to the Jews in the Rhineland, Swabia, Moravia, and Hungary, urging them to move to Turkey because of the favorable treatment there. A massive migration to Ottoman lands followed. When Ferdinand and Isabella of Spain expelled the Jews in 1492 and later, many migrated to the Ottoman Empire.

The Safavid authorities made efforts to convert Armenian Christians in the Caucasus, and many seem to have embraced Islam, some more voluntarily than others. Nevertheless, the Armenian Christian Church retained its vitality, and under the Safavids Armenian Christians were prominent merchants in long-distance trade. (See "Thinking Like a Historian: Forced Relocation of Armenians to Persia," page 486.)

Babur and his successors acquired even more non-Muslim subjects with their conquests in India, which included not only Hindus but also substantial numbers of Jains, Zoroastrians, Christians, and Sikhs.

Forced Relocation of Armenians to Persia

Many times over the course of history, people have been forced to move, often by new conquerors. Such was the fate of the Christian Armenian population when in 1603 Shah Abbas of Persia captured much of Armenia from the Ottomans. One group of Armenian merchants, moved from the town of Julfa to a new suburb of Isfahan, named New Julfa, fared relatively well, in part because Shah Abbas employed them as royal merchants and financiers.

1 **Iskandar Munshi, a Persian account of the Armenian deportation, 1616.** The court historian Iskandar Munshi (ca. 1560–ca. 1652) not surprisingly put a positive spin on Shah Abbas's deportation of the Armenians.

■ When [the Ottoman commander] Jegal-oglu reached Erivan, the Shah was camped near the . . . River. From there he dispatched Maqsud Sultan Kangarluy, . . . to transfer the civilian population of . . . Julfa to Isfahan. . . . There they were allotted land along the banks of the Zayanda, and houses with small gardens gradually grew up there; the properties were exempt from extraordinary taxes. Today, there are three thousand families living there, safe from the vicissitudes of fortune; the beauty of their new home had caused them to forget their former one.

2 **Arakel of Tabriz, an Armenian account of the deportation, 1658.** The Armenian historian Arakel of Tabriz (d. ca. 1670) presents the forced migration of perhaps a half million Armenians as a tragedy.

■ On the way, when they reached the small town of Julfa, the large and diverse population of the town, who had prepared themselves earlier, came out to greet the shah, as befitting a king. Old and young dressed and equipped, robed in magnificent garments of golden cloth, walked in a procession to greet the shah. Young lads carried sweet and precious wine in golden cups. With lit candles, frankincense and incense, and singing fine hymns, Armenian priests walked in front and sang with beautiful voices. . . .

After accomplishing all the tasks and undertakings that he had begun, the shah, together with his entire army, left Erevan and advanced toward Kars. . . . There, he informed his confidants about a plan that he had had in mind for a long time: to deport the Christian population and to destroy the land of Armenia. . . . Not one soul was to be left behind, be he a Christian or a Muslim, willing to leave or not. . . .

The Persian troops dispatched to drive the people forced them out and drove them from villages and towns; they set the places on fire, burning all the houses and dwellings without pity. The hay and straw, the wheat and barley, and other supplies stored by the people were all destroyed and burned as well. . . . For the Persians looked at the throng of people and their own army and saw that it was huge in numbers. It would take many days to transfer such a large mass across the river. . . . The numbers of people were great and there were not enough boats and rafts. . . .

The pitiless Persian soldiers drove the people and forced them to enter the water. When they waded into the river, fear made them wail and scream louder and louder. They began to cross, some grabbing a corner of a boat, others holding to rafts, others to the tails of horses, bulls, and oxen, and yet others by swimming. . . . Although some managed to swim across, many others perished by drowning.

[After being asked why he conferred favors on the Armenian merchants of New Julfa, Shah Abbas responded as follows.]

"Do not be angry over my fleeting and empty love toward them. Do not blame me, for I have brought them by force to our land. I have spent much money, effort, and tricks, not for their benefit, but for ours. They shall benefit our land and shall increase our population. If you kill the Christians who were driven from their land into ours, none will accept our faith. It would only make them fear us and secretly escape, one by one, to their own land."

ANALYZING THE EVIDENCE

1. Based on Sources 1 and 2, do you think it is plausible that Persian merchants complained to Shah Abbas that he was treating the Armenians too well?
2. Based on Sources 1–4, how well did the Armenian merchants adjust to their new circumstances? Do these texts give evidence of any continuing grievances?
3. Chardin (Source 3) and Fryer (Source 4) were in Persia in much the same period. What might account for their rather different understandings of the relations between the Safavid rulers and the Armenian merchants?
4. Why would Armenian merchants give the Russian tsar a gift as expensive as the throne in Source 5?

3 Jean Chardin, a French merchant's account of his travels, 1686. The French jewelry merchant Jean Chardin (1643–1713) spent several years in Persia between 1669 and 1677. His account of his travels proved popular and was quickly translated into English.

■ [Shah Abbas] was a just and equitable prince, and all his endeavors had this one tendency, to render the kingdom flourishing and his people happy. He found his empire all torn to pieces and usurped, and the greatest part of it impoverished and pillaged. But it is scarce to be believed, what effect his good government had, throughout his dominions. To give the reader but barely one single instance of it; he brought into the capital city a colony of Armenians, who were a laborious and industrious people, and had nothing in the world when they came there; but in the space of thirty years they grew so exceeding rich, that there were above threescore merchants among them, who, one with another, were worth from an hundred thousand crowns, to two millions, in money and merchandize.

4 John Fryer, an English physician's travels in Persia and India, 1681. John Fryer (ca. 1650–1733) was a surgeon for the British East India Company. His account of his travels included information on natural history as well as social customs.

■ The Armenians being skilled in all the intricacies and subtleties of trade at home, and travelling with these into the remotest kingdoms, become by their own industry, and by being factors of their own kindred's honesty, the wealthiest men, being expert at bargains wherever they come, evading thereby brokerage; and studying all the arts of thrift, will travel for fifty shillings, where we cannot for fifty thomands.... From such beginnings

do they raise sometimes great fortunes for themselves and masters....

For so it was provided by Shah Abbas when he deprived them of their own princes, and redeemed them from the Turkish slavery; between whose arms and the Persians, they hung miserably harassed, according to the successes of either's forces, for a long time; removing them from Erevan, Tabriz, and Syria, their native soil,... by which they became not only safe from their enemies, but they improved the glory of Isfahan by their unwearied industry, there being many of them credible merchants at this time, accounted worth an hundred thousand thomand (each thomand being three pound and a noble); so mightily do they increase under this umbrage, in riches and freedom; for whilst they sit lazily at home, their factors abroad in all parts of the earth return to their hives laden with honey....

They have sumptuous houses, enriched either by being merchants, or interpreters to foreign ministers, they being addicted to learn languages; few care for manual arts, or mechanic trades, though some apply themselves to husbandry.

(Armory of the Kremlin, Moscow, Russia/Scala/Art Resource, NY)

5 A throne given to the Russian tsar. When merchants in the Armenian Trading Company petitioned the Russian tsar for tax-exempt status in 1659, they presented this heavily bejeweled throne as a gift.

PUTTING IT ALL TOGETHER

Using the sources above, along with what you have learned in class and in this chapter, write a short essay that examines the experiences of the deported Armenians, perhaps comparing their experiences to those of other communities forced to leave their homes in earlier or later times (such as the Israelites in the ancient Middle East or the Cherokees and other Native Americans in North America).

Sources: (1) Iskandar Munshi, *History of Shah Abbas the Great,* trans. Roger Savory, Persian Heritage Series 28, 2 vols. (Boulder: Westview, 1979), pp. 859–860; (2) *The History of Vardapet Arak'el of Tabriz,* trans. George A. Bournoutian (Costa Mesa, CA: Mazda Publishers, 2005), pp. 25, 36–40, 55–56. Used by permission of George A. Bournoutian; (3) *Sir John Chardin's Travels in Persia* (New York: Cosimo Classics, 2010), p. 139; (4) John Fryer, *A New Account of East-India and Persia, in Eight Letters, Being Nine Years Travels, Begun 1672 and Finished 1681* (London: Chiswell, 1698), pp. 263–264, 268–269.

Emperor Akbar in the City of Fatehpur Sikri In 1569 Akbar founded the city of Fatehpur Sikri (the City of Victory) to honor the Muslim holy man Sheik Salim Chishti, who had foretold the birth of Akbar's son and heir Jahangir. Akbar is shown here seated on the cushion in the center overseeing the construction of the city. The image is contained in the *Akbarnama*, a book of illustrations Akbar commissioned to officially chronicle his reign. (Victoria & Albert Museum, London, UK/Bridgeman Images)

Some of Akbar's successors, above all Aurangzeb, were less tolerant. Aurangzeb appointed censors of public morals in important cities to enforce Islamic laws against gambling, prostitution, drinking, and the use of narcotics. He forbade sati—the self-immolation of widows on their husbands' funeral pyres—and the castration of boys to be sold as eunuchs. He also abolished all taxes not authorized by Islamic law. Aurangzeb's reversal of Akbar's religious tolerance and cultural cosmopolitanism extended further. He ordered the destruction of some Hindu temples and tried to curb Sikhism. He also required Hindus to pay higher customs duties than Muslims. Out of fidelity to Islamic law, he even criticized his mother's tomb, the Taj Mahal: "The lawfulness of a solid construction over a grave is doubtful, and there can be no doubt about the extravagance involved."[3] Aurangzeb's attempts to enforce rigid Islamic norms proved highly unpopular and aroused resistance that weakened Mughal rule.

Shifting Trade Routes and European Penetration

How were the Islamic empires affected by the gradual shift toward trade routes that bypassed their lands?

Over time, the number of Indians who converted to Islam increased, but the Mughal rulers did not force conversion. Akbar went the furthest in promoting Muslim-Hindu accommodation. He celebrated important Hindu festivals, such as Diwali, the festival of lights, and he wore his uncut hair in a turban as a concession to Indian practice. Also, Akbar twice married Hindu princesses, one of whom became the mother of his heir, Jahangir, and he appointed the Spanish Jesuit Antonio Monserrate (1536–1600) as tutor to one of his sons. Eventually, Hindus totaled 30 percent of the imperial bureaucracy.

It has widely been thought that a decline in the wealth and international importance of the Muslim empires could be directly attributed to the long-term shift in trading patterns that resulted from the discoveries of Columbus, Magellan, and other European explorers. The argument is that new sea routes enabled Europeans to acquire goods from the East without using Muslim intermediaries, so that the creation of European colonial powers beginning in the sixteenth century led directly and indirectly to the eclipse of the Ottomans, Safavids, and Mughals. Recent scholars have challenged these ideas as too simplistic. First, it was not until the eighteenth century that political decline became evident in the three Islamic empires. Second, Turkish, Persian, and Indian merchants remained very active as long-distance traders into the eighteenth century and opened up many new routes themselves. It is true that in the Islamic empires New World crops like potatoes and sweet potatoes fueled population increases less rapidly than in western Europe and East Asia. By 1800 the population of India was about 190 million, that of Safavid lands about 8 million, and that of Ottoman lands about 24 million. (By comparison, China's population stood at about 300 million in 1800 and Russia's about 35 million.)

European Rivalry for Trade in the Indian Ocean

Shortly before Babur's invasion of India, the Portuguese had opened the subcontinent to Portuguese trade. In 1510 they established the port of Goa on the west coast of India as their headquarters and through an aggressive policy took control of Muslim shipping in the Indian Ocean and Arabian Sea, charging high fees to let ships through. The Portuguese historian Barrões attempted to justify Portugal's seizure of commercial traffic that the Muslims had long dominated:

> It is true that there does exist a common right to all to navigate the seas and in Europe we recognize the rights which others hold against us; but the right does not extend beyond Europe and therefore the Portuguese as Lords of the Sea are justified in confiscating the goods of all those who navigate the seas without their permission.[4]

In short, the Portuguese decided that Western principles of international law should not restrict them in Asia. As a result, they controlled the spice trade over the Indian Ocean for almost a century.

In 1602 the Dutch formed the Dutch East India Company with the stated goal of wresting the enormously lucrative spice trade from the Portuguese. In 1685 they supplanted the Portuguese in Ceylon (Sri Lanka). The scent of fabulous profits also attracted the English. With a charter signed by Queen Elizabeth, eighty London merchants organized the British East India Company. In 1619 Emperor Jahangir granted a British mission important commercial concessions. Soon, by offering gifts, medical services, and bribes to Indian rulers, the British East India Company was able to set up twenty-eight coastal forts/trading posts. By 1700 the company had founded the cities that became Madras and Calcutta (today called Chennai and Kolkata) and had taken over Bombay (today Mumbai), which had been a Portuguese possession (Map 17.3).

The British called their trading posts factory-forts. The term *factory* did not signify manufacturing; it designated the walled compound containing the residences, gardens, and offices of British East India Company officials and the warehouses where goods were stored before being shipped to Europe. The company president exercised political authority over all residents.

Factory-forts existed to make profits from Asian-European trade, which was robust due to the popularity of Indian and Chinese wares in Europe in the late seventeenth and early eighteenth centuries. The European middle classes wanted Indian textiles, which were colorful, durable, cheap, and washable. The upper classes desired Chinese wallpaper and porcelains and Indian silks and cottons. Other Indian goods in demand included pepper and other spices, sugar, and opium. To pay for these goods, the British East India Company sold silver, copper, zinc, lead, and fabrics to the Indians. Profits grew even larger after 1700, when the company began to trade with China.

Merchant Networks in the Islamic Empires

The shifting trade patterns associated with European colonial expansion brought no direct benefit to the Ottomans and the Safavids, whose merchants could now be bypassed by Europeans seeking goods from India, Southeast Asia, or China. Yet merchants from these Islamic empires often proved adaptable, finding ways to benefit from the new trade networks.

In the case of India, the appearance of European traders led to a rapid increase in overall trade, helping Indian merchants and the Indian economy. Some Indian merchants in Calcutta and Bombay, for instance, made gigantic fortunes from trade within Asia carried on European ships. Block-printed cotton cloth, produced by artisans working at home, was India's chief export.

Within India the demand for cotton cloth, as well as for food crops, was so great that Akbar had to launch a wide-scale road-building campaign. From the Indian region of Gujarat, Indian merchant bankers shipped their cloth worldwide: across the Indian Ocean to Aden and the Muslim-controlled cities on the east coast of Africa; across the Arabian Sea to Muscat and Hormuz and up the Persian Gulf to the cities of Persia; up the Red Sea to the Mediterranean; by sea also to Malacca, Indonesia, China, and Japan; by land across Africa to Ghana on the west coast; and to Astrakhan, Poland, Moscow, and even the Russian cities on the distant Volga River. Indian businessmen had branch offices in many of these places, and all this activity produced fabulous wealth for some Indian merchants.

MAP 17.3 India, 1707–1805

In the eighteenth century Mughal power gradually yielded to the Hindu Marathas and to the British East India Company.

Indian merchants were often devout Hindus, Muslims, Buddhists, or Jains, evidence that undermines the argument of some Western writers, notably Karl Marx (see "The Birth of Socialism" in Chapter 24), that religion retarded Asia's economic development.

Throughout Muslim lands both Jews and Christians were active in commerce. A particularly interesting case involves the Armenian Christians in the sixteenth to eighteenth centuries. Armenian merchants had been trading from their base in Armenia for centuries and were especially known for their trade in Persian silk. When the Portuguese first appeared on the western coast of India in 1498 and began to settle in south India, they found many Armenian merchant communities already there. A few decades later Akbar invited Armenians to settle in his new capital, Agra. In 1603 Shah Abbas captured much of Armenia, taking it from the Ottomans, and forcing the Armenians to move more deeply into Persia. (See "Thinking Like a Historian: Forced Relocation of Armenians to Persia," page 486.)

Armenian merchant networks stretched from Venice and Amsterdam in western Europe, Moscow in Russia, and Ottoman-controlled Aleppo and Smyrna to all the major trading cities of India and even regions farther east, including Guangzhou in southern China and Manila in the Philippines. Many Armenian communities in these cities became quite substantial, built churches, and recruited priests. The merchant about to take a journey would borrow a sum of money to purchase goods and would contract to pay it back with interest on his return. Using couriers, these Armenian merchants sent long letters describing the trade environment and the prices that could be realized for given goods.

From the British East India Company to the British Empire in India

Britain's presence in India began with the British East India Company and its desire to profit from trade. Managers of the company in London discouraged all

English Dress Made of Indian Printed Cotton Cloth Early British traders in India were impressed with the quality of the textiles made there and began ordering designs that would be popular with the English. This dress, created around 1770–1780 in England, is made of printed cotton (chintz) from the southeastern part of India. Chintz became so popular in England that it was eventually banned because it was threatening local textile industries. (Victoria and Albert Museum, London, UK/ V & A Images/Art Resource, NY)

unnecessary expenses and financial risks and thus opposed missionary activities or interference in local Indian politics. Nevertheless, the company responded to political instability in India in the early eighteenth century by extending political control. When warlords appeared or an uprising occurred, people from the surrounding countryside flocked into the company's factory-forts, which gradually came to exercise political authority over the territories around them. The company's factories evolved into defensive installations manned by small garrisons of native troops—known as **sepoys**—trained in Western military weapons and tactics.

Britain eventually became the dominant foreign presence in India, despite challenges from the French. From 1740 to 1763 Britain and France were engaged in a tremendous global struggle, and India, like North America in the Seven Years' War (see Chapter 22), became a battlefield and a prize. The French won land battles, but English sea power proved decisive by preventing the landing of French reinforcements. The Treaty of Paris of 1763 recognized British control of much of India, marking the beginning of the British Empire in India.

How was Britain to govern so large a territory? Eventually, the East India Company was pushed out of its governing role because the English Parliament distrusted the company, believing it was corrupt. The Regulating Act of 1773 created the office of governor general to exercise political authority over the territory controlled by the company. The East India Company Act of 1784 required that the governor general be chosen from outside the company, and it made company directors subject to parliamentary supervision.

Implementation of these reforms fell to three successive governors: Warren Hastings (r. 1774–1785), Lord Charles Cornwallis (r. 1786–1794), and the marquess Richard Wellesley (r. 1797–1805). Hastings sought allies among Indian princes, laid the foundations for the first Indian civil service, abolished tolls to facilitate internal trade, placed the salt and opium trades under government control, and planned a codification of Muslim and Hindu laws. Cornwallis intro- duced the British style of property relations, in which the rents of tenant farmers supported the landlords. Wellesley was victorious over local rulers who resisted British rule, vastly extending British influence in India. Like most nineteenth-century British governors of India, Wellesley believed that British rule strongly benefited the Indians. With supreme condescension, he wrote that British power should be established over the Indian princes in order "to deprive them of the means of prosecuting any measure or of forming any confederacy hazardous to the security of the British empire, and to enable us to preserve the tranquility of India by exercising a general control over the restless spirit of ambition and violence which is characteristic of every Asiatic government."[5]

sepoys The native Indian troops who were trained as infantrymen.

Political Decline

What common factors led to the decline of central power in the Islamic empires in the seventeenth and eighteenth centuries?

By the end of the eighteenth century all three of the major Islamic empires were on the defensive and losing territory (Map 17.4). They faced some common problems—succession difficulties, financial strain, and loss of military superiority—but their circumstances differed in significant ways as well.

The first to fall was the Safavid Empire. Persia did not have the revenue base to maintain the sort of standing armies that the Ottomans and the Mughals had. Decline in the strength of the army encouraged increased foreign aggression. In 1722 the Afghans invaded from the east, seized Isfahan, and were able to repulse an Ottoman invasion from the west. In Isfahan thousands of officials and members of the shah's family were executed. In the following century no leaders emerged capable of reuniting all of Persia. In this political vacuum, Shi'a religious institutions grew stronger.

The Ottoman Empire also suffered from poor leadership. Early Ottoman practice had guaranteed that the sultans would be forceful men. The sultan's sons gained administrative experience as governors of provinces and military experience on the battlefield as part of their education. After the sultan died, any son who wanted to succeed had to contest his brothers to claim the throne, after which the new sultan would have his defeated brothers executed. Although bloody, this system led to the succession of capable, determined men. After Suleiman's reign, however, the tradition was abandoned. To prevent threats of usurpation, sons of the sultan were brought up in the harem, confined there as adults, and denied roles in government. The result was a series of rulers who were minor children or incompetent adults, leaving power in the hands of high officials and the mothers of the heirs. Political factions formed around viziers, military leaders, and palace women. In the contest for political favor, the devshirme was abandoned, and political and military ranks were filled by Muslims.

The Ottoman Empire's military strength also declined. The defeat of the Turkish fleet by the Spanish off the coast of Greece at Lepanto in 1571 marked the loss of Ottoman dominance in the Mediterranean. By the terms of a peace treaty with Austria signed at Karlowitz (1699), the Ottomans lost the major European provinces of Hungary and Transylvania, along with the tax revenues they had provided. Also, the Ottoman armies were depending more on mercenaries, and they did not keep up with the innovations in drill, command, and control that were then transforming European armies. From the late seventeenth century Ottoman armies began losing wars and territory along both northern and eastern borders. In 1774 the empire lost the lands on the northern bank of the Black Sea to Russia. In North Africa the local governors came to act more independently, sometimes starting hereditary dynasties.

In Mughal India the old Turkish practice of letting heirs fight for the throne persisted, leading to frequent struggles over succession, but also to strong rulers. Yet military challenges proved daunting there as well. After defeating his father and brothers, Aurangzeb made it his goal to conquer the south. The stiffest opposition came from the Marathas, a militant Hindu group centered in the western Deccan. From 1681 until his death in 1707, Aurangzeb led repeated sorties through the Deccan. He took many forts and won several battles, but total destruction of the Maratha guerrilla bands eluded him.

Aurangzeb's death led to thirteen years of succession struggles, shattering the empire. His eighteenth-century successors were less successful than the Ottomans in making the dynasty the focus of loyalty. Mughal provincial governors began to rule independently, giving only minimal allegiance to the throne at Delhi. Meanwhile, the Marathas pressed steadily northward, constituting the gravest threat to Mughal authority. Threats also came from the west. In 1739 the Persian adventurer Nadir Shah invaded India, defeated the Mughal army, looted Delhi, and, after a savage massacre, carried off a huge amount of treasure, including the Peacock Throne. Constant skirmishes between the Afghans and the Marathas for control of the Punjab and northern India ended in 1761 at Panipat, where the Marathas were crushed by the Afghans. At that point, India no longer had a state strong enough to impose order on the subcontinent or check the penetration of the Europeans. Not until 1857, however, did the Mughal Dynasty come to a formal end.

In all three empires fiscal difficulties contributed to strain on the state. A long period of peace in the late sixteenth century and again in the mid-eighteenth century, as well as a decline in the frequency of visits of the plague, led to a doubling of the population. Increased population, coupled with the "little ice age" of the mid-seventeenth century, meant that the land could not sustain so many people, nor could the towns provide jobs for the thousands of agricultural workers who fled to them. The return of demobilized soldiers aggravated the problem. Inflation, famine, and widespread uprisings resulted. Power was seized by local notables and military strongmen at the expense of central government officials.

MAP 17.4 The Muslim World, ca. 1700 The three great Islamic empires were adjacent to each other and of similar physical size. Many of their other neighbors were Muslim as well.

Chapter Summary

After the decline of the Mongols in Central Asia and Persia, many small Turkic-ruled states emerged in the region from Anatolia through Afghanistan. Three of them went on to establish large empires: the Ottomans in Anatolia, the Safavids in Persia, and the Mughals in India. The Ottoman Empire's political system reached its classic form under Suleiman I. All authority flowed from the sultan to his public servants: provincial governors, police officers, military generals, heads of treasuries, and viziers. In Persia for some time Turkish lords competed for power, with no single one dominant until 1501, when a fourteen-year-old military leader declared himself shah. The strength of this Safavid state rested in part on the skills of urban bureaucrats, who were vital to the civil machinery of government. Babur, from his base in Afghanistan, founded the Mughal Empire in India. His grandson

Akbar extended Mughal rule far into India. Whereas the Ottoman sultans and Safavid shahs used slaves acquired from non-Muslim lands for military and administrative positions, Akbar relied on the services of royal princes, nobles, and warrior-aristocrats. All three empires quickly adapted to new gunpowder technologies.

Each of the three Islamic empires presided over an extraordinary artistic and intellectual flowering in everything from carpetmaking and book illustration to architecture and gardening, from geography and astronomy to medicine. Each of these empires drew legitimacy from its support for Islam. There were, however, key differences: the Ottomans and Mughals supported the Sunni tradition, the Safavids the Shi'a tradition.

The three Islamic empires all had a substantial number of non-Muslim subjects. The Ottomans ruled over the Balkans, where most of the people were Christian, and Muslims in India were greatly outnumbered by Hindus.

European exploration opened new trade routes and enabled Europeans to trade directly with India and China, bypassing Muslim intermediaries in the Middle East. Within India British merchants increased their political control in politically unstable areas, leading before the end of the eighteenth century to a vast colonial empire in India.

By the end of the eighteenth century all three of the major Islamic empires were losing territory. The first to fall was the Safavid Empire. From the late seventeenth century Ottoman armies began losing wars along the northern and eastern borders, resulting in substantial loss of territory. Military challenges proved daunting in Mughal India as well. In all three empires, as central power declined, local notables and military strongmen seized power.

NOTES

1. *Memoirs of Zehir-Ed-Din Muhammed Baber: Emperor of Hindustan*, trans. John Leyden and William Erskine (London: Longman and Cadell, 1826), p. 333.
2. Quoted in M. C. Beach, *The Imperial Image: Paintings for the Mughal Court* (Washington, D.C.: Freer Gallery of Art, Smithsonian Institution, 1981), pp. 9–10.
3. Quoted in S. K. Ikram, *Muslim Civilization in India* (New York: Columbia University Press, 1964), p. 202.
4. Quoted in K. M. Panikkar, *Asia and Western Domination* (London: George Allen & Unwin, 1965), p. 35.
5. Quoted in W. Bingham, H. Conroy, and F. W. Iklé, *A History of Asia*, vol. 2 (Boston: Allyn and Bacon, 1967), p. 74.

CONNECTIONS

From 1300 to 1800 and from North Africa to India, Islamic civilization thrived under three dynastic houses: the Ottomans, the Safavids, and the Mughals. All three empires had a period of expansion when territory was enlarged, followed by a high point politically and culturally, and later a period of contraction, when territories broke away. Two of the empires had large non-Muslim populations. India, even under Mughal rule, remained a predominantly Hindu land, and the Ottomans, in the process of conquering the Balkans, acquired a population that was largely Greek Orthodox Christians. Though all three states supported Islam, the Safavids took Shi'a teachings as orthodox, while the other two favored Sunni teachings. At the cultural level, the borders of these three states were porous, and people, ideas, art motifs, languages, and trade flowed back and forth.

In East Asia the fifteenth through eighteenth centuries also saw the creation of strong, prosperous, and expanding states, though in the case of China (under the Qing Dynasty) and Japan (under the Tokugawa Shogunate) the eighteenth century was a cultural high point, not a period of decline. The Qing emperors were Manchus, from the region northeast of China proper, reminiscent of the Mughals, who began in Afghanistan. As in the Islamic lands, during these centuries the presence of European powers became an issue in East Asia, though the details were quite different. Although one of the commodities that the British most wanted was the tea produced in China, Britain did not extend political control in China the way it did in India. Japan managed to refuse entry to most European traders after finding their presence and their support for missionary activity disturbing. Chapter 21 takes up these developments in East Asia.

In the next three chapters the focus is on two other regions of the world, Europe and Africa. To fully understand what Britain was doing in India requires more background on what was happening in Europe from 1500 to 1800, a period when religious differences were causing strife between European states that were at the same time beginning to build overseas empires. By the eighteenth century the Scientific Revolution and the Enlightenment were having a major impact on people's lives in Europe, and the slave trade was tying Europe to both Africa and the Americas.

CHAPTER 17   **Review and Explore**

Identify Key Terms

Identify and explain the significance of each item below.

Ottomans (p. 470)   shah (p. 473)

sultan (p. 470)   Safavid (p. 473)

viziers (p. 473)   Qizilbash (p. 475)

devshirme (p. 473)   ulama (p. 475)

janissaries (p. 473)   Mughal (p. 476)

concubine (p. 473)   sepoys (p. 491)

Review the Main Ideas

Answer the focus questions from each section of the chapter.

1. How were the three Islamic empires established, and what sorts of governments did they set up? (p. 470)

2. What cultural advances occurred under the rule of the Ottoman, Safavid, and Mughal Empires? (p. 478)

3. How did Christians, Jews, Hindus, and other non-Muslims fare under these Islamic states? (p. 484)

4. How were the Islamic empires affected by the gradual shift toward trade routes that bypassed their lands? (p. 488)

5. What common factors led to the decline of central power in the Islamic empires in the seventeenth and eighteenth centuries? (p. 492)

Make Comparisons and Connections

Analyze the larger developments and continuities within and across chapters.

1. In what sense were the states of the Ottomans, Safavids, and Mughals empires rather than large states? Do all three equally deserve the term "empire"? Why or why not?

2. How did the expansion of European presence in the Indian Ocean after 1450 impinge on the societies and economies of each of the Islamic empires?

3. What made it possible for Islamic rulers to tolerate more religious difference than European Christian rulers of the same period did (Chapters 14 and 15)?

TIMELINE

WESTERN AND SOUTH ASIA		

1299–1326 Reign of Osman, founder of the Ottoman Dynasty

1299–1922 Ottoman Empire

1336–1405 Life of Timur

◆ **ca. mid-1400s** Coffeehouses become center of Islamic male social life

◆ **1453** Ottoman conquest of Constantinople

EAST ASIA

1368–1644 Ming Dynasty in China **(Ch. 21)**

1405–1433 Zheng He's naval expeditions **(Ch. 21)**

EUROPE

ca. 1350–1520 Italian Renaissance **(Ch. 15)**

AFRICA

AMERICAS

ca. 1428–1521 Aztec Empire dominates Mesoamerica **(Ch. 11)**

ca. 1438–1532 Inca Empire dominates the Andes **(Ch. 11)**

1300	1400

Suggested Resources

BOOKS

Barkey, Karen. *Empire of Difference*. 2008. Places the history of the Ottomans in comparative perspective.

Casale, Giancarlo. *The Ottoman Age of Exploration*. 2011. Lively account of Ottoman rivalry with the Portuguese in the Indian Ocean in the sixteenth century.

Dale, Stephen Frederic. *The Garden of the Eight Paradises: Babur and the Culture of Empire in Central Asia, Afghanistan and India, 1483–1750*. 2004. A scholarly biography that draws on and analyzes Babur's autobiography.

Dale, Stephen Frederic. *The Muslim Empires of the Ottomans, Safavids, and Mughals*. 2010. A comparative study of the three empires, with much on religion and culture.

Findley, Carter Vaughn. *The Turks in World History*. 2005. Takes a macro look at the three Islamic empires as part of the history of the Turks.

Finkel, Caroline. *Osman's Dream: A History of the Ottoman Empire*. 2006. A new interpretation that views the Ottomans from their own perspective.

Inalcik, Halil, and Günsel Renda. *Ottoman Civilization*. 2002. A huge, beautifully illustrated, government-sponsored overview, with an emphasis on the arts and culture.

Jackson, Peter, and Lawrence Lockhart, eds. *The Cambridge History of Iran*. Vol. 6: *The Timurid and Safavid Periods*. 1986. A set of essays by leading scholars on the social and cultural, as well as the political and economic, history of Iran.

Lapidus, Ira M. *A History of Islamic Societies*, 2d ed. 2002. A comprehensive yet lucid survey.

Mukhia, Harbans. *The Mughals of India: A Framework for Understanding*. 2004. A short but thoughtful analysis of the Mughal society and state.

Parker, Charles H. *Global Interactions in the Early Modern Age, 1400–1800*. 2010. Places the Islamic empires in a global context.

Parthasarathi, Prasannan. *Why Europe Grew Rich and Asia Did Not: Global Economic Divergence, 1600–1850*. 2011. Focuses on India and how it compared to Britain in producing cotton and coal and making scientific advances.

1501–1722 Safavid Empire in Persia

1520–1566 Reign of Ottoman sultan Suleiman I

1631–1648 Construction of Taj Mahal under Shah Jahan in India

1526–1857 Mughal Empire in India

1763
Treaty of Paris recognizes British control over much of India

1556–1605 Reign of Akbar in Mughal Empire

1517 Luther's Ninety-five Theses **(Ch. 15)**

ca. **1690–1789**
European Enlightenment **(Ch. 19)**

ca. **1464–1591** Songhai kingdom dominates the western Sudan **(Ch. 20)**

1492 Columbus lands on San Salvador **(Ch. 16)**

| 1500 | 1600 | 1700 |

Peirce, Leslie P. *The Imperial Harem: Women and Sovereignty in the Ottoman Empire.* 1993. A fresh look at the role of elite women under the Ottomans.

Richards, John F. *The Mughal Empire.* 1993. A coherent narrative history of the period 1526–1720.

Ruthven, Malise, and Azim Nanji. *Historical Atlas of Islam.* 2004. Provides numerous maps illustrating the shifting political history of Islamic states.

DOCUMENTARIES

The Great Moghuls (Ecosse Films, 1990). A British documentary (with six episodes) that tells the story of the Mughal Empire.

Ottoman Empire: The War Machine (History Channel, 2006). An overview of the Ottoman Empire, with lots of dramatizations.

Sufi Soul: The Mystic Music of Islam (MWTV/Riverboat, 2005). An introduction to the music to which the whirling dervishes whirl, with footage of many musicians.

Warrior Empire: The Mughals of India (History Channel, 2006). Covers the period from the founder Babar through the death of Aurangzeb in 1707.

FEATURE FILMS

The Day of the Siege: September Eleven 1683 (Renzo Martinelli, 2012). A Polish and Italian film (in English) on the Ottoman attack on Vienna, full of battle scenes.

Jodhaa Akbar (Ashutosh Gowariker, 2008). The story of Mughal emperor Akbar and Rajput princess Jodhaa, who married in the sixteenth century for political reasons and fell in love.

WEBSITES

Archnet. A rich collection of photos and videos on the architecture of Islamic societies, with a useful timeline. **archnet.org**

Gardens of the Mughal Empire. Sites and sounds of many of the major gardens dating to the Mughal period. **www.mughalgardens.org**

The Ottomans. This site on the Ottomans pays special attention to the military and wars, but also covers art and culture. **www.theottomans.org/english/history/index.asp**

18

European Power and Expansion

1500–1750

The two centuries that opened the early modern era witnessed crisis and transformation in Europe. What one historian has described as the long European "struggle for stability" originated with conflicts sparked by the Protestant and Catholic Reformations in the early sixteenth century and continued with economic and social breakdown into the late seventeenth century.[1] To consolidate their authority and expand their territories, European rulers increased the size of their armies, imposed higher taxes, and implemented bureaucratic forms of government. By the end of the seventeenth century they had largely succeeded in restoring order and securing increased power for the state.

The growth of state power within Europe raised a series of questions: Who held supreme power? What made it legitimate? Conflicts over these questions led to rebellions and at times outright civil war. Between roughly 1589 and 1715 two basic patterns of government emerged from these conflicts: absolute monarchy and the constitutional state. Almost all subsequent European governments were modeled on one of these patterns, which have also greatly influenced the rest of the world.

Whether a government was constitutional or absolutist, an important foundation of state power was empire and colonialism. Jealous of the riches and prestige the Iberian powers gained from their overseas holdings, England, France, and the Netherlands vied for territory in Asia and the Americas, while Russia pushed its borders east to the Pacific and west into central Europe. This was a distinctive moment in world history when exchange within and among empires produced constant movement of people, goods, and culture, with no one region or empire able to dominate the others entirely.

Louis XIV

In this painting, King Louis XIV receives foreign ambassadors to celebrate a peace treaty. The king grandly occupied the center of his court, which in turn served as the pinnacle for the French people and, at the height of his glory, for all of Europe.

Peace Treaty of Nijmegen, 1678/Museum of Fine Arts, Budapest, Hungary/Erich Lessing/Art Resource, NY

CHAPTER PREVIEW

THE PROTESTANT AND CATHOLIC REFORMATIONS
How did the Protestant and Catholic Reformations change power structures in Europe and shape European colonial expansion?

SEVENTEENTH-CENTURY CRISIS AND REBUILDING
How did seventeenth-century European rulers overcome social and economic crisis to build strong states?

ABSOLUTIST STATES IN WESTERN AND CENTRAL EUROPE
What was absolutism, and how did it evolve in seventeenth-century Spain, France, and Austria?

CONSTITUTIONALISM AND EMPIRE IN ENGLAND AND THE DUTCH REPUBLIC
Why and how did the constitutional state triumph in England and the Dutch Republic?

COLONIAL EXPANSION AND EMPIRE
How did European nations compete for global trade and empire in the Americas and Asia?

THE RUSSIAN EMPIRE
How did Russian rulers build a distinctive absolutist monarchy and expand into a vast and powerful empire?

The Protestant and Catholic Reformations

How did the Protestant and Catholic Reformations change power structures in Europe and shape European colonial expansion?

As a result of a movement of religious reform known as the **Protestant Reformation**, Western Christendom broke into many divisions in the sixteenth century. This splintering happened not only for religious reasons but also because of political and social factors. Religious transformation provided a source of power for many rulers and shaped European colonial expansion.

The Protestant Reformation

In early-sixteenth-century western Europe, calls for reform in the church came from many quarters, both within and outside the church. Critics of the church concentrated their attacks on clerical immorality, ignorance, and absenteeism. Charges of immorality were aimed at a number of priests who were drunkards, neglected the rule of celibacy, gambled, or indulged in fancy dress. Charges of ignorance applied to barely literate priests who delivered poor-quality sermons.

In regard to absenteeism, many clerics, especially higher ecclesiastics, held several benefices (offices) simultaneously. However, they seldom visited the communities served by the benefices. Instead they collected revenues from all the benefices assigned to them and hired a poor priest to fulfill their spiritual duties.

There was also local resentment of clerical privileges and immunities. Priests, monks, and nuns were exempt from civic responsibilities, such as defending the city and paying taxes. Yet religious orders frequently held large amounts of urban property. City governments were increasingly determined to integrate the clergy into civic life. This brought city leaders into opposition with bishops and the papacy, which for centuries had stressed the independence of the church from lay control.

This range of complaints helps explain why the ideas of Martin Luther (1483–1546), a priest and professor of theology from the German University of Wittenberg, found a ready audience. Luther and other Protestants—the word comes from a "protest" drawn up by a group of reforming princes in 1529—developed a new understanding of Christian doctrine in which salvation came through God's grace by faith alone and religious authority rested solely in the Bible. These ideas directly contradicted the teachings of the Catholic Church, but

Domestic Scene The Protestant notion that the best form of Christian life was marriage and a family helps explain the appeal of Protestantism to middle-class urban men and women, such as those shown in this domestic scene. The large covered bed at the back was both a standard piece of furniture in urban homes and a symbol of proper marital sexual relations. (© Mary Evans Picture Library/The Image Works)

they were attractive to educated people and urban residents, and they spread rapidly through preaching, hymns, and the printing press.

Luther lived in the Holy Roman Empire, a loose collection of largely independent states in which the emperor had far less authority than did the monarchs of western Europe. The Habsburg emperor, Charles V, was a staunch supporter of Catholicism, but the ruler of the territory in which Luther lived protected the reformer. Although Luther appeared before Charles V when he was summoned, he was not arrested and continued to preach and write.

Luther's ideas appealed to the local rulers of the empire for a variety of reasons. Though Germany was not a nation, people did have an understanding of being German because of their language and traditions. Luther frequently used the phrase "we Germans" in his attacks on the papacy, and his appeal to national feeling influenced many rulers. Also, while some German rulers were sincerely attracted to Lutheran ideas, material considerations swayed many others. The adoption of Protestantism would mean the legal confiscation of church properties. Thus many political authorities in the empire used the religious issue to extend their power and to enhance their independence from the emperor. Luther worked closely with political

Protestant Reformation A religious reform movement that began in the early sixteenth century and split the Western Christian Church.

authorities, viewing them as fully justified in reforming the church in their territories. Thus, just as in the Ottoman and Safavid Empires, rulers drew their legitimacy in part from their support for religion. By 1530 many parts of the Holy Roman Empire and Scandinavia had broken with the Catholic Church.

In England the issue of the royal succession triggered that country's break with Rome, and a Protestant Church was established during the 1530s under King Henry VIII (r. 1509–1547) and reaffirmed under his daughter Elizabeth I (r. 1558–1603). Church officials were required to sign an oath of loyalty to the monarch, and people were required to attend services at the state church, which became known as the Anglican Church.

Protestant ideas also spread into France, the Netherlands, Scotland, and eastern Europe. In all these areas, a second generation of reformers built on earlier ideas to develop their own theology and plans for insti-tutional change. The most important of the second-generation reformers was the Frenchman John Calvin (1509–1564), who reformed the city of Geneva, Switzerland. Calvin believed that God was absolutely sovereign and omnipotent and that humans had no free will. Thus men and women could not actively work to achieve salvation, because God had decided at the beginning of time who would be saved and who damned, a theological principle called predestination.

The church in Geneva served as the model for the Presbyterian Church in Scotland, the Huguenot (HYOO-guh-naht) Church in France, and the Puritan Churches in England and New England. Calvinism became the compelling force in international Protestantism, first in Europe and then in many Dutch and English colonies around the world. Calvinism was also the dominant form of Protestantism in France (Map 18.1).

MAP 18.1 Religious Divisions, ca. 1555 In the mid-sixteenth century, much of Europe remained Catholic. The Peace of Augsburg (1555) allowed the ruler of each territory in the Holy Roman Empire to determine the religion of its people. The northern territories of the empire became Lutheran, as did Scandinavia, while much of the southern empire remained Catholic. Sizable Calvinist populations existed in Scotland, the Netherlands, and central Europe. Eastern Europe was dominated by Orthodox Christianity, and the Ottoman Empire to the south and southeast was Muslim.

The Catholic Reformation

In response to the Protestant Reformation, by the 1530s the papacy was leading a movement for reform within the Roman Catholic Church. Many historians see the developments within the Catholic Church after the Protestant Reformation as two interrelated movements, one a drive for internal reform linked to earlier reform efforts and the other a Counter-Reformation that opposed Protestantism spiritually, politically, and militarily.

Pope Paul III (pontificate 1534–1549) established the Supreme Sacred Congregation of the Roman and Universal Inquisition, often called the Holy Office, with judicial authority over all Catholics and the power to imprison and execute. He also called a general council of the church, which met intermittently from 1545 to 1563 at the city of Trent. The Council of Trent laid

Jesuits in China This European image depicts early Jesuit missionaries baptizing converts in south China. (Archiv Gerstenberg — ullstein bild/Granger, NYC — All rights reserved.)

a solid basis for the spiritual renewal of the Catholic Church. It gave equal validity to the Scriptures and to tradition as sources of religious truth and tackled problems that had disillusioned many Christians. Bishops were required to live in their dioceses and to establish a seminary for educating and training clergy. Finally, it placed great emphasis on preaching to and instructing the laity. For four centuries the Council of Trent served as the basis for Roman Catholic faith, organization, and practice.

Just as seminaries provided education, so did new religious orders, which aimed to raise the moral and intellectual level of the clergy and people. The Ursuline (UHR-suh-luhn) order of nuns, founded by Angela Merici (1474–1540), attained enormous prestige for its education of women.

Another important new order was the Society of Jesus, or **Jesuits**. Founded by Ignatius Loyola (1491–1556) in 1540, this order played a powerful international role in strengthening Catholicism in Europe and spreading the faith around the world. Recruited primarily from wealthy merchant and professional families, the Society of Jesus developed into a highly centralized organization. It established well-run schools to educate the sons of the nobility as well as the poor. The Jesuits achieved phenomenal success for the papacy and the reformed Catholic Church, carrying Christianity to South and Central America, India, and Japan before 1550 and to Brazil, North America, and the Congo in the seventeenth century. Also, as confessors and spiritual directors to kings, Jesuits exerted great political influence.

Religious Violence

Religious differences led to riots, civil wars, and international conflicts in Europe during the sixteenth century. In the Holy Roman Empire fighting began in 1546. The empire was a confederation of hundreds of principalities, independent cities, duchies, and other polities loosely united under an elected emperor. The initial success of Emperor Charles V led to French intervention on the side of the Protestants, lest the emperor acquire even more power. In 1555 Charles agreed to the Peace of Augsburg, which officially recognized Lutheranism and ended religious war in Germany for many decades. Under this treaty, the political authority in each territory of the Holy Roman Empire was permitted to decide whether the territory would be Catholic or Lutheran. His hope of uniting his empire under a single church dashed, Charles V abdicated in 1556, transferring power over his Spanish and Dutch holdings to his son Philip II and his imperial power to his brother Ferdinand.

In France armed clashes between Catholic royalists and Calvinist antiroyalists occurred in many parts of the country. A savage Catholic attack on Calvinists in Paris on August 24, 1572—Saint Bartholomew's Day—occurred at the marriage of the king's sister Margaret of Valois to the Protestant Henry of Navarre. The Saint Bartholomew's Day massacre initiated a civil war that dragged on for fifteen years, destroying agriculture and commercial life in many areas.

In the Netherlands the movement for church reform developed into a struggle for Dutch independence. In the 1560s Spanish authorities attempted to suppress Calvinist worship and raised taxes. Civil war broke out from 1568 to 1578 between Catholics and Protestants in the Netherlands and between the provinces of the Netherlands and Spain. Eventually the ten southern provinces came under the control of the Spanish Habsburg forces. The seven northern provinces, led by Holland, formed the Union of Utrecht (United Provinces of the Netherlands) and in 1581 declared their independence from Spain. The north was Protestant, and the south remained Catholic. Hostilities continued until 1609, when Spain agreed to a truce that recognized the independence of the northern provinces.

The era of religious wars was also the time of the most extensive witch persecutions in European history, with between 100,000 and 200,000 people officially tried for witchcraft in the sixteenth and seventeenth centuries. Both Protestants and Catholics persecuted accused witches, with church officials and secular authorities acting together. The heightened sense of God's power and divine wrath in the Reformation era was an important factor in the witch-hunts, as were new demonological ideas, legal procedures involving torture, and neighborhood tensions. Though the gender balance of the accused varied widely in different parts of Europe, between 75 and 85 percent of those tried and executed were women, whom some demonologists viewed as weaker and so more likely to give in to the Devil.

Seventeenth-Century Crisis and Rebuilding

How did seventeenth-century European rulers overcome social and economic crisis to build strong states?

Historians often refer to the seventeenth century as an "age of crisis" because Europe was challenged by population losses, economic decline, and social and political unrest. These difficulties were partially due to climate changes that reduced agricultural productivity. But they also resulted from military competition among European powers, the religious divides of the Reformations, increased taxation, and war. Peasants and the urban poor were especially hard hit by the economic problems, and they frequently rioted against high food prices.

The atmosphere of crisis encouraged governments to take emergency measures to restore order, measures that they successfully turned into long-term reforms that strengthened the power of the state. In the long run, European states proved increasingly able to impose their will on the populace.

The Social Order and Peasant Life

Peasants occupied the lower tiers of a society organized in hierarchical levels. In much of Europe, the monarch occupied the summit and was celebrated as a semi-divine being chosen by God to embody the state. The clergy generally constituted the first order of society, due to its sacred role interceding with God on behalf of its flocks. Next came nobles, whose privileged status derived from their ancient bloodlines and leadership in battle. Many prosperous mercantile families had bought their way into the nobility through service to the monarchy in the fifteenth and sixteenth centuries, and they constituted a second tier of nobles. Those lower on the social scale, the peasants and artisans who formed the vast majority of the population, were expected to show deference to their betters. This was the "Great Chain of Being" that linked God to his creation in a series of ranked social groups.

In addition to being rigidly hierarchical, European societies were patriarchal. Religious and secular law commanded a man's wife, children, servants, and apprentices to respect and obey him. Fathers were entitled to use physical violence, imprisonment, and other forceful measures to impose their authority. These powers were balanced by expectations that a good father would care benevolently for his dependents.

In the seventeenth century the vast majority of Europeans lived in the countryside, as was the case in most parts of the world. In western Europe a small number of peasants owned enough land to feed themselves and possessed the livestock and plows necessary to work their land. Independent farmers were leaders of the peasant village. Below them were small landowners and tenant farmers who did not have enough land to be self-sufficient. At the bottom were villagers who worked as dependent laborers and servants. Private landowning among peasants was a distinguishing feature of western Europe. In central and eastern Europe the vast majority of peasants toiled as serfs for noble landowners, while in the Ottoman Empire all land belonged to the sultan.

Jesuits Members of the Society of Jesus, founded by Ignatius Loyola in 1540, whose goal was the spread of the Roman Catholic faith through schools and missionary activity.

The Young Beggar The mid-seventeenth century was a harsh period for many Europeans, who faced meager harvests, unemployment, high taxation, and social unrest. (Louvre, Paris, France/Bridgeman Images)

Economic Crisis and Popular Revolts

In the seventeenth century a period of colder and more variable climate afflicted much of the globe. Dubbed the "little ice age" by historians, this period of cold weather accompanied by both too much rain and episodes of severe drought resulted in shorter growing seasons with lower yields. A bad harvest created food shortages; a series of bad harvests could lead to famine. Recurrent famines significantly diminished the population of Europe and Asia in this period, through reduced fertility, increased susceptibility to disease, and outright starvation.

Industry also suffered. In Europe the output of woolen textiles, the most important industrial sector, declined sharply. Food prices were high, wages stagnated, and unemployment soared. This economic crisis was not universal: it struck various regions at different times and to different degrees. In the middle decades

of the century, for example, Spain, France, Germany, and the British Isles all experienced great economic difficulties, as did China, but these years were the golden age of the Netherlands (see "The Dutch Republic"). Japan also emerged relatively unscathed, as did South Asia and the Americas.

The urban poor and peasants were the hardest hit. When the price of bread rose beyond their capacity to pay, they frequently expressed their anger by rioting. Women often led these actions, since their role as mothers gave them some impunity in authorities' eyes. Historians have used the term **moral economy** for this vision of a world in which community needs predominate over competition and profit and in which necessary goods should thus be sold at a fair price.

During the middle years of the seventeenth century, harsh conditions transformed neighborhood bread riots into armed uprisings across much of Europe. Popular revolts were common in England, France, and throughout the Spanish Empire, particularly during the 1640s. At the same time that he struggled to put down an uprising in Catalonia, the economic center of the realm, Spanish king Philip IV faced revolt in Portugal, the northern provinces of the Netherlands, and Spanish-occupied Sicily. France suffered an uprising in the same period that won enthusiastic support from both nobles and peasants, while the English monarch was tried and executed by his subjects and Russia experienced an explosive rebellion. In China a series of popular revolts culminated in the fall of the Ming empire in 1644, demonstrating the global reach of the seventeenth-century crisis.

Municipal and royal authorities struggled to overcome popular revolt in the mid-seventeenth century. They feared that stern repressive measures, such as sending in troops to fire on crowds, would create martyrs and further inflame the situation, while full-scale occupation of a city would be very expensive and detract from military efforts elsewhere. The limitations of royal authority gave some leverage to rebels. To quell riots, royal edicts were sometimes suspended, prisoners released, and discussions initiated. By the beginning of the eighteenth century rulers had gained much greater control over their populations, as a result of the achievements in state-building discussed below (see "European Achievements in State-Building").

The Thirty Years' War

In addition to harsh economic conditions, popular unrest was greatly exacerbated by the impact of the decades-long conflict known as the **Thirty Years' War** (1618–1648), a war that drew in almost every European state. The background to the war was a shift in the balance between the population of Protestants and Catholics in the Holy Roman Empire that led to the deterioration of the Peace of Augsburg. Lutheran princes felt

MAP 18.2 Europe After the Thirty Years' War Which country emerged from the Thirty Years' War as the strongest European power? What dynastic house was that country's major rival in the early modern period?

Map legend:
- Austrian Habsburg lands
- Spanish Habsburg lands
- Other German states
- Swedish lands by 1648
- Ottoman Empire and tributary states
- Boundary of the Holy Roman Empire

compelled to form the Protestant Union (1608), and Catholics retaliated with the Catholic League (1609). Dynastic interests were also involved; the Spanish Habsburgs strongly supported the goals of their Austrian relatives: the unity of the empire and the preservation of Catholicism within it.

The war began with a conflict in Bohemia (part of the present-day Czech Republic) between the Catholic League and the Protestant Union but soon spread through the Holy Roman Empire, drawing in combatants from across Europe. After a series of initial Catholic victories, the tide of the conflict turned due to the intervention of Sweden, under its king Gustavus Adolphus (r. 1594–1632), and then France, whose prime minister, Cardinal Richelieu (REESH-uh-lyuh), inter-

vened on the side of the Protestants to undermine Habsburg power.

The 1648 Peace of Westphalia that ended the Thirty Years' War marked a turning point in European history. The treaties that established the peace not only ended conflicts fought over religious faith but also recognized the independent authority of more than three hundred German princes (Map 18.2), reconfirming

moral economy The early modern European view that community needs predominated over competition and profit and that necessary goods should thus be sold at a fair price.

Thirty Years' War A large-scale conflict extending from 1618 to 1648 that pitted Protestants against Catholics in central Europe, but also involved dynastic interests, notably of Spain and France.

the emperor's severely limited authority. The Augsburg agreement of 1555 became permanent, adding Calvinism to Catholicism and Lutheranism as legally permissible creeds. The United Provinces of the Netherlands, known as the Dutch Republic, won official freedom from Spain.

The Thirty Years' War was probably the most destructive event in central Europe prior to the world wars of the twentieth century. Perhaps one-third of urban residents and two-fifths of the rural population died, and agriculture and industry withered. Across Europe, states increased taxes to meet the cost of war, further increasing the suffering of a traumatized population.

European Achievements in State-Building

In this context of warfare, economic crisis, popular revolt, and demographic decline, rulers took urgent measures to restore order and rebuild their states. In some states, absolutist models of government prevailed. In others, constitutionalist forces dominated. Despite their political differences, all these states sought to protect and expand their frontiers, raise taxes, consolidate central control, establish social welfare programs, and compete for colonies and trade in the New and Old Worlds. In so doing, they followed a broad pattern of state-building and consolidation of power found across Eurasia in this period.

Rulers who wished to increase their authority encountered formidable obstacles, including poor communications, entrenched local power structures, and ethnic and linguistic diversity. Nonetheless, over the course of the seventeenth century both absolutist and constitutional governments achieved new levels of power and national unity. They did so by transforming emergency measures of wartime into permanent structures of government and by subduing privileged groups through the combined use of force and economic and social incentives. Increased state authority may be seen in four areas in particular: a tremendous growth in the size and professionalism of armies; much higher taxes; larger and more efficient bureaucracies; and territorial expansion both within Europe and overseas. A fifth important area of European state growth—

government sponsorship of scientific inquiry—will be discussed in Chapter 19.

Over time, centralized power added up to something close to **sovereignty**. A state may be termed sovereign when it possesses a monopoly over the instruments of justice and the use of force within clearly defined boundaries. In a sovereign state, no nongovernmental system of courts competes with state courts in the dispensation of justice. Also, private armies present no threat to central authority. While seventeenth-century states did not acquire full sovereignty, they made important strides toward that goal.

Absolutist States in Western and Central Europe

What was absolutism, and how did it evolve in seventeenth-century Spain, France, and Austria?

Rulers in absolutist states asserted that, because they were chosen by God, they were responsible to God alone. Under the rule of **absolutism**, monarchs claimed exclusive power to make and enforce laws, denying any other institution or group the authority to check their power. This system was limited in practice by the need to maintain legitimacy and compromise with elites. Spain, France, and Austria provide three key examples of the development of the absolutist state.

Spain

The discovery of silver at Potosí in 1545 had produced momentous wealth for Spain, allowing it to dominate Europe militarily (see "Spanish Silver and Its Economic Effects" in Chapter 16). Yet Spain had inherent weaknesses that the wealth of empire had hidden. When Philip IV took the throne in 1621, he inherited a vast and overstretched empire, which combined different kingdoms with their own traditions and loyalties. Spanish silver had created great wealth but also dependency. While Creoles undertook new industries in the colonies and European nations targeted Spanish colonial trade, industry and finance in Spain itself remained undeveloped.

Spain's limitations became apparent during the first half of the seventeenth century. Between 1610 and 1650 Spanish trade with the colonies in the New World fell 60 percent due to competition from colonial industries and from Dutch and English traders. To make matters worse, in 1609 the Crown expelled some three hundred thousand Moriscos, or former Muslims, significantly reducing the pool of skilled workers and merchants. At the same time, disease decimated the enslaved

sovereignty Authority of states that possess a monopoly over the instruments of justice and the use of force within clearly defined boundaries and in which private armies present no threat to central control; seventeenth-century European states made important advances toward sovereignty.

absolutism A political system common to early modern Europe in which monarchs claimed exclusive power to make and enforce laws, without checks by other institutions; this system was limited in practice by the need to maintain legitimacy and compromise with elites.

workers who toiled in South American silver mines. Moreover, the mines started to run dry, and the quantity of metal produced steadily declined after 1620 and Dutch privateers seized the entire silver fleet in 1628.

In Madrid the expenses of war and imperial rule constantly exceeded income. Despite the efforts of Philip's able chief minister, Gaspar de Guzmán, Count-Duke of Olivares, it proved impossible to force the kingdoms of the empire to shoulder the cost of its defense. To meet state debt, the Spanish crown repeatedly devalued the coinage and declared bankruptcy, which resulted in the collapse of national credit and steep inflation.

Spanish aristocrats, attempting to maintain an extravagant lifestyle they could no longer afford, increased the rents on their estates. High rents and heavy taxes drove the peasants from the land, leading to a decline in agricultural productivity. In cities wages and production stagnated. Spain also ignored new scientific methods that might have improved agricultural or manufacturing techniques because they came from the heretical nations of Holland and England.

Spain's situation worsened with internal rebellions and fresh military defeats during the Thirty Years' War and the remainder of the seventeenth century. The Treaty of Westphalia, which ended the Thirty Years' War, compelled Spain to recognize the independence of the Dutch Republic, and another treaty in 1659 granted extensive territories to France. Finally, in 1688 the Spanish crown reluctantly recognized the independence of Portugal. With these losses, the era of Spanish dominance in Europe ended.

The Foundations of French Absolutism

Although France was the largest and most populous state in western Europe, its position at the beginning of the seventeenth century appeared extremely weak. Struggling to recover from decades of religious civil war, France posed little threat to Spain's predominance in Europe. By the end of the century the countries' positions were reversed.

Henry IV (r. 1589–1610) inaugurated the Bourbon dynasty, defusing religious tensions and rebuilding France's economy. He issued the Edict of Nantes in 1598, allowing Huguenots (French Protestants) the right to worship in 150 traditionally Protestant towns

Diego Rodriguez de Silva y Velázquez, *Las Meninas*, 1656 The royal princess Margaret Theresa is shown here surrounded by her ladies-in-waiting. The painter Velázquez has portrayed himself working on a canvas, while her parents, the king and queen of Spain, are reflected in the mirror behind the princess. (Museo del Prado, Madrid, Spain/Bridgeman Images)

throughout France. He invested in infrastructure and raised revenue by selling royal offices instead of charging high taxes. Despite his efforts at peace, Henry was murdered in 1610 by a Catholic zealot.

Cardinal Richelieu (1585–1642) became first minister of the French crown on behalf of Henry's young son Louis XIII (r. 1610–1643). Richelieu designed his domestic policies to strengthen royal control. He extended the use of intendants, commissioners for each of France's thirty-two districts who were appointed by and were responsible to the monarch. By using the intendants to gather information and ensure royal edicts were enforced, Richelieu reduced the power of provincial nobles. Richelieu also viewed France's Huguenots as potential rebels, and he laid seige to La Rochelle, a Protestant stronghold. Richelieu's main foreign policy goal was to destroy the Habsburgs' grip on territories that surrounded France. Consequently, Richelieu supported Habsburg enemies, including Protestants, during the Thirty Years' War (see "The Thirty Years' War").

Cardinal Jules Mazarin (1602–1661) succeeded Richelieu as chief minister for the next child-king, the four-year-old Louis XIV, who inherited the throne from his father in 1643. Mazarin's struggle to increase royal revenues to meet the costs of the Thirty Years' War led to the uprisings of 1648–1653 known as the Fronde. In Paris magistrates of the Parlement of Paris, the nation's most important law court, were outraged by the Crown's autocratic measures. These so-called robe nobles (named for the robes they wore in court) encouraged violent protest by the common people. As rebellion spread outside Paris and to the sword nobles (the traditional warrior nobility), civil order broke down completely, and young Louis XIV had to flee Paris.

Much of the rebellion faded, however, when Louis XIV was declared king in his own right in 1651, ending the regency of his mother, Anne of Austria. The French people were desperate for peace and stability after the disorders of the Fronde and were willing to accept a strong monarch who could restore order. Louis pledged to do just that, insisting that only his absolute authority stood between the French people and a renewed descent into chaos.

Louis XIV and Absolutism

During the long reign of Louis XIV (r. 1643–1715), known as the Sun King, the French monarchy overcame weakness and division to become the most powerful nation in western Europe. Louis based his authority on the **divine right of kings**: God had established kings as his rulers on earth, and they were answerable

ultimately to him alone. However, Louis also recognized that kings could not simply do as they pleased. They had to obey God's laws and rule for the good of the people.

Like his counterpart, the Kangxi emperor of China, who inherited his realm only two decades after the Sun King did (see "Competent and Long-Lived Emperors" in Chapter 21), Louis XIV impressed his subjects with his discipline and hard work. (See "Global Viewpoints: Descriptions of Louis XIV of France and the Kangxi Emperor of China," at right.) He ruled his realm through several councils of state and insisted on taking a personal role in many of the councils' decisions. Despite increasing financial problems, Louis never called a meeting of the Estates General, the traditional French representative assembly composed of the three estates of clergy, nobility, and commoners. The nobility, therefore, had no means of united expression or action. To further restrict their political power, he excluded them from his councils and chose instead capable men of modest origins.

Although personally tolerant, Louis hated division. He insisted that religious unity was essential to the security of the state. In 1685 Louis revoked the Edict of Nantes. Around two hundred thousand Protestants, including some of the kingdom's most highly skilled artisans, fled France. Louis's insistence on "one king, one law, one religion" contrasts sharply with the religious tolerance exhibited by Muslim empires in the Middle East and South Asia (see "Non-Muslims Under Muslim Rule" in Chapter 17).

Despite his claims to absolute authority, there were multiple constraints on Louis's power. As a representative of divine power, he was obliged to rule in a way that seemed consistent with virtue and paternal benevolence. He had to uphold the laws issued by his royal predecessors. Moreover, he also relied on the collaboration of nobles. Without their cooperation, it would have been impossible for Louis to extend his power throughout France or wage his many foreign wars. (See "Thinking Like a Historian: What Was Absolutism?" page 510.)

The Wars of Louis XIV

Louis XIV kept France at war for thirty-three of the fifty-four years of his personal rule. Under the leadership of François le Tellier, marquis de Louvois, Louis's secretary of state for war, France acquired a huge professional army. The French army almost tripled in size. Uniforms and weapons were standardized, and a system of training and promotion was devised. As in so many other matters, Louis's model was emulated across Europe, resulting in a continent-wide transformation in military capability that scholars have referred to as a "military revolution."

divine right of kings The belief propagated by absolutist monarchs in Europe that they derived their power from God and were only answerable to him.

Descriptions of Louis XIV of France and the Kangxi Emperor of China

King Louis XIV of France (1638–1715) and the Kangxi emperor of Qing China (1654–1722) lived remarkably parallel lives. They both inherited realms in childhood and learned to rule from powerful women, in Louis's case his mother, Queen Anne of Austria, and in Kangxi's case his grandmother, Grand Empress Dowager Xiaozhuang. Both rulers built magnificent palaces and demonstrated hard work, discipline, and a thirst for glory and power. Louis sent Jesuits to the Chinese court to spread European scientific knowledge and Catholicism. The emperor originally welcomed them and was fascinated by their learning and technology, but he eventually banned them and Christianity from his realm. The following descriptions of Louis XIV and the Kangxi emperor, written by a French courtier and a Jesuit missionary, respectively, underline the similar qualities observers noted in the two rulers.

The Duke of Saint-Simon, *Memoirs of Louis XIV, His Court, and the Regency, 1739–1749.*

■ [He was] the very figure of a hero, so impregnated with a natural but most imposing majesty that it appeared even in his most insignificant gestures and movements, without arrogance but with simple gravity. . . . He was as dignified and majestic in his dressing gown as when dressed in robes of state, or on horseback at the head of his troops.

He excelled in all sorts of exercise and liked to have every facility for it. No fatigue nor stress of weather made any impression on that heroic figure and bearing; drenched with rain or snow, pierced with cold, bathed in sweat or covered with dust, he was always the same. . . .

[He had] the ability to speak well and to listen with quick comprehension; much reserve of manner adjusted with exactness to the quality of different persons; a courtesy always grave, always dignified, always distinguished, and suited to the age, rank, and sex of each individual, and, for the ladies, always an air of natural gallantry. . . .

Nothing could be regulated with greater exactitude than were his days and hours. In spite of all his variety of places, affairs, and amusements, with an almanac and a watch one might tell, three hundred leagues away, exactly what he was doing. . . . If he administered reproof, it was rarely, in few words, and never hastily. He did not lose control of himself ten times in his whole life, and then only with inferior persons, and not more than four or five times seriously.

Father Joachim Bouvet, *The History of Cang-Hy, the Present Emperour of China, 1699*

■ His whole Deportment is very Majestick, being well proportion'd in his Limbs, and pretty Tall, the Feature of his Face very exact, with a large and brisk Eye, beyond what is observable among others of that Nation; He is a little crooked Nosed, and pitted with the Small-pox, but not so as to be in the least disfigur'd by them.

But the rare Accomplishments of his Mind, surpass infinitely those of his Body. His Natural Genius is such as can be parallel'd but by few, being endow'd with a Quick and piercing Wit, a vast Memory, and Great Understanding; His Constancy is never to be shaken by any sinister Event, which makes him the fittest Person in the World, not only to undertake, but also to accomplish Great Designs.

To be short, his inclinations are so Noble, and in all respects so Answerable to the High Station of so Great a Prince, that his People stand in Admiration of his Person, being equally Charm'd with his Love and Justice, and the Tenderness he shews for his Subjects, and with his virtuous Inclinations; which as they are always guided by the Dictates of Reason, so, they render him an Absolute Master of his Passions.

QUESTIONS FOR ANALYSIS

1. What qualities did the Duke of Saint-Simon and Father Bouvet admire in Louis XIV and the Kangxi emperor? What similarities do you find among the qualities they describe?

2. Based on what you have read in this chapter, why was it important for an absolute ruler to possess the qualities the authors describe? What weaknesses do these excerpts suggest a would-be ruler should avoid, and why?

Sources: J. H. Robinson, ed., *Readings in European History*, vol. 2 (Boston: Ginn, 1906), pp. 285–286; Father Joachim Bouvet, *The History of Cang-Hy, the Present Emperor of China* (London: F. Coggan, 1699), p. 2.

What Was Absolutism?

Historians have long debated the nature of "absolutism" in seventeenth-century Europe. While many historians have emphasized the growth of state power in this period, especially under Louis XIV of France, others have questioned whether such a thing as "absolutism" ever existed. The following documents will allow you to draw your own conclusions about absolutism.

1 **Jacques-Bénigne Bossuet, political treatise, 1709.** In 1670 Louis XIV appointed Bishop Bossuet tutor to his son and heir, known as the dauphin. In *Politics Drawn from the Very Words of Holy Scripture*, Bossuet argued that royal power was divine and absolute, but not without limits.

■ It appears from all this that the person of the king is sacred, and that to attack him in any way is sacrilege. God has the kings anointed by his prophets with the holy unction in like manner as he has bishops and altars anointed. But even without the external application in thus being anointed, they are by their very office the representatives of the divine majesty deputed by Providence for the execution of his purposes. Accordingly God calls Cyrus his anointed. "Thus saith the Lord to his anointed, to Cyrus, whose right hand I have holden, to subdue nations before him." Kings should be guarded as holy things, and whosoever neglects to protect them is worthy of death.... There is something religious in the respect accorded to a prince. The service of God and the respect for kings are bound together. St. Peter unites these two duties when he says, "Fear God. Honour the king."... But kings, although their power comes from on high, as has been said, should not regard themselves as masters of that power to use it at their pleasure;... they must employ it with fear and self-restraint, as a thing coming from God and of which God will demand an account.

2 **Letter of the prince of Condé, royal governor of the province of Burgundy, to Controller General Jean-Baptiste Colbert, June 18, 1662.** In this letter, the king's representative in the province of Burgundy reports on his efforts to compel the leaders of the province to pay taxes levied by the royal government. The Estates of Burgundy comprised representatives of the three orders, or estates, of society: the clergy, the nobility, and the commoners.

■ Since then the Estates have deliberated every day, persuaded that the extreme misery in this province—caused by the great levies it has suffered, the sterility [of the land] in recent years, and the disorders that have recently occurred—would induce the king to give them some relief. That is why they offered only 500,000 for the free gift. Then, after I had protested this in the appropriate manner, they raised it to 600,000, then 800,000, and finally 900,000 livres. Until then I had stood firm at 1.5 million, but when I saw that they were on the verge of deciding not to give any more... I finally came down to the 1.2 million livres contained in my instructions and invited them to deliberate again, declaring that I could not agree to present any other proposition to the king and that I believed that there was no better way to serve their interests than to obey the king blindly. They agreed with good grace and came this morning to offer me a million. They begged me to leave it at that and not to demand more from them for the free gift; and since I told them they would have to do a little better to satisfy the king completely on this occasion, they again exaggerated their poverty and begged me to inform the king of it, but said that, rather than not please him, they preferred to make a new effort, and they would leave it up to me to declare what they had to do. I told them that I believed His Majesty would have the goodness to be satisfied with 1.05 million livres for the free gift, and they agreed.... So Monsieur, there is the deed done.

ANALYZING THE EVIDENCE

1. What elements of royal authority does the portrait of Louis XIV in Source 4 present to viewers? How would you compare this depiction of political power with images of modern-day politicians? How would you explain the differences?
2. What justification do the sources offer for Louis's claim to exercise "absolute" political authority? Based on his own words in Source 3, how do you think Louis would have viewed the constitutional governments of England and the Dutch Republic?
3. Compare and contrast the evidence for Louis's power given in these sources with evidence for limitations on it. What resources would a king have to muster to enlarge his army drastically (Source 5)? What insight do the negotiations over taxation (Source 2) give you into the ways the royal government acquired those resources?

3 **Louis XIV, *Memoir for the Instruction of the Dauphin*.** In 1670 Louis XIV finished a memoir he had compiled for the education of his son and heir. Presented in the king's voice — although cowritten with several royal aides — the memoir recounts the early years of Louis's reign and explains his approach to absolute rule.

■ For however it be held as a maxim that in every thing a Prince should employ the most mild measures and first, and that it is more to his advantage to govern his subjects by persuasive than coercive means, it is nevertheless certain that whenever he meets with impediments or rebellion, the interest of his crown and the welfare of his people demand that he should cause himself to be indispensably obeyed; for it must be acknowledged there is nothing can so securely establish the happiness and tranquility of a country as the perfect combination of all authority in the single person of the Sovereign. The least division in this respect often produces the greatest calamities; and whether it be detached into the hands of individuals or those of corporate bodies, it always is there in a state of fermentation.

. . . [B]esides the insurrections and the intestine commotions which the ambition of power infallibly produces when it is not repressed, there are still a thousand other evils created by the inactivity of the Sovereign. Those who are nearest his person are the first to observe his weakness, and are also the first who are desirous of profiting by it. Every one of those persons have necessarily others who are subservient to their avaricious views, and to whom they at the same time give the privilege of imitating them. Thus, from the highest to the lowest is a systematic corruption communicated, and it becomes general in all classes.

(Louis XIV in Royal Costume, 1701, by Hyacinthe François Rigaud [1659–1743] [oil on canvas]/ Musée du Louvre, Paris, France/Bridgeman Images)

4 **Hyacinthe Rigaud, portrait of Louis XIV, 1701.** This was one of Louis XIV's favorite portraits of himself. He liked it so much that he had many copies of the portrait made; his successors had their own portraits painted in the same posture with the same clothing and accoutrements.

5 **Growth of the French army.**

Time Period	Size of Army
Middle Ages	10,000 men
1635 (Louis XIII and Richelieu enter Thirty Years' War)	125,000 men
1670s (Louis XIV wages Dutch War)	280,000 men
1690s (Louis XIV wages Nine Years' War)	340,000 men

PUTTING IT ALL TOGETHER

Using the sources above, along with what you have learned in class and in this chapter, what was "absolutism"? Write a brief essay explaining what contemporaries thought absolute power entailed and the extent to which Louis XIV achieved such power.

Sources: (1) J. H. Robinson, ed., *Readings in European History,* vol. 2 (Boston: Ginn, 1906), p. 274; (2) William Beik, ed., *Louis XIV and Absolutism: A Brief Study with Documents* (Boston: Bedford/St. Martin's, 2000), pp. 127–128; (3) *Memoirs of Lewis the Fourteenth, Written by Himself, and Addressed to His Son,* vol. 1 (London: Longman, Hurst, Rees and Orme, 1806), pp. 13–14; (5) Based on information from John A. Lynn, *The Wars of Louis XIV, 1667–1714* (London: Routledge, 2013), pp. 5–51.

MAPPING THE PAST

MAP 18.3 Europe After the Peace of Utrecht, 1715 The series of treaties commonly called the Peace of Utrecht ended the War of the Spanish Succession and redrew the map of Europe. A French Bourbon king succeeded to the Spanish throne. France surrendered the Spanish Netherlands (later Belgium), then in French hands, to Austria and recognized the Hohenzollern rulers of Prussia. Spain ceded Gibraltar to Great Britain, for which it has been a strategic naval station ever since. Spain also granted Britain the *asiento*, the contract for supplying African slaves to America.

ANALYZING THE MAP Identify the areas on the map that changed hands as a result of the Peace of Utrecht. How did these changes affect the balance of power in Europe?

CONNECTIONS How and why did so many European countries possess scattered or discontiguous territories? What does this suggest about European politics in this period? Does this map suggest potential for future conflict?

During this long period of warfare, Louis's goal was to expand France to what he considered its natural borders and to win glory for the Bourbon dynasty. His results were mixed. During the 1660s and 1670s, French armies won a number of important victories. The wars of the 1680s and 1690s, however, brought no additional territories and placed unbearable strains on French resources.

Louis's last war, the War of the Spanish Succession (1701–1713), was endured by a French people suffer-

ing high taxes, crop failure, and widespread malnutrition and death. This war was the result of Louis's unwillingness to abide by a previous agreement to divide Spanish possessions between France and the Holy Roman emperor upon the death of the childless Spanish king Charles II (r. 1665–1700). In 1701 the English, Dutch, Austrians, and Prussians formed the Grand Alliance against Louis XIV. War dragged on until 1713, when it was ended by the Peace of Utrecht (Map 18.3).

The Peace of Utrecht marked the end of French expansion. Thirty-three years of war had given France the rights to all of Alsace and some commercial centers in the north. But at what price? At the time of Louis's death in 1715, an exhausted France hovered on the brink of bankruptcy.

The Economic Policy of Mercantilism

France's ability to build armies and fight wars depended on a strong economy. Fortunately for Louis, Jean-Baptiste Colbert (1619–1683) brilliantly occupied the position of controller general of finance from 1665 to 1683. Colbert's central principle was that the wealth and the economy of France should serve the state. To this end, Colbert rigorously applied mercantilist policies to France.

Mercantilism is a collection of governmental policies for the regulation of economic activities by and for the state, with the aim of increasing state power. It derives from the idea that a nation's international power is based on its wealth, specifically its supply of gold and silver. To accumulate wealth, a country always had to sell more goods abroad than it bought from foreign countries.

To increase exports, Colbert supported old industries and created new ones. He enacted new production regulations, created guilds to boost quality standards, and encouraged foreign craftsmen to immigrate to France. To encourage the purchase of French goods, he abolished many domestic tariffs and raised tariffs on foreign products. In 1664 Colbert founded the Company of the East Indies with hopes of competing with the Dutch for Asian trade. Colbert also sought to increase France's control over and presence in New France (Canada) (see "Colonial Empires of England and France").

During Colbert's tenure as controller general, Louis was able to pursue his goals without massive tax increases and without creating a stream of new offices. The constant pressure of warfare after Colbert's death, however, undid many of his economic achievements.

The Austrian Habsburgs

Absolutism was also the dominant form of monarchical rule among the more than one thousand states that composed the Holy Roman Empire. Prussia, a minor power with scattered holdings, emerged in the seventeenth and eighteenth centuries under the Hohenzollern dynasty as a major rival to the Austrian Habsburg dynasty (see "Enlightened Absolutism and Its Limits" in Chapter 19). Like all of central Europe, the Austrian Habsburgs emerged from the Thirty Years' War impoverished and exhausted. Their efforts to destroy Protestantism in the German lands and to turn the weak Holy Roman Empire into a real state had failed. Defeat in central Europe encouraged the Austrian Habsburgs to turn away from a quest for imperial dominance and to focus inward and eastward in an attempt to unify their diverse holdings.

Habsburg victory over Bohemia during the Thirty Years' War was an important step in this direction. Ferdinand II (r. 1619–1637) drastically reduced the power of the Bohemian Estates, the largely Protestant representative assembly. He also confiscated the landholdings of Protestant nobles and gave them to his supporters. After 1650 a large portion of the Bohemian nobility was of recent origin and owed its success to the Habsburgs.

With the support of this new nobility, the Habsburgs established direct rule over Bohemia. Under their rule, the condition of the serfs worsened substantially. The Habsburgs also successfully eliminated Protestantism in Bohemia. These changes were important steps in creating absolutist rule.

Ferdinand III (r. 1637–1657) continued to build state power. He centralized the government in the empire's German-speaking provinces, which formed the core Habsburg holdings, and established a permanent standing army. The Habsburg monarchy then turned east toward Hungary, which had been divided between the Ottomans and the Habsburgs in the early sixteenth century. Between 1683 and 1699 the Habsburgs pushed the Ottomans from most of Hungary and Transylvania. The recovery of all of the former kingdom of Hungary was completed in 1718.

Austrian Habsburg territory in 1648

Lands taken from Ottomans by Austrian Habsburgs, to 1699

Austrian Expansion, to 1699

Despite its reduced strength, the Hungarian nobility effectively thwarted the full development of Habsburg absolutism. Throughout the seventeenth century Hungarian nobles periodically rose in revolt against the Habsburgs. In 1703, with the Habsburgs bogged down in the War of the Spanish Succession, the Hungarians rose in one last patriotic rebellion under Prince Francis Rákóczy (RAH-coht-see). Rákóczy and his forces

mercantilism A system of economic regulations aimed at increasing the power of the state derived from the belief that a nation's international power was based on its wealth, specifically its supply of gold and silver.

were eventually defeated, but the Habsburgs agreed to restore many of the traditional privileges of the Hungarian aristocracy in return for the country's acceptance of Habsburg rule.

Elsewhere, the Habsburgs made significant achievements in state-building by forging consensus with the church and the nobility. A sense of common identity and loyalty to the monarchy grew among elites in Habsburg lands. German became the language of the state, and Vienna became the political and cultural center of the empire.

The Absolutist Palace

In 1682 Louis moved his court and government to the newly renovated palace at Versailles (vayr-SIGH), in the countryside southwest of Paris. The themes of the interior paintings and the sculptures in the gardens hailed Louis's power, with images of the Roman gods Apollo (the sun god) and Neptune (the sea god) making frequent appearances. The gardens' rational orderliness and symmetry showed that Louis's force extended even to nature, while their terraces and waterworks served as showcases for the latest techniques in military and civil engineering.

The palace quickly became the center of political, social, and cultural life, and all high-ranking nobles were required to spend at least part of the year in residence. Louis established an elaborate set of etiquette rituals for courtiers that encompassed every moment of his day, from waking up and dressing in the morning to removing his clothing and retiring at night. These rituals were far from meaningless or trivial. The king controlled immense resources and privileges; access to him meant favored treatment for government offices, military and religious posts, state pensions, honorary titles, and a host of other benefits.

A system of patronage—in which a higher-ranked individual protected a lower-ranked one in return for loyalty and services—flowed from the court to the provinces. Through this mechanism Louis gained cooperation from powerful nobles. Although they were denied public offices and posts, women played a central role in the patronage system. At court the king's wife, mistresses, and other female relatives recommended individuals for honors, advocated policy decisions, and brokered alliances between noble factions.

With Versailles as the center of European politics, French culture grew in international prestige. French became the language of polite society and international diplomacy, and France inspired a cosmopolitan European culture in the late seventeenth century that looked to Versailles as its center. Moreover, Louis's rival European monarchs soon followed his example, and palace building became a Europe-wide phenomenon.

Constitutionalism and Empire in England and the Dutch Republic

Why and how did the constitutional state triumph in England and the Dutch Republic?

While most European nations emerged from the crises of the seventeenth century with absolutist forms of government, England and the Netherlands evolved toward **constitutionalism**, which is the limitation of government by law. Constitutionalism also implies a balance between the authority and power of the government, on the one hand, and the rights and liberties of the subjects, on the other.

After decades of civil war, the English briefly adopted **republicanism**, a form of government in which there is no monarch and power rests in the hands of the people as exercised through elected representatives. Finally, in 1688 the English settled on a lasting political solution, constitutional monarchy. Under this system of government, England retained a monarch as the titular head of government but vested sovereignty in an elected parliament. For their part, the Dutch rejected monarchical rule in 1648, when their independence from Spain was formally recognized. Instead they adopted a republican form of government in which elected Estates (assemblies) held supreme power. Neither the English nor the Dutch were democratic by any standard, but to other Europeans, they were shining examples of the restraint of arbitrary power and the rule of law.

Religious Divides and Civil War

In 1603 beloved Queen Elizabeth was succeeded by her Scottish cousin James Stuart, who ruled England as James I (r. 1603–1625). Like Louis XIV, James believed that a monarch had a divine right to his authority and was responsible only to God. James I and his son Charles I (r. 1625–1649) considered any legislative constraint on their power a threat to their divine-right

constitutionalism A form of government in which power is limited by law and balanced between the authority and power of the government, on the one hand, and the rights and liberties of the subject or citizen, on the other; it includes constitutional monarchies and republics.

republicanism A form of government in which there is no monarch and power rests in the hands of the people as exercised through elected representatives.

Puritans Members of a sixteenth- and seventeenth-century reform movement within the Church of England that advocated purifying it of Roman Catholic elements, such as bishops, elaborate ceremonials, and wedding rings.

prerogative. Consequently, at every meeting of Parliament between 1603 and 1640, bitter squabbles erupted between the Crown and the House of Commons.

Religious issues also embittered relations between the king and the House of Commons. In the early seventeenth century many English people felt dissatisfied with the Church of England. Calvinist **Puritans** wanted to take the Reformation further by "purifying" the Anglican Church of Roman Catholic elements, including crown-appointed bishops, elaborate ceremonials, and wedding rings. James I responded to such ideas by declaring, "No bishop, no king." His son and successor, Charles I, further antagonized subjects by marrying a French Catholic princess and supporting the high-handed policies of archbishop of Canterbury William Laud (1573–1645). Political and religious conflict in this period was exacerbated by economic distress caused by severe weather conditions and periodic bouts of plague.

Charles avoided direct confrontation with his subjects by refusing to call Parliament into session from 1629 to 1640, instead financing the realm through extraordinary stopgap levies considered illegal by most English people. However, when Scottish Calvinists revolted against his religious policies, Charles was forced to summon Parliament to obtain funding for an army to put down the revolt. Angry with the king's behavior and sympathetic with the Scots' religious beliefs, the House of Commons passed the Triennial Act in 1641, which compelled the king to call Parliament every three years. The Commons also impeached Archbishop Laud and then threatened to abolish bishops. King Charles, fearful of a Scottish invasion, reluctantly accepted these measures. The next act in the conflict was precipitated by the outbreak of rebellion in Ireland. In 1641 the Catholic gentry of Ireland led an uprising in response to a feared invasion by British anti-Catholic forces.

Without an army, Charles I could neither come to terms with the Scots nor respond to the Irish rebellion. After a failed attempt to arrest parliamentary leaders, Charles left London and began to raise an army. In response, Parliament formed its own army, the New Model Army.

The English civil war (1642–1649) pitted the power of the king against that of Parliament. After three years of fighting, Parliament's army defeated the king's forces at the Battles of Naseby and Langport in the summer of 1645. Charles refused to concede defeat, and both sides waited for a decisive event. This arrived in the form of the army under the leadership of Oliver Cromwell, a member of the House of Commons

Puritan Occupations These twelve engravings depict typical Puritan occupations and show that the Puritans came primarily from the artisan and lower middle classes. The governing classes and peasants made up a much smaller percentage of Puritans, and most generally adhered to the traditions of the Church of England. (Visual Connection Archive)

The English Civil War, 1642–1649

Legend:
- Parliamentarians
- Royalists
- Major battle

and a devout Puritan. In 1647 Cromwell's troops captured the king and dismissed members of the Parliament who opposed Cromwell's actions. In 1649 the remaining representatives, known as the Rump Parliament, put Charles on trial for high treason. Charles was found guilty and beheaded on January 30, 1649.

The Puritan Protectorate

With the execution of Charles, the monarchy was abolished and a commonwealth, or republican government, was proclaimed. Theoretically, legislative power rested in the surviving members of Parliament, and executive power was lodged in a council of state. In fact, the army that had defeated the king controlled the government, and Oliver Cromwell controlled the army. Though called the Protectorate, the rule of Cromwell (1653–1658) was a form of military dictatorship. Reflecting Puritan ideas of morality, Cromwell's state forbade sports, kept the theaters closed, and rigorously censored the press.

On the issue of religion, Cromwell favored some degree of tolerance, and all Christians except Roman Catholics had the right to practice their faiths. Cromwell had long associated Catholicism in Ireland with sedition and heresy, and he led an army there to reconquer the country in August 1649. Following Cromwell's reconquest, the English banned Catholicism in Ireland, executed priests, and confiscated land from Catholics for English and Scottish settlers.

The Protectorate collapsed when Cromwell died in 1658 and his ineffectual son succeeded him. Fed up with military rule, the English longed for a return to civilian government. By 1660 they were ready to restore the monarchy.

Constitutional Monarchy

The Restoration of 1660 brought to the throne Charles II (r. 1660–1685), the eldest son of Charles I. Both houses of Parliament were also restored, as was the Anglican Church. However, Charles was succeeded by his Catholic brother James II, arousing fears of a return of Catholicism. A group of eminent persons in Parliament and the Church of England wrote to James's

Protestant daughter Mary and her Dutch husband, Prince William of Orange, inviting them to invade and take the throne of England. In November 1688 William arrived on the English coast with five hundred ships and over twenty thousand soldiers, causing James II, his queen, and their infant son to flee for France. Early in 1689 William and Mary were jointly crowned as king and queen of England.

The English called the events of 1688 and 1689 the Glorious Revolution because they believed it replaced one king with another with barely any bloodshed. In truth, William's arrival sparked riots and violence across the British Isles and in North American cities such as Boston and New York. Uprisings by supporters of James, known as Jacobites, occurred in 1689 in Scotland. In Ireland the two sides waged outright war from 1689 to 1691. William's victory at the Battle of the Boyne (1690) and the subsequent Treaty of Limerick (1691) sealed his accession to power.

In England the revolution represented the final destruction of the idea of divine-right monarchy. The men who brought about the revolution framed their opposition to Stuart-style absolutism in the **Bill of Rights of 1689**, which was passed by Parliament and formally accepted by William and Mary. Law was to be made in Parliament; once made, it could not be suspended by the Crown. Parliament had to be called at least once every three years. The Bill of Rights also established the independence of the judiciary and mandated that there be no standing army in peacetime. Protestants could possess arms, but the Catholic minority could not. Catholics could not inherit the throne. Additional legislation granted freedom of worship to Protestant dissenters but not to Catholics.

The Glorious Revolution and the concept of representative government found its best defense in political philosopher John Locke's *Second Treatise of Civil Government* (1690). Locke (1632–1704) maintained that a government that oversteps its proper function — protecting the natural rights of life, liberty, and property — becomes a tyranny. Under a tyrannical government, he argued, the people have the natural right to rebellion.

Although the events of 1688 and 1689 brought England closer to Locke's ideal, they did not constitute a democratic revolution. The Glorious Revolution placed sovereignty in Parliament, and Parliament represented the upper classes.

The Dutch Republic

In the late sixteenth century the seven northern provinces of the Netherlands fought for and won their independence from Spain. The independence of the Republic of the United Provinces of the Netherlands was recognized in 1648 in the treaty that ended the Thirty Years' War. In this period, often called the

Bill of Rights of 1689 A bill passed by Parliament and accepted by William and Mary that limited the powers of British monarchs and affirmed those of Parliament.

"golden age of the Netherlands," Dutch ideas and attitudes played a profound role in shaping a new and modern worldview. At the same time, the United Provinces developed its own distinctive model of a constitutional state.

Rejecting the rule of a monarch, the Dutch established a republic, a state in which power rested in the hands of the people and was exercised through elected representatives. Other examples of republics in early modern Europe included the Swiss Confederation and several autonomous city-states of Italy and the Holy Roman Empire. Among the Dutch, an oligarchy of wealthy businessmen called regents handled domestic affairs in each province's Estates, or assemblies. The provincial Estates held virtually all the power. A federal assembly, or States General, handled foreign affairs and war, but all issues had to be referred back to the local Estates for approval, and each of the seven provinces could veto any proposed legislation. Holland, the province with the largest navy and the most wealth, usually dominated the republic and the States General.

In each province, the Estates appointed an executive officer, known as the stadholder. Although in theory the stadholder was freely chosen by the Estates, in practice the reigning prince of Orange usually held the office of stadholder in several of the seven provinces of the republic. Tensions persisted between supporters of the House of Orange and those of the staunchly republican Estates, who suspected the princes of harboring monarchical ambitions. (See "Analyzing the Evidence: Gonzales Coques, *The Young Scholar and His Wife*," page 518.)

Global trade and commerce brought the Dutch the highest standard of living in Europe, perhaps in the world. Salaries were high, and all classes of society ate well. Consequently, the Netherlands experienced very few of the riots and popular revolts that characterized the rest of Europe.[2] The moral and ethical bases of Dutch commercial wealth were thrift, frugality, and religious tolerance. Jews enjoyed a level of acceptance and assimilation in Dutch business and general culture unique in early modern Europe. (See "Individuals in Society: Glückel of Hameln," page 520.) In the Dutch Republic tolerance not only seemed the right way but also contributed to profits by attracting a great deal of foreign capital and investment.

Colonial Expansion and Empire

How did European nations compete for global trade and empire in the Americas and Asia?

For much of the sixteenth century the Spanish and Portuguese dominated European overseas trade and colonization (see "Conquest and Settlement" in Chapter 16). In the early seventeenth century, however, England, France, and the Netherlands challenged Spain's monopoly. They eventually succeeded in creating overseas empires, consisting of settler colonies in North America, slave plantations in the Caribbean, and scattered trading posts in West Africa and Asia. Competition among them was encouraged by mercantilist economic doctrine, which dictated that foreign trade was a zero-sum game in which one country's gains necessarily entailed another's loss.

The Dutch Trading Empire

The so-called golden age of the Dutch Republic in the seventeenth century was built on its commercial prosperity and its highly original republican system of government. The Dutch came to dominate the European shipping business by putting profits from their original industry—herring fishing—into shipbuilding. They then took aim at Portugal's immensely lucrative Asian trade empire.

In 1599 a Dutch fleet returned to Amsterdam from a voyage to South East Asia carrying a huge cargo of spices. Those who had invested in the expedition received a 100 percent profit. The voyage led to the establishment in 1602 of the Dutch East India Company, founded with the stated intention of capturing the spice trade from the Portuguese.

In return for assisting Indonesian princes in local conflicts and disputes with the Portuguese, the Dutch won broad commercial concessions. Through agreements, seizures, and outright military aggression, they gained control of the western access to the Indonesian archipelago in the first half of the seventeenth century. Gradually, they acquired political domination over the archipelago itself. The Dutch were willing to use force more ruthlessly than the Portuguese were and had superior organizational efficiency. These factors allowed them to expel the Portuguese from Ceylon and other East Indian islands in the 1660s and henceforth dominate the production and trade of spices. The company also established the colony of Cape Town on the southern tip of Africa as a provisioning point for its Asian fleets.

The Dutch also aspired to a role in the Americas (Map 18.4). Founded in 1621, the Dutch West India Company aggressively sought to open trade with North and South America and capture Spanish territories there. The company captured or destroyed hundreds of Spanish ships, seized the Spanish silver fleet in 1628, and claimed portions of Brazil and the Caribbean. The Dutch also successfully interceded in the transatlantic slave trade, establishing a large number of trading stations on the west coast of Africa. Ironically, the nation that was known as a bastion of tolerance and freedom came to be one of the principal operators of the slave trade starting in the 1640s.

Gonzales Coques, *The Young Scholar and His Wife*

During the seventeenth century much of Europe was gripped by economic, social, and political crisis. A long period of cold, wet weather destroyed crops, while religious and political conflicts contributed to the outbreak of the highly destructive Thirty Years' War. A shining exception to this grim picture was the Netherlands, which saw increased agricultural productivity, growing involvement in world trade, and a thriving urban culture. The bustling cities of the Dutch Republic and Flanders gave birth in this period to a new style of painting, now known as "genre painting," that celebrated the virtues of everyday life, family, and the domestic sphere.

Although earlier generations of artists had reserved their highest praise for paintings that re-created great historical and mythological events, genre painters depicted realistic scenes set in family homes, taverns, and other prosaic locales. They eschewed representing idealized heroes and dramatic imagery in favor of the earthly pleasures of eating, drinking, and gathering with friends and family in cozy interiors, often furnished with the exotic wares pouring in from the East. Genre paintings thus reflected the values and pastimes of the wealthy bourgeois merchants and other urban elites who commissioned them. This painting style of the Dutch golden age became extremely popular and spread to the rest of northern Europe.

Gonzales Coques, the painter of this image, was born in Antwerp (part of modern Belgium) around 1615. He apprenticed with the Flemish artist Pieter Brueghel the Younger and became a master of the Antwerp painters' guild in 1640, the same year he produced this painting. Specializing in portraits of individuals and families — such as this fine rendition of an affluent young scholar and his wife — Coques contributed to the development of genre painting.

(*The Young Scholar and His Wife*, 1640, by Gonzales Coques [1614–1684] [oil on panel]/Gemaeldegalerie Alte Meister, Kassel, Germany/ © Museumslandschaft Hessen Kassel/Bridgeman Images)

QUESTIONS FOR ANALYSIS

1. What social and cultural values does this painting seem to celebrate? List the details in the painting that provide evidence for your answer.
2. What insight does the painter offer into the roles of men and women in this society and the attributes of masculinity and femininity? Why do you think the husband and wife are standing separately and not together, as they probably would in a modern family portrait?
3. How does the artist's use of color help convey meaning in the painting?

MAP 18.4 Seventeenth-Century Dutch Commerce Dutch wealth rested on commerce, and commerce depended on the huge Dutch merchant marine, manned by perhaps forty-eight thousand sailors. The fleet carried goods from all parts of the globe to the port of Amsterdam.

Colonial Empires of England and France

England and France followed the Dutch in challenging Iberian dominance overseas. Unlike the Iberian powers, whose royal governments financed exploration and directly ruled the colonies, England, France, and the Netherlands conducted the initial phase of colonization through chartered companies with monopolies over settlement and trade in a given area.

Just as the Spanish explorers had learned from the Reconquista, English expansion drew on long experience at home conquering and colonizing Ireland. After an unsuccessful first colony at Roanoke (in what is now North Carolina), the English colony of Virginia, founded at Jamestown in 1607, gained a steady hold by producing tobacco for a growing European market. Indentured servants obtained free passage to the colony in exchange for several years of work and the promise of greater opportunity than could be found in England. In the 1670s English colonists from the Caribbean island of Barbados settled Carolina, where conditions were suitable for large rice plantations. During the late seventeenth century enslaved Africans replaced indentured servants as laborers on tobacco

and rice plantations, and a harsh racial divide was imposed.

For the first settlers on the coast of New England, the reasons for seeking a new life in the colonies were more religious than economic. Many of these colonists were radical Protestants escaping Anglican repression. The small and struggling Puritan outpost of Plymouth Colony (1620) was followed by Massachusetts Bay Colony (1630), which grew into a prosperous settlement. Religious disputes in Massachusetts led to the dispersion of settlers into the new communities of Providence, Connecticut, Rhode Island, and New Haven. Because New England lacked the conditions for plantation agriculture, slavery was always a minor factor there.

Whereas the Spanish established wholesale dominance over Mexico and Peru and its indigenous inhabitants, English settlements hugged the Atlantic coastline and expelled indigenous people from their lands, leading to attacks by displaced groups and wars of reprisal and extermination. In place of the unified rule exerted by the Spanish crown, English colonization was haphazard and decentralized in nature, leading to greater colonial autonomy and diversity. As the English crown grew more interested in colonial expansion,

INDIVIDUALS IN SOCIETY

Glückel of Hameln

IN 1690 A JEWISH WIDOW IN THE SMALL GERMAN TOWN of Hameln in Lower Saxony sat down to write her autobiography. She wanted to distract her mind from the terrible grief she felt over the death of her husband and to provide her twelve children with a record. She told them that she was writing her memoirs "so you will know from what sort of people you have sprung, lest today or tomorrow your beloved children or grandchildren came and know naught of their family." Out of her pain and heightened consciousness, Glückel (1646–1724) produced an invaluable source for scholars.

She was born in Hamburg two years before the end of the Thirty Years' War. In 1649 the merchants of Hamburg expelled the Jews, who moved to nearby Altona, then under Danish rule. When the Swedes overran Altona in 1657–1658, the Jews returned to Hamburg "purely at the mercy of the Town Council." Glückel's narrative unfolds against a background of the constant harassment to which Jews were subjected—special papers, permits, bribes—and in Hameln she wrote, "And so it has been to this day and, I fear, will continue in like fashion."

When Glückel was "barely twelve," her father betrothed her to Chayim Hameln, and they married when she was fourteen. She describes him as "the perfect pattern of the pious Jew," a man who stopped his work every day for study and prayer, fasted, and was scrupulously honest in his business dealings. Only a few years older than Glückel, Chayim earned his living dealing in precious metals and in making small loans on pledges (pawned goods). This work required constant travel to larger cities, markets, and fairs, often in bad weather, always over dangerous roads. Chayim consulted his wife about all his business dealings. As he lay dying, a friend asked if he had any last wishes. "None," he replied. "My wife knows everything. She shall do as she has always done." For thirty years Glückel had been his friend, full business partner, and wife. They had thirteen children, twelve of whom survived their father, eight then unmarried. As Chayim had foretold, Glückel succeeded in launching the boys in careers and in providing dowries for the girls.

Glückel's world was her family, the Jewish community of Hameln, and the Jewish communities into which her children married. Her social and business activities took her across Europe, from Amsterdam to Berlin, from Danzig to Vienna; thus her world was far from narrow or provincial. She took great pride that Prince Frederick of Cleves, later king of Prussia, danced at the wedding of her eldest daughter. The rising prosperity of Chayim's businesses allowed the couple to maintain up to six servants.

Glückel was deeply religious, and her culture was steeped in Jewish literature, legends, and mystical and secular works. Above all, she relied on the Bible. Her language, heavily sprinkled with scriptural references, testifies to a rare familiarity with the Scriptures.

Students who wish to learn about seventeenth-century business practices, the importance of the dowry in marriage, childbirth, Jewish life, birthrates, family celebrations, and even the meaning of life can gain a good deal from the memoirs of this extraordinary woman who was, in the words of one of her descendants, the poet Heinrich Heine, "the gift of a world to me."

Rembrandt, *The Jewish Bride.* (Rijksmuseum, Amsterdam, The Netherlands/ Bridgeman Images)

QUESTIONS FOR ANALYSIS

1. Consider the ways in which Glückel of Hameln was both an ordinary and an extraordinary woman of her times. Would you call her a marginal or a central person in her society? Why?
2. How might Glückel's successes be attributed to the stabilizing force of absolutism in the seventeenth century?

Source: *The Memoirs of Glückel of Hameln* (New York: Schocken Books, 1977).

efforts were made to acquire the territory between New England in the north and Virginia in the south. The goal was to unify English holdings and minimize French and Dutch competition on the Atlantic seaboard. The results of these efforts were the mid-Atlantic colonies: the Catholic settlement of Maryland (1632); New York, captured from the Dutch in 1664; and the Quaker colony of Pennsylvania (1681).

The French represented yet another model of settlement and interaction, somewhat akin to the Portuguese in Asia and Africa. While the Spanish incorporated the large populations of pre-existing empires and the English expelled indigenous groups to provide agricultural land for their numerous colonists, the French focused on establishing trade and diplomatic relations with tribes that remained largely autonomous. In 1605 the French founded the settlement of Port-Royal on the Bay of Fundy in Acadia, as a base for fishing and the fur trade. In the following years, under the leadership of Samuel de Champlain the French moved west into the St. Lawrence River Valley, establishing the forts of Quebec (1608), Three Rivers (1634), and Montreal (1642). The French formed trade and military alliances with several tribes, including the Montagnais, Hurons, and Algonquins, which allowed them to acquire valuable furs throughout the Great Lakes region. Contact with French traders, settlers, and missionaries resulted in devastating epidemics for their indigenous

allies as well as increased political instability and violent conflict.

In the 1660s Louis XIV's capable controller general, Jean-Baptiste Colbert, established direct royal control over New France (Canada) and tried to enlarge its population by sending colonists. Nevertheless, immigration to New Canada remained minuscule compared with the stream of settlers who came to British North America. The Jesuits, who were the most active missionary orders in New France, established a college in Quebec as early as 1635.

Following the waterways of the St. Lawrence River, the Great Lakes, and the Mississippi River, the French ventured into much of North America in the 1670s and 1680s. In 1673 the Jesuit Jacques Marquette and the merchant Louis Joliet sailed down the Mississippi as far as present-day Arkansas. In 1682 Robert de La Salle traveled the Mississippi to the Gulf of Mexico, opening the way for French occupation of Louisiana.

In the first decades of the seventeenth century, English and French captains also challenged Spain's hold over the Caribbean, seizing a number of islands. These islands acquired new importance after 1640, when the Portuguese brought sugar plantations to Brazil. Sugar and slaves quickly followed in the West Indies (see "Sugar and Early Transatlantic Slavery" in Chapter 16), making the Caribbean plantations the most lucrative of all colonial possessions.

The Fur Trade In the early seventeenth century European fur traders relied on Native Americans' expertise and experience, leading to the equal relations depicted in this scene from the colony of New Sweden (in modern-day Pennsylvania). The action in the background shows violence among indigenous groups, rivalries exacerbated by contact with Europeans and their trade goods. Hudson's Bay Company, the English colonial trading company, issued its own tokens as currency in the fur trade. This token, dating from the mid-nineteenth century, displays the company's crest, which says "a skin for a skin" in Latin. Two stags face each other, with a fox at the top and four beavers on the shield. Traders received tokens for the pelts they sold and could use them to purchase goods from the company's store. European demand for beaver hats, made from the felted pelts of beavers, drove the tremendous expansion of the North American fur trade in the beginning of the seventeenth century.

(engraving: From *Geographia Americae with An Account of the Delaware Indians, Based on Surveys and Notes Made 1654–1656*, by Peter Lindestrom, published by The Swedish Colonial Society/Visual Connection Archive; token: © National Maritime Museum, London, UK/The Image Works)

European Claims in North America, 1714

HUDSON'S BAY COMPANY

Newfoundland

QUEBEC

NEW FRANCE

NOVA SCOTIA

THIRTEEN COLONIES

ATLANTIC OCEAN

LOUISIANA

SPANISH FLORIDA

Claims
- British
- French
- Spanish

The northern European powers also expanded in Africa and Asia. During the seventeenth century, France and England—along with Denmark and other northern European powers—established fortified trading posts, or factory-forts, in West Africa as bases for purchasing slaves and in India and the Indian Ocean for spices and other luxury goods. Thus, by the end of the seventeenth century, a handful of European powers possessed overseas empires that truly spanned the globe.

Mercantilism and Colonial Wars

Trade to and among European overseas possessions was governed by mercantilist economic policy (see "The Economic Policy of Mercantilism"). The acquisition of colonies was intended to increase the wealth and power of the mother country, and to that end, European states—starting with Spain in the sixteenth century—imposed trading monopolies on their overseas colonies and factories. The mercantilist notion of a "zero-sum game," in which any country's gain must come from another country's loss, led to hostile competition and outright warfare among European powers over their colonial possessions.

In England Oliver Cromwell established the first of a series of **Navigation Acts** in 1651, and the restored monarchy of Charles II extended them in 1660 and 1663. The acts required most goods imported into England and Scotland (Great Britain after 1707) to be carried on British-owned ships with British crews or on ships of the country producing the article. Moreover, these laws gave British merchants and shipowners a virtual monopoly on trade with British colonies. These economic regulations were intended to eliminate foreign competition and to encourage the development of a British shipping industry whose seamen could serve when necessary in the Royal Navy.

The Navigation Acts were a form of economic warfare against the Dutch, who were far ahead of the English in shipping and foreign trade in the mid-seventeenth century. In conjunction with three Anglo-Dutch wars between 1652 and 1674, the Navigation Acts seriously damaged Dutch shipping and commerce. By the late seventeenth century the Nether-

lands was falling behind England in shipping, trade, and settlement.

Thereafter France was England's most serious rival in the competition for overseas empire. France was continental Europe's leading military power. It was already building a powerful fleet and a worldwide system of rigidly monopolized colonial trade. But the War of the Spanish Succession, the last of Louis XIV's many wars (see "The Wars of Louis XIV") tilted the balance in favor of England. The 1713 Peace of Utrecht forced France to cede its North American holdings in Newfoundland, Nova Scotia, and the Hudson Bay territory to Britain. Spain was compelled to give Britain control of its West African slave trade and to let Britain send one ship of merchandise into the Spanish colonies annually. These acquisitions primed Britain to take a leading role in the growing Atlantic trade of the eighteenth century, including the transatlantic slave trade (see Chapter 19).

People Beyond Borders

As they seized new territories, European nations produced maps proudly outlining their possessions. The situation on the ground, however, was often much more complicated than the lines on those maps would suggest. Many groups of people lived in the contested frontiers between empires, habitually crisscrossed their borders, or carved out niches within empires where they carried out their own lives in defiance of the official rules.

Restricted from owning land and holding many occupations in Europe, Jews were eager participants in colonial trade and established closely linked mercantile communities scattered across many different empires. Similarly, a community of Christian Armenians in Isfahan in the Safavid Empire (modern-day Iran) formed the center of a trade network extending from London to Manila and Acapulco (see "Merchant Networks in the Islamic Empires" in Chapter 17). Family ties and trust within these minority groups were a tremendous advantage in generating the financial credit and cooperation necessary for international commerce. Yet Jews and Armenians were minorities where they settled and vulnerable to persecution.

The nomadic Cossacks and Tartars who inhabited the steppes of the Don River basin that bordered the Russian and Ottoman Empires are yet another example of "in-between" peoples. The Cossacks and the Tartars maintained considerable political and cultural autonomy through the seventeenth century and enjoyed a degree of peaceful interaction. By the eighteenth century, however, both Ottoman and Russian rulers had expanded state control in their frontiers and had reined in the raiding and migration of nomadic steppe peoples. As their example suggests, the assertion of state authority in the seventeenth and eighteenth centuries made it progressively harder for all of these groups to retain autonomy from the grip of empire.

Navigation Acts Mid-seventeenth-century English mercantilist laws that greatly restricted other countries' rights to trade with England and its colonies.

The Russian Empire

How did Russian rulers build a distinctive absolutist monarchy and expand into a vast and powerful empire?

Russia occupied a unique position among Eurasian states. With borders straddling eastern Europe and northwestern Asia, its development into a strong imperial state drew on elements from both continents. As in the Muslim empires in Central and South Asia and the Ming Dynasty in China, the expansion of Russia was a result of the weakening of the great Mongol and Timurid Empires. After declaring independence from the Mongols, the Russian tsars conquered a vast empire, extending through North Asia all the way to the Pacific Ocean. State-building and territorial expansion culminated during the reign of Peter the Great, who turned Russia toward the West by intervening in western European wars and politics and forcing his people to adopt elements of Western culture.

Mongol Rule in Russia and the Rise of Moscow

In the thirteenth century the Mongols had conquered Kievan Rus, the medieval Slavic state that included most of present-day Ukraine, Belarus, and part of northwest Russia. For two hundred years the Mongols forced the Slavic princes to submit to their rule. The princes of the Grand Duchy of Moscow, a principality within Kievan Rus, became particularly adept at serving the Mongols. Eventually the Muscovite princes were able to destroy the other princes who were their rivals for power. Ivan III (r. 1462–1505), known as Ivan the Great, greatly expanded the principality of Moscow, claiming large territories in the north and east to the Siberian frontier.

By 1480 Ivan III was strong enough to declare the autonomy of Moscow. To legitimize his new position, Ivan and his successors borrowed elements of Mongol rule. They forced weaker Slavic principalities to render tribute and adopted Mongol institutions such as the tax system, postal routes, and census. Loyalty from the highest-ranking nobles, or boyars, helped the Muscovite princes consolidate their power.

Another source of legitimacy lay in Moscow's claim to the political and religious inheritance of the Byzantine Empire. After the empire's capital, Constantinople, fell to the Ottomans in 1453, the princes of Moscow saw themselves as heirs of the Byzantine caesars (emperors) and guardians of the Orthodox Christian Church.

Building the Russian Empire

Developments in Russia took a chaotic turn with the reign of Ivan IV (r. 1533–1584), the famous Ivan the Terrible, who ascended to the throne at age three. His mother died when he was eight, leaving Ivan to suffer insults and neglect from the boyars at court. At age sixteen he pushed aside his advisers and crowned himself tsar.

Russian Peasants An eighteenth-century French artist visiting Russia recorded his impressions of the daily life of the Russian people in this etching of a fish merchant pulling his wares on a sleigh through a snowy village. Two caviar vendors behind him make a sale to a young mother standing at her doorstep with her baby in her arms. (From Jean-Baptiste le Prince's second set of Russian etchings, 1765. Private Collection/Gérard PIERSON/www.amis-paris-petersbourg.org)

Peter the Great and Foreign Experts

John Deane, an eminent English shipbuilder, was one of the many foreign artisans and experts brought to Russia by Peter the Great after his foreign tour of 1697. Several months after arriving in Russia, Deane sent a glowing account of the tsar's technical prowess to his patron in England, the marquess of Carmarthen, admiral of the English fleet.

■ I Have deferr'd writing, till I could be able to give Your Lordship a true Account (from my own Knowledge) of the *Czar* (our Master's) Navy, which being a New Thing in the World as yet, I believe is variously talk'd of in *England, &c.* First, at *Voronize* there is already in the Water and Rigg'd, 36, and to be Launch'd in the Spring 20 more stout Ships, from 30 to 60 Guns. Next, 18 very large Gallies (built after the *Venetian* manner by *Italian* Masters) are already compleated; and 100 smaller Gallies or Brigantines are equipt for the Sea; 7 Bomb-Ships are Launch'd and Rigg'd, and 4 Fireships are Building against the Spring, when they are all to go down to *Azoph*. The Ships are chiefly built by the *Dutch* and *Danes*.

The 25th of *August* last his Majesty came to *Moscow, incognito*; immediately he took in hand the rewarding of General *Gordon*'s Soldiers, that fought against the Rebels he defeated in *June* last, and next day gave Orders to fetch up all those of the Rebels who were dispersed by way of Banishment, which were in all then left about 2700. I suppose Your Lordship has been inform'd by Publick News, how they are hung round the Walls of this City, some hundreds beheaded,

some broke upon the Wheel, *&c.* to the whole Number of them, which was in all 3000.

At my arrival in Moscow, I fell very ill of the Bloody-Flux, which made me be in Moscow when his Majesty came home: About the latter end of October I was somewhat recovered, his Majesty then carried me down to Voronize [site of the naval shipyard] with him. Voronize is about 400 English Miles South-East from Moscow. There the Czar immediately set up a ship of 60 guns, where he is both Foreman and Master-Builder; and not to flatter him, I'll assure your Lordship it will be the best ship among them, and 'tis all from his own Draught; How he fram'd her together and how he made the Mould, and in so short a time as he did is really wonderful: But he is able at this day to put his own notions into practice, and laugh at his Dutch and Italian builders for their ignorance. There are several pieces of workmanship, as in the keel, stem, and post, which are all purely his own invention, and sound good work, and would be approved of by all the shipwrights of England if they saw it he has a round Tuck, and a narrow Floor, a good tumbling Home, and Circular Side; none are to exceed 11 Dutch Foot Draught of Water. He has not run into any Extreme, But taken the Mediums of all good Sailing Properties, which seem best. One may, methinks, call her an Abstract of his own private Observations whilst Abroad, strengthened by Your Lordship's Improving Discourses to him on that Subject, and his own extraordinary Notion of Sailing. One thing as to her Keel is, That should it wholly be beat out, yet it is so ordered,

---

After the sudden death of his wife, however, Ivan began a campaign of persecution against those he suspected of opposing him. He executed members of leading boyar families, along with their families, friends, servants, and peasants. To replace them, Ivan created a new service nobility, whose loyalty was guaranteed by their dependence on the state for land and titles.

As landlords demanded more from the serfs who survived the persecutions, growing numbers of peasants fled toward recently conquered territories to the east and south. There they joined free groups and warrior bands, known as **Cossacks**, who had been living on the borders of Russian territory since the fourteenth century. Ivan responded by tying serfs ever more firmly to the land. Simultaneously, he ordered that urban dwellers be bound to their towns and jobs so that he could tax them more heavily. These restrictions checked the growth of the Russian middle classes and stood in sharp contrast to economic and social developments in western Europe.

Ivan's reign was successful in defeating the remnants of Mongol power, adding vast new territories to the realm, and laying the foundations for the huge multiethnic Russian Empire. In the 1550s, strengthened by an alliance with Cossack bands, Ivan conquered the Muslim khanates of Kazan and Astrakhan and brought the fertile steppe region around the Volga River under Russian control. In the 1580s Cossacks fighting for the Russian state crossed the Ural Mountains and began the long conquest of Siberia. Because of the size and distance of the new territories, the Russian state did not initially seek to impose the Orthodox religion and maintained local elites in positions of honor and lead-

Cossacks Free groups and outlaw armies living on the borders of Russian territory from the fourteenth century onward. In the mid-sixteenth century they formed an alliance with the Russian state.

that the Ship will be tight and safe, and may continue so at Sea afterwards.

I likewise made a Suit of Moulds for a Ship of Sixty Guns, but after fell sick again; and at Christmas, when his Majesty came to Moscow, he brought me back again for recovery of my health, where I am at present; notwithstanding both our Ships go forward, having put things in such a posture, as that a *Grecian* (who has been in *England*) carries on the Business. Mr. *Ney* is Building of a 60 Gun Ship there too; besides, there are four of that Size (near built) upon the *Done*, two of 40 Guns already at *Azoph*, carried down some time since, and a great many Galleys, *&c.*

The Rivers *Vorona*, at *Voronitz*, when I was there, was hardly so broad as the Ships are long; but in the Spring about the latter End of *April*, or beginning of *May*, when the Snow melts, there is 16 Foot Water in that little River, and continues this height about 12 or 14 days, with a Rapid Torrent, with that force, that though it be 1000 Miles down to *Azoph* [Azov], yet the Ships will easily be there in 9 or 10 days. There is 30000 Soldiers at *Voronize*, to defend the Ships from the *Tartars*, who are very mischievous, and very swift in setting a place on Fire, and running away again. Those Ships that are Launcht lie fast in Ice about two Foot thick, so that the River is now as firm as Land, although this is reckoned a very mild Winter; for I remember in *January* one Afternoon with a *Southerly* Wind it thaw'd and rain'd for 3 or 4 hours, which is rare enough for an Almanack. The Ground is covered with Snow about a Yard deep, and 'tis mighty clear, piercing cold Weather, such as in *England* we can't imagine.

. . . His Majesty was at my Chamber two days of last Week, with Mr. *Styles* as Interpreter (who gives his humble duty to Your Lordship). You may guess what His Majesty came to be inform'd in whilst he was there; I shew'd him a Model of a Machine to bring up the *Royal Transport* to the *Volga*, at 17 Inches Draught of Water; he was pleas'd to like it, but gave no Orders for putting it in Execution, so I believe she will lie where she is now, and perish. Here are Three Envoys, *viz.* the *Emperor's*, the *Danes*, and *Brandenburgs*, in this *Slabado*, (as it is call'd), which lies from *Moscow*, as *Lambeth* does from *London*. The whole place is inhabited by the Dutch; I believe there may be 400 families. Last Sunday and Monday the strangers were invited to the consecration of General La Fort's house, which is the noblest building in Russia, and finely furnisht. There were all the envoys, and as near as I could guess 200 gentlemen, English, French, and Dutch, and about as many ladies; each day were dancing and musick. All the envoys, and all the lords (but three in Moscow) are going to Voronize to see the fleet, I suppose. His majesty went last Sunday to Voronize with Prince Alexander and I am to go down (being something recovered) with the Vice-Admiral about six days hence.

QUESTIONS FOR ANALYSIS

1. According to Deane, what evidence did Peter the Great give of his skills in shipbuilding? Based on this document, how would you characterize the relationship between Peter and his foreign experts?
2. What evidence does Dean provide of the impact of foreigners on life in Russia?
3. What image of Peter as a ruler emerges from this document? How does Deane characterize the tsar and his rule?

Source: John Deane, "A Letter from Moscow to the Marquess of Carmarthen, Relating to the Czar of Muscovy's Forwardness in His Great Navy, &c. Since His Return Home," in Sir John Barrow, *A Memoir of the Life of Peter the Great* (New York: Harper & Brothers, 1834), pp. 110–113.

---

ership, buying their loyalty with grants of land. In relying on cooperation from local elites and ruthlessly exploiting the common people, the Russians followed the pattern of the Spanish and other early modern European imperial states.

Following Ivan's death, Russia entered a chaotic period known as the Time of Troubles (1598–1613). While Ivan's relatives struggled for power, the Cossacks and peasants rebelled against nobles and officials. This social explosion from below brought the nobles together. They crushed the Cossack rebellion and elected Ivan's grandnephew, Michael Romanov (r. 1613–1645), the new hereditary tsar.

Despite the turbulence of the period, the Romanov tsars, like their western European counterparts, made further achievements in territorial expansion and state-building. After a long war, Russia gained land to the west in Ukraine in 1667. By the end of the century it had completed the conquest of Siberia to the east. This vast territorial expansion brought Russian power to the Pacific Ocean and was only checked by the powerful Qing Dynasty. Like the French in Canada, the basis of Russian wealth in Siberia was furs, which the state collected by forced annual tribute payments from local peoples. Profits from furs and other natural resources, especially mining in the eighteenth century, funded expansion of the Russian bureaucracy and the army.

The growth of state power did nothing to improve the lot of the common people. In 1649 a new law code extended serfdom to all peasants in the realm, giving lords unrestricted rights over their serfs and establishing penalties for harboring runaways. The new code also removed the privileges that non-Russian elites had enjoyed within the empire and required conversion to Russian orthodoxy. Henceforth, Moscow maintained strict control of trade and administration throughout the empire.

The peace imposed by harsh Russian rule was disrupted in 1670 by a failed rebellion led by the Cossack Stenka Razin, who attracted a great army of urban poor and peasants. The ease with which Moscow crushed the rebellion by the end of 1671 testifies to the success of the Russian state in unifying and consolidating its empire.

Peter the Great and Russia's Turn to the West

Heir to Romanov efforts at state-building, Peter the Great (r. 1682–1725) embarked on a tremendous campaign to accelerate and complete these processes. Peter built on the service obligations of Ivan the Terrible and his successors and continued their tradition of territorial expansion. Peter's ambitions hinged on gaining access to the sea by extending Russia's borders to the Black Sea (controlled by the Ottomans) and to the Baltic Sea (dominated by Sweden).

Peter embarked on his first territorial goal by conquering the Ottoman fort of Azov in 1696 and quickly built Russia's first navy base nearby. In 1697 the tsar went on an eighteen-month tour of western European capitals. Peter was fascinated by foreign technology, and he hoped to forge an anti-Ottoman alliance to strengthen his hold on the Black Sea. Peter failed to secure a military alliance, but he did learn his lessons from the growing power of the Dutch and the English. He also engaged more than a hundred foreign experts to return with him to Russia to help build the navy and improve Russian infrastructure. (See "Analyzing the Evidence: Peter the Great and Foreign Experts," page 524.)

To realize his second goal, Peter entered the Great Northern War (1700–1721) against Sweden. After a humiliating defeat at the Battle of Narva in 1700, Peter responded with measures designed to increase state power, strengthen his military, and gain victory. He required all nobles to serve in the army or in the civil administration—for life. Peter also created schools of navigation and mathematics, medicine, engineering, and finance to produce skilled technicians and experts. Furthermore, he established an interlocking military-civilian bureaucracy with fourteen ranks, and he decreed that everyone had to start at the bottom and work toward the top. He sought talented foreigners and placed them in his service. These measures gradually combined to make the army and government more powerful and efficient.

Peter the Great The compelling portrait above captures the strength and determination of the warrior-tsar in 1723, after more than three decades of personal rule. In his hand Peter holds the scepter, symbol of royal sovereignty, and across his breastplate is draped an ermine fur, a mark of honor. In the background are the battleships of Russia's new Baltic fleet and the famous St. Peter and St. Paul Fortress that Peter built in St. Petersburg. The image on the right portrays Peter dressed as a ship carpenter's apprentice during his incognito tour of western Europe. (tsar portrait: Hermitage, St. Petersburg, Russia/Bridgeman Images; carpenter's apprentice: Universal Images Group/UIG via Getty Images)

MAP 18.5 **The Expansion of Russia, 1462–1689** In little more than two centuries, Russia expanded from the small principality of Muscovy to an enormous multiethnic empire, stretching from the borders of western Europe through northern Asia to the Pacific.

Peter also greatly increased the service requirements of commoners. He established a regular standing army of peasant-soldiers, drafted for life. In addition, he created special regiments of Cossacks and foreign mercenaries. To fund the army, taxes on peasants increased threefold during Peter's reign. Serfs were also arbitrarily assigned to work in the growing number of factories and mines that supplied the military.

In 1709 Peter's new war machine was able to crush Sweden's army in Ukraine at Poltava (Map 18.5). Russia's victory against Sweden was conclusive in 1721, and Estonia and present-day Latvia came under Russian rule for the first time. The cost was high: warfare consumed 80 to 85 percent of all revenues. But Russia became the dominant power in the Baltic and very much a great European power.

After his victory at Poltava, Peter channeled enormous resources into building a new Western-style capital on the Baltic. The city of St. Petersburg was designed to reflect modern urban planning with wide, straight avenues; buildings set in a uniform line; and large parks. Each summer, twenty-five thousand to forty

thousand peasants were sent to provide construction labor in St. Petersburg without pay.

There were other important consequences of Peter's reign. For Peter, modernization meant westernization, and both Westerners and Western ideas flowed into Russia for the first time. He required nobles to shave their heavy beards and wear Western clothing. He also required them to attend parties where young men and women would mix together and freely choose their own spouses. From these efforts a new elite class of Western-oriented Russians began to emerge.

Peter's reforms were unpopular with many Russians. For nobles, one of Peter's most detested reforms was the imposition of unigeniture—inheritance of land by one son alone. For peasants, the reign of the tsar saw a significant increase in the bonds of serfdom. Nonetheless, Peter's modernizing and westernizing of Russia paved the way for it to move somewhat closer to the European mainstream in its thought and institutions during the Enlightenment, especially under Catherine the Great (see "Enlightened Absolutism and Its Limits" in Chapter 19).

Chapter Summary

Most parts of Europe experienced the first centuries of the early modern era as a time of crisis. Following the religious divides of the sixteenth-century Protestant and Catholic Reformations, Europeans in the seventeenth century suffered from economic stagnation, social upheaval, and renewed military conflict. Overcoming these obstacles, both absolutist and constitutional European states emerged from the seventeenth century with increased powers and more centralized control.

Monarchs in Spain, France, and Austria used divine right to claim they possessed absolute power and were not responsible to any representative institutions. Absolute monarchs overcame the resistance of the nobility both through military force and by confirming existing economic and social privileges. England and the Netherlands defied the general trend toward absolute monarchy, adopting distinctive forms of constitutional rule.

As Spain's power weakened, other European nations bordering the Atlantic Ocean sought their own profits and glory from overseas empires, with England emerging in the early eighteenth century with a distinct advantage over its rivals. Henceforth, war among European powers would include conflicts over territories and trade in the colonies. European rulers' increased control over their own subjects thus went hand in glove with the expansion of European power in the world.

In Russia, Mongol conquest and rule set the stage for a harsh tsarist autocracy that was firmly in place by the time of the reign of Ivan the Terrible in the sixteenth century. The reign of Ivan and his successors saw a great expansion of Russian territory, laying the foundations for a huge multiethnic empire. Peter the Great forcibly turned Russia toward the West by adopting Western technology and culture.

NOTES

1. Theodore K. Rabb, *The Struggle for Stability in Early Modern Europe* (Oxford: Oxford University Press, 1975), p. 10.
2. Simon Schama, *The Embarrassment of Riches: An Interpretation of Dutch Culture in the Golden Age* (New York: Alfred A. Knopf, 1987), pp. 165–170.

CONNECTIONS

The seventeenth century represented a difficult passage between two centuries of dynamism and growth in Europe. On one side lay the sixteenth century's religious enthusiasm and strife, overseas discoveries, rising populations, and vigorous commerce. On the other side stretched the eighteenth century's renewed population growth, economic development, and cultural flourishing. The first half of the seventeenth century was marked by harsh climate conditions and violent conflict across Europe and much of the world. Recurring crop failure, famine, and epidemic disease contributed to a stagnant economy and population loss. In the middle decades of the seventeenth century, the very survival of the European monarchies established in the Renaissance appeared in doubt.

With the re-establishment of order in the second half of the century, maintaining stability was of paramount importance to European rulers. While a few nations placed their trust in constitutionally limited governments, many more were ruled by monarchs proclaiming their absolute and God-given authority. Despite their political differences, most European states emerged from the period of crisis with shared achievements in state power, territorial expansion, and long-distance trade. In these achievements, they resembled the Qing in China and the Mughals in India, who also saw the consolidation of imperial authority in this period; by contrast, the Ottoman Empire recovered more slowly from the crises of the seventeenth century.

The eighteenth century was to see these power politics thrown into question by new Enlightenment aspirations for human society, which themselves derived from the inquisitive and self-confident spirit of the Scientific Revolution. These movements are explored in the next chapter. By the end of the eighteenth century demands for real popular sovereignty, colonial self-rule, and slave emancipation challenged the very bases of order so painfully achieved in the seventeenth century. Chapter 22 recounts the revolutionary movements that swept the late-eighteenth-century Atlantic world, while Chapters 25, 26, and 27 follow the story of European imperialism and the resistance of colonized peoples in Africa, Asia, and the Americas into the nineteenth century.

CHAPTER 18 Review and Explore

Identify Key Terms

Identify and explain the significance of each item below.

Protestant Reformation (p. 500)   absolutism (p. 506)   Puritans (p. 515)

Jesuits (p. 502)   divine right of kings (p. 508)   Bill of Rights of 1689 (p. 516)

moral economy (p. 504)   mercantilism (p. 513)   Navigation Acts (p. 522)

Thirty Years' War (p. 504)   constitutionalism (p. 514)   Cossacks (p. 524)

sovereignty (p. 506)   republicanism (p. 514)

Review the Main Ideas

Answer the focus questions from each section of the chapter.

1. How did the Protestant and Catholic Reformations change power structures in Europe and shape European colonial expansion? (p. 500)

2. How did seventeenth-century European rulers overcome social and economic crisis to build strong states? (p. 503)

3. What was absolutism, and how did it evolve in seventeenth-century Spain, France, and Austria? (p. 506)

4. Why and how did the constitutional state triumph in England and the Dutch Republic? (p. 514)

5. How did European nations compete for global trade and empire in the Americas and Asia? (p. 517)

6. How did Russian rulers build a distinctive absolutist monarchy and expand into a vast and powerful empire? (p. 523)

Make Comparisons and Connections

Analyze the larger developments and continuities within and across chapters.

1. This chapter has argued that, despite their political differences, rulers in absolutist and constitutionalist nations faced similar obstacles in the mid-seventeenth century and achieved many of the same goals. Based on the evidence presented here, do you agree with this argument? Why or why not?

2. Proponents of absolutism in western Europe believed that their form of monarchical rule was fundamentally different from and superior to what they saw as the "despotism" of Russia and the Ottoman Empire (Chapter 17). What was the basis of this belief, and how accurate do you think it was?

3. What common features did the Muslim empires of the Middle East and India (Chapter 17) share with European empires? How would you characterize interaction among these Eurasian empires?

TIMELINE

EUROPE

1533–1584 Reign of Ivan the Terrible in Russia

1598–1613
Time of Troubles
in Russia

1589–1610 Reign of
Henry IV in France

ASIA

1556–1605 Akbar expands Mughal Empire **(Ch. 17)**

MIDDLE EAST

← **1501–1722** Safavid Empire in Persia **(Ch. 17)**

AFRICA

← **ca. 1464–1591** Songhai Empire **(Ch. 20)**

1550	1575	1600

Suggested Resources
BOOKS

Beik, William. *A Social and Cultural History of Early Modern France.* 2009. An overview of early modern French history, by one of the leading authorities on the period.

Elliott, John H. *Imperial Spain, 1469–1716,* 2d ed. 2002. An authoritative account of Spain's rise to imperial greatness and its slow decline.

Gaunt, Peter, ed. *The English Civil War: The Essential Readings.* 2000. A collection showcasing leading historians' interpretations of the civil war.

Goldgar, Anne. *Tulipmania: Money, Honor, and Knowledge in the Dutch Golden Age.* 2007. A fresh look at the speculative fever for tulip bulbs in the early-seventeenth-century Dutch Republic.

Hughes, Lindsey, ed. *Peter the Great and the West: New Perspectives.* 2001. Essays by leading scholars on the reign of Peter the Great and his opening of Russia to the West.

Ingrao, Charles W. *The Habsburg Monarchy, 1618–1815,* 2d ed. 2000. An excellent synthesis of the political and social development of the Habsburg empire in the early modern period.

Kettering, Sharon. *Patronage in Sixteenth- and Seventeenth-Century France.* 2002. A collection of essays on courtly patronage, emphasizing the role of women in noble patronage networks.

Parker, Geoffrey. *Global Crisis: War, Climate Change and Catastrophe in the Seventeenth Century.* 2013. A sweeping account of the worldwide crisis of the seventeenth century, which the author argues was largely caused by climatic changes known as the "little ice age."

Romaniello, Matthew. *The Elusive Empire: Kazan and the Creation of Russia, 1552–1671.* 2012. A study of the conquest of Kazan by Ivan the Terrible in 1552 and the Russian Empire built in its aftermath.

Rountree, Helen C. *Pocahontas, Powhatan, Opechancanough: Three Indian Lives Changed by Jamestown.* 2005. Biographies of three important Native Americans involved in the Jamestown settlement; a rich portrait of the life of the Powhatan people and their encounter with the English.

Wilson, Peter H. *The Thirty Years War: Europe's Tragedy.* 2011. An overview of the origins and outcomes of the Thirty Years' War, focusing on political and economic issues in addition to religious conflicts.

◆ **1660** Restoration of English monarchy under Charles II

1682–1725 Reign of Peter the Great in Russia

1642–1649 English civil war, ending with the execution of Charles I

1653–1658 Oliver Cromwell's military rule in England (the Protectorate)

1688–1689 Glorious Revolution in England

1643–1715 Reign of Louis XIV in France

1651 ◆ First of the Navigation Acts

1665–1683 Jean-Baptiste Colbert applies mercantilism to France

1670–1671 Cossack revolt led by Stenka Razin

1701–1713 War of the Spanish Succession

1683–1718 Habsburgs push the Ottoman Turks from Hungary

1603–1867 Tokugawa Shogunate in Japan **(Chs. 21, 26)**

◆ **1652** East India Company settles Cape Town **(Ch. 20)**

| 1625 | 1650 | 1675 | 1700 |

FEATURE FILMS AND TELEVISION DRAMAS

Alatriste (Agustín Díaz Yanes, 2006). Set in the declining years of Spain's imperial glory, this film follows the violent adventures of an army captain who takes the son of a fallen comrade under his care.

Black Robe (Bruce Beresford, 1991). A classic film about French Jesuit missionaries among Algonquin and Huron Indians in New France in the seventeenth century.

Charles II: The Power and the Passion (BBC, 2003). An award-winning television miniseries about the son of executed English king Charles I and the Restoration that brought him to the throne in 1660.

Cromwell (Ken Hughes, 1970). The English civil war from its origin to Oliver Cromwell's victory, with battle scenes as well as personal stories of Cromwell and other central figures.

Girl with a Pearl Earring (Peter Webber, 2003). The life and career of painter Johannes Vermeer told through the eyes of a young servant girl who becomes his assistant and model.

Molière (Laurent Tirard, 2007). A film about the French playwright Molière, a favorite of King Louis XIV, which fancifully incorporates characters and plotlines from some of the writer's most celebrated plays.

The New World (Terrence Malick, 2005). Set in 1607 at the founding of the Jamestown settlement, this film retells the story of John Smith and Pocahontas.

WEBSITES

Chateau de Versailles. The official website of the palace of Versailles, built by Louis XIV and inhabited by French royalty until the revolution of 1789. **en.chateauversailles.fr/homepage**

The Invitation to a Funeral Tour: A Free-Style Jaunt around Restoration London. A website offering information on the places, food, and people of Restoration London, inspired by the novel *Invitation to a Funeral* by Molly Brown (1999). **www.okima.com/**

The Jesuit Relations and Allied Documents. Contains a complete English translation of *The Jesuit Relations and Allied Documents*, the reports submitted by Jesuit missionaries in New France to authorities in the home country. **puffin.creighton.edu/jesuit/relations/**

The Plymouth Colony Archive Project. A site hosted by the University of Illinois with searchable primary and secondary sources relating to the Plymouth colony, including court records, laws, journals and memoirs, wills, maps, and biographies of colonists. **www.histarch.uiuc.edu/Plymouth/index.html**

19

New Worldviews and Ways of Life
1540–1790

From the mid-sixteenth century on, age-old patterns of knowledge and daily life were disrupted by a series of transformative developments. Just as European explorers and conquerors overturned ancient models of the globe, so scholars challenged, and eventually discarded, ancient frameworks for understanding the heavens. The resulting conception of the universe and its laws remained in force until Albert Einstein's discoveries in the first half of the twentieth century. Accompanied by new discoveries in botany, zoology, chemistry, and other domains, these developments constituted a fundamental shift in the basic framework for understanding the natural world and the methods for examining it known collectively as the "Scientific Revolution."

In the eighteenth century philosophers extended the use of reason from nature to human society. Self-proclaimed members of an "Enlightenment" movement, they wished to bring the same progress to human affairs that their predecessors had brought to the understanding of the natural world. The Enlightenment created concepts of human rights, equality, progress, and tolerance that still guide Western societies. At the same time, some Europeans used their new understanding of reason to explain their own superiority, thus rationalizing attitudes now regarded as racist and sexist. Despite these biases, European intellectual change drew on contact and exchange with non-European peoples, ideas, and natural organisms.

Changes in the material world encouraged the emergence of new ideas. With the growth of population, the revitalization of industry, and growing world trade, Europeans began to consume at a higher level. Feeding the growth of consumerism was the expansion of transatlantic trade and lower prices for colonial goods, often produced by slaves. During the eighteenth century ships crisscrossing the Atlantic circulated commodities, ideas, and people to all four continents bordering the ocean. As trade became more integrated and communication intensified, an Atlantic world of mixed identities and vivid debates emerged.

Free People of Color

A sizable mixed-race population emerged in many European colonies in the Americas, including descendants of unions between masters and enslaved African women. The wealthiest of the free people of color, as they were called, were plantation owners with slaves of their own.

Portrait of a Young Woman, by an unknown artist, previously attributed to Jean-Etienne Liotard (1702–1789) (pastel on paper)/Saint Louis Art Museum/Bridgeman Images

CHAPTER PREVIEW

THE SCIENTIFIC REVOLUTION
What revolutionary discoveries were made in the sixteenth and seventeenth centuries, and what was their global context?

IMPORTANT CHANGES IN SCIENTIFIC THINKING AND PRACTICE
What intellectual and social changes occurred as a result of the Scientific Revolution?

THE RISE AND SPREAD OF THE ENLIGHTENMENT
How did the Enlightenment emerge, and what were major currents of Enlightenment thought?

KEY ISSUES OF ENLIGHTENMENT DEBATE
How did Enlightenment thinkers address issues of cultural and social difference and political power?

ECONOMIC CHANGE AND THE ATLANTIC WORLD
How did economic and social change and the rise of Atlantic trade interact with Enlightenment ideas?

The Scientific Revolution

What revolutionary discoveries were made in the sixteenth and seventeenth centuries, and what was their global context?

Building on developments in the Middle Ages and the Renaissance, tremendous advances in Europeans' knowledge of the natural world and techniques for establishing such knowledge took place between 1500 and 1700. Collectively known as the "Scientific Revolution," these developments emerged because many more people studied the natural world, using new methods to answer fundamental questions about the universe and how it operated. The authority of ancient Greek texts was replaced by a conviction that knowledge should be acquired by observation and experimentation and that mathematics could be used to understand and represent the workings of the physical world. By 1700 precise laws governing physics and astronomy were known, and a new emphasis on the practical uses of knowledge had emerged.

Hailed today as pioneers of a modern worldview, the major figures of the Scientific Revolution were for the most part devout Christians who saw their work as heralding the glory of creation and who combined older traditions of magic, astrology, and alchemy with their pathbreaking experimentation. Their discoveries took place in a broader context of international trade, imperial expansion, and cultural exchange. Alongside developments in modern science and natural philosophy, the growth of natural history in this period is now recognized by historians as a major achievement of the Scientific Revolution.

Why Europe?

In 1500 scientific activity flourished in many parts of the world. With the expansion of Islam into the lands of the Byzantine Empire in the seventh and eighth centuries, Muslim scholars inherited ancient Greek learning, which itself was built on centuries of borrowing from older civilizations in Egypt, Babylonia, and India. The interaction of peoples and cultures across the vast Muslim world, facilitated by religious tolerance and the common scholarly language of Arabic, was highly favorable to advances in learning.

In a great period of cultural and intellectual flourishing from 1000 to 1500, Muslim scholars thrived in cultural centers such as Baghdad and Córdoba. They established the world's first universities. In this fertile atmosphere, scholars surpassed the texts they had inherited in areas such as mathematics, physics, astronomy, and medicine. Arab and Persian mathematicians, for example, invented algebra, the concept of the algorithm, and decimal point notation, while Arab

astronomers improved on measurements recorded in ancient works.

China was also a vital center of scientific activity, which reached a peak in the mid-fourteenth century. Among its many achievements, papermaking, gunpowder, and the use of the compass in navigation would be the most influential for the West. In Mesoamerica, civilizations such as the Maya and the Aztecs devised complex calendar systems based on astronomical observations and developed mathematics and writing.

Given the multiple world sites of learning and scholarship, it was by no means inevitable that Europe would take the lead in scientific thought. In world history, periods of advancement produced by intense cultural interaction, such as those that occurred after the spread of Islam, are often followed by stagnation and decline during times of conflict and loss of authority. This is what happened in western Europe after the fall of the Western Roman Empire in the fifth century and in the Maya civilization after the collapse of its cultural and political centers around 900.

The re-establishment of stronger monarchies and the growth of trade in the High Middle Ages contributed to a renewal of learning in western Europe. As Europeans began to encroach on Islamic lands in Iberia, Sicily, and the eastern Mediterranean, they became aware of the rich heritage of Greek learning in these regions and the ways scholars had improved upon ancient knowledge. In the twelfth century many ancient Greek texts were translated into Latin, along with the commentaries of Arab scholars. A number of European cities created universities in which Aristotle's works dominated the curriculum.

As Europe recovered from the ravages of the Black Death in the late fourteenth and fifteenth centuries, the intellectual and cultural movement known as the Renaissance provided a crucial foundation for the Scientific Revolution. Scholars called humanists emphasized the value of acquiring knowledge for the practical purposes of life. The quest to restore the glories of the ancient past led to the rediscovery of a host of important classical texts. The fall of Constantinople to the Ottomans in 1453 resulted in a great influx of little-known Greek works, as Christian scholars fled to Italy with their precious texts.

In this period, western European universities established new professorships of mathematics, astronomy, and natural philosophy. The prestige of the new fields was low, especially mathematics, which was reserved for practical problems but not used as a tool to understand the functioning of the physical world itself. Nevertheless, these professorships eventually enabled the union of mathematics with natural philosophy that was to be a hallmark of the Scientific Revolution.

European overseas expansion in the fifteenth and sixteenth centuries provided another catalyst for new thought about the natural world. In particular, the navigational problems of long oceanic voyages in the age of expansion stimulated scientific research and invention. To help solve these problems, inventors developed many new scientific instruments, such as the telescope, barometer, thermometer, pendulum clock, microscope, and air pump. Better instruments, which permitted more accurate observations, often led to important new knowledge. Another crucial technology in this period was printing, which provided a faster and less expensive way to circulate knowledge.

Political and social conflicts were widespread in Eurasia in the sixteenth and early seventeenth centuries, but they had different results. The three large empires of the Muslim world (see "The Turkish Ruling Houses: The Ottomans, Safavids, and Mughals" in Chapter 17) that arose in the wake of the Mongol Empire sought to restore order and assert legitimacy in part by imposing Islamic orthodoxy. Their failure to adopt the printing press can be seen as part of a wider reaction against earlier traditions of innovation. Similarly, in China after the Manchu invasion of 1644, the new Qing Dynasty legitimized its authority through stricter adherence to Confucian tradition. By contrast, western Europe remained politically fragmented into smaller competitive nations, divisions that were augmented by the religious fracturing of the Protestant Reformation. These conditions made it impossible for authorities to impose one orthodox set of ideas and thus allowed individuals to question dominant patterns of thinking.

Scientific Thought to 1550

For medieval scholars, philosophy was the path to true knowledge about the world, and its proofs consisted of the authority of ancients (as interpreted by Christian theologians) and their techniques of logical argumentation. Questions about the physical nature of the universe and how it functioned belonged to a minor branch of philosophy called natural philosophy. Natural philosophy was based primarily on the ideas of Aristotle, the great Greek philosopher of the fourth century B.C.E. According to the Christianized version of Aristotle, a motionless earth stood at the center of the universe and was encompassed by ten separate concentric crystal spheres in which were embedded the moon, sun, planets, and stars. Beyond the spheres was Heaven with the throne of God and the souls of the saved.

Aristotle's views also dominated thinking about physics and motion on earth. Aristotle had distinguished between the world of the celestial spheres and that of the earth—the sublunar world. The sublunar realm was made up of four imperfect, changeable elements: air, fire, water, and earth. Aristotle and his followers also believed that a uniform force moved an object at a constant speed and that the object would stop as soon as that force was removed. The ancient Greek scholar Ptolemy amended Aristotle's physics by positing that the planets moved in small circles, called epicycles, each of which moved in turn along a larger circle, or deferent. This theory accounted for the apparent backward motion of the planets (which in fact occurs as planets closer to the sun overtake the

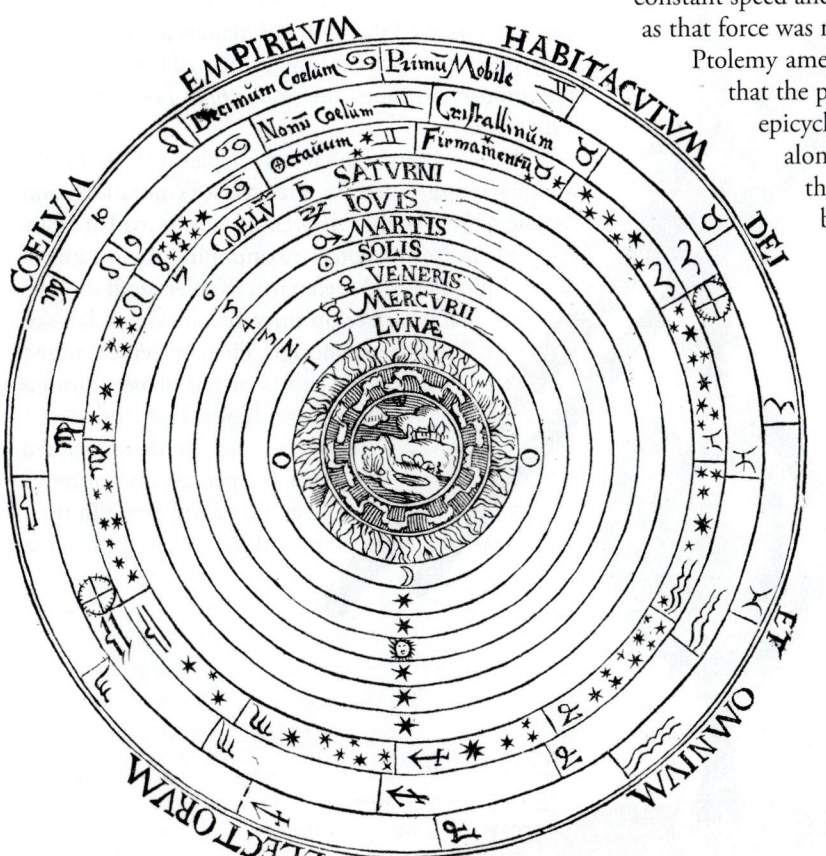

The Aristotelian Universe as Imagined in the Sixteenth Century A round earth is at the center, surrounded by spheres of water, air, and fire. Beyond this small nucleus, the moon, the sun, and the five planets were embedded in their own rotating crystal spheres, with the stars sharing the surface of one enormous sphere. Beyond, the heavens were composed of unchanging ether.
(Image Select/Art Resource, NY)

earth on their orbits) and provided a surprisingly accurate model for predicting planetary motion.

Ptolemy's work also provided the basic foundation of knowledge about the earth. Rediscovered around 1410, his *Geography* presented crucial advances on medieval cartography by representing a round earth divided into 360 degrees with the major latitude marks. However, Ptolemy's map reflected the limits of ancient knowledge, showing only the continents of Europe, Africa, and Asia, with land covering three-quarters of the world.

Galileo's Telescopic Observations of the Moon

Among the many mechanical devices Galileo invented was a telescope that could magnify objects twenty times (other contemporary telescopes could magnify objects only three times). Using this telescope, he obtained the empirical evidence that proved the Copernican system. He sketched many illustrations of his observations, including the six phases of the moon, two of which are shown here. (moon: Biblioteca Nazionale, Florence, Italy/Rabatti-Domingi/akg-images; telescope: Museo delle Scienze, Florence, Italy/akg-images)

Astronomy and Physics

The first great departure from the medieval understanding of cosmology was the work of the Polish cleric Nicolaus Copernicus (1473–1543). Copernicus came to believe that Ptolemy's cumbersome rules detracted from the majesty of a perfect creator. He preferred an idea espoused by some ancient Greek and Arab scholars: that the sun, rather than the earth, was at the center of the universe. Without questioning the Aristotelian belief in crystal spheres, Copernicus theorized that the stars and planets, including the earth, revolved around a fixed sun. Fearing the ridicule of other astronomers, Copernicus did not publish his *On the Revolutions of the Heavenly Spheres* until 1543, the year of his death.

One astronomer who agreed with the **Copernican hypothesis** was the Danish astronomer Tycho Brahe (TEE-koh BRAH-hee) (1546–1601). Brahe established himself as Europe's leading astronomer with his detailed observations of a new star that appeared suddenly in 1572 and shone very brightly for almost two years. The new star, which was actually a distant exploding star, challenged the idea that the heavenly spheres were unchanging and therefore perfect. Aided by grants from the king of Denmark, Brahe built the most sophisticated observatory of his day. After falling out with the king, Brahe acquired a new patron in the Holy Roman emperor Rudolph II, who built him a new observatory in Prague. For twenty years Brahe and his assistants observed the stars and planets with the naked eye in order to create new and improved tables of planetary motions, dubbed the *Rudolphine Tables* in honor of his patron.

Brahe's assistant, Johannes Kepler (1571–1630), carefully re-examined his predecessor's notations and came to believe that they could not be explained by Ptolemy's astronomy. Abandoning the notion of epicycles and deferents, Kepler used Brahe's data to develop three revolutionary laws of planetary motion. First, he demonstrated that the orbits of the planets around the sun are elliptical rather than circular. Second, he demonstrated that the planets do not move at a uniform speed in their orbits. When a planet is close to the sun it accelerates, and it slows as it moves farther away from the sun. Finally, Kepler's third law stated that the time a planet takes to make its complete orbit is precisely related to its distance from the sun.

Kepler's contribution was monumental. Whereas Copernicus had speculated, Kepler used mathematics to prove the precise relations of a sun-centered (solar) system. He thus united for the first time the theoretical cosmology of natural philosophy with mathematics. His work demolished the old system of Aristotle and Ptolemy, and with his third law he came close to formulating the idea of universal gravitation. In 1627 he also completed Brahe's *Rudolphine Tables*, which were used by astronomers for many years.

While Kepler was unraveling planetary motion, a young Florentine named Galileo Galilei (1564–1642) was challenging Aristotelian ideas about motion on earth. He measured the movement of a rolling ball across a surface, repeating the action again and again to verify his results. In his famous acceleration experiment, he showed that a uniform force—in this case, gravity—produced a uniform acceleration. Through another experiment, he formulated the **law of inertia**. He found that rest was not the natural state of objects. Rather, an object continues in motion forever unless stopped by some external force. His discoveries proved Aristotelian physics wrong.

On hearing details about the invention of the telescope in Holland, Galileo made one for himself in 1609. He quickly discovered the first four moons of Jupiter, which clearly demonstrated that Jupiter could not possibly be embedded in an impenetrable crystal sphere as Aristotle and Ptolemy maintained. This discovery provided concrete evidence for the Copernican theory.

Newton's Synthesis

By about 1640 the work of Brahe, Kepler, and Galileo had been largely accepted by the scientific community despite opposition from religious leaders (see "Science and Religion"). But the new findings failed to explain what forces controlled the movement of the planets and objects on earth. That challenge was taken up by English scientist Isaac Newton (1642–1727).

Newton arrived at some of his most basic ideas about physics in 1666 at age twenty-four but was unable to prove them mathematically. In 1684, after years of studying optics, Newton returned to physics for eighteen intensive months. The result was his towering accomplishment, a single explanatory system that integrated the astronomy of Copernicus, as corrected by Kepler's laws, with the physics of Galileo and his predecessors. Newton did this through a set of mathematical laws that explain motion and mechanics. These laws were published in 1687 in Newton's *Mathematical*

Principles of Natural Philosophy (also known as the *Principia*).

The key feature of the Newtonian synthesis was the **law of universal gravitation**. According to this law, each body in the universe attracts every other body in a precise mathematical relationship, whereby the force of attraction is proportional to the quantity of matter of the objects and inversely proportional to the square of the distance between them. The whole universe was unified in one majestic system. Matter moved on earth and throughout the heavens according to the same laws, which could be understood and expressed in mathematical terms.

Natural History and Empire

At the same time that they made advances in astronomy and physics, Europeans embarked on the pursuit of knowledge about unknown geographical regions. Because they were the first to acquire a large overseas empire, the Spanish pioneered these efforts. The Spanish crown sponsored many scientific expeditions to gather information and specimens, out of which emerged new discoveries that reshaped the fields of botany, zoology, cartography, and metallurgy, among others.

Plants were a particular source of interest because they offered tremendous profits in the form of spices, medicines, dyes, and cash crops. King Philip II of Spain sent his personal physician, Francisco Hernández, to New Spain for seven years in the 1560s. Hernández filled fifteen volumes with illustrations of three thousand plants previously unknown in Europe. He interviewed local healers about the plants' medicinal properties, thereby benefiting from centuries of Mesoamerican botanical knowledge.

Other countries followed the Spanish example as their global empires expanded, relying both on official expeditions and the private initiative of merchants, missionaries, and settlers. Over time, the stream of new information about plant and animal species overwhelmed existing intellectual frameworks. Carl Linnaeus (1707–1778) of Sweden sent his students on exploratory voyages around the world and, based on their observations and the specimens they collected, devised a system of naming and classifying living organisms still used today (with substantial revisions).

Copernican hypothesis The idea that the sun, not the earth, was the center of the universe.

law of inertia A law formulated by Galileo stating that motion, not rest, is the natural state of an object and that an object continues in motion forever unless stopped by some external force.

law of universal gravitation Newton's law that all objects are attracted to one another and that the force of attraction is proportional to the object's quantity of matter and inversely proportional to the square of the distance between them.

Metamorphoses of the Caterpillar and Moth Maria Sibylla Merian (1647–1717), the stepdaughter of a Dutch painter, became a celebrated scientific illustrator in her own right. Her finely observed pictures of insects in the South American colony of Suriname introduced many new species. For Merian, science was intimately tied with art: she not only painted but also bred caterpillars and performed experiments on them. Her two-year stay in Suriname, where she was accompanied by a teenage daughter, was a daring feat for a seventeenth-century woman. (bpk Bildagentur/Manuscript Division, Staatsbibliothek zu Berlin, Germany; Stiflung Preussischer Kulturbesitz/Photo: Ruth Schaut/Art Resource, NY)

empiricism A theory of inductive reasoning that calls for acquiring evidence through observation and experimentation rather than reason and speculation.

Magic and Alchemy

Recent historical research on the Scientific Revolution has focused on the contribution of ideas and practices that no longer belong to the realm of science, such as astrology and alchemy. Many of the most celebrated astronomers were also astrologers. Used as a diagnostic tool in medicine, astrology formed a regular part of the curriculum of medical schools.

Centuries-old practices of magic and alchemy also remained important traditions for natural philosophers. Early modern practitioners of magic strove to understand and control hidden connections they perceived among different elements of the natural world, such as that between a magnet and iron. The idea that objects possessed hidden or "occult" qualities that allowed them to affect other objects was a particularly important legacy of the magical tradition.

Johannes Kepler exemplifies the interaction among these different strands of interest in the natural world. His duties as court mathematician included casting horoscopes for the royal family, and he based his own life on astrological principles. He also wrote at length on cosmic harmonies and explained elliptical motion through ideas about the beautiful music created by the combined motion of the planets. Another example of the interweaving of ideas and beliefs is Sir Isaac Newton, who was both intensely religious and also fascinated by alchemy, whose practitioners believed (among other things) that base metals could be turned into gold.

Important Changes in Scientific Thinking and Practice

What intellectual and social changes occurred as a result of the Scientific Revolution?

The Scientific Revolution was not accomplished by a handful of brilliant individuals working alone. Advancements occurred in many fields as scholars developed new methods to seek answers to long-standing problems with the collaboration and assistance of skilled craftsmen who invented new instruments and helped conduct experiments. These results circulated in an international intellectual community from which women were usually excluded.

The Methods of Science

The English politician and writer Francis Bacon (1561–1626) was the greatest early propagandist for the experimental method. Rejecting the Aristotelian and medieval method of using speculative reasoning to build general theories, Bacon argued that new knowledge had to be pursued through empirical research. The researcher who wants to learn more about leaves or rocks, for example, should not speculate about the subject but should rather collect a multitude of specimens and then compare and analyze them to derive general principles. Bacon's contribution was to formalize the empirical method, which had already been used by Brahe and Galileo, into the general theory of inductive reasoning known as **empiricism**.

On the continent more speculative methods retained support. In 1619 the French philosopher René Descartes (day-KAHRT) (1596–1650) experienced a life-changing intellectual vision. Descartes saw that there was a perfect correspondence between geometry and algebra and that geometrical spatial figures could be expressed as algebraic equations and vice versa. A major step forward in mathematics, Descartes's discovery of analytic geometry provided scientists with an important new tool.

Descartes used mathematics to elaborate a highly influential vision of the workings of the cosmos. Drawing on ancient Greek atomist philosophies, Descartes developed the idea that matter was made up of identical "corpuscules" (tiny particles) that collided together in an endless series of motions, akin to the working of a machine. All occurrences in nature could be analyzed as matter in motion, and, according to Descartes, the total "quantity of motion" in the universe was constant. Descartes's mechanistic philosophy of the universe depended on the idea that a vacuum was impossible, which meant that every action had an equal reaction, continuing in an eternal chain reaction.

Descartes's greatest achievement was to develop his initial vision into a whole philosophy of knowledge and science. When experiments proved that sensory impressions could be wrong, Descartes decided it was necessary to doubt them and everything that could reasonably be doubted, and then, as in geometry, to use deductive reasoning from self-evident truths, which he called "first principles," to ascertain scientific laws. Descartes's reasoning ultimately reduced all substances to "matter" and "mind"—that is, to the physical and the spiritual. His view of the world as consisting of two fundamental entities is known as Cartesian dualism.

Both Bacon's inductive experimentalism and Descartes's deductive mathematical reasoning had flaws. Bacon's inability to appreciate the importance of mathematics and his obsession with practical results illustrated the limitations of antitheoretical empiricism. Likewise, some of Descartes's positions demonstrated the inadequacy of rigid, dogmatic rationalism. He believed, for example, that it was possible to deduce the whole science of medicine from first principles. Although insufficient on their own, Bacon's and Descartes's extreme approaches are combined in the modern scientific method, which began to crystallize in the late seventeenth century.

MAJOR CONTRIBUTORS TO THE SCIENTIFIC REVOLUTION

Nicolaus Copernicus (1473–1543)	Published *On the Revolutions of the Heavenly Spheres* (1543); theorized that the sun, rather than the earth, was the center of the galaxy
Paracelsus (1493–1541)	Pioneered the use of chemicals and drugs to address perceived chemical imbalances
Andreas Vesalius (1514–1564)	Published *On the Structure of the Human Body* (1543)
Tycho Brahe (1546–1601)	Built observatories and compiled data for the *Rudolphine Tables*, improved tables of planetary motions
Francis Bacon (1561–1626)	Advocated experimental method, formalizing theory of inductive reasoning known as empiricism
Galileo Galilei (1564–1642)	Used telescopic observation to provide evidence for Copernican hypothesis; experimented to formulate laws of physics, such as inertia
Johannes Kepler (1571–1630)	Used Brahe's data to mathematically prove the Copernican hypothesis; his new laws of planetary motion united for the first time natural philosophy and mathematics; completed the *Rudolphine Tables* in 1627
William Harvey (1578–1657)	Discovered blood circulation (1628)
René Descartes (1596–1650)	Used deductive reasoning to formulate theory of Cartesian dualism
Robert Boyle (1627–1691)	Founded the modern science of chemistry; created the first vacuum; discovered Boyle's law on the properties of gases
Isaac Newton (1642–1727)	Introduced the law of universal gravitation, synthesizing the theories of Copernicus and Galileo

Medicine, the Body, and Chemistry

The Scientific Revolution, which began with the study of the cosmos, soon transformed the understanding of the human body. For many centuries the ancient Greek physician Galen's explanation of the body carried the same authority as Aristotle's account of the universe. According to Galen, the body contained four humors: blood, phlegm, black bile, and yellow bile. Illness was believed to result from an imbalance of these humors.

Swiss physician and alchemist Paracelsus (1493–1541) was an early proponent of the experimental

Frontispiece to *De Humani Corporis Fabrica* (*On the Structure of the Human Body*)
The frontispiece to Vesalius's pioneering work, published in 1543, shows him dissecting a corpse before a crowd of students. This was a revolutionary new hands-on approach for physicians, who usually worked from a theoretical, rather than a practical, understanding of the body. Based on direct observation, Vesalius replaced ancient ideas drawn from Greek philosophy with a much more accurate account of the structure and function of the body. (© SSPL/Science Museum/The Image Works)

kind in creation as stated in Genesis. All religions derived from the Old Testament thus faced difficulties accepting the Copernican system. The leaders of the Catholic Church were initially less hostile than Protestant and Jewish religious leaders, but in the first decades of the sixteenth century Catholic attitudes changed. In 1616 the Holy Office placed the works of Copernicus and his supporters, including Kepler, on a list of books Catholics were forbidden to read.

Out of caution Galileo Galilei silenced his views on heliocentrism for several years, until 1623 saw the ascension of Pope Urban VIII, a man sympathetic to the new science. However, Galileo's 1632 *Dialogue on the Two Chief Systems of the World* went too far. Published in Italian and widely read, it openly lampooned the Aristotelian view and defended Copernicus. In 1633 Galileo was tried for heresy by the papal Inquisition. Imprisoned and threatened with torture, the aging Galileo recanted.

method in medicine and pioneered the use of chemicals and drugs to address what he saw as chemical, rather than humoral, imbalances. Another experimentalist, Flemish physician Andreas Vesalius (1514–1564), studied anatomy by dissecting human bodies. In 1543, the same year Copernicus published *On the Revolutions of the Heavenly Spheres*, Vesalius issued *On the Structure of the Human Body*. Its two hundred precise drawings revolutionized the understanding of human anatomy, disproving Galen. The experimental approach also led English royal physician William Harvey (1578–1657) to discover the circulation of blood through the veins and arteries in 1628.

The work of Irishman Robert Boyle (1627–1691) led to the development of modern chemistry. Following Paracelsus's lead, he undertook experiments to discover the basic elements of nature, which he believed was composed of infinitely small atoms. Boyle was the first to create a vacuum, thus disproving Descartes's belief that a vacuum could not exist in nature, and he discovered Boyle's law (1662), which states that the pressure of a gas varies inversely with volume.

Science and Religion

It is sometimes assumed that the relationship between science and religion is fundamentally hostile and that the pursuit of knowledge based on reason and proof is incompatible with faith. Yet during the Scientific Revolution most practitioners were devoutly religious and saw their work as contributing to the celebration of God's glory. However, the concept of heliocentrism, which displaced the earth from the center of the universe, threatened the understanding of the place of man-

Science and Society

The rise of modern science had many consequences. First, it led to the rise of a new and expanding social group—the international scientific community. Members of this community were linked together by common interests and values as well as by journals and scientific societies. The personal success of scientists and scholars depended on making new discoveries, and as a result science became competitive. Second, as governments intervened to support and sometimes direct research, the new scientific community became closely tied to the state and its agendas. National academies of science were created under state sponsorship in London in 1662, Paris in 1666, Berlin in 1700, and later across Europe.

It was long believed that the Scientific Revolution was the work of exceptional geniuses. More recently, historians have emphasized the importance of skilled craftsmen in the rise of science, particularly in the development of the experimental method. Many artisans developed a strong interest in emerging scientific ideas, and, in turn, the practice of science in the seventeenth century relied heavily on artisans' expertise in making instruments and conducting precise experiments.

Popularizing Science The frontispiece illustration of Fontenelle's *Conversations on the Plurality of Worlds* (1686) invites the reader to share the pleasures of astronomy with an elegant lady and an entertaining teacher. The drawing shows the planets revolving around the sun. (© Roger-Viollet/The Image Works)

Some things did not change in the Scientific Revolution. For example, scholars willing to challenge received ideas about the natural universe did not question traditional inequalities between the sexes. Instead the emergence of professional science may have worsened the inequality in some ways. When Renaissance courts served as centers of learning, talented noblewomen could find niches in study and research. But the rise of a scientific community raised barriers for women because the universities and academies that furnished professional credentials refused them entry.

There were, however, a number of noteworthy exceptions. In Italy universities and academies did accept women. Across Europe women worked as makers of wax anatomical models and as botanical and zoological illustrators. They were also very much involved in informal scientific communities, attending salons (see "Women and the Enlightenment"), conducting experiments, and writing learned treatises.

The Rise and Spread of the Enlightenment

How did the Enlightenment emerge, and what were major currents of Enlightenment thought?

The political, intellectual, and religious developments of the early modern period that gave rise to the Scientific Revolution further contributed to a series of debates about key issues in late-seventeenth- and eighteenth-century Europe and the wider world that came to be known as the **Enlightenment**. By shattering the unity of Western Christendom, the conflicts of the Reformation brought old religious certainties into question; the strong states that emerged to quell the disorder soon inspired questions about political sovereignty and its limits. Increased movement of peoples, goods, and ideas within and among the states of Asia, Africa, Europe, and its colonies offered examples of shockingly different ways of life and values. Finally, the tremendous achievements of the Scientific Revolution inspired intellectuals to believe that answers to all the questions being asked could be found through the use of rational and critical thinking. Progress was possible in human society as well as science.

The Early Enlightenment

Loosely united by certain key questions and ideas, the European Enlightenment (ca. 1690–1789) was a broad intellectual and cultural movement that gained strength gradually and did not reach its maturity until about 1750. Its origins in the late seventeenth century lie in a combination of developments, including political opposition to absolutist rule, religious conflicts between Protestants and Catholics and within Protestantism, and the attempt to apply principles and practices from the Scientific Revolution to human society.

A key crucible for Enlightenment thought was the Dutch Republic, with its proud commitments to religious tolerance and republican rule. When Louis XIV demanded that all Protestants convert to Catholicism, many Huguenots fled the country and resettled in the Dutch Republic. From this haven of tolerance, French Huguenots and their supporters began to publish tracts denouncing religious intolerance and suggesting that only a despotic monarch would deny religious freedom. Their challenge to authority thus combined religious and political issues.

Enlightenment An intellectual and cultural movement in late-seventeenth- and eighteenth-century Europe and the wider world that used rational and critical thinking to debate issues such as political sovereignty, religious tolerance, gender roles, and racial difference.

These dual concerns drove the career of one important early Enlightenment writer, Pierre Bayle (1647–1706), a Huguenot who took refuge from government persecution in the Dutch Republic. Bayle critically examined the religious beliefs and persecutions of the past in his *Historical and Critical Dictionary* (1697). Demonstrating that human beliefs had been extremely varied and very often mistaken, he concluded that nothing can ever be known beyond all doubt, a view known as skepticism.

The Dutch Jewish philosopher Baruch Spinoza (1632–1677) was a key figure in the transition from the Scientific Revolution to the Enlightenment. Deeply inspired by advances in the Scientific Revolution, Spinoza sought to apply natural philosophy to thinking about human society. He borrowed Descartes's emphasis on rationalism and his methods of deductive reasoning but rejected the French thinker's mind-body dualism. Instead Spinoza came to espouse monism, the idea that mind and body are united in one substance and that God and nature were merely two names for the same thing. He envisioned a deterministic universe in which good and evil were merely relative values, and human actions were shaped by outside circumstances, not free will. Spinoza was excommunicated by the relatively large Jewish community of Amsterdam for his controversial religious ideas, but he was heralded by his Enlightenment successors as a model of personal virtue and courageous intellectual autonomy.

German philosopher and mathematician Gottfried Wilhelm von Leibniz (1646–1716) refuted both Cartesian dualism and Spinoza's monism. Instead he adopted the idea of an infinite number of substances, or "monads," from which all matter is composed according to a harmonious divine plan. His *Theodicy* (1710) declared that ours must be "the best of all possible worlds" because it was created by an omnipotent and benevolent God.

Out of this period of intellectual turmoil came John Locke's *Essay Concerning Human Understanding* (1690), perhaps the most important text of the early Enlightenment. In this work Locke (1632–1704) set forth a new theory about how human beings learn and form their ideas. Whereas Descartes based his deductive logic on the conviction that certain first principles, or innate ideas, are imbued in humans by God, Locke insisted that all ideas are derived from experience. According to Locke, the human mind at birth is like a blank tablet, or tabula rasa, on which understanding and beliefs are inscribed by experience. Human development is therefore determined by external forces, like education and social institutions, not innate characteristics. Locke's essay contributed to the theory of **sensationalism**, the idea that all human ideas and thoughts are produced as a result of sensory impressions.

The Influence of the Philosophes

Divergences among the early thinkers of the Enlightenment show that, while they shared many of the same premises and questions, the answers they found differed widely. The spread of this spirit of inquiry and debate owed a great deal to the work of the **philosophes**, a group of influential French intellectuals who proclaimed that they were bringing the light of knowledge to their fellow humans.

To appeal to the public and get around the censors, the philosophes wrote novels and plays, histories and philosophies, and dictionaries and encyclopedias, all filled with satire and double meanings to spread their message. One of the greatest philosophes, the baron de Montesquieu (mahn-tuhs-KYOO) (1689–1755), pioneered this approach in *The Persian Letters* (1721). This work consists of letters supposedly written by two Persian travelers, Usbek and Rica, who as outsiders see European customs in unique ways and thereby allow Montesquieu a vantage point for criticizing existing practices and beliefs.

Disturbed by the growth in royal power under Louis XIV and inspired by the example of the physical sciences, Montesquieu set out to apply the critical method to the problem of government in *The Spirit of Laws* (1748). Arguing that forms of government were shaped by history, geography, and customs, Montesquieu identified three main types: monarchies, republics, and despotisms. A great admirer of the English parliamentary system, Montesquieu argued for a separation of powers, with political power divided among different classes and legal estates holding unequal rights and privileges. Decades later, his theory of separation of powers had a great impact on the constitutions of the United States in 1789 and of France in 1791.

The most famous philosophe was François-Marie Arouet, known by the pen name Voltaire (1694–1778). In his long career, Voltaire wrote more than seventy witty volumes, hobnobbed with royalty, and died a millionaire through shrewd speculations. His early career, however, was turbulent, and he was twice arrested for insulting noblemen. To avoid a prison term, Voltaire moved to England for three years, and there he came to share Montesquieu's enthusiasm for English liberties and institutions.

Returning to France, Voltaire met Gabrielle-Emilie Le Tonnelier de Breteuil, marquise du Châtelet (1706–1749), a gifted noblewoman. Madame du Châtelet invited Voltaire to live in her country house at Cirey in Lorraine. Passionate about science, she studied physics and mathematics and published the first French translation of Newton's *Principia*. Excluded from the Royal Academy of Sciences because she was a woman, Madame du Châtelet had no doubt that women's limited role in science was due to their unequal education.

While living at Cirey, Voltaire wrote works praising England and popularizing English scientific progress. Yet, like almost all the philosophes, Voltaire was a reformer, not a revolutionary. He pessimistically concluded that the best form of government was a good monarch, since human beings "are very rarely worthy to govern themselves." Nor did Voltaire believe in social and economic equality. The only realizable equality, Voltaire thought, was that "by which the citizen only depends on the laws which protect the freedom of the feeble against the ambitions of the strong."[1]

Voltaire's philosophical and religious positions were much more radical. Voltaire believed in God, but, like many Enlightenment thinkers, he rejected the established church in favor of **deism**, belief in a distant, noninterventionist deity. Above all, Voltaire and most of the philosophes hated religious intolerance, which they believed led to fanaticism and cruelty.

The strength of the philosophes lay in their number, dedication, and organization. Their greatest achievement was a group effort—the seventeen-volume *Encyclopedia: The Rational Dictionary of the Sciences, the Arts, and the Crafts*, edited by Denis Diderot (1713–1784) and Jean le Rond d'Alembert (1717–1783). Completed in 1765 despite opposition from the French state and the Catholic Church, the *Encyclopedia* contained hundreds of thousands of articles by leading scientists, writers, skilled workers, and progressive priests. Science and the industrial arts were exalted, religion and immortality questioned. Intolerance, legal injustice, and out-of-date social institutions were openly criticized.

After about 1770 a number of thinkers and writers began to attack the philosophes' faith in reason and progress. The most famous of these was the Swiss intellectual Jean-Jacques Rousseau (1712–1778). Like other Enlightenment thinkers, Rousseau was passionately committed to individual freedom. Unlike them, however, he attacked rationalism and civilization as destroying, rather than liberating, the individual. Warm, spontaneous feeling, Rousseau believed, had to complement and correct cold intellect. Rousseau's ideals greatly influenced the early Romantic movement, which rebelled against the culture of the Enlightenment in the late eighteenth century.

Rousseau's contribution to political theory in *The Social Contract* (1762) was based on two fundamental concepts: the general will and popular sovereignty. According to Rousseau, the **general will** is sacred and absolute, reflecting the common interests of all people, who have displaced the monarch as the holder of sovereign power. The general will is not necessarily the will of the majority, however. At times the general will may be the authentic, long-term needs of the people as correctly interpreted by a farseeing minority.

Enlightenment Movements Across Europe

The Enlightenment was a movement of international dimensions, with thinkers traversing borders in a constant exchange of visits, letters, and printed materials. The Republic of Letters, as this international group of scholars and writers was called, was a truly cosmopolitan set of networks stretching from western Europe to its colonies in the Americas, to Russia and eastern Europe, and along the routes of trade and empire to Africa and Asia.

Within this broad international conversation, scholars have identified regional and national particularities. Outside France, many strains of Enlightenment thought sought to reconcile reason with faith, rather than emphasizing the errors of religious fanaticism and intolerance. Some scholars point to a distinctive "Catholic Enlightenment" that aimed to renew and reform the church from within, looking to divine grace rather than human will as the source of social progress.

The Scottish Enlightenment, centered in Edinburgh, was marked by an emphasis on common sense and scientific reasoning. A central figure in Edinburgh was David Hume (1711–1776). Building on Locke's writings on learning, Hume argued that the human mind is really nothing but a bundle of impressions. These impressions originate only in sensory experiences and our habits of joining these experiences together. Since our ideas ultimately reflect only our sensory experiences, our reason cannot tell us anything about questions that cannot be verified by sensory experience (in the form of controlled experiments or mathematics), such as the origin of the universe or the existence of God. Hume further argued, in opposition to Descartes, that reason alone could not supply moral principles and that they derived instead from emotions and desires, such as feelings of approval or shame. Hume's rationalistic inquiry thus ended up undermining the Enlightenment's faith in the power of reason by emphasizing the superiority of the passions over reason in driving human behavior.

---

sensationalism An idea, espoused by John Locke, that all human ideas and thoughts are produced as a result of sensory impressions.

philosophes A group of French intellectuals who proclaimed that they were bringing the light of knowledge to their fellow humans.

deism Belief in a distant, noninterventionist deity, shared by many Enlightenment thinkers.

general will A concept associated with Rousseau, referring to the common interests of all the people, who have displaced the monarch as the holder of sovereign power.

MAJOR FIGURES OF THE ENLIGHTENMENT

Baruch Spinoza (1632–1677)	Early Enlightenment thinker excommunicated from the Jewish community for his concept of a deterministic universe
John Locke (1632–1704)	*Essay Concerning Human Understanding* (1690)
Gottfried Wilhelm von Leibniz (1646–1716)	Early German philosopher and mathematician
Pierre Bayle (1647–1706)	*Historical and Critical Dictionary* (1697)
Montesquieu (1689–1755)	*The Persian Letters* (1721); *The Spirit of Laws* (1748)
Voltaire (1694–1778)	Renowned French philosopher and author of more than seventy works
Gabrielle-Emilie Le Tonnelier de Breteuil, marquise du Châtelet (1706–1749)	French scholar and supporter of equal education for women
David Hume (1711–1776)	Central figure of the Scottish Enlightenment
Jean-Jacques Rousseau (1712–1778)	*The Social Contract* (1762)
Denis Diderot (1713–1784) and **Jean le Rond d'Alembert** (1717–1783)	Editors of *Encyclopedia: The Rational Dictionary of the Sciences, the Arts, and the Crafts* (1765)
Adam Smith (1723–1790)	*Theory of Moral Sentiments* (1759); *An Inquiry into the Nature and Causes of the Wealth of Nations* (1776)
Immanuel Kant (1724–1804)	*On the Different Races of Man* (1775); *What Is Enlightenment?* (1784)

Hume's ideas had a formative influence on another major figure of the Scottish Enlightenment, Adam Smith (1723–1790). In his *Theory of Moral Sentiments* (1759), Smith argued that social interaction produced feelings of mutual sympathy that led people to behave in ethical ways, despite inherent tendencies toward

economic liberalism The theory, associated with Adam Smith, that the pursuit of individual self-interest in a competitive market would lead to rising prosperity and greater social equality, rendering government intervention unnecessary and undesirable.

self-interest. Smith believed that the thriving commercial life of the eighteenth century was likely to produce civic virtue through the values of competition, fair play, and individual autonomy. In *An Inquiry into the Nature and Causes of the Wealth of Nations* (1776), Smith attacked the laws and regulations created by mercantilist governments that, he argued, prevented commerce from reaching its full capacity (see "Mercantilism and Colonial Wars" in Chapter 18). For Smith, ordinary people were capable of forming correct judgments based on their own experience and should therefore not be hampered by government regulations. Instead, the pursuit of individual self-interest in a competitive market would lead to rising prosperity and greater social equality. Smith's **economic liberalism** became the dominant form of economic thought in the early nineteenth century.

Inspired by philosophers of moral sentiments, like Hume and Smith, as well as by physiological studies of the role of the nervous system in human perception, the celebration of sensibility became an important element of eighteenth-century culture. Sensibility referred to an acute sensitivity of the nerves and brain to outside stimuli that produced strong emotional and physical reactions. Novels, plays, and other literary genres depicted moral and aesthetic sensibility as a particular characteristic of women and the upper classes. The proper relationship between reason and the emotions became a key question.

After 1760 Enlightenment ideas were hotly debated in the German-speaking states, often in dialogue with Christian theology. Immanuel Kant (1724–1804) was the greatest German philosopher of his day. Kant posed the question of the age when he published a pamphlet in 1784 titled *What Is Enlightenment?* He answered, "*Sapere Aude* (dare to know)! 'Have the courage to use your own understanding' is therefore the motto of enlightenment." He argued that if intellectuals were granted the freedom to exercise their reason publicly in print, enlightenment would surely follow. Kant was no revolutionary; he also insisted that in their private lives, individuals must obey all laws, no matter how unreasonable. Like other Enlightenment figures in central and east-central Europe, Kant thus tried to reconcile absolutism and religious faith with a critical public sphere.

Important developments in Enlightenment thought also took place in the Italian peninsula. After achieving independence from Habsburg rule (1734), the kingdom of Naples entered a period of intellectual flourishing. In northern Italy a central figure was Cesare Beccaria (1738–1794). His *On Crimes and Punishments* (1764) was a passionate plea for reform of the penal system that decried the use of torture, arbitrary imprisonment, and capital punishment and advocated the prevention of crime over its punishment.

Key Issues of Enlightenment Debate

How did Enlightenment thinkers address issues of cultural and social difference and political power?

The Scientific Revolution and the political and religious conflicts of the late seventeenth century were not the only developments that influenced European thinkers. Europeans' increased interactions with non-European peoples and cultures also helped produce the Enlightenment spirit. Enlightenment thinkers struggled to assess differences between Western and non-Western cultures, often adopting Eurocentric views, but sometimes expressing admiration for other societies. These same thinkers focused a great deal of attention on other forms of cultural and social difference, developing new ideas about race, gender, and political power. Although new "scientific" ways of thinking often served to justify inequality, the Enlightenment did see a rise in religious tolerance, a particularly crucial issue for Europe's persecuted Jewish population.

Shifting Views of the Non-Western World

In the wake of the great discoveries of the fifteenth and sixteenth centuries, the rapidly growing travel literature taught Europeans that the peoples of China, India, Africa, and the Americas had very different beliefs and customs. Educated Europeans began to look at truth and morality in relative, rather than absolute, terms.

The powerful and advanced nations of Asia were obvious sources of comparison with the West. Seventeenth-century Jesuit missionaries served as a conduit for transmission of knowledge to the West about Chinese history and culture. The philosopher and mathematician Leibniz corresponded with Jesuits stationed in China, coming to believe that Chinese ethics and political philosophy were superior but that Europeans had equaled China in science and technology; some scholars believe his concept of monads was influenced by Confucian teaching on the inherent harmony between the cosmic order and human society.[2]

During the eighteenth century Enlightenment opinion on China was divided. Voltaire and some other philosophes revered China—without ever visiting or seriously studying it—as an ancient culture replete with wisdom and learning, ruled by benevolent absolutist monarchs. They enthusiastically embraced Confucianism as a natural religion in which universal moral truths were uncovered by reason. By contrast, Montesquieu and Diderot criticized China as a despotic land ruled by fear.

Attitudes toward Islam and the Muslim world were similarly mixed. As the Ottoman military threat receded at the end of the seventeenth century, some Enlightenment thinkers assessed Islam favorably. Others, including Spinoza, saw Islamic culture as superstitious and favorable to despotism. In most cases, writing about Islam and Muslim cultures served primarily as a means to reflect on Western values and practices.

One writer with considerable personal experience in a Muslim country was Lady Mary Wortley Montagu, wife of the English ambassador to the Ottoman Empire.

Portrait of Mary Wortley Montagu in Turkish Attire
Lady Mary Wortley Montagu accompanied her husband, the British ambassador to the Ottoman Empire, on his diplomatic mission from 1717 to 1719. Her letters to friends and relatives provide a rare glimpse of the sultan's court and an unusually sympathetic depiction of life in the Muslim empire, including a positive appreciation of the status of Ottoman women. Lady Montagu had several portraits painted of herself in Ottoman dress, reflecting her fascination with Ottoman culture. (NYPL/Science Source/Getty Images)

Denis Diderot, "Supplement to Bougainville's Voyage"

Denis Diderot was born in a provincial town in eastern France and educated in Paris. Rejecting careers in the church and the law, he devoted himself to literature and philosophy. In 1749, sixty years before Charles Darwin's birth, Diderot was jailed by Parisian authorities for publishing an essay questioning God's role in the creation and suggesting the autonomous evolution of species. Following these difficult beginnings, Diderot's editorial work and writing on the *Encyclopedia* were the crowning intellectual achievements of his life and, according to some, of the Enlightenment itself.

Like other philosophes, Diderot disseminated Enlightenment ideas through various types of writing, ranging from scholarly articles in the *Encyclopedia* to philosophical treatises, novels, plays, book reviews, and erotic stories. His "Supplement to Bougainville's Voyage" (1772) was a fictional account of a European voyage to Tahiti inspired by the writings of traveler Louis-Antoine de Bougainville. In this passage, Diderot expresses his own loathing of colonial conquest and exploitation through the voice of an elderly Tahitian man. The character's praise for his own culture allows Diderot to express his Enlightenment idealization of natural man, free from the vices of civilized societies.

■ He was the father of a numerous family. At the time of the Europeans' arrival, he cast upon them a look that was filled with scorn, though it revealed no surprise, no alarm and no curiosity. They approached him; he turned his back on them and retired into his hut. His thoughts were only too well revealed by his silence and his air of concern, for in the privacy of his thoughts he groaned inwardly over the happy days of his people, now gone forever. At the moment of Bougainville's departure, when all the natives ran swarming onto the beach, tugging at this clothing and throwing their arms around his companions and weeping, the old man stepped forward and solemnly spoke:

"Weep, wretched Tahitians, weep—but rather for the arrival than for the departure of these wicked and grasping men! The day they will return, bearing in one hand that piece of wood you see suspended from this one's belt and in the other the piece of steel that hangs at the side of his companion. They will load you with chains, slit your throats and enslave you to their follies and vices. Someday you will be slaves to them, you will be as corrupt, as vile, as wretched as they are. But I have this consolation—my life is drawing to its close, and I shall not see the calamity that I foretell. O Tahitians, O my friends! You have the means of warding off a terrible fate, but I would die before I would advise you to make sure of it. Let them leave, and let them live."

Then turning to Bougainville, he went on, "And you, leader of these brigands who obey you, take your vessel swiftly from our shores. We are innocent and happy, and you can only spoil our happiness. We follow the pure instinct of nature, and you have tried to efface her imprint from our hearts. Here all things are for all, and you have preached to us I know not what distinctions between mine and thine. . . . If some day a Tahitian should land on your shores and if he

---

Her letters challenged prevailing ideas by depicting Turkish people as sympathetic and civilized. Montagu also disputed the notion that women were more oppressed in Ottoman society than at home in Europe.

Apart from debates about Asian and Muslim lands, the "discovery" of the New World and subsequent explorations in the Pacific Ocean also destabilized existing norms and values in Europe. One popular idea, among Rousseau and others, was that indigenous peoples of the Americas were living examples of "natural man," who embodied the essential goodness of humanity uncorrupted by decadent society.

New Definitions of Race

As scientists developed taxonomies of plant and animal species in response to discoveries in the Americas, they also began to classify humans into hierarchically ordered "races" and to speculate on the origins of perceived racial differences. The French naturalist Georges-Louis Leclerc, comte de Buffon (1707–1788), argued that humans originated with one species that then developed into distinct races due largely to climatic conditions.

Enlightenment thinkers such as David Hume and Immanuel Kant helped popularize these ideas. In *Of Natural Characters* (1748), Hume expressed his conviction that "negroes and in general all other species of men" were "naturally inferior to the whites."[3] In *On the Different Races of Man* (1775), Kant claimed that there were four human races, each of which derived from an original race. According to Kant, the closest descendants of the original race were the white inhabitants of northern Germany. (Scientists now know that humans originated in Africa.)

Using the word *race* to designate biologically distinct groups of humans was new in European thought. Previously, Europeans had grouped other peoples into should engrave on one of your stones or on the bark of one of your trees, *This land belongs to the people of Tahiti*, what would you think? You are stronger than we are! And what does that signify? When one of our lads carried off some of the miserable trinkets with which your ship is loaded, what an uproar you made, and what revenge you took! And at that very moment you were plotting, in the depths of your heart, to steal a whole country! You are not slaves; you would suffer death rather than be enslaved, yet you want to make slaves of us! Do you believe then, that the Tahitian does not know how to die in defense of his liberty? This Tahitian, whom you want to treat as a chattel, as a dumb animal—this Tahitian is your brother. You are both children of Nature—what right do you have over him that he does not have over you?

"You came; did we attack you? Did we plunder your vessel? Did we seize you and expose you to the arrows of our enemies? Did we force you to work in the fields alongside our beasts of burden? We respected our own image in you. Leave us our customs, which are wiser and more decent than yours. We have no wish to barter what you call our ignorance for your useless knowledge. We possess already all that is good or necessary for our existence. Do we merit your scorn because we have not been able to create superfluous wants for ourselves? When we are hungry, we have something to eat; when we are cold, we have clothing to put on. You have entered our huts—what is lacking there in your opinion? You are welcome to drive yourselves as hard as you please in pursuit of what you call the comforts of life, but allow sensible people to stop when they see they have nothing to gain but imaginary benefits from the continuation of their painful labors. If you persuade us to go beyond the bounds of strict necessity, when shall we come to the end of our labor? When shall we have time for enjoyment? We have reduced our daily and yearly labors to the least possible amount, because to us nothing seemed more desirable than leisure. Go and bestir yourselves in your own country; there you may torment yourselves as much as you like; but leave us in peace, and do not fill our heads with a hankering after your false needs and imaginary virtues.

QUESTIONS FOR ANALYSIS

1. On what grounds does the speaker argue for the Tahitians' basic equality with the Europeans?
2. What is the good life, according to the speaker, and how does it contrast with the European way of life? Which do you think is the better path, and why?
3. In what ways could Diderot's thoughts here be seen as representative of Enlightenment ideas? Are there ways in which they are not?
4. How realistic do you think this account is? Does it matter? How might defenders of colonial expansion respond to Diderot's criticism?

Source: Barzun, *Rameau's Nephew and Other Works: Diderot*, 1st Ed., © 1964. Reprinted by permission of Pearson Education, Inc., New York, New York.

"nations" based on their historical, political, and cultural affiliations, rather than on supposedly innate physical differences. While Europeans had long believed they were culturally superior to people from other nations, the new idea that racial difference was physical and innate rather than cultural taught them they were biologically superior as well. In turn, scientific racism helped legitimize and justify the tremendous growth of slavery that occurred during the eighteenth century.

Racist ideas did not go unchallenged. The abbé Raynal's *History of the Two Indies* (1770) fiercely attacked slavery and the abuses of European colonization. *Encyclopedia* editor Denis Diderot adopted Montesquieu's technique of criticizing European attitudes through the voice of outsiders in his dialogue between Tahitian villagers and their European visitors. (See "Analyzing the Evidence: Denis Diderot, 'Supplement to Bougainville's Voyage,'" above.) Former slaves, like Olaudah Equiano and Ottobah Cugoano, published eloquent memoirs testifying to the horrors of slavery and the innate equality of all humans. These challenges to racism, however, were in the minority. More often, Enlightenment thinkers supported racial inequality.

Women and the Enlightenment

Dating back to the Renaissance debate about women, the question of women's proper role in society and the nature of gender differences fascinated Enlightenment thinkers. Some philosophes championed greater rights and expanded education for women, claiming that the position and treatment of women were the best indicators of a society's level of civilization and decency. In the 1780s the marquis de Condorcet, a celebrated mathematician and contributor to the *Encyclopedia*, went so far as to urge that women should share equal rights with men. This was a rare position; most philosophes espoused modest reforms and did not challenge male superiority over women.

From the first years of the Enlightenment, women writers made crucial contributions both to debates about women's rights and to the broader Enlightenment discussion. In 1694 Mary Astell published *A Serious Proposal to the Ladies*, which encouraged women to aspire to the life of the mind and proposed the creation of a women's college. Astell also harshly criticized the institution of marriage. Echoing arguments made against the absolute authority of kings during the Glorious Revolution (see "Constitutional Monarchy" in Chapter 18), she argued that husbands should not exercise absolute control over their wives in marriage. Yet Astell, like most female authors of the period, was careful to acknowledge women's God-given duties to be good wives and mothers.

The explosion of printed literature over the eighteenth century (see "Urban Life and the Public Sphere") brought significant numbers of women writers into print, but they remained a small proportion of published authors. In the second half of the eighteenth century, women produced some 15 percent of published novels, the genre in which they enjoyed the greatest success. They represented a much smaller percentage of nonfiction authors.[4]

If they remained marginal in the world of publishing, women played a much more active role in the informal dimensions of the Enlightenment: conversation, letter writing, travel, and patronage of artists and writers. A key element of their informal participation was as salon hostesses, or *salonnières* (sah-lahn-ee-EHRZ). **Salons**, which began in the early seventeenth century and reached their peak from 1740 to 1789, were weekly meetings held in wealthy households. They brought together writers, aristocrats, financiers, and noteworthy foreigners for meals and witty discussions of the latest trends in literature, science, and philosophy. (See "Analyzing the Evidence: Enlightenment Culture," at right.)

Women's prominent role as society hostesses and patrons of the arts and letters outraged some Enlightenment thinkers. According to Rousseau, women and men were radically different beings and should play diametrically opposed roles in life. Destined by nature to assume the active role in sexual relations, men were naturally suited for the rough-and-tumble worlds of politics and public life. Women's role was to attract male sexual desire in order to marry and have children. For Rousseau, women's love for displaying themselves in public, attending salons, and pulling the strings of power was unnatural and had a corrupting effect on both politics and society.

Rousseau's emphasis on the natural laws governing women echoed a wider shift in ideas about gender during this period, as doctors, scientists, and philosophers increasingly agreed that women's essential characteristics were determined by their sexual organs and reproductive functions. This turn to nature, rather than tradition or scripture, as a means to understand human society had parallels in contemporary views on racial difference.

Enlightened Absolutism and Its Limits

Enlightenment thinkers' insistence on questioning long-standing traditions and norms inevitably led to issues of power and politics. Most philosophes were political moderates, who distrusted the uneducated masses and hoped for reform, not revolution. As Enlightenment ideas reached from Parisian salons to the centers of government, some absolutist rulers, without renouncing their own absolute authority, took up the call to reform their governments in accordance with the rational and humane principles of the Enlightenment. The result was what historians have called the **enlightened absolutism** of the later eighteenth century. This concept was reflected in programs of reform in Prussia, Russia, and Austria. (Similar programs in France and Spain will be discussed in Chapter 22.)

Frederick II (r. 1740–1786) of Prussia, known as Frederick the Great, promoted religious tolerance and free speech and improved the educational system. Under his reign, Prussia's laws were simplified, torture of prisoners was abolished, and judges decided cases quickly and impartially. However, Frederick did not free the serfs of Prussia; instead he extended the privileges of the nobility over them.

Frederick's reputation as an enlightened prince was rivaled by that of Catherine the Great of Russia (r. 1762–1796). Catherine pursued three major goals. First, she worked hard to continue Peter the Great's efforts to bring the culture of western Europe to Russia (see "Peter the Great and Russia's Turn to the West" in Chapter 18). Catherine's second goal was domestic reform. Like Frederick, she restricted the practice of torture, allowed limited religious tolerance, and tried to improve education and local government. The philosophes applauded these measures and hoped more would follow.

These hopes were dashed by a massive uprising of serfs in 1733 under the leadership of a Cossack soldier

salons Regular social gatherings held by talented and rich Parisian women in their homes, where philosophes and their followers met to discuss literature, science, and philosophy.

enlightened absolutism Term coined by historians to describe the rule of eighteenth-century monarchs who, without renouncing their own absolute authority, took up the call to reform their governments in accordance with the rational and humane principles of the Enlightenment.

Enlightenment Culture

Salons originated in seventeenth-century Paris and became social institutions during the cultural flourishing encouraged by French king Louis XIV. They were gatherings hosted by wealthy women for discussion of the latest literary publications, theatrical performances, and scientific discoveries. During the eighteenth century salons became centers for the dissemination of the new ideas of the Enlightenment. The female hostesses of the salons, known as *salonnières*, opened their homes once or twice a week to carefully cultivated groups of guests that included aristocrats, rich financiers, high-ranking officials, and noteworthy foreigners. The *salonnières* guided the discussion and supervised the guests' social interaction. Madame du Deffand, a prominent *salonnière,* hosted such guests as Montesquieu, d'Alembert, and Benjamin Franklin, then serving as the first United States ambassador to France. Invitations to salons were highly coveted; introductions to the rich and powerful could make the career of an ambitious writer, and, in turn, the social elite found amusement and cultural prestige in their ties to up-and-coming artists and men of letters.

   Salons did not keep formal records, but historians have learned about them from letters and memoirs written by *salonnières* and their guests. One of the few visual representations of the salons is this painting, which depicts an actor performing the first reading of a new play by Voltaire at a 1755 meeting of the salon of Madame Geoffrin. The painter, Anicet Charles Gabriel Lemonnier, was a regular guest at Geoffrin's salon and benefited from her patronage. Virtually all the individuals he has depicted here are recognizable members of Parisian salon society, including Enlightenment writers Diderot, d'Alembert, and Rousseau. Lemonnier created the work in 1812 as a commission for the empress Josephine; thus it must be seen as an imaginative reconstruction of the salon, created several decades after it took place.

(*The First Reading at Madame Geoffrin's of Voltaire's Tragedy "L'Orphelin de la Chine,"* 1755, by Gabriel Lemonnier [1743–1824] [oil on canvas]/Musée National du Château de Malmaison, France/DEA/Gianni Dagli Orti/Getty Images)

QUESTIONS FOR ANALYSIS

1. Which of these people do you think is the hostess, Madame Geoffrin, and why? What can we learn about Geoffrin from this painting of the salon hosted in her home?
2. Given that the salon was a central institution of the Enlightenment, what does this painting tell you about who belonged to the Enlightenment movement? How would you describe attendees in terms of social status, gender, and age?
3. Why would government ministers and wealthy nobles wish to socialize on a regular basis with philosophes, who were critical of French politics and society? How does this image help you understand the way that Enlightenment ideas were perceived by the elite of society?

MAPPING THE PAST

MAP 19.1 The Partition of Poland, 1772–1795 In 1772 the threat of war between Russia and Austria arose over Russian gains from the Ottoman Empire. To satisfy desires for expansion without fighting, Prussia's Frederick the Great proposed dividing parts of Poland among Austria, Prussia, and Russia. In 1793 and 1795 the three powers partitioned the remainder, and Poland ceased to exist as an independent nation.

ANALYZING THE MAP Of the three powers that divided the kingdom of Poland, which benefited the most? How did the partition affect the geographical boundaries of each state, and what was the significance of these geographical boundaries? What border with the former Poland remained unchanged? Why do you think this was the case?

CONNECTIONS Why was Poland vulnerable to partition in the later half of the eighteenth century? What does the fact that a country could simply cease to exist on the map say about European politics at the time? Could such an event happen today? Why or why not?

named Emelian Pugachev. Although Pugachev was ultimately captured and executed, his rebellion shocked Russian rulers. After 1775 Catherine gave nobles absolute control of their serfs and extended serfdom into new areas. In 1785 she formally freed nobles from taxes and state service. Under Catherine the Russian nobility thus attained its most exalted position, and serfdom entered its most oppressive phase.

Catherine's third goal was territorial expansion. Her armies subjugated the last descendants of the Mongols and the Crimean Tartars and began the conquest of the Caucasus on the border between Europe

and Asia. Her greatest coup was the partition of Poland, which took place in stages from 1772 to 1795 (Map 19.1).

Joseph II (r. 1780–1790), the Austrian Habsburg emperor, was perhaps the most sincere proponent of enlightened absolutism. Joseph abolished serfdom in 1781, and in 1789 he decreed that peasants could pay landlords in cash rather than through compulsory labor. When Joseph died at forty-nine, the Habsburg empire was in turmoil. His brother Leopold II (r. 1790–1792) canceled Joseph's radical edicts in order to re-establish order.

Perhaps the best example of the limitations of enlightened absolutism is the debates surrounding the possible emancipation of the Jews. For the most part, Jews in Europe were confined to tiny, overcrowded ghettos; were excluded by law from most occupations; and could be ordered out of a kingdom at a moment's notice.

In the eighteenth century an Enlightenment movement known as the **Haskalah** emerged from within the European Jewish community, led by the Prussian philosopher Moses Mendelssohn (1729–1786). Christian and Jewish Enlightenment philosophers, including Mendelssohn, began to advocate for freedom and civil rights for European Jews. (See "Thinking Like a Historian: The Enlightenment Debate on Religious Tolerance," page 552.)

Arguments for tolerance won some ground, especially under Joseph II of Austria. Most monarchs, however, refused to entertain the idea of emancipation. In 1791 Catherine the Great established the Pale of Settlement, a territory encompassing modern-day Belarus, Lithuania, Latvia, Moldova, Ukraine, and parts of Poland, in which most Jews were required to live until the Russian Revolution of 1917.

The Pale of Settlement, 1791

Economic Change and the Atlantic World

How did economic and social change and the rise of Atlantic trade interact with Enlightenment ideas?

Enlightenment debates took place within a rapidly evolving material world. Agricultural reforms contributed to a rise in population that in turned fueled substantial economic growth in eighteenth-century Europe. A new public sphere emerged in the growing cities of Europe and its colonies in which people exchanged opinions in cafés, bookstores, and other spaces. A consumer revolution brought fashion and imported foods into the reach of common people for the first time.

These economic and social changes were fed by an increasingly integrated Atlantic economy that circulated finished European products, raw materials from the colonies, and enslaved people from Africa. Over time, the people, goods, and ideas that crisscrossed the ocean created distinctive Atlantic communities and identities.

Economic and Demographic Change

The seventeenth century saw important gains in agricultural productivity in northwestern Europe that slowly spread throughout the continent. Using new scientific techniques of observation and experimentation, a group of scientists, government officials, and a few big landowners devised agricultural practices and tools that raised crop yields dramatically, especially in England and the Netherlands. These included new forms of crop rotation, better equipment, and selective breeding of livestock. The controversial process of **enclosure**, fencing off common land to create privately owned fields, allowed a break with traditional methods but at the cost of reducing poor farmers' access to land.

Colonial plants also provided new sources of calories and nutrition. Introduced into Europe from the Americas—along with corn, squash, tomatoes, and many other useful plants—the potato provided an excellent new food source and offset the lack of fresh vegetables and fruits in common people's winter diet. The potato had become an important dietary supplement in much of Europe by the end of the eighteenth century.

Increases in agricultural productivity and better nutrition, combined with the disappearance of bubonic plague after 1720 and improvements in sewage and water supply, contributed to the tremendous growth of the European population in the eighteenth century. The explosion of population was a major phenomenon in all European countries, leading to a doubling of the number of Europeans between 1700 and 1835.

Population growth increased the number of rural workers with little or no land, and this in turn contributed to the development of industry in rural areas. The poor in the countryside increasingly needed to supplement their agricultural earnings with other types of work. **Cottage industry**, which consisted of manufacturing with hand tools in peasant cottages and work sheds, grew markedly in the eighteenth century, particularly in England and the Low Countries.

Haskalah A Jewish Enlightenment movement led by Prussian philosopher Moses Mendelssohn.

enclosure The controversial process of fencing off common land to create privately owned fields that increased agricultural production at the cost of reducing poor farmers' access to land.

cottage industry Manufacturing with hand tools in peasant cottages and work sheds, a form of economic activity that became important in eighteenth-century Europe.

The Enlightenment Debate on Religious Tolerance

Enlightenment philosophers questioned many aspects of European society, including political authority, social inequality, and imperialism. A major focus of their criticism was the dominance of the established church and the persecution of minority faiths. While many philosophers defended religious tolerance, they differed widely in their approaches to the issue.

1 **Moses Mendelssohn, "Reply to Lavater," 1769.** In 1769 Johann Caspar Lavater, a Swiss clergyman, called on Moses Mendelssohn to either refute proofs of Christianity publicly or submit to baptism. Mendelssohn's reply is both a call for toleration and an affirmation of his religious faith.

■ It is, of course, the natural obligation of every mortal to diffuse knowledge and virtue among his fellow men, and to do his best to extirpate their prejudices and errors. One might think, in this regard, that it was the duty of every man publicly to oppose the religious opinions that he considers mistaken. But not all prejudices are equally harmful, and hence the prejudices we may think we perceive among our fellow men must not all be treated in the same way. Some are directly contrary to the happiness of the human race. . . . These must be attacked outright by every friend of humanity. . . . Of this kind are all people's errors and prejudices that disturb their own or their fellows' peace and contentment and kill every seed of the true and the good in man before it can germinate. On the one hand, fanaticism, misanthropy, and the spirit of persecution, and on the other, frivolity, luxury, and libertinism.

Sometimes, however, the opinions of my fellow men, which in my belief are errors, belong to the higher theoretical principles which are too remote from practical life to do any direct harm; but, precisely because of their generality, they form the basis on which the nation that upholds them has built its moral and social system, and thus happen to be of great importance to this part of the human race. To oppose such doctrines in public, because we consider them prejudices, is to dig up the ground to see whether it is solid and secure, without providing any other support for the building that stands on it. Anyone who cares more for the good of humanity than for his own fame will be slow to voice his opinion about such prejudices, and will take care not to attack them outright without extreme caution.

2 **Voltaire, *Treatise on Toleration*, 1763.** Voltaire, the prominent French philosophe, began his *Treatise on Toleration* by recounting the infamous trial of Jean Calas. Although all the evidence pointed toward suicide, the judges concluded that Calas had killed his son in order to prevent him from converting to Catholicism, and Calas was brutally executed in 1762. For Voltaire, the Calas affair was a battle between fanaticism and reason, extremism and moderation.

■ Some fanatic in the crowd cried out that Jean Calas had hanged his son Marc Antoine. The cry was soon repeated on all sides; some adding that the deceased was to have abjured Protestantism on the following day, and that the family and young Lavaisse had strangled him out of hatred of the Catholic religion. In a moment all doubt had disappeared. The whole town was persuaded that it is a point of religion with the Protestants for a father and mother to kill their children when they wish to change their faith.

. . . There was not, and could not be, any evidence against the family; but a deluded religion took the place of proof. . . . [The judges] were confounded when the old man, expiring on the wheel, prayed God to witness his innocence, and begged him to pardon his judges.

The daughters were taken from the mother and put in a convent. The mother, almost sprinkled with the blood of her husband, her eldest son dead, the younger banished, deprived of her daughters and all her property, was alone in the world, without bread, without hope, dying of the intolerable misery. Certain persons, having carefully examined the circumstances of this horrible adventure, were so impressed that they urged the widow, who had retired into solitude, to go and demand justice at the feet of the throne. . . . She reached Paris almost at the point of death. She was astonished at her reception, at the help and the tears that were given to her.

At Paris reason dominates fanaticism, however powerful it be; in the provinces fanaticism almost always overcomes reason.

ANALYZING THE EVIDENCE

1. Based on these sources, what attitudes did eighteenth-century Europeans manifest toward religions other than their own? Were such attitudes always negative?
2. What justifications did Enlightenment philosophers use to argue in favor of religious tolerance? Were arguments in favor of religious tolerance necessarily antireligious?
3. Why did Judaism figure so prominently in debates about religious tolerance in eighteenth-century Europe? In what ways do you think Mendelssohn's experience as a Jew (Source 1) shaped his views on religious tolerance?

3 **Bernard Picart, "Jewish Meal During the Feast of the Tabernacles,"** from *Ceremonies and Customs of All the Peoples of the World*, 1724. Eighteenth-century travel literature provided eager audiences with images and descriptions of religious practices from around the world. This image emphasizes the prosperity and warm family relations of a Jewish family enjoying a holiday meal, echoing the tolerant mind-set of the author.

(Heritage Images/Hulton Archives/Getty Images)

4 **Gotthold Ephraim Lessing, *Nathan the Wise*, 1779.** In this excerpt from *Nathan the Wise*, a play by German writer Gotthold Ephraim Lessing, the sultan Saladin asks a Jewish merchant named Nathan to tell him which is the true religion: Islam, Christianity, or Judaism. Nathan responds with a parable about a man who promised to leave the same opal ring, a guarantor of divine favor, to each of his three beloved sons. He then had two exact replicas of the ring made so that each son would believe he had inherited the precious relic.

■ **NATHAN:** Scarce was the father dead.
When each one with his ring appears
Claiming each the headship of the house.
Inspections, quarrelling, and complaints ensue;
But all in vain, the veritable ring
Was not distinguishable —
(*After a pause, during which he expects the Sultan's answer*)
Almost as indistinguishable as to us,
Is now — the true religion.

SALADIN: What? Is that meant as answer to my question?

NATHAN: 'Tis meant but to excuse myself, because
I lack the boldness to discriminate between the rings,
Which the father by express intent had made
So that they might not be distinguished.

SALADIN: The rings! Don't play with me.
I thought the faiths which I have named

Were easily distinguishable,
Even to their raiment, even to meat and drink.

NATHAN: But yet not as regards their proofs:
For do not all rest upon history, written or traditional?
And history can also be accepted
Only on faith and trust. Is it not so?
Now, whose faith and confidence do we least misdoubt?
That of our relatives? Of those whose flesh and blood we are,
Of those who from our childhood
Have lavished on us proofs of love,
Who ne'er deceived us, unless 'twere wholesome for us so?
How can I place less faith in my forefathers
Than you in yours? or the reverse?
Can I desire of you to load your ancestors with lies,
So that you contradict not mine? Or the reverse?
And to the Christian the same applies.
Is that not so?

PUTTING IT ALL TOGETHER

Using the sources above, along with what you have learned in class and in this chapter, compare and contrast the views on religious toleration presented in the sources. On what would the authors of these works have agreed? How did their arguments in favor of toleration differ? What explanation can you offer for the differences you note?

Sources: (1) Ritchie Robertson, ed., *The German-Jewish Dialogue: An Anthology of Literary Texts, 1749–1993* (New York: Oxford University Press, 1999), 308 words from pp. 41–42. Used by permission of Oxford University Press; (2) Voltaire, *A Treatise on Toleration and Other Essays*, trans. Joseph McCabe (Amherst, N.Y.: Prometheus Books, 1994), pp. 147–149, 152–153; (4) Crane Brinton, ed., *The Portable Age of Reason Reader* (New York: Viking Press, 1956), pp. 383–389.

Cottage Industry Many steps went into making textiles. This 1791 illustration of the different tasks involved in spinning yarn is based on the artist's observations of linen manufacture in the north of Ireland. The yarn was spun on the wheel and then wound on the clock reel to measure it into "hanks" of set length. After being boiled in a pot over the fire and dried, the yarn was ready for weaving. (The British Library, London, UK/ © British Library Board. All Rights Reserved/Bridgeman Images)

Despite the rise in rural industry, life in the countryside was insufficient to support the rapidly growing population. Many people thus left their small villages to join the tide of migration to the cities, especially after 1750. London and Paris swelled to over five hundred thousand people, while Naples and Amsterdam had populations of more than one hundred thousand. It was in the bustling public life of these cities that the Enlightenment emerged and took root.

The Atlantic Economy

European economic growth in the eighteenth century was spurred by the expansion of trade across the Atlantic Ocean. Commercial exchange in the Atlantic is often referred to as the triangle trade, designating a three-way transport of goods: European commodities to Africa; enslaved Africans to the colonies; and colonial goods back to Europe. This model highlights some of the most important flows of trade but significantly oversimplifies the picture. For example, a brisk intercolonial trade existed, with the Caribbean slave colonies importing food from other American colonies in exchange for sugar and slaves (Map 19.2).

Moreover, the Atlantic economy was inextricably linked to trade with the Indian and Pacific Oceans. The rising economic and political power of Europeans in the eighteenth century thus drew on the connections they established between the long-standing Asian and Atlantic trade worlds.

Over the course of the eighteenth century the economies of European nations bordering the Atlantic Ocean relied more and more on colonial exports. In England sales to the mainland colonies of North America and the West Indian sugar islands soared from £500,000 to £4 million (Figure 19.1). Exports to England's colonies in Ireland and India also rose substantially from 1700 to 1800.

At the core of this Atlantic world was the misery and profit of the Atlantic slave trade (see "The African Slave Trade" in Chapter 20). The brutal practice intensified dramatically after 1700 and especially after 1750 with the growth of trade and the increase in demand for slave-produced goods. English dominance of the slave trade provided another source of large profits to the home country. (See "Global Viewpoints: Malachy Postlethwayt and Olaudah Equiano on the Abolition of Slavery," page 557.)

The French also profited enormously from colonial trade in the eighteenth century, even after losing their vast North American territories to England in 1763. The Caribbean colonies of Saint-Domingue (modern-day Haiti), Martinique, and Guadeloupe provided immense fortunes from slave-based plantation agriculture. The wealth generated from colonial trade fostered the confidence of the merchant classes in Nantes, Bordeaux, and other large cities, and merchants soon joined other elite groups clamoring for more political power.

The third major player in the Atlantic economy, Spain, also saw its colonial fortunes improve during the eighteenth century. Its mercantilist goals were boosted by a recovery in silver production. Spanish territory in North America expanded significantly in the second half of the eighteenth century. At the close of the Seven Years' War (1756–1763) (see "The Seven Years' War" in Chapter 22), Spain gained Louisiana from the French, and its influence extended westward all the way to northern California through the efforts of Spanish missionaries and ranchers.

Conflict among European powers in the late seventeenth century led to the rise of privateers in the

MAP 19.2 The Atlantic Economy, 1701 The growth of trade encouraged both economic development and military conflict in the Atlantic basin. Four continents were linked together by the exchange of goods and slaves.

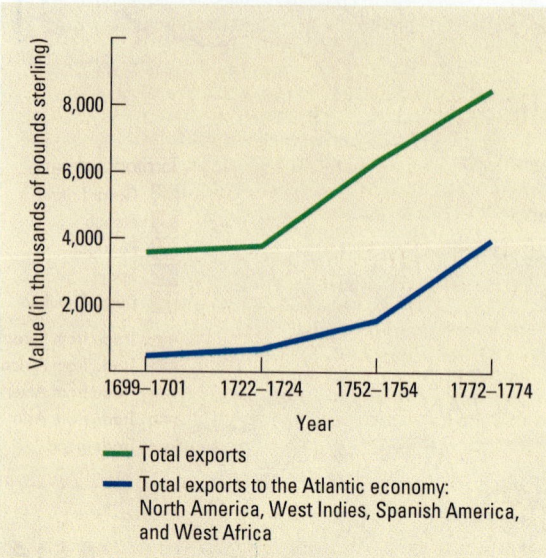

FIGURE 19.1 Exports of English Manufactured Goods, 1700–1774 While trade between England and Europe stagnated after 1700, English exports to Africa and the Americas boomed and greatly stimulated English economic development.

(Source: Data from R. Davis, "English Foreign Trade, 1700–1774," *Economic History Review*, 2nd ser., 15 [1962]: 302–303.)

Caribbean and elsewhere in the Atlantic world; these were ships sanctioned by their home government to attack and pillage those of enemy powers. Privateers operated with some semblance of legality, whereas the many pirates active in the Caribbean were outlaws subject to brutal punishment. The late seventeenth and early eighteenth centuries constituted the "golden age" of piracy, drawing poor European sailors and escaped slaves into the dangerous but lucrative activity.

Urban Life and the Public Sphere

Urban life in the Atlantic world gave rise to new institutions and practices that encouraged the spread of Enlightenment thought. From about 1700 to 1789 the production and consumption of books grew significantly. Lending libraries, bookshops, cafés, salons, and Masonic lodges provided spaces in which urban people debated new ideas. Together these spaces and institutions helped create a new **public sphere** that celebrated open debate informed by critical reason.

The public sphere was an idealized space where members of society came together to discuss the social, economic, and political issues of the day. Although Enlightenment thinkers addressed their ideas to educated and prosperous readers, even poor and illiterate people learned about such issues as they were debated at the marketplace or tavern.

Economic growth in the second half of the eighteenth century also enabled a significant rise in the consumption of finished goods and new foodstuffs that historians have labeled a "consumer revolution." A boom in textile production and cheap reproductions of luxury items meant that the common people could afford to follow fashion for the first time. Colonial trade made previously expensive and rare foodstuffs, such as sugar, tea, coffee, chocolate, and tobacco, widely available.

Culture and Community in the Atlantic World

As contacts among the Atlantic coasts of the Americas, Africa, and Europe became more frequent, and as European settlements grew into well-established colonies, new identities and communities emerged. The term *Creole* referred to people of Spanish or other European ancestry born in the Americas. Wealthy Creoles throughout the Atlantic colonies prided themselves on following European ways of life.

Over time, however, the colonial elite came to feel that their circumstances gave them different interests and characteristics from people of their home countries. Creoles adopted native foods, like chocolate, chili peppers, and squash, and sought relief from tropical disease in native remedies. Also, they began to turn against restrictions from their home countries: Creole traders and planters, along with their counterparts in English colonies, increasingly resented the regulations and taxes imposed by colonial bureaucrats, and such resentment would eventually lead to revolutions against colonial powers (see Chapter 22).

Not all Europeans in the colonies were wealthy or well educated. Numerous poor and lower-middle-class whites worked as clerks, shopkeepers, craftsmen, and laborers. With the exception of the English colonies of North America, white Europeans made up a minority of the population, outnumbered by indigenous peoples in Spanish America and, in the Caribbean, by the growing numbers of enslaved people of African descent. Since most European migrants were men, much of the colonial population of the Atlantic world descended from unions—forced or through consent—of European men and indigenous or African women. Colonial attempts to identify and control racial categories greatly influenced developing Enlightenment thought on racial differences.

In the Spanish and French Caribbean, as in Brazil, many slave masters acknowledged and freed their mixed-race children, leading to sizable populations of free people of color. In the second half of the eighteenth century the prosperity of some free people of

public sphere An idealized intellectual space that emerged in Europe during the Enlightenment. Here, the public came together to discuss important social, economic, and political issues.

Malachy Postlethwayt and Olaudah Equiano on the Abolition of Slavery

As Britain came to dominate transatlantic commerce during the eighteenth century, debate arose over the morality of the slave trade and the country's involvement in it. Malachy Postlethwayt, an economist, rejected criticism of slavery by arguing that African nations treated their subjects much worse than slave traders did and that the benefits of Christianity by far outstripped any disadvantages slaves might endure. In his famous autobiography, former slave Olaudah Equiano (oh-lah-OO-dah ay-kwee-AH-noh) emphasized the cruelties of slavery. He argued, against authors like Postlethwayt, that trade with free peoples in Africa promised much more economic benefit to Britain than did slavery.

Malachy Postlethwayt, *The National and Private Advantages of the African Trade Considered*

■ Many are prepossessed against this trade, thinking it a barbarous, inhuman and unlawful traffic for a Christian country to trade in Blacks; to which I would beg leave to observe; that though the odious appellation of slaves is annexed to this trade, it being called by some the slave-trade, yet it does not appear from the best enquiry I have been able to make, that the state of those people is changed for the worse, by being servants to our British planters in America; they are certainly treated with great lenity and humanity: and as the improvement of the planter's estates depends upon due care being taken of their healths and lives, I cannot but think their condition is much bettered to what it was in their own country.

Besides, the negro princes in Africa, 'tis well known, are in perpetual war with each other, and since before they had this method of disposing of their prisoners of war to Christian merchants, they were wont not only to be applied to inhuman sacrifices, but to extreme torture and barbarity, their transportation must certainly be a melioration [improvement] of their condition; provided living in a civilized Christian country, is better than living among savages; Nay, if life be preferable to torment and cruel death, their state cannot, with any color or reason, be presumed to be worsened.

Olaudah Equiano, Appeal for the Abolition of Slavery

■ Tortures, murder, and every other imaginable barbarity and iniquity, are practiced upon the poor slaves with impunity. I hope the great slave trade will be abolished. I pray it may be an event at hand. The great body of manufacturers, uniting in the cause, will considerably facilitate and expedite it; and as I have already stated, it is most substantially their interest and advantage, and as such the nation's at large (except those persons concerned in the manufacturing neck yokes, collars, chains, handcuffs, leg bolts, drags, thumb screws, iron muzzles, and coffins; cats, scourges, and other instruments of torture used in the slave trade). In a short time one sentiment will alone prevail, from motives of interest as well as justice and humanity. . . . If the blacks were permitted to remain in their own country, they would double themselves every fifteen years. In proportion to such increase will be the demand for manufactures. Cotton and indigo grow spontaneously in most parts of Africa; a consideration this of no small consequence to the manufacturing towns of Great Britain. It opens a most immense, glorious and happy prospect — the clothing, &c. of a continent ten thousand miles in circumference, and immensely rich in productions of every denomination in return for manufactures.

QUESTIONS FOR ANALYSIS

1. What contrast does Postlethwayt draw between the treatment of African people under slavery and in their home countries? What conclusion does he draw from this contrast?
2. To whom does Equiano address his appeal for abolition of the slave trade? What economic reasons does he provide for trading goods rather than slaves with Africa?

Sources: Malachy Postlethwayt, *The National and Private Advantages of the African Trade Considered* (London: Jon and Paul Knapton, 1746), pp. 4–5; Olaudah Equiano, *The Interesting Narrative of the Life of Olaudah Equiano*, 2d ed., ed. Robert J. Allison (Boston: Bedford/St. Martin's, 2007), pp. 194–195.

---

color brought a backlash from the white population of Saint-Domingue in the form of new race laws prohibiting nonwhites from marrying whites and forcing them to adopt distinctive attire. In the British colonies of the Caribbean and the southern mainland, by contrast, masters tended to leave their mixed-race progeny in slavery, maintaining a stark discrepancy between free whites and enslaved people of color.[5]

The identities inspired by the Atlantic world were equally complex. In some ways, the colonial encounter helped create new and more fixed forms of identity. Inhabitants of distinct regions of European nations came to see themselves as "Spanish" or "English" when they crossed the Atlantic; similarly, their colonial governments imposed the identity of "Indian" and "African" on peoples with vastly different linguistic, cultural,

The Consumer Revolution From the mid-eighteenth century on, the cities of western Europe witnessed a new proliferation of consumer goods. Items once limited to the wealthy few — such as fans, watches, snuffboxes, umbrellas, ornamental containers, and teapots — were now reproduced in cheaper versions for middling and ordinary people. The fashion for wide hoopskirts was so popular that the armrests of the chairs of the day, known as Louis XV chairs (left), were specially designed to accommodate them. Enlightenment fascination with Chinese culture was reflected in the tremendous popularity of *chinoiserie*, objects (such as the plate shown here) decorated in imitation of Chinese motifs and techniques. (chair: Louvre, Paris, France/© RMN–Grand Palais/Art Resource, NY; plate: Musée des Beaux-Arts, Moulins, France/Bridgeman Images)

and political origins. The result was the creation of new Creole communities that melded cultural and social elements of various groups of origin with the new European cultures.

Mixed-race people represented complex mixtures of indigenous, African, and European ancestry, so their status was ambiguous. Spanish administrators applied purity of blood (*limpieza de sangre*) laws — originally used to exclude Jews and Muslims during the reconquista — to indigenous and African peoples. Some mixed-race people sought to enter Creole society and obtain its many official and unofficial privileges by passing as white. Over time, where they existed in any number, mestizos and free people of color established their own communities and social hierarchies based on wealth, family connections, occupation, and skin color. (See "Individuals in Society: Rebecca Protten," at right.)

Restricted from owning land and holding many occupations in Europe, Jews were eager participants in the new Atlantic economy and established a network of mercantile communities along its trade routes. As in the Old World, Jews in European colonies faced discrimination. Jews were considered to be white Europeans and thus ineligible to be slaves, but they did not enjoy equal status with Christians. The status of Jews adds one more element to the complexity of Atlantic identities.

The Atlantic Enlightenment

The colonies of British North America were deeply influenced by the Scottish Enlightenment, with its emphasis on pragmatic approaches to the problems of life. Following the Scottish model, leaders in the colonies adopted a moderate, "commonsense" version of the Enlightenment that emphasized self-improvement and ethical conduct. In most cases, this version of the Enlightenment was perfectly compatible with religion and was chiefly spread through the growing colleges and universities of the colonies.

Northern Enlightenment thinkers often depicted Spain and its American colonies as the epitome of the superstition and barbarity they contested. Nonetheless, the dynasty that took power in Spain in the early eighteenth century followed its own course of enlightened absolutism, just like its counterparts in the rest of Europe. Under King Carlos III (r. 1759–1788) and his son Carlos IV (r. 1788–1808), Spanish administrators attempted to strengthen colonial rule and improve government efficiency. Enlightened administrators debated the status of indigenous peoples and whether it would be better for these peoples if they maintained their distinct legal status or were integrated into Spanish society.

Educated Creoles were well aware of the new currents of thought, and the universities, newspapers, and

Rebecca Protten

IN THE MID-1720s A YOUNG GIRL WHO CAME TO BE known as Rebecca traveled from Antigua to the small Danish sugar colony of St. Thomas, today part of the U.S. Virgin Islands. Eighty-five percent of St. Thomas's four thousand inhabitants were of African descent, almost all enslaved.

Surviving documents refer to Rebecca as a "mulatto," indicating a mixed European and African ancestry. A wealthy Dutch-speaking planter named van Beverhout purchased the girl as a servant, sparing her work in the grueling and deadly sugar fields. Rebecca won the family's favor, and they taught her to read, write, and speak Dutch. They also shared with her their Protestant faith and took the unusual step of freeing her.

As a free woman, she continued to work for the van Beverhouts and to study the Bible and spread its message of spiritual freedom. In 1736 she met missionaries for the Moravian Church, a German-Protestant sect that emphasized emotion and community in worship and devoted its mission work to the enslaved peoples of the Caribbean. The missionaries were struck by Rebecca's piety and her potential to assist their work. As one wrote: "She researches diligently in the Scriptures, loves the Savior, and does much good for other Negro women because she does not simply walk alone with her good ways but instructs them in the Scriptures as well." A letter Rebecca sent to Moravian women in Germany declared: "Oh! Help me to praise him, who has pulled me out of the darkness. I will take up his cross with all my heart and follow the example of his poor life."*

Rebecca soon took charge of the Moravians' female missionary work. Every Sunday and every evening after work, she would walk for miles to lead meetings with enslaved and free black women. The meetings consisted of reading and writing lessons, prayers, hymns, a sermon, and individual discussions in which she encouraged her new sisters in their spiritual growth.

In 1738 Rebecca married a German Moravian missionary, Matthaus Freundlich, a rare but not illegal case of mixed marriage. The same year, her husband bought a plantation, with slaves, to serve as the headquarters of their mission work. The Moravians—and presumably Rebecca herself—wished to spread Christian faith among slaves and improve their treatment, but did not oppose the institution of slavery itself.

Authorities nonetheless feared that baptized and literate slaves would agitate for freedom, and they imprisoned Rebecca and Matthaus. Only the unexpected arrival of German aristocrat and Moravian leader Count Zinzendorf saved the couple. Exhausted, they left for Germany in 1741, but Matthaus and the couple's young daughter died soon after their arrival.

A portrait of Rebecca Protten with her second husband and their daughter, Anna-Maria. (Courtesy of Jon F. Sensbach. Used by permission of the Moravian Archives [Unity Archives, Herrnhut, Germany], GS-393.)

In Marienborn, a German center of the Moravian faith, Rebecca encountered other black Moravians, who lived in equality alongside their European brethren. In 1746 she married another missionary, Christian Jacob Protten, son of a Danish sailor and, on his mother's side, grandson of a West African king. She and another female missionary from St. Thomas were ordained as deaconesses, probably making them the first women of color to be ordained in the Western Christian Church.

In 1763 Rebecca and her husband set out for her husband's birthplace, the Danish slave fort at Christiansborg (in what is now Accra, Ghana) to establish a school for mixed-race children. Her husband died in 1769, leaving Rebecca a widow once more. She died in obscurity near Christiansborg in 1780.

QUESTIONS FOR ANALYSIS

1. Why did Moravian missionaries assign such an important leadership role to Rebecca? What particular attributes did she offer?
2. Why did Moravians, including Rebecca, accept the institution of slavery instead of fighting to end it?
3. What does Rebecca's story teach us about the Atlantic world of the mid-eighteenth century? What might a philosophe have to say about her life story and its relationship to the ideals of the Enlightenment?

*Quotations from Jon F. Sensbach, *Rebecca's Revival: Creating Black Christianity in the Atlantic World* (Cambridge, Mass.: Harvard University Press, 2006), pp. 61, 63.

salons of Spanish America produced their own reform ideas. As in other European colonies, one effect of Enlightenment thought was to encourage Creoles to criticize the policies of the mother country and aspire toward greater autonomy.

Chapter Summary

Decisive breakthroughs in astronomy and physics in the seventeenth century demolished the medieval synthesis of Aristotelian philosophy and Christian theology. The impact of these scientific breakthroughs on intellectual life was enormous, nurturing a new critical attitude in many disciplines. In addition, an international scientific community arose, and state-sponsored academies, which were typically closed to women, advanced scientific research.

Believing that all aspects of life were open to debate and skepticism, Enlightenment thinkers asked challenging questions about religious tolerance, political power, and racial and sexual difference. Enlightenment thinkers drew inspiration from the new peoples and cultures encountered by Europeans and devised new ideas about race as a scientific and biological category. The ideas of the Enlightenment inspired absolutist rul-

ers in central and eastern Europe, but real reforms were limited.

In the second half of the eighteenth century agricultural reforms helped produce tremendous population growth. Economic growth and urbanization favored the spread of Enlightenment thought by producing a public sphere in which ideas could be debated. The expansion of transatlantic trade made economic growth possible, as did the lowering of prices on colonial goods due to the growth of slave labor. Atlantic trade involved the exchange of commodities among Europe, Africa, and the Americas, but it was also linked with trade in the Indian and Pacific Oceans. The movement of people and ideas across the Atlantic helped shape the identities of colonial inhabitants.

NOTES

1. Quoted in G. L. Mosse et al., eds., *Europe in Review* (Chicago: Rand McNally, 1964), p. 156.
2. D. E. Mungello, *The Great Encounter of China and the West, 1500–1800*, 2d ed. (Lanham, Md.: Rowman & Littlefield, 2005), p. 98.
3. Quoted in Emmanuel Chukwudi Eze, ed., *Race and the Enlightenment: A Reader* (Oxford: Blackwell, 1997), p. 33.
4. Aurora Wolfgang, *Gender and Voice in the French Novel, 1730–1782* (Aldershot, U.K.: Ashgate, 2004), p. 8.
5. Orlando Patterson, *Slavery and Social Death* (Cambridge, Mass.: Harvard University Press, 1982), p. 255.

CONNECTIONS

Hailed as the origin of modern thought, the Scientific Revolution must also be seen as a product of its past. With curriculum drawn from Islamic cultural achievements, medieval universities gave rise to important new scholarship in mathematics and natural philosophy. In turn, the ambition and wealth of Renaissance patrons nurtured intellectual curiosity and encouraged scholarly research and foreign exploration. Natural philosophers pioneered new methods of explaining and observing nature while drawing on centuries-old traditions of astrology, alchemy, and magic. A desire to control and profit from empire led the Spanish, followed by their European rivals, to explore and catalogue the flora and fauna of their American colonies. These efforts resulted in new frameworks in natural history.

Enlightenment ideas of the eighteenth century were a similar blend of past and present, progressive and traditional, inward-looking and cosmopolitan. Enlightenment thinkers advocated universal rights and liberties but also preached the biological inferiority of non-Europeans and women. Their principles often served as much to bolster absolutist regimes as to inspire revolutionaries to fight for human rights.

New notions of progress and social improvement would drive Europeans to embark on world-changing revolutions in politics and industry (see Chapters 22 and 23) at the end of the eighteenth century. These revolutions provided the basis for modern democracy and unprecedented scientific advancement. Yet some critics have seen a darker side. For them, the mastery over nature enabled by the Scientific Revolution now threatens to overwhelm the earth's fragile equilibrium, and the Enlightenment belief in the universal application of reason can lead to intolerance of other people's spiritual, cultural, and political values.

As the era of European exploration and conquest gave way to empire building, the eighteenth century witnessed increased consolidation of global markets and bitter competition among Europeans. The eighteenth-century Atlantic world thus tied the shores of Europe, the Americas, and Africa in a web of commercial and human exchange, including the tragedy of slavery, discussed in Chapter 20. The Atlantic world maintained strong ties with trade in the Pacific and the Indian Ocean.

CHAPTER 19 Review and Explore

Identify Key Terms

Identify and explain the significance of each item below.

Copernican hypothesis (p. 536)

law of inertia (p. 537)

law of universal gravitation (p. 537)

empiricism (p. 539)

Enlightenment (p. 541)

sensationalism (p. 542)

philosophes (p. 542)

deism (p. 543)

general will (p. 543)

economic liberalism (p. 544)

salons (p. 548)

enlightened absolutism (p. 548)

Haskalah (p. 551)

enclosure (p. 551)

cottage industry (p. 551)

public sphere (p. 556)

Review the Main Ideas

Answer the focus questions from each section of the chapter.

1. What revolutionary discoveries were made in the sixteenth and seventeenth centuries, and what was their global context? (p. 534)

2. What intellectual and social changes occurred as a result of the Scientific Revolution? (p. 538)

3. How did the Enlightenment emerge, and what were major currents of Enlightenment thought? (p. 541)

4. How did Enlightenment thinkers address issues of cultural and social difference and political power? (p. 545)

5. How did economic and social change and the rise of Atlantic trade interact with Enlightenment ideas? (p. 551)

Make Comparisons and Connections

Analyze the larger developments and continuities within and across chapters.

1. How did medieval and Renaissance developments contribute to the Scientific Revolution? Should the Scientific Revolution be seen as a sharp break with the past or as the culmination of long-term, gradual change?

2. The eighteenth century was the period of the European Enlightenment, which celebrated tolerance and human liberty. Paradoxically, it was also the era of a tremendous increase in slavery, which brought suffering and death to millions. How can you explain this paradox?

3. How did developments in population, global trade, and intellectual life affect each other in the eighteenth century? How and why did developments in one region affect other regions?

TIMELINE

EUROPE			
	← ca. 1500–1700 Scientific Revolution		
	ca. 1600–1789 French salons led by elite women		
MIDDLE EAST	← 1453 Ottoman conquest of Constantinople (Ch. 17)		
	← 1501–1722 Safavid Empire in Persia (Ch. 17)		
EAST ASIA	1582–1610 Jesuit Matteo Ricci in China (Ch. 21)	1644–1911 Manchus establish Qing Dynasty in China (Ch. 21)	
AFRICA			
AMERICAS			
AUSTRALIA			
	1600	1650	1700

Suggested Resources

BOOKS

Allen, Robert, et al., eds. *Living Standards in the Past: New Perspectives on Well-Being in Asia and Europe.* 2004. Offers rich comparative perspectives on population growth and living standards among common people

Cañizares-Esguerra, Jorge. *Nature, Empire, and Nation: Explorations of the History of Science in the Iberian World.* 2006. Explores the role of Spain and Spanish America in the development of science in the early modern period.

Curran, Andrew S. *The Anatomy of Blackness: Science and Slavery in an Age of Enlightenment.* 2011. Examines how Enlightenment thinkers transformed traditional thinking about people of African descent into ideas about biological racial difference.

Delbourgo, James, and Nicholas Dew, eds. *Science and Empire in the Atlantic World.* 2008. A collection of essays examining the relationship between the Scientific Revolution and the imperial expansion of European powers across the Atlantic.

Ellis, Markman. *The Coffee House: A Cultural History.* 2004. An engaging study of the rise of the coffeehouse and its impact on European cultural and social life.

Manning, Susan, and Francis D. Cogliano. *The Atlantic Enlightenment.* 2008. A series of essays examining the exchange of Enlightenment ideas, authors, and texts across the Atlantic Ocean.

Massie, Robert K. *Catherine the Great: Portrait of a Woman.* 2011. Recounts the life story of Catherine, from obscure German princess to enlightened ruler of Russia.

McMahon, Darrin M. *Happiness: A History.* 2006. Discusses how worldly pleasure became valued as a duty of individuals and societies in the Enlightenment.

Messbarger, Rebecca. *The Lady Anatomist: The Life and Work of Anna Morandi Manzolini.* 2010. The biography of an Italian woman artist and scientist whose life reflected the opportunities and constraints for eighteenth-century women.

Robertson, John. *The Case for the Enlightenment: Scotland and Naples, 1680–1760.* 2005. A comparative study of Enlightenment movements in Scotland and Naples, emphasizing commonalities between these two small kingdoms on the edges of Europe.

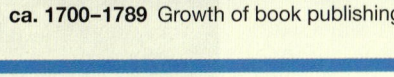

ca. 1700–1789 Growth of book publishing

ca. 1690–1789 Enlightenment

1740–1786 Reign of Frederick the Great of Prussia

1762–1796 Reign of Catherine the Great of Russia

◆ **1765** Philosophes publish *Encyclopedia: The Rational Dictionary of the Sciences, the Arts, and the Crafts*

◆ **1791** Establishment of the Pale of Settlement

1780–1790 Reign of Joseph II of Austria

1789–1807 Ottoman ruler Selim III introduces reforms **(Ch. 25)**

1738–1756 Major famine in West Africa **(Ch. 20)**

1756–1763 Seven Years' War **(Ch. 22)**

◆ **1770** Cook claims land in Australia for Britain **(Ch. 26)**

1780–1820 Peak of transatlantic slave trade **(Ch. 20)**

| 1750 | 1800 | 1850 |

Shapin, Steven. *The Scientific Revolution.* 1996. A concise and well-informed general introduction to the Scientific Revolution.

Sorkin, David. *Moses Mendelssohn and the Religious Enlightenment.* 1996. A brilliant study of the Jewish philosopher and of the role of religion in the Enlightenment.

DOCUMENTARIES

Blackbeard: Terror at Sea (National Geographic, 2006). A documentary recounting the exploits of the most famous eighteenth-century pirate.

Galileo's Battle for the Heavens (PBS, 2002). Recounts the story of Galileo's struggle with the Catholic Church over his astronomical discoveries, featuring re-enactments of key episodes in his life.

Newton's Dark Secrets (PBS, 2005). Explores Isaac Newton's fundamental scientific discoveries alongside his religious faith and practice of alchemy.

FEATURE FILMS AND TELEVISION DRAMAS

Amazing Grace (Michael Apted, 2006). An idealistic Briton's struggle to end his country's involvement in the slave trade alongside allies Olaudah Equiano and a repentant former slave-ship captain.

Catherine the Great (A&E, 1995). A made-for-television movie starring Catherine Zeta-Jones as the German princess who becomes Catherine the Great.

Ridicule (Patrice Leconte, 1996). When a provincial nobleman travels to the French court in the 1780s to present a project to drain a malarial swamp in his district, his naïve Enlightenment ideals incur the ridicule of decadent courtiers.

WEBSITES

The Bubble Project. A website presenting historical and modern resources on the South Sea Bubble of 1720, one of the first major international financial crises. **david-mcneil.ca/bubble/bubble.html**

The Encyclopedia of Diderot & d'Alembert Collaborative Translation Project. A collaborative project to translate the *Encyclopedia* edited by Denis Diderot and Jean le Rond d'Alembert into English, with searchable entries submitted by students and scholars and vetted by experts. **quod.lib.umich.edu/d/did/**

Mapping the Republic of Letters. A site hosted by Stanford University showcasing projects using mapping software to create spatial visualizations based on correspondence and travel of members of the eighteenth-century Republic of Letters. **republicofletters.stanford.edu/**

20

Africa and the World
1400–1800

A frican states and societies of the early modern period — from the fifteenth through the eighteenth centuries — included a wide variety of languages, cultures, political systems, and levels of economic development. Kingdoms and stateless societies coexisted throughout Africa, from small Senegambian villages to the Songhai (song-GAH-ee) kingdom and its renowned city of Timbuktu in West Africa, and from the Christian state of Ethiopia to the independent Swahili city-states along the East Africa coast. By the fifteenth century Africans had developed a steady rhythm of contact and exchange. Across the vast Sahara, trade goods and knowledge passed back and forth from West Africa to North Africa, and beyond to Europe and the Middle East. The same was true in East Africa, where Indian Ocean traders touched up and down the African coast to deliver goods from Arabia, India, and Asia and to pick up the ivory, gold, spices, and other products representing Africa's rich natural wealth. In the interior as well, extensive trading networks linked African societies across the vast continent.

Modern European intrusion into Africa beginning in the fifteenth century profoundly affected these diverse societies and ancient trading networks. The intrusion led to the transatlantic slave trade, one of the greatest forced migrations in world history, through which Africa made a substantial, though involuntary, contribution to the building of the West's industrial civilization. In the seventeenth century an increasing desire for sugar in Europe resulted in an increasing demand for slave labor in South America and the West Indies, where sugar was produced. In the eighteenth century Western technological changes created a demand for cotton and other crops that required extensive human labor, thus intensifying the West's "need" for African slaves.

Hip Ornament: Portuguese Face, 16th–19th century. Brass, iron. Gift of Mr. and Mrs. Klaus G. Perls, 1991 (1991.162.9)/
The Metropolitan Museum of Art, New York/Image copyright © The Metropolitan Museum of Art/Image source: Art Resource, NY

Waist Pendant of Benin Worn by Royalty

European intrusion in Africa during the early modern period deeply affected the diverse societies of Africa. The facial features, the beard, and the ruffled collar on this Edo peoples' artifact dating from the sixteenth to the nineteenth centuries are clearly Portuguese, but the braided hair is distinctly African, probably signifying royalty.

CHAPTER PREVIEW

WEST AFRICA IN THE FIFTEENTH AND SIXTEENTH CENTURIES

What types of economic, social, and political structures were found in the kingdoms and states along the west coast and in the Sudan?

CROSS-CULTURAL ENCOUNTERS ALONG THE EAST AFRICAN COAST

How did the arrival of Europeans and other foreign cultures affect the East African coast, and how did Ethiopia and the Swahili city-states respond to these incursions?

THE AFRICAN SLAVE TRADE

What role did slavery play in African societies before the transatlantic slave trade began, and what was the effect of European involvement?

West Africa in the Fifteenth and Sixteenth Centuries

What types of economic, social, and political structures were found in the kingdoms and states along the west coast and in the Sudan?

In mid-fifteenth-century Africa, Benin (buh-NEEN) and a number of other kingdoms flourished along the two-thousand-mile west coast between Senegambia and the northeastern shore of the Gulf of Guinea. Further inland, in the region of the Sudan (soo-DAN), the kingdoms of Songhai, Kanem-Bornu (KAH-nuhm BOR-noo), and Hausaland benefited from the trans-Saharan caravan trade, which along with goods brought Islamic culture to the region. Stateless societies such as those in the region of Senegambia (modern-day Senegal and the Gambia) existed alongside these more centralized states. Despite their political differences and whether they were agricultural, pastoral, or a mixture of both, West African cultures all faced the challenges presented by famine, disease, and the slave trade.

The West Coast: Senegambia and Benin

The Senegambian states possessed a homogeneous culture and a common history. For centuries Senegambia—named for the Senegal and Gambia Rivers—served as an important entrepôt for desert caravan contact with North African and Middle Eastern Islamic civilizations (Map 20.1). Through the transatlantic slave trade, Senegambia came into contact with Europe and the Americas. Thus Senegambia felt the impact of Islamic culture to the north and of European influences from the maritime West.

The Senegambian peoples spoke Wolof, Serer, and Pulaar, which all belong to the West African language group. Both the Wolof-speakers and the Serer-speakers had clearly defined social classes: royalty, nobility, warriors, peasants, low-caste artisans such as blacksmiths and leatherworkers, and enslaved persons. The enslaved class consisted of individuals who were pawned for debt, house servants who could not be sold, and people who were acquired through war or purchase. Senegambian slavery varied from society to society. In some

The Oba of Benin The oba's palace walls were decorated with bronze plaques that date from about the sixteenth to eighteenth centuries. This plaque vividly conveys the oba's power, majesty, and authority. The two attendants holding his arms also imply that the oba needs the support of his people. The oba's legs are mudfish, which represent fertility, peace, well-being, and prosperity, but their elongation, suggesting electric eels, relates the oba's terrifying and awesome power to the eel's jolting shock. (National Museum, Lagos, Nigeria/ photo: André Held/akg-images)

MAPPING THE PAST

MAP 20.1 West African Societies, ca. 1500–1800 The coastal region of West Africa witnessed the rise of a number of kingdoms in the sixteenth century.

ANALYZING THE MAP What geographical features defined each of the kingdoms shown here? Consider rivers, lakes, oceans, deserts, and forests. How might they have affected the size and shape of these kingdoms?

CONNECTIONS Compare this map to the small map on page 581 called "The Slave Coast of West Africa." Consider the role that rivers and other geographical factors played in the development of the West African slave trade. Why were Luanda and Benguela the logical Portuguese sources for slaves?

places slaves were considered chattel property and were treated as harshly as they would be later in the Western Hemisphere.

The word **chattel** originally comes from a Latin word meaning "head," as in "so many head of cattle." It reflects the notion that enslaved people are not human, but subhuman, like beasts of burden or other animals. Thus they can be treated like animals. But in Senegambia and elsewhere in Africa, many enslaved people were not considered chattel property and could not be bought and sold. Some even served as royal advisers and enjoyed great power and prestige.[1] Unlike in the Americas, where slave status passed forever from one generation to the next, in Africa the enslaved person's descendants were sometimes considered free.

Senegambia was composed of stateless societies, culturally homogeneous ethnic populations living in small groups of villages without a central capital. Among these stateless societies, **age-grade systems** evolved. Age-grades were groups of teenage males and females whom the society initiated into adulthood at the same time. Age-grades cut across family ties, created community-wide loyalties, and provided a means of local law enforcement, because each age-grade was responsible for the behavior of all its members.

The typical Senegambian community was a small, self-supporting agricultural village of closely related families. The average six- to eight-acre farm supported a moderate-size family. Millet and sorghum were the staple grains in northern Senegambia; farther south, forest dwellers cultivated yams as a staple. Social life centered on the family, and government played a limited role, interceding mostly to resolve family disputes and conflicts between families.

Alongside West African stateless societies like Senegambia were kingdoms and states ruled by kings who governed defined areas through bureaucratic hierarchies. The great forest kingdom of Benin emerged in the fifteenth and sixteenth centuries in what is now southern Nigeria (see Map 20.1). Over time, the position of its **oba**, or king, was exalted, bringing stability to the state. In the later fifteenth century the oba Ewuare strengthened his army and pushed Benin's borders as far as the Niger River in the east, westward into Yoruba

---

chattel An item of personal property; a term used in reference to enslaved people that conveys the idea that they are subhuman, like animals, and therefore may be treated like animals.

age-grade systems Among the societies of Senegambia, groups of teenage males and females whom the society initiated into adulthood at the same time.

oba The title of the king of Benin.

country, and south to the Gulf of Guinea. During the late sixteenth and seventeenth centuries the office of the oba evolved from a warrior-kingship to a position of spiritual leadership.

At its height in the late sixteenth century, Benin controlled a vast territory, and European visitors described a sophisticated society. A Dutch visitor in the early 1600s, possibly Dierick Ruiters, described the capital, Benin City, as possessing a great, wide, and straight main avenue down the middle, with many side streets crisscrossing it. The visitor entered the city through a high, well-guarded gate framed on each side by a very tall earthen bulwark, or wall, with an accompanying moat. There was also an impressive royal palace, with at least four large courtyards surrounded by galleries leading up to it. William Bosman, another Dutch visitor writing a hundred years later, in 1702, described the prodigiously long and broad streets "in which continual Markets are kept, either of Kine [cattle], Cotton, Elephants Teeth, European Wares; or, in short, whatever is to be come at in this Country."[2] Visitors also noted that Benin City was kept scrupulously clean and had no beggars and that public security was so effective that theft was unknown. The period also witnessed remarkable artistic creativity in ironwork, carved ivory, and especially bronze portrait busts. Over nine hundred brass plaques survive, providing important information about Benin court life, military triumphs, and cosmological ideas.

In 1485 Portuguese and other Europeans began to appear in Benin in pursuit of trade, and over the next couple of centuries Benin grew rich from the profits made through the slave trade and the export of tropical products, particularly pepper and ivory. Its main European trading partners along this stretch of the so-called slave coast were the Dutch and Portuguese. In the early eighteenth century tributary states and stronger neighbors nibbled at Benin's frontiers, challenging its power. Benin, however, survived as an independent entity until the British conquered and burned Benin City in 1898 as part of the European imperialist seizure of Africa (see "The Scramble for Africa, 1880–1914" in Chapter 25).

The Sudan: Songhai, Kanem-Bornu, and Hausaland

The Songhai kingdom, a successor state of the kingdoms of Ghana (ca. 900–1100) and Mali (ca. 1200–1450), dominated the whole Niger region of the western and central Sudan (see Map 20.1). The imperial expansion of Songhai began during the reign of the Songhai king Sonni Ali (r. ca. 1464–1492) and continued under his eventual successor, Muhammad Toure

(TOO-ray) (r. 1493–1528). From his capital at Gao, Toure extended his rule as far north as the salt-mining center at **Taghaza** (tah-GAHZ-ah) in the western Sahara and as far east as Agadez (AH-gah-dez) and Kano (KA-no). A convert to Islam, Toure returned from a pilgrimage to Mecca impressed by what he had seen there. He tried to bring about greater centralization in his own territories by building a strong army, improving taxation procedures, and replacing local Songhai officials with more efficient Arabs in an effort to substitute royal institutions for ancient kinship ties.

We know little about daily life in Songhai society because of the paucity of written records and surviving artifacts. Some information is provided by Leo Africanus (ca. 1493–1554), a Moroccan who published an account in 1526 of his many travels, which included a stay in the Songhai kingdom.

As a scholar, Africanus was naturally impressed by Timbuktu, the second-largest city of the empire, which he visited in 1513. "Here [is] a great store of doctors, judges, priests, and other learned men, that are bountifully maintained at the King's court," he reported.[3] Many of these Islamic scholars had studied in Cairo and other Muslim learning centers. They gave Timbuktu a reputation for intellectual sophistication, religious piety, and moral justice. (See "Global Viewpoints: European Descriptions of Timbuktu and Jenne," page 569.)

Songhai under Muhammad Toure seems to have enjoyed economic prosperity. Leo Africanus noted the abundant food supply, which was produced in the southern savanna and carried to Timbuktu by a large fleet of canoes. The elite had immense wealth, and expensive North African and European luxuries — clothes, copperware, glass and stone beads, perfumes, and horses — were much in demand. The existence of many shops and markets implies the development of an urban culture. In Timbuktu merchants, scholars, judges, and artisans constituted a distinctive bourgeoisie, or middle class. The presence of many foreign merchants, including Jews and Italians, gave the city a cosmopolitan atmosphere.

Slavery played an important role in Songhai's economy. On the royal farms scattered throughout the kingdom, enslaved people produced rice for the royal granaries. Slaves could possess their own slaves, land, and cattle, but they could not bequeath any of this property; the king inherited all of it. Muhammad Toure greatly increased the number of royal slaves. He bestowed slaves on favorite Muslim scholars, who thus gained a steady source of income. Slaves were also sold at the large market at Gao, where traders from North Africa bought them to resell later in Cairo, Constantinople, Lisbon, Naples, Genoa, and Venice.

Despite its considerable economic and cultural strengths, Songhai had serious internal problems. Islam

Taghaza A settlement in the western Sahara, the site of the main salt-mining center.

European Descriptions of Timbuktu and Jenne

Timbuktu and Jenne were important cities in the West African empires of Ghana, Mali, and Songhai. The writings of al-Hassan Ibn Muhammad al-Wezaz al-Fasi, also known as Leo Africanus (ca. 1493–1554), provide the most authoritative accounts of West Africa between the writings of Ibn Battuta in the fourteenth century and the writings of European travelers in the nineteenth century. The *Tarikh al-Sudan* (*History of the Sudan*), written by Abd al-Rahman al-Sadi (1594–after 1656), is one of the most important histories of the Mali and Songhai Empires in the fifteenth, sixteenth, and seventeenth centuries.

Leo Africanus on Timbuktu

■ [Timbuktu] is situated within twelve miles of a certaine branch of Niger [River], all the houses whereof are now changed into cottages built of chalke, and covered with thatch. There is a most stately temple to be seene, the wals thereof are made of stone and lime; and a princely palace . . . built by a most excellent workeman of Granada. Here are many shops of artificiers, and merchants, and especially of such as weave linen and cotton cloth. And hither do the Barbarie-merchants bring cloth of Europe. All the women of this region except maid-servants go with their faces covered. . . .

The inhabitants, & especially strangers there residing, are exceeding rich, insomuch, that the king that now is, married both his daughters unto two rich merchants. Here are many wels, containing most sweete water; and so often as the river Niger overfloweth, they conveigh the water thereof by certaine sluces into the towne.

Corne, cattle, milke, and butter this region yeeldeth in great abundance: but salt is verie scarce here; for it is brought hither by land from Tegaza, which is five hundred miles distant. When I myself was here, I saw one camels loade of salt sold for 80 ducates. The rich king of Tombuto hath many plates and scepters of gold, some whereof weigh 1300 pounds: and he keeps a magnificent and well furnished court. . . .

Here are great store of doctors, judges, priests, and other learned men, that are bountifully maintained at the kings cost and charges. And hither are brought divers manuscripts or written books out of Barbarie, which are sold for more money than any other merchandize.

Al-Sadi on Jenne

■ Jenne is a large . . . city, characterized by prosperity, good fortune and compassion. . . . It is the nature of Jenne's inhabitants to be kind and charitable, and solicitous for one another. . . .

Jenne is one of the great markets of the Muslims. Those who deal in salt from the mine of Taghaza meet there with those who deal in gold from the mine of Bitu. These two blessed mines have no equal in the entire world. . . . Jenne is the reason why caravans come to Timbuktu from all quarters—north, south, east and west. Jenne is situated to the south and west of Timbuktu beyond the two rivers. . . .

Jenne was founded as a pagan town in the middle of the second century of the *hijira* of the Prophet [150 anno hegirae (A.H.), the Islamic calendar, or 767–768 C.E.]. . . . Its people became Muslims at the end of the sixth century [A.H., or eleventh to twelfth century C.E.]. First, Sultan Kunburu became a Muslim, then people followed his example. When he made up his mind to embrace Islam he ordered that all the Muslim scholars within the city should be assembled. They totaled 4,200, and he made a profession of Islam before them, and told them to call upon God Most High to grant the city three things: firstly, that anyone who fled there from his homeland in poverty and distress should have this translated by God into luxury and ease, so that he may forget his homeland; secondly, that more strangers than local folk should settle there; and thirdly, that those who came to trade there should lose patience and grow weary over selling their goods, and so dispose of them cheaply, allowing the people of Jenne to make a profit.

QUESTIONS FOR ANALYSIS

1. During the colonial era, and even to the present day, Africa and its inhabitants were described in the most denigrating terms, such as pagan, savage, illiterate, poor, and uncivilized. How do the descriptions of these two African market and learning centers conform to those characterizations?
2. How important was Islam to the success of these two cities? In what ways?

Sources: Al-Hassan ibn-Mohammad al-Wezaz al-Fasi, *The History and Description of Africa.* Done into English in 1600 by John Pory. Robert Brown, ed. (London: Hakluyt Society, 1896), vol. 3, pp. 824–825; John O. Hunwick, *Timbuktu and the Songhay Empire: Al-Sadi's Tarikh al-Sudan Down to 1613 and Other Contemporary Documents.* Reproduced by permission of BRILL ACADEMIC PUBLISHERS in the format Republish in a book via Copyright Clearance Center.

never took root in the countryside, and Muslim officials alienated the king from his people. Muhammad Toure's reforms were a failure. He governed diverse peoples—Tuareg, Mandinka, and Fulani as well as Songhai—who were often hostile to one another, and no cohesive element united them. Finally, the Songhai never developed an effective method of transferring power. Revolts, conspiracies, and palace intrigues followed the death of every king, and only three of the nine rulers in the dynasty begun by Muhammad Toure died natural deaths. Muhammad Toure himself was murdered by one of his sons. His death began a period of political instability that led to the kingdom's slow disintegration. The empire came to an end in 1591 when a Moroccan army of three thousand soldiers—many of whom were slaves of European origin equipped with European muskets—crossed the Sahara and inflicted a crushing defeat on the Songhai at Tondibi.

East of Songhai lay the kingdoms of Kanem-Bornu and Hausaland (see Map 20.1). Under the dynamic military leader Idris Alooma (IH-dris ah-LOW-mah) (r. 1571–1603), Kanem-Bornu subdued weaker peoples and gained jurisdiction over an extensive area. Well drilled and equipped with firearms, his standing army and camel-mounted cavalry decimated warriors fighting with spears and arrows. Idris Alooma perpetuated a form of feudalism by granting land to able fighters in return for loyalty and the promise of future military assistance. Kanem-Bornu also shared in the trans-Saharan trade, shipping eunuchs and young girls to North Africa in return for horses and firearms.

A devout Muslim, Idris Alooma elicited high praise from ibn-Fartura, who wrote a history of his reign called *The Kanem Wars*:

> Among the most surprising of his acts was the stand he took against obscenity and adultery, so that no such thing took place openly in his time. Formerly the people had been indifferent to such offences. . . . In fact he was a power among his people and from him came their strength.
>
> The Sultan was intent on the clear path laid down by the Qur'an . . . in all his affairs and actions.[4]

Idris Alooma built mosques at his capital city of N'gazargamu and substituted Muslim courts and Islamic law for African tribunals and ancient customary law. His eighteenth-century successors lacked his vitality and military skills, however, and the empire declined.

Between Songhai and Kanem-Bornu were the lands of the Hausa (HOUSE-uh). Hausa merchants carried on a sizable trade in slaves and kola nuts with North African communities across the Sahara. Obscure trading posts evolved into important Hausa city-states like Kano and Katsina (kat-SIN-ah), through which Islamic

influences entered the region. Kano and Katsina became Muslim intellectual centers and in the fifteenth century attracted scholars from Timbuktu. The Muslim chronicler of the reign of King Muhammad Rimfa (RIMP-fah) (r. 1463–1499) of Kano records that the king introduced the Muslim practices of purdah (PUR-dah), or seclusion of women; Eid al-Fitr (eed-al-FITR), the festival after the fast of Ramadan; and the assignment of eunuchs to high state offices.[5] As in Songhai and Kanem-Bornu, however, Islam made no strong imprint on the Hausa masses until the nineteenth century.

The Lives of the People of West Africa

Wives and children were highly desired in African societies because they could clear and cultivate the land and because they brought prestige, social support, and security in old age. The results were intense competition for women, inequality of access to them, an emphasis on male virility and female fertility, and serious tension between male generations. Polygyny was almost universal.

Men acquired wives in two ways. In some cases, couples simply eloped and began their union. More commonly, a man's family gave bride wealth to the bride's family as compensation for losing the fruits of her productive and reproductive abilities. She was expected to produce children, to produce food through her labor, and to pass on the culture in the raising of her children. Because it took time for a young man to acquire the bride wealth, all but the richest men delayed marriage until about age thirty. Women married at about the onset of puberty.

The easy availability of land in Africa reduced the kinds of generational conflict that occurred in western Europe, where land was scarce. Competition for wives between male generations, however, was fierce. On the one hand, myth and folklore stressed respect for the elderly, and the older men in a community imposed their authority over the younger ones. On the other hand, young men possessed the powerful asset of their labor, which could easily be turned into independence where so much land was available.

"Without children you are naked" goes a Yoruba (YORE-uh-bah) proverb, and children were the primary goal of marriage. Just as a man's virility determined his honor, so barrenness damaged a woman's status. A wife's infidelity was considered a less serious problem than her infertility. A woman might have six widely spaced pregnancies in her fertile years; the universal practice of breast-feeding infants for two, three, or even four years may have inhibited conception. Long intervals between births due to food short-

Queen Mother and Attendants As in Ottoman, Chinese, and European societies, the mothers of African rulers sometimes exercised considerable political power because of their influence on their sons. African kings granted the title Queen Mother as a badge of honor. In this figure, the long beaded cap, called "chicken's beak," symbolizes the mother's rank, as do her elaborate neck jewelry and attendants.

(Culture: Edo peoples. Culture: Court of Benin. Altar Tableau: Queen Mother and Attendants, 18th century. Brass. Front, view #1. Gift of Mr. and Mrs. Klaus G. Perls, 1991 [1991.17.111]. The Metropolitan Museum of Art, New York/Image copyright © The Metropolitan Museum of Art/Image source: Art Resource, NY)

ages also may have limited pregnancies and checked population growth. Harsh climate, poor nutrition, and infectious diseases also contributed to a high infant mortality rate.

Both nuclear and extended families were common in West Africa. Nuclear families averaged only five or six members, but the household of a Big Man (a local man of power) included his wives, married and unmarried sons, unmarried daughters, poor relations, dependents, and scores of children. Extended families were common among the Hausa and Mandinka peoples. On the Gold Coast in the seventeenth century, a well-to-do man's household might number 150 people; in the Kongo region in west-central Africa, several hundred.

In agriculture men did the heavy work of felling trees and clearing the land; women then planted, weeded, and harvested. Between 1000 and 1400, cassava (manioc), bananas, and plantains came to West Africa from Asia. In the sixteenth century the Portuguese introduced maize (corn), sweet potatoes, and new varieties of yams from the Americas. Fish supplemented the diets of people living near bodies of water. According to former slave Olaudah Equiano, the Ibo people in the mid-eighteenth century ate plantains, yams, beans, and Indian corn, along with stewed poultry, goat, or bullock (castrated steer) seasoned with peppers.[6] However, such a protein-rich diet was probably exceptional.

Disease posed perhaps the biggest obstacle to population growth. Malaria, spread by mosquitoes and rampant in West Africa, was the greatest killer, especially of infants. West Africans developed a relatively high degree of immunity to malaria and other parasitic diseases. Acute strains of smallpox introduced by Europeans certainly did not help population growth, nor did venereal syphilis, which possibly originated in Latin America. As in Chinese and European communities in the early modern period, the sick depended on folk medicine. African medical specialists administered a variety of treatments. Still, disease was common where the diet was poor and lacked adequate vitamins.

The devastating effects of famine represented another major check on population growth. Drought, excessive rain, swarms of locusts, and rural wars that prevented land cultivation all meant later food shortages. In the 1680s famine extended from the Senegambian coast to the Upper Nile, and many people sold themselves into slavery for food. In the eighteenth century "slave exports" reached their peak in times of famine, and ships could fill their cargo holds simply by offering food. The worst disaster occurred from 1738 to 1756, when, according to one chronicler, the poor were reduced literally to cannibalism, also considered a metaphor for the complete collapse of civilization.[7]

Because the Americas had been isolated from the Eurasian-African landmass for thousands of years, parasitic diseases common in Europe, Africa, and Asia were unknown in the Americas before the Europeans' arrival. Enslaved Africans taken to the Americas brought with them the diseases common to tropical West Africa, such as yellow fever, dengue fever, malaria, and hookworm. Thus the hot, humid disease environment in the American tropics, where the majority of enslaved Africans lived and worked, became more "African." On the other hand, cold-weather European diseases, such as chicken pox, mumps, measles, and influenza, prevailed in the northern temperate zone in North America and the southern temperate zone in South America. This difference in disease environment partially explains why Africans made up the majority of the unskilled labor force in the tropical areas of the Americas, and Europeans made up the majority of the unskilled labor force in the Western Hemisphere temperate zones, such as the northern United States and Canada.

Trade and Industry

As in all premodern societies, West African economies rested on agriculture. There was some trade and industry, but population shortages encouraged local self-sufficiency, slowed transportation, and hindered exchange. There were very few large markets, and their relative isolation from the outside world and failure to attract large numbers of foreign merchants limited technological innovation.

For centuries black Africans had exchanged goods with North African merchants in centers such as Gao and Timbuktu. This long-distance trans-Saharan trade was conducted and controlled by Muslim-Berber merchants using camels. The two primary goods exchanged were salt, which came from salt mines in North Africa, and gold, which came mainly from gold mines in modern-day Mali, and later, modern Ghana.

As elsewhere around the world, water was the cheapest method of transportation, and many small dugout canoes and larger trading canoes plied the Niger and its delta region (see Map 20.1). On land West African peoples used pack animals (camels or donkeys) rather than wheeled vehicles; only a narrow

West African Trade Routes

Taghaza

Timbuktu · Gao

S A H A R A

Niger R.

Benin City

NIGER DELTA

→ Trade route

belt of land in the Sudan was suitable for animal-drawn carts. When traders reached an area infested with tsetse flies, they transferred each animal's load to human porters. Such difficulties in transport severely restricted long-distance trade, so most people relied on the regional exchange of local specialties.

West African communities had a well-organized market system. At informal markets on riverbanks, fishermen bartered fish for local specialties. More formal markets existed within towns and villages or on neutral ground between them. Markets also rotated among neighboring villages on certain days. Local sellers were usually women; traders from afar were men.

Salt had long been one of Africa's most critical trade items. Salt is essential to human health; the Hausa language has more than fifty words for it. The salt trade dominated the West African economies in the fifteenth, sixteenth, and seventeenth centuries. The main salt-mining center was at Taghaza (see Map 20.1) in the western Sahara. In the most wretched conditions, slaves dug the salt from desiccated lakes and loaded heavy blocks onto camels' backs. Nomadic **Tuareg** (Berber) peoples and later Moors (peoples of Berber and Arab descent) traded their salt south for gold, grain, slaves, and kola nuts. **Cowrie** (COW-ree) **shells**, imported from the Maldives in the Indian Ocean and North Africa, served as the medium of exchange. Gold continued to be mined and shipped from Mali until South American bullion flooded Europe in the sixteenth century. Thereafter, gold production in Mali steadily declined until the late twentieth and early twenty-first centuries, when it revived.

West African peoples engaged in many crafts, but the textile industry had the greatest level of specialization. The earliest fabric in West Africa was made of vegetable fiber. Muslim traders introduced cotton and its weaving in the ninth century. By the fifteenth century the Wolof and Mandinka regions had professional weavers producing beautiful cloth, but this cloth was too expensive to compete in the Atlantic and Indian Ocean markets after 1500. Although the relatively small quantities of cloth produced on very narrow looms (one to two inches wide) could not compete in a world market, they are the source of the famous multicolored African kente cloth made from threads of cotton, or cotton and silk, by the Akan people of Ghana and the Ivory Coast. The area around Kano, in northern Nigeria, is famous for the deeply dyed blue cloth produced on the narrowest looms in the world and favored by the Tuareg Berber peoples of North Africa.

Salt Making in the Central Sahara For centuries camel caravans transported salt south across the Sahara to the great West African kingdoms, where it was exchanged for gold. Here at Tegguida-n-Tessum, Niger, in the central Sahara, salt is still collected by pouring spring water into small pools dug out of the saline soil. The water leaches out the salt before evaporating in the desert sun, leaving deposits of pure salt behind, which are then shaped into blocks for transport. (Visual Connection Archive)

Cross-Cultural Encounters Along the East African Coast

How did the arrival of Europeans and other foreign cultures affect the East African coast, and how did Ethiopia and the Swahili city-states respond to these incursions?

East Africa in the early modern period faced repeated incursions from foreign powers. At the beginning of the sixteenth century Ethiopia faced challenges from the Muslim state of Adal, and then from Europeans. Jesuit attempts to substitute Roman Catholic liturgical forms for the Coptic Christian liturgies (see below) met with fierce resistance and ushered in a centuries-long period of hostility to foreigners. The wealthy Swahili city-states along the southeastern African coast also resisted European intrusions in the sixteenth century, with even more disastrous results. Cities such as Mogadishu, Kilwa, and Sofala used Arabic as the language of communication, and their commercial economies had long been tied to the Indian Ocean trade. The arrival of the Portuguese in 1498 proved catastrophic for those cities, and the Swahili coast suffered economic decline as a result.

Muslim and European Incursions in Ethiopia, ca. 1500–1630

At the beginning of the sixteenth century the powerful East African kingdom of Ethiopia extended from Massawa in the north to several tributary states in the south (Map 20.2), but the ruling Solomonic dynasty in Ethiopia, in power since the thirteenth century, faced serious external threats. Alone among the states in northeast and eastern Africa, Ethiopia was a Christian kingdom that practiced **Coptic Christianity**, an orthodox form of the Christian faith that originated in Egypt in about 42–45. By the early 1500s Ethiopia was an island of Christianity surrounded by a sea of Muslim states.

Adal, a Muslim state along the southern base of the Red Sea, began incursions into Ethiopia, and in 1529 the Adal general Ahmad ibn-Ghazi inflicted a disastrous defeat on the Ethiopian emperor Lebna Dengel (r. 1508–1540). Ibn-Ghazi followed up his victory with systematic devastation of the land; destruction of many Ethiopian artistic and literary works, churches, and

Tuareg Major branch of the nomadic Berber peoples who controlled the north-south trans-Saharan trade in salt.

cowrie shells Imported from the Maldives, they served as the medium of exchange in West Africa.

Coptic Christianity Orthodox form of Christianity from Egypt practiced in Ethiopia.

MAP 20.2 East Africa in the Sixteenth Century
In early modern times, the Christian kingdom of Ethiopia, first isolated and then subjected to Muslim and European pressures, played an insignificant role in world affairs. But the East African city-states, which stretched from Sofala in the south to Mogadishu in the north, had powerfully important commercial relations with Mughal India, China, the Ottoman world, and southern Europe.

monasteries; and the forced conversion of thousands to Islam. Lebna Dengel fled to the mountains and appealed to Portugal for assistance. The Portuguese came to his aid, but Dengel was killed in battle before the Portuguese arrived. The Muslim occupation of Christian Ethiopia, which began around 1531, ended in 1543, after a joint Ethiopian and Portuguese force defeated a larger Muslim army at the Battle of Wayna Daga.

In the late twelfth century tales of Prester John, rumored to be a powerful Christian monarch ruling a vast and wealthy African empire, reached western Europe. The search for Prester John, as well as for gold and spices, spurred the Portuguese to undertake a series of trans-African expeditions that reached Timbuktu and Mali in the 1480s and the Ethiopian court by 1508. Although Prester John was a mythical figure, Portuguese emissaries triumphantly but mistakenly identified the Ethiopian emperor as Prester John.[8] It was their desire to convert Ethiopians from Coptic Christianity to Roman Catholicism that motivated the Portuguese to aid the Ethiopians in defeating Adal's Muslim forces in 1543.

No sooner had the Muslim threat ended than Ethiopia encountered three more dangers. The Galla, now known as the Oromo, moved northward in great numbers in the 1530s, occupying portions of Harar, Shoa, and Amhara. The Ethiopians could not defeat them militarily, and the Galla were not interested in assimilation. For the next two centuries the two peoples lived together in an uneasy truce. Simultaneously, the Ottoman Turks seized Massawa and other coastal cities. Then the Jesuits arrived and attempted to force Roman Catholicism on a proud people whose Coptic form of Christianity long antedated the European version. Since Ethiopian national sentiment was closely tied to Coptic Christianity, violent rebellion and anarchy ensued.

In 1633 the Jesuit missionaries were expelled. For the next two centuries hostility to foreigners, weak political leadership, and regionalism characterized Ethiopia. Civil conflicts between Galla and Ethiopians erupted continually. The Coptic Church, though lacking strong authority, survived as the cornerstone of Ethiopian national identity.

The Swahili City-States and the Arrival of the Portuguese, ca. 1500–1600

The word **Swahili** means "People of the Coast" and refers to the people living along the East African coast and on the nearby islands. Although predominantly a Bantu-speaking people, the Swahili have incorporated significant aspects of Arab culture. The Arabic alphabet was used for the first written works in Swahili (although the Latin alphabet is now standard), and roughly 35 percent of Swahili words come from

Swahili Meaning "People of the Coast," the term used for the people living along the East African coast and on nearby islands.

Saint George in Ethiopian Art This wall painting of Saint George slaying a dragon resides in the stone-carved Church of Saint George in Lalibela, Ethiopia, and attests to the powerful and pervasive Christian influence on Ethiopian culture. (Galen R. Frysinger)

Arabic. Surviving texts in Swahili—from the earliest known Swahili documents dating from 1711—provide historians with a glimpse of early Swahili history that is not possible when studying early nonliterate African societies. By the eleventh century the Swahili had accepted Islam, which provided a common identity and unifying factor for all the peoples along coastal East Africa. Living on the Indian Ocean coast, the Swahili also felt the influences of Indians, Indonesians, Persians, and even the Chinese.

Swahili civilization was overwhelmingly maritime. A fertile, well-watered, and intensely cultivated stretch of land extending down the coast yielded valuable crops. The region's considerable prosperity, however, rested on trade and commerce. The Swahili acted as middlemen in an Indian Ocean–East African economy that might be described as early capitalism. They exchanged cloves, ivory, rhinoceros horn, tortoise shells, inlaid ebony chairs, copra (dried coconut meat that yields coconut oil), and inland slaves for Arabian and Persian perfumes, toilet articles, ink, and paper; for Indian textiles, beads, and iron tools; and for Chinese porcelains and silks. In the fifteenth century the cosmopolitan city-states of Mogadishu, Pate, Lamu, Mombasa, and especially Kilwa enjoyed a worldwide reputation for commercial prosperity and high living standards.[9] (See "Analyzing the Evidence: Lamu Old Town, Lamu Island, Kenya," page 576.)

The arrival of the Portuguese explorer Vasco da Gama (VAS-ko dah GAH-ma) (see Map 16.2) in 1498 spelled the end of the Swahili cities' independence. Lured by the spice trade, da Gama wanted to build a Portuguese maritime empire in the Indian Ocean. Some Swahili rulers, such as the sultan of Malindi (ma-LIN-dee), quickly agreed to a trading alliance with the Portuguese. Others, such as the sultan of Mombasa (mahm-BAHS-uh), were tricked into commercial agreements. Swahili rulers who rejected Portuguese overtures saw their cities bombarded and attacked. To secure alliances made between 1502 and 1507, the Portuguese erected forts at the southern port cities of Kilwa, Zanzibar (ZAN-zuh-bahr), and Sofala. These fortified markets and trading posts served as the foundation of Portuguese commercial power on the Swahili coast. (See "Analyzing the Evidence: Duarte Barbosa on the Swahili City-States," page 578.) The better-fortified northern cities, such as Mogadishu, survived as important entrepôts for goods to India.

Lamu Old Town, Lamu Island, Kenya

The old town of Lamu is the oldest and best-preserved Swahili community along the East African coast, and it is a wonderful example of the mixture of African, Arab, and European influences that shaped Swahili culture. Lamu was founded in 1370 by Arab traders, and the majority of its inhabitants are Muslims. It became wealthy from the East African slave trade, as evidenced by a few remaining large merchants' houses, made from coral stone and fitted with elaborately carved wooden doors. These homes had running water and indoor plumbing three hundred or more years ago, at a time when Europeans were still tossing the contents of chamber pots out into the street. Some houses were three stories or more high, like some of the buildings in this photo, with open-walled rooms at the top through which cool breezes blew. The upper stories of some houses had passageways connecting to other buildings so that Muslim women could visit neighbors without going out into the street. On display inside were costly Indian Ocean trade items, including fine porcelain from China, set into elaborate recesses in the walls.

(© Thomas Cockrem/Alamy Stock Photo)

Besides Arab and African influences, there is also evidence of the European presence on the island. The Portuguese controlled Lamu's trade from 1505 to 1652. The Germans claimed Lamu as part of their East German Protectorate in 1885, and the island fell under British colonial rule in 1890. The British closed the slave market and built a number of buildings along the waterfront, some of which you can see in this image, including the residence and offices of the local British colonial administrator. During the British colonial period, the road along the harbor, seen in this photo, was the only proper road on the island, and the colonial officer owned the only car. Each day he would drive his car from one end of the harbor to the other along this road in a grand display of the imperial presence.

QUESTIONS FOR ANALYSIS

1. How many different examples of the varying Arab, African, and European influences on Lamu can you identify in this image?
2. The buildings in this image are all set very close together, with only a narrow alley between them. Why do you think this was so? What would be the advantages of such an arrangement?

The Portuguese presence in the south did not yield the expected commercial fortunes. Rather than accept Portuguese commercial restrictions, the residents deserted the towns, and the town economies crumbled. Large numbers of Kilwa's people, for example, immigrated to northern cities. The gold flow from inland mines to Sofala (so-FALL-ah) slowed to a trickle. Swahili noncooperation successfully prevented the Portuguese from gaining control of the local coastal trade.

In the late seventeenth century pressures from the northern European maritime powers—the Dutch, French, and English, aided greatly by Omani Arabs—combined with local African rebellions to bring about the collapse of Portuguese influence in Africa. A Portuguese presence remained only at Mozambique in the far south and Angola (ahng-GO-luh) on the west coast.

The African Slave Trade

What role did slavery play in African societies before the transatlantic slave trade began, and what was the effect of European involvement?

The exchange of peoples captured in local and ethnic wars within sub-Saharan Africa, the trans-Saharan slave trade with the Mediterranean Islamic world beginning in the seventh century, and the slave traffic across the Indian Ocean all testify to the long tradition and continental dimensions of the African slave trade before European intrusion. The enslavement of human beings was practiced in some form or another all over Africa—indeed, all over the world. Sanctioned by law and custom, enslaved people served critical and well-defined roles in the social, political, and economic organization of many African societies. Domestically these roles ranged from concubines and servants to royal guards and advisers. As was the case later in the Americas, some enslaved people were common laborers. In terms of economics, slaves were commodities for trade, no more or less important than other trade items, such as gold and ivory.

Over time, the trans-Saharan slave trade became less important than the transatlantic trade, which witnessed an explosive growth during the seventeenth and eighteenth centuries. The millions of enslaved Africans forcibly exported to the Americas had a lasting impact on African society and led ultimately to a wider use of slaves within Africa itself.

The Institution of Slavery in Africa

Islamic practices strongly influenced African slavery. African rulers justified enslavement with the Muslim argument that prisoners of war could be sold and that captured people were considered chattel, or personal possessions, to be used any way the owner saw fit. Between 650 and 1600 Muslims transported perhaps as many as 4.82 million black slaves across the trans-Saharan trade route.[10] In the fourteenth and fifteenth centuries the rulers and elites of Mali and Benin imported thousands of white Slavic slave women, symbols of wealth and status, who had been seized in slave raids from the Balkans and Caucasus regions of the eastern Mediterranean by Turks, Mongols, and others.[11] In 1444, when Portuguese caravels landed 235 slaves at Algarve in southern Portugal, a contemporary observed that they seemed "a marvelous (extraordinary) sight, for, amongst them, were some white enough, fair enough, and well-proportioned; others were less white, like mulattoes; others again were black as Ethiops."[12]

Meanwhile, the flow of black people to Europe, begun during the Renaissance, continued. In the seventeenth and eighteenth centuries as many as two hundred thousand Africans entered European societies. Some arrived as slaves, others as servants; the legal distinction was not always clear. Eighteenth-century London, for example, had more than ten thousand blacks, most of whom arrived as sailors on Atlantic crossings or as personal servants brought from the West Indies. In England most were free, not slaves. Initially, a handsome black person was a fashionable accessory, a rare status symbol. Later, English aristocrats considered black servants too ordinary. The duchess of Devonshire offered her mother an eleven-year-old boy, explaining that the duke did not want a Negro servant because "it was more original to have a Chinese page than to have a black one; everybody had a black one."[13]

London's black population constituted a well-organized, self-conscious subculture, with black pubs, black churches, and black social groups assisting the black poor and unemployed. Some black people attained wealth and position, the most famous being Francis Barber, manservant of the sixteenth-century British literary giant Samuel Johnson and heir to Johnson's papers and to most of his sizable fortune.

In 1658 the Dutch East India Company began to allow the importation of slaves into the Cape Colony, which the company had founded on the southern tip of Africa at the Cape of Good Hope in 1652. Over the next century and a half about 75 percent of the slaves brought into the colony came from Dutch East India Company colonies in India and Southeast Asia or from Madagascar; the remaining 25 percent came from Africa. Most worked long and hard as field hands and at any

Cape Colony, ca. 1750

Duarte Barbosa on the Swahili City-States

The Portuguese writer, government agent, and traveler Duarte Barbosa made two voyages to India. Arriving first in 1500, he acted for five years as an interpreter and translator in Cochin and Cannanore in Kerala (in southwestern India on the Malabar coast), returning to Lisbon in 1506. On his second trip to India in 1511, he served the Portuguese government as chief scribe in the factory of Cannanore (a factory was a warehouse for the storage of goods, not a manufacturing center) and as the liaison with the local Indian rajah (prince). Barbosa returned to Portugal around 1516. In September 1519 he began his greatest adventure, setting off with Ferdinand Magellan to circumnavigate the globe. After Magellan was killed in a battle with native forces in the Philippines, Barbosa took joint command of the expedition, but was himself killed in the Philippines less than a week after Magellan, on May 1, 1521.

On the basis of his trips around the Indian Ocean in 1518, Barbosa completed his *Libro de Duarte Barbosa* (*The Book of Duarte Barbosa*), a geographical and ethnographic survey of peoples, lands, and commerce from the Cape of Good Hope to China. It was based largely on his personal observations. First published in Italian, the book won wide acclaim in Europe, and modern scholars consider its geographical information very accurate. The excerpts below describe some of the Swahili city-states along the East African coast.

Sofala

■ And the manner of their traffic was this: they came in small vessels named *zambucos* from the kingdoms of Kilwa, Mombasa, and Malindi, bringing many cotton cloths, some spotted and others white and blue, also some of silk, and many small beads, grey, red, and yellow, which things come to the said kingdoms from the great kingdom of Cambaya [in northwest India] in other greater ships. And these wares the said Moors who came from Malindi and Mombasa paid for in gold at such a price that those merchants departed well pleased; which gold they gave by weight.

The Moors of Sofala kept these wares and sold them afterwards to the Heathen of the Kingdom of Benametapa, who came thither laden with gold which they gave in exchange for the said cloths without weighing it. These Moors collect also great store of ivory which they find hard by Sofala, and this also they sell in the Kingdom of Cambaya at five or six cruzados the quintal. They also sell some ambergris, which is brought to them from the Hucicas, and is exceeding good. These Moors are black, and some of them tawny; some of them speak Arabic, but the more part use the language of the country. They clothe themselves from the waist down with cotton and silk cloths, and other cloths they wear over their shoulders like capes, and turbans on their heads. Some of them wear small caps dyed in grain in chequers and other woollen clothes in many tints, also camlets and other silks.

Their food is millet, rice, flesh and fish. In this river as far as the sea are many sea horses, which come out on the land to graze, which horses always move in the sea like fishes; they have tusks like those of small elephants in size, and the ivory is better than that of elephants, being whiter and harder, and it never loses colour. In the country near Sofala are many wild elephants, exceeding great (which the country-folk know not how to tame) lions, ounces [African lynx], deer and many other wild beasts. It is a land of plains and hills with many streams of sweet water.

---

other menial or manual forms of labor needed by their European masters. The Dutch East India Company was the single largest slave owner in the Cape Colony, employing its slaves on public works and company farms, but by 1780 half of all white men at the Cape had at least one slave. Slave ownership fostered a strong sense of racial and economic solidarity in the white master class.

Although in the seventeenth and eighteenth centuries Holland enjoyed a Europe-wide reputation for religious tolerance and intellectual freedom, in the Cape Colony the Dutch used a strict racial hierarchy and heavy-handed paternalism to maintain control over enslaved native and foreign-born peoples. In Muslim society the offspring of a free man and an enslaved woman were free, but in southern Africa such children remained enslaved. Because enslaved males greatly outnumbered enslaved females in the Cape Colony, marriage and family life were almost nonexistent for slaves. Because there were few occupations requiring special skills, those enslaved in the colony lacked opportunities to earn manumission, or freedom. And in contrast with North and South America and with Muslim societies, in the Cape Colony only a very small number of those enslaved won manumission; most of these were women.[14]

Kilwa

■ Going along the coast from this town of Mozambique, there is an island hard by the mainland which is called Kilwa, in which is a Moorish town with many fair houses of stone and mortar, with many windows after our fashion, very well arranged in streets, with many flat roofs. The doors are of wood, well carved, with excellent joinery. Around it are streams and orchards and fruit-gardens with many channels of sweet water. It has a Moorish king over it. From this place they trade with Sofala, whence they bring back gold, and from here they spread all over . . . the seacoast [which] is well-peopled with villages and abodes of Moors.

Before the King our Lord sent out his expedition to discover India the Moors of Sofala, Cuama, Angoya and Mozambique were all subject to the King of Kilwa, who was the most mighty king among them. And in this town was great plenty of gold, as no ships passed towards Sofala without first coming to this island. . . .

This town was taken by force from its king by the Portuguese, as, moved by arrogance, he refused to obey the King our Lord. There they took many prisoners and the king fled from the island, and His Highness ordered that a fort should be built there, and kept it under his rule and governance. Afterwards he ordered that it should be pulled down, as its maintenance was of no value nor profit to him, and it was destroyed by Antonio de Saldanha.

Malindi

■ Journeying along the coast towards India, there is a fair town on the mainland lying along a strand, which is named Malindi. It pertains to the Moors and has a Moorish king over it; the which place has many fair stone and mortar houses of many storeys, with great plenty of windows and flat roofs, after our fashion. The place is well laid out in streets. The folk are both black and white; they go naked, covering only their private parts with cotton and silk cloths. Others of them wear cloths folded like cloaks and waist-bands, and turbans of many rich stuffs on their heads.

They are great barterers, and deal in cloth, gold, ivory, and divers other wares with the Moors and Heathen of the great kingdom of Cambaya; and to their haven come every year many ships with cargoes of merchandize, from which they get great store of gold, ivory and wax. In this traffic the Cambay merchants make great profits, and thus, on one side and the other, they earn much money. There is great plenty of food in this city (rice, millet, and some wheat which they bring from Cambaya), and divers sorts of fruit, inasmuch as there is here abundance of fruit-gardens and orchards. Here too are plenty of round-tailed sheep, cows and other cattle and great store of oranges, also of hens.

The king and people of this place ever were and are friends of the King of Portugal, and the Portuguese always find in them great comfort and friendship and perfect peace, and there the ships, when they chance to pass that way, obtain supplies in plenty.

QUESTIONS FOR ANALYSIS

1. What seems to have impressed Barbosa? What was his attitude toward the various peoples he saw? What Portuguese or Western prejudices do you discern?
2. What was the Portuguese relationship to the Swahili city-states at the time Barbosa saw them?
3. What was the source of Sofala's gold? Of Sofala's and Malindi's ivory? What did the Indian kingdom of Cambaya use ivory for?

Source: Mansel Longworth Dames, trans., *The Book of Duarte Barbosa*, vol. 1 (London: Bedford Press, 1918).

The slave trade expanded greatly in East Africa's savanna and Horn regions in the late eighteenth century and the first half of the nineteenth century. Why this increased demand? Merchants and planters wanted slaves to work the sugar plantations on the Mascarene Islands, located east of Madagascar; the clove plantations on Zanzibar and Pemba; and the food plantations along the Kenyan coast. The eastern coast also exported enslaved people to the Americas, particularly to Brazil. In the late eighteenth and early nineteenth centuries, precisely when the slave trade to North America and the Caribbean declined, the Arabian and Asian markets expanded.

The Transatlantic Slave Trade

Although the trade in African people was a worldwide phenomenon, the transatlantic slave trade involved the largest number of enslaved Africans. This forced migration of millions of human beings, extending from the early sixteenth to the late nineteenth centuries, represents one of the most inhumane, unjust, and shameful tragedies in human history. It also immediately provokes a troubling question: why, in the seventeenth and eighteenth centuries, did enslavement in the Americas become almost exclusively African?

harsh brutality. These and other possible examples contradict the existence of a pan-European ideology or culture that opposed the enslavement of white Europeans. Moreover, the flow of white enslaved Slavic peoples from the Balkans into the eastern Mediterranean continued unabated during the same period.

Another theory holds that in the Muslim and Arab worlds by the tenth century, an association had developed between blackness and menial slavery. The Arab word *abd*, or "black," had become synonymous with *slave*. Although the great majority of enslaved persons in the Islamic world were white, a racial element existed in Muslim perceptions: not all slaves were black, but blacks were identified with slavery. In Europe, after the arrival of tens of thousands of sub-Saharan Africans in the Iberian Peninsula during the fifteenth century, Christian Europeans also began to make a strong association between slavery and black Africans. Therefore, Africans seemed the "logical" solution to the labor shortage in the Americas.[16]

Another important question relating to the African slave trade is this: why were African peoples enslaved in a period when serfdom was declining in western Europe, and when land was so widely available and much of the African continent had a labor shortage? The answer seems to lie in a technical problem related to African agriculture. Partly because of the tsetse fly, which causes sleeping sickness and other diseases, and partly because of easily leached lateritic soils (containing high concentrations of oxides), farmers had great difficulty using draft animals. Tropical soils responded poorly to plowing, and most work had to be done with the hoe. Productivity, therefore, was low. Thus, in precolonial Africa the individual's agricultural productivity was low, so his or her economic value to society was less than the economic value of a European peasant in Europe. Enslaved persons in the Americas were more productive than free producers in Africa. And European slave dealers were very willing to pay a price higher than the value of an African's productivity in Africa.

The incidence of disease in the Americas also helps explain African enslavement. Smallpox took a terrible toll on Native Americans, and between 30 and 50 percent of Europeans exposed to malaria succumbed to that sickness. Africans had developed some immunity to both diseases, and in the Americas they experienced the lowest mortality rate of any people, making them, ironically, the most suitable workers for the environment.

Portuguese colonization of Brazil began in the early 1530s, and in 1551 the Portuguese founded a sugar colony at Bahia. Between 1551 and 1575, before the North American slave traffic began, the Portuguese delivered more African slaves to Brazil than ever reached British North America (Figure 20.1). Portugal essen-

Below Stairs The prints and cartoons of Thomas Rowlandson (1756–1827) testify to the sizable numbers of blacks in eighteenth-century London, where they worked in naval and military service as well as domestic service. Here the household cook, maid, and footman relax before the kitchen fire. Interracial marriages were not uncommon. (© The Trustees of The British Museum/Art Resource, NY)

European settlers first enslaved indigenous peoples, the Amerindians, to work on the sugar plantations in the New World (see "Sugar and Early Transatlantic Slavery" in Chapter 16). When they proved ill suited to the harsh rigors of sugar production, the Spaniards brought in Africans.

One scholar has argued that a pan-European insider-outsider ideology prevailed across Europe. This cultural attitude permitted the enslavement of outsiders but made the enslavement of white Europeans taboo. Europeans could not bear the sight of other Europeans doing plantation slave labor. According to this theory, a similar pan-African ideology did not exist, as Africans had no problem with selling Africans to Europeans.[15] Several facts argue against the validity of this theory. English landlords exploited their Irish peasants with merciless severity, French aristocrats often looked on their peasantry with cold contempt, and Russian boyars treated their serfs with casual indifference and tially monopolized the slave trade until 1600 and continued to play a significant role in the seventeenth century, though the trade was increasingly taken over by the Dutch, French, and English. From 1690 until the British House of Commons abolished the slave trade in 1807, England was the leading carrier of African slaves.

Population density and supply conditions along the West African coast and the sailing time to New World markets determined the sources of slaves. As the demand for slaves rose, slavers moved down the West African coast from Senegambia to the more densely populated hinterlands of the Bight of Benin and the Bight of Biafra. The abundant supply of Africans to enslave in Angola, the region south of the Congo River, and the quick passage from Angola to Brazil and the Caribbean established that region as the major coast for Portuguese slavers.

Transatlantic wind patterns partly determined exchange routes. Shippers naturally preferred the swiftest crossing — that is, from the African port nearest the latitude of the intended American destination. Thus Portuguese shippers carried their cargoes from Angola to Brazil, and British merchants sailed from the Bight of Benin to the Caribbean. The great majority

The Slave Coast of West Africa

of enslaved Africans were intended for the sugar and coffee plantations extending from the Caribbean islands to Brazil. Angola produced 26 percent of all African slaves and 70 percent of all Portuguese slaves. Trading networks extending deep into the interior culminated at two major ports on the Angolan coast, Luanda (loo-AHN-da) and Benguela. The Portuguese acquired a few slaves through warfare but secured the vast majority through trade with African dealers. Whites did not participate in the inland markets, which were run solely by Africans.

Almost all Portuguese shipments went to satisfy the virtually insatiable Brazilian demand for slaves. The so-called **Middle Passage** was the horrific voyage under appalling and often deadly conditions of enslaved Africans across the Atlantic to the Americas.

Olaudah Equiano (see "Individuals in Society: Olaudah Equiano," page 582) describes the experience of his voyage as a captured slave from Benin to Barbados in the Caribbean:

> The stench of the hold while we were on the coast was so intolerably loathsome that it was dangerous to remain there for any time, and some of us had been

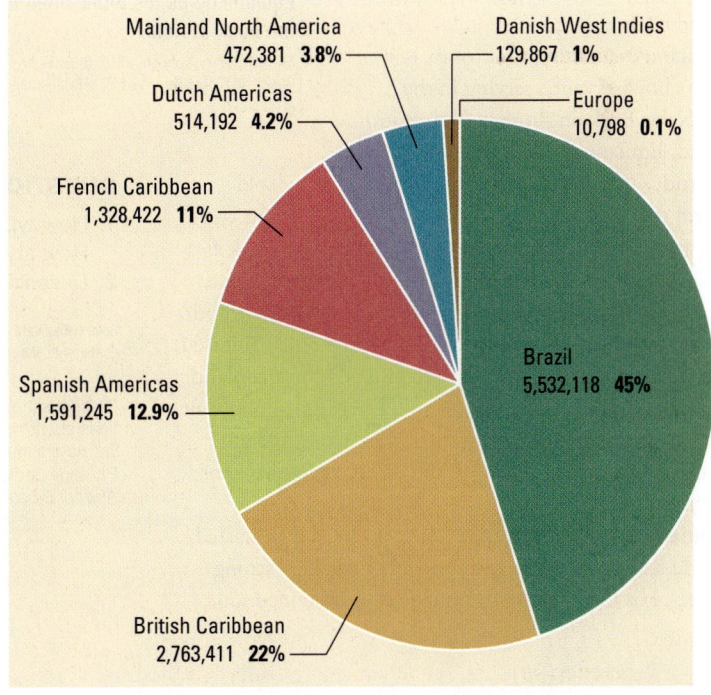

FIGURE 20.1 Estimated Slave Imports by Destination, 1501–1866 Brazil was the single largest importer of African slaves from 1501 to 1866. But when taken cumulatively, the British, French, Dutch, and Danish colonies of the Caribbean rivaled the much larger colony of Brazil for numbers of slaves imported from Africa.

(Source: Data from Emory University. "Assessing the Slave Trade: Estimates," in *Voyages: The Trans-Atlantic Slave Trade Database.* 2009. http://www.slavevoyages.org.)

Mainland North America 472,381 **3.8%**
Danish West Indies 129,867 **1%**
Dutch Americas 514,192 **4.2%**
Europe 10,798 **0.1%**
French Caribbean 1,328,422 **11%**
Spanish Americas 1,591,245 **12.9%**
Brazil 5,532,118 **45%**
British Caribbean 2,763,411 **22%**

Middle Passage Enslaved Africans' horrific voyage across the Atlantic to the Americas, under appalling and often deadly conditions.

INDIVIDUALS IN SOCIETY

Olaudah Equiano

MOST OF THE LIVES OF PEOPLE TRAFFICKED IN THE transatlantic slave trade remain hidden to us. Olaudah Equiano (1745–1797) is probably the best-known African slave. His autobiography, *The Interesting Narrative of the Life of Olaudah Equiano* (1789), represents a rare window into the slaves' obscurity.

In his autobiography, Equiano says that he was born in Benin (modern Nigeria) of Ibo ethnicity.* In his village all people shared in the cultivation of family lands. One day, when the adults were in the fields, strangers broke into the family compound and kidnapped the eleven-year-old Olaudah and his sister. As it took six months to walk to the coast, Olaudah's home must have been far inland. The sea, the slave ship, and the strange appearance of the white crew terrified the boy. Equiano's first master took him to Jamaica, to Virginia, and then to England, where he placed him in the custody of a kind family. They gave him the rudiments of an education, and he was baptized a Christian.

Equiano eventually went to sea as a captain's boy (servant), serving in the Royal Navy. Back on shore in Portsmouth, England, Equiano's master urged him to read, study, and learn basic mathematics. He later sold Equiano to a Philadelphia Quaker, Robert King, who was a rum and sugar merchant. King paid Equiano to work as a clerk in King's warehouse, as a longshoreman loading and unloading cargo ships, and at sea where he developed good navigational skills. Equiano became an entrepreneur himself, buying and selling small goods in the islands and mainland ports. Equiano had amassed enough money by 1766 to buy his freedom, and King signed the deed of manumission. Equiano was twenty-one years old; he had been a slave for ten years.

Equiano's *Narrative* reveals a complex and sophisticated man. He had a strong constitution and an equally strong character. His Christian faith undoubtedly sustained him.

In this 1789 portrait, Olaudah Equiano holds his Bible, open to the book of Acts.

(British Library, London, UK/© British Library Board. All Rights Reserved./The Bridgeman Art Library)

On his book's title page, he cited a verse from Isaiah (12:2): "The Lord Jehovah is my strength and my song."

Equiano loathed the brutal slavery he saw in the West Indies and the vicious racism he experienced in the North American colonies. He respected Robert King's fairness, admired British navigational and industrial technologies, and had many close white friends. He once described himself as "almost an Englishman." He was also involved in the black communities in the West Indies and in London.

Olaudah Equiano's *Narrative*, with its horrific descriptions of slavery, proved influential, and after its publication Equiano became active in the abolition movement. He spoke to large crowds in the industrial cities of Manchester and Birmingham in England, arguing that it was in the business interests of manufacturers to support abolition, as Africa was a huge, virtually untapped market for English cloth. Though he died in 1797, ten years before its passage, Equiano significantly advanced the abolitionist cause that led to the Slave Trade Act of 1807.

QUESTIONS FOR ANALYSIS

1. How typical was Olaudah Equiano's life as a slave? How atypical?
2. Describe Equiano's culture and his sense of himself.

Source: *Equiano's Travels: The Interesting Narrative of the Life of Olaudah Equiano*, ed. Paul Edwards (Portsmouth, N.H.: Heinemann, 1996).

*Recent scholarship has re-examined Equiano's life and raised some questions about his African origins and his experience of the Middle Passage. To explore the debate over Equiano's authorship of the African and Middle Passage portions of his autobiography, see Vincent Carretta, *Equiano, the African: Biography of a Self-Made Man* (New York: Penguin, 2007).

Peddlers in Rio de Janeiro A British army officer sketched this early-nineteenth-century scene of everyday life in Rio de Janeiro, Brazil. The ability to balance large burdens on the head meant that the person's hands were free for other use. Note the player (on the left) of a musical instrument originating in the Congo. On the right a woman gives alms to the man with the holy image in return for being allowed to kiss the image as an act of devotion. We do not know whether the peddlers were free and self-employed or were selling for their owners. (From *Drawings Taken by Lieutenant Henry Chamberlain, During the Years 1819 and 1820* [London: Columbian Press, 1822]/Visual Connection Archive)

permitted to stay on the deck for the fresh air; but now that the whole ship's cargo were confined together it became absolutely pestilential. The closeness of the place and the heat of the climate, added to the number in the ship, which was so crowded that each had scarcely room to turn himself, almost suffocated us. This produced copious perspirations, so that the air soon became unfit for respiration from a variety of loathsome smells, and brought on a sickness among the slaves, of which many died. . . . This wretched situation was again aggravated by the galling of the chains, now become insupportable, and the filth of the necessary tubs [of human waste], into which the children often fell and were almost suffocated. The shrieks of the women and the groans of the dying rendered the whole a scene of horror almost inconceivable.[17]

Although the demand was great, Portuguese merchants in Angola and Brazil sought to maintain only a steady trickle of slaves from the African interior to Luanda and across the ocean to Bahia and Rio de Janeiro: a flood of slaves would have depressed the American market. Planters and mine operators from the provinces traveled to Rio to buy slaves. Between 1795 and 1808 approximately 10,000 Angolans per year stood in the Rio slave market. In 1810 the figure rose to 18,000; in 1828 it reached 32,000.[18]

The English ports of London, Bristol, and particularly Liverpool dominated the British slave trade. In the eighteenth century Liverpool was the world's greatest slave-trading port. In all three cities, small and cohesive merchant classes exercised great public influence. The cities also had huge stores of industrial products for export, growing shipping industries, and large amounts of ready cash for investment abroad.

Slaving ships from Bristol plied back and forth along the Gold Coast, the Bight of Benin, Bonny, and Calabar looking for African traders who were willing to supply them with slaves. Liverpool's ships drew enslaved people from Gambia, the Windward Coast, and the Gold Coast. British ships carried textiles, gunpowder and flint, beer and spirits, British and Irish linens, and woolen cloth to Africa. A collection of goods was grouped together into what was called the **sorting**. An English sorting might include bolts of cloth, firearms, alcohol, tobacco, and hardware; this batch of goods was traded for an enslaved individual or a quantity of gold, ivory, or dyewood.[19]

European traders had two systems for exchange. First, especially on the Gold Coast, they established factory-forts. (For more on factory-forts, see "European Rivalry for Trade in the Indian Ocean" in Chapter 17.) These fortified trading posts were expensive to maintain but proved useful for fending off European rivals. Second, they used **shore trading**, in which European ships sent boats ashore or invited African dealers to bring traders and enslaved Africans out to the ships.

---

sorting A collection or batch of British goods that would be traded for a slave or for a quantity of gold, ivory, or dyewood.

shore trading A process for trading goods in which European ships sent boats ashore or invited African dealers to bring traders and slaves out to the ships.

The African Slave Trade A European slave trader discusses the exchange of goods for slaves brought to him by the African on the right at Gorée Island off the coast of Senegal. (The British Library, London, UK/akg-images)

(See "Thinking Like a Historian: Perspectives on the African Slave Trade," page 586.)

The shore method of buying slaves allowed the ship to move easily from market to market. The final prices of those enslaved depended on their ethnic origin, their availability when the shipper arrived, and their physical health when offered for sale in the West Indies or the North or South American colonies.

The supply of slaves for the foreign market was controlled by a small, wealthy African merchant class or by a state monopoly. By contemporary standards, slave raiding was a costly operation, and only black African entrepreneurs with sizable capital and labor could afford to finance and direct raiding drives.

The transatlantic slave trade that the British, as well as the Dutch, Portuguese, French, Americans, and others, participated in was part of a much larger trading network that is known as the triangle trade. European merchants sailed to Africa on the first leg of the voyage to trade European manufactured goods for enslaved Africans. When they had filled their ships' holds with enslaved people, they headed across the Atlantic on the second leg of the voyage, the Middle Passage. When they reached the Americas, the merchants unloaded and sold their human cargoes and used the profits to

purchase raw materials—such as cotton, sugar, and indigo—that they then transported back to Europe, completing the third leg of the commercial triangle.

Enslaved African people had an enormous impact on the economies and cultures of the Portuguese and Spanish colonies of South America and the Dutch, French, and British colonies of the Caribbean and North America. For example, on the sugar plantations of Mexico and the Caribbean; on the North American cotton, rice, and tobacco plantations; and in Peruvian and Mexican silver and gold mines, enslaved Africans not only worked in the mines and fields but also filled skilled, supervisory, and administrative positions and performed domestic service. In the United States enslaved Africans and their descendants influenced many facets of American culture, such as language, music (ragtime and jazz), dance, and diet. Even the U.S. White House and Capitol building, where Congress meets, were built partly by slave labor.[20] But the importance of the slave trade extended beyond the Atlantic world. Both the expansion of capitalism and the industrialization of Western societies; Egypt; and the nations of West, Central, and South Africa were related in one way or another to the traffic in African people.

Impact on African Societies

What economic impact did European trade have on African societies? Africans possessed technology well suited to their environment. Over the centuries they had cultivated a wide variety of plant foods; developed plant and animal husbandry techniques; and mined, smelted, and otherwise worked a great variety of metals. Apart from a handful of items, most notably firearms, American tobacco and rum, and Portuguese brandy, European goods presented no novelty to Africans, but were desirable because of their low prices. Africans exchanged slaves, ivory, gold, pepper, and animal skins for those goods. African states eager to expand or to control commerce bought European firearms, although the difficulty of maintaining guns often gave gun owners only marginal superiority over skilled bowmen.[21]

The African merchants who controlled the production of exports gained the most from foreign trade. The king of Dahomey (duh-HO-mee) (modern-day Benin in West Africa), for example, had a gross income in 1750 of £250,000 (almost U.S. $33 million today) from the overseas export of his fellow Africans. A portion of his profit was spent on goods that improved his people's living standard. Slave-trading entrepôts, which provided opportunities for traders and for farmers who supplied foodstuffs to towns, caravans, and slave ships, prospered. But such economic returns did not spread very far.[22] International trade did not lead to Africa's economic development. Africa experienced neither technological growth nor the gradual spread of economic benefits in early modern times.

As in the Islamic world, women in sub-Saharan Africa also engaged in the slave trade. In Guinea these women slave merchants and traders were known as *nhara*. They acquired considerable riches, often by marrying the Portuguese merchants and serving as go-betweens for these outsiders who were not familiar with the customs and languages of the African coast. One of them, Mae Aurélia Correia (1810?–1875?), led a life famous in the upper Guinea coastal region for its wealth and elegance. Between the 1820s and 1840s she operated her own trading vessels and is said to have owned several hundred slaves. Some of them she hired out as skilled artisans and sailors. She

and her sister (or aunt) Julia amassed a fortune in gold, silver jewelry, and expensive cloth while living in European-style homes. Julia and her husband, a trader from the Cape Verde Islands, also owned their own slave estates where they produced peanuts.

The intermarriage of French traders and Wolof women in Senegambia created a métis, or mulatto, class. In the emerging urban centers at Saint-Louis, members of this small class adopted the French language, the Roman Catholic faith, and a French manner of life, and they exercised considerable political and economic power. However, European cultural influences did not penetrate West African society beyond the seacoast.

The political consequences of the slave trade varied from place to place. The trade enhanced the power and wealth of some kings and warlords in the short run but promoted conditions of instability and collapse over the long run. In the Kongo kingdom the perpetual Portuguese search for Africans to enslave undermined the monarchy, destroyed political unity, and led to constant disorder and warfare; power passed to the village chiefs. Likewise in Angola, the slave trade decimated and scattered the population and destroyed the local economy. By contrast, the military kingdom of Dahomey, which entered into the slave trade in the eighteenth century and made it a royal monopoly, prospered enormously. Dahomey's economic strength rested on the slave trade. The royal army raided deep into the interior, and in the late eighteenth century Dahomey became one of the major West African sources of slaves. When slaving expeditions failed to yield sizable catches and when European demand declined, the resulting

Sapi-Portuguese Saltcellar Contact with the Sapi people of present-day Sierra Leone in West Africa led sixteenth-century Portuguese traders to commission this ivory saltcellar, for which they brought Portuguese designs. But the object's basic features — a spherical container and separate lid on a flat base, with men and/or women supporting, or serving as, beams below — are distinctly African. Here a Portuguese caravel sits on top with a man in the crow's nest. Four men stand below: two finely carved, regally dressed, and fully armed noblemen facing forward and two attendants in profile. (© akg-images/The Image Works)

Perspectives on the African Slave Trade

Before enslaved Africans began their horrific Middle Passage across the Atlantic, they were captured by African slavers in the interior and then traded to European merchants and slave-ship captains along the coast. Some African kingdoms, such as Benin or initially the Kongo, made enormous profits from the slave trade, while other societies, such as the Ibo, were the unfortunate victims.

1 Nzinga Mbemba (Affonso I), letter to the king of Portugal, July 6, 1526. Portuguese priests brought Christianity to the Kongo Kingdom in 1491, and King Affonso I (r. 1509–1543) of the Kongo and the entire royal family converted. Nevertheless, slavery had existed in the Kongo before the Portuguese arrived. King Affonso I initially profited from the transatlantic slave trade, but by the 1520s the trade threatened the kingdom's survival. Here Affonso begs the Portuguese king, João VI, to halt the trade.

◾ July 6, 1526

To Dom João, King our Brother

Sir, Your Highness should know how our Kingdom is being lost . . . caused by the excessive freedom given by your factors and officials to the men and merchants who are allowed to come to this Kingdom. . . .

And we cannot reckon how great the damage is, since the mentioned merchants are taking every day our natives, . . . they grab them and get them to be sold; and . . . our country is being completely depopulated. . . . We beg of Your Highness to help and assist us in this matter, . . . because it is *our will that in these Kingdoms there should not be any trade of slaves nor outlet for them*. . . . Otherwise we cannot remedy such an obvious damage. Pray Our Lord in His mercy to have Your Highness under His guard. . . . I kiss your hands many times.

At the town of Congo,
The King, Dom Affonso

2 William Bosman, description of the coast of Guinea, 1705. William Bosman, who arrived in West Africa in 1688, was employed by the Dutch East India Company at Elmina Castle (in modern Elmina, Ghana). He provides a detailed, first-person account of the African slave trade around the port city of Fida (modern Ouidah in Benin).

◾ The first business of one of our Factors when he comes to Fida, is to satisfie the Customs of the King . . . , about 100 Pounds in Guinea value. . . . After which we have free License to Trade. . . .

Before we can deal with any Person, we are obliged to buy the King's whole stock of Slaves at a set price; which is commonly one third or one fourth higher than ordinary: After which we [may] deal with all his Subjects. . . . But if there happen to be no stock of Slaves, the Factor must [trust] the Inhabitants with Goods to the value of one or two hundred Slaves; which Commodities they send into the In-land Country, in order to buy with them Slaves at all Markets, and that sometimes two hundred Miles deep in the Country. . . . Most of the Slaves that are offered to us are Prisoners of War, which are sold by the Victors as their Booty.

The Invalides . . . being thrown out, . . . the remainder are numbered, and it is entered who delivered them. In the meanwhile, a burning Iron, with the Arms or Name of the Companies, lies in the Fire; with which ours are marked on the Breast . . . that we may distinguish them from the Slaves of the English, French, or others (which are also marked with their Mark).

ANALYZING THE EVIDENCE

1. According to King Affonso's letter in Source 1, how were Portuguese merchants and foreign goods weakening his control over his people and depopulating his country?
2. In Sources 2 and 3, William Bosman and John Adams describe some of the rules and procedures followed by Africans and Europeans while engaging in the slave trade. What were some of these, and how did they advantage one side or the other, or both?
3. According to Adams's account in Source 3, how did the European ship captains and the African traders work together to obtain slaves?
4. Based on these sources, what assumptions can you make about how Africans viewed the slave trade?
5. In the image in Source 5, how do the African traders ensure that their captives, especially the men, will not rebel or run away?

3

John Adams, description of the shore trade at Bonny, 1822. John Adams, an English ship captain who made ten voyages to Africa between 1786 and 1800, describes the shore method of trading at Bonny.

■ This place is the wholesale market for slaves, as not fewer than 20,000 are annually sold here; 16,000 of whom are natives of one nation called Ibo....

Fairs where the slaves of the Ibo nation are obtained are held every five or six weeks at several villages, which are situated on the banks of the rivers and creeks in the interior, and to which the African traders of Bonny resort to purchase them.

...The [African] traders augment the quantity of their merchandise by obtaining from their friends, the captains of the slave ships, a considerable quantity of goods on credit.... Evening is the period chosen for the time of departure, when they proceed in a body, accompanied by the noise of drums, horns, and gongs. At the expiration of the sixth day, they generally return, bringing with them 1,500 or 2,000 slaves, who are sold to Europeans the evening after their arrival, and taken on board the ships.

4

Portuguese doctor, report on the slave trade in Luanda, 1793. An anonymous Portuguese doctor offers a detailed account of the conditions of enslaved Africans in Luanda. Be sure to note how the enslaved peoples are clearly considered, and treated, as chattel.

■ The dwelling place of the slave is simply the dirt floor of the compound, and he remains there exposed to harsh conditions and bad weather, and at night there are only a lean-to and some sheds ..., which they are herded into like cattle.

Their food continues scarce as before,... limited at times to badly cooked beans, at other

(Pictures from History/Bridgeman Images)

5

Gang of captives met at Mbame's on their way to Tette. This engraving is based on a sketch made by the Scottish missionary David Livingstone, who observed these enslaved African men, women, and children. Captured in the interior, the slaves were passing through the village of an African chief, Mbame, on their way to Tete, in modern Mozambique. Their African captors carry guns obtained from Europeans in the slave trade. Livingstone included the image in his account of his travels in central east Africa, *Narrative of an Expedition to the Zambesi...1858–1864*. The engraving was published in 1865–1866 in *Harper's New Monthly Magazine*.

times to corn.... And when they reach a port... they are branded on the right breast with the coat of arms of the king and nation, of whom they have become vassals.... This mark is made with a hot silver instrument in the act of paying the king's duties, and this brand mark is called a *carimbo*....

In this miserable and deprived condition the terrified slaves remain for weeks and months, and the great number of them who die is unspeakable. With some ten or twelve thousand arriving at Luanda each year, it often happens that only six or seven thousand are finally transported to Brazil.

PUTTING IT ALL TOGETHER

Using the sources above, along with what you have learned in class and in this chapter, write a short essay about the nature of the slave trade along the African coast. How did it operate, and what were the different roles that Europeans and Africans played in it?

Sources: (1) Basil Davidson, ed. *The African Past: Chronicles from Antiquity to Modern Times* (Boston: Little, Brown and Company, 1964), pp. 191–192; Copyright © 1964 by Basil Davidson. Reprinted by permission of Curtis Brown, Ltd.; (2) William Bosman, *A New and Accurate Description of the Coast of Guinea, Divided into the Gold, the Slave, and the Ivory Coasts* (London: J. Knapton, 1705), pp. 363–365; (3) John Adams, *Sketches Taken During Ten Voyages to Africa Between the Years 1786 and 1800* (London: Hurst, Robinson, and Co., 1822), pp. 38–39; (4) R. E. Conrad, *Children of God's Fire: A Documentary History of Black Slavery in Brazil* (Princeton, N.J.: Princeton University Press, 1983), pp. 20–23.

Queen Nzinga of Ndongo and Matamba Queen Ana Nzinga (ca. 1583–1663) ruled the Ndongo and Matamba kingdoms of the Mbundu people in modern-day Angola. Here she meets with the Portuguese governor at his offices in Luanda in 1622. Tradition says that the governor offered her only a floor mat to sit on, which would have placed her in a subordinate position to him, so she ordered one of her servants down onto the floor so she could sit on his back. She is recognized as a brilliant military strategist who personally led her troops into battle against the Portuguese. (Private Collection/Bridgeman Images)

depression in the Dahomean economy caused serious political unrest. Iboland, inland from the Niger Delta, from whose great port cities of Bonny and Brass the British drained tens of thousands of enslaved Africans, experienced minimal political effects. A high birthrate kept pace with the incursions of the slave trade, and Ibo societies remained demographically and economically strong.

What demographic impact did the slave trade have on Africa? Between approximately 1501 and 1866 more than 12 million Africans were forcibly exported to the Americas, 6 million were traded to Asia, and 8 million were retained as slaves within Africa. Figure 20.2 shows the estimated number of slaves shipped to the Americas in the transatlantic slave trade. Export figures do not include the approximately 10 to 15 percent who died during procurement or in transit.

The early modern slave trade involved a worldwide network of relationships among markets in the Middle East, Africa, Asia, Europe, and the Americas. But Africa

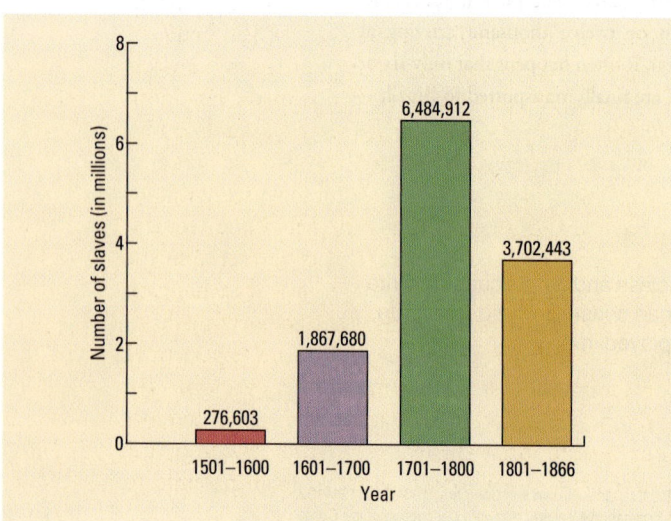

FIGURE 20.2 The Transatlantic Slave Trade, 1501–1866 The volume of slaves involved in the transatlantic slave trade peaked during the eighteenth century. These numbers show the slaves who embarked from Africa and do not reflect the 10 to 15 percent of enslaved Africans who died in transit.

(Source: Data from Emory University. "Assessing the Slave Trade: Estimates," in *Voyages: The Trans-Atlantic Slave Trade Database*. 2009. http://www.slavevoyages.org.)

was the crucible of the trade. There is no small irony in the fact that Africa, which of all the continents was most desperately in need of population because of its near total dependence on labor-intensive agriculture and pastoralism, lost so many millions to the trade. Although the British Parliament abolished the slave trade in 1807 and traffic in Africans to Brazil and Cuba gradually declined, within Africa the trade continued at the levels of the peak years of the transatlantic trade, 1780–1820. In the later nineteenth century developing African industries, using slave labor, produced a variety of products for domestic consumption and export. Again, there is irony in the fact that in the eighteenth century European demand for slaves expanded the trade (and wars) within Africa, yet in the nineteenth century European imperialists defended territorial aggrandizement by arguing that they were "civilizing" Africans by abolishing slavery. But after 1880 European businessmen (and African governments) did not push abolition; they wanted cheap labor.

Markets in the Americas generally wanted young male slaves. Asian and African markets preferred young females. Women were sought for their reproductive value, as sex objects, and because their economic productivity was not threatened by the possibility of physical rebellion, as might be the case with young men. Consequently, two-thirds of those exported to the Americas were male, one-third female. As a result, the population on Africa's western coast became predominantly female; the population in the East African savanna and Horn regions was predominantly male. The slave trade therefore had significant consequences for the institutions of marriage, the local trade in enslaved people (as these local populations became skewed with too many males or too many females), and the sexual division of labor. Although Africa's overall population may have shown modest growth from roughly 1650 to 1900, that growth was offset by declines in the Horn and on the eastern and western coasts. While Europe and Asia experienced considerable demographic and economic expansion in the eighteenth century, Africa suffered a decline.[23]

The political and economic consequences of the African slave trade are easier to measure than the human toll taken on individuals and societies. While we have personal accounts from many slaves, ships' captains and crews, slave masters, and others of the horrors of the slave-trading ports along Africa's coasts, the brutality of the Middle Passage, and the inhuman cruelty enslaved Africans endured once they reached the Americas, we know much less about the beginning of the slave's journey in Africa. Africans themselves carried out much of the "man stealing," the term used by Africans to describe capturing enslaved men, women, and children and marching them to the coast, where they were traded to Arabs, Europeans, or others.

Therefore, we have few written firsthand accounts of the pain and suffering these violent raids inflicted, either on the person being enslaved or on the families and societies they left behind.

Chapter Summary

In the early modern world, West African kingdoms and stateless societies existed side by side. Both had predominantly agricultural economies. Stateless societies revolved around a single village or group of villages without a central capital or ruler. Kings ruled over defined areas through bureaucratic hierarchies. The Sudanic empires controlled the north-south trans-Saharan trade in gold, salt, and other items. Led by predominantly Muslim rulers, these kingdoms belonged to a wider Islamic world, allowing them access to vast trade networks and some of the most advanced scholarship in the world. Still, Muslim culture affected primarily the royal and elite classes, seldom reaching the masses.

Europeans believed a wealthy (mythical) Christian monarch named Prester John ruled the Christian kingdom of Ethiopia. This fable attracted Europeans to Ethiopia, and partly explains why the Portuguese helped the Ethiopians fight off Muslim incursions. Jesuit missionaries tried to convert Ethiopians to Roman Catholicism but were fiercely resisted and expelled in 1633.

Swahili city-states on Africa's southeastern coast possessed a Muslim and mercantile culture. The Swahili acted as middlemen in the East African–Indian Ocean trade network, which in the late fifteenth and early sixteenth centuries Portugal sought to conquer and control. Swahili rulers who refused to form trading alliances with the Portuguese were attacked. The Portuguese presence caused the economic decline and death of many Swahili cities.

Slavery existed across Africa before Europeans arrived. Enslaved people were treated relatively benignly in some societies but elsewhere as chattel possessions, suffering harsh and brutal treatment. European involvement in the slave trade began around 1550, when the Portuguese purchased Africans to work in Brazil. The Dutch East India Company used enslaved Africans and southeast Asians in their Cape Colony. African entrepreneurs and merchants partnered in the trade, capturing people in the interior and exchanging them for firearms, liquor, and other goods with European slave ships. Though some kingdoms experienced a temporary rise of wealth and power, over time the slave trade was largely destabilizing. The individual suffering and social disruption in Africa caused by the enslavement of millions of Africans is impossible to estimate.

NOTES

1. P. D. Curtin, *Economic Change in Precolonial Africa: Senegambia in the Era of the Slave Trade* (Madison: University of Wisconsin Press, 1975), pp. 34–35; J. A. Rawley, *The Transatlantic Slave Trade: A History* (Lincoln: University of Nebraska Press, 2005).

2. Pieter de Marees, *Description of the Gold Kingdom of Guinea*, trans. and ed. Albert van Dantzig and Adam Jones (1602; repr., Oxford: Oxford University Press, 1987), pp. 226–228; William Bosman, *A New Description of the Coast of Guinea*, ed. John Ralph Willis (London: Frank Cass, 1967), p. 461.

3. Quoted in R. Hallett, *Africa to 1875* (Ann Arbor: University of Michigan Press, 1970), p. 151.

4. A. ibn-Fartura, "The Kanem Wars," in *Nigerian Perspectives*, ed. T. Hodgkin (London: Oxford University Press, 1966), pp. 111–115.

5. "The Kano Chronicle," quoted in *Nigerian Perspectives*, ed. T. Hodgkin (London: Oxford University Press, 1966), pp. 89–90.

6. *Equiano's Travels: The Interesting Narrative of the Life of Olaudah Equiano*, ed. P. Edwards (Portsmouth, N.H.: Heinemann, 1996), p. 4.

7. J. Iliffe, *Africans: The History of a Continent* (Cambridge: Cambridge University Press, 2007), p. 68.

8. See A. J. R. Russell-Wood, *The Portuguese Empire: A World on the Move* (Baltimore: Johns Hopkins University Press, 1998), pp. 11–13.

9. Ibid., pp. 35–38.

10. P. E. Lovejoy, *Transformations in Slavery: A History of Slavery in Africa* (Cambridge: Cambridge University Press, 1992), p. 25, Table 2.1, "Trans-Saharan Slave Trade, 650–1600."

11. Iliffe, *Africans*, p. 77.

12. Quoted in H. Thomas, *The Slave Trade* (New York: Simon and Schuster, 1997), p. 21.

13. G. Gerzina, *Black London: Life Before Emancipation* (New Brunswick, N.J.: Rutgers University Press, 1995), pp. 29–66 passim; quotation from p. 53.

14. R. Shell, *Children of Bondage: A Social History of the Slave Society at the Cape of Good Hope, 1652–1838* (Hanover, N.H.: University Press of New England, 1994), pp. 285–289.

15. See D. Eltis, *The Rise of African Slavery in the Americas* (Cambridge: Cambridge University Press, 2000), chap. 3; and the review/commentary by J. E. Inikori, *American Historical Review* 106.5 (December 2001): 1751–1753.

16. R. Blackburn, *The Making of New World Slavery: From the Baroque to the Modern, 1492–1800* (New York: Verso, 1998), pp. 79–80.

17. *Equiano's Travels*, pp. 23–26.

18. Rawley, *The Transatlantic Slave Trade*, pp. 45–47.

19. Robert W. July, *A History of the African People* (Prospect Heights, Ill.: Waveland Press, 1998), p. 171.

20. J. Thornton, *Africa and Africans in the Making of the Atlantic World* (New York: Cambridge University Press, 1992), pp. 138–142.

21. Robert W. July, *Precolonial Africa: An Economic and Social History* (New York: Scribner's, 1975), pp. 269–270.

22. A. G. Hopkins, *An Economic History of West Africa* (New York: Columbia University Press, 1973), p. 119.

23. P. Manning, *Slavery and African Life: Occidental, Oriental, and African Slave Trades* (New York: Cambridge University Press, 1990), pp. 22–23 and chap. 3, pp. 38–59.

CONNECTIONS

During the period from 1400 to 1800 many parts of Africa experienced a profound transition with the arrival of Europeans all along Africa's coasts. Ancient trade routes, such as those across the Sahara Desert or up and down the East African coast, were disrupted. In West Africa trade routes that had been purely internal now connected with global trade networks at European coastal trading posts. Along Africa's east coast the Portuguese attacked Swahili city-states in their effort to take control of the Indian Ocean trade nexus.

The most momentous consequence of the European presence along Africa's coast, however, was the introduction of the transatlantic slave trade. For more than three centuries Europeans, with the aid of African slave traders, enslaved millions of African men and women. Although many parts of Africa were untouched by the transatlantic slave trade, at least directly, areas where Africans were enslaved experienced serious declines in agricultural production, little progress in technological development, and significant increases in violence.

As we saw in Chapter 17 and will see in Chapter 21, early European commercial contacts with the empires of the Middle East and of South and East Asia were similar in many ways to those with Africa. Initially, the Portuguese, and then the English, Dutch, and French, did little more than establish trading posts at port cities and had to depend on the local people to bring them trade goods from the interior. Tropical diseases, particularly in India and Southeast Asia, took heavy death tolls on the Europeans, as they did in tropical Africa. What is more, while it was possible for the Portuguese to attack and conquer the individual Swahili city-states, Middle Eastern and Asian empires — such as the Ottomans in Turkey, the Safavids in Persia, the Mughals in India, and the Ming and Qing Dynasties in China — were, like the West African kingdoms, economically and militarily powerful enough to dictate terms of trade with the Europeans.

Resistance to enslavement took many forms on both sides of the Atlantic. In Haiti, as discussed in Chapter 22, resistance led to revolution and independence, marking the first successful uprising of non-Europeans against a colonial power. At the end of the nineteenth century, as described in Chapter 25, Europeans used the ongoing Arab-Swahili slave raids from Africa's eastern coast far into the interior as an excuse to invade and eventually colonize much of central and eastern Africa. The racial discrimination that accompanied colonial rule in Africa set the stage for a struggle for equality that led to eventual independence after World War II.

CHAPTER 20 Review and Explore

Identify Key Terms

Identify and explain the significance of each item below.

chattel (p. 567)

age-grade systems (p. 567)

oba (p. 567)

Taghaza (p. 568)

Tuareg (p. 572)

cowrie shells (p. 572)

Coptic Christianity (p. 573)

Swahili (p. 574)

Middle Passage (p. 581)

sorting (p. 583)

shore trading (p. 583)

Review the Main Ideas

Answer the focus questions from each section of the chapter.

1. What types of economic, social, and political structures were found in the kingdoms and states along the west coast and in the Sudan? (p. 566)

2. How did the arrival of Europeans and other foreign cultures affect the East African coast, and how did Ethiopia and the Swahili city-states respond to these incursions? (p. 573)

3. What role did slavery play in African societies before the transatlantic slave trade began, and what was the effect of European involvement? (p. 577)

Make Comparisons and Connections

Analyze the larger developments and continuities within and across chapters.

1. In what ways did Islam enrich the Sudanic empires of West Africa?

2. Discuss the ways in which Africa came into greater contact with a larger world during the period discussed in this chapter.

3. How did the transatlantic slave trade affect West African society?

AFRICA

← **1400–1600s** Salt trade dominates West African economy

← **ca. 1464–1591** Songhai kingdom dominates the western Sudan

1493–1528 Muhammad Toure governs and expands kingdom of Songhai

1571–1603 Idris Alooma governs kingdom of Kanem-Bornu

◆ **1485** Portuguese and other Europeans first appear in Benin

◆ **1498** Portuguese explorer Vasco da Gama sails around Africa

◆ **1591** Moroccan army defeats Songhai

1502–1507 Portuguese erect forts at Kilwa, Zanzibar, and Sofala on Swahili coast

◆ **1529** Adal defeats Ethiopian emperor; begins systematic devastation of Ethiopia

◆ **1543** Joint Ethiopian and Portuguese force defeats Muslims in Ethiopia

MIDDLE EAST

← **1299–1922** Ottoman Empire (Chs. 17, 25, 28)

EUROPE

← **1350–1520** European Renaissance (Ch. 15)

EAST ASIA

← **1368–1644** Ming Dynasty in China (Ch. 21)

AMERICAS

◆ **1521** ◆ **1533** Spanish conquest of Aztecs, then Incas (Ch. 16)

SOUTH ASIA

1526–1761 Era of Mughal India (Ch. 17)

1500	1550	1600

Suggested Resources

BOOKS

Berger, Iris, E. Frances White, and Cathy Skidmore-Heiss. *Women in Sub-Saharan Africa: Restoring Women to History.* 1999. Necessary reading for a complete understanding of African history.

Cooper, Frederick. *Plantation Slavery on the East Coast of Africa.* 1997. Useful study of slavery as practiced in Africa.

Fredrickson, G. M. *Racism: A Short History.* 2002. Contains probably the best recent study of the connection between African slavery and Western racism.

Klein, Martin, and Claire C. Robertson. *Women and Slavery in Africa.* 1997. Written from the perspective that most slaves in Africa were women.

Law, Robin. *Oyo Empire, c. 1600–c. 1836: A West African Imperialism in the Era of the Atlantic Slave Trade.* 1977. Remains the definitive study of the powerful Oyo Empire in what is today southwestern Nigeria.

Lovejoy, Paul E. *Transformations in Slavery: A History of Slavery in Africa,* 3d ed. 2012. Essential for an understanding of slavery in an African context.

Middleton, John. *The World of the Swahili: An African Mercantile Civilization.* 1992. Introduction to East Africa and the Horn region.

Northrup, David. *Africa's Discovery of Europe, 1450–1850,* 3d ed. 2013. Offers a unique perspective on African-European contact.

Oliver, Roland, and Anthony Atmore. *Medieval Africa, 1250–1800.* 2001. A history of premodern Africa by two renowned historians of the continent.

Pearson, Michael N. *Port Cities and Intruders: The Swahili Coast, India, and Portugal in the Early Modern Era.* 2002. Comprehensive introduction to the Swahili coast and the Indian Ocean trade network.

Powell, Eve Troutt, and John O. Hunwick. *The African Diaspora in the Mediterranean Lands of Islam.* 2002. Important study of Islam and the African slave trade.

Robinson, David. *Muslim Societies in African History.* 2004. Valuable introduction to Islam in Africa by a renowned Africanist.

Shell, Robert C.-H. *Children of Bondage: A Social History of the Slave Society at the Cape of Good Hope, 1652–1838.* 1994. A massive study of Cape slave society filled with much valuable statistical data.

1652 Dutch East India Company establishes colony at Cape of Good Hope

1658 Dutch East India Company allows importation of slaves into Cape Colony

1680s Famine from Senegambian coast to Upper Nile

1738–1756 Major famine in West Africa

1789 Olaudah Equiano publishes autobiography

1688–1689 English Glorious Revolution (Ch. 18)

1644–1911 Qing Dynasty in China (Chs. 21, 26)

1603–1867 Tokugawa Shogunate in Japan (Ch. 21)

| 1650 | 1700 | 1750 |

Shillington, Kevin. *History of Africa*, 3d ed. 2012. A soundly researched, highly readable, and well-illustrated survey.

Thornton, John. *Africa and Africans in the Making of the Atlantic World, 1400–1680*, 2d ed. 1998. Places African developments in an Atlantic context.

DOCUMENTARY

Africa: A Voyage of Discovery with Basil Davidson (Home Vision, 1984). An eight-part series about African history and society. See particularly episode 2, "Mastering the Continent"; episode 3, "Caravans of Gold"; and episode 4, "Kings and Cities." Run times are about fifty minutes for each program.

FEATURE FILMS

Amistad (Steven Spielberg, 1997). An award-winning film recounting the true story of a successful slave rebellion aboard *La Amistad*, a slave ship that was later seized by the United States, and the resulting legal battle over the status of the enslaved Africans that eventually reached the U.S. Supreme Court.

12 Years a Slave (Steve McQueen, 2013). Critically acclaimed, Academy Award–winning film adaptation of an 1853 slave narrative by Solomon Northup, a freeborn African American who was kidnapped and sold into slavery.

WEBSITES

Internet African History Sourcebook. A valuable reference site for historical sources on African history. **sourcebooks.fordham.edu/halsall/africa/africasbook .asp**

The Story of Africa. Some of the world's top Africanists have contributed to this BBC website's discussion of African history from an African perspective. **www.bbc.co.uk/worldservice/africa/features /storyofafrica/**

Voyages: The Trans-Atlantic Slave Trade Database. The premier database site for information about the transatlantic slave trade, including information and maps about nearly 36,000 slaving voyages, estimates of the number of enslaved Africans, and the identity of 91,491 Africans found in the slave records. **www.slavevoyages.org**

21

Continuity and Change in East Asia

1400–1800

The four centuries from 1400 to 1800 were a time of growth and dynamic change throughout East Asia. Although both China and Japan suffered periods of war, each ended up with expanded territories. The age of exploration brought New World crops to the region, leading to increased agricultural output and population growth. It also brought new opportunities for foreign trade and new religions. Another link between these countries was the series of massive Japanese invasions of Korea in the late sixteenth century, which led to war between China and Japan.

In China the native Ming Dynasty (1368–1644) brought an end to Mongol rule. Under the Ming, China saw agricultural reconstruction, commercial expansion, and the rise of a vibrant urban culture. In the early seventeenth century, after the Ming Dynasty fell into disorder, the non-Chinese Manchus founded the Qing Dynasty (1644–1911) and added Taiwan, Mongolia, Tibet, and Xinjiang to their realm. The Qing Empire thus was comparable to the other multiethnic empires of the early modern world, such as the Ottoman, Russian, and Habsburg Empires. In China itself the eighteenth century was a time of peace and prosperity.

In the Japanese islands the fifteenth century saw the start of civil war that lasted a century. At the end of the sixteenth century the world seemed to have turned upside down when a commoner, Hideyoshi, became the supreme ruler. He did not succeed in passing on his power to an heir, however. Power was seized by Tokugawa Ieyasu. Under the Tokugawa Shogunate (1603–1867), Japan restricted contact with the outside world and social mobility among its own people. Yet Japan thrived, as agricultural productivity increased and a lively urban culture developed.

Detail, *Portrait of the Imperial Bodyguard Zhanyinbao*, China, 18th century, Qing Dynasty (1644–1911). Hanging scroll; ink and color on silk. Purchase, The Dillon Fund Gift, 1986 (1986.206)/The Metropolitan Museum of Art, New York/Image copyright © The Metropolitan Museum of Art/Image source Art Resource, NY

The Manchu Imperial Bodyguard Zhanyinbao

Commissioned by the Qianlong emperor (r. 1736–1796), this portrait of imperial bodyguard Zhanyinbao was part of a large set that hung in the hall where the emperor received foreign emissaries.

CHAPTER PREVIEW

Ming China, 1368–1644

What sort of state and society developed in China after the Mongols were ousted?

The founding of the Ming Dynasty ushered in an era of peace and prosperity. By the beginning of the seventeenth century, however, the Ming government was beset by fiscal, military, and political problems.

The Rise of Zhu Yuanzhang and the Founding of the Ming Dynasty

The founder of the **Ming Dynasty**, Zhu Yuanzhang (JOO yoowan-JAHNG) (1328–1398), began life in poverty during the last decades of the Mongol Yuan Dynasty. His home region was hit by drought and then plague in the 1340s, and when he was only sixteen years old, his father, oldest brother, and that brother's wife all died, leaving two penniless boys with three bodies to bury. With no relatives to turn to, Zhu Yuanzhang asked a monastery to accept him as a novice. The monastery itself was short of funds, and the monks soon sent Zhu out to beg for food. For three or four years he wandered through central China. Only after he returned to the monastery did he learn to read.

A few years later, in 1351, members of a religious sect known as the Red Turbans rose in rebellion against the government. Red Turban teachings drew on Manichaean ideas about the incompatibility of the forces of good and evil as well as on the cult of the Maitreya Buddha, who according to believers would in the future bring his paradise to earth to relieve human suffering. When the temple where Zhu Yuanzhang was living was burned down in the fighting, Zhu joined the rebels and rose rapidly.

Ming China, ca. 1600

Zhu and his followers developed into brilliant generals, and gradually they defeated one rival after another. In 1356 Zhu took the city of Nanjing and made it his base. In 1368 his armies took Beijing, which the Mongol emperor and his closest followers had vacated just days before. Then forty years old, Zhu Yuanzhang declared himself emperor of the Ming (Bright) Dynasty. As emperor, he is known as Taizu (TIGH-dzoo) or the Hongwu emperor.

Taizu started his reign wanting to help the poor. To lighten the weight of government taxes and compulsory labor, he ordered a full-scale registration of cultivated land and population so that these burdens could be assessed more fairly. He also tried persuasion. He issued instructions to be read aloud to villagers, telling them to be obedient to their parents, live in harmony with their neighbors, work contentedly at their occupations, and refrain from evil.

Although in many ways anti-Mongol, Taizu retained some Yuan practices. One was setting up provinces as the administrative layer between the central government and the prefectures (local governments a step above counties). Another was the hereditary service obligation for both artisan and military households.

Garrisons were concentrated along the northern border and near the capital at Nanjing. Each garrison was allocated a tract of land that the soldiers took turns cultivating to supply their own food. Although in theory this system should have provided the Ming with a large but inexpensive army, the reality was less satisfactory. Garrisons were rarely self-sufficient. Furthermore, men compelled to become soldiers did not necessarily make good fighting men, and desertion was difficult to prevent. Consequently, like earlier dynasties, the Ming turned to non-Chinese northerners for much of its armed forces.

Taizu had deeply ambivalent feelings about men of education and sometimes brutally humiliated them in open court. His behavior was so erratic that it is most likely that he suffered from some form of mental illness. When literary men began to avoid official life, Taizu made it illegal to turn down appointments or to resign from office. He began falling into rages that only the empress could stop, and after her death in 1382 no one could calm him. In 1376 Taizu had thousands of officials killed because they were found to have taken shortcuts in their handling of paperwork for the grain tax. In 1380 Taizu concluded that his chancellor was plotting to assassinate him, and thousands only remotely connected to the chancellor were executed. From then on, Taizu acted as his own chancellor, dealing directly with the heads of departments and ministries.

The next important emperor, called Chengzu or the Yongle emperor (r. 1403–1425), was also a military man. One of Taizu's younger sons, he took the throne by force from his nephew and often led troops into battle against the Mongols. Like his father, Chengzu was willing to use terror to keep government officials in line.

Early in his reign, Chengzu decided to move the capital from Nanjing to Beijing, which had been his own base as a prince and the capital during Mongol times. Constructed between 1407 and 1420, Beijing was a planned city. Like Chang'an in Sui and Tang times (581–907), it was arranged like a set of boxes within boxes and built on a north-south axis. The main

Ming Dynasty The Chinese dynasty in power from 1368 to 1644; it marked a period of vibrant urban culture.

Forbidden City The palace complex in Beijing, commonly called the Forbidden City, was built in the early fifteenth century when the capital was moved from Nanjing to Beijing. Audience halls and other important state buildings are arranged on a north-south axis with huge courtyards between them, where officials would stand during ceremonies. (View Stock/age-fotostock)

outer walls were forty feet high and nearly fifteen miles around. Inside was the Imperial City, with government offices, and within that the palace itself, called the Forbidden City, with close to ten thousand rooms.

The areas surrounding Beijing were not nearly as agriculturally productive as those around Nanjing. To supply Beijing with grain, the Yuan Grand Canal connecting the city to the rice basket of the Yangzi River regions was broadened, deepened, and supplied with more locks and dams. The 15,000 boats and the 160,000 soldiers of the transport army who pulled loaded barges from the towpaths along the canal became the lifeline of the capital.

Problems with the Imperial Institution

Taizu had decreed that succession should go to the eldest son of the empress or to the son's eldest son if the son predeceased his father, the system generally followed by earlier dynasties. In Ming times, the flaws in this system became apparent as one mediocre, obtuse, or erratic emperor followed another.

Because Taizu had abolished the position of chancellor, emperors turned to secretaries and eunuchs to manage the paperwork. Eunuchs were essentially slaves who had been captured as boys and castrated. Society considered eunuchs the basest of servants, and Confucian scholars heaped scorn on them. Yet Ming emperors, like rulers in earlier dynasties, often preferred the always-compliant eunuchs to high-minded, moralizing civil service officials.

In Ming times, the eunuch establishment became huge. By the late fifteenth century the eunuch bureaucracy had grown as large as the civil service, with each having roughly twelve thousand positions. After 1500 the eunuch bureaucracy grew even more rapidly, and by the mid-sixteenth century seventy thousand eunuchs were in service throughout the country, with ten thousand in the capital. Tension between the two bureaucracies was high. In 1420 Chengzu set up a eunuch-run secret service to investigate cases of suspected corruption and sedition in the regular bureaucracy. Eunuch control over vital government processes became a severe problem.

In hope of persuading emperors to make reforms, many Ming officials risked their careers and lives by speaking out. To give an example, in 1519, when an emperor announced plans to make a tour of the southern provinces, over a hundred officials staged a protest by kneeling in front of the palace. The emperor ordered the officials to remain kneeling for three days, then had them flogged; eleven died. Rarely, however, did such acts move an emperor to change his mind.

Although the educated public complained about the performance of emperors, no one proposed or even imagined alternatives to imperial rule. High officials were forced to find ways to work around uncooperative emperors, but they were not able to put in place institutions that would limit the damage an emperor could do.

The Mongols and the Great Wall

The early Ming emperors held Mongol fighting men in awe and feared they might form another great military machine of the sort Chinggis Khan (ca. 1162–1227) had put together two centuries earlier. Although in Ming times the Mongols were never united in a pan-Mongol federation, groups of Mongols could and did raid. Twice they threatened the dynasty: in 1449 the khan of the western Mongols captured the Chinese emperor, and in 1550 Beijing was surrounded by the forces of the khan of the Mongols in Inner Mongolia. Fearful of anything that might strengthen the Mongols, Ming officials were reluctant to grant any privileges to Mongol leaders, such as trading posts along the borders. Instead they wanted the different groups of Mongols to trade only through the formal tribute system. When trade was finally liberalized in 1570, friction was reduced.

Two important developments shaped Ming-Mongol relations: the construction of the Great Wall and closer relations between Mongolia and Tibet. The Great Wall, much of which survives today, was built as a compromise when Ming officials could agree on no other way to manage the Mongol threat. The wall extends about 1,500 miles from northeast of Beijing into Gansu province. In the eastern 500 miles, the wall averages about 35 feet high and 20 feet across, with lookout towers every half mile.

Whether the wall did much to protect Ming China from the Mongols is still debated. Perhaps of more significance was the spread of Tibetan Buddhism among the Mongols. Tibet in this period was dominated by the major Buddhist monasteries, which would turn to competing Mongol leaders when they needed help. In 1577 the third Dalai Lama accepted the invitation of Altan Khan to visit Mongolia, and the khan declared Tibetan Buddhism to be the official religion of all the Mongols. The Dalai Lama gave the khan the title "King of Religion," and the khan swore that the Mongols would renounce blood sacrifice. When the third Dalai Lama's reincarnation was found to be the great-grandson of Altan Khan, the ties between Tibet and Mongolia, not surprisingly, became even stronger. From the perspective of Ming China, the growing influence of Buddhism among the Mongols seemed a positive development, as Buddhist emphasis on nonviolence was expected to counter the Mongols' love of war (though in fact the development of firearms was probably more crucial in the Mongols' loss of military advantage over their neighbors).

The Examination Life

In sharp contrast to Europe in this era, Ming China had few social barriers. It had no hereditary aristocracy that could have limited the emperor's absolute power. Although China had no titled aristocracy, it did have an elite whose status was based above all on government office acquired through education. Unlike in many European countries of the era, China's merchants did not become a politically articulate class of the well-to-do. Instead the politically active class was that of the scholars who Confucianism taught should aid the ruler in running the state. Merchants tried to marry into the scholar class in order to rise in the world.

Thus, despite the harsh and arbitrary ways in which the Ming emperors treated their civil servants, educated men were eager to enter the government. Reversing the policies of the Mongol Yuan Dynasty, the Ming government recruited almost all its officials through **civil service examinations**. Candidates had to study the Confucian classics and the interpretations of them

Portrait of a Scholar-Official The official Jiang Shunfu arranged to have his portrait painted wearing an official robe and hat and followed by two boy attendants, one holding a lute wrapped in cloth. During Ming and Qing times, the rank of an official was made visible by the badges he wore on his robes. The pair of cranes on Jiang's badge shows he held a first-rank post in the civil service hierarchy. (Visual Connection Archive)

by the twelfth-century Neo-Confucian scholar Zhu Xi (joo shee) (1130–1200), whose teachings were declared orthodox. To become officials, candidates had to pass examinations at the prefectural, the provincial, and the capital levels. To keep the wealthiest areas from dominating the exams, quotas were established for the number of candidates that each province could send on to the capital.

Of course, boys from well-to-do families had a significant advantage because their families could start their education with tutors at age four or five, though less costly schools were becoming increasingly available as well. Families that for generations had pursued other careers—for example, as merchants or physicians—had more opportunities than ever for their sons to become officials through the exams. (See "Individuals in Society: Tan Yunxian, Woman Doctor," page 600.) Clans sometimes operated schools for their members. Most of those who attended school stayed only a few years, but students who seemed most promising moved on to advanced schools where they practiced essay writing and studied the essays of men who had succeeded in the exams.

The examinations at the prefecture level lasted a day and drew hundreds if not thousands of candidates. The government compound would be taken over to give all candidates places to sit and write. The provincial and capital examinations were given in three sessions spread out over a week. In the first session, candidates wrote essays on passages from the classics. In the second and third sessions, candidates had to write essays on practical policy issues and on a passage from the *Classic of Filial Piety* (a brief text celebrating devotion to parents and other superiors). In addition, they had to show that they could draft state papers such as edicts, decrees, and judicial rulings. Reading the dynastic histories was a good way to prepare for policy questions and state paper exercises.

The provincial examinations were major local events. From five thousand to ten thousand candidates descended on the city and filled up its hostels. To prevent cheating, no written material could be taken into the cells, and candidates were searched before being admitted. Anyone caught wearing a cheat-sheet (an inner gown covered with the classics in minuscule script) was thrown out of the exam and banned from the next session as well. During the sessions candidates had time to write rough drafts of their essays, correct them, and then copy neat final versions. Throughout this time, tension was high.

After the papers were handed in, clerks recopied them and assigned them numbers to preserve anonymity. Proofreaders checked the copying before handing the papers to the assembled examiners, who divided them up to grade, which generally took about twenty days. Those 2 to 10 percent who passed could not spend long celebrating, however, because they had to begin preparing for the capital exams, less than a year away.

Everyday Life in Ming China

For civil servants and almost everyone else, everyday life in Ming China followed patterns established in earlier periods. The family remained central to most people's lives, and almost everyone married. Beyond the family, people's lives were shaped by the type of work they did and where they lived.

Large towns and cities proliferated in Ming times and became islands of sophistication in the vast sea of rural villages. In these urban areas small businesses manufactured textiles, paper, and luxury goods such as silks and porcelains. The southeast became a center for the production of cotton and silks; other areas specialized in the grain and salt trades and in silver.

Printing reached the urban middle classes by the late Ming period, when publishing houses were putting out large numbers of books aimed at general audiences. To make their books attractive in the marketplace, entrepreneurial book publishers commissioned artists to illustrate them. By the sixteenth century more and more books were being published in the vernacular language (the language people spoke), especially short stories, novels, and plays. Ming vernacular short stories depicted a world much like that of their readers, full of shop clerks and merchants, monks and prostitutes, students and matchmakers. (See "Global Viewpoints: Chinese and European Commentators on Urban Amusements," page 602.)

The full-length novel made its first appearance during the Ming period. The plots of the early novels were heavily indebted to story cycles developed by oral storytellers over the course of several centuries. Competing publishers brought out their own editions of these novels, sometimes adding new illustrations or commentaries.

The Chinese found recreation and relaxation in many ways besides reading. The affluent indulged in an alcoholic drink made from fermented and distilled rice, and once tobacco was introduced from the Americas, both men and women took up pipes. Plays were also very popular. Owners of troupes would purchase young children and train them to sing and perform. Jesuit missionary Matteo Ricci, who lived in China from 1582 to 1610, thought too many people were addicted to these performances:

> These groups of actors are employed at all imposing banquets, and when they are called they come prepared to enact any of the ordinary plays. The host at the banquet is usually presented with a volume of

civil service examinations A highly competitive series of written tests held at the prefecture, province, and capital levels in China to select men to become officials.

Tan Yunxian, Woman Doctor

THE GRANDMOTHER OF TAN YUNXIAN (1461–1554) WAS the daughter of a physician, and her husband had married into her home to learn medicine himself. At least two of their sons—including Yunxian's father—passed the civil service examination and became officials, raising the social standing of the family considerably. The grandparents wanted to pass their medical knowledge down to someone, and because they found Yunxian very bright, they decided to teach it to her.

Tan Yunxian married and raised four children but also practiced medicine, confining her practice to women. At age fifty she wrote an autobiographical account, *Sayings of a Female Doctor*. In the preface she described how, under her grandmother's tutelage, she had first memorized the *Canon of Problems* and the *Canon of the Pulse*. Then when her grandmother had time, she asked her granddaughter to explain particular passages in these classic medical treatises.

Tan Yunxian began the practice of medicine by treating her own children, asking her grandmother to check her diagnoses. When her grandmother was old and ill, she gave Yunxian her notebook of prescriptions and her equipment for making medicines, telling her to study them carefully. Later, Yunxian herself became seriously ill and dreamed of her grandmother telling her on what page of which book to find the prescription that would cure her. When she recovered, she began her medical career in earnest.

Tan Yunxian's book records the cases of thirty-one patients she treated, most of them women with chronic complaints rather than critical illnesses. Many of the women had what the Chinese classed as women's complaints, such as menstrual irregularities, repeated miscarriages, barrenness, and postpartum fatigue. Some had ailments that men too could suffer, such as coughs, nausea, insomnia, diarrhea, rashes, and swellings. Like other literati physicians, Yunxian regularly prescribed herbal medications. She also practiced moxibustion, the technique of burning moxa (dried artemisia) at specified points on the body with the goal of stimulating the circulation of qi (life energy). Because the physician applying the moxa had to touch the patient, male physicians could not perform moxibustion on women.

Yunxian's patients included working women, and Yunxian seems to have thought that their problems often sprang from overwork. One woman came to her because she had had vaginal bleeding for three years. When questioned, the woman told Yunxian that she worked all day with her husband at their kiln making bricks and tiles. Yunxian's diagnosis was overwork, and she gave the woman pills to replenish her yin energies. A boatman's wife came to her complaining of

Tan Yunxian would have consulted traditional herbals, like this one, with sketches of plants of medicinal value and descriptions of their uses. (Wellcome Library, London, UK)

numbness in her hands. When the woman told Yunxian that she worked in the wind and rain handling the boat, the doctor advised some time off. In another case Yunxian explained to a servant girl that she had gone back to work too soon after suffering a wind damage fever.

By contrast, when patients came from upper-class families, Tan Yunxian believed negative emotions were the source of their problems, particularly if a woman reported that her mother-in-law had scolded her or that her husband had recently brought a concubine home. Yunxian told two upper-class women who had miscarried that they lost their babies because they had hidden their anger, causing fire to turn inward and destabilize the fetus.

Tan Yunxian herself lived a long life, dying at age ninety-three.

QUESTIONS FOR ANALYSIS

1. Why do you think Tan Yunxian treated only women? Why might she have been more effective with women patients than a male physician would have been?
2. What do you think of Yunxian's diagnoses? Do you think she was able to help many of her patients?

Source: Based on Charlotte Furth, *A Flourishing Yin: Gender in China's Medical History, 960–1665* (Berkeley: University of California Press, 1999), pp. 285–295.

Popular Romance Literature Women were among the most avid readers of the scripts for plays, especially romantic ones like *The Western Chamber*, a story of a young scholar who falls in love with a well-educated girl he encounters by chance. In this scene, the young woman looks up at the moon as her maid looks at its reflection in the pond. Meanwhile, her young lover scales the wall. This multicolor woodblock print, made in 1640, was one of twenty-one created to illustrate the play. (Pictures from History/CPA Media)

plays and he selects the one or several he may like. The guests, between eating and drinking, follow the plays with so much satisfaction that the banquet at times may last for ten hours.[1]

Rice supplied most of the calories of the population in central and south China. (In north China, wheat, made into steamed or baked bread or into noodles, served as the dietary staple.) Farmers began to stock the rice paddies with fish, which continuously fertilized the rice fields, destroyed malaria-bearing mosquitoes, and enriched the diet. Farmers also grew cotton, sugarcane, and indigo as commercial crops. New methods of crop rotation allowed for continuous cultivation and for more than one harvest per year from a single field.

The Ming rulers promoted the repopulation and colonization of war-devastated regions through reclamation of land and massive transfers of people. Immigrants to these areas received large plots and exemption from taxation for many years. Reforestation played a dramatic role in the agricultural revolution. In 1391 the Ming government ordered 50 million trees planted in the Nanjing area to produce lumber for the construction of a maritime fleet. In 1392 each family holding a land grant in Anhui province had to plant two hundred mulberry, jujube, and persimmon trees. In

1396 peasants in the present-day provinces of Hunan and Hubei in central China planted 84 million fruit trees. Historians have estimated that 1 billion trees were planted during Taizu's reign.

Increased food production led to steady population growth and the multiplication of markets, towns, and small cities. Larger towns had permanent shops; smaller towns had periodic markets convening every five or ten days. They sold essential goods—such as pins, matches, oil for lamps, candles, paper, incense, and tobacco—to country people from the surrounding hamlets. Markets usually offered essential goods such as lamp oil and matches as well as the services of moneylenders, pawnbrokers, and craftsmen such as carpenters, barbers, joiners, and locksmiths.

Ming Decline

Beginning in the 1590s the Ming government was beset by fiscal, military, and political problems. The government went nearly bankrupt helping defend Korea against a Japanese invasion (see "Piracy and Japan's Overseas Adventures"). Then came a series of natural disasters: floods, droughts, locusts, and epidemics ravaged one region after another. At the same time, a "little ice age" brought a drop in average temperatures that shortened the growing season and reduced harvests. In

Chinese and European Commentators on Urban Amusements

Zhang Dai (1597–1684?) lived the life of a well-to-do urban aesthete in Nanjing in the last decades of the Ming Dynasty, and then saw that life destroyed by the Manchu invasion. In later years, in much reduced circumstances, he wrote with nostalgia about the pleasures of his youth. His account of a popular storyteller can be compared to a Swiss visitor's account of the London theater scene in 1599.

Zhang Dai on a Nanjing Storyteller

■ Pockmarked Liu of Nanjing . . . is an excellent storyteller.

He tells one episode a day, and his fee is one ounce of silver. To engage him you have to make your booking, and forward his retainer, ten days in advance, and even then you may be out of luck. . . . I heard him tell the story of Wu Song killing the tiger on Jingyang Ridge. His version diverged greatly from the original text. He will describe things in the minutest particular, but his choice of what to put in and leave out is nice and neat, and he is never wordy. His bellow is like the boom of a mighty bell, and when he gets to some high point in the action he will let loose such a peal of thunder that the building will shake on its foundations. I remember that when Wu Song goes into the inn to get a drink and finds no one there to serve him, he suddenly gave such a roar as to set all the empty vessels humming and vibrating. To make dull patches come to life like this is typical of his passion for detail.

When he goes to perform in someone's house, he will not loosen his tongue until his hosts sit quietly, hold their breath, and give him their undivided attention. If he spots the servants whispering, or if his listeners yawn or show any signs of fatigue, he will come to an abrupt halt, and be impervious to persuasion to continue. He will often talk till past midnight, still keeping up an unhurried flow, while the servants wipe the tables, trim the lamp, and silently serve tea in cups of tasteful porcelain. His pacing and his inflexions, his articulation and his cadences, are exactly suited to the situation, and lay bare the very body and fibre of the matter. If one

plucked all the other storytellers alive by the ear and made them listen to him, I do not doubt but they would be struck dumb with wonder and give up the ghost on the spot.

Thomas Platter on London Theater

■ On September 21st after lunch, about two o'clock, I and my party crossed the water, and there in the house with the thatched roof witnessed an excellent performance of the tragedy of the first Emperor Julius Caesar with a cast of some fifteen people; when the play was over, they danced very marvelously and gracefully together as is their wont, two dressed as men and two as women. . . . Thus daily at two in the afternoon, London has two, sometimes three plays running in different places, competing with each other, and those which play best obtain most spectators. The playhouses are so constructed that they play on a raised platform, so that everyone has a good view. There are different galleries and places, however, where the seating is better and more comfortable and therefore more expensive. For whoever cares to stand below only pays one English penny, but if he wishes to sit he enters by another door and pays another penny, while if he desires to sit in the most comfortable seats, which are cushioned, where he not only sees everything well, but can also be seen, then he pays yet another English penny at another door. And during the performance food and drink are carried round the audience, so that for what one cares to pay one may also have refreshment.

QUESTIONS FOR ANALYSIS

1. What similarities do you see in the way the performers in these descriptions entertained their audiences? What differences do you see?
2. What makes foreign visitors' accounts useful? What advantage do local observers have?

Sources: David Pollard, trans. and ed., *The Chinese Essay* (New York: Columbia University Press, 2000), pp. 89–90. Reproduced with permission of C. HURST & CO. LTD. in the format Book via Copyright Clearance Center; Clare Williams, trans., *Thomas Platter's Travels in England, 1599* (London: J. Cape, 1937), pp. 166–167.

---

areas of serious food shortages, gangs of army deserters and laid-off soldiers began scouring the countryside in search of food. Once the gangs had stolen all their grain, hard-pressed farmers joined them just to survive. The Ming government had little choice but to try to increase taxes to deal with these threats, but the last thing people needed was heavier taxes.

Adding to the hardship was a sudden drop in the supply of silver. In place of the paper money that had circulated in Song and Yuan times, silver ingots came into general use as money in Ming times. Much of this silver originated in either Japan or the New World and entered China as payment for the silk and porcelains exported from China. When events in Japan and the Philippines led to disruption of trade, silver imports dropped. This led to deflation in China, which caused real rents to rise. Soon there were riots among urban workers and tenant farmers. In 1642 a group of rebels cut the dikes on the Yellow River, causing massive flooding. A smallpox epidemic soon added to the death toll. In 1644 the last Ming emperor, in despair, took his own life when rebels entered Beijing, opening the way for the start of a new dynasty.

The Manchus and Qing China, to 1800

Did the return of alien rule with the Manchus have any positive consequences for China?

The next dynasty, the **Qing Dynasty** (1644–1911), was founded by the Manchus, a non-Chinese people who were descended from the Jurchens. In the late sixteenth century the Manchus began expanding their territories, and in 1644 they founded the Qing (CHING) Dynasty, which brought peace and in time prosperity. Successful Qing military campaigns extended the borders into Mongol, Tibetan, and Uighur regions, creating a multiethnic empire that was larger than any earlier Chinese dynasty.

The Rise of the Manchus

In the Ming period, the Manchus lived in dispersed communities in what is loosely called Manchuria (the northeast of modern-day China). In the more densely populated southern part of Manchuria, the Manchus lived in close contact with Mongols, Koreans, and Chinese (Map 21.1). They were not nomads but rather hunters, fishers, and farmers. Like the Mongols, they also were excellent horsemen and archers and had a strongly hierarchical social structure, with elites and slaves. Slaves, often Korean or Chinese, were generally acquired through capture. Manchu villages were often at odds with each other over resources, and men did not leave their villages without arming themselves with bows and arrows or swords. Interspersed among these Manchu settlements were groups of nomadic Mongols who lived in tents.

The Manchus credited their own rise to Nurhaci (1559–1626). Over several decades, he united the Manchus and expanded their territories. Like Chinggis Khan, who had reorganized the Mongol armies to reduce the importance of tribal affiliations, Nurhaci created a new social basis for his armies in units called **banners**. Each banner was made up of a set of military companies and included the families and slaves of the soldiers. Each company had a hereditary captain, often from Nurhaci's own lineage. When new groups were

defeated, their members were distributed among several banners to lessen their potential for subversion.

The Manchus entered China by invitation of the distinguished Ming general Wu Sangui, who was near the eastern end of the Great Wall when he heard that the rebels had captured Beijing. The Manchus proposed to Wu that they join forces and liberate Beijing. Wu opened the gates of the Great Wall to let the Manchus in, and within a couple of weeks they occupied Beijing. When the Manchus made clear that they intended to conquer the rest of the country and take the throne themselves, Wu and many other Chinese generals joined forces with them. Before long, China was again under alien rule.

In the summer of 1645 the Manchus ordered all Chinese men to shave the front of their heads and braid the rest in the Manchu fashion, an order many refused to comply with. Their resistance led Manchu commanders to order the slaughter of defiant cities. After quelling resistance, the Qing put in place policies and institutions that gave China a respite from war and disorder. Most of the political institutions of the Ming Dynasty were taken over relatively unchanged, including the examination system.

After peace was achieved, population growth took off. Between 1700 and 1800 the Chinese population seems to have nearly doubled, from about 150 million to over 300 million. Population growth during the eighteenth century has been attributed to many factors: global warming that extended the growing season, expanded use of New World crops, slowing of the spread of new diseases that had accompanied the sixteenth-century expansion of global traffic, and the efficiency of the Qing government in providing relief in times of famine.

Some scholars have recently argued that China's overall standard of living in the mid-eighteenth century was comparable to Europe's and that the standards of China's most developed regions, such as the lower Yangzi region, compared favorably to those of the most developed regions of Europe at the time, such as England and the Netherlands. Life expectancy, food consumption, and even facilities for transportation were at similar levels.

Competent and Long-Lived Emperors

For more than a century, China was ruled by only three rulers, each of them hard-working, talented, and committed to making the Qing Dynasty a success.

Qing Dynasty The dynasty founded by the Manchus that ruled China from 1644 to 1911.

banners Units of the Manchu army, composed of soldiers, their families, and slaves.

MAP 21.1 The Qing Empire, ca. 1800 The sheer size of the Qing Empire in China almost inevitably led to its profound cultural influence on the rest of Asia.

ANALYZING THE MAP How many different cultural groups are depicted? Which occupied the largest territories? Where was crop agriculture most prevalent?

CONNECTIONS What geographical and political factors limited the expansion of the Qing Empire?

Two, the Kangxi and Qianlong emperors, had exceptionally long reigns.

Kangxi (KAHNG-shee) (r. 1661–1722) proved adept at meeting the expectations of both the Chinese and the Manchu elites. Kangxi could speak, read, and write Chinese and made efforts to persuade educated Chinese that the Manchus had a legitimate claim to rule, even trying to attract Ming loyalists who had been unwilling to serve the Qing. He undertook a series of tours of the south, where Ming loyalty had been strongest, and he held a special exam to select men to compile the official history of the Ming Dynasty.

Qianlong (chyan-luhng) (r. 1736–1796) understood that the Qing's capacity to hold the multiethnic empire together rested on their ability to appeal to all those they ruled. Besides speaking Manchu and Chinese, Qianlong learned to converse in Mongolian, Uighur, Tibetan, and Tangut, and he addressed envoys in their own languages. He became as much a patron

of Tibetan Buddhism as of Chinese Confucianism. He initiated a massive project to translate the Tibetan Buddhist canon into Mongolian and Manchu and had huge multilingual dictionaries compiled.

To demonstrate to the Chinese scholar-official elite that he was a sage emperor, Qianlong worked on affairs of state from dawn until early afternoon and then turned to reading, painting, and calligraphy. He was ostentatious in his devotion to his mother, visiting her daily and tending to her comfort with all the devotion of the most filial Chinese son. He took several tours down the Grand Canal to the southeast, in part to emulate his grandfather, in part to entertain his mother, who accompanied him on these tours.

Despite these displays of Chinese virtues, the Qianlong emperor was alert to any signs of anti-Manchu thoughts or actions. He ordered full searches for books with disparaging references to the Manchus or to previous alien conquerors like the Jurchens and Mongols.

Presenting a Horse to the Emperor This detail from a 1757 hand scroll shows the Qianlong emperor, seated, receiving envoys from the Kazakhs. Note how the envoy, presenting a pure white horse, is kneeling to the ground performing the kowtow, which involved lowering his head to the ground as an act of reverence. The artist was Giuseppe Castiglione, an Italian who worked as a painter in Qianlong's court. (Musée des Arts Asiatiques-Guimet, Paris, France/© RMN–Grand Palais/Art Resource, NY)

Sometimes passages were deleted or rewritten, but when an entire book was offensive, it was destroyed.

Throughout Qianlong's reign, China remained an enormous producer of manufactured goods and led the way in assembly-line production. The government operated huge textile factories, but some private firms were even larger. Hangzhou had a textile firm that gave work to 4,000 weavers, 20,000 spinners, and 10,000 dyers and finishers. The porcelain kilns at Jingdezhen employed the division of labor on a large scale and were able to supply porcelain to much of the world. The growth of the economy benefited the Qing state, and the treasury became so full that the Qianlong emperor was able to cancel taxes on several occasions.

Imperial Expansion

The Qing Dynasty put together a multiethnic empire that was larger than that of any earlier Chinese dynasty. Taiwan was acquired in 1683. In 1696 Kangxi led an army of eighty thousand men into Mongolia, and within a few years Manchu supremacy was accepted there. Cannon and muskets gave Qing forces military superiority over the Mongols, who were armed only with bows and arrows. Thus the Qing could dominate the steppe cheaply, effectively ending two thousand years of Inner Asian military advantage.

In the 1720s the Qing established a permanent garrison of banner soldiers in Tibet. By this time, the expanding Qing and Russian Empires were nearing each other. In 1689 the Manchu and the Russian rulers approved a treaty—written in Russian, Manchu,

Chinese, and Latin—defining their borders in Manchuria and regulating trade. Another treaty in 1727 allowed a Russian ecclesiastical mission to reside in Beijing and a trade caravan to make a trip from Russia to Beijing once every three years.

The last region to be annexed was Chinese Turkestan (the modern province of Xinjiang). Both the Han and the Tang Dynasties had stationed troops in the region, exercising loose overlordship, but neither the Song nor the Ming had tried to control the area. The Qing won the region in the 1750s through a series of campaigns against Uighur and Dzungar Mongol forces.

Japan's Middle Ages, ca. 1400–1600

How did Japan change during this period of political instability?

In the twelfth century Japan entered an age dominated by military men, an age that can be compared to Europe's feudal age. The Kamakura Shogunate (1185–1333) had its capital in the east, at Kamakura. It was succeeded by the Ashikaga Shogunate (1338–1573), which returned the government to Kyoto (KYOH-toh) and helped launch, during the fifteenth century, the great age of Zen-influenced Muromachi culture. The sixteenth century brought civil war over succession to the shogunate, leading to the building of massive castles and the emergence of rulers of obscure origins who eventually unified the realm.

Muromachi Culture

The headquarters of the Ashikaga shoguns were on Muromachi Street in Kyoto, and the refined and elegant style that they promoted is often called Muromachi culture. The shoguns patronized Zen Buddhism, the school of Buddhism associated with meditation and mind-to-mind transmission of truth.

Zen ideas of simplicity permeated the arts. The Silver Pavilion built by the shogun Yoshimasa (r. 1449–1473) epitomizes Zen austerity. Yoshimasa was also influential in the development of the tea ceremony, which celebrated the beauty of imperfect objects, such as plain or misshapen cups or pots. Spare monochrome paintings fit into this aesthetic, as did simple asymmetrical flower arrangements.

The shoguns were also patrons of the **Nō theater**. Nō drama originated in popular forms of entertainment, including comical skits and dances directed to the gods. It was transformed into high art by Zeami (1363–1443), an actor and playwright. Nō was performed on a bare stage with a pine tree painted across the backdrop. One or two actors wearing brilliant brocade robes performed, using stylized gestures and stances, one wearing a mask. The actors were accompanied by a chorus and a couple of musicians playing drums and flute. Many of the stories concerned ghosts consumed by jealous passions or the desire for revenge. The performers conveyed emotions and ideas as much through gestures, stances, and dress as through words. Zeami argued that the most meaningful moments came during silence, when the actor's spiritual presence allowed the audience to catch a glimpse of the mysterious and inexpressible.

Civil War

Civil war began in Kyoto in 1467 as a struggle over succession to the shogunate. Rival claimants and their followers used arson as their chief weapon and burned down temples and mansions, destroying much of the city and its treasures. Once Kyoto was laid waste, war spread to outlying areas. When the shogun could no longer protect cities, merchants banded together to hire mercenaries. In the political vacuum, the Lotus League, a commoner-led religious sect united by faith in the saving power of the Lotus Sutra, set up a commoner-run government that collected taxes and settled disputes. In 1536, during eight days of fighting, the powerful Buddhist monastery Enryakuji

Hideyoshi's Campaigns in Japan and Korea, 1592–1598

attacked the League and its temples, burned much of the city, and killed men, women, and children who were thought to be believers.

In these confused and violent circumstances, power devolved to the local level, where warlords, from the **daimyo** (DIGH-myoh) class of regional lords, built their power bases. Many of the most successful daimyo were self-made men who rose from obscurity.

The violence of the period encouraged castle building. The castles were built not on mountaintops but on level plains, and they were surrounded by moats and walls made from huge stones. Inside a castle was an elegantly decorated many-storied keep. Though relatively safe from incendiary missiles, the keeps were vulnerable to Western-style cannon, introduced in the 1570s.

The Victors: Nobunaga and Hideyoshi

The first daimyo to gain a predominance of power was Oda Nobunaga (1534–1582). A samurai of the lesser daimyo class, he recruited followers from masterless samurai who had been living by robbery and extortion. After he won control of his native province in 1559, he immediately set out to extend his power through central Japan. A key step was destroying the military power of the great monasteries. To increase revenues, he minted coins, the first government-issued money in Japan since 958. He also eliminated customs barriers and opened the little fishing village of Nagasaki to foreign commerce; it soon became Japan's largest port.

In 1582, in an attempted coup, Nobunaga was forced by one of his vassals to commit suicide. His general and staunchest adherent, Toyotomi Hideyoshi (1537–1598), avenged him and continued the drive toward unification of the daimyo-held lands, finally completed in 1590.

Like the Ming founder, Hideyoshi (HEE-deh-YOH-shee) was a peasant's son who rose to power through military talent. A series of campaigns brought all of Japan under Hideyoshi's control. Hideyoshi soothed the vanquished daimyo as Nobunaga had done—with lands and military positions—but he also required them to swear allegiance and to obey him down to the smallest particular. For the first time in over two centuries, Japan had a single ruler.

Hideyoshi did his best to ensure that future peasants' sons would not be able to rise as he had. His great sword hunt of 1588 collected weapons from farmers, who were no longer

Matsumoto Castle Hideyoshi built Matsumoto Castle between 1594 and 1597. Designed to be impregnable, it was surrounded by a moat and had a base constructed of huge stones. In the sixteenth and early seventeenth centuries Spanish and Portuguese missionaries compared Japanese castles favorably to European castles of the period. (Adina Tovy/Robert Harding World Imagery)

allowed to wear swords. Restrictions were also placed on samurai; they were prohibited from leaving their lord's service or switching occupations. To improve tax collection, Hideyoshi ordered a survey of the entire country that tied each peasant household to the land. With the country pacified, Hideyoshi embarked on an ill-fated attempt to conquer Korea and China that ended only with his death, discussed later in this chapter.

The Tokugawa Shogunate, to 1800

What was life like in Japan during the Tokugawa peace?

On his deathbed, Hideyoshi set up a council of regents to govern during the minority of his infant son. The strongest regent was Hideyoshi's long-time supporter Tokugawa Ieyasu (toh-koo-GAH-wuh ee-eh-YAH-soo) (1543–1616). In 1600 at Sekigahara, Ieyasu smashed a coalition of daimyo defenders of the heir and began building his own government—thus ending the long period of civil war. In 1603 he took the title "shogun." The **Tokugawa Shogunate** that Ieyasu fashioned lasted until 1867. This era is also called the Edo (AY-doh) period after the location of the shogunate in the city of Edo (now called Tokyo), starting Tokyo's history as Japan's most important city (Map 21.2).

Tokugawa Government

Over the course of the seventeenth century the Tokugawa shoguns worked to consolidate relations with the daimyo. In a scheme resembling the later residency requirements imposed by Louis XIV in France (see "The Absolutist Palace" in Chapter 18), Ieyasu set up the **alternate residence system**, which compelled the lords to live in Edo every other year and to leave their wives and sons there—essentially as hostages.

The peace imposed by the Tokugawa Shogunate brought a steady rise in population to about 30 million people by 1800. To maintain stability, the early Tokugawa shoguns froze social status. Daimyo were prohibited from moving troops outside their frontiers, making alliances, and coining money. Samurai and peasants were kept strictly apart. Samurai were defined as those permitted to carry swords. Prohibited from owning land, they had to live in castles (which evolved into

---

Nō theater A type of Japanese theater performed on a bare stage by one or two actors wearing brilliant brocade robes, one actor wearing a mask. The performers conveyed emotions and ideas as much through gestures, stances, and dress as through words.

daimyo Regional lords in Japan, many of whom were self-made men.

Tokugawa Shogunate The Japanese government in Edo founded by Tokugawa Ieyasu. It lasted from 1603 to 1867.

alternate residence system Arrangement in which Japanese lords were required to live in Edo every other year and left their wives and sons there as hostages to the Tokugawa Shogunate.

MAP 21.2 Tokugawa Japan, 1603–1867 The lands that the shogunate directly controlled were concentrated near its capital at Edo. The daimyo of distant places, such as the island of Kyushu, were required to make long journeys to and from Edo every year.

castle-towns), and they depended on stipends from their lords, the daimyo. Likewise, merchants and artisans had to live in towns and could not own land.

After 1639 Japan limited its contacts with the outside world because of concerns both about the loyalty of subjects converted to Christianity by European missionaries and about the imperialist ambitions of European powers (discussed below). However, China remained an important trading partner and source of ideas. The Edo period also saw the development of a school of native learning that rejected Buddhism and Confucianism as alien and tried to identify a distinctly Japanese sensibility.

Commercialization and the Growth of Towns

During the civil war period, warfare seems to have promoted social and economic change, much as it had in China during the Warring States Period (403–221 B.C.E.). Trade grew, and greater use was made of coins imported from Ming China. Markets began appearing at river crossings, at the entrances to temples and shrines, and at other places where people congregated. Towns and cities sprang up all around the country, some of them around the new castles. Traders and artisans dealing in a specific product began forming guilds. Foreign trade also flourished, despite chronic problems with pirates who raided the Japanese, Korean, and Chinese coasts (see "Piracy and Japan's Overseas Adventures").

In most cities, merchant families with special privileges from the government controlled the urban econ-omy. Frequently, a particular family dominated the trade in a particular product and then branched out into other businesses. Japanese merchant families also devised distinct patterns and procedures for their business operations.

In the seventeenth century underemployed farmers and samurai, not to mention the ambitious and adventurous, thronged to the cities. As a result, Japan's cities grew tremendously. Kyoto became the center for the manufacture of luxury goods like lacquer, brocade, and fine porcelain. Osaka was the chief market, especially for rice. Edo was a center of consumption by the daimyo, their vassals, and government bureaucrats. Both Osaka and Edo reached about a million residents.

Two hundred fifty towns came into being in this period. Most ranged in size from 3,000 to 20,000 people, but a few, such as Hiroshima, Kagoshima, and Nagoya, had populations of between 65,000 and 100,000. In addition, perhaps two hundred towns along the main road to Edo emerged to meet the needs of men traveling on the alternate residence system. In the eighteenth century perhaps 4 million people, 15 percent of the Japanese population, resided in cities or towns.

The Life of the People in the Edo Period

The Tokugawa shoguns brought an end to civil war by controlling the military. Stripped of power and required to spend alternate years at Edo, many of the daimyo and samurai passed their lives in idle pursuit

Daimyo Procession The system of alternate residence meant that some daimyo were always on the road. The constant travel of daimyo with their attendants between their domains and Edo, the shogun's residence, stimulated construction of roads, inns, and castle-towns.

(*Daimyo's Processions Passing Along the Tokaido*, by Utagawa Sadahide [1807–1873]/triptych of polychrome woodblock prints; ink and color on paper, Edo period [1615–1868]. Bequest of William S. Lieberman, 2005, accession 2007.49.290a–c/Metropolitan Museum of Art, New York/Image copyright © The Metropolitan Museum of Art/Image source: Art Resource, NY)

of pleasure. They spent extravagantly on paintings, concubines, boys, the theater, and the redecoration of their castles. These temptations, as well as more sophisticated pleasures and the heavy costs of maintaining alternate residences at Edo, gradually bankrupted the warrior class.

All major cities contained places of amusement for men—teahouses, theaters, restaurants, and houses of prostitution. Desperately poor parents sometimes sold their daughters to entertainment houses (as they did in China and medieval Europe), and the most attractive or talented girls, trained in singing, dancing, and conversational arts, became courtesans, later called geishas (GAY-shahz), "accomplished persons."

Cities were also the center for commercial publishing. The art of color woodblock printing also was perfected during this period. As in contemporary China, the reading public eagerly purchased fiction and the scripts for plays. Ihara Saikaku (1642–1693) wrote stories of the foibles of townspeople in such books as *Five Women Who Loved Love* and *The Life of an Amorous Man*. One of the puppet plays of Chikamatsu Monzaemon (1653–1724) tells the story of the son of a business owner who, caught between duty to his family and love of a prostitute, decides to resolve the situation by double suicide. Similar stories were also performed in Kabuki theater, where plays could go on all day, actors wore elaborate makeup, and men trained

to impersonate women performed female roles. (See "Analyzing the Evidence: Interior View of a Kabuki Theater," page 610.)

Almost as entertaining as attending the theater was watching the long processions of daimyo, their retainers, and their luggage as they passed back and forth to and from Edo every year. The shogunate prohibited most travel by commoners, but they could get passports to take pilgrimages, visit relatives, or seek the soothing waters of medicinal hot springs. Setting out on foot, groups of villagers would travel to such shrines as Ise, often taking large detours to visit Osaka or Edo to sightsee or attend the theater.

During the seventeenth and eighteenth centuries daimyo and upper-level samurai paid for their extravagant lifestyles by raising taxes on their subordinate peasants from 30 or 40 percent of the rice crop to 50 percent. Not surprisingly, this angered peasants, and peasant protests became chronic during the eighteenth century. Natural disasters also added to the peasants' misery. In 1783 Mount Asama erupted, spewing volcanic ash that darkened the skies all summer; the resulting crop failures led to famine. When famine recurred again in 1787, commoners rioted for five days in Edo, smashing merchants' stores and pouring sake and rice into the muddy streets. The shogunate responded by trying to control the floating population of day laborers without families in the city. At one

Interior View of a Kabuki Theater

In the Edo period, kabuki theater was one of the most popular forms of entertainment in Japanese cities, where it was patronized by merchants, samurai, and other townspeople. It originated in crude, bawdy skits dealing with love and romance and performed by women. Because actresses were thought to corrupt public morals, the Tokugawa government banned them from the stage in 1629. From that time on, men played all the parts. Male actors in female dress and makeup performed as seductively as possible to entice the men who thronged the theaters. Some moralists complained from time to time about the licentiousness of kabuki, but the Tokugawa government decided to accept both kabuki and prostitution as necessary evils.

Kabuki performances generally took all day and consisted of several short plays or one long five-act play. Historical plays were very popular but were always set far enough in the past so that the government would not see them as a form of political protest. The main characters of historical plays were usually samurai. Ordinary townsmen or farmers could be the main characters in dramas and love stories, which were also popular. Some of these revolved around lovers who cannot overcome the obstacles to life together, leading them to decide to be together in death through double suicide.

(*Kabuki* Theatre by Okumara Masanobu [1686–1764] [color woodblock print]/Private Collection/Bridgeman Images)

The makeup worn by kabuki actors allowed the audience to see from a distance the sort of person being portrayed. Black generally suggested villainy, red passion or heroism, and green the supernatural. Actors became quite famous, and their stage names tied them to lineages of actors known for certain roles or acting styles.

Kabuki theaters had not only a central stage but also a walkway that projected out into the audience and was used for dramatic entrances and exits and other important scenes. Movable scenery and lighting effects made possible the staging of storms, fires, and hurricanes. The theater was not darkened, so the audience also got to see who else was attending the theater and what they were wearing.

Kabuki had a close connection to the art of the colored woodblock print, both of which flourished in the eighteenth century. Artists created not only prints like this one, showing the inside of a theater, but also single-sheet portraits of actors, which increased the performers' fame.

QUESTIONS FOR ANALYSIS

1. How many people are performing in this scene? What are they doing?
2. Are there more men or women in the audience? How do you distinguish them? Are any of the men samurai? How can you tell?
3. What is going on in the audience? Is everyone looking at the actors?

point they were rounded up and transported to work the gold mines in an island off the north coast, where most of them died within two or three years.

This picture of peasant hardship tells only part of the story. Agricultural productivity increased substantially during the Tokugawa period. Peasants who improved their lands and increased their yields continued to pay the same assessed tax and could pocket the surplus as profit. They could also take on other work. At Hirano near Osaka, for example, 61.7 percent of all arable land was sown in cotton. The peasants ginned the cotton locally before transporting it to wholesalers in Osaka. In many rural places, as many peasants worked in the manufacture of silk, cotton, or vegetable oil as in the production of rice.

In comparison to farmers, merchants had a much easier life, even if they had no political power. In 1705 the shogunate confiscated the property of a merchant in Osaka "for conduct unbecoming a member of the commercial class" (but more likely because too many samurai owed him money). The government seized 50 pairs of gold screens, 360 carpets, several mansions, 48 granaries and warehouses scattered around the country, and hundreds of thousands of gold pieces. Few merchants possessed such fabulous wealth, but many lived very comfortably. (See "Thinking Like a Historian: Attention to Dress in Edo Japan," page 612.)

Within a village, some families would be relatively well-off, others barely able to get by. The village headman generally came from the richest family, but he consulted a council of elders on important matters. Women in better-off families were much more likely to learn to read than women in poor families. Daughters of wealthy peasants studied penmanship, the Chinese classics, poetry, and the proper forms of correspondence, and they rounded out their education with travel. By contrast, girls from middle-level peasant families might have had from two to five years of formal schooling, focused on moral instruction.

By the fifteenth and sixteenth centuries Japan's family and marriage systems had evolved in the direction of a patrilocal, patriarchal system more like China's, and Japanese women had lost the prominent role in high society that they had occupied during the Heian period. It became standard for women to move into their husbands' homes, where they occupied positions subordinate to both their husbands and their mothers-in-law. In addition, elite families stopped dividing their property among all their children; instead they retained it for the sons alone or increasingly for a single son who would continue the family line. Wedding rituals involved both the exchange of betrothal gifts and the movement of the bride from her parents' home to her husband's home. She brought with her a trousseau that provided her with clothes and other items she would need for daily life, but not with land, which

Interior of Nijo Castle To assert control over the imperial court and the city of Kyoto, Tokugawa Ieyasu built palace-like Nijo Castle there in 1601–1603. He had the sliding doors painted by leading artists of the period, making the castle as elegant as the imperial palace. (© Iberfoto/The Image Works)

would have given her economic autonomy. On the other hand, her position within her new family was more secure, for it became more difficult for a husband to divorce his wife. If her husband fathered children with concubines, she was their legal mother.

A peasant wife shared responsibility for the family's economic well-being with her husband. If of poor or middling status, she worked alongside her husband in the fields, doing the routine work while he did the heavy work. If they were farm hands and worked for wages, the wife invariably earned a third or a half less than her husband. Wives of prosperous farmers never worked in the fields, but they reeled silk, wove cloth, helped in any family business, and supervised the maids. When cotton growing spread to Japan in the sixteenth century, women took on the jobs of spinning and weaving it. Families were growing smaller in this period in response to the spread of single-heir inheritance. Japanese families restricted the number of children they had by practicing abortion and infanticide, turning to adoption when no heir survived.

Widows and divorcées of the samurai elite—where female chastity was the core of fidelity—were not expected to remarry. Among the peasant classes, by contrast, divorce seems to have been fairly common—the divorce rate was at least 15 percent in the villages near Osaka in the eighteenth century. A poor woman wanting a divorce could simply leave her husband's home. Sometimes Buddhist temple priests served as divorce brokers: they went to the village headman and had him force the husband to agree to a divorce. News of the coming of temple officials was usually enough to produce a letter of separation.

Attention to Dress in Edo Japan

Japanese woodblock prints of the Edo period show a fascination with the patterns and colors of the clothes that people wore. Textual sources of the period largely confirm this attention to dress among the residents of the large cities, especially Edo (Tokyo), Kyoto, and Osaka. Both moralists and the government saw fine or elaborate clothes as inappropriate for ordinary city residents such as merchants and their employees, who were often rich enough to dress well but expected to display humility in the fixed status system of the time.

1 **Law regulating dress, 1683.** The government issued repeated sumptuary laws to regulate the kinds of clothing townsmen were allowed to wear. This law was issued in 1683.

■ Thin silk crepe
Embroidery
Dapple tie-dye

These materials are prohibited hereafter in women's clothing. Unusual weaving and dyeing must not be done. One length of outer material for a padded robe may not be bought or sold for a higher price than 200 me of silver.

2 **Ihara Saikaku on fashion, 1688 and 1686.** Ihara Saikaku (1642–1693), a member of an Osaka merchant family, wrote about the world he knew in many literary forms. The first passage here is from an essay published in 1688; the second is from a fictional story published in 1686.

■ Ostentation

Fashions have changed from those of the past and have become increasingly ostentatious. In everything people have a liking for finery above their station. Women's clothes in particular go to extremes. Because they forget their proper place, extravagant women should be in fear of divine punishment. Even the robes of the awesome high-ranking families used to be of nothing finer than Kyoto habutae. Black clothing with five crests cannot be called inappropriate to anyone from daimyo down to commoner. But in recent years, certain shrewd Kyoto people have started to lavish every manner of magnificence on men's and women's clothes and to put out design books in color. With modish fine-figured patterns, palace style hundred-color prints, and bled dapple tie-dye, they go the limit for unusual designs to suit any taste. Such behavior by wives and the marriages of daughters have drained the household finances and impaired the family business of countless merchants. Prostitutes make a daily display of beautiful clothes toward earning a living. But beautiful wives of commoners, when they are not blossom-viewing in spring or maple-viewing in autumn or going to weddings, should forego these many layers of conspicuous garments....

[Commenting on a clothier's shop in Kyoto] When we look at these garments, we see that the outer material of white figured silk gauze has been folded over and used as the lining as well, with a layer of crimson silk crepe between, making a three-layered summer kimono. Sleeves and collar are padded with silk wadding. There was nothing like this in olden times. To go further than this, they would have to use various materials of Chinese-style weaving as everyday clothes. The recent clothing laws were for all the provinces and all the people. If we give this some thought we realize that we can be grateful for them. It is distressing to see a merchant wearing good silks. Pongee [a light-weight fabric] suits him better and looks better on him. But fine clothes are essential to a samurai's status, and therefore even a samurai who is without attendants should not dress like an ordinary person.

The Beauty Contest

There was in the capital a band of four inseparable young men who were known for their handsome appearance and riotous living. Thanks to large inheritances they could spend every day in the year seeking their own pleasure....

After the theatre one evening they were lounging around a tea shop called Matsuya and one of them remarked, "I have never seen so many good-looking local girls as I did today. Do you suppose we could find others who would seem just as beautiful now?" They thought they might, and decided to watch for pretty girls among the people who had gone to see the wisteria blossoms and were now returning to their homes. After a worldly actor in the group had been chosen as chief judge, a "beauty contest" was conducted until

ANALYZING THE EVIDENCE

1. In the print in Source 4, how is each of the dancers dressed? How many different patterns and colors are shown?
2. Why would the government and moralists object to people's wearing beautiful clothes (Sources 1 and 3)?
3. Based on Saikaku's writings in Source 2, what distinguished men's and women's clothes? What sorts of observations did people make about clothes? How did they evaluate style?
4. What sort of connection existed between the fixed social hierarchy of Edo period Japan and the emphasis on fashion and style in clothes during the period?

the twilight hours, providing a new source of amusement for the jaded gentlemen....

Next they spied a lady of thirty-four or thirty-five with a graceful long neck and intelligent-looking eyes, above which could be seen a natural hairline of rare beauty. Her nose, it was true, stood a little high, but that could easily be tolerated. Underneath she wore white satin, over that light blue satin, and outside — reddish-yellow satin. Each of these garments was luxuriously lined with the same material. On her left sleeve was a hand-painted likeness of the Yoshida monk, along with his passage, "To sit alone under a lamp, and read old books..." Assuredly, this was a woman of exquisite taste.

Her sash was of folded taffeta bearing a tile design. Around her head she had draped a veil like that worn by court ladies; she wore stockings of pale silk and sandals with triple-braided straps. She walked noiselessly and gracefully, moving her hips with a natural rhythm. "What a prize for some lucky fellow!" a young buck exclaimed. But these words were hardly uttered when the lady, speaking to an attendant, opened her mouth and disclosed that one of her lower teeth was missing, to the complete disillusionment of her admirers.

4 **Ippitsusai Buncho, woodblock print of entertainers, 1769.** Here the artist Ippitsusai Buncho (active 1755–1790) depicts two shrine dancers, Ohatsu and Onami. The performers' fans could purchase colorful prints like these for relatively small sums.

(*The Shrine Dancers [Miko] Ohatsu and Onami,* 1769, by Ippitsusai Buncho [1725–1794] [color woodblock print]/Art Institute of Chicago/Clarence Buckingham Collection/Bridgeman Images)

3 **Ishida Baigan, Dialogues for the City and the Countryside.** Ishida Baigan (1685–1744), a townsman who had worked for years as a clerk in a dry goods store, committed himself to popular instruction, often giving public sermons. His followers gathered together their records of conversations with him and published them. In this example he argues that it is not only imprudent for ordinary people to spend a lot on clothes but also morally wrong for them to act above their station.

■ Ostentatious people of the present world not only wear fine clothes themselves but dress their maids in clothing made of thin damask and figured satin with embroidery and applique. Someone from the country seeing them would take them for court nobles or feudal dignitaries, but would wonder why they were not being attended by samurai followers. Lowly townsmen who are so ostentatious are criminals who violate moral principles.... They put in disorder the propriety of noble and humble, of honored and despised.

PUTTING IT ALL TOGETHER

Using the sources above, along with the other Japanese woodblock prints in this chapter, as well as what you have learned in class and in this chapter, write a short essay that analyzes the place of clothing in urban culture in seventeenth- and eighteenth-century Japan and compares Japanese moralists' positions on clothing to those of moralists in other societies who have objected to clothing that attracts attention.

Sources: (1) Donald H. Shively, "Sumptuary Regulation and Status in Early Tokugawa Japan," *Harvard Journal of Asiatic Studies* 25 (1964–1965): 126. Used by permission of Mary Elizabeth Berry; (2) "Ostentation" from Shively, "Sumptuary Regulation and Status," 124–125; "The Beauty Contest" from Donald Keene, ed., *Anthology of Japanese Literature.* Copyright © 1955 by Grove Press. Used by permission of Grove/Atlantic, Inc. Any third party use of this material, outside of this publication, is prohibited; (3) Shively, "Sumptuary Regulation and Status," 158.

Edo Craftsman at Work Less than 3 inches tall, this ivory figure shows a parasol maker seated on the floor (the typical Japanese practice) eating his lunch, his tools by his side. (Private Collection/ Photo © Boltin Picture Library/ Bridgeman Images)

Maritime Trade, Piracy, and the Entry of Europe into the Asian Maritime Sphere

How did the sea link the countries of East Asia, and what happened when Europeans entered this maritime sphere?

In the period 1400–1800 maritime trade and piracy connected China and Japan to each other and also to Korea, Southeast Asia, and Europe. Both Korea and Japan relied on Chinese coinage, and China relied on silver from Japan. During the fifteenth century China launched overseas expeditions. Japan was a major base for pirates. In the sixteenth century European traders appeared, eager for Chinese porcelains and silks. Christian missionaries followed. Political changes in Europe changed the international makeup of the European traders in East Asia, with the dominant groups first the Portuguese, next the Dutch, and then the British.

Zheng He's Voyages

Early in the Ming period, the Chinese government tried to revive the tribute system of the Han (206 B.C.E.–

220 C.E.) and Tang (618–907) Dynasties, when China had dominated East Asia and envoys had arrived from dozens of distant lands. To invite more countries to send missions, the third Ming emperor (Chengzu, or Yongle) authorized an extraordinary series of voyages to the Indian Ocean under the command of the Muslim eunuch Zheng He (juhng huh) (1371–1433).

Zheng He's father had made the trip to Mecca, and the seven voyages that Zheng led between 1405 and 1433 followed old Arab trade routes. The first of the seven was made by a fleet of 317 ships, of which 62 were huge, 440 feet long. Each expedition involved from twenty thousand to thirty-two thousand men. Their itineraries included stops in Vietnam, Malaysia, Indonesia, Sri Lanka, India, and, in the later voyages, Hormuz (on the coast of Persia) and East Africa (see Map 16.1). At each stop Zheng He went ashore to visit rulers, transmit messages of China's peaceful intentions, and bestow lavish gifts. Rulers were invited to come to China or send envoys and were offered accommodation on the return voyages. Near the Straits of Malacca, Zheng's fleet battled Chinese pirates, bringing them under control. Zheng He made other shows of force as well, deposing rulers deemed unacceptable in Java, Sumatra, and Sri Lanka.

On the return of these expeditions, the Ming emperor was delighted by the exotic things the fleet brought back, such as giraffes and lions from Africa, fine cotton cloth from India, and gems and spices from Southeast Asia. Ma Huan, an interpreter who accompanied Zheng He, collected data on the plants, animals, peoples, and geography that they encountered and wrote a book titled *The Overall Survey of the Ocean's Shores*. Still, these expeditions were not voyages of discovery; they followed established routes and pursued diplomatic rather than commercial goals.

Why were these voyages abandoned? Officials complained about their cost and modest returns. As a consequence, after 1474 all the remaining ships with three or more masts were broken up and used for lumber. Chinese did not pull back from trade in the South China Sea and Indian Ocean, but the government no longer promoted trade, leaving the initiative to private merchants and migrants.

Piracy and Japan's Overseas Adventures

One goal of Zheng He's expeditions was to suppress piracy, which had become a problem all along the China coast. Already in the thirteenth century social disorder and banditry in Japan had expanded into seaborne banditry, which occurred within the Japanese islands around the Inland Sea (Map 21.3), in the straits between Korea and Japan, and along the Korean and Chinese coasts. Pirates not only looted settlements but often captured people and held them for ransom. As maritime trade throughout East Asia grew more lively, sea bandits also took to attacking ships to steal their cargo. Although the pirates were called the "Japanese pirates" by both the Koreans and the Chinese, pirate gangs in fact recruited from all countries. The Ryūkyū (ryoo-kyoo) Islands and Taiwan became major bases.

Possibly encouraged by the exploits of these bandits, Hideyoshi, after his victories in unifying Japan, decided to extend his territory across the seas. In 1590, after receiving congratulations from Korea on his victories, Hideyoshi sent a letter asking the Koreans to allow his armies to pass through their country, declaring that his real target was China. He also sent demands for submission to countries of Southeast Asia and to the Spanish governor of the Philippines.

In 1592 Hideyoshi mobilized 158,000 soldiers and 9,200 sailors for his invasion and equipped them with muskets and cannon, which had recently been introduced into Japan. His forces overwhelmed Korean defenders and reached Seoul within three weeks and Pyongyang in two months. A few months later, in the middle of winter, Chinese armies arrived to help defend

Korea, and Japanese forces were pushed back from Pyongyang. A stalemate remained in place until 1597, when Hideyoshi sent out new Japanese troops. This time the Ming army and the Korean navy were more successful in resisting the Japanese. In 1598, after Hideyoshi's death, the Japanese army withdrew from Korea, but Korea was left devastated. (See "Analyzing the Evidence: Keinen's Poetic Diary of the Korea Campaign," page 616.)

After recovering from the setbacks of these invasions, Korea began to advance socially and economically. During the Chosŏn (joe-sun) Dynasty (1392–1910), the Korean elite (the yangban) turned away from Buddhism and toward strict Neo-Confucian orthodoxy. As agricultural productivity improved, the population grew from about 4.4 million in 1400 to about 8 million in 1600, 10 million in 1700, and 14 million in 1810 (or about half the size of Japan's population and one-twentieth of China's). With economic advances, slavery declined. When slaves ran away, landowners found that it was less expensive to replace them with sharecroppers than to recapture them.

MAP 21.3 East Asia, ca. 1600 Pirates and traders often plied the same waters as seaborne trade grew in the sixteenth century. The Portuguese were especially active in setting up trading ports.

ANALYZING THE EVIDENCE

Keinen's Poetic Diary of the Korea Campaign

The Buddhist priest Keinen (1534?–1611) was ordered in 1597 to accompany the local daimyo on Hideyoshi's second campaign in Korea and spent seven months there. As a Buddhist, he did not revel in military feats but rather deplored the death and suffering that he observed. Adopting the time-honored form of the poetic diary, Keinen ends each day's entry with a short poem. The excerpt quoted here begins about six weeks after he left home.

■ Eighth month, 4th day. Every one is trying to be the first off the ship; no one wants to lag behind. They fall over each other in trying to get at the plunder, to kill people. It is a sight I cannot bear to see.

> A hubbub rises
> as from roiling clouds and mist
> where they swarm about
> in their rage for the plunder
> of innocent people's goods.

VIII.5.
They are burning the houses. As I watched them go up in smoke, I thought that my own existence was like this and was seized by sympathy.

> The "Red Country" is
> what they call it, but black is
> the smoke that rises
> from the burning houses
> where you see flames flying high.

VIII.6.
The very fields and hillsides have been put to the fire, not to speak of the forts. People are put to the sword, or they are shackled with chains and bamboo tubes choking the neck. Parents sobbing for their children, children searching for their parents—never before have I seen such a pitiable sight.

The hills are ablaze
with the cries of soldiers
intoxicated
with their pyrolatry —
the battleground of demons.

VIII.7.
Looking at the various kinds of plunder amassed by them all, I formed a desire for such things. Could I really be like this, I thought, and felt ashamed. How can I attain salvation like this, I thought.

> How ashamed I am!
> For everything that I see
> I form desires —
> a creature of delusions,
> my mind full of attachments.

On the same day, as I exerted myself in reflections on my spiritual state, I felt myself more and more ashamed. And yet the Buddha has vowed not to give weight to the weightiest of evil deeds, not to abandon the most abandoned and intemperate!

> Unless it be through
> reliance on the vow of
> Amida Buddha,
> who could obtain salvation
> with such wicked thoughts as mine?

VIII.8.
They are carrying off Korean children and killing their parents. Never shall they see each other again. Their mutual cries—surely this is like the torture meted out by the fiends of hell.

> It is piteous;
> when the four fledglings parted,*
> it must have been thus —

Between 1750 and 1790 the slave population dropped from 30 percent to 5 percent of the population. The hold of the yangban elite, however, remained strong. Through the eighteenth century about two dozen yangban families dominated the civil service examinations, leaving relatively few slots for commoners to rise to through study.

Europeans Enter the Scene

In the sixteenth century Portuguese, Spanish, and Dutch merchants and adventurers began to participate in the East Asian maritime world (see "The European Voyages of Discovery" in Chapter 16). The trade among Japan, China, and Southeast Asia was very profitable, and the European traders wanted a share of it. They also wanted to develop trade between Asia and Europe.

The Portuguese and Dutch were not reluctant to use force to gain control of trade, and they seized many outposts along the trade routes, including Taiwan. Moreover, they made little distinction between trade, smuggling, and piracy. In 1521 the Ming tried to ban the Portuguese from China. Two years later an expeditionary force commissioned by the Portuguese king to negotiate a friendship treaty defeated its mission by firing on Chinese warships near Guangzhou. In 1557, without informing Beijing, local Chinese officials decided that the way to regulate trade was to allow the

I see the parents' lament
over their sobbing children.

VIII.11.
As night fell, I saw people's houses go up in smoke. They have lost everything to the fire, all their grain and all their property.

How wretched it is!
Smoke lingers still where the grain
was burned and wasted;
so that is where I lay my
head tonight: on the scorched earth.

. . . .

VIII.15.
The fortress is to be stormed before dawn tomorrow. Fascines of bamboo have been distributed to the assault troops. The sun was about to set as they worked their way close in, right up against the edge of the castle's bulwarks, and gunfire opened up from the several siege detachments, accompanied by arrows shot from short-bows. Unthinkable numbers of men were killed. As I saw them dying:

From the fortress, too,
from their short-bows, too.
How many killed? Beyond count
is the number of the dead.

The castle fell to the assault in the course of the night. Lord Hishu's troops were the first inside the walls. Needless to say, he is to get a vermilion-seal letter of commendation.

VIII.16.
All in the fortress were slaughtered, to the last man and woman. No prisoners were taken. To be sure, a few were kept alive for exchange purposes.

How cruel! This world
of sorrow and inconstancy

does have one constant —
men and women, young and old
die and vanish; are no more.

VIII.17.
Until yesterday they did not know that they would have to die; today, they are transformed into the smoke of impermanence, as is the way of this world of constant change. How can I be unaffected by this!

Look! Everyone, look!
Is this, then, to be called the human condition? —
a life with a deadline,
a life with a limit: today.

QUESTIONS FOR ANALYSIS

1. Buddhism teaches the impermanence of phenomena and the need to let go of attachments, and it opposes the taking of life. Which of Keinen's responses can be identified as specifically Buddhist?
2. Does Keinen's use of poetry seem natural, or do you think it seems forced? Explain your response.
3. What would be the purpose of bringing a Buddhist priest opposed to killing on a military campaign?

Source: *Sources of Japanese Tradition*, by Wm. Theodore de Bary, Donald Keene, George Tanabe, and Paul Varley. Reproduced with permission of COLUMBIA UNIVERSITY PRESS in the format Book via Copyright Clearance Center.

*An allusion to the proverbial tale of a mother bird's sorrow at her fledglings' departure to the four directions.

Portuguese to build a trading post on uninhabited land near the mouth of the Pearl River. The city they built there — Macao — became the first destination for Europeans going to China until the nineteenth century, and it remained a Portuguese possession until 1999.

European products were not in demand in China, but silver was. Japan had supplied much of China's silver, but with the development of silver mines in the New World, European traders began supplying large quantities of silver to China, allowing the expansion of China's economy.

Chinese were quick to take advantage of the new trading ports set up by European powers. Manila, under Spanish control, and Taiwan and Batavia, both under Dutch control, all attracted thousands of Chinese colonists. In Batavia harbor (now Jakarta, Indonesia) Chinese ships outnumbered those from any other country by two or three to one. Local people felt the intrusion of Chinese more than of Europeans, and riots against Chinese led to massacres on several occasions.

A side benefit of the appearance of European traders was New World crops. Sweet potatoes, maize, peanuts, tomatoes, chili peppers, tobacco, and other crops were quickly adopted in East Asia. Sweet potatoes and maize in particular facilitated population growth because they could be grown on land previously thought too sandy or too steep to cultivate. Sweet potatoes became a common poor people's food.

The Jesuit Presence in China

This French engraving shows three generations of European Jesuits active at the Chinese court, Matteo Ricci (1552–1610) and two mathematicians and astronomers, Johann Adam Schall von Bell (1592–1666) and Ferdinand Verbiest (1623–1688). Below them are two prominent Chinese converts, the official Xu Guangqi and his granddaughter. (Private Collection/Bridgeman Images)

Christian Missionaries

The Spanish and Portuguese kings supported missionary activity, and merchant vessels soon brought Catholic missionaries to East Asia. The Jesuit priest Francis Xavier had worked in India and the Indies before China and Japan attracted his attention. In 1549 he was the first Christian missionary to arrive in Japan, landing on Kyushu, Japan's southernmost island (see Map 21.2). After he was expelled by the local lord, he traveled throughout western Japan as far as Kyoto, proselytizing wherever warlords allowed. He soon made many converts among the poor and even some among the daimyo. Xavier then set his sights on China but died on an uninhabited island off the China coast in 1552.

Other missionaries carried on his work, and by 1600 there were three hundred thousand baptized Christians in Japan. Most of them lived on Kyushu, where the shogun's power was weakest and the loyalty of the daimyo most doubtful. In 1615 bands of Christian samurai supported Tokugawa Ieyasu's enemies at the fierce Battle of Osaka. A couple of decades later, thirty thousand peasants in the heavily Catholic area of northern Kyushu revolted. The Tokugawa Shogunate thus came to associate Christianity with domestic disorder and insurrection and in 1639 stepped up its repression of Christianity. Foreign priests were expelled and thousands of Japanese Christians crucified.

Meanwhile, in China the Jesuits concentrated on gaining the linguistic and scholarly knowledge they would need to convert the educated class. The Jesuit Matteo Ricci studied for years in Macao before setting himself up in Nanjing and trying to win over members of the educated class. In 1601 he was given permission to reside in Beijing, where he made several high-placed conversions. He also interested educated Chinese men in Western geography, astronomy, and Euclidean mathematics.

Ricci and his Jesuit successors believed that Confucianism was compatible with Christianity. The Jesuits thought that both faiths shared similar concerns for morality and virtue, and they viewed the Confucian practice of making food offerings to ancestors as an expression of filial reverence rather than as a form of worship. The Franciscan and Dominican friars, who had taken a vow of poverty, disagreed with the Jesuit position. In 1715 religious and political quarrels in Europe led the pope to decide that the Jesuits' accommodating approach was heretical. Angry at this insult, the Kangxi emperor forbade all Christian missionary work in China.

Learning from the West

Although both China and Japan ended up prohibiting Christian missionary work, other aspects of Western culture were seen as impressive and worth learning. The closed-country policy that Japan instituted in 1639 restricted Japanese from leaving the country and kept European merchants in small enclaves. Still, Japanese interest in Europe did not disappear. Through the Dutch enclave of Deshima on a tiny island in Nagasaki harbor, a stream of Western ideas, arts, and inventions trickled into Japan in the eighteenth century.

Dutch in Japan The Japanese were curious about the appearance, dress, and habits of the Dutch who came to the enclave of Deshima to trade. In this detail from a long hand scroll, Dutch traders are shown interacting with a Japanese samurai in a room with Japanese tatami mats on the floor. Note also the Western musical instrument.

(Private Collection/Bridgeman Images)

In China, too, both scholars and rulers showed an interest in Western learning. The Kangxi emperor frequently discussed scientific and philosophical questions with the Jesuits at court. When he got malaria, he accepted the Jesuits' offer of the medicine quinine. The court was impressed with the Jesuits' skill in astronomy and quickly appointed them to the Board of Astronomy. In 1674 the emperor asked them to re-equip the observatory with European instruments. In the visual arts the emperor and his successors employed Italian painters to make imperial portraits. Firearms and mechanical clocks were also widely admired. The court established its own clock and watch factory, and in 1673 the emperor insisted that the Jesuits manufacture cannon for him and supervise gunnery practice.

Admiration was not one-sided. In the early eighteenth century China enjoyed a positive reputation in Europe. The French philosopher Voltaire wrote of the rationalism of Confucianism and saw advantages to the Chinese political system because the rulers did not put up with parasitical aristocrats or hypocritical priests. Chinese medical practice also drew European interest. One Chinese practice that Europeans adopted was "variolation," an early form of smallpox inoculation.

The Shifting International Environment in the Eighteenth Century

The East Asian maritime world underwent many changes from the sixteenth to the eighteenth centuries. As already noted, the Japanese pulled back their own traders and limited opportunities for Europeans to trade in Japan. In China the Qing government limited trading contacts with Europe to Guangzhou in the far south in an attempt to curb piracy. Portugal lost many of its bases to the Dutch, and by the eighteenth century the British had become as active as the Dutch. In the seventeenth century the British and Dutch sought primarily porcelains and

Porcelain Vase Among the objects produced in China that were in high demand in Europe in the seventeenth and eighteenth centuries were colorful porcelains. In this period Chinese potters perfected the use of overglaze enamels, which allowed the application of many colors to a single object. Blue, green, yellow, orange, and red all appear on this 18-inch-tall vase.

(Vase, Qing Dynasty, Kangxi period [1662–1722], late 17th–early 18th century. Porcelain painted in overglaze famille verte enamels and gold. Bequest of John D. Rockefeller Jr., 1960 [61.200.66]/The Metropolitan Museum of Art/Image source: Art Resource, NY)

silk, but in the eighteenth century tea became the commodity in most demand.

By the late eighteenth century Britain had become a great power and did not see why China should be able to dictate the terms of trade. Wanting to renegotiate relations, King George III sent Lord George Macartney to China in 1793 with six hundred cases of British goods, ranging from clocks and telescopes to Wedgwood pottery and landscape paintings. The Qianlong emperor was, however, not impressed. As he pointed out in his formal reply, the Qing Empire "possesses all things in prolific abundance and lacks no product within its own borders"; thus trading with Europe was a kindness, not a necessity.[2]

Chapter Summary

After the fall of the Mongols, China was ruled by the native Ming Dynasty for nearly three centuries. The dynasty's founder ruled for thirty years, becoming more paranoid and despotic over time. Very few of his successors were particularly good rulers, yet China thrived in many ways. Population grew as food production increased. Educational levels were high as more and more men prepared for the civil service examinations. Urban culture was lively, and publishing houses put out novels, short stories, and plays in the vernacular language for large audiences.

In 1644 the Ming Dynasty fell to the non-Chinese Manchus. The Manchu rulers proved more competent than the Ming emperors and were able to both maintain peace and expand the empire to incorporate Mongolia, Tibet, and Central Asia. Population grew steadily under Manchu rule.

During the fifteenth and sixteenth centuries Japan was fragmented by civil war. As daimyo attacked and defeated each other, power was gradually consolidated, until Hideyoshi gained control of most of the country. Japan also saw many cultural developments during this period, including the increasing influence of Zen ideas on the arts and the rise of Nō theater.

After Hideyoshi's death, power was seized by Tokugawa Ieyasu, the founder of the Tokugawa Shogunate. During the seventeenth and eighteenth centuries Japan reaped the rewards of peace. The early rulers tried to create stability by freezing the social structure and limiting foreign contact to the city of Nagasaki. As the wealth of the business classes grew, the samurai, now dependent on fixed stipends, became progressively poorer. Samurai and others in search of work and pleasure streamed into the cities.

Between 1400 and 1800 maritime trade connected the countries of Asia, but piracy was a perpetual problem. Early in this period China sent out naval expeditions looking to promote diplomatic contacts, reaching as far as Africa. In the sixteenth century European traders arrived in China and Japan and soon developed profitable trading relationships. The Chinese economy became so dependent on huge imports of silver acquired through this trade that a cutoff in supplies caused severe hardship. Trade with Europe also brought New World crops and new ideas. The Catholic missionaries who began to arrive in Asia introduced Western science and learning as well as Christianity, until they were banned in both Japan and China. Although the shogunate severely restricted trade, some Western scientific ideas and technology entered Japan through the port of Nagasaki. Chinese, too, took an interest in Western painting, astronomy, and firearms. Because Europeans saw much to admire in East Asia in this period, ideas also flowed from East to West.

NOTES

1. L. J. Gallagher, trans., *China in the Sixteenth Century: The Journals of Matthew Ricci, 1583–1610* (New York: Random House, 1953), p. 23.
2. Pei-kai Cheng and M. Lestz, with J. Spence, eds., *The Search for Modern China: A Documentary History* (New York: W. W. Norton, 1999), p. 106.

CONNECTIONS

During the four centuries from 1400 to 1800, the countries of East Asia became increasingly connected. On the oceans trade and piracy linked them, and for the first time a war involved China, Korea, and Japan. At the same time, their cultures and social structures were in no sense converging. The elites of China and Japan were very different: in Japan elite status was hereditary, while in China the key route to status and power involved doing well on a written examination. In Japan the samurai elite were expected to be skilled warriors, but in China the highest prestige went to men of letters. The Japanese woodblock prints that capture many features of the entertainment quarters in Japanese cities show a world distinct from anything in China.

By the end of this period, East Asian countries found themselves in a rapidly changing international environment, mostly because of revolutions occurring far from their shores. The next two chapters take up the story of these revolutions, first the political ones in America, France, and Haiti, and then the Industrial Revolution that began in Britain. In time, these revolutions would profoundly alter East Asia as well.

CHAPTER 21   Review and Explore

Identify Key Terms

Identify and explain the significance of each item below.

Ming Dynasty (p. 596)

civil service examinations (p. 598)

Qing Dynasty (p. 603)

banners (p. 603)

Nō theater (p. 606)

daimyo (p. 606)

Tokugawa Shogunate (p. 607)

alternate residence system (p. 607)

Review the Main Ideas

Answer the focus questions from each section of the chapter.

1. What sort of state and society developed in China after the Mongols were ousted? (p. 596)

2. Did the return of alien rule with the Manchus have any positive consequences for China? (p. 603)

3. How did Japan change during this period of political instability? (p. 605)

4. What was life like in Japan during the Tokugawa peace? (p. 607)

5. How did the sea link the countries of East Asia, and what happened when Europeans entered this maritime sphere? (p. 614)

Make Comparisons and Connections

Analyze the larger developments and continuities within and across chapters.

1. How does the Qing Dynasty compare as an empire to other Eurasian empires of its day (Chapters 17 and 18)?

2. How were the attractions of city life in China and Japan of this period similar to those in other parts of Eurasia (Chapters 17 and 18)?

3. Can you think of any other cases in world history in which a farmer's son rose to the top of the power structure the way that Zhu Yuanzhang and Hideyoshi did? Why was this uncommon?

TIMELINE

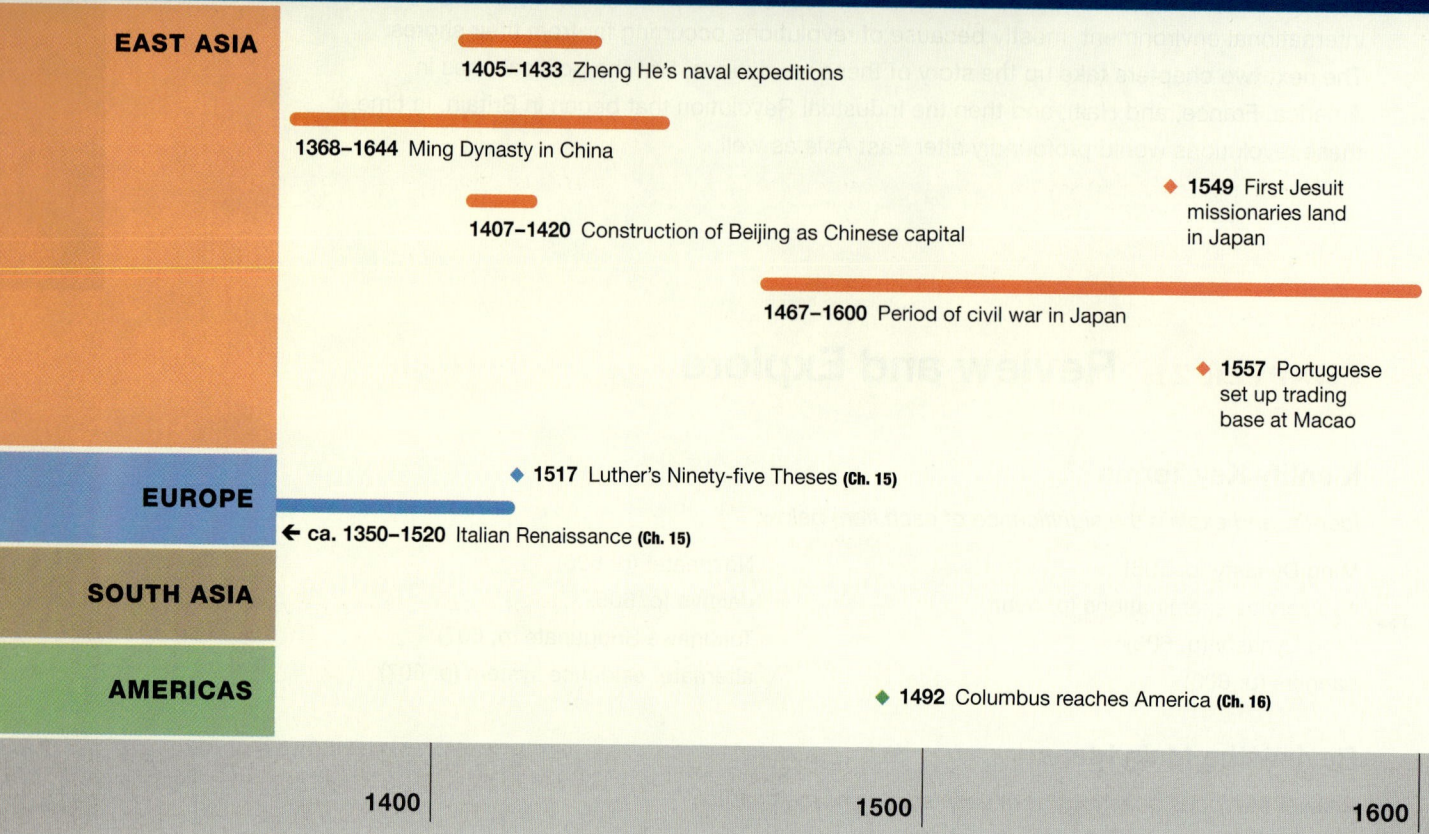

EAST ASIA

1405–1433 Zheng He's naval expeditions

1368–1644 Ming Dynasty in China

1549 First Jesuit missionaries land in Japan

1407–1420 Construction of Beijing as Chinese capital

1467–1600 Period of civil war in Japan

1557 Portuguese set up trading base at Macao

EUROPE

1517 Luther's Ninety-five Theses **(Ch. 15)**

← **ca. 1350–1520** Italian Renaissance **(Ch. 15)**

SOUTH ASIA

AMERICAS

1492 Columbus reaches America **(Ch. 16)**

1400   1500   1600

Suggested Resources

BOOKS

Berry, Mary Elizabeth. *The Culture of Civil War in Kyoto*. 1994. Uses diaries and other records to examine how people made sense of violence and social change.

Crossley, Pamela. *The Manchus*. 2002. A lively account that lets one think about Qing history from the rulers' point of view.

Dardess, John W. *Ming China, 1368–1644*. 2012. A short but informative look at Ming China from its emperors at the top to its outlaws at the bottom.

Elliott, Mark C. *Emperor Qianlong: Son of Heaven, Man of the World*. 2009. Examines the Qing Dynasty at its height from the perspective of a remarkable emperor.

Elvin, Mark. *The Pattern of the Chinese Past*. 1973. Offers an explanation of China's failure to maintain its technological superiority in terms of a "high-level equilibrium trap."

Hanley, Susan B. *Everyday Things in Premodern Japan*. 1999. Shows that the standard of living during the Edo period was comparable to that in the West at the same time.

Hegel, Robert E., ed. and trans. *True Crimes in Eighteenth-Century China: Twenty Case Histories*. 2009.

Describes various crimes (including neighborhood feuds, murder, and sedition) and how the Chinese government dealt with them at several levels.

Keene, Donald. *Yoshimasa and the Silver Pavilion: The Creation of the Soul of Japan*. 2003. A lively introduction to the aesthetic style associated with Zen and its connection to shogunate patrons.

Mann, Susan. *Precious Records: Women in China's Long Eighteenth Century*. 1997. A well-written analysis of women's lives in the educated class.

McDermott, Joseph. *A Social History of the Chinese Book: Books and Literati Culture in Late Imperial China*. 2006. Places Chinese printing in a comparative perspective.

Mungello, David. *The Great Encounter of China and the West, 1500–1800*. 1999. A short but stimulating examination of the various dimensions of the first phase of Chinese-European relations.

Pomeranz, Kenneth. *The Great Divergence: China, Europe, and the Making of the Modern World Economy*. 2000. Argues that the most advanced areas of China were on a par with the most advanced regions of Europe through the eighteenth century.

1644–1911 Manchus' Qing Dynasty in China

◆ **1639** Japan restricts contact with the outside world and intensifies suppression of Christianity

◆ **1793** Lord Macartney's diplomatic visit to China

1603–1867 Tokugawa Shogunate in Japan

ca. 1690–1789 The Enlightenment in Europe (Ch. 19)

1631–1648 Construction of Taj Mahal under Shah Jahan in India (Ch. 17)

◆ **1763** Treaty of Paris recognizes British control over much of India (Ch. 17)

| 1700 | 1800 | 1900 |

Rowe, William T. *China's Last Empire: The Great Qing.* 2009. An up-to-date and thoughtful narrative of the Manchu rulers and the empire over which they presided.

Stanley, Amy. *Selling Women: Prostitution, Markets, and the Household in Early Modern Japan.* 2012. Connects the state, the family, and the market.

Totman, Conrad. *A History of Japan.* 2000. An excellent, well-balanced survey.

Vaporis, Constantine Komitos. *Breaking Barriers: Travel and the State in Early Modern Japan.* 1994. An examination of recreational and religious travel.

Waldron, Arthur. *The Great Wall of China: From History to Myth.* 1990. Places the construction of the current Great Wall in the context of Ming-Mongol relations.

DOCUMENTARY

Presenting River Elegy. (Deep Dish TV, 1990). A condensed version of a controversial Chinese documentary contrasting Chinese civilization, tied to the Yellow River, to other civilizations connecting more to the ocean.

FEATURE FILMS

Rikyu (Hiroshi Teshigahara, 1989). An award-winning movie that brings together the famous tea master Sen no Rikyu and Toyotomi Hideyoshi, the warlord who united Japan in the late sixteenth century.

Silence (Martin Scorsese, 2016). A dramatization of the experience of Jesuit missionaries in Japan after the government began persecuting Christians.

The Sino-Dutch War 1661 (Ziniu Wu, 2000). A dramatization of the conflict between the Ming loyalists in Taiwan and the Dutch, in which some see reflections of the conflicts between the Nationalists in Taiwan and the Communists in the twentieth century.

WEBSITES

Asian Topics: Tokugawa Japan. Videos of scholars discussing many issues concerning the Tokugawa period; part of Columbia University's Asian Topics website. **afe.easia.columbia.edu/at/tokugawa/tj01.html**

Golden Ornaments Decorate Tomb of Ming Dynasty Duchess. History Channel site on a recent archaeological find of a Ming tomb. **www.history.com/news/golden-ornaments-decorate-tomb-of-ming-dynasty-duchess**

22

Revolutions in the Atlantic World

1775–1825

A great wave of revolution rocked the Atlantic world from 1775 to 1825. As trade goods, individuals, and ideas circulated in ever-greater numbers across the Atlantic Ocean, debates and events in one locale soon influenced those in another. With changing social realities challenging the old order of life and the emergence of Enlightenment ideals of freedom and equality, reformers in many places demanded fundamental changes in politics and government. At the same time, wars fought for dominance of the Atlantic economy burdened European governments with crushing debts, making them vulnerable to calls for reform.

The revolutionary era began in 1775 in North America, where the United States of America won freedom from Britain in 1783. Then in 1789 France became the leading revolutionary nation. It established first a constitutional monarchy, then a radical republic, and finally a new empire under Napoleon that would last until 1815. Inspired both by the ideals of the revolution on the continent and by internal colonial conditions, the slaves in the French colony of Saint-Domingue rose up in 1791, followed by colonial settlers, indigenous people, and slaves in Latin America. Their rebellion would eventually lead to the creation of independent nations in the Caribbean, Mexico, and South America. In Europe and its colonies abroad, the world of modern politics was born.

Jean-Baptiste Belley

Born in Senegal and enslaved in the colony of Saint-Domingue, Jean-Baptiste Belley fought in the American War of Independence and was elected as a deputy to the French National Convention. His career epitomizes the transnational connections of the era of Atlantic revolutions.

Jean-Baptiste Belley (1747–1805), Deputy of Santo Domingo at the French Convention, 1797, by Anne-Louis Girodet de Roussy-Trioson (1767–1824) (oil on canvas). Inv. MV4616. Photo: Gerard Blot/Château de Versailles, France/© RMN–Grand Palais/Art Resource, NY

CHAPTER PREVIEW

BACKGROUND TO REVOLUTION   What were the factors behind the age of revolution in the Atlantic world?

THE AMERICAN REVOLUTIONARY ERA, 1775–1789
Why and how did American colonists forge a new, independent nation?

REVOLUTION IN FRANCE, 1789–1799
Why and how did revolutionaries in France transform the nation first into a constitutional monarchy and then into a republic that entered war with European powers?

NAPOLEON'S EUROPE, 1799–1815
How did Napoleon Bonaparte assume control of France and much of Europe, and what factors led to his downfall?

THE HAITIAN REVOLUTION, 1791–1804
How did a slave revolt on colonial Saint-Domingue lead to the creation of the independent nation of Haiti in 1804?

REVOLUTIONS IN LATIN AMERICA
Why and how did the Spanish and Portuguese colonies of North and South America shake off European domination and develop into national states?

Background to Revolution

What were the factors behind the age of revolution in the Atlantic world?

The origins of revolutions in the Atlantic world were complex. No one cause lay behind them, nor was revolution inevitable or certain of success. However, a series of shared factors helped set the stage for reform. They included fundamental social and economic changes and political crises that eroded state authority; the impact of political ideas derived from the Enlightenment; and, perhaps most important, imperial competition and financial crises generated by the expenses of imperial warfare.

Social Change

Eighteenth-century European society was legally divided into groups with special privileges, such as the nobility and the clergy, and groups with special burdens, such as the peasantry. Nobles were the largest landowners. They enjoyed exemption from many taxes and exclusive rights such as hunting and bearing swords. In most countries, various middle-class groups—professionals, merchants, and guild masters—enjoyed privileges that allowed them to monopolize all sorts of economic activity.

Traditional prerogatives persisted in societies undergoing dramatic change. Due to increased agricultural production, Europe's population rose rapidly after 1750, and its cities and towns swelled in size. Inflation kept pace with demography, making it increasingly difficult for urban people to find affordable food and living space. One way they kept up, and even managed to participate in the new consumer revolution (see "Urban Life and the Public Sphere" in Chapter 19), was by working harder and for longer hours. More positive developments were increased schooling and a rise in literacy rates, particularly among urban men.

Economic growth created new inequalities between rich and poor. While the poor struggled with rising prices, investors grew rich from the spread of rural manufacture and overseas trade. Old distinctions between the landed aristocracy and city merchants began to fade as enterprising nobles put money into trade and rising middle-class bureaucrats and merchants bought landed estates and noble titles. Marriages between nobles and wealthy, educated commoners (called the *bourgeoisie* [boorzh-wah-ZEE] in France) served both groups' interests, and a mixed-caste elite began to take shape.

Another social change involved the racial regimes established in European colonies. By the late eighteenth century European law accepted that only Africans and people of African descent were subject to slavery. Even free people of color—a term for nonslaves of African or mixed African-European descent—were subject to significant restrictions on their legal rights. Racial privilege conferred a new dimension of entitlement on European settlers in the colonies, and they used extremely brutal methods to enforce it.

In Spanish America and Brazil, people of European and African descent intermingled with the very large

The Awakening of the Third Estate French inhabitants were legally divided into three orders, or estates: the clergy, the nobility, and everyone else. This cartoon from July 1789 represents the third estate as a common man throwing off his chains and rising up against his oppression during the French Revolution, as the first estate (the clergy) and the second estate (the nobility) look on in fear. (Musée de la Ville de Paris, Musée Carnavalet, Paris, France/Bridgeman Images)

indigenous population. Demographers estimate that indigenous people accounted for 60 to 75 percent of the population of Latin America at the end of the colonial period, in spite of tremendous population losses in the sixteenth and seventeenth centuries. The colonies that became Peru and Bolivia had indigenous majorities; the regions that became Argentina and Chile had European majorities. Until the reforms of Charles III, indigenous people and Spaniards were required by law to live in separate communities, although many of the former secretly fled to Spanish cities and haciendas to escape forced labor obligations. Mestizos (meh-STEE-zohz), people of mixed European and indigenous descent, held a higher social status than other nonwhites, but a lower status than Europeans who could prove the "purity" of their blood.

Demands for Liberty and Equality

In addition to destabilizing social changes, the ideals of liberty and equality helped fuel revolutions in the Atlantic world. The call for liberty was first of all a call for individual human rights. Supporters of the cause of individual liberty (who became known as "liberals" in the early nineteenth century) demanded freedom to worship according to the dictates of their consciences, an end to censorship, and freedom from arbitrary laws and from judges who simply obeyed orders from the government.

The call for liberty was also a call for a new kind of government. Reformers believed that the people had sovereignty—that is, that the people alone had the authority to make laws limiting an individual's freedom of action. In practice, this system of government meant choosing legislators who represented the people and were accountable to them. Monarchs might retain their thrones, but their rule should be constrained by the will of the people.

Equality was a more ambiguous idea. Eighteenth-century liberals argued that, in theory, all citizens should have identical rights and liberties. However, they accepted a number of distinctions. First, most male eighteenth-century liberals believed that equality between men and women was neither practical nor desirable. Women played an important informal role in the Atlantic revolutions, but in each case male legislators limited formal political rights—the right to vote, to run for office, to participate in government—to men. Second, few questioned the superiority of people of European descent over those of indigenous or African origin. Even those who believed that the slave trade was unjust and should be abolished, such as Thomas Jefferson, usually felt that emancipation was so socially and economically dangerous that it must be undertaken slowly and gradually, if at all.

Finally, liberals never believed that everyone should be equal economically. Great differences in wealth and income between rich and poor were perfectly acceptable, so long as every free white male had a legally equal chance at economic gain. However limited they appear to modern eyes, these demands for liberty and equality were revolutionary, given that a privileged elite had long existed with little opposition.

The two most important Enlightenment influences for late-eighteenth-century liberals were John Locke and the baron de Montesquieu. Locke maintained that England's long political tradition rested on "the rights of Englishmen" and on representative government through Parliament. He argued that if a government oversteps its proper function of protecting the natural rights of life, liberty, and private property, it becomes a tyranny. Montesquieu was also an admirer of England's Parliament. He believed that powerful "intermediary groups"—such as the judicial nobility of which he was a proud member—offered the best defense of liberty against despotism.

The Atlantic revolutions began with aspirations for equality and liberty among the social elite. Soon, however, dissenting voices emerged as some revolutionaries became frustrated with the limitations of liberal notions of equality and liberty and clamored for a fuller realization of these concepts. Depending on location, their demands included political rights for women and free people of color, the emancipation of slaves, better treatment of indigenous people, and government regulations to reduce economic inequality. The age of revolution was thus characterized by bitter conflicts over how far reform should go and to whom it should apply. (See "Thinking Like a Historian: The Rights of Which Men?" page 628.)

The Seven Years' War

The roots of revolutionary ideology could be found in Enlightenment texts, but it was by no means inevitable that such ideas would result in revolution. Instead events—political, economic, and military—created crises that opened the door for radical action. One of the most important was the global conflict known as the Seven Years' War (1756–1763).

The war's battlefields stretched from central Europe to India to North America, pitting a new alliance of England and Prussia against the French, Austrians, and, later, Spanish. Its origins were in conflicts left unresolved at the end of the War of the Austrian Succession in 1748, during which Prussia had seized the Austrian territory of Silesia. In central Europe, Austria's monarch Maria Theresa vowed to win back Silesia and to crush Prussia. By the end of the Seven Years' War, Maria Theresa had almost succeeded, but Prussia survived with its boundaries intact.

The Rights of Which Men?

In August 1789 the legislators of the French Revolution adopted the Declaration of the Rights of Man and of the Citizen, enshrining full legal equality under the law for French citizens. Who exactly could become a citizen and what rights they might enjoy quickly became contentious issues.

1 Robespierre on the distinction between active and passive citizenship, 1789. In a November 1789 letter, Maximilien Robespierre denounced the decision to limit political participation to those with a certain amount of wealth. In 1792 a new law installed universal suffrage, but wealth restrictions returned under the Directory in 1795.

■ No doubt you know that a specific sum of money is being demanded of citizens for them to exercise the rights of citizens; that they must pay a tax equivalent to three days' work in order to participate in the primary assemblies; ten days' to be a member of the secondary assemblies which are called departments; finally 54 livres tax and possession of landed property to be eligible for the national assembly. These provisions are the work of the aristocratic party in the Assembly which has not even permitted the others to defend the rights of the people and has constantly shouted them down; so that the most important of all our deliberations was taken without discussion, carried off in tumult. . . .

[I]t seems to me that a representation founded on the bases I have just indicated could easily raise up an aristocracy of riches on the ruins of the feudal aristocracy; and I do not see that the people which should be the aim of every political institution will gain much from this kind of arrangement. Moreover I fail to see how representatives who derive their power from their constituents, that is to say from all the citizens without distinction of wealth, have the right to despoil the major part of these constituents of the power which they have confided to them.

2 Petition of the French Jews, 1790. After granting civil rights to Protestants in December 1789, the National Assembly began to consider the smaller but more controversial population of French Jews. Eager to become citizens in their own right, the Jews of Paris, Alsace, and Lorraine presented a joint petition to the National Assembly in January 1790.

■ A great question is pending before the supreme tribunal of France. *Will the Jews be citizens or not?* . . .

In general, civil rights are entirely independent from religious principles. And all men of whatever religion, whatever sect they belong to, whatever creed they practice, provided that their creed, their sect, their religion does not offend the principles of a pure and severe morality, all these men, we say, equally able to serve the fatherland, defend its interests, contribute to its splendor, should all equally have the title and the rights of citizen. . . .

Reflect, then, on the condition of the Jews. Excluded from all the professions, ineligible for all the positions, deprived even of the capacity to acquire property, not daring and not being able to sell openly the merchandise of their commerce, to what extremity are you reducing them? You do not want them to die, and yet you refuse them the means to live: you refuse them the means, and you crush them with taxes. You leave them therefore really no other resource than usury [lending money with interest]. . . .

Everything is changing; the lot of the Jews must change at the same time; and the people will not be more surprised by this particular change than by all those which they see around them everyday.

3 Free men of color address the National Assembly, 1789. In the first years of the Revolution, debate raged over the question of political equality in Saint-Domingue. In October 1789 a group of free men of color appeared before the National Assembly to present an appeal for political rights for themselves (but not for the enslaved).

■ [C]itizens of all classes have been called to the great work of public regeneration; all have contributed to writing complaints and nominating deputies to defend their rights and set forth their interests.

The call of liberty has echoed in the other hemisphere.

ANALYZING THE EVIDENCE

1. Both the citizenship distinction discussed by Robespierre in Source 1 and the petition by the Jews of France in Source 2 raise the issue of the relationship between economic status and citizenship rights. How would you compare the relationships in each case?
2. Compare the arguments made by the free men of color in Source 3 and Etta Palm d'Aelders in Source 4. Why did the free men insist on the strong contributions they had already made while d'Aelders emphasized women's weakness and humiliation? What do these rhetorical strategies tell you about contemporary ideas about masculinity and femininity?
3. What does Source 5 tell you about claims made for emancipating Caribbean slaves? How would you compare this image's implicit arguments for emancipation with the claims for rights voiced in the other sources? What can images do that written texts cannot?

It should certainly have erased even the memory of these outrageous distinctions between citizens of the same land; instead, it has brought forth even more appalling ones.... In this strange system, the citizens of color find themselves represented by the white colonists' deputies, although they have still never been included in their partial assemblies and they have not entrusted any power to these deputies. Their opposition interests, which sadly are only too obvious, make such representation absurd and contradictory.... The citizens of color are clearly as qualified as the whites to demand this representation.

Like them they are all citizens, free and French; the edict of March 1685 accords them all such rights and guarantees them all such privileges.... Like them they are property owners and farmers; like them they contribute to the relief of the state by paying the levies and bearing all expenses that they and the whites share. Like them they have already shed their blood and are prepared to spill it again for the defense of the fatherland. Like them, finally, though with less encouragement and means, they have proven their patriotism again and again.

4 Etta Palm d'Aelders on the rights of women, 1791.
During the Revolution, Dutch-born Etta Palm d'Aelders became an outspoken advocate for women's rights. In her *Address of French Citizenesses to the National Assembly*, she addresses the National Assembly in opposition to a proposed law reserving for husbands the capacity to seek legal redress for adultery.

■ It is a question of your duty, your honor, your interest, to destroy down to their roots these gothic laws which abandon the weakest but [also] the most worthy half of humanity to a humiliating existence, to an eternal slavery.

You have restored to man the dignity of his being in recognizing his rights; you will no longer allow woman to groan beneath an arbitrary authority; that would be to overturn the fundamental principles on which rests the stately edifice you are raising by your untiring labors for the happiness of Frenchmen. It is too late to equivocate. Philosophy has drawn truth from the darkness; the time has come; justice, sister of liberty, calls all individuals to the equality of rights, without discrimination of sex; the laws of a free people must be equal for all beings, like the air and the sun....

[T]he powers of husband and wife must be equal and separate. The law cannot establish any difference between these two authorities; they must give equal protection and maintain a perpetual balance between the two married people....

You will complete your work by giving girls a moral education equal to that of their brothers; for education is for the soul what watering is for plants; it makes it fertile, causes it to bloom, fortifies it, and carries the germ productive of virtue and talents to a perfect maturity.

(Bibliothèque des Arts Décoratifs, Paris, France/Archives Charmet/Bridgeman Images)

5 "I Am Free," allegorical portrait of the liberation of Caribbean slaves, ca. 1794.
Celebrating the abolition of slavery by the French revolutionary government in 1794, this print depicts a freed slave dressed in the national colors of red, white, and blue and wearing the Liberty cap, an important symbol of the Revolution. The adoption of the cap in France was inspired by the bonnet given by Roman slave owners to their slaves in the ritual of manumission.

MOI LIBRE

PUTTING IT ALL TOGETHER

Using the sources above, along with what you have learned in class and in this chapter, write a short essay exploring how different groups drew on the events, language, and principles of the French Revolution to make their claims. Keep in mind both differences and similarities in their rhetorical strategies as well as any additional sources of legitimation they employed.

Sources: (1) John Hardman, *The French Revolution Sourcebook* (London: Arnold, 2002), pp. 120–121; (2) Excerpt from pp. 93, 95–97 in *The French Revolution and Human Rights: A Brief Documentary History,* edited, translated, and with an introduction by Lynn Hunt. © 1996 by Bedford/St. Martin's. Used by permission of Bedford/St. Martin's; (3) Laurent Dubois and John D. Garrigus, *Slave Revolution in the Caribbean, 1789–1804: A Brief History with Documents* (Boston: Bedford/St. Martin's, 2006), pp. 68–69; (4) Darline Gay Levy, Harriet Branson Applewhite, and Mary Durham Johnson, eds., *Women in Revolutionary Paris, 1789–1795* (Champaign-Urbana: University of Illinois Press, 1981), pp. 75–77.

In North America the encroachment of English settlers into territory claimed by the French in the Ohio Valley resulted in skirmishes that soon became war. Although the inhabitants of New France were greatly outnumbered by British colonists, their forces achieved major victories until 1758. Both sides relied on the participation of Native American tribes with whom they had long-standing trade contacts and actively sought new indigenous allies during the conflict. The tide of the conflict turned when the British diverted resources from the war in Europe, using superior sea power to destroy the French fleet and choke French commerce around the world.

British victory on all colonial fronts was ratified in the 1763 **Treaty of Paris**. Canada and all French

territory east of the Mississippi River passed to Britain, and France ceded Louisiana to Spain as compensation for Spain's loss of Florida to Britain. France also gave up most of its holdings in India, opening the way to British dominance on the subcontinent (Map 22.1).

The war was costly for all participants, and in its aftermath British, French, and Spanish governments had to increase taxes to repay loans, raising a storm of protest and demands for political reform. Since the Caribbean colony of Saint-Domingue (san-doh-MANGH) remained French, revolutionary turmoil in the mother country would directly affect its population. The seeds of revolutionary conflict in the Atlantic world were thus sown.

MAP 22.1 The Seven Years' War in Europe, North America, and India, 1755–1763
As a result of the war, France lost its vast territories in North America and India. In an effort to avoid costly conflicts with Native Americans living in the newly conquered territory, the British government in 1763 prohibited colonists from settling west of the Appalachian Mountains. One of the few remaining French colonies in the Americas, Saint-Domingue (on the island of Hispaniola) was the most profitable plantation in the New World.

The American Revolutionary Era, 1775–1789

Why and how did American colonists forge a new, independent nation?

Increased taxes and government control sparked colonial protests in the New World, where the era of liberal political revolution began. After revolting against their home country, the thirteen mainland colonies of British North America succeeded in establishing a new unified government. Participants in the revolution believed they were demanding only the traditional rights of English men and women. But those traditional rights were liberal rights, and in the American context they had strong democratic and popular overtones. Yet the revolution was a grievous disappointment to the one-fifth of the American population living in slavery who were denied freedom under the new government, despite its liberal principles.

The Origins of the Revolution

The high cost of the Seven Years' War doubled the British national debt. Anticipating further expenses to defend newly conquered territories, the British government broke with tradition and announced that it would maintain a large army in North America and tax the colonies directly. In 1765 Parliament passed the Stamp Act, which levied taxes on a long list of commercial and legal documents, diplomas, newspapers, almanacs, and playing cards. These measures seemed perfectly reasonable to the British, for a much heavier stamp tax already existed in Britain, and proceeds from the tax were to fund the defense of the colonies. Nonetheless, the colonists vigorously protested the Stamp Act by rioting and by boycotting British goods. Thus Parliament reluctantly repealed it.

This dispute raised an important political issue. The British government believed that Americans were represented in Parliament, albeit indirectly (like most British people), and that Parliament ruled throughout the empire. Many Americans felt otherwise, and came to see British colonial administration and parliamentary supremacy as grave threats to existing American liberties.

Americans' resistance to these threats was fed by the great degree of independence they had long enjoyed. In British North America, unlike in England and Europe, religious freedom was taken for granted. Colonial assemblies made the important laws, which were seldom overturned by the British government. Also, the right to vote was much more widespread than in England.

Moreover, greater political equality was matched by greater social and economic equality, at least for the free population. There was no hereditary nobility, and independent farmers dominated colonial society. This was particularly true in the northern colonies, where the revolution originated.

In 1773 disputes over taxes and representation flared up again. Under the Tea Act of that year, the East India Company secured a profitable monopoly on the tea trade, and colonial merchants were excluded. The price on tea was actually lowered for colonists, but the act generated a great deal of opposition because of its impact on local merchants.

In protest, Boston men disguised as Native Americans held a rowdy Tea Party in which they boarded East India Company ships and threw tea from them into the harbor. In response, the so-called Coercive Acts of 1774 instated a series of harsh measures. County conventions in Massachusetts urged that the acts be "rejected as the attempts of a wicked administration to enslave America." Other colonial assemblies joined in the denunciations. In September 1774 the First Continental Congress met in Philadelphia. The more radical members of this assembly argued successfully against concessions to the English crown. The British Parliament also rejected compromise, and in April 1775 fighting between colonial and British troops began at Lexington and Concord.

Independence from Britain

As fighting spread, the colonists moved slowly toward open calls for independence. The uncompromising attitude of the British government and its use of German mercenaries did much to dissolve loyalties to the home country and to unite the separate colonies. *Common Sense* (1775), a brilliant attack by the recently arrived English radical Thomas Paine (1737–1809), also mobilized public opinion in favor of independence.

On July 4, 1776, the Second Continental Congress adopted the **Declaration of Independence**. Written by Thomas Jefferson and others, this document boldly listed the tyrannical acts committed by George III (r. 1760–1820) and proclaimed the natural rights of mankind and the sovereignty of the American states. The Declaration of Independence in effect universalized the traditional rights of English people and made them the rights of all mankind.

After the Declaration of Independence, the conflict often took the form of a civil war pitting patriots

Treaty of Paris The 1763 peace treaty that ended the Seven Years' War, according vast French territories in North America and India to Britain and Louisiana to Spain.

Declaration of Independence The 1776 document in which the American colonies declared independence from Great Britain and recast traditional English rights as universal human rights.

The Signing of the Declaration of Independence, July 4, 1776 John Trumbull's famous painting shows the dignity and determination of America's revolutionary leaders. An extraordinarily talented group, they succeeded in rallying popular support without losing power to more radical forces in the process. (U.S. Capitol Collection/Photo © Boltin Picture Library/Bridgeman Images)

against Loyalists, those who maintained an allegiance to the Crown. The Loyalists, who numbered up to 20 percent of the total white population, tended to be wealthy and politically moderate. They were few in number in New England and Virginia, but more common in the Deep South and on the western frontier. British commanders also recruited Loyalists from enslaved people by promising freedom to any slave who left his master to fight for the mother country.

On the international scene, the French wanted revenge against the British for the humiliating defeats of the Seven Years' War. Thus they sympathized with the rebels and supplied guns and gunpowder from the beginning of the conflict. In 1778 the French government offered the

Loyalist Strength in the Colonies, ca. 1774–1776

Americans a formal alliance, and in 1779 and 1780 the Spanish and Dutch declared war on Britain. Catherine the Great of Russia helped organize the League of Armed Neutrality to protect neutral shipping rights and succeeded in hampering Britain's naval power.

Thus by 1780 Britain was engaged in an imperial war against most of Europe as well as the thirteen colonies. In these circumstances, and in the face of severe reverses in India, in the West Indies, and at Yorktown in Virginia, a new British government decided to cut its losses and end the war. Under the Treaty of Paris of 1783, Britain recognized the independence of the thirteen colonies and ceded all its territory between the Allegheny Mountains and the Mississippi River to the Americans.

KEY EVENTS OF THE AMERICAN REVOLUTION

1765	Britain passes the Stamp Act
1773	Britain passes the Tea Act
1774	Britain passes the Coercive Acts in response to the Tea Party in the colonies; the First Continental Congress refuses concessions to the English crown
April 1775	Fighting begins between colonial and British troops
July 4, 1776	The Second Continental Congress adopts the Declaration of Independence
1778–1780	The French, Spanish, and Dutch side with the colonists against Britain
1783	The Treaty of Paris recognizes the independence of the American colonies
1787	The U.S. Constitution is signed
1791	The first ten amendments to the Constitution are ratified (the Bill of Rights)

Framing the Constitution

The liberal program of the American Revolution was consolidated by the federal Constitution, the Bill of Rights, and the creation of a national republic. Assembling in Philadelphia in the summer of 1787, the delegates to the Constitutional Convention were determined to end the period of economic depression, social uncertainty, and leadership under a weak central government that had followed independence. The delegates thus decided to grant the federal, or central, government important powers: regulation of domestic and foreign trade, the right to tax, and the means to enforce its laws.

The central government would operate in Montesquieu's framework of checks and balances, under which authority was distributed across three different branches — the executive, legislative, and judicial branches — which would prevent one interest from gaining too much power. The power of the federal government would in turn be checked by that of the individual states.

When the results of the Constitutional Convention were presented to the states for ratification, a great public debate began. The opponents of the proposed Constitution — the **Antifederalists** — charged that the framers of the new document had taken too much power from the individual states and made the federal government too strong. Moreover, many Antifederalists feared for the individual freedoms for which they had fought. To overcome these objections, the Federalists promised to spell out these basic freedoms as soon as the new Constitution was adopted. The result was the first ten amendments to the Constitution, which the first Congress passed shortly after it met in New York in March 1789. These amendments, ratified in 1791, formed an effective Bill of Rights to safeguard the individual.

Limitations of Liberty and Equality

The American Constitution and the Bill of Rights exemplified the strengths and the limits of what came to be called classical liberalism. Liberty meant individual freedoms and political safeguards. Liberty also meant representative government, but it did not mean democracy, with its principle of one person, one vote. Equality meant equality before the law, not equality of political participation or wealth. It did not mean equal rights for slaves, Native Americans, or women.

A vigorous abolitionist movement during the 1780s led to the passage of emancipation laws in all northern states, but slavery remained prevalent in the South, and discord between pro- and antislavery delegates roiled the Constitutional Convention of 1787. The result was a set of compromises that ensured that slavery would endure in the United States for the foreseeable future.

The new republic also failed to protect the Native American tribes whose lands fell within or alongside the territory ceded by Britain at the Treaty of Paris. The 1787 Constitution promised protection to Native Americans and guaranteed that their land would not be taken without consent. Nonetheless, the rights and interests of Native Americans were generally ignored as a growing colonial population pushed westward.

Women played a vital role in the American Revolution. They were essential participants in boycotts of British goods, which squeezed profits from British merchants and fostered the revolutionary spirit. After the outbreak of war, women raised funds for the Continental Army and took care of homesteads, workshops, and other businesses when their men went off to fight. Women did not, however, receive the right to vote in the new Constitution, an omission confirmed by a clause added in 1844.

Antifederalists Opponents of the American Constitution who felt it diminished individual rights and accorded too much power to the federal government at the expense of the states.

Revolution in France, 1789–1799

Why and how did revolutionaries in France transform the nation first into a constitutional monarchy and then into a republic that entered war with European powers?

Although inspired in part by events in North America, the French Revolution did not mirror the American example. It was more radical and more complex, more influential and more controversial. For Europeans and most of the rest of the world, it was the great revolution of the eighteenth century, the revolution that opened the modern era in politics.

Breakdown of the Old Order

As did the American Revolution, the French Revolution had its immediate origins in the financial difficulties of the government. The efforts of the ministers of King Louis XV (r. 1715–1774) to raise taxes to meet the expenses of the War of the Austrian Succession and the Seven Years' War were thwarted by the high courts, known as the parlements. The noble judges of the parlements resented this threat to their exemption from taxation and decried the government's actions as a form of royal despotism.

When renewed efforts to reform the tax system similarly failed in 1776, the government was forced to finance its enormous expenditures during the American war with borrowed money. As a result, the national debt soared. In 1786 the finance minister informed King Louis XVI (r. 1774–1792) that the nation was on the verge of bankruptcy.

Louis XVI's minister of finance convinced the king to call an assembly of notables in 1787 to gain support for major fiscal reforms. The assembled notables declared that sweeping tax changes required the approval of the **Estates General**, the representative body of all three estates. Louis XVI's efforts to reject their demands failed, and in July 1788 he reluctantly called the Estates General into session.

The National Assembly

The Estates General was a legislative body with representatives from the three orders of society: the clergy, nobility, and commoners. On May 5, 1789, the twelve hundred newly elected delegates of the three estates gathered in Versailles for the opening session of the Estates General. They met in an atmosphere of deepening economic crisis, triggered by a poor grain harvest in 1788.

The Estates General was almost immediately deadlocked by arguments about voting procedures. The government insisted that each estate should meet and vote separately. Critics had demanded instead a single assembly dominated by the third estate. In his famous pamphlet *What Is the Third Estate?* the abbé Emmanuel Joseph Sieyès argued that the nobility was a tiny, overprivileged minority and that commoners constituted the true strength of the French nation. (See "Analyzing the Evidence: Abbé Sieyès, *What Is the Third Estate?*" page 636.) The issue came to a crisis in June 1789 when delegates of the third estate refused to meet until the king ordered the clergy and nobility to sit with them in a single body. A few parish priests began to go over to the third estate, which on June 17 voted to call itself the **National Assembly**. On June 20 the delegates of the third estate, excluded from their hall because of "repairs," moved to a large indoor tennis court where they swore the famous Oath of the Tennis Court, pledging not to disband until they had been recognized as a National Assembly and had written a new constitution.

The king's response was disastrously ambivalent. Although he made a conciliatory speech accepting the deputies' demands, he called a large army toward the capital to bring the Assembly under control, and on July 11 he dismissed his finance minister and other liberal ministers. On July 14, 1789, several hundred common people, angered by the king's actions, stormed the Bastille (ba-STEEL), a royal prison. Ill-judged severity on the part of the Crown thus led to the first episodes of popular violence.

Uprisings also rocked the countryside. In July and August 1789 peasants throughout France began to rise in insurrection against their lords. Fear of marauders and vagabonds hired by vengeful landlords—called the Great Fear by contemporaries—seized the rural poor and fanned the flames of rebellion.

The National Assembly responded to the swell of popular anger with a surprise maneuver on the night of August 4, 1789. By a decree of the Assembly, all the old noble privileges—peasant serfdom where it still existed, exclusive hunting rights, the right to collect fees for having legal cases judged in the lord's court, the right to make peasants work on the roads, and a host of other entitlements—were abolished along with tithes paid to the church. On August 27, 1789, the Assembly further issued the Declaration of the Rights of Man and of the Citizen. This clarion call of the liberal revolutionary ideal guaranteed equality before the

Estates General Traditional representative body of the three estates of France that met in 1789 in response to imminent state bankruptcy.

National Assembly French representative assembly formed in 1789 by the delegates of the third estate and some members of the clergy, the second estate.

The Tennis Court Oath, June 20, 1789 Painted two years after the event shown, this dramatic painting by Jacques-Louis David depicts a crucial turning point in the early days of the Revolution. On June 20 delegates of the third estate arrived at their meeting hall in the Versailles palace to find the doors closed and guarded. Fearing the king was about to dissolve their meeting by force, the deputies reassembled at a nearby indoor tennis court and swore a solemn oath not to disperse until they had been recognized as the National Assembly. (Musée de la Ville de Paris, Musée Carnavalet, Paris, France/Bridgeman Images)

law, representative government for a sovereign people, and individual freedom. It was quickly disseminated throughout France, the rest of Europe, and around the world.

The National Assembly's declaration had little practical effect for the poor and hungry people of Paris. The economic crisis worsened after the fall of the Bastille, as aristocrats fled the country and the luxury market collapsed. Foreign markets also shrank, and unemployment among the urban working class grew.

Constitutional Monarchy

The next two years, until September 1791, saw the consolidation of the liberal revolution. In June 1790 the National Assembly abolished the nobility, and in July the king swore to uphold the as-yet-unwritten constitution. The king remained the head of state, but all lawmaking power now resided in the National Assembly, elected by the wealthiest half of French males. The constitution finally passed in September 1791 was the first in French history. It legalized divorce and broadened women's rights to inherit property and to obtain financial support for illegitimate children from fathers, but excluded women from political office and voting.

In addition to ruling on women's rights, the National Assembly replaced the patchwork of historic provinces with eighty-three departments of approximately equal size. The deputies prohibited monopolies, guilds, and workers' associations and abolished barriers to trade within France. Thus the National Assembly applied the spirit of the Enlightenment in a thorough reform of France's laws and institutions.

Abbé Sieyès, *What Is the Third Estate?*

In the flood of pamphlets that appeared after Louis XVI's call for a meeting of the Estates General, the most influential was written in 1789 by a Catholic priest named Emmanuel Joseph Sieyès. In *What Is the Third Estate?* the abbé Sieyès vigorously condemned the system of privilege that lay at the heart of French society. The term *privilege* combined the Latin words for "private" and "law." In Old Regime France, no one set of laws applied to all; over time, the monarchy had issued a series of particular laws, or privileges, that enshrined special rights and entitlements for select individuals and groups. Noble privileges were among the weightiest.

Sieyès rejected this entire system of legal and social inequality. Deriding the nobility as a foreign parasite, he argued that the common people of the third estate, who did most of the work and paid most of the taxes, constituted the true nation. His pamphlet galvanized public opinion and played an important role in convincing representatives of the third estate to proclaim themselves a "National Assembly" in June 1789. Sieyès later helped bring Napoleon Bonaparte to power, abandoning the radicalism of 1789 for an authoritarian regime.

■ 1. What is the Third Estate? Everything.
  2. What has it been until now in the political order? Nothing.
  3. What does it want? To become something.

. . . What is a Nation? A body of associates living under a *common* law and represented by the same *legislature*.

Is it not more than certain that the noble order has privileges, exemptions, and even rights that are distinct from the rights of the great body of citizens? Because of this, it [the noble order] does not belong to the common order, it is not covered by the law common to the rest. Thus its civil rights already make it a people apart inside the great Nation. It is truly *imperium in imperio* [a law unto itself].

As for its *political* rights, the nobility also exercises them separately. It has its own representatives who have no mandate from the people. Its deputies sit separately, and even when they assemble in the same room with the deputies of the ordinary citizens, the nobility's representation still remains essentially distinct and separate: it is foreign to the Nation by its very principle, for its mission does not emanate from the people, and by its purpose, since it consists in defending, not the general interest, but the private interests of the nobility.

The Third Estate therefore contains everything that pertains to the Nation and nobody outside of the Third Estate can claim to be part of the Nation. What is the Third Estate? EVERYTHING. . . .

By Third Estate is meant the collectivity of citizens who belong to the common order. Anybody who holds a legal privilege of any kind leaves that common order, stands as an exception to the common law, and in consequence does not belong to the Third Estate. . . . It is certain that the moment a citizen acquires privileges contrary to common law, he no longer belongs to the common order. His new interest is opposed to the general interest; he has no right to vote in the name of the people. . . .

The National Assembly also imposed a radical reorganization on religious life. It granted religious freedom to the small minority of French Jews and Protestants. Furthermore, in November 1789 it nationalized the property of the Catholic Church and abolished monasteries.

In July 1790 the Civil Constitution of the Clergy established a national church with priests chosen by voters. The National Assembly then forced the Catholic clergy to take an oath of loyalty to the new government. The pope formally condemned this measure, and only half the priests of France swore the oath. Many sincere Christians, especially those in the countryside, were also upset by these changes in the religious order. The attempt to remake the Catholic Church, like the abolition of guilds and workers' associations, sharpened the conflict between the educated classes and the common people that had been emerging in the eighteenth century.

The National Convention

The outbreak and progress of revolution in France produced great excitement and a sharp division of opinion in Europe and the United States. Liberals and radicals saw a triumph of liberty over despotism, while conservative leaders were deeply troubled by the aroused spirit of reform. In 1790 Edmund Burke published *Reflections on the Revolution in France*, one of the great expressions of European conservatism. He derided abstract principles of "liberty" and "rights" and insisted on the importance of inherited traditions and privileges as a bastion of social stability.

In vain can anyone's eyes be closed to the revolution that time and the force of things have brought to pass; it is none the less real. Once upon a time the Third Estate was in bondage and the noble order was everything that mattered. Today the Third is everything and nobility but a word. Yet under the cover of this word a new and intolerable aristocracy has slipped in, and the people has every reason to no longer want aristocrats. . . .

What is the will of a Nation? It is the result of individual wills, just as the Nation is the aggregate of the individuals who compose it. It is impossible to conceive of a legitimate association that does not have for its goal the common security, the common liberty, in short, the public good. No doubt each individual also has his own personal aims. He says to himself, "protected by the common security, I will be able to peacefully pursue my own personal projects, I will seek my happiness where I will, assured of encountering only those legal obstacles that society will prescribe for the common interest, in which I have a part, and with which my own personal interest is so usefully allied." . . .

Advantages which differentiate citizens from one another lie outside the purview of citizenship. Inequalities of wealth or ability are like the inequalities of age, sex, size, etc. In no way do they detract from the *equality* of citizenship. These individual advantages no doubt benefit from the protection of the law; but it is not the legislator's task to create them, to give privileges to some and refuse them to others. The law grants nothing; it protects what already exists until such time that what exists begins to harm the common interest. These are the only limits on individual freedom. I imagine the law as being at the center of a large globe; we the citizens without exception, stand equidistant from it on the surface and occupy equal places; all are equally dependent on the law, all present it with their liberty and their property to be protected; and this is what I call the *common rights* of citizens, by which they are all alike. All these individuals communicate with each other, enter into contracts, negotiate, always under the common guarantee of the law. If in this general activity somebody wishes to get control over the person of his neighbor or usurp his property, the common law goes into action to repress this criminal attempt and puts everyone back in their place at the same distance from the law. . . .

It is impossible to say what place the two privileged orders [the clergy and the nobility] ought to occupy in the social order: this is the equivalent of asking what place one wishes to assign to a malignant tumor that torments and undermines the strength of the body of a sick person. It must be *neutralized*. We must re-establish the health and working of all organs so thoroughly that they are no longer susceptible to these fatal schemes that are capable of sapping the most essential principles of vitality.

QUESTIONS FOR ANALYSIS

1. What criticism of noble privileges does Sieyès offer? Why does he believe nobles are "foreign" to the nation?
2. How does Sieyès define the nation, and why does he believe that the third estate constitutes the nation?
3. What relationship between citizens and the law does Sieyès envision? What limitations on the law does he propose?

Source: Excerpt from pp. 65–70 in *The French Revolution and Human Rights: A Brief Documentary History*, edited, translated, and with an introduction by Lynn Hunt. Copyright © 1996 by Bedford Books of St. Martin's Press. Used by permission of the publisher.

The kings and nobles of continental Europe, who had at first welcomed the revolution in France as weakening a competing power, now feared its impact. In June 1791 the royal family was arrested and returned to Paris after a failed attempt to escape France. To the monarchs of Austria and Prussia, the arrest of a crowned monarch was unacceptable. Two months later they issued the Declaration of Pillnitz, proclaiming their willingness to intervene in France to restore Louis XVI's rule, if necessary.

The new French representative body, called the Legislative Assembly, was dominated by members of the **Jacobin club**, one of the many political clubs that had formed to debate the issues of the day. The Jacobins and other deputies reacted with patriotic fury to the Declaration of Pillnitz, and in April 1792 France declared war on Francis II of Austria, the Habsburg monarch.

France's crusade against tyranny went poorly at first. Prussian forces joined Austria against the French, who broke and fled at their first military encounter with this First Coalition of antirevolutionary foreign powers. The Legislative Assembly declared the country in danger, and volunteers rallied to the capital. In August the Assembly suspended the king from all his functions and imprisoned him.

The fall of the monarchy marked a rapid radicalization of the Revolution. In late September 1792 a new assembly, called the National Convention, was elected by universal manhood suffrage. The Convention proclaimed France a republic, a nation in which the people, instead of a monarch, held sovereign power. Under the

Jacobin club A political club during the French Revolution to which many of the deputies of the Legislative Assembly belonged.

leadership of the **Mountain**, the radical faction of the Jacobin club led by Maximilien Robespierre (ROHBZ-pyayr) and Georges Jacques Danton, the Convention tried and convicted the king for treason. On January 21, 1793, Louis was executed. His wife, Marie Antoinette, suffered the same fate later that year.

In February 1793 the National Convention declared war on Britain, the Dutch Republic, and Spain. Republican France was now at war with almost all of Europe, and it faced mounting internal opposition. Peasants in western France revolted against being drafted into the army, with the Vendée region of Brittany emerging as the epicenter of revolt. Devout Catholics, royalists, and foreign agents encouraged their rebellion.

By March 1793 the National Convention was locked in struggle between two factions of the Jacobin club, the radical Mountain and the more moderate **Girondists** (juh-RON-dist). With the middle-class delegates so bitterly divided, the laboring poor of Paris once again emerged as the decisive political factor. The laboring poor and the petty traders were often known as the **sans-culottes** (san-koo-LAHT) ("without breeches") because their men wore trousers instead of the knee breeches of the wealthy. (See "Analyzing the Evidence: Contrasting Visions of the Sans-Culottes," at right.) They demanded radical political action to guarantee them their daily bread. The Mountain, sensing an opportunity to outmaneuver the Girondists, joined with sans-culotte activists to engineer a popular uprising. On June 2, 1793, armed sans-culottes invaded the Convention and forced its deputies to arrest twenty-nine Girondist deputies for treason. All power passed to the Mountain.

Areas of French Insurrection, 1793

This military and political crisis led to the most radical period of the Revolution, which lasted from spring 1793 until summer 1794. To deal with threats from within and outside France, the Convention formed the Committee of Public Safety in April 1793. Led by Robespierre, the Committee advanced on several fronts in 1793 and 1794. First, in September 1793 Robespierre and his colleagues established a planned economy. Rather than let supply and demand determine prices, the government set maximum allowable prices for key products. Though the state was too weak to enforce all its price regulations, it did fix the price of bread in Paris at levels the poor could afford.

The government also put the people to work producing arms, munitions, and uniforms for the war effort. The government told craftsmen what to produce, nationalized many small workshops, and requisitioned raw materials and grain. These economic reforms amounted to an emergency form of socialism, which thoroughly frightened Europe's propertied classes and greatly influenced the subsequent development of socialist ideology.

Second, the **Reign of Terror** (1793–1794) enforced compliance with republican beliefs and practices. Special revolutionary courts tried "enemies of the nation" for political crimes. As a result, some forty thousand French men and women were executed or died in prison. Presented as a necessary measure to save the republic, the Terror was a weapon directed against all suspected of opposing the revolutionary government.

In their efforts to impose unity, the Jacobins also took actions to suppress women's participation in political debate, which they perceived as disorderly and a distraction from women's proper place in the home. On October 30, 1793, the National Convention declared, "The clubs and popular societies of women, under whatever denomination are prohibited."

The third element of the Committee's program was to bring about a cultural revolution that would transform former royal subjects into republican citizens. The government sponsored revolutionary art and songs as well as secular holidays and open-air festivals to celebrate republican virtues. It also attempted to rationalize daily life by adopting the decimal system for weights and measures and a new calendar based on ten-day weeks. A campaign of de-Christianization aimed to eliminate Catholic symbols and beliefs. Fearful of the hostility aroused in rural France, however, Robespierre called for a halt to de-Christianization measures in mid-1794.

The final element in the program of the Committee of Public Safety was its appeal to a new sense of national identity and patriotism. With a common language and a common tradition reinforced by the revolutionary ideals of popular sovereignty and democracy,

Mountain Led by Robespierre, the French National Convention's radical faction, which led the Convention in 1793.

Girondists A moderate group that fought for control of the French National Convention in 1793.

sans-culottes The laboring poor of Paris, so called because the men wore trousers instead of the knee breeches of the wealthy; the term came to refer to the militant radicals of the city.

Reign of Terror The period from 1793 to 1794, during which Robespierre's Committee of Public Safety tried and executed thousands suspected of political crimes and a new revolutionary culture was imposed.

Contrasting Visions of the Sans-Culottes

These two images offer profoundly different representations of a sans-culotte woman. The image on the left was created by a French artist, while the image on the right is English. The French words above the image on the right read in part, "Heads! Blood! Death! . . . I am the Goddess of Liberty! . . . Long Live the Guillotine!" Both of these illustrations underline the importance of gendered imagery in the French Revolution. Although women were denied active participation in the political life of the new republic, both supporters and opponents of the Revolution used representations of women to depict the events that unfolded after 1789. Proponents of traditional social order and hierarchy employed images of bloodthirsty radical women to suggest that the Revolution had turned the *world upside down* and perverted women's naturally docile and domestic character. By contrast, those who supported the Revolution were eager to emphasize the down-to-earth virtue of common women.

In both images, the artists have focused attention on clothing and physical appearance as a way to convey their messages about the political and moral character of the sans-culotte woman. During the Revolution, French women themselves clashed over the issue of how to use clothing to support the Revolution. The woman on the right is wearing the cockade, a tricolor rosette of ribbons that was adopted in 1789 as a revolutionary symbol. During the Terror in 1793, the Society of Revolutionary Republican Women, a club of radical women associated with the sans-culotte movement, successfully demanded that all women be required by law to wear the cockade, a measure that led to violent protests by other women. Brawls between competing groups of women over the cockade helped persuade the National Convention to outlaw all female clubs and any political participation by women in October 1793.

(Musée de la Ville de Paris, Musée Carnavalet, Paris, France/ Archives Charmet/Bridgeman Images)

(By James Gillray [1757–1815]/© Courtesy of the Warden and Scholars of New College, Oxford, UK/Bridgeman Images)

QUESTIONS FOR ANALYSIS

1. How would you describe the woman on the left? What qualities does the artist seem to ascribe to her, and how do you think these qualities relate to the sans-culottes and the Revolution?
2. How would you characterize the facial expression and attire of the woman on the right? How does the inclusion of the text contribute to your impressions of her?
3. What does the contrast between these two images suggest about differences between French and English perceptions of the sans-culottes and of the French Revolution? Why do you think the artists have chosen to depict women? How did the artists use the women's clothing and appearances to support their implicit arguments about the sans-culottes?

KEY EVENTS OF THE FRENCH REVOLUTION

May 5, 1789	Estates General meets at Versailles
June 20, 1789	Oath of the Tennis Court
July 14, 1789	Storming of the Bastille
July–August 1789	Great Fear
August 4, 1789	National Assembly abolishes noble privileges
August 27, 1789	National Assembly issues Declaration of the Rights of Man and of the Citizen
July 1790	Civil Constitution of the Clergy establishes a national church; Louis XVI agrees to a constitutional monarchy
June 1791	Royal family is arrested while attempting to flee France
August 1791	Austria and Prussia issue the Declaration of Pillnitz
April 1792	France declares war on Austria
August 1792	Legislative Assembly takes Louis XVI prisoner and suspends him from functions
September 1792	National Convention declares France a republic and abolishes monarchy
January 21, 1793	Louis XVI is executed
February 1793	France declares war on Britain, the Dutch Republic, and Spain; revolts in some provinces
March 1793	Struggle between Girondists and the Mountain
June 1793	Sans-culottes invade the National Convention; Girondist leaders are arrested
September 1793	Price controls are instituted to aid the poor
1793–1794	Reign of Terror
Spring 1794	French armies are victorious on all fronts
July 1794	Robespierre is executed; Thermidorian reaction begins
1795	Economic controls are abolished, and suppression of the sans-culottes begins
1795–1799	Directory rules
1798–1799	Austria, Britain, and Russia form the Second Coalition against France
1799	Napoleon Bonaparte overthrows the Directory and seizes power

many French people developed an intense emotional attachment to the nation. This was the birth of modern nationalism, the strong identification with one's nation, which would have a profound effect on subsequent European history.

To defend the nation, a decree of August 1793 imposed a draft on all unmarried young men. By January 1794 French armed forces outnumbered those of their enemies almost four to one. By spring 1794 French armies were victorious on all fronts and domestic revolt was largely suppressed. The republic was saved.

The Directory

The success of French armies led the Committee of Public Safety to relax emergency economic controls, but they extended the political Reign of Terror. The revolutionary tribunals sent many critics to the guillotine, including long-standing collaborators whom Robespierre believed had turned against him. A group of radicals and moderates in the Convention, knowing that they might be next, organized a conspiracy. They howled down Robespierre when he tried to speak to the National Convention on July 27, 1794—a date known as 9 Thermidor according to France's newly adopted republican calendar. The next day it was Robespierre's turn to be guillotined.

The respectable middle-class lawyers and professionals who had led the liberal Revolution of 1789 then reasserted their authority. This period of **Thermidorian reaction**, as it was called, harkened back to the moderate beginnings of the Revolution. In 1795 the National Convention abolished many economic controls and severely restricted local political organizations. In addition, the middle-class members of the National Convention wrote a new constitution restricting eligibility to serve as a deputy to men of substantial means. To prevent a new Robespierre from monopolizing power, the new Assembly granted executive power to a five-man body, called the Directory.

The Directory continued to support military expansion abroad, but war was no longer so much a crusade as a response to economic problems. Large, victorious armies reduced unemployment at home. However, the French people quickly grew weary of the corruption and ineffectiveness that characterized the Directory. This general dissatisfaction revealed itself clearly in the national elections of 1797, which returned a large number of conservative and even monarchist deputies. Fearing for its survival, the Directory used the army to nullify the elections and began to govern dictatorially. Two years later Napoleon Bonaparte ended the Directory in a coup d'état (koo day-TAH) and substituted a strong dictatorship for a weak one. While claiming to uphold revolutionary values, Napoleon would install authoritarian rule.

The Execution of Robespierre

Completely wooden except for the heavy iron blade, the guillotine was devised by a French revolutionary doctor named Guillotin as a humane method of execution. The guillotine was painted red for Robespierre's execution. Large crowds witnessed the execution in a majestic public square in central Paris, then known as the Place de la Revolution and now called the Place de la Concorde (Harmony Square).

(Robespierre: National Library, Madrid, Spain/Photo © Tarker/ Bridgeman Images; guillotine: Musée de la Ville de Paris, Musée Carnavalet, Paris, France/Bridgeman Images)

Napoleon's Europe, 1799–1815

How did Napoleon Bonaparte assume control of France and much of Europe, and what factors led to his downfall?

For almost fifteen years, from 1799 to 1814, France was in the hands of a keen-minded military dictator of exceptional ability. Napoleon Bonaparte (1769–1821) realized the need to put an end to civil strife in France in order to create unity and consolidate his rule. And he did. But Napoleon saw himself as a man of destiny, and the glory of war and the dream of universal empire proved irresistible.

Napoleon's Rule of France

Born on the Mediterranean island of Corsica into an impoverished noble family, Napoleon left home and became a lieutenant in the French artillery in 1785. Rising rapidly in the new army, Napoleon was placed in command of French forces in Italy and won brilliant victories there in 1796 and 1797. His next campaign, in Egypt, was a failure, but Napoleon returned to France before the fiasco was generally known. French aggression in Egypt and elsewhere provoked the British to organize a new alliance in 1798, the Second Coalition, which included Austria and Russia.

Napoleon soon learned that some prominent members of the legislature were plotting against the Directory. The dissatisfaction of these plotters stemmed not

Thermidorian reaction A reaction in 1794 to the violence of the Reign of Terror, resulting in the execution of Robespierre and the loosening of economic controls.

so much from the fact that the Directory was a dictatorship as from the fact that it was a weak dictatorship.

The young Napoleon, nationally revered for his heroism, was an ideal figure of authority. On November 9, 1799, Napoleon and his conspirators ousted the Directors, and the following day soldiers disbanded the legislature. Napoleon was named first consul of the republic, and a new constitution consolidating his position was overwhelmingly approved in a plebiscite in December 1799. Republican appearances were maintained, but Napoleon became the real ruler of France.

Napoleon worked to maintain order and end civil strife by appeasing powerful groups in France, offering them favors in return for loyal service. Napoleon's bargain with the middle class was codified in the Civil Code of March 1804, also known as the **Napoleonic Code**, which reasserted two of the fundamental principles of the Revolution of 1789: equality of all male citizens before the law and absolute security of wealth and private property. Napoleon and the leading bankers of Paris established the privately owned Bank of France in 1800, which served the interests of both the

state and the financial oligarchy. Napoleon won over peasants by defending the gains in land and status they had won during the Revolution.

At the same time, Napoleon consolidated his rule by recruiting disillusioned revolutionaries for the network of government officials. Nor were members of the old nobility slighted. In 1800 and again in 1802 Napoleon granted amnesty to noble émigrés on the condition that they return to France and take a loyalty oath. Members of this returning elite soon occupied high posts in the expanding centralized state. Napoleon also created a new imperial nobility to reward his most talented generals and officials.

Furthermore, Napoleon sought to restore the Catholic Church in France so that it could serve as a bulwark of social stability. Napoleon and Pope Pius VII (pontificate 1800–1823) signed the Concordat of 1801. Under this agreement the pope gained the right for French Catholics to practice their religion freely, but Napoleon's government now nominated bishops, paid the clergy, and exerted great influence over the church in France.

Order and unity had a price: authoritarian rule. Women lost many of the gains they had made in the 1790s. Under the Napoleonic Code, women were dependents of either their fathers or their husbands, and they could not make contracts or have bank accounts in their own names. Napoleon also curtailed free speech and freedom of the press and manipulated voting in the occasional elections. After 1810 political suspects were held in state prisons, as they had been during the Terror.

Napoleon's Expansion in Europe

After coming to power in 1799, Napoleon sent peace feelers to Austria and Britain, the dominant powers of the Second Coalition. When these overtures were rejected, French armies led by Napoleon decisively defeated the Austrians. Subsequent treaties with Austria in 1801 and Britain in 1802 consolidated France's hold on the territories its armies had won up to that point.

Jacques-Louis David, *Napoleon Bonaparte, First Consul, Crossing the Alps at Great St. Bernard Pass, 20 May 1800* Napoleon Bonaparte commissioned this portrait by the great painter David to immortalize his crossing of the Alps with the French army on the way to conquer Italy. Napoleon was a master at the use of visual imagery as a form of propaganda to disseminate the legend of his military prowess and extraordinary charisma. (Château de Versailles, France/Bridgeman Images)

In 1802 Napoleon was secure but still driven to expand his power. Aggressively redrawing the map of German-speaking lands so as to weaken Austria and encourage the secondary states of southwestern Germany to side with France, Napoleon tried to restrict British trade with all of Europe. He then plotted to attack Britain, but his Mediterranean fleet was destroyed by Lord Nelson at the Battle of Trafalgar on October 21, 1805.

Austria, Russia, and Sweden joined with Britain to form the Third Coalition against France shortly before the Battle of Trafalgar. Yet the Austrians and the Russians were no match for Napoleon, who scored a brilliant victory over them at the Battle of Austerlitz in December 1805. Russia decided to pull back, and Austria accepted large territorial losses in return for peace as the Third Coalition collapsed.

Napoleon then reorganized the German states to his liking. In 1806 he abolished many tiny German states as well as the Holy Roman Empire and established by decree the German Confederation of the Rhine, a union of fifteen German states minus Austria, Prussia, and Saxony.

Napoleon's intervention in German affairs alarmed the Prussians, who mobilized their armies. In October 1806 Napoleon attacked them and won two more victories at Jena and Auerstädt. The war with Prussia, now joined by Russia, continued into the following spring. After Napoleon won another victory, Alexander I of Russia was ready to negotiate for peace. In the treaties of Tilsit in 1807, Prussia lost half its population through land concessions, while Russia accepted Napoleon's reorganization of western and central Europe and promised to enforce Napoleon's economic blockade against British goods.

The Grand Empire and Its End

Napoleon's so-called **Grand Empire** encompassed virtually all of Europe except Great Britain. It consisted of three parts. The core, or first part, was an ever-expanding France (Map 22.2). The second part consisted of a number of dependent satellite kingdoms. The third part comprised the independent but allied states of Austria, Prussia, and Russia. After 1806 both satellites and allies were expected to support Napoleon's **Continental System**, a blockade in which no ship coming from Britain or her colonies was permitted to

German
Confederation
of the Rhine, 1806

dock at any port that was controlled by the French. The blockade was intended to destroy the British economy and, thereby, its ability to wage war.

In the areas incorporated into France and in the satellites, French rule sparked patriotic upheavals and encouraged the growth of reactive nationalism. The first great revolt occurred in Spain. In 1808 Napoleon deposed Spanish king Ferdinand VII and placed his own brother Joseph on the throne. A coalition of Catholics, monarchists, and patriots rebelled against this attempt to turn Spain into a satellite of France. French armies occupied Madrid, but the foes of Napoleon fled to the hills and waged guerrilla warfare. Events in Spain sent a clear warning: resistance to French imperialism was growing.

Yet Napoleon pushed on. In 1810, when the Grand Empire was at its height, Britain still remained at war with France, helping the guerrillas in Spain and Portugal. The Continental System was a failure. Instead of harming Britain, the system provoked the British to set up a counterblockade, which created hard times for French consumers. Perhaps looking for a scapegoat, Napoleon turned on Alexander I of Russia, who in 1811 openly repudiated Napoleon's prohibitions against British goods.

Napoleon's invasion of Russia began in June 1812 with a force that eventually numbered 600,000. Originally planning to winter in the Russian city of Smolensk, Napoleon recklessly pressed on toward Moscow (see Map 22.2). The Battle of Borodino that followed was a draw. Alexander ordered the evacuation of Moscow, which the Russians then burned in part, and he refused to negotiate. Finally, after five weeks in the scorched city, Napoleon ordered a disastrous retreat. When the frozen remnants of Napoleon's army staggered into Poland and Prussia in December, 370,000 men had died and another 200,000 had been taken prisoner.[1]

Napoleonic Code French civil code promulgated in 1804 that reasserted the 1789 principles of the equality of all male citizens before the law and the absolute security of wealth and private property.

Grand Empire The empire over which Napoleon and his allies ruled, encompassing virtually all of Europe except Great Britain.

Continental System A blockade imposed by Napoleon in which no ship coming from Britain or its colonies was permitted to dock at any port controlled by the French.

Map legend:
- French empire
- Dependent states
- Allied with Napoleon
- ★ French victory
- ★ French defeat

KINGDOM OF NORWAY AND DENMARK

KINGDOM OF SWEDEN

St. Petersburg

Stockholm

North Sea

Copenhagen

Baltic Sea

SWEDISH POMERANIA

Königsberg

Tilsit

Vilna

Napoleon's invasion of Russia, June–Sept. 1812

Borodino 1812

Moscow

GREAT BRITAIN

Hamburg

Lübeck

Bremen

PRUSSIA

Danzig

Friedland 1807

Smolensk

Maloyaroslavets 1812

French retreat, Oct.–Dec. 1812

Neman R.

RUSSIAN EMPIRE

London

Berlin

Rhine

Elbe

GRAND DUCHY OF WARSAW

Kiev

WESTPHALIA

Brussels

Auerstädt 1806

SAXONY

Waterloo 1815

Amiens

Jena 1806

CONFEDERATION OF THE RHINE

Paris

Lunéville

BAVARIA

Austerlitz 1805

Wagram 1804

Vienna

Pressburg

WÜRTTEMBERG

Zurich

BADEN

Buda

Pest

ATLANTIC OCEAN

FRANCE

Marengo 1800

Milan

Genoa

KINGDOM OF ITALY

ILLYRIAN PROVINCES

AUSTRIAN EMPIRE

Danube R.

Black Sea

PORTUGAL

Marseilles

Elba

Corsica

Lisbon

Madrid

SPAIN

Rome

Sardinia

Naples

OTTOMAN EMPIRE

Trafalgar 1805

GIBRALTAR (Gr. Br.)

Mediterranean Sea

KINGDOM OF NAPLES

Palermo

Ionian Is. (Gr. Br.)

Athens

KINGDOM OF SICILY

0 100 200 miles
0 100 200 kilometers

Malta (Gr. Br.)

MAPPING THE PAST

MAP 22.2 Napoleonic Europe in 1812 At the height of the Grand Empire in 1810, Napoleon had conquered or allied with every major European power except Britain. But in 1812, angered by Russian repudiation of his ban on trade with Britain, Napoleon invaded Russia with disastrous results. Compare this map with Map 18.3, which shows the division of Europe in 1715.

ANALYZING THE MAP How had the balance of power shifted in Europe from 1715 to 1812? What changed, and what remained the same? What was the impact of Napoleon's wars on Germany, the Italian peninsula, and Russia?

CONNECTIONS Why did Napoleon achieve vast territorial gains where Louis XIV did not?

Francisco Goya, *The Third of May 1808* Spanish master Francisco Goya created a passionate and moving indictment of the bruality of war in this painting from 1814, which depicts the close-range execution of Spanish rebels by Napoleon's forces in May 1808. Goya's painting evoked the bitterness and despair of many Europeans who suffered through Napoleon's invasions. It forms a devastating counterpoint to the glorious portrait of Napoleon by David earlier in the chapter. (Museo del Prado, Madrid, Spain/Bridgeman Images)

Leaving his troops to their fate, Napoleon raced to Paris to raise another army. Meanwhile, Austria and Prussia deserted Napoleon and joined Russia and Britain in the Treaty of Chaumont in March 1814, by which the four powers formed the Quadruple Alliance to defeat the French emperor. Less than a month later, on April 4, 1814, a defeated Napoleon abdicated his throne. The victorious allies then exiled Napoleon to the island of Elba off the coast of Italy.

In February 1815 Napoleon staged a daring escape from Elba. Landing in France, he issued appeals for support and marched on Paris. But Napoleon's gamble was a desperate long shot, for the allies were united against him. At the end of a frantic period known as the Hundred Days, they crushed his forces at Waterloo on June 18, 1815, and imprisoned him on the island of St. Helena, off the western coast of Africa. The restored Bourbon dynasty took power under Louis XVIII, a younger brother of Louis XVI.

The Haitian Revolution, 1791–1804

How did a slave revolt on colonial Saint-Domingue lead to the creation of the independent nation of Haiti in 1804?

The events that led to the creation of the independent nation of Haiti constitute the third, and perhaps most extraordinary, chapter of the revolutionary era in the Atlantic world. The French colony that was to become Haiti reaped huge profits through a ruthless system of slave-based plantation agriculture. News of revolution in France lit a powder keg of contradictory aspirations among white planters, free people of color, and slaves. Free people of color and, later, the enslaved rose up to claim their freedom. They succeeded, despite invasion by the British and Spanish and Napoleon Bonaparte's

KEY EVENTS OF THE HAITIAN REVOLUTION

1760s	Colonial administrators begin rescinding the rights of free people of color
July 1790	Vincent Ogé leads a failed rebellion to gain rights for free people of color
August 1791	Slave revolts begin
April 4, 1792	National Assembly enfranchises all free men of African descent
September 1793	British troops invade Saint-Domingue
February 4, 1794	National Convention ratifies the abolition of slavery and extends it to all French territories
May 1796	Toussaint L'Ouverture is named lieutenant governor of Saint-Domingue
1800	After invading the south of Saint-Domingue, L'Ouverture gains control of the entire colony
1802	French general Charles-Victor-Emmanuel Leclerc arrests L'Ouverture and deports him to France
1803	L'Ouverture dies
1804	After defeating French forces, Jean Jacques Dessalines declares the independence of Saint-Domingue and the creation of the sovereign nation of Haiti

bid to reimpose French control. In 1804 Haiti became the only nation in history to claim its freedom through slave revolt.

Revolutionary Aspirations in Saint-Domingue

On the eve of the French Revolution, Saint-Domingue was inhabited by a variety of social groups who resented and mistrusted one another. The European population included French colonial officials, wealthy plantation owners and merchants, and poor artisans and clerks. Individuals of European descent born in the colonies were called **Creoles**, and over time they had developed their own interests, distinct from those of metropolitan France. Vastly outnumbering the white population were the colony's five hundred thousand enslaved people, along with a sizable population of some forty thousand free people of African and mixed African and European descent. Members of this last group referred to themselves as "free people of color."

Most of the island's enslaved population performed grueling toil in the island's sugar plantations. The highly outnumbered planters used extremely harsh methods, such as beating, maiming, and executing slaves, to maintain their control. The 1685 Code Noir (Black Code) that legally regulated slavery was intended to provide minimal standards of humane treatment, but its tenets were rarely enforced. Masters calculated that they could earn more by working slaves ruthlessly and purchasing new ones when they died than by providing the food, rest, and medical care needed to allow the enslaved population to reproduce naturally. This meant that a constant inflow of newly enslaved people from Africa was necessary to work the plantations.

Despite their brutality, slaveholders on Saint-Domingue freed a certain number of their slaves, mostly their own mixed-race children, thereby producing one of the largest populations of free people of color in any slaveholding colony. The Code Noir had originally granted free people of color the same legal status as whites. From the 1760s on, however, colonial administrators began rescinding these rights, and by the time of the French Revolution free people of color were subject to many discriminatory laws.

The political and intellectual turmoil of the 1780s, with its growing rhetoric of liberty, equality, and fraternity, raised new challenges and possibilities for each of Saint-Domingue's social groups. For enslaved people, news of abolitionist movements in France led to hopes that the mother country might grant them freedom. Free people of color looked to reforms in Paris as a means of gaining political enfranchisement and reasserting equal status with whites. The white Creole elite, however, was determined to protect its way of life, including slaveholding. They hoped to gain control of their own affairs, as had the American colonists before them.

The National Assembly frustrated the hopes of all these groups. Cowed by colonial representatives who claimed that support for free people of color would result in slave insurrection, the Assembly refused to extend French constitutional safeguards to the colonies. At the same time, however, the Assembly also reaffirmed French monopolies over colonial trade, thereby angering planters as well.

In July 1790 Vincent Ogé (aw-ZHAY) (ca. 1750–1791), a free man of color, returned to Saint-Domingue from Paris determined to win rights for his people. He raised an army and sent letters to the new Provincial Assembly of Saint-Domingue demanding political rights for all free citizens. When Ogé's demands were refused, he and his followers turned to armed insurrection. After initial victories, his army was defeated, and Ogé was executed by colonial officials. Revolutionary leaders in Paris were more sympathetic to Ogé's cause. In May 1791 the National Assembly granted political

Creoles People of European descent born in the Americas.

MAP 22.3 The War of Haitian Independence, 1791–1804 Neighbored by the Spanish colony of Santo Domingo, Saint-Domingue was the most profitable European colony in the Caribbean. In 1791 slave revolts erupted in the north near Le Cap, which had once been the capital. In 1770 the French had transferred the capital to Port-au-Prince, which in 1804 became the capital of the newly independent Haiti.

rights to free people of color born to two free parents who possessed sufficient property. When news of this legislation arrived in Saint-Domingue, the colonial governor refused to enact it. Violence then erupted between groups of whites and free people of color in parts of the colony.

The Outbreak of Revolt

Just as the sans-culottes helped push forward more radical reforms in France, the second stage of revolution in Saint-Domingue also resulted from decisive action from below. In August 1791 slaves took events into their own hands. Groups of slaves held a series of nighttime meetings to plan a mass insurrection. In doing so, they drew on their own considerable military experience; the majority of slaves had been born in Africa, and many had served in the civil wars of the kingdom of Kongo and other conflicts before being taken into slavery.[2] They also drew on a long tradition of slave resistance prior to 1791, which had ranged from work slowdowns, to running away, to taking part

in African-derived religious rituals and dances known as *vodou* (or voodoo). According to some sources, the August 1791 pact to take up arms was sealed by such a voodoo ritual.

Revolts began on a few plantations on the night of August 22. As the uprising spread, rebels joined together in an ever-growing slave army. During the next month enslaved combatants attacked and destroyed hundreds of sugar and coffee plantations.

On April 4, 1792, as war loomed with the European states, the National Assembly issued a decree extending full citizenship rights to free men of African descent. The Assembly hoped this measure would win their political loyalty and their aid in defeating the slave rebellion.

Warfare in Europe soon spread to Saint-Domingue (Map 22.3). Since the beginning of the slave insurrection, the Spanish colony of Santo Domingo, on the eastern side of the island of Hispaniola, had supported rebel slaves. In early 1793 the Spanish began to bring slave leaders and their soldiers into the Spanish army. Toussaint L'Ouverture (TOO-sahn LOO-

French Forces Under Napoleon Attack Saint-Domingue In 1802 an expedition of French forces sent by Napoleon Bonaparte arrived in Saint-Domingue. Its mission was to regain French control of the colony and re-establish slavery (which had been abolished in 1794 by the National Convention). French soldiers — including the leader of the expedition — succumbed to yellow fever and to the strong resistance of armies composed of former slaves and free people of color. In 1804 France recognized the independence of Haiti. (Bibliothèque Nationale, Paris, France/Bridgeman Images)

vair-toor) (1743–1803), a freed slave who had joined the revolt, was named a Spanish officer. In September the British navy blockaded the colony, and invading British troops captured French territory on the island. For the Spanish and British, revolutionary chaos provided a tempting opportunity to capture a profitable colony.

Desperate for forces to oppose France's enemies, commissioners sent by the newly elected National Convention promised freedom to slaves who fought for France. By October 1793 the commissioners had abolished slavery throughout the colony. On February 4, 1794, the Convention ratified the abolition of slavery and extended it to all French territories.

The tide of battle began to turn when Toussaint L'Ouverture switched sides. By 1796 the French had regained control of the colony, and L'Ouverture had emerged as a key military leader. (See "Individuals in Society: Toussaint L'Ouverture," at right.) In March 1796, after he rescued the French colonial governor

from hostile forces, L'Ouverture was named lieutenant governor of Saint-Domingue.

The War of Haitian Independence

With Toussaint L'Ouverture acting increasingly as an independent ruler of the western province of Saint-Domingue, another general, André Rigaud (ree-GO) (1761–1811), set up his own government in the southern peninsula. Tensions mounted between L'Ouverture and Rigaud. While L'Ouverture was a freed slave of African descent, Rigaud belonged to the elite group of free people of color. This elite resented the growing power of former slaves like L'Ouverture, who in turn accused the elite of adopting the prejudices of white settlers. Civil war broke out between the two sides in 1799, when L'Ouverture's forces, led by his lieutenant, Jean Jacques Dessalines (1758–1806), invaded the south. Victory over Rigaud in 1800 gave L'Ouverture control of the entire colony.

Toussaint L'Ouverture

LITTLE IS KNOWN OF THE EARLY LIFE OF SAINT-Domingue's brilliant military and political leader Toussaint L'Ouverture. He was born in 1743 on a plantation outside Le Cap owned by the Count de Bréda. According to tradition, L'Ouverture was the eldest son of a captured African prince from modern-day Benin. Toussaint Bréda, as he was then called, occupied a privileged position among slaves. Instead of performing backbreaking labor in the fields, he served his master as a coachman and livestock keeper. He also learned to read and write French and some Latin, but he was always more comfortable with the Creole dialect.

During the 1770s the plantation manager emancipated L'Ouverture, who subsequently leased his own small coffee plantation, worked by slaves. He married Suzanne Simone, who already had one son, and the couple had another son during their marriage. In 1791 he joined the slave uprisings that swept Saint-Domingue, and he took on the *nom de guerre* (war name) L'Ouverture, meaning "the opening." L'Ouverture rose to prominence among rebel slaves allied with Spain and by early 1794 controlled his own army. A devout Catholic who led a frugal and ascetic life, L'Ouverture impressed others with his enormous physical energy, intellectual acumen, and air of mystery. In 1794 he defected to the French side and led his troops to a series of victories against the Spanish. In 1795 the National Convention promoted L'Ouverture to brigadier general.

Over the next three years L'Ouverture successively eliminated rivals for authority on the island. First he freed himself of the French commissioners sent to govern the colony. With a firm grip on power in the northern province, L'Ouverture defeated General André Rigaud in 1800 to gain control in the south. His army then marched on the capital of Spanish Santo Domingo on the eastern half of the island, meeting little resistance. The entire island of Hispaniola was now under his command.

With control in his hands, L'Ouverture was confronted with the challenge of building a post-emancipation society, the first of its kind. The task was made even more difficult by the chaos wreaked by war, the destruction of plantations, and bitter social and racial tensions. For L'Ouverture the most pressing concern was to re-establish the plantation economy. Without revenue to pay his army, the gains of the rebellion could be lost. He therefore encouraged white planters to return and reclaim their property. He also adopted harsh policies toward former slaves, forcing them back to their plantations and restricting their ability to acquire land. When they resisted, he sent troops across the island to enforce submission. L'Ouverture's 1801 constitution reaffirmed his draconian labor policies and named L'Ouverture governor for life, leaving Saint-Domingue as a colony in name alone. In June 1802 French forces arrested L'Ouverture and jailed him at Fort de Joux in France's Jura Mountains near the Swiss border. He died of pneumonia on April 7, 1803, leaving his lieutenant, Jean Jacques Dessalines, to win independence for the new Haitian nation.

Equestrian portrait of Toussaint L'Ouverture. (Bibliothèque Nationale, Paris, France/Archives Charmet/Bridgeman Images)

QUESTIONS FOR ANALYSIS

1. Toussaint L'Ouverture was both slave and slave owner. How did each experience shape his life and actions?
2. What did L'Ouverture and Napoleon Bonaparte have in common? How did they differ?

This victory was soon challenged by Napoleon, who had his own plans for using the profits from a re-established system of plantation slavery as a basis for expanding the French empire. In 1802 French forces under the command of Napoleon's brother-in-law, General Charles-Victor-Emmanuel Leclerc, arrested L'Ouverture and deported him to France, where the revolutionary leader died in 1803.

It was left to L'Ouverture's lieutenant, Jean Jacques Dessalines (duh-sah-LEEN), to unite the resistance, and he led it to a crushing victory over French forces. On January 1, 1804, Dessalines formally declared the independence of Saint-Domingue and the creation of the new sovereign nation of Haiti, the name used by the pre-Columbian inhabitants of the island.

Haiti, the second independent state in the Americas and the first in Latin America, was born from the only successful large-scale slave revolt in history. This event spread shock and fear through slaveholding societies in the Caribbean and the United States, bringing to life their worst nightmares of the utter reversal of power and privilege. Fearing the spread of slave rebellion to the United States, President Thomas Jefferson refused to recognize Haiti. The liberal proponents of the American Revolution thus chose to protect slavery at the expense of revolutionary ideals of universal human rights. Yet Haitian independence had fundamental repercussions for world history, helping spread the idea that liberty, equality, and fraternity must apply to all people. The next phase of Atlantic revolution soon opened in the Spanish-American colonies.

Revolutions in Latin America

Why and how did the Spanish and Portuguese colonies of North and South America shake off European domination and develop into national states?

In 1800 the Spanish Empire in the Americas stretched from the headwaters of the Mississippi River in present-day Minnesota to the tip of Cape Horn in the Antarctic (Map 22.4). Portugal controlled the vast territory of Brazil. Spain and Portugal believed that the great wealth of the Americas existed for the benefit of the Iberian powers, a stance that fostered bitterness and a thirst for independence in the colonies. Between 1806 and 1825 the colonies in Latin America were convulsed by upheavals that ultimately resulted in their independence. For Latin American republicans, their struggles were a continuation of the transatlantic wave of democratic revolution.

The Origins of the Revolutions Against Colonial Powers

Spain's humiliating defeat in the War of the Spanish Succession (1701–1713) (see "The Wars of Louis XIV" in Chapter 18) prompted demands for sweeping reform of all of Spain's institutions, including its colonial policies and practices. The new Bourbon dynasty initiated a decades-long effort known as the Bourbon reforms, which aimed to improve administrative efficiency and increase central control. Under Charles III (r. 1759–1788), Spanish administrators drew on Enlightenment ideals of rationalism and progress to strengthen colonial rule and thereby increase the fortunes and power of the Spanish state. They created a permanent standing army and enlarged colonial militias, sought to bring the church under tighter control, and dispatched intendants (government commissioners) with extensive new powers to oversee the colonies.

Additionally, Spain ended its policy of insisting that all colonial trade pass through its own ports and instead permitted free trade within the Spanish Empire. This was intended to favor Spain's competition with Great Britain and Holland by stimulating trade and thereby increasing the imperial government's tax revenues. In Latin America these actions stimulated the production and export of agricultural commodities that were in demand in Europe. Colonial manufacturing, however, which had been growing steadily, suffered a heavy blow under free trade. Colonial textiles and china, for example, could not compete with cheap Spanish products.

Madrid's tax reforms also aggravated discontent. Like Great Britain, Spain believed its colonies should bear some of the costs of their own defense. Accordingly, Madrid raised the prices of its monopoly products—tobacco and liquor—and increased sales taxes on many items. War with revolutionary France in the 1790s led to additional taxes and forced loans, all of which were widely resented. Moreover, high prices and heavier taxes imposed a great burden on indigenous communities, which bore the brunt of all forms of taxation and suffered from the corruption and brutality of tax collectors.

Political conflicts beyond the colonies also helped drive aspirations for independence. The French Revolution and the Napoleonic Wars, which involved France's occupation of Spain and Britain's domination of the seas, isolated Spain and weakened its control over its Latin American colonies.

Racial and ethnic divisions further fueled discontent. At this time, Creoles numbered approximately 3 million of a population of roughly 14 million. They resented the economic and political dominance of the roughly 200,000 **peninsulares** (puh-nihn-suh-LUHR-ayz), as the colonial officials and other natives of Spain

---

peninsulares A term for natives of Spain and Portugal.

MAP 22.4 Latin America, ca. 1780 and 1830 By 1830 almost all of Central America, South America, and the Caribbean islands had won independence. Note that the many nations that now make up Central America were unified when they first won independence from Mexico. Similarly, modern Venezuela, Colombia, and Ecuador were still joined in Gran Colombia.

or Portugal were called. The Creoles wanted to free themselves from Spain and Portugal and to rule the colonies themselves. They had little interest in improving the lot of the Indians, who constituted by far the largest population group, or that of the mestizos of mixed Spanish and Indian background and the mulattos of mixed Spanish and African heritage.

Slavery was practiced throughout Latin America, but unevenly. The Andes, Mexico, and Central America had relatively small enslaved populations. By contrast, regions dominated by plantation agriculture — especially the Caribbean islands and Brazil — relied on massive numbers of enslaved laborers. Sizable populations of free people of color existed throughout colonial Latin America, greatly outnumbering slaves in many cities. Despite prejudicial laws, they played an important role in urban public life, serving in large numbers in the militia units of cities such as Havana, Mexico City, Lima, and Buenos Aires. As in Saint-Domingue, white Creoles spurred a backlash against the rising social prominence of free people of color in the last decades of the eighteenth century.

A final factor contributing to rebellion was cultural and intellectual ideas. One set of such ideas was Enlightenment thought, which had been trickling into Latin America for decades (see "The Atlantic Enlightenment" in Chapter 19). By 1800 the Creole elite throughout Latin America was familiar with Enlightenment political thought and its role in inspiring colonial demands for independence. Another important set of ideas consisted of indigenous traditions of justice and reciprocity, which often looked back to an idealized precolonial past. Local people thus perceived Spanish impositions as an assault on the traditional moral communities that bound them to each other and to the Crown. Creoles took advantage of indigenous symbols as a source of legitimacy, but this did not mean they were prepared to view Indians and mestizos as equals.

Resistance, Rebellion, and Independence

The mid-eighteenth century witnessed frequent Andean Indian rebellions against increased taxation and the Bourbon crown's other impositions. In 1780, under the leadership of a descendant of the Inca rulers who took the name Tupac Amaru II, a massive insurrection exploded in the Cuzco region (see Map 22.4). Indian chieftains from the region gathered a powerful force of Indians and people of mixed race. Rebellion swept across highland Peru, where many Spanish officials were executed. Creoles joined forces with Spaniards and Indian nobles to crush the rebellion, shocked by the radical social and economic reforms promised by

its leaders. The government was obliged to concede to some of the rebels' demands by abolishing the repartimiento system, which required Indians to buy goods solely from tax collectors, and establishing assemblies of local representatives in Cuzco.

As news of the rebellion of Tupac Amaru II trickled northward, it helped stimulate the 1781 Comuneros Revolt in the New Granada viceroyalty (see Map 22.4). In this uprising, an Indian and mestizo peasant army commanded by Creole captains marched on Bogotá to protest high taxation, loss of communal lands, and state monopolies on liquor and tobacco. Dispersed by the ruling Spanish, who made promises they did not intend to keep, the revolt in the end did little to improve the Indians' lives.

Authorities were shaken by these revolts and the many smaller uprisings that broke out through the eighteenth century, including slave rebellions in Venezuela in the 1790s. But the uprisings did not give rise directly to the independence movements that followed. Led from below, they did not question monarchical rule or the colonial relationship between Spain and Spanish America.

Two events outside of Spanish America did much to shape the ensuing struggle for independence. First, the revolution on Saint-Domingue and the subsequent independence of the nation of Haiti in 1804 convinced Creole elites, many of whom were slaveholders, of the dangers of slave revolt and racial warfare (see Map 22.3). Their plans and strategies would henceforth be shaped by their determination to avoid a similar outcome in Spanish America.

Second, in 1808 Napoleon Bonaparte deposed Spanish king Ferdinand VII and placed his own brother on the Spanish throne (see "The Grand Empire and Its End"). Spanish leaders meeting in exile defiantly began work on the nation's first constitution. Completed in 1812, the Constitution of Cadiz enshrined universal manhood suffrage, freedom of the press, limited monarchy, and other liberal principles. Colonial deputies obtained the right to representation in future assemblies, but not proportional to their population. Many future founding fathers of Latin American republics participated actively in the constitutional congress, which thus greatly influenced the spread of liberal ideas.

In the colonies, the political crisis engendered by Napoleon's coup encouraged movements for self-governance. In cities like Buenos Aires and Caracas, town councils, known as cabildos, took power into their own hands, ostensibly on behalf of the deposed king, Ferdinand. In July 1811 a regional congress in Caracas declared the independence of the United States of Venezuela and drafted a liberal constitution guaranteeing basic freedoms and abolishing the slave trade but restricting political participation to property owners. (See "Global Viewpoints: Declarations of Independence: The United States and Venezuela," page 654.) The republic failed after only one year, but patriots continued to fight royalist forces for the next eight years under the leadership of Simón Bolívar (1783–1830), who belonged to a wealthy land- and slave-owning family.

Bolívar and other Creole elites fighting for independence were forced to acknowledge that victory against Spain would require support from the nonwhites they had previously despised and who had often supported sympathetic royalist leaders against slave-owning Creoles. In return for promising to abolish slavery after independence, Bolívar received military and financial aid from the new Haitian nation. He granted immediate emancipation to slaves who joined the revolutionary struggle and named former slaves and free people of color to positions of authority in the army.

Triumph of Bolívar Bolívar was treated as a hero everywhere he went in South America. (Sammlung Archiv für Kunst und Geschichte, Berlin, Germany/akg-images)

His victories over Spanish armies won Bolívar the presidency of the new republic of Gran Colombia (formerly the New Granada viceroyalty) in 1819. The republic passed laws for the gradual emancipation of slavery and issued a liberal constitution, similar to that of 1811. Bolívar and other military leaders continued attacks against the Spanish, eventually freeing or helping to liberate the future nations of Colombia, Ecuador, Peru, Chile, and Bolivia (named after the great liberator). Bolívar encouraged the new states to begin the process of manumission, a suggestion that met with great success in the Republic of Chile, which abolished slavery in 1823, but elsewhere encountered resistance from Creole slaveholders.

Dreaming of a continental political union, Bolívar summoned a conference of the new American republics in 1826 in Panama City. The meeting achieved little, however. The territories of Gran Colombia soon splintered (see Map 22.4), and a sadly disillusioned Bolívar went into exile.

Events in Mexico followed a different course. Under Spain, Mexico had been united with Central America as the Viceroyalty of New Spain. In 1808, after Napoleon's coup, the Spanish viceroy assumed control of the government of New Spain from its capital in Mexico City. Meanwhile, groups of rebels plotted to overthrow royalist power. Under the leadership of Miguel Hidalgo, a Jesuit priest who espoused racial and social equality, poor Creoles and indigenous and mestizo peasants rose up against the Spanish in 1810. Although Hidalgo was quickly caught and executed by the combined forces of Spain and Creole elites, popular revolts spread across Mexico.

By 1820 the desire for autonomy from Spain had spread among Creole elites. They joined forces with rebellious armies to make common cause against Spain and succeeded in winning over many royalist troops. In 1821 they issued a declaration of Mexican independence. Originally established as a constitutional monarchy, the new state became a republic in 1823. Gradual steps toward the abolition of slavery culminated in the freeing of all slaves by the end of the 1820s and the election of a president of African descent in 1829.

Portuguese Brazil followed a less turbulent path to independence than the Spanish-American republics. When Napoleon's troops entered Portugal, the royal family fled to Brazil and made Rio de Janeiro the capital of the Portuguese Empire. The king returned to Portugal in 1821, leaving his son Pedro in Brazil as regent. Under popular pressure, Pedro proclaimed Brazil's independence in 1822, issued a constitution, and even led resistance against Portuguese troops. He accepted the title Emperor Pedro I (r. 1822–1831). Although Brazil remained a monarchy, Creole elites dominated society in Brazil, as they did elsewhere in Latin America.

GLOBAL VIEWPOINTS

Declarations of Independence:
The United States and Venezuela

Within fifty years of the drafting of the Declaration of Independence by Thomas Jefferson and others in 1776, some twenty other independence movements in Europe and the Americas had issued similar proclamations. The rapid spread of this new type of political declaration testifies to the close connections among transatlantic revolutionary movements in this period. Many of the later declarations of independence modeled themselves self-consciously on the language and arguments of the 1776 text, excerpted below, but they also reflected the unique circumstances in which they were created, as demonstrated by the Venezuelan declaration, also excerpted below.

A Declaration by the Representatives of the United States of America, July 4, 1776

■ We hold these Truths to be self-evident, that all Men are created equal, that they are endowed by their Creator with certain unalienable Rights, that among these are Life, Liberty, and the Pursuit of Happiness—That to secure these Rights, Governments are instituted among Men, deriving their just Powers from the Consent of the Governed, that whenever any Form of Government becomes destructive of these Ends, it is the Right of the People to alter or to abolish it, and to institute new Government, laying its Foundation on such Principles, and organizing its Powers in such Form, as to them shall seem most likely to effect their Safety and Happiness. Prudence, indeed, will dictate that Governments long established should not be changed for light and transient Causes; and accordingly all Experience hath shewn, that Mankind are more disposed to suffer, while Evils are sufferable, than to right themselves by abolishing the Forms to which they are accustomed. But when a long Train of Abuses and Usurpations, pursuing invariably the same Object, evinces a Design to reduce them under absolute Despotism, it is their Right, it is their Duty, to throw off such Government, and to provide new Guards for their future Security. . . . The History of the present King of Great-Britain is a History of repeated Injuries and Usurpations, all having in direct Object the Establishment of an Absolute Tyranny over these States.

Venezuelan Declaration of Independence, July 5, 1811

■ In the Name of the All-powerful God, We, the Representatives of the united Provinces . . . , forming the American Confederation of Venezuela, in the South Continent, in Congress assembled, considering the full and absolute possession of our Rights, which we recovered justly and legally from the 19th of April, 1810, in consequence of the occurrences in Bayona,* and the occupation of the Spanish Throne by conquest, and the succession of a new Dynasty, constituted without our consent, . . . calling on the SUPREME BEING to witness the justice of our proceedings and the rectitude of our intentions, do implore his divine and celestial help; and ratifying, at the moment in which we are born to the dignity which his Providence restores to us, the desire we have of living and dying free, and of believing and defending the holy Catholic and Apostolic Religion of Jesus Christ. We, therefore, in the name and by the will and authority which we hold from the virtuous People of Venezuela, DO declare solemnly to the world, that its united Provinces are, and ought to be, from this day, by act and right, Free, Sovereign, and Independent States; and that they are absolved from every submission and dependence on the Throne of Spain . . . and that a free and independent State, thus constituted, has full power to take that form of Government which may be conformable to the general will of the People, to declare war, make peace, form alliances, regulate treaties of commerce, limits, and navigation; and to do and transact every act, in like manner as other free and independent States.

QUESTIONS FOR ANALYSIS

1. What justification does the first declaration offer for the independence of the United States of America from Great Britain? What influences from Enlightenment thought are evident in this text?
2. What similarities and differences do you find between the declaration of the United States of America and that of Venezuela?

Sources: The Declaration of Independence (1776); *Interesting Official Documents Relating to the United Provinces of Venezuela* (London: Longman and Co., 1812), pp. 3, 18–19.

*The forced abdication of Spanish king Ferdinand VII in favor of Joseph Bonaparte.

KEY EVENTS IN EARLY LATIN AMERICAN REVOLUTIONS

1759–1788	Reign of Charles III, who instituted administrative and economic reforms
July 1811	Regional congress in Caracas declares independence of the United States of Venezuela
1822	Proclamation of Brazil's independence from Portugal
1826	Call by Simón Bolívar for Panama conference on Latin American union
1830s	New Spain breaks up into five separate countries
1888	Emancipation of slaves in Brazil

Because they had gained independence without military struggle, Brazil's Creole elites avoided making common cause with poor whites and people of color, and they refused to consider ending slavery once independence arrived.

The Aftermath of Revolution in the Atlantic World

The Atlantic revolutions shared many common traits. They had common origins in imperial competition, war debt, social conflict, and Enlightenment ideals. Over the course of revolution, armed struggle often took the form of civil war, in which the participation of ordinary people — sans-culottes, slaves, free people of color, mestizos, and Indians — played a decisive role. Perhaps their most important similarity was in the democratic limitations of the regimes these revolutions created and the frustrated aspirations they bequeathed to subsequent generations of marginalized citizens.

For the most part, the elite liberals who led the revolutions were not democrats and had no intention of creating regimes of full economic or social equality. The constitutions they wrote generally restricted political rights to landowners and middle-class men. Indigenous people may have gained formal equality as citizens, yet they found that the actual result was the removal of the privileged status they had negotiated with their original conquerors. Thus they suffered the loss of rights over their land and other resources. Moreover, none of the postrevolutionary constitutions gave women a role in political life.

The issue of slavery, by contrast, divided the revolutions. The American Revolution was led in part by slaveholding landowners, who were determined to retain slavery in its aftermath, while the more radical French republic abolished it throughout the French empire (a measure soon reversed by Napoleon). The independent nation of Haiti was built on the only successful slave revolt in history, but the need for revenue from plantation agriculture soon led to the return of coercive labor requirements, if not outright slavery. In Latin America independence speeded the abolition of slavery, bringing an immediate ban on the slave trade and gradual emancipation from the 1820s to the 1850s. Still, Cuba and Brazil, which had enormous slave populations, did not end slavery until 1886 and 1888, respectively.

The aftermath of the Atlantic revolutions brought extremely different fortunes to the new nations that emerged from them. France returned to royal rule with the restoration of the Bourbon monarchy in 1815. A series of revolutionary crises ensued in the nineteenth century as succeeding generations struggled over the legacies of monarchicism, republicanism, and Bonapartism. It was not until 1871 that republicanism finally prevailed (see "Republican France" in Chapter 24). The transition to an independent republic was permanent and relatively smooth in the United States. Nevertheless, the unresolved conflict over slavery would lead to catastrophic civil war in 1860. Haiti faced crushing demands for financial reparations from France and the hostility of the United States and other powers.

The newly independent nations of Latin America had difficulty achieving economic and political stability when the wars of independence ended. In the 1830s regional separatism caused New Spain to break up into five separate countries. The failure of political union in New Spain and Gran Colombia isolated individual countries, prevented collective action, and later paved the way for the political and economic intrusion of the United States and other powers. Spain's Caribbean colonies of Puerto Rico and Cuba remained loyal, in large part due to fears that slave revolt would spread from neighboring Haiti.

The Creole leaders of the revolutions had little experience in government, and the wars left a legacy of military, not civilian, leadership. Despite these disappointments, liberal ideals of political and social equality born of the revolutionary era left a crucial legacy for future generations in Latin America (see Chapter 27).

Chapter Summary

From 1775 to 1825 a wave of revolution swept through the Atlantic world. Its origins included long-term social and economic changes, Enlightenment ideals of liberty and equality, and the costs of colonial warfare.

British efforts to raise taxes after the Seven Years' War aroused violent protest in the American colonies. In 1776 the Second Continental Congress issued the Declaration of Independence, and by 1783 Britain had recognized the independence of the thirteen colonies.

In 1789 delegates to the Estates General defied royal authority to declare themselves a National Assembly, which promulgated France's first constitution in 1791. Led by the Jacobin club, the Assembly waged war on Austria and Prussia and proclaimed France a republic. From the end of 1793, under the Reign of Terror, the Revolution pursued internal and external enemies ruthlessly and instituted economic controls to aid the poor. The weakness of the Directory government after the fall of Robespierre enabled Napoleon Bonaparte to claim control of France. Napoleon's relentless military ambitions allowed him to spread French power through much of Europe but ultimately led to his downfall.

After a failed uprising by free men of color, slaves rose in revolt in the French colony of Saint-Domingue in August 1791. Their revolt, combined with the outbreak of war and the radicalization of the French Revolution, led to a sequence of conflicts and rebellions that culminated in independence for the new Haitian nation in 1804.

Latin American independence movements drew strength from Spain's unpopular policies and the political crisis engendered by Napoleon's invasion of Portugal and Spain. Under the leadership of Simón Bolívar, the United States of Venezuela claimed independence in 1811. Led by Creole officers but reliant on nonwhite soldiers, rebel armies successfully fought Spanish forces over the next decade. Despite Bolívar's efforts to build a unified state, in the 1830s New Spain split into five separate countries. In Brazil the royal regent proclaimed independence in 1822 and reigned as emperor of the new state.

NOTES

1. Donald Sutherland, *France, 1789–1815: Revolution and Counterrevolution* (New York: Oxford University Press, 1986), p. 420.
2. John K. Thornton, "'I Am the Subject of the King of Congo': African Political Ideology and the Haitian Revolution," *Journal of World History* 4.2 (Fall 1993): 181–214.

CONNECTIONS

The Atlantic world was the essential context for a great revolutionary wave in the late eighteenth and early nineteenth centuries. The movement of peoples, commodities, and ideas across the Atlantic Ocean in the eighteenth century created a world of common debates, conflicts, and aspirations. Moreover, the high stakes of colonial empire heightened competition among European states, leading to a series of wars that generated crushing costs for overburdened treasuries. For the British and Spanish in their American colonies and the French at home, the desperate need for new taxes weakened government authority and opened the door to rebellion. In turn, the ideals of the French Revolution inspired slaves and free people of African descent in Saint-Domingue and Latin America to rise up and claim the promise of liberty, equality, and fraternity for people of all races.

The chain reaction did not end with the liberation movements in Latin America that followed the Haitian Revolution. Throughout the nineteenth and early twentieth centuries periodic convulsions occurred in Europe, the Americas, and elsewhere as successive generations struggled over political rights first proclaimed by late-eighteenth-century revolutionaries (see Chapters 24 and 27). Meanwhile, as dramatic political events unfolded, a parallel economic revolution was gathering steam. This was the Industrial Revolution, the topic of the next chapter, which originated around 1780 and accelerated through the end of the eighteenth century. After 1815 the twin forces of industrialization and democratization would combine to transform Europe and the world.

CHAPTER 22 **Review and Explore**

Identify Key Terms

Identify and explain the significance of each item below.

Treaty of Paris (p. 630)

Declaration of Independence (p. 631)

Antifederalists (p. 633)

Estates General (p. 634)

National Assembly (p. 634)

Jacobin club (p. 637)

Mountain (p. 638)

Girondists (p. 638)

sans-culottes (p. 638)

Reign of Terror (p. 638)

Thermidorian reaction (p. 640)

Napoleonic Code (p. 642)

Grand Empire (p. 643)

Continental System (p. 643)

Creoles (p. 646)

peninsulares (p. 650)

Review the Main Ideas

Answer the focus questions from each section of the chapter.

1. What were the factors behind the age of revolution in the Atlantic world? (p. 626)

2. Why and how did American colonists forge a new, independent nation? (p. 631)

3. Why and how did revolutionaries in France transform the nation first into a constitutional monarchy and then into a republic that entered war with European powers? (p. 634)

4. How did Napoleon Bonaparte assume control of France and much of Europe, and what factors led to his downfall? (p. 641)

5. How did a slave revolt on colonial Saint-Domingue lead to the creation of the independent nation of Haiti in 1804? (p. 645)

6. Why and how did the Spanish and Portuguese colonies of North and South America shake off European domination and develop into national states? (p. 650)

Make Comparisons and Connections

Analyze the larger developments and continuities within and across chapters.

1. What was revolutionary about the age of revolution? How did the states that emerged out of the eighteenth-century revolutions differ from the states that predominated in previous centuries?

2. To what extent would you characterize the revolutions discussed in this chapter as Enlightenment movements? (See "The Atlantic Enlightenment" in Chapter 19.) How did the increased circulation of goods, people, and ideas across the Atlantic in the eighteenth century contribute to the outbreak of revolution on both sides of the ocean?

3. In what sense did the age of revolution mark the beginning of modern politics in Europe and the Americas?

TIMELINE

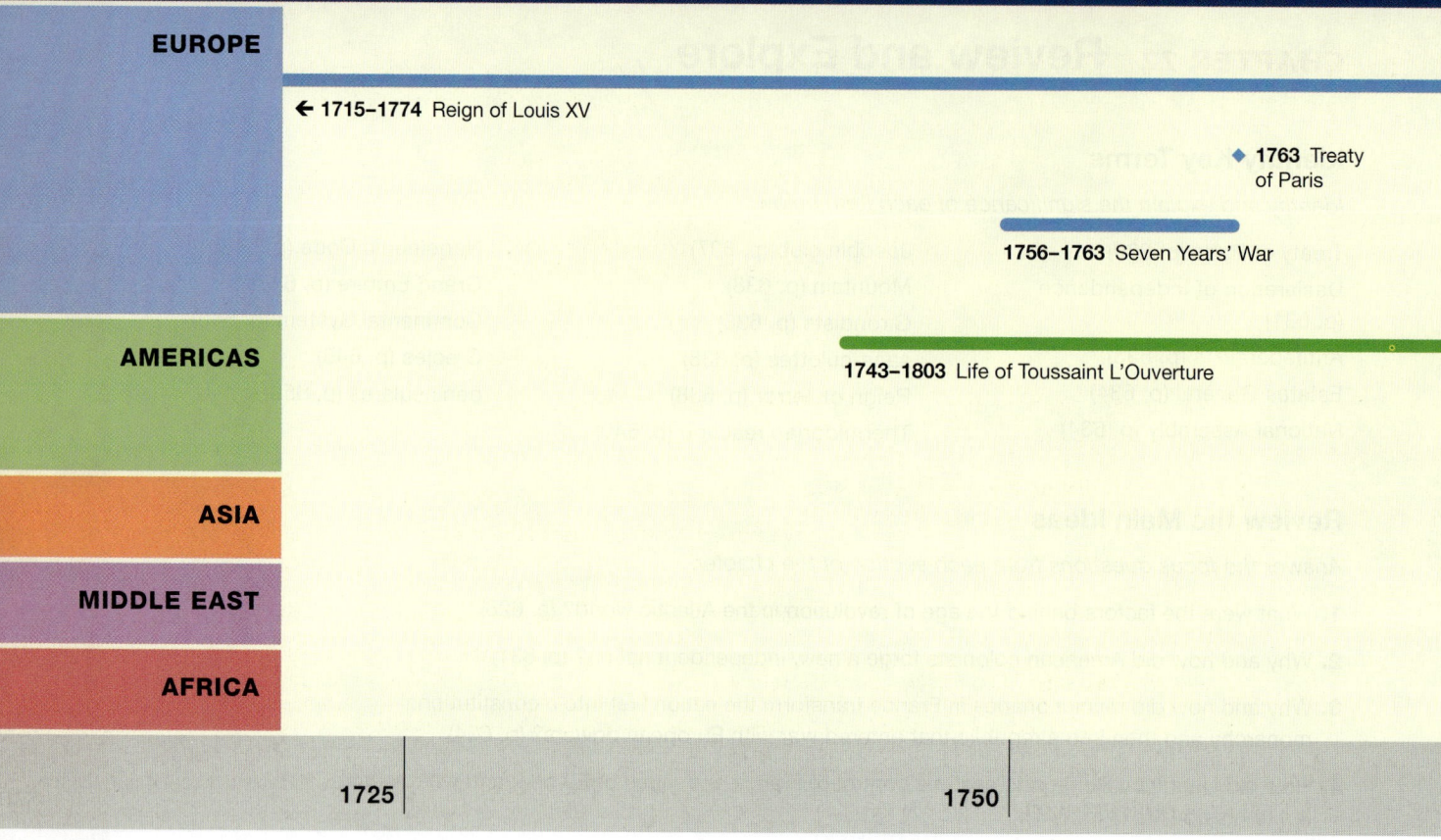

EUROPE

← **1715–1774** Reign of Louis XV

◆ **1763** Treaty of Paris

1756–1763 Seven Years' War

AMERICAS

1743–1803 Life of Toussaint L'Ouverture

ASIA

MIDDLE EAST

AFRICA

1725

1750

Suggested Resources

BOOKS

Armitage, David, and Sanjay Subrahmanyam, eds. *The Age of Revolutions in Global Context, c. 1760–1840.* 2009. Presents the international causes and consequences of the age of revolutions.

Bell, David A. *The First Total War: Napoleon's Europe and the Birth of Warfare as We Know It.* 2007. Argues that the French Revolution created a new form of "total" war that prefigured the world wars of the twentieth century.

Calloway, Colin G. *The Scratch of a Pen: 1763 and the Transformation of North America.* 2006. A study of the dramatic impact of the Seven Years' War on the British and French colonies of North America.

Desan, Suzanne. *The Family on Trial in Revolutionary France.* 2004. Studies the effects of revolutionary law on the family, including the legalization of divorce.

Dubois, Laurent. *Avengers of the New World: The Story of the Haitian Revolution.* 2004. An excellent and highly readable account of the revolution that transformed the French colony of Saint-Domingue into the independent state of Haiti.

Gould, Eliga H., and Peter S. Onuf, eds. *Empire and Nation: The American Revolution in the Atlantic World.* 2005. A collection of essays placing the American Revolution in its wider Atlantic context, including studies of its impact on daily life in the new republic and the remaining British Empire.

Klooster, Wim. *Revolutions in the Atlantic World: A Comparative History.* 2009. An accessible and engaging comparison of the revolutions in North America, France, Haiti, and Spanish America.

McPhee, Peter, ed. *A Companion to the French Revolution.* 2013. A wide-ranging collection of essays on the French Revolution, written by experts in the field.

Schechter, Ronald. *Obstinate Hebrews: Representations of Jews in France, 1715–1815.* 2003. An illuminating study of Jews and attitudes toward them in France, from the Enlightenment to emancipation.

Sepinwall, Alyssa, ed. *Haitian History: New Perspectives.* 2013. A collection of essays showcasing the most important new scholarship on the Haitian Revolution.

Van Young, Eric. *The Other Rebellion: Popular Violence, Ideology, and the Mexican Struggle for Independence, 1810–1821.* 2001. Authoritative study of why ordinary Mexicans joined the fight for independence from Spain.

Wood, Gordon S. *The American Revolution: A History.* 2003. A concise introduction to the American Revolution by a Pulitzer Prize–winning historian.

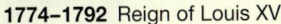

1774–1792 Reign of Louis XVI

1799–1814 Reign of Napoleon Bonaparte

1789–1799 French Revolution

◆ **1790** Edmund Burke publishes
Reflections on the Revolution in France

1775–1783 American Revolution

1791–1804 Haitian Revolution

◆ **1775** Thomas Paine publishes *Common Sense*

◆ **1784** British pass East India Company Act **(Ch. 17)**

◆ **1793** British diplomatic visit to China **(Ch. 21)**

1789–1807 Ottoman Ruler Selim III introduces reforms **(Ch. 25)**

1780–1820 Peak of transatlantic slave trade **(Ch. 20)**

◆ **1807** Slave trade declared
illegal in British Empire **(Ch. 25)**

1775	1800	1825

DOCUMENTARIES

Égalité for All: Toussaint Louverture and the Haitian Revolution (PBS, 2009). Uses music, interviews, voodoo rituals, and dramatic re-enactments to explore the Haitian Revolution and its fascinating leader, Toussaint L'Ouverture.

Liberty! The American Revolution (PBS, 1997). A dramatic documentary about the American Revolution, consisting of six hour-long episodes that cover events from 1763 to 1788.

The War That Made America (PBS, 2006). This miniseries about the Seven Years' War (known as the French and Indian War in North America) focuses on alliances between Native Americans and the French and British; it also examines George Washington's role in the conflict as a young officer.

FEATURE FILMS AND TELEVISION DRAMAS

Farewell, My Queen (Benoît Jacquot, 2012). A fictional view of the final days of the French monarchy, from the perspective of a female servant whose job is to read to Queen Marie Antoinette.

John Adams (HBO, 2008). An award-winning miniseries on the life of one of the Founding Fathers of the United States.

The Liberator (Alberto Arvelo, 2014). The first Venezuelan film to be nominated for an Oscar presents an epic survey of the life and battles of Simón Bolívar, hero of the Spanish-American wars of independence.

Master and Commander: The Far Side of the World (Peter Weir, 2003). A British navy captain pursues a French vessel along the coast of South America during the Napoleonic Wars.

WEBSITES

French Revolution Digital Archive. A website hosted by Stanford University that includes fourteen thousand digital images from the French Revolution. **frda.stanford.edu/**

Haiti Digital Library. A guide to online primary sources, articles, and websites related to Haitian history, from the revolution to modern times; sponsored by the Haiti Laboratory at Duke University. **sites.duke.edu/haitilab/english/**

Liberty, Equality, Fraternity: Exploring the French Revolution. Features a large image and document collection from the era of the French Revolution, as well as songs, maps, and thematic essays written by scholars in the field. **chnm.gmu.edu/revolution/**

The Papers of George Washington. A site with online versions of many documents pertaining to and written by George Washington, accompanied by articles on themes related to Washington's life and views. **gwpapers.virginia.edu**

23

The Revolution in Energy and Industry
1760–1850

While the revolutions of the Atlantic world were opening a new political era, another revolution was beginning to transform economic and social life. The Industrial Revolution began in Great Britain around 1780 and soon began to influence continental Europe and the United States. Quite possibly only the development of agriculture during Neolithic times had a comparable impact and significance in world history. Non-Western nations began to industrialize after 1860.

Industrialization profoundly modified human experience. It changed patterns of work, transformed the social structure, and eventually altered the international balance of political power in favor of the most rapidly industrialized nations, especially Great Britain. What was revolutionary about the Industrial Revolution was not its pace or that it represented a sharp break with the previous period. On the contrary, the Industrial Revolution built on earlier developments, and the rate of progress was slow. What was remarkable about the Industrial Revolution was that it inaugurated a period of sustained economic and demographic growth that has continued to the present. Although it took time, the Industrial Revolution eventually helped ordinary people in the West gain a higher standard of living.

(*Interior of a Furnace*, 1865 [oil on canvas] [detail] by Charles Housez [1822–1888]/BOURNE GALLERY ARCHIVE/
© Bourne Gallery, Reigate, Surrey, UK/ Bridgeman Images)

Young Factory Worker

Children composed a substantial element of the workforce in early factories, where they toiled long hours in dangerous and unsanitary conditions. Until a mechanized process was invented at the end of the nineteenth century, boys working in glass-bottle factories, like the youth pictured here, stoked blazing furnaces with coal and learned to blow glass.

CHAPTER PREVIEW

THE INDUSTRIAL REVOLUTION IN BRITAIN
Why did the Industrial Revolution begin in Britain, and how did it develop between 1780 and 1850?

INDUSTRIALIZATION IN EUROPE AND THE WORLD
How did countries in Europe and around the world respond to the challenge of industrialization after 1815?

NEW PATTERNS OF WORKING AND LIVING
How did work evolve during the Industrial Revolution, and how did daily life change for working people?

RELATIONS BETWEEN CAPITAL AND LABOR
How did the changes brought about by the Industrial Revolution lead to new social classes, and how did people respond to the new structure?

The Industrial Revolution in Britain

Why did the Industrial Revolution begin in Britain, and how did it develop between 1780 and 1850?

The Industrial Revolution began in Great Britain, the nation created by the formal union of Scotland, Wales, and England in 1707. The transformation in industry was something new in history, and it was unplanned. It originated from a unique combination of possibilities and constraints in late-eighteenth-century Britain. With no models to copy and no idea of what to expect, Britain pioneered not only in industrial technology but also in social relations and urban living.

Why Britain?

Perhaps the most important debate in economic history focuses on why the Industrial Revolution originated in western Europe, and Britain in particular, rather than in other parts of the world, such as Asia. Historians continue to debate this issue, but the best answer seems to be that Britain possessed a unique set of possibilities and constraints—abundant coal, high wages, a relatively peaceful and centralized government, well-developed financial systems, innovative culture, highly skilled craftsmen, and a strong position in empire and global trade, including slavery—that spurred its people to adopt a capital-intensive, machine-powered system of production.

Thus a number of factors came together over the long term to give rise to the Industrial Revolution in Britain. The Scientific Revolution and the Enlightenment fostered a new worldview that embraced progress and the role of research and experimentation in understanding and mastering the natural world. Moreover, Britain's intellectual culture emphasized the public sharing of knowledge, including that of scientists and technicians from other countries.

In the economic realm, the seventeenth-century expansion of rural industry produced a surplus of English woolen cloth. Exported throughout Europe, English cloth brought commercial profits and high wages. By the eighteenth century the expanding Atlantic economy and trade with India and China were also serving Britain well. The mercantilist colonial empire Britain aggressively built, augmented by a strong position in Latin America and in the transatlantic slave trade, provided raw materials like cotton and a growing market for British manufactured goods (see "The Atlantic Economy" in Chapter 19). Strong demand for British manufacturing meant that British workers earned high wages compared to the rest of the world's laborers.

Agriculture also played an important role in bringing about the Industrial Revolution. English farmers were second only to the Dutch in productivity in 1700, and they were continually adopting new methods of farming. Because of increasing efficiency, landowners were able to produce more food with a smaller workforce. The enclosure movement had deprived many small landowners of their land, leaving the landless poor to work as hired agricultural laborers or in rural industry. These groups created a pool of potential laborers for the new factories.

Abundant food and high wages in turn meant that the ordinary English family no longer had to spend almost everything it earned just to buy bread. Thus the family could spend more on manufactured goods. They could also pay to send their children to school. Britain's populace enjoyed high levels of education compared to that of the rest of Europe. Moreover, in the eighteenth century the members of the average British family—including women and girls—were redirecting their labor away from unpaid work for household consumption and toward work for wages that they could spend on goods.

Britain also benefited from rich natural resources and a well-developed infrastructure. In an age when it was much cheaper to ship goods by water than by land, no part of England was more than fifty miles from navigable water. Beginning in the 1770s a canal-building boom enhanced this advantage. Rivers and canals facilitated easy movement of England and Wales's enormous deposits of iron and coal. The abundance of coal combined with high wages in manufacturing placed Britain in a unique position among the nations of the world: its manufacturers had extremely strong incentives to develop technologies to draw on the power of coal to increase workmen's productivity. In regions with lower wages, such as India and China, the costs of mechanization outweighed potential gains in productivity.

Cottage Industry and Transportation in Great Britain in the 1700s

Industrial areas
- Coal deposit
- Metal goods
- Woolen cloth
- Canals, 1800
- Navigable rivers

SCOTLAND

Newcastle

North Sea

Manchester

Sheffield

Birmingham

Iron

WALES

ENGLAND

Iron

Bath

London

Iron

Exeter

English Channel

A final factor favoring British industrialization was the heavy hand of the British state and its policies. Britain's parliamentary system taxed its population aggressively and spent the money on a navy to protect imperial commerce and on an army that could be used to quell uprisings by disgruntled workers. Starting with the Navigation Acts under Oliver Cromwell (see "Mercantilism and Colonial Wars" in Chapter 18), the British state also adopted aggressive tariffs, or duties, on imported goods to protect its industries.

All these factors combined to initiate the **Industrial Revolution**, a term first coined to describe the burst of major inventions and technical changes that took place in certain industries. This technical revolution went hand in hand with an impressive quickening in the annual rate of industrial growth in Britain. Whereas industry had grown at only 0.7 percent between 1700 and 1760 (before the Industrial Revolution), it grew at the much higher rate of 3 percent between 1801 and 1831, when industrial transformation was in full swing.[1]

Technological Innovations and Early Factories

The pressure to produce more goods for a growing market and to reduce the labor costs of manufacturing was directly related to the first decisive breakthrough of the Industrial Revolution: the creation of the world's first machine-powered factories in the British cotton textile industry. Technological innovations in the manufacture of cotton cloth led to a new system of production and social relationships.

The putting-out system that developed in the seventeenth-century textile industry involved a merchant who loaned, or "put out," raw materials to cottage workers who processed the raw materials in their own homes and returned the finished products to the merchant. There was always a serious imbalance in textile production based on cottage industry: the work of four or five spinners was needed to keep one weaver steadily employed. During the eighteenth century the putting-out system grew across Europe, but most extensively in Britain. The growth of demand only increased pressures on the supply of thread.

Many a tinkering worker knew that devising a better spinning wheel promised rich rewards. It proved hard to spin the traditional raw materials—wool and flax—with improved machines, but cotton was different. Cotton textiles had first been imported into Britain from India by the East India Company as a rare and delicate luxury for the upper classes. In the eighteenth century a lively market for cotton cloth emerged in West Africa, where the English and other Europeans traded it for enslaved people. By 1760 a tiny domestic cotton industry had emerged in northern England

based on imported raw materials, but it could not compete with cloth produced by workers in India and other parts of Asia. International competition thus drove English entrepreneurs to invent new technologies to bring down labor costs.

After many experiments over a generation, a carpenter and jack-of-all-trades, James Hargreaves, invented his cotton-spinning jenny about 1765. At almost the same moment, a barber-turned-manufacturer named Richard Arkwright invented (or possibly pirated) another kind of spinning machine, the water frame. These breakthroughs produced an explosion in the infant cotton textile industry in the 1780s and made some inventors, like Richard Arkwright, extremely wealthy. By 1790 the new machines were producing ten times as much cotton yarn as had been made in 1770.

Hargreaves's **spinning jenny** was simple, inexpensive, and powered by hand. In early models from six to twenty-four spindles were mounted on a sliding carriage, and each spindle spun a fine, slender thread. The machines were usually worked by women, who moved the carriage back and forth with one hand and turned a wheel to supply power with the other. Now it was the male weaver who could not keep up with the vastly more efficient female spinner.

Arkwright's **water frame** employed a different principle. It quickly acquired a capacity of several hundred spindles and demanded much more power than a single operator could provide. A solution was found in waterpower. The water frame required large specialized mills located beside rivers, factories that employed as many as one thousand workers. The major drawback of the water frame was that it could spin only a coarse, strong thread. Around 1780 a hybrid machine invented by Samuel Crompton proved capable of spinning very fine and strong thread in large quantities. (See "Individuals in Society: Samuel Crompton," page 665.) Gradually, all cotton spinning was concentrated in large-scale factories.

These revolutionary developments in the textile industry allowed British manufacturers to compete successfully in international markets in both fine and coarse cotton thread. At first, the machines were too expensive to build and did not provide enough savings in labor to be adopted in continental Europe or

---

Industrial Revolution A term first coined in the 1830s to describe the burst of major inventions and economic expansion that took place in certain industries, such as cotton textiles and iron, between 1780 and 1850.

spinning jenny A simple, inexpensive, hand-powered spinning machine created by James Hargreaves about 1765.

water frame A spinning machine created by Richard Arkwright that had a capacity of several hundred spindles and used waterpower; it therefore required a larger and more specialized mill — a factory.

Woman Working a Spinning Jenny The loose cotton strands on the slanted bobbins shown in this illustration of Hargreaves's spinning jenny passed up to the sliding carriage and then on to the spindles (inset) in back for fine spinning. The worker, almost always a woman, regulated the sliding carriage with one hand, and with the other she turned the crank on the wheel to supply power. By 1783 one woman could spin a hundred threads at a time. (spinning jenny: © Mary Evans Picture Library/The Image Works; spindle: Picture Research Consultants & Archives)

elsewhere. Where wages were low and investment capital was scarce, there was little point in adopting mechanized production until the machines' productivity increased significantly and the cost of manufacturing the machines dropped, both of which occurred in the first decades of the nineteenth century.[2]

Families using cotton in cottage industry were freed from their constant search for adequate yarn from scattered part-time spinners, because all the thread needed could be spun in the cottage on the jenny or obtained from a nearby factory. The income of weavers, now hard-pressed to keep up with the spinners, rose markedly until about 1792. In response, mechanics and capitalists sought to invent a power loom to save on labor costs. This Edmund Cartwright achieved in 1785. But the power looms of the factories worked poorly at first and did not fully replace handlooms until the 1820s.

Working conditions in the early cotton factories were so poor that adult workers were reluctant to work in them. Factory owners often turned to orphans and abandoned children instead. By placing them in "apprenticeship" with factory owners, parish officers charged with caring for such children saved money.

The owners gained workers over whom they exercised almost the authority of slave owners. Housed, fed, and locked up nightly in factory dormitories, the young workers labored thirteen or fourteen hours a day, six days a week, for little or no pay.

The Steam Engine Breakthrough

Well into the eighteenth century, Europe, like other areas of the world, relied mainly on wood for energy, and human beings and animals performed most work. This dependence meant that Europe and the rest of the world remained poor in energy and power.

By the eighteenth century wood was in ever-shorter supply in Britain. Processed wood (charcoal) was mixed with iron ore in blast furnaces to produce pig iron that could be processed into steel, cast iron, or wrought iron. The iron industry's appetite for wood was enormous, and by 1740 the British iron industry was stagnating. As wood became ever more scarce, the British looked to coal as an alternative. They had first used coal in the late Middle Ages as a source of heat. By 1640 most homes in London were heated with coal, and it was also used in industry to provide heat for

Samuel Crompton

SAMUEL CROMPTON'S LIFE STORY ILLUSTRATES the remarkable ingenuity and determination of the first generation of inventors in the Industrial Revolution as well as the struggles they faced in controlling and profiting from their inventions. Crompton was born in 1753 in Bolton-in-the Moors, a Lancashire village active in the domestic production of cotton thread and cloth. Crompton descended from small landowners and weavers, but his grandfather had lost the family land and his father died shortly after his birth.

Crompton's mother was a pious and energetic woman who supported the family by tenant farming and spinning and weaving cotton. Crompton spent years spinning in childhood until he was old enough to begin weaving. His mother ensured that he was well educated at the local school, and as a teenager he attended night classes, studying algebra, mathematics, and trigonometry.

This was the period when John Kay's invention of the flying shuttle doubled the speed of handloom weaving, leading to a drastic rise in the demand for thread. Crompton's family acquired one of the new spinning jennies—invented by James Hargreaves—and he saw for himself how they increased productivity. He was also acquainted with Richard Arkwright, inventor of the water frame, who then operated a barbershop in Bolton.

In 1774 Crompton began work on the spinning machine that would consume what little free time, and spare money, he possessed over the next five years. Solitary by nature and fearful of competition, Crompton worked alone and in secret. He earned a little extra money playing violin in the Bolton theater orchestra, and he possessed a set of tools left over from his father's own mechanical experiments.

The result of all this effort was the spinning mule, so called because it combined the rollers of Arkwright's water frame with the moving carriage of Hargreaves's spinning jenny. With the mule, spinners could produce very fine and strong thread in large quantities, something no previous machine had permitted. The mule effectively ended England's reliance on India for the finest muslin cloth.

In 1780, possessed of a spectacular technological breakthrough and a beloved bride, Crompton seemed poised for a prosperous and happy life. Demand surged for the products of his machine, and manufacturers were desperate to learn its secrets. Too poor and naïve to purchase a patent for his invention, Crompton shared it with manufacturers through a subscription agreement. Unfortunately, he received little of the promised money in return.

Once exposed to the public, the spinning mule quickly spread across Great Britain. Crompton continued to make high-quality yarn, but had to compete with all the other

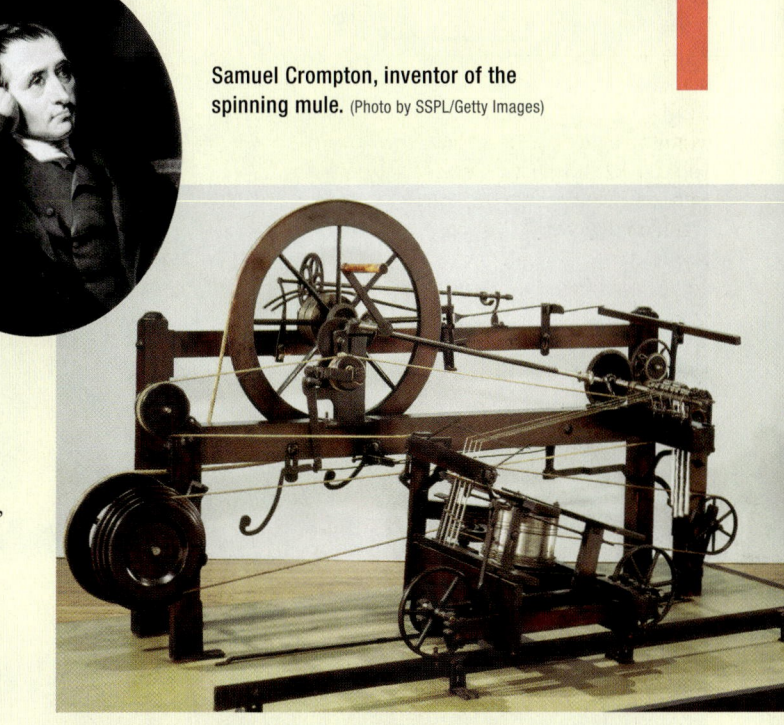

Samuel Crompton, inventor of the spinning mule. (Photo by SSPL/Getty Images)

Replica of the spinning mule, a hybrid machine that combined features from Hargreaves's spinning jenny and Arkwright's water frame. (Photo by SSPL/Getty Images)

workshops using his machine. Moreover, he could not keep skilled workers, since they were constantly lured away by his competitors' higher wages.

As others earned great wealth with the mule, Crompton grew frustrated by his relative poverty. In 1811 he toured Great Britain to document his invention's impact. He estimated that 4,600,000 mules were then in operation that directly employed 70,000 people. Crompton's supporters took these figures to Parliament, which granted him a modest reward of £5,000. However, this boost did little to improve his fortunes, and his subsequent business ventures failed. In 1824 local benefactors took up a small subscription to provide for his needs, but he died in poverty in 1827 at the age of seventy-four.

QUESTIONS FOR ANALYSIS

1. What factors in Crompton's life enabled him to succeed as an inventor?
2. Why did Crompton fail to profit from his inventions?
3. What does the contrast between Richard Arkwright's financial success and Crompton's relative failure tell us about innovation and commercial enterprise in the Industrial Revolution?

Source: Gilbert James France, *The Life and Times of Samuel Crompton, Inventor of the Spinning Machine Called the Mule* (London: Simpkin Marshall, 1859).

James Nasmyth's Mighty Steam Hammer Nasmyth's invention was the forerunner of the modern pile driver, and its successful introduction in 1832 epitomized the rapid development of steam-power technology in Britain. In this painting by the inventor himself, workers manipulate a massive iron shaft being hammered into shape at Nasmyth's foundry near Manchester. (Ann Ronan Pictures/Print Collector/Getty Images)

making beer, glass, soap, and other products. The breakthrough came when industrialists began to use coal to produce mechanical energy and to power machinery.

To produce more coal, mines had to be dug deeper and deeper and were constantly filling with water. Mechanical pumps, usually powered by animals walking in circles at the surface, had to be installed. Animal power was expensive and bothersome. In an attempt to overcome these disadvantages, Thomas Savery in 1698 and Thomas Newcomen in 1705 invented the first primitive **steam engines**. Both engines burned coal to produce steam that drove the water pumps.

In 1763 a gifted young Scot named James Watt (1736–1819) was drawn to a critical study of the steam engine. Watt worked at the University of Glasgow as a skilled craftsman making scientific instruments. In 1763 Watt was called on to repair a Newcomen engine being used in a physics course. Watt discovered that the Newcomen engine could be significantly improved by adding a separate condenser. This invention, patented in 1769, greatly increased the efficiency of the steam engine.

To make his invention a practical success, Watt needed skilled workers, precision parts, and capital, and the relatively advanced nature of the British economy

steam engines A breakthrough invention by Thomas Savery in 1698 and Thomas Newcomen in 1705 that burned coal to produce steam, which was then used to operate a pump; the early models were superseded by James Watt's more efficient steam engine, patented in 1769.

Rocket The name given to George Stephenson's effective locomotive that was first tested in 1829 on the Liverpool and Manchester Railway and reached a maximum speed of 35 miles per hour.

proved essential. A partnership in 1775 with Matthew Boulton, a wealthy English industrialist, provided Watt with adequate capital and exceptional skills in salesmanship. Among Britain's highly skilled locksmiths, tinsmiths, and millwrights, Watt found mechanics who could install, regulate, and repair his sophisticated engines. From ingenious manufacturers, Watt was gradually able to purchase precision parts. By the late 1780s the firm of Boulton and Watt had made the steam engine a practical and commercial success in Britain.

The coal-burning steam engine of Watt and his followers was the Industrial Revolution's most fundamental advance in technology. For the first time in history, humanity had, at least for a few generations, almost unlimited power at its disposal. For the first time, inventors and engineers could devise and implement all kinds of power equipment to aid people in their work. Steam power began to replace waterpower in cotton-spinning mills during the 1780s, contributing greatly to that industry's phenomenal rise. Steam also took the place of waterpower in flour mills, in the malt mills used in breweries, in the flint mills supplying the pottery industry, and in the mills exported by Britain to the West Indies to crush sugarcane.

The British iron industry was also radically transformed. After 1770 the adoption of steam-driven bellows in blast furnaces allowed for great increases in the quantity of pig iron produced by British ironmakers. In the 1780s Henry Cort developed the puddling furnace, which allowed pig iron to be refined with coke, a smokeless and hot-burning fuel produced by heating coal to rid it of impurities.

Cort also developed steam-powered rolling mills, which were capable of spewing out finished iron in every shape and form. The economic consequence of these technical innovations was a great boom in the British iron industry. In 1740 annual British iron production was only 17,000 tons. With the spread of coke smelting and the impact of Cort's inventions, production had reached 260,000 tons by 1806. In 1844 Britain produced 3 million tons of iron. Once expensive, iron became the cheap, basic, indispensable building block of the British economy.

Steam-Powered Transportation

The first steam locomotive was built by Richard Trevithick after much experimentation. George Stephenson's locomotive named ***Rocket*** sped down the track of the just-completed Liverpool and Manchester Railway at a maximum speed of 35 miles per hour in 1829. The line from Liverpool to Manchester was the first modern railroad, using steam-powered locomotives to carry customers to the new industrial cities. It was a financial as well as a technical success, and many private companies were organized to build more rail lines. Within

MAP 23.1 The Industrial Revolution in Great Britain, ca. 1850 Industry concentrated in the rapidly growing cities of the north and the center of England, where rich coal and iron deposits were close to one another.

twenty years they had completed the main trunk lines of Great Britain (Map 23.1). Other countries were quick to follow, with the first steam-powered trains operating in the United States in the 1830s and in Brazil, Chile, Argentina, and the British colonies of Canada, Australia, and India in the 1850s (Figure 23.1).

The arrival of the railroad had many significant consequences. It dramatically reduced the cost and uncertainty of shipping freight over land. Previously, markets had tended to be small and local; as the barrier of high transportation costs was lowered, markets became larger and even nationwide. Larger markets encouraged manufacturers to build larger factories with more sophisticated machinery in a growing number of industries. Such factories could make goods more

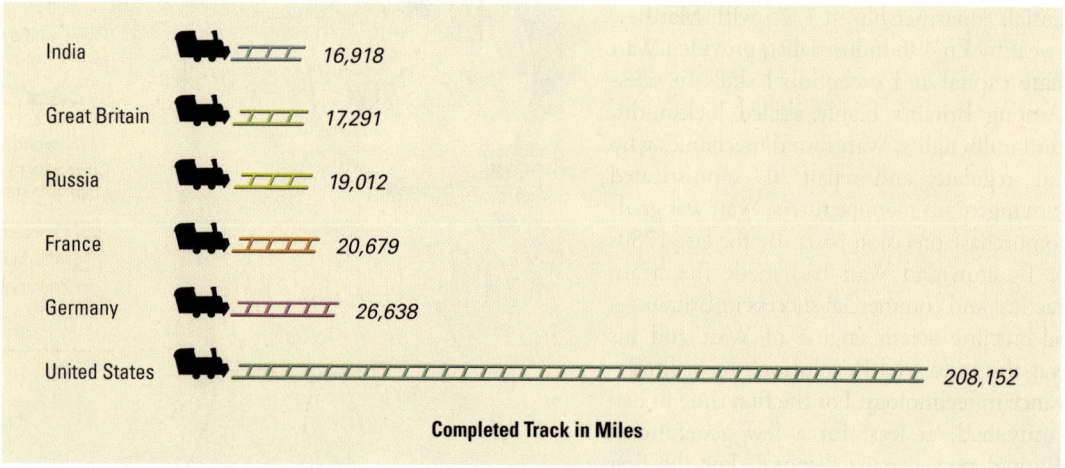

	Completed Track in Miles
India	16,918
Great Britain	17,291
Russia	19,012
France	20,679
Germany	26,638
United States	208,152

FIGURE 23.1 Railroad Track Mileage, 1890 Steam railroads were first used by the general public for shipping in England in the 1820s, and they quickly spread to other countries. The United States was an early adopter of railroads and by 1890 had surpassed all other countries in miles of track, as shown in this figure.

cheaply and gradually subjected most cottage workers and many urban artisans to severe competitive pressures. In all countries, the construction of railroads created a strong demand for unskilled labor and contributed to the growth of a class of urban workers.

The railroad also had a tremendous impact on cultural values and attitudes. The last and culminating invention of the Industrial Revolution, the railroad dramatically revealed the power and increased the speed of the new age. (See "Analyzing the Evidence: *Rain, Steam, and Speed—the Great Western Railway*," at right.)

The steam engine also transformed water travel. French engineers completed the first steamships in the 1770s, and the first commercial steamships came into use in North America several decades later. The *Clermont*, designed by Robert Fulton, began to travel the Hudson River in New York State in 1807, shortly followed by ships belonging to brewer John Molson on the St. Lawrence River. The steamship brought the advantages of the railroad—speed, reliability, efficiency—to water travel.

Industry and Population

In 1851 London hosted an industrial fair called the Great Exhibition in the newly built **Crystal Palace**. More than 6 million visitors from all over Europe marveled at the gigantic new exhibition hall set in the middle of a large, centrally located park. The building was made entirely of glass and iron, both of which were now cheap and abundant. Sponsored by the British royal family, the exhibition celebrated the new era

of industrial technology and the kingdom's role as world economic leader.

Britain's claim to be the "workshop of the world" was no idle boast, for it produced two-thirds of the world's coal and more than half of its iron and cotton cloth. More generally, in 1860 Britain produced a remarkable 20 percent of the entire world's output of industrial goods, whereas it had produced only about 2 percent of the world total in 1750.[3] As the British economy significantly increased its production of manufactured goods, the gross national product (GNP) rose roughly fourfold at constant prices between 1780 and 1851. At the same time, the population of Britain boomed, growing from about 9 million in 1780 to almost 21 million in 1851. Thus growing numbers consumed much of the increase in total production.

Rapid population growth in Great Britain was key to industrial development. More people meant a more mobile labor force, with a wealth of young workers in need of employment and ready to go where the jobs were. Sustaining the dramatic increase in population, in turn, was possible only through advances in agriculture and industry. Many contemporaries feared that the rapid growth in population would inevitably lead to disaster. In his *Essay on the Principle of Population* (1798), Thomas Malthus (1766–1834) argued that population would always tend to grow faster than the food supply. Malthus concluded that the only hope of warding off such "positive checks" to population growth as war, famine, and disease was "prudential restraint."[4] That is, young men and women had to limit the growth of population by marrying late in life. But Malthus was not optimistic about this possibility. The powerful attraction of the sexes would cause most people to marry early and have many children.

Crystal Palace The location of the Great Exhibition in 1851 in London, an architectural masterpiece made entirely of glass and iron.

Rain, Steam, and Speed—the Great Western Railway

The last and culminating invention of the Industrial Revolution, the railroad dramatically revealed the power and increased the speed of the new age. Until the coming of the railroad, travel was largely measured by the distance that a human or a horse could cover before becoming exhausted. Steam power created a revolution in human transportation, allowing a constant, rapid rate of travel with no limits on its duration. Time and space suddenly and drastically contracted, as far-away places could be reached in one-third the time or less. As the poet Heinrich Heine proclaimed in 1843, "What changes must now occur, in our way of looking at things, in our notions! . . . I feel as if the mountains and forests of all countries were advancing on Paris. Even now, I can smell the German linden trees; the North Sea's breakers are rolling against my door."*

Racing down the track at speeds that reached 50 miles per hour by 1850 was an overwhelming experience. Some great artists succeeded in expressing this sense of power and awe. An outstanding example of this is depicted here in the painting by Joseph M. W.

(National Gallery, London, UK/Bridgeman Images)

Turner (1775–1851): *Rain, Steam, and Speed — the Great Western Railway*. Contemporary novelists also recorded their impressions of early train travel, as in this striking passage by Charles Dickens: "Through the hollow, on the height, by the heath, by the orchard, by the park, by the garden, over the canal, across the river, where the sheep are feeding, where the mill is going, where the barge is floating, where the dead are lying, where the factory is smoking, where the stream is running, where the village clusters . . . away with a strike and a roar and a rattle, and no trace to leave behind but dust and vapour."† The increase in speed also led doctors to worry about the effects of the constant noise and vibration on passengers and crew.

Despite these concerns, the railroad quickly became a central institution of society. So did the massive new train stations, the cathedrals of the industrial age. Leading railway engineers such as Isambard Kingdom Brunel and Thomas Brassey, whose tunnels pierced mountains and whose bridges spanned valleys, became public idols — the astronauts of their day.

QUESTIONS FOR ANALYSIS

1. What impression of train travel does this painting convey to the viewer? What techniques did Turner employ to create this impression? Would you describe Turner's painting as a negative or a positive depiction?
2. How would you compare this representation of travel by train to images you have seen in current media of travel by automobile or airplane? How would you account for any similarities or differences in nineteenth-century and contemporary depictions of travel?

*Quoted in Wolfgang Schivelbusch, *The Railway Journey: The Industrialization of Time and Space in the Nineteenth Century* (Berkeley: University of California Press, 1986), p. 37.

†Charles Dickens, *Dombey and Son* (Ware, U.K.: Wordsworth Editions, 1999), p. 262.

Interior View of the Crystal Palace Built for the Great Exhibition of 1851, the Crystal Palace was a spectacular achievement in engineering, prefabricated from three hundred thousand sheets of glass. With almost fifteen thousand exhibitors, the event constituted the first international industrial exhibition, showcasing manufactured products from Britain, its empire, and the rest of the world. Later, the building was disassembled and moved to another site in London, where it stood until destroyed by fire in 1936. (London Metropolitan Archives, City of London, UK/Bridgeman Images)

Economist David Ricardo (1772–1823) spelled out the pessimistic implications of Malthus's thought. Ricardo's depressing **iron law of wages** posited that, because of the pressure of population growth, wages would always sink to subsistence level. That is, wages would be just high enough to keep workers from starving.

Malthus, Ricardo, and their followers were proved wrong in the long run. However, until the 1820s, or even the 1850s, contemporary observers might reasonably have concluded that the economy and the total population were racing neck and neck, with the outcome very much in doubt. There was another problem as well. Perhaps workers, farmers, and ordinary people did not get their rightful share of the new wealth. Perhaps only the rich got richer, while the poor got poorer or made no progress. We will turn to this great issue after situating the process of industrialization in its European and global context.

Industrialization in Europe and the World

How did countries in Europe and around the world respond to the challenge of industrialization after 1815?

As new technologies and a new organization of labor began to revolutionize production in Britain, other countries took notice and began to emulate its example. With the end of the Napoleonic Wars, the nations of the European continent quickly adopted British inventions and achieved their own pattern of technological innovation and economic growth. By the last decades of the nineteenth century, western European countries as well as the United States and Japan had industrialized their economies to a considerable, albeit varying, degree.

Industrialization in other parts of the world proceeded more gradually, with uneven jerks and national and regional variations. Scholars are still struggling to explain these variations as well as the dramatic advan-

iron law of wages Theory proposed by English economist David Ricardo suggesting that the pressure of population growth prevents wages from rising above the subsistence level.

tage in economic production that Western nations gained for the first time in history over non-Western ones. These questions are especially important because they may offer valuable lessons for poor countries that today are seeking to improve their material condition through industrialization and economic development. The latest findings on the nineteenth-century experience are encouraging. They suggest that there were alternative paths to the industrial world and that there was and is no need to follow a rigid, predetermined British model.

National and International Variations

Comparative data on industrial production in different countries over time help give us an overview of what happened. One set of data, the work of a Swiss scholar, compares the level of industrialization on a per capita basis in several countries from 1750 to 1913. These data are far from perfect, but they reflect basic trends and are presented in Table 23.1 for closer study.

Table 23.1 presents a comparison of how much industrial product was produced, on average, for each person in a given country in a given year. All the numbers are expressed in terms of a single index number of 100, which equals the per capita level of industrial goods in Great Britain and Ireland in 1900. Every number in the table is thus a percentage of the 1900 level in Britain and is directly comparable with other

numbers. The countries are listed in roughly the order that they began to use large-scale, power-driven technology.

What does this overview tell us? First, one sees in the first column that in 1750 all countries were fairly close together, including non-Western areas such as China and India. However, the column headed 1800 shows that Britain had opened up a noticeable lead over all countries by 1800, and that gap progressively widened as the British Industrial Revolution accelerated through 1830 and reached full maturity by 1860.

Second, the table shows that Western countries began to emulate the British model successfully over the nineteenth century, with significant variations in the timing and in the extent of industrialization. Belgium led in adopting Britain's new technology, and it experienced a truly revolutionary surge between 1830 and 1860. France developed factory production more gradually and did not experience "revolutionary" growth in industrial output. Slow but steady economic growth in France was overshadowed by the spectacular rise of Germany and the United States after 1860 in what has been termed the "Second Industrial Revolution." In general, eastern and southern Europe began the process of industrialization later than northwestern and central Europe. Nevertheless, these regions made real progress in the late nineteenth century, as growth after 1880 in Austria-Hungary, Italy, and Russia suggests. This meant that all European states as well as the

TABLE 23.1 Per Capita Levels of Industrialization, 1750–1913

	1750	1800	1830	1860	1880	1900	1913
Great Britain	10	16	25	64	87	100	115
Belgium	9	10	14	28	43	56	88
United States	4	9	14	21	38	69	126
France	9	9	12	20	28	39	59
Germany	8	8	9	15	25	52	85
Austria-Hungary	7	7	8	11	15	23	32
Italy	8	8	8	10	12	17	26
Russia	6	6	7	8	10	15	20
China	8	6	6	4	4	3	3
India	7	6	6	3	2	1	2

Note: All entries are based on an index value of 100, equal to the per capita level of industrialization in Great Britain in 1900. Data for Great Britain include Ireland, England, Wales, and Scotland.

Source: Data from P. Bairoch, "International Industrialization Levels from 1750 to 1980," *Journal of European Economic History* 11 (Spring 1982): 294, U.S. Journals at Cambridge University Press.

United States managed to raise per capita industrial levels in the nineteenth century.

These increases stood in stark contrast to the decreases that occurred at the same time in many non-Western countries, most notably in China and India, as Table 23.1 shows. European countries industrialized to a greater or lesser extent even as most of the non-Western world stagnated. Japan, which is not included in this table, stands out as an exceptional area of non-Western industrial growth in the second half of the nineteenth century. After the forced opening of the country to the West in the 1850s, Japanese entrepreneurs began to adopt Western technology and manufacturing methods, resulting in a production boom by the late nineteenth century (see "Industrialization" in Chapter 26). Differential rates of wealth- and power-creating industrial development, which heightened disparities within Europe, also greatly magnified existing inequalities between Europe and the rest of the world (see "The Rise of Global Inequality" in Chapter 25).

Industrialization in Continental Europe

Throughout Europe the eighteenth century was an era of agricultural improvement, population increase, expanding foreign trade, and growing cottage industry. Thus, when the pace of British industry began to accelerate in the 1780s, continental businesses began to adopt the new methods as they proved their profitability. During the period of the revolutionary and Napoleonic Wars, from 1793 to 1815, however, western Europe experienced tremendous political and social upheaval that temporarily halted economic development. With the return of peace in 1815, however, western European countries again began to play catch-up.

They faced significant challenges. In the newly mechanized industries, British goods were being produced very economically, and these goods had come to dominate world markets. In addition, British technology had become so advanced that very few engineers or skilled technicians outside England understood it. Moreover, the technology of steam power involved large investments in the iron and coal industries and, after 1830, required the existence of railroads. Continental business people had great difficulty amassing the large sums of money the new methods demanded, and laborers bitterly resisted the move to working in factories. All these factors slowed the spread of mechanization (Map 23.2).

Nevertheless, western European nations possessed a number of advantages that helped them respond to these challenges. First, most had rich traditions of putting-out enterprise, merchant capitalism, and skilled urban trades. These assets gave their firms the ability to adapt and survive in the face of new market conditions. Second, continental capitalists did not need to develop their own advanced technology. Instead they could "borrow" the new methods developed in Great Britain, as well as the engineers and some of the financial resources they lacked. Finally, European countries had strong, independent governments that were willing to use the power of the state to promote industry and catch up with Britain.

Agents of Industrialization

Western European success in adopting British methods took place despite the best efforts of the British to prevent it. The British realized the great value of their technical discoveries and tried to keep their secrets to themselves. Until 1825 it was illegal for artisans and skilled mechanics to leave Britain; until 1843 the export of textile machinery and other equipment was forbidden. Many talented, ambitious workers, however, slipped out of the country illegally and introduced the new methods abroad.

Thus British technicians and skilled workers were a powerful force in the spread of early industrialization. A second agent of industrialization consisted of talented European entrepreneurs such as Fritz Harkort (1793–1880). Serving in England as a Prussian army officer during the Napoleonic Wars, Harkort was impressed with what he saw. Harkort set up shop building steam engines in the Ruhr Valley, on the western border with France. In spite of problems obtaining skilled workers and machinery, Harkort succeeded in building and selling engines. However, his ambitious efforts failed to turn a profit. His career illustrates both the great efforts of a few important business leaders to duplicate the British achievement and the difficulty of the task.

National governments played an even more important role in supporting industrialization in continental Europe than in Britain. **Tariff protection** was one such support. The French, for example, responded to a flood of cheap British goods in 1815, after the Napoleonic Wars, by laying high taxes on imported goods. Customs agreements emerged among some German states starting in 1818, and in 1834 a number of states signed a treaty creating a customs union, or *Zollverein*. The treaty allowed goods to move between member states without tariffs, while erecting a single uniform tariff against other nations.

After 1815 continental governments also bore the cost of building roads, canals, and railroads to improve

tariff protection A government's way of supporting and aiding its own economy by laying high taxes on imported goods from other countries, as when the French responded to the flood of cheaper British goods in their country by imposing high tariffs on some imported products.

MAPPING THE PAST

MAP 23.2 **Continental Industrialization, ca. 1850** Although continental countries were beginning to make progress by 1850, they still lagged far behind Britain. For example, continental railroad building was still in an early stage, whereas the British rail system was essentially complete (see Map 23.1). Coal played a critical role in nineteenth-century industrialization, both as a power source for steam engines and as a raw material for making iron and steel.

ANALYZING THE MAP Locate the major exposed (that is, known) coal deposits in 1850. Which countries and areas appear rich in coal resources, and which appear poor? Is there a difference between northern and southern Europe?

CONNECTIONS What is the relationship between known coal deposits and emerging industrial areas in continental Europe? In England?

transportation. Belgium led the way in the 1830s and 1840s, building a state-owned railroad network that stimulated the development of heavy industry and made the country an early industrial leader. In France the state shouldered all the expense of acquiring and laying roadbed, including bridges and tunnels.

Finally, banks, like governments, also played a larger and more creative role on the continent than in Britain. Previously, almost all banks in Europe had been private. Because of the possibility of unlimited financial loss, the partners of private banks generally avoided industrial investment as being too risky.

In the 1830s two important Belgian banks pioneered in a new direction. They received permission from the growth-oriented government to establish themselves as corporations enjoying limited liability. That is, if the bank went bankrupt, stockholders would lose only their original investments in the bank's common stock, and they could not be forced to pay for additional losses out of other property they owned. Limited liability helped these banks attract investors. They mobilized impressive resources for investment in big companies, became industrial banks, and successfully promoted industrial development. Similar corporate

The Circle of the Rue Royale, Paris, 1868 The Circle of the Rue Royale was an exclusive club of aristocrats, bankers, railway owners, and other members of Parisian high society. This group portrait projects the wealth and elegance of the club's members, who are gathered on the balcony of a hotel. (Fine Art Images/Heritage Images/Getty Images)

banks became important in France and Germany in the 1850s and 1860s.

The combined efforts of skilled workers, entrepreneurs, governments, and industrial banks meshed successfully between 1850 and the financial crash of 1873. In Belgium, France, and the German states key indicators of modern industrial development increased at average annual rates of 5 to 10 percent. As a result, rail networks were completed in western Europe and much of central Europe, and the leading continental countries mastered the industrial technologies that had first been developed in Great Britain. In the early 1870s Britain was still Europe's most industrial nation, but a select handful of countries were closing the gap.

The Global Picture

The Industrial Revolution did not have a transformative impact beyond Europe prior to the 1860s, with the exception of the United States and Japan. In many countries, national governments and pioneering entrepreneurs promoted industrialization, but fell short of transitioning to an industrial economy. For example, in Russia the imperial government brought steamships to the Volga River and a railroad to the capital, St. Petersburg, in the first decades of the nineteenth century. By midcentury ambitious entrepreneurs had established steam-powered cotton factories

using imported British machines. However, these advances did not lead to overall industrialization of the country. Instead Russia confirmed its role as provider of raw materials, especially timber and grain, to the hungry West.

Egypt, a territory of the Ottoman Empire, similarly began an ambitious program of modernization after a reform-minded viceroy took power in 1805. This program included the use of imported British technology and experts in textile manufacture and other industries (see "Egypt: From Reform to British Occupation" in Chapter 25). These industries, however, could not compete with lower-priced European imports. Like Russia, Egypt fell back on agricultural exports, such as sugar and cotton, to European markets.

Such examples of faltering efforts at industrialization could be found in many other places in the Middle East, Asia, and Latin America. Where European governments maintained direct or indirect control, they acted to maintain colonial markets as sources of raw materials and consumers for their own products, rather than encouraging the spread of industrialization. In India millions of poor textile workers lost their livelihood because they could not compete with industrially produced British cotton. The British charged stiff import duties on Indian cottons entering the kingdom, but prohibited the Indians from doing the same to British imports. (See "Global Viewpoints:

Indian Cotton Manufacturers

The mechanization of spinning and weaving in Britain led to tremendous increases in productivity, which in turn allowed British manufacturers to produce large volumes of cloth at low prices. The East India Company sold this cloth in India at prices lower than those for locally produced cotton, but imposed a stiff tariff on Indian cloth imported to Britain. This unequal situation and its destructive impact on Indian cloth manufacturers — who had previously led the world in cotton cloth production — quickly became apparent. Despite appeals from the manufacturers themselves, defenders of this policy claimed that it would be better for Indians to focus on producing raw cotton, which could then be brought to Britain to be finished. The two documents excerpted below exemplify the two sides of the dispute.

Petition of Natives of Bengal to the British Privy Council for Trade, 1831

■ The humble Petition of the undersigned Manufacturers and Dealers in Cotton and Silk Piece-Goods, the fabrics of Bengal;

Sheweth,

That of late years your Petitioners have found their business nearly superseded by the introduction of the fabrics of Great Britain into Bengal, the importation of which augments every year, to the great prejudice of the native manufactures.

That the fabrics of Great Britain are consumed in Bengal without any duties being levied thereon to protect the native fabrics.

That the fabrics of Bengal are charged with the following duties when they are used in Great Britain:

On manufactured cottons, 10 per cent
On manufactured silks, 24 per cent . . .

They therefore pray to be admitted to the privilege of British subjects, and humbly entreat your Lordships to allow the cotton and silk fabrics of Bengal to be used in Great Britain "free of duty," or at the same rate which may be charged on British fabrics consumed in Bengal.

Your Lordships must be aware of the immense advantages the British manufacturers derive from their skill in constructing and using machinery, which enables them to undersell the unscientific manufacturers of Bengal in their own country; . . . such an instance of justice to the natives of India would not fail to endear the British Government to them.

Robert Rickards, Testimony to the Select Committee of the House of Lords, 1821

■ I think it very likely that the further introduction of our cheap cotton manufactures into India may supersede, as they have done already to a certain degree, the use and consumption of many of the cotton manufactures of the country; but I am not aware of any injury to the population of India that is likely to result from this state of things; probably, the most beneficial trade that can be carried on between India and this country will be found to consist in the exchange of the raw produce of the East for the manufactured goods of Britain. I believe the native Indians have it in their power, from the cheapness of labour and food in that country, and the great fertility of the soil, to produce raw articles calculated for the manufactures of Britain, at a cheaper rate than perhaps any other country in the world; and if their industry should be directed to this point, instead of to local manufactures, it will interfere the less with their present occupations and employments; inasmuch as the weavers generally throughout India are cultivators of the soil also, and are occupied to the full as much in their fields as at their looms.

QUESTIONS FOR ANALYSIS

1. Why did Robert Rickards believe that Indians would not be harmed if their cloth manufacturing industry was destroyed by cheap British imports?
2. What response might the Bengal cotton and silk manufacturers have made to Rickards?

Sources: Appendix to the Report from the Select Committee of the House of Commons on the Affairs of the East-India Company, 16th August 1832 (London: J. L. Cox and Son, 1833), pp. 774–775; Third Report from the Select Committee Appointed to Consider the Means of Improving and Maintaining the Foreign Trade of the Country, East Indies, and China, 1821 (746), VI.340.

Indian Cotton Manufacturers," above.) The arrival of railroads in India in the mid-nineteenth century served the purpose of agricultural rather than industrial development.

Latin American economies were disrupted by the early-nineteenth-century wars of independence (see "The Aftermath of Revolution in the Atlantic World"

in Chapter 22). As these countries' economies recovered in the mid-nineteenth century, they increasingly adopted steam power for sugar and coffee processing and for transportation. Like elsewhere, this technology first supported increased agricultural production for export and only later drove domestic industrial production.

Press for Packing Indian Cotton, 1864 British industrialization destroyed a thriving Indian cotton textile industry, whose weavers could not compete with cheap British imports. India continued to supply raw cotton to British manufacturers. (Granger, NYC—All rights reserved.)

The rise of industrialization in Britain, western Europe, and the United States thus caused other regions of the world to become increasingly economically dependent. Instead of industrializing, many territories underwent a process of deindustrialization or delayed industrialization. In turn, relative economic weakness made them vulnerable to the new wave of imperialism undertaken by industrialized nations in the second half of the nineteenth century (see "The New Imperialism, 1880–1914" in Chapter 25).

As for China, it did not adopt mechanized production until the end of the nineteenth century, but continued as a market-based, commercial society with a massive rural sector and industrial production based on traditional methods. In the 1860s and 1870s, when Japan was successfully adopting industrial methods, the Chinese government showed similar interest in Western technology and science. However, in the mid-nineteenth century China faced widespread uprisings, which drained attention and resources to the military; moreover, after the Boxer Uprising of 1900 (see "Republican Revolution" in Chapter 26), Western powers forced China to pay massive indemnities, further reducing its capacity to promote industrialization.

New Patterns of Working and Living

How did work evolve during the Industrial Revolution, and how did daily life change for working people?

Having first emerged in the British countryside in the late eighteenth century, factories and industrial labor began migrating to cities by the early nineteenth century. For some people, the Industrial Revolution brought improvements, but living and working conditions for the poor stagnated or even deteriorated until around 1850, especially in overcrowded industrial cities.

Work in Early Factories

The first factories of the Industrial Revolution were cotton mills, which began functioning in the 1770s along fast-running rivers and streams and were often located in sparsely populated areas. Cottage workers, accustomed to the putting-out system, were reluctant to work in the new factories even when they received relatively good wages. In a factory, workers had to keep up with the machine and follow its relentless tempo. Moreover, they had to show up every day, on time, and work long, monotonous hours under the constant supervision of demanding overseers.

Cottage workers were not used to that way of life. All members of the family worked hard and long, but in spurts, setting their own pace. Women and children could break up their long hours of spinning with other tasks. On Saturday afternoon the head of the family delivered the week's work to the merchant manufacturer and got paid. Saturday night was a time of relaxation and drinking, especially for men.

Also, early factories resembled English poorhouses, where totally destitute people went to live at public expense. The similarity between large brick factories and large stone poorhouses increased the cottage workers' fear of factories and their hatred of factory discipline. It was cottage workers' reluctance to work in factories that prompted early cotton mill owners to turn to pauper children.

Working Families and Children

By the 1790s the early labor pattern was rapidly changing. The use of pauper apprentices was in decline, and in 1802 it was forbidden by Parliament. Many more textile factories were being built, mainly in urban areas, where they could use steam power rather than waterpower and attract a workforce more easily than in the countryside. People came from near and far to work in the cities. Collectively, these wage laborers came to be known as the "working class," a term first used in the late 1830s.

In some cases, workers accommodated to the system by carrying over familiar working traditions. Some came to the mills and the mines as family units, as they had worked on farms and in the putting-out system. The mill or mine owner bargained with the head of the family and paid him or her for the work of the whole family.

Ties of kinship were particularly important for newcomers, who often traveled great distances to find work. Many urban workers in Great Britain were from Ireland. They were forced out of rural Ireland by population growth and deteriorating economic conditions from 1817. Their numbers increased dramatically during the desperate years of the potato famine, from 1845 to 1851. Like many other immigrant groups held together by ethnic and religious ties, the Irish worked together, formed their own neighborhoods, and maintained their cultural traditions.

In the early decades of the nineteenth century, however, technical changes made it less and less likely that workers could continue to labor in family groups. As control and discipline passed into the hands of impersonal managers and overseers, adult workers began to protest against inhuman conditions on behalf of their

children. Some enlightened employers and social reformers in Parliament agreed that more humane standards were necessary, and they used widely circulated parliamentary reports to influence public opinion. For example, Robert Owen (1771–1858), a successful textile manufacturer, testified in 1816 before an investigating committee on the basis of his experience. He argued that employing children under ten years of age as factory workers was "injurious to the children, and not beneficial to the proprietors."[5] Workers also provided graphic testimony at such hearings as the reformers pressed Parliament to pass corrective laws.

These efforts resulted in a series of British Factory Acts from 1802 to 1833 that progressively limited the workday of child laborers and set minimum hygiene and safety requirements. The **Factory Act of 1833** stated that children between ages nine and thirteen could work a maximum of eight hours per day, not including two hours for education. Teenagers aged fourteen to eighteen could work up to twelve hours, while those under nine were banned from employment. The act also installed a system of full-time professional inspectors to enforce labor regulations. The Factory Acts constituted significant progress in preventing the exploitation of children. One unintended drawback of restrictions on child labor, however, was that they broke the pattern of whole families working together in the factory, because efficiency required standardized shifts for all workers. After 1833 the number of children employed in industry declined rapidly.

The Sexual Division of Labor

With the restriction of child labor and the collapse of the family work pattern in the 1830s came a new sexual division of labor. By 1850 the man was emerging as the family's primary wage earner, while the married woman found only limited job opportunities. Generally denied good jobs at high wages in the growing urban economy, wives were expected to concentrate on their duties at home. Evolving gradually, but largely in place by 1850, this new pattern of **separate spheres** in Britain constituted a major development in the history of women and of the family.

Several factors combined to create this new sexual division of labor. First, the new and unfamiliar discipline of the clock and the machine was especially hard on married women of the laboring classes. Factory discipline conflicted with child care in a way that labor on the farm or in the cottage had not.

Factory Act of 1833 English law that led to a sharp decline in the employment of children by limiting the hours that children over age nine could work and banning employment of children younger than nine.

separate spheres A gender division of labor with the wife at home as mother and homemaker and the husband as wage earner.

Workers at a U.S. Mill Female workers at a U.S. cotton mill in 1890 take a break from operating belt-driven weaving machines to pose for this photograph, accompanied by their male supervisor. The first textile mills, established in the 1820s in Massachusetts, employed local farm girls. As competition intensified, conditions deteriorated and the mills increasingly relied on immigrant women who had few alternatives to the long hours, noise, and dangers of factory work. By 1900 more than 1 million women worked in factories in the United States. (Courtesy of George Eastman Museum, accession number 1966:0039:0013)

Second, running a household in conditions of urban poverty was an extremely demanding job in its own right. There were no supermarkets or public transportation. Shopping and feeding the family constituted a never-ending challenge. Taking on a brutal job outside the house had limited appeal for the average married woman from the working class. Thus many women might well have accepted the emerging division of labor as the best available strategy for family survival in the industrializing society.

Third, to a large degree the young, generally unmarried women who did work for wages outside the home were segregated from men and confined to certain "women's jobs" because the new sexual division of labor replicated long-standing patterns of gender segregation and inequality. In the preindustrial economy, a small sector of the labor market had always been defined as "women's work," especially tasks involving needlework, spinning, food preparation, child care, and nursing. This traditional sexual division of labor took on new overtones, however, in response to the factory system. The growth of factories and mines brought unheard-of opportunities for girls and boys to mix on the job, free of familial supervision. Such opportunities led to more unplanned pregnancies and fueled the illegitimacy explosion that had begun in the late eighteenth century and that gathered force until at least 1850. Thus segregation of jobs by gender was partly an effort by older people to help control the sexuality of working-class youths.

Investigations into the British coal industry before 1842 provide a graphic example of this concern. (See "Analyzing the Evidence: The Testimony of Young Mine Workers," page 680.) The middle-class men leading the inquiry professed horror at the sight of girls and women working without shirts, which was a common practice because of the heat, and they quickly assumed the prevalence of licentious sex with the male miners. In fact, most girls and married women worked for related males in a family unit that provided considerable protection and restraint. Yet many witnesses from the working class also believed that the mines

Mines Act of 1842 English law prohibiting underground work for all women and girls as well as for boys under ten.

were inappropriate and dangerous places for women and girls. Some miners stressed particularly the danger of sexual aggression for girls working past puberty. As one explained, "I consider it a scandal for girls to work in the pits. Till they are 12 or 14 they may work very well but after that it's an abomination. . . . The work of the pit does not hurt them, it is the effect on their morals that I complain of."[6] The **Mines Act of 1842** prohibited underground work for all women and girls as well as for boys under ten.

A final factor encouraging working-class women to withdraw from paid labor was the domestic ideals emanating from middle-class women, who had largely embraced the "separate spheres" ideology. Middle-class reformers published tracts and formed societies to urge poor women to devote more care and attention to their homes and families.

Living Standards for the Working Class

Although the evidence is complex and sometimes contradictory, most historians now agree that overall living standards for the working class did not rise substantially until 1850. Factory wages began to rise after 1815, but these gains were modest and were offset by a decline in married women's and children's participation in the labor force, meaning that many households had less total income than before. Moreover, many people still worked outside the factories as cottage workers or rural laborers, and in those sectors wages declined. Thus the increase in the productivity of industry did not lead to an increase in the purchasing power of the British working classes. Only after 1830, and especially after 1840, did real wages rise substantially, so that the average worker earned roughly 30 percent more in real terms in 1850 than in 1770.

Up to that point, the harshness of labor in the new industries probably outweighed their benefits as far as working people were concerned. With industrialization, workers toiled longer and harder at jobs that were often more grueling and more dangerous. (See "Thinking Like a Historian: Making the Industrialized Worker," page 682.) In England nonagricultural workers labored about 250 days per year in 1760 as compared to 300 days per year in 1830, while the normal workday remained an exhausting eleven hours throughout the entire period.[7]

As the factories moved to urban areas, workers followed them in large numbers, leading to an explosion in the size of cities, especially in the north of England. By the end of the nineteenth century England had become by far the most urbanized country in Europe. Life in the new industrial cities, such as Manchester and Liverpool, was grim. Given extremely high rates of infant mortality, average life expectancy was around

only twenty-five to twenty-seven years, some fifteen years less than the national average.[8] Migrants to the booming cities found expensive, hastily constructed, overcrowded apartments and inadequate sanitary systems.

Another way to consider the workers' standard of living is to look at the goods they purchased, which also suggest stagnant or declining living standards until the middle of the nineteenth century. One important area of improvement was in the consumption of cotton goods, which became much cheaper and could be enjoyed by all classes. However, in other areas, food in particular, the modest growth in factory wages was not enough to compensate for rising prices.

From the 1850s onward, matters improved considerably as wages made substantial gains and the prices of many goods dropped. A greater variety of foods became available, including the first canned goods. Some of

Working-Class Housing in Glasgow, 1868 Like other British cities, Glasgow experienced a population boom in the nineteenth century. Migrant workers from Ireland and the Highlands were housed in cramped, damp, and dark tenements without running water and were thus vulnerable to infectious disease. This photograph was taken as part of a campaign to expose the dismal living conditions of industrial workers. (Private Collection/The Stapleton Collection/Bridgeman Images)

The Testimony of Young Mine Workers

The use of child labor in British industrialization quickly attracted the attention of humanitarians and social reformers. This interest led to investigations by parliamentary commissions, which resulted in laws limiting the hours and the ages of children working in large factories. Designed to build a case for remedial legislation, parliamentary inquiries gave large numbers of workers a rare chance to speak directly to contemporaries and to historians.

The moving passages that follow are taken from testimony gathered in 1841 and 1842 by the Ashley Mines Commission. Interviewing employers and many male and female workers, the commissioners focused on the physical condition of the youths and on the sexual behavior of workers far underground. The subsequent Mines Act of 1842 sought to reduce immoral behavior and sexual bullying by prohibiting underground work for all women and girls (and for boys younger than ten).

Mr. Payne, Coal Master

■ That children are employed generally at nine years old in the coal pits and sometimes at eight. In fact, the smaller the vein of coal is in height, the younger and smaller are the children required; the work occupies from six to seven hours per day in the pits; they are not ill-used or worked beyond their strength; a good deal of depravity exists but they are certainly not worse in morals than in other branches of the Sheffield trade, but upon the whole superior; the morals of this district are materially improving; Mr. Bruce, the clergyman, has been zealous and active in endeavoring to ameliorate their moral and religious education. . . .

Ann Eggley, Hurrier, 18 Years Old

■ I'm sure I don't know how to spell my name. We go at four in the morning, and sometimes at half-past four. We begin to work as soon as we get down. We get out after four, sometimes at five, in the evening. We work the whole time except an hour for dinner, and sometimes we haven't time to eat. I hurry [move coal wagons underground] by myself, and have done so for long. I know the corves [small coal wagons] are very heavy, they are the biggest corves anywhere about. The work is far too hard for me; the sweat runs off me all over sometimes. I am very tired at night. Sometimes when we get home at night we have not power to wash us, and then we go to bed. Sometimes we fall asleep in the chair. Father said last night it was both a shame and a disgrace for girls to work as we do, but there was naught else for us to do. I began to hurry when I was seven and I have been hurrying ever since. . . . The girls are always tired. I was poorly twice this winter; it was with headache. . . . We don't always get enough to eat and drink, but we get a good supper. I have known my father go at two in the morning to work . . . and he didn't come out till four. I am quite sure that we work constantly 12 hours except on Saturdays. We wear trousers and our shifts in the pit and great big shoes clinkered and nailed. The girls never work naked to the waist in our pit. The men don't insult us in the pit. The conduct of the girls in the pit is good enough sometimes and sometimes bad enough. I never went to a day-school. I went a little to a Sunday-school, but I soon gave it over. I thought it too bad to be confined both Sundays and week-days. I walk about and get the fresh air on Sundays. I have not learnt to read. I don't know my letters. I never learnt naught. I never go to church

the most important advances were in medicine. Smallpox vaccination became routine, and surgeons began to use anesthesia in the late 1840s. By 1850 trains and steamships had revolutionized transportation for the masses, while the telegraph made instant communication possible for the first time in human history. Gaslights greatly expanded the possibilities of nighttime activity.

In addition to the technical innovations that resulted from industrialization, other, less tangible changes were also taking place. As young men and women migrated away from their villages to seek employment in urban factories, many close-knit rural communities were destroyed. The loss of skills and work autonomy, along with the loss of community, must be included in the assessment of the Industrial Revolution's impact on the living conditions of the poor.

Relations Between Capital and Labor

How did the changes brought about by the Industrial Revolution lead to new social classes, and how did people respond to the new structure?

In Great Britain industrial development led to the creation of new social groups and intensified long-standing problems between capital and labor. A new class of factory owners and industrial capitalists arose. The demands of modern industry regularly brought the interests of the middle-class industrialists into conflict with those of the people who worked for them— the working class. As observers took note of these changes, they raised new questions about how indus-

or chapel. . . . I never heard of Christ at all. Nobody has ever told me about him, nor have my father and mother ever taught me to pray. I know no prayer; I never pray.

Patience Kershaw, Age 17

■ My father has been dead about a year; my mother is living and has ten children, five lads and five lasses; the oldest is about thirty, the youngest is four; three lasses go to mill; all the lads are colliers, two getters and three hurriers; one lives at home and does nothing; mother does nought but look after home.

All my sisters have been hurriers, but three went to the mill. Alice went because her legs swelled from hurrying in cold water when she was hot. I never went to day-school; I go to Sunday-school, but I cannot read or write; I go to pit at five o'clock in the morning and come out at five in the evening; I get my breakfast of porridge and milk first; I take my dinner with me, a cake, and eat it as I go; I do not stop or rest any time for the purpose; I get nothing else until I get home, and then have potatoes and meat, not every day meat. I hurry in the clothes I have now got on, trousers and ragged jacket; the bald place upon my head is made by thrusting the corves; my legs have never swelled, but sisters' did when they went to mill; I hurry the corves a mile and more under ground and back; they weigh 300 cwt.;* I hurry 11 a day; I wear a belt and chain at the workings to get the corves out; the putters [miners] that I work for are *naked* except their caps; they pull off all their clothes; I see them at work when I go up; sometimes they beat me, if I am not quick enough, with their hands; they strike me upon my back; the boys take liberties with me, sometimes, they pull me about; I am the only girl in the pit; there are about 20 boys and 15 men; all the men are naked; I would rather work in mill than in coal-pit.

Isabel Wilson, Coal Putter, 38 Years Old

■ When women have children thick [fast] they are compelled to take them down early. I have been married 19 years and have had 10 bairns [children]; seven are in life. When on Sir John's work was a carrier of coals, which caused me to miscarry five times from the strains, and was gai [very] ill after each. Putting is no so oppressive; last child was born on Saturday morning, and I was at work on the Friday night.

Once met with an accident; a coal brake my cheek-bone, which kept me idle some weeks. I have wrought below 30 years, and so has the guid man; he is getting touched in the breath now.

QUESTIONS FOR ANALYSIS

1. How does Payne's testimony compare with that of Ann Eggley and Patience Kershaw?
2. Describe the work of Eggley, Kershaw, and Wilson. What strikes you most about the testimonies of these workers?
3. The witnesses were responding to questions from middle-class commissioners. What did the commissioners seem interested in? Why?

Source: *Voices of the Industrial Revolution: Selected Readings from the Liberal Economists and Their Critics*, pp. 87–90, edited by J. Bowditch and C. Ramsland. Copyright © 1961, 1989 by the University of Michigan. Reprinted by permission of the publisher.

*An old English unit of weight equaling 112 pounds.

trialization affected social relationships. Meanwhile, enslaved laborers in European colonies contributed to the industrialization process in multiple ways.

The New Class of Factory Owners

Early industrialists operated in a highly competitive economic system. There were countless production problems, and success and large profits were by no means certain. Manufacturers therefore waged a constant battle to cut their production costs and stay afloat. Much of the profit had to go back into the business for new and better machinery.

Most early industrialists drew upon their families and friends for labor and capital, but they came from a variety of backgrounds. Many were from well-established merchant families with rich networks of contacts and support. Others were of modest means, especially in the early days. Artisans and skilled workers of exceptional ability had unparalleled opportunities. Members of ethnic and religious groups who had been discriminated against in the traditional occupations controlled by the landed aristocracy jumped at the new chances and often helped each other.

As factories and firms grew larger, and opportunities declined, it became harder for a gifted but poor young mechanic to start a small enterprise and end up as a wealthy manufacturer. Expensive, formal education became more important for young men as a means of success and advancement. In Britain by 1830 and in France and Germany by 1860, leading industrialists were more likely to have inherited their well-established enterprises, and they were financially much more secure than their struggling parents had been.

Making the Industrialized Worker

Looking back from the vantage point of the 1820s and 1830s, contemporary observers saw in early industrialization a process that was as much about social transformation as it was about techno-logical transformation—a process in which changes in work conditions were closely tied to changes in workers' family lives, values, and mental habits.

1 **Peter Gaskell,** *The Manufacturing Population of England: Its Moral, Social, and Physical Conditions, and the Changes Which Have Arisen from the Use of Steam Machinery,* **1833.** In this excerpt, Peter Gaskell sketches the moral, social, and physical conditions of English workers *before* industrialization took hold, linking these characteristics to preindustrial work conditions.

■ Prior to the year 1760, manufactures were in a great measure confined to the demands of the home market. At this period, and down to 1800 . . . the majority of the artisans engaged in them had laboured in their own houses, and in the bosoms of their families. . . .

These were, undoubtedly, the golden times of manufactures, considered in reference to the char-acter of the labourers. By all the processes being carried on under a man's own roof, he retained his individual respectability; he was kept apart from associations that might injure his moral worth, whilst he generally earned wages which were suffi-cient not only to live comfortably upon, but which enabled him to rent a few acres of land; thus join-ing in his own person two classes, that are now daily becoming more and more distinct. . . .

Thus, removed from many of those causes which universally operate to the deterioration of the moral character of the labouring man, when brought into large towns . . . the small farmer, spin-ner, or hand-loom weaver presents as orderly and respectable an appearance as could be wished. It is true that the amount of labour gone through was but small; that the quantity of cloth or yarn pro-duced was but limited—for he worked by the rule of his strength and convenience. They were, how-ever, sufficient to clothe and feed himself and fam-ily decently, and according to their station; to lay

by a penny for an evil day, and to enjoy those amusements and bodily recreations then in being. He was a respectable member of society; a good father, a good husband, and a good son.

2 **Richard Guest,** *A Compendious History of the Cotton-Manufacture,* **1823.** Like Peter Gaskell, Richard Guest, one of the earliest historians of the English textile industry, believed that industrialization had "introduced great changes into the manners and habits of the people." Unlike Gaskell, however, Guest was convinced that these changes had been for the better. Where Gaskell saw moral decline, Guest saw moral awakening.

■ The progress of the Cotton Manufacture intro-duced great changes into the manners and habits of the people. The operative workmen being thrown together in great numbers had their facul-ties sharpened and improved by constant commu-nication. Conversation wandered over a variety of topics not before essayed; the questions of Peace and War, which interested them importantly, inas-much as they might produce a rise or fall of wages, became highly interesting, and this brought them into the vast field of politics and discussions on the character of their Government, and the men who composed it. They took a greater interest in the defeats and victories of their country's arms, and from being only a few degrees above their cattle in the scale of intellect, they became Political Citizens. . . .

The facility with which the Weavers changed their masters, the constant effort to find out and obtain the largest remuneration for their labour, the excitement to ingenuity which the higher wages for fine manufactures and skillful workmanship produced, and a conviction that they depended

ANALYZING THE EVIDENCE

1. How does Richard Guest's characterization of preindustrial workers and conditions in Source 2 compare to Peter Gaskell's in Source 1? Why did Gaskell think industrialization would harm workers' morals while Guest saw it as a force for moral improvement?
2. Early-nineteenth-century artists produced many images of the new factories. How would you describe the textile mill shown in Source 4?
3. According to the German doctor in Source 3, what challenges confronted working-class women in their daily lives? To what extent does he seem to blame the women themselves for their situation? How might observations like these have affected the new sexual division of labor discussed in the text?
4. In what ways were Robert Owen's innovations (Source 5) a response to the negative impacts of industrialization highlighted by the German doctor (Source 3)?

mainly on their own exertions, produced in them that invaluable feeling, a spirit of freedom and independence, and that guarantee for good conduct and improvement of manners, a consciousness of the value of character and of their own weight and importance.

3 **Living conditions of the working class, 1845.** As middle-class reformers began to investigate working-class living conditions, they were shocked at what they found. This excerpt comes from an 1845 interview of doctors in a German industrial city.

■ QUESTION: What is your usual experience regarding the cleanliness of these classes?

DR. BLUEMNER: Bad! Mother has to go out to work, and can therefore pay little attention to the domestic economy, and even if she makes an effort, she lacks time and means. A typical woman of this kind has four children, of whom she is still suckling one, she has to look after the whole household, to take food to her husband at work, perhaps a quarter of a mile away on a building site; she therefore has no time for cleaning and then it is such a small hole inhabited by so many people. The children are left to themselves, crawl about the floor or in the streets, and are always dirty; they lack the necessary clothing to change more often, and there is no time or money to wash these frequently. There are, of course, gradations; if the mother is healthy, active and clean, and if the poverty is not too great, then things are better.

(The LIFE Picture Collection/Time Life Pictures/Getty Images)

4 **Power loom weaving, 1834.** This engraving shows adult women operating power looms under the supervision of a male foreman, and it accurately reflects both the decline of family employment and the emergence of a gender-based division of labor in many British factories. The jungle of belts and shafts connecting the noisy looms to the giant steam engine on the ground floor created a constant din.

5 **Robert Owen,** *A New View of Society*, **1831.** Manufacturer and social reformer Robert Owen was also interested in the lessons of the early years of industrialization. He wished not to defend or decry industrialization, but to apply those lessons to the design and operation of his textile factory at New Lanark, Scotland.

■ The system of receiving apprentices from public charities was abolished; permanent settlers with large families were encouraged, and comfortable houses built for their accommodation. The practice of employing children in the mills, of six, seven, and eight years of age, was discontinued, and their parents advised to allow them to acquire health and education until they were ten years old.... The children were taught reading, writing, and arithmetic during five years, that is, from five to ten, in the village school, without expense to their parents....

[A]ttention was given to the domestic arrangements of the community. Their houses were rendered more comfortable, their streets were improved, the best provisions were purchased, and sold to them at low rates.... They were taught to be rational, and they acted rationally. Thus both parties experienced the incalculable advantages of the system which had been adopted. Those employed became industrious, temperate, healthy, faithful to their employers, and kind to each other; while the proprietors were deriving services ... far beyond those which could be obtained by any other means than those of mutual confidence and kindness.

PUTTING IT ALL TOGETHER

Using the sources above, along with what you have learned in class and in this chapter, create a comparison of industrial and preindustrial conditions, written from the perspective of a nineteenth-century observer. Your observer can come from any social background: he or she could be a scholar like Peter Gaskell or Richard Guest, a factory owner like Robert Owen, or an actual factory worker. As you write, be sure to consider the influence of your observer's background on his or her characterization of the changes brought by industrialization. What differences would your observer highlight? Why?

Sources: (1) Peter Gaskell, *The Manufacturing Population of England: Its Moral, Social, and Physical Conditions, and the Changes Which Have Arisen from the Use of Steam Machinery* (London: Baldwin and Cradock, 1833), pp. 15–16, 18; (2 and 5) E. Royston Pike, *Human Documents of the Industrial Revolution in Britain.* Copyright © 1966 Routledge. Published by Allen & Unwin. Reproduced by permission of Taylor & Francis Books UK. (3) Laura L. Frader, ed., *The Industrial Revolution: A History in Documents* (Oxford: Oxford University Press, 2006), pp. 85–86.

Just like working-class women, the wives and daughters of successful businessmen also found fewer opportunities for active participation in Europe's business world. Rather than contributing as vital partners in a family-owned enterprise, as so many middle-class women had done before, these women were increasingly valued for their ladylike gentility.

Responses to Industrialization

From the beginning, the British Industrial Revolution had its critics. Among the first were the Romantic poets, including William Blake (1757–1827) and William Wordsworth (1770–1850). Some handicraft workers—notably the **Luddites**, who attacked factories in northern England in 1811 and later—smashed the new machines, which they believed were putting them out of work. Doctors and reformers wrote of problems in the factories and new towns, while Malthus and Ricardo concluded that workers would earn only enough to stay alive.

This pessimistic view was accepted and reinforced by Friedrich Engels (1820–1895), the future revolutionary and colleague of Karl Marx (see "The Birth of Socialism" in Chapter 24). After studying conditions in northern England, this young son of a wealthy Prussian cotton manufacturer published in 1844 *The Condition of the Working Class in England*, a blistering indictment of the capitalist classes. Engels's extremely influential account of capitalist exploitation and increasing worker poverty was embellished by Marx and later socialists.

Analysis of industrial capitalism, often combined with reflections on the French Revolution, led to the development of a new overarching interpretation—a new paradigm—regarding social relationships. Briefly, this paradigm argued that individuals were members of separate classes based on their relationship to the means of production, that is, the machines and factories that dominated the new economy. As owners of expensive industrial machinery and as dependent laborers in their factories, the two main groups of society had separate and conflicting interests. Accordingly, the comfortable, well-educated "public" of the eighteenth century came increasingly to be defined as the middle class, and the "people" gradually began to perceive themselves as composing a modern working class. And

while the new class interpretation was open to criticism, it appealed to many because it seemed to explain what was happening. Therefore, conflicting classes existed, in part, because many individuals came to believe they existed and developed an awareness that they belonged to a particular social class—this awareness is what Karl Marx called **class-consciousness**.

Meanwhile, other observers believed that conditions were improving for the working people. In his 1835 study of the cotton industry, Andrew Ure (yoo-RAY) wrote that conditions in most factories were not harsh and were even quite good. Edwin Chadwick, a government official well acquainted with the problems of the working population, concluded that the "whole mass of the laboring community" was increasingly able "to buy more of the necessities and minor luxuries of life."[9] Nevertheless, those who thought, correctly, that conditions were stagnating or getting worse for working people were probably in the majority.

The Early Labor Movement in Britain

Not everyone worked in large factories and coal mines during the Industrial Revolution. In 1850 more British people still worked on farms than in any other single occupation. The second-largest occupation was domestic service, with more than 1 million household servants, 90 percent of whom were women.

Within industry itself, the pattern of artisans working with hand tools in small shops remained unchanged in many trades, even as others were revolutionized by technological change. For example, the British iron industry was completely dominated by large-scale capitalist firms by 1850. Yet the firms that fashioned iron into small metal goods employed on average fewer than ten wage workers who used handicraft skills.

Working-class solidarity and class-consciousness developed in small workshops as well as in large factories. In the northern factory districts, anticapitalist sentiments were frequent by the 1820s. Commenting in 1825 on a strike in the woolen center of Bradford and the support it had gathered from other regions, one newspaper claimed with pride that "it is all the workers of England against a few masters of Bradford."[10]

Such sentiments ran contrary to the liberal tenets of economic freedom. Liberal economic principles were embraced by statesmen and middle-class business owners in the late eighteenth century and continued to gather strength in the early nineteenth century. In 1799 Parliament passed the **Combination Acts**, which outlawed unions and strikes. In 1813 and 1814 Parliament repealed an old law regulating the wages of artisans and the conditions of apprenticeship. As a result of these and other measures, certain skilled artisan workers found aggressive capitalists ignoring traditional work rules and trying to flood their trades with unorganized women workers and children to beat down wages.

Luddites Group of handicraft workers who attacked factories in northern England in 1811 and after, smashing the new machines that they believed were putting them out of work.

class-consciousness An individual's sense of class differentiation, a term introduced by Karl Marx.

Combination Acts English laws passed in 1799 that outlawed unions and strikes, favoring capitalist business owners over skilled artisans. Bitterly resented and widely disregarded by many craft guilds, the acts were repealed by Parliament in 1824.

Union Membership Certificate This handsome membership certificate belonged to Arthur Watton, a properly trained and certified papermaker of Kings Norton in Birmingham, England. Members of such unions proudly framed their certificates and displayed them in their homes, showing that they were skilled workers. (Courtesy, Sylvia Waddell)

after 1851 in the direction of craft unions. These unions won real benefits for members by fairly conservative means and thus became an accepted part of the industrial scene.

British workers also engaged in direct political activity in defense of their interests. After the collapse of Owen's national trade union, many working people went into the Chartist movement, which fought for universal manhood suffrage. Workers were also active in campaigns to limit the workday in factories to ten hours and to permit duty-free importation of wheat into Great Britain to secure cheap bread. Thus working people developed a sense of their own identity and played an active role in shaping the new industrial system. They were neither helpless victims nor passive beneficiaries.

The Impact of Slavery

Another mass labor force of the Industrial Revolution was composed of the millions of enslaved men, women, and children who toiled in European colonies in the Caribbean and in the nations of North and South America. Historians have long debated the extent to which revenue from slavery contributed to Britain's achievements in the Industrial Revolution.

Most now agree that profits from colonial plantations and slave trading were a small portion of British national income in the eighteenth century. Nevertheless, the impact of slavery on Britain's economy was much broader than direct profits alone. In the mid-eighteenth century the need for items to exchange for colonial cotton, sugar, tobacco, and slaves stimulated demand for British manufactured goods in the Caribbean, North America, and West Africa. Britain's dominance in the slave trade also led to the development of finance and credit institutions that would help early industrialists obtain capital for their businesses.

The British Parliament abolished the slave trade in 1807 and freed all slaves in British territories in 1833, but by 1850 most of the cotton processed by British mills was supplied by the coerced labor of slaves in the southern United States. Thus the Industrial Revolution was integrally connected to the Atlantic world and the misery of slavery.

The capitalist attack on artisan guilds and work rules was bitterly resented by many craftworkers, who subsequently played an important part in Great Britain and in other countries in gradually building a modern labor movement. The Combination Acts were widely disregarded by workers. Craftsmen continued to take collective action, and societies of skilled factory workers also organized unions. Unions sought to control the number of skilled workers, to limit apprenticeship to members' own children, and to bargain with owners over wages. In the face of widespread union activity, Parliament repealed the Combination Acts in 1824, and unions were tolerated, though not fully accepted, after 1825.

The next stage in the development of the British trade-union movement was the attempt to create a single large national union. This effort was led not so much by working people as by social reformers such as Robert Owen. Owen, a self-made cotton manufacturer, had pioneered in industrial relations by combining firm discipline with concern for the health, safety, and hours of his workers. After 1815 he experimented with cooperative and socialist communities. Then in 1834 Owen organized one of the largest and most visionary of the early national unions, the Grand National Consolidated Trades Union.

When Owen's and other grandiose schemes collapsed, the British labor movement moved once again

Chapter Summary

As markets for manufactured goods increased both domestically and overseas, Britain was able to respond with increased production, largely because of its stable government, abundant natural resources, and flexible labor force. The first factories arose as a result of innovations in the textile industry. The demand for improvements in energy led to innovations and improvements in the steam engine, which transformed the iron industry, among others. In the early nineteenth century transportation of goods was greatly enhanced with the adoption of steam-powered trains and ships.

After 1815 continental European countries gradually built on England's technical breakthroughs. Entrepreneurs set up their own factories and hired skilled local artisans along with English immigrants experienced in the new technologies. Newly established corporate banks worked in conjunction with government interventions in finance and tariff controls to promote railroads and other industries. Beginning around 1850 Japan and the United States also began to rapidly industrialize, but generally the Industrial Revolution spread more slowly outside Europe, as many countries were confined to producing agricultural goods and other raw materials to serve European markets.

The rise of modern industry had a profound impact on society, beginning in Britain in the late eighteenth century. Industrialization led to the growing size and wealth of the middle class and the rise of a modern industrial working class. Rigid rules, stern discipline, and long hours weighed heavily on factory workers, and improvements in the standard of living came slowly, but they were substantial by 1850. Married women withdrew increasingly from wage work and concentrated on child care and household responsibilities. The era of industrialization also fostered new attitudes toward child labor, encouraged protective factory legislation, and called forth a new sense of class feeling and an assertive labor movement. Slave labor in European colonies contributed to the rise of the Industrial Revolution by increasing markets for European goods, supplying raw materials, and encouraging the development of financial systems.

NOTES

1. N. F. R. Crafts, *British Economic Growth During the Industrial Revolution* (Oxford: Oxford University Press, 1985), p. 32.
2. John Allen, *The British Industrial Revolution* (Cambridge: Cambridge University Press, 2009), pp. 1–2.
3. P. Bairoch, "International Industrialization Levels from 1750 to 1980," *Journal of European Economic History* 11 (Spring 1982): 269–333.
4. Quoted in J. Bowditch and C. Ramsland, eds., *Voices of the Industrial Revolution* (Ann Arbor: University of Michigan Press, 1961), p. 55, from Thomas Malthus, *Essay on the Principle of Population*, 4th ed. (1807).
5. Quoted in E. R. Pike, *"Hard Times": Human Documents of the Industrial Revolution* (New York: Praeger, 1966), p. 109.
6. Quoted in J. Humphries, ". . . 'The Most Free from Objection' . . . : The Sexual Division of Labor and Women's Work in Nineteenth-Century England," *Journal of Economic History* 47 (December 1987): 941.
7. H.-J. Voth, *Time and Work in England, 1750–1830* (Oxford: Oxford University Press, 2000), pp. 268–270; also pp. 118–133.
8. Joel Mokyr, *The Enlightened Economy: An Economic History of Britain, 1700–1850* (New Haven: Yale University Press, 2009), p. 455.
9. Quoted in W. A. Hayek, ed., *Capitalism and the Historians* (Chicago: University of Chicago Press, 1954), p. 126.
10. Quoted in D. Geary, ed., *Labour and Socialist Movements in Europe Before 1914* (Oxford: Berg, 1989), p. 29.
11. Kenneth Pomeranz, *The Great Divergence: China, Europe, and the Making of the Modern World Economy* (Princeton, N.J.: Princeton University Press, 2000).

CONNECTIONS

For much of its history, Europe lagged behind older and more sophisticated civilizations in China and the Middle East. And yet by 1800 Europe had broken ahead of the other regions of the world in terms of wealth and power, a process historians have termed "the Great Divergence."[11]

One prerequisite for the rise of Europe was its growing control over world trade, first in the Indian Ocean in the sixteenth and seventeenth centuries and then in the eighteenth-century Atlantic world. A second crucial factor behind the Great Divergence was the Industrial Revolution, which dramatically increased the pace of production and distribution while reducing their cost, thereby allowing Europeans to control other countries first economically and then politically. By the middle of the nineteenth century the gap between Western industrial production and standards of living and those of the non-West had grown dramatically, bringing with it the economic dependence of non-Western nations, meager wages for their largely impoverished populations, and increasingly aggressive Western imperial ambitions (see "The World Market" in Chapter 25). In the late nineteenth century non-Western countries began to experience their own processes of industrialization. Today's world is witnessing a surge in productivity in China, India, and other non-Western nations, with uncertain consequences for the global balance of power.

CHAPTER 23 **Review and Explore**

Identify Key Terms

Identify and explain the significance of each item below.

Industrial Revolution (p. 663)	Crystal Palace (p. 668)	Mines Act of 1842 (p. 679)
spinning jenny (p. 663)	iron law of wages (p. 670)	Luddites (p. 684)
water frame (p. 663)	tariff protection (p. 672)	class-consciousness (p. 684)
steam engines (p. 666)	Factory Act of 1833 (p. 677)	Combination Acts (p. 684)
Rocket (p. 667)	separate spheres (p. 677)	

Review the Main Ideas

Answer the focus questions from each section of the chapter.

1. Why did the Industrial Revolution begin in Britain, and how did it develop between 1780 and 1850? (p. 662)

2. How did countries in Europe and around the world respond to the challenge of industrialization after 1815? (p. 670)

3. How did work evolve during the Industrial Revolution, and how did daily life change for working people? (p. 676)

4. How did the changes brought about by the Industrial Revolution lead to new social classes, and how did people respond to the new structure? (p. 680)

Make Comparisons and Connections

Analyze the larger developments and continuities within and across chapters.

1. Why did Great Britain take the lead in industrialization, and when did other countries begin to adopt the new techniques and organization of production?

2. How did historical developments between 1600 and 1800 contribute to the rise of Europe to world dominance in the nineteenth century? Argue for or against the following proposition: "Given contemporary trends, the dominance of the West in the nineteenth and twentieth centuries should be seen as a temporary aberration, rather than as a fundamental and permanent shift in the global balance of power."

3. How would you compare the legacy of the political revolutions of the late eighteenth century (Chapter 22) with that of the Industrial Revolution? Which seems to you to have created the most important changes, and why?

TIMELINE

EUROPE

ca. 1780–1850 Industrial Revolution and accompanying population boom in Great Britain

1769 Watt patents modern steam engine

1799 Combination Acts passed in England

ca. 1765 Hargreaves invents spinning jenny; Arkwright creates water frame

1802–1833 Factory Acts passed in England

AMERICAS

ASIA

MIDDLE EAST

1780   1800

Suggested Resources

BOOKS

Allen, Robert C. *The British Industrial Revolution in Global Perspective.* 2009. Explains the origins of the Industrial Revolution and why it took place in Britain and not elsewhere.

Davidoff, Leonore, and Catherine Hall. *Family Fortunes: Men and Women of the English Middle Class, 1750–1850*, rev. ed. 2003. Examines both economic activities and cultural beliefs with great skill.

Griffin, Emma. *A Short History of the British Industrial Revolution.* 2010. An accessible and lively introduction to the subject.

Horn, Jeff, Leonard N. Rosenband, and Merritt Roe Smith. *Reconceptualizing the Industrial Revolution.* 2010. A collection of essays by leading scholars that re-examines the most contentious debates in the field.

Humphries, Jane. *Childhood and Child Labour in the British Industrial Revolution.* 2010. A moving account of the experience of children during the Industrial Revolution, based on numerous autobiographies.

James, Harold. *Family Capitalism.* 2006. A study of the entrepreneurial dynasties of the British Industrial Revolution.

Mokyr, Joel. *The Enlightened Economy: An Economic History of Britain, 1700–1850.* 2009. A masterful explanation of industrialization and economic growth in Britain that emphasizes the impact of Enlightenment openness and curiosity.

Morris, Charles R. *The Dawn of Innovation: The First American Industrial Revolution.* 2012. Tells the story of the individuals, inventions, and trade networks that transformed the United States from a rural economy to a global industrial power.

Prados de la Escosura, Leandro, ed. *Exceptionalism and Industrialisation: Britain and Its European Rivals, 1688–1815.* 2004. Compares the path toward economic development in Britain and the rest of Europe.

Rosenthal, Jean-Laurent, and R. Bin Wong, *Before and Beyond Divergence: The Politics of Economic Change in China and Europe.* 2011. A study of the similarities and differences between Europe and China that led to the origins and growth of industrialization in Europe.

Stearns, Peter N. *The Industrial Revolution in World History*, 4th ed. 2012. A useful brief survey.

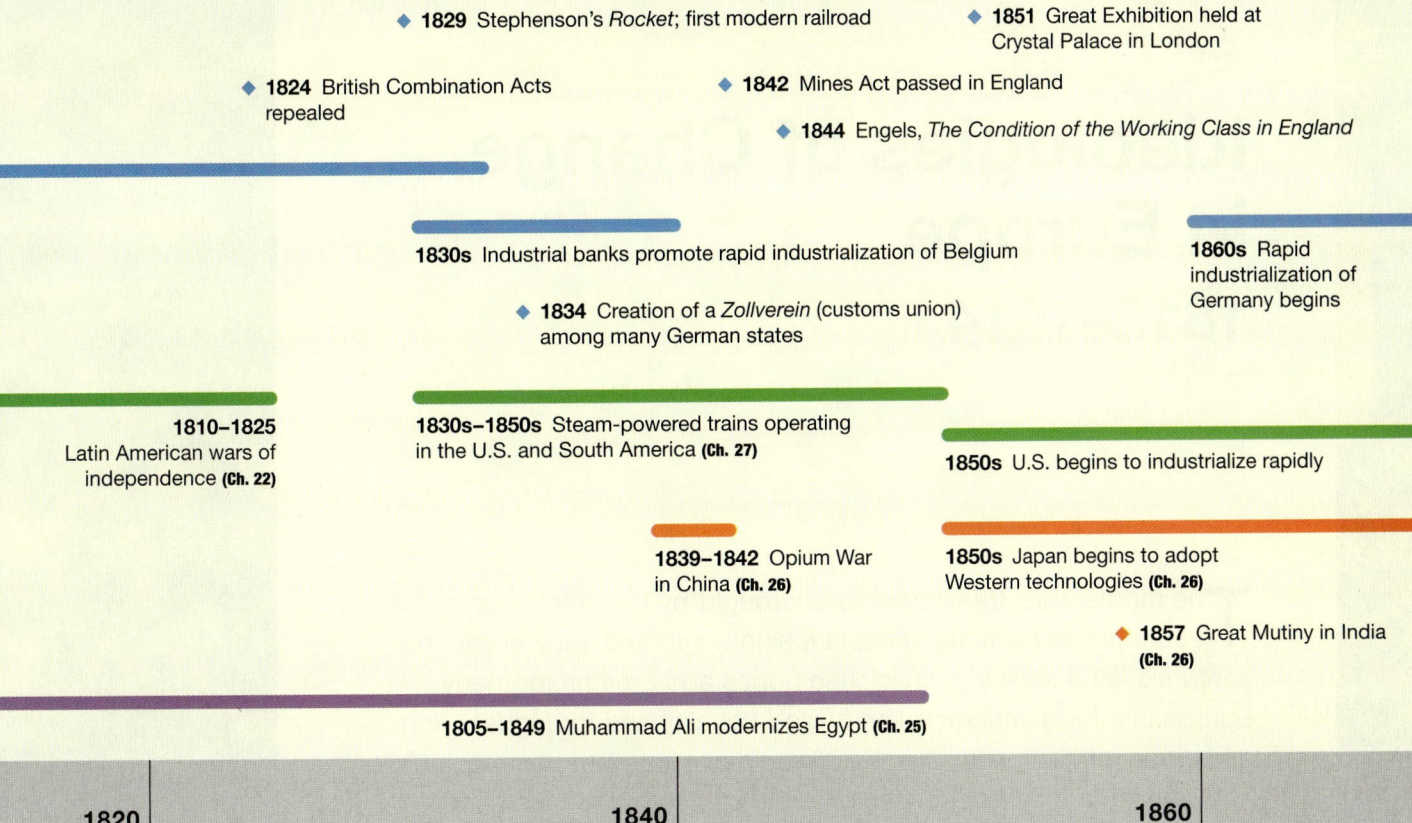

1829 Stephenson's *Rocket*; first modern railroad

1851 Great Exhibition held at Crystal Palace in London

1824 British Combination Acts repealed

1842 Mines Act passed in England

1844 Engels, *The Condition of the Working Class in England*

1830s Industrial banks promote rapid industrialization of Belgium

1860s Rapid industrialization of Germany begins

1834 Creation of a *Zollverein* (customs union) among many German states

1810–1825 Latin American wars of independence **(Ch. 22)**

1830s–1850s Steam-powered trains operating in the U.S. and South America **(Ch. 27)**

1850s U.S. begins to industrialize rapidly

1839–1842 Opium War in China **(Ch. 26)**

1850s Japan begins to adopt Western technologies **(Ch. 26)**

1857 Great Mutiny in India **(Ch. 26)**

1805–1849 Muhammad Ali modernizes Egypt **(Ch. 25)**

1820   1840   1860

DOCUMENTARIES

The Children Who Built Victorian Britain (BBC, 2011). An account of the role of child labor in the Industrial Revolution, based on written testimonies from children of that era.

The Men Who Built America (History Channel, 2013). A miniseries on the bankers and industrialists who created modern America from the Civil War to the Great Depression.

Mill Times (PBS, 2006). A combination of documentary video and animated re-enactments that tells the story of the mechanization of the cotton industry in Britain and the United States.

FEATURE FILMS AND TELEVISION DRAMAS

Germinal (Claude Berri, 1993). In a European coal-mining town during the Industrial Revolution, exploited workers go on strike and encounter brutal repression from the authorities.

Hard Times (Granada TV, 1977). A four-hour miniseries adaptation of Charles Dickens's famous novel about the bitter life of mill workers in England during the Industrial Revolution.

Oliver Twist (Roman Polanski, 2005). A film based on a novel by Charles Dickens depicting the harsh conditions of life for orphans and poor children in nineteenth-century London.

WEBSITES

Images of the Industrial Revolution in Britain. A collection of annotated images from the eighteenth and nineteenth centuries covering various aspects of the Industrial Revolution. **www.netnicholls.com /neh2001/index.html**

Spinning the Web. A website offering comprehensive information on the people, places, industrial processes, and products involved in the mechanization of the British cotton industry. **www.spinningtheweb .org.uk/industry**

Women Working, 1800–1930. A digital collection of the Harvard University Library, with sources and links related to women's labor in the nineteenth and early twentieth centuries. **ocp.hul.harvard.edu/ww**

24

Ideologies of Change in Europe

1815–1914

The momentous transformations wrought by the political and economic revolutions of the late eighteenth and early nineteenth centuries left a legacy of unfinished hopes and dreams for many Europeans: for democracy, liberty, and equality and for higher living standards for all. These aspirations would play out with unpredictable and tumultuous consequences over the course of the nineteenth century. After 1815 the powers that defeated Napoleon united under a revived conservatism to stamp out the spread of liberal and democratic reforms. But the political and social innovations made possible by the unfinished revolutions proved difficult to contain.

In politics, powerful ideologies — liberalism, nationalism, and socialism — emerged to oppose conservatism. All played critical roles in the political and social battles of the era and the great popular upheaval that eventually swept across Europe in the revolutions of 1848. These revolutions failed, however, and gave way to more sober — and more successful — nation building in the 1860s. European political leaders and middle-class nationalists also began to deal effectively with the challenges of the emerging urban society. One way they did so was through nationalism — mass identification with a nation-state that was increasingly responsive to the needs of its people. At the same time, the triumph of nationalism promoted bitter rivalries between states and peoples, spurred a second great wave of imperialism, and in the twentieth century brought an era of tragic global conflict.

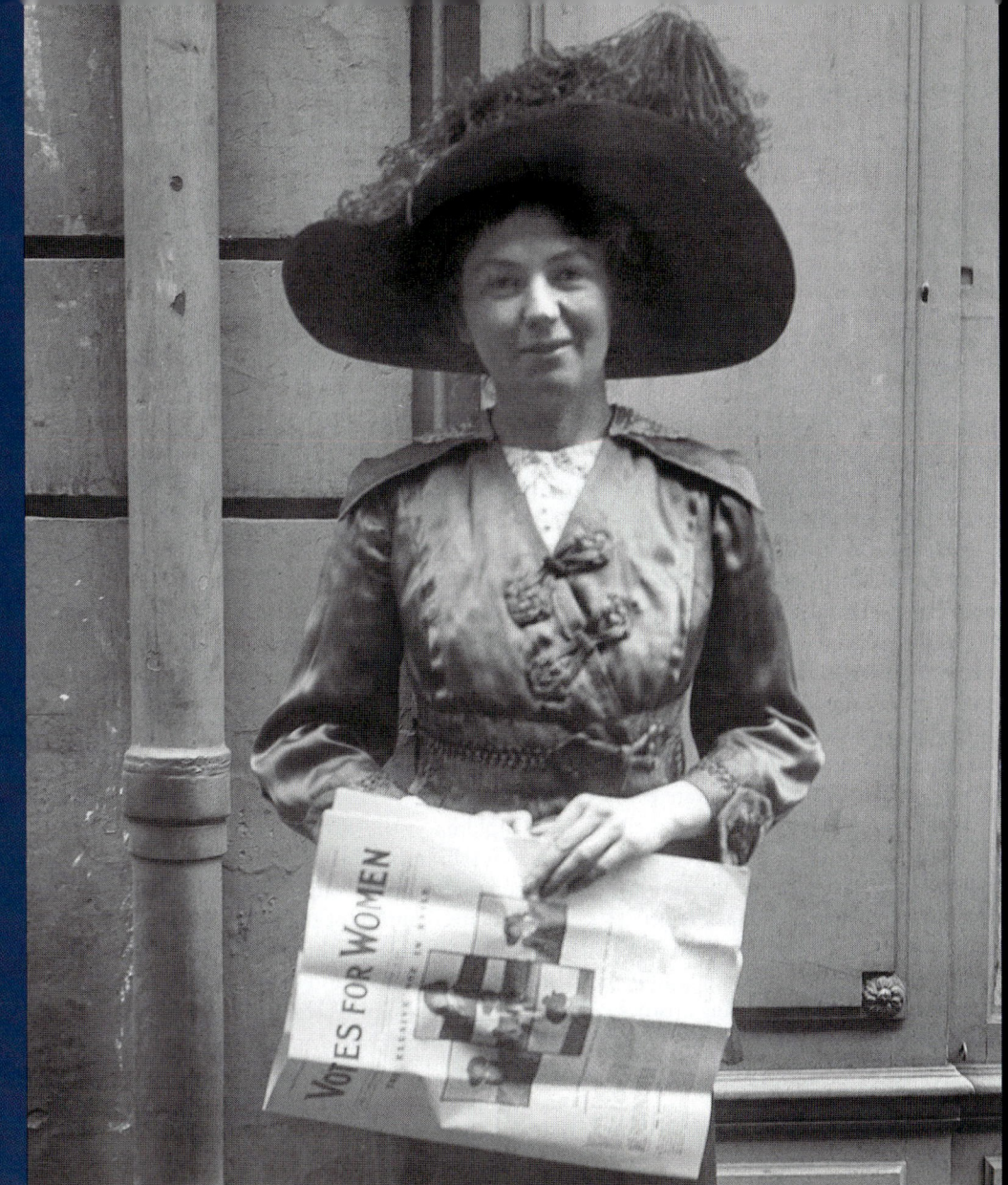

Christabel Pankhurst, Militant Suffragette

Christabel Pankhurst led the British Women's Social and Political Union, whose motto was "deeds, not words." This photo was taken in 1912 in Paris, where Pankhurst was living to avoid arrest for her increasingly violent actions to obtain the vote for women, including bombing the home of the future prime minister. Women in Britain and many other countries gained the right to vote in the years immediately after World War I.

© Maurice Branger/Roger-Viollet/The Image Works

CHAPTER PREVIEW

A Conservative Peace Gives Way to Radical Ideas

How did the allies fashion a peace settlement in 1815, and what radical ideas emerged between 1815 and 1848?

After finally defeating Napoleon, the conservative aristocratic monarchies of Russia, Prussia, Austria, and Great Britain — known as the Quadruple Alliance (see "The Grand Empire and Its End" in Chapter 22) — reaffirmed their determination to hold France in line and to defeat the intertwined dangers of war and revolution. At the **Congress of Vienna** (1814–1815), they fashioned a lasting peace settlement that helped produce fifty years without major warfare in Europe. On the domestic front, they sought to restore order and limit the spread of revolutionary ideas.

Despite the congress's success on the diplomatic front, many observers at the time were frustrated by the high-handed dictates of the Great Powers and their refusal to adopt social reforms. After 1815 such critics sought to harness the radical ideas of the revolutionary age to new political movements. Many rejected **conservatism**, a political philosophy that stressed retaining traditional values and institutions, including hereditary monarchy and a strong landowning aristocracy. Radical thinkers developed alternative ideologies and tried to convince society to act on them.

The Political and Social Situation After 1815

When the Quadruple Alliance, along with representatives of minor powers, met together at the Congress of Vienna they combined leniency toward France with strong defensive measures. The Low Countries — Belgium and Holland — were united under an enlarged Dutch monarchy capable of opposing France more effectively. Prussia received considerably more territory along France's eastern border to stand as a "sentinel on the Rhine" against renewed French aggression. The congress recognized the neutrality of certain territories — for example, the cantons of Switzerland — as a means of creating buffer zones between potentially hostile states. The first Peace of Paris returned France to the boundaries it possessed in 1792, which were larger than those of 1789. Even after Napoleon's brief return to power tested the allies' patience, France did not have to give up much additional territory and had to pay only modest reparations.

In their moderation toward France, the allies were motivated by self-interest and traditional ideas about the balance of power. To the peacemakers, especially to Klemens von Metternich (1773–1859), Austria's foreign minister, the balance of power meant an international equilibrium of political and military forces that would discourage aggression by any state or combination of states. This required, among other measures, ensuring the internal stability of France. The Quadruple Alliance members also agreed to meet periodically to discuss their common interests and to consider appropriate measures to maintain peace in Europe. This agreement represented a transformation of European diplomacy; the "congress system" it inaugurated lasted long into the nineteenth century.

The leaders of the congress reached their decisions with little recognition of the interests of smaller states and subject peoples within multiethnic states. They also left aside the question of the European territories of the Ottoman Empire, which Napoleon had schemed to divide between France and Russia. With the rise of nationalism, these neglected issues would pose serious threats to the post-1815 order. On a more positive note, the leading powers of the congress, led by Britain, issued a declaration condemning the slave trade and calling on European states to begin the process of abolition.

Conservatism After 1815

In 1815, under Metternich's leadership, Austria, Prussia, and Russia formed the Holy Alliance, dedicated to crushing the ideas and politics of the revolutionary era. Metternich's policies dominated the entire German Confederation of thirty-eight independent German states (Map 24.1). It was through the German Confederation that Metternich had the repressive Karlsbad Decrees issued in 1819. These decrees required the member states to root out radical ideas in their universities and newspapers, and a permanent committee was established to investigate and punish any liberal or radical organizations.

Adhering to a conservative political philosophy, Metternich believed that strong governments were needed to protect society from its worst instincts. Like many European conservatives of his time, Metternich believed that liberalism (see the next section), as embod-

---

Congress of Vienna A meeting of the Quadruple Alliance (Russia, Prussia, Austria, Great Britain) and France held in 1814–1815 to fashion a general peace settlement after the defeat of Napoleonic France.

conservatism A political philosophy that stressed retaining traditional values and institutions, including hereditary monarchy and a strong landowning aristocracy.

liberalism A philosophy whose principal ideas were equality and liberty; liberals demanded representative government and equality before the law as well as such individual freedoms as freedom of the press, freedom of speech, freedom of assembly, and freedom from arbitrary arrest.

The Congress of Vienna A French political cartoon shows the rulers of Europe dividing the map of Europe among themselves at the Congress of Vienna. Meanwhile, Napoleon (who had escaped from Elba at the time) removes the section with France on it, and the English representative holds a set of scales loaded with gold coins, a reference to the English role in financing the allies. (Musée de la Ville de Paris, Musée Carnavalet, Paris, France/ Archives Charmet/Bridgeman Images)

ied in revolutionary America and France, had been responsible for a generation of war with untold bloodshed and suffering. He blamed liberal revolutionaries for stirring up the lower classes, which he believed desired nothing more than peace and quiet.

Another belief that Metternich opposed, which was often allied with liberalism, was nationalism, the idea that each national group had a right to establish its own independent government. The Habsburg's Austrian Empire was a dynastic state dominated by Germans but containing many other national groups. This multinational state was both strong and weak. It was strong because of its large population and vast territories, but weak because of its many and potentially dissatisfied nationalities. In these circumstances, Metternich opposed both liberalism and nationalism, for Austria could not accommodate those ideologies and remain a powerful empire. Metternich's antinationalist efforts were supported by the two great multinational empires on Austria's borders, Russia and the Ottoman Empire.

Liberalism and the Middle Class

The principal ideas of **liberalism**—liberty and equality—were by no means defeated in 1815. First realized in the American Revolution and then achieved in part in the French and Latin American Revolutions, liberalism demanded representative government and equality before the law. The idea of liberty also meant specific individual freedoms: freedom of the press, freedom of speech, freedom of assembly, and freedom from arbitrary arrest. In Europe only France, with Louis XVIII's Constitutional Charter, and Great Britain, with its Parliament and historic liberties of English men and women, had realized much of the liberal program in 1815. Even in those countries, liberalism had only begun to succeed

Liberalism faced more radical ideological competitors in the early nineteenth century. Opponents of liberalism especially criticized its economic principles, which called for unrestricted private enterprise and no government interference in the economy. This philosophy

MAPPING THE PAST

MAP 24.1 Europe in 1815 In 1815 Europe contained many different states, but after the defeat of Napoleon international politics was dominated by the five Great Powers: Russia, Prussia, Austria, Great Britain, and France. (The number rises to six if one includes the Ottoman Empire.)

ANALYZING THE MAP Trace the political boundaries of each Great Power, and compare their geographical strengths and weaknesses. What territories did Prussia and Austria gain as a result of the war with Napoleon?

CONNECTIONS How did Prussia's and Austria's territorial gains contribute to the balance of power established at the Congress of Vienna? What other factors enabled the Great Powers to achieve such a long-lasting peace?

was popularly known as the doctrine of **laissez faire** (lay-say FEHR). In early-nineteenth-century Britain economic liberalism was embraced most enthusiastically by business groups and thus became a doctrine associated with corporate interests.

In the early nineteenth century liberal political ideals also became more closely associated with narrow

class interests. Early-nineteenth-century liberals favored representative government, but they generally wanted property qualifications attached to the right to vote and to serve in Parliament.

As liberalism became increasingly identified with the middle class after 1815, some intellectuals and foes of conservatism felt that liberalism did not go nearly

Popular Image of the National Anthem of Germany In the late nineteenth and early twentieth centuries, patriotic nationalism swept European populations. This attitude was encouraged by printed images such as this trading card (distributed in packets of beef bouillon cubes) that showed the words and music for the new German national anthem, flanked by a female embodiment of the new nation and a pair of happy peasants in folkloric dress. (Private Collection/© Look and Learn/Bridgeman Images)

far enough. They called for replacing monarchical rule with republics, for democracy through universal male suffrage, and for greater economic and social equality. These democrats and republicans were more radical than the liberals, and they were more willing to endorse violence to achieve goals. As a result, liberals and radical republicans could join forces against conservatives only up to a point.

The Growing Appeal of Nationalism

Nationalism was a radical new ideology that emerged in the years after 1815—an idea destined to have an enormous influence in the modern world. Early advocates of the "national idea" argued that the members of what we would call today an ethnic group had their own spirit and their own cultural unity, which were manifested especially in a common language, history, and territory. In fact, such cultural unity was more a dream than a reality as local dialects abounded, historical memory divided the inhabitants of the different states as much as it unified them, and a variety of ethnic groups shared the territory of most states.

Nevertheless, many European nationalists sought to make the territory of each people coincide with well-defined boundaries in an independent nation-state. It was this political goal that made nationalism so explosive in central and eastern Europe after 1815, when there were either too few states (Austria, Russia, and the Ottoman Empire) or too many (the Italian peninsula and the German Confederation), and when different peoples overlapped and intermingled.

Between 1815 and 1850 most people who believed in nationalism also believed in either liberalism or radical democratic republicanism. A common faith in the creativity and nobility of the people was perhaps the single most important reason for the linking of these two concepts. Liberals and especially democrats saw the people as the ultimate source of all good government. They agreed that the benefits of self-government would be possible only if the people were united by common traditions that transcended class and local interests. Thus individual liberty and love of a free nation overlapped greatly.

laissez faire A doctrine of economic liberalism advocating unrestricted private enterprise and no government interference in the economy.

nationalism The idea that each people had its own spirit and its own cultural unity, which manifested itself especially in a common language and history and could serve as the basis for an independent political state.

Yet early nationalists also stressed the differences among peoples, and they developed a strong sense of "we" and "they." Thus, while European nationalism's main thrust was liberal and democratic, below the surface lurked ideas of national superiority and national mission.

The Birth of Socialism

Socialism, a second radical doctrine after 1815, began in France. Early French socialists shared a sense of disappointment in the outcome of the French Revolution. They were also alarmed by the rise of laissez faire and the emergence of modern industry, which they saw as fostering inequality and selfish individualism. There was, they believed, an urgent need for a further reorganization of society to establish cooperation and a new sense of community.

Early French socialists felt an intense desire to help the poor, whose conditions had not been improved by industrial advances, and they preached greater economic equality between the rich and the poor. Inspired by the economic planning implemented in revolutionary France (see "The National Convention" in Chapter 22), they argued that the government should rationally organize the economy to control prices and prevent unemployment. Socialists also believed that government should regulate private property or that private property should be abolished and replaced by state or community ownership.

Up to the 1840s France was the center of socialism, as it had been the center of revolution in Europe, but in the following decades the German intellectual Karl Marx (1818–1883) would weave the diffuse strands of social thought into a distinctly modern ideology. Marx had studied philosophy at the University of Berlin before turning to journalism and economics. In 1848 the thirty-year-old Karl Marx and the twenty-eight-year-old Friedrich Engels published *The Communist Manifesto*, which became the guiding text of socialism.

Marx argued that middle-class interests and those of the industrial working class were inevitably opposed to each other. According to the *Manifesto*, the "history of all previously existing society is the history of class struggles." In Marx's view, one class had always exploited the other, and, with the advent of modern industry, society was split more clearly than ever before: between

the well-educated and prosperous middle class—the **bourgeoisie**—and the modern working class—the **proletariat**.

Just as the bourgeoisie had triumphed over the feudal aristocracy in the French Revolution, Marx predicted that the proletariat would conquer the bourgeoisie in a new revolution. While a tiny majority owned the means of production and grew richer, the ever-poorer proletariat was constantly growing in size and in class-consciousness. Marx believed that the critical moment when class conflict would result in revolution was very near, as the last lines of *The Communist Manifesto* make clear:

> Germany . . . is on the eve of a bourgeois revolution, that is bound to be . . . the prelude to an immediately following proletarian revolution. . . .
>
> Let the ruling classes tremble at a Communist revolution. The proletarians have nothing to lose but their chains. They have a world to win. WORKING MEN OF ALL COUNTRIES, UNITE!

Marx drew on the arguments of Adam Smith and David Ricardo, who taught that labor was the source of all value. He went on to argue that profits were really wages stolen from the workers. Moreover, Marx incorporated Friedrich Engels's account of the terrible oppression of the new class of factory workers in England. Thus Marx pulled together powerful ideas and insights to create one of the great secular religions out of the intellectual ferment of the early nineteenth century.

Reforms and Revolutions, 1815–1850

Why did revolutions triumph briefly throughout most of Europe in 1848, and why did they fail?

As liberal, nationalist, and socialist forces battered the conservatism of 1815, social and economic conditions continued to deteriorate for many Europeans, adding to the mounting pressures. In some countries, such as Great Britain, change occurred gradually and largely peacefully, but in 1848 radical political and social ideologies combined with economic crisis to produce revolutionary movements that demanded an end to repressive government. Between 1815 and 1848 many European countries, including France, Austria, and Prussia, experienced variations on this basic theme.

Social and Economic Conflict

The slow and uneven spread of industrialization in Europe after 1815 meant that the benefits of higher productivity were not felt by many. In Great Britain,

socialism A radical political doctrine that opposed individualism and that advocated cooperation and a sense of community; key ideas were economic planning, greater economic equality, and state regulation of property.

bourgeoisie The well-educated, prosperous, middle-class groups.

proletariat The Marxist term for the working class of modern industrialized society.

the earliest adopter of industrial methods, living standards only began to rise after 1850, and this trend took longer to spread to the continent. Indeed, for many people in the cities and countryside, the first half of the nineteenth century brought a decline in the conditions of daily life. In Europe's rapidly growing cities, migrants encountered overcrowding, shoddy housing, and poor sanitation, ideal conditions for the spread of infectious disease.

Despite booming urbanization, much of the continent remained agricultural, and the traditional social hierarchy, dominated by a landowning aristocracy, persisted. Serfdom still existed in the Hungarian provinces of the Austrian Empire, Prussian Silesia, and Russia. In the early nineteenth century, however, the pressures of a rapidly growing population, the adoption of new forms of agriculture, and the spread of exploitative rural industry destabilized these existing patterns. Many peasants lost access to collective land due to enclosure and the adoption of more efficient farming techniques. Meanwhile, the growing number of cottage workers resisted exploitation by merchant capitalists, and journeymen battled masters in urban industries.

Social malaise was exacerbated by the fact that the retracing of borders at the Congress of Vienna had placed many populations in new and unfamiliar states. Lack of loyalty to the central government only worsened popular anger over rising tax rates and other burdens. These simmering tensions broke to the surface in the 1840s, as widespread crop failure in 1845–1846 led to economic crisis.

In spring 1848 many people's grievances about enclosure and taxation resembled those of the eighteenth century. What transformed these conflicts was the political ideologies born from the struggles and unfulfilled hopes of the French Revolution—liberalism, nationalism, and socialism—as well as the newly invigorated conservatism that stood against them. These ideologies helped turn economic and social conflicts into the revolutions of 1848.

Liberal Reform in Great Britain

The English parliamentary system guaranteed basic civil rights, but only about 8 percent of the population could vote for representatives to Parliament. By the 1780s there was growing interest in reform, but the French Revolution threw the British aristocracy into a panic. After 1815 the British government put down popular protests over unemployment and the high cost of grain caused by the Napoleonic Wars with repressive legislation and military force.

By the early 1830s the social and economic changes created by industrialization began to be felt in politics. In 1832 continuous pressure from the liberal middle classes and popular unrest convinced the king and the House of Lords that they needed to act. The Reform Bill of 1832 moved British politics in a more democratic direction by giving new industrial areas increased representation in the House of Commons and by increasing the number of voters by about 50 percent. For the first time, comfortable middle-class urban groups, the main beneficiaries of industrialization, as well as some substantial farmers, received the vote. Two years later, the New Poor Law called for unemployed and indigent families to be placed in harsh workhouses rather than receiving aid from local parishes to remain in their own homes. With this act, Britain's rulers sought to relieve middle-class taxpayers of the burden of poor relief and to encourage unemployed rural workers to migrate to cities and take up industrial work.

Thus limited democratic reform was counterbalanced by harsh measures against the poor, both linked to the new social and economic circumstances of the Industrial Revolution. Many working people protested their exclusion from voting and the terms of the New Poor Law. Between 1838 and 1848 they joined the Chartist movement (see "The Early Labor Movement in Britain" in Chapter 23), which demanded universal male suffrage. In 1847 the ruling conservative party, known as the Tories, sought to appease working people with the Ten Hours Act, which limited the workday for women and young people in factories to ten hours. Tory aristocrats championed such legislation in order to compete with the middle class for working-class support.

This competition meant that the Parliamentary state relied on eliciting support from its people and thereby succeeded in managing unrest without the outbreak of revolution. Another factor favoring Great Britain's largely peaceful evolution in the nineteenth century was the fact that living standards had begun to rise significantly by the late 1840s, as the benefits of industrialization finally began to be felt. Thus England avoided the violence and turmoil of the revolutions of 1848 that shook continental Europe.

The people of Ireland did not benefit from these circumstances. Long ruled as a conquered people, the population was mostly composed of Irish Catholic peasants who rented their land from a tiny minority of Protestant landowners, many of whom resided in England. Ruthlessly exploited and growing rapidly in numbers, the rural population around 1800 lived under abominable conditions.

In spite of terrible conditions, Ireland's population doubled from 4 million to 8 million between 1780 and 1840, fueled in large part by the calories and nutritive qualities of the potato. However, the potato crop failed in 1845, 1846, 1848, and 1851 in Ireland and throughout much of Europe. Many suffered in

Europe, but in Ireland, where dependency on the potato was much more widespread, the result was starvation and death. The British government, committed to laissez-faire economic policies, reacted slowly and utterly inadequately. One and a half million people died, while another million fled between 1845 and 1851, primarily to the United States and Great Britain. The Great Famine, as this tragedy came to be known, intensified anti-British feeling and promoted Irish nationalism.

Revolutions in France

Louis XVIII's Constitutional Charter of 1814 was essentially a liberal constitution. It protected economic and social gains made by the middle class and the peasantry in the French Revolution, recognized intellectual and artistic freedom, and created a parliament with upper and lower houses. The charter was anything but democratic, however. Only a tiny minority of males had the right to vote for the legislative deputies who, with the king and his ministers, made the nation's laws.

Louis's conservative successor, Charles X (r. 1824–1830), wanted to re-establish the old order in France. To rally French nationalism and gain popular support, he exploited a long-standing dispute with Muslim Algeria, a vassal state of the Ottoman Empire. In June 1830 a French force crossed the Mediterranean and took the capital of Algiers. The French continued to wage war against Algerian resistance until 1847, when they finally subdued the country. Bringing French and other European settlers to Algeria and expropriating large amounts of Muslim-owned land, the conquest of Algeria marked the rebirth of French colonial expansion.

Buoyed by this success, Charles overplayed his hand and repudiated the Constitutional Charter. After three days of uprisings in Paris, which sparked a series of revolts by frustrated liberals and democrats across Europe, Charles fled. His cousin Louis Philippe (r. 1830–1848) accepted the Constitutional Charter of 1814 and assumed the title of the "king of the French people." Still, the situation in France remained fundamentally unchanged. Political and social reformers and the poor of Paris were bitterly disappointed.

During the 1840s this sense of disappointment was worsened by bad harvests and the slow development of industrialization, which meant that living conditions for the majority of the working classes were deteriorating rather than improving. Similar conditions prevailed across continental Europe, which was soon rocked by insurrections. In February full-scale revolution broke out in France, and its shock waves rippled across the continent.

Louis Philippe had refused to approve social legislation or consider electoral reform. Frustrated desires for change, high-level financial scandals, and crop failures in 1845 and 1846 united diverse groups of the king's opponents, including merchants, intellectuals, shopkeepers, and workers. In February 1848, as popular revolt broke out, barricades went up and Louis Philippe abdicated. (See "Analyzing the Evidence: The Triumph of Democratic Republics," at right.)

The revolutionaries quickly drafted a democratic, republican constitution for France's Second Republic, granting the right to vote to every adult male. Slaves in the French colonies were freed, the death penalty was abolished, and national workshops were established for unemployed Parisian workers.

Yet there were profound differences within the revolutionary coalition in Paris. The socialism promoted by radical republicans frightened not only the liberal middle and upper classes but also the peasants, many of whom owned land. When the French masses voted for delegates to the new Constituent Assembly in late April 1848, the monarchists won a clear majority. When the new government dissolved the national workshops in Paris, workers rose in a spontaneous insurrection. After three terrible "June Days" and the death or injury of more than ten thousand people, the republican army stood triumphant in a sea of working-class blood and hatred.

The revolution in France thus ended in failure. The middle and working classes had turned against each other. In place of a generous democratic republic, the Constituent Assembly completed a constitution featuring a strong executive. This allowed Louis Napoleon, nephew of Napoleon Bonaparte, to win a landslide victory in the December 1848 election based on promises to lead a strong government in favor of popular interests.

President Louis Napoleon at first shared power with a conservative National Assembly. But in 1851 Louis Napoleon dismissed the Assembly and seized power in a coup d'état. A year later he called on the French to make him hereditary emperor, and 97 percent voted to do so in a national plebiscite. Louis Napoleon then ruled France's Second Empire as Napoleon III, initiating policies favoring economic growth and urban development to appease the populace.

The Revolutions of 1848 in Central Europe

Throughout central Europe, social conflicts were exacerbated by the economic crises of 1845 to 1846. News of the upheaval in France in 1848 provoked the outbreak of revolution. Liberals demanded written constitutions, representative government, and greater civil liberties from authoritarian regimes. When governments hesitated, popular revolts followed. Urban workers and students allied with middle-class liberals and peasants.

The Triumph of Democratic Republics

In spring 1848 French artist Frédéric Sorrieu completed a series of four lithographs celebrating the democratic and republican forces sweeping across Europe. This image shows the nations of Europe assembled carrying their flags and wearing distinctive national costumes. They are shown joyfully marching past the statue of a woman, who holds the torch of Enlightenment and the 1789 Declaration of the Rights of Man and of the Citizen. The statue also echoes the first French Revolution by depicting liberty as a woman. In the foreground, symbols of absolutism and the church are shown in crumbled ruins.

(*Universal Democratic and Social Republics*, 1848, by Frédéric Sorrieu [1807–ca. 1861] [lithograph]/Musée de la Ville de Paris, Musée Carnavalet, Paris, France/Bridgeman Images)

Sorrieu arranged the nations based on his perception of their progress toward democracy and freedom. The United States and Switzerland, two pre-existing free republics, have already passed the Statue of Liberty (shown behind the French flag on the left). France is shown passing the statue, suggesting that Sorrieu's homeland was at that moment in the process of achieving liberty and equality. Right behind France comes Germany, with its people carrying a black, red, and gold flag. Germany was not unified as a nation-state until 1871; this image reveals a dream of German national unification decades before it took place.

As this image suggests, radical visions of democracy and republicanism often went hand in hand with nationalist fervor. For Sorrieu, the political ideal consisted of distinct and peaceful nation-states whose people were united by shared national pride and culture. Despite apparent differences of wealth and social status, each nation is joined under its flag and marching together toward greater freedom. The appearance of Christ, who stands beneath the banner of "brotherhood" surrounded by angels, reveals divine support for this vision.

QUESTIONS FOR ANALYSIS

1. How many different flags can you count and identify? What message do the flags send to viewers of the lithograph? Is this an image about nationalism or republicanism?
2. How would you characterize the types of people marching and the mood of the crowd? What does the composition of the crowd tell us about the gathered nations?
3. What do the angels, Statue of Liberty, and discarded crowns suggest about the artist's view of the events of 1848? Do you think this illustration was created before or after the collapse of the revolution in France? Why?

In the face of these coalitions, monarchs made hasty concessions. Soon, however, popular revolutionary fronts broke down as they had in France.

Compared with the situation in France, where political participation by working people reached its peak, revolts in central Europe tended to be dominated by social elites. They were also more sharply divided between moderate constitutionalists and radical republicans. The revolution in the Austrian Empire began in 1848 in Hungary, when nationalistic Hungarians demanded national autonomy, full civil liberties, and universal suffrage. When Viennese students and workers also took to the streets and peasant disorders broke out, the Habsburg emperor Ferdinand I (r. 1835–1848) capitulated and promised reforms and a liberal constitution. The coalition of revolutionaries was not stable, however. When the monarchy abolished serfdom, the

newly free peasants lost interest in the political and social questions agitating the cities.

The revolutionary coalition was also weakened and ultimately destroyed by conflicting national aspirations. In March the Hungarian revolutionary leaders pushed through an extremely liberal constitution, but they also sought to create a unified Hungarian nation. The minority groups, including Romanians, Serbs, and Croats, that formed half the population objected that such unification would hinder their own political autonomy and cultural independence. Likewise, Czech (CHEK) nationalists based in Bohemia and the city of Prague came into conflict with German nationalists. Thus nationalism within the Austrian Empire enabled the monarchy to play off one ethnic group against the other.

The monarchy's first breakthrough came in June when the army crushed a working-class revolt in Prague.

Street Fighting in Berlin, 1848 This contemporary lithograph portrays a street battle on March 18, 1848, between Prussian troops loyal to King Frederick William IV and civilian men and women demonstrators. The king withdrew his troops the following day rather than kill any more of his "beloved Berliners." Revolutionaries across Europe often dug up paving stones and used them as weapons. The tricolor flag achieved prominence during the revolution as the symbol of a united and democratic Germany. (akg-images)

In October the predominantly peasant troops of the regular Austrian army attacked the student and working-class radicals in Vienna and retook the city. When Ferdinand I abdicated in favor of his young nephew, Franz Joseph (see "Great Britain and the Austro-Hungarian Empire"), only Hungary had yet to be brought under control. Fearing the spread of liberal ideas to his realm, Nicholas I of Russia (r. 1825–1855) obligingly lent his support. In June 1849, 130,000 Russian troops poured into Hungary and subdued the country. For a number of years the Habsburgs ruled Hungary as a conquered territory.

After Austria, Prussia was the largest and most influential kingdom in the German Confederation. Prior to 1848 middle-class Prussian liberals had sought to reshape Prussia into a liberal constitutional monarchy, which would lead the confederation's thirty-eight states into a unified nation. When artisans and factory workers in Berlin exploded in revolt in March 1848 and joined with middle-class liberals against the monarchy, Prussian king Frederick William IV (r. 1840–1861) caved in. On March 21 he promised to grant Prussia a liberal constitution and to merge Prussia into a new national German state.

Elections were held across the German Confederation for a national parliament, which convened to write a federal constitution for a unified German state. Members of the new parliament completed drafting a liberal constitution in March 1849 and elected King Frederick William of Prussia emperor of the new German national state. By early 1849, however, Frederick William had reasserted his royal authority, contemptuously refusing to accept the "crown from the gutter." When Frederick William tried to get the small monarchs of Germany to elect him emperor on his own terms, with authoritarian power, Austria balked. Supported by Russia, Austria forced Prussia to renounce all its unification schemes in late 1850.

Thus, across Europe, the uprisings of 1848, which had been inspired by the legacy of the late-eighteenth-century revolutionary era, were unsuccessful. Reform movements splintered into competing factions, while the forces of order proved better organized and more united, on both a domestic and international level.

Nation Building in Italy, Germany, and Russia

How did strong leaders and nation building transform Italy, Germany, and Russia?

Louis Napoleon's triumph in 1848 and his authoritarian rule in the 1850s provided Europe's victorious forces of order with a new political model. To what extent might the expanding urban middle classes and even portions of the working classes rally to a strong and essentially conservative national state that also promised change? This was one of the great political questions in the 1850s and 1860s. In central Europe a resounding answer came with the national unification of Germany and Italy. (See "Global Viewpoints: German and Italian Views on Nationalism," page 702.)

The Russian Empire also experienced profound political crises in this period, but they were unlike those in Germany or Italy because Russia was already a vast multinational state. It became clear to Russian leaders that they had to embrace the process of **modernization**, defined narrowly as the changes that enable a country to compete effectively with the leading countries at a given time.

Cavour, Garibaldi, and the Unification of Italy

Italy had never been a united nation prior to 1850. A battleground for the Great Powers after 1494, Italy was reorganized in 1815 at the Congress of Vienna. Austria received the rich northern provinces of Lombardy and Venetia (vih-NEE-shuh). Sardinia and Piedmont fell under the rule of an Italian monarch, and Tuscany shared north-central Italy with several smaller states. The papacy ruled over central Italy and Rome, while a branch of the Bourbons ruled Naples and Sicily (Map 24.2).

After 1815 the goal of a unified Italian nation captivated many Italians, but there was no agreement on how it could be achieved. In 1848 the efforts of idealistic nationalist Giuseppe Mazzini (joo-ZEP-pay maht-SEE-nee) to form a democratic Italian republic were crushed by Austrian forces. Temporarily driven from Rome during the upheavals of 1848, a frightened Pope Pius IX (pontificate 1846–1878) turned against most modern trends, including national unification. At the same time, Victor Emmanuel, king of independent Sardinia, retained the moderate liberal constitution granted under duress in March 1848. To the Italian middle classes, Sardinia (see Map 24.2) appeared to be a liberal, progressive state ideally suited to drive Austria out of northern Italy and achieve the goal of national unification.

Sardinia had the good fortune of being led by Count Camillo Benso di Cavour. Cavour's national goals were limited and realistic. Cavour came from a noble family and embraced the economic doctrines and business activities associated with the prosperous middle class. Until 1859 he sought unity only for the states of northern and perhaps central Italy in a greatly expanded kingdom of Sardinia.

---

modernization The changes that enable a country to compete effectively with the leading countries at a given time.

German and Italian Views on Nationalism

German philosopher Johann Gottfried von Herder's *Ideas for the Philosophy of History of Humanity* (1784–1791) described the long evolution of human communities. According to Herder, this process had produced distinct national communities in Europe, each united by a common language and shared traditions. Herder respected these cultural traditions but did not believe they should lead to distinct nation-states. Instead he celebrated the common spirit that existed among Europeans based on their centuries-old history of interaction. By contrast, Giuseppe Mazzini, the leading prophet of Italian nationalism before 1848, believed fervently that nations should exist as sovereign states. He founded a secret society to fight for the unification of the Italian states in a democratic republic. The excerpt below was written in 1858 and addressed to Italian workingmen.

Johann Gottfried von Herder, *Ideas for the Philosophy of History of Humanity*

■ This is more or less a picture of the peoples of Europe. What a multicolored and composite picture! . . . Sea voyages and long migrations of people finally produced on the small continent of Europe the conditions for a great league of nations. Unwittingly the Romans had prepared it by their conquests. Such a league of nations was unthinkable outside of Europe. Nowhere else have people intermingled so much, nowhere else have they changed so often and so much their habitats and thereby their customs and ways of life. In many European countries it would be difficult today for the inhabitants, especially for single families and individuals, to say, from which people they descend, whether from Goths, Moors, Jews, Carthaginians or Romans, whether from Gauls, Burgundians, Franks, Normans, Saxons, Slavs, Finns or Illyrians, or how in the long line of their ancestors their blood had been mixed. Hundreds of causes have tempered and changed the old tribal composition of the European nations in the course of the centuries; without such an intermingling the common spirit of Europe could hardly have been awakened.

Giuseppe Mazzini, "Duties Towards Your Country"

■ God gave you the means of multiplying your forces and your powers of action indefinitely when he gave you a Country, when, like a wise overseer of labor, who distributes the different parts of the work according to the capacity of the workmen, he divided Humanity into distinct groups upon the face of our globe, and thus planted the seeds of nations. Evil governments have disfigured the design of God, which you may see clearly marked out, as far, at least, as regards Europe, by the courses of the great rivers, by the lines of the lofty mountains, and by other geographical conditions; they have disfigured it by conquest, by greed, by jealousy of the just sovereignty of others; disfigured it so much that today there is perhaps no nation except England and France whose confines correspond to this design.

[These evil governments] did not, and they do not, recognize any country except their own families and dynasties, the egoism of caste. But the divine design will infallibly be fulfilled. Natural divisions, the innate spontaneous tendencies of the peoples will replace the arbitrary divisions sanctioned by evil governments. The map of Europe will be remade. The Countries of the People will rise, defined by the voice of the free, upon the ruins of the Countries of Kings and privileged castes. . . .

Without Country you have neither name, voice, nor rights, no admissions as brothers into the fellowships of the Peoples. You are the bastards of Humanity. Soldiers without a banner, . . . you will find neither faith nor protection. . . . Do not beguile yourselves with the hope of emancipation from unjust social conditions if you do not first conquer a Country for yourselves; where there is no Country there is no common agreement to which you can appeal; . . . and he who has the upper hand keeps it, since there is no common safeguard for the interests of all.

QUESTIONS FOR ANALYSIS

1. How does Herder describe the "common spirit" of Europe, and what is his explanation for how it came into being?
2. How does Mazzini explain and justify the existence of individual countries (or nations)? According to Mazzini, why have Italians been prevented from having their own nation, and why is it so important that they obtain one?
3. How would you compare the views of Herder and Mazzini?

Sources: Hans Kohn, *Nationalism: Its Idea and History* (Princeton, N.J.: D. Van Nostrand Company, 1955), pp. 108–110; G. Mazzini, *The Duties of Man and Other Essays* (London: M. M. Dent and Sons, 1907), pp. 51–54.

MAP 24.2 The Unification of Italy, 1859–1870
The leadership of Sardinia-Piedmont, nationalist fervor, and Garibaldi's attack on the Kingdom of the Two Sicilies were decisive factors in the unification of Italy.

In the 1850s Cavour worked to consolidate Sardinia as a liberal constitutional state capable of leading northern Italy. He entered a secret alliance with Napoleon III, and in July 1858 he goaded Austria into attacking Sardinia. The combined Franco-Sardinian forces were victorious, but Napoleon III decided on a compromise peace with the Austrians in July 1859 to avoid offending French Catholics by supporting an enemy of the pope. Sardinia would receive only Lombardy, the area around Milan. Cavour resigned in protest.

Popular revolts and Italian nationalism salvaged Cavour's plans. While the war against Austria raged in the north, dedicated nationalists in central Italy had risen and driven out their rulers. Cavour returned to power in early 1860, and the people of central Italy voted overwhelmingly to join a greatly enlarged kingdom of Sardinia. Cavour had achieved his original goal of a north Italian state (see Map 24.2).

For superpatriots such as Giuseppe Garibaldi (1807–1882), the job of unification was still only half done. A poor sailor's son, Garibaldi personified the romantic revolutionary nationalism of 1848. Having led a unit of volunteers to several victories over Austrian troops in 1859, Garibaldi emerged in 1860 as an independent force in Italian politics. (See "Individuals in Society: Giuseppe Garibaldi," page 704.)

Secretly supported by Cavour, Garibaldi landed on the shores of Sicily in May 1860. His guerrilla band captured the imagination of the Sicilian peasantry, which rose in rebellion. Garibaldi captured Palermo and crossed to the mainland. When Garibaldi and Victor Emmanuel rode through Naples to cheering crowds, they symbolically sealed the union of north and south, of monarch and people.

The new kingdom of Italy, which did not include Venice until 1866 or Rome until 1870, was a parliamentary monarchy under Victor Emmanuel, neither radical nor democratic. Only a small minority of Italian males could vote. Despite political unity, the propertied classes and the common people were divided. A great social and cultural gap separated the industrializing north from the agrarian south.

INDIVIDUALS IN SOCIETY

Giuseppe Garibaldi

WHEN GIUSEPPE GARIBALDI VISITED ENGLAND in 1864, he received the most triumphant welcome ever given to any foreigner. Honored and fêted by politicians and high society, he also captivated the masses. An unprecedented crowd of a half million people cheered his carriage through the streets of London. These ovations were no fluke. In his time, Garibaldi was probably the most famous and most beloved figure in the world.* How could this be?

A rare combination of wild adventure and extraordinary achievement partly accounted for his demigod status. Born in Nice, Garibaldi went to sea at fifteen and sailed the Mediterranean for twelve years. At seventeen his travels took him to Rome, and he was converted in an almost religious experience to the "New Italy, the Italy of all the Italians." As he later wrote in his bestselling *Autobiography*, "The Rome that I beheld with the eyes of youthful imagination was the Rome of the future—the dominant thought of my whole life."

Sentenced to death in 1834 for his part in a revolutionary uprising in Genoa, Garibaldi barely escaped to South America. For twelve years he led a guerrilla band in Uruguay's struggle for independence from Argentina. "Shipwrecked, ambushed, shot through the neck," he found in a tough young woman, Anna da Silva, a mate and companion in arms. Their first children nearly starved in the jungle while Garibaldi, clad in his long red shirt, fashioned a legend as a fearless freedom fighter.

After he returned to Italy in 1848, the campaigns of his patriotic volunteers against the Austrians in 1848 and 1859 mobilized democratic nationalists. The stage was set for his volunteer army to liberate Sicily against enormous odds, astonishing the world and creating a large Italian state. Garibaldi's achievement matched his legend.

A brilliant fighter, the handsome and inspiring leader was an uncompromising idealist of absolute integrity. He never drew personal profit from his exploits, continuing to milk his goats and rarely possessing more than one change of clothing. When Victor Emmanuel offered him lands and titles after his great victory in 1860, even as the left-leaning volunteers were disbanded and humiliated, Garibaldi declined, saying he could not be bought off. Returning to his farm on a tiny rocky island, he denounced the government without hesitation when he concluded that it was betraying the dream of unification with its ruthless rule in the south.

Giuseppe Garibaldi, the charismatic leader, shown in a portrait painted in 1850.

(*Giuseppe Garibaldi*, 1850, by Auguste Etienne [1794–1865] [oil on panel]/Musée de l'Armée, Paris, France/akg-images)

Yet even after a duplicitous Italian government caused two later attacks on Rome to fail, his faith in the generative power of national unity never wavered. Garibaldi showed that ideas and ideals count in history.

Above all, millions of ordinary men and women identified with Garibaldi because they believed that he was fighting for them. They recognized him as one of their own and saw that he remained true to them in spite of his triumphs, thereby ennobling their own lives and aspirations. Welcoming runaway slaves as equals in Latin America, advocating the emancipation of women, introducing social reforms in the south, and pressing for free education and a broader suffrage in the new Italy, Garibaldi the national hero fought for freedom and human dignity. The common people understood and loved him for it.

QUESTIONS FOR ANALYSIS

1. Why was Garibaldi so famous and popular?
2. Nationalism evolved and developed in the nineteenth century. How did Garibaldi fit into this evolution? What kind of a nationalist was he?

*Denis Mack Smith, *Garibaldi: A Great Life in Brief* (New York: Alfred A. Knopf, 1956), pp. 136–147; Denis Mack Smith, "Giuseppe Garibaldi," *History Today*, August 1991, pp. 20–26.

MAP 24.3 The Unification of Germany, 1866–1871 This map shows how Prussia expanded and a new German Empire was created through two wars, the Austro-Prussian War of 1866 and the Franco-Prussian War of 1870–1871.

Bismarck and German Unification

In the aftermath of 1848 the German states, particularly Austria and Prussia, were locked in a political stalemate, each seeking to block the power of the other within the German Confederation. At the same time, powerful economic forces were undermining the political status quo. Modern industry was growing rapidly within the German customs union, or *Zollverein*. By 1853 all the German states except Austria had joined the customs union, and a new Germany excluding Austria was becoming an economic reality. Rising prosperity from the rapid growth of industrialization after 1850 gave new impetus to middle-class liberals.

By 1859 liberals had assumed control of the parliament that emerged from the upheavals of 1848 in Prussia. The national uprising in Italy in 1859, however, convinced Prussia's tough-minded Wilhelm I (r. 1861–1888) that political change and even war with Austria or France was possible. Wilhelm I pushed to raise taxes and increase the defense budget to double the army's size. The Prussian parliament, reflecting the middle class's desire for a less militaristic society, rejected the military budget in 1862, and the liberals triumphed in new elections. King Wilhelm then called on Count Otto von Bismarck (1815–1898) to head a new ministry and defy the parliament.

Born into the Prussian landowning aristocracy, Bismarck (BIZ-mark) loved power, but he was also extraordinarily flexible and pragmatic in pursuing his goals. When Bismarck took office as chief minister in 1862, he declared that government would rule without parliamentary consent. Bismarck had the Prussian bureaucracy continue to collect taxes even though the parliament refused to approve the budget, and he reorganized the army. For their part, the voters of Prussia continued to express their opposition to Bismarck's policies by sending large liberal majorities to the parliament from 1862 to 1866.

In 1866 Bismarck launched the Austro-Prussian War with the intent of expelling Austria from German politics. The war lasted only seven weeks, as the reorganized Prussian army defeated Austria decisively. Bismarck forced Austria to withdraw from German affairs and dissolved the existing German Confederation. The mainly Protestant states north of the Main River were grouped in the new North German Confederation, led by an expanded Prussia (Map 24.3, page 705). Each state retained its own local government, but the federal government—Wilhelm I and Bismarck—controlled the army and foreign affairs.

To make peace with the liberal middle class and the nationalist movement, Bismarck asked the Prussian parliament to approve after the fact all the government's "illegal" spending between 1862 and 1866. Overawed by Bismarck's achievements, middle-class liberals now jumped at the chance to cooperate, opting for national unity and military glory over the battle for truly liberal institutions. Bismarck also followed Napoleon III's example by creating a legislature with members of the lower house elected by universal male suffrage, allowing him to bypass the middle class and appeal directly to the people if necessary. The constitutional struggle in Prussia was over, and the German middle class was respectfully accepting the monarchical authority and aristocratic superiority that Bismarck represented.

The final act in the drama of German unification followed quickly with a patriotic war against France. The apparent issue—whether a distant relative of Prussia's Wilhelm I might become king of Spain—was only a diplomatic pretext. By 1870, alarmed by Prussia's growing power, French leaders had decided on a war to teach Prussia a lesson.

As soon as war against France began in 1870, Bismarck had the wholehearted support of the south German states. The Germans quickly defeated Louis Napoleon's armies at Sedan on September 1, 1870. Three days later French patriots in Paris proclaimed yet another French republic and vowed to continue fighting. But after five months, in January 1871, a starv-

ing Paris surrendered, and France accepted Bismarck's harsh peace terms. By this time the south German states had agreed to join a new German Empire.

The Franco-Prussian War released an enormous surge of patriotic feeling in Germany. The new German Empire had become Europe's most powerful state, and most Germans were enormously proud. Semi-authoritarian nationalism and a "new conservatism," which was based on an alliance of the propertied classes and sought the active support of the working classes, had triumphed in Germany.

The Modernization of Russia

In the 1850s Russia was a poor agrarian society with a rapidly growing population. Almost 90 percent of the population lived off the land, and serfdom was still the basic social institution. Then the Crimean War of 1853 to 1856 arose from the breakdown of the balance of power established at the Congress of Vienna, European competition over influence in the Middle East, and Russian desires to expand into European territories held by the Ottoman Empire. France and Great Britain, aided by Sardinia and the Ottoman Empire, inflicted a humiliating defeat on Russia.

Russia's military defeat showed that it had fallen behind the industrializing nations of western Europe. Moreover, the war had caused hardship and raised the specter of massive peasant rebellion. Military disaster thus forced the new tsar, Alexander II (r. 1855–1881), and his ministers along the path of rapid social change and general modernization.

The Crimean War, 1853–1856

The first and greatest of the reforms was the freeing of the serfs in 1861. The emancipated peasants received, on average, about half of the land, which was to be collectively owned by peasant villages. The prices for the land were high, and collective ownership limited the possibilities of agricultural improvement and migration to urban areas. Thus the effects of the reform were limited. More successful was reform of the legal system, which established independent courts and equality before the law. The government also relaxed censorship and partially liberalized policies toward Russian Jews.

Russia's greatest strides toward modernization were economic rather than political. Rapid, government-subsidized railroad construction to 1880 enabled agricultural Russia to export grain and thus earn money for further industrialization. Industrial suburbs grew up around Moscow and St. Petersburg, and a class of modern factory workers began to take shape. Russia began seizing territory in far eastern Siberia, on the border with China; in Central Asia, north of Afghanistan; and in the Islamic lands of the Caucasus.

In 1881 an anarchist assassinated Alexander II, and the reform era came to an abrupt end. Political modernization remained frozen until 1905, but economic modernization sped forward in the massive industrial surge of the 1890s. The key leader was Sergei Witte (suhr-GAY VIH-tuh), the energetic minister of finance. Under Witte's leadership, the government doubled Russia's railroad network by the end of the century and promoted Russian industry with high protective tariffs.

By 1900 Russia was catching up with western Europe and expanding its empire in Asia. By 1903 Russia had established a sphere of influence in Chinese Manchuria and was eyeing northern Korea. When the protests of equally imperialistic Japan were ignored, the Japanese launched a surprise attack on Russian forces in Manchuria in February 1904. After Japan scored repeated victories, Russia was forced in September 1905 to accept a humiliating defeat.

Military disaster in East Asia brought political upheaval at home. On January 22, 1905, workers peacefully protesting for improved working conditions and higher wages were attacked by the tsar's troops outside the Winter Palace. This event, known as Bloody Sunday, set off a wave of strikes, peasant uprisings, and troop mutinies across Russia. The revolutionary surge culminated in October 1905 in a paralyzing general strike, which forced the government to capitulate. The

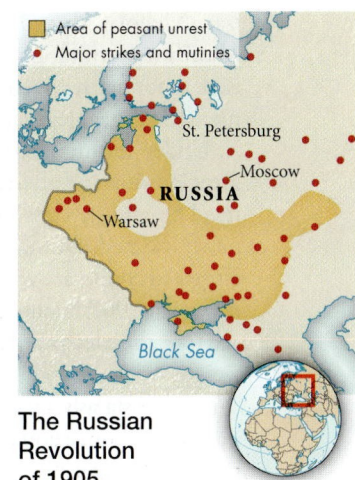

The Russian Revolution of 1905

Bloody Sunday, Russia, 1905 On January 22, 1905, Russian troops fired on striking workers who had peacefully assembled in front of the Winter Palace in St. Petersburg, hoping to present their grievances to the tsar. Over a hundred demonstrators died and many hundreds more were injured in the ensuing massacre. The event, known as Bloody Sunday, helped rouse resistance to the imperial government. (Laski Diffusion/Newsmakers/Getty Images) tsar, Nicholas II (r. 1894–1917), issued the **October Manifesto**, which granted full civil rights and promised a popularly elected Duma (DOO-muh) (parliament) with real legislative power.

Under the new constitution, Nicholas II retained great powers and the Duma had only limited authority. The middle-class liberals, the largest group in the newly elected Duma, were badly disappointed, and efforts to cooperate with the tsar's ministers soon broke down. In 1907 Nicholas II and his reactionary advisers rewrote the electoral law so as to greatly increase the weight of the propertied classes. On the eve of World War I, Russia was a partially modernized nation, a conservative constitutional monarchy with an agrarian but industrializing economy.

Urban Life in the Age of Ideologies

What was the impact of urban growth on cities, social classes, families, and ideas?

By 1900 western Europe was urban and industrial as surely as it had been rural and agrarian in 1800. Rapid urban growth in the nineteenth century worsened long-standing overcrowding and unhealthy living conditions, lending support to voices calling for revolutionary change. In response, government leaders, city planners, reformers, and scientists urgently sought solutions to these challenges. Over the long term, success in improving the urban environment and the introduction of social welfare measures encouraged people to put their faith in a responsive national state.

Urban Development

Since the Middle Ages, European cities had been centers of government, culture, and large-scale commerce. They had also been congested, dirty, and unhealthy. Industrialization greatly worsened these conditions. The steam engine freed industrialists from dependence on the energy of streams and rivers so that by 1800 there was every incentive to build new factories in cities, which had better shipping facilities and a large and ready workforce. Therefore, as industry grew, overcrowded and unhealthy cities expanded rapidly.

In the 1820s and 1830s people in Britain and France began to worry about the condition of their cities. Parks and open areas were almost nonexistent, and narrow houses were built wall to wall in long

rows. Highly concentrated urban populations lived in extremely unsanitary conditions, with open drains and sewers flowing alongside or down the middle of unpaved streets. Infected water contributed to a European cholera epidemic in 1831–1832, killing hundreds of thousands and contributing to social unrest.

The urban challenge—and the pressure of radical ideas including those of the revolutions of 1848—eventually brought an energetic response from a generation of reformers. The most famous early reformer was Edwin Chadwick, a British official. Collecting detailed reports from local officials and publishing his findings in 1842, Chadwick concluded that the stinking excrement of communal outhouses could be carried off by water through sewers at less than one-twentieth the cost of removing it by hand. In 1848 Chadwick's report became the basis of Great Britain's first public health law, which created a national health board and gave cities broad authority to build modern sanitary systems. Such sanitary movements won dedicated supporters in the United States, France, and Germany from the 1840s on.

Early sanitary reformers were handicapped by the prevailing miasmatic theory of disease—the belief that people contract disease when they breathe foul odors. In the 1840s and 1850s keen observation by doctors and public health officials suggested that contagion spread through physical contact with filth and not by its odors, thus weakening the miasmatic idea. An understanding of how this occurred came out of the work of Louis Pasteur (1822–1895), who developed the **germ theory** of disease. By 1870 the work of Pasteur and others had demonstrated that specific living organisms caused specific diseases and that those organisms could be controlled. These discoveries led to the development of a number of effective vaccines. Surgeons also applied the germ theory in hospitals, sterilizing not only the wound but everything else that entered the operating room.

The achievements of the bacterial revolution coupled with the public health movement saved millions of lives, particularly after about 1890. In England, France, and Germany death rates declined dramatically, and diphtheria, typhoid, typhus, cholera, and yellow fever became vanishing diseases in the industrializing nations.

More effective urban planning after 1850 also improved the quality of urban life. France took the lead during the rule of Napoleon III (r. 1848–1870), who believed that rebuilding Paris would provide employment, improve living conditions, and glorify and strengthen his empire. Baron Georges Haussmann (HOWSS-mun) (1809–1884), whom Napoleon III placed in charge of Paris, destroyed the old medieval core of Paris to create broad tree-lined boulevards, long

October Manifesto The result of a great general strike in Russia in October 1905, it granted full civil rights and promised a popularly elected Duma (parliament) with real legislative power.

germ theory The idea that disease is caused by the spread of living organisms that can be controlled.

Buenos Aires Postcard, ca. 1908 Between 1880 and 1910 the modern city of Buenos Aires, the capital of Argentina, emerged. City planners adopted the wide boulevards, monuments, and long vistas that Baron Haussmann had brought to Paris in the mid-nineteenth century. (© Mary Evans Picture Library/Grenville Collins Postcard Collection/The Image Works)

open vistas, monumental buildings, middle-class housing, parks, and improved sewers and aqueducts. In addition to easing traffic and providing impressive vistas, the broad boulevards were intended to prevent a recurrence of the easy construction and defense of barricades by revolutionary crowds that had occurred in 1848. The rebuilding of Paris stimulated urban development throughout Europe, particularly after 1870.

Mass public transportation was also of great importance in the improvement of urban living conditions. In the 1890s countries in North America and Europe adopted an American transit innovation, the electric streetcar. Millions of riders hopped on board during the workweek. On weekends and holidays streetcars carried city people on outings to parks and the countryside, racetracks, and music halls.[1] Electric streetcars also gave people of modest means access to improved housing, as the still-crowded city was able to expand and become less congested.

Industrialization and the growth of global trade led to urbanization outside of Europe. The tremendous appetite of industrializing nations for raw materials, food, and other goods caused the rapid growth of port cities and mining centers across the world. These included Alexandria in Egypt, the major port for trans-porting Egyptian cotton, and mining cities like San Francisco in California and Johannesburg in South Africa. Many of these new cities consciously emulated European urban planning. For example, from 1880 to 1910 the Argentine capital of Buenos Aires modernized rapidly. The development of Buenos Aires was greatly stimulated by the arrival of many Italian and Spanish immigrants, part of a much larger wave of European migration in this period (see "Immigration" in Chapter 27).

Social Inequality and Class

By 1850 at the latest, the wages and living conditions of the working classes were finally improving. Greater economic rewards, however, did not significantly narrow the gap between rich and poor. In fact, economic inequality worsened in Europe over the course of the nineteenth century and reached its height on the eve of World War I. In every industrialized country around 1900, the richest 20 percent of households received anywhere from 50 to 60 percent of all national income, whereas the bottom 30 percent of households received 10 percent or less of all income. Despite the promises of the political and economic revolutions of the late

Hudson's Soap Advertising Postcard, ca. 1903 Early-twentieth-century advertisements, such as this one for Hudson's Soap, reflected the strict class divisions of society.
(Collection/REX/Shutterstock)

eighteenth century, the gap between rich and poor in the early twentieth century was thus as great as or even wider than it had been in the eighteenth-century age of agriculture and aristocracy.

Despite extreme social inequality, society had not split into two sharply defined opposing classes, as Marx had predicted. Instead economic specialization created an almost unlimited range of jobs, skills, and earnings; one group or subclass blended into another in a complex, confusing hierarchy.

Between the tiny elite of the very rich and the sizable mass of the dreadfully poor existed a range of subclasses, each filled with individuals struggling to rise or at least to hold their own in the social order. A confederation of middle classes was loosely linked by occupations requiring mental, rather than physical, skill. As the upper middle class, composed mainly of successful business families, gained in income and progressively lost all traces of radicalism after the trauma of 1848, they were drawn toward the aristocratic lifestyle.

One step below was a much larger group of moderately successful industrialists and merchants, professionals in law and medicine, and midlevel managers of large public and private institutions. The expansion

of industry and technology called for experts with specialized knowledge, and the most valuable of the specialties became solid middle-class professions. Next came independent shopkeepers, small traders, and tiny manufacturers — the lower middle class. Industrialization and urbanization also diversified the lower middle class and expanded the number of white-collar employees. White-collar employees were propertyless, but generally they were fiercely committed to the middle class and to the ideal of moving up in society.

Food, housing, clothes, and behavior all expressed middle-class values. Employment of at least one full-time maid was the clearest sign that a family had crossed the divide from the working classes into the middle classes. Freed from domestic labor, the middle-class wife directed her servants, supervised her children's education, and used her own appearance and that of her home to display the family's status. The middle classes shared a code of expected behavior and morality, which stressed hard work, self-discipline, and personal achievement.

At the beginning of the twentieth century about four out of five Europeans belonged to the working classes — that is, people whose livelihoods depended primarily on physical labor. Many of them were small landowning peasants and hired farm hands, especially in eastern Europe. The urban working classes were even less unified than the middle classes. Economic development and increased specialization during the nineteenth century expanded the traditional range of working-class skills, earnings, and experiences. Skilled, semiskilled, and unskilled workers accordingly developed widely divergent lifestyles and cultural values, and their differences contributed to a keen sense of social status and hierarchy within the working classes.

Highly skilled workers, who made up about 15 percent of the working classes, became known as the labor aristocracy. They were led by construction bosses and factory foremen. The labor aristocracy also included members of the traditional highly skilled handicraft trades that had not transitioned to mechanized production, as well as new kinds of skilled workers such as shipbuilders and railway locomotive engineers.

Below the labor aristocracy stood the complex world of semiskilled and unskilled urban workers. A large number of the semiskilled were factory workers who earned good wages and whose relative importance in the labor force was increasing. Below the semiskilled workers was a larger group of unskilled workers that included day laborers and domestic servants.

To make ends meet, many working-class wives had to join the ranks of working women in the "sweated industries." These industries resembled the old putting-out and cottage industries of earlier times, and they were similar to what we call sweatshops today. The women normally worked at home and were paid by the piece, often making clothing after the advent of the sewing machine in the 1850s.

Despite their harsh lives, the urban working classes found outlets for fun and recreation. Across Europe drinking remained a favorite working-class leisure-time activity along with sports and music halls. Religion continued to provide working people with solace and meaning, although church attendance among the urban working classes declined in the late nineteenth century, especially among men.

The Changing Family

Industrialization and the growth of modern cities also brought great changes to the lives of women and families. As economic conditions improved, only women in poor families tended to work outside the home. The ideal became separate spheres, the strict division of labor by sex. This rigid division meant that married women faced great obstacles if they needed or wanted to move into the world of paid employment outside the home. Well-paying jobs were off-limits to women, and a woman's wage was almost always less than a man's, even for the same work.

Because they needed to be able to support their wives, middle-class men did not marry until they were well established in their careers. The system encouraged marriages between older men and younger women with little experience with adult life. Men were encouraged to see themselves as the protectors of their fragile and vulnerable wives.

As the ideology and practice of rigidly separate spheres narrowed women's horizons, their control and influence in the home became increasingly strong throughout Europe in the late nineteenth century. The comfortable home run by the middle-class wife was idealized as a warm shelter in a hard and impersonal urban world. By 1900 working-class families had adopted many middle-class values, but they did not have the means to fully realize the ideals of domestic comfort or separate spheres. Nevertheless, the working-class wife generally determined how the family's money was spent and took charge of all major domestic decisions. The woman's guidance of the household went hand in hand with the increased emotional importance of home and family for all social groups.

Ideas about sexuality within marriage varied. Many French marriage manuals of the late nineteenth century stressed that women had legitimate sexual needs. In the more puritanical United States, however, sex manuals recommended sexual abstinence for unmarried men and limited sexual activity for married men. Respectable women were thought to experience no sexual pleasure at all from sexual activity, and anything vaguely sexual was to be removed from their surroundings; even the legs of pianos were to be covered. (See "Analyzing the Evidence: Stefan Zweig on Middle-Class Youth and Sexuality," page 712.)

Medical doctors in both Europe and the United States began to study sexual desires and behavior more closely, and to determine what was considered "normal" and "abnormal." Same-sex attraction, labeled "homosexuality" for the first time, was identified as a "perversion." Governments increasingly regulated prostitution, the treatment of venereal disease, and access to birth control in ways that were shaped by class and gender hierarchies. Medical science also turned its attention to motherhood, and a wave of books instructed middle-class women on how to be better mothers.

Ideas about sexuality and motherhood were inextricably tied up with ideas about race. As European nations embarked on imperialist expansion in the second half of the nineteenth century, the need to maintain the racial superiority that justified empire led to increased concerns about the possible dilution or weakening of the European races. Maintaining healthy bodies, restricting sexuality, preventing interracial marriages, and ensuring that women properly raised

Stefan Zweig on Middle-Class Youth and Sexuality

Growing up in Vienna in a prosperous Jewish family, Stefan Zweig (1881–1942) became an influential voice calling for humanitarian values and international culture in early-twentieth-century Europe. Passionately opposed to the First World War, Zweig wrote poetry, plays, and novels. But he was most famous for his biographies: shrewd psychological portraits of historical figures such as Magellan and Marie Antoinette. After Hitler came to power in 1933, Zweig lived in exile until his death in 1942. Zweig's last work was *The World of Yesterday* (1943), one of the truly fascinating autobiographies of the twentieth century. In the following passage, Zweig recalls the romantic experiences and sexual separation of middle-class youth before the First World War.

■ During the eight years of our higher schooling [beyond grade school], something had occurred which was of great importance to each one of us: we ten-year-olds had grown into virile young men of sixteen, seventeen, and eighteen, and Nature began to assert its rights. . . . It did not take us long to discover that those authorities in whom we had previously confided—school, family, and public morals—manifested an astonishing insincerity in this matter of sex. But what is more, they also demanded secrecy and reserve from us in this connection. . . .

This "social morality," which on the one hand privately presupposed the existence of sexuality and its natural course, but on the other would not recognize it openly at any price, was doubly deceitful. While it winked one eye at a young man and even encouraged him with the other "to sow his wild oats," as the kindly language of the home put it, in the case of a woman it studiously shut both eyes and acted as if it were blind. That a man could experience desires, and was permitted to experience them, was silently admitted by custom. But to admit frankly that a woman could be subject to similar desires, or that creation for its eternal purposes also required a female polarity, would have transgressed the conception of the "sanctity of womanhood." In the pre-Freudian era, therefore, the axiom was agreed upon that a female person could have no physical desires as long as they had not been awakened by man, and that, obviously, was officially permitted only in marriage. But even in those moral times, in Vienna in particular, the air was full of dangerous erotic infection, and a girl of good family had to live in a completely sterilized atmosphere, from the day of her birth until the day when she left the altar on her husband's arm. In order to protect young girls, they were not left alone for a single moment. . . . Every book which they read was inspected, and above all else, young girls were constantly kept busy to divert their attention from any possible dangerous thoughts. They had to practise the piano, learn singing and drawing, foreign languages, and the history of literature and art. They were educated and overeducated. But while the aim was to make them as educated and as socially correct as possible, at the same time society anxiously took great pains that they should remain innocent of all natural things to a degree unthinkable today. A young girl of good family was not allowed to have any idea of how the male body was formed, or to know how children came into the world, for the angel was to enter into matrimony not only physically untouched, but completely "pure" spiritually as well. "Good breeding," for a young girl of that time, was identical with ignorance of life; and this ignorance ofttimes lasted for the rest of their lives. . . .

What possibilities actually existed for a young man of the middle-class world? In all the others, in the so-called lower classes, the problem was no problem at all. . . . In most of our Alpine villages the number of natural children greatly exceeded the legitimate ones. Among the proletariat, the worker, before he could get married, lived with another worker in free love. . . . It was only in our middle-class society that such a remedy as an early marriage was scorned. . . . And so there was an artificial interval of six, eight, or ten years between actual manhood and manhood as society accepted it; and in this interval the young man had to take care of his own "affairs" or adventures.

their children were all components of racial strength, in the eyes of many European thinkers.

Women in industrializing countries also began to limit the number of children they bore. This revolutionary reduction in family size, in which the comfortable and well-educated classes took the lead, was founded on parents' desire to improve their economic and social position and that of their children. By having fewer youngsters, parents could give those they had advantages, from music lessons to expensive university educations.

The ideal of separate spheres and the rigid gender division of labor meant that middle-class women lacked legal rights and faced discrimination in education and employment. Organizations founded by middle-class feminists campaigned for legal equality as

Those days did not give him too many opportunities. Only a very few particularly rich young men could afford the luxury of keeping a mistress, that is, taking an apartment and paying her expenses. And only a very few fortunate young men achieved the literary ideal of love of the times—the only one which it was permitted to describe in novels—an affair with a married woman. The others helped themselves for the most part with shopgirls and waitresses, and this offered little inner satisfaction. . . . But, generally speaking, prostitution was still the foundation of the erotic life outside of marriage; in a certain sense it constituted a dark underground vault over which rose the gorgeous structure of middle-class society with its faultless, radiant façade.

The present generation has hardly any idea of the gigantic extent of prostitution in Europe before the [First] World War. Whereas today it is as rare to meet a prostitute on the streets of a big city as it is to meet a wagon in the road, then the sidewalks were so sprinkled with women for sale that it was more difficult to avoid than to find them. To this was added the countless number of "closed houses," the night clubs, the cabarets, the dance parlours with their dancers and singers, and the bars with their "come-on" girls. At that time female wares were offered for sale at every hour and at every price. . . . And this was the same city, the same society, the same morality, that was indignant when young girls rode bicycles, and declared it a disgrace to the dignity of science when Freud in his calm, clear, and penetrating manner established truths that they did not wish to be true. The same world that so pathetically defended the purity of womanhood allowed this cruel sale of women, organized it, and even profited thereby.

We should not permit ourselves to be misled by sentimental novels or stories of that epoch. It was a bad time for youth. The young girls were hermetically locked up under the control of the family, hindered in their free bodily as well as intellectual development. The young men were forced to secrecy and reticence by a morality which fundamentally no one believed or obeyed. Unhampered, honest relationships—in other words, all that could have made youth happy and joyous according to the laws of Nature—were permitted only to the very few.

QUESTIONS FOR ANALYSIS

1. According to Zweig, how did the sex lives of young middle-class women and young middle-class men differ? What accounted for these differences?
2. What were the differences between the sex lives of the middle class and those of the so-called lower classes? What was Zweig's opinion of these differences?
3. Zweig ends with a value judgment: "It was a bad time for youth." Do you agree or disagree? Why?

Source: Excerpts from *World of Yesterday* by Stefan Zweig, translated by Helmut Ripperger and B. W. Huebsch, translation copyright 1943, renewed © 1971 by the Viking Press, Inc. Used by permission of Viking Books, an imprint of Penguin Publishing Group, a division of Penguin Random House LLC. All rights reserved. Any third party use of this material, outside of this publication, is prohibited. Interested parties must apply directly to Penguin Random House LLC for permission.

well as for access to higher education and professional employment. In the late nineteenth century middle-class women scored some significant victories, such as the 1882 law giving British married women full property rights. Rather than contesting existing notions of women as morally superior guardians of the home, feminists drew on these ideas for legitimacy in speaking out about social issues.

Socialist women leaders usually took a different path. They argued that the liberation of working-class women would come only with the liberation of the entire working class. In the meantime, they championed the cause of working women and won some practical improvements. In a general way, these different approaches to women's issues reflected the diversity of classes and political views in urban society.

Paris Brothel, ca. 1900
This photograph of a Parisian brothel at the turn of the twentieth century shows the efforts made to create a luxurious and glamorous atmosphere for its patrons. (Musée de la Ville de Paris, Musée Carnavalet, Paris, France/Archives Charmet/Bridgeman Images)

Science for the Masses

Breakthroughs in industrial technology stimulated basic scientific inquiry as researchers sought to explain how such things as steam engines and blast furnaces actually worked. The result from the 1830s onward was an explosive growth of fundamental scientific discoveries that were increasingly transformed into material improvements for the general population.

A perfect example of the translation of better scientific knowledge into practical human benefits was the development of the branch of physics known as thermodynamics, the study of the relationship between heat and mechanical energy. By midcentury physicists had formulated the fundamental laws of thermodynamics, which were then applied to mechanical engineering, chemical processes, and many other fields. Electricity was transformed from a curiosity in 1800 to a commercial form of energy. (See "Thinking Like a Historian: The Promise of Electricity," page 716.) By 1890 the internal combustion engine fueled by petroleum was an emerging competitor to steam and electricity.

Everyday experience and innumerable articles in newspapers and magazines impressed the importance of science on the popular mind. The methods of science acquired unrivaled prestige after 1850. Many educated people came to believe that the union of careful experiment and abstract theory was the only reliable route to truth and objective reality. The Enlightenment idea that natural processes were determined by rigid laws, leaving little room for either divine intervention or human will, won broad acceptance.

Living in an era of rapid change, nineteenth-century thinkers in Europe were fascinated with the idea of evolution and dynamic development. The most influential of all nineteenth-century evolutionary thinkers was Charles Darwin (1809–1882). Darwin believed that all life had gradually evolved from a common ancestral origin in an unending "struggle for survival." Darwin's theory of **evolution** is summarized in the title of his work *On the Origin of Species by the Means of Natural Selection* (1859). He argued that small variations within individuals in one species enabled them to acquire more food and better living conditions and made them more successful in reproducing, thus allowing them to pass their genetic material to the next generation. When a number of individuals within a species became distinct enough that they could no longer interbreed successfully with others, they became a new species.

evolution The idea, developed by Charles Darwin, that all life had gradually evolved from a common origin through a process of natural selection.

Social Darwinism The application of the theory of biological evolution to human affairs, it sees the human race as driven to ever-greater specialization and progress by an unending economic struggle that determines the survival of the fittest.

Darwin's theory of natural selection provoked resistance, particularly because he extended the theory to humans. His findings reinforced the teachings of secularists such as Marx, who scornfully dismissed religious belief in favor of agnostic or atheistic materialism. Many writers also applied the theory of biological evolution to human affairs. Herbert Spencer (1820–1903), an English philosopher, saw the human race as driven forward to ever-greater specialization and progress by a brutal economic struggle that determines the "survival of the fittest." The idea that human society also evolves, and that the stronger will become powerful and prosperous while the weaker will be conquered or remain poor, became known as **Social Darwinism**. Powerful nations used this ideology to justify nationalism and expansion, and colonizers to justify imperialism.

Not only did science shape society, but society also shaped science. As nations asserted their differences from one another, they sought "scientific" proof for those differences, which generally meant proof of their own superiority. European and American scientists, anthropologists, and physicians sought to prove that Europeans and those of European descent were more intelligent than other races, and that northern Europeans were more advanced than southern Europeans. Africans were described and depicted as "missing links" between chimpanzees and Europeans. This scientific racism extended to Jews, who were increasingly described as a separate and inferior race, not a religious group.

Madrid in 1900 This wistful painting of a Spanish square on a rainy day, by Enrique Martínez Cubells y Ruiz (1874–1917), includes a revealing commentary on how scientific discoveries transformed urban life. Coachmen wait atop their expensive hackney cabs for a wealthy clientele, while modern electric streetcars that carry the masses converge on the square from all directions. In this way the development of electricity brought improved urban transportation and enabled the city to expand to the suburbs. (Museo Municipal, Madrid, Spain/Bridgeman Images)

The Promise of Electricity

The commercialization and widespread use of electricity around 1900 made possible a broad spectrum of new technologies in the late nineteenth century, including telephones and telegraphs; radio; electric lights in public and private space; electric railroads, trams, and subways; electrochemistry and electrometallurgy; power plants, generators, and batteries; and electric motors and machines. How did the arrival of electricity change people's lives?

1 **The Palace of Electricity, 1900 Universal Exhibition, Paris.** The ever-popular world fairs and expositions organized around the turn of the century typically included a pavilion dedicated to the wonders of electricity, with spectacular electric light displays, sponsored by local electric power companies. This engraving shows spectators in the magnificent "Palace of Electricity" at the 1900 Universal Exhibition in Paris.

(akg-images)

(Russian Master State History Museum, Moscow, Russia/Fine Art Images/Getty Images)

2 **"Luks' — The Least Expensive and Brightest Lighting for All Occasions,"** **ca. 1900.** This Russian poster advertising lighting systems from the Luks' (Deluxe) lighting company in Riga portrays a princess of light, with flowing locks and diaphanous gown, holding an electric bulb that illuminates first the Russian Empire and then the rest of the globe. The small scene at the bottom shows the historic Tauride Palace in St. Petersburg — "illuminated by Luks' lights" — and suggests the revolutionary effect of electric light on public spaces.

ANALYZING THE EVIDENCE

1. What aspects of electrification do the images in Sources 1 and 2 portray to viewers? How would you compare the visual evocation of electricity in those images with the textual description of the benefits of "electrical progress" in Source 3?
2. How did the adoption of electricity for transportation and communication (Sources 4 and 5) change the way time and space were experienced both in cities and across the globe?
3. Why do you think Source 2 uses a female figure to personify electricity? Consider also Sources 1, 4, and 5. Do the benefits of electricity seem different for members of each sex? Or for people of different social classes?
4. Do the sources suggest any negative consequences related to electrification? Are there elements of these sources that might have been disturbing to contemporary observers?

3 **"Electrical Progress in Great Britain During 1909."** An American journal for electricians offered glowing approval of the electrification of Great Britain. Along with the United States, Britain was a world leader in electrification around 1900; other European nations were not far behind.

■ The most noticeable and at the same time the most hopeful, feature of the year 1909 in the United Kingdom, has been the great progress made in bringing electricity within the compass of the "small man." This movement, which means so much for the future of all electrical industry, has occupied the close attention of a large proportion of the electricity works managers and engineers and of most manufacturing and importing businesses. . . .

[T]he forward movement [of the filament lamp] is now in full swing. The wire lamp is everywhere working wonders in reducing the cost of electric lighting on existing installations and that fact together with the very strong support that is being given by other influences, is making it easier to get electrical applications adopted in many places where it seemed impossible before. . . .

[The London power companies] are now jointly using the daily press in an advertising campaign so conducted as to command the attention of all who read, educating them as to the rightful claims of electricity. One of the companies has opened a model "Electric Home" in its area, fitted throughout with electric lighting, heating, and small power. The house is occupied by a tenant who is under special arrangement to admit the public between certain hours every day, to demonstrate to them the manifold domestic applications of electricity and their convenience and cleanliness. Neither coal nor gas is used for any purpose whatsoever in the house. . . . This popularizing work is still very necessary indeed, for really the public does not know yet much that it ought to know. . . .

[The report then describes a number of technological advances, including newly built electric-generating plants, electric-powered steel mills, and the use of electric motors in a variety of industrial applications.]

4 **"General Map of Large-Scale World Telegraph Communications, 1901/03."** After some equipment failures, British and U.S. engineers successfully completed the first transatlantic telegraph cable, fired by electric current, in 1858. By 1900 telegraph cables circled the globe. (Boston Public Library/Bridgeman Images)

5 **Electric trams and lines in Piazza del Duomo, Milan, Italy, ca. 1900.** Electric streetcar and subway systems made quick travel through urban spaces accessible and inexpensive. In Milan, the tracks and streetcars, and the installation of electric streetlights, strike a modern contrast to the Gothic cathedral and Neoclassical triumphal arch that frame the central square.

(DEA Picture Library/Getty Images)

PUTTING IT ALL TOGETHER

Using the sources above, along with what you have learned in class and in Chapters 23 and 24, write a short essay that describes the effects of electrification on European society. Was electricity a fundamental driving force in the history of Western society?

Source: (3) Albert H. Bridge, "Electrical Progress in Great Britain in 1909," *Electrical Review and Western Electrician*, January 1, 1910, 17–19.

Théodore Géricault, *The Raft of the Medusa*, 1819 In 1816 the *Medusa*, a French navy frigate on a colonizing expedition to Senegal, ran aground on a sandbank. This painting, by the Romantic master Théodore Géricault, evokes the horror and despair of sailors stranded on a makeshift raft who vainly hail a passing ship. Only 10 of the 150 men who took refuge on the raft ultimately survived. (Louvre, Paris, France/Bridgeman Images)

Cultural Shifts

The French Revolution kindled the belief that radical reconstructions of politics and society were also possible in cultural and artistic life. The most significant expression of this belief in the early nineteenth century was the Romantic movement. In part a revolt against what was perceived as the cold rationality of the Enlightenment, **Romanticism** was characterized by a belief in emotional exuberance, unrestrained imagination, and spontaneity in both art and personal life. Preoccupied with emotional excess, Romantic works explored the awesome power of love and desire and of hatred, guilt, and despair. Where Enlightenment thinkers embraced secularization and civic life, Romantics delved into religious ecstasy and the hidden recesses of the self. The Romantics were passionately

moved by nature and decried the growth of modern industry and industrial cities.

The French Romantic painter Eugène Delacroix (oo-ZHEHN deh-luh-KWAH) (1798–1863) depicted dramatic, colorful scenes that stirred the emotions. He frequently painted non-European places and people, whether lion hunts in Morocco or women in a sultan's harem. Like other Romantic works, Delacroix's art reveals the undercurrents of desire and fascination within Europe's imperial ambitions in "exotic" and "savage" places in the nineteenth century.

It was in music that Romanticism realized most fully and permanently its goals of free expression and emotional intensity. Abandoning well-defined structures, the great Romantic composers used a wide range of forms to create musical landscapes and evoke powerful emotion. The first great Romantic composer is among the most revered today, Ludwig van Beethoven (1770–1827).

Romanticism A movement in art, literature, and music characterized by a belief in emotional exuberance, unrestrained imagination, and spontaneity in both art and personal life.

Romanticism also found a distinctive voice in poetry. In 1798 William Wordsworth (1770–1850) and his fellow Romantic poet Samuel Taylor Coleridge (1772–1834) published their *Lyrical Ballads*, which abandoned flowery classical conventions for the language of ordinary speech. Wordsworth described his conception of poetry as the "spontaneous overflow of powerful feeling recollected in tranquility."

Victor Hugo's (1802–1885) powerful novels exemplified the Romantic fascination with fantastic characters, strange settings, and human emotions. The hero of Hugo's famous *Hunchback of Notre Dame* (1831) is the great cathedral's deformed bell-ringer, a "human gargoyle" overlooking the teeming life of fifteenth-century Paris.

The study of history became a Romantic passion. History was the key to a universe that was now perceived to be organic and dynamic, not mechanical and static as the Enlightenment thinkers had believed. Historical studies supported the development of national aspirations and encouraged entire peoples to seek in the past their special destinies.

In central and eastern Europe, in particular, literary Romanticism and early nationalism reinforced each other. Romantics turned their attention to peasant life and transcribed the folk songs, tales, and proverbs that the cosmopolitan Enlightenment had disdained. The brothers Jacob and Wilhelm Grimm were particularly successful at rescuing German fairy tales from oblivion. In the Slavic lands Romantics played a decisive role in converting spoken peasant languages into modern written languages.

Beginning in the 1840s Romanticism gave way to a new artistic genre, Realism. Influenced by the growing prestige of science in this period, Realist writers believed that literature should depict life exactly as it is. Forsaking poetry for prose and replacing the personal, emotional viewpoint of the Romantics with strict scientific objectivity, the Realists simply observed and recorded.

Realist writers focused on creating fiction based on contemporary everyday life. Beginning with a dissection of the middle classes, from which most of them sprang, many Realists eventually focused on the working classes, especially the urban working classes, which had been neglected in literature before this time. The Realists put a microscope to unexplored and taboo topics — sex, strikes, violence, alcoholism — shocking middle-class critics.

The Realists' claims of objectivity did not prevent the elaboration of a definite worldview. Realists such as the famous French novelist Émile Zola (1840–1902) and English novelist Thomas Hardy (1840–1928) were determinists. They believed that human beings, like atoms, are components of the physical world and

that all human actions are caused by unalterable natural laws: heredity and environment determine human behavior; good and evil are merely social conventions. They were also critical of the failures of industrial society; by depicting the plight of poor workers, they hoped to bring about positive social change.

Nationalism and Socialism, 1871–1914

How did nationalism and socialism shape European politics in the decades before the Great War?

After 1871 Europe's heartland was organized into strong national states. Only on Europe's borders — in Ireland and Russia, in Austria-Hungary and the Balkans — did people still strive for national unity and independence. Nationalism served, for better or worse, as a new unifying political principle. At the same time, socialist parties grew rapidly. Governing elites manipulated national feeling to create a sense of unity to divert attention from underlying class conflicts, and increasingly channeled national sentiment in an antiliberal and militaristic direction, tolerating anti-Semitism and waging wars in non-Western lands. This policy helped manage domestic conflicts, but only at the expense of increasing the international tensions that erupted in World War I.

Trends in Suffrage

There were good reasons why ordinary people felt increasing loyalty to their governments in central and western Europe by the turn of the twentieth century. Ordinary men felt they were becoming "part of the system," quite simply, because more of them could vote. By 1914 universal male suffrage had become the rule rather than the exception.

Women also began to demand the right to vote. The first important successes occurred in Scandinavia and Australia. In Sweden taxpaying single women and widows could vote in municipal elections after 1862. Australia and Finland gave women the right to vote in national elections and stand for parliament in 1902 and 1906, respectively (although restrictions on Aboriginal women's voting rights in Australia continued until the 1960s). In the western United States, women could vote in twelve states by 1913. One example among the thousands of courageous "suffragettes" was French socialist Hubertine Auclert (ew-ber-TEEN o-CLAIR), who in 1880–1881 led demonstrations, organized women in a property-tax boycott, and created the first suffragist newspaper in France.[2] Auclert and her counterparts elsewhere in Europe had little success before 1914, but they prepared the way for the female vote in many countries immediately after World War I.

As the right to vote spread, politicians and parties in national parliaments usually represented the people more responsively. The multiparty system prevailing in most countries meant that parliamentary majorities were built on shifting coalitions, which gave political parties leverage to obtain benefits for their supporters. Governments also passed laws to alleviate general problems, thereby acquiring greater legitimacy and appearing more worthy of support.

The German Empire

The new German Empire was a federal union of Prussia and twenty-four smaller states. The separate states conducted much of the everyday business of government. Unifying the whole was a strong national government with a chancellor—Bismarck until 1890—and a popularly elected parliament called the Reichstag (RIGHKS-tahg). Although Bismarck repeatedly ignored the wishes of the parliamentary majority, he nonetheless preferred to win the support of the Reichstag to lend legitimacy to his policy goals.

Bismarck was a fierce opponent of socialism. In 1878 he pushed through a law outlawing the German Social Democratic Party, but he was unable to force socialism out of existence. Bismarck then urged the Reichstag to enact new social welfare measures to gain the allegiance of the working classes. In 1883 the Reichstag created national health insurance, followed in 1884 by accident insurance and in 1889 by old-age pensions and retirement benefits. Together, these laws created a national social security system that was the first of its kind anywhere, funded by contributions from wage earners, employers, and the state.

Under Kaiser Wilhelm I (r. 1861–1888), Bismarck had managed the domestic and foreign policies of the state. In 1890 the new emperor, Wilhelm II (r. 1888–1918), eager to rule in his own right and to earn the workers' support, forced Bismarck to resign. Following Bismarck's departure, the Reichstag passed new laws to aid workers and to legalize socialist political activity.

Although Wilhelm II was no more successful than Bismarck in getting workers to renounce socialism, in the years before World War I the Social Democratic Party broadened its base and adopted a more patriotic tone. German socialists identified increasingly with the German state and concentrated on gradual social and political reform.

Republican France

Although Napoleon III's reign made some progress in reducing antagonisms between classes, the Franco-Prussian War undid these efforts, and in 1871 France seemed hopelessly divided once again. The republicans who proclaimed the Third Republic in Paris refused to admit defeat by the Germans. They defended Paris with great heroism for weeks, until they were starved into submission by German armies in January 1871. When national elections then sent a large majority of conservatives and monarchists to the National Assembly, France's leaders decided they had no choice but to achieve peace by surrendering Alsace and Lorraine to Germany. Parisians exploded in patriotic frustration and proclaimed the Paris Commune in March 1871.

Commune leaders wanted to govern Paris without interference from the conservative French countryside. The National Assembly, led by conservative politician Adolphe Thiers, ordered the French army into Paris and brutally crushed the Commune. Twenty thousand people died in the fighting. As in June 1848, it was Paris against the provinces, French against French. Out of this tragedy France slowly formed a new national unity, achieving considerable stability before 1914.

The moderate republicans who governed France sought to preserve their creation by winning the loyalty of the next generation. Trade unions were fully legalized, and France acquired a colonial empire (see "The Scramble for Africa" in Chapter 25 and "Mainland Southeast Asia" in Chapter 26). A series of laws between 1879 and 1886 established free compulsory elementary education for both girls and boys, thereby greatly reducing the role of parochial Catholic schools, which had long been hostile to republicanism. In France and throughout the world, the general expansion of public education served as a critical nation- and nationalism-building tool in the late nineteenth century.

Although the educational reforms of the 1880s disturbed French Catholics, many of them rallied to the republic in the 1890s, and tensions between church and state eased. Unfortunately, the **Dreyfus affair** changed all that. In 1894 Alfred Dreyfus (DRY-fuss), a Jewish captain in the French army, was falsely accused and convicted of treason. In 1898 and 1899 the case split France apart. On one side was the army, which had manufactured evidence against Dreyfus, joined by anti-Semites and most of the Catholic establishment. On the other side stood the civil libertarians and most of the more radical republicans.

Dreyfus affair A divisive case in which Alfred Dreyfus, a Jewish captain in the French army, was falsely accused and convicted of treason. The Catholic Church sided with the anti-Semites against Dreyfus; after Dreyfus was declared innocent, the French government severed all ties between the state and the church.

Le Petit Journal

SUPPLÉMENT ILLUSTRÉ

Huit pages : CINQ centimes

DIMANCHE 13 JANVIER 1895

LE TRAITRE

The Traitor: Degradation of Alfred Dreyfus
After being arrested and convicted in a secret court martial for treason, Captain Dreyfus bravely stood at attention during a public degradation ceremony. While the officer on duty tore off his stripes, ripped off his honors, and broke his sword in two, Dreyfus shouted out, "You are degrading an innocent man! Long live France! Long live the army!" (Private Collection/Bridgeman Images)

This battle, which eventually led to Dreyfus's being declared innocent, revived militant republican feeling against the church. Between 1901 and 1905 the government severed all ties between the state and the Catholic Church after centuries of close relations.

Great Britain and the Austro-Hungarian Empire

The development of Great Britain and Austria-Hungary, two leading but quite different powers, throws a powerful light on the dynamics of nationalism in Europe before 1914. At home Britain made more of its citizens feel a part of the nation by passing consecutive voting rights bills that culminated with the establishment of universal male suffrage in 1884. Moreover, overdue social welfare measures were passed in a spectacular rush between 1906 and 1914. The ruling Liberal Party substantially raised taxes on the rich to pay for national health insurance, unemployment benefits, old-age pensions, and a host of other social measures. The state was integrating the urban masses socially as well as politically.

On the eve of World War I, however, the unanswered question of Ireland brought Great Britain to the brink of civil war. The terrible Irish famine of the 1840s and early 1850s had fueled an Irish revolutionary movement. The English slowly granted concessions, and in 1913 the British Parliament passed a bill granting Ireland self-government, or home rule.

The Irish Catholic majority in the southern counties ardently desired home rule. Irish Protestants in the northern counties of Ulster, however, vowed to resist home rule, fearing they would fall under the control of the majority Catholics. Unable to resolve the conflict as World War I started in August 1914, the British government postponed indefinitely the whole question of Irish home rule.

The Irish dilemma helps one appreciate how desperate the situation in the Austro-Hungarian Empire had become by the early twentieth century. Reacting to the upheaval of 1848, Austrian emperor Franz Joseph (r. 1848–1916) and his bureaucracy ruled Hungary as a conquered territory. This was part of broader efforts to centralize Austria and Germanize the language and culture of the different nationalities.

After its defeat by Prussia in 1866, however, a weakened Austria was forced to establish the so-called dual monarchy. The empire was divided in two, and the nationalistic Magyars gained virtual independence for Hungary. The two states were joined only by a shared monarch and common ministries for finance, defense, and foreign affairs. Still, the disintegrating force of competing nationalisms continued unabated, and the Austro-Hungarian Empire was progressively weakened and eventually destroyed by the conflicting national aspirations of its different ethnic groups. It was these ethnic conflicts in the Balkans that touched off the Great War in 1914 (see "The Outbreak of War" in Chapter 28).

Jewish Emancipation and Modern Anti-Semitism

Revolutionary changes in political principles and the triumph of the nation-state brought equally revolutionary changes in Jewish life in western and central Europe. Beginning in France in 1791, Jews gradually gained civil rights. In the 1850s and 1860s liberals in Austria, Italy, and Prussia pressed successfully for legal equality for all regardless of religion. In 1871 the constitution of the new German Empire abolished restrictions on Jewish marriage, choice of occupation, place of residence, and property ownership.

By 1871 a majority of Jews in western and central Europe had improved their economic situations and entered the middle classes. Most Jews identified strongly with their respective nation-states and considered themselves patriotic citizens. Exclusion from government employment and discrimination in social relations continued, however, in central Europe.

"The Expulsion of the Jews from Russia" So reads this postcard, correctly suggesting that Russian government officials often encouraged popular anti-Semitism and helped drive many Jews out of Russia in the late nineteenth century. The road signs indicate that these poor Jews are crossing into Germany, where they will find a grudging welcome and a meager meal at the Jolly Onion Inn. Other Jews from eastern Europe settled in France and Britain, thereby creating small but significant Jewish populations in both countries for the first time since they had expelled most of their Jews in the Middle Ages. (Alliance Israélite Universelle, Paris, France/Archives Charmet/Bridgeman Images)

Vicious anti-Semitism reappeared after the stock market crash of 1873, beginning in central Europe. Drawing on long traditions of religious intolerance, this hostility also drew on modern, supposedly scientific ideas about Jews as a separate race (see "Science for the Masses" in Chapter 24). Anti-Semitic beliefs were particularly popular among conservatives, extremist nationalists, and people who felt threatened by Jewish competition.

Anti-Semites also created modern political parties. In Austrian Vienna in the early 1890s, Karl Lueger (LOO-guhr), the popular mayor of Vienna from 1897 to 1910, combined fierce anti-Semitic rhetoric with his support of municipal ownership of basic services. In response to spreading anti-Semitism, a Jewish journalist named Theodor Herzl (1860–1904) turned from German nationalism to advocate Jewish political nationalism, or **Zionism**, and the creation of a Jewish state.

Before 1914 anti-Semitism was most oppressive in eastern Europe, where Jews also suffered from terrible poverty. In the Russian Empire, where there was no Jewish emancipation and 4 million of Europe's 7 million Jewish people lived in 1880, officials used anti-Semitism to channel popular discontent away from the government. In 1881–1882 a wave of violent pogroms commenced in southern Russia. The police and the army stood aside for days while peasants assaulted Jews and looted and destroyed their property. Official harassment continued in the following decades, and many Russian Jews emigrated to western Europe and the United States.

The Socialist Movement

Socialism appealed to large numbers of working men and women in the late nineteenth century, and the growth of socialist parties after 1871 was phenomenal. By 1912 the German Social Democratic Party, which espoused Marxist principles, had millions of followers and was the Reichstag's largest party. Socialist parties also grew in other countries, and Marxist socialist parties were linked together in an international organization.

As socialist parties grew and attracted large numbers of members, they looked more and more toward gradual change and steady improvement for the working class and less and less toward revolution. Workers themselves were progressively less inclined to follow radical programs for several reasons. As workers gained the right to vote and won real benefits, their attention focused more on elections than on revolutions. Workers were also not immune to nationalistic patriotism. Nor were workers a unified social group. Perhaps most important of all, workers' standard of living rose steadily after 1850, and the quality of life improved substantially in urban areas.

The growth of labor unions reinforced this trend toward moderation. In Great Britain new unions that formed for skilled workers after 1850 avoided radical politics and concentrated on winning better wages and hours for their members through collective bargaining and compromise. After 1890 unions for unskilled workers developed in Britain.

German unions were not granted important rights until 1869, and until the Anti-Socialist Laws were repealed in 1890 the government frequently harassed them as socialist fronts. But after most legal harassment was eliminated, union membership skyrocketed.

The German trade unions and their leaders were thoroughgoing revisionists. **Revisionism** was an effort by various socialists to update Marxist doctrines to reflect the realities of the time. The socialist Eduard Bernstein (1850–1932) argued in his *Evolutionary Socialism* in 1899 that Marx's predictions of ever-greater poverty for workers had been proved false. Therefore, Bernstein suggested, socialists should reform their doctrines and win gradual evolutionary gains for workers through legislation, unions, and further economic development.

Socialist parties in other countries had clear-cut national characteristics. Russians and socialists in the Austro-Hungarian Empire tended to be the most radical. In Great Britain the socialist but non-Marxist Labour Party formally committed to gradual reform. In Spain and Italy anarchism, seeking to smash the state rather than the bourgeoisie, dominated radical thought and action.

In short, socialist policies and doctrines varied from country to country. Socialism itself was to a large extent "nationalized." This helps explain why almost all socialist leaders supported their governments when war came in 1914.

Chapter Summary

In 1814 the victorious allied powers sought to restore peace and stability in Europe. The conservative powers used intervention and repression as they sought to prevent the spread of subversive ideas and radical changes in politics. After 1815 ideologies of liberalism, nationalism, and socialism all developed to challenge the new order. The growth of these forces culminated in the liberal and nationalistic revolutions of 1848, revolutions that were crushed by resurgent conservative forces. In the second half of the nineteenth century Italy and Germany became unified nation-states, while

Zionism The movement toward Jewish political nationhood started by Theodor Herzl.

revisionism An effort by various socialists to update Marxist doctrines to reflect the realities of the time.

Russia undertook a modernization program and struggled with popular discontent.

Living conditions in rapidly growing industrial cities declined until the mid-nineteenth century, when governments undertook major urban development, including new systems of sewerage, water supply, and public transportation. Major changes in the class structure and family life occurred, as the separate spheres ideology strengthened, and the class structure became more complex and diversified. The prestige of science grew tremendously, and scientific discoveries, such as Darwin's theory of natural selection, challenged the traditional religious understanding of the world. In the realm of literature and the arts, the Romantic movement reinforced the spirit of change. Romanticism gave way to Realism in the 1840s.

Western society became increasingly nationalistic as well as urban and industrial in the late nineteenth century. Nation-states became more responsive to the needs of their people, and they enlisted widespread support as political participation expanded, educational opportunities increased, and social security systems took shape. Even socialism became increasingly national in orientation, gathering strength as a champion of working-class interests in domestic politics. Yet even though nationalism served to unite peoples, it also drove them apart and contributed to the tragic conflicts of the twentieth century.

NOTES

1. J. McKay, *Tramways and Trolleys: The Rise of Urban Mass Transport in Europe* (Princeton, N.J.: Princeton University Press, 1976), p. 81.
2. "*La Citoyenne* in the World: Hubertine Auclert and Feminist Imperialism," *French Historical Studies* 31.1 (Winter 2009): 63–84.

CONNECTIONS

Much of world history in the past two centuries can be seen as a struggle over the unfinished legacies of the late-eighteenth-century revolutions in politics and economics. Although defeated in 1848, the new political ideologies associated with the French Revolution re-emerged decisively after 1850. Nationalism, with its commitment to the nation-state, became the most dominant of the new ideologies. National movements brought about the creation of unified nation-states in two of the most fractured regions in Europe, Germany and Italy.

After 1870 nationalism and militarism, its frequent companion, touched off increased competition between the major European powers for raw materials and markets for manufactured goods. As discussed in the next two chapters, during the last decades of the nineteenth century Europe colonized nearly all of Africa and large areas in Asia. In Europe itself nationalism promoted bitter competition between states, threatening the very progress and unity it had helped to build. In 1914 the power of unified nation-states turned on itself, unleashing an unprecedented conflict among Europe's Great Powers. Chapter 28 tells the story of this First World War.

Nationalism also sparked worldwide challenges to European dominance by African and Asian leaders who fought to liberate themselves from colonialism, and it became a rallying cry in nominally independent countries like China and Japan, whose leaders sought freedom from European and American influence and a rightful place among the world's leading nations. Chapters 25, 26, and 33 explore these developments. Likewise, Chapter 33 discusses how the problems of rapid urbanization and the huge gaps between rich and poor caused by economic transformations in America and Europe in the nineteenth century are now the concern of policymakers in Africa, Asia, and Latin America.

Another important ideology of change, socialism, remains popular in Europe, which has seen socialist parties democratically elected to office in many countries. Marxist revolutions that took absolute control of entire countries, as in Russia, China, and Cuba, occurred in the twentieth century.

CHAPTER 24   Review and Explore

Identify Key Terms

Identify and explain the significance of each item below.

Congress of Vienna (p. 692)

conservatism (p. 692)

liberalism (p. 693)

laissez faire (p. 694)

nationalism (p. 695)

socialism (p. 696)

bourgeoisie (p. 696)

proletariat (p. 696)

modernization (p. 701)

October Manifesto (p. 708)

germ theory (p. 708)

evolution (p. 714)

Social Darwinism (p. 715)

Romanticism (p. 718)

Dreyfus affair (p. 720)

Zionism (p. 723)

revisionism (p. 723)

Review the Main Ideas

Answer the focus questions from each section of the chapter.

1. How did the allies fashion a peace settlement in 1815, and what radical ideas emerged between 1815 and 1848? (p. 692)

2. Why did revolutions triumph briefly throughout most of Europe in 1848, and why did they fail? (p. 696)

3. How did strong leaders and nation building transform Italy, Germany, and Russia? (p. 701)

4. What was the impact of urban growth on cities, social classes, families, and ideas? (p. 708)

5. How did nationalism and socialism shape European politics in the decades before the Great War? (p. 719)

Make Comparisons and Connections

Analyze the larger developments and continuities within and across chapters.

1. How did the spread of radical ideas and the movements for reform and revolution explored in this chapter draw on the "unfinished" political and industrial revolutions of the late eighteenth century (Chapters 22, 23)?

2. How and why did the relationship between the state and its citizens change in the last decades of the nineteenth century?

3. How did the emergence of a society divided into working and middle classes affect the workplace, homemaking, and family values and gender roles?

TIMELINE

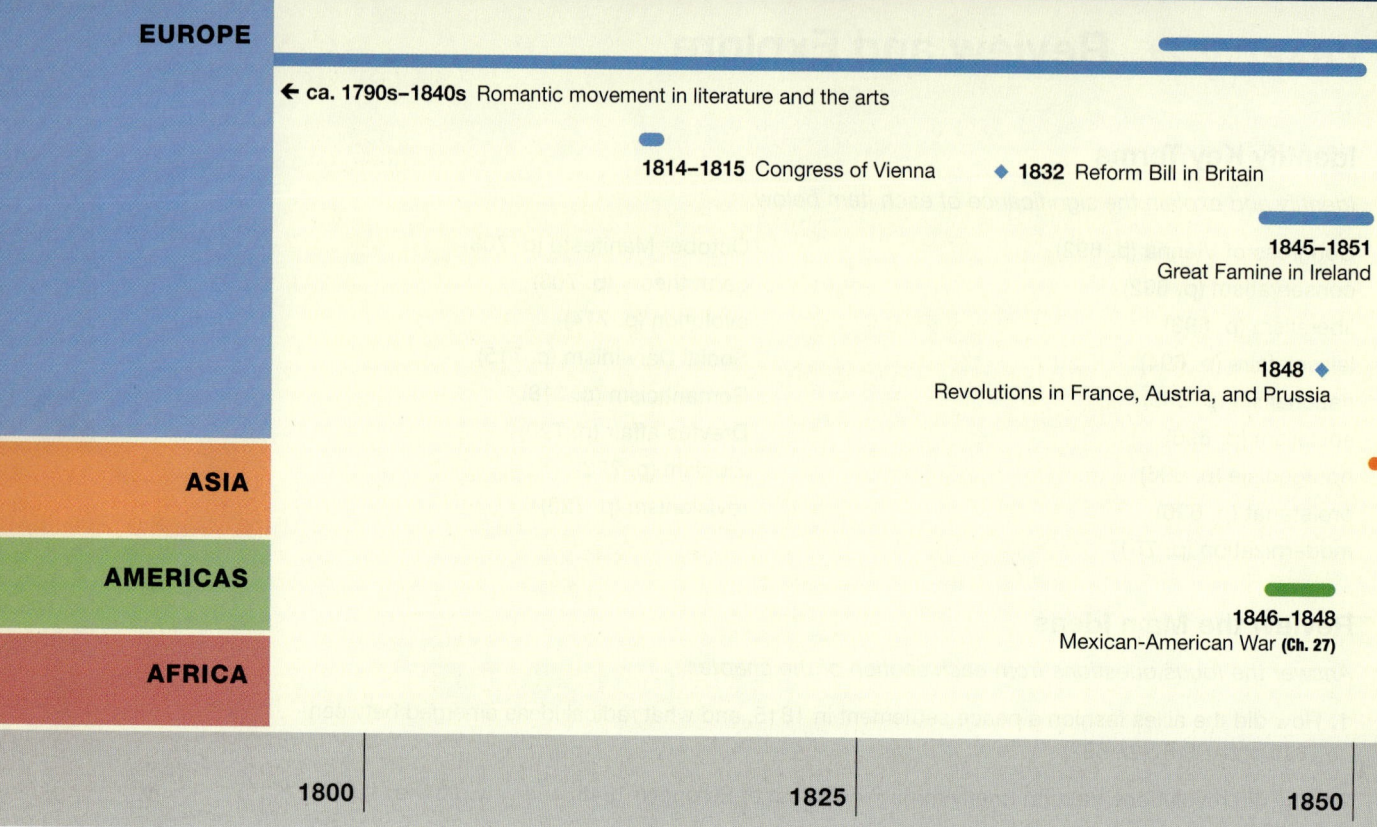

EUROPE

← ca. 1790s–1840s Romantic movement in literature and the arts

1814–1815 Congress of Vienna   ◆ **1832** Reform Bill in Britain

1845–1851
Great Famine in Ireland

1848 ◆
Revolutions in France, Austria, and Prussia

ASIA

AMERICAS

1846–1848
Mexican-American War **(Ch. 27)**

AFRICA

1800   1825   1850

Suggested Resources

BOOKS

Barnes, David S. *The Great Stink of Paris and the Nineteenth-Century Struggle Against Filth and Germs.* 2006. An outstanding introduction to sanitary developments and attitudes toward public health.

Baycroft, Timothy, and Mark Hewitson, eds. *What Is a Nation? Europe 1789–1914.* 2009. A sweeping study of nationalism in all its forms and all the processes that affected its evolution.

Berger, Stefan, ed. *A Companion to Nineteenth-Century Europe, 1789–1914.* 2006. A useful study with an up-to-date bibliography.

Coontz, Stephanie. *Marriage, A History: From Obedience to Intimacy, or How Love Conquered Marriage.* 2005. A lively inquiry into the historical background to current practice.

Fuchs, Rachel. *Gender and Poverty in Nineteenth-Century Europe.* 2005. A history of the transformation of poor women's daily lives in the nineteenth century, dealing with sexuality, death, work, and family.

Gildea, Robert. *Barricades and Borders: Europe, 1800–1914,* 2d ed. 1996. A recommended general study.

Koven, Seth. *Slumming: Sexual and Social Politics in Victorian London.* 2006. A provocative, in-depth account of middle-class encounters with the London working class in the late nineteenth century.

Malia, Martin, and Terrence Emmons. *History's Locomotives: Revolutions and the Making of the Modern World.* 2006. An ambitious comparative work of high quality.

Merriman, John. *Massacre: The Life and Death of the Paris Commune.* 2014. A gripping account of a revolutionary uprising in nineteenth-century Paris.

Otis, Laura. *Literature and Science in the Nineteenth Century: An Anthology.* 2009. A fascinating selection of writings from a time when humanities and science were not considered separate disciplines.

Sperber, Jonathan. *Karl Marx: A Nineteenth-Century Life.* 2013. An even-handed, cradle-to-grave biography of the famous revolutionary theorist.

Winks, Robin W., and Joan Neuberger. *Europe and the Making of Modernity: 1815–1914.* 2005. A grand narrative of the forces that shaped modern Europe from the Congress of Vienna to the Great War.

ca. 1840s–1890s Realism dominates Western literature

1853–1856 Crimean War

1859–1870 Unification of Italy

1866–1871 Unification of Germany

◆ **1859** Darwin, *On the Origin of Species by the Means of Natural Selection*

◆ **1861** Russian serfs freed

1851–1864 Taiping Rebellion **(Ch. 26)**

◆ **1857** Great Mutiny / Great Revolt in India **(Ch. 26)**

1861–1865 U.S. Civil War **(Ch. 27)**

◆ **1905** Revolution in Russia

1906–1914 Social reform in Britain

1904–1905 Russo-Japanese War

◆ **1898** Spanish-American War **(Ch. 27)**

1880–1914 European "scramble for Africa" **(Ch. 25)**

1875   **1900**   **1925**

DOCUMENTARIES

English Poetry Anthology: The Romantic Poets (Kultur Video, 2006). Documents the Romantic poetry movement in England, featuring Wordsworth, Byron, and Keats.

Landmarks of Western Art: Romanticism (Kultur Video, 2003). Documents the Romantic movement in painting, highlighting artists such as Turner, Constable, Goya, and Géricault.

The Rise, from *Heaven on Earth: The Rise and Fall of Socialism* (PBS, 2005). The first of a three-part series, this documentary follows the rise of the socialist movement.

FEATURE FILMS

Bright Star (Jane Campion, 2009). A drama about the British Romantic poet John Keats and his relationship with Fanny Brawne, which was cut short by Keats's early death.

Frankenstein (James Whale, 1931). Based on the classic Romantic novel by Mary Shelley, the film tells the story of an obsessed scientist who creates a living being in a bizarre science experiment.

Les Misérables (Tom Hooper, 2012). Adapted from Victor Hugo's epic novel, the film portrays ex-convict Jean Valjean's pursuit of redemption. The film is also a commentary on social unrest in early-nineteenth-century France and depicts the student uprising in Paris in 1832.

WEBSITES

Heilbrunn Timeline of Art History: Romanticism. The Metropolitan Museum of Art's overview of the Romantic movement within art, along with a slide show of eighteen pieces of artwork from the period. **www.metmuseum.org/toah/hd/roma/hd_roma.htm**

Marxists Internet Archive. This archive offers a vast amount of material and sources related to Karl Marx, communism, and Communist revolutions. **marxists.org/index.htm**

25

Africa, the Ottoman Empire, and the New Imperialism

1800–1914

While industrialization and nationalism were transforming society in Europe and the neo-European countries (the United States, Canada, Australia, New Zealand, and, to an extent, South Africa), Western society itself was reshaping the world. European commercial interests went in search of new sources of raw materials and markets for their manufactured goods. At the same time, millions of Europeans and Asians emigrated abroad. What began as a relatively peaceful exchange of products with Africa and Asia in the early nineteenth century had transformed by century's end into a frenzy of imperialist occupation and domination that had a profound impact on both colonizer and colonized.

The political annexation of territory in the 1880s — the "New Imperialism," as it is often called by historians — was the capstone of Western society's underlying economic and technological transformation. More directly, Western imperialism rested on a formidable combination of superior military might and strong authoritarian rule, and it posed a brutal challenge to African and Asian peoples. Indigenous societies met this Western challenge in different ways and with changing tactics. By 1914 local elites in many lands were rallying their peoples and leading an anti-imperialist struggle for dignity and genuine independence that would triumph after 1945.

Sengbe Pieh

Enslaved in 1839, Pieh (later known as Joseph Cinqué) led a famous revolt on the slave ship *Amistad*. He and his fellow slaves were charged with mutiny and murder, but in March 1840 the U.S. Supreme Court found them innocent because they had been illegally captured and sold. They returned to their native Sierra Leone as free men.

Portrait, 1839, by Nathaniel Jocelyn (1796–1881) (oil on canvas)/Granger, NY —All rights reserved

CHAPTER PREVIEW

AFRICA: FROM THE SLAVE TRADE TO EUROPEAN COLONIAL RULE
What were the most significant changes in Africa during the nineteenth century, and why did they occur?

THE NEW IMPERIALISM, 1880–1914
What were the causes and consequences of European empire building after 1880?

THE ISLAMIC HEARTLAND UNDER PRESSURE
How did the Ottoman Empire and Egypt try to modernize themselves, and what were the most important results?

THE EXPANDING WORLD ECONOMY
What were the global consequences of European industrialization between 1800 and 1914?

THE GREAT GLOBAL MIGRATION
What fueled migration, and what was the general pattern of this unprecedented movement of people?

Africa: From the Slave Trade to European Colonial Rule

What were the most significant changes in Africa during the nineteenth century, and why did they occur?

In the nineteenth and early twentieth centuries the different regions of Africa experienced gradual but monumental change. The transatlantic slave trade declined and practically disappeared by the late 1860s. In the early nineteenth century Islam expanded its influence south of the Sahara Desert, and Africa still generally remained free of European political control. After about 1880 further Islamic expansion to the south stopped, but the pace of change accelerated as France and Britain led European nations in the "scramble for Africa," dividing and largely conquering the continent. By 1900 the foreigners were consolidating their authoritarian empires.

Trade and Social Change

The most important development in West Africa before the European conquest was the decline of the Atlantic slave trade and the simultaneous rise in exports of **palm oil** and other commodities. This shift in African foreign trade marked the beginning of modern economic development in sub-Saharan Africa.

Although the trade in enslaved Africans was a global phenomenon, the transatlantic slave trade between Africa and the Americas became the most extensive and significant portion of it (see "The Transatlantic Slave Trade" in Chapter 20). Until 1700, and perhaps even 1750, most Europeans considered the African slave trade a legitimate business activity. After 1775 a broad campaign to abolish slavery developed in Britain and grew into one of the first peaceful mass political movements based on the mobilization of public opinion in British history. British women played a critical role in this movement, denouncing the immorality of human bondage and stressing the cruel treatment of female slaves and slave families. Abolitionists also argued for a transition to legitimate (nonslave) trade to end both the transatlantic slave trade and the internal African slave systems. In 1807 Parliament declared the

slave trade illegal. Britain then began using its navy to seize slave runners' ships, liberate the captives, and settle them in the British port of Freetown, in Sierra Leone, as well as in Liberia (see Map 25.1, page 733). Freed American slaves had established the colony of Liberia in 1821–1822.

British action had a limited impact at first. Britain's navy intercepted fewer than 10 percent of all slave ships, and the demand for slaves remained high on the sugar and coffee plantations of Cuba and Brazil until the 1850s and 1860s. The United States banned slave importation from January 1, 1808. From that time on, natural increase (slaves having children) mainly accounted for the subsequent growth of the African American slave population before the Civil War. Strong financial incentives remained, however, for Portuguese and other European slave traders and for those African rulers who relied on profits from the trade for power and influence.

As more nations joined Britain in outlawing the slave trade, shipments of human cargo slackened along the West African coast (see Map 25.1). At the same time the ancient but limited shipment of slaves across the Sahara and from the East African coast into the Indian Ocean and through the Red Sea expanded dramatically. Only in the 1860s did this trade begin to decline rapidly. As a result, total slave exports from all regions of sub-Saharan Africa declined only marginally, from 7.4 million in the eighteenth century to 6.1 million in the nineteenth century.[1] Abolitionists failed to achieve their vision that "legitimate trade" in tropical products would quickly replace illegal slave exports.

Nevertheless, beginning in West Africa, a legitimate trade did make steady progress for several reasons. First, with Britain encouraging palm tree cultivation as an alternative to the slave trade, palm oil sales from West Africa to Britain surged, from only one thousand tons in 1810 to more than forty thousand tons in 1855. Second, the sale of palm oil admirably served the self-interest of industrializing Europe. Manufacturers used palm oil to lubricate their giant machines and to make cheap soap and other cosmetics. Third, peanut production for export also grew rapidly, in part because both small, independent African family farmers and large-scale enterprises could produce peanuts for the substantial American and European markets.

Finally, powerful West African rulers and warlords who had benefited from the Atlantic slave trade redirected some of their slaves' labor into the production of legitimate goods for world markets. This was possible because local warfare and slave raiding continued to enslave large numbers of people in sub-Saharan Africa, so slavery and slave markets remained strong. Although some enslaved captives might still be sold abroad, now women were often kept as wives, con-

---

palm oil A West African tropical product often used to make soap; the British encouraged its cultivation as an alternative to the slave trade.

jihad Religious war waged by Muslim scholars and religious leaders against both animist rulers and Islamic states that they deemed corrupt.

Sokoto caliphate Founded in 1809 by Uthman dan Fodio, this African state was based on Islamic history and law.

cubines, or servants, while men were used to transport goods, mine gold, grow crops, and serve in slave armies. Thus the transatlantic slave trade's slow decline coincided with the most intensive use of slaves within Africa.

All the while, a new group of African merchants was emerging to handle legitimate trade, and some grew rich. Women were among the most successful of these merchants. There is a long tradition of West African women's active involvement in trade, but the arrival of Europeans provided new opportunities. The African wife of a European trader served as her husband's interpreter and learned all aspects of his business. When the husband died, as European men invariably did in the hot, humid, and mosquito-infested conditions of tropical West Africa, the African wife inherited his commercial interests, including his inventory and his European connections. Many such widows used their considerable business acumen to make small fortunes.

By the 1850s and 1860s legitimate African traders, flanked by Western-educated African lawyers, teachers, and journalists, had formed an emerging middle class in the West African coastal towns. Unfortunately for West Africans, in the 1880s and 1890s African business leadership gave way to imperial subordination.

Islamic Revival and Expansion in Africa

The Sudanic savanna is that vast belt of flat grasslands stretching across Africa below the Sahara's southern fringe (the Sahel). By the early eighteenth century Islam had been practiced throughout this region for five hundred to one thousand years, depending on the area. City dwellers, political rulers, and merchants in many small states were Muslim. Yet the rural peasant farmers and migratory cattle raisers—the vast majority of the population—generally held on to traditional animist practices, worshipping ancestors, praying at local shrines, and invoking protective spirits. Since many Muslim rulers shared some of these beliefs, they did not try to convert their subjects in the countryside or enforce Islamic law.

A powerful Islamic revival began in the eighteenth century and gathered strength in the early nineteenth century. In essence, Muslim scholars and fervent religious leaders arose to wage successful **jihads** (JEE-hahds), or religious wars, against both animist rulers and Islamic states they deemed corrupt. The new reformist rulers believed African cults and religious practice could no longer be tolerated, and they often effected mass conversions of animists to Islam.

The most important of these revivalist states, the **Sokoto caliphate** (SOH-kuh-toh KAL-uh-fate), illus-

trates the pattern of Islamic revival in Africa. It was founded by Uthman dan Fodio (AHTH-mun dahn FOH-dee-oh) (1754–1817), a Muslim teacher who first won followers among both the Fulani herders and in the Muslim state of Gobir in the northern Sudan. After his religious community was attacked by Gobir's rulers, Uthman launched the jihad of 1804, one of the most important events in nineteenth-century West Africa. Uthman claimed the Hausa rulers of Muslim Gobir "worshipped many places of idols, and trees, and rocks, and sacrificed to them," killing and plundering their subjects without any regard for Islamic law.[2] He recruited young religious students and discontented Fulani cattle raisers to form the backbone of his jihadi fighters and succeeded in overthrowing the Hausa rulers and expanding Islam into the Sudan. In 1809 Uthman established the new Sokoto caliphate (see Map 20.1).

The triumph of the Sokoto caliphate had profound consequences for Africa and the Sudan. First, the caliphate was governed by a sophisticated written constitution based on Islamic history and law. This government of laws, rather than men, provided stability and made Sokoto one of the most prosperous regions in tropical Africa. Second, because of Sokoto and other revivalist states, Islam became much more widely and deeply rooted in sub-Saharan Africa than ever before. Finally, as one historian explained, Islam had always approved of slavery for non-Muslims and Muslim heretics, and "the *jihads* created a new slaving frontier on the basis of rejuvenated Islam."[3] In 1900 the Sokoto caliphate had at least 1 million and perhaps as many as 2.5 million slaves.

Islam also expanded in East Africa. From the 1820s on, Arab merchants and adventurers pressed far into the interior in search of slaves and ivory, converting and intermarrying with local Nyamwezi (nyahm-WAY-zee) elites and establishing small Muslim states. The Arab immigrants brought literacy, administrative skills, and increased trade and international contact, as well as the intensification of slavery, to East Africa. In 1837 Sayyid Said (sa-EED sa-EED) (r. 1804–1856), the sultan of Oman, conquered Mombasa, the great port city in modern Kenya. After moving his capital from southern Arabia to the island of Zanzibar in 1840, Said gained control of most of the Swahili-speaking East African coast. He then routed all slave shipments from the coast to the Ottoman Empire and Arabia through Zanzibar. He also successfully encouraged Indian merchants to develop slave-based clove plantations in his territories. In 1870, before Christian missionaries and Western armies began to arrive in force and halt Islam's spread, it appeared that most of the East and Central African populations would accept Islam within a generation.[4]

The Scramble for Africa, 1880–1914

Between 1880 and 1914 Britain, France, Germany, Belgium, Spain, and Italy, worried that they would not get "a piece of that magnificent African cake" (in Belgian king Leopold II's graphic words), scrambled for African possessions as if their national livelihoods were at stake. In 1880 Europeans controlled barely 20 percent of the African continent, mainly along the coast; by 1914 they controlled over 90 percent. Only Ethiopia in northeast Africa and Liberia on the West African coast remained independent (Map 25.1).

In addition to the general causes underlying Europe's imperialist burst after 1880, certain events and individuals stand out. First, as the antislavery movement succeeded in shutting down the Atlantic slave trade by the late 1860s, slavery's persistence elsewhere attracted growing attention in western Europe and the Americas. Missionaries played a key role in publicizing the horrors of slave raids and the suffering of thousands of enslaved Africans. The public was led to believe that European conquest and colonization would end this human tragedy by bringing, in Scottish missionary David Livingstone's famous phrase, "Commerce, Christianity, and Civilization" to Africa.

Second, King Leopold II (r. 1865–1909) of Belgium also played a crucial role. His agents signed treaties with African chiefs and planted Leopold's flag along the Congo River. In addition, Leopold intentionally misled other European leaders to gain their support by promising to promote Christianity and civilization in his proposed Congo Free State. By 1883 Europe had caught "African fever," and the race for territory was on. Third, to lay down some rules for this imperialist competition, French premier Jules Ferry and German chancellor Otto von Bismarck arranged a European conference on sub-Saharan Africa in Berlin in 1884–1885. The **Berlin Conference**, to which Africans were not invited, established the principle that European claims to African territory had to rest on "effective occupation" in order to be recognized by other states. A nation could establish a colony only if it had effectively taken possession of the territory through signed treaties with local leaders and had begun to develop it economically. The representatives at the conference recognized Leopold's rule over the Congo Free State.

In addition to developing rules for imperialist competition, participants at the Berlin Conference agreed to care for the native peoples' moral and material well-being, bring Christianity and civilization to Africa, and suppress slavery and the slave trade. These rules

and agreements were contained in the General Act of the conference:

> All the Powers exercising sovereign rights or influence in the aforesaid territories bind themselves to watch over the preservation of the native tribes, and to care for the improvement of the conditions of their moral and material well-being, and to help in suppressing slavery, and especially the slave trade.
>
> They shall, without distinction of creed or nation, protect and favour all religious, scientific or charitable institutions and undertakings created and organized for the above ends, or which aim at instructing the natives and bringing home to them the blessings of civilization.[5]

In truth, however, these ideals ran a distant second to, and were not allowed to interfere with, the nations' primary goal of commerce—holding on to their old markets and exploiting new ones.

Fourth, the Berlin Conference coincided with Germany's emergence as an imperial power. In 1884 and 1885 Bismarck's Germany established **protectorates** (autonomous states or territories partly controlled and protected by a stronger outside power) over a number of small African kingdoms and societies (see Map 25.1). In acquiring colonies, Bismarck cooperated with France's Jules Ferry against the British. The French expanded into West Africa and also formed a protectorate on the Congo River. Meanwhile, the British began enlarging their West African enclaves and pushed northward from the Cape Colony and westward from the East African coast.

The British also moved southward from Egypt, which they had seized in 1882 (see "Egypt: From Reform to British Occupation"), but were blocked in the eastern Sudan by fiercely independent Muslims. In 1881 a pious Sudanese leader, Muhammad Ahmad (AH-mad) (1844–1885), proclaimed himself the "Mahdi" (MAH-dee) (a messianic redeemer of Islam) and led a revolt against foreign control of Egypt. In 1885 his army massacred a British force and took the city of Khartoum (khar-TOUM), forcing the British to retreat to Cairo. Ten years later a British force returned, building a railroad to supply arms and reinforcements as it went. In 1898 these troops, under the command of Field Marshal Horatio Hubert Kitchener, met their foe at Omdurman (AHM-dur-man), where Sudanese Muslims armed with spears were cut down by the recently invented machine gun. In the end eleven thousand Muslim fighters lay dead, while only twenty-eight Britons had been killed. Their commander received the title of "Lord Kitchener of Khartoum."

All European nations resorted to some violence in their colonies to retain control, subdue the population, appropriate land, and force African laborers to work long hours at physically demanding, and often

---

Berlin Conference A meeting of European leaders held in 1884–1885 to lay down basic rules for imperialist competition in sub-Saharan Africa.

protectorate An autonomous state or territory partly controlled and protected by a stronger outside power.

Colonial presence, 1914

British	Belgian
French	Spanish
German	Independent African states
Italian	
Portuguese	Afrikaner republic

Colonial presence, 1878

MAPPING THE PAST

MAP 25.1　The Partition of Africa　The European powers carved up Africa after 1880 and built vast political empires.

ANALYZING THE MAP　What European countries were leading imperialist states in Africa, and what lands did they hold? What countries maintained political independence?

CONNECTIONS　The late nineteenth century was the high point of European imperialism. What were the motives behind the rush for land and empire in Africa?

Brutality in the Congo No Africans suffered more violent and brutal treatment under colonial rule than those living in Belgian king Leopold II's Congo Free State. When not having their hands, feet, or heads cut off as punishment, Africans were whipped with *chicottes*, whips made of dried hippopotamus hide. Some Congolese were literally whipped to death.
(© TopFoto/The Image Works)

dangerous, jobs. In no colony, however, was the violence and brutality worse than in Leopold II's Congo Free State. Rather than promoting Leopold's promised Christianity and civilization, the European companies operating in the Congo Free State introduced slavery, unimaginable savagery, and terror. Missionaries and others were not even allowed into the colony, to prevent them from reporting the horrors they would witness there.

Profits in the Congo Free State came first from the ivory trade, but in the 1890s, after many of the Congo's elephant herds had been decimated, a new cash crop arose to take ivory's place. In the mid-1880s Scottish-born John Dunlop developed a process to make inflatable rubber tires. A worldwide boom in the demand for raw rubber soon followed, as new uses for rubber were found. By the mid-1890s rubber had surpassed ivory as the Congo Free State's major income producer, as more than half the colony possessed wild rubber vines growing thickly in the equatorial rain forest. The companies Leopold allowed to make profits in the Congo soon could not get enough rubber. Violence and brutality increased exponentially as Europeans and their well-armed mercenaries terrorized entire regions, cutting off hands, feet, and heads, and wiping out whole villages to send the message that Africans must either work for the Europeans or die. The shed African

blood is recalled in the colony's frightening nickname—the "red rubber colony." In the first years of the nineteenth century, human rights activists such as Edmund Morel (moh-REHL) exposed the truth about the horrific conditions in the Congo Free State. In 1908 Leopold was forced to turn over his private territory to Belgium as a colony, the Belgian Congo. (See "Global Viewpoints: The Congo Free State," at right.)

Southern Africa in the Nineteenth Century

The development of southern Africa diverged from that of the rest of sub-Saharan Africa in important ways. Whites settled in large numbers, modern capitalist industry took off, and British imperialists had to wage all-out war.

When the British took possession of the Dutch Cape Colony during the Napoleonic Wars, there were about twenty thousand free Dutch citizens and twenty-five thousand African slaves, with substantial mixed-race communities on the northern frontier of white settlement. After 1815 powerful African chiefdoms; the Boers, or **Afrikaners** (descendants of the original Dutch settlers); and British colonial forces waged a complicated three-cornered battle to build strong states in southern Africa.

While the British consolidated their rule in the Cape Colony, the talented Zulu king Shaka (SHAHK-ah) (r. 1818–1828) was creating the largest and most pow-

Afrikaners Descendants of the Dutch settlers in the Cape Colony in southern Africa.

The Congo Free State

One historian estimates that between 1890 and 1910 the African population of the Congo Free State declined by nearly 10 million souls.* The public learned of the brutal conditions in the Congo through the efforts of reformers and journalists. George Washington Williams (1849–1891), an African American Baptist minister, lawyer, and historian, was dazzled, as were many others, by the noble humanitarian goals that Leopold II claimed to have for the Congo, but when Williams visited the Congo in 1890 he was sickened by what he saw. His public letter to King Leopold, excerpted below, offers one of the earliest firsthand accounts of the horrors of the Congo. Edmund Morel (1873–1924), a British clerk, was similarly galvanized to undertake a campaign against Leopold after noticing that nearly 80 percent of the goods that his shipping firm sent to the Congo were weapons, shackles, and ammunition, while arriving ships were filled with cargoes of rubber, ivory, and other high-value goods.

George Washington Williams, "An Open Letter to His Serene Majesty Leopold II," 1890

■ Your Majesty's Government has been, and is now, guilty of waging unjust and cruel wars against natives, with the hope of securing slaves and women, to minister to the behests of the officers of your Government. . . . I have no adequate terms with which to depict to your Majesty the brutal acts of your soldiers upon such raids as these. The soldiers who open the combat are usually the bloodthirsty cannibalistic Bangalas, who give no quarter to the aged grandmother or nursing child at the breast of its mother. There are instances in which they have brought the heads of their victims to their white officers on the expeditionary steamers, and afterwards eaten the bodies of slain children. In one war two Belgian Army officers saw, from the deck of their steamer, a native in a canoe some distance away. He was not a combatant and was ignorant of the conflict . . . upon the shore, some distance away. The officers made a wager of £5 that they could hit the native with their rifles. Three shots were fired and the native fell dead, pierced through the head, and the trade canoe was transformed into a funeral barge and floated silently down the river.

Edmund Morel, from *King Leopold's Rule in Africa*, 1904

■ One of the most atrocious features of the persistent warfare of which year in year out the Congo territories are the scene, is the mutilation both of the dead and of the living which goes on under it. . . . The first intimation that Congo State troops were in the habit of cutting off the hands of men, women, and children in connection with the rubber traffic reached Europe through the Rev. J. B. Murphy, of the American Baptist Missionary Union, in 1895. He described how the State soldiers had shot some people on Lake Mantumba . . . , "cut off their hands and took them to the Commissaire." The survivors of the slaughter reported the matter to a missionary at Irebu, who went down to see if it were true, and was quickly convinced by ocular demonstration. Among the mutilated victims was a little girl, not quite dead, who subsequently recovered. In a statement which appeared in the [London] *Times*, Mr. Murphy said, "These hands — the hands of men, women, and children — were placed in rows before the Commissary, who counted them to see that the soldiers had not wasted cartridges."

QUESTIONS FOR ANALYSIS

1. What factors might have allowed such horrible atrocities to be committed without greater public awareness and outcry?
2. How do these two readings exemplify the theory that the colonial experience brutalized both colonized and colonizer?

Sources: George Washington Williams, "An Open Letter to Leopold II, King of the Belgians and Sovereign of the Independent State of Congo, July 18, 1890," in John Hope Franklin, *George Washington Williams: A Biography* (Chicago: University of Chicago Press, 1985), pp. 245–246, 250–251; Edmund D. Morel, *King Leopold's Rule in Africa* (New York: Funk and Wagnalls, 1905), pp. 110–111.

*Adam Hochschild, *King Leopold's Ghost* (Boston: Houghton Mifflin, 1999), pp. 225–234.

erful kingdom in southern Africa in the nineteenth century. Shaka's warriors, drafted by age groups and placed in highly disciplined regiments, perfected the use of a short stabbing spear in deadly hand-to-hand combat. The Zulu armies often destroyed their African enemies completely, sowing chaos and sending refugees fleeing in all directions. Shaka's wars led to the creation of Zulu, Tswana (TSWAH-nah), Swazi (SWAH-zee), Ndebele (n-deh-BELL-ee), and Sotho (SOO-too, not SOH-thoh) states in southern Africa. By 1890 these states were largely subdued by Dutch and British invaders, but only after many hard-fought frontier wars.

Between 1834 and 1838 the British abolished slavery in the Cape Colony and introduced racial equality before the law to protect African labor. In 1836 about ten thousand Afrikaner cattle ranchers and farmers, resentful of equal treatment of blacks by British colonial officials and missionaries after the abolition of slavery, began to make their so-called Great Trek northward into the interior. In 1845 another group of Afrikaners joined them north of the Orange River. Over the next thirty years Afrikaner and British settlers reached a mutually advantageous division of southern Africa. The British ruled the strategically valuable colonies of Cape Colony and Natal (nuh-TAHL) on the coast, and the Afrikaners controlled the ranch-land republics of Orange Free State and the Transvaal (TRANS-vahl) in the interior. The Zulu, Xhosa, Sotho, Ndebele, and other African peoples lost much of their land but remained the majority—albeit an exploited majority.

The discovery of incredibly rich deposits of diamonds in 1867 near Kimberley, and of gold in 1886 in the Afrikaners' Transvaal Republic around modern Johannesburg, revolutionized the southern African economy, making possible large-scale industrial capitalism and transforming the lives of all its peoples. The extraction of these minerals, particularly the deep-level gold deposits, required big foreign investment, Euro-

pean engineering expertise, and an enormous labor force. Thus small-scale miners soon gave way to powerful financiers, particularly Cecil Rhodes (1853–1902). Rhodes came from a large middle-class British family and at seventeen went to southern Africa to seek his fortune. By 1888 Rhodes's firm, the De Beers mining company, monopolized the world's diamond industry and earned him fabulous profits. The "color bar" system of the diamond fields gave whites the well-paid skilled positions and put black Africans in the dangerous, low-wage jobs far below the earth's surface. Southern Africa became one of the world's leading diamond and gold producers, pulling in black migratory workers from all over the region (as it does to this day).

The mining bonanza whetted the appetite of British imperialists led by the powerful Rhodes, who was considered the ultimate British imperialist. He once famously observed that the British "happen to be the best people in the world, with the highest ideals of decency and justice and liberty and peace, and the more of the world we inhabit, the better for humanity."[6] Between 1888 and 1893 Rhodes used missionaries and

Republic Gold Mining Company, South Africa, ca. 1888 This early photo, taken only a couple of years after the discovery of gold and the beginning of the Witwatersrand gold rush, shows both black and white miners at a gold mine. By this time, twenty-one years after the discovery of diamonds at Kimberley, labor segregation had become a regular feature of mine work. White workers claimed the supervisory jobs, while blacks were limited to dangerous low-wage labor. (Bettmann Collection/Getty Images)

his British South Africa Company, chartered by the British government, to force African chiefs to accept British protectorates, and he managed to add Southern and Northern Rhodesia (modern-day Zimbabwe and Zambia) to the British Empire.

Southern Rhodesia is one of the most egregious examples of a region where Europeans misled African rulers to take their land. In 1888 the Ndebele (or Matabele) king, Lobengula (loh-ben-GUL-ah) (1845–1894), ruler over much of modern southwestern Zimbabwe, met with three of Rhodes's men, led by Charles Rudd, and signed the Rudd Concession. Lobengula believed he was simply allowing a handful of British fortune hunters a few years of gold prospecting in Matabeleland. Lobengula had been misled, however, by the resident London Missionary Society missionary (and Lobengula's supposed friend), the Reverend Charles Helm, as to the document's true meaning and Rhodes's hand behind it. Even though Lobengula soon repudiated the agreement, he opened the way for Rhodes's seizure of the territory.

In 1889 Rhodes's British South Africa Company received a royal charter from Queen Victoria to occupy Matabeleland on behalf of the British government. Though Lobengula died in early 1894, his warriors bravely fought Rhodes's private army in the First and Second Matabele Wars (1893–1894, 1896–1897), but were decimated by British Maxim guns. By 1897 Matabeleland had ceased to exist; it had been replaced by the British-ruled settler colony of Southern Rhodesia. Before his death, Lobengula asked Reverend Helm, "Did you ever see a chameleon catch a fly? The chameleon gets behind the fly and remains motionless for some time, then he advances very slowly and gently, first putting forward one leg and then the other. At last, when well within reach, he darts his tongue and the fly disappears. England is the chameleon and I am that fly."[7]

The Transvaal gold fields still remained in Afrikaner hands, however, so Rhodes and the imperialist clique initiated a series of events that sparked the South African War of 1899–1902 (also known as the Anglo-Boer War). The British needed 450,000 troops to crush the Afrikaners, who never had more than 30,000 men in the field. Often considered the first "total war," this conflict witnessed the British use of a scorched-earth strategy to destroy Afrikaner property, and concentration camps to detain Afrikaner families and their servants, thousands of whom died of illness. Africans were sometimes forced and sometimes volunteered to work for one side or the other; estimates of their number range from 15,000 to 40,000

for each side. They did everything from scouting and guard duty to heavy manual labor, driving wagons, and guarding the livestock.

The long and bitter war divided whites in South Africa, but South Africa's blacks were the biggest losers. The British had promised the Afrikaners representative government in return for surrender in 1902, and they made good on their pledge. In 1910 the Cape Colony, Natal, the Orange Free State, and the Transvaal formed a new self-governing Union of South Africa. After the peace settlement, because the white minority held almost all political power in the new union, and because Afrikaners outnumbered English-speakers, the Afrikaners began to regain what they had lost on the battlefield. South Africa, under a joint British-Afrikaner government within the British Empire, began the creation of a modern segregated society that culminated in an even harsher system of racial separation, or apartheid (uh-PAHRT-ayte), after World War II.

Colonialism's Impact After 1900

By 1900 much of Africa had been conquered and a system of colonial administration was taking shape. In general, this system weakened or shattered the traditional social order.

The self-proclaimed political goal of the French and the British—the principal colonial powers—was to provide good government for their African subjects, especially after World War I. "Good government" meant, above all, law and order. It meant a strong, authoritarian government, which maintained a small army, built up an African police force, and included a modern bureaucracy capable of taxing and governing the population. Many African leaders and their peoples had chosen not to resist the invaders' superior force, and others stopped fighting and turned to other, less violent means of resisting colonial rule. Thus the goal of law and order was widely achieved.

Colonial governments demonstrated much less interest in providing basic social services. Education, public health, hospital, and other social service expenditures increased after the Great War but still remained limited. Europeans feared the political implications of mass education and typically relied instead on the modest efforts of state-subsidized mission schools. Moreover, they tried to make even their poorest colonies pay for themselves through taxation.

Economically, the colonial goal was to draw the African interior into the world economy on terms favorable to the dominant Europeans. Railroads linking

The South African War, 1899–1902

Missionary School, South Africa, 1910 In this photo, African students are taught by a Roman Catholic nun. In the early days of a mission station, before a school building had been erected, nuns and priests held classes outside. Sometimes they also traveled to surrounding African villages and held classes outside there. The students were generally given a mixture of academic subject matter and religious instruction. (© Sz Photo/Scherl/The Image Works)

coastal trading centers to interior outposts facilitated easy shipment of raw materials out and manufactured goods in. Railroads had two other important outcomes: they allowed quick troop movements to put down local unrest, and they allowed many African peasants to earn wages for the first time.

The focus on economic development and low-cost rule explains why colonial governments were reluctant to move decisively against slavery within Africa. Officials feared that an abrupt abolition of slavery where it existed would disrupt production and lead to costly revolts by powerful slaveholding elites, especially in Muslim areas. Thus colonial regimes settled for halfway measures designed to satisfy humanitarian groups in Europe and also make all Africans, free or enslaved, participate in a market economy and work for wages. Even this cautious policy emboldened many slaves to run away, thereby facilitating a rapid decline of slavery within Africa.

Colonial governments also often imposed taxes. Payable only in labor or European currency, these taxes compelled Africans to work for their white overlords. Africans despised no aspect of colonialism more than forced labor, widespread until about 1920. In some regions, particularly in West Africa, African peasants

continued to respond freely to the new economic opportunities by voluntarily shifting to export crops on their own farms. Overall, the result of these developments was an increase in wage work and production geared to the world market and a decline in nomadic herding and traditional self-sufficient farming of sustainable crops. In sum, the imposition of bureaucratic Western rule and the gradual growth of a world-oriented cash economy after 1900 had a revolutionary impact on large parts of Africa.

The New Imperialism, 1880–1914

What were the causes and consequences of European empire building after 1880?

Western expansion into Africa and Asia reached its apex between about 1880 and 1914. In those years the leading European nations sent streams of money and manufactured goods to both continents and also rushed to create or enlarge vast overseas political empires. This frantic activity differed sharply from the limited economic penetration of non-Western territories between 1816 and 1880, which had left a China or a Japan "opened" but politically independent. By contrast, late-nineteenth-century empires recalled the

New Imperialism The late-nineteenth-century drive by European countries to create vast political empires abroad.

old European colonial empires of the seventeenth and eighteenth centuries and led contemporaries to speak of the **New Imperialism**.

Characterized by a frenzied rush to plant the flag over as many people and as much territory as possible, the most spectacular manifestation of the New Imperialism was the seizure of almost all of Africa. Less striking but equally important was Europe's extension of political control in Asia, the subject of Chapter 26.

Causes of the New Imperialism

Many factors contributed to the West's late-nineteenth-century rush for territory in Africa and Asia, and controversies continue to rage over interpretation of the New Imperialism. Despite complexity and controversy, however, basic causes are clearly identifiable.

Economic motives played an important role in the extension of political empires, especially of the British Empire. By the 1870s France, Germany, and the United States were rapidly industrializing. For a century Great Britain had been the "workshop of the world," the dominant modern industrial power. Now it was losing its industrial leadership, as its share of global manufacturing output dropped from 33 percent to just 14 percent between 1870 and 1914, and facing increasingly tough competition in foreign markets. In this changing environment of widening economic internationalism, the world experienced one of the worst economic depressions in history, the Long Depression of 1873 to 1879 (originally called the Great Depression until the Great Depression of the 1930s supplanted it). To protect home industries, America and Europe (except for Britain and the Netherlands) raised tariff barriers, abandoning the century-long practice of free trade and laissez-faire capitalism. Unable to export their goods and faced with excess production, market saturation, and high unemployment, Britain, the other European powers, and the United States turned to imperial expansion, seeking African and Asian colonies to sell their products and acquire cheap raw materials. The Long Depression was arguably the single most important spark touching off the age of New Imperialism.

Economic gains from the New Imperialism proved limited, however, before 1914. The new colonies were too poor to buy much, and they offered few immediately profitable investments. Nonetheless, colonies became important for political and diplomatic reasons. Each leading European country considered them crucial to national security, military power, and international prestige. (See "Analyzing the Evidence: A French Leader Defends Imperialism," page 740.)

Colonial rivalries reflected the increasing aggressiveness of Social Darwinian theories of brutal competition among races. As one prominent English economist argued in 1873, the "strongest nation has always

Tools for Empire Building Western technological advances aided imperialist ambitions in Africa. The Maxim gun was highly mobile and could lay down a continuous barrage that decimated charging enemies, as in the slaughter of Muslim tribesmen at the Battle of Omdurman in Sudan. Quinine, first taken around 1850 to prevent the contraction of malaria, enabled Europeans to move safely into the African interior and overwhelm native peoples. And the development of the electromagnetic telegraph in the 1840s permitted rapid long-distance communications for the first time in history.

(quinine bottle: Science Museum, London, UK/Wellcome Images; gun: Private Collection/Peter Newark Military Pictures/Bridgeman Images; telegraph: John D. Jenkins, The Spark Museum of Electrical Invention, www.sparkmuseum.com)

been conquering the weaker . . . and the strongest tend to be best."[8] Thus European nations, considered as racially distinct parts of the dominant white race, had to seize colonies to prove their strength and virility. Moreover, since racial struggle was nature's inescapable law, the conquest of "inferior" peoples was just. Social Darwinism and harsh racial doctrines fostered imperialist expansion.

A French Leader Defends Imperialism

Although Jules Ferry (1832–1893) first gained political prominence as an ardent champion of secular public education, he was most famous for his empire building. While he was French premier in 1880–1881 and again in 1883–1885, France occupied Tunisia, extended its rule in Indonesia, seized Madagascar, and penetrated the Congo. Criticized by conservatives, socialists, and some left-wing republicans for his colonial expansion, Ferry defended his policies before the French National Assembly and also elaborated a philosophy of imperialism in his writings.

In a speech to the Assembly on July 28, 1883, portions of which follow, Ferry answered his critics and summarized his three main arguments with brutal honesty. Note that Ferry adamantly insisted that imperial expansion did not weaken France in its European struggle with Germany, as some opponents charged, but instead increased France's grandeur and power. Imperialists needed the language of patriotic nationalism to be effective.

■ *M. Jules Ferry*: Gentlemen, . . . I believe that there is some benefit in summarizing and condensing, in the form of arguments, the principles, the motives, and the various interests by which a policy of colonial expansion may be justified; it goes without saying that I will try to remain reasonable, moderate, and never lose sight of the major continental interests which are the primary concern of this country. What I wish to say, to support this proposition, is that in fact, just as in word, the policy of colonial expansion is a political and economic system; I wish to say that one can relate this system to three

orders of ideas: economic ideas, ideas of civilization in its highest sense, and ideas of politics and patriotism.

In the area of economics, I will allow myself to place before you, with the support of some figures, the considerations which justify a policy of colonial expansion from the point of view of that need, felt more and more strongly by the industrial populations of Europe and particularly those of our own rich and hard working country: the need for export markets. Is this some kind of chimera? Is this a view of the future or is it not rather a pressing need, and, we could say, the cry of our industrial population? I will formulate only in a general way what each of you, in the different parts of France, is in a position to confirm. Yes, what is lacking for our great industry, drawn irrevocably on to the path of exportation by the [free trade] treaties of 1860, what it lacks more and more is export markets. Why? Because next door to us Germany is surrounded by barriers, because beyond the ocean, the United States of America has become protectionist, protectionist in the most extreme sense. . . .

Gentlemen, there is a second point, . . . the humanitarian and civilizing side of the question. On this point the honorable M. Camille Pellatan has jeered in his own refined and clever manner; he jeers, he condemns, and he says "What is this civilization which you impose with cannonballs? What is it but another form of barbarism? Don't these populations, these inferior races, have the same rights as you? Aren't they masters of their own houses? Have they called upon you? You come to them against their will, you offer them violence, but not civilization." There, gentlemen, is the thesis; I do not

So, too, did the industrial world's unprecedented technological and military superiority. Three developments were crucial. First, the rapidly firing machine gun was an ultimate weapon in many unequal battles. Second, newly discovered **quinine** (KWIGH-nighn) effectively controlled malaria attacks, which had previously decimated Europeans in the tropics. Third, the introduction of steam power strengthened the Western powers in two ways. Militarily, they could swiftly transport their armies by sea or rail where they were most needed. Economically, steamships with ever-larger cargoes now made round-trip journeys to far-flung colonies much more quickly and economically. Small steamboats could travel back and forth along the coast and also carry goods up and down Africa's great rivers, as portrayed in the classic American film

The African Queen (1951). Likewise, freight cars pulled by powerful steam engines—immune to disease, unlike animals and humans—replaced the thousands of African porters hitherto responsible for carrying raw materials from the interior to the coast. Never before—and never again after 1914—would the technological gap between the West and the non-Western regions of the world be so great.

Domestic political and class conflicts also contributed to overseas expansion. Conservative political leaders often manipulated colonial issues in order to divert popular attention from domestic problems and to create a false sense of national unity. Imperial propagandists relentlessly stressed that colonies benefited workers as well as capitalists, and they encouraged the masses to savor foreign triumphs and imperial glory.

Finally, special-interest groups in each country were powerful agents of expansion. Shipping companies wanted lucrative subsidies. White settlers wanted more

quinine An agent that proved effective in controlling attacks of malaria, which had previously decimated Europeans in the tropics.

hesitate to say that this is not politics, nor is it political metaphysics. ("Ah, Ah" *on far left*.)

. . . Gentlemen, I must speak from a higher and more truthful plane. It must be stated openly that, in effect, superior races have rights over inferior races. (*Movement on many benches on the far left.*)

M. Jules Maigne: Oh! You dare to say this in the country which has proclaimed the rights of man!

M. de Guilloutet: This is a justification of slavery and the slave trade! . . .

M. Jules Ferry: I repeat that superior races have a right, because they have a duty. They have the duty to civilize inferior races. . . . (*Approval from the left. New interruptions from the extreme left and from the right.*)

Gentlemen, there are certain considerations which merit the attention of all patriots. The conditions of naval warfare have been profoundly altered. ("Very true! Very true!")

At this time, as you know, a warship cannot carry more than fourteen days' worth of coal, no matter how perfectly it is organized, and a ship which is out of coal is a derelict on the surface of the sea, abandoned to the first person who comes along. Thence the necessity of having on the oceans provision stations, shelters, ports for defense and revictualling. (*Applause at the center and left. Various interruptions.*) And it is for this that we needed Tunisia, for this that we needed Saigon and the Mekong Delta, for this that we need Madagascar, that we are at Diégo-Suarez and Vohemar [two Madagascar ports] and will never leave them! (*Applause from a great number of benches.*) Gentlemen, in Europe as it is today, in this competition of so many rivals which we see growing around us, some by perfecting their military or maritime forces, others by the prodigious development of an ever growing population; in a Europe, or rather in a universe of this sort, a policy of peaceful seclusion or abstention is simply the highway to decadence! Nations are great in our times only by means of the activities which they develop; it is not simply "by the peaceful shining forth of institutions" (*interruptions on the extreme left and right*) that they are great at this hour.

. . . [The Republican Party] has shown that it is quite aware that one cannot impose upon France a political ideal conforming to that of nations like independent Belgium and the Swiss Republic; that something else is needed for France: that she cannot be merely a free country, that she must also be a great country, exercising all of her rightful influence over the destiny of Europe, that she ought to propagate this influence throughout the world and carry everywhere that she can her language, her customs, her flag, her arms, and her genius. (*Applause at center and left.*)

QUESTIONS FOR ANALYSIS

1. What was Jules Ferry's economic argument for imperial expansion? Why had colonies recently gained greater economic value?
2. How did Ferry's critics attack the morality of foreign expansion? How did Ferry try to claim the moral high ground in his response?
3. What political arguments did Ferry advance? How would you characterize his philosophy of politics and national development?

Source: Speech before the French National Assembly, July 28, 1883. Reprinted in R. A. Austen, ed., *Modern Imperialism: Western Overseas Expansion and Its Aftermath, 1776–1965* (Lexington, Mass.: D. C. Heath, 1969), pp. 70–73.

land. Missionaries and humanitarians wanted to spread religion and stop the slave trade. Military men and colonial officials foresaw rapid advancement and high-paid positions in growing empires. The actions of such groups pushed the course of empire forward.

A "Civilizing Mission"

To rationalize their aggressive and racist actions, Europeans and Americans argued they could and should "civilize" supposedly primitive non-Western peoples. According to this view, Africans and Asians would benefit from Western educations, modern economies, cities, advanced medicine, and higher living standards and eventually might be ready for self-government and Western democracy.

European imperialists also argued that imperial government protected colonized peoples from ethnic warfare, the slave trade within Africa, and other forms of exploitation by white settlers and business people. Thus the French spoke of their sacred "civilizing mission." In 1899 Rudyard Kipling (1865–1936), perhaps the most influential British writer of the 1890s, exhorted Westerners to unselfish service in distant lands (while warning of the high costs involved) in his poem "The White Man's Burden."

Take up the White Man's Burden —
Send forth the best ye breed —
Go bind your sons to exile
To serve your captives' need,
To wait in heavy harness,
On fluttered folk and wild —
Your new-caught, sullen peoples
Half-devil and half-child.[9]

Kipling's poem, written in response to America's seizure of the Philippines after the Spanish-American War, and his concept of a **white man's burden** won wide acceptance among American imperialists. This principle was an important factor in the decision to rule, rather than liberate, the Philippines after the Spanish-American War (see "The Philippines" in Chapter 26). Like their European counterparts, these Americans believed their civilization had reached unprecedented heights, enabling them to bestow unique benefits on all "less advanced" peoples. (See "Analyzing the Evidence: Pears' Soap Advertisement," at right.)

Imperialists also claimed that peace and stability under European or American dominion permitted the spread of Christianity. In Africa Catholic and Protestant missionaries competed with Islam south of the Sahara, seeking converts and building schools. Many Africans' first real contact with Europeans and Americans was in mission schools. Some peoples, such as the Ibo in Nigeria, became highly Christianized. Such successes in black Africa contrasted with the general failure of missionary efforts in the Islamic world and in much of Asia.

Critics of Imperialism

Imperial expansion aroused sharp, even bitter, critics. One forceful attack was delivered in 1902, after the unpopular South African War, by radical English economist J. A. Hobson (1858–1940) in his *Imperialism*. Hobson contended that the rush to acquire colonies resulted from the economic needs of unregulated (by governments) capitalism. Moreover, Hobson argued, the quest for empire diverted popular attention away from domestic reform and the need to reduce the great gap between rich and poor at home. These and similar arguments had limited appeal because most people fervently believed imperialism was economically profitable for the homeland. Both Hobson and public opinion were wrong, however. Most British and European investors put the bulk of their money in the United States, Canada, Russia, and other industrializing countries. Sub-Saharan Africa accounted for less than 5 percent of British exports in 1890, and British investments in Africa flowed predominantly to the mines in southern African. Thus, while some sectors of the British economy did profit from imperial conquests, and trade with these conquests was greater just before the Great War than in 1870, overall profits from imperialism were marginal at best.

Hobson and many Western critics struck home, however, with their moral condemnation of whites' imperiously ruling nonwhites. Kipling and his kind were lampooned as racist bullies whose rule rested on brutality, racial contempt, and the Maxim machine gun. Polish-born novelist Joseph Conrad (1857–1924), in *Heart of Darkness* (1902), castigated the "pure selfishness" of Europeans in "civilizing" Africa.

Critics charged Europeans with applying a degrading double standard and failing to live up to their own noble ideals. At home Europeans had won or were winning representative government, individual liberties, and a certain equality of opportunity. In their empires Europeans imposed military dictatorships on Africans and Asians, forced them to work involuntarily, and discriminated against them shamelessly.

African and Asian Resistance

To African and Asian peoples, Western expansion represented a profoundly disruptive assault, which threatened traditional ruling classes, economies, and ways of life. Christian missionaries and European secular ideologies challenged established beliefs and values. African and Asian societies experienced crises of identity, although the details of each people's story varied substantially. (See "Thinking Like a Historian: African Views of the Scramble for Africa," page 744.)

Initially African and Asian rulers often responded to imperialist incursions by trying to drive the unwelcome foreigners away, as in China and Japan (see "The Opium War" and "The 'Opening' of Japan" in Chapter 26). Violent antiforeign reactions exploded elsewhere again and again, but the industrialized West's superior military technology almost invariably prevailed. In addition, Europeans sought to divide and conquer by giving special powers and privileges to some individuals and groups from among the local population, including traditional leaders such as chiefs, landowners, and religious figures; and Western-educated professionals and civil servants, including police officers and military officers. These local elites recognized the imperial power realities in which they were enmeshed and manipulated them to maintain or gain authority over the masses. Some concluded that the West was superior in certain ways and that they needed to reform and modernize their societies by copying some European achievements. By ruling indirectly through a local elite (backed by the implied threat of force), relatively small numbers of Europeans could maintain control over much larger populations without constant rebellion and protest. European empires were won by force, but they were maintained by cultural as well as military and political means.

Nevertheless, imperial rule was in many ways an imposing edifice built on sand. Acceptance of European rule was shallow and weak among the colonized masses. They were often quick to follow determined charismatic personalities who came to oppose the Europeans. Such leaders always arose, both when Europe-

---

white man's burden The idea that Europeans could and should civilize more primitive nonwhite peoples and that imperialism would eventually provide nonwhites with modern achievements and higher standards of living.

Pears' Soap Advertisement

Andrew Pears began making his transparent soap in London in 1789. Starting in the late nineteenth century, it was marketed worldwide as a product symbolizing progress in advancing Europe's "civilizing mission." Massive quantities of palm oil were shipped from Africa to Europe, where palm oil replaced whale oil as the preferred oil for oiling machinery and producing cosmetics. In 1910 the Lever brothers, William and James, bought Pears's company and sold Pears' Soap along with their own brands, including Sunlight, Lifebuoy, and Lux, under the name Lever Brothers (now Unilever). These soaps were made with palm oil from Lever plantations in the Congo and the Solomon Islands. Pears' Soap is still made today in India. Refined petroleum eventually supplanted palm oil, but contemporary brand names like Palmolive and Lever are vestiges of the days when palm oil was king.

Interestingly, the idea of cleanliness through using soap and taking baths was a relatively new "civilized" phenomenon in England. The soapmaking industry had its beginnings in the late eighteenth century. Only with the rise of the urbanized middle class in the mid-nineteenth century did cleanliness join with other Victorian values like morality, elitism, industrialism, mental and physical improvement, and Christianity. Thus using soap and taking frequent baths were practices still relatively new in England when manufacturers started advertising soap throughout the empire.

QUESTIONS FOR ANALYSIS

1. Which elements or words in this advertisement suggest the Western ideal of "civilization"? Which elements or words are used to describe non-Europeans?
2. How does this advertisement relate to Europe's "civilizing mission" and the English maxim "Cleanliness is next to godliness"?
3. How can Pears' Soap lighten "the white man's burden" and brighten "the dark corners of the earth"? To whom does the phrase "the cultured of all nations" refer?

The first step towards lightening

The White Man's Burden

is through teaching the virtues of cleanliness.

Pears' Soap

is a potent factor in brightening the dark corners of the earth as civilization advances, while amongst the cultured of all nations it holds the highest place—it is the ideal toilet soap.

(© North Wind Picture Archives/Alamy Stock Photo)

---

ans ruled directly, or indirectly through native governments, for at least two basic reasons.

First, the nonconformists—the eventual anti-imperialist leaders—developed a burning desire for human dignity. They felt such dignity was incompatible with, and impossible under, foreign rule. Second, potential leaders found in the Western world the necessary ideologies and justification for their protest, such as liberalism, with its credo of civil liberty and political self-determination. Above all, they found themselves attracted to the nineteenth-century Western ideology of nationalism, which asserted that every people had the right to control their own destiny. After 1917 anti-imperialist revolt found another weapon in Lenin's version of Marxist socialism.

African Views of the Scramble for Africa

There are always two sides to any historical event, but often the only voices that are heard are those of the victors. There is an African proverb that underscores this point: "Until the lions have their historians, tales of hunting will always glorify the hunter." Historians should try to gather evidence from both sides, and for no event is this more true than in Europe's colonization of the African continent.

1 **King Moshoeshoe, letter to Sir George Grey, 1858.** King Moshoeshoe (r. 1786?–1870) gathered his Basotho peoples and others around him in what is now Lesotho. When neighboring Afrikaners threatened to take his territory and Basotho independence, he asked the British for help.

■ Thaba Bosigo, June 1858

I know . . . you have heard with pain of the horrors occasioned by the war [between the Orange Free State and myself], at present suspended in the hopes that peace may be restored by Your Excellency's mediation.

Allow me, however, to bring to your remembrance the following circumstances: About twenty-five years ago my knowledge of the White men and their laws was very limited. I knew merely that mighty nations existed, and among them was the English. These, the blacks who were acquainted with them, praised for their justice. Unfortunately it was not with the English Government that my first intercourse with the whites commenced. People who had come from the Colony first presented themselves to us, they called themselves Boers. I thought all white men were honest. Some of these Boers asked permission to live upon our borders. I . . . believe[d] they would live with me as my own people lived, that is, looking to me as to a father and a friend. . . .

We were at peace for a time. In the commencement of the present year (1858) my people living near farmers received orders to remove from their places. . . . We tried to keep all quiet, but the Boers went further . . . in troubling the Basutos and threatening war. . . . Still I tried to avert war. . . . I had given orders that no farms should be burnt, and my orders were obeyed till my people saw village after village burnt off, and the corn destroyed, they then carried destruction among the enemy's homes. . . . My bands were getting ready to make a descent upon them, when the Boers . . . request[ed] . . . a cessation of hostilities. I knew what misery I should bring upon the country by leaving the Basutos to ravage the Boer places, and therefore I have agreed. . . . I cannot say that I do so with the consent of my people, for many of those who suffered by the enemy were anxious to recover their losses.

If they have remained quiet, it has been owing to my persuasions and my promises that they might have good hope of justice—Your Excellency having consented to act as arbitrator between the Boers and Basutos.

Moshesh, Chief of the Basutos

2 **King Lobengula, letter to Queen Victoria, 1889.** Realizing the Rudd Concession threatened Ndebele independence, Ndebele king Lobengula sent two envoys to Cape Town and London in January–February 1889 to meet with Queen Victoria and seek her advice. On April 26, 1889, he wrote to the queen, repudiating the Rudd Concession.

■ To Her Majesty Queen Victoria

Some time ago a party of men came into my country, the principal one appearing to be a man called Rudd. They asked me for a place to dig for gold, and said they would give me certain things for the right to do so. I told them to bring what they would give and I would show them what I would give. A document was written and presented to me for signature. I asked what it contained, and was told that in it were my words and the words of those men. I put my hand to it. About three months afterwards I heard from other sources that I had given by that document the right to all the minerals of my country. I called a meeting of my Indunas [chiefs] and also of the white men and demanded a copy of the document. It was proved to me that I had signed away the mineral rights of my whole country to Rudd and his friends.

I have since had a meeting of my Indunas and they will not recognize the paper, as it contains neither my words nor the words of those who got it from me.

From Lobengula

ANALYZING THE EVIDENCE

1. What one word in Moshoeshoe's letter in Source 1 best describes his impression of the English?
2. Do any of these sources suggest Africans were treated fairly in their dealings with Europeans during the scramble for Africa?
3. European imperialists partly justified their invasion of Africa by saying they were ridding the continent of bloodthirsty tyrants. Do any of the African leaders cited in Sources 1–4 appear to fit that description?
4. In what ways might the British and Zulu figures depicted in Source 5 be perceived in Great Britain? How might they be perceived by the Zulu?

(Universal History Archive/Universal Images Group/Getty Images)

5 **Battle of Isandlwana, 1879.** On January 22, 1879, about 22,000 Zulu warriors defeated around 1,350 British and indigenous troops at the beginning of the Anglo-Zulu War. It remains the single greatest defeat the British ever suffered against a non-European force. Here British lieutenants Teignmouth Melvill and Nevill Coghill make a last stand against the Zulu. This painting was created by the English war artist Charles Edwin Fripp shortly after the war.

3 **Queen Mother Yaa Asantewaa rallies the Asante people, 1900.** In 1900 the governor general of the British Gold Coast, Frederick Hodgson, deported Asante king Prempeh I to the Seychelles. Hodgson then demanded the Golden Stool, the symbol of the Asante nation. Queen Mother Yaa Asantewaa rallied the Asante and led the Asante rebellion against the British in the War of the Golden Stool.

■ Now I have seen that some of you fear to go forward to fight for our king. If it were in the brave days, . . . chiefs would not sit down to see their king taken away without firing a shot. No white man could have dared to speak to a chief of the Asante nation the way the governor spoke to your chiefs this morning.

Is it true that the bravery of the Asante is no more? I cannot believe it. It cannot be! I must say this: if you, the men of the Asante, will not go forward, then we will. We, the women. I shall call upon my fellow women—we will fight the white men. We will fight till the last of us fall in the battlefields.

4 **King Wobogo refuses to negotiate with the French, 1895.** In 1895, in what is modern Burkina Faso, Wobogo, the Moro Naba, or king, of the Mosi refused to negotiate with a French officer, Captain Destenave. The following year the French deposed the king, seized his capital, and installed a Mosi ruler of their choosing.

■ I know the whites wish to kill me in order to take my country, and yet you claim that they will help me to organize my country. But I find my country good just as it is. I have no need of them. I know what is necessary for me and what I want: I have my own merchants: also, consider yourself fortunate that I do not order your head to be cut off. Go away now, and above all, never come back.

PUTTING IT ALL TOGETHER

Using the sources above, along with what you have learned in class and in this chapter, write a short essay about the different types of African resistance to European colonization. Why would some African leaders choose to fight wars, some simply refuse to cooperate, and some cooperate?

Sources: (1) George McCall Theal, ed., *Basutoland Records. Vol. 2: 1853–1861* (Cape Town: W. A. Richards & Sons, Government Printers, 1883), pp. 384–388; (2) Edmund D. Morel, *The Black Man's Burden* (New York: B. W. Huebsch, 1920), pp. 34–35; (3) Elias Yussif, *The Facet of Black Culture,* vol. 1 (Bloomington, Ind.: Trafford, 2013), pp. xxi–xxii; (4) A. Adu Boahen, ed., *UNESCO General History of Africa. Vol. 7: Africa Under Colonial Domination, 1880–1935,* abridged ed. (Berkeley: University of California Press, 1990), p. 1.

The Islamic Heartland Under Pressure

How did the Ottoman Empire and Egypt try to modernize themselves, and what were the most important results?

Stretching from West Africa into southeastern Europe and across Southwest Asia to the East Indies, Islamic civilization competed successfully with western Europe for centuries. Beginning in the late seventeenth century, however, the rising absolutist states of Austria and Russia began to challenge the Ottoman Empire and gradually to reverse Ottoman rule in southeastern Europe. In the nineteenth century European industrialization and nation building further altered the long-standing balance of power, and Western expansion eventually posed a serious challenge to Muslims everywhere.

Decline and Reform in the Ottoman Empire

Although the Ottoman Empire began a slow decline after Suleiman (SOO-lay-man) the Magnificent in the sixteenth century, the relationship between the Ottomans and the Europeans in about 1750 was still one of roughly equal strength. This parity began to change quickly and radically, however, in the later eighteenth century, as the Ottomans fell behind western Europe in science, industrial skill, and military technology.

A transformation of the army was absolutely necessary to battle the Europeans more effectively and enhance the sultanate's authority within the empire. There were two primary obstacles to change, however. First, Ottoman military weakness reflected the decline of the sultan's "slave army," the janissary corps. With time, the janissaries — boys and other slaves raised in Turkey as Muslims, then trained to serve in the Ottoman infantry's elite corps — became a corrupt and privileged hereditary caste, absolutely opposed to any military innovations that might undermine their high status. Second, the empire was no longer a centralized military state. Instead local governors were becoming increasingly independent, pursuing their own interests and even seeking to establish their own governments and hereditary dynasties.

Sultan Selim III (r. 1789–1807) understood these realities, but when he tried to reorganize the army, the janissaries refused to use any "Christian" equipment. In 1807 they revolted and executed Selim in a palace revolution, one of many that plagued the Ottoman state. Selim's successor, the reform-minded Mahmud II (r. 1808–1839), proceeded cautiously, picking loyal officers and building his dependable artillery corps. In 1826 his council ordered the janissaries to drill in the European manner. As expected, the janissaries revolted and charged the palace, where they were mowed down by the waiting artillery.

The destruction and abolition of the janissaries cleared the way for building a new army, but it came too late to stop the rise of Muhammad Ali, the Ottoman governor in Egypt. In 1831 his French-trained forces occupied the Ottoman province of Syria and appeared ready to depose Mahmud II. The Ottoman sultan survived, but only with help from Britain, Russia, and Austria. The Ottomans were saved again in 1839, after their forces were routed trying to drive Muhammad Ali from Syria. In the last months of 1840 Russian diplomatic efforts, British and Austrian naval blockades, and threatened military action convinced Muhammad Ali to return Syria to the Ottomans. European powers preferred a weak and dependent Ottoman state to a strong and revitalized Muslim entity under a leader such as Muhammad Ali.

In 1839, realizing their precarious position, liberal Ottoman statesmen launched an era of radical reforms, which lasted until 1876 and culminated in a constitution and a short-lived parliament. Known as the **Tanzimat** (TAHN-zee-maht) (literally, "regulations" or "orders"), these reforms were designed to remake the empire on a western European model. The new decrees called for Muslim, Christian, and Jewish equality before the law and in business, security of life and property, and a modernized administration and military. New commercial laws allowed free importation of foreign goods, as British advisers demanded, and permitted foreign merchants to operate freely throughout an economically dependent empire. Under British pressure, slavery in the empire was drastically curtailed, though not abolished completely. Of great significance, growing numbers among the elite and the upwardly mobile embraced Western education, adopted Western manners and artistic styles, and accepted secular values to some extent.

Intended to bring revolutionary modernization such as that experienced by Russia under Peter the Great (see "Peter the Great and Russia's Turn to the West" in Chapter 18) and by Japan in the Meiji era (see "The Meiji Restoration" in Chapter 26), the Tanzimat achieved only partial success. The Ottoman state and society failed to regain its earlier power and authority for several reasons. First, implementation of the reforms required a new generation of well-trained and trustworthy officials, and that generation did not exist. Second, the liberal reforms failed to halt the growth of nationalism among Christian subjects in the Balkans (discussed below), which resulted in crises and defeats that undermined all reform efforts. Third, the Ottoman initiatives did not curtail the appetite of Western imperialism, and European bankers gained a stranglehold on Ottoman finances. In 1875 the Ottoman state

Tanzimat A set of radical reforms designed to remake the Ottoman Empire on a western European model.

Pasha Halim Receiving Archduke Maximilian of Austria As this painting suggests, Ottoman leaders became well versed in European languages and culture. They also mastered the game of power politics, playing one European state against another and securing the Ottoman Empire's survival. The black servants on the right may be slaves from the Sudan. (Miramare Palace, Trieste, Italy/De Agostini Picture Library/Gianni Dagli Orti/Bridgeman Images)

had to declare partial bankruptcy and place its finances in the hands of European creditors.

Finally, the elaboration—at least on paper—of equal rights for citizens and religious communities failed to create greater unity within the state. Religious disputes increased, worsened by the Great Powers' relentless interference. This development embittered relations between religious communities, distracted the government from its reform mission, and split Muslims into secularists and religious conservatives. Islamic conservatives became the most dependable supporters of Sultan Abdülhamid II (ahb-DUHL-ah-mid) (r. 1876–1909), who abandoned the model of European liberalism in his long and repressive reign.

Meanwhile, the Ottoman Empire gradually lost control of its vast territories. Serbian nationalists rebelled and forced the Ottomans to grant Serbia local autonomy in 1816. The Greeks revolted against Ottoman rule in 1821 and won their national independence in 1830. As the Otto-

mans dealt with these uprisings by their Christian subjects in Europe, they failed to defend their Islamic provinces in North Africa. In 1830 French armies began their conquest of the Arabic-speaking province of Algeria.

Finally, during the Russo-Turkish War (1877–1878), absolutist Russia and a coalition of Balkan countries pushed southward into Ottoman lands and won a decisive victory. At the Congress of Berlin in 1878, the European Great Powers and the Ottoman Empire met to formally recognize Bulgarian, Romanian, Serbian, and Montenegrin independence. The Ottomans also lost territory to the Russians in the Caucasus, Austria-Hungary occupied the Ottoman provinces of Bosnia-Herzegovina (BAHZ-nee-uh HERT-suh-go-vee-nuh) and Novi Pazar (NOH-vi PAH-zar), and Great Britain took over Cyprus (SIGH-pruhs). The Ottoman Empire, now labeled the "sick man of Europe" in the European press, left the meeting significantly weakened and humiliated.

Ottoman Decline in the Balkans, 1818–1830

The combination of declining international power and conservative tyranny eventually led to a powerful resurgence of the modernizing impulse among idealistic Turkish exiles in Europe and young army officers in Istanbul. These fervent patriots, the so-called **Young Turks**, seized power in the 1908 revolution, overthrowing Sultan Abdülhamid II. They made his brother Mehmed V (r. 1909–1918) the figurehead sultan and forced him to implement reforms. The Young Turks helped prepare the way for the birth of modern secular Turkey after the defeat and collapse of the Ottoman Empire in World War I.

Egypt: From Reform to British Occupation

The ancient land of the pharaohs had been ruled by a succession of foreigners from 525 B.C.E. to the Ottoman conquest in the early sixteenth century. In 1798, as France and Britain prepared for war in Europe, Napoleon Bonaparte invaded Egypt, thereby threatening British access to India, and occupied the territory for three years. Into the power vacuum left by the French withdrawal stepped an extraordinary Albanian-born Turkish general, Muhammad Ali (1769–1849).

Appointed Egypt's governor by Sultan Selim III in 1805, Muhammad Ali set out to build his own state on the strength of a large, powerful army organized along European lines. He also reformed the government and promoted modern industry. (See "Individuals in Society: Muhammad Ali," at right.) For a time Muhammad Ali's ambitious strategy seemed to work, but it eventually foundered when his armies occupied Syria and he threatened the Ottoman sultan, Mahmud II. In the face of European military might and diplomatic entreaties, Muhammad Ali agreed to peace with his Ottoman overlords and withdrew. In return he was given unprecedented hereditary rule over Egypt and Sudan. By his death in 1849, Muhammad Ali had established a strong and virtually independent Egyptian state within the Ottoman Empire.

To pay for a modern army and industrialization, Muhammad Ali encouraged the development of commercial agriculture geared to the European market, which had profound social implications. Egyptian peasants had been largely self-sufficient, growing food on state-owned land allotted to them by tradition.

The Suez Canal, 1869

High-ranking officials and members of Muhammad Ali's family began carving private landholdings out of the state domain, and they forced the peasants to grow cash crops for European markets.

Muhammad Ali's modernization policies attracted growing numbers of Europeans to the banks of the Nile. Europeans served as army officers, engineers, doctors, government officials, and police officers. Others worked in trade, finance, and shipping. Above all, Europeans living in Egypt combined with landlords and officials to continue steering commercial agriculture toward exports. As throughout the Ottoman Empire, Europeans enjoyed important commercial and legal privileges and formed an economic elite.

In 1863 Muhammad Ali's grandson Ismail began his sixteen-year rule (r. 1863–1879) as Egypt's khedive (kuh-DEEV), or prince. He was a westernizing autocrat who received his education at France's leading military academy and dreamed of European technology and capital to modernize Egypt and build a vast empire in northwestern Africa. He promoted cotton production, and exports to Europe soared. Ismail also borrowed large sums, and with his support the Suez Canal was completed by a French company in 1869, shortening the voyage from Europe to Asia by thousands of miles. Cairo acquired modern boulevards and Western hotels. As Ismail proudly declared, "My country is no longer in Africa, we now form part of Europe."[10]

Major cultural and intellectual changes accompanied the political and economic ones. The Arabic of the masses, rather than the conqueror's Turkish, became the official language, and young, European-educated Egyptians helped spread new skills and ideas in the bureaucracy. A host of writers, intellectuals, and religious thinkers responded to the novel conditions with innovative ideas that had a powerful impact in Egypt and other Muslim societies.

Three influential figures who represented broad families of thought were especially significant. The teacher and writer Jamal al-Din al-Afghani (jah-MAL al-DIN al-af-GHAN-ee) (1838/39–1897) argued for the purification of Islamic religious belief, Muslim unity, and a revolutionary overthrow of corrupt Muslim rulers and foreign exploiters. The more moderate Muhammad Abduh (AHB-duh) (1849–1905) launched the modern Islamic reform movement. Abduh concluded that Muslims should adopt a flexible, reasoned approach to change, modernity, science, social questions, and foreign ideas and not reject these out of hand.

Young Turks Fervent patriots who seized power in the revolution of 1908, forcing the conservative sultan to implement reforms; they helped pave the way for the birth of modern secular Turkey.

INDIVIDUALS IN SOCIETY

Muhammad Ali

THE DYNAMIC LEADER MUHAMMAD Ali stands across the history of modern Egypt like a colossus. Yet the essence of the man remains a mystery, and historians vary greatly in their interpretations of him. Sent by the Ottomans, with Albanian troops, to oppose the French occupation of Egypt in 1799, Muhammad Ali maneuvered skillfully after the French withdrawal in 1802. In 1805 he was named pasha, or Ottoman governor, of Egypt. Only the Mamluks remained as rivals. Originally an elite corps of Turkish slave soldiers, the Mamluks had become a semifeudal military ruling class living off the Egyptian peasantry. In 1811 Muhammad Ali offered to make peace, and he invited the Mamluk chiefs and their retainers to a banquet in Cairo's Citadel. As the unsuspecting guests processed through a narrow passage, his troops opened fire, slaughtering all the Mamluk leaders.

Muhammad Ali, the Albanian-born ruler of Egypt, in 1839. (Mary Evans Picture Library/The Image Works)

After eliminating his foes, Muhammad Ali embarked on a program of radical reforms. He reorganized agriculture and commerce, reclaiming most of the cultivated land for the state domain, which he controlled. He also established state agencies to monopolize, for his own profit, the sale of agricultural goods. Commercial agriculture geared to exports to Europe developed rapidly, especially after the successful introduction of high-quality cotton in 1821. Canals and irrigation systems along the Nile were rebuilt and expanded.

Muhammad Ali used his growing revenues to recast his army along European lines. He recruited French officers to train the soldiers. As the military grew, so did the need for hospitals, schools of medicine and languages, and secular education. Young Turks and some Egyptians were sent to Europe for advanced study. The ruler boldly financed factories to produce uniforms and weapons, and he prohibited the importation of European goods so as to protect Egypt's infant industries. In the 1830s state factories were making one-fourth of Egypt's cotton into cloth. Above all, Muhammad Ali drafted Egyptian peasants into the military for the first time, thereby expanding his army to one hundred thousand men. It was this force that conquered the Ottoman province of Syria, threatened the sultan in Istanbul, and triggered European intervention. Grudgingly recognized by his Ottoman overlord as Egypt's hereditary ruler in 1841, Muhammad

Ali nevertheless had to accept European and Ottoman demands to give up Syria and abolish his monopolies and protective tariffs. The old ruler then lost heart; his reforms languished, and his factories disappeared.

In the attempt to understand Muhammad Ali and his significance, many historians have concluded that he was a national hero, the "founder of modern Egypt." His ambitious state-building projects — hospitals, schools, factories, and the army — were the basis for an Egyptian reawakening and eventual independence from the Ottomans' oppressive foreign rule. Similarly, state-sponsored industrialization promised an escape from poverty and Western domination, which was foiled only by European intervention and British insistence on free trade.

A growing minority of historians question these views. They see Muhammad Ali primarily as an Ottoman adventurer. In their view, he did not aim for national independence for Egypt, but rather "intended to carve out a small empire for himself and for his children after him."* Paradoxically, his success, which depended on heavy taxes and brutal army service, led to Egyptian nationalism among the Arabic-speaking masses, but that new nationalism was directed against Muhammad Ali and his Turkish-speaking entourage. Continuing research into this leader's life will help resolve these conflicting interpretations.

QUESTIONS FOR ANALYSIS

1. Which of Muhammad Ali's actions support the interpretation that he was the founder of modern Egypt? Which actions support the opposing view?
2. After you have studied Chapter 26, compare Muhammad Ali and the Meiji reformers in Japan. What accounts for the similarities and differences?

*K. Fahmy, *All the Pasha's Men: Mehmed Ali, His Army, and the Making of Modern Egypt* (Cambridge: Cambridge University Press, 1997), p. 310.

Finally, the writer Qasim Amin (KAH-zim ah-MEEN) (1863–1908) represented those who found inspiration in the West in the late nineteenth century. In his influential book *The Liberation of Women* (1899), Amin argued forcefully that superior education for European women had contributed greatly to the Islamic world's falling far behind the West. In his view, the rejuvenation of Muslim societies required greater equality for women:

> History confirms and demonstrates that the status of women is inseparably tied to the status of a nation. Where the status of a nation is low, reflecting an uncivilized condition for that nation, the status of women is also low, and when the status of a nation is elevated, reflecting the progress and civilization of that nation, the status of women in that country is also elevated.[11]

Egypt changed rapidly during Ismail's rule, but his projects were reckless and enormously expensive. By 1876 the Egyptian government could not pay the interest on its colossal debt. Rather than let Egypt go bankrupt and repudiate its loans, France and Great Britain intervened, forcing Ismail to appoint French and British commissioners to oversee Egyptian finances. This meant that Europeans would determine the state budget and in effect rule Egypt.

Foreign financial control evoked a violent nationalistic reaction. Continuing diplomatic pressure, which forced Ismail to abdicate in favor of his weak son, Tewfiq (teh-FEEK) (r. 1879–1892), resulted in bloody anti-European riots in Alexandria in 1882. In response, the British fleet bombarded Alexandria, and a British expeditionary force occupied all of Egypt. British armies remained in Egypt until 1956.

Initially the British maintained the fiction that Egypt was an autonomous province of the Ottoman Empire, but the khedive was a mere puppet. In reality, the British consul, General Evelyn Baring, later Lord Cromer, ruled the country after 1883. Baring was a paternalistic reformer. He initiated tax reforms and made some improvements to conditions for peasants. Foreign bondholders received their interest payments, while Egyptian nationalists chafed under foreign rule.

Egyptian Travel Guide Ismail's efforts to transform Cairo were fairly successful. As a result, European tourists could more easily visit the country that their governments dominated. Ordinary Europeans were lured to exotic lands by travel books like this colorful "Official Guide" to an exhibition on Cairo held in Berlin.
(Private Collection/Archives Charmet/Bridgeman Images)

The Expanding World Economy

What were the global consequences of European industrialization between 1800 and 1914?

Over the course of the nineteenth century the Industrial Revolution expanded and transformed economic relations across the face of the earth. As a result, the world's total income grew as never before, and international trade boomed. Western nations used their superior military power to force non-Western nations to open their doors to Western economic interests. Consequently, the largest share of the ever-increasing gains from trade flowed to the West, resulting in a stark division between rich and poor countries.

The Rise of Global Inequality

From a global perspective, the ultimate significance of the Industrial Revolution was that it allowed those world regions that industrialized in the nineteenth century to increase their wealth and power enormously in comparison with those that did not. A gap between the industrializing regions (Europe, North America, Japan) and the nonindustrializing regions (mainly Africa, Asia, and Latin America) opened and grew steadily throughout the nineteenth century (Figure 25.1). Moreover, this pattern of uneven global development became institutionalized, built into the structure of the world economy. Thus evolved a world of

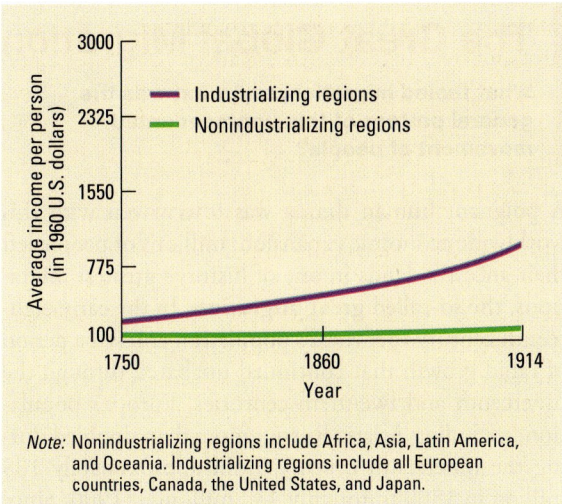

FIGURE 25.1 The Growth of Average Income per Person Worldwide, 1750–1914

(Source of data: P. Bairoch and M. Lévy-Leboyer, eds., *Disparities in Economic Development Since the Industrial Revolution* [New York: Macmillan, 1980].)

economic haves and have-nots, with the have-not peoples and nations far outnumbering the haves.

In 1750 the average living standard was no higher in Europe as a whole than in the rest of the world. By 1914 the average person in the wealthiest countries had an income four or five times as great (and in Great Britain nine or ten times as great) as an average person's income in the poorest countries of Africa and Asia. The rise in average income and well-being reflected the rising level of industrialization in Great Britain and then in the other developed countries before World War I.

The reasons for these enormous income disparities have generated a great deal of debate. One school of interpretation stresses that the West used science, technology, capitalist organization, and even its critical worldview to create its wealth and greater physical well-being. An opposing school argues that the West used its political, economic, and military power to steal much of its riches through its rapacious colonialism in the nineteenth and twentieth centuries.

These issues are complex, and there are few simple answers. As noted in Chapter 23, the wealth-creating potential of technological improvement and more intensive capitalist organization was great. At the same time, the initial breakthroughs in the late eighteenth century rested in part on Great Britain's having already used political force to dominate a substantial part of the world economy. In the nineteenth century other industrializing countries joined with Britain to extend Western dominion over the entire world economy. Unprecedented wealth was created, but the lion's share of that new wealth flowed to the West and its propertied classes and to a tiny indigenous elite of cooperative rulers, landowners, and merchants.

The World Market

World trade was a powerful stimulus to economic development in the nineteenth century. In 1913 the value of world trade was about twenty-five times what it had been in 1800, even though prices of manufactured goods and raw materials were lower in 1913 than in 1800. In a general way, this enormous increase in international commerce summed up the growth of an interlocking world economy centered in Europe.

Great Britain played a key role in using trade to tie the world together economically. In 1815 Britain already possessed a colonial empire, including India, Canada, and Australia. The technological breakthroughs of the Industrial Revolution encouraged British manufacturers to seek export markets around the world. After Parliament repealed laws restricting grain importation in 1846, Britain also became the world's leading importer of foreign goods. Free access to Britain's market stimulated the development of mines and plantations in Africa and Asia.

The conquest of distance facilitated the growth of trade. Wherever railroads were built, they drastically reduced transportation costs, opened new economic opportunities, and called forth new skills and attitudes.

Much of the railroad construction undertaken in Africa, Asia, and Latin America connected seaports with inland cities and regions, as opposed to linking and developing cities and regions within a country. Thus railroads dovetailed with Western economic interests, facilitating the inflow and sale of Western manufactured goods and the export and development of local raw materials.

Steam power also revolutionized transportation by sea. Steam power was first used to supplant sails on the world's oceans in the late 1860s. Passenger and freight rates tumbled, and the shipment of low-priced raw materials from one continent to another became feasible.

The revolution in land and sea transportation helped European settlers seize vast, thinly populated territories and produce agricultural products and raw materials for sale in Europe. Improved transportation enabled Asia, Africa, and Latin America to export not only the traditional tropical products—spices, dyes, tea, sugar, coffee—but also new raw materials for industry, such as jute, rubber, cotton, and peanut and coconut oil. Intercontinental trade was enormously facilitated by the Suez Canal in Egypt and the Panama Canal in Central America. Of great importance, too, was large and continual investment in modern port facilities, which made loading and unloading cheaper, faster, and more dependable. Finally, transoceanic telegraph cables inaugurated rapid communications among the world's financial centers and linked world commodity prices in a global network.

The growth of trade and the conquest of distance encouraged Europeans to make massive foreign investments beginning about 1840, but not to European colonies or protectorates in Asia and Africa. About three-quarters of total European investment went to other European countries, the United States and Canada, Australia and New Zealand, and Latin America. Here booming, industrializing economies offered the most profitable investment opportunities. Much of this investment was peaceful and mutually beneficial for lenders and borrowers. The victims were Native Americans, Australian Aborigines (AB-or-ij-uh-nees), New Zealand Maoris (MAO-reez), and other native peoples who were displaced and decimated by the diseases, liquor, and weapons of an aggressively expanding Western society.

British East African Railway Poster Europeans constructed railroads in most of their African colonies to haul raw materials from the interior to coastal ports and to transport colonial officials, white settlers, and foreign tourists. Britain's East African railroad line from Kampala, Uganda, to the Kenyan port city of Mombasa was one of the most famous and most romanticized. Indians from British India did much of the construction and then remained in Kenya to form substantial Indian communities. President Theodore Roosevelt rode this train while on his 1909 African safari. (Advertising Archive/Courtesy, Everett Collection)

The Great Global Migration

What fueled migration, and what was the general pattern of this unprecedented movement of people?

A poignant human drama was interwoven with this worldwide economic expansion: millions of people left their ancestral lands in one of history's greatest migrations, the so-called **great migration**. In the early eighteenth century the world's population entered a period of rapid growth that continued unabated through the nineteenth and twentieth centuries. Europe's population (including Asiatic Russia) more than doubled during the nineteenth century, from approximately 188 million in 1800 to roughly 432 million in 1900. Since African and Asian populations increased more slowly than those in Europe, Europeans and peoples of predominantly European origin jumped from about 22 percent of the world's total in 1850 to a high of about 38 percent in 1930.

Rapid population growth led to relative overpopulation in area after area in Europe and was a driving force behind emigration and Western expansion. Millions of country folk moved to nearby cities, and the more adventuresome went abroad, in search of work and economic opportunity. Some governments encouraged their excess populations to emigrate, even paying part of their expenses. Wars, famine, poverty, and, particularly in the case of Russian and eastern European Jews, bigotry and discrimination were also leading causes for emigrants to leave their ancestral homelands. More than 60 million people left Europe over the course of the nineteenth century, primarily for the rapidly growing "areas of European settlement" — North and South America, Australia, New Zealand, and Siberia. European emigration crested in the first decade of the twentieth century, when more than five times as many men and women departed as in the 1850s.

The European migrant was most often a small peasant landowner or a village craftsman whose traditional way of life was threatened by too little land, estate agriculture, and cheap factory-made goods. Determined to maintain or improve their precarious status, the vast majority of migrants were young and often unmarried. Many European migrants eventually returned home after some time abroad. Moreover, when the economic situation improved at home or when people began to win basic political and social reforms, migration slowed.

Ties of family and friendship played a crucial role in the movement of peoples. Over several years a given province or village might lose significant numbers of its inhabitants to migration. These people then settled together in rural enclaves or tightly knit urban neighborhoods in foreign lands thousands of miles away. Very often a strong individual — a businessman, a reli-

Mulberry Street, New York, ca. 1900 This photo captures the vibrancy and energy of Manhattan's Lower East Side at the height of new immigration to America from around the 1880s to the early 1920s. Mulberry Street, and many others such as Delancey, Bowery, Orchard, and Hester, were home to millions of newly arrived immigrants from all over the world. Leaving their small, crowded tenement rooms, they would fill the streets with a cacophony of languages, dress, music, and the smell of exotic foods. (Image Asset Management/ IAM/akg-images)

gious leader — blazed the way, and others followed, forming a **migration chain**.

A substantial number of Asians — especially Chinese, Japanese, Indians, and Filipinos — also responded to population pressure and rural hardship with temporary or permanent migration. At least 3 million Asians moved abroad before 1920. Most went as indentured laborers to work on the plantations or in the gold mines of Latin America, southern Asia, Africa, California, Hawaii, and Australia. White estate owners often used Asians to replace or supplement black Africans after the suppression of the Atlantic slave trade.

Asian migration would undoubtedly have been much greater if planters and mine owners desiring cheap labor had had their way. But usually they did not. Asians fled the plantations and gold mines as soon as possible, seeking greater opportunities in trade and towns. Here, however, they came into conflict with white settlers, who demanded a halt to Asian immigration. By the 1880s Americans and Australians were building **great white walls** — discriminatory laws designed to keep Asians out.

The general policy of "whites only" in the lands of large-scale European settlement meant that Europeans and people of European ancestry reaped the main benefits of the great migration. By 1913 people in Austra-

lia, Canada, and the United States all had higher average incomes than did people in Great Britain, still Europe's wealthiest nation. This, too, contributed to Western dominance in the increasingly lopsided world.

Within Asia and Africa the situation was different. Migrants from south China frequently settled in Dutch, British, and French colonies of Southeast Asia, where they established themselves as peddlers and small shopkeepers. These "overseas Chinese" gradually emerged as a new class of entrepreneurs and office workers. Traders from India and modern-day Lebanon performed the same function in much of sub-Saharan Africa after European colonization in the late nineteenth century. Thus in some parts of Asia and Africa the business class was both Asian and foreign, protected and tolerated by Western imperialists who found these business people useful.

great migration The mass movement of people from Europe in the nineteenth century; one reason that the West's impact on the world was so powerful and complex.

migration chain The movement of peoples in which one strong individual blazes the way and others follow.

great white walls Discriminatory laws passed by Americans and Australians to keep Asians from settling in their countries in the 1880s.

Chapter Summary

Following Europe's Industrial Revolution in the late eighteenth and early nineteenth centuries, European demands for raw materials and new markets reoriented Africa's economy. The transatlantic slave trade declined dramatically as Africans began producing commodities for export. This legitimate trade in African goods proved profitable and led to the emergence of a small black middle class. Islam revived and expanded until about 1870.

After 1880 a handful of Western nations seized most of Africa and parts of Asia and rushed to build authoritarian empires. The reasons for this empire building included trade rivalries, competitive nationalism in Europe, and self-justifying claims of a civilizing mission. European nations' unprecedented military superiority enabled them to crush resistance and impose their will.

The Ottoman Empire and Egypt prepared to become modern nation-states in the twentieth century by introducing reforms to improve the military, provide technical and secular education, and expand personal liberties. They failed, however, to defend themselves from Western imperialism. The Ottoman Empire lost territory but survived in a weakened condition. Egypt's Muhammad Ali reformed the government and promoted modern industry, but Egypt went bankrupt and was conquered and ruled by Britain. Western domination was particularly bitter for most Muslims because they saw it as profaning Islam and taking away their political independence.

Population pressures at home and economic opportunities abroad caused millions of European emigrants to resettle in the sparsely populated areas of European settlement in North and South America, Australia, and Asiatic Russia. Migration from Asia was much more limited, mainly because European settlers raised high barriers to prevent the settlement of Asian immigrants.

NOTES

1. P. Lovejoy, *Transformations in Slavery: A History of Slavery in Africa*, 2d ed. (Cambridge: Cambridge University Press, 2000), p. 142.
2. Quoted in J. Iliffe, *Africans: The History of a Continent* (Cambridge: Cambridge University Press, 1995), p. 169.
3. Lovejoy, *Transformations in Slavery*, p. 15.
4. R. Oliver, *The African Experience* (New York: Icon Editions, 1991), pp. 164–166.
5. Quoted in H. Wheaton, *Elements of International Law* (London: Stevens & Sons, 1889), p. 804.
6. Quoted in Bernard Porter, *The Lion's Share: A Short History of British Imperialism, 1850–1970* (London: Longman, 1975), p. 134.
7. Quoted in Anthony Thomas, *Rhodes* (New York: St. Martin's Press, 1996), p. 194.
8. Walter Bagehot, *Physics and Politics, or Thoughts on the Application of the Principle of "Natural Selection" and "Inheritance" to Political Society* (New York: D. Appleton, 1873), pp. 43, 49.
9. Rudyard Kipling, *The Five Nations* (London, 1903).
10. Quoted in Earl of Cromer, *Modern Egypt* (London, 1911), p. 48.
11. Qasim Amin, *The Liberation of Women and The New Woman* (The American University of Cairo Press, 2000), p. 6.

CONNECTIONS

By the end of the nineteenth century broader industrialization across Europe increased the need for raw materials and markets, and with it came a rush to create or enlarge vast political empires abroad. The New Imperialism was aimed primarily at Africa and Asia, and in the years before 1914 the leading European nations not only created empires abroad, but also continued to send massive streams of migrants, money, and manufactured goods around the world. (The impact of this unprecedented migration is taken up in the next two chapters.) This political empire building contrasted sharply with the economic penetration of non-Western territories between 1816 and 1880, which had allowed Africa to develop a "legitimate trade" and end the transatlantic slave trade, and which left China and Japan "opened" but politically independent, as Chapter 26 will show.

European influence also grew in the Middle East. Threatened by European military might, modernization, and Christianity, Turks and Arabs tried to implement reforms that would assure their survival and independence but also endeavored to retain key aspects of their cultures, particularly Islam. Although they made important advances in the modernization of their economies and societies, their efforts were not enough to overcome Western imperialism. With the end of World War I and the collapse of the Ottoman Empire, England and France divided much of the Middle East into colonies and established loyal surrogates as rulers in other, nominally independent, countries. Chapter 29 will take up the story of these developments.

Easy imperialist victories over weak states and poorly armed non-Western peoples encouraged excessive pride and led Europeans to underestimate the fragility of their accomplishments. Imperialism also made nationalism more aggressive and militaristic. As European imperialism was dividing the world after the 1880s, the leading European states were also dividing themselves into two opposing military alliances. As Chapter 28 will show, when the two armed camps stumbled into war in 1914, the results were disastrous. World War I set the stage for a new anti-imperialist struggle in Africa and Asia for equality and genuine independence, the topic of Chapters 31 and 32.

CHAPTER 25 Review and Explore

Identify Key Terms

Identify and explain the significance of each item below.

palm oil (p. 730)
jihad (p. 731)
Sokoto caliphate (p. 731)
Berlin Conference (p. 732)
protectorate (p. 732)

Afrikaners (p. 734)
New Imperialism (p. 739)
quinine (p. 740)
white man's burden (p. 742)
Tanzimat (p. 746)

Young Turks (p. 748)
great migration (p. 752)
migration chain (p. 753)
great white walls (p. 753)

Review the Main Ideas

Answer the focus questions from each section of the chapter.

1. What were the most significant changes in Africa during the nineteenth century, and why did they occur? (p. 730)

2. What were the causes and consequences of European empire building after 1880? (p. 738)

3. How did the Ottoman Empire and Egypt try to modernize themselves, and what were the most important results? (p. 746)

4. What were the global consequences of European industrialization between 1800 and 1914? (p.750)

5. What fueled migration, and what was the general pattern of this unprecedented movement of people? (p. 752)

Make Comparisons and Connections

Analyze the larger developments and continuities within and across chapters.

1. Explain the transitions in Africa from the slave trade to legitimate trade to colonialism in the late eighteenth and nineteenth centuries. How was Europe's Industrial Revolution (Chapter 23) related to these transitions?

2. Europeans had been visiting Africa's coasts for four hundred years before colonizing the entire continent in thirty years in the second half of the nineteenth century. Why hadn't they colonized Africa earlier, and what factors allowed them to do it then?

3. What were the causes of the great migration in the late nineteenth and early twentieth centuries?

AFRICA

1805–1848 Muhammad Ali modernizes Egypt

1808–1839 Mahmud II rules Ottoman state and enacts reforms

◆ 1809 Uthman dan Fodio founds Sokoto caliphate

◆ 1830 France begins conquest of Algeria

GLOBAL

AMERICAS

1806–1825 Latin American wars of independence (Ch. 22)

ASIA

| 1800 | 1820 | 1840 |

Suggested Resources

BOOKS

Bagachi, Amiya Kumar. *Perilous Passage: Mankind and the Ascendancy of Capital.* 2005. A spirited radical critique of Western imperialism.

Conklin, Alice. *A Mission to Civilize: The French Republican Ideal and West Africa, 1895–1930.* 1997. An outstanding examination of French imperialism.

Cook, Scott B. *Colonial Encounters in the Age of High Imperialism.* 1996. A stimulating and very readable overview.

Coquery-Vidrovitch, Catherine. *Africa and the Africans in the Nineteenth Century: A Turbulent History.* 2009. English translation of a highly regarded history by a premier African scholar.

Findley, C. *The Turks in World History.* 2005. An exciting reconsideration of the Turks in long-term perspective.

Harper, Marjory, and Stephen Constantine. *Migration and Empire.* 2010. A comparative study of migration throughout the British Empire.

Headrick, Daniel R. *Tools of Empire.* 1991. Stresses technological superiority in Western expansion.

Hochschild, Adam. *King Leopold's Ghost: A Story of Greed, Terror, and Heroism in Colonial Africa.* 1999. The definitive account of King Leopold II's Congo and the human rights crusaders who exposed its horrors.

Hourani, Albert. *A History of the Arab Peoples*, 2d ed. 2010. Offers brilliant insights on developments in the nineteenth century.

Law, Robin, ed. *From Slave Trade to "Legitimate" Commerce: The Commercial Transition in Nineteenth-Century West Africa.* 2002. Leading scholars describe the transition to legitimate trade from an African perspective.

Lovejoy, P. *Transformations in Slavery: A History of Slavery in Africa*, 3d ed. 2012. A fine synthesis of current knowledge.

Medard, Henri, and Shane Doyle. *Slavery in the Great Lakes Region of East Africa.* 2007. A significant contribution to the understudied story of slavery in East Africa, mainly in the nineteenth and early twentieth centuries.

Meredith, Martin. *Diamonds, Gold, and War: The British, the Boers, and the Making of South Africa.* 2007. An excellent account of the British scramble

1884–1885 Berlin Conference   **1899–1902** South African War

1880–1914 Most of Africa falls under European rule; height of New Imperialism in Asia and Africa

1839–1876 Western-style reforms (Tanzimat) in Ottoman Empire

1899 Kipling, "The White Man's Burden"; Amin, *The Liberation of Women*

1869 Completion of Suez Canal

1902 Conrad, *Heart of Darkness*; Hobson, *Imperialism*

1908 Young Turks seize power in Ottoman Empire

1870s–1914 Second Industrial Revolution **(Ch. 23)**

1861–1865 U.S. Civil War **(Ch. 27)**

1898 Spanish-American War **(Ch. 27)**

1859–1885 French conquest of Vietnam **(Ch. 26)**

1858 Completion of British rule over India **(Ch. 26)**

1867 Meiji Restoration in Japan **(Ch. 26)**

1911 Chinese revolution **(Ch. 26)**

1860   **1880**   **1900**

---

for South Africa from 1806 to the South African War (1899–1902).

Nugent, Walter. *Crossings: The Great Transatlantic Migrations, 1870–1914.* 1992. A classic study of migration history.

Wright, John. *The Trans-Saharan Slave Trade.* 2007. A well-researched study of slavery in a long-neglected region of Africa.

DOCUMENTARIES

Africa: A Voyage of Discovery with Basil Davidson (Home Vision, 1984). An eight-part series about African history and society. See particularly episode 5, "The Bible and the Gun"; and episode 6, "The Magnificent African Cake."

King Leopold's Ghost (Pippa Scott and Oreet Rees, 2006). Based on Adam Hochschild's bestselling book by the same title, this documentary recounts the history of King Leopold II's Congo in all its brutality and horror.

The Ottomans: Europe's Muslim Emperors (BBC, 2013). A three-part BBC documentary that tells the history of the Ottoman Empire from its founding in the late thirteenth century to its downfall in the Great War.

FEATURE FILM

Mountains of the Moon (Bob Rafelson, 1990). A beautifully filmed telling of the efforts by two English explorers, Sir Richard Burton and John Speke, to find the source of the Nile River in the late 1850s and early 1860s.

WEBSITE

"Imperialism" in the *Internet Modern History Sourcebook.* A valuable reference site for historical sources on New Imperialism, from a global perspective, including primary sources, analyses, and links to other related websites.
sourcebooks.fordham.edu/halsall/mod /modsbook34.asp

26

Asia and the Pacific in the Era of Imperialism
1800–1914

During the nineteenth century the societies of Asia underwent enormous changes as a result of population growth, social unrest, and the looming presence of Western imperialist powers. At the beginning of the century Spain, the Netherlands, and Britain had colonies in the Philippines, modern Indonesia, and India, respectively. By the end of the century much more land — most of the southern tier of Asia, from India to the Philippines — had been made colonies of Western powers. Most of these colonies became tied to the industrializing world as exporters of agricultural products or raw materials, including timber, rubber, tin, sugar, tea, cotton, and jute. The Western presence brought benefits, especially to educated residents of major cities, where the colonizers often introduced modern public health, communications, and educational systems. Still, cultural barriers between the colonizers and the colonized were huge, and the Western presence rankled.

Not all the countries in Asia were reduced to colonies. Although Western powers put enormous pressures on China and exacted many concessions from it, China remained politically independent. Much more impressively, Japan became the first non-Western nation to meet the many-sided challenge of Western expansion. Japan emerged from the nineteenth-century crisis stronger than any other Asian nation, becoming the first non-Western country to industrialize successfully. By the end of this period Japan had become an imperialist power itself.

Rammohun Roy

The expansion of British power in India posed intellectual and cultural challenges to the native elite. Among those who rose to this challenge was writer and reformer Rammohun Roy, depicted here.

Victoria and Albert Museum, London, UK/V&A Images/Art Resource, NY

CHAPTER PREVIEW

INDIA AND THE BRITISH EMPIRE IN ASIA
In what ways did India change as a consequence of British rule?

COMPETITION FOR SOUTHEAST ASIA
Why were most but not all Southeast Asian societies reduced to colonies?

CHINA UNDER PRESSURE
Was China's decline in the nineteenth century due more to internal problems or to Western imperialism?

JAPAN'S RAPID TRANSFORMATION
How was Japan able to quickly master the challenges posed by the West?

THE PACIFIC REGION AND THE MOVEMENT OF PEOPLE
What were the causes and consequences of the vast movement of people in the Pacific region?

THE COUNTRIES OF ASIA IN COMPARATIVE PERSPECTIVE
What explains the similarities and differences in the experiences of Asian countries in this era?

India and the British Empire in Asia

In what ways did India change as a consequence of British rule?

Arriving in India on the heels of the Portuguese in the seventeenth century, the British East India Company outmaneuvered French and Dutch rivals and was there to pick up the pieces as the Mughal Empire decayed during the eighteenth century (see "From the British East India Company to the British Empire in India" in Chapter 17). By 1757 the company had gained control over much of India. During the nineteenth century the British government replaced the company, progressively unified the subcontinent, and harnessed its economy to British interests.

Travel and communication between Britain and India became much faster, safer, and more predictable in this period. The time it took to travel to India from Britain dropped from six months to three weeks, due both to the development of steamships and the 1869 opening of the Suez Canal. Whereas at the beginning of the nineteenth century someone in England had to wait a year or more to get an answer to a letter sent to India, by 1870 it took only a couple of months—or, if the matter was urgent, only a few hours by telegraph.

The Evolution of British Rule

In India the British ruled with the cooperation of local princely allies, whom they could not afford to offend. To assert their authority, the British disbanded and disarmed local armies, introduced simpler private property laws, and enhanced the powers of local princes and religious leaders, both Hindu and Muslim. The British administrators were on the whole competent and concerned about the welfare of the Indian peasants. Slavery was outlawed and banditry suppressed, and new laws designed to improve women's position in society were introduced. Sati (widow suicide) was outlawed in 1829, legal protection of widow remarriage was extended in 1856, and infanticide (disproportionately of female newborns) was banned in 1870.

The last armed resistance to British rule occurred in 1857.

The Great Mutiny / Great Revolt, 1857

By that date the British military presence in India had grown to include two hundred thousand Indian sepoy troops and thirty-eight thousand British officers. In 1857 groups of sepoys, especially around Delhi, revolted in what the British called the **Great Mutiny** and the Indians called the **Great Revolt**. The sepoys' grievances were many, ranging from the use of fat from cows (sacred to Hindus) and pigs (regarded as filthy by Muslims) to grease rifle cartridges to high tax rates and the incorporation of low-caste soldiers into the army. The insurrection spread rapidly throughout northern and central India before it was finally crushed, primarily by native troops from other parts of India loyal to the British. Thereafter, although princely states were allowed to continue, Britain ruled India much more tightly. Moreover, the British in India acted more like an occupying power and mixed less with the Indian elite.

After 1858 India was ruled by the British Parliament in London and administered by a civil service in India, the upper echelons of which were all white. In 1900 this elite consisted of fewer than 3,500 top officials for a population of 300 million.

The Socioeconomic Effects of British Rule

The impact of British rule on the Indian economy was multifaceted. In the early stages, the British East India Company expanded agricultural production, creating large plantations. Early crops were opium to export to China (see "The Opium War") and tea to substitute for imports from China. India gradually replaced China as the leading exporter of tea to Europe. Clearing land for tea and coffee plantations, along with massive commercial logging operations, led to extensive deforestation.

To aid the transport of goods, people, and information, the colonial administration invested heavily in India's infrastructure. By 1855 India's major cities had all been linked by telegraph and railroads, and postal service was being extended to local villages. By 1900 the rail network extended 25,000 miles, serving 188 million passengers. By then over 370,000 Indians worked for the railroads. Irrigation also received attention, and by 1900 India had the world's most extensive irrigation system.

At the same time, Indian production of textiles suffered a huge blow. Britain imported India's raw cotton but exported machine-spun yarn and machine-woven cloth, displacing millions of Indian hand-spinners and hand-weavers. By 1900 India was buying 40 percent of Britain's cotton exports. Not until 1900 were small steps taken toward industrializing India. By 1914 about a million Indians worked in factories.

Breakfast at Home In India the families of British civil servants could live more comfortably than they could back home. The artist Augustus Jules Bouvier captured their lifestyle in this 1842 engraving. (Private Collection/The Stapleton Collection/Bridgeman Images)

Although the economy expanded, the poor did not see much improvement in their standard of living. Tenant farming and landlessness increased with the growth in plantation agriculture. Increases in production were eaten up by increases in population, which, as noted, had reached approximately 300 million by 1900. There was also a negative side to improved transportation. As Indians traveled more widely on the convenient trains, disease spread, especially cholera, which is transmitted by exposure to contaminated water. Pilgrims customarily bathed in and drank from sacred pools and rivers, worsening this problem. Despite improvements made to sanitation, in 1900 four out of every one thousand residents of British India still died of cholera each year.

The British and the Indian Educated Elite

The Indian middle class probably gained more than the poor from British rule, because they were the ones to benefit from the English-language educational system Britain established in India. (See "Thinking Like a Historian: English-Language Education for Indians," page 762.) Missionaries also established schools with Western curricula, and 790,000 Indians were attending some 24,000 schools by 1870. High-caste Hindus came to form a new elite profoundly influenced by Western thought and culture.

By creating a well-educated, English-speaking Indian elite and a bureaucracy aided by a modern communication system, the British laid the groundwork for a unified, powerful state. Britain placed under the same general system of law and administration the various Hindu and Muslim peoples of the subcontinent who had resisted one another for centuries. University graduates tended to look on themselves as Indians more than as residents of separate states and kingdoms, a necessary step for the development of Indian nationalism.

Some Indian intellectuals sought to reconcile the values of the modern West and their own traditions. Rammohun Roy (1772–1833), who had risen to the top of the native ranks in the British East India Company, founded a college that offered instruction in Western languages and subjects. He also founded a society to reform traditional customs, especially child marriage, the caste system, and restrictions on widows. He espoused a modern Hinduism founded on the *Upanishads* (oo-PAH-nih-shadz), the ancient sacred texts of Hinduism.

The more that Western-style education was developed in India, the more the inequalities of the system became apparent to educated Indians. Indians were eligible to take the examinations for entry into the elite **Indian Civil Service**, the bureaucracy that administered the Indian government, but the exams were given in England. Since few Indians could travel such a long distance to take the test, in 1870 only 1 of the 916 members of the service was Indian. In other words, no matter how Anglicized educated Indians became, they could never become the white rulers' equals. The top jobs, the best clubs, the modern hotels, and even certain railroad compartments were sealed off to brown-skinned men and women. Most of the British elite considered the jumble of Indian peoples and castes to

Great Mutiny / Great Revolt The terms used by the British and the Indians, respectively, to describe the last armed resistance to British rule in India, which occurred in 1857.

Indian Civil Service The bureaucracy that administered the government of India. Entry into its elite ranks was through examinations that Indians were eligible to take, but these tests were offered only in England.

English-Language Education for Indians

In 1813, when the British Parliament renewed the charter of the East India Company for twenty years, it required the company to apply 100,000 rupees per year to support learning among the natives of India. Most of this went to traditional schools for either Hindus or Muslims. By the early 1820s, however, some were arguing that rather than support local traditions of "oriental learning," it would be better to introduce useful subjects, including science and English.

1 Rammohun Roy, letter to Lord Amherst, 1823. In December 1823 the leading Indian intellectual, Rammohun Roy, who was well educated in both traditional Indian subjects and English, responded negatively to a British proposal to establish a school teaching Sanskrit and Hindu literature in a letter addressed to the governor general, Lord Amherst.

■ When this Seminary of learning was proposed, we understood that the Government in England had ordered a considerable sum of money to be annually devoted to the instruction of its Indian Subjects. We were filled with sanguine hopes that this sum would be laid out in employing European Gentlemen of talents and education to instruct the natives of India in Mathematics, Natural Philosophy, Chemistry, Anatomy, and other useful Sciences, which the Nations of Europe have carried to a degree of perfection that has raised them above the inhabitants of other parts of the world. . . .

We now find that the Government are establishing a Sanskrit school under Hindu Pundits to impart such knowledge as is already current in India. This Seminary (similar in character to those which existed in Europe before the time of Lord Bacon) can only be expected to load the minds of youth with grammatical niceties and metaphysical distinctions of little or no practicable use to the possessors or to society. . . . The Sanskrit language, so difficult that almost a life time is necessary for its perfect acquisition, is well known to have been for ages a lamentable check on the diffusion of knowledge; and the learning concealed under this almost impervious veil is far from sufficient to reward the labour of acquiring it.

2 John Tytler, letter to Lord Macaulay, January 26, 1835. Based on his experience both practicing medicine in India and supervising a medical school in Calcutta, the physician John Tytler argued in favor of using the local languages to teach "useful knowledge."

■ There is no instance of any Native making much progress in Science except through the medium of its own language, and I am decidedly of opinion, that knowledge can be generally diffused through a people by means of its Vernacular language only.

And hence every plan of education from which the Native languages are excluded must ultimately fail and every attempt to cultivate foreign languages while the indigenous are neglected must be imperfect and unsatisfactory. . . .

The Sum of the whole is that English should be taught thoroughly to as many as have opportunities to learn it, but that Science is to be diffused generally by means of the languages of the Country and these it is the Natives' duty to cultivate and ours to learn.

3 Thomas Babington Macaulay on education in India, 1833 and 1835. The English statesman Thomas Babington Macaulay (1800–1859) touched on the larger goals of government education in India in a speech in Parliament in 1833. Here an excerpt from this speech is followed by the decision he issued two years later on February 2, 1835.

■ EXCERPT FROM SPEECH

Are we to keep the people of India ignorant in order that we may keep them submissive? Or do we think that we can give them knowledge without awakening ambition? . . .

It may be that the public mind of India may expand under our system till it has outgrown that system; that by good government we may educate

ANALYZING THE EVIDENCE

1. Do Rammohun Roy (Source 1) and Thomas Babington Macauley (Source 3) prefer instruction in English for the same reasons? In what ways do they differ?
2. How would Roy (Source 1) or Macaulay (Source 3) respond to John Tytler (Source 2) on the issue of teaching modern medicine? Are they talking about different kinds of education?
3. If you were writing a history of the British Empire in India, how would you cast the debate on the introduction of English as a language of instruction (Sources 1–4)? Does the debate reflect a colonial sense of superiority over the local people, or does it indicate a commitment to the improvement of the lives of Indians? How do you factor in the construction of school buildings (Source 5)?
4. Source 4 is a secondary source, a very early appraisal by someone who witnessed the movement's outcome. What does it offer that the contemporary sources (Sources 1–3) cannot?

our subjects into a capacity for better government, that, having become instructed in European knowledge, they may, in some future age, demand European institutions. Whether such a day will ever come I know not. But never will I attempt to avert or to retard it. Whenever it comes, it will be the proudest day in English history. To have found a great people sunk in the lowest depths of slavery and superstition, to have so ruled them as to have made them desirous and capable of all the privileges of citizens would indeed be a title to glory all our own. . . .

Minute on Education

What then shall that language [of instruction] be? One half of the committee maintain that it should be the English. The other half strongly recommend the Arabic and Sanskrit. The whole question seems to me to be which language is the best worth knowing? . . .

It will hardly be disputed, I suppose, that the department of literature in which the Eastern writers stand highest is poetry. . . . But when we pass from works of imagination to works in which facts are recorded and general principles investigated, the superiority of the Europeans becomes absolutely immeasurable. . . .

It is taken for granted by the advocates of oriental learning that no native of this country can possibly attain more than a mere smattering of English. . . . This is not merely an assumption, but an assumption contrary to all reason and experience. . . . I have heard the very question on which I am now writing discussed by native gentlemen with a liberality and an intelligence which would do credit to any member of the Committee of Public Instruction. . . .

In one point I fully agree with the gentlemen to whose general views I am opposed. I feel with them that it is impossible for us, with our limited means, to attempt to educate the body of the people. We must at present do our best to form a class who may be interpreters between us and the millions whom we govern, a class of persons Indian in blood and color, but English in tastes, in opinions, in morals and in intellect. To that class we may leave it to refine the vernacular dialects of the country, to enrich those dialects with terms of science borrowed from the Western nomenclature, and to render them by degrees fit vehicles for conveying knowledge to the great mass of the population.

4 James Kerr on whom to educate in India, 1851. Sixteen years after Macauley's decision in favor of the use of English as a language of instruction, the educator James Kerr wrote a history of the movement.

■ Perhaps we must be content in India, as has happened elsewhere, to leave the learned classes, as they are called, behind, and to raise up new men who will adopt our views more heartily than the Pundits are likely to do. Those whose interests are so intimately connected with the old system, whose influence and importance are derived from it, will be the very last, except in rare instances, to come over to the side of improvement.

(Haeckel Collection/ullstein bild via Getty Images)

5 Elphinstone College in Mumbai. The British also invested in the bricks and mortar of university buildings in India. Elphinstone College, seen in this late-nineteenth-century photo, was built in 1856.

PUTTING IT ALL TOGETHER

Using the sources above, along with what you have learned in class and in this chapter, write a short essay that analyzes the British decision to offer higher education in English in India.

Sources: (1) Bureau of Education, *Selections from Educational Records, Part I (1781–1839)*, ed. H. Sharp (Calcutta: Superintendent Government Printing, 1920; reprint: Delhi: National Archives of India, 1965), pp. 98–101; (2) Quoted in Natalie Robinson Sirkin and Gerald Sirkin, "The Battle of Indian Education: Macaulay's Opening Salvo Newly Discovered," *Victorian Studies* 14.4 (June 1971): 421–426; (3) *Speeches of Lord Macaulay* (London: Longman et al., 1860), pp. 162–163; Bureau of Education, *Selections from Educational Records, Part I*, pp. 107–117; (4) James Kerr, *A Review of Public Instruction in the Bengal Presidency from 1835 to 1851* (Calcutta: Baptist Mission Press, 1852), p. 144.

be racially inferior. For example, when the British Parliament in 1883 was considering a bill to allow Indian judges to try white Europeans in India, the British community rose in protest and defeated the measure. As Lord Kitchener, one of the most distinguished British military commanders in India, stated:

> It is this consciousness of the inherent superiority of the European which has won for us India. However well educated and clever a native may be, and however brave he may prove himself, I believe that no rank we can bestow on him would cause him to be considered an equal of the British officer.[1]

The peasant masses might accept such inequality as the latest version of age-old class and caste hierarchies, but the well-educated, English-speaking elite eventually could not. They had studied not only Milton and Shakespeare but also English traditions of democracy, liberty, and national pride.

In the late nineteenth century the colonial ports of Calcutta, Bombay, and Madras, now all linked by railroads, became centers of intellectual ferment. In these and other cities, newspapers in English and in regional languages gained influence. Lawyers trained in English law began agitating for Indian independence. By 1885, when a group of educated Indians came together to found the **Indian National Congress**, demands were increasing for the equality and self-government that Britain had already granted white-settler colonies such as Canada and Australia. The Congress Party called for more opportunities for Indians in the Indian Civil Service and reallocation of the government budget from military expenditures to the alleviation of poverty. The party advocated unity across religious and caste lines, but most members were upper-caste, Western-educated Hindus.

Defending British possessions in India became a key element of Britain's foreign policy during the nineteenth century and led to steady expansion of the territory Britain controlled in Asia. By 1852 the British had annexed Burma (now Myanmar), administering it as a province of India (Map 26.1). The establishment of a British base in Singapore was followed by expansion into Malaya (now Malaysia) in the 1870s and 1880s. In both Burma and Malaya, Britain tried to foster economic development, building railroads and promoting trade. Burma became a major exporter of timber and rice, Malaya of tin and rubber. So many laborers were brought into Malaya for the expanding mines and plantations that its population came to be approximately one-third Malay, one-third Chinese, and one-third Indian.

Wooden Model of a Colonial Courtroom
The presiding judge, an officer with the British East India Company, is seated on a chair with his top hat on the table. The Indian assistants are seated on the floor, and the plaintiffs and defendants in the case are standing. Notice the attention the Indian craftsman paid to the details of the dress and hats of each of the figures in this 20-inch-long wooden model. (Victoria and Albert Museum, London, UK/V&A Images/Art Resource, NY)

Indian National Congress A political association formed in 1885 that worked for Indian self-government.

MAPPING THE PAST

MAP 26.1 Asia in 1914 India remained under British rule, while China precariously preserved its political independence. The Dutch Empire in modern-day Indonesia was old, but French control of Indochina was a product of the New Imperialism.

ANALYZING THE MAP Consider the colonies of the different powers on this map. What European countries were leading imperialist states, and what lands did they hold? Can you see places where colonial powers were likely to come into conflict with each other?

CONNECTIONS Do the sizes of the various colonial territories as seen on this map adequately reflect their importance to the countries that possessed them? If not, what else should be taken into account in thinking about the value of these sorts of colonial possessions?

Competition for Southeast Asia

Why were most but not all Southeast Asian societies reduced to colonies?

At the beginning of the nineteenth century only a small part of Southeast Asia was under direct European control. By the end of the century most of the region would be in foreign hands.

The Dutch East Indies

Although Dutch forts and trading posts in the East Indies dated back to the seventeenth century, in 1816 the Dutch ruled little more than the island of Java. Thereafter they gradually brought almost all of the 3,000-mile-long archipelago under their political authority. In extending their rule, the Dutch, like the British in India, brought diverse peoples with different languages and distinct cultural traditions into a single political entity (see Map 26.1).

Taking over the Dutch East India Company in 1799, the Dutch government modified the company's loose control of Java and gradually built a modern bureaucratic state. Javanese resistance to Dutch rule led to the bloody **Java War** (1825–1830). In 1830, after the war, the Dutch abolished the combination of tribute from rulers and forced labor from peasants that they had used to obtain spices, and they established instead a particularly exploitive policy called the Culture System. Under this system, Indonesian peasants were forced to plant a fifth of their land in export crops, especially coffee and sugar, to turn over to the Dutch as tax.

At the end of the nineteenth century the Dutch began to encourage Western education in the East Indies. The children of local rulers and privileged elites, much like their counterparts in India, encountered new ideas in Dutch-language schools. They began to question the long-standing cooperation of local elites with Dutch colonialism, and they searched for a new national identity. Thus anticolonial nationalism began to take shape in the East Indies in the early twentieth century, and it would blossom after World War I.

Mainland Southeast Asia

Unlike India and Java, mainland Southeast Asia had escaped European rule during the eighteenth century. In 1802 the **Nguyen Dynasty** (1802–1945) came to power in Vietnam, putting an end to thirty years of peasant rebellion and civil war. For the first time in the country's history, a single Vietnamese monarchy ruled the entire country. Working through a centralizing scholar bureaucracy fashioned on the Chinese model, the Nguyen (GWIHN) Dynasty energetically built irrigation canals, roads and bridges, and impressive palaces in Hue (HWAY), the new capital city. Construction placed a heavy burden on the peasants drafted to do the work, and this hardship contributed to a resurgence of peasant unrest.

Roman Catholic missionaries from France posed a second, more dangerous threat to Vietnam's Confucian ruling elite. The king and his advisers believed that Christianity would undermine Confucian moral values and the unity of the Vietnamese state. In 1825 King Minh Mang (r. 1820–1841) outlawed the teaching of Christianity, and soon his government began executing Catholic missionaries and Vietnamese converts. As many as thirty thousand Vietnamese Christians were executed in the 1850s. In response, in 1859–1860 a French naval force seized Saigon and three surrounding provinces in southern Vietnam, making that part

The French Governor General and the Vietnamese Emperor The twelfth emperor of the Nguyen Dynasty, Khai Dinh (1885–1925), had to find ways to get along with the French governor general (in this picture, Albert Sarraut) if he wished to preserve his dynasty. Seen here in 1917 or 1918, he had adopted Western leather shoes but otherwise tried to keep a distinct Vietnamese identity in his dress. (Maurice-Louis Branger/Roger-Viollet/Getty Images)

of Vietnam a French colony. In 1884–1885 France launched a second war against Vietnam and conquered the rest of the country. Laos and Cambodia were added to form French Indochina in 1887. In all three countries the local rulers were left on their thrones, but France dominated and tried to promote French culture.

After the French conquest, Vietnamese patriots continued to resist the colonial occupiers. After Japan's victory over Russia in 1905 (see "Japan as an Imperial Power"), a new generation of nationalists saw Japan as a model for Vietnamese revitalization and freedom. They went to Japan to study and planned for anticolonial revolution in Vietnam.

Java War The 1825–1830 war between the Dutch government and the Javanese, fought over the extension of Dutch control of the island.

Nguyen Dynasty The last Vietnamese ruling house, which lasted from 1802 to 1945.

In all of Southeast Asia, only Siam (today Thailand) succeeded in preserving its independence. Siam was sandwiched between the British in Burma and the French in Indochina. Siam's very able king, Chula-longkorn (r. 1868–1910), took advantage of this situation to balance the two competitors against each other. Chulalongkorn had studied Greek and Latin and Western science and kept up with Western news by reading British newspapers from Hong Kong and Singapore. He outlawed slavery and implemented modernizing reforms that centralized the government so that it could more effectively control outlying provinces coveted by the imperialists. Independent Siam gradually developed a modern centralizing state similar to those constructed by Western imperialists in their Asian possessions.

The Philippines

The United States became one of the imperialist powers in Asia when it took the Philippines from Spain in 1898. When the Spanish established rule in the Philippines in the sixteenth century, the islands had no central government or literate culture; order was maintained by village units dominated by local chiefs. Under the Spanish, Roman Catholic churches were established, and Spanish priests able to speak the local languages became the most common intermediaries between local populations, who rarely could speak Spanish, and the new rulers. The government of Spain encouraged Spaniards to colonize the Philippines through the encomienda system (see "Indigenous Population Loss and Economic Exploitation" in Chapter 16); Spaniards who had served the Crown were rewarded with grants giving them the exclusive right to control public affairs and collect taxes in a specific locality of the Philippines. A local Filipino elite also developed, aided by the Spanish introduction of private ownership of land. Manila developed into an important entrepôt in the galleon trade between Mexico and China, and this trade also attracted a large Chinese community, which handled much of the trade within the Philippines.

In the late nineteenth century wealthy Filipinos began to send their sons to study abroad, and a movement to press Spain for reforms emerged among those who had been abroad. When the Spanish cracked down on critics, a rebellion erupted in 1896. (See "Individuals in Society: José Rizal," page 768.)

In 1898 war between Spain and the United States broke out in Cuba (see "The Spanish-American War" in Chapter 27), and in May the American naval commodore George Dewey sailed into Manila Bay and sank the Spanish fleet anchored there. Dewey called on the Filipino rebels to help defeat the Spanish forces, but when the rebels declared independence, the U.S. government refused to recognize them. U.S. forces fought the Filipino rebels, and by the end of the insurrection in 1902 the war had cost the lives of five thousand Americans and about two hundred thousand Filipinos. In the following years the United States introduced a form of colonial rule that included public works and economic development projects, improved education and medicine, and, in 1907, an elected legislative assembly.

China Under Pressure

Was China's decline in the nineteenth century due more to internal problems or to Western imperialism?

In 1800 most Chinese had no reason to question the concept of China as the central kingdom. A century later China's world standing had sunk precipitously. In 1900 foreign troops marched into China's capital to protect foreign nationals, and more and more Chinese had come to think that their government, society, and cultural values needed to be radically changed.

The Opium War

Seeing little to gain from trade with European countries, the Qing (Manchu) emperors, who had been ruling China since 1644 (see "The Rise of the Manchus" in Chapter 21), permitted Europeans to trade only at the port of Guangzhou (Canton) and only through licensed Chinese merchants. Initially, the balance of trade was in China's favor. Great Britain and the other Western nations used silver to pay for tea, since they had not been able to find anything the Chinese wanted to buy. By the 1820s, however, the British had found something the Chinese would buy: opium. Grown legally in British-occupied India, opium was smuggled into China, where its use and sale were illegal. Huge profits and the cravings of addicts led to rapid increases in sales, from 4,500 chests a year in 1810 to 10,000 in 1830 and 40,000 in 1838. At this point it was China that suffered a drain of silver, since it was importing more than it was exporting.

To deal with this crisis, the Chinese government dispatched Lin Zexu to Guangzhou in 1839. He dealt harshly with Chinese who purchased opium and seized the opium stores of British merchants. Lin even wrote to Queen Victoria: "Suppose there were people from another country who carried opium for sale to England and seduced your people into buying and smoking it; certainly your honorable ruler would deeply hate it

José Rizal

IN THE MID-SEVENTEENTH CENTURY a Chinese merchant immigrated to the Philippines and married a woman who was half Chinese, half Filipino. Because of anti-Chinese animosity, he changed his name to Mercado, Spanish for "merchant."

Mercado's direct patrilineal descendant José Rizal (1861–1896) was born into a well-to-do family that leased a plantation from Dominican friars. Both of his parents were educated, and he was a brilliant student himself. In 1882, after completing his studies at the Jesuit-run college in Manila, he went to Madrid to study medicine. During his ten years in Europe he not only earned a medical degree in Spain and a Ph.D. in Germany but also found time to learn several European languages and make friends with scientists, writers, and political radicals.

While in Europe, Rizal became involved with Filipino revolutionaries and contributed numerous articles to their newspaper, *La Solidaridad*, published in Barcelona. Rizal advocated making the Philippines a province of Spain, giving it representation in the Spanish parliament, replacing Spanish friars with Filipino priests, and making Filipinos and Spaniards equal before the law. He spent a year at the British Museum doing research on the early phase of the Spanish colonization of the Philippines. He also wrote two novels.

The first novel, written in Spanish, was fired by the passions of nationalism. In satirical fashion, it depicts a young Filipino of mixed blood who studies for several years in Europe before returning to the Philippines to start a modern secular school in his hometown and to marry his childhood sweetheart. The church stands in the way of his efforts, and the colonial administration proves incompetent. The novel ends with the hero being gunned down after the friars falsely implicate him in a revolutionary conspiracy. Rizal's own life ended up following this narrative surprisingly closely.

José Rizal. (The Library of Congress, Prints and Photographs Division, LC-USZ62-43453)

In 1892 Rizal left Europe, stopped briefly in Hong Kong, and then returned to Manila to help his family with a lawsuit. Though he secured his relatives' release from jail, he ran into trouble himself. Because his writings were critical of the power of the church, he made many enemies, some of whom had him arrested. He was sent into exile to a Jesuit mission town on the relatively primitive island of Mindanao. There he founded a school and a hospital, and the Jesuits tried to win him back to the church. He kept busy during his four years in exile, not only teaching English, science, and self-defense, but also maintaining his correspondence with scientists in Europe. When a nationalist secret society rose in revolt in 1896, Rizal, in an effort to distance himself, volunteered to go to Cuba to help in an outbreak of yellow fever. Although he had no connections with the secret society and was on his way across the ocean, Rizal was arrested and shipped back to Manila.

Tried for sedition by the military, Rizal was found guilty. When handed his death certificate, Rizal struck out the words "Chinese half-breed" and wrote "pure native." He was publicly executed by a firing squad in Manila at age thirty-five, making him a martyr of the nationalist cause.

QUESTIONS FOR ANALYSIS

1. How did Rizal's comfortable family background contribute to his becoming a revolutionary?
2. How would Rizal's European contemporaries have reacted to his opposition to the Catholic Church?

---

and be bitterly aroused."[2] Although for years the little community of foreign merchants had accepted Chinese rules, by 1839 the British, the dominant group, were ready to flex their muscles. British merchants wanted to create a market for their goods in China and get tea more cheaply by trading closer to its source in central China. They also wanted a European-style diplomatic relationship with China, with envoys and ambassadors, commercial treaties, and published tariffs. With the encouragement of their merchants in China, the British sent an expeditionary force from India with forty-two warships.

Treaty of Nanjing The settlement reached by Britain and China in 1842 was written in both English and Chinese. The chief negotiators of both sides signed the document, and the seals of both countries were placed on it. The Chinese seal was impressed with red ink in the traditional way, while the British used wax. (National Archives, UK/Photo © Mary Evans Picture Library/The Image Works)

With its control of the seas, the British easily shut down key Chinese ports and forced the Chinese to negotiate. Dissatisfied with the resulting agreement, the British sent a second, larger force, which took even more coastal cities, including Shanghai. This **Opium War** was settled at gunpoint in 1842. The Treaty of Nanjing and subsequent agreements opened five ports to international trade, fixed the tariff on imported goods at 5 percent, imposed an indemnity of 21 million ounces of silver on China to cover Britain's war expenses, and ceded the island of Hong Kong to Britain. Through the clause on **extraterritoriality** (the legal principle that exempts individuals from local law), British subjects in China became answerable only to British law, even in disputes with Chinese. The treaties also had a "most-favored nation" clause, which meant that whenever one nation extracted a new privilege from China, it was extended automatically to Britain.

The treaties satisfied neither side. China continued to refuse to accept foreign diplomats at its capital in Beijing, and the expansion of trade fell far short of Western expectations. Between 1856 and 1860 Britain and France renewed hostilities with China. British and French troops occupied Beijing and set the emperor's summer palace on fire. Another round of harsh treaties gave European merchants and missionaries greater privileges and forced the Chinese to open several more cities to foreign trade.

Internal Problems

China's problems in the nineteenth century were not all of foreign origin. By 1850 China, for centuries the world's most populous country, had more than 400 million people. As the population grew, farm size shrank, forests were put to the plow, surplus labor suppressed wages, and conflicts over rights to water and tenancy increased. Hard times also led to increased female infanticide, as families felt that they could not afford to raise more than two or three children and saw sons as necessities. (See "Global Viewpoints: Chinese and British Efforts to Reduce Infant Deaths," page 771.)

These economic and demographic circumstances led to some of the most destructive rebellions in China's history. The worst was the **Taiping Rebellion** (1851–1864), in which some 20 million people lost their lives, making it one of the bloodiest wars in world history.

Opium War The 1839–1842 war between the British and the Chinese over limitations on trade and the importation of opium into China.

extraterritoriality The legal principle that exempts individuals from local law, applicable in China because of the agreements reached after China's loss in the Opium War.

Taiping Rebellion A massive rebellion by believers in the religious teachings of Hong Xiuquan, begun in 1851 and not suppressed until 1864.

Chinese Rebellions, 1851–1911

Taiping Rebellion, 1851–1864
Boxer uprising, 1900
Revolt of 1911

The Taiping (TIGH-ping) Rebellion was initiated by Hong Xiuquan (hong shoh-chwan) (1814–1864). After reading a Christian tract given to him by a missionary, Hong interpreted visions he had had to mean he was Jesus's younger brother and had a mission to wipe out evil in China. He soon gathered followers, whom he instructed to destroy idols and ancestral temples, give up opium and alcohol, and renounce foot binding and prostitution. In 1851 he declared himself king of the Heavenly Kingdom of Great Peace (Taiping), an act of open insurrection.

By 1853 the Taiping rebels, as Hong's followers were known, had moved north and established their capital at the major city of Nanjing, which they held on to for a decade. From this base they set about creating a utopian society based on the equalization of land-holdings and the equality of men and women. To suppress the Taipings, the Manchus had to turn to Chinese scholar-officials, who raised armies on their own, revealing the Manchus' military weakness.

The Self-Strengthening Movement

After the various rebellions were suppressed, forward-looking reformers began addressing the Western threat. Under the slogan "self-strengthening," they set about modernizing the military along Western lines. Some of the most progressive reformers also initiated new industries, which in the 1870s and 1880s included railway lines, steam navigation companies, coal mines, telegraph lines, and cotton spinning and weaving factories.

These measures drew resistance from conservatives, who thought copying Western practices was compounding defeat. A highly placed Manchu official objected that "from ancient down to modern times"

Hong Kong Tailors In 1872 the newspaper *Shenbao* was founded in Shanghai, and in 1884 it added an eight-page weekly pictorial supplement. Influenced by the pictorial press then popular in Europe, it depicted both news and human interest stories, both Chinese and foreign, helping readers understand all of the social and cultural changes then taking place. This scene shows a tailor shop in Hong Kong where Chinese tailors use sewing machines and make women's clothes in current Western styles. To Chinese readers, men making women's clothes and placing them on bamboo forms would have seemed as peculiar as the style of the dresses. (From *Dianshizhai huabao*, a Shanghai picture magazine, 1885 or later/Visual Connection Archive)

Chinese and British Efforts to Reduce Infant Deaths

In the premodern world, infant survival was precarious. Chinese scholars knew that one reason was infanticide among the poor. In the first document, from the 1840s, the Chinese scholar You Zhi describes setting up a private charity to provide small payments to poverty-stricken parents so that they would not kill a newborn child. This charitable practice can be compared to the foundling hospitals put in place in England in the 1760s. Jonas Hanway, the English author of the second document, does not accuse parents of deliberately killing babies but observes that abandoned children die in high numbers.

You Zhi, "The Society to Save Babies"

■ When poor families have too many children, their difficult circumstances often compel them to drown newborn babies, a practice which has already become so widespread that no one considers it strange. Not only are baby girls drowned, at times even baby boys are; not only do the poor drown their children, even the well-to-do do it. . . .

Those making the effort to accumulate good deeds will buy live animals just to release them! Aren't human lives even more precious? . . .

We have formed a society named "The Society to Save Babies." Every time a baby is born to a truly poor family unable to raise it, our society will as a rule grant them money and rice to cover six months. Only when it is absolutely impossible for them to keep the child at home will the society send the child to an orphanage as a way to save its life. The parents may at first keep the baby for the subsidy, but they will come to love it more every day and so eventually will keep it out of love. . . .

In the area we serve, any family too destitute to keep a newborn should report to the Society, accompanied by neighbors who are willing to serve as witnesses. The Society's inspector will then go personally to the home to assess the situation, and if it is as reported, will give the parents one peck of white rice and two hundred coins. For the next five months they can claim the same amount each month, identifying themselves with a ticket. . . . After five months, if they definitely cannot afford to keep the child, the Society will arrange for it to be taken to an orphanage. . . .

With the passage of time, people will find ways to cheat. Once a payment system is started, there inevitably will be people who could support their children but pretend to be poor to obtain the money and rice. . . .

As to babies born from illicit relations, making it difficult for the mother to keep them, we should tell midwives that they will receive four hundred to five hundred cash as a reward if they secretly bring such babies to the Society. In this way we will be able to save quite a few additional lives.

Jonas Hanway, *An Earnest Appeal for Mercy to the Children of the Poor*

■ One of our most important inquietudes, especially in time of war, is that we want people, and yet many lives are lost by the grossest negligence in our police. . . .

Many children instead of being nourished with care, by the fostering hand or breast of a wholesome country nurse, are thrust into the impure air of a workhouse, into the hands of some careless, worthless young female, or decrepit old woman, and inevitably lost for want of such means as the God of nature, their father as well as ours, has appointed for their preservation. . . .

[W]e ought no more to suffer a child to die for want of the common necessaries of life, though he is born to labor, than one who is the heir to a dukedom. The extinction of those who labor would be more fatal to the community than if the number of the highest ranks of the people were reduced. . . .

Never shall I forget the evidence given at Guild-Hall, upon occasion of a master of a workhouse of a large parish, who was challenged for forcing a child from the breast of the mother, and sending it to the Foundling Hospital. He alleged this in his defense, "We send all our children to the Foundling Hospital; we have not saved one alive for fourteen years. We have no place fit to preserve them in; the air is too confined."

QUESTIONS FOR ANALYSIS

1. How similar are the two authors' goals? How do their religious values shape their goals?
2. How do the two authors view the poor?
3. What differences between their countries might account for the differences in the authors' strategies?

Sources: *Deyi lu*, 2. 32, 40, 41, 55, http://ctext.org/wiki.pl?if=gb&chapter=276413, trans. Patricia Ebrey; Jonas Hanway, *An Earnest Appeal for Mercy to the Children of the Poor* (London: Dodsley, 1766), pp. 1–9.

there had never been "anyone who could use mathematics to raise a nation from a state of decline or to strengthen it in times of weakness."[3] Yet knowledge of the West gradually improved with more translations and travel in both directions. Newspapers covering world affairs began publication in Shanghai and Hong Kong. By 1880 China had embassies in London, Paris, Berlin, Madrid, Washington, Tokyo, and St. Petersburg.

Despite the enormous effort put into trying to catch up, China was humiliated yet again at the end of the nineteenth century. First came the discovery that Japan had so successfully modernized that it posed a threat to China. Then in 1894 Japanese efforts to separate Korea from Chinese influence led to the brief Sino-Japanese War, in which China was decisively defeated the next year. China's helplessness in the face of aggression led to a scramble among the European powers for concessions and protectorates in China. At the high point of this rush in 1898, it appeared that the European powers might actually divide China among themselves, the way they had recently divided Africa.

Republican Revolution

China's humiliating defeat in the Sino-Japanese War in 1895 led to a renewed drive for reform. In 1898 a group of educated young reformers gained access to the twenty-seven-year-old Qing emperor. They warned him of the fate of Poland (divided by the European powers in the eighteenth century; see "Enlightened Absolutism and Its Limits" in Chapter 19) and regaled him with the triumphs of the Meiji reformers in Japan. They proposed redesigning China as a constitutional monarchy with modern financial and educational systems. For three months the emperor issued a series of reform decrees. But the Manchu establishment and the empress dowager felt threatened and not only suppressed the reform movement but imprisoned the emperor as well. Hope for reform from the top was dashed.

A period of violent reaction swept the country, reaching its peak in 1900 with the uprising of a secret society that foreigners dubbed the **Boxers**. The Boxers blamed China's ills on foreigners, especially Christian missionaries. After the Boxers laid siege to the foreign legation quarter in Beijing, a dozen nations, including Japan, sent twenty thousand troops to lift the siege. In the negotiations that followed, China had to agree to cancel civil service examinations and pay a staggering indemnity.

After this defeat, gradual reform lost its appeal. More and more Chinese were studying abroad and learning about Western political ideas, including democracy

Foreign Soldiers in Shanghai In this photo taken in 1900, British, French, German, and Japanese officers pose for a portrait. The foreign armies that suppressed the Boxer Uprising stayed for months in China. (Private Collection/Bridgeman Images)

and revolution. The most famous was Sun Yatsen (1866–1925). Sent by his peasant family to Hawaii, he learned English and then continued his education in Hong Kong. From 1894 on, he spent his time abroad organizing revolutionary societies. He joined forces with Chinese student revolutionaries studying in Japan, and together they sparked the **1911 Revolution**, which brought China's long history of monarchy to an end, to be replaced by a Western-style republic. China had escaped direct foreign rule but would never be the same.

Japan's Rapid Transformation

How was Japan able to quickly master the challenges posed by the West?

During the eighteenth century Japan (much more effectively than China) kept foreign merchants and missionaries at bay. It limited trade to a single port (Nagasaki), where only the Dutch were allowed, and forbade Japanese to travel abroad. Because Japan's land and population were so much smaller than China's, the Western powers never expected much from Japan as a trading partner and did not press it as urgently. Still, the European threat was part of what propelled Japan to modernize.

The "Opening" of Japan

Wanting to play a greater role in the Pacific, the United States decided to force the Japanese to open to trade. In 1853 Commodore Matthew Perry steamed into Edo (now Tokyo) Bay and demanded diplomatic negotiations with the emperor. Under threat of **gunboat diplomacy**, and after consulting with the daimyo (major lords), the officials signed a treaty with the United States that opened two ports and permitted trade.

Japan at this time was a complex society. The emperor in Kyoto had no effective powers. For more than two hundred years real power had been in the hands of the Tokugawa shogun in Edo (AY-doh) (see "Tokugawa Government" in Chapter 21). The country was divided into numerous domains, each under a daimyo (DIGH-myoh). Each daimyo had under him samurai, warriors who had hereditary stipends and privileges, such as the right to wear a sword. Peasants and merchants were also legally distinct classes, and in theory social mobility from peasant to merchant or merchant to samurai was impossible. After two centuries of peace, there were many more samurai than were needed to administer or defend the country, and many lived very modestly. They were proud, however,

and felt humiliated by the sudden American intrusion and the unequal treaties that the Western countries imposed. Some began agitating against the shogunate under the slogan "Revere the emperor and expel the barbarians."

When foreign diplomats and merchants began to settle in Yokohama after 1858, radical samurai reacted with a wave of antiforeign terrorism and antigovernment assassinations. The response from Western powers was swift and unambiguous. They sent an allied fleet of American, British, Dutch, and French warships to demolish key Japanese forts, further weakening the power and prestige of the shogun's government.

The Meiji Restoration

In 1867 a coalition of reform-minded daimyo led a coup that ousted the Tokugawa Shogunate. The samurai who led this coup declared a return to direct rule by the emperor, which had not been practiced in Japan for more than six hundred years. This emperor was called the Meiji (MAY-jee) emperor and this event the **Meiji Restoration**, a great turning point in Japanese history.

The domain leaders who organized the coup, called the Meiji Oligarchs, moved the boy emperor to Tokyo castle. They used the young sovereign to win over both the lords and the commoners. Real power remained in the hands of the oligarchs.

The battle cry of the Meiji reformers had been "strong army, rich nation." How were these goals to be accomplished? Convinced that they could not beat the West until they had mastered the secrets of its military and industrial might, they initiated a series of measures to reform Japan along modern Western lines. Within four years a delegation was traveling the world to learn what made the Western powers strong. Its members examined everything from the U.S. Constitution to the factories, shipyards, and railroads that made the European landscape so different from Japan's.

Japan under the shoguns had been decentralized, with most of the power over the population in the hands of the many daimyo. By elevating the emperor, the oligarchs were able to centralize the government. In 1871 they abolished the domains and merged the domain armies. Following the example of the French

Boxers A Chinese secret society that blamed the country's ills on foreigners, especially missionaries, and rose in rebellion in 1900.

1911 Revolution The uprising that brought China's monarchy to an end.

gunboat diplomacy The imposition of treaties and agreements under threat of military violence, such as the opening of Japan to trade after Commodore Perry's demands.

Meiji Restoration The 1867 ousting of the Tokugawa Shogunate that "restored" the power of the Japanese emperors.

Fukuzawa Yukichi, "Escape from Asia"

Fukuzawa Yukichi was one of the most prominent intellectuals and promoters of westernization in Meiji Japan. His views on domestic policy were decidedly liberal, but he took a hard-line approach to foreign affairs. His ruthless criticism of Korea and China published on March 16, 1885, can be read as inviting colonialism. In 1895, ten years after writing this call to action, he rejoiced at Japan's victory over China in the conflict over Korea.

■ Civilization is like an epidemic of measles. The current measles in Tokyo, which has advanced eastwards from Nagasaki in western Japan, seems to have begun to claim more victims with the arrival of springtime. Will we be able now to find a means of checking this epidemic? It is obvious that we have no way to do so. We cannot put up effective resistance, even against an epidemic that carries with it only harm; much less against civilization, which is always accompanied by both harm and good, but by more good than harm.

Though our land of Japan is situated on the Eastern edge of Asia, the spirit of its people has already shaken off the backwardness of Asia to accept the civilization of the West. Unfortunately, however, we have two neighboring countries, one being called China, the other called Korea. The people of these two countries are no different from us Japanese people in having been brought up since olden times in the Asian culture and customs, and yet, whether because they are of another racial origin, or because, while similar in culture and customs, differ from us in the main lines of their traditional education, a comparison of the three countries, Japan, China, and Korea, reveals that the latter two resemble each other more closely than they do Japan. The people of those two countries do not know how to go about reforming and making progress, whether individually or as a country. It is not that they have not seen or heard of civilized things in the present world of facile communication; yet what their eyes and ears perceive have failed to stimulate their minds, and their emotional attachment to ancient manners and customs has changed little for the past hundreds and thousands of years. In this lively theater of civilization, where things change daily, they still speak of education in terms of Confucianism, cite humanity, justice, civility, and wisdom as their principles of school education, are completely obsessed only with outward appearance, are in reality not only ignorant of truths and principles but so extreme in their cruelty and shamelessness that for them morality is completely nonexistent, and yet are as arrogant as if they never gave a thought to self-examination.

In our view, these countries have no likelihood of maintaining their independence in the current tide of civilization's eastward advance. Let there not be the slightest doubt that, unless they are fortunate enough to have motivated men appear in their lands who, as a first step to improve the condition of their countries will plan such a great enterprise of overall reform of their governments as our Restoration was, and succeed in altering their people's minds through political reforms, those countries will meet their doom in but a few years, with their territories divided among the civilized countries of the world. The reason is that China and Korea, confronted by an epidemic of civilization comparable to measles, are impossibly trying to ward it off, despite its

---

Revolution, they dismantled the four-class legal system and declared everyone equal. This amounted to stripping the samurai (7 to 8 percent of the population) of their privileges. Even their monopoly on the use of force was eliminated: the new army recruited commoners along with samurai. Not surprisingly, some samurai rose up against their loss of privileges. None of these uncoordinated uprisings made any difference.

Several leaders of the Meiji Restoration, in France on a fact-finding mission during the Franco-Prussian War of 1870–1871, were impressed by the active participation of French citizens in the defense of Paris. For Japan to survive in the hostile international environment, they concluded, ordinary people had to be trained to fight. Consequently, a conscription law, modeled on the French law, was issued in 1872. To improve the training of soldiers, the new War College was organized along German lines, and German instructors were recruited to teach there. Young samurai were trained to form the new professional officer corps.

Many of the new institutions established in the Meiji period reached down to the local level. Schools open to all were rapidly introduced beginning in 1872. Teachers were trained in newly established teachers' colleges, where they learned to inculcate discipline, patriotism, and morality. Another modern institution that reached the local level was a national police force. In 1884 police training schools were established in every prefecture, and within a few years one- or two-man police stations were set up throughout the country. These policemen came to act as local agents of the central government. They not only dealt with crime but also enforced public health rules, conscription laws, and codes of behavior.

inevitability, by shutting themselves up in a room, with the result being that they are cutting off their supply of fresh air and asphyxiating themselves. Though mutual help between neighboring countries has been likened to the relationship between the lips and the teeth, China and Korea of today cannot be of any assistance at all to our country of Japan.

Civilized western man is not without a tendency to regard all three countries as identical because of their geographic proximity and to apply his evaluation of China and Korea to Japan also. For example, when he finds that the governments of China and Korea are old-fashioned autocracies without abiding laws, the western man will suppose Japan too to be a lawless country. When he finds that the gentlemen of China and Korea are too deeply infatuated to know what science is, the western scholar will think that Japan too is a land of Yin-Yang and the Five Elements. When the Chinese display their servility and shamelessness, they obscure the chivalrous spirit of the Japanese. When the Koreans employ cruel means of physical punishment, the Japanese too are surmised to be just as inhuman. Such examples are too numerous to count. This may be compared to the case in which most of those in a string of houses within a village or town are foolish, lawless, cruel, and inhuman; an occasional family that heeds what is just and right will be eclipsed by the other's evil and its virtue will never be noticed. It is indeed not infrequent that something similar happens in our foreign relations and indirectly interferes with them. This should be regarded a great misfortune for our country of Japan.

To plan our course now, therefore, our country cannot afford to wait for the enlightenment of our neighbors and to cooperate in building Asia up. Rather, we should leave their ranks to join the camp of the civilized countries of the West.

Even when dealing with China and Korea, we need not have special scruples simply because they are our neighbors, but should behave toward them as the westerners do. One who befriends an evil person cannot avoid being involved in his notoriety. In spirit, then, we break with our evil friends of Eastern Asia.

QUESTIONS FOR ANALYSIS

1. What does Fukuzawa mean by "civilization"?
2. How does Fukuzawa's justification of colonialism compare to Europeans' justification of it during the same period?

Source: Centre for East Asian Cultural Studies, comp., *Meiji Japan Through Contemporary Sources.* Vol. 3: *1869–1894* (Tokyo: Centre for East Asian Cultural Studies, 1972), pp. 129–133, modified. Used by permission of the Center for East Asian Cultural Studies.

In 1889 Japan became the first non-Western country to adopt the constitutional form of government. A commission sent abroad to study European constitutional governments had come to the conclusion that the German constitutional monarchy would provide the best model for Japan, rather than the more democratic governments of the British, French, and Americans. Japan's new government had a two-house parliament, called the Diet. The upper house of lords was drawn largely from former daimyo and nobles, and the lower house was elected by a limited electorate (about 5 percent of the adult male population in 1890). Although Japan now had a government based on laws, it was authoritarian rather than democratic. The emperor was declared "sacred and inviolable." He had the right to appoint the prime minister and cabinet. He did not have to ask the Diet for funds because wealth assigned to the imperial house was entrusted to the Imperial Household Ministry, which was outside the government's control.

Cultural change during the Meiji period was as profound as political change. For more than a thousand years China had been the major source of ideas and technologies introduced into Japan. But in the late nineteenth century China, beset by Western pressure, had become an object lesson on the dangers of stagnation. The influential author Fukuzawa Yukichi began urging Japan to pursue "civilization and enlightenment," by which he meant Western civilization. (See "Analyzing the Evidence: Fukuzawa Yukichi, 'Escape from Asia,'" above.) Soon Japanese were being told to conform to Western taste, eat meat, wear Western-style clothes, and drop customs that Westerners found odd, such as married women's blackening their teeth.

Ito Hirobumi and His Family The statesman Ito Hirobumi posed for this picture with his wife, son, and two grandsons at his country residence in 1908. Although as an official he promoted rapid political and economic change, at home he kept to many traditional practices, such as wearing traditional dress.
(Popperfoto/Getty Images)

Industrialization

The leaders of the Meiji Restoration, wanting to strengthen Japan's military capacity, promoted industrialization. The government paid large salaries to attract foreign experts to help with industrialization, and Japanese were encouraged to go abroad to study science and engineering.

The government played an active role in getting railroads, mines, and factories started. Early on, the Japanese government decided to compete with China in the export of tea and silk to the West. Introducing the mechanical reeling of silk gave Japan a strong price advantage in the sale of silk, and Japan's total foreign trade increased tenfold from 1877 to 1900. The next stage was to develop heavy industry. A huge indemnity exacted from China in 1895, as part of the peace agreement, was used to establish the Yawata Iron and Steel Works. The third stage of Japan's industrialization would today be called import substitution. Factories such as cotton mills were set up to help cut the importation of Western consumer goods (See "Analyzing the Evidence: Japan's First Skyscraper," at right).

Most of the great Japanese industrial conglomerates known as *zaibatsu* (zigh-BAHT-dzoo), such as Mitsubishi, got their start in this period, often founded by men with government connections. Sometimes the government set up plants that it then sold to private investors at bargain prices. Successful entrepreneurs were treated as patriotic heroes.

As in Europe, the early stages of industrialization brought hardship to the countryside. Farmers often rioted as their incomes failed to keep up with prices or as their tax burdens grew. Workers in modern industries were no happier, and in 1898 railroad workers went on strike for better working conditions and overtime pay. Still, rice production increased, death rates dropped as public health was improved, and the population grew from about 33 million in 1868 to about 45 million in 1900.

Japan as an Imperial Power

During the course of the Meiji period, Japan became an imperial power, making Taiwan and Korea into its colonies. The conflicts that led to Japanese acquisition of both of them revolved around Korea.

Japan's First Skyscraper

The title in the upper right of this woodblock print identifies the subject as the Pavilion That Pierces the Clouds, a well-known building completed in 1890 and popularly known as "Twelve Stories." It was designed by a Scottish engineer soon after his arrival in Japan and was the first building in Japan with an elevator. All its floors were equipped with electric lighting, adding to its modern allure. At 225 feet tall, it was the tallest building in Tokyo for decades and was visible from almost anywhere in the city. It was also the best place to look down on Tokyo, either from the lounge on the tenth floor or the observation deck equipped with telescopes on the twelfth floor. On a clear day one could see Mount Fuji.

Inside, Twelve Stories offered many kinds of amusement. On its second to seventh floors, it housed forty-six stores selling goods from around the world, including one that sold woodblock prints used in a popular board game. Art exhibitions were held on the ninth floor. There was also room for cultural events, including Western music concerts, photograph exhibitions, and beauty contests. The Great Kanto Earthquake of 1923 damaged the tower so severely that it had to be completely demolished, and it was never rebuilt, but in its heyday it was one of the best-known landmarks in Tokyo.

Utagawa Kunimasa IV (1838–1920), the artist who made this print, was trained by two former heads of the Utagawa line of woodblock print artists, and, like them, he supported himself largely though selling pictures of popular actors. With the rapid introduction of Western culture in the Meiji period, he and other artists of the period turned their attention to all that was modern and exotic, including foreigners and their odd clothing, vehicles, and buildings.

QUESTIONS FOR ANALYSIS

1. Locate all the people in this picture. How are they dressed? What are they doing?
2. Keeping in mind that the building in this picture was built in 1890, what connections can you draw between the politics of the period and this visual celebration of a new style of architecture?
3. How did the artist, Utagawa Kunimasa IV, adapt traditional woodblock print artistic conventions to the portrayal of new features of life in Tokyo? Would a visiting artist from the West have painted this scene the same way, or is there something distinctively Japanese about this picture?

(*Pavilion Above the Clouds*, Suroroku 1890, by Utagawa Kunimasa IV [1838–1920] [woodblock print with collage elements]/Mead Art Museum, Amherst College/Bridgeman Images)

The Chosŏn Dynasty had been on the throne in Korea since 1392. In the second half of the nineteenth century Korea found itself caught between China, Japan, and Russia, each trying to protect or extend its sphere of influence. Westerners also began demanding that Korea be "opened." Korea's first response was to insist that its foreign relations be handled through Beijing. Matters were complicated by the rise in the 1860s of a religious cult, the Tonghak movement, that had strong xenophobic elements. Although the government executed the cult founder in 1864, this cult continued to gain support, especially among impoverished peasants. Thus, like the Chinese government in the same period, the Korean government faced simultaneous internal and external threats.

In 1871 the U.S. minister to China took five warships to try to open Korea, but left after exchanges of fire resulted in 250 Koreans dead without any progress in getting the Korean government to make concessions. Japan tried next and in 1876 forced the Korean government to sign an unequal treaty and open three ports to Japanese trade. On China's urging, Korea also signed treaties with the European powers in an effort to counterbalance Japan.

Over the next couple of decades reformers in China and Japan tried to encourage Korea to adopt its own self-strengthening movement, but Korean conservatives did their best to undo reform efforts. In 1894, when the religious cult rose in a massive revolt, both China and Japan sent military forces, claiming to come to the Korean government's aid. They ended up fighting each other instead in what is known as the Sino-Japanese War (see "The Self-Strengthening Movement"). With its decisive victory, Japan gained Taiwan from China and was able to make Korea a protectorate. In 1910 Korea was formally annexed as a province of Japan.

Japan also competed aggressively with the leading European powers for influence and territory in China, particularly in the northeast (Manchuria). There Japanese and Russian imperialism met and collided. In 1904 Japan attacked Russian forces and, after its 1905 victory in the bloody **Russo-Japanese War**, emerged with a valuable foothold in China—Russia's former protectorate over Port Arthur (see Map 26.1).

Japanese Expansion, 1875–1914

Japan's victories over China and Russia changed the way European nations looked at Japan. Through negotiations Japan was able to eliminate extraterritoriality in 1899 and gain control of its own tariffs in 1911. Within Japan, the success of the military in raising Japan's international reputation added greatly to its political influence.

The Pacific Region and the Movement of People

What were the causes and consequences of the vast movement of people in the Pacific region?

The nineteenth century was marked by extensive movement of people into, across, and out of Asia and the broad Pacific region. Many of these migrants moved from one Asian country to another, but there was also a growing presence of Europeans in Asia, a consequence of the increasing integration of the world economy (see "The Expanding World Economy" in Chapter 25).

Settler Colonies in the Pacific: Australia and New Zealand

The largest share of the Europeans who moved to the Pacific region in the nineteenth century went to the settler colonies in Australia and New Zealand (Map 26.2). In 1770 the English explorer James Cook visited New Zealand, Australia, and Hawaii. All three of these places in time became destinations for migrants.

Between 200 and 1300 C.E. Polynesians settled numerous islands of the Pacific, from New Zealand in the south to Hawaii in the north and Easter Island in the east. Thus most of the lands that explorers like Cook encountered were occupied by societies with chiefs, crop agriculture, domestic animals such as chickens and pigs, excellent sailing technology, and often considerable experience in warfare. Australia had been settled millennia earlier by a different population. When Cook arrived in Australia, it was occupied by about three hundred thousand Aborigines who lived entirely by food gathering, fishing, and hunting. Like the Indians of Central and South America, the people in all these lands fell victim to Eurasian diseases and died in large numbers.

Australia was first developed by Britain as a penal colony. Between 1787 and 1869, when the penal colony system was abolished, a total of 161,000 convicts were transported to Australia. After the end of the Napoleonic Wars in 1815, a steady stream of nonconvicts chose to relocate to Australia. Raising sheep proved suitable to Australia's climate, and wool exports steadily

Russo-Japanese War The 1904–1905 war between Russia and Japan fought over imperial influence and territory in northeast China (Manchuria).

MAP 26.2 Australia Because of the vast deserts in western Australia, cities and industries developed mainly in the east. Australia's early geographical and cultural isolation bred a sense of inferiority. Air travel, the communications revolution, and the massive importation of Japanese products and American popular culture have changed that.

increased, from 75,400 pounds in 1821 to 24 million pounds in 1845. To encourage migration, the government offered free passage and free land to immigrants. By 1850 Australia had five hundred thousand inhabitants. The discovery of gold in Victoria in 1851 quadrupled that number in a few years. The gold rush also provided the financial means for cultural development. Public libraries, museums, art galleries, and universities opened in the thirty years after 1851. These institutions dispensed a distinctly British culture.

Not everyone in Australia was of British origin, however. Chinese and Japanese built the railroads and ran the shops in the towns and the market gardens nearby. Filipinos and Pacific Islanders did the hard work in the sugarcane fields. Afghans and their camels

The "Life of Emigration" Puzzle, ca. 1840 Some of the advertising designed to attract people to move to Australia was aimed at children, such as this wooden puzzle depicting the life of a family moving from Britain to Australia. (Photograph courtesy of the State Library of South Australia, S.A. Memory website)

Maori Chief, 1885 This photograph depicts Chief Wahanui of the Ngati Maniapoto tribe with his family and friends. The chief had fought in the Maori wars against the British in 1864–1865. Twenty years later, he and his family had adopted many elements of Western material culture. (By Alfred Burton [1834–1914] [albumen print]/ Private Collection/© Michael Graham-Stewart/Bridgeman Images)

controlled the carrying trade in some areas. But fear that Asian labor would lower living standards and undermine Australia's distinctly British culture led to efforts to keep Australia white.

Australia gained independence in stages. In 1850 the British Parliament passed the Australian Colonies Government Act, which allowed the four most populous colonies — New South Wales, Tasmania, Victoria, and South Australia — to establish colonial legislatures, determine the franchise, and frame their own constitutions. In 1902 Australia became one of the first countries in the world to give women the vote.

By 1900 New Zealand's population had reached 750,000, only a fifth of Australia's. One major reason more people had not settled these fertile islands was the resistance of the native Maori people. They quickly mastered the use of muskets and tried for decades to keep the British from taking their lands.

Foreign settlement in Hawaii began gradually. Initially, whalers stopped there for supplies, as they did at other Pacific Islands. Missionaries and businessmen came next, and soon other settlers followed, both whites and Asians. A plantation economy developed centered on sugarcane. In the 1890s leading settler families overthrew the native monarchy, set up a republic, and urged the United States to annex Hawaii, which it did in 1898.

Asian Emigration

Like Europeans, Asians left their native countries in unprecedented numbers in the nineteenth century (Map 26.3). As in Europe, both push and pull factors prompted people to leave home. Between 1750 and 1900 world population grew rapidly, in many places tripling. China and India were extremely densely populated countries — China with more than 400 million people in the mid-nineteenth century, India with more than 200 million. Not surprisingly, these two giants were the leading exporters of people in search of work or land. On the pull side were the new opportunities created by the flow of development capital into previously underdeveloped areas. In many of the European colonies in Asia the business class came to consist of

MAP 26.3 Emigration Out of Asia, 1820–1914 As steamships made crossing oceans quicker and more reliable, many people in Asia left their home countries to find new opportunities elsewhere. European imperialism contributed to this flow, especially by recruiting workers for newly established plantations or mines. Many emigrants simply wanted to work a few years to build their savings and planned to return home. Often, however, they ended up staying in their new countries and forming families there.

both Asian and European migrants. Asian diasporas formed in many parts of the world, with the majority in Asia itself, especially Southeast Asia.

By the nineteenth century Chinese formed key components of mercantile communities throughout Southeast Asia. Chinese often assimilated in Siam and Vietnam, but they rarely did so in Muslim areas such as Java, Catholic areas such as the Philippines, and primitive tribal areas such as northern Borneo. In these places distinct Chinese communities emerged, usually dominated by speakers of a single Chinese dialect.

With the growth in trade that accompanied the European imperial expansion, Chinese began to settle in the islands of Southeast Asia in larger numbers. After Singapore was founded by the British in 1819, Chinese rapidly poured in, soon becoming the dominant ethnic group. In British-controlled Malaya, some Chinese built great fortunes in the tin business, while

others worked in the mines. Chinese also settled in the Spanish-controlled Philippines and in Dutch-controlled Indonesia.

Discovery of gold in California in 1848, Australia in 1851, and Canada in 1858 encouraged Chinese to book passage to those places. In California few arrived soon enough to strike gold, but they quickly found work building railroads, and others took up mining in Wyoming and Idaho.

Indian entrepreneurs were similarly attracted by the burgeoning commerce of the growing British Empire. The bulk of Indian emigrants were **indentured laborers**, recruited under contract. The rise of indentured labor from Asia was a direct result of the outlawing of the African slave trade in the early nineteenth century by Britain and the United States. Sugar plantations in

indentured laborers Laborers who agreed to a term of employment, specified in a contract.

Canadian Immigration Certificate

This certificate proved that the eleven-year-old boy in the photograph had a legal right to be in Canada, as the $500 head tax required for immigration of Chinese had been paid. The head tax on Chinese immigrants introduced in 1885 started at $50, but it was raised to $100 in 1900 and to $500 in 1903. Equal to about what a laborer could earn in two years, the tax succeeded in its goal of slowing the rate of Asian immigration to Canada.

(Head tax certificate for Jung Bak Hun, issued January 3, 1919/ © Government of Canada. Reproduced with the permission of the Minister of Public Works and Government Services Canada [2016]. Source: Library and Archives Canada/Department of Employment and Immigration fonds/Vol. 712, C.I.5 certificate 88103)

the Caribbean and elsewhere needed new sources of workers, and planters in the British colonies discovered that they could recruit Indian laborers to replace blacks. After the French abolished slavery in 1848, they recruited workers from India as well. Later in the century many Indians emigrated to British colonies in Africa, the largest numbers to South Africa.

Indentured laborers secured as substitutes for slaves were often treated little better than slaves. In response to such abuse, the Indian colonial government established regulations stipulating a maximum indenture period of five years, after which the migrant would be entitled to passage home. Even though government "protectors" were appointed at the ports of embarkation, exploitation of indentured workers continued largely unchecked.

In areas outside the British Empire, China offered the largest supply of ready labor. Starting in the 1840s contractors arrived at Chinese ports to recruit labor for plantations and mines in Cuba, Peru, Hawaii, Sumatra, South Africa, and elsewhere. Chinese laborers did not have the British government to protect them and seem to have suffered even more than Indian workers.

India and China sent more people abroad than any other Asian countries during this period, but they were not alone. As Japan started to industrialize, its cities could not absorb all those forced off the farms, and people began emigrating in significant numbers, many to Hawaii and later to South America. Emigration from the Philippines also was substantial, especially after it became a U.S. territory in 1898.

Asian migration to the United States, Canada, and Australia—the primary destinations of European emigrants—would undoubtedly have been greater if it had not been so vigorously resisted by the white settlers in those regions. In 1882 Chinese were barred from becoming American citizens, and the immigration of Chinese laborers was suspended. Australia also put a stop to Asian immigration with the Commonwealth Immigration Restriction Act of 1901, which established the "white Australia policy" that remained on the books until the 1970s.

Most of the Asian migrants discussed so far were illiterate peasants or business people, not members of traditional educated elites. By the beginning of the twentieth century, however, another group of Asians was going abroad in significant numbers: students. Most of these students traveled abroad to learn about Western science, law, and government in the hope of strengthening their own countries. On their return they contributed enormously to the intellectual life of their societies, increasing understanding of the modern Western world and also becoming the most vocal advocates of overthrowing the old order and driving out the colonial masters.

Among the most notable of these foreign-educated radicals were Mohandas Gandhi (1869–1948) (see "Gandhi's Resistance Campaign in India" in Chapter 29) and Sun Yatsen. Sun developed his ideas about the republican form of government while studying in Hawaii and Hong Kong. Gandhi, after studying law in Britain, took a job in South Africa, where he became involved in trying to defend the interests of the Indians who lived and worked there. It was there that he gradually elaborated his idea of passive resistance.

The Countries of Asia in Comparative Perspective

What explains the similarities and differences in the experiences of Asian countries in this era?

At the start of the nineteenth century the societies of Asia varied much more than those of any other part of the world. In the temperate zones of East Asia, the old established monarchies of China, Japan, and Korea were all densely populated and boasted long literary traditions and traditions of unified governments. They had ties to each other that dated back many centuries and shared many elements of their cultures. South of them, in the tropical and subtropical regions, cultures were more diverse. India was just as densely populated as China, Japan, and Korea, but politically and culturally less unified, with several major languages and dozens of independent rulers reigning in kingdoms large and small, not to mention the growing British presence. In both India and Southeast Asia, Islam was much more important than it was in East Asia. All the countries with long written histories and literate elites were at a great remove from the thinly populated and relatively primitive areas without literate cultures and sometimes even without agriculture, such as Australia and some of the islands of the Philippines and Indonesia.

The nineteenth century gave the societies of Asia more in common in that all of them in one way or another had come into contact with the expanding West. Still, the Western powers did not treat all the countries the same way. Western powers initially wanted manufactured goods from the more developed Asian societies, especially Indian cotton textiles and Chinese porcelains. At the beginning of the nineteenth century Britain had already gained political control over large parts of India and was intent on forcing China to trade on terms more to its benefit. It paid virtually no attention to Korea and Japan, not seeing in them the same potential for profit. The less developed parts of Asia also attracted increasing Western interest, not because they could provide manufactured goods, but because they offered opportunities for Western development, much as the Americas had earlier.

The West that the societies of Asia faced during the nineteenth century was itself rapidly changing, and the steps taken by Western nations to gain power in Asia naturally also changed over time. Western science and technology were making rapid advances, which gave European armies progressively greater advantages in weaponry. The Industrial Revolution made it possible for countries that industrialized early, such as Britain, to produce huge surpluses of goods for which they had to find markets; this development shifted their interest in Asia from a place to buy goods to a place to sell goods. Britain had been able to profit from its colonization of India, and this profit both encouraged it to consolidate its rule and invited its European rivals to look for their own colonies. For instance, rivalry with Britain led France to seek colonies in Southeast Asia not only for its own sake but also as a way to keep Britain from extending its sphere of influence any farther.

There were some commonalities in the ways Asian countries responded to pressure from outside. In the countries with long literary traditions, often the initial response of the established elite was to try to drive the unwelcome foreigners away. This was the case in China, Japan, and Korea in particular. Violent antiforeign reactions exploded again and again, but the superior military technology of the industrialized West almost invariably prevailed. Some Asian leaders insisted on the need to preserve their cultural traditions at all costs. Others came to the opposite conclusion that the West was indeed superior in some ways and that they would have to adopt European ideas or techniques for their own purposes. This can be seen both among Indians who acquired education in English and in many of the Meiji reformers in Japan. The struggles between the traditionalists and the westernizers were often intense. As nationalism took hold in the West, it found a receptive audience among the educated elites in Asia. How could the assertion that every people had the right to control its own destiny not appeal to the colonized?

Whether they were colonized or not, most countries in Asia witnessed the spread of new technologies between 1800 and 1914. Railroads, telegraphs, modern sanitation, and a wider supply of inexpensive manufactured goods brought fundamental changes in everyday life not only to lands under colonial rule, such as India and Vietnam, but also, if less rapidly, to places that managed to remain independent, such as China and Japan. In fact, the transformation of Japan between 1860 and 1900 was extraordinary. By 1914 Japan had urban conveniences and educational levels comparable to those in Europe.

Chapter Summary

In the nineteenth century the countries of Asia faced new challenges. In India Britain extended its rule to the whole subcontinent, though often the British ruled indirectly through local princes. Britain brought many modern advances to India, such as railroads and schools. Slavery was outlawed, as was widow suicide and infanticide. Resistance to British rule took several forms. In 1857 Indian soldiers in the employ of the British rose in a huge revolt, and after Britain put down this rebellion it ruled India much more tightly. Indians who received English education turned English ideas of liberty and representative rule against the British and founded the Indian National Congress, which called for Indian independence.

In Southeast Asia by the end of the nineteenth century most countries, from Burma to the Philippines, had been made colonies of Western powers, which developed them as exporters of agricultural products or raw materials, including rubber, tin, sugar, tea, cotton, and jute. The principal exception was Siam (Thailand), whose king was able to play the English and French off against each other and institute centralizing reforms. In the Philippines more than three centuries of Spanish rule ended in 1898, but Spain was replaced by another colonial power: the United States.

In the nineteenth century China's world standing declined as a result of both foreign intervention and internal unrest. The government's efforts to suppress opium imports from Britain led to military confrontation with the British and to numerous concessions that opened China to trade on Britain's terms. Within its borders, China faced unprecedented population pressure and worsening economic conditions that resulted in uprisings in several parts of the country. Further humiliations by the Western powers led to concerted efforts to modernize, but China never quite caught up. Inspired by Western ideas of republican government, revolutionaries tried to topple the dynasty, finally succeeding in 1911–1912.

Japan was the one Asian country to quickly transform itself when confronted by the military strength of the West. It did this by overhauling its power structure. The Meiji centralized and strengthened Japan's power by depriving the samurai of their privileges, writing a constitution, instituting universal education, and creating a modern army. At the same time they guided Japan toward rapid industrialization. By the

early twentieth century Japan had become an imperialist power with colonies in Korea and Taiwan.

The nineteenth century was also a great age of migration. Citizens of Great Britain came east in large numbers, many to join the Indian civil service or army, others to settle in Australia or New Zealand. Subjects of Asian countries also went abroad, often leaving one Asian country for another. Asian students traveled to Europe, Japan, or the United States to continue their educations. Millions more left in search of work. With the end of the African slave trade, recruiters from the Americas and elsewhere went to India and China to secure indentured laborers. Asian diasporas formed in many parts of the world.

By the turn of the twentieth century the countries in the Asia and Pacific region varied greatly in wealth and power. There are several reasons for this. The countries did not start with equivalent circumstances. Some had long traditions of unified rule; others did not. Some had manufactured goods that Western powers wanted; others offered raw materials or cheap labor. The timing of the arrival of Western powers also made a difference, especially because Western military superiority increased over time. European Great Power rivalry had a major impact, especially after 1860. Similarities in the experiences of Asian countries are also notable and include many of the benefits (and costs) of industrialization seen elsewhere in the world, such as modernizations in communication and transportation, extension of schooling, and the emergence of radical ideologies.

NOTES

1. Quoted in K. M. Panikkar, *Asia and Western Dominance: A Survey of the Vasco da Gama Epoch of Asian History* (London: George Allen & Unwin, 1959), p. 116.
2. Ssu-yu Teng and J. K. Fairbank, *China's Response to the West: A Documentary Survey* (New York: Atheneum, 1971), p. 26.
3. Ibid., p. 76, modified.

CONNECTIONS

The nineteenth century brought Asia change on a much greater scale than did any earlier century. Much of the change was political — old political orders were ousted or reduced to tokens by new masters, often European colonial powers. Old elites found themselves at a loss when confronted by the European powers with their modern weaponry and modern armies. Cultural change was no less dramatic as the old elites pondered the differences between their traditional values and the ideas that seemed to underlie the power of the European states. In several places ordinary people rose in rebellion, probably in part because they felt threatened by the speed of cultural change. Material culture underwent major changes as elites experimented with Western dress and architecture and ordinary people had opportunities to travel on newly built railroads. Steamships, too, made long-distance travel easier, facilitating the out-migration of people seeking economic opportunities far from their countries of birth.

In the Americas, too, the nineteenth century was an era of unprecedented change and movement of people. Colonial empires were being overturned there, not imposed as they were in Asia in the same period. The Americas were on the receiving end of the huge migrations taking place, while Asia, like Europe, was much more an exporter of people. The Industrial Revolution brought change to all these areas, both by making available inexpensive machine-made products and by destroying some old ways of making a living. Intellectually, in both Asia and the Americas the ideas of nationalism and nation building shaped how people, especially the more educated, thought about the changes they were experiencing.

CHAPTER 26   Review and Explore

Identify Key Terms

Identify and explain the significance of each item below.

Great Mutiny / Great Revolt (p. 760)

Indian Civil Service (p. 761)

Indian National Congress (p. 764)

Java War (p. 766)

Nguyen Dynasty (p. 766)

Opium War (p. 769)

extraterritoriality (p. 769)

Taiping Rebellion (p. 769)

Boxers (p. 772)

1911 Revolution (p. 773)

gunboat diplomacy (p. 773)

Meiji Restoration (p. 773)

Russo-Japanese War (p. 778)

indentured laborers (p. 781)

Review the Main Ideas

Answer the focus questions from each section of the chapter.

1. In what ways did India change as a consequence of British rule? (p. 760)

2. Why were most but not all Southeast Asian societies reduced to colonies? (p. 765)

3. Was China's decline in the nineteenth century due more to internal problems or to Western imperialism? (p. 767)

4. How was Japan able to quickly master the challenges posed by the West? (p. 773)

5. What were the causes and consequences of the vast movement of people in the Pacific region? (p. 778)

6. What explains the similarities and differences in the experiences of Asian countries in this era? (p. 783)

Make Comparisons and Connections

Analyze the larger developments and continuities within and across chapters.

1. How quickly was Asia affected by the Industrial Revolution in Europe (Chapter 23)? Explain your answer.

2. How do the experiences of European colonies in Asia compare to those in Africa (Chapter 25)?

3. How does China's response to the challenge of European pressure compare to that of the Ottoman Empire (Chapter 25) during the same period?

TIMELINE

Suggested Resources

BOOKS

Bayly, C. A. *Indian Society and the Making of the British Empire*. 1990. A synthesis of recent research that provides a complex portrait of the interaction of Indian society and British colonial administration.

Bose, Sugata, and Ayesha Jalal. *Modern South Asia: History, Culture, Political Economy*. 1998. Incorporates recent scholarship with postcolonial perspective in a wide-ranging study.

Duus, Peter. *The Abacus and the Sword: The Japanese Penetration of Korea, 1895–1910*. 1995. Analyzes the interplay of business interests (the abacus) and military interests (the sword) in Japan's push for colonial possessions.

Fairbank, John King, and Merle Goldman. *China: A New History*, 2d ed. 2006. A treatment of China's experiences in the nineteenth century that is rich in interesting detail.

Hane, Mikiso. *Peasants, Rebels, Women, and Outcastes: The Underside of Modern Japan*, 2d ed. 2003. Draws on wide-ranging sources to provide a fuller picture of Japanese history.

Hopper, Helen. *Fukuzawa Yukichi: From Samurai to Capitalist*. 2005. A brief account of the life of a key westernizing intellectual.

Irokawa, Daikichi. *The Culture of the Meiji Period*. 1988. Makes excellent use of letters, diaries, and songs to probe changes in the ways ordinary people thought during a crucial period of political change.

Kuhn, Philip A. *Chinese Among Others: Emigration in Modern Times*. 2008. A history of Chinese emigration that is global in scope and vividly written.

Metcalf, Barbara D., and Thomas Metcalf. *A Concise History of Modern India*. 2012. A well-crafted overview.

Pruitt, Ida. *A Daughter of Han: The Autobiography of a Chinese Working Woman*. 1967. A highly revealing glimpse of Chinese society fashioned by journalist Ida Pruitt in the 1930s based on what a Chinese woman born in 1867 told Pruitt of her life.

Rowe, William T. *China's Last Empire: The Great Qing*. 2009. An overview of the Qing Empire by a major historian.

Spence, Jonathan. *God's Chinese Son*. 1997. Tells the story of the Taipings as much as possible from their own perspective.

Steinberg, David Joel, ed. *In Search of Southeast Asia: A Modern History*, rev. ed. 1987. An impressive work on Southeast Asia by seven specialists.

1857 Great Mutiny / Great Revolt by Indian sepoys against British rule

1867 Meiji Restoration in Japan

1872 Universal public schools established in Japan

1885 Indian National Congress founded

1859–1885 Vietnam becomes a colony of France

1861–1865 U.S. Civil War **(Ch. 27)**

1861 Serfs freed in Russia **(Ch. 24)**

1895 Japan defeats China, gains Taiwan

1898 U.S. takes control of Philippines from Spain

1904–1905 Japan attacks and defeats Russia

1910 Korea becomes a province of Japan

1912 China's monarchy replaced by a republic

1860	1880	1900

Walthall, Anne. *Japan: A Cultural, Social, and Political History.* 2006. A concise overview with good coverage of local society and popular culture.

Yeh, Catherine. *Shanghai Love: Courtesans, Intellectuals, and Entertainment Culture: 1850–1910.* 2006. An engaging account of the culture that developed in the treaty ports of China.

DOCUMENTARIES

The Meiji Revolution (PBS, 1992). Part of the award-winning *Pacific Century* series. Makes extensive use of photographs and woodblock prints as well as feature films.

The Two Coasts of China: Asia and the Challenge of the West (PBS, 1992). Part of the award-winning *Pacific Century* series. Focuses mostly on the elite response to the shift in foreign threat from the north to the seacoast.

FEATURE FILMS

Burning of the Imperial Palace (Han Hsiang Li, 1983). This joint Hong Kong–Chinese film dramatizes the events that culminated in the looting and destruction of the imperial Old Summer Palace by invading English and French troops in 1860.

Mangal Pandey: The Rising (Ketan Mehta, 2005). A fictional story of friendship and betrayal during the time of the 1857 uprising in India.

The Man Who Would Be King (John Huston, 1975). In this popular film based on a Rudyard Kipling story, two rogue ex-noncommissioned officers of the Indian army set off from late-nineteenth-century British India in search of adventure. The actors include Sean Connery, Michael Caine, and Christopher Plummer.

The Opium War (Jin Xie, 1997). The Chinese view of the Opium War, dramatized.

WEBSITES

British India and the "Great Rebellion." A good overview of the 1857 conflict in India. www.bbc.co.uk/history /british/victorians/indian_rebellion_01.shtml

Early Photography of Japan. A well-organized, easy-to-use portal to more than two thousand early photos of Japan in Harvard collections. hcl.harvard.edu/collections/epj/index.cfm

27

The Americas in the Age of Liberalism

1810–1917

Independence brought striking change and stubborn continuities to the Americas. With the exception of Haiti's revolution, American nations gained independence with their colonial social orders mostly intact. Slavery endured in the United States, Cuba, and Brazil until the second half of the nineteenth century. In Spanish America land remained concentrated in the hands of colonial elites. Territorial expansion displaced most of the indigenous communities that had withstood colonialism. By 1900 millions of immigrants from Europe, the Middle East, and Asia had settled in the Americas.

Though new political systems and governing institutions emerged, political rivals struggled to share power. Liberal republicanism became the most common form of government. But there were exceptions, such as the monarchy that ruled Brazil until 1889 and the parliamentary system tied to Britain that developed in Canada, which retained a symbolic role for the British monarch. Economically, the United States nurtured expanding internal markets and assumed an influential place in Atlantic and Pacific trade. Across Latin America, new nations with weak internal markets and often poorly consolidated political systems struggled to accumulate capital or industrialize.

Yaqui Woman

Indians across the Americas found their world under assault during the nineteenth century as new nation-states completed the process of territorial consolidation begun in the colonial era. Yaqui people like the woman depicted here faced the dual pressures of the United States' westward expansion and Mexico's integration of northern borderlands.

Edward S. Curtis Collection/Library of Congress, Prints and Photographs Division, Washington, D.C./LC-USZ62-1044492

CHAPTER PREVIEW

NEW NATIONS   How and why did the process of nation-state consolidation vary across the Americas?

SLAVERY AND ABOLITION
Why did slavery last longer in the United States, Brazil, and Cuba than in the other republics of the Americas? How did resistance by slaves shape abolition?

EXPORT-LED GROWTH AND SOCIAL UNREST
As Latin America became more integrated into the world economy, how did patterns of economic growth shape political culture and social reactions?

IMMIGRATION   What factors shaped patterns of immigration to the Americas? How did immigrants shape — and how were they shaped by — their new settings?

A NEW AMERICAN EMPIRE
In what ways did U.S. policies in the Caribbean and Central America resemble European imperialism? How did U.S. foreign policy depart from European imperialism?

New Nations

How and why did the process of nation-state consolidation vary across the Americas?

After American nations gained their independence between 1783 and 1825, each began a long and often-violent process of state-building and consolidating its eventual national territory. In countries such as Mexico and Argentina new governments failed to establish the trust needed for political stability. In the United States long-standing tensions culminated in the Civil War, while in Cuba nationalists fought a long struggle for independence from Spain.

Liberalism and Caudillos in Spanish America

To establish political and economic frameworks, American nations reached for ideologies that circulated in the Atlantic in the age of revolution (see "Demands for Liberty and Equality" in Chapter 22). The dominant ideology of the era was liberalism. Liberals sought to create representative republics with strong central governments framed by constitutions that defined and protected individual rights, in particular the right to freely own and buy and sell private property. Beginning with the United States, colonies that became independent nations in the Americas all adopted liberal constitutions.

The U.S. Constitution, in its earliest form, is an example of classic liberalism: it defined individual rights, but those individual rights were subordinated to property rights. Slaves were considered property rather than individuals with constitutional rights. Only property owners could vote, only men could own property, and the new government did not recognize the property of Indians. Liberalism mainly served and protected **oligarchs**—the small number of individuals and families who had monopolized political power and economic resources since the colonial era. Liberalism preserved slavery, created tools that allowed the wealthy and powerful to continue to concentrate landownership in the countryside, gave industrialists a free hand over their workers, and concentrated political power in the hands of those who held economic power.

By the end of the nineteenth century liberalism commingled with other ideologies such as Social Darwinism and scientific racism (see "Science for the Masses" in Chapter 24). This combination also inspired the imperial ambitions of the United States toward Mexico and the **Circum-Caribbean**, the region that includes the Antilles as well as the lands that bound the Caribbean Sea in Central America and northern South America.

The implementation of liberalism took different shapes. The United States deferred questions about centralized federal power over local state authority, as well as the legality of slavery, until its Civil War (1861–1865). After the North prevailed, liberal economic growth gave rise to business and industrial empires and stimulated the immigration of millions of people to provide cheap labor for the booming economy. In Spanish America wars of independence left behind a weak consensus about government, which led to long cycles of civil war across many countries.

The lack of a shared political culture among powerful groups in Spanish America created a crisis of confidence. Large landowners held great local power that they refused to yield to politicians in a distant capital. Political factions feared that if a rival faction won power, it would not abide by the rules and limits framed by the constitution, or that a rival would use its governing authority to crush its opponents. The power vacuum that resulted was often filled by caudillos, strong leaders who came to power and governed through their charisma and leadership abilities. This form of leadership is known as **caudillismo** (COW-deeh-is-moh).

The rule of a caudillo often provided temporary stability amid the struggles between liberals and conservatives, but caudillos cultivated their own prestige at the expense of building stable political institutions.

Mexico and the United States

The rumblings of independence first stirred Mexico in 1810. A century later, in 1910, the country was engulfed in the first great social upheaval of the twentieth century, the Mexican Revolution. In the century between these events, Mexico declined politically and economically from its status as the most prosperous and important colony of the Spanish Empire. It lost most of its national territory as Central American provinces broke away and became independent republics and as the United States expanded westward and captured or purchased Mexico's northern lands.

Mexicans experienced political stabilization and economic growth again in the second half of the nineteenth century when liberal leaders, especially the dic-

oligarchs In Latin America, the small number of individuals and families that had monopolized political power and economic resources since the colonial era.

Circum-Caribbean The region encompassing the Antilles as well as the lands that bound the Caribbean Sea in Central America and northern South America.

caudillismo Government by figures who rule through personal charisma and the support of armed followers in Latin America.

manifest destiny The doctrine that the United States should absorb the territory spanning from the original Atlantic states to the Pacific Ocean.

Caudillo Juan Manuel de Rosas of Argentina Frees a Group of Enslaved Women, 1841 One of the best-known caudillos, Rosas ruled Argentina from 1829 to 1852. To maintain his power, Rosas relied on the loyalty of his armed followers and his ability to cultivate a popular following through measures like the gradual abolition of slavery. (Pictures from History/CPA Media)

tator Porfirio Díaz (r. 1876–1911), imposed order and attracted foreign investment. But as Díaz himself is said to have remarked, "Poor Mexico, so far from God, so close to the United States."[1] The United States pursued territorial expansion under the doctrine of **manifest destiny**, by which the United States would absorb all the territory spanning from its original Atlantic states to the Pacific Ocean. To do so, the United States took lands from Indian nations and Mexico (Map 27.1).

Mexico's woes after independence resulted mainly from the inability of its political leaders to establish a consensus about how to govern the new nation. The general who led the war against Spain, Agustín de Iturbide, proclaimed himself emperor in 1822. When he was deposed a year later, the country's southern provinces broke away, becoming Guatemala, Honduras, Nicaragua, El Salvador, and Costa Rica. Power in Mexico rested in the hands of regional caudillos and local bosses. The presidency changed hands frequently as rival factions competed against each other. Antonio López de Santa Anna, the most powerful of Mexico's caudillos, held the presidency ten times between 1833 and 1854—three separate times in 1833 alone.

By contrast, the United States established a clearer vision of government embodied in the 1789 Constitution. Deep disagreements remained over questions such as the power of the federal government relative to state governments, which played out in debates about

the future of slavery and westward expansion. These tensions lasted well into the nineteenth century and culminated in the Civil War (1861–1865).

Economically, the United States remained integrated into the expanding and industrializing British Empire, so U.S. merchants retained access to Atlantic markets and credit. But the United States faced deepening regional differences: in the first half of the nineteenth century the North grew fastest, becoming the center of immigration, banking, and industrialization. In the South slavery and tenant farming kept much of the population at the economic margins and weakened internal markets. Slavery also inhibited immigration, since immigrants avoided settling in areas where they had to compete with unfree labor.

The dichotomy between the economies of the U.S. North and South repeated itself in the difference between the economies of the United States and Latin America. Latin American economies were organized around the export of agricultural and mineral commodities like sugar and silver, not around internal markets as in the United States, and these export economies were disrupted by the independence process.

The fate of the major silver mine in Mexico illustrates the challenges presented by independence. La Valenciana in central Mexico was the most productive silver mine in the world. It was one of the first places where the steam engine was used to pump water out of shafts, allowing the mine to reach below the water table. The machinery was destroyed during Mexico's war of independence (1810–1821), and the flooded mine ceased operation. Neither private investors nor the new government had the capital necessary to reactivate the mine after independence.

Mexico entered a vicious cycle: without capital and economic activity, tax revenues evaporated, public administration disintegrated, and the national government became unmanageable. The lack of political stability, in turn, drove investors away. The consequences are striking: in 1800 Mexico produced half the goods and services that the United States did; by 1845 production had dropped to only 8 percent. Per capita income fell by half.[2]

Politically and economically weakened after independence, Mexico was vulnerable to expansionist pressure from the United States. At independence, Mexico's

northern territories included much of what is today the U.S. Southwest and West. These territories attracted the interest of U.S. politicians, settlers, and land speculators. In the 1820s settlers from the U.S. South petitioned the Mexican government for land grants in the province of Texas, in return for which they would adopt Mexican citizenship. The U.S. government encouraged these settlers to declare the independence of Texas in 1836.

After Texas and Florida became U.S. states in 1845, President James Polk expanded the nation's border westward, precipitating the Mexican-American War (1846–1848). (See "Global Viewpoints: Perspectives on the Mexican-American War," page 794.) In the **Treaty of Guadalupe Hidalgo** (1848), Mexico ceded half its territory to the United States. With the U.S. acquisition of Florida from Spain in 1819 and the conquest of Mexican territory, many Latinos—U.S. citi-

MAP 27.1 Displacement of Indigenous Peoples, 1780s–1910s The United States and Mexico waged repeated wars to claim the lands of Native American nations. This was the last stage of the process of conquest and dispossession that began with the arrival of Europeans in the Americas three centuries earlier. As national armies seized native lands, displaced native peoples were forcibly removed, leading to the deaths of thousands and the destruction of cultures.

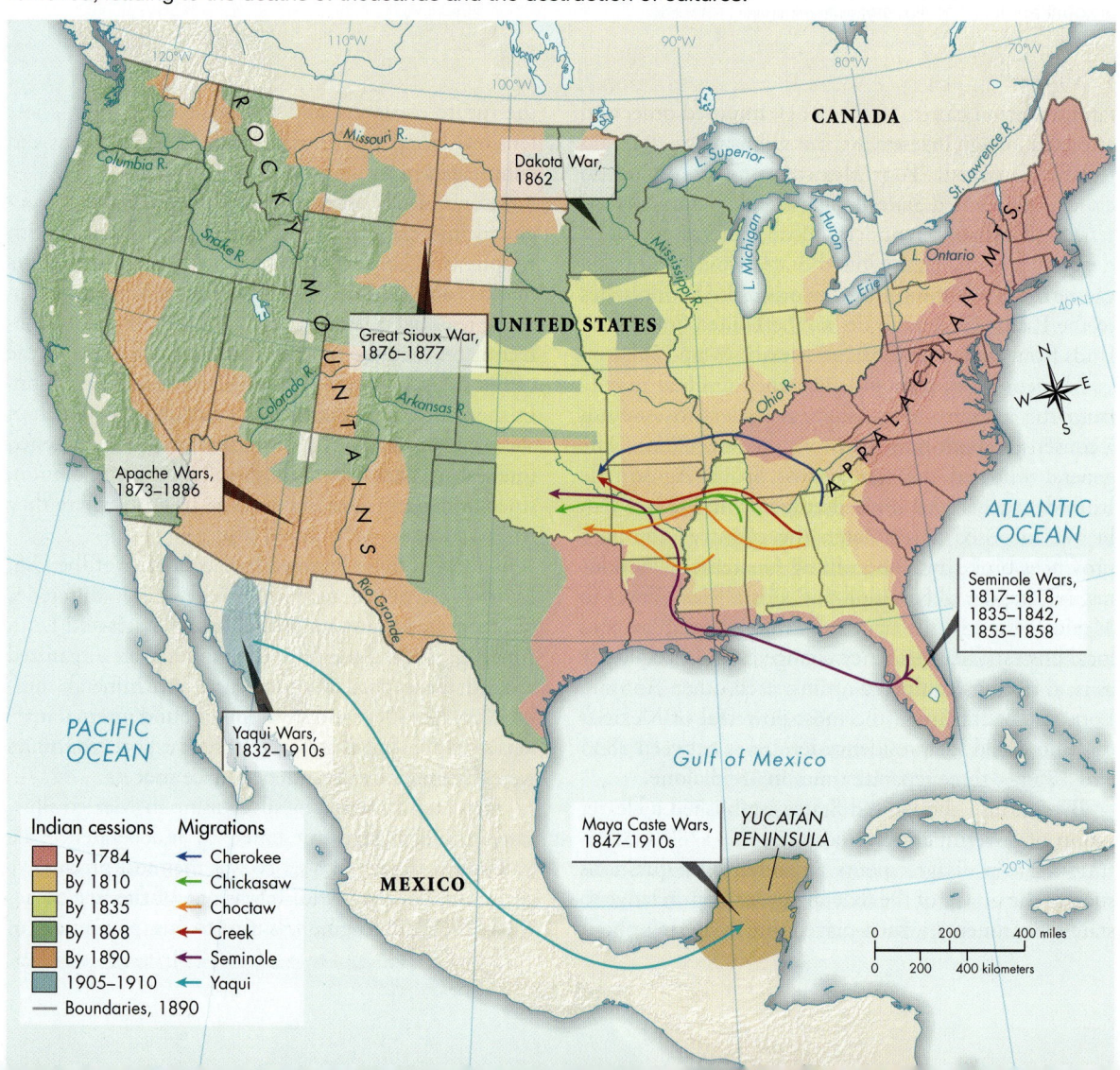

zens or residents of Latin American origin or descent—became U.S. citizens not because they moved to the United States but because the United States moved to them.

Liberal Reform in Mexico

In 1853 Mexican president Santa Anna unintentionally ushered in a new era of liberal consolidation and economic reform by triggering a backlash against his sale of Mexican territory along the northern border to the United States in a deal known as the Gadsden Purchase. Many Mexicans thought Santa Anna betrayed the nation and threw their support behind a new generation of liberal leaders. Beginning with the presidency of Ignacio Comonfort (pres. 1855–1858), these liberals carried out sweeping legal and economic changes called *La Reforma*, or "the reform."

Liberal reformers sought to make all individuals equal under the law and established property ownership as a basic right and national goal. The first major step in La Reforma was the Juárez Law (1855), which abolished old legal privileges for military officers and members of the clergy. The law was written by Minister of Justice Benito Juárez (hoo-AH-rehs), an Indian from Oaxaca (whah-HAH-kah) whose first language was Zapotec. Juárez began life as a farmer but earned a law degree and became the most important force in consolidating Mexico's political system in the decades after independence. An even more consequential measure, the **Lerdo Law** (1856), banished another legacy of colonialism: "corporate lands," meaning lands owned by groups or institutions, such as the Catholic Church, a major landowner, rather than by individual property owners. Liberals saw those landholdings as backward and inefficient and wanted to replace them with small rural farm owners.

These reforms triggered a backlash from conservative landowners and the church. When liberals ratified a new constitution in 1857, the Catholic Church threatened to excommunicate anyone who swore allegiance to it. Conservatives revolted, triggering a civil war called the Wars of Reform (1857–1861). Liberal forces led by Benito Juárez defeated the conservatives, who then conspired with French emperor Napoleon III to invite a French invasion of Mexico. Napoleon III saw an opportunity to re-establish France's American empire. His propaganda gave currency to the term "Latin America," used to assert that France had a natural role to play in Mexico because of a common "Latin" origin.

The French army invaded Mexico in 1862. Its main resistance was the defense mounted by a young officer named Porfirio Díaz, who blocked the invaders' advance through the city of Puebla on their way to Mexico City. The day of the Battle of Puebla, May 5, became a national holiday (known in the United States as "Cinco de Mayo"). Mexican conservatives and Napoleon III installed his Austrian cousin Maximilian of Habsburg as emperor of Mexico.

The deposed Juárez led a guerrilla war against the French troops backing Maximilian. When the U.S. Civil War ended in 1865, the U.S. government sought to root out France's influence on its border. The United States threw its support behind Juárez and pressured France to remove its troops. Bolstered by surplus Civil War armaments that flooded across the border into Mexico, Juárez's nationalists prevailed and executed Maximilian. Conservatives had been completely discredited: they had conspired with another country to install a foreign leader through a military invasion.

We can compare Benito Juárez, who governed the restored republic until 1876, with Abraham Lincoln. Both rose from humble rural origins to become able liberal lawyers. They became agile political and military leaders who prevailed in civil wars. The decade between the Wars of Reform and Juárez's restoration of the republic in 1867 can also be compared to the U.S. Civil War: both were watersheds in which questions that had lingered since independence were violently resolved and liberalism emerged as the dominant political philosophy.

Brazil: A New World Monarchy

Brazil gained independence in 1822 as a monarchy ruled by Emperor Pedro I, the son and heir of the Portuguese emperor. The creation of a Brazilian monarchy marked the culmination of a process that began in 1808, when Napoleon's armies crossed the Pyrenees from France to invade the Iberian Peninsula. Napoleon toppled the Spanish crown, but the Portuguese royal family, many of the government's bureaucrats, and most of the aristocracy fled aboard British warships to Portugal's colony of Brazil. This would be the first and only time a European empire would be ruled from one of its colonies.

Before the seat of Portuguese power relocated to Brazil, colonial policies had restricted many activities in Brazil in order to keep the colony dependent and subordinate to Portugal. It was only with the arrival of the imperial court that Brazil gained its first printing press, library, and military and naval academies, as well as schools for engineering, medicine, law, and the arts.

With the flight of the emperor to Brazil in 1808 and the declaration of independence by his son in 1822, Brazil achieved something that had eluded

---

Treaty of Guadalupe Hidalgo The 1848 treaty between the United States and Mexico in which Mexico ceded large tracts of land to the United States.

Lerdo Law An 1856 Mexican law that barred corporate landholdings.

Perspectives on the Mexican-American War

The Mexican-American War (1846–1848) was fought over U.S. control of northern Mexico, which became the Southwest and West of the United States. But the war was not fought only on the border: the U.S. Army and Navy fought far less armed and prepared Mexican forces from the Pacific to the borderlands and the Caribbean, going so far as to capture Mexico City.

José Joaquín de Herrera, President of Mexico, on the Loss of Texas, December 1845

■ In order to start a war, politicians agree that three questions must be examined: 1st, that of justice, 2nd, that of availability of resources, 3rd, that of convenience. . . . If, for launching war, one would only have to consider our justice, any hesitation in this matter would be either a crime or a lack of common sense. But next come the questions of feasibility and convenience for starting and maintaining hostilities with firmness and honor and all the consequences of a war of this nature.

A foreign war against a powerful and advanced nation that possesses an impressive navy and a . . . population that increases every day because of immigrants attracted to its great . . . prosperity, would imply immense sacrifices of men and money—not to assure victory, but simply to avoid defeat. Are such sacrifices possible for the Mexican Republic in her present state of exhaustion, after so many years of error and misadventure?

Manuel Crescencio Rejón, Minister of the Interior and Foreign Affairs Under Two Mexican Presidents, Arguing Against Ratification of the Treaty of Guadalupe Hidalgo, 1848

■ The social advantages which would accrue to us by accepting a peace now have been exaggerated, as well as the ease with which we would be able to maintain our remaining territories. It would be necessary, in order to sustain such illusions, to underestimate the spirit of enterprise of the North American people in industrial and commercial pursuits, to misunderstand their history and their tendencies, and also to presuppose in our own spirit less resistance than we have already shown toward the sincere friends of progress. Only through such illusions might one maintain that the treaty would bring a change that would be advantageous to us—as has been claimed.

Walt Whitman, Editorial in Favor of the War in the *Brooklyn Daily Eagle*, May 11, 1846

■ We are justified in the face of the world, in having treated Mexico with more forbearance than we have ever yet treated an enemy—for Mexico, though contemptible in many respects, is an enemy deserving a vigorous "lesson." . . . Let our arms now be carried with a spirit which shall teach the world that, while we are not forward for a quarrel, America knows how to crush, as well as how to expand!

Ulysses S. Grant, Looking Back on His Participation in the War, 1885

■ I was bitterly opposed to the measure, and to this day regard the war, which resulted, as one of the most unjust ever waged by a stronger against a weaker nation. It was an instance of a republic following the bad example of European monarchies, in not considering justice in their desire to acquire additional territory. . . . The occupation, separation and annexation [of Mexico] were, from the inception of the movement to its final consummation, a conspiracy to acquire territory out of which slave states might be formed for the American Union.

QUESTIONS FOR ANALYSIS

1. What issues do the Mexican politicians raise? What are their areas of disagreement?
2. How does the knowledge that Whitman's piece was a newspaper editorial shape your reading of it?
3. What might the implications have been for the U.S. forces if many officers had disapproved of the war the way Grant did?

Sources: Carol and Thomas Christensen, *The U.S. Mexican War* (San Francisco: Bay Books, 1998), p. 50; Ernesto Chávez, *The U.S. War with Mexico: A Brief History with Documents* (Boston: Bedford/St. Martin's, 2008), pp. 127, 83; Ulysses S. Grant, *Memoirs*, chap. 3, accessed through Project Gutenberg, http://www.gutenberg.org/files/5860/5860-h/5860-h.htm.

A Government Functionary Leaving Home with His Family and Servants, 1839 This lithograph is a depiction of Brazilian patriarchal and slave society social hierarchies that are shown through differences of gender, race, and age. The male patriarch is followed by members of the household ordered by their diminishing rank. (Bibliothèque Nationale, Paris, France/Archives Charmet/Bridgeman Images)

Spanish-American nations: it retained territorial unity under relative political stability. A liberal constitution adopted in 1824 lasted until a republican military coup in 1889. It established a two-chamber parliamentary system and a role for the emperor as a guide and intermediary in political affairs. Pedro I was not adept in this role and abdicated in 1831, leaving behind a regency governing in the name of his young son, Pedro II. In 1840, at the age of fourteen, Pedro II declared himself an adult and assumed the throne, ruling Brazil for the next forty-nine years.

Independent Brazil had many continuities with its colonial past. It remained the society with the largest number of African slaves in the Americas. It also continued to be economically and militarily dependent on Britain, as its mother-country, Portugal, had been in the eighteenth century. Britain negotiated with Brazil a "Friendship Treaty" that allowed British industrial goods to enter the country with very low tariffs. The flood of cheap British imports inhibited Brazilian industrialization. British economic and political influence, as well as special privileges enjoyed by British citizens in Brazil, were examples of **neocolonialism**, the influence that European powers and the United States exerted over politically and economically weaker countries after independence.

Slavery and Abolition

Why did slavery last longer in the United States, Brazil, and Cuba than in the other republics of the Americas? How did resistance by slaves shape abolition?

In former Spanish-American colonies, the abolition of slavery quickly followed independence. In British colonies, slavery ended in 1834, and the British navy suppressed the Atlantic slave trade. But in the United States, Cuba, and Brazil slavery endured well into the nineteenth century. In each of these countries the question of abolition became entwined with the disputes over the nature of government and authority—federal unionism versus states' rights in the United States, independence for Cuba, and monarchy versus republicanism in Brazil.

Slave Societies in the Americas

Africans and their descendants were enslaved in every country of the Americas. The experiences in slavery

---

neocolonialism The establishment of political and economic influence over regions after they have ceased to be formal colonies.

and freedom of Africans and African Americans, defined here as the descendants of slaves brought from Africa anywhere in the New World, varied considerably. Several factors shaped their experiences: the nature of slave regimes in different economic regions, patterns of manumission (individual slaves' gaining their freedom), the nature of abolition (the ending of the institution of slavery), and the proportion of the local population they represented.

The settlement of Africans as slaves was the most intense in areas that relied on plantation agriculture. (See "Analyzing the Evidence: Slaves Sold South from Richmond, 1853," at right.) Plantations cultivated a single crop—especially sugar, coffee, tobacco, and cotton—on a vast scale that supplied distant global markets. Cotton from Alabama was spun by looms in New England or Britain; sugar and coffee from Brazil were consumed in European salons. Enslaved Africans played many other roles as well. From Buenos Aires to Boston, slavery was widespread in port cities, where it was fed by easy access to the slave trade and the demand for street laborers such as porters. And across the Americas, enslaved women were forced into domestic service, a role that conferred social prestige on their masters, but which also added sexual abuse to the miseries that enslaved people endured.

Independence and Abolition

Slavery and abolition became intertwined with the process of political independence. The different relationships between independence and abolition in the United States and Haiti shaped perceptions across the rest of the continent. In Haiti independence was achieved in a revolution in which slaves turned against their oppressors. By contrast, the United States gained its independence in a war that did not result in widespread slave revolt, and it created a liberal political regime that preserved the institution of slavery. When elites in other American colonies contemplated independence, they weighed whether the U.S. or the Haitian experience awaited them. As a result, in colonies where the subordinated population was the largest, independence movements proceeded the slowest. News of the Haitian Revolution spread briskly through slave communities. Slaves far from the Caribbean wore pendants with images of Haitian revolutionary leader Toussaint L'Ouverture. (See "Individuals in Society: Toussaint L'Ouverture" in Chapter 22.)

British efforts to keep their North American colonies, as well as a combination of moral and economic appeals for the abolition of slavery in British territories, hastened the end of the slave trade to the Americas. When British forces fought to prevent the independence of the United States, they offered freedom to slaves who joined them. Many slaves did so, and after the British defeat and withdrawal, they dispersed to Spanish Florida, the Caribbean, and West Africa.

In 1807 British abolitionists pressured the British Parliament to end the Atlantic slave trade to British colonies, and in 1833 Parliament voted to abolish slavery the following year in Canada and Britain's Caribbean colonies. To reduce economic competition, the British government pressured other nations to follow suit. A British naval squadron patrolled the Atlantic to suppress the slave trade. The squadron captured slave ships, freed the slaves they carried, and resettled them in a colony the British government established in Sierra Leone in 1787 to settle former slaves who had sided with Britain in the American Revolution.

In Spanish America independence forces enlisted the participation of slaves and offered freedom in return. Thousands gained manumission by siding with rebel forces, and new national governments enacted gradual abolition. The first step toward abolition was often through **free womb laws** that freed children born to slave women. These laws, passed across independent Spanish America between 1811 and 1825, created gradual abolition but did not impose an immediate financial loss on slaveholders: to the contrary, the free children of slaves remained apprenticed to their masters until they reached adulthood. Similar laws hastened the abolition of slavery in the Northern states of the United States.

The combination of free womb laws and manumission as a reward for military service meant that unlike in the United States, by the time slavery was abolished in Latin American countries, most peoples of African descent had already gained their freedom (Map 27.2).

In the United States the questions of nation building and slavery remained connected. The determination of Southern states to protect the slave regime was enshrined in the Constitution, which granted individual states autonomy in matters such as slavery. As slavery was abolished in Northern states, westward expansion tested the political compromise between the North and South, culminating in the Civil War. In 1854, even as slavery was abolished in the last Spanish-American republics, armed confrontations erupted in Kansas over whether that territory would be incorporated as a state permitting slavery. Tensions between the North and the South reached a breaking point when Abraham Lincoln, opposed to the spread of slavery, was elected president in 1860. Southern political leaders, fearing that Lincoln might abolish slavery, seceded and formed a new nation, the Confederate States of America. Lincoln declared the secession illegal and waged war to preserve the territorial integrity of the United States. The ensuing civil war resulted in the deaths of over 750,000 combatants and civilians.

free womb laws Laws passed across the nineteenth-century Americas that instituted a gradual form of abolition through which children born to slaves gained their freedom.

ANALYZING THE EVIDENCE

Slaves Sold South from Richmond, 1853

This scene was painted by a British artist, based on events he witnessed in the U.S. South twenty years after slavery was abolished in the British Empire. Being "sold south," as this image depicts, was a terrifying fate. In addition to having their families ripped apart, those who were sold were sent to plantations where the labor regimes were famously harsh. Note the ways in which the artist depicts not only the slave families but also the white, mixed, and free black traders.

(*After the Sale: Slaves Going South from Richmond*, 1853, by Eyre Crowe [1824–1910] [oil on canvas]/© Chicago History Museum, Illinois, USA/Bridgeman Images)

The experience of being "sold south" in the United States had its equivalents in other slave societies. In Cuba the dreaded destination was the easternmost province of Oriente, with the fearsome intensity of its sugar plantation regime. In Brazil slaves faced the threat of being sent across the Atlantic to Portuguese colonies in west and central Africa. The threat of being sent to a more grueling and often-lethal region was a terrible power masters wielded over slaves, but so too was the power to destroy a family by selling away husbands or wives, or separating parents from young children. Slave regimes in the Americas endured in part because of the terror that masters wielded over slaves, and these threats were powerful tools in maintaining slave owners' domination over enslaved people.

QUESTIONS FOR ANALYSIS

1. How does the artist try to provoke a reaction against slavery?
2. How are whites and free blacks represented in the image?
3. Can you think of other examples of art with social or political messages? How would this painting compare in its effectiveness?

MAPPING THE PAST

MAP 27.2 Abolition in the Americas The process of abolition in the Americas was gradual and varied across regions. In some areas, such as Mexico and parts of New England, slavery was abolished soon after independence, while in the U.S. South it lasted until the end of the Civil War. In Texas slavery was abolished by the Mexican government, but when Texas became part of the United States, slavery was legally reinstated. In British territories slavery was abolished in 1834. Across Latin America the abolition of slavery was hastened by civil wars that mobilized slaves as combatants. The last country to abolish slavery, Brazil, did so only in 1888.

ANALYZING THE MAP How did the United States resemble Latin America in its patterns of abolition?

CONNECTIONS Why did some countries abolish slavery earlier, and why did others do so much later?

In 1862 Lincoln sought to pressure the Confederate states to rejoin the Union by issuing the Emancipation Proclamation. The proclamation, which became effective January 1, 1863, abolished slavery in all states that remained opposed to the Union. It was intended as leverage to bring the rebel states back, not to abolish slavery altogether; consequently it freed slaves only in states that had seceded. Nevertheless, the proclamation hastened the demise of slavery. In 1865 Southern rebel states surrendered after Northern armies decimated their industrial, agricultural, and military capacity. Months later, the Thirteenth Amendment to the Constitution fully abolished slavery. Subsequent amendments recognized the citizenship and rights of people formerly enslaved.

Two aspects made slavery in the United States different from slavery in Latin America: gradual abolition in the North made it a regional rather than a national institution; and the Civil War, followed by military occupation of the South (1865–1877), created a last-ing regional backlash that codified racial segregation. This did not make the South entirely racist and the North entirely antiracist: segregation is a form of racism but hardly the only one. Instead race relations in the northern and western states of the United States resembled those of Latin America, where racial prejudice and the marginalization of African Americans were perpetuated through largely informal practices, such as discrimination in employment, housing, and lending. Meanwhile, the U.S. South erected a distinct legal edifice preserving white privilege that best resembled the oppressive white-minority regimes of South Africa and Rhodesia (see "Resistance to White Rule in Southern Africa" in Chapter 32).

Abolition in Cuba and Brazil

Cuba and Brazil followed long paths to abolition. In Cuba nationalist rebels fought for independence from Spain in the Ten Years' War (1868–1878). Many slaves and free blacks joined the failed anticolonial struggle, and rebel leaders expressed support for abolition. Spanish authorities sought to defuse the tensions feeding that struggle by granting freedom to slaves who fought on the Spanish side in the war, to the children of slaves born since 1868, and to slaves over age sixty. By 1878 Spanish forces had defeated the nationalists, but the conflict had set in motion an irreversible process of abolition.

In Brazil an 1871 law granted freedom to children born to slaves, and an 1885 law granted freedom to slaves over age sixty. At best, these laws were half measures, aimed at placating abolitionists without disrupting the economic reliance on slave labor. At worst, they mocked the meaning of abolition: children freed under the free womb laws remained apprenticed to their mother's master until they reached adulthood. These laws preserved masters' access to the labor of the children of slaves, while freeing masters from their obligations to care for elderly slaves. Slavery was finally abolished in Cuba in 1886 and in Brazil in 1888, making them the last regions of the Americas to end slavery. Abolition did not come about solely through laws from the top down. Pressure exerted by slaves contributed to abolition. Slave resistance, in its many forms, intensified in the later years of the nineteenth century. Slaves escaped in growing numbers. In many cases, they settled in communities of runaway slaves, particularly in Brazil, where the vast interior offered opportunities to resettle out of the reach of slave society. (See "Thinking Like a Historian: The Abolition of Slavery in Brazil, from Above and Below," page 800.) In the years preceding abolition, in some regions of Brazil slave flight became so widespread that slaves might simply leave their plantation and hire themselves out to a nearby planter whose own slaves had also run away. In the end, the costs of slavery had become unsustainable.

Export-Led Growth and Social Unrest

As Latin America became more integrated into the world economy, how did patterns of economic growth shape political culture and social reactions?

Beginning in the 1850s and accelerating through conflicts like Mexico's Wars of Reform, the U.S. Civil War, and the Paraguay War in South America, the consolidation of liberalism in the Americas created conditions for a return of foreign investment that brought economic growth. But liberal reforms created new economic pressures against rural workers and indigenous communities who led reform and resistance movements such as those unleashed by the Mexican Revolution.

Latin America Re-enters the World Economy

The wars of independence in Spanish America disrupted the trade networks that had sustained the region's economies, while civil war and rule by caudillos delayed the consolidation of liberal regimes. In the first decades of independence, Latin America's economic integration with the world decreased. For rural peasants and indigenous communities, this was a benefit in disguise: the decline of trade made lands less valuable. The rents landowners could charge tenant farmers decreased, making it easier for peasants to gain access to land.

By the second half of the nineteenth century Latin American elites reached a compromise that combined liberal political ideas about the way national government should be structured with liberal economic policies that favored large landowners. Political stability and economic growth returned. Foreign investment intensified. By the turn of the twentieth century Latin American countries were firmly tied to the world economy. Indigenous and rural communities paid a high price for this return to economic growth: as the value of agricultural exports increased, so did the value of land. Governments, foreign investors, and large landowners seized indigenous lands through war, legal action, or coercion at a dizzying rate.

For example, in the late 1880s the Argentine government sold off lands it took from indigenous communities. The land was inexpensive, but because it was sold in such large parcels, the few who could purchase it did so by mortgaging existing landholdings. Though reformers had imagined the creation of a class of small farmers, the result was the opposite: more than 20 million acres were sold to just 381 landowners who created vast estates known as **latifundios**.[3]

Liberal economic policies and the intensification of foreign trade concentrated land in the hands of wealthy exporters. Governments represented the interests of large landowners by promoting commodity exports and industrial imports, following the liberal economic principle of comparative advantage (that countries should export what they could produce the most efficiently and import what other countries could produce more cheaply and efficiently). Brazil became the world's largest exporter of coffee and experienced a brief but intense boom in rubber production. Argentina became one of the most efficient and profitable exporters of grains and beef. Chile and Peru served the international market for fertilizers by exporting nitrates and bat guano.

These export booms depended on imported capital and technology. In the Circum-Caribbean this came mostly from investors in the United States, while in South America it often came from Britain. (See

---

latifundios Vast landed estates in Latin America.

The Abolition of Slavery in Brazil, from Above and Below

The abolition of slavery in the Americas was a gradual process that involved pressure applied by slaves and free blacks, as well as abolitionist politics practiced by powerful groups and individuals. Sources on abolition can offer very different versions of how abolition came to pass. In many cases, planters and politicians credited themselves for abolition, which they presented as a sign of their virtue and enlightenment. The experiences of slaves often tell a different story in which abolition was hastened by their flight and resistance.

1 Joaquim Nabuco, argument for the benefits of abolition, 1883. Joaquim Nabuco was a wealthy Brazilian landowner who became one of the political leaders in favor of the abolition of slavery. In his most famous work, *Abolitionism,* Nabuco points out the ways the nation would benefit from ending slavery.

■ Only after slaves and masters are both liberated from the yoke that keeps them equally from free life can we apply ourselves to this serious program of reforms—among which those that can be passed into law, though of tremendous importance, are insignificant alongside those that we must achieve ourselves by means of education, fellowship, the press, through voluntary immigration, by a cleansed spiritual life, and through a new vision of the State. . . .

Compare the Brazil of today, with its slavery, to the ideal of the Fatherland that we Abolitionists uphold: a nation in which all are free; where, lured by the honesty of our institutions and by the freedom of our system, European immigration will bring to the tropics a ceaseless current of vibrant, energetic, and healthy Caucasian blood which we will be able to absorb without danger, unlike that Chinese wave with which the large property owners aspire to corrupt and debase our race even further; a nation that could labor with originality toward the good of humanity and the advancement of South America.

2 Antônio Manuel Bueno de Andrada on slaves' struggles for freedom, 1918. Antônio Manuel Bueno de Andrada, a Brazilian abolitionist, recalled the efforts of slaves to free themselves in the last years of slavery by escaping en masse from their plantations.

■ A large group of slaves fled from the outskirts of Capivarí [in the state of São Paulo]. The large group included more than one hundred able-bodied men, women, old people, and children, led by a black man named Pio. They marched to the city of Porto Feliz. Police units surrounded them on the road, but the fugitive slaves resisted and fended off their attackers. They marched calmly through the city's streets in the full light of day. Farther ahead, they prevailed in two or three more skirmishes with the police. His forces having been beaten, the police chief asked the Army to intervene. Under the command of junior officer Gasparino Carneiro Leão, fifty cavalrymen set out to surround and detain the resolute rebels. By this time the National Army refused to serve as "bloodhounds," as slave hunters. The noble young Gasparino made no secret of his abolitionist sentiments. He set out on the shameful mission intending to not attack the unfortunate slaves. From atop a hill near Santo Amaro he spotted the slaves, who were descending the opposite side of the pass. The commander sent out a corporal who was also an abolitionist to urge the blacks to disperse into the forest. The corporal dismounted and set out on foot. The leader of the fugitives, the black man Pio, did not know the corporal's humanitarian intentions, so he charged at the soldier and killed him with the blow of a scythe. The soldiers spontaneously responded with shots that killed the black man. Despite the moment's agitation, the abolitionist officer did not allow the slaughter of

ANALYZING THE EVIDENCE

1. In Source 1, to whom is Joaquim Nabuco addressing his appeal? According to Nabuco, who suffers because of the existence of slavery? What interests are served by abolition?
2. In the painting in Source 4, what symbols are used to explain abolition? For instance, what is the architectural style? What color and what gender are the different figures, and what significance do you think these details have?
3. How do Antônio Manuel Bueno de Andrada's account in Source 2 and the government report in Source 3 shape our understanding of how slavery came to an end in Brazil?
4. Compare the vision of abolition offered by the appeal in Source 1 and the painting in Source 4 with the vision of abolition offered by the accounts of slave flight in Sources 2 and 3. What does the disparity between the visions tell us about abolition?

4 **Pedro Américo, *Liberation of the Slaves,* 1889.** This allegorical painting by Brazilian artist Pedro Américo depicts a slave family kneeling before a figure representing liberty. Behind the family, a demon representing slavery lies vanquished.

© Pictures from History/The Image Works

the terrified fugitives. He returned to São Paulo to face a military tribunal that absolved him unanimously.

The slaves continued on their painful journey to the city of Santos. At the edge of the Serra do Mar, near the peaks where the Cubatão River flows [over 100 miles from Capivarí], they were hunted down like wild animals. The bush captains and police mercilessly killed men, women, and children. Fewer than twenty fugitives made it to Santos. The body of the black man Pio was taken to São Paulo and opened up at a police station. The coroner's report showed that he had not eaten for more than three days!

The autopsy revealed that this black leader, who fought off organized forces, and who marched with a commanding presence through wealthy towns, suffered from hunger at the moment in which he gave his life for the freedom of his race.

3 **Government of São Paulo province, report on slave flight, 1888.** The coffee-planting province of São Paulo was one of Brazil's most important regions economically and a site of intense slave labor. In this document, provincial officials report on the disintegration of the slave labor system through massive slave resistance.

■ [G]rave and unforseen events precipitated the conclusion of slavery in the province. We refer to the flight en masse of slaves from a large number of agricultural establishments and the consequent abandonment of agriculture. These events, assuming ever more alarming proportions, partly because of the effects of the sudden withdrawal of workers from the plantations, partly because of the dangers posed to public security on the highways and in the towns through which the bands of fleeing slaves passed, could not fail to alarm the public spirit, inspiring apprehension and disquiet.

PUTTING IT ALL TOGETHER

Using the sources above, along with what you have learned in class and in this chapter, write a short essay that compares Brazilian slaves' resistance to bondage through flight with examples of popular resistance in other parts of the world.

Sources: (1) Joaquim Nabuco, *O Abolicionismo* (São Paulo: Companhia Editora Nacional, 1938), pp. 243–246, trans. Jerry Dávila; (2) Antônio Manuel Bueno de Andrada, "A abolição em São Paulo: Depoimento de um testemunha," May 13, 1918, p. 3, trans. Jerry Dávila; (3) Quoted in George Reid Andrews, *Blacks and Whites in São Paulo, Brazil, 1888–1988* (Madison: University of Wisconsin Press, 1991), p. 40.

Barranquilla, Colombia, ca. 1910 Like port cities across Latin America, Barranquilla in Colombia began as a center of trade, and by the early twentieth century it was a bustling center of immigration and industrialization. (© Mary Evans Picture Library/Grenville Collins Postcard Collection/The Image Works)

"Individuals in Society: Henry Meiggs, Promoter and Speculator," at right.)

British capital and technology built Argentina's network of railroads and refrigerated meatpacking plants. Chile's nitrate-mining industry was expanded through the War of the Pacific (1879–1883), a conflict in which Chile seized territory in bordering Peru and Bolivia. As a result, Bolivia lost its access to the Pacific and became a landlocked nation. The war and its outcomes revealed British influence as well: to finance the war, the Chilean government issued bonds bought by British investors. The bonds were repaid through the sale of concessions for mining the nitrate-rich lands that Chile conquered from Bolivia. In 1878 British companies controlled 13 percent of nitrate mining. By 1890 they controlled 90 percent.

Liberal Consolidation in South America

As in the United States and Mexico, the process of liberal nation-state consolidation in South America took place through military conflict. The War of the Triple Alliance, or Paraguay War (1865–1870), in which Paraguay fought Brazil, Argentina, and Uruguay, played a similar role to Mexico's Wars of Reform and the U.S. Civil War in consolidating liberalism. In 1865 Paraguayan leader Francisco Solano López declared war against the three neighboring countries after political competition between Argentina and Brazil threatened Paraguay's use of Uruguay's port of Montevideo. Land-locked Paraguay depended on Montevideo as a shipping point for its imports and exports.

The war was devastating for Paraguay, which lost more than half its national population, including most adult men. But victory, too, was traumatic for Argentina and Brazil: why had it taken five years to defeat a much smaller neighbor? The war prompted debates about the need for economic modernization and the reform of national governments.

In Brazil, where Emperor Pedro II's calls for volunteers to enlist in the army fell on deaf ears, the army enlisted slaves who, if they served honorably and survived, would be granted freedom. What did it mean that the free citizens of a nation would not mobilize to defend it, and that the nation prevailed only through the sacrifices borne by its slaves? For many, especially officers who were veterans of the conflict, the lesson was that being a monarchy that relied on slavery made Brazil a weak and backward nation. Veteran officers and liberal opponents of the war formed a movement to create a liberal republic and abolish slavery. These republicans overthrew monarchy in 1889 and created a liberal republic.

In Argentina, after the war with Paraguay, liberal leaders beginning with Domingo Sarmiento (pres. 1868–1874) pressed modernizing reforms. These included a military campaign called the Conquest of the Desert (1878–1885), in which Argentine troops took control of the lands of Mapuche Indians in the southern region of Patagonia and opened new lands for sale to ranchers. The wars were accompanied by ambitious railroad

Henry Meiggs, Promoter and Speculator

ALL THROUGHOUT THE AMERICAS IN THE NINETEENTH century, opportunities beckoned. Henry Meiggs, born in upstate New York in 1811, responded to several of them, building and losing fortunes in Brooklyn, San Francisco, Chile, and Peru.

Meiggs, with only an elementary school education, began work at his father's shipyard. He soon started his own lumber business and did well until he lost everything in the financial panic of 1837. He rebuilt his business, and when gold was discovered in California in 1848, he filled a ship with lumber and sailed around Cape Horn to San Francisco, where he sold his cargo for $50,000, twenty times what he had paid for it. He then entered the lumber business, organizing crews of five hundred men to fell huge California redwoods and bring them to his steam sawmills. As his business flourished, he began speculating in real estate, which led to huge debts when the financial crisis of 1854 hit. In an attempt to save himself and his friends, Meiggs forged warrants for more than $900,000; when discovery of the fraud seemed imminent, he sailed with his wife and children for South America.

Although at one point Meiggs was so strapped for cash that he sold his watch, within three years of arriving in Chile, he had secured his first railway contract, and by 1867 he had built about 200 miles of rail lines in that country. In 1868 he went to Peru, which had less than 60 miles of track at the time. In the next nine years he would add 700 more.

Meiggs was not an engineer, but he was a good manager. He recruited experienced engineers from abroad and arranged the purchase of foreign rolling stock, rails, and ties, acting as a promoter and developer. Much of the funding came from international investors in Peruvian bonds.

The most spectacular of the rail lines Meiggs built was Peru's Callao-Lima-Oroya line, which crosses the Andes at about seventeen thousand feet above sea level, making it the highest standard-gauge railway in the world. Because water was scarce in many areas along the construction site, it had to be transported up to workers, who were mostly local people. Dozens of bridges and tunnels had to be built, and casualties were high. Eight hundred people were invited to the banquet that marked the beginning of work on the Oroya Railway. Meiggs drummed up enthusiasm at the event by calling the locomotive the "irresistible battering ram of modern civilization."

In Peru Meiggs became known for his extravagance and generosity, and some charged that he bribed Peruvian officials on a large scale to get his projects approved. He was a good speaker and loved to entertain lavishly. In one example of his generosity, he distributed thousands of pesos and soles to the victims of the earthquake of 1868. He also contributed to the beautification of Lima by tearing down an old wall and putting a seven-mile-long park in its place.

The challenges in building the Callao-Lima-Oroya railroad across the Andes can be imagined from this picture of one of its many bridges. (Michael Maslan/Corbis/VCG via Getty Images)

Always the speculator, Meiggs died poor in 1877, with his debts exceeding his assets. He was beloved, however, and more than twenty thousand Peruvians, many of whom had labored on his projects, attended his funeral at a Catholic church in Lima.

QUESTIONS FOR ANALYSIS

1. What accounts for the changes in fortune that Meiggs experienced?
2. Were the Latin American governments that awarded contracts to Meiggs making reasonable decisions?
3. Should it matter whether Meiggs had to bribe officials to get the railroads built? Why or why not?

construction that linked inland areas to the coast to transport goods, which brought the introduction of barbed wire fencing that intensified ranching capabilities and the development of new strains of cattle and wheat that increased production.

The Porfiriato and Liberal Stability in Mexico

When Porfirio Díaz became president of Mexico in 1876, the hero of the Battle of Puebla inherited a country in which much had been achieved: President Juárez had established national unity against the French invasion. His generation of liberal leaders had also created a legal and political framework based on the 1857 constitution. But it was a country that faced enormous challenges: per capita income was less than it had been at independence in 1821. The country had barely four hundred miles of railroads, compared to more than seventy thousand miles in the United States. Díaz's first challenge was to attract foreign investment.

Porfirio Díaz built a regime—the **Porfiriato**—with unprecedented stability and ruled, with a single term out of power, from 1876 to 1911. He ruled by the mantra "*pan o palo*," bread or the stick, rewarding supporters and ruthlessly punishing opponents. The political stability he created made Mexico a haven for foreign investment, particularly from the United States. Foreign trade increased tenfold, and the country became the third-largest oil producer in the world. Railroads rapidly expanded, reaching fifteen thousand miles of track by 1910, much of it connecting Mexico to the United States. Railroads also connected regions long isolated from each other and sustained national markets for the first time since the colonial era.

The Porfiriato was a modernizing regime. The government swelled with technocrats called *científicos* (see-en-TEE-fee-kohs), to whom Díaz granted great autonomy and lavish rewards. By contrast, the Porfiriato considered indigenous peoples racially inferior and suppressed them. This was the case of the Yaqui Indians of Sonora, at the border with Arizona (see Map 27.1). Díaz's army vanquished Yaqui communities, seized their land, and dispatched survivors to the Yucatán, where they worked as slaves on plantations cultivating *henequén* (hen-eh-KEN), a plant whose fibers were used in the hay-baling machines increasingly used by U.S. farmers. The Porfiriato used the mission of modernization and economic development to justify a range of abuses.

Economic progress enriched Díaz and his allies but proved perilous to rural communities. As the rise in foreign investment and economic activity made land valuable, small landholders became vulnerable. Large landowners and speculative investors used the Lerdo Law to usurp the lands of peasants across the countryside. In addition, the 1883 Law of Barren Lands allowed real estate companies to identify land that was not being cultivated (often land that communities allowed to lie fallow as they rotated crops) so it could be surveyed and auctioned off. The abuse of these laws by land speculators had devastating consequences: by 1910, 80 percent of rural peasants had no land.

The Growth of Industry in Mexico Workers at a textile mill in Mexico around 1900. (© akg-images/ The Image Works)

Emiliano Zapata and Pancho Villa in Mexico's Presidential Palace, 1914 Villa sits in the presidential chair topped with the golden eagle, and Zapata appears next to him on the right, holding a sombrero. Two small children peer over their shoulders as each leader insists he will not claim the presidency since his goal was reform and not power.
(Universal History Archive/UIG/Bridgeman Images)

The Porfiriato and its liberal ideology favored the needs of foreign investors over its own citizens. Most of Mexico's 1910 population of 12 million remained tied to the land. The expansion of railroads into that land made it valuable, and liberal reforms provided the tools to transfer that value from peasants to capitalists. Given Mexico's proximity to the United States, that process was swifter and more intense than it was elsewhere in Latin America, and it led to the first great social upheaval of the twentieth century.

The Mexican Revolution

Porfirio Díaz declared himself the unanimous winner of Mexico's 1910 elections. His defeated challenger, wealthy landowner and liberal lawyer Francisco Madero, issued a manifesto calling the election illegitimate and pronouncing himself the provisional president of Mexico. Madero's call to arms was the spark that ignited a powder keg of grievances from peasants whose lands had been taken or threatened, and from exploited urban workers.

Peasants and workers across the country rose up, drove out Díaz, and annointed Madero provisional president. Madero proved to be a weak reformer, and armed peasant groups rose up again, this time against him. The U.S. ambassador, who considered Madero to be inadequate in his defense of U.S. business interests, con-

spired with the commander of Madero's army to assassinate him in 1912. Mexico's revolution now deepened, as factions around the country joined the fighting.

The ideological leadership of the Mexican Revolution came from Emiliano Zapata and his supporters, who hailed from rural communities south of Mexico City whose lands were threatened. The Zapatistas made their demands in a document called the **Plan de Ayala** (ai-YAH-lah) that called for the return of all land, forests, and waters taken from rural communities. Their pledge to fight until these demands were met was taken up by many armed groups across Mexico, particularly the army commanded by the charismatic Pancho Villa (pahn-choh VEE-yah). They found allies as well in the Red Brigades of anarchist and socialist workers who controlled the capital, Mexico City, during much of the war.

Supporters of the Plan de Ayala were gradually beaten back by the faction that would eventually prevail, a group called the Constitutionalists, led by politician Venustiano Carranza and Álvaro Obregón, a skilled general who emulated tactics and strategies employed in Europe in the First World War. But to consolidate

Porfiriato The regime of Porfirio Díaz, who presided in Mexico from 1876 to 1880 and again from 1884 to 1911.

Plan de Ayala Document written by Zapatistas during the Mexican Revolution that demanded the government return all land, forests, and waters taken from rural communities.

political control and to convince rebels like those supporting Zapata and Villa to put down their arms, their constitution included key demands from the Plan de Ayala and from urban workers.

In meeting the demands of peasants and workers, Mexico's 1917 constitution imposed the most significant limits to liberalism yet attempted in the Americas. It broke the fundamental liberal embrace of private property by asserting that all land, water, and subsoil resources belong to the nation, which allows their use for the public good. This clause allowed the government to expropriate lands from large estates to make grants of collective land called *ejidos* (eh-HEE-dohz) to rural communities. Over 80 million acres of farmland and forests would be redistributed as ejidos. The constitution included the most advanced labor code in the world at the time, guaranteeing workers the right to unionize and strike, an eight-hour workday, a minimum wage, and protections for women workers, including maternity leave.

By agreeing to these social demands, the Constitutionalist faction was able to consolidate control over a new political order that would enjoy remarkable stability: the political party that emerged from the Constitutionalists would hold presidential power for almost all of the next one hundred years.

Immigration

What factors shaped patterns of immigration to the Americas? How did immigrants shape — and how were they shaped by — their new settings?

During the late nineteenth and early twentieth centuries unprecedented numbers of people from Europe, Asia, and the Middle East settled across North and South America. The largest wave of immigrants — some 28 million between 1860 and 1914 — settled in the United States. Another 8 million had settled in Argentina and Brazil by 1930. This cycle of immigration was a product of liberal political and economic reforms that abolished slavery, established stable political systems, and created a framework for integrating immigrants as factory and farm laborers.

Immigration to Latin America

In 1852 the Argentine political philosopher Juan Bautista Alberdi published *Bases and Points of Departure for Argentine Political Organization*, in which he argued that the development of his country depended on immigration. Drawing on the Social Darwinist theory that whites were racially more advanced than

Indians and blacks, Alberdi maintained that black and indigenous Argentines lacked basic skills, and it would take too long to train them. Thus he pressed for massive immigration from northern Europe and the United States:

> Each European who comes to our shores brings more civilization in his habits, which will later be passed on to our inhabitants, than many books of philosophy. . . . Do we want to sow and cultivate in America English liberty, French culture, and the diligence of men from Europe and from the United States? Let us bring living pieces of these qualities.[4]

Alberdi's ideas, guided by the aphorism "to govern is to populate," won immediate acceptance and were even incorporated into the Argentine constitution, which declared, "The Federal government will encourage European immigration." Other countries of the Americas, also influenced by Social Darwinism, adopted similar immigration policies.

Coffee barons in Brazil, *latifundiarios* (owners of vast estates) in Argentina, or investors in nitrate and copper mining in Chile made enormous profits that they reinvested in new factories. Latin America had been tied to the Industrial Revolution in Britain and northern Europe from the outset as a provider of raw materials and as a consumer of industrial goods. In the major exporting countries of Argentina, Brazil, and Mexico, domestic industrialization now began to take hold in the form of textile mills, food-processing plants, and mechanized transportation such as modern ports and railroads.

By the turn of the twentieth century an industrial working class had begun to emerge. In Brazil and Argentina these workers, who were mainly European immigrants, proved unexpectedly contentious: they brought with them radical ideologies that challenged liberalism, particularly anarchism and **anarcho-syndicalism**, a version of anarchism that advocated placing power in the hands of workers' unions. These workers clashed with bosses and political leaders who rejected the idea that workers had rights. The authorities suppressed worker organizations such as unions, and they resisted implementing labor laws such as a minimum wage, restrictions on child labor, the right to strike, or factory safety regulations.

Radicalized workers mounted labor actions that at times grew into general strikes with over one hundred thousand workers picketing. But outside of Mexico, the movements of urban workers did not merge with rural unrest in the formula that produced revolution.

Although Europe was a significant source of immigrants to Latin America, so were Asia and the Middle East. In the late nineteenth and early twentieth centuries large numbers of Japanese arrived in Brazil, most settling in São Paulo state, creating the largest Japanese

anarcho-syndicalism A version of anarchism that advocated placing power in the hands of workers' unions.

community in the world outside of Japan. From the Middle East, Lebanese, Turks, and Syrians also entered Brazil. South Asian laborers went to Trinidad, Jamaica, Guyana, and other British territories in the Caribbean, mostly as indentured servants under five-year contracts. Perhaps one-third returned to India, but the rest stayed, saved money, and bought small businesses or land. After slavery was abolished in Cuba in 1886, some work in the cane fields was done by Chinese indentured laborers. Likewise, the abolition of slavery in Mexico led to the arrival of thousands of Chinese bonded servants.

Thanks to the influx of new arrivals, Buenos Aires, São Paulo, Mexico City, Montevideo, Santiago, and Havana experienced spectacular growth. By 1914 Buenos Aires had emerged as one of the most cosmopolitan cities in the world, with a population of 3.6 million. As Argentina's political capital, the city housed its government bureaucracies and agencies. The meat-packing, food-processing, flour-milling, and wool industries were concentrated there as well. Half of all overseas tonnage passed through the city, which was also the heart of the nation's railroad network. Elegant shops near the Plaza de Mayo catered to the expensive tastes of the elite upper classes that constituted about 5 percent of the population. By contrast, the thousands of immigrants who toiled twelve hours a day, six days a week, on docks and construction sites and in meat-packing plants were crowded into the city's one-room tenements.

Immigrants brought wide-ranging skills that helped develop industry and commerce. In Argentina, Italian and Spanish settlers stimulated the expansion of cattle ranching, meat processing, wheat farming, and the shoe industry. In Brazil, Italians gained a leading role in the coffee industry, and Japanese farmers made the country self-sufficient in rice production. Chinese laborers built Peruvian railroads, and in sections of large cities such as Lima, the Chinese dominated the ownership of shops and restaurants.

Immigrants in the Americas Indian immigrants at a Jamaican banana plantation (right) and German immigrants in Brazil (below) at the turn of the twentieth century. Immigrants brought new cultures and worldviews to the Americas. (Jamaica: © The Print Collector/Heritage/The Image Works; Brazil: © SZ Photo/Sherl/The Image Works)

Immigration to the United States

After the Civil War ended in 1865, the United States underwent an industrial boom powered by exploitation of the country's natural resources. The federal government turned over vast amounts of land and mineral resources to private industrialists for development. In particular, railroad companies—the foundation of industrial expansion—received 130 million acres. By 1900 the U.S. railroad system was 193,000 miles long, connected every part of the nation, and represented 40 percent of the railroad mileage in the world, and it was all built by immigrant labor.

Between 1860 and 1914, 28 million immigrants came to the United States. Though many became rural homesteaders, industrial America developed through the labor of immigrants. Chinese, Scandinavian, and Irish immigrants laid railroad tracks. At the Carnegie Steel Corporation, Slavs and Italians produced one-third of the world's total steel supply in 1900. As in South America, immigration fed the growth of cities. In 1790 only 5.1 percent of Americans were living in centers of twenty-five hundred or more people. By 1860 this figure had risen to 19.9 percent, and by 1900 almost 40 percent of the population lived in cities. Also by 1900, three of the largest cities in the world were in the United States—New York City with 3.4 million people, Chicago with 1.7 million, and Philadelphia with 1.4 million.

Working conditions for new immigrants were often deplorable. Industrialization had created a vast class of workers who depended entirely on wage labor. Employers paid women and children much less than men. Some women textile workers earned as little as $1.56 for seventy hours of work, while men received from $7 to $9 for the same work. Because business owners resisted government efforts to install costly safety devices, working conditions in mines and mills were frightful. In 1913 alone, even after some safety measures had been instituted, twenty-five thousand people died in industrial accidents. Between 1900 and 1917 seventy-two thousand railroad workers died on the job. Workers responded to these conditions with strikes, violence, and, gradually, unionization.

Immigrants faced more than economic exploitation: they were also subjected to harsh ethnic stereotypes and faced pressure to culturally assimilate. An economic depression in the 1890s increased resentment toward immigrants. Powerful owners of mines, mills, and factories fought the organization of labor unions, fired thousands of workers, slashed wages, and ruthlessly exploited their workers. Workers in turn feared that immigrant labor would drive salaries lower. Some of this antagonism sprang from racism, some from old Protestant prejudice against Catholicism, the faith of many of the new arrivals. Anti-Semitism against Jewish immigrants from eastern Europe intensified, while increasingly violent agitation against Asians led to race riots in California and finally culminated in the Chinese Exclusion Act of 1882, which denied Chinese laborers entrance to the country. Japanese immigration to the United States was restricted in 1907, so later Japanese immigrants settled in South America.

Immigrants were received very differently in Latin America, where oligarchs encouraged immigration from Europe, the Middle East, and Japan because they believed these "whiter" workers were superior to black or indigenous workers. By contrast, in the United States

"The Chinese Must Go!"
Anti-immigrant sentiment intensified as immigration to the United States accelerated in the late nineteenth and early twentieth centuries. This 1880 campaign advertisement presented Chinese immigrants as a threat to native-born workers. (Sarin Images/Granger, NY— All rights reserved.)

the descendants of northern European Protestants developed prejudices and built social barriers out of their belief that Catholic Irish, southern and eastern European, or Jewish immigrants were not white enough.

Immigration to Canada

Canada was sparsely populated in the nineteenth century relative to other areas of the Americas. Provinces of the British colony gained governing autonomy after 1840 and organized a national government, the Dominion of Canada, in 1867 (Map 27.3). British authorities agreed to grant the provinces political independence in order to avoid the disruption and loss of influence that followed U.S. independence, and in return the Dominion retained a symbolic role for the British monarchy. By 1900 Canada still had only a little over 5 million people (as compared to 13.6 million in Mexico and 76 million in the United States). As in the United States and Latin America, native peoples were pushed aside by Canada's development plans, and their population dropped by half or more during the century, many succumbing to the newcomers' diseases.

By 1900 there were only about 127,000 indigenous people left in Canada. French Canadians were the largest minority in the population, and they remained different in language, law, and religion.

Immigration to Canada increased in the 1890s. Between 1897 and 1912, 961,000 people entered Canada from the British Isles, 594,000 from Europe, and 784,000 from the United States. Some immigrants went to work in the urban factories of Hamilton, Toronto, and Montreal. However, most immigrants from continental Europe—Poles, Germans, Scandinavians, and Russians—flooded the midwestern plains and soon transformed the prairies into one of the world's greatest grain-growing regions. Between 1891 and 1914 wheat production soared from 2 million bushels per year to 150 million bushels. Mining expanded, and British Columbia, Ontario, and Quebec produced large quantities of wood pulp, much of it sold to the United States. Canada's great rivers were harnessed to supply hydroelectric power for industrial and domestic use. But Canada remained a predominantly agricultural country, with less than 10 percent of its population engaged in manufacturing.

MAP 27.3 The Dominion of Canada, 1871 Shortly after the Dominion of Canada came into being as a self-governing nation within the British Empire in 1867, new provinces were added. Vast areas of Canada were too sparsely populated to achieve provincial status. Alberta and Saskatchewan did not become part of the Dominion until 1905; Newfoundland was added only in 1949.

Promoting European Immigration and Settlement
A Canadian Pacific Railway advertisement seeking British farmers to immigrate to Canada reflects patterns seen across the Americas: in lands wrested from indigenous communities, the arrival of railroads integrated territories into the national and global economy, while making those lands available for white European settlement. (Private Collection/Peter Newark American Pictures/Bridgeman Images)

A New American Empire

In what ways did U.S. policies in the Caribbean and Central America resemble European imperialism? How did U.S. foreign policy depart from European imperialism?

By 1890 the United States had claimed the contiguous territories it acquired through purchase, war, and displacement. Its frontier was closed. The United States redirected its expansionist pressures outward, beginning with the remnants of the Spanish Empire: Cuba and Puerto Rico in the Caribbean, and the Philippine Islands and Guam in the Pacific.

The United States emulated the imperialism of European nations like Britain and France by claiming control of land and people that served its economic interests and justifying its domination by arguing that it was advancing civilization.

U.S. Intervention in Latin America

Between 1898 and 1932 the U.S. government intervened militarily thirty-four times in ten nations in the Caribbean and Central America to extend and protect its economic interests. U.S. influence in the Circum-Caribbean was not new, however, and stretched back to the early nineteenth century. In 1823 President James Monroe proclaimed in the **Monroe Doctrine** that the United States would keep European influence out of Latin America. This doctrine asserted that Latin America was part of the U.S. sphere of influence. U.S. intervention in Latin America was also a byproduct of the manifest destiny ideal of consolidating national territory from the Atlantic to the Pacific. Often the easiest way to connect the two sides of the continent was through Latin America.

The California gold rush of the 1840s created pressure to move people and goods quickly and inexpensively between the eastern and western parts of the United States decades before its transcontinental railroad was completed in 1869. It was cheaper, faster, and safer to travel to the east or west coast of Mexico and Central America, traverse the continent where it was narrower, and continue the voyage by sea. The Panama Railway, the first railroad constructed in Central America, served exactly this purpose and was built with U.S. investment in 1855.

Facing pressure from abolitionists against expanding the slave regime westward, planters and politicians in the U.S. South responded by seeking opportunities to annex new lands in Latin America and the Caribbean. They eyed Cuba, the Dominican Republic, El Salvador, and Nicaragua. In Nicaragua, Tennessean William Walker employed a mercenary army to depose the government and install himself as president (1856–1857). One of his first acts was to reinstate slavery. He was overthrown by armies sent from Costa Rica, El Salvador, and Honduras.

By the end of the nineteenth century U.S. involvement in Latin America had intensified, first through private investment and then through military force. In 1893 a group of U.S. investors formed the Santo Domingo Improvement Company, which bought the foreign debt of the Dominican Republic and took control of its customs houses in order to repay investors and creditors. After the government propped up by the U.S. company fell, President Theodore Roosevelt introduced what would be known as the **Roosevelt Corollary** to the Monroe Doctrine, which stated that the United States, as a civilized nation, would correct the "chronic wrongdoing" of its neighbors, such as failure to protect U.S. investments.

To this end, in 1903 and 1904 Roosevelt deployed Marines to the Dominican Republic to protect the investments of U.S. firms. Marines occupied and governed the Dominican Republic again from 1916 to 1924. The violent and corrupt dictator Rafael Trujillo (troo-HEE-yo) ruled from 1930 to 1961 with the support of the United States. When he eventually defied the United States, he was assassinated by rivals acting with the encouragement of the Central Intelligence Agency.

Versions of the Dominican Republic's experience played out across the Circum-Caribbean. U.S. Marines occupied Haiti from 1915 to 1934 and Nicaragua from 1912 to 1934. These military occupations followed a similar pattern of using military force to protect private U.S. companies' investments in banana and sugar plantations, railroads, mining, ports, and utilities. And as U.S. forces departed, they left power in the hands of dictators who served U.S. interests. These dictators governed not through popular consent but through force, corruption, and the support of the United States.

The Spanish-American War

In Cuba a second war of independence erupted in 1895 after it had failed to gain freedom from Spain in the Ten Years' War (1868–1878). A brutal war of attrition ensued, and by 1898 the countryside was in ruins and Spanish colonial control was restricted to a handful of cities. Cuban nationalists were on the verge of defeating the Spanish forces and gaining independence. But before they could realize this goal, the United States intervened, resulting in the Spanish-American War (1898).

The U.S. intervention began with a provocative act: sailing the battleship *Maine* into Havana harbor. This was an aggressive act because the battleship was capable of bombarding the entire city. But soon after it laid anchor, the *Maine* exploded and sank, killing hundreds of sailors. The U.S. government accused Spain of sinking the warship, a charge Spain denied, and demanded that the Spanish government provide restitution. Later investigations determined that a kitchen fire spread to the main munitions storage and blew up the ship. The sinking of the *Maine* led to war between Spain and the United States over control of Cuba and the Philippines. The U.S. Navy and Marines fought and defeated Spanish forces in the Pacific and the Caribbean. With its victory, the United States acquired Guam and Puerto Rico and launched a military occupation of Cuba and the Philippines.

Puerto Rico and Guam became colonies directly ruled by U.S. administrators, and residents of both island territories did not gain the right to elect their own leaders until after the Second World War. They remained commonwealths (territories that are not states) of the United States. The U.S. government also established direct rule in the Philippines, brushing aside the government established by Filipino nationalists who had fought for freedom from Spain. Nationalists then fought against the United States in the Philippine-American War (1899–1902) in an unsuccessful effort to establish an independent government.

Cuba alone gained independence, but U.S. pressure limited that independence. The Platt Amendment, which the United States imposed as a condition of Cuban independence, gave the U.S. Senate the power to cancel laws passed by the Cuban congress, withheld the Cuban government's right to establish foreign treaties, and granted the United States control over Guantanamo Bay, where it established a permanent naval base. In addition to imposing legal limits on Cuban independence, the United States militarily occupied Cuba in 1899–1902, 1906–1908, and 1912. Between 1917 and 1922 U.S. administrator Enoch Crowder governed the island from his staterooms on the battleship *Minnesota*.

The constraints that the U.S. government imposed on Cuban politics, along with its willingness to deploy troops and periodically establish military rule, created a safe and fertile environment for U.S. investment. As the first U.S. commander of Cuba, General Leonard Wood equated good government with investor confidence: "When people ask me what I mean by stable government, I tell them 'money at six percent.'"[5] Cuban farmers had been bankrupted by the war of independence that had raged since 1895. One hundred thousand farms and three thousand ranches were destroyed. U.S. investors flooded in. By 1919 half of the island's sugar mills were owned by U.S. businesses. Small farms were consolidated into estates as twenty-two companies took hold of 20 percent of Cuba's national territory. U.S. companies like Coca-Cola and Hershey were among the new landowners that took control of their most important ingredient: sugar.

The United States exported its prevailing racial prejudices to its new Caribbean territories. In Cuba, U.S. authorities encouraged political parties to exclude black Cubans. Black war veterans established the Independent Party of Color in 1908 in order to press for political inclusion. Party leaders Evaristo Estenoz and Pedro Ivonet sought to use the party's potential electoral weight to incorporate black Cubans into government and education. The party was banned in 1910, and in 1912 its leaders organized a revolt that led to a violent backlash by the army and police, supported by U.S. Marines. The campaign against members of the

Monroe Doctrine An 1823 proclamation that established a U.S. sphere of influence over the Americas by opposing European imperialism on the continent.

Roosevelt Corollary A corollary to the Monroe Doctrine stating that the United States would correct what it saw as "chronic wrongdoing" in neighboring countries.

Reyita Castillo Bueno on Slavery and Freedom in Cuba

Reyita Castillo Bueno was born in Cuba in 1902. When she narrated her life to her granddaughter, she reflected on her own grandmother, an Angolan woman brought to Cuba in the illicit slave trade of the mid-nineteenth century. Her memories captured both the slow process of abolition (her mother worked like a slave for her family's master, even though she was born after the free womb law) and the difficulties black Cubans faced after the United States intervened in the independence struggle.

My Grandma Flew Away

■ My grandmother's name was Antonina, although everyone called her Tatica. . . . Tatica told us her family came from a little village in a place called Cabinda [at the border between Angola and Congo], they were Quicongos and they grew manioc and coffee and also wove with raffia. The men of the village made canoes, drums and various wooden utensils. . . .

One evening, when the family was at home, having finished working in the fields, and the children were playing, they suddenly heard explosions and shouting. It was a group of white men with guns who were attacking the village, burning the houses and capturing women and men, killing children and old people. It was a terrible massacre. My great-grandmother saw her son and her husband vanish; she tried as hard as she could to defend the girls, but they beat her and took the three oldest. . . .

After such horror came the long march to the steamer — as she used to say — she never managed to figure out how long it lasted. They tied them to each other so they couldn't escape. . . . On the way they'd be beaten if they fell down from exhaustion or thirst.

The ship that took them from Africa was crammed with men, women and even children, though not many. . . . She said they were the ones the whites couldn't wrench out of their mothers' arms. Since it was so full, there was some problem, and although Tatica didn't know precisely what was wrong, they started throwing men overboard — the oldest, the most frail. What an outrage! Just hearing about it made you want to cry, and even now my eyes well up with tears and you feel tremendously indignant because they threw them overboard alive, with no compassion whatsoever.

When they reached land, Tatica and my aunts didn't know where they were, it was much later that they found out this was Cuba. They took them to a big hut where they were fed and had water thrown over them. . . . A person from the Hechavarría family bought all three of them. . . . The Hechavarrías also bought other Africans, there were about fifteen or twenty altogether on the plantation. One of them was young and strong and not from my grandmother's village. His name was Basilio and he and Tatica fell in love.

They lived together secretly so that the masters wouldn't find out. Although my grandmother didn't want to have children — and she took preventative infusions of herbs and roots — she got pregnant and had a daughter they named Socorro, who had to work very hard from a very young age. Later my mother was born, she had to work as a slave doing housework for the masters, even though this was after the law of free wombs.

My mother wasn't Basilio's daughter, but one of my grandmother's masters was her father. The slaves couldn't resist when the masters wanted to take advantage of them. It would have cost them a whipping and the stocks. There

---

party was followed by a wave of lynchings of black Cubans across the island. (See "Analyzing the Evidence: Reyita Castillo Bueno on Slavery and Freedom in Cuba," above.)

In Puerto Rico the influence of U.S. racism was more direct. In 1913, as the U.S. Congress debated granting Puerto Ricans U.S. citizenship, the federal judge for Puerto Rico appointed by President Woodrow Wilson objected and wrote to the president that Puerto Ricans "have the Latin American excitability and I think Americans should go slowly in granting them anything like autonomy. Their civilization is not at all like ours yet." Later the judge declared, "The mixture of black and white in Porto Rico threatens to create a race of mongrels of no use to anyone, a race of Spanish American talkers. A governor of the South, or with

knowledge of southern remedies for that trouble could, if a wise man, do much."[6]

The United States instituted the "remedies" to which the judge alluded, such as the sterilization of thousands of Puerto Rican women as part of a policy aimed at addressing what the government saw as overpopulation on the island. In addition, Puerto Rican men drafted into U.S. military service were organized into segregated units, as African Americans were.

The Panama Canal

U.S. imperialism in the Caribbean extended beyond Cuba and Puerto Rico to the prize the United States had pursued for decades: a canal to connect the Atlantic and Pacific Oceans. The canal would transport cargo was an immoral hypocrisy in those men: on the one hand they looked down on them, but when it came to rape they didn't care what colour their skin was.

After the abolition of slavery in 1886, Tatica went to live in a little hut which Basilio built on a tiny piece of land he was given. . . . When Basilio joined up with the independence forces in the war of 1895, Tatica took to the hills with him. . . .

Tatica didn't like Catholicism, she was very superstitious and believed in life after death. I remember what my grandmother used to say about Africans who lived far away from their countries. She said their spirits returned to their lands when they died. I couldn't go to her funeral because I didn't live in La Maya anymore. . . . I cried so much! But when I calmed down and closed my eyes I seemed to see her rise up to the sky and fly through the clouds, on the way back to her native land, towards her beloved, never forgotten Africa, which I learned to love too from all the stories she told us.

The 1912 Afro-Cuban Revolt

■ Many people gathered in my uncle's house. They'd get me to stand guard at the door; they'd shut themselves into the little room off the patio where they kept the things for making candies. One day several men came, among them Pedro Ivonet and Evaristo Estenoz. When my aunt Mangá went to greet them, Estenoz put his arm around me and kissed me. Ivonet too; Estenoz was very handsome. There was another one, another handsome black man—I can't remember his name—who made speeches; he spoke beautifully.

Back then I didn't know how important they were in the movement. They were leaders of the Independent Coloured Party; but I had heard that a senator called Morúa Delgado had voted in a law against the creation of political parties for blacks, or rather, for people of only one race. "Coloured" people considered this law unjust, because they realized they needed a political organization that would allow them to look for their own solutions to problems, because the white ones weren't helping at all. . . . Estenoz met with the President of the Republic, who said he'd support them in gaining this right, that they should pretend to take up arms against the government so he could get the Assembly and the Senate to believe there would be war between blacks and whites and to avoid it they must vote down the Morúa law, and thus the Party would be approved.

[President Gómez's] real interest lay in securing the black vote, because he wanted to be re-elected President. When he couldn't achieve anything, he sent a commission into the hills with a message for the blacks: "Don't surrender, I'll keep trying to solve the problem." And to prevent them from finding out what he'd promised the blacks, what he did was send the army under General Monteagudo against them.

Just imagine! How were they to defend themselves? With old shotguns? With machetes? Since they didn't have enough weapons—and moreover they weren't intending to wage war—they were hunted town and captured. Poor souls! I saw them when they brought them down from the hills, tied up. They killed them, threw them in pots and set them on fire. Many of those who surrendered were taken to a place called Arroyo Blanco and there they were murdered.

QUESTIONS FOR ANALYSIS

1. How does Reyita Castillo Bueno understand race?
2. How does culture change for the different generations in Castillo Bueno's narrative?
3. How does Castillo Bueno convey the abolition of slavery and the wars of independence to readers?

Source: Maria de los Reyes Castillo Bueno, *Reyita: The Life of a Black Cuban Woman in the Twentieth Century* (Durham, N.C.: Duke University Press, 2000), pp. 23–26, 49–51. Copyright, Latin American Bureau (Research & Action) Ltd., London. First published in the UK, September 2000. Used by permission of the Latin American Bureau/The Practical Action.

between the east and west of the United States much less expensively than rail. In the mid-nineteenth century the U.S. railroad tycoon Cornelius Vanderbilt tried but failed to build a canal through Nicaragua. Later in the century, a consortium of French investors pursued the construction of a canal in the Colombian province of Panama, encouraged by the success of the Suez Canal that connected the Mediterranean to the Red Sea and the Indian Ocean, completed in 1869. Engineers and laborers completed some excavation before the French company went bankrupt.

After the Spanish-American War gave the U.S. more direct control of the Caribbean, U.S. authorities negotiated with the Colombian government for the right to continue the project started by the French company. When the Colombian congress balked at the U.S. government's demand that it should have territorial control of the canal, the U.S. government encouraged an insurrection in Panama City and recognized the rebels as leaders of the new country of Panama. The new Panamanian government gave the United States permanent control over the canal in 1904 and the land upon which it was built, which became known as the Canal Zone. The Canal Zone became an unincorporated U.S. territory, similar in status to Puerto Rico and Guam. It housed canal workers as well as U.S. military installations.

Tens of thousands of migrant workers from around the Caribbean provided labor for construction of the canal, which opened in 1914. U.S. authorities instituted the same segregationist policies applied in their other Caribbean territories. Workers were divided into a "gold roll" of highly paid white U.S. workers and a "silver role" of mostly black workers, who came from Barbados, Panama, Nicaragua, Colombia, and other parts of the Caribbean. They were paid lower wages, faced much higher rates of death and injury, and lived in less healthy conditions. The Canal Zone itself functioned as a segregated enclave: U.S. residents could move freely between it and Panamanian territory, but it was closed to Panamanians except those who entered through labor contracts.

Chapter Summary

In the century after independence, political consolidation and economic integration varied across the Americas. The North of the United States became the continent's main engine of capital accumulation, immigration, and industrialization. In the U.S. South and Brazil reliance on slavery weakened internal markets, inhibited immigration, and slowed industrialization. In Spanish America the lack of a governing consensus until the second half of the nineteenth century resulted in "lost decades" after independence, in which new countries fell behind not only relative to other regions of the world, but even relative to their past colonial experiences.

The cycle of war that began in the 1850s and continued for the next two decades reshaped the Americas politically and economically, consolidating a liberal order that placed great wealth in few hands while dealing misery and dislocation to many others. Liberalism had a modernizing influence on trade and industry, but it further concentrated wealth. Just as the United States waged wars against the Indians and pushed its frontier westward, so Brazil, Venezuela, Ecuador, Peru,

and Bolivia expanded into the Amazonian frontier at the expense of indigenous peoples. Likewise, Mexico, Chile, and Argentina had their own "Indian wars" and frontier expansion. Racial prejudice kept most African Americans at the social and economic margins.

By the beginning of the twentieth century, the economies of American nations were tightly integrated into the world economy, and powerful currents of immigration further deepened ties between continents. Industrialization that began in the northeast of the United States developed elsewhere in the continent, but the lead in industrialization held by the United States allowed it to increasingly impose its will over other nations. The economic and social dislocations produced by the liberal model of export-oriented economic growth also awoke growing social demands by the rural and urban poor. These boiled over the most dramatically in Mexico's 1910 revolution, but in cities to the south such as Buenos Aires, Argentina, and Santiago, Chile, workers' demands for the right to organize for better wages and for political representation also became too insistent to ignore.

NOTES

1. Jürgen Buchenau, *Mexican Mosaic: A Brief History of Mexico* (Wheeling, Ill.: Harlan-Davidson, 2008), p. 2.
2. Jaime E. Rodriguez O., *Down from Colonialism: Mexico's Nineteenth Century Crisis* (Los Angeles: Chicano Studies Center Research Publications, UCLA, 1983), p. 15.
3. David Rock, *Argentina, 1516–1987: From Spanish Colonization to Alfonsín* (Berkeley: University of California Press, 1987), p. 154.
4. Quoted in Nicolas Shumway, *The Invention of Argentina* (Berkeley: University of California Press, 1991), p. 147.
5. Quoted in Luis A. Pérez, *The War of 1898: The United States and Cuba in History and Historiography* (Chapel Hill: University of North Carolina Press, 1998), p. 32.
6. Quoted in Arturo Morales Carrión, *Puerto Rico: A Political and Cultural History* (New York: W. W. Norton, 1983), pp. 187–188.

CONNECTIONS

In the Americas the century or so between independence and World War I was a time of nation building. Colonial governments were overthrown, new constitutions were written, settlement was extended, slavery was ended, and immigrants from around the world settled across the continent. Although wealth was very unevenly distributed, in most of these countries it was not hard to find signs of progress: growing cities, expanding opportunities for education, modern conveniences. This progress came with harsh costs for indigenous communities, rural peasants, and the growing ranks of urban industrial workers. The great upheaval of the Mexican Revolution was a reaction against these costs, and resulted in a society that curbed some of the excesses facilitated by liberalism.

World War I, the topic of the next chapter, affected these countries in a variety of ways. Canada followed Britain into the war in 1914 and sent six hundred thousand men to fight, losing many in some of the bloodiest battles of the war. The United States did not join the war until 1917, but quickly mobilized several million men and in 1918 began sending soldiers and materials in huge numbers. Even countries that maintained neutrality, as all the Latin American countries other than Brazil did, felt the economic impact of the war deeply, especially the increased demand for food and manufactured goods. For the working class the global demand for exported foods drove up the cost of living, but the profits that oligarchs accumulated fueled the process of industrialization.

CHAPTER 27   Review and Explore

Identify Key Terms

Identify and explain the significance of each item below.

oligarchs (p. 790)	free womb laws (p. 796)
Circum-Caribbean (p. 790)	latifundios (p. 799)
caudillismo (p. 790)	Porfiriato (p. 804)
manifest destiny (p. 791)	Plan de Ayala (p. 805)
Treaty of Guadalupe Hidalgo (p. 792)	anarcho-syndicalism (p. 806)
Lerdo Law (p. 793)	Monroe Doctrine (p. 810)
neocolonialism (p. 795)	Roosevelt Corollary (p. 810)

Review the Main Ideas

Answer the focus questions from each section of the chapter.

1. How and why did the process of nation-state consolidation vary across the Americas? (p. 790)

2. Why did slavery last longer in the United States, Brazil, and Cuba than in the other republics of the Americas? How did resistance by slaves shape abolition? (p. 795)

3. As Latin America became more integrated into the world economy, how did patterns of economic growth shape political culture and social reactions? (p. 799)

4. What factors shaped patterns of immigration to the Americas? How did immigrants shape — and how were they shaped by — their new settings? (p. 806)

5. In what ways did U.S. policies in the Caribbean and Central America resemble European imperialism? How did U.S. foreign policy depart from European imperialism? (p. 810)

Make Comparisons and Connections

Analyze the larger developments and continuities within and across chapters.

1. How did the embrace of liberalism in Latin America resemble or differ from its expression in other parts of the world?

2. How did factors that influenced the Mexican Revolution express themselves in other parts of the Americas?

3. In what ways did the United States come to resemble European powers in building overseas empires (Chapters 25, 26)? How did U.S. expansionism and the colonialism practiced by Britain and France differ?

4. How did neocolonialism make Latin America after independence resemble regions of Asia and Africa (Chapters 25, 26) that were subjected to direct colonial rule?

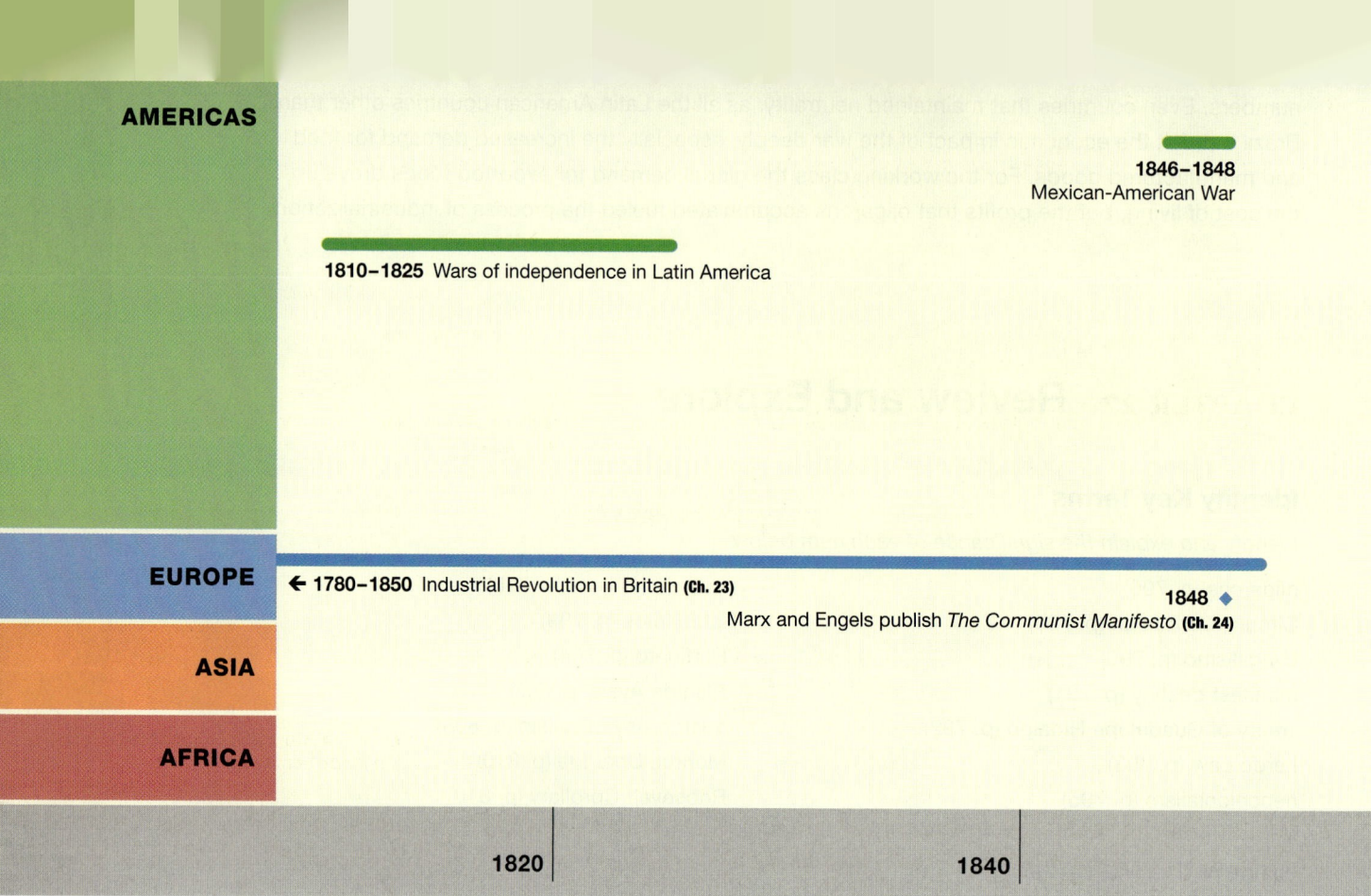

AMERICAS

1846–1848
Mexican-American War

1810–1825 Wars of independence in Latin America

EUROPE ← **1780–1850** Industrial Revolution in Britain (Ch. 23)

1848 ◆
Marx and Engels publish *The Communist Manifesto* (Ch. 24)

ASIA

AFRICA

1820   1840

Suggested Resources

BOOKS

Baptist, Edward E. *The Half Has Never Been Told: Slavery and the Making of American Capitalism.* 2014. Examines how the development of the United States shaped the experiences of slaves.

Bayly, C. A. *The Birth of the Modern World, 1780–1914.* 2003. Useful for viewing the countries of the Americas in the context of global developments.

Beckert, Sven. *Empire of Cotton: A Global History.* 2014. A history of the commodity that shows the global connections forged around a plantation slave regime.

Beezley, William. *Judas at the Jockey Club and Other Episodes of Porfirian Mexico,* 2d ed. 2004. A provocative study of Mexico under the Porfiriato.

Bender, Thomas. *A Nation Among Nations: America's Place in World History.* 2006. Shows that key events in American history are best seen in global context.

Da Costa, Emilia Viotti. *The Brazilian Empire: Myths and Histories.* 2000. Examines nation building, liberalism, and abolition in the largest slave society of the Americas.

Fernandez-Armesto, Felipe. *The Americas: A Hemispheric History.* 2003. Provocative and engagingly written.

Goldfield, David. *Still Fighting the Civil War: The American South and Southern History,* updated ed. 2013. Examines the Civil War and its enduring legacies for the U.S. South.

Helg, Aline. *Our Rightful Share: The Afro-Cuban Struggle for Equality, 1886–1912.* 1995. An insightful reading of race relations amid Cuban independence and the abolition of slavery.

Knight, Alan. *The Mexican Revolution: A Very Short Introduction.* 2016. A concise interpretation of the Mexican Revolution by one of its leading scholars.

Lesser, Jeffrey. *Immigration, Ethnicity, and National Identity in Brazil, 1808 to the Present.* 2013. A broad-ranging social history.

Morton, Desmond. *A Short History of Canada,* 6th ed. 2006. A well-written popular history.

1857–1861
Mexican Wars of Reform

1868–1878 Cuban Ten Years' War

◆ **1886** Abolition of slavery in Cuba

◆ **1898** Spanish-American War

1861–1865 U.S. Civil War

1904 ◆
U.S. secures the rights to build and
control the Panama Canal

1865–1870 Paraguay War
(War of the Triple Alliance)

◆ **1888** Abolition of slavery in Brazil

◆ **1867** Dominion of Canada formed

◆ **1889** Brazilian monarchy overthrown and
republic established

1910 ◆
Mexican Revolution erupts

1879–1883 War of the Pacific

◆ **1858** British Parliament begins
to rule India **(Ch. 26)**

◆ **1867** Japan's Meiji Restoration promotes
reforms and industrialization **(Ch. 26)**

1884–1885 Berlin Conference formalizes
European colonization in Africa **(Ch. 25)**

1860	1880	1900

DOCUMENTARIES

The Civil War (PBS, 1990). A documentary by Ken
Burns offering a gripping account of the conflict.

The Storm That Swept Mexico (Raymond Telles, 2011).
A PBS documentary that explores the Mexican
Revolution.

FEATURE FILMS

Lincoln (Steven Spielberg, 2012) and *Django Unchained*
(Quentin Tarantino, 2012). As a pair, these films
reflect stylized visions of ending slavery from above
and from below.

El Otro Francisco (Sergio Giral, 1975). Re-examines
the Cuban abolitionist novel *Francisco*, by Anselmo
Suárez y Romero, from a Marxist viewpoint on
slavery and resistance.

WEBSITES

A Guide to the Mexican War. This Library of Congress
site compiles documents, maps, and music related to
the war. **www.loc.gov/rr/program/bib/mexicanwar/**

Topics in Chronicling America. This Library of Congress
project has a wealth of material on the Spanish-
American War and the creation of the Panama Canal.
www.loc.gov/rr/news/topics/spanishAmWar.html
www.loc.gov/rr/news/topics/panama.html

28

World War and Revolution
1914–1929

In summer 1914 the nations of Europe went willingly to war. They believed they had no other choice, but everyone confidently expected a short war leading to a decisive victory. Such a war, they believed, would "clear the air." Then European society could continue as before. They were wrong. The First World War was long, global, indecisive, and tremendously destructive. It quickly degenerated into a senseless military stalemate lasting four years. To the shell-shocked generation of survivors, it became simply the Great War.

In March 1917, as Russia suffered horrendous losses on the eastern front, its war-weary people rebelled against their tsar, Nicholas II, forcing him to abdicate. Moderate reformists established a provisional government but made the fatal decision to continue the war against Germany. In November Vladimir Lenin and his Communist Bolshevik Party staged a second revolution, this time promising an end to the war. The Germans forced a harsh peace on the Russians, but Lenin believed this a small price to pay for the establishment of history's first Communist state. Few then could have realized how profoundly this event would shape the course of the twentieth century.

When the Great War's victorious Allies, led by Great Britain, France, and the United States, gathered in Paris in 1919 to write the peace, they were well aware of the importance of their decisions. Some came to Paris seeking revenge, some came looking for the spoils of war, and some promoted nationalist causes, while a few sought an idealistic end to war. The process was massive and complex, but in the end few left Paris satisfied with the results. The peace and prosperity the delegates had so earnestly sought lasted barely a decade.

Private Collection/Archives Charmet/Bridgeman Images

Senegalese Soldier

A *tirailleur* (literally, "skirmisher") from French West Africa who fought in Europe during the Great War. Across the bottom of this postcard image from the era, the soldier proclaimed his loyalty with the phrase "Glory to the Greater France," meaning France and its colonies. Note the two German *pickelhaube* (spike helmets) he wears on his head.

CHAPTER PREVIEW

THE FIRST WORLD WAR, 1914–1918
What were the long-term and immediate causes of World War I, and how did the conflict become a global war?

THE HOME FRONT   How did total war affect the home fronts of the major combatants?

THE RUSSIAN REVOLUTION   What factors led to the Russian Revolution, and what was its outcome?

THE WAR'S CONSEQUENCES   What were the global consequences of the First World War?

THE SEARCH FOR PEACE AND POLITICAL STABILITY, 1919–1929
How did leaders deal with the political dimensions of uncertainty and try to re-establish peace and prosperity in the interwar years?

THE AGE OF ANXIETY
In what ways were the anxieties of the postwar world expressed or heightened by revolutionary ideas in modern thought, art, and science and in new forms of communication?

The First World War, 1914–1918

What were the long-term and immediate causes of World War I, and how did the conflict become a global war?

The First World War clearly marked a major break in the course of world history. The maps of Europe and southwest Asia were redrawn, nationalist movements took root and spread across Asia (the subject of the next chapter), America consolidated its position as a global power, and the world experienced, for the first time, industrialized, total war. Europe's Great Powers started the war and suffered the most—in casualties, in costs, in destruction, and in societal and political upheaval. Imperialism also brought the conflict to the Middle East, Africa, and Asia, making this a global war of unprecedented scope. The young soldiers who went to war believed in the pre-1914 world of order, progress, and patriotism. Then, in the words of German soldier and writer Erich Remarque (rih-MAHRK), the "first bombardment showed us our mistake, and under it the world as they had taught it to us broke in pieces."[1]

Origins and Causes of the Great War

Scholars began arguing over the Great War's origins soon after it began, and the debate continues a century after its end. The victorious Allied powers expressed their opinion—that Germany caused the war—in the Versailles treaty. But history seldom offers such simple answers, particularly to questions so complex. The war's origins lie in the nineteenth century, and its immediate causes lie in the few years and months before the war, especially one particular morning in June 1914.

Any study of the Great War's origins must begin with nationalism (see "The Growing Appeal of Nationalism" in Chapter 24), one of the major ideologies of the nineteenth century, and its armed companion, **militarism**, the glorification of the military as the supreme ideal of the state with all other interests subordinate to it. European concerns over national security, economies, welfare, identities, and overseas empires set nation against nation, alliance against alliance, and army against army until they all went to war at once.

Competition between nations intensified greatly when Germany became a unified nation-state and

Yanitza, the Albanian "Joan of Arc" Tringe Smajli, known as Yanitza, was an Albanian guerrilla fighter who, following the death of her father and two brothers in battle, took a vow of chastity, adopted male clothing, and joined Albanian rebels revolting against the Ottoman Empire in 1911–1912. She is recognized as a People's Hero of Albania. (Private Collection/Archives Charmet/Bridgeman Images)

the most powerful country in Europe in 1871. A new era in international relations began, as Chancellor Bismarck declared Germany a "satisfied" power, having no territorial ambitions within Europe and desiring only peace.

But how to preserve the peace? Bismarck's first concern was to keep rival France diplomatically isolated and without military allies. His second concern was to prevent Germany from being dragged into a war between the two rival empires, Austria-Hungary and Russia, as they sought to fill the power vacuum created in the Balkans by the Ottoman Empire's decline (see "Decline and Reform in the Ottoman Empire" in Chapter 25). To these ends, Bismarck brokered a series of treaties and alliances, all meant to ensure the balance of power in Europe and to prevent the outbreak of war.

In 1890 Germany's new emperor, Wilhelm II, forced Bismarck to resign and then abandoned many of Bismarck's efforts to ensure German security through promoting European peace and stability. Wilhelm

militarism The glorification of the military as the supreme ideal of the state with all other interests subordinate to it.

Triple Entente The alliance of Great Britain, France, and Russia in the First World War.

Triple Alliance,
1882–1915
Triple Entente,
1907–1917
Neutral

MAP 28.1 European Alliances at the Outbreak of World War I, 1914 By the time war broke out, Europe was divided into two opposing alliances: the Triple Entente of Britain, France, and Russia and the Triple Alliance of Germany, Austria-Hungary, and Italy. Italy switched sides and joined the Entente in 1915.

refused to renew a nonaggression pact Bismarck had signed with Russia in 1887, for example, which prompted France to court the tsar, offering loans and arms, and sign a Franco-Russian Alliance in 1892. With France and Russia now allied against Germany, Austria, and Italy, Great Britain's foreign policy became increasingly crucial. Many Germans and some Britons felt that the ethnically related Germanic and Anglo-Saxon peoples were natural allies. However, the good relations that had prevailed between Prussia and Great Britain since the mid-eighteenth century gave way after 1890 to a bitter Anglo-German rivalry.

There were several reasons for this development. Germany and Great Britain's commercial rivalry in world markets and Kaiser Wilhelm's publicly expressed intention to create a global German empire unsettled the British. German nationalist militarists saw a large navy as the legitimate mark of a great world power, and their decision in 1900 to add a fleet of big-gun battleships to their already expanding navy heightened tensions. British leaders considered this expansion a military challenge to their long-standing naval supremacy.

Thus British leaders set about shoring up their exposed position with their own alliances and agree-ments. Britain improved its relations with the United States, concluded an alliance with Japan in 1902, and in the Anglo-French Entente (ahn-TAHNT) of 1904 settled all outstanding colonial disputes with France. Frustrated by Britain's closer relationship with France, Germany's leaders decided to test the entente's strength by demanding an international conference to challenge French control over Morocco. At the Algeciras (al-jih-SIR-uhs) (Spain) Conference in 1906, Germany's crude bullying only forced France and Britain closer together, and Germany left the meeting empty-handed.

The Moroccan crisis was something of a diplomatic revolution. Britain, France, Russia, and even the United States began to view Germany as a potential threat. At the same time, German leaders began to suspect sinister plots to encircle Germany and block its development as a world power. In 1907 Russia and Britain settled their outstanding differences and signed the Anglo-Russian Agreement. This treaty, together with the earlier Franco-Russian Alliance of 1892 and Anglo-French Entente of 1904, served as a catalyst for the **Triple Entente**, the alliance of Great Britain, France, and Russia in the First World War (Map 28.1).

MAP 28.2 The Balkans, 1878–1914 The Ottoman Empire suffered large territorial losses after the Congress of Berlin in 1878 but remained a power in the Balkans. By 1914 ethnic boundaries that did not follow political boundaries had formed, and Serbian national aspirations threatened Austria-Hungary.

By 1909 Europe's leading nations were divided into two hostile blocs, both ill-prepared to deal with upheaval in the Balkans.

The Outbreak of War

In 1897, the year before he died, the prescient Bismarck is reported to have remarked, "One day the great European War will come out of some damned foolish thing in the Balkans."[2] By the early twentieth century a Balkans war seemed inevitable. The reason was simple: nationalism was destroying the Ottoman Empire in Europe and threatening to break up the Austro-Hungarian Empire.

Serbia led the way, becoming openly hostile to both Austria-Hungary and the Ottoman Empire. The Slavic Serbs looked to Slavic Russia for support of their national aspirations. In 1908, to block Serbian expansion, Austria formally annexed Bosnia and Herzegovina, with their large Serbian, Croatian (kroh-AY-shuhn),

and Muslim populations. Serbia erupted in rage but could do nothing without Russia's support.

Then two nationalist wars, the first and second Balkan wars in 1912 and 1913, finally destroyed the centuries-long Ottoman presence in Europe (Map 28.2). This sudden but long-expected event elated Balkan nationalists but dismayed Austria-Hungary's leaders, who feared that Austria-Hungary might next be broken apart.

Within this tense context, Serbian nationalist Gavrilo Princip (gah-VRIH-loh prin-SIP) assassinated Archduke Franz Ferdinand, heir to the Austro-Hungarian throne, and his wife, Sophie, on June 28, 1914, during a state visit to the Bosnian capital of Sarajevo (sar-uh-YAY-voh). Austria-Hungary's leaders held Serbia responsible and on July 23 presented Serbia with an unconditional ultimatum that included demands amounting to Austrian control of the Serbian state. When Serbia replied moderately but evasively, Austria declared war on Serbia on July 28 (Map 28.3).

MAP 28.3 The First World War in Europe The trench war on the western front was concentrated in Belgium and northern France (inset), while the war in the east encompassed an enormous territory.

Legend (main map):
- Triple Entente and allies
- Central Powers and allies
- Greatest extent of territory gained by Germany-Austria
- German submarine war zone
- Neutral nations
- Farthest advance by Central Powers on date marked
- Farthest advance by Entente Powers on date marked
- British naval blockade
- Major battle

The Western Front

Legend (inset):
- Germany, 1914
- Greatest extent of territory gained by Germany, Sept. 1914
- Front at beginning of 1915
- German offensive, Summer 1918
- Major battle

Of prime importance in Austria-Hungary's fateful decision was Germany's unconditional support. Kaiser Wilhelm II and his chancellor, Theobald von Bethmann-Hollweg (THEE-uh-bawld von BAYT-mahn-hawl-vayk), realized that war between Austria and Russia was likely, for Russia could not stand by and watch the Serbs be crushed. Yet Bethmann-Hollweg hoped that while Russia (and its ally France) might go to war, Great Britain would remain neutral.

Anticipating a possible conflict, Europe's military leaders had been drawing up war plans and timetables for years, and now these, rather than diplomacy, began to dictate policy. On July 28, as Austrian armies bombarded Belgrade, Tsar Nicholas II ordered a partial mobilization against Austria-Hungary but almost immediately found this was impossible. Russia had assumed a war with both Austria and Germany, and it could not mobilize against one without mobilizing against the other. Therefore, on July 29 Russia ordered full mobilization and in effect declared general war. The German general staff had also prepared for a two-front war. Its Schlieffen (SHLEE-fuhn) plan, first drafted in 1905, called for first knocking out France with a lightning attack through neutral Belgium to capture Paris before turning on a slower-to-mobilize Russia. On August 3 German armies invaded Belgium. Great Britain declared war on Germany the following day. In each country the great majority of the population rallied to defend its nation and enthusiastically embraced war in August 1914.

The Schlieffen Plan

Planned German offensive
Actual German offensive
Neutral nations

GREAT BRITAIN
NETHERLANDS
BELGIUM
Brussels
GERMANY
Rhine R.
LUX.
Reims
Paris
Metz
Seine R.
Marne R.
FRANCE
SWITZ.
0   100   200 mi.
0   100   200 km

Stalemate and Slaughter

When the Germans invaded Belgium in August 1914, the Belgian army defended its homeland and then fell back to join a rapidly landed British army corps near the Franco-Belgian border. Instead of quickly capturing Paris in a vast encircling movement, German soldiers were advancing slowly along an enormous front. On September 6 the French attacked the German line at the Battle of the Marne (MAHRN). For three days France threw everything into the attack, forcing the Germans to fall back (see Map 28.3).

The two stalled armies then dug in behind rows of trenches, mines, and barbed wire. A "no-man's land" of one hundred to three hundred yards lay between the two combatants. Eventually an unbroken line of parallel zigzag trenches stretched over four hundred miles from the Belgian coast to the Swiss frontier. By November 1914 the slaughter on the western front had begun in earnest. For four years battles followed the same plan: after ceaseless heavy artillery shelling to "soften up" the enemy, young soldiers went "over the top" of the trenches in frontal attacks on the enemy's line.

German writer Erich Remarque described a typical attack in his celebrated novel *All Quiet on the Western Front* (1929):

> We see men living with their skulls blown open; we see soldiers run with their two feet cut off. . . . Still the little piece of convulsed earth in which we lie is held. We have yielded no more than a few hundred yards of it as a prize to the enemy. But on every yard there lies a dead man.[3]

The human cost of **trench warfare** was staggering, while territorial gains were minuscule. In the Battle of the Somme (SAWM) in summer 1916, the British and French gained an insignificant 125 square miles at a cost of 600,000 dead or wounded. The Germans lost 500,000 men. That same year the unsuccessful German attack on Verdun (vehr-DUHN) cost 700,000 lives on both sides. The slaughter was made even greater by new weapons of war—including chemical gases, tanks, airplanes, flamethrowers, and the machine gun. British poet Siegfried Sassoon (1886–1967) wrote of the Somme offensive, "I am staring at a sunlit picture of Hell."[4] (See "Global Viewpoints: British and Canadian Poetry of the Great War," at right.) The year 1917 was equally terrible.

On the eastern front, the Russians moved into eastern Germany but suffered appalling losses against the Germans at the Battles of Tannenberg and the Masurian Lakes in August and September 1914 (see Map 28.3). German and Austrian forces then reversed the Russian advances of 1914 and forced the Russians to retreat deep into their own territory in the 1915 eastern campaign. A staggering 2.5 million Russians were killed, wounded, or taken prisoner.

These changing tides of victory and hopes of territorial gains brought neutral countries into the war. Italy, a member of the Triple Alliance since 1882, declared its neutrality in 1914. Then, in May 1915, Italy joined the Triple Entente of Great Britain, France, and Russia in return for promises of Austrian territory. In September Bulgaria joined the Triple Alliance in order to settle old scores with Serbia.

trench warfare Fighting behind rows of trenches, mines, and barbed wire; used in World War I with a staggering cost in lives and minimal gains in territory.

British and Canadian Poetry of the Great War

Some of the finest and most memorable literature and poetry of the twentieth century came from the generation who experienced the Great War. These are three of the most famous poems of the Great War, all written by soldiers during the war. Rupert Brooks's "The Soldier" is the most famous of a series of sonnets he wrote in 1914. Brooks died on April 23, 1915, at the age of twenty-seven while traveling with the British Mediterranean Expeditionary Force to Gallipoli. John McCrae, a Canadian doctor, published "In Flanders Fields" in December 1915. He died of pneumonia while serving at a Canadian field hospital in northern France on January 28, 1918. British poet Wilfred Owen wrote "Dulce et Decorum Est" in 1917. He was killed in battle a week before the armistice on November 4, 1918.

Rupert Brooks, "The Soldier," 1914

If I should die, think only this of me:
    That there's some corner of a foreign field
That is for ever England. There shall be
    In that rich earth a richer dust concealed;
A dust whom England bore, shaped, made aware,
    Gave, once, her flowers to love, her ways to roam,
A body of England's, breathing English air,
    Washed by the rivers, blest by suns of home.

And think this heart, all evil shed away,
    A pulse in the eternal mind, no less
        Gives somewhere back the thoughts by England given;
Her sights and sounds; dreams happy as her day;
    And laughter, learnt of friends; and gentleness,
        In hearts at peace, under an English heaven.

John McCrae, "In Flanders Fields," 1915

In Flanders fields the poppies blow
        Between the crosses, row on row,
    That mark our place; and in the sky
    The larks, still bravely singing, fly
Scarce heard amid the guns below.

We are the Dead. Short days ago
We lived, felt dawn, saw sunset glow,
    Loved and were loved, and now we lie
        In Flanders fields.

Take up our quarrel with the foe:
To you from falling hands we throw
    The torch; be yours to hold it high.
    If ye break faith, with us who die
We shall not sleep, though poppies grow
        In Flanders fields.

Wilfred Owen, "Dulce et Decorum Est," 1917

Bent double, like old beggars under sacks,
Knock-kneed, coughing like hags, we cursed through sludge,
Till on the haunting flares we turned our backs
And towards our distant rest began to trudge.
Men marched asleep. Many had lost their boots
But limped on, blood-shod. All went lame; all blind;
Drunk with fatigue, deaf even to the hoots
Of gas shells dropping softly behind.

Gas! Gas! Quick, boys!—An ecstasy of fumbling,
Fitting the clumsy helmets just in time;
But someone still was yelling out and stumbling,
And floundering like a man in fire or lime . . .
Dim, through the misty panes and thick green light,
As under a green sea, I saw him drowning.

In all my dreams, before my helpless sight,
He plunges at me, guttering, choking, drowning.

If in some smothering dreams you too could pace
Behind the wagon that we flung him in,
And watch the white eyes writhing in his face,
His hanging face, like a devil's sick of sin;
If you could hear, at every jolt, the blood
Come gargling from the froth-corrupted lungs,
Obscene as cancer, bitter as the cud
Of vile, incurable sores on innocent tongues —
My friend, you would not tell with such high zest
To children ardent for some desperate glory,
The old Lie: *Dulce et decorum est* [It is sweet and fitting]
Pro patria mori. [To die for one's country.]

QUESTIONS FOR ANALYSIS

1. Which of these poems would you describe as the most idealistic and patriotic? Why?
2. What do you think explains the obvious antiwar nature of Owen's poem compared to the poems of Brooks and McCrae?

Source: Jon Silkin, ed., *The Penguin Book of First World War Poetry*, 2d ed. rev. (New York: Penguin Putnam, 1996), pp. 81–82, 85, 192–193.

John Nash, *Over the Top* John Nash was an English artist who served as a soldier with the First Battalion Artists' Rifles from 1916 to 1918 and then served as an official war artist in 1918. This painting depicts the Artists' Rifles leaving their trench to attack at Welsh Ridge in France on December 30, 1917. In a unit of eighty men, Nash was one of only twelve soldiers not wounded or killed by German shelling and gunfire; many of the casualties occurred during the first few minutes of the advance.

(*Over the Top, 1st Artists' Rifles at Marcoing, 30th December 1917*, 1918, by John Nash [1893–1977] [oil on canvas]/Imperial War Museum, London, UK/© IWM [Art.IWM. ART 1656]/Bridgeman Images)

The War Becomes Global

In October 1914 the Ottoman Empire joined with Austria and Germany, by then known as the Central Powers. A German alliance permitted the Turks to renounce the limitations on Ottoman sovereignty imposed by Europeans in the nineteenth century and also to settle old grievances with Russia, the Turks' historic enemy.

The entry of the Ottoman Turks pulled the entire Middle East into the war and made it truly a global conflict. While Russia attacked the Ottomans in the Caucasus, the British protected their rule in Egypt. In 1915, at the Battle of Gallipoli (guh-LIP-uh-lee), British forces tried to take the Dardanelles (dahr-duh-NELZ) and Constantinople from the Ottoman Turks but were badly defeated. Casualties were high on both

sides and included thousands of Australians and New Zealanders. Deeply loyal to the mother country, Australia sent 329,000 men and vast economic aid to Britain during the war. Over 100,000 New Zealanders also served in the war, almost a tenth of New Zealand's entire population, and they suffered a 58 percent casualty rate—one of the highest of any country. Nearly 4,000 native New Zealand Maori soldiers also fought at Gallipoli and on the western front. Ormond Burton, a New Zealand infantryman, later observed that "somewhere between the landing at Anzac [a cove on the Gallipolian peninsula] and the end of the battle of the Somme, New Zealand very definitely became a nation."[5] The British had more success inciting Arabs to revolt against their Turkish overlords. The foremost Arab leader was Hussein ibn-Ali (1856–1931), who governed much of the Ottoman Empire's territory along the Red Sea (see Map 29.1, page 858). In 1915 Hussein won vague British commitments for an independent Arab kingdom, with himself as king of the Arabs. In return, he joined forces with the British under T. E. Lawrence, who in 1917 led Arab tribesmen and Indian soldiers in a successful guerrilla war against the Turks on the Arabian peninsula. In the Ottoman province of Iraq, Britain occupied Basra (BAHS-rah) in 1914 and captured Baghdad in 1917. In 1918 British armies, aided by imperial forces from Egypt, India, Australia, and New Zealand, smashed the old Ottoman state. Thus war brought revolutionary change to the Middle East.

Japan, allied with the British since 1902, joined the Triple Entente on August 23, 1914, and began attacking German-controlled colonies and territories in the Pacific. Later that year Japan seized Germany's holdings on the Shandong (shan-dawng) Peninsula in China.

War also spread to colonies in Africa and East Asia. Colonized peoples provided critical supplies and fought in Europe, Africa, and the Ottoman Empire.

More than a million Africans and Asians served in the various armies of the warring powers, with more than double that number serving as porters to carry equipment. Drawn primarily from Senegal, French West Africa, and British South Africa, over 140,000 Africans fought on the western front, and 31,000 of them died there.

Many of these men joined up to get clothes (uniforms), food, and money for enlisting. Others did so because colonial recruiters promised them better lives when they returned home. Most were illiterate and had no idea of why they were going or what they would experience. One West African infantryman, Kande Kamara, later wrote:

> We black African soldiers were very sorrowful about the white man's war. . . . I didn't really care who was right—whether it was the French or the Germans— I went to fight with the French army and that was all I knew. The reason for war was never disclosed to any soldier. . . . We just fought and fought until we got exhausted and died.[6]

Indian Soldiers Convalescing in England Over 130,000 Indian soldiers served on the western front during the Great War, mostly during the first year of battle before being transferred to the Middle East to fight at Gallipoli and in the Mesopotamian campaign. Wounded Indian troops convalesced at the Royal Pavilion at Brighton, a former royal residence built in a faux-Oriental style that drew on several elements of Indian and Islamic architecture. In this posed piece, one of a series of photos of the Indian "martial races" distributed as postcards and used for slide-show lectures, some men sit playing cards, while others watch. Such photos reassured British and Indians alike that Britain took good care of its loyal imperial soldiers. (© Mary Evans Picture Library/ The Image Works)

The war had a profound impact on these colonial troops. Fighting against and killing Europeans destroyed the impression that the Europeans were superhuman. New concepts like nationalism and individual freedoms—ideals for which the Europeans were supposedly fighting—were carried home to become rallying cries for future liberation struggles.

A crucial turning point in the expanding conflict came in April 1917 when the United States declared war on Germany. American intervention grew out of the war at sea and sympathy for the Triple Entente. At the beginning of the war Britain and France established a naval blockade to strangle the Central Powers. In early 1915 Germany launched a counter-blockade using the new and deadly effective submarine. In May a German submarine sank the British passenger liner *Lusitania* (loo-sih-TAY-nee-uh) (which, besides regular passengers, was secretly and illegally carrying war materials to Britain). More than a thousand people died, including 139 U.S. citizens. President Woodrow Wilson protested vigorously. Germany was forced to restrict its submarine warfare for almost two years or face almost certain war with the United States.

Early in 1917 the German military command—confident that improved submarines could starve Britain into submission before the United States could come to its rescue—resumed unrestricted submarine warfare. This was a reckless gamble. The United States declared war on Germany and eventually tipped the balance in favor of the Triple Entente.

The Home Front

How did total war affect the home fronts of the major combatants?

The war's impact on civilians was no less massive than on the men crouched in trenches. Total war mobilized entire populations, led to increased state power, and promoted social equality. It also led to dissent and a growing antiwar movement.

Mobilizing for Total War

Within months of the outbreak of the First World War, national unity governments began to plan and control economic and social life in order to wage **total war**. Governments imposed rationing, price and wage controls, and even restrictions on workers' freedom of movement. These total-war economies blurred the old distinction between soldiers on battlefields and civil-

ians at home. (See "Analyzing the Evidence: The Experience of War," page 830.) The ability of central governments to manage and control highly complicated economies increased and strengthened their powers, often along socialist lines.

Germany went furthest in developing a planned economy to wage total war. Soon after war began, the Jewish industrialist Walter Rathenau (RAHT-uh-now) convinced the German government to set up the War Raw Materials Board to ration and distribute raw materials. Food was also rationed, and the board successfully produced substitutes, such as synthetic rubber and synthetic nitrates, for scarce war supplies. Following the terrible Battles of Verdun and the Somme in 1916, military leaders forced the Reichstag (RIGHKS-tahg) to accept the Auxiliary Service Law, which required all males between seventeen and sixty to work only at jobs considered critical to the war effort. Women also worked in war factories, mines, and steel mills.

As mature liberal democracies, France and Great Britain mobilized economically for total war less rapidly and less completely than autocratic Germany, aided by the fact that they could import materials from their colonies and from the United States. When it became apparent that the war was not going to end quickly, however, the Western Allies all passed laws giving their governments sweeping powers over all areas of the nation's daily life—including industrial and agricultural production, censorship, education, health and welfare, the curtailment of civil liberties, labor, and foreign aliens.

The Social Impact of War

The social impact of total war was no less profound than the economic impact, though again there were important national variations. The military's insatiable needs—nearly every belligerent power resorted to conscription to put soldiers in the field—created a tremendous demand for workers at home. This situation brought about momentous changes.

One such change was increased power and prestige for labor unions. Unions cooperated with war governments in return for real participation in important decisions. This entry of labor leaders into policymaking councils paralleled the entry of socialist leaders into the war governments.

Women's roles also changed dramatically. In every belligerent country, large numbers of women went to work in industry, transportation, and offices. A former parlor maid reportedly told her boyfriend as he prepared to leave for France:

> While you are at the front firing shells, I am going into a munitions factory to make shells. The job will

total war Practiced by countries fighting in World War I, a war in which the government plans and controls all aspects of economic and social life in order to make the greatest possible military effort.

Women Working at a Munitions Factory These women, working at the Woolwich munitions factory in southeast London, are shoveling thousands of cartridge shells into wooden boxes to be shipped to the front in France. Women worked in munitions factories in all the warring nations, handling highly explosive materials and toxic chemicals and operating dangerous machines. Women's war efforts were rewarded in some countries after the war when they received the right to vote. (© TopFoto/The Image Works)

not be as well paid as domestic service, it will not be as comfortable as domestic service; it will be much harder work, but it will be my bit, and every time you fire your gun you can remember I am helping to make the shells.[7]

Moreover, women became highly visible — not only as munitions workers but as bank tellers, mail carriers, and even police officers. Women also served as nurses and doctors at the front. (See "Individuals in Society: Vera Brittain," page 832.) In general, the war greatly expanded the range of women's activities and changed attitudes toward women. Although at war's end most women were quickly let go and their jobs were given back to the returning soldiers, their many-sided war effort caused Britain, Germany, the United States, and Austria to grant them the right to vote after the war.

Recent scholarship has shown, however, that traditional views of gender — of male roles and female roles — remained remarkably resilient and that there was a significant conservative backlash in the postwar years. Even as the war progressed, many men, particularly soldiers, grew increasingly hostile toward women. Some were angry at mothers, wives, and girlfriends for urging them to enlist and fight in the horrible war. Soldiers with wives and girlfriends back home grew increasingly convinced that they were cheating on them. Others worried that factory or farm jobs had been taken by women and there would be no work when they returned home. Men were also concerned that if women received the vote at war's end, they would vote themselves into power. These concerns, as well as the fear that women would lose their femininity, are reflected in a letter from Private G. F. Wilby,

The Experience of War

World War I was a total war: it enlisted the efforts of male and female adults and children, both at home and on the battlefield. It was a terrifying and painful experience for all those involved, not the romantic endeavor it was purported to be. The documents below offer two different wartime experiences. The first is from a letter written by a German soldier fighting in the trenches. The second is from the diary of a Viennese woman. As you read both passages, think about the different ways war and its consequences were made real for these two people.

A German Soldier Writes from the Trenches, March 1915

■ *Souchez, March 11th, 1915*
"So fare you well, for we must now be parting," so run the first lines of a soldier-song which we often sang through the streets of the capital. These words are truer than ever now, and these lines are to bid farewell to you, to all my nearest and dearest, to all who wish me well or ill, and to all that I value and prize.

Our regiment has been transferred to this dangerous spot, Souchez. No end of blood has already flowed down this hill. A week ago the 142nd attacked and took four trenches from the French. It is to hold these trenches that we have been brought here. There is something uncanny about this hill-position. Already, times without number, other battalions of our regiment have been ordered here in support, and each time the company came back with a loss of twenty, thirty or more men. In the days when we had to stick it out here before, we had 22 killed and 27 wounded. Shells roar, bullets whistle; no dugouts, or very bad ones; mud, clay, filth, shell-holes so deep that one could bathe in them.

This letter has been interrupted no end of times. Shells began to pitch close to us—great English 12-inch ones—and we had to take refuge in a cellar. One such shell struck the next house and buried four men, who were got out from the ruins horribly mutilated. I saw them and it was ghastly!

Everybody must be prepared now for death in some form or other. Two cemeteries have been made up here, the losses have been so great. I ought not to write that to you, but I do so all the same, because the newspapers have probably given you quite a different impression. They tell only of our gains and say nothing about the blood that has been shed, of the cries of agony that never cease. The newspaper doesn't give any description either of *how* the "heroes" are laid to rest, though it talks about "heroes' graves" and writes poems and such-like about them. Certainly in Lens I have attended funeral-parades where a number of dead were buried in one large grave with pomp and circumstance. But up here it is pitiful the way one throws the dead bodies out of the trench and lets them lie there, or scatters dirt over the remains of those which have been torn to pieces by shells.

I look upon death and call upon life. I have not accomplished much in my short life, which has been chiefly occupied with study. I have commended my soul to the Lord God. It bears His seal and is altogether His. Now I am free to dare anything. My future life belongs to God, my present one to the Fatherland, and I myself still possess happiness and strength.

A Viennese Woman Remembers Home-Front Life

■ Ten dekagrammes [3½ ounces] of horse-flesh per head are to be given out to-day for the week. The cavalry horses held in reserve by the military authorities are being slaughtered for lack of fodder, and the people of Vienna are for a change to get a few mouthfuls of meat of which they have so long been deprived. Horse-flesh! I should like to know whether my instinctive repugnance to horse-flesh as food is personal,

serving in East Africa, to his fiancée in London, Ethel Baxter, in August 1918:

> Whatever you do, don't go in Munitions or anything in that line—just fill a Woman's position and remain a woman. . . . I want to return and find the same loveable little woman that I left behind—not a coarse thing more of a man than a woman.[8]

War also promoted social equality, blurring class distinctions and lessening the gap between rich and poor. Greater equality was reflected in full employment, rationing according to physical needs, and a sharing of hardships. Society became more uniform and more egalitarian.

Growing Political Tensions

During the war's first two years, belief in a just cause and patriotic nationalism united soldiers and civilians behind their various national leaders. Each government employed censorship and propaganda to maintain popular support. (See "Analyzing the Evidence: 'Never Forget!'" page 833.)

By spring 1916, however, cracks were appearing under the strain of total war. In April Irish nationalists in Dublin unsuccessfully rose up against British rule in the Easter Rebellion. Strikes and protest marches over inadequate food flared up on every home front. In April 1917 nearly half the French infantry divisions or whether my dislike is shared by many other housewives. My loathing of it is based, I believe, not on a physical but on a psychological prejudice.

I overcame my repugnance, rebuked myself for being sentimental, and left the house. A soft, steady rain was falling, from which I tried to protect myself with galoshes, waterproof, and umbrella. As I left the house before seven o'clock and the meat distribution did not begin until nine o'clock, I hoped to get well to the front of the queue.

No sooner had I reached the neighbourhood of the big market hall than I was instructed by the police to take a certain direction. I estimated the crowd waiting here for a meagre midday meal at two thousand at least. Hundreds of women had spent the night here in order to be among the first and make sure of getting their bit of meat. Many had brought with them improvised seats—a little box or a bucket turned upside down. No one seemed to mind the rain, although many were already wet through. They passed the time chattering, and the theme was the familiar one: What have you had to eat? What are you going to eat? One could scent an atmosphere of mistrust in these conversations: they were all careful not to say too much or to betray anything that might get them into trouble.

At length the sale began. Slowly, infinitely slowly, we moved forward. The most determined, who had spent the night outside the gates of the hall, displayed their booty to the waiting crowd: a ragged, quite freshly slaughtered piece of meat with the characteristic yellow fat. [Others] alarmed those standing at the back by telling them that there was only a very small supply of meat and that not half the people waiting would get a share of it. The crowd became very uneasy and impatient, and before the police on guard could prevent it, those standing in front organized an attack on the hall which the salesmen inside were powerless to repel. Everyone seized whatever he could lay his hands on, and in a few moments all the eatables had vanished. In the confusion stands were overturned, and the police forced back the

aggressors and closed the gates. The crowds waiting outside, many of whom had been there all night and were soaked through, angrily demanded their due, whereupon the mounted police made a little charge, provoking a wild panic and much screaming and cursing. At length I reached home, depressed and disgusted, with a broken umbrella and only one galosh.

We housewives have during the last four years grown accustomed to standing in queues; we have also grown accustomed to being obliged to go home with empty hands and still emptier stomachs. Only very rarely do those who are sent away disappointed give cause for police intervention. On the other hand, it happens more and more frequently that one of the pale, tired women who have been waiting for hours collapses from exhaustion. The turbulent scenes which occurred to-day inside and outside the large market hall seemed to me perfectly natural. In my dejected mood the patient apathy with which we housewives endure seemed to me blameworthy and incomprehensible.

QUESTIONS FOR ANALYSIS

1. What is the soldier's view of the war? Would you characterize the letter as optimistic or pessimistic? Why?
2. What similarities and differences do you see in the experiences of the soldier and the Viennese woman?
3. Why does the Viennese woman describe the housewives as "blameworthy" and "incomprehensible"?

Sources: Alfons Ankenbrand, in *German Students' War Letters*, ed. A. F. Wedd (London: Methuen, 1929), pp. 72–73; *Blockade: The Diary of an Austrian Middle-Class Woman, 1914–1924*, trans. Winifred Ray (New York: Ray Long & Richard Smith, 1932), pp. 63–68.

mutinied for two months after suffering enormous losses in the Second Battle of the Aisne. Later that year there was a massive mutiny of Russian soldiers supporting the revolution.

The Central Powers experienced the most strain. In October 1916 a young socialist assassinated Austria's chief minister. By 1917 German political unity was also collapsing, and prewar social conflicts were re-emerging. A coalition of Socialists and Catholics in the Reichstag called for a compromise "peace without annexations or reparations." Thus Germany, like its ally Austria-Hungary and its enemy France, began to crack in 1917. But it was Russia that collapsed first and saved the Central Powers—for a time.

The Russian Revolution

What factors led to the Russian Revolution, and what was its outcome?

The 1917 Russian Revolution, directly related to the Great War, opened a new era with a radically new prototype of state and society that changed the course of the twentieth century.

The Fall of Imperial Russia

Imperial Russia in 1914 was still predominantly a rural and nonurbanized society. Industrialization came late

INDIVIDUALS IN SOCIETY

Vera Brittain

ALTHOUGH THE GREAT WAR UPENDED millions of lives, it struck Europe's young people with the greatest force. For Vera Brittain (1893–1970), as for so many in her generation, the war became life's defining experience, which she captured forever in her famous autobiography, *Testament of Youth* (1933).

Raised in a wealthy business family in northern England, Brittain bristled at small-town conventions and discrimination against women. She read voraciously and dreamed of being a successful writer. After finishing boarding school and against her father's objections, Brittain passed Oxford's rigorous entry exams and won a scholarship to its women's college. She also fell in love with Roland Leighton, an equally brilliant student from a literary family and the best friend of her younger brother, Edward. All three, along with two more close friends, Victor Richardson and Geoffrey Thurlow, confidently prepared to enter Oxford in late 1914.

But war intervened and Brittain shared with millions of Europeans a thrilling surge of patriotic support for her government. She wrote in her diary that her "great fear" was that England would declare its neutrality and commit the "grossest treachery" toward France.* She supported Roland's decision to enlist, agreeing with her sweetheart's romantic view of war as "very ennobling and very beautiful." Later, exchanging anxious letters with Roland in France in 1915, Brittain began to see the conflict in more personal, human terms, and wondered if any victory or defeat could be worth Roland's life.

Struggling to quell her doubts, Brittain redoubled her commitment to England's cause and volunteered as an army nurse. For the next three years she served with distinction in military hospitals in London, Malta, and northern France, repeatedly torn between the vision of noble sacrifice and the reality of human tragedy. She lost her sexual inhibitions caring for mangled male bodies, and she longed to consummate her love with Roland. Awaiting his return on leave on Christmas Day, 1915, she was greeted instead with a telegram: Roland had been killed two days before.

Roland's death was the first of several devastating blows that eventually overwhelmed Brittain's idealistic patriotism.

Vera Brittain was marked forever by her wartime experiences. (Hulton Archive/ Getty Images)

In 1917 first Geoffrey and then Victor died from gruesome wounds. In early 1918, as the last great German offensive filled her war-zone hospital with maimed and dying German prisoners, the bone-weary Vera felt a common humanity and saw only more victims. Weeks later, her brother Edward died in action. When the war ended, she was, she said, a "complete automaton," with her "deepest emotions paralyzed if not dead."

Returning to Oxford and finishing her studies, Brittain gradually recovered. She formed a deep, restorative friendship with another talented woman writer, Winifred Holtby; published novels and articles; and became a leader in the feminist campaign for gender equality. She also married and had children. But her wartime memories remained. Finally, Brittain succeeded in coming to grips with them in *Testament of Youth*, her powerful antiwar autobiography. The unflinching narrative spoke to the experiences of an entire generation and became a runaway bestseller. Above all, perhaps, Brittain captured the ambivalent, contradictory character of the war, in which millions of young people found excitement, courage, and common purpose but succeeded only in destroying their lives with their superhuman efforts and futile sacrifices. Becoming ever more committed to pacifism, Brittain opposed England's entry into World War II.

QUESTIONS FOR ANALYSIS

1. What were Brittain's initial feelings toward the war? How and why did they change as the conflict continued?
2. Why did Brittain volunteer as a nurse, as many women did? How might wartime nursing have influenced women of her generation?
3. In portraying the ambivalent, contradictory character of World War I for Europe's youth, was Brittain describing the contradictory character of all modern warfare? Explain your answer.

*Quoted in the excellent study by P. Berry and M. Bostridge, *Vera Brittain: A Life* (London: Virago Press, 2001), p. 59; additional quotations are from pp. 80 and 136.

"Never Forget!"

Belgium's neutrality had been guaranteed in the Treaty of London (1839), but when the Schlieffen plan called for Germany to violate this neutrality, the German chancellor famously referred to the treaty as just a "scrap of paper." This 1915 French poster with a passionate headline (meaning "Never Forget!") dramatizes Germany's brutal invasion of Belgium in 1914 and its treatment of civilians. The "Rape of Belgium" featured prominently — and effectively — in anti-German propaganda.

Many historians on both sides at the time and for some time after dismissed the more extreme accounts of the horrors of the invasion as exaggerated Allied propaganda. It is true that British and American propaganda publicists at the time did dwell on gruesome reports of child abuse and the rape and perverse mutilation of women perpetuated by German soldiers more than on accounts of their deliberate acts of arson and destruction of priceless archives, homes, buildings, and factories. Recent scholarship, however, has confirmed that the Germans did commit large-scale atrocities, which would now be considered war crimes, including the extensive abuse and rape of women. It is estimated that in Belgium the Germans were responsible for killing 23,700 civilians, injuring more than 30,000 civilians, and making more than 18,000 children orphans. The Germans also carried out the wanton mass destruction of civilian property, and much of Belgium's industrial infrastucture was either destroyed or looted and taken back to Germany. The "Rape of Belgium," in the opinion of scholars today, was very real.

(© Mary Evans Picture Library/The Image Works)

QUESTIONS FOR ANALYSIS

1. How is neutral Belgium personified? What do you think the artist's purpose was?
2. How did governments use propaganda and other means to unite people for the war effort?

to Russia and, although rapidly expanding, was still in its early stages. Peasants still made up perhaps 80 percent of the population. Besides the royal family and the nobility, the rest of Russian society consisted of the bourgeoisie (the elite, educated upper and middle classes, such as liberal politicians, propertied and professional classes, military officer corps, and landowners) and the proletariat (the urban working class, which remained small, and rank-and-file soldiers and sailors). These two factions contended for power when the tsar abdicated in 1917.

Like their allies and their enemies, Russians embraced war with patriotic enthusiasm in 1914. For a moment Russia was united, but soon the war began to take its toll. Russia quickly exhausted its supplies of shells and ammunition, and better-equipped German armies inflicted terrible losses—1.5 million casualties and nearly 1 million

"The Russian Ruling House" This wartime cartoon captures the ominous, spellbinding power of Rasputin over Tsar Nicholas II and his wife, Alexandra. Rasputin's manipulations disgusted the Russian public and contributed to the monarchy's collapse. (© INTERFOTO/Alamy Stock Photo)

His departure was a fatal turning point. His German-born wife, Tsarina Alexandra, took control of the government and the home front. She tried to rule absolutely in her husband's absence with an uneducated Siberian preacher, Rasputin (ra-SPOO-tin), as her most trusted adviser. In a desperate attempt to right the situation, three members of the high aristocracy murdered Rasputin in December 1916. In this convulsive atmosphere, the government slid steadily toward revolution.

Large-scale strikes, demonstrations, and protest marches were now commonplace, as were bread shortages. On March 8, 1917, a women's bread march in Petrograd (formerly St. Petersburg) started riots, which spread throughout the city. While his ministers fled the city, the tsar ordered that peace be restored, but discipline broke down, and the soldiers and police joined the revolutionary crowd. The Duma declared a provisional government on March 12, 1917. Three days later, Nicholas abdicated.

The Provisional Government

The **March Revolution** was joyfully accepted throughout the country. A new government formed in May 1917, with the understanding that an elected democratic government, ruling under a new constitution drafted by a future Constituent Assembly, would replace it when circumstances permitted. The provisional government established equality before the law; freedom of religion, speech, and assembly; the right of unions to organize and strike; and other classic liberal measures.

The provisional government soon made two fatal decisions, however, that turned the people against it. First, it refused to confiscate large landholdings and give them to peasants, fearing that such drastic action in the countryside would only complete the disintegration of Russia's peasant army. Second, the government decided that the continuation of war was still the all-important national duty and that international alliances had to be honored. Neither decision was popular. The peasants believed that when the tsar's autocratic rule ended, so too did the nobles' title to the land, which was now theirs for the taking. The army believed that the March Revolution meant the end of the war.

captured in 1915 alone. Russian soldiers were sent to the front without rifles; they were told to find their arms among the dead. The Duma (DOO-muh), Russia's lower house of parliament, and *zemstvos* (ZEMST-vohs), local governments, led the effort toward full mobilization on the home front. These efforts improved the military situation, but overall Russia mobilized less effectively for total war than did the other warring nations.

Although limited industrial capacity was a serious handicap in a war against highly industrialized Germany, Russia's real problem was leadership. A kindly, slightly dull-witted man, Tsar Nicholas II (r. 1894–1917) distrusted the moderate Duma and rejected any democratic sharing of power. As a result, the Duma, whose members came from the elite classes, and the popular masses became increasingly critical of the tsar's leadership and the appalling direction of the war. In response, Nicholas (who had no military background) traveled to the front in September 1915 to lead Russia's armies—and thereafter received all the blame for Russian losses.

From its first day, the provisional government had to share power (dual power) with a formidable rival that represented the popular masses — the **Petrograd Soviet** (or council) of Workers' and Soldiers' Deputies, a huge, fluctuating mass organization composed of two to three thousand workers, soldiers, and socialist intellectuals. This counter-government, or half government, issued its own radical orders, further weakening the provisional government. Most famous of these was Army Order No. 1, issued in March 1917, which stripped officers of their authority and gave power to elected committees of common soldiers. (See "Thinking Like a Historian: Russian Views of War and Revolution," page 836.)

Order No. 1 led to a total collapse of army discipline. Peasant soldiers began "voting with their feet," to use Lenin's graphic phrase, returning to their villages to get a share of the land that peasants were seizing from landowners, either through peasant soviets (councils) or by force, in a great agrarian upheaval. Through the summer of 1917, the provisional government, led from July by the socialist Alexander Kerensky, became increasingly more conservative and authoritarian as it tried to maintain law and order and protect property (such as nobles' land and factories). The government was being threatened from one side by an advancing German army and from the other by proletarian forces, urban and rural alike, shouting "All power to the soviets!" and calling for an even more radical revolution.

Lenin and the Bolshevik Revolution

According to most traditional twentieth-century accounts of the two Russian revolutions in 1917 written by both anti-Soviet Russian and Western scholars, in March Russia successfully overthrew the tsar's autocratic rule and replaced it with a liberal, Western-style democracy. Then in November a small group of hardcore radicals, led by Vladimir Lenin, somehow staged a second revolution and installed an atheistic Communist government. More recently, however, and especially since the Soviet archives were opened in the 1990s following the dissolution of the Soviet Union, a different picture has emerged. Scholars are recognizing that the second revolution had widespread popular support and that Lenin was often following events as much as leading them.

Born into the middle class, Vladimir Ilyich Lenin (1870–1924) became an enemy of imperial Russia when his older brother was executed for plotting to kill the tsar in 1887. As a law student Lenin studied Marxist doctrines with religious ferocity. Exiled to Siberia for three years because of socialist agitation, Lenin lived in western Europe after his release for seventeen years and developed his own revolutionary interpretations of Marxist thought (see "The Birth of Socialism" in Chapter 24).

Three interrelated ideas were central for Lenin. First, he stressed that only violent revolution could destroy capitalism. Second, Lenin believed that a socialist revolution was possible even in an agrarian country like Russia. According to classical Marxist theory, a society must reach the capitalist, industrial stage of development before its urban workers, the proletariat, can rise up and create a Communist society. Lenin thought that although Russia's industrial working class was small, the peasants, who made up the bulk of the army and navy, were also potential revolutionaries. Third, Lenin believed that at a given moment revolution was determined more by human leadership than by vast historical laws. He called for a highly disciplined workers' party, strictly controlled by a dedicated elite of intellectuals and full-time revolutionaries like him. This "vanguard of the proletariat" would not stop until revolution brought it to power.

Lenin's ideas did not go unchallenged by other Russian Marxists. At a Social Democratic Labor Party congress in London in 1903, Lenin demanded a small, disciplined, elitist party; his opponents wanted a more democratic party with mass membership. The Russian Marxists split into two rival factions. Because his side won one crucial vote at the congress, Lenin's camp became known as **Bolsheviks**, or "majority group"; his opponents were Mensheviks, or "minority group."

In March 1917 Lenin and nearly all the other leading Bolsheviks were living in exile abroad or in Russia's remotest corners. After the March Revolution, the German government provided safe passage for Lenin from his exile in Switzerland across Germany and back into Russia, hoping he would undermine Russia's sagging war effort. They were not disappointed. Arriving in Petrograd on April 16, Lenin attacked at once, issuing his famous April Theses. To the Petrograd Bolsheviks' great astonishment, he rejected all cooperation with what he called the "bourgeois" provisional government and instead called for exactly what the popular masses themselves were demanding: "All power to the soviets!" and "Peace, Land, Bread!" Bolshevik support increased through the summer, culminating in mass demonstrations in Petrograd on July 16–20 by

March Revolution The first phase of the Russian Revolution of 1917, in which unplanned uprisings led to the abdication of the tsar and the establishment of a provisional democratic government that was then overthrown in November by Lenin and the Bolsheviks.

Petrograd Soviet A counter-government to the 1917 Russian provisional government, this organization was a huge, fluctuating mass meeting of two to three thousand workers, soldiers, and socialist intellectuals.

Bolsheviks The "majority group"; this was Lenin's camp of the Russian party of Marxist socialism.

Russian Views of War and Revolution

The provisional government's fatal decision to continue the war to protect Mother Russia after Tsar Nicholas's abdication was initially greeted with some enthusiasm. As casualties continued to mount, however, the Russian army turned against Alexander Kerensky and his government. By the summer of 1917 women and children were being recruited as soldiers, the countryside was in turmoil, and the army was in open rebellion.

1 **U.S. Army, intelligence report on conditions of the troops at the front, October 2–13, 1917.** After America entered the war in April 1917, intelligence reports about the war were more important than ever. In late summer to early fall of 1917 the U.S. Army intelligence service reported that the majority of Russian soldiers had abandoned all loyalty to the provisional government and had lost all respect for its authority.

■ *Northern Front.* The situation in the army has not changed and may be described as a complete lack of confidence in the officers and the higher commanding personnel. The belief is growing among the soldiers that they cannot be punished for what they do.... The influence of Bolshevik ideas is spreading very rapidly. To this must be added a general weariness, an irritability, and a desire for peace at any price....

12th Army. The press of the political parties is no longer influencing the soldier masses. Again and again one hears the orders of the Provisional Government severely criticized. The committee of the 95th Regiment...declared Kerensky a traitor....

Apart from the Bolshevik not a single [political] movement has any popularity. Those who read moderate newspapers are looked upon as [followers of the] "bourgeoisie" and "counter-revolutionists." An intensive agitation is being conducted in favor of an immediate cessation of military operations on all fronts. Whenever a whole regiment or battalion refuses to carry out a military order, the fact is immediately made known to other parts of the army through special agitators....

Western Front.... Because of general war weariness, bad nourishment, mistrust of officers, etc., there has developed an intense defeatist agitation accompanied by refusals to carry out orders, threats to the commanding personnel, and attempts to fraternize with Germans. Everywhere one hears voices calling for immediate peace, because, they say, no one will stay in the trenches during the winter.... [The rank and file hold] a deep-rooted conviction...that fraternization with the enemy is a sure way of attaining peace....

The following general conclusions may be drawn from the reports of the commissars: The approaching winter campaign has accelerated the disintegration of the army and increased the longing for peace. It is necessary to leave nothing undone which might supply the soldiers with food, shoes, and winter clothing; to see that the army is reduced in numbers; to improve the discipline in the reserve regiments. Otherwise the ranks will be filled with such material as will lead to the complete demoralization and destruction of the army.

2 **Rural landowners, letter on revolt in the Russian countryside, June 1917.** In June 1917, following the March Revolution and the abdication of the tsar, landowners in a rural county in the Russian countryside sent this memorandum on the current situation to the Chief Land Committee in Petrograd. It reports that the peasants are taking the issue of land and agricultural reform into their own hands, rather than waiting for action by the provisional government.

■ The old men, the sick, and the women remaining in the countryside have accepted the overthrow calmly, and consider it to be the result of the Tsar's foolish management of the country. It might have been expected that the demand for a social revolution would not penetrate into the countryside soon and would at first remain only the demand of the army and the workers. But the replacement of the entire local administration, the elimination of the police and the usual authorities in the villages, and the amnesty granted criminals hastened the advent of the revolution....

ANALYZING THE EVIDENCE

1. According to the U.S. Army's report in Source 1, what problems did the Russian military leadership face in early October 1917? How were these problems related to political events in Russia at the time?
2. What was the peasants' main concern in the countryside, as described in the landowners' letter in Source 2? How did the peasants handle this issue?
3. What were the Petrograd Garrison's major demands, as outlined in the resolutions in Source 3? How did these reflect Lenin and the Bolsheviks' revolutionary principles?
4. How might the recruitment of child soldiers, like those shown in Source 4, have affected the morale of the Russian people and their support for the war at home and at the front?
5. Why would the provisional government specifically recruit all-female combat units, as in Source 5? What effect might their presence on the battlefield have had on the male troops?

The county committee destroyed the right to property, the right to the management and use of one's belongings, contractual rights, without first consulting the landowners. Thus the county committee lowered rental prices on land by 25 per cent. . . . The district committee went even further and lowered prices by 60 per cent. In some localities the peasants seized the land free.

3 **Resolutions of the Petrograd Garrison, November 1917.** On November 3, at a meeting of the Petrograd Soviet, which Trotsky attended, the Petrograd military garrison passed resolutions that sound like a Bolshevik revolutionary manifesto.

■ Welcoming all the decisions of the Petrograd Soviet the Petrograd Garrison hereby declares:

The time for words is past. The country is on the verge of ruin. The army demands peace, the peasants land, and the workers bread and work. The Coalition Government is against the people. It became the tool of the enemies of the people. The time for words is past. The All-Russian Congress of Soviets must take the power into its own hands in order to give to the people peace, land, and bread. Only thus can the safety of the revolution and of the people be insured.

All power to the Soviets!
An immediate armistice on all fronts!
The land to the peasants!
An honest and prompt convocation of the Constituent Assembly!

The Petrograd Garrison gives its solemn promise to place at the disposal of the All-Russian Congress its entire strength even to the last man.

You may count on us—you who are the legitimate representatives of the soldiers, workers, and peasants. We are all at our posts ready *to conquer or to die!*

4 **Boy soldiers of the Russian army, ca. 1917.** Eager young boys have always lied about their age to serve in wars, and boy soldiers fought for all the opposing forces in the Great War. Usually, however, they were sent home when discovered. Toward the end of the war, Russia sent young boys off to fight in their exhausted and depleted armies.

(Private Collection/Peter Newark Military Pictures/Bridgeman Images)

(Private Collection/The Stapleton Collection/Bridgeman Images)

5 **First Russian Women's Battalion of Death, 1917** After the March Revolution overthrew Tsar Nicholas, the provisional government tried to rally the exhausted Russian soldiers by creating all-female combat units. They were known as the Battalions of Death because they were expected to lead the way into battle.

PUTTING IT ALL TOGETHER

Using the sources above, along with what you have learned in class and in this chapter, write a short essay about the state of Russian society in late summer to early fall of 1917. Why might the majority of Russians have been ready for another revolution? What major issues—economic, social, the war, government—were the people most upset about?

Sources: (1) James Bunyan and H. H. Fisher, *The Bolshevik Revolution, 1917–1918: Documents and Materials* (Stanford, Calif.: Stanford University Press, 1934), pp. 24–25; (2) Thomas Riha, ed., *Readings in Russian Civilization,* 2d ed. Vol. 3: *Soviet Russia, 1917–1963* (Chicago: University of Chicago Press, 1969): pp. 507, 509. (3) Bunyan and Fisher, *The Bolshevik Revolution,* p. 79.

Lenin and Stalin at Lenin's Country House at Gorki
This controversial photo, supposedly taken by Lenin's sister in 1922, two years before Lenin's death, has stirred much scholarly debate. Some argue that Stalin had himself airbrushed into the photo later to support his claim as Lenin's legitimate successor. Even if the photo is authentic, it appears to have been retouched later, on Stalin's orders, to clear his severely pockmarked face; to make his shorter and stiffer left arm, injured in a childhood accident, appear normal; and to make him taller (he was only 5 feet 4 inches tall) and larger than the smaller and more passive-looking Lenin. (Gorki Haynes Archive/Popperfoto/Getty Images)

soldiers, sailors, and workers. Lenin and the Bolshevik Central Committee had not planned these demonstrations and were completely unprepared to support them. Nonetheless, the provisional government labeled Lenin and other leading Bolsheviks traitors and ordered them arrested. Lenin had to flee to Finland.

Meanwhile, however, the provisional government itself was collapsing. The coalition between liberals and socialists was breaking apart as their respective power bases—bourgeoisie and proletariat—demanded they move further to the right or left. Prime Minister Kerensky's unwavering support for the war lost him all credit with the army, the only force that might have saved him and democratic government in Russia. In early September an attempted right-wing military coup failed as Petrograd workers organized themselves as Red Guards to defend the city and then convinced the coup's soldiers to join them. Lenin, from his exile in Finland, now called for an armed Bolshevik insurrection before the Second All-Russian Congress of Soviets met in early November.

In October the Bolsheviks gained a fragile majority in the Petrograd Soviet. Lenin did not return to Russia until mid-October and even then remained in hiding. It was Lenin's supporter Leon Trotsky (1879–1940)

who brilliantly executed the Bolshevik seizure of power. On November 6 militant Trotsky followers joined with trusted Bolshevik soldiers to seize government buildings and arrest provisional government members. That evening Lenin came out of hiding and took control of the revolution. The following day revolutionary forces seized the Winter Palace, and Kerensky capitulated. At the Congress of Soviets, a Bolshevik majority declared that all power had passed to the soviets and named Lenin head of the new government.

The Bolsheviks came to power for three key reasons. First, by late 1917 democracy had given way to anarchy as the popular masses no longer supported the provisional government. Second, in Lenin and Trotsky the Bolsheviks had truly superior leaders who were utterly determined to provoke a Marxist revolution. Third, the Bolsheviks appealed to soldiers, urban workers, and peasants who were exhausted by war and eager for socialism.

Dictatorship and Civil War

The Bolsheviks' true accomplishment was not taking power but keeping it and conquering the chaos they had helped create. Once again, Lenin was able to profit from developments over which he and the Bolsheviks had no control. Since summer 1917 an unstoppable peasant revolution had swept across Russia, as peasants divided among themselves the estates of the landlords and the church. Thus Lenin's first law, which supposedly gave land to the peasants, actually merely approved what peasants were already doing. Lenin then met urban workers' greatest demand with a decree giving local workers' committees direct control of individual factories.

The Bolsheviks proclaimed their regime a "provisional workers' and peasants' government," promising that a freely elected Constituent Assembly would draw up a new constitution. However, when Bolshevik delegates won fewer than one-fourth of the seats in free elections in November, the Constituent Assembly was permanently disbanded by Bolshevik soldiers acting under Lenin's orders.

Lenin then moved to make peace with Germany, at any price. That price was very high. Germany demanded the Soviet government surrender all its western territories in the Treaty of Brest-Litovsk (BREHST lih-TAWFSK) in March 1918. With Germany's defeat eight months later, the treaty was nullified, but it allowed Lenin time to escape the disaster of continued war and pursue his goal of absolute political power for the Bolsheviks—now renamed Communists—within Russia.

The war's end and the demise of the democratically elected Constituent Assembly revealed Bolshevik rule as a dictatorship. "Long live the [democratic] soviets; down with the Bolsheviks" became a popular slogan. Officers of the old army organized so-called White opposition to the Bolsheviks in southern Russia, Ukraine, Siberia, and west of Petrograd and plunged the country into civil war from November 1917 to October 1922. The Whites came from many political factions and were united only by their hatred of the Bolsheviks—the Reds. In almost five years of fighting, 125,000 Reds and 175,000 Whites and Poles were killed before the Red Army, formed in March 1918 under Trotsky's command, claimed final victory.

The Bolsheviks' Red Army won for several reasons. Strategically, they controlled the center, while the disunited Whites attacked from the fringes. Moreover, the Whites' poorly defined political program failed to unite all of the Bolsheviks' foes under a progressive democratic banner. Most important, the Communists developed a better army, against which the divided Whites were no match.

The Bolsheviks also mobilized the home front. Establishing **War Communism**—the application of the total-war concept to a civil conflict—they seized grain from peasants, introduced rationing, nationalized all banks and industry, and required everyone to work. Although these measures contributed to a breakdown of normal economic activity, they also served to maintain labor discipline and to keep the Red Army supplied.

Revolutionary terror also contributed to the Communist victory. The old tsarist secret police was re-established as the Cheka (CHEHK-kah), which hunted down and executed thousands of real or supposed foes, including the tsar and his family. During the so-called Red Terror of 1918–1920, the Cheka sowed fear, silenced opposition, and executed an estimated 250,000 "class enemies."

Finally, foreign military intervention in the civil war ended up helping the Communists. The Allies sent troops to prevent war materiel that they had sent to the provisional government from being captured by the Germans. After the Soviet government nationalized all foreign-owned factories without compensation and refused to pay foreign debts, Western governments began to support White armies. While these efforts did little to help the Whites' cause, they did permit the Communists to appeal to the ethnic Russians' patriotic nationalism.

The Russian Civil War, 1917–1922

- Ceded after Treaty of Brest-Litovsk, 1918
- Bolshevik territory, 1919
- Occupied by Allies, 1919
- → White Army forces
- — Boundary of U.S.S.R., 1921

KEY EVENTS OF THE RUSSIAN REVOLUTION

1914	Russia enters World War I
1916–1917	Tsarist government in crisis
March 1917	March Revolution; Duma declares a provisional government; tsar abdicates; Petrograd Soviet issues Army Order No. 1
April 1917	Lenin returns from exile
October 1917	Bolsheviks gain a majority in the Petrograd Soviet
November 7, 1917	Bolsheviks seize power; Lenin named head of new Bolshevik government
1917–1922	Civil war
March 1918	Treaty of Brest-Litovsk; Trotsky becomes head of the Red Army
1922	Civil war ends; Lenin and the Bolshevik Communists take control of Russia

War Communism The application of the total-war concept to a civil conflict; the Bolsheviks seized grain from peasants, introduced rationing, nationalized all banks and industry, and required everyone to work.

The War's Consequences

What were the global consequences of the First World War?

In spring 1918 the Germans launched their last major attack against France and failed. A defeated Germany finally ageed to an armistice on November 11, following ones already signed by the Austrian-Hungarian (November 3) and Ottoman (October 30) leaders. All three monarchies fell and their empires broke apart. In January 1919 the victorious Western Allies came together in Paris hoping to establish a lasting peace.

Laboring intensively, the Allies soon worked out peace terms with Germany, created the peacekeeping League of Nations, and reorganized eastern Europe and southwest Asia. The 1919 peace settlement, however, failed to establish a lasting peace or to resolve the issues that had brought the world to war. World War I and the treaties that ended it shaped the course of the twentieth century, often in horrible ways. Surely this was the ultimate tragedy of the Great War that cost $332 billion and left 10 million people dead and another 20 million wounded.

The End of the War

Peace and an end to the war did not come easily. Victory over revolutionary Russia had temporarily boosted sagging German morale, and in spring 1918 the German army attacked France once more. The German offensive was turned back in July at the Second Battle of the Marne, where 140,000 fresh American soldiers saw action. Adding 2 million men in arms to the war effort by August, the late but massive American intervention decisively tipped the scales in favor of Allied victory.

By September British, French, and American armies were advancing steadily on all fronts. On October 4 the German emperor formed a new, more liberal German government to sue for peace. As negotiations over an armistice dragged on, the frustrated German people rose up. On November 3 sailors in Kiel (KEEL) mutinied, and throughout northern Germany soldiers and workers established revolutionary councils on the Russian soviet model. With army discipline collapsing, Kaiser Wilhelm abdicated and fled to Holland. Socialist leaders in Berlin proclaimed a German republic on November 9 and agreed to tough Allied terms of surrender. The armistice went into effect at 11 o'clock on November 11, 1918.

The Paris Peace Treaties

Seventy delegates from twenty-seven nations attended the opening of the Paris Peace Conference at the Versailles (vayr-SIGH) Palace on January 18, 1919. By August 1920 five major treaties with the defeated powers had been agreed upon. The most well-known, the Treaty of Versailles, laid out peace terms with Germany and also included the Covenant of the League of Nations and an article establishing the International Labour Organization. The conference also yielded a number of minor treaties, unilateral declarations, bilateral treaties, and League of Nations mandates (Map 28.4). The delegates had met with great expectations. A young British diplomat later wrote that the victors "were journeying to Paris . . . to found a new order in Europe. We were preparing not Peace only, but Eternal Peace."[9]

This idealism was strengthened by President Wilson's January 1918 peace proposal, his Fourteen Points. Wilson stressed national self-determination and the rights of small countries and called for the creation of a **League of Nations**, a permanent international organization designed to protect member states from aggression and avert future wars.

The real powers at the conference were the "Big Three": the United States, Great Britain, and France. Germany and Russia were excluded, and Italy's role was limited. President Wilson wanted to immediately deal with the establishment of a League of Nations, while Prime Ministers Lloyd George of Great Britain and, especially, Georges Clemenceau (klem-uhn-soh) of France were primarily concerned with punishing Germany.

Although personally inclined to make a somewhat moderate peace with Germany, Lloyd George felt pressured for a victory worthy of the sacrifices of total war. As Rudyard Kipling summed up the general British feeling at war's end, the Germans were "a people with the heart of beasts."[10] For his part, Clemenceau wanted revenge and lasting security for France, which, he believed, required the creation of a buffer state between France and Germany, Germany's permanent demilitarization, and vast German reparations. Wilson, supported by Lloyd George, would hear none of this. In the end, Clemenceau agreed to a compromise, abandoning the French demand for a Rhineland buffer state in return for a formal defensive alliance with the United States and Great Britain.

On June 28, 1919, in the great Hall of Mirrors at Versailles (where Germany had forced France to sign the armistice ending the Franco-Prussian War), German representatives of the ruling moderate Social Democrats and the Catholic Party reluctantly signed the treaty.

League of Nations A permanent international organization established during the 1919 Paris Peace Conference to protect member states from aggression and avert future wars.

MAPPING THE PAST

MAP 28.4 Territorial Changes in Europe After World War I The Great War brought tremendous changes to eastern Europe. Empires were shattered, new nations were established, and a dangerous power vacuum was created by the relatively weak states established between Germany and Soviet Russia.

ANALYZING THE MAP What territory did Germany lose, and to whom? What new independent states were formed from the old Russian Empire?

CONNECTIONS How were the principles of national self-determination applied to the redrawing of Europe after the war? Did this theory work out?

Germany's African colonies were mandated to Great Britain, France, South Africa, and Belgium. Germany's hold over the Shandong Peninsula in China passed to Japan, provoking an eruption of outrage among Chinese nationalists (see "The Rise of Nationalist China" in Chapter 29). Germany's territorial losses within Europe were minor: Alsace-Lorraine was returned to France, and parts of Germany were ceded to the new Polish state (see Map 28.4). The treaty limited Germany's army to one hundred thousand men and allowed no new military fortifications in the Rhineland.

More harshly, the Allies demanded that Germany (with Austria) accept responsibility for the war and pay reparations equal to all civilian damages caused by the war, although the Allies left the actual reparations figure to be set at a later date when tempers had cooled. These much-criticized "war-guilt" and "reparations" clauses reflected British and French popular demands for revenge, but were bitterly resented by the German people.

The **Treaty of Versailles** and the other agreements reached in Paris were seen as the first steps toward re-establishing international order, albeit ones that favored the victorious Allies, and they would have far-reaching consequences for the remainder of the twentieth century and beyond.

In eastern Europe, Poland regained its independence (see Map 19.1), and the independent states of Austria, Hungary, Czechoslovakia, and a larger Romania were created out of the Austro-Hungarian Empire (see Map 28.4). A greatly expanded Serbian monarchy united Slavs in the western Balkans and took the name Yugoslavia.

Promises of independence made to Arab leaders were largely brushed aside, and Britain and France extended their power in the Middle East, taking advantage of the breakup of the Ottoman Empire. As League of Nations mandates, the French received Lebanon and Syria, and Britain took Iraq and Palestine. Palestine was to include a Jewish national homeland first promised by Britain in 1917 in the Balfour Declaration (see "Nationalist Movements in the Middle East" in Chapter 29). Only Hussein's Arab kingdom of Hejaz (hee-JAZ) received independence. These Allied acquisitions, although officially League of Nations mandates, were simply colonialism under another name. They left colonized peoples in the Middle East, Asia (see Chapter 29), and Africa bitterly disappointed and demonstrated that the age of Western and Eastern imperialism lived on.

Treaty of Versailles The 1919 peace settlement that ended World War I; it declared Germany responsible for the war, limited Germany's army to one hundred thousand men, and forced Germany to pay huge reparations.

American Rejection of the Versailles Treaty

The 1919 peace settlement was not perfect, but for war-shattered Europe it was an acceptable beginning. Moreover, Allied leaders wanted a quick settlement for another reason: they detested Lenin and feared his Bolshevik Revolution might spread. The remaining problems could be worked out in the future.

Such hopes were dashed, however, when the United States quickly reverted to its prewar preferences for isolationism and the U.S. Senate, led by Republican Henry Cabot Lodge, rejected the Versailles treaty on November 19, 1919. Wilson obstinately rejected all attempts at compromise on the treaty, ensuring that it would never be ratified in any form and that the United States would never join the League of Nations. Moreover, the Senate refused to ratify Wilson's defensive alliance with France and Great Britain. Using U.S. action as an excuse, Great Britain also refused to ratify its defensive alliance with France. Betrayed by its allies, France stood alone, and the great hopes of early 1919 had turned to ashes by year's end.

The Search for Peace and Political Stability, 1919–1929

How did leaders deal with the political dimensions of uncertainty and try to re-establish peace and prosperity in the interwar years?

The pursuit of real and lasting peace in the first half of the interwar years proved difficult for many reasons. Germany hated the Treaty of Versailles. France was fearful and isolated. Britain was undependable, and the United States had turned its back on Europe's problems. Eastern Europe was in ferment, and no one could predict Communist Russia's future. Moreover, the international economic situation was poor and was greatly complicated by war debts and disrupted patterns of trade. Yet for a time, from 1925 to late 1929, it appeared that peace and stability were within reach.

Germany and the Western Powers

Nearly all Germans and many other observers immediately and for decades after believed the Versailles treaty represented a harsh dictated peace and should be revised or repudiated as soon as possible. Many right-wing Germans, including Adolf Hitler, believed there had been no defeat; instead they believed German soldiers had been betrayed (*Dolchstoss*—"stabbed in the back") by liberals, Marxists, Jews, and other "November criminals" who had surrendered in order to seize power.

Historians have recently begun to reassess the treaty's terms, however, and many scholars currently view them as relatively reasonable. They argue that much of the German anger toward the Allies was based more on perception than reality. With the collapse of Austria-Hungary, the dissolution of the Ottoman Empire, and the revolution in Russia, Germany emerged from the war an even stronger power in eastern Europe than before, and an economically stronger and more populated nation than France or Great Britain. Moreover, when contrasted with the extremely harsh Treaty of Brest-Litovsk that Germany had forced on Lenin's Russia, and the peace terms Germany had intended to impose on the Allies if it won the war, the Versailles treaty was far from being a vindictive and crippling peace. Had it been, Germany could hardly have become the economic and military juggernaut that it was only twenty years later.

This is not to say, however, that France did not seek some degree of revenge on Germany for both the Franco-Prussian War (see "Bismarck and German Unification" and Map 24.3 in Chapter 24) and the Great War. Most of the war on the western front had been fought on French soil. The expected reconstruction costs and the amount of war debts France owed to the United States were staggering. Thus the French believed that heavy German reparations were an economic necessity that could hold Germany down indefinitely and would enable France to realize its goal of security.

The British felt differently. Prewar Germany had been Great Britain's second-best market, and after the war a healthy, prosperous Germany appeared to be essential to the British economy. In addition, the British were suspicious of France's army—the largest in Europe—and the British and French were at odds over their League of Nations mandates in the Middle East.

While France and Britain drifted in different directions, the Allied reparations commission completed its work and announced in April 1921 that Germany had to pay the enormous sum of 132 billion gold marks ($33 billion) in annual installments of 2.5 billion gold marks. The young German republic—known as the Weimar Republic—made its first reparations

French Occupation of the Ruhr, 1923–1925

payment in that year. Then in 1922, wracked by rapid inflation and political assassinations, and motivated by hostility and arrogance as well, the Weimar Republic announced its inability to pay more and proposed a reparations moratorium for three years.

The British were willing to accept a moratorium, but the French were not. Led by their prime minister, Raymond Poincaré (pwan-kah-RAY) (1860–1934), the French decided they had to either call Germany's bluff or see the entire peace settlement dissolve to their great disadvantage. In January 1923 French and Belgian armies occupied the Ruhr (ROO-uhr) district, industrial Germany's heartland, creating the most serious international crisis of the 1920s.

Strengthened by a wave of patriotism, the German government ordered the people of the Ruhr to stop working and to resist French occupation nonviolently. The French responded by sealing off not only the Ruhr but also the entire Rhineland from the rest of Germany, letting in only enough food to prevent starvation.

By summer 1923 France and Germany were engaged in a great test of wills. French armies could not collect reparations from striking workers at gunpoint. But French occupation was paralyzing Germany and its economy, and the German government was soon forced to print money to pay its bills. Prices soared, and German money rapidly lost all value. In 1919 one American dollar equaled nine German marks; by November 1923 it took over 4.2 trillion German marks to purchase one American dollar. As retired and middle-class people saw their savings wiped out, many Germans felt betrayed. They hated and blamed for their misfortune the Western governments, their own government, big business, the Jews, the workers, and the Communists. The crisis left them psychologically prepared to follow radical right-wing leaders.

In August 1923, as the mark's value fell and political unrest grew throughout Germany, Gustav Stresemann (GOOS-tahf SHTRAY-zuh-mahn) (1878–1929) became German chancellor. Stresemann adopted a compromising attitude. He called off the peaceful resistance campaign in the Ruhr and in October agreed in principle to pay reparations but asked first for a re-examination of Germany's ability to pay. Poincaré accepted. Thus, after five years of hostility and tension, Germany and France, with British and American help, decided to try compromise and cooperation.

Hope in Foreign Affairs

In 1924 an international committee of financial experts headed by American banker Charles G. Dawes met to re-examine reparations. Under the terms of the resulting **Dawes Plan** (1924), Germany's yearly reparations were reduced and linked to the level of German economic prosperity. Germany would also receive large loans from the United States to promote German recovery, as well as to pay reparations to France and Britain, thus enabling those countries to repay the large sums they owed the United States. This circular flow of international payments was complicated and risky, but it worked for a while, facilitating a worldwide economic recovery in the late 1920s.

This economic settlement was matched by a political settlement. In 1925 European leaders met in Locarno, Switzerland. Germany and France solemnly pledged to accept their common border, and both Britain and Italy agreed to fight either France or Germany if one invaded the other. Stresemann also agreed to settle boundary disputes with Poland and Czechoslovakia by peaceful means, and France promised those countries military aid if Germany attacked them. Other developments also strengthened hopes for international peace. In 1926 Germany joined the League of Nations, and in 1928 fifteen countries signed the Kellogg-Briand Pact. The signing nations "condemned and renounced war as an instrument of national policy."

The pact fostered the cautious optimism of the late 1920s and also encouraged the hope that the United States would accept its international responsibilities.

Hope in Democratic Government

European domestic politics also offered reason for hope. During the Ruhr occupation and the great inflation, Germany's republican government appeared ready to collapse. But the moderate businessmen who tended to dominate the various German coalition governments believed that economic prosperity demanded good relations with the Western powers, and they supported parliamentary government at home. Elections were held regularly, and as the economy boomed in the aftermath of the Dawes Plan, republican democracy appeared to have growing support among a majority of Germans.

There were, however, sharp political divisions in the country. Many unrepentant nationalists and monarchists populated the right and the army. In November 1923 an obscure politician named Adolf Hitler, who had become leader of an obscure workers party, the National Socialist German Workers Party, in July 1921, proclaimed a "national socialist revolution" in a Munich beer hall. Hitler's plot to seize government control was poorly organized and easily crushed. Hitler was sentenced to prison, where he outlined his theories and program in his book **Mein Kampf** (*My Struggle*, 1925). Members of Germany's Communist Party received directions from Moscow, and they accused the Social Democrats of betraying the revolution. The working classes were divided politically, but a majority supported the socialist, but nonrevolutionary, Social Democrats.

France's situation was similar to Germany's. Communists and socialists battled for the workers' support. After 1924 the democratically elected government rested mainly in the hands of moderate coalitions, and business interests were well represented. France's great accomplishment was the rapid rebuilding of its war-torn northern region, and good times prevailed until 1930.

Britain, too, faced challenges after 1920. The great problem was unemployment, which hovered around 12 percent throughout the 1920s. The state provided unemployment benefits and a range of additional social services. These and other measures kept living standards from seriously declining, defused class tensions, and pointed the way to the welfare state Britain established after World War II.

The wartime trend toward greater social equality also continued, helping to maintain social harmony. Relative social harmony was accompanied by the rise of the Labour Party, which, under Prime Minister Ramsay MacDonald (1866–1937), governed the country in 1924 and 1929–1935. The Labour Party sought a gradual and democratic move toward socialism, so that the middle classes were not overly frightened as the working classes won new benefits.

The British Conservatives under Stanley Baldwin (1867–1947) showed the same compromising spirit on social issues, and Britain experienced only limited social unrest in the 1920s and 1930s. In 1922 Britain granted southern, Catholic Ireland full autonomy after a bitter guerrilla war, thereby removing another source of prewar friction. Thus developments in both international relations and domestic politics gave the leading democracies cause for cautious optimism in the late 1920s.

Dawes Plan The product of the 1924 World War I reparations commission, accepted by Germany, France, and Britain, that reduced Germany's yearly reparations, made payment dependent on German economic prosperity, and granted Germany large loans from the United States to promote recovery.

Mein Kampf Adolf Hitler's autobiography, published in 1925, which also contains Hitler's political ideology.

existentialism The name given to a highly diverse and even contradictory philosophy that stresses the meaninglessness of existence and the search for moral values in a world of terror and uncertainty.

The Age of Anxiety

In what ways were the anxieties of the postwar world expressed or heightened by revolutionary ideas in modern thought, art, and science and in new forms of communication?

Many people hoped that happier times would return after the war, along with the familiar prewar ideals of peace, prosperity, and progress. The war had caused such social, economic, and psychological upheaval, however, that great numbers of men and women felt themselves increasingly adrift in an age of anxiety and continual crisis.

Uncertainty in Philosophy and Religion

Before 1914 most people in the West still believed in Enlightenment philosophies of progress, reason, and individual rights. As the century began, progress was a daily reality, apparent in the rising living standard, the taming of the city, the spread of political rights to women and workers, and the growth of state-supported social programs. Just as there were laws of science, many thinkers felt, there were laws of society that rational human beings could discover and wisely act on. Even before the war, however, some philosophers, such as the German Friedrich Nietzsche (NEE-chuh) (1844–1900), called such faith in reason into question. The First World War accelerated the revolt against established philosophical certainties. Logical positivism, often associated with Austrian philosopher Ludwig Wittgenstein (VIHT-guhn-shtighn) (1889–1951), rejected most concerns of traditional philosophy—from God's existence to the meaning of happiness—as nonsense and argued that life must be based on facts and observation. Others looked to **existentialism** for answers. Highly diverse and even contradictory, existential thinkers were loosely united in a search for moral values in a terrifying and uncertain world. They did not believe that a supreme being had established humanity's fundamental nature and given life its meaning. In the words of the French existentialist Jean-Paul Sartre (1905–1980), "Man's existence precedes his essence. . . . To begin with he is nothing. He will not be anything until later, and then he will be what he makes of himself."[11]

In contrast, the loss of faith in human reason and in continual progress led to a renewed interest in Christianity. After World War I several thinkers and theologians began to revitalize Christian fundamentals, and intellectuals increasingly turned to religion between about 1920 and 1950. Sometimes described as Christian existentialists because they shared the loneliness and despair of atheistic existentialists, these believers felt that religion was one meaningful answer to terror and anxiety. In the words of a famous Roman Catholic convert, English novelist Graham Greene, "One began to believe in heaven because one believed in hell."[12]

The New Physics

For people no longer committed to traditional religious beliefs, a belief in unchanging natural laws offered some comfort. These laws seemed to determine physical processes and permit useful solutions to more and more problems. A series of discoveries beginning around the turn of the century, however, challenged the established certainties of Newtonian physics (see "Newton's Synthesis" in Chapter 19).

An important first step toward the new physics was the British physicist J. J. Thomson's 1897 discovery of subatomic particles, which proved that atoms were not stable and unbreakable. The following year Polish-born physicist Marie Curie (1867–1934) and her French husband, Pierre (1859–1906), discovered radium and demonstrated that it constantly emits subatomic particles and thus does not have a constant atomic weight. Building on this, German physicist Max Planck (1858–1947) showed in 1900 that subatomic energy is emitted in uneven little spurts, which he called "quanta," and not in a steady stream, as previously believed.

In 1905 the German-Jewish genius Albert Einstein (1879–1955) further undermined Newtonian physics. His theory of special relativity postulated that time and space are relative to the observer's viewpoint and that only the speed of light is constant for all frames of reference in the universe. In addition, Einstein's theory that matter and energy are interchangeable and that even a particle of matter contains enormous levels of potential energy, would later become the scientific basis for the atomic bomb.

The 1920s opened the "heroic age of physics," in the apt words of one of its leading pioneers, Ernest Rutherford (1871–1937). In 1919 Rutherford first split the atom. Breakthrough followed breakthrough, but some discoveries raised new doubts about reality. In 1927 German physicist Werner Heisenberg (VEHR-nuhr HIGH-zuhn-burg) theorized his "uncertainty principle," whereby any act of measurement in quantum physics is affected by, and blurred by, the experimenter. Thus, if experiments in an exact science like physics can be distorted by human observation, what other areas of human knowledge are similarly affected? Is ultimate truth unknowable?

The implications of the new theories and discoveries were disturbing to millions of people in the 1920s and 1930s. The new universe was strange and troubling, and, moreover, science appeared distant from human experience and human problems.

Unlocking the Power of the Atom Many of the fanciful visions of science fiction came true in the twentieth century, although not exactly as first imagined. This 1927 cartoon satirizes a professor who has split the atom and has unwittingly destroyed his building and neighborhood in the process. In the Second World War scientists harnessed the atom in bombs and decimated faraway cities and their inhabitants. (© Mary Evans Picture Library/The Image Works)

En amerikansk tecknares bekymmer för framtiden.

Då professorn äntligen efter årslånga experiment lyckades sönderdela en atom.

Freudian Psychology

With physics presenting an uncertain universe so unrelated to ordinary human experience, questions about the power and potential of the human mind assumed special significance. The findings and speculations of psychologist Sigmund Freud (1856–1939) were particularly disturbing.

Before Freud, most psychologists assumed that human behavior resulted from rational thinking by the conscious mind. By analyzing dreams and hysteria, Freud developed a very different view of the human psyche. Freud concluded that human behavior was governed by three parts of the self: the **id**, **ego**, and **superego**. The primitive, irrational unconscious, which he called the id, was driven by sexual, aggressive, and pleasure-seeking desires and was locked in constant battle with the mind's two other parts: the rationalizing conscious—the ego—which mediates what a person can do, and ingrained moral values—the superego—which specify what a person should do. Thus, for Freud, human behavior was a product of a fragile compromise between instinctual drives and the controls of rational thinking and moral values.

id, ego, superego Freudian terms for the primitive, irrational unconscious (id), the rationalizing conscious that mediates what a person can do (ego), and the ingrained moral values that specify what a person should do (superego).

modernism A variety of cultural movements at the end of the nineteenth century and beginning of the twentieth that rebelled against traditional forms and conventions of the past.

Twentieth-Century Literature

Western literature was also influenced by the general intellectual climate of pessimism, relativism, and alienation. In the twentieth century many writers adopted the limited, often confused viewpoint of a single individual. Like Freud, these novelists focused on the complexity and irrationality of the human mind.

Some novelists used the stream-of-consciousness technique with its reliance on internal monologues to explore the psyche. The most famous stream-of-consciousness novel is *Ulysses*, published by Irish novelist James Joyce (1882–1941) in 1922. Abandoning conventional grammar and blending foreign words, puns, bits of knowledge, and scraps of memory together in bewildering confusion, the language of *Ulysses* was intended to mirror modern life itself.

Creative writers rejected the idea of progress; some even described "anti-utopias," nightmare visions of things to come. In 1918 Oswald Spengler (1880–1936) published *The Decline of the West*, in which he argued that Western civilization was in its old age and would soon be conquered by East Asia. Likewise, T. S. Eliot (1888–1965) depicted a world of growing desolation in his famous poem *The Waste Land* (1922). Franz Kafka's (1883–1924) novels *The Trial* (1925) and *The Castle* (1926) portrayed helpless individuals crushed by inexplicably hostile forces.

Modern Architecture, Art, and Music

Like scientists and intellectuals, creative artists rebelled against traditional forms and conventions at the end of the nineteenth century and beginning of the twentieth. This **modernism** in architecture, art, and music, which grew more influential after the war, meant constant experimentation and a search for new kinds of expression.

The United States pioneered in the new architecture. In the 1890s the Chicago School of architects, led by Louis H. Sullivan (1856–1924), used cheap steel, reinforced concrete, and electric elevators to build skyscrapers and office buildings lacking almost any exterior

Eiffel Tower, 1926 The works of the French artist Robert Delaunay (1885–1941) represent most of the major art styles of the early twentieth century, including modernism, abstraction, Futurism, Fauvism, Cubism, and Orphism. His early renderings of the Eiffel Tower (1909–1912), the iconic symbol of urbanization, the machine age, and, as a radio tower, limitless communication, possess features drawn from several of these styles. His later paintings of the Eiffel Tower, such as the one shown here, draw on a much wider palette of brilliant colors, reflecting aspects of a style known as Orphism, with which he is most closely identified. (Private Collection/Photo © Christie's Images/Bridgeman Images)

ornamentation. The buildings of Frank Lloyd Wright (1867–1959) were renowned for their sometimes-radical design, their creative use of wide varieties of materials, and their appearance of being part of the landscape.

In Europe architectural leadership centered in German-speaking countries. In 1919 Walter Gropius (1883–1969) merged the schools of fine and applied arts at Weimar into a single interdisciplinary school, the Bauhaus. Throughout the 1920s the Bauhaus movement stressed good design for everyday life and **functionalism**—that is, a building should serve the purpose for which it is designed. The movement attracted enthusiastic students from all over the world.

Art increasingly took on a nonrepresentational, abstract character. In 1907 in Paris the famous Spanish painter Pablo Picasso (1881–1973), along with Georges Braque (BRAHK), Marcel Duchamp, and other artists, established Cubism—an artistic approach concentrated on a complex geometry of zigzagging lines and sharply angled overlapping planes. Since the Renaissance, artists had represented objects from a single viewpoint and had created unified human forms. In his first great Cubist work, *Les Demoiselles d'Avignon* (lay dehm-wuh-ZEHL da-vee-NYAWN) (1907), Picasso's figures present a radical new view of reality with a strikingly non-Western depiction of the human form. Their faces resemble carved African masks, reflecting the growing importance of non-Western artistic traditions in Europe in the early twentieth century.

The ultimate stage in the development of abstract, nonrepresentational art occurred around 1910. Artists such as the Russian-born Wassily Kandinsky (1866–1944) turned away from nature completely. "The observer," said Kandinsky, "must learn to look at [my] pictures . . . as form and color combinations . . . as a representation of mood and not as a representation of *objects*."[13]

Radicalization accelerated after World War I. The most notable new developments were New Objectivity (*Sachlichkeit* [SAHK-leech-kight] in German), Dadaism (DAH-dah-ihz-uhm), and Surrealism. New Objectivity emerged from German artists' experiences in the Great War and the Weimar Republic. Paintings by artists like George Grosz (GRAWSH) and Otto Dix were provocative, emotionally disturbing, and harshly satirical. Dadaism attacked all accepted standards of art and behavior, delighting in outrageous conduct. After 1924 many Dadaists were attracted to Surrealism. Surrealists, such as Salvador Dalí (1904–1989), painted fantastic worlds of wild dreams and complex symbols.

Developments in modern music were strikingly parallel to those in painting. Attracted by the emo-tional intensity of expressionism, composers depicted unseen inner worlds of emotion and imagination. Just as abstract painters arranged lines and color but did not draw identifiable objects, so modern composers arranged sounds atonally without creating recognizable harmonies. Led by composers such as the Austrian Arnold Schönberg (SHUHN-buhrg) (1874–1951) and the Russian Igor Stravinsky (1882–1971), modern composers turned their backs on long-established musical conventions. The pulsating, dissonant rhythms and the dancers' earthy representation of lovemaking in Stravinsky's ballet *The Rite of Spring* nearly caused a riot when first performed in Paris in 1913.

Movies and Radio

In the decades following the First World War, motion pictures became the main entertainment of the masses worldwide. During the First World War the United States became the dominant force in the rapidly expanding silent-film industry, and Charlie Chaplin (1889–1978), an Englishman working in Hollywood, demonstrated that in the hands of a genius the new medium could combine mass entertainment and artistic accomplishment.

Motion pictures also became powerful tools of indoctrination, especially in countries with dictatorial regimes. Lenin encouraged the development of Soviet film making, and Sergei Eisenstein (1898–1948), the most famous of his film makers, and others dramatized the Communist view of Russian history. In Germany Hitler, who rose to power in 1933, turned to a talented woman film maker, Leni Riefenstahl (REE-fuhn-shtahl) (1902–2003), for a masterpiece of documentary propaganda, *Triumph of the Will*, based on the 1934 Nazi Party rally at Nuremberg. Her film was a brilliant and all-too-powerful depiction of Germany's rebirth as a great power under Nazi leadership.

Whether foreign or domestic, motion pictures became the main entertainment of the masses worldwide until after the Second World War. Motion pictures offered ordinary people a temporary escape from the hard realities of international tensions, uncertainty, unemployment, and personal frustrations.

Radio also dominated popular culture after the war. In 1920 the first major public broadcasts were made in Great Britain and the United States. Every major country quickly established national broadcasting networks. LOR, Radio Argentina, became the first formal radio station in the world when it made its first broadcast in August 1920. Radios were revolutionary in that they were capable of reaching all of a nation's citizens at once, offering them a single perspective on current events and teaching them a single national language and pronunciation.

---

functionalism The principle that buildings, like industrial products, should serve the purpose for which they were made as well as possible.

The International Appeal of Cinema A movie house in Havana, Cuba, in 1933 showing two American films made in 1932: *El Rey de la Plata* (*Silver Dollar*), starring Edward G. Robinson, and *6 horas de Vida* (*Six Hours to Live*), featuring Warner Baxter. The partially visible poster in the upper right is advertising *El último varon sobre la Tierra* (*The Last Man on Earth*), an American-produced Spanish-language movie starring Raul Roulien, first released in Spain in January 1933.

(Walker Evans [1903–1975]/*Cinema*, 1933, printed ca. 1970. Gelatin silver print, The Metropolitan Museum of Art. Gift of Arnold H. Crane, 1971 [1971.646.12]/© Walker Evans Archive, The Metropolitan Museum of Art, New York/Image copyright © The Metropolitan Museum of Art/Image source: Art Resource, NY)

Chapter Summary

Nationalism, militarism, imperialism, and the alliance system increased political tensions across Europe at the end of the nineteenth century. Franz Ferdinand's assassination in 1914 sparked a regional war that soon became global. Four years of stalemate and slaughter followed. Entire societies mobilized for total war, and government powers greatly increased. Women earned greater social equality, and labor unions grew. Many European countries adopted socialism as a realistic economic blueprint.

Horrible losses on the eastern front led to Russian tsar Nicholas II's abdication in March 1917. A provisional government controlled by moderate social democrats replaced him but refused to withdraw Russia from the war. A second Russian revolution followed in November 1917, led by Lenin and his Bolshevik Party. The Bolsheviks established a radical Communist regime, smashed existing capitalist institutions, and posed an ongoing challenge to Europe and its colonial empires.

The "war to end all wars" brought only a fragile truce. The Versailles treaty took away Germany's colonies, limited its military, and demanded admittance of war guilt and exorbitant war reparations. Separate treaties redrew the maps of Europe and the Middle East. Allied wartime solidarity faded, and Germany remained unrepentant, setting the stage for World War II. Globally, the European powers refused to extend self-determination to their colonies, instead creating a mandate system that sowed further discontent among colonized peoples.

In the 1920s moderate political leaders sought to create an enduring peace and rebuild prewar prosperity through compromise. By decade's end they seemed to have succeeded: Germany experienced an economic recovery, France rebuilt its war-torn regions, and Britain's Labour Party expanded social services. Ultimately, however, these measures were short-lived.

The war's horrors, particularly the industrialization of war that slaughtered millions, shattered Enlightenment ideals and caused widespread anxiety. In the interwar years philosophers, artists, and writers portrayed these anxieties in their work. Movies and the radio initially offered escape but soon became powerful tools of indoctrination and propaganda.

NOTES

1. Erich Maria Remarque, *All Quiet on the Western Front*, trans. A. W. Wheen (New York: Fawcett, 1996), p. 13.
2. Winston Churchill, *The World Crisis, 1911–1918* (New York: Free Press, 2005), p. 96.
3. Remarque, *All Quiet*, pp. 134–135.
4. Siegfried Sassoon, *The Memoirs of George Sherston: Memoirs of an Infantry Officer* (New York: Literary Guild of America, 1937), p. 74.
5. Quoted in Keith Sinclair, *The Growth of New Zealand Identity, 1890–1980* (Auckland, N.Z.: Longman Paul, 1987), p. 24.
6. Svetlana Palmer and Sarah Wallis, eds., *Intimate Voices from the First World War* (New York: William Morrow, 2003), p. 221.
7. Ethel Alec-Tweedie, *Women and Soldiers*, 2d ed. (London: John Lane, 1918), p. 29.
8. Janet S. K. Watson, "Khaki Girls, VADS, and Tommy's Sisters: Gender and Class in First World War Britain," *The International History Review* 19 (1997): 49.
9. Quoted in H. Nicolson, *Peacemaking 1919* (New York: Grosset & Dunlap Universal Library, 1965), pp. 8, 31–32.
10. Quoted ibid., p. 24.
11. Quoted in John Macquarrie, *Existentialism* (New York: Penguin Books, 1972), p. 15.
12. G. Greene, *Another Mexico* (New York: Viking Press, 1939), p. 3.
13. Quoted in A. H. Barr, Jr., *What Is Modern Painting?* 9th ed. (New York: Museum of Modern Art, 1966), p. 25.

CONNECTIONS

The Great War continues to influence global politics and societies, nearly a century after the guns went silent in November 1918. To understand the origins of many modern world conflicts, one must study first the intrigues and treaties and the revolutions and upheavals that were associated with this first truly world war.

In Chapter 30 we will see how the conflict contributed to a worldwide depression, the rise of totalitarian dictatorships, and a Second World War more global and destructive than the first. In the Middle East the Ottoman Empire came to an end, allowing France and England to carve out mandated territories — including modern Iraq, Palestine/Israel, and Lebanon — that remain flash points for violence and political instability in the twenty-first century. Nationalism, the nineteenth-century European ideology of change, took root in Asia, partly driven by Wilson's promise of self-determination. In Chapter 29 the efforts of various nationalist leaders — Atatürk in Turkey, Gandhi in India, Mao Zedong in China, Ho Chi Minh in Vietnam, and others — to throw off colonial domination will be examined, as well as the rise of ultranationalism in Japan, which led it into World War II and to ultimate defeat.

America's entry into the Great War placed it on the world stage, a place it has not relinquished as a superpower in the twentieth and twenty-first centuries. Russia, too, eventually became a superpower, but this outcome was not so clear in 1919 as its leaders fought for survival in a vicious civil war. By the outbreak of World War II Joseph Stalin had solidified Communist power, and the Soviet Union and the United States would play leading roles in defeating totalitarianism in Germany and Japan. But at war's end, as explained in Chapter 31, the two superpowers found themselves opponents in a Cold War that lasted for much of the rest of the twentieth century.

CHAPTER 28 Review and Explore

Identify Key Terms

Identify and explain the significance of each item below.

militarism (p. 820)

Triple Entente (p. 821)

trench warfare (p. 824)

total war (p. 828)

March Revolution (p. 834)

Petrograd Soviet (p. 835)

Bolsheviks (p. 835)

War Communism (p. 839)

League of Nations (p. 840)

Treaty of Versailles (p. 842)

Dawes Plan (p. 844)

Mein Kampf (p. 844)

existentialism (p. 845)

id, ego, superego (p. 846)

modernism (p. 847)

functionalism (p. 848)

Review the Main Ideas

Answer the focus questions from each section of the chapter.

1. What were the long-term and immediate causes of World War I, and how did the conflict become a global war? (p. 820)

2. How did total war affect the home fronts of the major combatants? (p. 828)

3. What factors led to the Russian Revolution, and what was its outcome? (p. 831)

4. What were the global consequences of the First World War? (p. 840)

5. How did leaders deal with the political dimensions of uncertainty and try to re-establish peace and prosperity in the interwar years? (p. 842)

6. In what ways were the anxieties of the postwar world expressed or heightened by revolutionary ideas in modern thought, art, and science and in new forms of communication? (p. 845)

Make Comparisons and Connections

Analyze the larger developments and continuities within and across chapters.

1. The war between Austria and Serbia should have been a small regional conflict in one corner of Europe. How did nationalism, militarism, and the New Imperialism contribute to its expansion into a global conflict?

2. In what ways would someone transported in time from 1900 to 1925 have been shocked and surprised at the changes that had occurred in that short time?

3. How did the mandate system established by the League of Nations reflect the Social Darwinian ideas of the late nineteenth century (Chapter 24)?

WORLD WAR I

1914–1918 World War I

◆ **June 28, 1914** Assassination of Archduke Franz Ferdinand of Austria-Hungary

◆ **August 1914** Japan joins the Triple Entente

◆ **October 1914** Ottoman Empire joins Central Powers

◆ **May 1915** Italy joins the Triple Entente; Germans sink the *Lusitania*

◆ **April 1917** U.S. declares war on Germany

◆ **1919** Treaty of Versailles

◆ **March 1918** Treaty of Brest-Litovsk

◆ **November 1918** Armistice ends the war; revolution in Germany

RUSSIA

1917–1922 Russian civil war

◆ **1917** March Revolution; tsar abdicates; Bolsheviks seize power; Lenin heads new government

MIDDLE EAST

◆ **1915** Armenian genocide in the Ottoman Empire begins **(Ch. 29)**

◆ **1916** Arab revolt against Ottoman rule begins **(Ch. 29)**

ASIA

1920 ◆ Gandhi launches nonviolent campaign against British rule in India **(Ch. 29)**

AMERICAS

← **1910** Mexican Revolution **(Ch. 27))**

◆ **1914** Panama Canal opens **(Ch. 27)**

GLOBAL

1915   **1920**

Suggested Resources

BOOKS

Andelman, David A. *A Shattered Peace: Versailles 1919 and the Price We Pay Today.* 2007. A clearly written study of the Paris Peace Conference and how it has shaped world history to the present day.

Camus, Albert. *The Stranger* and *The Plague.* 1942 and 1947. The greatest existential novelist at his unforgettable best.

Eksteins, Modris. *Rites of Spring: The Great War and the Birth of the Modern Age.* 1989. An imaginative cultural investigation that has won critical acclaim.

Figes, Orlando. *A People's Tragedy: The Russian Revolution, 1891–1924.* 1996. Massive but accessible, this masterful synthesis traces the revolution from its origins to Lenin's death in 1924.

Fitzpatrick, Sheila. *The Russian Revolution*, 3d ed. 2008. A concise history that incorporates previously inaccessible Russian archives and the latest research. Fitzpatrick argues that the revolution ended only with the Stalinist purges in the late 1930s.

Fromkin, David. *Europe's Last Summer: Who Started the Great War?* 2004. A well-argued, compulsively readable discussion of responsibility for the war by a master historian.

Fromkin, David. *A Peace to End All Peace: The Fall of the Ottoman Empire and the Creation of the Modern Middle East,* 2d ed. 2009. A brilliant account of the Middle East in the critical years between 1914 and 1922.

Gay, Peter. *Modernism: The Lure of Heresy.* 2007. A personal perspective on twentieth-century high culture by a leading intellectual and cultural historian.

Gilbert, Martin. *The First World War: A Complete History.* 1994. A comprehensive study in one volume by a major military historian.

Isaacson, Walter. *Einstein: His Life and Universe.* 2007. A well-received introduction to Einstein's life and work.

Macmillan, Margaret. *Paris, 1919: Six Months That Changed the World.* 2001. A masterful account of the negotiations and issues at the Paris Peace Conference.

Reed, John. *Ten Days That Shook the World.* 1919. The classic eyewitness account of the Russian Revolution by a young, pro-Bolshevik American.

Young, Louise. *Japan's Total Empire: Manchuria and the Culture of Wartime Imperialism.* 1998. A fascinating pioneering work on Japanese imperialism.

DOCUMENTARY

The First World War (Channel Four, 2003). Based on the book by the distinguished Great War historian Hew Strachan, this ten-episode series is a powerful and comprehensive account of all aspects of the Great War.

The Great War and the Shaping of the 20th Century. (BBC, PBS, 1996) A well-organized and comprehensive introduction to the Great War. An eight-part series on each stage of the war, how the war shaped the twentieth century, and historians' views of the war, as well as a timeline and maps.

FEATURE FILMS

All Quiet on the Western Front (Lewis Milestone, 1930). Based on the famous novel by Erich Maria Remarque, this cinematic masterpiece portraying the horrors of World War I trench warfare is one of the most powerful war, and antiwar, films of all time. It won the Academy Award for Best Picture in 1930 and was restored and rereleased in 2011.

Paths of Glory (Stanley Kubrick, 1957). Considered one of the best war movies of all time, this story of the trial of three French soldiers accused of cowardice on the battlefield is based on a real-life event during the Great War.

Suffragette (Sarah Gavron, 2015). Set in the years just before the Great War, this film is a powerful portrayal of the efforts by militant suffragettes in England to gain the vote for women.

WEBSITES

"Russian Revolution" in the *Internet Modern History Sourcebook.* An excellent reference site for the Russian Revolution, with many primary documents and several links to other related websites. **sourcebooks.fordham.edu/halsall/mod /modsbook39.asp**

Spartacus Educational: Causes and Events of WW I. A comprehensive introduction to the Great War, including a glossary, statistics, and a bibliography. **spartacus-educational.com/FWW.htm**

29

Nationalism in Asia

1914–1939

From Asia's perspective, the First World War was largely a European civil war that shattered Western imperialism's united front, underscored the West's moral bankruptcy, and convulsed prewar relationships throughout Asia. Most crucially, the war sped the development of modern Asian nationalism. Before 1914 the nationalist gospel of anti-imperialist political freedom and racial equality had already won converts among Asia's westernized, educated elites. In the 1920s and 1930s it increasingly won the allegiance of the masses. Nationalism in Asia between 1914 and 1939 became a mass movement with potentially awesome power.

The modern nationalism movement was never monolithic. In Asia especially, where the new and often narrow ideology of nationalism was grafted onto old, rich, and complex civilizations, the shape and eventual outcome of nationalist movements varied enormously. Between the outbreaks of the First and Second World Wars, each Asian country developed a distinctive national movement rooted in its own unique culture and history. Each nation's people created their own national reawakening, which reinvigorated thought and culture as well as politics and economics. Nationalist movements gave rise in Asia to conflict both within large, multiethnic states and between independent states.

The Asian nationalist movement witnessed the emergence of two of the true giants of the twentieth century. Mohandas Gandhi in India and Mao Zedong in China both drew their support from the peasant masses in the world's two most populous countries. Gandhi successfully used campaigns of peaceful nonviolent resistance to British colonial rule to gain Indian independence. Mao, on the other hand, used weapons of war and socialist promises of equality to defeat his westernized nationalist opponents and establish a modern Communist state.

Kasturba Gandhi

Wife of Indian political leader Mohandas Gandhi, Kasturba was barely fourteen years old and he thirteen when their marriage took place. Kasturba (1869–1944) supported Gandhi through decades of struggle for Indian independence. Here she spins cotton on a *charkha*, or spinning wheel, part of Gandhi's campaign for Indians to become self-sufficient by making their own cloth and freeing themselves from imported British goods.

© Dinodia Photo Library/The Image Works

CHAPTER PREVIEW

THE FIRST WORLD WAR'S IMPACT ON NATIONALIST TRENDS
Why did modern nationalism develop in Asia between the First and Second World Wars, and what was its appeal?

NATIONALIST MOVEMENTS IN THE MIDDLE EAST
How did the Ottoman Empire's collapse in World War I shape nationalist movements in the Middle East?

TOWARD SELF-RULE IN INDIA
What role did Gandhi and his campaign of militant nonviolence play in leading India to independence from the British?

NATIONALIST STRUGGLES IN EAST AND SOUTHEAST ASIA
How did nationalism shape political developments in East and Southeast Asia?

The First World War's Impact on Nationalist Trends

Why did modern nationalism develop in Asia between the First and Second World Wars, and what was its appeal?

In the late nineteenth and early twentieth centuries the peoples of Asia adapted the European ideology of nationalism to their own situations. The First World War profoundly affected Asian nationalist aspirations by altering relations between Asia and Europe. For four years Asians watched Kipling's haughty bearers of "the white man's burden" (see "A 'Civilizing Mission'" in Chapter 25) vilify and destroy each other. Japan's defeat of imperial Russia in 1905 (see "Japan as an Imperial Power" in Chapter 26) had shown that an Asian power could beat a European Great Power; Asians now saw the entire West as divided and vulnerable.

Asian Reaction to the War in Europe

The Great War was a global conflict, but some peoples were affected more significantly than others. The Japanese and Ottoman Turks were directly involved, fighting with the Allies and Central Powers, respectively. The Chinese, who overthrew their emperor in 1911, were more concerned with internal events and the threat from Japan than with the war in Europe. In British India and French Indochina the war's impact was unavoidably greater. Total war required the British and the French to draft their colonial subjects into the conflict. An Indian or Vietnamese soldier who fought in France and came in contact there with democratic and republican ideas, however, was less likely to accept foreign rule when he returned home. The British and the French therefore had to make rash promises to gain the support of these colonial peoples and other allies during the war. After the war the nationalist genie the colonial powers had called on refused to slip meekly back into the bottle.

U.S. president Wilson's war aims also raised the hopes of peoples under imperial rule. In January 1918 Wilson proposed his Fourteen Points (see "The Paris Peace Treaties" in Chapter 28), whose key idea was national self-determination for the peoples of Europe and the Ottoman Empire. Wilson recommended in Point 5 that in all colonial questions "the interests of native populations be given equal weight with the desires of European governments," and he seemed to call for national self-rule. This message had enormous appeal for educated Asians, fueling their hopes of freedom.

The Mandates System

After winning the war, the Allies tried to re-establish or increase their political and economic domination of their Asian and African colonies. Although fatally weakened, Western imperialism remained very much alive in 1918, partly because President Wilson was no revolutionary. At the Paris Peace Conference Wilson compromised on colonial questions in order to achieve some of his European goals and create the League of Nations.

The compromise at the Paris Peace Conference between Wilson's vague, moralistic idealism and the European determination to maintain control over colonial empires was a system of League of Nations mandates over Germany's former colonies and the old Ottoman Empire. Article 22 of the League of Nations Covenant, which was part of the Treaty of Versailles, assigned territories "inhabited by peoples incapable of governing themselves" to various "developed nations." "The well-being and development of such peoples" was declared "a sacred trust of civilization." The **Permanent Mandates Commission**, whose members came from European countries with colonies, was created to oversee the developed nations' fulfillment of their international responsibility. Thus the League elaborated a new principle—development toward the eventual goal of self-government—but left its implementation to the colonial powers themselves. Industrialized Japan was the only Asian state to obtain mandates.

The mandates system demonstrated that Europe was determined to maintain its imperial power and influence. Bitterly disappointed patriots throughout Asia saw the system as an expansion of the imperial order. Yet they did not give up. They preached national self-determination and struggled to build mass movements capable of achieving freedom and independence.

In this struggle Asian nationalists were encouraged by Soviet communism. After seizing power in 1917, Lenin declared that the Asian inhabitants of the new Soviet Union were complete equals of the Russians with a right to their own development. The Communists also denounced European and American imperialism and pledged to support revolutionary movements in colonial countries. The example, ideology, and support of Soviet communism exerted a powerful influence in the 1920s and 1930s, particularly in China and French Indochina (see "China's Intellectual Revolution" and "Striving for Independence in Southeast Asia").

Permanent Mandates Commission A commission created by the League of Nations to oversee the developed nations' fulfillment of their international responsibility toward their mandates.

Nationalism's Appeal

There were at least three reasons for the upsurge of nationalism in Asia. First and foremost, nationalism provided the most effective means of organizing anti-imperialist resistance both to direct foreign rule and to indirect Western domination. Second, nationalism called for fundamental changes and challenged old political and social practices and beliefs. As in Russia after the Crimean War, in Turkey after the Ottoman Empire's collapse, and in Japan after the Meiji Restoration, the nationalist creed after World War I went hand in hand with acceptance of modernization by the educated elites, who used modernization to contest the influence and power of conservative traditionalists. Third, nationalism offered a vision of a free and prosperous future and provided an ideology to ennoble the sacrifices the struggle would require.

Nationalism also had a dark side. As in Europe (see "The Growing Appeal of Nationalism" in Chapter 24), Asian nationalists developed a strong sense of "we" and "they." "They" were often the enemy. European imperialists were just such a "they," and nationalist feelings generated the will to challenge European domination. But, as in Europe, Asian nationalism also stimulated bitter conflicts and wars between peoples, in three different ways.

First, as when the ideology of nationalism first developed in Europe in the early 1800s, Asian (and African) elites were often forced to create a national identity in colonies that Europeans had artificially created, or in multiethnic countries held together by authoritarian leaders but without national identities based on shared ethnicities or histories. Second, nationalism stimulated conflicts between relatively homogeneous peoples in large states, rallying, for example, Chinese against Japanese and vice versa. Third, nationalism often heightened tensions between ethnic or religious groups within states. In nearly all countries there were ancient ethnic and religious differences and rivalries. Imperial rulers of colonial powers (like the British and French) and local authoritarian rulers (like the Chinese emperor) exploited these ethnic and religious differences to "divide and conquer" the peoples in their empires. When the rigid imperial rule ended, the different national, religious, or even ideological (communists versus capitalists) factions turned against each other, each seeking to either seize control of or divide the existing state, and to dominate the enemy "they" within its borders. This habit of thinking in terms of "we" versus "they" was, and still is, a difficult frame of mind to abandon, and these divisions made it difficult for nationalist leaders to unite people under a common national identity.

Nationalism's appeal in Asia was not confined to territories under direct European rule. Europe and the United States had forced even the most solid Asian states, China and Japan, to accept humiliating limitations on their sovereignty. Thus the nationalist promise of genuine economic independence and true political equality with the West appealed as powerfully in old but weak states like China as in colonial territories like British India.

Nationalist Movements in the Middle East

How did the Ottoman Empire's collapse in World War I shape nationalist movements in the Middle East?

The most flagrant attempt to expand Western imperialism occurred in southwest Asia (Map 29.1). There the British and the French successfully encouraged an Arab revolt in 1916 and destroyed the Ottoman Empire. Europeans then sought to replace Turks as principal rulers throughout the region. Turkish, Arab, and Persian nationalists, as well as Jewish nationalists arriving from Europe, reacted violently. They struggled to win nationhood, and as the Europeans were forced to make concessions, they sometimes came into sharp conflict with each other, most notably in Palestine.

The Arab Revolt

Long subject to European pressure, the Ottoman Empire failed to reform and modernize in the late nineteenth century (see "The Islamic Heartland Under Pressure" in Chapter 25). Declining international stature and domestic tyranny led idealistic exiles to engage in revolutionary activity and motivated army officers to seize power and save the Ottoman state. These patriots, the so-called Young Turks, succeeded in the 1908 revolution, and subsequently they were determined to hold together the remnants of the vast multiethnic empire. Defeated in the Balkan war of 1912 and stripped of practically all territory in Europe, the Young Turks redoubled their efforts in southwest Asia. The most important of their possessions were Syria — consisting of modern-day Lebanon, Syria, Israel, the West Bank, the Gaza Strip, and Jordan — and Iraq. The Ottoman Turks also claimed the Arabian peninsula but exercised only loose control there.

For centuries the largely Arab populations of Syria and Iraq had been tied to their Ottoman rulers by their common faith in Islam (though there were Christian Arabs as well). Yet beneath the surface, ethnic and linguistic tensions simmered between Turks and Arabs.

Young Turk actions after 1908 made the embryonic "Arab movement" a reality. The majority of Young Turks promoted a narrow Turkish nationalism. They

MAPPING THE PAST

MAP 29.1 The Partition of the Ottoman Empire, 1914–1923 By 1914 the Ottoman Turks had been pushed out of the Balkans, and their Arab provinces were on the edge of revolt. That revolt erupted in the First World War and contributed greatly to the Ottomans' defeat. When the Allies then attempted to implement their plans, including independence for the Armenian people, Mustafa Kemal arose to forge in battle the modern Turkish state.

ANALYZING THE MAP What new countries were established as a result of the partition of the Ottoman Empire? Where were mandates established? What might you conclude about European views of the Middle East based on how Europe divided up the region?

CONNECTIONS How might the collapse of the Ottoman Empire in World War I have contributed to the current situation in the Middle East?

Refugees from the Armenian Genocide An estimated 1.5 million Armenians were killed, or died from hunger and exhaustion, during forced deportation marches carried out by the Ottoman Turks in 1915–1917. This photo shows some of the 100,000 to 200,000 Armenians who survived. They had been driven into the Syrian Desert and were later discovered at As-Salt in northern Jordan. The refugees were later taken by the British to Jerusalem, and some of their descendants still live in the Armenian Quarter there.
(Pictures from History/Bridgeman Images)

further centralized the Ottoman Empire and extended the sway of Turkish language and culture. In 1909 the Turkish government brutally slaughtered thousands of Armenian Christians, a prelude to the wholesale massacre of more than a million Armenians during the First World War. Meanwhile, Arab discontent grew.

During World War I the Turks aligned themselves with Germany and Austria-Hungary (see "The War Becomes Global" in Chapter 28). As a result, the Young Turks drew all of the Middle East into what had been up to that point a European war. Arabs opposed to Ottoman rule found themselves allied with the British, who encouraged the alliance with vague promises of an independent Arab kingdom. After British victories on the Arab peninsula in 1917 and 1918, many Arab patriots expected a large, unified Arab state to rise from the dust of the Ottoman collapse. Within two years,

however, Arab nationalists felt bitterly betrayed by Great Britain and its allies.

Arab bitterness was partly directed at secret wartime treaties between Britain and France to divide and rule the old Ottoman Empire. In the 1916 **Sykes-Picot Agreement**, Britain and France secretly agreed that France would receive modern-day Lebanon, Syria, and much of southern Turkey, and Britain would receive Palestine, Jordan, and Iraq. The Sykes-Picot Agreement contradicted British promises concerning Arab independence after the war and left Arab nationalists feeling cheated and betrayed.

> **Sykes-Picot Agreement** The 1916 secret agreement between Britain and France that divided up the Arab lands of Lebanon, Syria, southern Turkey, Palestine, Jordan, and Iraq.

ANALYZING THE EVIDENCE

Resolution of the General Syrian Congress at Damascus

Great Britain and France had agreed to divide up the Arab lands, and the British had also made conflicting promises to Arab and Jewish nationalists. However, President Wilson insisted at the Paris Peace Conference that the right of self-determination should be applied to the conquered Ottoman territories, and he sent an American commission of inquiry to Syria, even though the British and French refused to participate. The commission canvassed political views throughout greater Syria, and its long report with many documents reflected public opinion in the region in 1919.

To present their view to the Americans, Arab nationalists from present-day Syria, Lebanon, Israel, the West Bank, the Gaza Strip, and Jordan came together in Damascus as the General Syrian Congress, and they passed the following resolution on July 2, 1919. In addition to the Arab call for political independence, the delegates addressed the possibility of French rule under a League of Nations mandate and the establishment of a Jewish national home.

■ We the undersigned members of the General Syrian Congress, meeting in Damascus on Wednesday, July 2nd, 1919, . . . provided with credentials and authorizations by the inhabitants of our various districts, Moslems, Christians, and Jews, have agreed upon the following statement of the desires of the people of the country who have elected us to present them to the American Section of the International Commission; the fifth article was passed by a very large majority; all the other articles were accepted unanimously.

1. We ask absolutely complete political independence for Syria within these boundaries. [Describes the area including the present-day states of Syria, Lebanon, Israel, the West Bank, the Gaza Strip, and Jordan.]

2. We ask that the Government of this Syrian country should be a democratic civil constitutional Monarchy on broad decentralization principles, safeguarding the rights of minorities, and that the King be the Emir Faisal, who carried on a glorious struggle in the cause of our liberation and merited our full confidence and entire reliance.

3. Considering the fact that the Arabs inhabiting the Syrian area are not naturally less gifted than other more advanced races and that they are by no means less developed than the Bulgarians, Serbians, Greeks, and Roumanians at the beginning of their independence, we protest against Article 22 of the Covenant of the League of Nations, placing us among the nations in their middle stage of development which stand in need of a mandatory power.

4. In the event of the rejection by the Peace Conference of this just protest for certain considerations that we may not understand, we, relying on the declarations of President Wilson that his object in waging war was to put an end to the ambition of conquest and colonization, can only regard the mandate mentioned in the Covenant of the League of Nations as equivalent to the rendering of economical and technical assistance that does not prejudice our complete independence. And desiring that our country should not fall a prey to colonization and believing that the American Nation is farthest from any thought of colonization and has no political ambition in our country, we will seek the technical and economical assistance from the United States of America, provided that such assistance does not exceed 20 years.

A related source of Arab frustration was Britain's wartime commitment to a Jewish homeland in Palestine. The **Balfour Declaration** of November 1917, made by the British foreign secretary Arthur Balfour, declared:

His Majesty's Government views with favour the establishment in Palestine of a national home for the Jewish People, and will use their best endeavors to facilitate the achievement of this object, it being clearly understood that nothing shall be done which may prejudice the civil and religious rights of existing non-Jewish communities in Palestine.[1]

As a careful reading reveals, the Balfour Declaration made contradictory promises to European Jews and Middle Eastern Arabs.

Some British Cabinet members believed the Balfour Declaration would appeal to German, Austrian, and American Jews and thus help the British war effort. Others sincerely supported the Zionist vision of a Jewish homeland (see "Jewish Emancipation and Modern Anti-Semitism" in Chapter 24), but also believed that Jews living in this homeland would be grateful to Britain and thus help maintain British control of the Suez Canal.

In 1914 Jews made up about 11 percent of the predominantly Arab population in the Ottoman territory

Balfour Declaration A 1917 statement by British foreign secretary Arthur Balfour that supported the idea of a Jewish homeland in Palestine.

5. In the event of America not finding herself in a position to accept our desire for assistance, we will seek this assistance from Great Britain, also provided that such assistance does not infringe the complete independence and unity of our country and that the duration of such assistance does not exceed that mentioned in the previous article.

6. We do not acknowledge any right claimed by the French Government in any part whatever of our Syrian country and refuse that she should assist us or have a hand in our country under any circumstances and in any place.

7. We oppose the pretensions of the Zionists to create a Jewish commonwealth in the southern part of Syria, known as Palestine, and oppose Zionist migration to any part of our country; for we do not acknowledge their title but consider them a grave peril to our people from the national, economical, and political points of view. Our Jewish compatriots shall enjoy our common rights and assume the common responsibilities.

8. We ask that there should be no separation of the southern part of Syria, known as Palestine, nor of the littoral western zone, which includes Lebanon, from the Syrian country. We desire that the unity of the country should be guaranteed against partition under whatever circumstances.

9. We ask complete independence for emancipated Mesopotamia [today's Iraq] and that there should be no economical barriers between the two countries.

10. The fundamental principles laid down by President Wilson in condemnation of secret treaties impel us to protest most emphatically against any treaty that stipulates the partition of our Syrian country and against any private engagement aiming at the establishment of Zionism in the southern part of Syria; therefore we ask the complete annulment of these conventions and agreements.

The noble principles enunciated by President Wilson strengthen our confidence that our desires emanating from the depths of our hearts, shall be the decisive factor in determining our future; and that President Wilson and the free American people will be our supporters for the realization of our hopes, thereby proving their sincerity and noble sympathy with the aspiration of the weaker nations in general and our Arab people in particular.

We also have the fullest confidence that the Peace Conference will realize that we would not have risen against the Turks, with whom we had participated in all civil, political, and representative privileges, but for their violation of our national rights, and so will grant us our desires in full in order that our political rights may not be less after the war than they were before, since we have shed so much blood in the cause of our liberty and independence.

We request to be allowed to send a delegation to represent us at the Peace Conference to defend our rights and secure the realization of our aspirations.

QUESTIONS FOR ANALYSIS

1. What kind of state did the delegates want?
2. How did the delegates want to modify an unwanted League of Nations mandate to make it less objectionable?
3. Did the delegates view their "Jewish compatriots" and the Zionists in different ways? Why?

Source: "Resolution of the General Syrian Congress at Damascus, 2 July 1919," from the *King-Crane Commission Report*, in *Foreign Relations of the United States: Paris Peace Conference, 1919*, 12: 780–781.

that became, under British control, Palestine. The "national home for the Jewish People" mentioned in the Balfour Declaration implied to the Arabs—and to the Zionist Jews as well—some kind of Jewish state that would be incompatible with majority rule.

After Faisal bin Hussein's failed efforts at the Paris Peace Conference to secure Arab independence, Arab nationalists met in Damascus at the General Syrian Congress in 1919 and unsuccessfully called again for political independence. (See "Analyzing the Evidence: Resolution of the General Syrian Congress at Damascus," above.) Ignoring Arab opposition, the British mandate in Palestine formally incorporated the Balfour Declaration and its commitment to a Jewish national home. In March 1920 the Syrian National Congress proclaimed Syria independent, with Faisal bin Hussein as king. A similar congress declared Iraq an independent kingdom.

Western reaction to events in Syria and Iraq was swift and decisive. A French army stationed in Lebanon attacked Syria, taking Damascus in July 1920. Faisal fled, and the French took over. Meanwhile, the British put down an uprising in Iraq and established effective control there. Western imperialism appeared to have replaced Turkish rule in the Middle East (see Map 29.1).

The Turkish Revolution

Days after the end of the First World War, French and then British troops entered Constantinople to begin a five-year occupation of the Ottoman capital. A young English official wrote that he found the Ottoman Empire "utterly smashed." The Turks were "worn out" from the war, and without bitterness they awaited the construction of a "new system."[2] The Allies' new system was blatant imperialism, which proved harsher for the defeated Turks than for the Arabs now free from Turkish rule. A treaty forced on the helpless sultan dismembered Turkey and reduced it to a puppet state. Great Britain and France occupied parts of Turkey, and Italy and Greece claimed shares as well. There was a

sizable Greek minority in western Turkey, and Greek nationalists cherished the "Great Idea" of a modern Greek empire modeled on long-dead Christian Byzantium. In 1919 Greek armies carried by British ships landed on the Turkish coast at Smyrna and advanced into the interior. Turkey seemed finished.

But Turkey produced a great leader and revived to become an inspiration to the entire Middle East. Mustafa Kemal (moo-STAH-fah kuh-MAHL) (1881–1938), considered the father of modern Turkey, was a military man sympathetic to the Young Turk movement. After the armistice, he watched with anguish the Allies' aggression and the sultan's cowardice. In early 1919 he began working to unify Turkish resistance.

The sultan, bowing to Allied pressure, initially denounced Kemal, but the cause of national liberation proved more powerful. The catalyst was the Greek invasion and attempted annexation of much of western Turkey. A young Turkish woman described feelings she shared with countless others:

> After I learned about the details of the Smyrna occupation by Greek armies, I hardly opened my mouth on any subject except when it concerned the sacred struggle. . . . I suddenly ceased to exist as an individual. I worked, wrote and lived as a unit of that magnificent national madness.[3]

Refusing to acknowledge the Allied dismemberment of their country, the Turks battled on through 1920 despite staggering defeats. The next year the Greeks advanced almost to Ankara, the nationalist stronghold in central Turkey. There Mustafa Kemal's forces took the offensive and won a great victory. The Greeks and their British allies sued for peace. The resulting **Treaty of Lausanne** (1923) recognized a truly independent Turkey, and Turkey lost only its former Arab provinces (see Map 29.1).

Mustafa Kemal believed Turkey should modernize and secularize along Western lines. His first moves, beginning in 1923, were political. Kemal called on the National Assembly to depose the sultan and establish a republic, and he had himself elected president. Kemal savagely crushed the demands for independence of ethnic minorities within Turkey like the Armenians and the Kurds, but he realistically abandoned all thought of winning back lost Arab territories. He then created a one-party system in order to work his will.

Kemal's most radical changes pertained to religion and culture. For centuries most believers' intellectual and social activities had been regulated by Islamic religious authorities. Profoundly influenced by the example of western Europe, Mustafa Kemal set out, like the philosophes of the Enlightenment, to limit religious influence in daily affairs, but, like Russia's Peter the Great, he employed dictatorial measures rather than reason and democracy to reach his goal. Kemal decreed a revolutionary separation of church and state. Secular

Mustafa Kemal Surnamed Atatürk, meaning "father of the Turks," Mustafa Kemal and his supporters imposed revolutionary changes aimed at modernizing and westernizing Turkish society and the new Turkish government. Dancing here with his adopted daughter at her high-society wedding, Atatürk often appeared in public in elegant European dress — a vivid symbol for the Turkish people of his radical break with traditional Islamic teaching and custom. (Hulton Archive/Getty Images)

law codes inspired by European models replaced religious courts. State schools replaced religious schools and taught such secular subjects as science, mathematics, and social sciences.

Mustafa Kemal also struck down many entrenched patterns of behavior. Women, traditionally secluded and inferior to males in Islamic society, received the right to vote. Civil law on a European model, rather than the Islamic code, now governed marriage. Women could seek divorces, and no man could have more than one wife at a time. Men were forbidden to wear the tall red fez of the Ottoman era as headgear; government employees were ordered to wear business suits and felt hats, erasing the visible differences between Muslims and "infidel" Europeans. The old Arabic script was replaced with a new Turkish alphabet based on Roman letters, which facilitated massive government efforts to spread literacy after 1928. Finally, in 1935, surnames on the European model were introduced. The National Assembly granted Mustafa Kemal the surname Atatürk, which means "father of the Turks."

By his death in 1938, Atatürk and his supporters had consolidated their revolution. Government-sponsored industrialization was fostering urban growth and new attitudes, encouraging Turks to embrace business and science. Poverty persisted in rural areas, as did some religious discontent among devout Muslims. But like the Japanese after the Meiji Restoration, the Turkish people had rallied around the nationalist banner to repulse European imperialism and were building a modern secular nation-state.

Modernization Efforts in Persia and Afghanistan

In Persia (renamed Iran in 1935) strong-arm efforts to build a unified modern nation ultimately proved less successful than in Turkey. In the late nineteenth century Persia had also been subject to extreme foreign pressure, which stimulated efforts to reform the government as a means of reviving Islamic civilization. In 1906 a nationalistic coalition of merchants, religious leaders, and intellectuals revolted. The despotic shah was forced to grant a constitution and establish a national assembly, the **Majlis** (MAHJ-lis).

Yet the 1906 Persian revolution was doomed to failure, largely because of European imperialism. Without consulting Iran, in 1907 Britain and Russia divided the country into spheres of influence. Britain's sphere ran along the Persian Gulf; the Russian sphere encompassed the whole northern half of Persia (see Map 29.1). Thereafter Russia intervened constantly. It blocked reforms, occupied cities, and completely dominated the country by 1912. When Russian power collapsed in the Bolshevik Revolution, British armies rushed into the power vacuum. By bribing corrupt Persians, Great Britain in 1919 negotiated a treaty allowing the

installation of British "advisers" in every government department.

The Majlis refused to ratify the treaty, and the blatant attempt to make Persia a British satellite aroused the national spirit. In 1921 reaction against the British brought to power a military dictator, Reza Shah Pahlavi (PAH-luh-vee) (1877–1944), who proclaimed himself shah in 1925 and ruled until 1941.

Inspired by Turkey's Mustafa Kemal, Reza Shah had three basic goals: to build a modern nation, to free Persia from foreign domination, and to rule with an iron fist. The challenge was enormous. Persia was a vast, undeveloped country. The rural population was mostly poor and illiterate, and among the Persian majority were sizable ethnic minorities with their own aspirations. Furthermore, Iran's powerful religious leaders hated Western (Christian) domination but were equally opposed to a more secular, less Islamic society.

To realize his vision of a strong Persia, the shah created a modern army, built railroads, and encouraged commerce. He won control over ethnic minorities such as the Kurds in the north and Arab tribesmen on the Iraqi border. He reduced the privileges granted to foreigners and raised taxes on the powerful Anglo-Persian Oil Company, which had been founded in 1909 to exploit the first great oil strike in the Middle East. Yet Reza Shah was less successful than Atatürk.

Because the European-educated elite in Persia was smaller than the comparable group in Turkey, the idea of re-creating Persian greatness on the basis of a secularized society attracted relatively few determined supporters. Many powerful religious leaders turned against Reza Shah, and he became increasingly brutal, greedy, and tyrannical.

Afghanistan, meanwhile, was nominally independent in the nineteenth century, but the British imposed political restrictions and constantly meddled in the country's affairs. In 1919 emir Amanullah Khan (1892–1960) declared war on the British government in India and won complete independence for the first time. Amanullah (ah-man-UL-lah) then decreed revolutionary modernizing reforms designed to hurl his primitive country into the twentieth century. He established modern, secular schools for both boys and girls, and adult education classes for

Afghanistan Under Amanullah Khan

Treaty of Lausanne The 1923 treaty that ended the Turkish war and recognized the territorial integrity of a truly independent Turkey.

Majlis The national assembly established by the despotic shah of Iran in 1906.

the predominantly illiterate population. He did away with seclusion and centuries-old dress codes for women, abolished slavery, created the country's first constitution in 1923, restructured and reorganized the economy, and established a legislative assembly and secular (rather than Islamic) court system. The result was tribal and religious revolt, civil war, and retreat from reform. Islam remained both religion and law. A powerful but primitive patriotism enabled Afghanistan to win political independence from the West, but not to build a modern society.

Gradual Independence in the Arab States

French and British mandates forced Arab nationalists to seek independence by gradual means after 1920. Arab nationalists were indirectly aided by Western taxpayers who wanted cheap — that is, peaceful — empires. As a result, Arabs won considerable control over local affairs in the mandated states, except Palestine, though the mandates remained European satellites in international and economic affairs.

In Iraq the British chose Faisal bin Hussein, whom the French had deposed in Syria, as king. Faisal obligingly gave British advisers broad behind-the-scenes control. The king also accepted British ownership of Iraq's oil fields, consequently giving the West a stranglehold on the Iraqi economy. Given the severe limitations imposed on him, Faisal (r. 1921–1933) proved to be an able ruler, gaining his peoples' support and encouraging moderate reforms. In 1932 he secured Iraqi independence at the price of a restrictive long-term military alliance with Great Britain.

Egypt had been occupied by Great Britain since 1882 (see "Egypt: From Reform to British Occupation" in Chapter 25) and had been a British protectorate since 1914. Following intense nationalist agitation after the Great War, Great Britain in 1922 proclaimed Egypt formally independent but continued to occupy the country militarily and control its politics. In 1936 the British agreed to restrict their troops to their bases in the Suez Canal Zone.

The French compromised less in their handling of their mandated Middle East territories. Following the Ottoman Empire's collapse after World War I, the French designated Lebanon as one of several ethnic enclaves within a larger area that became part of the French mandate of Syria. They practiced a policy of divide and rule and generally played off ethnic and religious minorities against each other. In 1926 Lebanon became a separate republic but remained under the control of the French mandate. Arab nationalists in

Syria finally won promises of Syrian independence in 1936 in return for a friendship treaty with France.

In short, the Arab states gradually freed themselves from Western political mandates but not from Western military threats or from pervasive Western influence. Since large Arab landowners and urban merchants increased their wealth and political power after 1918, they often supported the Western hegemony. Radical nationalists, on the other hand, recognized that Western control of the newly discovered Arab oil fields was proof that economic independence and genuine freedom had not yet been achieved.

Arab-Jewish Tensions in Palestine

Relations between the Arabs and the West were complicated by the tense situation in the British mandate of Palestine, and that situation deteriorated in the interwar years. Both Arabs and Jews denounced the British, who tried unsuccessfully to compromise with both sides. Arab nationalist anger, however, was aimed primarily at Jewish settlers. The key issue was Jewish migration from Europe to Palestine.

Jewish nationalism, known as Zionism, took shape in Europe in the late nineteenth century under Theodor Herzl's leadership (see "Jewish Emancipation and Modern Anti-Semitism" in Chapter 24). Herzl believed only a Jewish state could guarantee Jews dignity and security. The Zionist movement encouraged some of the world's Jews to settle in Palestine, but until 1921 the great majority of Jewish emigrants preferred the United States.

After 1921 the situation changed radically. An isolationist United States drastically limited immigration from eastern Europe, where war and revolution had kindled anti-Semitism. Moreover, the British began honoring the Balfour Declaration despite Arab protests. Thus Jewish immigration to Palestine from turbulent Europe in the interwar years grew rapidly, particularly after Adolf Hitler became German chancellor in 1933. By 1939 Palestine's Jewish population had increased almost fivefold since 1914 and accounted for about 30 percent of all inhabitants.

Jewish settlers in Palestine faced formidable difficulties. Although much of the land purchased by the Jewish National Fund was productive, the sellers of such land were often wealthy absentee Arab landowners who cared little for their Arab tenants' welfare. When the Jewish settlers replaced those long-time Arab tenants, Arab farmers and intellectuals burned with a sense of injustice. Moreover, most Jewish immigrants came from urban backgrounds and preferred to establish new cities like Tel Aviv or to live in existing towns, where they competed with the Arabs. The land issue combined with economic and cultural friction to harden Arab protest into hatred.

kibbutz A Jewish collective farm, first established by Zionists in Palestine, on which each member shared equally in the work, rewards, and defense.

Kibbutz Children Picking Grapes Many of the early kibbutzim, such as this one at Kfar Blum in Israel's northern Galilee, were agricultural settlements that produced cotton and fruits such as grapes, oranges, and apples, which were then packed and shipped around the world. They also produced most of the food eaten by the members. On the kibbutz, as these children illustrate, all did their share of the work. Collection boxes for the Zionist cause (below) date back to 1884, but donations became more standardized after the founding of the Jewish National Fund in 1901. The first Blue Box appeared in 1904, with the suggestion that a box be placed in every Jewish home around the world and contributed to as often as possible. Still collected today, Blue Box donations fund projects such as planting forests, establishing parks, and building roads and water reservoirs in the Israeli state. (kibbutz: Courtesy, Kibbutz Kfar Blum Archives; box: Courtesy National Jewish Fund)

The British gradually responded to Arab pressure and tried to slow Jewish immigration. This effort satisfied neither Jews nor Arabs, and between 1936 and 1939 the three communities (Arab, Jewish, and British) were engaged in an undeclared civil war. On the eve of the Second World War, the frustrated British proposed an independent Palestine with the number of Jews permanently limited to only about one-third of the total population. Zionists felt themselves in grave danger of losing their dream of an independent Jewish state.

Nevertheless, in the face of adversity Jewish settlers gradually succeeded in forging a cohesive community in Palestine. Hebrew, for centuries used only in religious worship, was revived as a living language in the 1920s–1930s to bind the Jews in Palestine together. Despite its slow beginnings, rural development achieved often remarkable results. The key unit of agricultural organization was the **kibbutz**, a collective farm on which each member shared equally in the work, rewards, and defense. An egalitarian socialist ideology also characterized industry, which grew rapidly. By 1939 a new but old nation was emerging in the Middle East.

Toward Self-Rule in India

What role did Gandhi and his campaign of militant nonviolence play in leading India to independence from the British?

The nationalist movement in British India grew out of two interconnected cultures, Hindu and Muslim. While the two joined together to challenge British rule, they also came to see themselves as fundamentally different. Nowhere has modern nationalism's power both to unify and to divide been more strikingly demonstrated than in India.

British Promises and Repression

Indian nationalism had emerged in the late nineteenth century (see "The British and the Indian Educated Elite" in Chapter 26), and when the First World War began, the British feared an Indian revolt. Instead Indians supported the war effort. About 1.2 million Indian soldiers and laborers voluntarily served in Europe, Africa, and the Middle East. The British government in India and the native Indian princes sent

British Man Fishing in India British colonial officials, such as this gentleman reposing in a wicker chair while fishing in India around 1925, enjoyed lifestyles that were often much more comfortable than would have been the case back in England. Gardeners, chauffeurs, maids, cooks, and other personal servants, like the three men helping the fisher, were commonly hired to wait on the colonists hand and foot. Some justified the lifestyle as demonstrating the refinements of civilization — part of the white man's burden.

(© Mary Evans Picture Library/The Image Works)

large supplies of food, money, and ammunition. In return, the British opened more good government jobs to Indians and made other minor concessions.

As the war in distant Europe ground on, however, inflation, high taxes, food shortages, and a terrible influenza epidemic created widespread suffering and discontent. The prewar nationalist movement revived, becoming stronger than ever, and moderates and radicals in the Indian National Congress Party joined forces. Moreover, in 1916 Hindu leaders in the Congress Party hammered out an alliance—the **Lucknow Pact**—with India's Muslim League. The Lucknow (LUHK-noh) Pact forged a powerful united front of Hindus and Muslims and called for putting India on an equal footing with self-governing British dominions like Canada, Australia, and New Zealand.

The British response to the Lucknow Pact was mixed. In August 1917 the British called for the "gradual development of self-governing institutions with a view to the progressive realization of responsible government in India."[4] But the proposed self-government was much more limited than that granted the British dominions. In late 1919 the British established a dual administration: part Indian and elected, part British and authoritarian. Such uncontroversial activities as

agriculture and health were transferred from British to Indian officials, but sensitive matters like taxes, police, and the courts remained solely in British hands.

Old-fashioned authoritarian rule also seriously undermined whatever positive impact this reform might have had. The 1919 Rowlatt Acts indefinitely extended wartime "emergency measures" designed to curb unrest and root out "conspiracy." The result was a wave of rioting across India.

Under these tense conditions a crowd of some ten thousand gathered to celebrate a Sikh religious festival in an enclosed square in the Sikh (SEEK) holy city of Amritsar (ahm-RIHT-suhr) in the northern Punjab province. Unknown to the crowd, the local English commander, General Reginald Dyer, had banned all public meetings that very day. Dyer marched his troops into the square and, without warning, ordered them to fire into the crowd until the ammunition ran out. Official British records of the Amritsar Massacre list 379 killed and 1,137 wounded, but these figures remain hotly contested as being too low. Tensions flared, and India stood on the verge of more violence and repression. That India took a different path to national liberation was due largely to Mohandas K. Gandhi (1869–1948), the most influential Indian leader of modern times.

The Roots of Militant Nonviolence

Gandhi grew up in a well-to-do family, and after his father's death he went to study law in England, where

Lucknow Pact A 1916 alliance between the Hindus leading the Indian National Congress Party and the Muslim League.

satyagraha Loosely translated as "soul force," which Gandhi believed was the means of striving for truth and social justice through love, suffering, and conversion of the oppressor.

he passed the English bar. Upon returning to India, he decided in 1893 to try a case for some wealthy Indian merchants in the British colony of Natal (part of modern South Africa). It was a momentous decision.

In Natal Gandhi took up the plight of the expatriate Indian community. White plantation owners had been importing thousands of poor Indians as indentured laborers since the 1860s. Some of these Indians, after completing their period of indenture, remained in Natal as free persons and economic competitors. In response, the Afrikaner (of Dutch descent) and British settlers passed brutally discriminatory laws. Poor Indians had to work on plantations or return to India. Rich Indians, who had previously had the vote in Natal, lost that right in 1896. Gandhi undertook his countrymen's legal defense.

Meanwhile, Gandhi was searching for a spiritual theory of social action. He studied Hindu and Christian teachings and gradually developed a weapon for the poor and oppressed that he called **satyagraha** (suh-TYAH-gruh-huh). Gandhi conceived of satyagraha, loosely translated as "soul force," as a means of striving for truth and social justice through love and a willingness to suffer the oppressor's blows, while trying to convert him or her to one's views of what is true and just. Its tactic was active nonviolent resistance.

When South Africa's white government severely restricted Asian immigration and internal freedom of movement, Gandhi put his philosophy into action and organized a nonviolent mass resistance campaign. Thousands of Indian men and women marched in peaceful protest and withstood beatings, arrest, and imprisonment.

In 1914 South Africa's exasperated whites agreed to many of the Indians' demands. They passed a law abolishing discriminatory taxes on Indian traders, recognized the legality of non-Christian marriages, and permitted the continued immigration of free Indians.

Gandhi's Resistance Campaign in India

In 1915 Gandhi returned to India a hero. The masses hailed him as a mahatma, or "great soul"—a Hindu title of veneration for a man of great knowledge and humanity. In 1920 Gandhi launched a national campaign of nonviolent resistance to British rule. He urged his countrymen to boycott British goods, jobs, and honors and told peasants not to pay taxes.

The nationalist movement had previously touched only the tiny, prosperous, Western-educated elite. Now both the illiterate masses of village India and the educated classes heard Gandhi's call for militant nonviolent resistance. It particularly appealed to the masses of Hindus who were not members of the warrior caste or the so-called military races and who were traditionally passive and nonviolent. The British had regarded

ordinary Hindus as cowards. Gandhi told them that they could be courageous and even morally superior:

> What do you think? Wherein is courage required—in blowing others to pieces from behind a cannon, or with a smiling face to approach a cannon and be blown to pieces? Who is the true warrior—he who keeps death always as a bosom-friend, or he who controls the death of others? Believe me that a man devoid of courage and manhood can never be a passive resister.[5]

Gandhi made the Indian National Congress into a mass political party, welcoming members from every ethnic group and cooperating closely with the Muslim minority.

In 1922 some Indian resisters turned to violence, murdering twenty-two policemen. Savage riots broke out, and Gandhi abruptly called off his campaign, observing that he had "committed a Himalayan blunder in placing civil disobedience before those who had never learnt the art of civil disobedience."[6] Arrested for fomenting rebellion, Gandhi served two years in prison. Upon his release Gandhi set up a commune, established a national newspaper, and set out to reform Indian society and improve the lot of the poor. For Gandhi moral improvement, social progress, and the national movement went hand in hand. Above all, Gandhi nurtured national identity and self-respect. He also tried to instill in India's people the courage to overcome their fear of their colonial rulers and to fight these rulers with nonviolence. (See "Global Viewpoints: Gandhi and Mao on Revolutionary Means," page 868.)

During Gandhi's time in prison (1922–1924) the Indian National Congress had splintered into various factions, and Gandhi spent the years after his release quietly trying to reunite the organization. In 1929 the radical nationalists, led by Jawaharlal Nehru (juh-WAH-hur-lahl NAY-roo) (1889–1964), pushed through the National Congress a resolution calling for virtual independence within a year. The British stiffened in their resolve against Indian independence, and Indian radicals talked of a bloody showdown.

India, ca. 1930

Gandhi and Mao on Revolutionary Means

India's Mohandas Gandhi and China's Mao Zedong successfully led two of the largest and most populous nations to independence in the late 1940s. Although both drew much of their support from the peasant masses, their political philosophies were exact oppposites.

Gandhi believed active nonviolent disobedience to British rule was the only way Indians could break free of British rule and gain independence. Mao, in his *Little Red Book*, argues that "power flows from the barrel of a gun," and that only through the use of violence can the Chinese masses rid themselves of corrupt warlords, cruel landowners, imperialist occupiers, and ruling elites.

Mohandas Gandhi

■ Complete civil disobedience is rebellion without the element of violence in it. An out-and-out resister simply ignores the authority of the State. He becomes an outlaw claiming to disregard every unmoral State law. Thus, for instance, he may refuse to pay taxes, he may refuse to recognize the authority in his daily intercourse. . . . In doing all this he never uses force and never resists force when it is used against him. In fact, he invites imprisonment and other uses of force against himself. This he does because and when he finds the bodily freedom he seemingly enjoys to be an intolerable burden. He argues to himself that a State allows personal freedom only in so far as the citizen submits to its regulations. Submission to the State law is the price a citizen pays for his personal liberty. Submission, therefore, to a State wholly or largely unjust is an immoral barter for liberty. . . .

A body of civil resisters is, therefore, like an army subject to all the discipline of a soldier. . . . And as a civil resistance army is or ought to be free from passion because free from the spirit of retaliation, it requires the fewest number of soldiers. Indeed, one *perfect* civil resister is enough to win the battle of Right against Wrong. [1921]

You might of course say that there can be no nonviolent rebellion and there has been none known to history. Well, it is my ambition to provide an instance, and it is my dream that my country may win its freedom through nonviolence. And, I would like to repeat to the world times without num-

ber, that I will not purchase my country's freedom at the cost of nonviolence. My marriage to nonviolence is such an absolute thing that I would rather commit suicide than be deflected from my position. I have not mentioned truth in this connection, simply because truth cannot be expressed except by nonviolence. [1931]

Mao Zedong

■ *War* is the highest form of struggle for resolving contradictions, when they have developed to a certain state, between classes, nations, states, or political groups, and it has existed ever since the emergence of private property and of classes.

The seizure of power by armed force, the settlement of the issue by war, is the central task and the highest form of revolution. This Marxist-Leninist principle of revolution holds good universally, for China and for all other countries.

According to the Marxist theory of the state, . . . whoever wants to seize and retain state power must have a strong army. Some people ridicule us as advocates of the "omnipotence of war." Yes, we are advocates of the omnipotence of revolutionary war; that is good, not bad, it is Marxist. Experience in the class struggle in the era of imperialism teaches us that it is only by the power of the gun that the working class and the laboring masses can defeat the armed bourgeoisie and landlords; in this sense we may say that only with guns can the whole world be transformed.

QUESTIONS FOR ANALYSIS

1. According to Gandhi, when should people resort to nonviolent disobedience in opposing their rulers?
2. According to Mao, what is the highest form of revolution? What theory does he draw on for this conclusion?

Sources: Mahatma Gandhi, "Young India, November 10, 1921" and "Young India, November 12, 1931," in *All Men Are Brothers: Autobiographical Reflections*, ed. Krishna Kripalani (New York: Continuum, 1997), pp. 81, 135–136. Reprinted by permission of the Navajivan Trust; Mao Tsetung, *Quotations from Chairman Mao Tsetung* (Peking: Foreign Languages Press, 1972), pp. 58, 61–63.

Into this tense situation Gandhi masterfully reasserted his leadership, taking a hard line toward the British but insisting on nonviolent methods. He organized a massive resistance campaign against the tax on salt, which gave the British a veritable monopoly on the salt that was absolutely necessary for survival in India's heat and humidity and affected every Indian family. From March 12 to April

6, 1930, Gandhi led tens of thousands of people in a spectacular march to the sea, where he made salt in defiance of the law. A later demonstration at the British-run Dharasana (dahr-AH-sahn-nah) salt works resulted in many of the 2,500 nonviolent marchers being beaten senseless by policemen in a brutal and well-publicized encounter. Over the next months the British arrested Gandhi and

Gandhi on the Salt March, March 1930 A small, frail man, Gandhi possessed enormous courage and determination. His campaign of nonviolent resistance to British rule inspired the Indian masses and mobilized a nation. Here he is shown walking on his famous march to the sea to protest the English-Indian government's monopoly on salt production. (© SZ Photo/Scherl/Bridgeman Images)

sixty thousand other protesters for making and distributing salt. But the protests continued, and in 1931 the frustrated and unnerved British released Gandhi from jail and sat down to negotiate with him over Indian self-rule. Negotiations resulted in a new constitution, the Government of India Act, in 1935, which greatly strengthened India's parliamentary representative institutions and gave Indians some voice in the administration of British India.

Despite his best efforts, Gandhi failed to heal a widening split between Hindus and Muslims. Indian nationalism, based largely on Hindu symbols and customs, increasingly disturbed the Muslim minority, represented by the Muslim League led by the Western-educated Bombay lawyer Muhammad Ali Jinnah (jee-NAH) (1876–1948). Tempers mounted, and both sides committed atrocities. By the late 1930s Muslim League leaders were calling for the creation of a Muslim nation in British India, a "Pakistan," or "land of the pure." As in Palestine, the rise of conflicting nationalisms in India based on religion would lead to tragedy (see "Independence in India, Pakistan, and Bangladesh" in Chapter 31).

Nationalist Struggles in East and Southeast Asia

How did nationalism shape political developments in East and Southeast Asia?

Because of the efforts of the Meiji reformers, nationalism and modernization were well developed in Japan by 1914. Japan competed politically and economically with the world's leading nations, building its own empire and proclaiming its special mission in Asia. Initially China lagged behind, but after 1912 the pace of nationalist development began to quicken.

By promoting extensive modernization in the 1920s, the Chinese nationalist movement managed to reduce the power and influence both of the warlords who controlled large territories in the interior and of the imperialist West. This achievement was soon undermined, however, by an internal civil war followed by war with an expanding Japan. Nationalism also flourished elsewhere in Asia, scoring a major victory in the Philippines.

The Rise of Nationalist China

The 1911 Revolution led by Sun Yatsen (1866–1925) overthrew the Qing (CHING) Dynasty, and after four thousand years of monarchy the last Chinese emperor, Puyi (1906–1967), abdicated in February 1912 (see "Republican Revolution" in Chapter 26). Sun Yatsen (soon yaht-SEHN) proclaimed China a republic and thereby opened an era of unprecedented change for Chinese society. In 1912 Sun Yatsen turned over leadership of the republican government to the other central figure in the revolution, Yuan Shigai (yoo-AHN shee-KIGH). Originally called out of retirement to save the Qing Dynasty, Yuan (1859–1916) betrayed its Manchu leaders and convinced the revolutionaries that he could unite the country peacefully and prevent foreign intervention. Once elected president of the republic, however, Yuan concentrated on building his own power. In 1913 he used military force to dissolve China's parliament and ruled as a dictator. China's first modern revolution had failed.

The extent of the failure became apparent only after Yuan's death in 1916, when the central government in Beijing almost disintegrated. For more than a decade thereafter, power resided in a multitude of local military leaders, the so-called warlords. Their wars, taxes, and corruption created terrible suffering.

Foreign imperialism intensified the agony of warlordism. Japan's expansion into Shandong and southern Manchuria during World War I angered China's growing middle class and enraged China's young patriots (see Map 29.2, page 878). On May 4, 1919, five thousand students in Beijing exploded against the decision of the Paris Peace Conference to leave the Shandong Peninsula in Japanese hands. This famous incident launched the **May Fourth Movement**, which opposed both foreign domination and warlord government. (See "Thinking Like a Historian: Interpreting the May Fourth Movement," page 874.)

The May Fourth Movement, which was both strongly pro-Marxist and passionately anti-imperialist, looked to the October 1917 Bolshevik Revolution in Russia as a model for its own nationalist revolution. In 1923 Sun Yatsen decided to ally his Nationalist Party, or Guomindang (gwoh-mihn-dang), with Lenin's Communist Third International and the newly formed Chinese Communist Party. The result was the first of many so-called national liberation fronts.

Sun, however, was no Communist. In his *Three Principles of the People*, elaborating on the official Nationalist Party ideology—nationalism, democracy, and people's livelihood—nationalism remained of prime importance:

> Compared to the other peoples of the world we have the greatest population and our civilization is four thousand years old; we should be advancing in the front rank with the nations of Europe and America. But the Chinese people . . . do not have national spirit. . . . If we do not earnestly espouse nationalism and weld together our four hundred million people into a strong nation, there is a danger of China's being lost and our people being destroyed. If we wish to avert this catastrophe, we must . . . bring this national spirit to the salvation of the country.[7]

Democracy, in contrast, had a less exalted meaning. Sun equated it with firm rule by the Nationalists, who would improve people's lives through land reform and welfare measures.

Sun planned to use the Nationalist Party's revolutionary army to crush the warlords and reunite China under a strong central government. When Sun unexpectedly died in 1925, Jiang Jieshi (known in the West as Chiang Kai-shek) (1887–1975) took his place. In 1926 and 1927 Jiang Jieshi (jee-ang jee-shee) led Nationalist armies in a successful attack on warlord governments in central and northern China. In 1928 the Nationalists established a new capital at Nanjing. Foreign states recognized the Nanjing government, and superficial observers believed China to be truly reunified.

In fact, national unification was only skin-deep. China remained a vast agricultural country plagued by foreign concessions, regional differences, and a lack of modern communications. Moreover, the uneasy alliance between the Nationalist Party and the Chinese Communist Party had turned into a bitter, deadly rivalry. Fearful of Communist subversion of the Nationalist government, Jiang decided in April 1927 to liquidate his left-wing "allies" in a bloody purge. Chinese Communists went into hiding and vowed revenge.

China's Intellectual Revolution

Nationalism was the most powerful idea in China between 1911 and 1929, but it was only one aspect of a complex intellectual revolution, generally known as the **New Culture Movement**, that hammered at traditional Chinese thought and custom, advocated cultural renaissance, and pushed China into the modern world. The New Culture Movement was founded around 1916 by young Western-oriented intellectuals in Beijing. These intellectuals attacked Confucian ethics, which subordinated subjects to rulers, sons to fathers, and wives to husbands. As modernists, they advocated new and anti-Confucian virtues: individu-

May Fourth Movement A Chinese nationalist movement against foreign imperialists and warlord rule; it began as a 1919 student protest against the decision of the Paris Peace Conference to leave the Shandong Peninsula in the hands of Japan.

New Culture Movement An intellectual revolution beginning in 1916 that attacked traditional Chinese, particularly Confucian, culture and promoted Western ideas of science, democracy, and individualism.

The Fate of a Chinese Patriot

On May 30, 1925, British municipal police in Shanghai opened fire on a group of Chinese demonstrators who were protesting unfair labor practices and wages and the foreign imperialist presence in their country. The police killed thirteen people and wounded many others, touching off nationwide and international protests and attacks on foreign offices and businesses. Merchants and workers across the country organized strikes and boycotts against Japanese and British goods and factories. The Chinese Communist Party in particular benefited significantly from the anti-imperialist sentiment stirred up by this incident, with party membership swelling from only a few hundred members to over twenty thousand. The unrest lasted for three months, until the British fired the policemen involved and paid a cash indemnity to the families of the wounded and dead.

This political cartoon shows the fate of the Chinese patriots at the hands of warlords and foreign imperialists. The Chinese characters on the plume of the soldier's hat say "Warlords," referring to the large private armies that many landowners employed to maintain control over the territory they had seized. The label on the chest of the fat, obviously Western man says, "Foreign Imperialism." The waistband on the patriot being choked reads, "Patriotic compatriot." In the upper left-hand corner the characters read, "Warlords and Imperialists' oppression of the Chinese people, before and after May 30, 1925." The "map" that the figures stand on represents "The Republic of China." Each place where there is a pile of skulls and blood is labeled with the name of a city where massacres occurred: Qingdao, Nanjing, Shanghai, Jiujiang, Guangzhou, Hankou, and Chongqing. The Chinese characters on the map in the lower left corner read, "The massacres of the entire country." The name of the organization producing the cartoon is written across the bottom: "Membership Drive of the Chinese Salvation Association."

(Library of Congress, Prints and Photographs Division, Washington, D.C./LC-USZ62-99451)

QUESTIONS FOR ANALYSIS

1. Which figures represent Chinese warlords, foreign imperialists, and Chinese patriots?
2. What does the cartoon suggest about the fate of the Chinese demonstrators?
3. What emotions are these images trying to evoke in the person viewing the cartoon?

alism, democratic equality, and the critical scientific method. They also promoted the use of simple, understandable written language as a means to clear thinking and mass education. China, they said, needed a whole new culture, a radically different worldview. (See "Thinking Like a Historian: Interpreting the May Fourth Movement," page 874.)

Many intellectuals thought the radical worldview China needed was Marxist socialism. It, too, was Western in origin, "scientific" in approach, and materialist in its denial of religious belief and Confucian family ethics. But while liberalism and individualism reflected the bewildering range of Western thought since the Enlightenment, Marxist socialism offered the certainty of a single all-encompassing creed. As one young Communist intellectual exclaimed, "I am now able to impose order on all the ideas which I could not reconcile; I have found the key to all the problems which appeared to me self-contradictory and insoluble."[8]

Marxism provided a means of criticizing Western dominance, thereby salving Chinese pride. Chinese Communists could blame China's pitiful weakness on rapacious foreign capitalistic imperialism. Thus Marxism, as modified by Lenin and applied by the Bolsheviks in the Soviet Union, appeared as a means of catching up with the hated but envied West. For Chinese believers, it promised salvation soon. (See "Analyzing the Evidence: The Fate of a Chinese Patriot," page 871.)

Chinese Communists could and did interpret Marxism-Leninism to appeal to the masses — the peasants. Mao Zedong (sometimes spelled Mao Tse-tung) in particular quickly recognized the impoverished Chinese peasantry's enormous revolutionary potential. (See "Global Viewpoints: Gandhi and Mao on Revolutionary Means," page 868.) A member of a prosperous, hard-working peasant family, Mao Zedong (maow-dzuh-dahng) (1893–1976) converted to Marxist socialism in 1918. He began his revolutionary career as an urban labor organizer. In 1925 protest strikes by Chinese textile workers against their Japanese employers unexpectedly spread from the big coastal cities to rural China, prompting Mao (like Lenin in Russia) to reconsider the peasants (see "Lenin and the Bolshevik Revolution" in Chapter 28). Investigating the rapid growth of radical peasant associations in Hunan province, Mao argued passionately in a 1927 report:

> The force of the peasantry is like that of the raging winds and driving rain. It is rapidly increasing in violence. No force can stand in its way. The peasantry will tear apart all nets which bind it and hasten along the road to liberation. They will bury beneath them all forces of imperialism, militarism, corrupt officialdom, village bosses and evil gentry.[9]

Mao's first experiment in peasant revolt — the Autumn Harvest Uprising of September 1927 — was not successful, but Mao learned quickly. He advocated

equal distribution of land and broke up his forces into small guerrilla groups. After 1928 he and his supporters built up a self-governing Communist soviet, centered at Jiangxi (jee-AHNG-shee) in southeastern China, and dug in against Nationalist attacks.

China's intellectual revolution also stimulated profound changes in popular culture and family life. (See "Individuals in Society: Ning Lao, a Chinese Working Woman," at right.) After the 1911 Revolution Chinese women enjoyed increasingly greater freedom and equality, and gradually gained unprecedented educational and economic opportunities. Thus rising nationalism and the intellectual revolution interacted with monumental changes in Chinese family life.

From Liberalism to Ultranationalism in Japan

The nearly total homogeneity of the Japanese population (98.5 percent ethnic Japanese) was a major factor in the Meiji reformers' efforts to build a powerful, nationalistic, modern state and resist Western imperialism. Their spectacular success deeply impressed Japan's fellow Asians. The Japanese, alone among Asia's peoples, had mastered modern industrial technology by 1910 and had fought victorious wars against both China and Russia. The First World War brought more triumphs. In 1915 Japan seized Germany's Asian holdings and retained most of them as League of Nations mandates. The Japanese economy expanded enormously. Profits soared as Japan won new markets that wartime Europe could no longer supply.

In the early 1920s Japan made further progress on all fronts. In 1922 Japan signed a naval arms limitation treaty with the Western powers and returned some of its control over the Shandong Peninsula to China. These conciliatory moves reduced tensions in East Asia. At home Japan seemed headed toward genuine democracy. The electorate expanded twelvefold between 1918 and 1925 as all males over twenty-five won the vote. Two-party competition was intense. Japanese living standards were the highest in Asia. Literacy was universal.

Japan's remarkable rise was accompanied by serious problems. Japan had a rapidly growing population but scarce natural resources. As early as the 1920s Japan was exporting manufactured goods in order to pay for imports of food and essential raw materials. Deeply enmeshed in world trade, Japan was vulnerable to every boom and bust. These economic realities broadened support for Japan's colonial empire. Before World War I Japanese leaders saw colonial expansion primarily in terms of international prestige and national defense. They believed that control of Taiwan, Korea, and Manchuria provided an essential "outer ring of defense" to protect the home islands from Russian attack and Anglo-American imperialism. Now, in the

Ning Lao, a Chinese Working Woman

THE VOICE OF THE POOR AND UNEDUCATED IS OFTEN muffled in history. Thus *A Daughter of Han*, a rare autobiography of an illiterate working woman as told to an American friend, Ida Pruitt, offers unforgettable insights into the evolution of ordinary Chinese life and family relations.

Ning Lao was born in 1867 to poor parents in the northern city of Penglai on the Shandong Peninsula. Her foot binding was delayed to age nine, since she "loved so much to run and play." She described the pain when the bandages were finally drawn tight: "My feet hurt so much that for two years I had to crawl on my knees."* Her arranged marriage at age fourteen was a disaster. She found that her husband was a drug addict ("in those days everyone took opium to some extent") who sold everything to pay for his habit. Yet "there was no freedom then for women," and "it was no light thing for a woman to leave her house" and husband. Thus Ning Lao endured her situation until her husband sold their four-year-old daughter to buy opium. Taking her remaining baby daughter, she fled.

Taking off her foot bandages, Ning Lao became a beggar. Her feet began to spread, quite improperly, but she walked without pain. And the beggar's life was "not the hardest one," she thought, for a beggar woman could go where she pleased. To better care for her child, Ning Lao became a servant and a cook in prosperous households. Some of her mistresses were concubines (secondary wives taken by rich men in middle age), and she concluded that concubinage resulted in nothing but quarrels and heartache. Hot tempered and quick to take offense and leave an employer, the hard-working woman always found a new job quickly. In time she became a peddler of luxury goods to wealthy women confined to their homes.

The two unshakable values that buoyed Ning Lao were a tough, fatalistic acceptance of life—"Only fortune that comes of itself will come. There is no use to seek for it"— and devotion to her family. She eventually returned to her husband, who had mellowed, seldom took opium, and was "good" in those years. She reflected, "But I did not miss him when he died. I had my newborn son and I was happy. My house was established. . . . Truly all my life I spent thinking of my family." Her lifelong devotion was reciprocated by her son and granddaughter, who cared for her well in her old age.

Ning Lao's remarkable life story encompasses both old and new Chinese attitudes toward family life. Her son moved to the capital city of Beijing, worked in an office, and had only one wife. Her granddaughter, Su Teh, studied in missionary schools and became a college teacher and a determined foe of arranged marriages. She personified the trend toward greater freedom for Chinese women.

The tough and resilient Ning Lao (right) with Ida Pruitt.
(Reproduced with permission of Eileen Hsu-Balzer)

Generational differences also highlighted changing political attitudes. When the Japanese invaded China and occupied Beijing in 1937, Ning Lao thought that "perhaps the Mandate of Heaven had passed to the Japanese . . . and we should listen to them as our new masters." Her nationalistic granddaughter disagreed. She urged resistance and the creation of a new China, where the people governed themselves. Leaving to join the guerrillas in 1938, Su Teh gave her savings to her family and promised to continue to help them. One must be good to one's family, she said, but one must also work for the country.

QUESTIONS FOR ANALYSIS

1. Compare the lives of Ning Lao and her granddaughter. In what ways were they different and similar?
2. In a broader historical perspective, what do you find most significant about Ning Lao's account of her life? Why?

*Ida Pruitt, *A Daughter of Han: The Autobiography of a Chinese Working Woman* (New Haven, Conn.: Yale University Press, 1945), p. 22. Other quotations are from pages 83, 62, 71, 182, 166, 235, and 246.

Interpreting the May Fourth Movement

On May 4, 1919, several thousand students at Peking (Beijing) University demonstrated against Japan's receipt of Germany's former territorial privileges in China's Shandong province. The protest soon acquired a much broader agenda, however, by incorporating the causes of the New Culture Movement that had begun in the mid-1910s. These included the promotion of democracy, science, equality, modernization, education reform, the revision of the land tenure system, women's emancipation, and opposition to foreign influences in China.

1 **Luo Jialun, "Notice from Beijing Educational Circles," May 4, 1919.** This notice, drafted by a Peking University student, was printed on a flyer that was circulated among the crowd during the student demonstration in Beijing on May 4, 1919. The students first listened to speeches and then began a march toward Beijing's diplomatic quarter.

■ The Japanese demands at the Peace Conference to annex Qingdao and to adminster all the rights to Shandong are going to succeed! Their diplomacy has triumphed! Our diplomacy has failed! If Shandong is lost, it will wreck China's territory! If China's territory is wrecked, China will perish! That is why we from the educational circles have lined up today to go to the various legations in order to ask the countries involved to do justice. We urge our country's industrial and commercial sectors to rise up and organize a national assembly, to fight for sovereignty abroad and to drive out the traitors at home. China's fate depends on this! Today we propose to our compatriots these two principles:

China's land may be conquered but it must not be forfeited!
China's people may be killed but they must not surrender!
The Country will perish! Countrymen arise!

2 **Chen Duxiu, excerpt from "Should We Be Patriotic After All?" 1922.** Chen Duxiu (too-shoe) was dean of humanities at Peking University. He was arrested and imprisoned on June 8, 1919, for his participation in the May Fourth Movement.

■ Since the outbreak of the Shandong crisis, patriotic chanting is heard everywhere. It is therefore all the more important to raise the question: should we be patriotic or not? To ask this rational question in the midst of an emotional upheaval is particularly important, since reason is frequently in conflict with mass psychology. . . . Nationalism is chiefly an emotional response. It can drive people to extreme, irrational behavior—take the example of the German and Japanese military. . . . [N]ationalism is just another excuse for harming people, making them blind, mad enough to sacrifice themselves. We uneducated, ignorant, disorganized Chinese people aren't fit for patriotism yet, much less for the long-range reflection about what kind of country we want. But this need not always be so.

3 **Tianjin Awakening Society, "Declaration on Marriage, Education, and Economics," 1919.** The Tianjin Awakening Society was formed during the New Culture Movement and included both male and female members. Participation in groups like this had a liberating effect on the women involved and allowed them to focus their activities on their foremost concerns: marriage, education, and economics.

■ Marriage is a matter which many young men and women earnestly hope can be satisfactorily revolved. Since most young men and women are under the oppression of headstrong parents, have no opportunity to fight back, and even submit to parents making decisions on their behalf, malignant outcomes are frequent and everywhere to be seen. . . . Oh, loveable and vivacious young women! Do not be afraid of offending your parents, do not be afraid of offending your parents-in-law, and do not be afraid of offending your husband or other kinfolk. If you feel the environment is unfit for your existence you should courageously break away from it. Society is replete with persons who sympathize with you and who are ready to assist you. Hurry up and join hands with them!

ANALYZING THE EVIDENCE

1. According to Source 1, what actions do the students intend to take to accomplish their goals? What are their guiding principles?
2. In Source 2, why is Chen Duxiu concerned about patriotism and nationalism? What kinds of actions does he say these two "isms" evoke?
3. According to Source 3, what kinds of actions should young women take in the changing China of 1919? Why might they be afraid of this change in Chinese society?
4. According to Hu Shih in Source 4, what kinds of changes still need to be carried out?
5. Why are the students burning Japanese goods in the photo in Source 5? What do the Japanese goods represent?

(© Pictures from History/The Image Works)

5 **Tsinghua University students burn Japanese goods, 1919.** One of the actions taken by the Chinese university students was to burn imported Japanese goods.

4 **Hu Shih on the work remaining, December 1919.** Hu Shih was a Western-educated Chinese philosopher and one of the leaders of the New Culture Movement. He coined the phrases "Mr. Democracy" and "Mr. Science" to encourage the adoption of these Western ideals. In this excerpt, Hu Shih mentions some of the actions that remain to be taken to modernize China and promote democracy and science.

◼ It was the nonpolitical forces—the students, the merchants, the demonstrations and street orations, and the boycott—that did the work and triumphed. This was a great revelation and produced a new optimism.

. . . [W]e still have the masses to educate, the women to emancipate, the schools to reform, the home industries to develop, the family system to reshape, the dead and antiquated ideas to combat, the false and harmful idols to dethrone, the many, many social and economic wrongs to redress. It is in these new channels of activity that Young China, with reawakened hope and vigor, is now working slowly but steadily to rebuild a new foundation for Chinese democracy.

PUTTING IT ALL TOGETHER

Using the sources above, along with what you have learned in class and in this chapter, write a short essay about the anti-imperialist, political, and cultural revolution initiated by the May Fourth and New Culture Movements. What were the students seeking to change? Why was Marxism an important ideology in the movement?

Sources: (1) "Notice from Beijing Educational Circles," quoted in Chen Pingyuan, *Touches of History: An Entry into "May Fourth" China,* Michel Hockx, trans. (Boston: Brill, 2011), p. 26; (2) Chen Duxiu, "Should We Be Patriotic After All?" quoted in Vera Schwarcz, *The Chinese Enlightenment: Intellectuals and the Legacy of the May Fourth Movement of 1919* (Berkeley: University of California Press, 1986), p. 23; (3) Quoted in Yunzhi Geng, *An Introductory Study on China's Cultural Transformation in Recent Time* (Berlin: Springer-Verlag, 2015), p. 286; (4) Hu Shih, "Intellectual China in 1919," quoted in Jerome B. Grieder, *Hu Shih and the Chinese Renaissance: Liberalism in the Chinese Revolution, 1917–1937* (Cambridge: Harvard University Press, 1970), p. 177.

Japanese Suffragists In the 1920s Japanese women pressed for political emancipation in demonstrations like this one, but they did not receive the right to vote until 1946. Like these suffragists, some young Japanese women adopted Western fashions. Most workers in modern Japanese textile factories were women. (Mansell/The LIFE Picture Collection/Getty Images)

1920s, Japan's colonies also seemed essential for markets, raw materials, and economic growth.

Japan's rapid industrial development also created an imbalanced "dualistic" economy. The modern sector consisted of a handful of giant conglomerate firms, the **zaibatsu** (zigh-BAHT-dzoo), or "financial combines." Zaibatsu firms wielded enormous economic power and dominated the other sector of the economy, an unorganized multitude of peasant farmers and craftsmen. The result was financial oligarchy, corruption of government officials, and a weak middle class.

Behind the façade of party politics, Japanese elites—the emperor, high government officials, big business and military leaders—jockeyed savagely for power. Cohesive leadership, which had played such an important role in Japan's modernization by the Meiji reformers, had ceased to exist. By far the most serious challenge to peaceful progress was fanatical nationalism. As in Europe, ultranationalism first emerged in Japan in the late nineteenth century but did not flower fully until the First World War and the 1930s.

Though their views were often vague, Japan's ultranationalists shared several fundamental beliefs. They were violently anti-Western, rejecting democracy, big business, and Marxist socialism. Reviving old myths, they stressed the emperor's godlike qualities and the samurai warrior's code of honor, obedience, and respon-

sibility. Despising party politics, they assassinated moderate leaders and plotted armed uprisings to achieve their goals. Above all else, the ultranationalists preached foreign expansion. Like Western imperialists shouldering "the white man's burden," Japanese ultranationalists thought their mission was a noble one. "Asia for the Asians" was their anti-Western rallying cry. As the famous ultranationalist Kita Ikki wrote in 1923, "Our seven hundred million brothers in China and India have no other path to independence than that offered by our guidance and protection."[10]

The ultranationalists were noisy and violent in the 1920s, but it took the Great Depression of the 1930s to tip the scales decisively in their favor. The worldwide depression (see "Worldwide Effects" in Chapter 30) hit Japan like a tidal wave in 1930. Exports and wages collapsed; unemployment and raw suffering soared. The ultranationalists blamed the system, and people listened.

Japan Against China

Among those who listened with particular care were young Japanese army officers in Manchuria, the under-populated, resource-rich province of northeastern China controlled by the Japanese army since its victory over Russia in 1905. The rise of Chinese nationalism embodied in the Guomindang unification of China challenged Japanese control over Manchuria. In response, junior Japanese officers in Manchuria, in cooperation with top generals in Tokyo, secretly manufactured an excuse for aggression in late 1931. They blew up some Japanese-owned railroad tracks near the city of

zaibatsu Giant conglomerate firms established in Japan beginning in the Meiji period and lasting until the end of World War II.

Long March The 6,000-mile retreat of the Chinese Communist army in 1934 to a remote region on the northwestern border of China, during which tens of thousands lost their lives.

Shenyang (Mukden) and then, with reinforcements rushed in from Korea, quickly occupied all of Manchuria in "self-defense."

In 1932 Japan proclaimed Manchuria an independent state, renaming it Manchukuo, and in 1934 installed Puyi, the last Qing emperor, as puppet emperor over the puppet state. When the League of Nations condemned Japanese aggression in Manchuria, Japan resigned in protest. Japanese aggression in Manchuria proved that the army, though reporting directly to the Japanese emperor, was an independent force subject to no outside control.

For China the Japanese conquest of Manchuria was disastrous. Japanese aggression in Manchuria drew attention away from modernizing efforts. The Nationalist government promoted a massive boycott of Japanese goods but lost interest in social reform. Above all, the Nationalist government after 1931 completely neglected land reform and the Chinese peasants' grinding poverty. A contemporaneous Chinese economist spelled out the revolutionary implications: "It seems clear that the land problem in China today is as acute as that of eighteenth-century France or nineteenth-century Russia."[11] Mao Zedong agreed.

Having abandoned land reform, partly because they themselves were often landowners, the Nationalists under Jiang Jieshi devoted their energies between 1930 and 1934 to great campaigns of encirclement and extermination of the Communists' rural power base in southeastern China. In 1934 they closed in for the kill, but, in one of the most incredible sagas of modern times, the main Communist army broke out, beat off attacks, and retreated 6,000 miles in twelve months to a remote region on the northwestern border (Map 29.2).

Of the estimated 100,000 men and women who began the **Long March**, only 8,000 to 10,000 reached the final destination in Yan'an (YEH-nahn).

There Mao built up his forces once again, established a new territorial base, and won local peasant support in five unprecedented ways. First, Mao's forces did not pillage and rape across the countryside as imperialist and warlord armies had always done. Second, Mao set up schools, albeit for Marxist education, so the nearly universally illiterate peasants could learn to read and write. Third, Mao established health clinics to provide the peasants with basic medical care. Fourth, Mao's armies, rather than stealing the peasants' produce, put down their weapons and helped the peasants plant and harvest their crops. Fifth, Communist courts tried the warlords and landlords for crimes against the peasants, who for the first time in Chinese history received economic and social justice.

In Japan politics became increasingly chaotic. In 1937 the Japanese military and the ultranationalists were in command. Unable to force China to cede more territory in northern China, they used a minor incident near Beijing as a pretext for a general attack. This marked the beginning of what became World War II in Asia, although Japan issued no declaration of war. The Nationalist government, which had just formed a united front with the Communists, fought hard, but Japanese troops quickly took Beijing and northern China. After taking the port of Shanghai, the Japanese launched an immediate attack up the Yangzi River.

Foretelling the horrors of World War II, the Japanese air force bombed Chinese cities and civilian populations with unrelenting fury. Nanjing, the capital, fell in December 1937. Entering the city, Japanese soldiers

Mao Zedong and the Chinese Long March Mao's Communist forces were welcomed by the peasants during the Long March and at the army's final destination at Yan'an because the soldiers treated them with respect. In Yan'an they set up schools and health clinics, helped the farmers with their crops, and tried and punished the warlords and landlords. Here Mao talks with some peasants while on the Long March. (akg-images)

MAP 29.2 The Chinese Communist Movement and the War with Japan, 1927–1938 After urban uprisings ordered by Stalin failed in 1927, Mao Zedong succeeded in forming a self-governing Communist soviet in mountainous southern China. Relentless Nationalist attacks between 1930 and 1934 finally forced the Long March to Yan'an, where the Communists were well positioned for guerrilla war against the Japanese.

went berserk and committed dreadful atrocities over seven weeks. They brutally murdered an estimated 200,000 to 300,000 Chinese civilians and unarmed soldiers, and raped 20,000 to 80,000 Chinese women. The "Rape of Nanjing" combined with other Japanese atrocities to outrage world opinion. The Western powers denounced Japanese aggression but, with tensions rising in Europe, took no action.

By late 1938 Japanese armies occupied sizable portions of coastal China (see Map 29.2). But the Nationalists and the Communists had retreated to the interior, and both refused to accept defeat. In 1939, as Europe edged toward another great war, China and Japan were bogged down in a savage stalemate. This undeclared war—called by historians the Second Sino-Japanese War (1937–1945)—provided a spectacular example of conflicting nationalisms.

Striving for Independence in Southeast Asia

The tide of nationalism was also rising in Southeast Asia. Nationalists in French Indochina and the Philippines urgently wanted genuine political independence and freedom from foreign rule. In French Indochina they ran up against an imperialist stone wall. The obstacle to Filipino independence came from America and Japan.

The French in Indochina, as in all their colonies, refused to export the liberal policies contained in the stirring words of their own Declaration of the Rights of Man and of the Citizen: liberty, equality, and fraternity (see "The National Assembly" in Chapter 22). This uncompromising attitude stimulated the growth of an equally stubborn Communist opposition under

Ho Chi Minh (hoh chee mihn) (1890–1969), which despite ruthless repression emerged as the dominant anti-French force in Indochina.

In the Philippines, however, a well-established nationalist movement achieved greater success. As in colonial Latin America, the Spanish in the Philippines had been indefatigable missionaries. By the late nineteenth century the Filipino population was 80 percent Catholic. Filipinos shared a common cultural heritage and a common racial origin. Education, especially for girls, was advanced for Southeast Asia, and already in 1843 a higher percentage of people could read in the Philippines than in Spain itself. Economic development helped to create a westernized elite, which turned first to reform and then to revolution in the 1890s.

Filipino nationalists were bitterly disillusioned when the United States, having taken the Philippines from Spain in the Spanish-American War of 1898, ruthlessly beat down a patriotic revolt and denied the universal Filipino desire for independence. The Americans claimed the Philippines was not ready for self-rule and might be seized by Germany or Britain if it could not establish a stable, secure government. As the imperialist power in the Philippines, the United States encouraged education and promoted capitalistic economic development. And as in British India, an elected legislature was given some real powers.

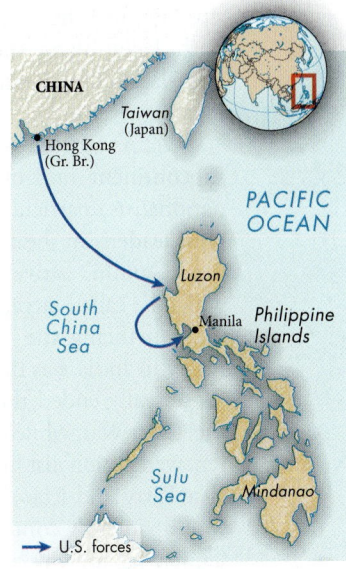

The Spanish-American War in the Philippines, 1898

As in India and French Indochina, demands for independence grew. One important contributing factor was American racial attitudes. Americans treated Filipinos as inferiors and introduced segregationist practices borrowed from the American South. American racism made passionate nationalists of many Filipinos. However, it was the Great Depression that had the most radical impact on the Philippines.

As the United States collapsed economically in the 1930s, the Philippines suddenly appeared to be a liability rather than an asset. American farm groups lobbied for protection from cheap Filipino sugar. To protect American jobs, labor unions demanded an end to Filipino immigration. Responding to public pressure, in 1934 Congress made the Philippines a self-governing commonwealth and scheduled independence for 1944. Sugar imports were reduced, and immigration was limited to only fifty Filipinos per year.

Some Filipino nationalists denounced the continued U.S. presence, but others were less certain that it was the immediate problem. Japan was fighting in China and expanding economically into the Philippines and throughout Southeast Asia. By 1939 a new threat to Filipino independence would come from Japan itself.

Uncle Sam as Schoolmaster In this cartoon that first appeared on the cover of *Harper's Weekly* in August 1898, unruly students from Spain's former colonies in Cuba and the Philippines, now living under American rule, are identified as a "Cuban Ex-patriot" and a "Guerilla." They are being disciplined with a switch by a stern Uncle Sam as he tries to teach them self-government. The gentleman to the left reading a book is José Miguel Gómez, one of Cuba's revolutionary heroes, while the Filipino insurrectionist Emilio Aguinaldo is made to wear a dunce cap and stand in the corner. The two well-behaved girls to the right represent Hawaii and Puerto Rico. (Sarin Images/Granger, NYC — All rights reserved.)

Chapter Summary

The Ottoman Empire's collapse in World War I left a power vacuum that both Western imperialists and Asian nationalists sought to fill. Strong leaders, such as Turkey's Mustafa Kemal, led successful nationalist movements in Turkey, Persia, and Afghanistan. British and French influence over the League of Nations–mandated

Arab states declined in the 1920s and 1930s as Arab nationalists pushed for complete independence. The situation in Palestine, where the British had promised both Palestinians and Jewish Zionists independent homelands, deteriorated in the interwar years as increasingly larger numbers of European Jews migrated there.

Britain's centuries-long colonial rule over the Indian subcontinent met increasing resistance from Indian nationalists, particularly from Indian National Congress leaders, in the first decades of the twentieth century. Gandhi's active, nonviolent resistance campaign, which he called satyagraha, was principally responsible for convincing the British that their colonial hegemony in India was doomed. China's 1911 Revolution successfully ended the ancient dynastic system before the Great War, while the 1919 May Fourth Movement renewed nationalist hopes after it. Jiang Jieshi's Nationalist Party and Mao Zedong's Communists, however, would violently contest who would rule over a unified China. Japan, unlike China, industrialized early and by the 1920s seemed headed toward genuine democracy, but militarists and ultranationalists then launched an aggressive campaign of foreign expansion based on "Asia for Asians," which contributed to the buildup to World War II. As the Great Depression took hold, Filipino nationalists achieved independence from the United States. The diversity of these nationalist movements, arising out of separate historical experiences and distinct cultures, helps explain why Asian nationalists, like European nationalists, developed a strong sense of "we" and "they." In Asia "they" included other Asians as well as Europeans.

NOTES

1. Howard M. Sachar, *A History of Israel: From the Rise of Zionism to Our Time* (New York: Alfred A. Knopf, 1985), p. 109.
2. H. Armstrong, *Turkey in Travail: The Birth of a New Nation* (London: John Lane, 1925), p. 75.
3. Quoted in Lord Kinross, *Atatürk: A Biography of Mustafa Kemal, Father of Modern Turkey* (New York: Morrow, 1965), p. 181.
4. Lawrence James, *Raj: The Making and Unmaking of British India* (New York: St. Martin's Press, 1998), p. 458.
5. Quoted in E. Erikson, *Gandhi's Truth: On the Origins of Militant Nonviolence* (New York: W. W. Norton, 1969), p. 225.
6. M. K. Gandhi, *Non-Violent Resistance (Satyagraha)* (New York: Schocken Books, 1961), p. 365.
7. Quoted in W. T. de Bary, W. Chan, and B. Watson, *Sources of Chinese Tradition* (New York: Columbia University Press, 1964), pp. 768–769.
8. Quoted in J. F. Fairbank, E. O. Reischauer, and A. M. Craig, *East Asia: Tradition and Transformation* (Boston: Houghton Mifflin, 1973), p. 774.
9. Quoted in B. I. Schwartz, *Chinese Communism and the Rise of Mao* (Cambridge, Mass.: Harvard University Press, 1951), p. 74.
10. Quoted in W. T. de Bary, R. Tsunoda, and D. Keene, *Sources of Japanese Tradition*, vol. 2 (New York: Columbia University Press, 1958), p. 269.
11. Institute of Pacific Relations, *Agrarian China: Selected Source Material from Chinese Authors* (Chicago: University of Chicago Press, 1938), p. 1.

CONNECTIONS

Just as nationalism drove politics and state-building in Europe in the nineteenth century, so it took root across Asia in the late nineteenth and early twentieth centuries. While nationalism in Europe developed out of a desire to turn cultural unity into political reality and create imagined communities out of millions of strangers, in Asia nationalist sentiments drew their greatest energy from opposition to European imperialism and domination. Asian modernizers, aware of momentous advances in science and technology and of politics and social practices in the West, also pressed the nationalist cause by demanding an end to outdated conservative traditions that they argued only held back the development of modern, independent nations capable of throwing off Western domination and existing as equals with the West.

The nationalist cause in Asia took many forms and produced some of the twentieth century's most remarkable leaders. In Chapter 32 we will discuss how nationalist leaders across Asia shaped the freedom struggle and the resulting independence according to their own ideological and personal visions. China's Mao Zedong is the giant among the nationalist leaders who emerged in Asia, but he replaced imperialist rule with one-party Communist rule. Gandhi's dream of a unified India collapsed with the partition of British India into Hindu India and Muslim Pakistan and Bangladesh. India and Pakistan remain bitter, and nuclear-armed, enemies today, as we will see in Chapter 33. Egypt assumed a prominent position in the Arab world after World War II under Gamal Nasser's leadership and, after a series of wars with Israel, began to play a significant role in efforts to find a peaceful resolution to the Israeli-Palestinian conflict. That conflict, however, continues unabated as nationalist and religious sentiments inflame feelings on both sides. Ho Chi Minh eventually forced the French colonizers out of

Vietnam, only to face another Western power, the United States, in a long and deadly war. As described in Chapter 31, a unified Vietnam finally gained its independence in 1975, but, like China, the country was under one-party Communist control.

Japan remained an exception to much of what happened in the rest of Asia. After a long period of isolation, the Japanese implemented an unprecedented program of modernization and westernization in the late nineteenth century. Japan continued to model itself after the West when it took control of former German colonies as mandated territories after the Great War and occupied territory in China, Korea, Vietnam, Taiwan, and elsewhere. In the next chapter we will see how ultranationalism drove national policy in the 1930s, ultimately leading to Japan's defeat in World War II.

CHAPTER 29　Review and Explore

Identify Key Terms

Identify and explain the significance of each item below.

Permanent Mandates Commission (p. 856)

Sykes-Picot Agreement (p. 859)

Balfour Declaration (p. 860)

Treaty of Lausanne (p. 862)

Majlis (p. 863)

kibbutz (p. 865)

Lucknow Pact (p. 866)

satyagraha (p. 867)

May Fourth Movement (p. 870)

New Culture Movement (p. 870)

zaibatsu (p. 876)

Long March (p. 877)

Review the Main Ideas

Answer the focus questions from each section of the chapter.

1. Why did modern nationalism develop in Asia between the First and Second World Wars, and what was its appeal? (p. 856)

2. How did the Ottoman Empire's collapse in World War I shape nationalist movements in the Middle East? (p. 857)

3. What role did Gandhi and his campaign of militant nonviolence play in leading India to independence from the British? (p. 865)

4. How did nationalism shape political developments in East and Southeast Asia? (p. 869)

Make Comparisons and Connections

Analyze the larger developments and continuities within and across chapters.

1. Asian leaders adopted several of the ideologies of change that evolved in nineteenth-century Europe (Chapter 24) to unite their peoples against European imperialism in the twentieth century. Give examples of some of these ideologies and where they were adopted.

2. How were Indian, Chinese, and Turkish responses to European imperialism in the twentieth century affected by the different individual histories of these nations (Chapters 25, 26)?

3. Compare and contrast Japan's actions as a modern, imperial power in the late nineteenth century and the first three decades of the twentieth century with those of the European imperial powers at the same time (Chapters 25, 26).

TIMELINE

ASIA

◆ **1916** New Culture Movement in China begins

◆ **1916** Lucknow Pact forms alliance between Hindus and Muslims in India

◆ **1916** Sykes-Picot Agreement divides Ottoman Empire between France and Britain

◆ **1917** Balfour Declaration expresses British support for Jewish homeland in Palestine

◆ **1919** Afghanistan achieves independence

◆ **1923** Treaty of Lausanne ends war in Turkey

AMERICAS

← **1910** Mexican Revolution (Ch. 27)

EUROPE

1919–1920 Paris Peace Conference and treaties (Ch. 28)

RUSSIA

1917–1922 Russian Revolution and civil war (Ch. 28)

GLOBAL

← **1898** Spanish-American War (Ch. 27)

← **1914–1918** World War I (Ch. 28)

1920   **1925**

Suggested Resources

BOOKS

Fenby, Jonathan, *The Penguin History of Modern China: The Fall and Rise of a Great Power, 1850 to the Present*, 2d ed. 2013. An up-to-date comprehensive account of China's fall and rise.

Fromkin, David. *A Peace to End All Peace: The Fall of the Ottoman Empire and the Creation of the Modern Middle East*, 20th anniversary ed. 2009. A thorough but readable introduction to the Middle East in the early twentieth century.

Gandhi, Rajmohan. *Gandhi: The Man, His People, and the Empire.* 2008. Monumental scholarly biography written by a university professor who is also Gandhi's grandson.

Hane, Mikiso, and Louis G. Perez. *Modern Japan: A Historical Survey*, 5th ed. 2012. Highly readable and comprehensive study of modern Japan.

Hourani, Albert. *A History of the Arab Peoples*, rev. ed. 2010. One of the best single-volume histories of the Arab peoples.

Kawamura, Noriko, *Emperor Hirohito and the Pacific War.* 2015. A new biography of the controversial emperor that draws on new and reappraised sources.

Mango, Andrew. *Atatürk.* 2000. Rich, well-researched biography of this complex Turkish leader.

Osborne, Milton. *Southeast Asia: An Introductory History*, 11th ed. 2013. Remains the classic introduction to the region's history.

Sachar, Howard M. *A History of Israel: From the Rise of Zionism to Our Time*, 3d ed. 2007. A detailed history of Zionism and the Jewish state.

Spence, Jonathan. *The Search for Modern China*, 3d ed. 2012. Important study of modern China by a leading Chinese scholar.

Wolpert, Stanley. *A New History of India*, 8th ed. 2008. An excellent introduction to India's history.

Young, Louise. *Japan's Total Empire: Manchuria and the Culture of Wartime Imperialism.* 1998. A fascinating pioneering work on Japanese imperialism.

◆ **1927** Jiang Jieshi, leader of Chinese Nationalist Party, purges Communist allies

◆ **1937** Japanese militarists launch attack on China

◆ **1930** Gandhi's march to the sea to protest the British salt tax

◆ **1932** Iraq gains independence in return for military alliance with Great Britain

◆ **1934** Mao Zedong leads Chinese Communists on Long March

◆ **1931** Japan occupies Manchuria

◆ **1934** Philippines gains self-governing commonwealth status from U.S.

◆ **1933** Hitler and Nazi Party take power in Germany **(Ch. 30)**

1929–1939 Great Depression **(Ch. 30)**

| 1930 | 1935 | 1940 |

DOCUMENTARIES

Mahatma Gandhi: Pilgrim of Peace (A&E, 2000). A brief examination of Gandhi's life; part of A&E's *Biography* series.

Mao Tse Tung: China's Peasant Emperor (A&E, 1998). An introduction to Mao Zedong's life as a revolutionary and as the leader of Communist China; part of A&E's *Biography* series.

FEATURE FILMS

Gandhi (Richard Attenborough, 1982). Nominated for eleven Academy Awards, and winner of Best Picture, Best Director (Richard Attenborough), and Best Actor (Ben Kingsley), this film received broadly positive critical acclaim, both in India and internationally.

The Last Emperor (Bernardo Bertolucci, 1987). Winner of nine Academy Awards, including Best Picture, this is a beautifully filmed epic biographical movie about the last Chinese emperor, Puyi, who ascended to the throne when he was two in 1908 and was then forced to abdicate in 1912. The Japanese made him puppet emperor of the puppet Manchukuo Empire from 1934 to 1945.

WEBSITES

East Asian History Sourcebook. Includes primary and secondary sources and links to other websites, for most of East Asia, including China, Japan, and Korea. **sourcebooks.fordham.edu/Halsall/eastasia /eastasiasbook.asp**

Internet Indian History Sourcebook. A good starting point for sources on India's history, including links to other sites. **sourcebooks.fordham.edu/Halsall/india /indiasbook.asp**

30

The Great Depression and World War II

1929–1945

The years of anxiety and political maneuvering in Europe after World War I were made much worse when a massive economic depression spread around the world following the American stock market crash of October 1929. An increasingly interconnected global economy now collapsed. Free-market capitalism appeared to have run its course. People everywhere looked for relief to new leaders, some democratically elected, many not. In Europe, on the eve of the Second World War, few liberal democratic governments survived. Worldwide, in countries such as Brazil, Japan, the Soviet Union, and others, as well as in Europe, dictatorships seemed the wave of the future.

The mid-twentieth-century era of dictatorship is a deeply disturbing chapter in the history of civilization. The key development was not only the resurgence of authoritarian rule, but also the rise of a particularly ruthless brand of totalitarianism that reached its fullest realization in the Soviet Union, Nazi Germany, and Japan in the 1930s. Stalin, Hitler, and Japan's military leaders intervened radically in society and ruled with unprecedented severity. Hitler's sudden attack on Poland in 1939 started World War II in Europe. His successes encouraged the Japanese to expand their stalemated Chinese campaign into a vast Pacific war. By war's end, millions had died on the battlefields and in the bombed-out cities. Millions more died in the Holocaust, in Stalin's Soviet Union from purges and forced imposition of communism, and during Japan's quest to create an "Asia for Asians."

Jewish Boy in Nazi-Controlled France

Israel Lichtenstein, wearing a Jewish star, was born in Paris in 1932. His father was one of an estimated 1 million Jews who died in the Auschwitz concentration camp. Israel and his mother were also sent to a concentration camp, but they escaped and survived the Holocaust by going into hiding until the end of the war. Israel later immigrated to the nation of Israel.

United States Holocaust Memorial Museum, courtesy of Israel Lichtenstein

CHAPTER PREVIEW

The Great Depression, 1929–1939

What caused the Great Depression, and what were its consequences?

Like the Great War, the Great Depression must be spelled with capital letters. Beginning in 1929 an exceptionally long and severe economic depression struck the entire world with ever-greater intensity, and recovery was uneven and slow. Only the Second World War brought it to an end.

The Economic Crisis

Though economic activity was already declining moderately in many countries by early 1929, the U.S. stock market crash in October of that year really started the Great Depression. The American stock market boom was built on borrowed money. Two factors explain why. First, the wealth gap (or income inequality) between America's rich and poor reached its greatest extent in the twentieth century in 1928–1929. One percent of Americans then held 70 percent of all America's wealth. Eventually, with not enough money to go around, the remaining 99 percent of Americans had to borrow to make even basic purchases—as a result, the cost of farm credit, installment loans, and home mortgages skyrocketed. Then a point was reached where the 99 percent could borrow no more, so they stopped buying.

Second, wealthy investors and speculators took increasingly greater investment risks. One such popular risk was to buy stocks by paying only a small fraction of the total purchase price and borrowing the remainder from their stockbrokers or from banks. Such buying "on margin" was extremely dangerous. When prices started falling, the hard-pressed margin buyers started selling to pay their debts. The result was a financial panic. Countless investors and speculators were wiped out in a matter of days or weeks, and the New York stock market's crash started a domino effect that hit most of the world's major stock exchanges.

The financial panic in the United States triggered a worldwide financial crisis. Throughout the 1920s American bankers and investors had lent large sums to many countries, and as panic spread, New York bankers began recalling their short-term loans. Frightened citizens around the world began to withdraw their bank savings, leading to general financial chaos. The recall of American loans also accelerated the collapse in world prices, as business people dumped goods in a frantic attempt to get cash to pay what they owed.

The financial chaos led to a drastic decline in production in country after country. Between 1929 and 1933 world output of goods fell by an estimated 38 percent. Countries now turned inward and tried to go it alone. Many followed the American example, in which protective tariffs were raised to their highest levels ever in 1930 to seal off shrinking national markets for American producers only.

Although historians' opinions differ, two factors probably best explain the relentless slide to the bottom from 1929 to early 1933. First, the international economy lacked leadership able to maintain stability when the crisis came. Neither the seriously weakened Britain nor the United States—the world's economic leaders—stabilized the international economic system in 1929. Instead Britain and the United States cut back international lending and erected high tariffs.

Second, in almost every country, governments cut their budgets and reduced spending instead of running large deficits to try to stimulate their economies. That is, governments needed to put large sums of money into the economy to stimulate job growth and spending. After World War II such a "counter-cyclical policy," advocated by the British economist John Maynard Keynes (1883–1946), became a well-established weapon against depression. But in the 1930s orthodox economists generally regarded Keynes's prescription with horror.

Mass Unemployment

The need for large-scale government spending was tied to mass unemployment. The 99 percent's halt in buying contributed to the financial crisis, which led to production cuts, which in turn caused workers to lose their jobs and have even less money to buy goods. This led to still more production cuts, and unemployment soared. In Britain unemployment had averaged 12 percent in the 1920s; between 1930 and 1935 it averaged more than 18 percent. Germany and Austria had some of the highest unemployment rates, 30–32 percent in 1932. The worst unemployment was in the United States. In the 1920s unemployment there had averaged only 5 percent; in 1933 it soared to about 33 percent of the entire labor force: 14 million people were out of work. This was the only time in American history when more people left America than immigrated in—including thousands of Mexican Americans who suffered increasing hostility, accused of stealing jobs from those who considered themselves to be "real Americans," and perhaps a hundred thousand Americans who migrated to the Soviet Union, attracted by communism's promises of jobs and a new life.

Mass unemployment created great social problems. Poverty increased dramatically, although in most industrialized countries unemployed workers generally received some meager unemployment benefits or pub-

Louisville Flood Victims, 1937 During the Great Depression, Louisville, Kentucky, was hit by the worst flood in its history. The famous documentary photographer Margaret Bourke-White captured this image of African American flood victims lining up for food. Not only does the billboard message mock the Depression-era conditions, but the smiling white family appears to be driving its car through the line of people, drawing attention to America's race and class differences. (Margaret Bourke-White/Time & Life Pictures/Getty Images)

lic aid that prevented starvation. Millions of unemployed people lost their spirit, and homes and ways of life were disrupted in countless personal tragedies. In 1932 workers in Manchester, England, appealed to their city officials — a typical appeal echoed throughout the Western world:

> We tell you that thousands of people . . . are in desperate straits. We tell you that men, women, and children are going hungry. . . . We tell you that great numbers are being rendered distraught through the stress and worry of trying to exist without work. . . .
>
> If you do not provide useful work for the unemployed — what, we ask, is your alternative? Do not imagine that this colossal tragedy of unemployment is going on endlessly without some fateful catastrophe. Hungry men are angry men.[1]

The New Deal in the United States

The Great Depression and the response to it marked a major turning point in American history. Herbert Hoover (U.S. pres. 1929–1933) and his administration initially reacted with limited action. When the financial crisis struck Europe with full force in summer 1931 and boomeranged back to the United States, banks failed and unemployment soared. In 1932 industrial production fell to about 50 percent of its 1929 level.

In these desperate circumstances Franklin Delano Roosevelt (U.S. pres. 1933–1945) won a landslide presidential victory in 1932 with promises of a "**New Deal** for the forgotten man." Roosevelt's basic goal was

New Deal Franklin Delano Roosevelt's plan to reform capitalism in the United States through forceful government intervention in the economy.

to preserve capitalism by reforming it. Rejecting socialism and government ownership of industry, Roosevelt advocated forceful federal government intervention in the economy. His commitment to national relief programs marked a profound shift from the traditional stress on family support and local community responsibility.

Roosevelt attacked mass unemployment by creating new federal agencies that launched a vast range of public works projects so the federal government could directly employ as many people as financially possible. The Works Progress Administration (WPA), set up in 1935, employed one-fifth of the entire U.S. labor force at some point in the 1930s, and these workers constructed public buildings, bridges, and highways.

In 1935 the U.S. government established a national social security system with old-age pensions and unemployment benefits. The 1935 National Labor Relations Act declared collective bargaining to be U.S. policy, and union membership more than doubled. In general, between 1935 and 1938 government rulings and social reforms chipped away at the privileges of the wealthy and tried to help ordinary people.

Despite undeniable accomplishments in social reform, the New Deal was only partly successful as a response to the Great Depression. Unemployment was still a staggering 10 million when war broke out in Europe in 1939. The New Deal brought fundamental reform, but it never did pull the United States out of the depression; only the Second World War did that.

The European Response to the Depression

The American stock market's collapse in October 1929 set off a chain of economic downturns that hit Europe, particularly Germany and Great Britain, the hardest. Postwar Europe had emerged from the Great War deeply in debt and in desperate need of investment capital to rebuild. The United States became the primary creditor and financier. Germany borrowed, for example, to pay Britain war reparations, and then Britain took that money and repaid its war debts and investment loans to America. When the American economy crashed, the whole circular system crashed with it.

Of all the Western democracies, the Scandinavian countries under socialist leadership responded most successfully to the challenge of the Great Depression. When the economic crisis struck in 1929, Sweden's socialist government pioneered the use of large-scale deficits to finance public works projects and thereby maintain

production and employment. Scandinavian governments also increased social welfare benefits. All this spending required a large bureaucracy and high taxes. Yet both private and cooperative enterprise thrived, as did democracy. Some observers considered Scandinavia's welfare socialism an appealing middle way between what they considered to be sick capitalism and cruel communism or fascism.

In Britain, Ramsay MacDonald's Labour government (1929–1931) and, after 1931, the Conservative-dominated coalition government followed orthodox economic theory. The budget was balanced, but unemployed workers received barely enough welfare support to live. Nevertheless, the economy recovered considerably after 1932, reflecting the gradual reorientation of the British economy. Britain concentrated increasingly on the national, rather than the international, market. Old export industries, such as textiles and coal, continued to decline, but new industries, such as automobiles and electrical appliances, grew. These developments encouraged British isolationism and often had devastating economic consequences for Britain's far-flung colonies and dominions, which depended heavily upon reciprocal trade with Great Britain and the United States. (See "Analyzing the Evidence: British Conservative Party Poster," at right.)

The Great Depression came late to France as it was relatively less industrialized and more isolated from the world economy. But once the depression hit, it stayed. Economic stagnation both reflected and heightened an ongoing political crisis, as liberals, democratic socialists, and Communists fought for control of the French government with conservatives and the far right. The latter groups agitated against parliamentary democracy and turned to Mussolini's Italy and Hitler's Germany for inspiration. At the same time, the Communist Party and many workers looked to Stalin's Russia for guidance.

Frightened by the growing popularity of Hitler- and Mussolini-style right-wing dictatorships at home and abroad, the Communist, Socialist, and Radical Parties in France formed an alliance—the **Popular Front**—for the May 1936 national elections. Following its clear victory, the Popular Front government launched a far-reaching New Deal–inspired program of social and economic reform. Popular with workers (because it supported unions) and the lower middle class, these measures were quickly sabotaged by rapid inflation, rising wages, a decline in overseas exports, and cries of socialist revolution from frightened conservatives. Politically, the Popular Front lost many left-wing supporters when it failed to back the republican cause in the Spanish Civil War while Hitler and Mussolini openly armed and supported Franco's nationalists. In June 1937, with the country hopelessly divided, the Popular Front collapsed.

Popular Front A party formed in 1936 in France that encouraged unions and launched a far-reaching New Deal–inspired program of social reform.

British Conservative Party Poster

In June 1930 the United States enacted a tariff (tax) on goods imported into the country. Lawmakers thought this action would force Americans to buy American products and would thereby revive American businesses and increase employment. By this time, however, the United States had long been a member of the global economy and depended as much on exporting goods as on importing them. The effect of the tariff was to reduce America's international trade and to cause other countries to turn to the same supposed economic remedy, further depressing international trade.

When the Great Depression hit, Great Britain, like many other countries, faced a financial crisis. In August 1930 the Labour government resigned and a new unity government drawn from Labour and Conservative members alike took over, but this soon collapsed as well. In October 1931 a general election was held, which resulted in a landslide victory for Conservative members of Parliament. Early in 1932 the Conservative-led government introduced tariffs on all imports (except those from members of the British Empire) at a rate of 10 percent. This campaign poster from the 1931 British general election portrays crates and bags of foreign goods being unloaded on English docks. It was these shiploads of foreign goods that the tariffs would block when the Conservatives triumphed.

QUESTIONS FOR ANALYSIS

1. Where are the goods on the dock from?
2. What do the Conservatives want stopped?
3. Was the attitude of this poster's creators toward foreign goods unique to England? What other countries held similar views? What effect did such attitudes have on the worldwide depression?

(The Conservative Party Archive/Getty Images)

Worldwide Effects

The Great Depression's magnitude was unprecedented, and its effect rippled well beyond Europe and the United States. Because many countries and colonies in Africa, Asia, and Latin America were nearly totally dependent on one or two commodities—such as coffee beans or cocoa—for income, the implementation of protectionist trade policies by the leading industrial nations had devastating effects.

The Great Depression hit the vulnerable commodity economies of Latin America especially hard. With foreign sales plummeting, Latin American countries could not buy the industrial goods they needed from abroad. The global depression provoked a profound shift toward economic nationalism after 1930, as popularly based governments worked to reduce foreign influence and gain control of their own economies and natural resources. These efforts were fairly successful. By the late 1940s factories in Argentina, Brazil, and

Chile could generally satisfy domestic consumer demand for the products of light industry. But as in Hitler's Germany, the deteriorating economic conditions in Latin America also gave rise to dictatorships, some of them modeled along European Fascist lines.

The Great Depression marked a decisive turning point in the development of African nationalism. For the first time, educated Africans faced widespread unemployment. African peasants and small business people who had been drawn into world trade, and who sometimes profited from booms, also felt the economic pain, as did urban workers. In some areas the result was unprecedented mass protest.

While Asians were somewhat affected by the Great Depression, the consequences varied greatly by country or colony and were not as serious generally as they were elsewhere. That being said, where the depression did hit, it was often severe. The price of rice fell by two-thirds between 1929 and 1932. Also crippling to the region's economies was Asia's heavy dependence on raw material exports. With debts to local money-lenders fixed in value and taxes to colonial governments hardly ever reduced, many Asian peasants in the 1930s struggled under crushing debt and suffered terribly. (See "Global Viewpoints: Socialism and the Working Class," at right.)

When the Great Depression reached China in the early 1930s, it hit the rural economy the hardest. China's economy depended heavily on cash-crop exports and these declined dramatically, while cheap foreign agricultural goods—such as rice and wheat—were dumped in China. While Chinese industrial production dropped off after 1931, it quickly recovered. Much of this growth was in the military sector, as China tried to catch up with the West and also prepare for war with Japan.

In Japan the terrible suffering caused by the Great Depression caused ultranationalists and militarists to call for less dependence on global markets and the expansion of a self-sufficient empire. Such expansion began in 1931 when Japan invaded Chinese Manchuria, which became a major source of the raw materials needed to feed Japanese industrial growth (see "Japan Against China" in Chapter 29). Japan recovered more quickly from the Great Depression than did any other major industrial power because of prompt action by the civilian democratic government, but the government and large corporations continued to be blamed for the economic downturn. By the mid-1930s this lack of confidence, combined with the collapsing international economic order, Europe's and America's increasingly isolationist and protectionist policies, and a growing admiration for Nazi Germany and its authoritarian, militaristic model of government, had led the Japanese military to topple the civilian authorities and dictate Japan's future.

Authoritarian States

What was the nature of the new totalitarian dictatorships, and how did they differ from conservative authoritarian states and from each other?

Both conservative and radical totalitarian dictatorships arose in Europe in the 1920s and the 1930s. Although they sometimes overlapped in character and practice, they were profoundly different in essence.

Conservative Authoritarianism

The traditional form of antidemocratic government in world history was conservative authoritarianism. Like Russia's tsars and China's emperors, the leaders of such governments relied on obedient bureaucracies, vigilant police departments, and trustworthy armies to control society. They forbade or limited popular participation in government and often jailed or exiled political opponents. Yet they had neither the ability nor the desire to control many aspects of their subjects' lives. As long as the people did not try to change the system, they often enjoyed considerable personal independence.

After the First World War, conservative authoritarianism revived, especially in Latin America. Conservative dictators also seized power in Spain and Portugal, and in the less-developed eastern part of Europe. There were several reasons for this development. These lands lacked strong traditions of self-government, and many new states, such as Yugoslavia, were torn by ethnic conflicts. Dictatorship appealed to nationalists and military leaders as a way to repress such tensions and preserve national unity. Large landowners and the church were still powerful forces in these predominantly agrarian areas and often looked to dictators to protect them from progressive land reform or Communist agrarian upheaval. Conservative dictatorships were concerned more with maintaining the status quo than with mobilizing the masses or forcing society into rapid change or war.

Radical Totalitarian Dictatorships

By the mid-1930s a new kind of radical dictatorship—termed totalitarian—had emerged in the Soviet Union, Germany, and, to a lesser extent, Italy. Scholars disagree over the definition of totalitarianism, its origins, and to what countries and leaders the term should apply. Moreover, when the Cold War began in the late 1940s (see "The World Remade" in Chapter 31), conservatives, particularly in the United States, commandeered the term as shorthand for the "evil" Communist regimes in the Soviet Union and its satellites.

Socialism and the Working Class

James Keir Hardie (1856–1915) was the first Socialist member of the British Parliament and a founder of the British Labour Party. His *From Serfdom to Socialism* (1907) was intended to make a "brief unadorned statement of the case for Socialism, easily understandable by plain folks."

In 1936–1937 George Orwell (1903–1950), famous for his novels *1984* and *Animal Farm*, lived in Wigan, a mill town in a coal-mining district near Manchester in the north of England. In *The Road to Wigan Pier*, he tried to explain why socialism did not have more support among the workers.

James Keir Hardie, *From Serfdom to Socialism*

■ But it is to the working-class itself that we must look for changing the system of production and making it a means of providing for the healthy human need of all the people. This is so not only because of their numbers but also because unless they consciously set themselves to win Socialism it can never be won. It is, in the fullest sense of a very much abused phrase, a People's Cause. When it has been won it will be their fight which has won it; should it never be won, and should our Western civilisation totter on until it falls into the depths of a merciful oblivion, that too will be their doing, and be due entirely to their not having had the courage and the intelligence to put up a fight strong enough to save it and themselves.

Somewhat dimly at present, but with growing clearness of vision, the worker begins to see that he will remain a menial, outcast and forlorn, until he has made himself master of the machine he tends and the soil he tills. Hence the growth of Socialism.

George Orwell, *The Road to Wigan Pier*

■ Socialism . . . is a theory confined entirely to the middle class. The typical Socialist is not, as tremulous old ladies imagine, a ferocious-looking workingman with greasy overalls and a raucous voice. He is either a youthful snob-Bolshevik who in five years' time will quite probably have made a wealthy marriage and been converted to Roman Catholicism; or, still more typically, a prim little man with

a white-collar job, usually a secret teetotaler . . . often with vegetarian leanings . . . and, above all, with a social position which he has no intention of forfeiting. . . . In addition to this there is the horrible . . . prevalence of cranks. . . . The mere words "Socialism" and "Communism" draw towards them . . . every fruit-juice drinker, nudist, sandal-wearer, sex-maniac, Quaker, "Nature Cure" quack, pacifist, and feminist in England. . . .

A working man, so long as he remains a genuine working man, is seldom or never a Socialist. . . . Very likely he votes Labour, or even Communist if he gets the chance, but his conception of Socialism is quite different from that of the book-trained Socialist. . . . To [him] . . . Socialism does not mean much more than better wages and shorter hours and nobody bossing you about. . . . Often . . . he is a truer Socialist than the orthodox Marxist, because he does remember, what the other so often forgets, that Socialism means justice and common decency. . . . His vision of the Socialist future is a vision of present society with the worst abuses left out, and with . . . the same things as at present—family life, the pub, football, and local politics. As for the philosophic side of Marxism, . . . I have yet to meet a *working* miner, steel-worker, cotton-weaver, docker, navvy, or whatnot who was "ideologically" sound.

QUESTIONS FOR ANALYSIS

1. Both Hardie and Orwell were writing about socialism in Great Britain, one in 1907 and the other in the 1930s. What aspects of Hardie's analysis of potential socialists would Orwell agree with, and what aspects would he disagree with?
2. What events occurred between 1907 and the 1930s that might have affected the socialist movement in Great Britain? Explain your answer.
3. Is one of these authors more pessimistic about the spread of socialism than the other is? Which one? Why?

Sources: James Keir Hardie, *From Serfdom to Socialism* (London: George Allen, 1907), pp. ix, 29–31; George Orwell, *The Road to Wigan Pier* (New York: Harcourt Brace, 1958), pp. 173–177. Copyright © 1958 and renewed by the Estate of Sonia B. Orwell. Reprinted by permission of Houghton Mifflin Harcourt Publishing Company. All rights reserved.

Liberals, especially in the 1960s, used the term more loosely to refer to every system they felt inhibited freedom—from local police to the U.S. Pentagon. Thus by the 1980s many scholars questioned the term's usefulness. More recently, with these caveats, scholars have returned to the term to explain and understand fascism, Nazism, and communism in the 1920s, 1930s, and 1940s.

It can be argued that **totalitarianism** began with the total war effort of 1914–1918 (see "Mobilizing for Total War" in Chapter 28), as governments acquired total control over all areas of society in order to achieve

> **totalitarianism** A radical dictatorship that exercises complete political power and control over all aspects of society and seeks to mobilize the masses for action.

one supreme objective: victory. This provided a model for future totalitarian states. As the French thinker Élie Halévy (AY-lee ah-LAY-vee) observed in 1936, the varieties of modern totalitarian tyranny—fascism, Nazism, and communism—could be thought of as "feuding brothers" with a common father: the nature of modern war.[2]

The consequences of the Versailles treaty (1919) and the severe economic and political problems that Germany and Italy faced in the 1920s left both those countries ripe for new leadership, but not necessarily totalitarian dictators. It was the Great Depression that must be viewed as the immediate cause of the modern totalitarian state.

In 1956 American historians Carl Friedrich and Zbigniew Brzezinski (z-BIG-nyef bzheh-ZIN-skee) identified at least six key features of modern totalitarian states: (1) an official ideology; (2) a single ruling party; (3) complete control of "all weapons of armed combat"; (4) complete monopoly of all means of mass communication; (5) a system of terror, physical and psychic, enforced by the party and the secret police; and (6) central control and direction of the entire economy.[3]

While all these features were present in Stalin's Communist Soviet Union and Hitler's Nazi Germany, there were some major differences. Most notably, Soviet communism seized private property for the state and sought to level society by crushing the middle classes. Nazi Germany also criticized big landowners and industrialists but, unlike the Communists, did not try to nationalize private property, so the middle classes survived. This difference in property and class relations led some scholars to speak of "totalitarianism of the left"—Stalinist Russia—and "totalitarianism of the right"—Nazi Germany.

Moreover, Soviet Communists ultimately had international aims: they sought to unite the workers of the world. Mussolini and Hitler claimed they were interested in changing state and society on a national level only, although Hitler envisioned a greatly expanded "living space," or *lebensraum* (LAY-buhns-rowm), for Germans in eastern Europe and Russia. Both Mussolini and Hitler used the term **fascism** (FASH-iz-uhm) to describe their movements' supposedly "total" and revolutionary character. Orthodox Marxist Communists argued that the Fascists were powerful capitalists

The Spread of Fascism in Spain, 1937 In the 1920s and 1930s most European countries had Fascist sympathizers. Between 1936 and 1939 Fascist nationalist forces led by General Francisco Franco, pictured here, fought a brutal war against the government of Spain's left-leaning, democratic Second Spanish Republic. Socialist and liberal volunteers from around the world came to Spain to fight against Franco's army, as recounted in Ernest Hemingway's novel *For Whom the Bell Tolls*. Pablo Picasso portrayed the destruction to one town caused by German Nazi and Italian Fascist warplanes, supporting Franco, in his famous painting *Guernica*. Following the nationalist victory, Franco ruled Spain as a dictator for thirty-six years. (© Imagno/Austrian Archives/The Image Works)

seeking to destroy the revolutionary working class and thus protect their enormous profits. So while Communists and Fascists both sought the overthrow of existing society, their ideologies clashed, and they were enemies.

European Fascist movements shared many characteristics, including extreme, often expanionist, nationalism; anti-socialism aimed at destroying working-class movements; a dynamic and violent leader; a crushing of human individualism; alliances with powerful capitalists and landowners; and glorification of war and the military. Fascists, especially in Germany, also embraced racial homogeneity. Indeed, while class was the driving force in communist ideology, race and racial purity were profoundly important to Nazi ideology.

Although 1930s Japan has sometimes been called a Fascist society, most recent scholars disagree with this label. Japanese political philosophers were attracted by some European Fascist ideas, such as Hitler's desire for eastward expansion, which would be duplicated by Japan's expansion to the Asian mainland. Other appealing concepts included nationalism, militarism, the corporatist economic model, and a single, all-powerful political party. The idea of a Japanese dictator, however, clashed with the emperor's divine status. There were also various ideologically unique forces at work in Japan, including ultranationalism, militarism (building on the historic role of samurai warriors in Japanese society), reverence for traditional ways, emperor worship, and the profound changes to Japanese society beginning with the Meiji Restoration in 1867 (see "The Meiji Restoration" in Chapter 26). These also contributed to the rise of a totalitarian, but not Fascist, state before the Second World War.

In summary, the concept of totalitarianism remains a valuable tool for historical understanding. It correctly highlights that in the 1930s Germany, the Soviet Union, and Japan made an unprecedented "total claim" on the beliefs and behaviors of their respective citizens.[4] However, none of these nations were successful in completely dominating their citizens. Thus totalitarianism is an idea never fully achieved.

Stalin's Soviet Union

How did Stalin and the Communist Party build a totalitarian order in the Soviet Union?

Joseph Stalin (1879–1953) consolidated his power following Lenin's death in 1924 and by 1927 was the de facto leader of the Soviet Union. In 1928 he launched the first **five-year plan**—a "revolution from above,"[5] as he so aptly termed it, to transform Soviet society along socialist lines, and to generate a Communist

society with new attitudes, new loyalties, and a new socialist humanity. Stalin and the Communist Party used constant propaganda, enormous sacrifice, and unlimited violence and state control to establish a dynamic, modern totalitarian state in the 1930s.

From Lenin to Stalin

By spring 1921 Lenin and the Bolsheviks had won the civil war, but they ruled a shattered and devastated land. Facing economic disintegration, the worst famine in generations, riots by peasants and workers, and an open rebellion by previously pro-Bolshevik sailors at Kronstadt (kruhn-SHTAHT), Lenin changed course. In March 1921 he announced the **New Economic Policy (NEP)**, which re-established limited economic freedom in an attempt to rebuild agriculture and industry. Peasant producers could sell their surpluses in free markets, as could private traders and small handicraft manufacturers. Heavy industry, railroads, and banks, however, remained wholly nationalized.

The NEP was successful both politically and economically. Politically, it was a necessary but temporary compromise with the Soviet Union's overwhelming peasant majority. Economically, the NEP brought rapid recovery. In 1926 industrial output surpassed prewar levels, and peasants were producing almost as much grain as before the war.

As the economy recovered, an intense power struggle began in the Communist Party's inner circles, for Lenin left no chosen successor when he died in 1924. The principal contenders were Stalin and Leon Trotsky. While Trotsky appeared to be the stronger of the two, in the end Stalin won because he gained the support of the party, the only genuine source of power in the one-party state.

Stalin gradually achieved absolute power between 1922 and 1927. He used the moderates to crush Trotsky and then turned against the moderates and destroyed them as well. Stalin's final triumph came at the party congress of December 1927, which condemned all deviation from the general party line as formulated by Stalin.

---

fascism A movement characterized by extreme, often expansionist nationalism, anti-socialism, a dynamic and violent leader, and glorification of war and the military.

five-year plan Launched by Stalin in 1928 and termed the "revolution from above," its goal was to modernize the Soviet Union and generate a Communist society with new attitudes, new loyalties, and a new socialist humanity.

New Economic Policy (NEP) Lenin's 1921 policy re-establishing limited economic freedom in the Soviet Union in an attempt to rebuild agriculture and industry in the face of economic disintegration.

The Five-Year Plans

The 1927 party congress marked the end of the NEP and the beginning of socialist five-year plans. The first five-year plan had staggering economic objectives. In just five years, total industrial output was to increase by 250 percent and agricultural production by 150 percent. By 1930 economic and social change was sweeping the country in a frenzied effort to modernize and industrialize, much like in Britain in the nineteenth century (see "The Industrial Revolution in Britain" in Chapter 23), and dramatically changing the lives of ordinary people, sometimes at great personal cost. One worker complained, "The workers . . . made every effort to fulfill the industrial and financial plan and fulfilled it by more than 100 percent, but how are they supplied? The ration is received only by the worker, except for rye flour, his wife and small children receive nothing. Workers and their families wear worn-out clothes, the kids are in rags, their naked bellies sticking out."[6]

Stalin unleashed his "second revolution" because, like Lenin, he was deeply committed to socialism. Stalin was also driven to catch up with the advanced and presumably hostile Western capitalist nations. In February 1931 Stalin famously declared:

It is sometimes asked whether it is not possible to slow down the tempo a bit. . . . No, comrades, it is not possible! The tempo must not be reduced! . . . To slacken the tempo would mean falling behind. And those who fall behind get beaten. No, we refuse to be beaten! . . . We are fifty or a hundred years behind the advanced countries. We must make good this distance in ten years. Either we do it, or we shall be crushed.[7]

Domestically, there was the peasant problem. For centuries peasants had wanted to own the land, and finally they had it. Sooner or later, the Communists reasoned, the peasants would become conservative capitalists and threaten the regime. Stalin therefore launched a preventive war against the peasantry to bring it under the state's absolute control.

That war was **collectivization**—the forcible consolidation of individual peasant farms into large, state-controlled enterprises. Beginning in 1929 peasants were ordered to give up their land and animals and become members of collective farms. As for the kulaks, the better-off peasants, Stalin instructed party workers to "break their resistance, to eliminate them as a class."[8] (See "Thinking Like a Historian: Peasant Resistance to Stalin's Collectivization Plan," page 896.) Stripped of land and livestock, many starved or were deported to forced-labor camps for "re-education."

Because almost all peasants were poor, the term *kulak* soon meant any peasant who opposed the new system. Whole villages were often attacked. One conscience-stricken colonel in the secret police confessed to a foreign journalist:

I am an old Bolshevik. I worked in the underground against the Tsar and then I fought in the Civil War. Did I do all that in order that I should now surround villages with machine guns and order my men to fire indiscriminately into crowds of peasants? Oh, no, no![9]

Forced collectivization led to disaster. Many peasants slaughtered their animals and burned their crops in protest. Nor were the state-controlled collective farms more productive. Grain output barely increased, and collectivized agriculture made no substantial financial contribution to Soviet industrial development during the first five-year plan.

In Ukraine Stalin instituted a policy of all-out collectivization with two goals: to destroy all expressions of Ukrainian nationalism, and to break the Ukrainian peasants' will so they would accept collectivization and Soviet rule. Stalin began by purging Ukraine of its intellectuals and political elite. He then set impossibly high grain quotas for the collectivized farms. This grain quota had to be turned over to the government before any peasant could receive a share. Many scholars and dozens of governments and international organizations have declared Stalin's and the Soviet government's policies a deliberate act of genocide. As one historian observed:

Grain supplies were sufficient to sustain everyone if properly distributed. People died mostly of terror-starvation (excess grain exports, seizure of edibles from the starving, state refusal to provide emergency relief, bans on outmigration, and forced deportation to food-deficit locales), not poor harvests and routine administrative bungling.[10]

The result was a terrible man-made famine, called in Ukrainian the *Holodomor* (HAU-lau-dau-mohr) (Hunger extermination), in Ukraine in 1932 and 1933, which probably claimed 3 to 5 million lives.

Collectivization was a cruel but real victory for Communist ideologues who were looking to institute their brand of communism and to crush opposition as much as improve production. By 1938, 93 percent of peasant families had been herded onto collective farms at a horrendous cost in both human lives and resources. Regimented as state employees and dependent on the state-owned tractor stations, the collectivized peasants were no longer a political threat.

The industrial side of the five-year plans was more successful. Soviet industry produced about four times

---

collectivization Stalin's forcible consolidation, beginning in 1929, of individual peasant farms in the Soviet Union into large, state-controlled enterprises.

as much in 1937 as in 1928. No other major country had ever achieved such rapid industrial growth. Heavy industry led the way, and urban development accelerated: more than 25 million people migrated to cities to become industrial workers during the 1930s.

The sudden creation of dozens of new factories demanded tremendous resources. Funds for industrial expansion were collected from the people through heavy hidden sales taxes. Firm labor discipline also contributed to rapid industrialization. Trade unions lost most of their power, and individuals could not move without police permission. When factory managers needed more hands, they were sent "unneeded" peasants from collective farms.

Foreign engineers were hired to plan and construct many of the new factories. Highly skilled American engineers, hungry for work in the depression years, were particularly important until newly trained Soviet experts began to replace them after 1932. Thus Stalin's planners harnessed the skill and technology of capitalist countries to promote the surge of socialist industry.

Life and Culture in Soviet Society

Daily life was hard in Stalin's Soviet Union. Despite these hardships, many Communists saw themselves as heroically building the world's first socialist society while capitalism crumbled and fascism rose in the West.

Offsetting the hardships were the important social benefits Soviet workers received, such as old-age pensions, free medical services and education, and day-care centers for children. Unemployment was almost unknown. Moreover, there was the possibility of personal advancement. Rapid industrialization required massive numbers of trained experts. Thus the Stalinist state broke with the egalitarian policies of the 1920s and provided tremendous incentives to those who acquired specialized skills. A growing technical and managerial elite joined the political and artistic elites in a new upper class, whose members were rich and powerful.

Soviet society's radical transformation profoundly affected women's lives. The Russian Bolshevik Revolution immediately proclaimed complete equality of rights for women. In the 1920s divorce and abortion were made easily available, and women were urged to work outside the home. After Stalin came to power, however, he encouraged a return to traditional family values.

The most lasting changes for women involved work and education. Peasant women continued to work on farms, and millions of women now toiled in factories and heavy construction. The more determined women entered the ranks of the better-paid specialists in industry and science. By 1950, 75 percent of all doctors in the Soviet Union were women.

Culture was thoroughly politicized through constant propaganda and indoctrination. Party activists lectured workers in factories and peasants on collective farms, while newspapers, films, and radio broadcasts recounted socialist achievements and warned of capitalist plots.

Stalinist Terror and the Great Purges

In the mid-1930s the push to build socialism and a new society culminated in ruthless police terror and a massive purging of the Communist Party. In August 1936 sixteen prominent "Old Bolsheviks"—party members before the 1917 revolution—confessed to all manner of plots against Stalin in spectacular public show trials in Moscow. Then in 1937 the secret police arrested a mass of lesser party officials and newer members, torturing them and extracting confessions for more show trials. In addition to the party faithful, union officials, managers, intellectuals, army officers, and countless ordinary citizens were struck down. One Stalin functionary admitted, "Innocent people were arrested: naturally—otherwise no one would be frightened. If people were arrested only for specific misdemeanors, all the others would feel safe and so become ripe for treason."[11] In all, at least 8 million people were arrested, and millions of these were executed. Those not immediately executed were sent to gulags (GOO-lagz)—labor camps from which few escaped. Many were simply worked to death as they provided convict labor for Stalin's industrialization drive in areas of low population.

Stalin recruited 1.5 million new members to replace those purged. Thus more than half of all Communist Party members in 1941 had joined since the purges. This new generation of Stalin-formed Communists served the leader effectively until his death in 1953 and then governed the Soviet Union until the early 1980s. Stalin's mass purges remain baffling, for most historians believe those purged posed no threat and confessed to crimes they had not committed. Some historians have challenged the long-standing interpretation that blames the great purges on Stalin's cruelty or madness. They argue that Stalin's fears were exaggerated but genuine and were shared by many in the party and in the general population. Investigations and trials snowballed into a mass hysteria, a new witch-hunt.[12] Historians who have accessed recently opened Soviet archives, however, continue to hold that Stalin was intimately involved with the purges and personally directed them, abetted by amenable informers, judges, and executioners. Oleg Khlevniuk, a Ukrainian historian familiar with these archives, writes, "Theories

Peasant Resistance to Stalin's Collectivization Plan

In 1929 Stalin ordered the forced collectivization of all peasants onto state-controlled farms, promising that large-scale industrialized agriculture would provide them all, equally, with better lives. The peasants generally would have none of it and resisted so successfully that the state resorted to violence, starvation, and genocide to force them out of their homes, off their lands, and onto the collective farms.

1 Maurice Hindus on peasant distrust of Soviet promises, 1929. Journalist Maurice Hindus wrote about peasant attitudes toward collective farms during a visit to his native village in central Russia in the summer of 1929.

■ These peasants never believed in anybody's words; they had always mistrusted the whole world. . . . And now they were to give up their individual land, their horses, their cows, their farm buildings—the things that had given them bread, protection against starvation, the very security they needed to hold body and soul together—all on the mere promise of a youthful agitator that this would enrich their lives!

2 Apocalyptic visions of collectivization, late 1929. Nightmarish rumors of what was to come spread from village to village across Russia among the generally illiterate but very religious peasants as the specter of collectivization approached.

■ In the collective farm, there will be a special stamp, [they] will close all the churches, not allow prayer, dead people will be cremated, the christening of children will be forbidden, invalids and the elderly will be killed, there won't be any husbands or wives, [all] will sleep under a one-hundred-meter blanket. Beautiful men and women will be taken and brought to one place to produce beautiful people. Children will be taken from their parents, there will be wholesale incest. . . . The collective farm—this is beasts in a single shed, people in a single barrack.

3 Stalingrad district administration, proclamation calling for open rebellion, 1930. In July 1930 a proclamation issued by the administration of the Stalingrad district in the lower Volga River region called for the peasants to rise up and overthrow the Soviet government.

■ Citizens of great Russia. The People's Democratic party calls on you to throw off the yoke of the unprecedented red terror. Citizens remember the slogans of the years of revolution—freedom of speech, press, conscience, religion; factories to the workers, land to the peasants, etc. And what have the people gotten from these slogans. A dictatorship of the ruinous communist party gave, instead of the promises, . . . a robbery of all the laboring population unprecedented in the history of humanity. Instead of freedom of conscience and religion, the mass closing of churches. . . . Instead of freedom of speech and the press—the brutal suppression of the thought and speech of people—terror for the workers, and instead of bread—hunger; instead of land, the peasantry gets taxes. . . .

Down with the thieving dictatorship of the . . . Communists, down with the red terror. . . . [D]own with collectivization which is a hidden form of slave labor.

ANALYZING THE EVIDENCE

1. In Source 1, who is the "youthful agitator," and what is he asking the peasants to give up?
2. What are the different effects of collectivization feared by the peasants in Source 2?
3. Who is the target of the peasants' anger in Source 3? In what ways are the peasants' lives threatened by collectivization?
4. To whom or what is the activist in Source 4 remaining loyal? What has he witnessed?
5. Why might the image in Source 5 be considered a propaganda piece created by the Soviet regime to promote collectivization? What might the effect of such an image be?

4 **A Soviet activist on performing his revolutionary duty, 1933.** One of the activists recruited to enforce the collectivization and gather the peasants' grain in the Ukraine recalls the horrors he witnessed while carrying out his duties in support of the socialist fatherland.

■ I firmly believed that the ends justified the means. Our great goal was the universal triumph of Communism, and for the sake of that goal everything was permissible—to lie, to steal, to destroy hundreds of thousands and even millions of people, . . . everyone who stood in the way. . . .

In the terrible spring of 1933 I saw people dying from hunger. I saw women and children with distended bellies, turning blue, still breathing but with vacant, lifeless eyes. And corpses—corpses in ragged sheepskin coats and cheap felt boots; corpses in peasant huts, in the melting snow. . . . I saw all this and did not go out of [my] mind or commit suicide. Nor did I curse those who had sent me out to take away the peasants' grain in the winter, and in the spring to persuade the barely walking, skeleton-thin or sickly-swollen people to go into the fields in order to "fulfil the bolshevik sowing plan in shock-worker style."

Nor did I lose my faith. As before, I believed because I wanted to believe.

(Universal Images Group/Sovfoto/akg-images)

5 **Dinner time on a collective farm, 1936.** Male and female peasants on a Soviet collective farm near Kiev take time to share a meal.

PUTTING IT ALL TOGETHER

Using the sources above, along with what you have learned in class and in this chapter, write a short essay on the Soviet government's efforts to promote collectivization and the peasants' reactions to collectivization.

Sources: (1) Maurice Gerschon Hindus, *Red Bread: Collectivization in a Russian Village*, quoted in R. W. Davies, *The Socialist Offensive: The Collectivisation of Soviet Agriculture, 1929–1930* (Cambridge, Mass.: Harvard University Press, 1980), pp. 209–210; (2) Russian State Archive of the Economy, quoted in Lynne Viola, *Peasant Rebels Under Stalin: Collectivization and the Culture of Peasant Resistance* (Oxford: Oxford University Press, 1996), p. 59; (3) Archives of the Internal Security Police, quoted in Viola, *Peasant Rebels Under Stalin,* p. 120; (4) Lev Kopelev, *The Education of a True Believer,* quoted in Robert Conquest, *The Harvest of Sorrow: Soviet Collectivization and the Terror—Famine* (New York: Oxford University Press, 1986), p. 233.

The Soviet Forced-Labor Camp at Arkhangelsk From 1929 to 1953 millions of Soviet citizens were sent to forced-labor prison camps such as this one, and over 1.5 million died. Ten to 20 percent of these prisoners were women, many of them found guilty of nothing more than being married to men considered enemies of the state. Here male and female prisoners work in a lumberyard in a cold and snowy climate near the Arctic Circle. (© SZ Photo/Bridgeman Images)

about the elemental, spontaneous nature of the terror, about a loss of central control over the course of mass repression, and about the role of regional leaders in initiating the terror are simply not supported by the historical record."[13] In short, a ruthless and paranoid Stalin found large numbers of willing collaborators for crime as well as for achievement.

Mussolini and Fascism in Italy

How did Italian fascism develop?

Benito Mussolini's Fascist movement and his seizure of power in 1922 were important steps in the rise of dictatorships between the two world wars. Mussolini and his supporters were the first to call themselves "Fascists." His dictatorship was brutal and theatrical, and it contained elements of both conservative authoritarianism and modern totalitarianism.

The Seizure of Power

In the early twentieth century Italy was a liberal state with civil rights and a constitutional monarchy. On the eve of the First World War, the parliamentary regime granted universal male suffrage. But there were serious problems. Poverty was widespread, and many peasants were more attached to their villages and local interests than to the national state. Church-state relations were often tense. Class differences were also extreme, and by 1912 the Socialist Party's radical wing led the powerful revolutionary socialist movement.[14]

World War I worsened the political situation. Having fought on the Allied side almost exclusively for purposes of territorial expansion, Italian nationalists were disappointed with Italy's modest gains at the Paris Peace Conference. Workers and peasants also felt cheated: to win their support during the war, the government had promised social and land reform, which it failed to deliver after the war.

The Russian Revolution inspired and energized Italy's revolutionary socialist movement, and radical workers and peasants began occupying factories and seizing land in 1920. These actions scared and mobilized the property-owning classes. Thus by 1921 revolutionary socialists, antiliberal conservatives, and frightened property owners were all opposed — though for different reasons — to the liberal parliamentary government.

Into these crosscurrents of unrest and fear stepped Benito Mussolini (1883–1945). Mussolini began his political career as a Socialist Party leader and radical newspaper editor before World War I. Expelled from the Italian Socialist Party for supporting the war, and wounded on the Italian front in 1917, Mussolini returned home and began organizing bitter war veterans into a band of Fascists — Italian for "a union of forces."

At first Mussolini's program was a radical combination of nationalist and socialist demands. As such, it competed directly with the well-organized Socialist Party and failed to attract followers. When Mussolini realized his violent verbal assaults on rival Socialists won him growing support from conservatives and the frightened middle classes, he began to shift gears and to exalt nation over class. By 1921 he was ridiculing and dismissing the Marxist interpretation of history:

> We deny the existence of two classes, because there are many more than two classes. We deny that human history can be explained in terms of economics. We deny your internationalism. That is a luxury article, which only the elevated can practice, because peoples are passionately bound to their native soil.[15]

Mussolini and his private army of **Black Shirts** also turned to physical violence. Few people were killed, but Socialist newspapers, union halls, and local Socialist Party headquarters were destroyed, eventually pushing Socialists out of the city governments of northern Italy. A skillful politician, Mussolini convinced his followers they were opposing the "Reds," while also promoting a real revolution of the little people against the established interests.

With the government breaking down in 1922, Mussolini stepped forward as the savior of order and property. In October 1922 thirty thousand Fascists marched on Rome, threatening the king and demanding he appoint Mussolini prime minister. Victor Emmanuel III (r. 1900–1946), forced to choose between Fascists or Socialists, asked Mussolini to form a new cabinet. Thus, after widespread violence and a threat of armed uprising, Mussolini seized power "legally."

The Regime in Action

In 1924 Mussolini declared his desire to "make the nation Fascist"[16] and imposed a series of repressive measures. Press freedom was abolished, elections were

Mussolini Leading a Parade in Rome Benito Mussolini was a master showman who drew on Rome's ancient heritage to promote Italian fascism. He wanted a grand avenue to stage triumphal marches with thousands of troops, so he had the Way of the Imperial Forums built through the old city. Here Mussolini rides at the head of a grand parade in 1932 to inaugurate the new road, passing the Roman Coliseum, one of the focal points along the route. (Stefano Bianchetti/Corbis via Getty Images)

fixed, and the government ruled by decree. Mussolini arrested his political opponents, disbanded all independent labor unions, and put dedicated Fascists in control of Italy's schools. He created a Fascist youth movement, Fascist labor unions, and many other Fascist organizations. He trumpeted his goal in a famous slogan of 1926: "Everything in the state, nothing outside the state, nothing against the state."[17] By year's end Italy was a one-party dictatorship under Mussolini's unquestioned leadership.

Black Shirts A private army under Mussolini in Italy that destroyed Socialist newspapers, union halls, and local Socialist Party headquarters, eventually pushing Socialists out of the city governments of northern Italy.

Mussolini was only primarily interested, however, in personal power. Rather than destroy the old power structure, he remained content to compromise with the conservative classes that controlled the army, the economy, and the state. He controlled labor but left big business to regulate itself, profitably and securely. There was no land reform.

Mussolini also drew increasing support from the Catholic Church. In the **Lateran Agreement** of 1929, he recognized the Vatican as a tiny independent state and agreed to give the church heavy financial support. The pope in return urged Italians to support Mussolini's government.

Like Stalin and Hitler, Mussolini favored a return of traditional roles for women. He abolished divorce and told women to stay at home and produce children. In 1938 women were limited by law to a maximum of 10 percent of the better-paying jobs in industry and government.

Mussolini's government passed no racial laws until 1938 and did not persecute Jews savagely until late in the Second World War, when Italy was under Nazi control. Nor did Mussolini establish a truly ruthless police state. Only twenty-three political prisoners were condemned to death between 1926 and 1944. Mussolini's Fascist Italy, though repressive and undemocratic, was never really totalitarian.

Hitler and Nazism in Germany

Why were Hitler and his Nazi regime initially so popular, and how did their actions lead to World War II?

The most frightening dictatorship developed in Nazi Germany. Here Nazism asserted an unlimited claim over German society and proclaimed the ultimate power of its leader, Adolf Hitler. Nazism's aspirations were truly totalitarian.

The Roots of Nazism

Nazism grew out of many complex concepts, of which the most influential were extreme nationalism and racism. These ideas captured the mind of the young Adolf Hitler (1889–1945) and evolved into Nazism.

Lateran Agreement A 1929 agreement in which Mussolini in Italy recognized the Vatican as an independent state and agreed to give the church heavy financial support in return for the pope's public support.

Nazism A movement born of extreme nationalism and racism and dominated by Adolf Hitler from 1933 until the end of World War II in 1945.

Enabling Act An act pushed through the Reichstag by the Nazis in 1933 that gave Hitler absolute dictatorial power for four years.

The son of an Austrian customs official, Hitler did poorly in high school and dropped out at age sixteen. He then headed to Vienna, where he was exposed to extreme Austro-German nationalists who believed Germans to be a superior people and central Europe's natural rulers. They advocated union with Germany and violent expulsion of "inferior" peoples from the Austro-Hungarian Empire.

From these extremists Hitler eagerly absorbed virulent anti-Semitism, racism, and hatred of Slavs. He developed an unshakable belief in the crudest distortions of Social Darwinism (see "Science for the Masses" in Chapter 24), the superiority of Germanic races, and the inevitability of racial conflict. The Jews, he claimed, directed an international conspiracy of finance capitalism and Marxist socialism against German culture, German unity, and the German race. Anti-Semitism and racism became Hitler's most passionate convictions.

Hitler greeted the Great War's outbreak as a salvation. The struggle and discipline of serving as a soldier in the war gave his life meaning, and when Germany suddenly surrendered in 1918, Hitler's world was shattered. Convinced that Jews and Marxists had "stabbed Germany in the back," he vowed to fight on.

In late 1919 Hitler joined a tiny extremist group in Munich called the German Workers' Party. By 1921 Hitler had gained absolute control of this small but growing party, now renamed the National Socialist German Worker's Party, or Nazi Party. A master of mass propaganda and political showmanship, Hitler worked his audiences into a frenzy with wild attacks on the Versailles treaty, the Jews, war profiteers, and Germany's Weimar Republic.

In late 1923 Germany under the Weimar Republic was experiencing unparalleled hyperinflation and seemed on the verge of collapse (see "Germany and the Western Powers" in Chapter 28). Hitler, inspired by Mussolini's recent victory, attempted an armed uprising in Munich. Despite the failure of the poorly organized plot and Hitler's arrest, Nazism had been born.

Hitler's Road to Power

At his trial Hitler violently denounced the Weimar Republic and attracted enormous publicity. During his brief prison term in 1924 he dictated *Mein Kampf* (*My Struggle*), in which he expounded on his basic ideas on race and anti-Semitism, the notion of territorial expansion based on "living space" for Germans, and the role of the leader-dictator, called the *Führer* (FYOOR-uhr).

The Nazis remained a small splinter group until the 1929 Great Depression shattered the economic prosperity and stability of the late 1920s. By the end of 1932, 32 percent or more of Germany's labor force was

Young People in Hitler's Germany This photo from 1930 shows Hitler admiring a young boy dressed in the uniform of Hitler's storm troopers, a paramilitary organization of the Nazi Party that supported Hitler's rise to power in the 1920s and early 1930s. Only a year after the founding of the storm troopers in 1921, Hitler began to organize Germany's young people into similar paramilitary groups in an effort to militarize all of German society. The young paramilitaries became the Hitler Youth, who eventually numbered in the millions. (Popperfoto/Getty Images)

unemployed. Industrial production fell by one-half between 1929 and 1932. No factor contributed more to Hitler's success than this economic crisis.

Hitler rejected free-market capitalism and advocated government programs to promote recovery. He pitched his speeches to middle- and lower-middle-class groups and to skilled workers. As the economy collapsed, great numbers of these people "voted their pocket-books"[18] and deserted the conservative and moderate parties for the Nazis. In the July 1932 election the Nazis won 14.5 million votes—38 percent of the total—and became the largest party in the Reichstag.

Hitler and the Nazis appealed strongly to German youth; Hitler himself was only forty in 1929. In 1931 almost 40 percent of Nazi Party members were under thirty, compared with 20 percent of Social Democrats. "National Socialism is the organized will of the youth,"[19] proclaimed the official Nazi slogan. National recovery, exciting and rapid change, and personal advancement made Nazism appealing to millions of German youths.

Hitler also came to power because of the breakdown of democratic government. Germany's economic collapse in the Great Depression convinced many voters that the country's republican leaders were incompetent and corrupt. Disunity on the left was another nail in the republic's coffin. The Communists refused to cooperate with the Social Democrats, even though the two parties together outnumbered the Nazis in the Reichstag.

Finally, Hitler excelled in backroom politics. In 1932 he succeeded in gaining support from key people in the army, big business, and politics, who thought they could manipulate and use him to their own advantage. Thus in January 1933 President Paul von Hindenburg (1847–1934) legally appointed Hitler, leader of Germany's largest party, as German chancellor.

The Nazi State and Society

Hitler quickly established an unshakable dictatorship. When the Reichstag building was partly destroyed by fire in February 1933, Hitler blamed the Communist Party. He convinced President von Hindenburg to sign dictatorial emergency acts that abolished freedom of speech and assembly and most personal liberties. He also called for new elections in an effort to solidify his political power.

When the Nazis won only 44 percent of the votes, Hitler outlawed the Communist Party and arrested its parliamentary representatives. Then on March 23, 1933, the Nazis forced through the Reichstag the so-called **Enabling Act**, which gave Hitler absolute dictatorial power for four years.

Hitler and the Nazis took over the government bureaucracy, installing many Nazis in top positions.

Hitler next outlawed strikes and abolished independent labor unions, which were replaced by the Nazi Labor Front. Professional people—doctors and lawyers, teachers and engineers—also saw their independent organizations swallowed up in Nazi associations. Publishing houses and universities were put under Nazi control, and students and professors publicly burned forbidden books. Modern art and architecture were ruthlessly prohibited. Life became violently anti-intellectual. As the cynical Joseph Goebbels, later Nazi minister of propaganda, put it, "When I hear the word 'culture' I reach for my gun."[20] By 1934 a brutal dictatorship characterized by frightening dynamism and total obedience to Hitler was already largely in place.

In 1934 Hitler also ordered that all civil servants and members of the German armed forces swear a binding oath of "unquestioning obedience" to Adolf Hitler. The SS—Hitler's elite personal guard—grew rapidly. Under Heinrich Himmler (1900–1945), the SS took over the political police (the Gestapo) and expanded its network of concentration camps.

From the beginning, German Jews were a special object of Nazi persecution. By late 1934 most Jewish lawyers, doctors, professors, civil servants, and musicians had been banned from their professions. In 1935 the infamous Nuremberg Laws classified as Jewish anyone having three or more Jewish grandparents and deprived Jews of all rights of citizenship. By 1938 roughly one-quarter of Germany's half million Jews had emigrated, sacrificing almost all their property in order to leave Germany.

In late 1938 the attack on the Jews accelerated and grew more violent. On November 9 and 10, 1938, the Nazis initiated a series of well-organized attacks against Jews throughout Nazi Germany and some parts of Austria. This infamous event is known as Kristallnacht (krees-TAHL-nahkht), or Night of Broken Glass, after the broken glass that littered the streets following the frenzied destruction of Jewish homes, shops, synagogues, and neighborhoods by German civilians and uniformed storm troopers. U.S. consul David Buffum reported of the Nazis in Leipzig:

> The most hideous phase of the so-called "spontaneous" action, has been the wholesale arrest and transportation to concentration camps of male German Jews between the ages of sixteen and sixty. . . . Having demolished dwellings and hurled most of the effects to the streets, the insatiably sadistic perpetrators threw many of the trembling inmates into a small stream that flows through the Zoological Park, commanding horrified spectators to spit at them, defile them with mud and jeer at their plight.[21]

Many historians consider this night the beginning of Hitler's Final Solution against the Jews, and after this event it became very difficult for Jews to leave Germany.

Some Germans privately opposed these outrages, but most went along or looked the other way. Although this lack of response reflected the individual's helplessness in a totalitarian state, it also reflected the strong popular support Hitler's government enjoyed.

Hitler's Popularity

Hitler had promised the masses economic recovery—"work and bread"—and he delivered. The Nazi Party launched a large public works program to pull Germany out of the depression. In 1935 Germany turned decisively toward rearmament. Unemployment dropped steadily, and by 1938 the Nazis boasted of nearly full employment. For millions of Germans economic recovery was tangible evidence that Nazi promises were more than show and propaganda.

For ordinary German citizens, in contrast to those deemed "undesirable" (Jews, Slavs, Gypsies, Jehovah's Witnesses, Communists, and homosexuals), Hitler's government offered greater equality and more opportunities. In 1933 class barriers in Germany were generally high. Hitler's rule introduced changes that lowered these barriers. The new Nazi elite included many young and poorly educated dropouts, rootless lower-middle-class people like Hitler who rose to the top with breathtaking speed. More generally, however, the Nazis tolerated privilege and wealth only as long as they served party needs.

Yet Hitler and the Nazis failed to bring about a real social revolution. The well-educated classes held on to most of their advantages, and only a modest social leveling occurred in the Nazi years. Significantly, the Nazis shared with the Italian Fascists the stereotypical view of women as housewives and mothers. Only when facing labor shortages during the war did they reluctantly mobilize large numbers of German women for office and factory work.[22]

Not all Germans supported Hitler, and a number of German groups actively resisted him after 1933. Tens of thousands of political enemies were imprisoned, and thousands were executed. In the first years of Hitler's rule, the principal resisters were trade-union Communists and Socialists. Catholic and Protestant churches produced a second group of opponents. Their efforts were directed primarily at preserving genuine religious life, however, not at overthrowing Hitler. Finally, in 1938 and again during the war, some high-ranking army officers, who feared the consequences of Hitler's reckless aggression, plotted, unsuccessfully, against him.

Aggression and Appeasement, 1933–1939

After Germany's economic recovery and Hitler's success in establishing Nazi control of society, Hitler turned to the next item on his agenda: aggressive territorial expansion. Germany's withdrawal from the League of Nations in October 1933 indicated its determination to rearm. When in March 1935 Hitler established a general military draft and declared the "unequal" Versailles treaty disarmament clauses null and void, leaders in Britain, France, and Italy issued a rather tepid joint protest and warned him against future aggressive actions.

But the emerging united front against Hitler quickly collapsed. Britain adopted a policy of appeasement, granting Hitler everything he could reasonably want (and more) in order to avoid war. British appeasement, which practically dictated French policy, had the support of many powerful British conservatives who, as in Germany, underestimated Hitler. The British people, still horrified by the memory, the costs, and the losses of the First World War, generally supported pacifism rather than war.

Some British leaders at the time, however, such as Winston Churchill, bitterly condemned appeasement as peace at any price. After the war, British appeasement came to be viewed as "the granting from fear or cowardice of unwarranted concessions in order to buy temporary peace at someone else's expense."[23] Beginning in the 1990s some historians have argued that British leaders had no real choice but to appease Hitler in the 1930s, because neither Great Britain nor France was prepared psychologically or militarily to fight another war.[24]

In March 1936 Hitler marched his armies without notice into the demilitarized Rhineland, violating the Treaties of Versailles and Locarno. France would not move without British support, and Britain refused to act. As Britain and France opted for appeasement, Hitler found powerful allies, particularly Mussolini, who in October 1935 had attacked the independent African kingdom of Ethiopia. Western

Italy's Ethiopian Campaign, 1935–1936

Hitler Playing with All the Statesmen This satirical cartoon from 1938 shows Hitler playing with all the statesmen attending the Four Power (Italy, Germany, England, France) Peace Conference that year in Munich. The Munich Agreement that came out of this meeting permitted Germany to annex the Sudetenland in Czechoslovakia, although representatives of that country were not invited to the conference. British prime minister Neville Chamberlain is portrayed in the lower right corner, under Hitler's boot. (Kelen Collection/Snark Archives © Photo12/The Image Works)

MAP 30.1 **The Growth of Nazi Germany, 1933–1939** Until March 1939 Hitler brought ethnic Germans into the Nazi state; then he turned on the Slavic peoples, whom he had always hated. He stripped Czechoslovakia of its independence and prepared for an attack on Poland in September 1939.

powers had condemned the Italian aggression, but Hitler supported Italy energetically. In October 1936 Italy and Germany established the so-called Rome-Berlin Axis. Japan, which wanted support for its occupation of Manchuria, joined the Axis alliance in 1940 (see "Japan Against China" in Chapter 29).

At the same time, Germany and Italy intervened in the Spanish Civil War (1936–1939), where their support helped General Francisco Franco's Fascist movement defeat republican Spain. Republican Spain's only official aid in the fight against Franco came from the Soviet Union.

In late 1937 Hitler moved forward with his plans to crush Austria and Czechoslovakia as the first step in his long-contemplated drive to the east for living

space. On March 12, 1938, German armies moved into Austria unopposed, and Austria became two provinces of Greater Germany (Map 30.1).

Simultaneously, Hitler demanded that the pro-Nazi, German-speaking territory of western Czechoslovakia—the Sudetenland—be turned over to Germany. Democratic Czechoslovakia was prepared to defend itself, but appeasement triumphed again. In September 1938 British prime minister Arthur Neville Chamberlain (1869–1940) and French negotiators met with Hitler in Munich and agreed with him that the Sudetenland should be ceded to Germany immediately. Returning to London from the Munich Conference, Chamberlain told cheering crowds that he had secured "peace with honour . . . peace for our time."[25] Sold out by the Western powers, Czechoslovakia gave in.

Hitler's armies occupied the remainder of Czechoslovakia, however, in March 1939. This time, there was no possible rationale of self-determination for Nazi aggression. When Hitler used the question of German minorities in Danzig as a pretext to confront Poland, Chamberlain declared that Britain and France would fight if Hitler attacked his eastern neighbor. Hitler did not take these warnings seriously and pressed on.

Through the 1930s Hitler had constantly referred to ethnic Slavs in the Soviet Union and other countries as *Untermenschen* (OON-ter-men-schen) (inferior people), and relations between the two countries had grown increasingly tense. War between Germany and the Soviet Union seemed inevitable, and, indeed, Stalin believed that Great Britain and France secretly hoped the Nazis and Bolsheviks would destroy each other. Then, in an about-face that stunned the world, sworn enemies Hitler and Stalin signed a nonaggression pact in August 1939. Each dictator promised to remain neutral if the other became involved in war. An attached secret protocol divided eastern Europe into German and Soviet zones "in the event of a political and territorial reorganization."[26] Stalin agreed to the pact for three reasons: he distrusted Western intentions, he needed more time to build up Soviet industry and military reserves, and Hitler offered territorial gain.

For Hitler, everything was now set. He told his generals on the day of the nonaggression pact, "My only fear is that at the last moment some dirty dog will come up with a mediation plan."[27] On September 1, 1939, the Germans attacked Poland from three sides. Two days later, Britain and France, finally true to their word, declared war on Germany. The Second World War in Europe had begun.

The Second World War, 1939–1945

How did Germany and Japan build empires in Europe and Asia, and how did the Allies defeat them?

World war broke out because Hitler's and Japan's ambitions were essentially unlimited. Nazi soldiers scored enormous successes in Europe until late 1942, establishing a vast empire of death and destruction. Japan attacked the United States in December 1941 and then moved to expand its empire throughout Asia and the Pacific Ocean. Eventually, the mighty Grand Alliance of Britain, the United States, and the Soviet Union overwhelmed the aggressors in manpower and military strength. Thus the Nazi and Japanese empires proved short-lived.

EVENTS LEADING TO WORLD WAR II

1919	Treaty of Versailles is signed
1921	Hitler heads National Socialist German Worker's Party (Nazis)
1922	Mussolini seizes power in Italy
1927	Stalin takes control of the Soviet Union
1929–1939	Great Depression
1931	Japan invades Manchuria
January 1933	Hitler is appointed chancellor of Germany
March 1933	Reichstag passes the Enabling Act, granting Hitler absolute dictatorial power
October 1933	Germany withdraws from the League of Nations
1935	Nuremberg Laws deprive Jews of all rights of citizenship
March 1935	Hitler announces German rearmament
October 1935	Mussolini invades Ethiopia and receives Hitler's support
March 1936	German armies move unopposed into the demilitarized Rhineland
1936–1939	Spanish Civil War
October 1936	Rome-Berlin Axis created
1937	Japan invades China
March 1938	Germany annexes Austria
September 1938	Munich Conference: Britain and France agree to German seizure of the Sudetenland from Czechoslovakia
March 1939	Germany occupies the rest of Czechoslovakia; appeasement ends in Britain
August 1939	Nazi-Soviet nonaggression pact is signed
September 1, 1939	Germany invades Poland
September 3, 1939	Britain and France declare war on Germany

Hitler's Empire in Europe, 1939–1942

Using planes, tanks, and trucks in the first example of a **blitzkrieg** (BLITZ-kreeg), or "lightning war," Hitler's armies crushed Poland in four weeks. The Soviet Union quickly took its share agreed to in the secret protocol—the eastern half of Poland and the Baltic states of Lithuania, Estonia, and Latvia. In spring 1940 the Nazi lightning war struck again. After occupying Denmark, Norway, and Holland, German motorized columns broke through southern Belgium and into France.

As Hitler's armies poured into France, aging marshal Henri-Philippe Pétain, a national hero of the Great War, formed a new French government—the so-called Vichy (VIH-shee) government—and accepted defeat. By July 1940 Hitler ruled practically all of western continental Europe; Italy was an ally, the Soviet Union a friendly neutral (Map 30.2). Only Britain, led by Winston Churchill (1874–1965), remained unconquered.

Vichy France, 1940

BELGIUM
LUX.
LORRAINE
Paris
FRANCE
ALSACE
SWITZ.
Vichy
VICHY
FRANCE
ITALY
Bay of Biscay
SPAIN
Mediterranean Sea

- Occupied by Germany
- Annexed by Germany

To prepare for an invasion of Britain, Germany first needed to gain control of the air. In the Battle of Britain, which began in July 1940, German planes attacked British airfields and key factories, dueling with British defenders high in the skies. In September Hitler began indiscriminately bombing British cities to break British morale. British aircraft factories increased production, and Londoners defiantly dug in. By September Britain was winning the air war, and Hitler abandoned his plans for an immediate German invasion of Britain.

Hitler now allowed his lifetime obsession of creating a vast eastern European empire for the "master race" to dictate policy. In June 1941 Germany broke the Nazi-Soviet nonaggression pact and attacked the Soviet Union. By October Leningrad was practically surrounded, Moscow was besieged, and most of Ukraine had been conquered. But the Soviets did not collapse, and when a severe winter struck German armies outfitted in summer uniforms, the invaders were stopped.

Although stalled in Russia, Hitler ruled an enormous European empire.

London Bomb Shelter, 1940 Hitler believed that his relentless terror bombing of London — the "blitz" — could break the will of the British people. He was wrong. The blitz caused enormous destruction, but Londoners went about their business with courage and calm determination, as this unforgettable image of people being entertained in a bomb shelter in the Tube (subway) suggests. (Bettmann/Getty Images)

Legend:
- Axis powers and their allies
- Occupied by Germany and its allies
- Allied powers and their allies
- Neutral nations
- Boundary of Greater Germany
- Major battle

Siege of Leningrad, Sept. 1941–Jan. 1944

Germans repulsed, Dec. 1941

Moscow Oct. 1941–Jan. 1942

Siege of Stalingrad, Aug. 21, 1942–Jan. 31, 1943

Russian front, spring 1944

Russian front, Nov. 1942

Kursk July–Aug. 1943

Dnieper Aug.–Dec. 1943

Russian front, Dec. 1941

Germany surrenders, May 8, 1945

Siege, Sept. 1939 Uprising, Aug.–Sept. 1944

Russian front, Feb. 1945

Battle of Britain, fall 1940

Invasion of Normandy June 6, 1944

Western front, Feb. 1945

Battle of the Bulge Dec. 1944

Axis troops occupy Vichy France, Nov. 10 and 11, 1942

Italian front Feb. 1945

Rome (Liberated June 1944)

Monte Cassino May 1944

Salerno Sept. 1943

Allies invade Sicily and Italy, July–Sept. 1943

Axis troops evacuated, May 1943

Casablanca Nov. 1942

Sicily July 1943

Battle for Crete, May 20–June 1, 1941

Joined Allies, Nov. 1942

El Alamein autumn 1942

0 200 400 miles
0 200 400 kilometers

MAP 30.2 World War II in Europe and Africa, 1939–1945 The map shows the extent of Hitler's empire at its height, before the Battle of Stalingrad in late 1942 and the subsequent advances of the Allies until Germany surrendered on May 7, 1945.

He now began building a **New Order** based on the guiding principle of Nazi totalitarianism: racial imperialism. Within the New Order, the Dutch, Norwegians, Swedes, and Danes received preferential treatment, for the Germans believed they were racially related to the German "Aryan" master race. The French, an "inferior" Latin people, occupied the middle position. At the bottom of the New Order were the harshly treated "subhumans," Jews and Slavs.

Hitler envisioned a vast eastern colonial empire where enslaved Poles, Ukrainians, and Russians would die or be killed off while Germanic peasants would resettle the abandoned lands. Himmler and the elite SS corps implemented a program of destruction in the occupied territories to create a "mass settlement space" for Germans.

blitzkrieg "Lightning war" using planes, tanks, and trucks, first used by Hitler to crush Poland in four weeks.

New Order Hitler's program, based on the guiding principle of racial imperialism, which gave preferential treatment to the Nordic peoples above "inferior" Latin peoples and, at the bottom, "subhuman" Slavs and Jews.

The Holocaust, 1941–1945

Prelude to Murder This photo captures the terrible inhumanity of Nazi racism. Frightened and bewildered families from the soon-to-be-destroyed Warsaw Ghetto are being forced out of their homes by German soldiers for deportation to concentration camps. There they faced murder in the gas chambers. (Keystone/Getty Images)

The Holocaust

Finally, the Nazi state condemned all European Jews to extermination in the **Holocaust**. After Warsaw fell in 1939, the Nazis forced Jews in the occupied territories to move to urban ghettos, while German Jews were sent to occupied Poland. After Germany attacked Russia in June 1941, forced expulsion spiraled into extermination. In late 1941 Hitler and the Nazi leadership ordered the SS to speed up planning for "the final solution of the Jewish question."[28] Throughout the Nazi empire Jews were systematically arrested, packed like cattle onto freight trains, and dispatched to extermination camps.

Arriving at their destination, small numbers of Jews were sent to nearby slave labor camps, where they were starved and systematically worked to death. (See "Individuals in Society: Primo Levi," at right.) Most victims were taken to "shower rooms," which were actually gas chambers. By 1945 about 6 million Jews had been murdered.

Who was responsible for this terrible crime? After the war, historians laid the guilt on Hitler and the Nazi leadership, arguing that ordinary Germans had little knowledge of the extermination camps, or that those who cooperated had no alternative given the brutality of Nazi terror and totalitarian control. Beginning in

the 1990s studies appeared revealing a much broader participation of German people in the Holocaust and popular indifference (or worse) to the Jews' fate.[29] In most occupied countries local non-German officials also cooperated in the arrest and deportation of Jews.

Japan's Asian Empire

By late 1938, 1.5 million Japanese troops were bogged down in China, holding a great swath of territory but unable to defeat the Nationalists and the Communists (see "Japan Against China" in Chapter 29). In 1939, as war broke out in Europe, the Japanese redoubled their ruthless efforts in China. Implementing a savage policy of "kill all, burn all, destroy all," Japanese troops committed shocking atrocities, including the so-called Rape of Nanjing. During Japan's war in China — the second Sino-Japanese War (1937–1945) — the Japanese are estimated to have killed 4 million Chinese people.

In August 1940 the Japanese announced the formation of a self-sufficient Asian economic zone. Although they spoke of liberating Asia from Western imperialism and of "Asia for the Asians," their true intentions were to eventually rule over a vast Japanese empire. Ultranationalists moved to convince Japan's youth that Japan had a sacred liberating mission in Asia. (See "Analyzing the Evidence: Ultranationalist Pamphlet for Japanese Students," page 910.)

For the moment, however, Japan needed allies. In September 1940 Japan signed a formal alliance (the

Holocaust The attempted systematic extermination of all European Jews and other "undesirables" by the Nazi state during World War II.

Primo Levi

MOST JEWS DEPORTED TO AUSCHWITZ were murdered as soon as they arrived, but the Nazis made some prisoners into slave laborers, and a few of these survived. Primo Levi (1919–1987), an Italian Jew, became one of the most influential witnesses to the Holocaust and its death camps.

Like many in Italy's small Jewish community, Levi's family belonged to the urban professional classes. The young Primo Levi graduated in 1941 from the University of Turin with highest honors in chemistry. Since 1938, when Italy introduced racial laws, he had faced growing discrimination, and two years after graduation he joined the antifascist resistance movement. Quickly captured, he was deported to Auschwitz with 650 Italian Jews in February 1944. Stone-faced SS men picked only ninety-six men and twenty-nine women to work in their respective labor camps. Levi was one of them.

Primo Levi, who never stopped thinking, writing, and speaking about the Holocaust. (Bernard Gotfryd/Getty Images)

Nothing had prepared Levi for what he encountered. The Jewish prisoners were kicked, punched, stripped, branded with tattoos, crammed into huts, and worked unmercifully. Hoping for some sign of prisoner solidarity in this terrible environment, Levi found only a desperate struggle of each against all and enormous status differences among prisoners. Many stunned and bewildered newcomers, beaten and demoralized by their bosses—the most privileged prisoners—collapsed and died. Others struggled to secure their own privileges, however small, because food rations and working conditions were so abominable that ordinary Jewish prisoners perished in two to three months.

Sensitive and noncombative, Levi found himself sinking into oblivion. But instead of joining the mass of the "drowned," he became one of the "saved"—a complicated surprise with moral implications that he would ponder all his life. As Levi explained in *Survival in Auschwitz* (1947), the usual road to salvation in the camps was some kind of collaboration with German power.* Savage German criminals were released from prison to become brutal camp guards; non-Jewish political prisoners competed for jobs entitling them to better conditions; and, especially troubling for Levi, a small number of Jewish men plotted and struggled for the power of life and death over other Jewish prisoners.

Though not one of these Jewish bosses, Levi believed that he himself, like almost all survivors, had entered the "gray zone" of moral compromise. Only a very few superior individuals, "the stuff of saints and martyrs," survived the death camps without shifting their moral stance.

For Levi, compromise and salvation came from his profession. Interviewed by a German technocrat for the camp's synthetic rubber program, Levi performed brilliantly in scientific German and savored his triumph as a Jew over Nazi racism. Work in the warm camp laboratory offered Levi opportunities to pilfer equipment that could then be traded to other prisoners for food and necessities. Levi also gained critical support from three saintly prisoners who refused to do wicked and hateful acts. And he counted "luck" as essential for his survival: in the camp infirmary with scarlet fever in February 1945 as advancing Russian armies prepared to liberate the camp, Levi was not evacuated by the Nazis and shot to death like most Jewish prisoners.

After the war Primo Levi was forever haunted by the nightmare that the Holocaust would be ignored or forgotten. Always ashamed that so many people whom he considered better than himself had perished, he wrote and lectured tirelessly to preserve the memory of Jewish victims and guilty Nazis. Wanting the world to understand the Jewish genocide in all its complexity so that never again would people tolerate such atrocities, he grappled tirelessly with his vision of individual choice and moral compromise in a hell designed to make the victims collaborate and persecute each other.

QUESTIONS FOR ANALYSIS

1. Describe Levi's experience at Auschwitz. How did camp prisoners treat each other? Why?
2. What does Levi mean by the "gray zone"? How is this concept central to his thinking?
3. Will a vivid historical memory of the Holocaust help prevent future genocide? Why or why not?

*Primo Levi, *Survival in Auschwitz: The Nazi Assault on Humanity*, rev. ed. 1958 (London: Collier Books, 1961), pp. 79–84, and *The Drowned and the Saved* (New York: Summit Books, 1988). These powerful testimonies are highly recommended.

Ultranationalist Pamphlet for Japanese Students

In August 1941, only four months before Japan's coordinated attacks on Pearl Harbor and colonial empires in Southeast Asia, Japan's Ministry of Education issued "The Way of Subjects." Required reading for high school and university students, this twenty-page pamphlet summed up the basic tenets of Japanese ultranationalism, which had become dominant in the 1930s.

As this selection suggests, ultranationalism in Japan combined a sense of mission with intense group solidarity and unquestioning devotion to a semidivine emperor. Thus Japanese expansion into Manchuria and the war in China were part of Japan's sacred calling to protect the throne and to free Asia from Western exploitation and misrule. Of course, an unknown percentage of students (and adults) did not believe that the myths of Japan's state religion were literally true. Nevertheless, they were profoundly influenced by extremist nationalism: Japanese soldiers' determination to fight to the death was a prime indicator of that influence.

■ The way of the subjects of the Emperor issues from the polity of the Emperor, and is to guard and maintain the Imperial Throne coexistent with the Heavens and the Earth. This is not the sphere of the abstract, but a way of daily practice based on history. The life and activities of the nation are all attuned to the task of giving great firmness to the foundation of the Empire. . . .

Modern history, in a nutshell, has been marked by the formation of unified nations in Europe and their contests for supremacy in the acquisition of colonies. Early in the modern period of history, the American continent was discovered and, stimulated by this, Europeans vigorously found their way to India and China by sounding the furrows of the oceans. Their march into all parts of the world paved the way for their subsequent world domination politically, economically, and culturally and led them to act freely as they pleased, and to believe that they alone were justified in their outrageous behavior. . . .

The industrial development propelled by invention of machines demanded a considerably large amount of materials and the consequent overseas markets for the disposal of manufactured goods. The result was that a severe contest for colonial acquisition and trade competition ensued naturally and that wars of the strong preying on the weak were repeated. The history of wars waged among Spain, Portugal, Holland, Britain, France, and other countries in the modern age, and the rise and fall of their influence, have close connections with their overseas aggression. . . .

The self-destruction in the shape of the World War finally followed. It was only natural that cries were raised even among men of those countries after the war that the Occidental [Western] civilization was crumbling. A vigorous movement was started by Britain, France, and the United States to maintain the status quo by all means. Simultaneously, a movement aiming at social revolution through class conflict on the basis of thoroughgoing materialism like communism also was developed with unremitting vigor. On the other hand, Nazism and Fascism arose with great force. The basic theories of these new racial principles and the totalitarianism in Germany and Italy are to remove and improve the evils of individualism and liberalism.

That these [totalitarian] principles show great concern for Oriental [Eastern] culture and spirit is a noteworthy fact that suggests the future of the Occidental civilization and the creation of a new culture. Thus the orientation of world history has made the collapse of the world of the old order an

---

Axis alliance) with Germany and Italy, and Vichy France granted the Japanese dominion over northern French Indochina. The United States, upset with Japan's occupation of Indochina and fearing embattled Britain would collapse if it lost its Asian colonies, froze scrap iron sales to Japan and applied further economic sanctions in October.

As 1941 opened, Japan's leaders faced a critical decision. At the time, the United States was the world's largest oil producer and supplied over 90 percent of Japan's oil needs. Japan had only a year and a half's worth of military and economic oil reserves, which the war in China and the Japanese military and merchant navies were quickly drawing down. The Netherlands' colonial possessions in Indonesia (Netherlands East Indies) could supply all of Japan's oil, rubber, and tin needs, but the Japanese feared an attack there would bring American reprisal. On July 26, 1941, President Roosevelt embargoed all oil exports to Japan and froze its assets in the United States. Japan now had to either recall its forces from China or go to war before running out of oil. It chose war.

On December 7, 1941, Japan launched a surprise attack on the U.S. fleet in Pearl Harbor in the Hawaiian Islands. Japan hoped to cripple its Pacific rival, gain time to build a defensible Asian empire, and eventually win an ill-defined compromise peace.

The Japanese attack was a limited success. The Japanese sank or crippled every American battleship, but by chance all the American aircraft carriers were at sea and escaped unharmed. Hours later the Japanese destroyed half of the American Far East Air Force staassured conclusion. Japan has hereby opened the start for the construction of a new world order based on moral principles.

The Manchurian Affair was a violent outburst of Japanese national life long suppressed. Taking advantage of this, Japan in the glare of all the Powers stepped out for the creation of a world based on moral principles and the construction of a new order. This was a manifestation of the spirit, profound and lofty, embodied in the Empire-founding, and an unavoidable action for its national life and world mission. . . .

Japan has a political mission to help various regions in the Greater East Asia Co-prosperity Sphere [the Japanese term for Japan's Asian empire], which are reduced to a state of quasi colony by Europe and America, so as to rescue them from their control. Economically, this country will have to eradicate the evils of their exploitation and then set up an economic structure for coexistence and co-prosperity. Culturally, Japan must strive to fashion East Asiatic nations to change their following of European and American culture and to develop Oriental culture for the purpose of contributing to the creation of a right world. The Orient has been left to destruction for the past several hundred years. Its rehabilitation is not an easy task. It is natural that unusual difficulties attend the establishment of a new order and the creation of a new culture. The conquest of these difficulties alone will do much to help in establishing a morally controlled world, in which all nations can cooperate and all people can secure their proper position. . . .

Japan, since the founding of the Empire, has been basking under a benign rule of a line of Emperors unbroken for ages eternal, and has been growing and developing in an atmosphere of great harmony as a nation, consisting of one large family. However diverse the Empire's structures in politics, economy, culture, military affairs, and others may be, all finally are unified under the Emperor, the center. The country has lived under the Imperial rule and glory.

The ideals of Japan are to manifest to the entire world the spirit of her Empire-founding represented by the principle that "the benevolent rule of the Emperor may be extended so as to embrace the whole world." There is virtually no country in the world other than Japan having such a superb and lofty mission bearing world significance. So it can be said that the construction of a new structure and a defense state is all in order that Japan may revive her proper national structure and come back to her original status of national strength and leaving no stone unturned in displaying her total power to the fullest extent. . . .

The Imperial Family is the fountain source of the Japanese nation, and national and private lives issue from this. . . .

The way of the subjects is to be loyal to the Emperor in disregard of self, thereby supporting the Imperial Throne coexistence with the Heaven and with the Earth. . . .

The great duty of the Japanese people to guard and maintain the Imperial Throne has lasted to the present since the Empire founding and will last forever and ever. To serve the Emperor is its key point. Our lives will become sincere and true when they are offered to the Emperor and the state. Our own private life is fulfillment of the way of the subjects; in other words, it is not private, but public, insofar as it is held by the subjects supporting the Throne.

QUESTIONS FOR ANALYSIS

1. How does "The Way of Subjects" interpret modern history? In what ways do Western thought and action threaten Japan?
2. What is Japan's mission in Asia?
3. What is the basis of Japanese sovereignty? What is the individual's proper role in society?

Source: "The Way of Subjects," in *Japan Times Advertiser*, August 1941. Reprinted in David J. Lu, *Japan: A Documentary History* (Armonk: N.Y.: M. E. Sharpe, 1997), pp. 435–440.

tioned at Clark Air Base in the Philippines. Americans were humiliated by these unexpected defeats, which soon overwhelmed American isolationism and brought the United States into the war.

Hitler immediately declared war on the United States. Simultaneously, Japanese armies successfully attacked European and American colonies in Southeast Asia. Small but well-trained Japanese armies defeated larger Dutch and British armies to seize the Netherlands East Indies and the British colonies of Hong Kong, Malaya, and Singapore. After American forces surrendered the Philippines in May 1942, Japan held a vast empire in Southeast Asia and the western Pacific (Map 30.3).

The Japanese claimed they were freeing Asians from Western imperialism, and they called their empire the Greater East Asian Co-Prosperity Sphere. Most local populations were glad to see the Western powers go, but Asian faith in "co-prosperity" and support for Japan steadily declined as the war progressed. Although the Japanese set up anticolonial governments and promised genuine independence, real power always rested with Japanese military commanders and their superiors in Tokyo. Moreover, the Japanese never treated local populations as equals, and the occupiers exploited local peoples for Japan's wartime needs.

The Japanese often exhibited great cruelty toward prisoners of war and civilians. Dutch, Indonesian, and perhaps as many as two hundred thousand Korean women were forced to provide sex for Japanese soldiers as "comfort women." Recurring cruel behavior aroused local populations against the invaders.

MAPPING THE PAST

MAP 30.3 World War II in the Pacific In 1942 Japanese forces overran an enormous amount of territory, which the Allies slowly recaptured in a long, bitter struggle.

ANALYZING THE MAP Locate the extent of the Japanese empire in 1942, and compare it to the Japanese-controlled territory at surrender in 1945. Where was the fighting in the Pacific concentrated?

CONNECTIONS How was the course of the war's end in Europe different from that of Asia, and what does this suggest about the difficulties that the Allies faced in fighting the Japanese?

The Grand Alliance

While the Nazis and the Japanese built their empires, Great Britain (the greatest colonial power), the United States (the greatest capitalist power), and the Soviet Union (the greatest Communist power) joined together in an unlikely military pact called the Grand Alliance. The vagaries of war, rather than choice, brought them together. Stalin had been cooperating with Hitler before Germany attacked Russia in June 1941, and the United States entered the war only after the Japanese attack on Pearl Harbor in December.

Grand Alliance leaders agreed to a **Europe first policy** set forth by Churchill and adopted by Roosevelt. Only after defeating Hitler would the Allies mount

Europe first policy The military strategy, set forth by Churchill and adopted by Roosevelt, that called for the defeat of Hitler in Europe before the United States launched an all-out strike against Japan in the Pacific.

an all-out attack on Japan. To encourage mutual trust, the Allies adopted the principle of the unconditional surrender of Germany and Japan, and no unilateral treaties (as Russia had signed with Germany in World War I). This policy cemented the Grand Alliance because it denied Germany and Japan any hope of dividing their foes.

The Grand Alliance's military resources were awesome. The United States possessed a unique capacity to wage global war with its large population and mighty industry, which it harnessed in 1943 to outproduce not only the Axis powers but also the rest of the world combined.[30] The British economy was totally and effectively mobilized, and the country became an important staging area for the war in Europe. As for the Soviet Union, so great was its economic strength that it might well have defeated Germany without Western help. Stalin drew on the massive support of the people for what the Soviets called the "Great Patriotic War of the Fatherland."

The War in Europe, 1942–1945

Halted at the gates of Moscow and Leningrad in 1941, the Germans renewed their offensive against the Soviet Union in 1942 and attacked Stalingrad in July. The Soviet armies counterattacked, quickly surrounding the entire German Sixth Army of 300,000 men. By late January 1943 only 123,000 soldiers were left to surrender. In summer 1943 the larger, better-equipped Soviet armies took the offensive and began to push the Germans back (see Map 30.2).

Not yet prepared to attack Germany directly through France, the Western Allies engaged in heavy fighting in North Africa (see Map 30.2). In autumn 1942 British forces defeated German and Italian armies at the Battle of El Alamein (el a-luh-MAYN) in Egypt. Shortly thereafter an Anglo-American force took control of the Vichy French colonies of Morocco and Algeria.

Having driven the Axis powers from North Africa by spring 1943, Allied forces invaded Italy. War-weary Italians deposed Mussolini, and the new Italian government accepted unconditional surrender in September 1943. Italy, it seemed, was liberated. But German commandos rescued Mussolini and made him head of a puppet government. German armies seized Rome and all of northern Italy. They finally surrendered only on April 29, 1945. Two days earlier Mussolini had been captured by partisan forces, and he was executed the next day.

On June 6, 1944, American and British forces under General Dwight Eisenhower landed on the beaches of Normandy, France, in history's greatest naval invasion. More than 2 million men and almost 0.5 million vehicles pushed inland and broke through the German lines.

Roosevelt, Churchill, and Stalin at Yalta In February 1945, three months before his death, President Roosevelt met with the other two leaders of the Grand Alliance, Churchill and Stalin, at the Crimean resort town of Yalta. With victory against Germany clearly in sight, they met to discuss the reconstruction of war-torn Europe, the treatment and occupation of Germany and eastern Europe after the war, and the Soviet Union's entry into the war in the Pacific. Although Stalin made some important concessions, many historians argue that Roosevelt was already too ill to join Churchill in demanding stronger guarantees from Stalin regarding self-determination for eastern Europe. (Franklin D. Roosevelt Presidential Library and Museum/National Archives and Records Administration/U.S. National Archives/photo CT53-70:5)

In early February 1945 a sick and feeble Franklin Roosevelt met with Stalin and Churchill at Yalta in the Russian Crimea to negotiate plans for the remainder of the war in Europe, Russia's participation in the war in Asia, and the postwar world. Roosevelt was later severely criticized by some for supposedly "handing over" eastern Europe and northeast Asia (North Korea in particular) to the Soviet Union. Other scholars have noted, however, that Stalin made substantial concessions as well.

In March 1945 American troops crossed the Rhine and entered Germany. The Soviets had been advancing steadily since July 1943, and on April 26, 1945, the Red Army met American forces on the Elbe River in Germany. As Soviet forces fought their way into Berlin, Hitler committed suicide in his bunker on April 30. On May 7 the remaining German commanders capitulated.

The War in the Pacific, 1942–1945

While gigantic armies clashed on land in Europe, the greatest naval battles in history decided the fate of the war in Asia. In April 1942 the Japanese devised a plan to take Port Moresby in New Guinea and also destroy U.S. aircraft carriers in an attack on Midway Island (see Map 30.3). Having broken the secret Japanese code, the Americans skillfully won a series of decisive naval victories. First, in the Battle of the Coral Sea in May 1942, an American carrier force halted the Japanese advance on Port Moresby. Then, in the Battle of Midway in June 1942, American pilots sank all four of the attacking Japanese aircraft carriers and established overall naval equality with Japan in the Pacific.

The United States gradually won control of the sea and air as it geared up its war industry. By 1943 the United States was producing one hundred thousand aircraft a year, almost twice as many as Japan produced in the entire war. In July 1943 the Americans and their Australian allies opened an "island-hopping" campaign toward Japan. By 1944 hundreds of American submarines were hunting in "wolf packs," decimating shipping and destroying economic links in Japan's far-flung, overextended empire.

The Pacific war was brutal—a "war without mercy"—and atrocities were committed on both sides.[31] Aware of Japanese atrocities in China and the Philippines, the U.S. forces seldom took Japanese prisoners after the Battle of Guadalcanal in August 1942, killing even those rare Japanese soldiers who offered to surrender. American forces moving across the central and western Pacific in 1943 and 1944 faced unyielding resistance, and this resistance hardened soldiers as American casualties kept rising. A product of spiraling violence, mutual hatred, and dehumanizing racial stereotypes, the war without mercy intensified as it moved toward Japan.

The War in the Philippines U.S. and Filipino forces held out on the Bataan peninsula until April 1942, when seventy-six thousand soldiers surrendered to the Japanese military. Most of the prisoners were sick, wounded, or suffering from malnutrition, and the Japanese systematically executed many of them. Other prisoners, such as those pictured here, were marched to exhaustion without water in the blazing sun on the infamous Bataan Death March, and many were bayoneted or beaten to death. (Mansell/The LIFE Picture Collection/ Getty Images)

A Hiroshima Survivor Remembers Yasuko Yamagata was seventeen when she saw the brilliant blue-white "lightning flash" that became a fiery orange ball consuming everything that would burn. Thirty years later Yamagata painted this scene, her most unforgettable memory of the atomic attack. An incinerated woman, poised as if running with her baby clutched to her breast, lies near a water tank piled high with charred corpses. (GE15-05 drawn by Yasuko Yamagata, Hiroshima Peace Memorial Museum)

In June 1944 U.S. bombers began a relentless bombing campaign of the Japanese home islands. In October 1944 American forces under General Douglas MacArthur landed on Leyte Island in the Philippines. In the ensuing Battle of Leyte Gulf, the Japanese lost 13 large warships, including 4 aircraft carriers, while the Americans lost only 3 small ships. The Japanese navy was practically finished.

In spite of massive defeats, Japanese troops continued to fight on. Indeed, the bloodiest battles of the Pacific war took place on Iwo Jima in February 1945 and on Okinawa in June 1945. American commanders believed that an invasion of Japan might cost 1 million American casualties and possibly 10 to 20 million Japanese lives. In fact, Japan was almost helpless, its industry and cities largely destroyed by intense American bombing. As the war in Europe ended in April 1945, Japanese leaders were divided. Hardliners argued that surrender was unthinkable; Japan had never been invaded or lost a war. A peace faction sought a negotiated end to the war.

On July 26 Truman, Churchill, and Stalin issued the Potsdam Declaration, which demanded unconditional surrender. The declaration left unclear whether the Japanese emperor would be treated as a war criminal. The Japanese, who considered Emperor Hirohito a god, sought clarification and amnesty for him. The Allies remained adamant that the surrender be unconditional. The Japanese felt compelled to fight on.

On August 6 and 9, 1945, the United States dropped atomic bombs on Hiroshima and Nagasaki in Japan. Also on August 9, Soviet troops launched an invasion of the Japanese puppet state of Manchukuo (Manchuria, China). To avoid a Soviet invasion and further atomic bombing, the Japanese announced their surrender on August 14, 1945. The Second World War, which had claimed the lives of more than 50 million soldiers and civilians, was over.

Chapter Summary

The 1929 American stock market crash triggered a global Great Depression. Western democracies expanded their powers and responded with relief programs. Authoritarian and Fascist regimes arose to replace some capitalist democracies. Only World War II ended the depression.

The radical totalitarian dictatorships of the 1920s and 1930s were repressive, profoundly antiliberal, and exceedingly violent. Mussolini set up the first Fascist government, a one-party dictatorship, but it was never truly a totalitarian state on the order of Hitler's Germany or Stalin's Soviet Union. In the Soviet Union Stalin launched a socialist "revolution from above" to modernize and industrialize the U.S.S.R. Mass purges of the Communist Party in the 1930s led to the imprisonment and deaths of millions.

Hitler and the Nazi elite rallied support by recalling the humiliation of World War I and the terms of the Versailles treaty, condemning Germany's leaders, building on racist prejudices against "inferior" peoples, and warning of a vast Jewish conspiracy to harm Germany and the German race. The Great Depression caused German voters to turn to Hitler for relief. After he declared the Versailles treaty disarmament clause null and void, British and French leaders tried appeasement. On September 1, 1939, his unprovoked attack on Poland forced the Allies to declare war, starting World War II.

Nazi armies first seized Poland and Germany's western neighbors and then turned east. Here Hitler planned to build a New Order based on racial imperialism. In the Holocaust that followed, millions of Jews and other "undesirables" were systematically exterminated. In Asia the Japanese created the Greater East Asian Co-Prosperity Sphere. This was a sham, as "Asia for the Asians" meant nothing but Japanese domination and control. After Japan attacked Pearl Harbor, the United States entered the war. In 1945 the Grand Alliance of the United States, Britain, and the Soviet Union defeated, outproduced, and outmanned Germany and Japan.

NOTES

1. Quoted in S. B. Clough et al., eds., *Economic History of Europe: Twentieth Century* (New York: Harper & Row, 1968), pp. 243–245.
2. E. Halévy, *The Era of Tyrannies* (Garden City, N.Y.: Doubleday, 1965), pp. 265–316, esp. p. 300.
3. Carl J. Friedrich and Zbigniew K. Brzezinski, *Totalitarian Dictatorship and Autocracy*, 2d ed. (Cambridge, Mass.: Harvard University Press, 1965), pp. 21–23.
4. I. Kershaw, *The Nazi Dictatorship: Problems and Perspectives of Interpretation*, 2d ed. (London: Edward Arnold, 1989), p. 34.
5. See Robert C. Tucker, *Stalin in Power: The Revolution from Above, 1928–1941* (New York: W. W. Norton, 1992).
6. Lewis Siegelbaum and Andrei Sokolov, *Stalinism as a Way of Life: A Narrative in Documents* (New Haven, Conn.: Yale University Press, 2000), pp. 38–39.
7. Joseph Stalin, "Speech to First All-Congress Conference of Managers of Socialist Industry, February 4, 1931," in Joseph Stalin, *Leninism* (London: George Allen & Unwin, 1940), pp. 365–366.
8. Robert Service, *Stalin: A Biography* (Cambridge, Mass.: Harvard University Press, 2005), p. 266.
9. Quoted in I. Deutscher, *Stalin: A Political Biography*, 2d ed. (New York: Oxford University Press, 1967), p. 325, fn. 1.
10. Steven Rosefielde, *Red Holocaust* (New York: Routledge, 2010), p. 259, fn. 12.
11. Malcolm Muggeridge, *Chronicles of Wasted Time. Chronicle 1: The Green Stick* (New York: William Morrow, 1973), pp. 234–235.
12. M. Malia, *The Soviet Tragedy: A History of Socialism in Russia, 1917–1991* (New York: Free Press, 1995), pp. 227–270; see also the controversial work by historian John Archibald Getty, *Origins of the Great Purges: The Soviet Communist Party Reconsidered, 1933–1938* (New York: Cambridge University Press, 1985).
13. Oleg V. Khlevniuk, *Master of the House: Stalin and His Inner Circle* (New Haven, Conn.: Yale University Press, 2009), p. xix.
14. R. Vivarelli, "Interpretations on the Origins of Fascism," *Journal of Modern History* 63 (March 1991): 41.
15. Ion Smeaton Munro, *Through Fascism to World Power: A History of the Revolution in Italy* (London: Alexander Maclehose, 1933), p. 120.
16. Christopher Seton-Watson, *Italy from Liberalism to Fascism, 1870–1925* (London: Methuen, 1967), p. 661.
17. Ibid.
18. W. Brustein, *The Logic of Evil: The Social Origins of the Nazi Party, 1925–1933* (New Haven, Conn.: Yale University Press, 1996), pp. 52, 182.
19. Karl Dietrich Bracher, *The German Dictatorship: The Origins, Structure, and Effects of National Socialism*, trans. Jean Steinberg (New York: Praeger, 1970), p. 146.
20. Quoted in R. Stromberg, *An Intellectual History of Modern Europe* (New York: Appleton-Century-Crofts, 1966), p. 393.
21. Quoted in R. Moeller, *The Nazi State and German Society: A Brief History with Documents* (Boston: Bedford/St. Martin's, 2010), p. 108.
22. See Claudia Koonz, *Mothers in the Fatherland: Women, the Family, and Nazi Politics* (New York: St. Martin's Press, 1987).
23. D. N. Dilks, "Appeasement Revisited," *University of Leeds Review* 15 (1972): 28–56.
24. See Frank McDonough, *Neville Chamberlain, Appeasement, and the British Road to War* (Manchester: Manchester University Press, 1998).
25. Winston Churchill, *The Second World War: The Gathering Storm* (Boston: Houghton Mifflin, 1948), p. 318.
26. Izidors Vizulis, *The Molotov-Ribbentrop Pact of 1939: The Baltic Case* (New York: Praeger, 1990), p. 16.
27. Anthony Read, *The Devil's Disciples: Hitler's Inner Circle* (New York: W. W. Norton, 2004), pp. 571–572.
28. Jeremy Noakes and Geoffrey Pridham, eds., "Message from Hermann Göring to Reinhard Heydrich, 31 July, 1941," in *Documents on Nazism, 1919–1945* (New York: Viking Press, 1974), p. 486.
29. See, for example, Christopher Browning, *Ordinary Men: Reserve Police Battalion 101 and the Final Solution in Poland* (New York: HarperCollins, 1992); Robert Gellately, *Backing Hitler: Consent and Coercion in Nazi Germany* (Oxford: Oxford University Press, 2001); Ian Kershaw, *Hitler, the Germans, and the Final Solution* (New Haven, Conn.: Yale University Press, 2008).
30. H. Willmott, *The Great Crusade: A New Complete History of the Second World War* (New York: Free Press, 1989), p. 255.
31. J. Dower, *War Without Mercy: Race and Power in the Pacific War* (New York: Pantheon, 1986).

CONNECTIONS

If anyone still doubted the interconnectedness of all the world's inhabitants following the Great War, those doubts faded as events on a truly global scale touched everyone as never before. First a Great Depression shook the financial foundations of the wealthiest capitalist economies and the poorest producers of raw materials and minerals. Another world war followed, bringing global death and destruction. At war's end, as we shall see in Chapter 31, the world's leaders revived Woodrow Wilson's idea of a League of Nations and formed the United Nations in 1946 to prevent such tragedies from ever reoccurring.

Although the United Nations was an attempt to bring nations together, the postwar world became more divided than ever. Chapter 31 will describe how two new superpowers — the United States and the Soviet Union — emerged from World War II to engage one another in the Cold War for nearly the rest of the century. Then in Chapters 32 and 33 we will see how less developed nations in Asia, Africa, and Latin America emerged after the war. Many of them did so by turning the nineteenth-century European ideology of nationalism against its creators, breaking the bonds of colonialism.

CHAPTER 30 Review and Explore

Identify Key Terms

Identify and explain the significance of each item below.

New Deal (p. 887)

Popular Front (p. 888)

totalitarianism (p. 891)

fascism (p. 892)

five-year plan (p. 893)

New Economic Policy (NEP) (p. 893)

collectivization (p. 894)

Black Shirts (p. 899)

Lateran Agreement (p. 900)

Nazism (p. 900)

Enabling Act (p. 901)

blitzkrieg (p. 906)

New Order (p. 907)

Holocaust (p. 908)

Europe first policy (p. 912)

Review the Main Ideas

Answer the focus questions from each section of the chapter.

1. What caused the Great Depression, and what were its consequences? (p. 886)

2. What was the nature of the new totalitarian dictatorships, and how did they differ from conservative authoritarian states and from each other? (p. 890)

3. How did Stalin and the Communist Party build a totalitarian order in the Soviet Union? (p. 893)

4. How did Italian fascism develop? (p. 898)

5. Why were Hitler and his Nazi regime initially so popular, and how did their actions lead to World War II? (p. 900)

6. How did Germany and Japan build empires in Europe and Asia, and how did the Allies defeat them? (p. 905)

Make Comparisons and Connections

Analyze the larger developments and continuities within and across chapters.

1. Compare the effects of the Great Depression on the peoples and economies of Europe, Latin America, and East Asia. How did governments in these regions and their citizens respond to this economic cataclysm?

2. Which ideologies of change from nineteenth-century Europe (Chapter 24) contributed to the outbreak of World War II? What new ideologies arose at this time that led the world to war?

3. Is it possible to compare the death and destruction of the Great War with that of World War II? Why or why not? Did the horrors of total war in World War I somehow make the greater scale of mass killing and devastation more acceptable in World War II? Explain.

TIMELINE

GLOBAL		**1929–1939** Great Depression
EUROPE	◆ **1922** Mussolini seizes power in Italy	
	1924–1929 Buildup of Nazi Party in Germany	
		◆ **1927** Stalin is de facto ruler of the Soviet Union
		◆ **1929** Start of collectivization in Soviet Union
MIDDLE EAST		
ASIA		**1931** ◆ Japan invades Manchuria
AMERICAS		
	1925	**1930**

Suggested Resources

BOOKS

Brendon, Piers. *The Dark Valley: A Panorama of the 1930s*. 2002. Masterful, sweeping account of this tumultuous decade.

Brooker, Paul. *Twentieth-Century Dictatorships: The Ideological One-Party State*. 1995. A comparative analysis.

Crowe, David M. *The Holocaust: Roots, History, and Aftermath*. 2008. Analyzes the origins and ghastly implementation of Nazi racial politics.

Geyer, Michael, and Sheila Fitzpatrick. *Beyond Totalitarianism: Stalinism and Nazism Compared*. 2009. Comparative studies of the two dictatorships based on archival sources that have only recently become available to historians.

Gilbert, Martin. *The Second World War: A Complete History*, rev. ed. 2004. Massively detailed global survey.

Glantz, David M., and Jonathan M. House. *When Titans Clashed: How the Red Army Stopped Hitler*, rev. ed. 2015. Authoritative account of the eastern front in World War II.

Hasegawa, Tsuyoshi. *Racing the Enemy: Stalin, Truman, and the Surrender of Japan*. 2005. Masterful diplomatic history with a controversial new account of the end of the war.

Kindleberger, Charles P. *The World in Depression, 1929–1939*, 40th anniversary ed. 2013. Perhaps the best analytical account of the global origins, events, and aftermath of the Great Depression.

Parker, Selwyn. *The Great Crash: How the Stock Market Crash of 1929 Plunged the World into Depression*. 2008. A lively and readable account of the global consequences of the Great Depression.

Spector, Ronald H. *Eagle Against the Sun: The American War with Japan*. 1985. Although this book focuses primarily on the war from the Japanese and American perspectives, many consider it the best single-volume history of the war in the Pacific.

Weinberg, Gerhard. *A World at Arms: A Global History of World War II*, 2d ed. 2005. Global survey with a political-diplomatic emphasis.

Wright, Gordon. *The Ordeal of Total War*, rev. ed. 1997. Explores the scientific, psychological, and economic dimensions of the war.

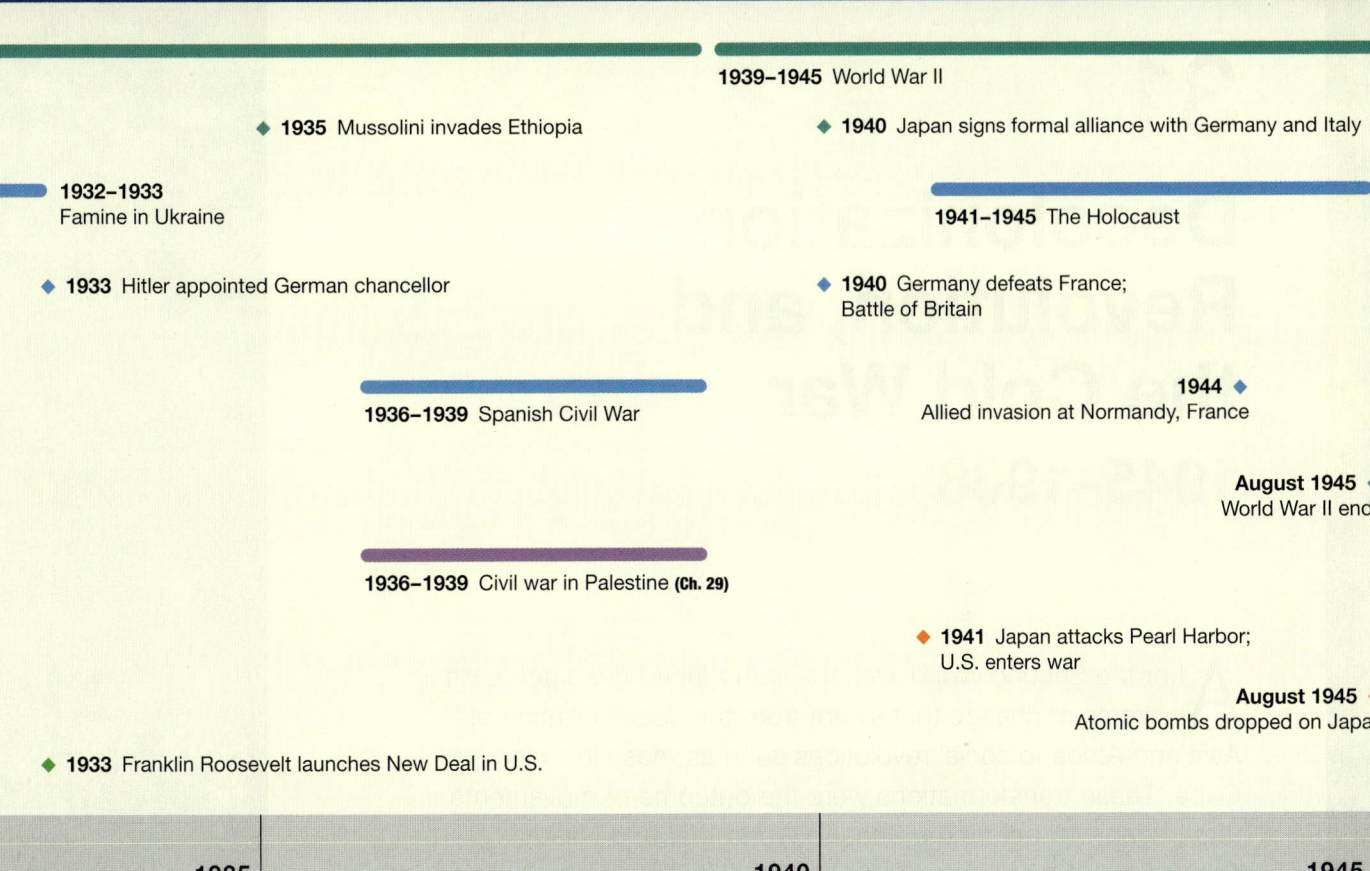

1939–1945 World War II

◆ **1935** Mussolini invades Ethiopia

◆ **1940** Japan signs formal alliance with Germany and Italy

1932–1933
Famine in Ukraine

1941–1945 The Holocaust

◆ **1933** Hitler appointed German chancellor

◆ **1940** Germany defeats France;
Battle of Britain

1944 ◆
Allied invasion at Normandy, France

1936–1939 Spanish Civil War

August 1945 ◆
World War II ends

1936–1939 Civil war in Palestine **(Ch. 29)**

◆ **1941** Japan attacks Pearl Harbor;
U.S. enters war

August 1945 ◆
Atomic bombs dropped on Japan

◆ **1933** Franklin Roosevelt launches New Deal in U.S.

| 1935 | 1940 | 1945 |

DOCUMENTARIES

Triumph of the Will (Leni Riefenstahl, 1935). The classic documentary/propaganda film directed by Hitler's cinema propagandist Leni Riefenstahl. It celebrates the birth of the thousand-year Reich through its portrayal of the 1934 Nuremberg Nazi rally.

The World at War (Thames Television, 1973–1974). Often called the definitive documentary on World War II, this twenty-six-episode chronicle of the war was produced in Britain and is narrated by Laurence Olivier.

FEATURE FILMS

Letters from Iwo Jima (Clint Eastwood, 2006). A joint Japanese-American production that tells the story of the Battle of Iwo Jima from the Japanese soldiers' perspective. Directed by American film director Clint Eastwood, the movie is in Japanese (with English subtitles) and has an all-Japanese cast. A companion film, *Flags of Our Fathers*, portrays the same battle from the American perspective.

Saving Private Ryan (Steven Spielberg, 1998). Generally recognized as one of the best war films of all time, this movie about the invasion of Normany is noted for its realistic portrayal of war, particularly the Allied assault on Omaha Beach on June 6, 1944.

Schindler's List (Steven Spielberg, 1993). Based on the true story of Oskar Schindler, a German businessman who rescued more than a thousand mainly Polish-Jewish refugees during the Holocaust.

WEBSITES

Spartacus Educational: The Second World War. One of the websites of the Spartacus Educational project, this site contains a large collection of entries about all aspects of World War II. **spartacus-educational.com/2WW.htm**

The World at War, History of WW 1939–1945. This well-organized and comprehensive website covers all aspects of World War II, includes a discussion forum and message board, and allows users to search the site by keyword. **www.euronet.nl/users/wilfried/ww2/ww2.htm**

31

Decolonization, Revolution, and the Cold War
1945–1968

After the Second World War, the world faced deep and swift currents of change that swept from the decolonization of Asia and Africa to social revolutions such as those in China and Cuba. These transformations were the outcome of movements that began well before the Second World War and were accelerated by the war's upheaval. The transformations took place in the international context of the Cold War, a rivalry between the United States and the Soviet Union.

As people in Asia and Africa pushed back against centuries of Western expansion and demanded national self-determination and racial equality, new nations emerged and nearly every colonial territory gained formal independence between 1945 and the early 1960s. A revolution in China consolidated Communist rule and initially followed the Soviet model, but then veered in new directions. Rather than form an allied Communist front, China and the Soviet Union became economic and political rivals.

The Cold War that emerged between the U.S. and U.S.S.R. following the world war did not involve armed conflict between the two nations. But it became a global experience in which each country backed rival factions in conflicts around the world. The Cold War also imposed a division between western European countries allied to the United States, and eastern European nations that the Soviet Union brought into its zone of influence.

好好學習
天天向上

Pictures from History/Bridgeman Images

Pictures from History/Bridgeman Images

China Charts a New Revolutionary Path

A member of the Red Guards, part of the mass mobilization known as the Proletarian Cultural Revolution, which was directed by Chinese leader Mao Zedong between 1966 and 1976.

CHAPTER PREVIEW

THE WORLD REMADE   How did the Cold War and decolonization shape the postwar world?

NATIONALISM IN SOUTH ASIA AND THE MIDDLE EAST
How did religion and the legacies of colonialism affect the formation of new nations in South Asia and the Middle East after World War II?

REVOLUTION AND RESURGENCE IN EAST AND SOUTHEAST ASIA
How did the Cold War shape reconstruction, revolution, and decolonization in East and Southeast Asia?

DECOLONIZATION IN AFRICA   What factors influenced decolonization in Africa after World War II?

POPULIST AND REVOLUTIONARY PATHWAYS IN LATIN AMERICA
Why did populism emerge as such a powerful political force in Latin America?

THE LIMITS OF POSTWAR PROSPERITY
Why did the world face growing social unrest in the 1960s?

The World Remade

How did the Cold War and decolonization shape the postwar world?

The rivalry between the United States and the Soviet Union divided postwar Europe and became a long, tense standoff, the **Cold War**. As the Cold War took shape, three events separated by barely two years foreshadowed the changes that would take place in the world following the Second World War: the independence of India and Pakistan in 1947; the establishment of the state of Israel in 1948; and the Communist revolution in China in 1949. All had their roots in the decades preceding the Second World War—and even predating the First World War. Yet each was shaped by the war and its outcomes.

The Cold War

The Cold War originated in disputes over the political outcome of the war. Soviet leader Joseph Stalin insisted that his country needed control of eastern Europe to guarantee military security from Germany. While U.S. president Franklin Roosevelt had been inclined to accommodate these demands, his successor, Harry Truman, demanded free elections throughout eastern Europe. Stalin refused.

The United States' status as the only country that possessed atomic weapons at the end of the war bolstered Truman's tough stance. Just as the U.S. sense of security came from having a monopoly on the atomic bomb, Stalin pursued security by militarily occupying eastern Europe and imposing compliant governments that would provide a buffer against the threat of western European aggression. These countries were considered Soviet satellites—nations whose politics and economics were modeled on and dictated by the Soviet Union.

President Truman misread these occupations as a campaign for world domination. Communist movements in Greece and China, beyond Stalin's occupation zone, fed these fears. In October 1945 Truman issued the **Truman Doctrine**, aimed at "containing" communism to areas already occupied by the Soviet army by providing military and economic support to governments threatened by Communist control. (His reference to regimes imposed by force applied only to Europe and countries threatened by communism, not to European colonial domination of Asia and Africa.)

Truman asked Congress for military aid for Greece and Turkey to prevent the spread of communism. Soon after, Secretary of State George C. Marshall proposed a broader package of economic and food aid—the **Marshall Plan**—to help Europe rebuild. Stalin refused Marshall Plan assistance for eastern Europe. The Soviet Union's support for the overthrow of the democratically elected Czechoslovakian government in 1948 and its replacement by a Communist govern-

Berlin Airlift Residents of Berlin watch a U.S. Air Force cargo plane land with supplies to support West Berliners during the Soviet blockade (1948–1949). (Courtesy CSU Archives/The Everett Collection)

MAP 31.1 Cold War Europe in the 1950s Europe was divided by an "iron curtain" during the Cold War. None of the Communist countries of eastern Europe were participants in the Marshall Plan.

ment shocked the U.S. Congress into approving the Marshall Plan in April 1948.

A lasting pattern of escalating reactions to real and perceived provocations was established between the U.S. and Soviet Union. Stalin retaliated by blocking road traffic through the Soviet zone of Germany to Berlin, prompting the U.S. and its allies to airlift millions of tons of provisions to the West Berliners. After 324 days the Soviets backed down: containment seemed to work. In 1949 the United States formed an anti-Soviet military alliance of Western governments: the North Atlantic Treaty Organization (**NATO**). Stalin countered by tightening his hold on his satellites, united in 1955 under the Warsaw Pact. Europe was divided into two hostile blocs. British prime minister Winston Churchill warned that an "iron curtain has descended across the Continent."

The Soviet Union, with its massive army arrayed across eastern Europe, and the United States, with its industrial strength and atomic weapons, emerged as superpowers whose might dwarfed that of other coun-

tries. Superpower status reached an awkward balance after the Soviet Union developed its own atomic weapons in 1949. Both nations pitched themselves into a military and geopolitical confrontation that stopped short of outright war: the Cold War (Map 31.1).

An ideological divide defined the rivalry between the United States and the Soviet Union. The United States saw itself as the defender of a "free world" governed by liberal principles such as free markets, private property, and individual rights protected by democratic constitutions. The Soviet Union defined itself as the defender of the rights of workers and peasants

Cold War The post–World War II conflict between the United States and the Soviet Union.

Truman Doctrine The 1945 American policy of preventing the spread of Communist rule.

Marshall Plan A 1948 American plan for providing economic aid to Europe to help it rebuild after World War II.

NATO The North Atlantic Treaty Organization, an anti-Soviet military alliance of Western nations, formed in 1949.

against their exploiters, the rights of colonial peoples against their colonizers, and economic development based on planning and equitable distribution. The Cold War sharpened the distinctions between these models, creating opposing paths that the superpowers pressured other countries to follow.

The United Nations

In 1945 representatives of fifty nations met in San Francisco to draft a charter for a new intergovernmental organization called the United Nations. Like that of its predecessor, the League of Nations (see "The Paris Peace Treaties" in Chapter 28), the immediate goal of the United Nations was to mediate international conflicts in order to preserve peace. But in 1945 the founders of the United Nations foresaw a more ambitious role than the League of Nations had played: the UN would also support decolonization; promote economic development; and expand access to health care, worker protections, environmental conservation, and gender equity.

United Nations Programs at Work, 1951 As part of a UN assistance program, the United Nations Children's Fund (UNICEF) provided milk to children in Greece in the aftermath of civil war in that country.
(© Amerika Haus/SZ Photo/The Image Works)

The United Nations was divided into two bodies: a General Assembly that met annually and included all nations that signed the UN Charter; and a Security Council made up of five regional powers, each of which held veto power over the council's decisions, making it a body that in effect functioned only through unanimous consent. Roosevelt intended the Security Council to include the United States, the Soviet Union, Great Britain, China, and Brazil. Because of U.S. influence over Latin America, British and Soviet leaders feared the Brazilian seat would simply be a second vote for the United States, so they insisted that France instead be the fifth member of the Security Council. After the Chinese Revolution in 1949, the government of Taiwan held China's seat until the United Nations transferred it to the People's Republic of China in 1971.

The UN gave critical support to decolonization efforts. Its charter defended the right of self-determination, and it served as a forum for liberation movements to make claims or negotiate the terms of independence. The UN also provided a platform for opponents of colonialism to condemn those colonial powers that resisted their calls for self-determination. In addition, UN member nations volunteered military forces to serve around the world as peacekeepers, who have provided a buffer to ease violent disputes and served as observers to ensure that agreements were being met or that abuses were not being committed in conflict areas.

In its early years, the United Nations mediated Indonesia's demand for independence from the Netherlands, which fought a four-year war to reoccupy the former colony. The UN deployed peacekeepers in the newly created border between India and Pakistan, and it helped determine the terms under which Britain relinquished control of Palestine and Jordan, as well as the terms for the creation of Israel in 1948. The agenda of the United Nations evolved as new member states joined. In 1960 alone, eighteen African nations were seated at the UN, forming part of an "Afro-Asian bloc" committed to rapidly completing the decolonization process and advancing postcolonial economic development.

The Politics of Liberation

The term *Third World* emerged in the 1950s among observers who viewed Africa, Asia, and Latin America as a single entity, different from both the capitalist, industrialized "First World" and the Communist, industrialized "Second World." The idea of a Third World had particular appeal amid the Cold War rivalry, because it allowed advocates to try to stake out an autonomous space outside of Cold War pressures. Despite deep differences between them, most so-called Third World countries in Africa, Asia, and Latin

America were poor and economically underdeveloped—meaning less industrialized—and were thus also referred to as "nonindustrial" or "industrializing" nations.

Many areas of the Third World were still colonies of European countries at the end of the Second World War, though this status was challenged by nationalist liberation movements. The roots of many liberation movements often reached back to the nineteenth century. Colonial powers repressed these movements, but after the Second World War those colonial powers were weaker and nationalist movements grew more insistent. The quest for liberation took many forms. Economically, nations emerging from colonialism sought industrialization and development to end dependence on former colonizers. Politically, they sought alliances with other industrializing nations to avoid the neocolonial influences of more powerful nations. Intellectually, they reacted against Western assumptions of white supremacy.

The former colonies faced intense pressure to align themselves ideologically and economically with either the United States or the Soviet Union, and few could resist the pressure or the incentives those powers brought to bear. Nonetheless, to varying degrees, they tried to operate independently from the two superpowers in a number of ways. In 1955 leaders of twenty-nine recently independent nations in Asia and Africa met in Bandung, Indonesia, to create a framework for political and economic cooperation so they could emerge from colonialism without having to resubordinate their nations either to their former colonizers or to pressures from the Cold War superpowers. The participants outlined principles for rejecting pressure from the superpowers and supporting decolonization. In 1961 nations participating in the Bandung Conference met in Yugoslavia, where Marxists who had come to power in the struggle against Nazi Germany zealously guarded their independence from the Soviet Union, to form a Non-Aligned Nations Movement.

Dependency and Development Theories

In 1948 the United Nations established the Economic Commission for Latin America (ECLA) in Santiago, Chile, to study economic development. Under the direction of Argentine economist Raúl Prebisch, ECLA produced Latin America's main intellectual contributions to the twentieth century: a diagnosis of reasons why less industrialized regions of the world lagged economically and technologically behind Europe and the United States. These ideas were known as **dependency theory**.

According to dependency theory, the first regions to industrialize in the nineteenth century—western Europe and the United States—locked in a lasting economic advantage magnified by colonialism and neocolonialism. This advantage trapped countries in Latin America, Africa, and Asia in roles as exporters of agricultural and mineral commodities and importers of capital and technology. According to this analysis, the prosperity of Europe and the United States was built on the impoverishment of other regions, an inequality that increased over time as the value of commodities decreased relative to the value of manufactured and technological goods.

How could this pattern be broken? Could a country that grew coffee become a country that manufactured cars? This question would be asked many times around the world in the second half of the twentieth century, and it would be answered in many ways.

One approach was **modernization theory**, which suggested that societies passed through phases of development from primitive to modern, and that adopting the political, economic, or cultural practices of places like the United States was the best remedy for poverty. (See "Global Viewpoints: U.S. and Latin American Views on Development," page 926.) This theory shaped U.S. foreign aid programs, which deployed armies of experts offering advice in areas ranging from revising legal codes to digging wells. These experts often did not understand local conditions, believing that the American way was always best. Regardless of their intentions, these projects were often riddled with unintended negative consequences, which led to mistrust of U.S. aid.

For peoples emerging from colonialism, dependency theory was more appealing. Newly independent nations faced enormous pressures: rural poverty pushed millions into cities where good jobs were scarce. Cities and the countryside alike had insufficient schools and health care. Dependency theorists favored state planning to both induce industrialization and distribute resources more equitably. A common tool to do this was **import substitution industrialization (ISI)**. Under ISI policies, countries imposed trade barriers to keep certain foreign products out and provided subsidies for domestic industries to make the same goods. Dependency suggested that even ISI was not enough, and that deep social reforms were needed, such as the redistribution of large farming estates to rural workers, as well as state control of major industries and banks.

---

dependency theory The belief, formulated in Latin America in the mid-twentieth century, that development in some areas of the world locks other nations into underdevelopment.

modernization theory The belief, held in countries such as the United States in the mid-twentieth century, that all countries evolved in a linear progression from traditional to mature.

import substitution industrialization (ISI) The use of trade barriers to keep certain foreign products out of one's country so that domestic industry can emerge and produce the same goods.

U.S. and Latin American Views on Development

Is economic development something all nations share democratically as it spreads from Great Powers to the industrializing world? By outlining a linear progression of economic growth, the American economist Walt Whitman Rostow used modernization theory to create a road map for countries to follow as they evolved from "traditional" to "mature" states. Brazilian dependency theorist Celso Furtado disagreed. For Furtado, economic development in the United States and Europe made the rest of the world dependent upon those regions and inhibited the spread of development. A key difference in these economists' interpretations concerns countries' relationships to the international economy.

Walt Whitman Rostow, 1960

■ It is possible to identify all societies, in their economic dimensions, as lying within one of five categories: the traditional society, the preconditions for take-off, the take-off, the drive to maturity, and the age of high mass-consumption. . . .

First, the traditional society. A traditional society is one whose structure is developed within limited production functions, based on pre-Newtonian science and technology, and on pre-Newtonian attitudes towards the physical world. Newton is here used as a symbol for that watershed in history when men came widely to believe that the external world was subject to a few knowable laws. . . .

The second stage of growth embraces societies in the process of transition; . . . it takes time to transform a traditional society in the ways necessary for it to exploit the fruits of modern science, to fend off diminishing returns, and thus to enjoy the blessings and choices opened up by the march of compound interest. . . .

We now come to the great watershed in the life of modern societies: . . . the take-off. . . . The forces making for economic progress, which yielded limited bursts and enclaves of modern activity, expand and come to dominate the society. . . .

After take-off there follows a long interval of sustained if fluctuating progress, as the now regularly growing economy drives to extend modern technology over the whole front of its economic activity. . . . The economy finds its place in the international economy: goods formerly imported are produced at home; new import requirements develop, and new export commodities to match them. . . .

We now come to the age of high mass-consumption, where, in time, the leading sectors shift towards durable consumers' goods and services: a phase from which Americans are beginning to emerge; whose not unequivocal joys Western Europe and Japan are beginning energetically to probe; and with which Soviet society is engaged in an uneasy flirtation. . . .

When technological maturity is reached, and the nation has at its command a modernized and differentiated industrial machine, to what ends should it be put, and in what proportions: to increase social security, through the welfare state; to expand mass-consumption into the range of durable consumers' goods and services; to increase the nation's stature and power on the world scene; or to increase leisure?

Celso Furtado, 1970

■ As a consequence of the rapid spread of new production methods from a small number of centers radiating technological innovations, there has come into existence a process tending to create a world-wide economic system. It is thus that underdevelopment is considered a creature of development, or rather, as a consequence of the impact of the technical processes and the international division of labor commanded by the small number of societies that espoused the Industrial Revolution of the nineteenth century. The resulting relations between these societies and the underdeveloped areas involve forms of dependence that can hardly be overcome. . . . [D]ependence [is] maintained by controlling the assimilation of new technological processes through the installation of productive activities within the dependent economies, all under the control of groups integrated into the dominant economies.

On the assumption of the foregoing, we infer that underdevelopment cannot be studied as a "phase" of the development process since such a "phase" would be overcome if certain factors came into play simultaneously. And, since the underdeveloped economies are contemporaries of—and in one way or another, dependent on—their developed counterparts, the former cannot retrace the experiences of the latter. Therefore, development and underdevelopment should be considered as two aspects of the same historical process involving the creation and the spread of modern technology.

QUESTIONS FOR ANALYSIS

1. Which model of economic development better explains the historical experiences of developing countries as described in this chapter, and why?
2. What alternative interpretations might better explain the histories of underdeveloped countries?

Sources: W. W. Rostow, *The Stages of Economic Growth* (Cambridge: Cambridge University Press, 1960), pp. 4–10, 16. © Cambridge University Press, 1960. Reprinted with permission of Cambridge University Press; Celso Furtado, *Obstacles to Development in Latin America*, trans. Charles Ekker (Garden City, N.Y.: Anchor Books, 1970), p. xvi.

The governments that attempted land redistribution or the nationalization of foreign firms faced a backlash by landowners, foreign corporations, and political conservatives. In many cases, reformist governments were deposed in military coups supported by the United States. One example was Guatemala, where a democratically elected government pursued the redistribution of land held by large U.S. companies. The government was overthrown in 1954 in a coup organized by the U.S. government.

The experience in Guatemala hardened Cold War views. The events led the United States to expand its containment doctrine to Latin America, where it stepped in to block governments whose reforms it interpreted as Communist. For Latin American reformers, the events in Guatemala suggested that peaceful, gradual change would be blocked by the U.S. and that more radical paths were needed. One person drawing this lesson was an Argentine medical student volunteering in Guatemala at the time of the coup. Ernesto "Che" Guevara (CHAY goo-eh-vahrah) (1928–1967) developed an approach to revolution using tactics he outlined in a manual called *Guerilla Warfare*. Guevara believed that private property and wage labor were forms of exploitation that could be overthrown by free workers volunteering their labor to help liberate others.

Within Catholicism, ideas of social reform and liberation crystallized into a movement called **liberation theology**. The movement emerged in Latin America amid reforms of the Catholic Church by Pope John XXIII (pontificate 1958–1963), who called on clergy to engage with the contemporary world—a world characterized by poverty and exclusion. In 1968 the Latin American Council of Bishops gathered in Medellín, Colombia, and invoked dependency theory as it called on clergy to exercise a "preferential option for the poor" by working toward "social justice," including land redistribution, the recognition of peasants' and labor unions, and condemnation of economic dependency and neocolonialism.

Drawing on dependency theory and sometimes verging on revolutionary Marxism, priests attracted to liberation theology challenged governments, fought against landowners and business owners they saw as oppressors, and formed community organizations, or ecclesiastical base communities, where the residents of poor neighborhoods could gather to discuss their problems and devise solutions. After the 1970s Popes John Paul II (pontificate 1978–2005) and Benedict XVI (pontificate 2005–2013) suppressed liberation theology and silenced its most outspoken thinkers. Advocates of liberation theology greeted the naming of a pope from Latin America, Francis, in 2013 as a return to the focus on fighting poverty and social exclusion within the Catholic Church.

Liberation Theology Participants at a meeting of ecclesiastical base communities in Brazil gather under a banner reading "Altar of Martyrs: Your Blood Nourishes Our Base Communities." This 1986 meeting, eighteen years after the Medellín Conference, shows the lasting impact of liberation theology in Latin America. (Bernard Bisson/Sygma via Getty Images)

Interpreting the Postcolonial Experience

Many intellectuals who came of age during and after the struggle for political emancipation embraced a vision of solidarity among peoples oppressed by colonialism and racism. Some argued that genuine freedom required a total rejection of Western values in addition to an economic and political break with the former colonial powers. Frantz Fanon (1925–1961) expressed these views in his powerful study of colonial peoples, *The Wretched of the Earth* (1961).

According to Fanon, a French-trained black psychiatrist from the Caribbean island of Martinique, decolonization is always a violent process whereby colonizers are replaced by an absolutely different species—the colonized, those he called "the wretched of the earth."

liberation theology A movement within the Catholic Church to support the poor in situations of exploitation that emerged with particular force in Latin America in the 1960s.

During decolonization the colonized masses mock colonial values, "insult them, and vomit them up" in a psychic purge. Fanon believed that throughout Africa and Asia the former imperialists and their local collaborators — the "white men with black faces" — remained the enemy:

> During the colonial period the people are called upon to fight against oppression; after national liberation, they are called upon to fight against poverty, illiteracy, and underdevelopment. The struggle, they say, goes on. . . . We are not blinded by the moral reparation of national independence; nor are we fed by it. The wealth of the imperial countries is our wealth too. . . . Europe is literally the creation of the Third World. The wealth which smothers her is that which was stolen from the underdeveloped peoples.[1]

Fanon gave voice to radicals attacking imperialism and struggling for liberation.

As countries gained independence, some writers looked beyond wholesale rejection of the industrialized powers. They, too, were anti-imperialist, but they were often also activists and cultural nationalists who celebrated the histories and cultures of their peoples. Many did not hesitate to criticize their own leaders or fight oppression and corruption.

The Nigerian writer Chinua Achebe (chee-NOO-ah ah-CHAY-beh) (1930–2013) sought to restore his people's self-confidence by reinterpreting the past. For Achebe, the "writer in a new nation" had first to embrace the "fundamental theme" that Africans had their own culture before the Europeans came and that it was the duty of writers to help Africans reclaim their past. In his 1958 novel *Things Fall Apart*, Achebe brings to life the men and women of an Ibo village at the beginning of the twentieth century, with all their virtues and frailties. Woven into the story are the proverbs and wisdom of a sophisticated people and the beauty of a vanishing world:

> [The white man] says that our customs are bad; and our own brothers who have taken up his religion also say that our customs are bad. How do you think we can fight when our own brothers have turned against us? The white man is very clever. He came quietly and peaceably with his religion. We were amused at his foolishness and allowed him to stay. Now he has won our brothers, and our clan can no longer act like one. He has put a knife on the things that held us together and we have fallen apart.[2]

In later novels Achebe portrayed the postindependence disillusionment of many writers and intellectuals, which reflected trends in many developing nations in the 1960s and 1970s. He developed a sharp critique of rulers who seemed increasingly estranged from national realities and corrupted by Western luxury.

Novelist V. S. Naipaul, born in Trinidad in 1932 of Indian parents, also castigated governments in the developing countries for corruption, ineptitude, and self-deception. Another of Naipaul's recurring themes is the poignant loneliness and homelessness of people uprooted by colonialism and Western expansion.

For peoples emerging from colonial domination, or confronting the poverty and social exclusion that was commonplace outside of industrialized nations, the postwar challenge of liberation was not simply political and economic, but also cultural and spiritual. The middle decades of the twentieth century saw a broad awakening of voices among peoples who had been rendered voiceless by their marginalization.

Nationalism in South Asia and the Middle East

How did religion and the legacies of colonialism affect the formation of new nations in South Asia and the Middle East after World War II?

The three South Asian countries created through independence from Britain and subsequent partition, India, Pakistan, and Bangladesh, reflected the dominant themes of cultural and economic nationalism that characterized the end of colonialism, but ethnic and religious rivalries greatly complicated their renewal and development.

Throughout the vast *umma* (world of Islam), nationalism became a powerful force after 1945, stressing modernization and the end of subordination to Western nations. The nationalists who guided the formation of modern states in the Arab world struggled to balance Cold War pressures from the United States and the Soviet Union, as well as the tension between secular modernization and Islam. At the heart of this world, Jewish nationalists founded the state of Israel following the Second World War. The Zionist claim to a homeland came into sharp, and often violent, conflict with the rights and claims of the Palestinian people displaced by the creation of Israel.

Independence in India, Pakistan, and Bangladesh

World War II accelerated the drive toward Indian independence begun by Mohandas Gandhi (see "Gandhi's Resistance Campaign in India" in Chapter 29). In 1942 Gandhi called on the British to "quit India" and threatened another civil disobedience campaign. He and the other Indian National Congress Party leaders were soon after arrested and were jailed for much of the war. Thus India's wartime support for Britain was substantial but not always enthusiastic. Meanwhile, the Congress Party's prime rival skillfully seized the opportunity to increase its influence.

The Congress Party's rival was the **Muslim League**, led by lawyer Muhammad Ali Jinnah (1876–1948). Jinnah feared that India's Hindu majority would dominate national power at the expense of Muslims. He proposed the creation of two separate countries divided along religious lines:

> The Hindus and Muslims have two different religions, philosophies, social customs, literatures. They neither inter-marry, nor dine together, and indeed, they belong to two different civilizations which are based mainly on conflicting ideas and conceptions. . . . To yoke together two such nations under a single State, one as a numerical minority and the other as majority, must lead to growing discontent and final destruction of any fabric that may be so built up for the government of such a State.[3]

Gandhi disagreed with Jinnah's two-nation theory, which he believed would lead to ethnic sectarianism rather than collaboration.

Britain agreed to speedy independence for India after 1945, but conflicts between Hindu and Muslim nationalists led to murderous clashes in 1946. When it became clear that Jinnah and the Muslim League would accept nothing less than an independent state of Pakistan, the British government mediated a partition that created a predominantly Hindu nation and a predominantly Muslim nation. In 1947 India and Pakistan gained political independence from Britain as two separate nations (Map 31.2).

Violence and mass expulsions followed independence. Perhaps a hundred thousand Hindus and Muslims were slaughtered, and an estimated 5 million became refugees. "What is there to celebrate?" exclaimed Gandhi in reference to independence, "I see nothing but rivers of blood."[4] Gandhi labored to ease tensions between Hindus and Muslims, but in the aftermath of riots in January 1948, he was killed by a Hindu gunman who resented what he saw as Gandhi's appeasement of Muslims.

After the ordeal of independence, relations between India and Pakistan remained tense. Fighting over the disputed area of Kashmir, a strategically important northwestern border state with a Muslim majority annexed by India, lasted until 1949 and broke out again in 1965–1966, 1971, and 1999 as tensions continued.

In India, Jawaharlal Nehru (1889–1964) and the Indian National Congress Party ruled for a generation and introduced major social reforms. Hindu women gained legal equality, including the right to vote, to seek divorce, and to marry outside their castes. The constitution abolished the untouchable caste. In practice, less discriminatory attitudes toward women and untouchables evolved slowly—especially in rural villages, where 85 percent of the people lived.

MAP 31.2 The Partition of British India, 1947 Violence and fighting were most intense where there were large Hindu and Muslim minorities — in Kashmir, the Punjab, and Bengal. The tragic result of partition, which occurred repeatedly throughout the world in the twentieth century, was a forced exchange of populations and greater homogeneity on both sides of the border.

The Congress Party pursued state-driven economic development, but population growth of about 2.4 percent per year consumed much of the increased output of economic expansion. The relocation of millions during the partition of India and Pakistan exacerbated poverty. The Congress Party maintained neutrality in the Cold War, distancing itself from both the United States and the Soviet Union. Instead India became one of the leading voices in the Non-Aligned Nations Movement.

At independence, Pakistan was divided between eastern and western provinces separated by more than a thousand miles of Indian territory, as well as by language, ethnic background, and social custom. The Bengalis of East Pakistan constituted a majority of Pakistan's population as a whole, but were neglected by the central government, which remained in the hands

Muslim League Political party founded in 1906 in colonial India that advocated for a separate Muslim homeland after independence.

The Non-Aligned Movement Indira Gandhi, daughter of Jawaharlal Nehru, became prime minister of India in 1966. She is shown here at a 1966 meeting of the Non-Aligned Nations Movement, seated between Yugoslav president Josip Tito (left) and Egyptian president Gamal Abdel Nasser (right). (© Sueddeutsche Zeitung Photo/The Image Works)

of West Pakistan's elite after Jinnah's death. In 1971 the Bengalis revolted and won their independence as the new nation of Bangladesh after a violent civil war. Bangladesh, a secular parliamentary democracy, struggled to find political and economic stability amid famines that resulted from monsoon floods, tornadoes, and cyclones in the vast, low-lying, and intensely farmed Ganges Delta.

Arab Socialism in the Middle East

In the postwar period, new Arab states in the Middle East emerged from colonial rule. For centuries the region had been dominated by the Ottoman Empire. After the First World War, France and Britain claimed protectorates in the former Ottoman territories. Britain already claimed Egypt as a protectorate and France controlled Algeria. New nations emerging from colonial rule in the Middle East embraced **Arab socialism**, a modernizing, secular, and nationalist project of nation building aimed at economic development, a strong military, and Pan-Arab unity.

Arab socialism held particular significance for women in Middle Eastern societies. It cast aside religious restrictions on women's education, occupations, public activities, and fashions. In countries like Egypt

and Iraq, the openness of education and access to professions enjoyed by urban, typically affluent women symbolized an embrace of Western modernity, although senior posts in government, the professions, and business were still dominated by men.

In 1952 army officers overthrew Egypt's monarchy and expelled the British military force that occupied the country. The movement's leader, Gamal Abdel Nasser (1918–1970), built a nationalist regime aimed at eradicating the vestiges of colonialism. Applying the principles of Arab socialism, Nasser pursued the secularization of Egyptian society, created an extensive social welfare network, redistributed rural lands, and promoted industrialization.

Nasser's National Charter called for the nationalization of transportation, mining, dams, banks, utilities, insurance, and heavy industry. In the countryside the size of landholdings was limited and estates were broken up. As Nasser declared, "When we started this revolution, we wanted to put an end to exploitation. Hence our struggle to put capital at the service of man, and to put land at the service of man, instead of leaving man at the service of the feudalist who owns the land."[5]

In 1956 Nasser took a symbolic and strategic step toward national sovereignty when he ordered the army to take control of the Suez Canal, still held by Britain and France. A coalition of British, French, and Israeli forces invaded to retake the canal. The Soviet Union offered support to Egypt. To prevent Soviet intervention and a Soviet-Egyptian alliance, the United States negotiated a cease-fire that granted Egypt control of the canal. Alongside control of the canal, Nasser's other main economic accomplishment was the Aswan Dam on the Nile River, which generated electricity for industrialization in northern Egypt while allowing southern Egypt to control flooding and increase agricultural production. Nasser negotiated the funding and technical expertise for the dam with both the United States and the Soviet Union, eventually settling on Soviet aid. The Suez crisis and the Aswan Dam were examples in which a nationalist leader like Nasser successfully played the superpowers against each other.

Military officers in other Arab countries emulated Nasser's nationalism and socialist developmentalism. In Syria and Iraq these nationalists formed the Pan-Arab socialist Ba'ath Party. For members of national Ba'ath parties, Egypt was a model for developing a single-party state that implemented nationalist and development aspirations. Syria briefly merged with Egypt from 1958 until 1961, forming the United Arab Republic. Officers who resented Nasser's control of Syria revolted against Egypt and established a separate Syrian government dominated by the Ba'ath Party. In Iraq the Ba'ath Party helped overthrow the British-backed monarchy in 1958, leading to Ba'ath Party rule that ended when a U.S. military invasion toppled Saddam Hussein in 2003.

Arab socialism A modernizing, secular, and nationalist project of nation building in the Middle East aimed at economic development and the development of a strong military.

Palestine Liberation Organization (PLO) Created in 1964, a loose union of Palestinian refugee groups opposed to Israel and united in the goal of establishing a Palestinian state.

The Arab-Israeli Conflict

Before the Second World War, Arab nationalists were loosely united in their opposition to the colonial powers and to Jewish migration to Palestine. In the aftermath of the Second World War, Palestinians and new Arab states emerging from British and French domination strenuously opposed Jewish settlement in Palestine (see "Arab-Jewish Tensions in Palestine" in Chapter 29). In 1947 the British government announced its intention to withdraw from Palestine in 1948. The difficult problem of a Jewish homeland was placed in the hands of the United Nations, which passed a plan to partition Palestine into two separate states—one Arab and one Jewish (Map 31.3). The Jews accepted, and the Arabs rejected, the partition of Palestine.

By early 1948 an undeclared civil war raged in Palestine. When the British mandate ended on May 14, 1948, the Jews proclaimed the state of Israel. Arab countries immediately attacked the new state, but Israeli forces drove off the invaders and conquered more territory. Roughly nine hundred thousand Palestinian refugees fled or were expelled from old Palestine. The war left an enormous legacy of Arab bitterness toward Israel and its political allies, Great Britain and the United States. In 1964 a loose union of Palestinian refugee groups opposed to Israel and seeking a Palestinian state joined together, under the leadership of Yasir Arafat (1929–2004), to form the **Palestine Liberation Organization (PLO)**.

Nationalist leaders in neighboring Syria and Egypt cultivated political support at home through opposition to Israel and threats to crush it militarily. This tension repeatedly erupted into war. On June 1, 1967, when Syrian and Egyptian armies massed on Israel's borders, the Israeli government went to war, launching air strikes that destroyed most of the Egyptian, Syrian, and Jordanian air forces. Over the next five days Israeli armies defeated Egyptian, Syrian, Jordanian, and Palestinian forces and took control of the Sinai Peninsula and the Gaza Strip from Egypt, the West Bank and East Jerusalem from Jordan, and the Golan Heights from Syria. In the Six-Day War (also known as the 1967 Arab-Israeli War), Israel proved itself to be the preeminent military force in the region, and it expanded the territory under its control threefold.

After the war Israel began to build large Jewish settlements in the Gaza Strip and the West Bank, home to millions of Palestinians. On November 22, 1967, the UN Security Council adopted Resolution 242, which contained a "land for peace" formula by which Israel was called upon to withdraw from the occupied territories, and in return the Arab states were to withdraw all claims to Israeli territory, cease hostilities, and recognize the sovereignty of the Israeli state. The tension between rival territorial claims persisted.

MAP 31.3
The Middle East After 1947 The partition of Palestine by the United Nations resulted in the creation in 1948 of Israel, which faced repeated conflicts with rival Arab states.

Legend:
- Jewish state after UN partition of Palestine, 1947
- Area added by Israel after War of 1948–1949
- Area controlled by Israel after Six-Day War, 1967
- Israeli-occupied area after Yom Kippur War, 1973
- Area united as United Arab Republic, 1958–1961

Revolution and Resurgence in East and Southeast Asia

How did the Cold War shape reconstruction, revolution, and decolonization in East and Southeast Asia?

In Asia Japan's defeat ended the Second World War, but other conflicts continued: nationalists in European colonies intensified their struggle for independence, and in China Nationalist and Communist armies that had cooperated against the Japanese invaders now confronted each other in a renewed civil war. In 1949 Communist forces under Mao Zedong triumphed and

established the People's Republic of China. The Communist victory in China shaped the nature of Japan's reconstruction, as its U.S. occupiers determined that an industrially and economically strong Japan would serve as a counterweight to Mao. U.S. fear of the spread of communism drew the country into conflicts in Korea and Vietnam, intensifying the stakes in the decolonization struggle across East and Southeast Asia.

The Communist Victory in China

When Japan surrendered to the Allies in August 1945, Communists and Nationalists both rushed to seize evacuated territory. Communists and Nationalists had fought each other before the Second World War, but had put aside their struggle to resist Japanese invasion. With the war over, the Nationalists and Communists resumed their conflict. By 1948 the Nationalist forces had disintegrated before the better-led, more determined Communists. The following year Nationalist leader Jiang Jieshi and 2 million mainland Chinese fled to Taiwan, and in October 1949 Mao Zedong proclaimed the People's Republic of China (Map 31.4).

Communism triumphed in China for many reasons. Mao Zedong and the Communists had avoided pitched battles and concentrated on winning peasant support and forming a broad anti-Japanese coalition. By reducing rents and promising land redistribution, they emerged in peasant eyes as China's true patriots. (See "Analyzing the Evidence: Poster Art in Communist China," at right.)

Between 1949 and 1954 the Communists consolidated their rule. They seized the vast landholdings of a minority of landlords and rich peasants and redistributed the land to 300 million poor peasants. Meanwhile, as Mao admitted in 1957, mass arrests led to the summary execution of eight hundred thousand "class enemies"; the true figure is probably much higher. Millions more were deported to forced-labor camps.

Mao and the party looked to the Soviet Union for inspiration in the early 1950s. China adopted collective agriculture and Soviet-style five-year plans to promote industrialization. The Soviet Union provided considerable economic aid, and Soviet technicians built factories. In the cultural and intellectual realms, too, the Chinese followed the Soviet example. Basic civil and political rights were abolished. Temples and churches were closed. The Chinese enthusiastically promoted Soviet Marxist ideas concerning women and the family. Full equality, work outside the home, and state-supported child care became primary goals.

In 1958 China broke from the Marxist-Leninist course of development and began to go its own way. Mao proclaimed a **Great Leap Forward** in which industrial growth would be based on small-scale backyard

MAP 31.4 Decolonization in Asia
After the Second World War, countries colonized by Britain, France, the Netherlands, Japan, Australia, and the United States gained their independence. In cases such as Vietnam and Indonesia, independence came through armed struggles against colonizers who were reluctant to leave.

Great Leap Forward Mao Zedong's acceleration of Chinese development in which industrial growth was to be based on small-scale backyard workshops run by peasants living in gigantic self-contained communes.

Poster Art in Communist China

One of the most popular art forms in Communist China was poster art, millions of copies of which were printed to adorn the walls of homes, offices, factories, and businesses. This uniquely Chinese form did not contain abstract, modern, or bourgeois elements and did not reflect classical Chinese art styles. Instead, such posters glorified the state, its leaders, and the heroes of the revolution. The two young women in this poster wear uniforms and caps bearing the Communist red star, the five points of which represent the five components of Communist society: the youth, the army, the peasants, the workers, and the intellectuals.

This poster, called "Lei Feng Is Everywhere," was part of an early 1960s campaign by China's People's Liberation Army. The campaign featured an ordinary soldier, Lei Feng, and celebrated his virtues of selflessness, modesty, and dedication to the Communist Party. Lei Feng appears in the small poster behind the woman on the telephone. By emphasizing the virtues of ordinary people, the campaign modeled behaviors for the public to follow. In this poster of a family, the presence of a poster about Lei Feng was meant to show how these messages are brought into the family's home. The main poster also shows us images of order and prosperity in family life under the Communist Party.

(© Pictures from History/The Image Works)

QUESTIONS FOR ANALYSIS

1. Who is depicted, and what are they doing? Describe the space the four figures are in and what appears in the space. What message do you think the artist seeks to convey with this image?
2. What social function or application might posters such as this one have?
3. Consider the people who are represented in the poster. What is the choice of figures intended to show? What roles do women play, based on their dress? And what do you infer from the different ages represented?

workshops and steel mills run by peasants living in gigantic self-contained communes. The plan led to economic disaster, as land in the countryside went untilled when peasants turned to industrial production. As many as 30 million people died in famines that swept the country in 1960–1961. When Soviet premier Nikita Khrushchev criticized Chinese policy in 1960, Mao condemned him and his Soviet colleagues as detestable "modern revisionists." Khrushchev cut off aid, splitting the Communist world apart.

Mao lost influence in the party after the Great Leap Forward fiasco and the Sino-Soviet split, but in 1965 he staged a dramatic comeback, launching the **Great Proletarian Cultural Revolution**. He sought to purge the party and to recapture the revolutionary fervor of the guerrilla struggle. The army and the nation's young people responded enthusiastically, organizing themselves into radical cadres called Red Guards. Students denounced their teachers and practiced rebellion in the name of revolution. Mao's thoughts, through his speeches and writings, were collected in the *Little Red Book*, which became scripture to the Red Guards. Here the young Red Guards learned the underlying maxim of Mao's revolution: "Every communist must grasp the truth, 'Political power grows out of the barrel of a gun.'"[6]

The Red Guards sought to erase all traces of "feudal" and "bourgeois" culture and thought. Ancient monuments and countless works of art, antiques, and books were destroyed. Party officials, professors, and intellectuals were exiled to remote villages to purify themselves with heavy labor. Universities were shut down for years. Thousands of people died, many of them executed, and millions more were sent to rural forced-labor camps. The Red Guards attracted enormous worldwide attention and served as an extreme model for the student rebellions in the West in the late 1960s.

Conflict in Korea

As Japanese forces were withdrawn after 1945, Korea was divided into Soviet and American zones of occupation, which in 1948 became Communist North Korea and anticommunist South Korea. When the Communists triumphed in China in late 1949, many fearful Americans saw new evidence of a powerful worldwide Communist conspiracy. When the Russian-backed Communist forces of North Korea invaded South Korea in 1950, President Tru-

man sent U.S. troops to lead a UN coalition force to stop what he interpreted as a coordinated Communist effort to dominate Asia.

The Korean War (1950–1953) ended in a stalemate with little more than symbolic gains for either side. North Korea conquered most of the peninsula, but the South Korean, American, and UN troops repelled their foes north to the Chinese border. At that point China intervened and pushed the South Koreans and Americans back south. In 1953 a fragile truce was negotiated, and the fighting stopped. The United States had extended its policy of containing communism to Asia, but drew back from invading Communist China and possibly provoking nuclear war.

Japan's American Reconstruction

When American occupation forces landed in the Tokyo-Yokohama area after Japan's surrender in August 1945, they found only smokestacks and large steel safes standing amid miles of rubble in what had been the heart of industrial Japan. Japan, like Germany, was formally occupied by all the Allies, but real power resided in American hands. U.S. general Douglas MacArthur exercised almost absolute authority. MacArthur and the Americans had a revolutionary plan for defeated Japan, introducing reforms designed to make Japan a free, democratic society along American lines.

Japan's sweeping American revolution began with demilitarization and a systematic purge of convicted war criminals and wartime collaborators. The American-dictated constitution of 1946 allowed the emperor to remain the "symbol of the State." Real power resided in the Japanese Diet, whose members were popularly elected. A bill of rights granted basic civil liberties and freed all political prisoners, including Communists. Article 9 of the new constitution abolished the Japanese armed forces and renounced war. The American occupation left Japan's powerful bureaucracy largely intact and used it to implement fundamental social and economic reforms. The occupation promoted the Japanese labor movement, introduced American-style antitrust laws, and "emancipated" Japanese women, granting them equality before the law. The occupation also imposed land reform that strengthened the small independent farmers, who became staunch defenders of postwar democracy.

The Korean War

SOVIET UNION

CHINA

Farthest UN advance Nov. 1950

Chosin Reservoir

Yalu R.

NORTH KOREA

Pyongyang

Sea of Japan

Demilitarized zone 1953

38th Parallel

Seoul

Inchon landing Sept. 15, 1950

SOUTH KOREA

UN defensive line Sept. 1950

Yellow Sea

Pusan

JAPAN

→ North Korean invasion, June–Sept. 1950
→ UN offensive, Sept.–Nov. 1950
→ Communist Chinese offensive, Nov. 1950–Jan. 1951

Baseball in Japan Though baseball arrived in Japan in the late nineteenth century, it increased in popularity during U.S. occupation. This photo from 1950 shows children in their baseball uniforms, with a U.S. Jeep in the background. (Courtesy CSU Archives/The Everett Collection)

America's efforts to remake Japan in its own image were powerful but short-lived. As Mao's forces prevailed in China, American leaders began to see Japan as a potential ally, not as an object of social reform. The American command began purging leftists and rehabilitating prewar nationalists. The Japanese prime minister during much of the occupation and early post-occupation period was Shigeru Yoshida. A former diplomat with a facility for negotiating with Western nations, Yoshida was the ideal leader in Western eyes for postwar Japan. He channeled all available resources to the rebuilding of Japan's industrial infrastructure, while he left the military defense of the country to the American occupying forces.

The occupation ended in 1952 with a treaty that restored Japan's independence and a role for Japan as the chief Asian ally of the United States in its efforts to contain the spread of communism. Japan's industry provided matériel used by the U.S. armed forces in Korea and Vietnam, and a Security Treaty provided territory for U.S. military installations, particularly the island of Okinawa.

The Vietnam War

French Indochina experienced the bitterest struggle for independence in Southeast Asia. With financial backing from the United States, France tried to reimpose imperial rule there after the Communist and nationalist guerrilla leader Ho Chi Minh (1890–1969) declared an independent republic in 1945. French forces were decisively defeated in the 1954 Battle of Dien Bien Phu. At an international peace conference later that year, French Indochina gained independence. Laos and Cambodia became separate states, and Vietnam was temporarily divided into separately governed northern and southern regions pending elections to select a single unified government within two years. The South Vietnamese government refused to hold the elections, and civil war between it and the Communist Democratic Republic of Vietnam, or North Vietnam, broke out in 1959.

Cold War fears and U.S. commitment to the ideology of containment drove the United States to get involved in Vietnam. The administration of President Dwight D. Eisenhower (elected in 1952) refused to sign the Geneva Accords that temporarily divided the country, and provided military aid to help the south resist North Vietnam. Eisenhower's successor, John F. Kennedy, increased the number of American "military advisers."

In 1964 U.S. president Lyndon Johnson greatly expanded America's role in the Vietnam conflict, seeking to "escalate" the war sufficiently to break the will of the North Vietnamese and their southern allies without resorting to "overkill," which might risk war with the entire Communist bloc. South Vietnam received massive U.S. military aid, and large numbers of American forces joined in combat. The United States bombed North Vietnam with ever-greater intensity, but it did not invade North Vietnam or launch a naval blockade of its ports.

The Vietnam War

U.S. and South Vietnamese forces

Major North Vietnamese supply route into South Vietnam

Important battle or action

Great Proletarian Cultural Revolution A movement launched in 1965 by Mao Zedong that attempted to recapture the revolutionary fervor of his guerrilla struggle.

Global Perspectives on the Vietnam War

The war between North and South Vietnam was both a local and a global struggle. The Vietnam War followed the Vietnamese fight for independence from France. It saw combat involving forces from the United States, South Korea, Australia, and New Zealand pitted against North Vietnam, which received aid from China and the Soviet Union. The conflict spurred antiwar movements around the world that melded with other struggles against imperialism or racism, or for the rights of women and minorities.

1 **Ho Chi Minh, Declaration of Independence of the Democratic Republic of Vietnam, 1945.** In 1945, after decades of French colonialism and Japanese occupation, Ho, a Marxist revolutionary and North Vietnam's prime minister, read Vietnam's Declaration of Independence to a Hanoi audience. Ho's declaration places the independence of Vietnam in the context of a global history of self-determination of peoples.

■ All men are created equal. They are endowed by their Creator with certain inalienable rights, among these are Life, Liberty, and the pursuit of Happiness. This immortal statement was made in the Declaration of Independence of the United States of America in 1776. In a broader sense, this means: All the peoples on the earth are equal from birth, all the peoples have a right to live, to be happy and free.

The Declaration of the French Revolution made in 1791 on the Rights of Man and the Citizen also states: "All men are born free and with equal rights and must always remain free and have equal rights." Those are undeniable truths.

Nevertheless, for more than eighty years, the French imperialists, abusing the standard of Liberty, Equality, and Fraternity, have violated our Fatherland and oppressed our fellow-citizens....

A people who have courageously opposed French domination for more than eighty years, a people who have fought side by side with the Allies against the Fascists during these last years, such a people must be free and independent. For these reasons, we ... solemnly declare to the world that Vietnam has the right to be a free and independent country.

(Interfoto/akg-images)

2 **Protesters in Japan, 1971.** Members of the Anti-Imperial Student Council participate in an anti–Vietnam War demonstration in Tokyo, in which activists combined protests against the U.S. role in Vietnam, opposition to the U.S. Security Treaty, and demands for university reforms.

ANALYZING THE EVIDENCE

1. Explain the rationale for Vietnam's independence offered by Ho Chi Minh in Source 1. What kinds of global connections does he make, and how do these support his argument?
2. What were the basic propositions underlying American policy in Southeast Asia according to Lyndon Johnson in Source 3?
3. How did Ho, Johnson, and Oda, like the protesters pictured in Sources 2 and 5, connect their stances to broader historic and contemporary struggles?

(Bettmann/Getty Images)

5 **Jeannette Rankin Brigade march in Washington, 1968.** In the United States the antiwar movement converged with other struggles such as the African American, American Indian, and Latino civil rights movements, as well as the movement for women's rights. The Jeannette Rankin Brigade brought together several antiwar groups formed by women, whose activism extended from opposition to the war to support for women's rights. The brigade took the name of the first woman elected to Congress, in 1916, a lifelong pacifist. Jeannette Rankin, age eighty-seven, holds the banner in the center.

3 **Lyndon Johnson, address to Congress regarding the Tonkin Gulf Resolution, 1964.** President Lyndon Johnson's request to Congress brought the deployment of U.S. troops in Vietnam. Over the following decade, the deployment of over five hundred thousand troops would not be enough for the United States to prevail militarily.

■ Our policy in southeast Asia has been consistent and unchanged since 1954. [It has] four simple propositions:

1. *America keeps her word.* Here as elsewhere, we must and shall honor our commitments.
2. *The issue is the future of southeast Asia as a whole.* A threat to any nation in that region is a threat to all, and a threat to us.
3. *Our purpose is peace.* We have no military, political, or territorial ambitions in the area.
4. *This is not just a jungle war, but a struggle for freedom on every front of human activity.*

...As President of the United States I... now ask the Congress, to join in affirming the national determination... that the United States will continue in its basic policy of assisting the free nations of the area to defend their freedom.

4 **Oda Makoto on opposition in Japan to the U.S. conflict in Vietnam, 1967.** The movement in Japan against the Vietnam War gave voice to the generation that reached adulthood after the Second World War. Opposition to the war created a space to question broader aspects of postwar Japan, such as the agreement that granted military bases to the United States as well as the profits Japanese companies garnered from supplying the U.S. armed forces. Antiwar movement leader Oda Makoto draws the connections between the war and Japanese society.

■ Realistically speaking, we are all guilty of complicity in the Vietnam War. We must recognize that each of us is among the perpetrators. In my opinion, this is why we must conduct our opposition movement all the more forcefully. But to put it less practically and more in terms of basic principles, if we don't take a clear position against the war and seek peace here and now, perhaps the hand [holding the gun] will be ours one day. To the extent that we don't firmly nail down our basic principles as individuals, perhaps we will have to fire the bullet on orders from the state.

PUTTING IT ALL TOGETHER

Using the sources above, along with what you have learned in class and in this chapter, write a short essay on how Ho Chi Minh's arguments for independence from France and Lyndon Johnson's rationale for military intervention in Vietnam relate to opposition to Japan's support for U.S. military involvement, such as that expressed by Oda Makoto.

Sources: (1) Ho Chi Minh, *Selected Works,* vol. 3 (Hanoi, 1960–1962), pp. 17–21; (3) Lyndon B. Johnson, "Special Message to the Congress on U.S. Policy in Southeast Asia, August 5, 1964," in *Public Papers of the Presidents of the United States: Lyndon B. Johnson, 1963–1964.* Vol. 2: *July 1 to December 31, 1964* (Washington, D.C.: Government Printing Office, 1965), pp. 930–932; (4) Quoted in Thomas Havens, *Fire Across the Sea: The Vietnam War and Japan, 1965–1975* (Princeton, N.J.: Princeton University Press, 1987), p. 120.

Most Americans first saw the war as a legitimate defense against communism, but the combined effect of watching the results of the violent conflict on the nightly television news and experiencing the widening military draft spurred a growing antiwar movement on U.S. college campuses. By the late 1960s growing numbers of critics in the U.S. and around the world denounced American involvement in the conflict. The north's Tet Offensive in January 1968, a major attack on South Vietnamese cities, shook Americans' confidence in their government's ability to manage the conflict. Within months President Johnson announced he would not stand for re-election, and he called for negotiations with North Vietnam. (See "Thinking Like a Historian: Global Perspectives on the Vietnam War," page 936.)

Elected in 1968, President Richard Nixon sought to disengage America from Vietnam. He intensified the bombardment of the enemy while simultaneously pursuing peace talks with the North Vietnamese. He also began a slow process of withdrawal from Vietnam in a process called "Vietnamization," which transferred the burden of the war to the South Vietnamese army, cutting American forces from 550,000 to 24,000 in four years. Nixon finally reached a peace agreement with North Vietnam in 1973 that allowed the remaining American forces to withdraw by 1975.

Despite U.S. efforts, the Communists proved victorious in 1975 and created a unified Marxist Vietnam. After more than thirty-five years of battle, the Communists turned to a nation-building process that had been delayed by decades of war against colonial rule and the U.S. effort to force a political and economic model on the country as part of its doctrine of containment of communism. Millions of Vietnamese civilians faced reprisals for aligning with the United States, including Hmong (ha-MUHNG) and Degar peoples, such as the Mnong (MUH-nong), and other ethnic minorities. They first fled to refugee camps elsewhere in Southeast Asia and later settled as refugees in the United States. (See "Individuals in Society: Sieng, a Mnong Refugee in an American High School" in Chapter 33.)

Decolonization in Africa

What factors influenced decolonization in Africa after World War II?

By 1964 most of Africa had gained independence (Map 31.5). Only Portugal's colonies and southern Africa remained under white minority rule, gaining their independence after long armed struggles that ended in 1975. Many national leaders saw socialism as the best way to sever colonial ties and erase exploitation within their new borders. But institutional barriers left over from the colonial era hampered

these efforts: new nations inherited inefficient colonial bureaucracies, economic systems that privileged the export of commodities, and colonial educational systems intended to build servants of empire. The range of actions available to new leaders was narrowed by former colonizers' efforts to retain their economic influence and by the political and ideological divisions of the Cold War.

The Growth of African Nationalism

African nationalism resembled similar movements in Asia and the Middle East in its reaction against colonialism, but there were important differences. First, because the imperial system and Western education did not solidify in Africa until after 1900 (see "Colonialism's Impact After 1900" in Chapter 25), national movements came of age in the 1920s and reached maturity after 1945. Second, Africa's multiplicity of ethnic groups, coupled with colonial boundaries that often bore no resemblance to existing ethnic geography, greatly complicated the development of political — as distinct from cultural — nationalism. Was a modern national state based on ethnic or clan loyalties? Was it to be a continent-wide union? Would the multiethnic territories carved out by European empires become the new African nations? Such questions were not fully addressed until after 1945. (See "Analyzing the Evidence: C. L. R. James on Pan-African Liberation," page 941.)

The first nationalist impetus came from the United States and the Caribbean. The most renowned participant in this "black nationalism" was W. E. B. Du Bois (1868–1963). Du Bois (doo-BOISS) was a cofounder of the National Association for the Advancement of Colored People (NAACP) in the United States and organized Pan-African congresses in Paris during the Paris Peace Conference in 1919 and in Brussels in 1921. **Pan-Africanists** sought black solidarity and a self-governing union of all African peoples. Jamaican-born Marcus Garvey (1887–1940) was the most influential Pan-Africanist, rallying young, educated Africans to his call of "Africa for the Africans."

In the 1920s a surge of anticolonial nationalism swept educated Africans in French and British colonies. African intellectuals in Europe formulated and articulated *négritude*, or blackness: pride, self-confidence, and joy in black creativity and the black spirit. This westernized African elite pressed for better access to government jobs, steps toward self-government, and an end to discrimination. They claimed the right to speak for ordinary Africans and denounced government-supported chiefs for subordinating themselves to white colonial leaders.

The mass protests that accompanied the deprivations of the Great Depression, in particular the **cocoa holdups** of 1930–1931 and 1937–1938, fueled the

MAPPING THE PAST

MAP 31.5 Decolonization in Africa, 1947 to the Present Most African territories achieved statehood by the mid-1960s, as European empires passed away, unlamented.

ANALYZING THE MAP How many African states achieved independence after 1945? How many experienced some sort of postcolonial conflict?

CONNECTIONS How did the imperialist legacy serve to complicate the transition to stable, independent nations in Africa, Asia, and Latin America?

new nationalism. Cocoa dominated the British colonial economy in the Gold Coast (which became Ghana). As prices plummeted after 1929, cocoa farmers refused to sell their beans to the British firms that fixed prices and monopolized exports. Farmers organized cooperatives to cut back production and sell their crops directly to European and American chocolate manufacturers. The cocoa holdups mobilized the population against the foreign companies and demonstrated the power of mass organization and protest.

The repercussions of the Second World War in Africa greatly accelerated the changes begun in the 1930s. Many African soldiers who served in India had been powerfully impressed by Indian nationalism. As African mines and plantations strained to meet wartime demands, towns mushroomed into cities, which became centers of discontent and hardship.

Western imperialism also changed. The principle of self-government was written into the United Nations charter and was supported by Great Britain's postwar Labour government. Thus the key question for Great Britain's various African colonies became the terms of self-government. Britain and France were in no rush. But a new type of African leader was emerging. Impatient and insistent, these spokesmen for modern

African nationalism were remarkably successful. These postwar African leaders formed an elite by virtue of their advanced European or American education, and they were influenced by Western thought. But compared with the interwar generation of educated Africans, they were more radical and had humbler social origins. Among them were former schoolteachers, union leaders, government clerks, lawyers, and poets.

Postwar African nationalists pragmatically accepted prevailing colonial boundaries to avoid border disputes and achieve freedom as soon as possible. Sensing a loss of power, traditional rulers sometimes became the new leaders' worst political enemies. Skillfully, the new leaders channeled postwar hope and discontent into support for mass political organizations that offset this traditional authority. These organizations staged gigantic protests and became political parties.

Pan-Africanists People who, through a movement beginning in 1919, sought black solidarity and envisioned a vast self-governing union of all African peoples.

cocoa holdups Mass protests in Africa's Gold Coast in the 1930s by producers of cocoa who refused to sell their beans to British firms and instead sold them directly to European and American chocolate manufacturers.

Kwame Nkrumah Visits China
Ghana's first prime minister, Kwame Nkrumah, faced challenges similar to those confronted by other leaders of newly independent African nations, which included building new nation-states, emerging from the structures of colonialism, and navigating the pressures of the Cold War. The experiences of other societies that underwent revolution or liberation offered a guide. Nkrumah, accompanied here by Chinese premier Zhou Enlai, visited China in 1961 to study its economic system.
(Keystone-France/Gamma-Rapho via Getty Images)

Ghana Shows the Way

The most charismatic of this generation of African leaders was Kwame Nkrumah (KWA-may ihn-CROO-mah) (1909–1972). Nkrumah spent ten years studying in the United States, where he was influenced by European socialists and Marcus Garvey. He returned to the Gold Coast after the Second World War and entered politics. Under his leadership the Gold Coast—which he renamed "Ghana"—became the first sub-Saharan state to emerge from colonialism.

Nkrumah built a radical party that appealed particularly to modern groups such as veterans, merchant women, union members, and cocoa farmers. He and his party injected the enthusiasm of religious revivals into their rallies and propaganda as they called for "Self-Government Now." Rejecting halfway measures, Nkrumah and his Convention People's Party staged strikes and riots.

After he was arrested in 1950, the "Deliverer of Ghana" campaigned from jail and saw his party win a smashing victory in the 1951 national elections. He was released from prison to head the transitional government. By 1957 now Prime Minister Nkrumah had achieved worldwide fame and influence as Ghana became independent. After Ghana's breakthrough, independence for other African colonies followed. The main problem in some colonies was the permanent white settlers, not the colonial officials: wherever white settlers were numerous, as in Algeria, Kenya, and Rhodesia, they fought to preserve their privileged position.

French-Speaking Regions

Decolonization took a different course in French-speaking Africa. The events in the French North African colony of Algeria in the 1950s and early 1960s help clarify France's attitude toward its sub-Saharan African colonies.

France attempted to retain Algeria, home to a large, mostly Catholic, European settler population, known as the pieds-noirs (black feet) because its members wore black shoes instead of sandals. In 1954 Algeria's anticolonial movement, the **National Liberation Front (FLN)**, began a war for independence, which the French colonial police and armed forces bitterly contested, leaving over 500,000 Algerians dead and millions more displaced. After the FLN won and created an independent Algerian state in 1962, an estimated 900,000 of the 1.25 million Europeans and indigenous Jews fled.

The war in Algeria and Indochina's military victory divided France and undermined its political stability. As a result, it was difficult for France to respond to nationalists in its other African colonies until Charles

National Liberation Front The anticolonial movement in Algeria, which began a war against the French in 1954 and won independence in 1962.

C. L. R. James on Pan-African Liberation

Trinidadian historian Cyril Lionel Robert James (1901–1989) was one of the most influential intellectual advocates of Pan-Africanism as a solution for colonialism and racial discrimination. In 1938 he published a moving, powerful, and meticulously documented history of the Haitian Revolution, *The Black Jacobins*, to present a history of successful black resistance to white domination that could inspire others. His aim was to demonstrate to his contemporary brethren that they stood atop a proud tradition of resistance as they fought for decolonization in the twentieth century. In 1969 James published *A History of Pan-African Revolt*, a revised edition of his 1938 *History of Negro Revolt*, to engage with the black freedom struggles reshaping Africa and the Americas. In the 1969 edition of *A History of Pan-African Revolt*, James reflected on the significance of black liberation movements and civil rights movements around the world.

Africa

■ The dozen years that have unfolded since the winning of independence by the Gold Coast in 1957 are some of the most far-ranging and politically intense that history has known. African state after African state has gained political independence in a tumultuous rush that was not envisaged by even the most sanguine of the early advocates of independence. . . . What is to be noted is that Kenyatta, Nkrumah, Banda, to take the best-known names, were all imprisoned by the British Government and *had to be released to head the independent states*. The British Government, as did the French and the Belgian, found that despite their soldiers, their guns and planes, they could not rule. The colonial mentality having been broken, the only way to restore some sort of order . . . was to transfer the man in jail to be the head of state. In no other way could the African people once more accommodate themselves to any social structure.

They accepted the African leader and his African colleagues. But that is precisely why in African state after African state, with almost the rapidity with which independence was gained, military dictatorship after military dictatorship has succeeded to power. . . . What are the reasons for this rapid decay and decline of African nationalism? . . .

The states which the African nationalist leaders inherited were not in any sense African. With the disintegration of the political power of the imperialist states in Africa, and the rise of militancy of the African masses, a certain political pattern took shape. Nationalist political leaders built a following,

they or their opponents gained support among the African civil servants who had administered the imperialist state, and the newly independent African state was little more than the old imperialist state only now administered and controlled by Black nationalists. That these men, western-educated and western-oriented, had or would have little that was nationalist or African to contribute to the establishment of a truly new and truly African order was seen most clearly by the late Frantz Fanon. . . .

The United States

■ Summer after summer has seen tremendous struggles by the Black masses, led by unknown, obscure, local leaders. Perhaps the most significant was that which followed the assassination of Dr. Martin Luther King, the world-famous Black leader. The American government placed a cordon of troops around the White House and government buildings and areas in Washington. They then abandoned the city, the capital of the United States, to the embittered and insurgent Blacks, who constitute a majority of the Washington population. The question to be asked: what else could the government have done?

One can only record the question most often and most seriously asked: can any government mobilize the white population, or a great majority of it, in defence of white racism against militant Blacks? The only legitimate answer lies in the continuing militancy or retreat of the Black population. This population is at least 30 million in number, strategically situated in the heart of many of the most important cities in the United States. If the Black population continues to resist racism, the militants and youth actively and the middle classes sympathetic or neutral, then the physical defeat of the Black struggle against racism will involve the destruction of the United States as it has held together since 1776.

QUESTIONS FOR ANALYSIS

1. How does James explain the rise of military dictators in Africa?
2. How does James equate the struggles in Africa and the United States?
3. What does James mean when he says that a defeat in the civil rights struggle would mean the destruction of the United States?

Source: C. L. R. James, *A History of Pan-African Revolt* (1969; repr. Chicago: Charles H. Kerr, 2005), pp. 127–129, 135–136. Used by permission of PM Press, Inc.

de Gaulle returned to power in 1958. Seeking to maximize France's influence over the future independent nations, de Gaulle devised a divide-and-rule strategy. He divided the French West Africa and French Equatorial Africa federations into thirteen separate governments, thus creating a "French commonwealth." Plebiscites were called in each territory to ratify the new arrangement. An affirmative vote meant continued ties with France; a negative vote signified immediate independence and a complete break with France.

De Gaulle's gamble was shrewd. The educated black elite—as personified by the influential poet-politician Léopold Sédar Senghor (LAY-o-pold SAY-dar SEHN-gohr) (1906–2001), who led Senegal's government—identified with France and dreaded an abrupt separation. They also wanted French aid to continue. France, in keeping with its ideology of assimilation, had given the vote to the educated colonial elite after the Second World War, and about forty Africans held French parliamentary seats after 1946. These factors moderated French African leaders' pursuit of independence.

In Guinea, however, a young nationalist named Sékou Touré (SAY-koo too-RAY) (1922–1984) led his people to overwhelmingly reject the new constitution in 1958. Inspired by Ghana's Nkrumah, Touré laid it out to de Gaulle face-to-face: "We have one prime and essential need: our dignity. But there is no dignity without freedom. . . . We prefer freedom in poverty to opulence in slavery."[7]

Weaker European nations such as Belgium and Portugal responded to decolonization in ways that were more destabilizing. Portugal's dictatorship fought to keep its colonies, such as Angola and Mozambique. To ensure this, the Portuguese regime intensified white settlement and repression of nationalist groups. Belgium, which had discouraged the development of an educated elite in the Congo, abruptly granted independence in 1959, leaving in place a weak government. Independence resulted in violent ethnic conflict and foreign intervention. The United States backed a dictatorship by Mobutu Sese Seko (Muh-BOO-too SEH-seh SEH-koh), who renamed the country Zaire. Poverty deepened as the tremendous wealth generated from mining went into the hands of foreign companies and Mobutu's family and cronies.

Populist and Revolutionary Pathways in Latin America

Why did populism emerge as such a powerful political force in Latin America?

In the decades after the Second World War, Latin American nations struggled to find a political balance that integrated long-excluded groups such as women, workers, and peasants. Populist politicians built a base of support among the urban and rural poor. They often combined charisma with promises of social change, particularly through national economic development that would create more and better job opportunities. In many cases, the conservative reaction against populists led the armed forces to seize power. Revolutionary leader Fidel Castro carved an alternative path in Cuba. Castro went beyond the reforms advocated by populists and sought an outright revolutionary transformation of Cuban society.

Economic Nationalism in Mexico

In the decades following the Mexican Revolution, a durable political and economic formula emerged under the Institutional Revolutionary Party (PRI), which dominated public life while adhering to the social goals demanded by the movements that had fought in the revolution, especially the redistribution of land. By the end of the Second World War, Mexico had embraced economic nationalism—the effort to promote economic development through substitution of imports with domestic manufacturing and through state control of key industries like the oil sector.

As before the revolution, Mexicans faced a curtailed democracy, though in this case the government was controlled by a single party rather than a single individual. The PRI came to control elected office at every level, as well as networks of patronage. The party was also an omnipresent intermediary between business and labor. Mexico's economy also grew consistently through the 1970s, in what was termed an "economic miracle." This was a time of rapid urbanization, with people leaving rural areas for jobs in factories or for lower-paying service jobs, such as maids and janitors. The embrace of economic nationalism softened some of the edges of economic change that Mexicans had experienced in the liberal era, but social inequities remained. The upper and middle classes reaped the lion's share of the benefits of this economic growth.

A housing and civic complex in the Tlatelolco (tlah-tehl-OL-koh) district of Mexico City symbolized both the promise of the Mexican economic miracle and also the limits to democracy in Mexico. In the 1960s the Mexican government built dozens of modernist apartment buildings and government ministries. Their centerpiece was the Plaza of the Three Cultures, which contained ruins from the Aztec Empire, a colonial Spanish church, and the contemporary nation reflected in modernist architecture. It was in Tlatelolco where government forces silenced political dissent in advance of the 1968 Olympics by opening fire on a student march.

The Plaza of the Three Cultures in Tlatelolco, Mexico City Modern apartment buildings rise behind Aztec ruins and a Spanish church built in 1536. Mexican authorities massacred student protesters at this plaza to suppress unrest before the 1968 Summer Olympics in the city. (© Macduff Everton/The Image Works)

Populism in Argentina and Brazil

Argentina and Brazil's postwar economic development was shaped by populist politicians who championed economic nationalism. These politicians sought support from millions of people who gained the right to vote for the first time as universal suffrage spread through Latin America. Universal male suffrage was achieved in Argentina in 1912 and in Mexico in 1917. Women gained the right to vote across Latin America in the decades that followed, beginning with Ecuador in 1929 and Brazil in 1932. In most cases voters still needed to be literate to vote. To appeal to these millions of new voters, populist candidates promised schools and hospitals, higher wages, and nationalist projects that would create more industrial jobs.

At the turn of the century Argentina's economy prospered through its liberal export boom (see "Latin America Re-enters the World Economy" in Chapter 27), but industrialization followed only haltingly and the economy faltered. Populist Juan Perón, an army colonel, was elected president in 1946 with the support of Argentina's unions. Juan Perón was charismatic, but his wife, Eva, known as Evita, was even more so, and played a vital role in promoting Perón. Once in power, Perón embarked on an ambitious scheme to transform Argentina's economy: The government would purchase all the country's agricultural exports in order to negotiate their sale abroad at a higher price. Perón would then reinvest the profits in industry and raise worker wages to stimulate demand.

Perón's scheme worked in the immediate postwar period, when European agricultural production had not yet recovered from the war. But as commodity prices declined, Perón reduced government payments to farmers, who ceased to bring their harvests to market. In the coming decades Argentina never returned to the high rates of economic growth it had enjoyed at the beginning of the century. Many blamed Perón for distorting the economy for his own political gain. Others saw Perón's efforts as halting a worse decline: Argentina's economy had long been dependent on Britain, and as Britain's capacity to import declined, so did Argentina's fortunes.

INDIVIDUALS IN SOCIETY

Eva Perón

OFTEN CALLED EVITA (THE SPANISH diminutive of Eva), Eva Duarte de Perón (1919–1952) was one of five children born outside of marriage to Juan Duarte and Juana Ibarguren, near Buenos Aires. Duarte returned to his legitimate wife and children when Eva was a year old, leaving Juana and her children destitute and dependent on Juana's sewing for their existence. As they grew older, all the children had to work.

At fifteen Eva Duarte moved to the cosmopolitan city of Buenos Aires. Although she had little formal education and no connections, she possessed beauty and charisma, and soon she joined a professional theater group. She also modeled, appeared in a few movies, and acted in a radio series. By 1943, although only twenty-three years old, she was one of the highest-paid actresses in the country.

In 1943 Eva met widowed Colonel Juan Perón, then secretary of labor and social welfare in the military government that had seized power that year. Juan Perón had grand ambitions, intending to run for president. Eva Duarte became his partner and confidante, and she won him support among the Argentine masses. In 1945 Juan Perón and Eva Duarte married.

A year later Perón won the presidency. Eva had campaigned for her husband and had organized support from *los descamisados* (the shirtless ones), her name for Argentina's poor. When Perón assumed the presidency, Eva, though not officially appointed, became the secretary of labor. Having come from a childhood of poverty herself, she now worked tirelessly for the poor, for the working classes, and with organized labor. She instituted a number of social welfare measures and promoted a new Ministry of Health, which resulted in the creation of new hospitals and disease-treatment programs. In 1948 she established the Eva Perón

Eva Perón waves to supporters from the balcony of the presidential palace, Casa Rosada, in Buenos Aires, on October 17, 1951. (Archivo Clarin/ AP Photo/AP Images)

Welfare Foundation, which grew into an immense semiofficial welfare agency, helping the poor throughout Argentina.

From early on, Eva Perón had supported women's suffrage, and in September 1947 Argentine women won the right to vote. Eva then formed the Female Perónist Party, which by 1951 had five hundred thousand members. In 1951 she seemed ready to run for vice president beside her husband. Her declining health, however, forced her to turn down the nomination. Juan Perón won the election by over 30 percent, but when Eva died the following year, his authoritarian rule and bad economic policies lost him support, and a military junta forced him into exile.

Eva Perón's life story is an amazing one, but what happened following her death is just as extraordinary. Before the massive monument intended to hold her embalmed body could be built, the military seized power and her body disappeared. Seventeen years later the generals finally revealed that it was in a tomb in Milan, Italy. Juan Perón, living in Spain with his third wife, had the body exhumed and brought to Spain, where he kept it in his house. Perón returned to Argentina in 1973 and won the presidential election, but died the following year. His wife, Isabelita Perón, succeeded him as president. Juan and Eva's bodies were briefly displayed together at his funeral and then, finally, buried.

QUESTIONS FOR ANALYSIS

1. Why do you think Eva Perón was adored by many Argentines when she died?
2. What were some of the welfare and government programs that Eva Perón promoted?

Source: Nicholas Fraser and Marysa Navarro, *Evita: The Real Life of Eva Perón* (New York: Norton, 1976).

Despite these economic setbacks, Perón initially remained highly popular, buoyed by the public appeals made by Evita. (See "Individuals in Society: Eva Perón," above.) After Evita died of cancer in 1952, much of the magic slipped away. Amid the stagnating economy even Perón's union supporters faltered, and he responded harshly to press criticism. In 1955 the armed forces deposed and exiled Perón. The military ruled Argentina for the next three years, conducting a process of "de-Perónization." It banned Perón's party and even forbade mention of his name. But Perón remained the most popular politician in the country. Presidential candidates could not win without discreetly winning the exiled Perón's endorsement, and this veiled support for Perón by civilian leaders prompted repeated military interventions in politics.

In Brazil, reacting against the economic and political liberalism through which coffee planters dominated the country, the armed forces installed Getúlio Vargas as president in 1930. Vargas initiated democratic reforms but veered into a nationalist dictatorship known as the "New State" (1937–1945), inspired by European fascism. Despite his harsh treatment of opponents, he was popular with workers and was elected in 1950 to a new term as president, now reinvented as a populist who promised nationalist economic reforms. The armed forces and conservatives mistrusted Vargas's appeals to workers and organized to depose him in 1954. Before they could act, Vargas killed himself.

The Vargas era saw rapid industrialization, the legalization of labor unions, and the creation of a minimum wage. Juscelino Kubitschek, elected in 1955, continued to build upon Vargas's populism and nationalism. Between 1956 and 1960 Kubitschek's government borrowed heavily from abroad to promote industry and build the futuristic new capital of Brasília in the midst of a wilderness. Kubitschek's slogan was "Fifty Years' Progress in Five."

In 1961 leftist populist João Goulart became Brazil's president. Goulart sought deeper reforms, including the redistribution of land and limits on the profits

Building a Modern Capital Architect Oscar Niemeyer at the site of the construction of the futuristic National Congress building in Brazil's new planned capital, Brasília, in 1960. (© Rene Burri/Magnum Photos)

multinational corporations could take out of the country. In 1964 the armed forces, backed by the United States, deposed Goulart and held on to power for the next twenty-one years.

Communist Revolution in Cuba

Cuba remained practically an American colony until the 1930s, when a series of rulers with socialist and Communist leanings seized and lost power. Cuba's political institutions were weak and its politicians corrupt. In March 1952 Fulgencio Batista (1901–1973) staged a coup with American support and instituted an authoritarian regime that favored wealthy Cubans and U.S. businesses.

The Cuban Revolution (1953–1959) brought Fidel Castro (1927–2016) to power through an armed insurgency that used guerrilla tactics crafted by Argentine revolutionary Ernesto "Che" Guevara. Castro pursued deep economic reforms such as land redistribution and rent caps to help the urban poor. Because Castro's nationalization of utilities and industries as well as land reform came at the expense of U.S. businesses, U.S. president John F. Kennedy staged an invasion of Cuba to topple Castro. When the invasion force, composed of Cuban exiles, landed at the Bay of Pigs, the Cuban revolutionary army, commanded by Castro, repelled it in an embarrassment to the United States.

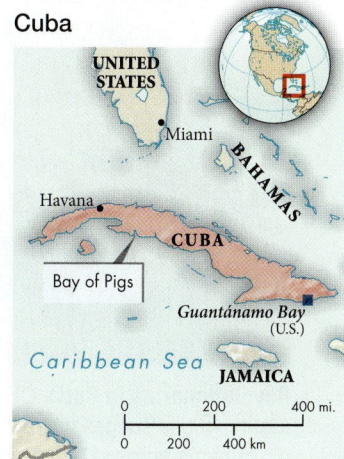

Castro had not come to power as a Communist: his main aim had been to regain control of Cuba's economy and politics from the United States. But U.S. efforts to overthrow him and to starve the Cuban economy drove him to form an alliance with the Soviet Union, which agreed to place nuclear missiles in Cuba to protect against another U.S. invasion. When Kennedy demanded the missiles be removed, the military and diplomatic brinksmanship of the 1962 Cuban missile crisis ensued. In 1963 the U.S. placed a complete commercial embargo on Cuba that remains in place although diplomatic relations were restored in 2015.

Castro now declared himself a Marxist-Leninist and relied on Soviet military and economic support, though Cuba retained a revolutionary mind-set that differed from the rest of the Soviet bloc. Castro was committed to spreading revolution to the rest of Latin America, and Guevara participated in armed struggles in the Congo and Bolivia before being assassinated by U.S.-trained Bolivian forces in 1967. Within Cuba

Revolutionaries in Cuba Che Guevara (left) and Fidel Castro (right), whose successful revolution in Cuba inspired armed movements across Latin America. (© United Archives/Topfoto/The Image Works)

activists swept into the countryside and taught people who were illiterate. Medical attention and education became free and widely accessible. The Cuban Revolution inspired young radicals across Latin America to believe in the possibility of swift revolution and brisk reforms to combat historic inequalities. But these reforms were achieved at great cost and through the suppression of political dissent. Castro declared in 1961, "Inside of the revolution anything, outside the revolution, nothing."[8] Political opponents were jailed or exiled.

The Limits of Postwar Prosperity

Why did the world face growing social unrest in the 1960s?

In the 1950s and 1960s the United States and the Soviet Union, as well as both western and eastern Europe, rebounded economically from the combined strains of the Great Depression and the Second World War. The postwar return of prosperity increased living standards but did not resolve underlying tensions and conflicts.

The Soviet Union Struggles to Move Beyond Stalin

The Cold War provided Stalin with the opportunity to revive many of the harshest aspects of the repression citizens of the Soviet Union had experienced in the 1930s, such as purges of soldiers and civilian officials and the revival of forced-labor camps. Stalin reasserted control of the government and society by reintroducing five-year plans to cope with the enormous task of reconstruction. He exported this system to eastern Europe. Rigid indoctrination, attacks on religion, and a lack of civil liberties became facts of life in the region's one-party states. Only Yugoslavia's Josip Tito (1892–1980), the popular resistance leader and Communist Party chief, could resist Soviet domination successfully because there was no Russian army in Yugoslavia.

After Stalin died in 1953, his successor Nikita Khrushchev (CROO-shehv) (1894–1971) realized that reforms were necessary because of widespread fear and hatred of Stalin's political terrorism. Khrushchev and the reformers in his administration curbed the secret police and gradually closed many forced-labor camps. Change was also necessary for economic reasons. Agriculture struggled, and shortages of consumer goods discouraged hard work. Moreover, Stalin's foreign policy had provoked a strong Western alliance, isolating the Soviet Union.

Khrushchev denounced Stalin and his crimes in a "secret speech" delivered to a closed session of the Twentieth Party Congress in 1956:

> It is clear that . . . Stalin showed in a whole series of cases his intolerance, his brutality, and his abuse of power. Instead of proving his political correctness and mobilizing the masses, he often chose the path of repression and physical annihilation, not only against actual enemies, but also against individuals who had not committed any crimes against the party and the Soviet Government.[9]

The liberalization of the Soviet Union—labeled de-Stalinization in the West—was genuine. Khrushchev declared that "peaceful coexistence" with capitalism was possible. The government shifted some economic resources to production of consumer goods, improving standards of living throughout the booming 1960s. De-Stalinization opened new space for creative work and for expressing dissent. The writer Aleksandr Solzhenitsyn (1918–2008) created a sensation when his *One Day in the Life of Ivan Denisovich* was published in the Soviet Union in 1962. Solzhenitsyn's novel portrayed life in a Stalinist concentration camp in grim detail and was a damning indictment of the Stalinist past.

De-Stalinization stimulated rebelliousness in the eastern European satellites. Poland won greater autonomy in 1956 after extensive protests forced the Soviets to allow a new Communist government. Led by students and workers, the people of Budapest, Hungary, installed a liberal Communist reformer as their new chief in October 1956. The rebellion was short-lived. After the government promised open elections and renounced Hungary's military alliance with Moscow, the Soviet army invaded and crushed the revolution, killing thousands. When the United States did not come to Hungary's aid, many eastern European reformers concluded that their best hope was to strive for incremental gains rather than broad change.

In August 1961 the East German government began construction of a twenty-seven-mile wall between East and West Berlin. It also built a ninety-mile-long barrier between the three allied sectors of West Berlin and East Germany, thereby completely cutting off West Berlin. Officially the wall was called the "Anti-Fascist Protection Wall." In reality the Berlin Wall prevented East Germans from "voting with their feet" by defecting to the West.

By late 1962 opponents had come to see Khrushchev's policies as a dangerous threat to party authority. Moreover, Khrushchev did not succeed in alleviating tensions with the West. In 1962 Khrushchev ordered missiles with nuclear warheads installed in Cuba to shield it from U.S. invasion, triggering the Cuban missile crisis. The hard line taken by the U.S. over the placement of the missiles put the superpowers on the brink of war until Khrushchev backed down and removed the missiles. Two years later, Communist Party leaders removed him. After Leonid Brezhnev (1906–1982) and his supporters took over in 1964, they stopped further liberalization and launched an arms buildup, determined not to repeat Khrushchev's humiliation by the United States.

Postwar Challenges in Western Europe and the United States

In 1945 much of western Europe was devastated by the war, and it faced mass unemployment, shortages of food and fuel, and the dislocation of millions of people. But in the decades that followed, western Europe experienced a dramatic recovery. Democratic governments thrived in an atmosphere of broadening civil liberties. Progressive Catholics and their Christian Democratic political parties were particularly influential. Socialists and Communists active in the resistance against Hitler returned with renewed prestige. In the immediate postwar years welfare measures such as family stipends, health insurance, and expanded public housing were enacted throughout much of Europe.

An immediate result of the Cold War was the partition between a Soviet-controlled German Democratic Republic (East Germany) and a Federal Republic of Germany (West Germany) that had been occupied by the United States, Britain, and France. With the support of the United States, which wanted to turn an economically resurgent West Germany into a bulwark

Guest Workers in Europe
In the 1950s and 1960s thousands of workers from Spain, Portugal, Italy, Greece, and Turkey immigrated into parts of Europe where the postwar growth in industrial production had created a scarcity of labor. Workers like this Italian seamstress and supervisor in a German factory fled a weak economy and high unemployment in their country of origin, seeking work in countries like Germany and France. (Max Scheler/Suddeutsche Zeitung Photo/Alamy Stock Photo)

against Soviet expansion, Chancellor Konrad Adenauer (1881–1967), brought Germany firmly into the Western capitalist camp. He forged close ties with the United States, Great Britain, and France. He also initiated dialogues with leaders of Europe's Jewish community and with Israel to encourage a reconciliation following the Holocaust. As Germany recovered from the war, it became Europe's leading economic power, a member of NATO, and an architect of efforts at European unity.

Amid the destruction and uncertainty brought by two world wars caused by Europeans and fought in Europe, many Europeans believed that only unity could forestall future European conflicts. The first steps toward economic unity were taken through close cooperation over Marshall Plan aid. These were followed by the creation in 1952 of a Coal and Steel Community, made up of France, West Germany, Italy, Belgium, the Netherlands, and Luxembourg. In 1957 these nations signed the Treaty of Rome, creating the European Economic Community, popularly known as the **Common Market**. The treaty's primary goal was to eliminate trade barriers between them and create a single market almost as large as that of the United States.

Migrant laborers, mainly from southern Italy, North Africa, Turkey, Greece, and Yugoslavia, also shaped western European societies and drove their economic recovery. Tens of millions of migrant workers made it possible for western European economies to continue to grow beyond their postwar labor capacity. This was especially important in Germany, where they filled gaps left by the wartime loss of a large proportion of the adult male population. Governments at first labeled the migrants as "guest workers" to signal their temporary status, though in practice many would remain in their new homes. As their communities became more settled, migrants faced a backlash from majority populations and came to resent and resist their treatment as second-class citizens.

In the United States the postwar era was also shaped by economic recovery and social pressures. The Second World War ended the Great Depression in the United States, bringing about an economic boom that increased living standards dramatically. By the end of the war, the United States had the strongest economy and held an advantage over its past commercial rivals: its industry and infrastructure had not been damaged by war. After the war, U.S. manufactured goods saturated markets around the world that had previously been dominated by Britain, France, and Germany.

Postwar America experienced a social revolution as well: after a long struggle African Americans began to experience major victories against the deeply entrenched system of segregation and discrimination. This civil rights movement advanced on several fronts, none more prominent than legal victories that ended the statutory segregation of schools. African American civil rights activists challenged inequality by using Gandhian methods of nonviolent resistance: as civil rights leader Martin Luther King, Jr. (1929–1968), said, "Christ furnished the spirit and motivation, while Gandhi furnished the method." He told the white power structure, "We will not hate you, but we will not obey your evil laws."[10]

The World in 1968

In 1968 pressures for social change boiled over into protests worldwide. The preceding two decades offered the world an example of how much people could change as decolonization swept much of the world. Revolutionary struggles stretched from Cuba to the remaining colonies in Africa and the war in Southeast Asia. The architecture of white supremacism and racial segregation was being dismantled in the United States. Young protesters drew upon recent history to appreciate how much could be achieved and looked at their world to see how much more was needed. Around the world, streets and squares filled with protesters.

In Czechoslovakia the "Prague Spring"—a brief period of liberal reform and loosening of political controls—unfolded as reformers in the Czechoslovakian Communist Party gained a majority and replaced a long-time Stalinist leader with Alexander Dubček (DOOB-chehk), whose new government launched

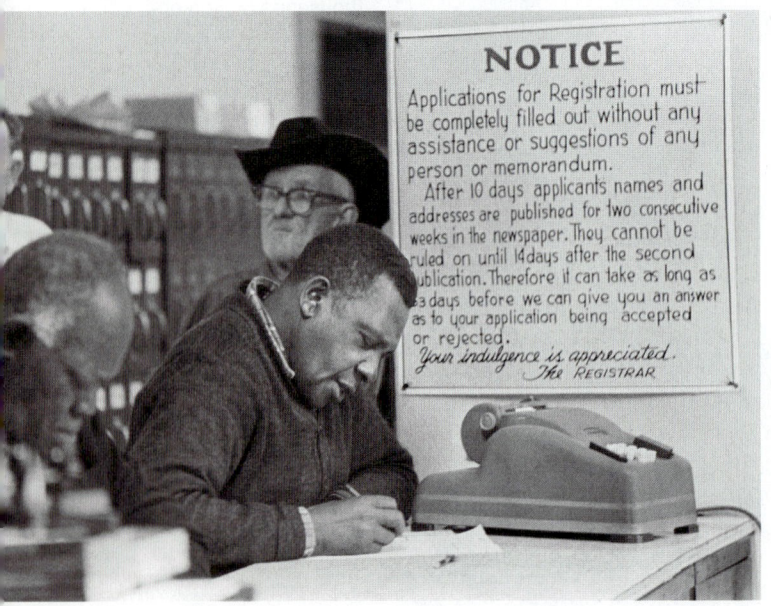

Registering to Vote African American residents of Hattiesburg, Mississippi, register to vote in 1964. The sign on the wall indicates that their names will be published in the newspaper for two consecutive weeks, making African Americans vulnerable to violent reprisals for registering to vote. (© 1976 Matt Herron/Take Stock/The Image Works)

dramatic reforms. Dubček and his allies called for "socialism with a human face," which meant rolling back many of the strictures imposed by Stalin. He restored freedom of speech and freedom of the press. Communist leaders in the Soviet Union and other eastern European states feared that they would face similar demands for reform from their own citizens. Protests against the excesses of Communist rule erupted in Poland and Yugoslavia.

In France students went on strike over poor university conditions. When government responded with harsh punishments, larger and more radical student protests erupted. Labor unions called a general strike. The strikes captured the anxieties of the generation that had been raised in postwar Europe. For many of them, their governments' postwar socialist reforms were incomplete and the time was now ripe for more far-ranging change—if not outright revolution. Similar student movements erupted across western Europe.

In Latin America students rose in protest as well. In Argentina students in the industrial city of Córdoba went on strike against the military dictatorship that had been in place since 1966. Joined by factory workers, the protesters took control of the city in an event known as the Cordobazo. In Brazil a national student strike challenged the military dictatorship that had been in power since 1964. In Mexico City, where the 1968 Olympic games would be held, students used the international visibility of the event to protest the heavy-handed ruling PRI Party. The Latin American students challenging their regimes were motivated by the example offered by revolutionary Cuba, which they saw as a model of swift social transformation.

The ongoing U.S. military intervention in Vietnam met with growing opposition worldwide. In Japan protesters denounced what they saw as the complicity of their government and businesses in the U.S. military intervention in Vietnam, and challenged the Security Treaty that bound Japan and the United States. As the continuation of the war depended increasingly on military drafts, protests against the Vietnam War and against the draft erupted on college campuses across the United States and in its ally in the conflict, Australia.

In the United States the antiwar movement marked an increase in popular mobilization: civil rights marches in the South now extended to protests against discrimination and police violence in cities like Boston and Chicago. Protesters around the world were aware of each other and felt empowered by the sense that they were participating in a worldwide movement against the abuses of the established order. Their actions echoed Che Guevara's call for "two, three or many Vietnams" of resistance against imperialism.

In 1968 it seemed that social movements worldwide were on the verge of opening the floodgates to a wave of

The Soviet Invasion of Prague, 1968 Czech demonstrators throw torches and wave flags in an attempt to stop a tank as the Soviet army crushes the protests of the Prague Spring in 1968. (Libo Hajsky/AFP/Getty Images)

radical change, but the opposite was more true. Protesters and reformers faced violent reactions from the powerful political and economic groups they challenged. Conservatives reacted against more than the protests of 1968: they sought to slow or sometimes reverse the dramatic changes that had taken place in the postwar era.

Around the world, protests were followed by violent crackdowns such as the Soviet deployment of tanks in Czechoslovakia in October 1968, which crushed the Prague Spring, unseated Dubček, and led to harsh persecutions of the Prague Spring's supporters. In Mexico, Argentina, and Brazil, military and paramilitary groups launched violent campaigns against protesting students and workers, such as the Mexican government's shooting of protesters in Tlatelolco before the Olympics. In the United States assassins killed Martin Luther King, Jr., and other civil rights leaders. In 1967 Che Guevara was executed by Bolivian troops trained and led by the U.S. government. Around the world, revolutionary violence was met with increasingly violent repression.

Common Market The European Economic Community created in 1957.

Chapter Summary

The decades after the Second World War were an era of rebuilding, a term that had different meanings for different peoples. In Europe, the Soviet Union, and Japan, rebuilding literally meant clearing the rubble from wartime devastation and restoring what had been destroyed. In Germany and Japan in particular, rebuilding meant charting political and economic paths different from the ones that nationalist fervor had forged.

For the United States and the Soviet Union, rebuilding meant developing a military and ideological complex with which to confront each other in the Cold War. In each country individually, rebuilding took other forms: in the Soviet Union it meant finding ways to reform the system of political terror and coercion through which Stalin had ruled; in the United States it meant struggling to overcome the structures of white supremacism and other forms of racial discrimination.

The idea of rebuilding took on its deepest meaning in Asia, Africa, and the Middle East, where rebuilding meant dismantling European colonialism to establish independent states. This required replacing not just colonial institutions but colonial mentalities, patterns of production, and forms of education, and developing ways of relating that were not based on terms dictated by colonizers. Intellectuals and artists strove to decolonize the mind as politicians worked to decolonize the state in a process that proved slow and difficult. In Latin America rebuilding meant finding the means to overcome patterns of social exclusion that were legacies of colonialism and neocolonialism. It also meant finding the means to industrialize, overcoming the patterns of dependency and underdevelopment diagnosed by Latin American intellectuals and social scientists.

The decades after 1945 showed how much was possible through mass movements, advancing industrialization, and political self-determination. But the balance of these years also showed how much more work remained to overcome poverty, underdevelopment, and neocolonialism.

NOTES

1. Frantz Fanon, *The Wretched of the Earth*, trans. Constance Farrington (New York: Grove Press, 1968), pp. 43, 93–94, 97, 102.
2. Chinua Achebe, *Things Fall Apart* (London: Heinemann, 2000), pp. 124–125.
3. Syed Sharifuddin Pirzada, ed., *Foundations of Pakistan: All-India Muslim League Documents.* Vol. 2: *1924–1947* (Karachi: National Publishing House, 1970), p. 338.
4. Quoted in K. Bhata, *The Ordeal of Nationhood: A Social Study of India Since Independence, 1947–1970* (New York: Atheneum, 1971), p. 9.
5. Cited in Sami Hanna and George Gardner, *Arab Socialism: A Documentary Survey* (Leiden: Brill, 1969), p. 106.
6. Mao Zedong, *Quotations from Chairman Mao Tsetung* (Peking: Foreign Language Press, 1972), p. 61.
7. Quoted in R. Hallett, *Africa Since 1875: A Modern History* (Ann Arbor: University of Michigan Press, 1974), pp. 378–379.
8. Quoted in Samuel Farber, *Cuba Since the Revolution of 1959: A Critical Assessment* (Chicago: Haymarket Books, 2011), p. 22.
9. *Congressional Record: Proceedings and Debates of the 84th Congress, 2nd Session* (May 22, 1956–June 11, 1956), C11, Part 7 (June 4, 1956), pp. 9389–9403.
10. Regarding Gandhi's methods: see M. L. King, Jr., *Stride Toward Freedom: The Montgomery Story* (New York: Perennial Library, 1964), p. 67. Regarding evil laws: quoted in S. E. Morison et al., *A Concise History of the American Republic* (New York: Oxford University Press), p. 697.

CONNECTIONS

The great transformations experienced by peoples around the world following the Second World War can best be compared to the age of revolution in the late eighteenth and early nineteenth centuries (see Chapter 22). In both eras peoples rose up to undertake the political, economic, social, and cultural transformation of their societies. In both eras, history seemed to accelerate, driven by events that had impacts across the globe. As in the age of revolution, which saw the independence of the United States and most of Spanish America as well as the Haitian and French Revolutions, people swept aside old notions of authority tied to kings and empires. In Asia the Chinese Revolution and the independence of India and Pakistan marked the accelerating pace of liberation movements that dismantled European colonialism and ushered in new political ideologies and economic systems.

Liberation movements spanning the globe sought not only to end imperial domination and remove social boundaries imposed by white racism, but also to make deeper changes in how peoples perceived themselves and their societies. As radical and new as these ideas were, they nonetheless owed much to the Enlightenment ideals about liberal individual rights that were promoted by the ideologues of the French and American Revolutions.

Though the social revolutions in countries like China and Cuba and the independence movements across Africa, Asia, and the Middle East brought unprecedented deep and fast changes, they were only the first steps in remaking societies that had been created by centuries of colonialism. Uprooting the legacies of colonialism — in the form of poverty, continued domination of economies by foreign powers, limited industrialization, and weak states — remained a daunting challenge that societies continued to face in the future.

CHAPTER 31 Review and Explore

Identify Key Terms

Identify and explain the significance of each item below.

Cold War (p. 922)

Truman Doctrine (p. 922)

Marshall Plan (p. 922)

NATO (p. 923)

dependency theory (p. 925)

modernization theory (p. 925)

import substitution industrialization (ISI) (p. 925)

liberation theology (p. 927)

Muslim League (p. 929)

Arab socialism (p. 930)

Palestine Liberation Organization (PLO) (p. 931)

Great Leap Forward (p. 932)

Great Proletarian Cultural Revolution (p. 934)

Pan-Africanists (p. 938)

cocoa holdups (p. 938)

National Liberation Front (p. 940)

Common Market (p. 948)

Review the Main Ideas

Answer the focus questions from each section of the chapter.

1. How did the Cold War and decolonization shape the postwar world? (p. 922)

2. How did religion and the legacies of colonialism affect the formation of new nations in South Asia and the Middle East after World War II? (p. 928)

3. How did the Cold War shape reconstruction, revolution, and decolonization in East and Southeast Asia? (p. 932)

4. What factors influenced decolonization in Africa after World War II? (p. 938)

5. Why did populism emerge as such a powerful political force in Latin America? (p. 942)

6. Why did the world face growing social unrest in the 1960s? (p. 946)

Make Comparisons and Connections

Analyze the larger developments and continuities within and across chapters.

1. What changes in the postwar world had their roots in developments that predated the war? How did the Second World War (Chapter 30) itself accelerate or spur changes in the postwar era?

2. What effect did the Cold War have on the process of decolonization?

3. How might the postwar era be compared to the age of revolution (Chapter 22)?

TIMELINE

GLOBAL

◆ **1945** United Nations established

1947–1975 Decolonization in Africa, Asia, and Middle East

ASIA

1950–1953 Korean War

◆ **1947** Independence of India

◆ **1949** Chinese Revolution

EUROPE

◆ **1948** Marshall Plan enacted

◆ **1949** Formation of NATO

MIDDLE EAST

◆ **1948** Creation of Israel

AMERICAS

1946–1955 Populist Juan Perón leads Argentina

AFRICA

← **1920s** Anticolonial nationalism sweeps Western-educated Africans in French and British colonies

← **1930–1931; 1937–1938** Cocoa holdups in the Gold Coast

1945   **1950**   **1955**

Suggested Resources

BOOKS

Borstelmann, Thomas. *The Cold War and the Color Line: American Race Relations in the Global Arena.* 2003. An incisive discussion of the connections between racial thought and policy.

Cleveland, William L., and Martin Bunton. *A History of the Modern Middle East*, 6th ed. 2016. Well-crafted survey introduction to the modern history and politics of the Middle East.

Collins, Robert O., and James M. Burns. *A History of Sub-Saharan Africa.* 2007. Clearly written introduction to the continent's history.

Gaddis, John Lewis. *The Cold War: A New History.* 2005. A concise, authoritative, and accessible account of the Cold War by one of its leading historians.

Guha, Ramachandra. *India After Gandhi: The History of the World's Largest Democracy.* 2007. In-depth study of the last sixty years of Indian history and development.

Halberstam, David. *The Coldest Winter: America and the Korean War.* 2007. The last, and perhaps best, history written by one of America's finest journalist-historians.

Kamrava, Mehran. *The Modern Middle East: A Political History Since the First World War*, 3d ed. 2013. A concise overview of modern Middle East history, economics, and politics.

Keddie, Nikki R. *Modern Iran: Roots and Results of Revolution.* 2006. A classic survey of Iranian history and politics by a leading scholar of modern Iran.

Meade, Teresa A. *A History of Modern Latin America, 1800 to the Present.* 2009. A comprehensive history and analysis of the continent and its peoples.

Meredith, Martin. *The Fate of Africa: A History of Fifty Years of Independence.* 2006. A very accessible study of modern independent Africa that spans the entire continent.

Moaddel, Mansoor. *Islamic Modernism, Nationalism, and Fundamentalism.* 2005. A scholarly historical introduction to the society and politics of the Middle East.

Osborne, Milton. *Southeast Asia: An Introductory History*, 12th ed. 2016. Classic introduction to the region.

1959–1975 War in Vietnam

1965 Great Proletarian Cultural Revolution in China

1956 Soviet invasion of Hungary

1961 East German government builds Berlin Wall

1957 Formation of Common Market

1953–1964 Khrushchev implements de-Stalinization in the Soviet Union

1956 Nasser nationalizes Suez Canal

1967 Six-Day War in Israel

1953–1959 Cuban Revolution

1962 Cuban missile crisis

1957 Ghana gains independence from colonial rule, marking the beginning of a rapid wave of decolonization in Africa

1960

1965

DOCUMENTARIES

China: A Century of Revolution (Sue Williams, 1997). This six-episode documentary explores the roots and course of China's Communist revolution.

The Cold War (CNN, 1998). A twenty-four-episode series that takes a detailed look at the Cold War's European origins, global reach, and resolution.

The 50 Years War: Israel and the Arabs (PBS/BBC, 1998). Examines the Arab-Israeli conflict beginning with the 1947 UN partition of Palestine.

FEATURE FILMS

The Battle of Algiers (Gillo Pontecorvo, 1966). Chronicling the Algerian war for independence from France, this film is a rich reflection on the practices of guerrilla warfare and the anticolonial struggle.

Fail Safe (Sidney Lumet, 1964). A thriller centered on the phone conversations between the U.S. president and Soviet premier as they seek to defuse a nuclear crisis.

Z and *State of Siege* (Costa-Gavras, 1969 and 1972). Two powerful films that explore Greece's descent into dictatorship in the 1960s and U.S. support for torture and repression in Latin America.

WEBSITES

Africana Age: African & African Diasporan Transformations in the 20th Century. The Schomburg Center for Research in Black Culture at the New York Public Library offers essays and research materials on topics such as "Négritude," "Black Power," and "African Decolonization."
exhibitions.nypl.org/africanaage/essay-landing.html

The United Nations and Decolonization. Documents on the founding of the United Nations and the question of decolonization.
www.un.org/en/decolonization/

Universal Newsreels. The Internet Archive contains many newsreels on subjects in this chapter.
**archive.org detailsuniversal_newsreels?&sort=
-downloads&page=2**

32

Liberalization
1968–2000s

In the 1970s two currents ran against each other in much of the world. The radicalism of liberation in decolonization, revolutions, and mass social movements continued. Women's movements achieved important successes in pressing for reproductive rights and equity in education, employment, and compensation, both in the West and in nationalist regimes around the world. The most dramatic phase of decolonization in Africa and black civil rights mobilization in the United States had succeeded, but the hard work of making new nations function, or of achieving racial equality, continued.

But alongside this current ran a different one whose influence was not easily apparent in the early 1970s but was undeniable by the 1990s: liberalization. Liberal political and economic ideology experienced a resurgence. After the Second World War, the United States had championed liberal economic policies and global free trade, but this objective ran against the desires of other countries to protect and promote their own industrialization and economic development. But in the last decades of the century, the U.S. drive for global liberalization of trade experienced greater success, while reform movements in the Eastern bloc and in Latin America pursued human rights and political liberalization.

Thalia Watmough/aliki image library/Alamy Stock Photo

Sandinista Soldier in Nicaragua

Street art in Jinotega, Nicaragua, shows an armed female soldier of the Sandinista National Liberation Front picking coffee beans in her military camouflage. The Sandinistas overthrew the U.S.-backed dictator Anastasio Somoza in 1979. After their victory, the socialist Sandinistas ruled Nicaragua until 1990 and then returned to power in 2006.

CHAPTER PREVIEW

Oil Shocks and Liberalization

What were the short-term and long-term consequences of the OPEC oil embargo?

In 1973 war erupted again between Israel and its neighbors Egypt and Syria. The conflict became known both as the Yom Kippur War because it coincided with the Jewish religious holiday of atonement, and as the Ramadan War because it occurred during the Muslim month of fasting. Armed with advanced weapons from the Soviet Union, Egyptian and Syrian armies came close to defeating Israel before the U.S. government airlifted sophisticated arms to Israel. Israel counterattacked, reaching the outskirts of both Cairo and Damascus before the fighting ended.

Arab oil-exporting countries retaliated against U.S. support for Israel by imposing an embargo on oil sales to countries that had aided Israel during the war. Amid the oil embargo, the war in Vietnam, and political conflict within the United States, U.S. political and economic influence as a global superpower seemed to decline.

The OPEC Oil Embargo

In 1960 oil-exporting countries formed a cartel called the **Organization of the Petroleum Exporting Countries (OPEC)** to coordinate production and raise prices. They aimed to increase national revenue to support economic development. Until the early 1970s OPEC had failed to control the market for oil. But in 1973 OPEC countries agreed to an embargo, withholding oil sales to the United States and western Europe in response to their support for Israel in the Yom Kippur War.

Since oil is a commodity that is traded globally, it remained available in Europe and the United States

despite the embargo. But the embargo disrupted the market and caused panic. The price of oil increased almost overnight from $3 to $12 per barrel, quadrupling energy costs. OPEC's ability to disrupt the world economy, and the U.S. government's powerlessness to reverse the disruption, suggested a new world order. Brazil's military leaders, for example, distanced themselves from their traditional alliance with the United States and built relations with OPEC countries. Fearing reprisal from Arab countries, Brazil quietly halted exports to Israel, while promoting arms sales and engineering services to Libya and Iraq. Brazil's foreign minister told U.S. secretary of state Henry Kissinger, "If you could supply us with a million barrels of oil a day, perhaps this shift would not be so abrupt."[1]

Oil prices remained high and peaked again in the second oil shock of 1979, which resulted from the Iranian revolution that ousted the secular government and brought religious leaders to power. In the United States energy costs sapped economic growth and triggered inflation, a combination dubbed stagflation. Europe and Japan, heavily dependent on oil imports, resorted to bicycles and mass transit to reduce their energy needs, as well as intense development of nuclear energy.

In the decade after the first oil shock, OPEC countries such as Saudi Arabia deposited their profits in international banks, particularly in the United States, which in turn reinvested these deposits as loans that governments around the world used to finance development. This money was known as **petrodollars**. In this economic cycle, consumers around the world paid higher prices for fuel, which generated profits for oil exporters, who invested the profits in large banks. In turn, these banks loaned this capital out to foreign governments. Many industrializing countries faced both high energy costs and heavy debts amassed through petrodollar loans.

In the United States, as stagflation and the 1979 second oil shock fueled inflation, the Federal Reserve Bank raised interest rates. Increased interest rates in the United States made it more expensive to borrow money, which slowed economic activity and led to an economic recession. The recession diminished consumer demand for goods, which reduced inflation. But the United States was not the only country to experience this recession: countries that exported to the United States faced reduced demand for their goods, and countries that borrowed from U.S. banks found that the interest on their debts increased as well. In industrializing nations the rapid increase in interest on their heavy debts became a crippling burden, triggering a global crisis. Countries facing soaring debts and interest rates became dependent on U.S. assistance to restructure unsustainable loans, allowing the U.S.

Organization of the Petroleum Exporting Countries (OPEC) A cartel formed in 1960 by oil-exporting countries designed to coordinate oil production and raise prices, giving those countries greater capacity for economic development and greater leverage in world affairs.

petrodollars The global recirculation by international banks of profits from the higher price of oil following the 1973 OPEC oil embargo.

neoliberalism A return beginning in the 1980s to policies intended to promote free markets and the free circulation of capital across national borders.

Washington Consensus Policies restricting public spending, lowering import barriers, privatizing state enterprises, and deregulating markets in response to the 1980s debt crisis in Latin America.

government to dictate terms that imposed neoliberal free-market reforms.

Beginning in the 1980s neoliberal policies increasingly shaped the world economy. **Neoliberalism** promoted free-market policies and the free circulation of capital across national borders. Debtor countries needed to continue to borrow in order to pay the interest on the debts they held, and their ability to secure loans now depended on their adherence to a set of liberal principles known as the **Washington Consensus**: policies that restricted public spending, lowered import barriers, privatized state enterprises, and deregulated markets.

The forces unleashed by the Yom Kippur War and the OPEC oil embargo of 1973 at first tipped the scale in favor of less industrialized nations, but by the 1980s the scale had swung back as debt and liberalization returned power to the most economically powerful countries, in particular the United States. The experiences of Mexico and Nigeria reflect the effects of the boom-and-bust cycle ignited by the oil embargo. In both cases, the oil boom of the 1970s fueled long-standing projects for development and industrialization. But as boom turned to bust, both countries were left with enduring challenges: ethnic and religious divisions continued to undermine Nigeria, while Mexico's one-party state struggled to retain power as it yielded to liberalizing pressure from the United States.

Mexico Under the PRI

By the 1970s Mexico's Institutional Revolutionary Party (PRI) had been in power since the revolution. PRI candidates held nearly every public office. The PRI controlled both labor unions and federations of businessmen. More than a party, it was a vast system of patronage. It was also the party of land reform, universal public education, industrialization, and state ownership of the country's oil reserves. Mexico's road from economic nationalism to the liberal reforms of the 1970s and 1980s is also the story of the PRI.

In the aftermath of the 1968 Tlatelolco massacre, the PRI chose and elected as president populist Luis Echeverría, who sought to reclaim the mantle of revolutionary reform by nationalizing utilities and increasing social spending. He and his successor, José López Portillo, embarked on development projects financed through projected future earnings of the state oil monopoly PEMEX. Amid the decline of oil prices during the global recession, in 1982 the Mexican government stopped payments on its foreign debt, nationalized the banks, and steeply devalued the peso.

The PRI was further undermined by its inept and corrupt response to a devastating earthquake that struck Mexico City in 1986. Two years later the PRI faced its first real presidential election challenge. Cuauhtémoc

The Power of the PRI A lottery board game with the Mexican Institutional Revolutionary Party (PRI) logo in the top left corner indicates its widespread presence in everyday Mexican life. (Courtesy, MODO, Museo del Objeto del Objeto, Mexico City)

(kwow-TAY-mokh) Cárdenas, who was the son of populist Lázaro Cárdenas and was named after the last Aztec ruler, ran against PRI candidate Carlos Salinas de Gortari. On election night, as the vote counting favored Cárdenas, the government declared that the computers tabulating the votes had crashed and declared Salinas the winner. The PRI-controlled congress ordered the ballots burned afterward.

As Mexican leaders found themselves hemmed in by the debt crisis, they were compelled to embrace the Washington Consensus, which meant restricted spending, opening trade borders, and privatization. They abandoned the economic nationalism that had driven development, and negotiated a free-trade agreement with the United States and Canada, the North American Free Trade Agreement (NAFTA), which went into effect in 1994.

Nigeria, Africa's Giant

Nigeria's boom-and-bust oil economy aggravated the challenges of nation building after independence. The British imposed the name "Nigeria" on a region of many ancient kingdoms and hundreds of ethnic groups (see Map 31.5, page 939). After the country gained independence from Britain in 1960, Nigeria's key constitutional question was the relationship between the central government and its ethnically distinct regions. Under the federal system created after independence, each region had a dominant ethnic group and a corresponding political party. After independence Nigeria's ethnic rivalries intensified, and in 1967 they erupted in the Biafran war in which the Igbo ethnic group in southeastern Nigeria fought unsuccessfully to form a separate nation. The war lasted three years and resulted in famine that left millions dead.

The wealth generated by oil exports in the 1970s had contradictory effects on Nigerian society. On one hand, a succession of military leaders who held power after a 1966 coup grew increasingly corrupt through-out the 1970s. When the dictator General Murtala Muhammad (1938–1976) sought to eradicate corruption, fellow officers assassinated him. On the other hand, oil wealth allowed the country to rebuild after the Biafran war. By the mid-1970s Nigeria had the largest middle and professional classes on the continent outside of South Africa. Nigeria's oil boom in the 1970s resembled Mexico's experience: the expectation of future riches led to growing indebtedness, and when global demand and oil prices collapsed amid the global recession of the early 1980s, Nigeria faced a debt crisis.

Oil wealth allowed Nigeria to develop one innovative solution to its ethnic divisions: the construction of a modernist new capital, Abuja, modeled on Brazil's project in Brasília (see "Populism in Argentina and Brazil" in Chapter 31). Located in the center of the country at the confluence of major regional and ethnic boundaries, Abuja symbolized equal representation in government. Urban planning reflected both the reality of ethnic divisions and the objective of integration: residential areas were divided by ethnicity, but shopping and services were located between them to encourage commingling.

Oil in Nigeria Nigeria's oil has brought great profits to some, but poorer Nigerians have been excluded from the profits and have borne the costs of oil production. This fisherman displays his nets, which have been fouled by spilled oil. (George Ojodi/Bloomberg via Getty Images)

Except for an early period of civilian rule, Muslim army officers ruled Nigeria until 1998, when the dictator General Sani Abacha suddenly died. Nigerians adopted a new constitution in 1999, and that same year they voted in free elections and re-established civilian rule. Subsequent elections in 2007 marked the first civilian-to-civilian transfer of power. Ethnic tensions remained. Since 2000 ethnic riots and violence by the fundamentalist Islamic group Boko Haram have left thousands dead in the predominantly Muslim northern Nigerian states. Much of the violence can be attributed to conflicts between Muslims and non-Muslim groups that resented the introduction of shari'a (Islamic law) in the state of Zamfara in 1999. Since then, another eleven northern Nigerian states have adopted shari'a, spurring resentment from the non-Muslim populations in these states.

War and Revolution in the Middle East

How did war and revolution reshape the Middle East?

The 1973 Yom Kippur War had a lasting effect across the Middle East. Egypt and Syria had again been defeated, but Israelis also felt more vulnerable after the war. The oil embargo empowered oil-exporting nations like Saudi Arabia, Libya, and Iraq. The Middle East faced deepening divisions, which added to the conflict between Israel and its neighbors. The region was reshaped by the increasing wealth of oil producers relative to other Arab states. Rising Islamic militancy led to revolution in Iran, as well as religious challenges to the rule of secular, modernizing dictatorships in countries like Egypt.

The Palestinian-Israeli Conflict

After the 1973 war, the United States intensified efforts to mediate a resolution to conflicts in the Middle East. Peacemaking efforts by U.S. president Jimmy Carter led to the 1978 Camp David Accords, which normalized relations between Israel and its neighbors Egypt and Jordan. With the prospect of border wars between Israel and its neighbors diminished, political attention turned to the conflict between Israel and Palestinian nationalist organizations. Tensions between Syria and Israel shifted from their border into Lebanon, where Syria backed the militia Hezbollah, or Party of God. Hezbollah condemned the 1978 and 1982 Israeli invasions of Lebanon aimed at eradicating the Palestine Liberation Organization's control of southern Lebanon, and had as one of its stated objectives the complete destruction of the state of Israel.

In 1987 young Palestinians in the occupied territories of the Gaza Strip and the West Bank began the **intifada**, a prolonged campaign of civil disobedience against Israeli soldiers. Inspired increasingly by Islamic fundamentalists, the Palestinian uprising eventually posed a serious challenge not only to Israel but also to the secular Palestine Liberation Organization (PLO), long led from abroad by Yasir Arafat. The result was an unexpected and mutually beneficial agreement in 1993 between Israel and the PLO. Israel agreed to recognize Arafat's organization and start a peace process that granted Palestinian self-rule in Gaza and called for self-rule throughout the West Bank in five years. In return, Arafat renounced violence and abandoned the demand that Israel must withdraw from all land occupied in the 1967 war.

The peace process increasingly divided Israel. In 1995 a right-wing Jewish extremist assassinated Prime Minister Yitzhak Rabin. In 1996 a coalition of opposition parties won a slender majority, charging the Palestinian leadership with condoning anti-Jewish violence. The new Israeli government limited Palestinian self-rule and expanded Jewish settlements in the West Bank. On the Palestinian side, dissatisfaction with the peace process grew. Between 1993 and 2000 the number of Jewish settlers in the West Bank doubled to two hundred thousand, and Palestinian per capita income declined by 20 to 25 percent.

Failed negotiations between Arafat and Israel in 2000 unleashed an explosion of violence between Israelis and Palestinians known as the Second Intifada. In 2003 the Israeli government began to build a barrier around the West Bank, which met with opposition from Israelis and Palestinians alike.

The death of Yasir Arafat, the PLO's long-time leader, in November 2004 marked a turning point in the Israeli-Palestinian conflict. Mahmoud Abbas, Arafat's pragmatic successor, found little room for negotiation. In January 2006 Hamas, a Sunni Muslim political party, won 72 of the 136 seats in the Palestinian legislature, seizing control from Abbas and the PLO. Considered by Israel to be a terrorist organization, Hamas had gained widespread support from many Palestinians for the welfare programs it established in the West Bank and Gaza Strip.

Immediately after the Hamas victory, Israel, the United States, and the European Union suspended aid to the Palestinian Authority, the governing body of the West Bank and Gaza Strip established by the 1994 peace agreement. Since then, economic and humanitarian conditions for Palestinians living in the Gaza Strip have deteriorated. In 2007 Hamas, a political organization committed to building an Islamic state in

intifada Beginning in 1987, a prolonged campaign of civil disobedience by Palestinian youth against Israeli soldiers; the Arabic word *intifada* means "shaking off."

Israel's Wall of Separation This wall, shown under construction in 2006, blocks off a Palestinian refugee camp in Arab East Jerusalem, limiting the camp inhabitants' access to the city they call home. (AWAD/Getty Images)

the area now composed of Israel, Gaza, and the West Bank, assumed control of the Gaza Strip, deepening political divisions in Palestinian territory. In 2010, 63 percent of the 1.5 million citizens of Gaza lived below the United Nations–defined poverty line.

Egypt: Arab World Leader

From the time of Gamal Nasser's seizure of power in 1956 to the mid-1970s, Egypt, due to its large military, its anti-imperialist rhetoric, and its support for Arab unity, was recognized as the leader of the Arab world. In 1978 Egypt's president, Anwar Sadat (1918–1981), negotiated a peace settlement with Israel known as the Camp David Accords. Though Egypt gained the return of the Sinai Peninsula from Israel, some Arab leaders denounced Sadat's initiative as treason.

After Sadat was assassinated by religious radicals in 1981, Egyptian relations with Israel deteriorated, but Egypt and Israel maintained their fragile peace as Sadat's successor, Hosni Mubarak, took office. Mubarak remained a consistent supporter of Israel and a mediator between Israel and the Arab world. In return for helping to stabilize the region, the United States gave Egypt billions of dollars in development, humanitar-

ian, and military aid. Domestically, this aid failed to yield economic development, and Mubarak ruled with an increasingly dictatorial hand. Many of the government's critics charged that massive fraud and corruption funneled Egypt's wealth to a privileged few. Over 40 percent of Egyptians lived in poverty.

Under Mubarak's thirty-year regime, an emergency law that had been in place since 1967 legalized censorship, suspended limited freedom of expression and assembly, allowed for the establishment of a special security court, and gave the government the right to arrest people without charge and detain prisoners indefinitely. Mubarak used the emergency law to create a wholly separate justice system in order to silence opposition and repress anyone perceived as a threat to his rule. Demonstrations, political organizations, and even financial donations that were not approved by the government were banned under the law. Thousands of people were arrested.

In December 2010 demonstrations broke out in Tunisia against the twenty-three-year authoritarian rule of President Zine Ben Ali, leading to his downfall in January 2011. This populist revolt soon spread across North Africa and the Middle East, including to the streets of Cairo and other cities in Egypt as

Egyptians of all ages united in revolt against Mubarak's dictatorial rule. After three weeks of growing demonstrations, coordinated through Facebook, Twitter, and other communications networks, Mubarak stepped down as president in 2011 and was arrested soon after. Libya, located between Tunisia and Egypt, also witnessed an uprising against its dictatorial leader of forty-two years, Muammar Gaddafi. Gaddafi struggled violently to remain in power, but was deposed and killed amid European and U.S. air strikes. That same year, a lengthy and intense civil war erupted in Syria, pitting opponents of ruler Bashar al-Assad against an army equipped and trained to oppose Israel.

The "Arab Spring" uprisings that swept the Middle East shook a political order that had rested in the hands of the armed forces and pursued secular, nationalist objectives. The deposed leaders were the ideological descendants of Nasser, though their regimes had come to rely more on force than on modernizing social reform. The reaction against these regimes was often religious and culturally conservative. The political transitions resulting from this upheaval tended to pit secular and religious factions against each other amid debates over the nature of government and social change. Among the countries where regimes were brought down by Arab Spring protesters, Egypt alone reversed course, returning to rule by the secular armed forces under the leadership of General Abdel Fattah el-Sisi.

Revolution and War in Iran and Iraq

In oil-rich Iran foreign powers competed for political influence in the decades after the Second World War, and the influence of the United States in particular helped trigger a revolutionary backlash. In 1953 Iran's prime minister, Muhammad Mossadegh (MOH-sah-dehk) (1882–1967), tried to nationalize the British-owned Anglo-Iranian Oil Company, forcing the pro-Western shah Muhammad Reza Pahlavi (r. 1941–1979) to flee to Europe. Mossadegh's victory was short-lived. Loyal army officers, with the help of the American CIA, quickly restored the shah to his throne.

Pahlavi set out to build a powerful modern nation to ensure his rule, and Iran's gigantic oil revenues provided the necessary cash. The shah pursued land reform, secular education, and increased power for the central government. Modernization was accompanied by corruption and dictatorship. The result was a violent reaction against secular values: an Islamic revolution in 1979 aimed at infusing Islamic principles into all aspects of personal and public life. Led by the cleric Ayatollah Ruholla Khomeini, the fundamentalists deposed the shah and tried to build their vision of a true Islamic state.

Iran's revolution frightened its neighbors. Iraq, especially, feared that Iran—a nation of Shi'ite (SHEE-ight) Muslims—would succeed in getting Iraq's Shi'ite majority to revolt against its Sunni leaders (Map 32.1). In September 1980 Iraq's ruler, Ba'ath Party leader Saddam Hussein (1937–2006), launched a surprise attack against Iran. With their enormous oil revenues and powerful armed forces, Iran and Iraq—Persians and Arabs, Islamists and nationalists—clashed in an eight-year conflict that killed hundreds of thousands of soldiers on both sides before ending in a modest victory for Iran in 1988.

In 1990, saddled with the costs of war, Hussein commanded an invasion of oil-rich Kuwait and proclaimed its annexation to Iraq. To Hussein's surprise, his troops were driven out of Kuwait by an American-led, United Nations–sanctioned military coalition, which included Arab forces from Egypt, Syria, and Saudi Arabia. The United Nations Security Council imposed economic sanctions on Iraq as soon as it invaded Kuwait, and these sanctions continued after the 1990–1991 Persian Gulf War, to force Iraq to destroy its stockpiles of chemical and biological weapons under United Nations supervision. Alleging that Iraq still had such weapons, the United States led an invasion of Iraq in 2003 that overthrew Saddam Hussein's regime. The invasion led to the Second Persian Gulf War, which involved a lengthy U.S. occupation and a violent insurgency against U.S. military forces, which remained in Iraq until 2011.

As secular Iraq staggered, Iran's revolutionary regime seemed to moderate. Executive power in Iran was divided between a Supreme Leader and twelve-member Guardian Council selected by high Islamic clerics, and a popularly elected president and parliament. After reformist leaders pressed for relaxation of strict Islamic decrees, the Supreme Leader, controlling the army and the courts, vetoed the reforms and jailed some of the religious leadership's most vocal opponents, creating a context for the election of conservative populist Mahmoud Ahmadinejad (ahh-MAH-deen-eh-jahd) (b. 1956).

Ahmadinejad engaged in brinksmanship over the development of a nuclear weapons program, called for Israel's destruction, and backed the Hamas Party in the Gaza Strip and Hezbollah in Lebanon. He won re-election in 2009 after a bitterly contested challenge from moderates. The government suppressed a "green revolution" of protests that echoed the Arab Spring. In 2013 opposition groups came together to support the election of Hassan Rouhani, a centrist cleric who promised civil rights reforms. In 2015 Rouhani reached an agreement with a group of world powers led by the United States to freeze the country's nuclear program in return for the lifting of economic sanctions that had sapped Iran's economy.

MAPPING THE PAST

MAP 32.1 Abrahamic Religions in the Middle East and Surrounding Regions Islam, Judaism, and Christianity, which all trace their origins back to the patriarch Abraham, have significant populations in the Middle East. Since the 1979 Iranian revolution, Shi'ites throughout the region have become more vocal in their demands for equality and power. One of the largest stateless ethnic groups, the Kurds, who follow various religions, has become a major player in the politics of the region, especially in Iraq and Turkey, where the group seeks Kurdish independence.

ANALYZING THE MAP Which religion dominates? Where are the largest concentrations of Jews and Christians in the Middle East located?

CONNECTIONS How have divisions between Shi'ite and Sunni Muslims contributed to war in the region?

Latin America: Dictatorship, Debt, and Democratization

What effect did the Cold War and debt crisis have on Latin America?

After the Cuban Revolution in 1959, the United States financed and armed military dictatorships to suppress any dissent that might lead to communism and to secure U.S. influence in the region. Many elected governments were toppled in military coups that brought right-wing military dictatorships to power with U.S. military and financial support.

Civil Wars in Central America

Central America experienced the greatest violence in Latin America during the Cold War. In the second half of the twentieth century reformers in Central America sought economic development that was less dependent on the United States and U.S. corporations, and groups of peasants and urban workers began to press for political rights and improved living standards. Through the lens of the Cold War, Central American conservatives and the U.S. government saw these nationalists, peasants, and workers as Communists who should be suppressed. In turn, many workers and peasants radicalized and formed Marxist revolutionary movements. The result of this conflict, and of U.S. support for right-wing governments, officers, and paramilitary groups, was hundreds of thousands of deaths.

In Guatemala, after reformist president Jacobo Arbenz was deposed in 1954 by a military coup organized by the CIA, subsequent Guatemalan leaders, backed by the U.S. government, violently suppressed peasant movements, killing over two hundred thousand mostly indigenous people. In 2013 former dictator José Efraín Ríos Montt was convicted of genocide against Maya communities, though the Guatemalan Constitutional Court annulled the conviction.

El Salvador and Nicaragua, too, faced civil wars. In 1979 the Sandinista movement overthrew dictator Anastasio Somoza Debayle in Nicaragua. The Sandinistas, who conducted a revolutionary transformation of Nicaragua inspired by Communist rule in Cuba, were undermined by war with a U.S.-trained and U.S.-financed insurgent army called the Contras. In El Salvador a right-wing death squad killed Archbishop Oscar Romero in 1980 for speaking out against their violence.

U.S. policies that encouraged one faction to fight against the other deepened political instability and repression and intensified these civil wars. Acting against U.S. wishes, Costa Rican president Oscar Arias mediated peace talks in 1986 among the warring factions in Nicaragua, El Salvador, and Guatemala, which ended the wars and initiated open elections in each country, with former armed rivals competing instead at the ballot box. Peace did not bring prosperity, and in the decades following the end of the civil wars both poverty and violence have remained intense, prompting many Central Americans to seek opportunity in Mexico and the United States.

Boom and Bust in Chile

In the 1960s Chilean voters pushed for greater social reforms, culminating in the election of the Marxist candidate Salvador Allende (ah-YEHN-day) as president in 1970. Allende redistributed land and nationalized foreign businesses, including the country's vast copper mines, drawing fiery opposition from conservative Chileans, foreign businesses, and the U.S. government. Allende used mining revenue to pay for housing, education, health care, and other social welfare projects. U.S. president Richard Nixon created a clandestine task force to organize an "invisible blockade" to disrupt the Chilean economy by withholding economic aid and quietly instructing U.S. companies not to trade with or invest in Chile. Nixon instructed his task force to "make [Chile's] economy scream."[2]

In 1973 Chile's armed forces deposed Allende, who killed himself when the military stormed the presidential palace. A **junta**, or council of commanders of the branches of the armed forces, took power. Its leader, General Augusto Pinochet (peen-oh-CHEHT) (1915–2006), instituted radical economic reforms, giving neoliberal economists a free hand to conduct what they

Genocide in Guatemala's Civil War The United Nations declared the systematic killing of indigenous Guatemalans during the country's civil war an act of genocide. In recent years investigators have worked to identify victims of the government's violence, such as six people who disappeared in 1982, whose remains have been returned to their community for burial. (Reuters/Newscom)

junta A government headed by a council of commanders of the branches of the armed forces.

called "shock treatment" to remake Chile as a free-market economy. Schools, health care, pensions, and public services were turned over to private companies. Regulatory protections for industry were slashed, and land was concentrated into the hands of large agricultural corporations. The U.S. government lavished Pinochet with economic aid.

The reforms created a boom-and-bust cycle in which Chile became especially vulnerable to global economic changes. At its peak, Chile's economy grew at 8 percent per year. The costs of the reforms were just as intense. Income inequality soared: a handful of Chileans tied to big business conglomerates and banks made fortunes, while workers faced job loss and an increasing cost of living. In 1975 the implementation of reforms that cut social programs and caused mass unemployment left half of the country's children malnourished. The 1982 recession in Chile put one-third of Chileans out of work.

Under Pinochet, thousands of Chileans disappeared, and tens of thousands were tortured. These abuses brought international condemnation and resistance within Chile. Women who had lost relatives gathered under the protection of the Catholic Church and embroidered quilts known as *arpilleras*, rendering images of their missing relatives or experiences with repression. Catholic leaders used the church's privileged position to investigate human rights abuses, uncovering mass graves that served as proof of the dictatorship's violence.

Amid the excesses of Pinochet's dictatorship, opponents and even many allies looked for ways to curb his power and find the path for redemocratization. After the 1982 economic crisis, businessmen joined opposition groups such as the Catholic Church to press for liberalization. These groups formed a coalition called Concertación, which proposed a return to democracy that maintained the major elements of free-market reforms. Concertación called on Chileans to vote "NO" in a 1988 plebiscite on whether Pinochet would remain in power. The "NO" vote won, and Chile held its first democratic elections in two decades.

The opposition alliance in Chile resembled many other alliances around the world that sought transitions from authoritarian rule: political opponents who advocated for human rights joined forces with business groups that sought markets in order to produce a post-dictatorship democracy founded on free-market principles and support for human rights.

The Dirty War in Argentina

The Argentine military intervened repeatedly in politics for decades after it deposed populist Juan Perón in 1955 (see "Populism in Argentina and Brazil" in Chapter 31). By 1973 the armed forces conceded that their efforts to erase Perón's legacy — to "de-Perónize" the country — had failed. They allowed Perón to return, and he was again elected president, with his wife Isabelita, a political novice, as vice president. Soon after the election, Juan Perón died. Isabelita Perón, the first woman to become president in Latin America, faced daunting circumstances: Marxist groups such as the Montoneros waged a guerrilla war against the regime, while the armed forces and death squads waged war on them.

In March 1976 a military junta took power and announced a Process of National Reorganization. Influenced by French military theorists who had been stung by their defeats in guerrilla wars in Vietnam and Algeria, the generals waged a "dirty war," seeking to kill and "disappear" people whom they considered a destructive "cancer" on the nation. Between fourteen and thirty thousand Argentines perished at the hands of the armed forces during the dirty war.

A handful of mothers whose children had disappeared began appearing in the Plaza de Mayo in front of the presidential palace holding pictures of their missing children and carrying signs reading "Where are they?" A growing organization of the Mothers of the Plaza de Mayo was soon joined by the Grandmothers, who demanded the whereabouts of children born to women who were detained and disappeared while pregnant. These mothers were only kept alive until they gave birth. Their children were placed with adoptive families tied to the police or armed forces. Unlike in Chile and Brazil, in Argentina senior Catholic clergy did not advocate for human rights or the protection of dissidents. Instead Argentine bishops praised the coup and defended the military regime until it ended in 1983.

In 1982, emboldened by its success in eradicating its opposition, the Argentine junta occupied a set of islands off its southern coast that were claimed by Britain. Known in Britain as the Falklands and in Argentina as the Malvinas, the islands were home to a small British settlement. Britain resisted the invasion, and the Falklands/Malvinas War resulted in a humiliating defeat for the Argentine junta. After the war the junta abruptly called for elections, and a civilian president took office in 1983.

The new president, Raúl Alfonsín, faced a debt crisis similar to Mexico's. He also struggled to find justice for the crimes committed by the junta. Prosecution and conviction of the junta leaders created a backlash in the armed forces: mid-ranking officers revolted out of fear that they, too, would be prosecuted, and they forced the government to halt prosecutions. Trapped by the economic and political crises, Alfonsín left office early. His successor, Carlos Menem, tried a different approach. Menem pardoned the junta members and embarked on free-market reforms, privatizing businesses and utilities and reducing trade barriers. Investment flooded in, and Argentina seemingly put the past to rest.

The Mothers of the Plaza de Mayo In a protest in Buenos Aires, mothers and grandmothers demand information about their children and grandchildren who were "disappeared" by the Argentine military junta. (Eduardo Di Baia/AP Photo/AP Images)

As the capacity to attract foreign investment through privatization ran out by the end of the century, Argentina faced economic crisis again. In 2001, amid a run on banks and a collapse of the Argentine peso, the country had five different presidents in a single month. Eventually, the economy stabilized during the presidency of Néstor Kirchner, succeeded by his wife, Cristina Fernández de Kirchner. Néstor Kirchner, who died in 2010 while Cristina Fernández de Kirchner was president, prosecuted those responsible for violence during the dirty war again, achieving convictions of not just the junta leaders but members of the armed forces and police who perpetrated human rights violations.

Development and Dictatorship in Brazil

Brazil's military dictatorship, in power since 1964, began with liberal reforms but moved to a nationalist project of industrialization and infrastructure development that resembled some of the prescriptions of dependency theorists: increased state control of industry, restrictions on imports, and heavy investments in infrastructure. They initially achieved annual growth rates averaging 11 percent between 1968 and 1973. This growth depended on cheap imported oil and harsh political repression. When the oil embargo threatened growth, the generals borrowed heavily from abroad to subsidize fuel costs and conducted costly alternative energy projects to substitute oil with hydroelectric dams and ethanol made from sugarcane.

The Brazilian cycle of borrowing petrodollars to subsidize oil imports and development projects was ruinous for the country. By the end of the 1970s Brazil had the largest foreign debt in the developing world. When the second oil shock hit in 1979 and the U.S. government raised interest rates, making Brazil's dollar-dominated debt more expensive to manage, the country entered what became known as a "lost decade" of recession and inflation. Many workers earned less in 1989 than they had in 1980.

The economic crisis set the tone for a transition to democracy: as the generals made painful cuts to public services and as Brazilians faced soaring inflation and recession, the public overwhelmingly turned against military rule and supported redemocratization. When the first civilian president took office in 1985, inflation stood at 235 percent per year and the foreign debt at $95 billion (compared to $3.2 billion when the military took power). Inflation peaked at 3,375 percent per year before being tamed by the introduction of a new currency linked to the U.S. dollar, coupled with high interest rates.

As in Chile, Brazil's transition to democracy was shaped by liberalization. Business groups, which had grown uneasy with the dictatorship's borrowing and central planning, joined forces with human rights advocates to return the "rule of law," rather than arbitrary rule by generals. The debt left behind by Brazil's military leaders drove liberal economic reforms. To sustain its debt payments, the Brazilian government accepted the Washington Consensus, reducing public spending and opening the economy to imports and foreign investment. Neoliberal reforms included privatizing state enterprises, reducing protections for domestic industry against foreign competition, and keeping interest rates high to control inflation. Inflation remained low, but Brazilians faced a high cost of living, and high interest rates reduced lending to businesses and suppressed economic growth.

Resistance to White Rule in Southern Africa

How did white-minority rule end in southern Africa?

The racially segregated system of apartheid in South Africa was part of a region of white-minority rule that included Portuguese Angola and Mozambique, the government of Ian Smith in Rhodesia, and South African control of the former German colony of Namibia. Wars of independence in Angola and Mozambique eroded the buffer of neighboring white-minority governments around South Africa, and domestic and foreign pressure brought a political transition to majority rule in Namibia and South Africa in the 1990s.

Portuguese Decolonization and Rhodesia

At the end of World War II Portugal was the poorest country in western Europe and was ruled by a dictatorship, but it still claimed an immense overseas empire that included Angola, Mozambique, Guinea-Bissau, and Cape Verde. Since the 1920s Portuguese dictator António Salazar (1889–1970) had relied on forced labor in Angola's diamond mines to finance his regime. To alleviate poverty in Portugal, Salazar also promoted colonial settlement in Angola and Mozambique, where the white population rose from seventy thousand in 1940 to over five hundred thousand in 1970.

Salazar was determined to resist decolonization, insisting that Portuguese territories were "overseas provinces," whose status he compared to Alaska and Hawaii's relationship to the United States. Without the ability to negotiate decolonization, nationalists in the colonies resorted to armed insurrections. By the early 1970s independence movements in Cape Verde, Guinea-Bissau, and Mozambique fought guerrilla wars against the Portuguese army and colonial militias. The human toll was immense. To stop the wars Portuguese officers returning from the colonies overthrew Portugal's government in 1974. Guinea-Bissau and Cape Verde became independent that same year, Angola and Mozambique a year later. The nationalist movements that took power were all Marxist. Their radicalism was a product of their long struggle against oppression, inequality, and lack of access to their countries' resources.

The end of colonialism in Angola and Mozambique shifted the political landscape of southern Africa. Mozambique helped rebels fighting white-minority rule in Rhodesia, while the South African government saw independent Angola as a threat to apartheid and to its control over Namibia. The bloc of white-minority rule had been shattered. But after more than a decade of war for independence, neither Angola nor Mozambique would soon find peace.

The new government of Mozambique faced a guerrilla movement financed by Rhodesia. As Angola became independent, it faced immediate invasions from Zaire (encouraged by the United States) and South Africa. The new president of Angola, Agostinho Neto (nay-TOH) (1922–1978), requested military aid from Cuba, which airlifted troops that repelled both invasions and kept the regime in place. Until the late 1980s tens of thousands of Cuban troops faced off with the South African Defense Force and mercenary armies to defend the government of Angola.

In the British colony of Rhodesia white settlers, a small minority of the population, declared independence on their own to avoid sharing power with the black majority. In 1965 they established a white-minority government under farmer and politician Ian Smith. The new Rhodesian state faced international condemnation for its treatment of black citizens, including the first economic sanctions imposed by the United Nations. The Rhodesian army and police dealt violently with black political activists who challenged white rule.

The Zimbabwe African People's Union (ZAPU) fought a guerrilla war against Rhodesia's white regime. Rebuffed by the United States and Britain, ZAPU turned to China and the Soviet Union for support. When Mozambique gained independence in 1974, its government allowed ZAPU and other guerrilla groups to use neighboring Mozambican territory as a staging ground to launch attacks on Rhodesia, making it impossible for Ian Smith's government to endure. Open elections were negotiated, and these were easily won in 1979 by ZAPU leader Robert Mugabe. The following year, the Mugabe government renamed the newly independent country Zimbabwe after an ancient city-state that predated colonial rule.

South Africa Under Apartheid

In 1948 the ruling South African National Party created a racist and segregationist system of discrimination known as **apartheid**, meaning "apartness" or "separation." The population was legally divided into racial groups: whites, blacks, Asians, and racially mixed "coloureds." Good jobs in the cities were reserved for whites, who lived in luxurious modern central neighborhoods. Blacks were restricted to precarious outlying townships plagued by poverty, crime, and mistreatment from white policemen.

In the 1950s black South Africans and their allies mounted peaceful protests. A turning point came in 1960, when police in the township of Sharpeville fired at demonstrators and killed sixty-nine black protesters. The main black political organization—the **African National Congress (ANC)**—was outlawed but continued in exile. Other ANC members, led by a young lawyer, Nelson Mandela (1918–2013), stayed in South Africa to mount armed resistance. In 1962 Mandela was captured, tried for treason, and sentenced to life imprisonment. (See "Thinking Like a Historian: The Struggle for Freedom in South Africa," page 968.)

In the 1970s the South African government fell into the hands of "securocrats," military and intelligence officers who adopted a policy known as the "total strategy," directing the state's resources into policing apartheid and dominating South Africa's neighbors by force. At the United Nations, African leaders denounced the South African government, and activists in countries around the world pressured their governments to impose economic sanctions against the South African regime. South Africa's white leaders responded with cosmetic reforms in 1984 to improve their international standing. The 3 million coloureds and the 1 million South Africans of Asian descent gained limited parliamentary representation, but no provision was made for any representation of the country's 22 million blacks.

The reforms provoked a backlash. In the segregated townships young black militants took to the streets, clashing with white security forces; these protests left five thousand dead and fifty thousand jailed without charges between 1985 and 1989. Across the Angolan border, South African troops fought escalating conflicts with Angolan, ANC, and Cuban forces. Mounting casualties and defeat in major battles shook white South Africans' confidence.

The Sharpeville Massacre In March 1960, South Africans flee the area around the Sharpeville police station, where police opened fire on protesters demonstrating against the apartheid policy of requiring blacks to carry pass books to restrict their movements. (World History Archive/Ann Ronan Collection/age-fotostock)

apartheid The system of racial segregation and discrimination that was supported by the Afrikaner government in South Africa.

African National Congress (ANC) The main black nationalist organization in South Africa, led by Nelson Mandela.

The Struggle for Freedom in South Africa

The movement to fight apartheid quickly went beyond South Africa's borders. In the 1950s and 1960s the government of India emerged as an outspoken critic, given the large population of Indian descent subject to apartheid in South Africa. Newly independent African and Asian nations also championed majority rule. In addition, movements against apartheid grew in Europe, the United States, the Caribbean, and Latin America. Consider the ways in which these sources define moral right and wrong in South Africa.

1 Nelson Mandela, opening statement at trial, 1964. In 1963 Nelson Mandela and several other ANC members were charged with sabotage and conspiracy and sentenced to life in prison. The passage below is taken from Mandela's opening statement in his 1964 trial. During his decades in prison, Mandela became one of the leading global symbols of the evils of apartheid.

■ At the outset, I want to say that the suggestion made by the state in its opening that the struggle in South Africa is under the influence of foreigners or communists is wholly incorrect. I have done whatever I did, both as an individual and as a leader of my people, because of my experience in South Africa and my own proudly felt African background, and not because of what any outsider might have said. . . .

Africans want to be paid a living wage. Africans want to perform work which they are capable of doing, and not work which the Government declares them to be capable of. We want to be allowed to live where we obtain work, and not be endorsed out of an area because we were not born there. We want to be allowed and not to be obliged to live in rented houses which we can never call our own. We want to be part of the general population, and not confined to living in our ghettoes. African men want to have their wives and children to live with them where they work, and not to be forced into an unnatural existence in men's hostels. Our women want to be with their men folk and not to be left permanently widowed in the reserves. We want to be allowed out after eleven o'clock at night and not to be confined to our rooms like little children. We want to be allowed to travel in our own country and to seek work where we want to, where we want to and not where the Labour Bureau tells us to. We want a just share in the whole of South Africa; we want security and a stake in society.

2 Mark Behr's character Marnus in *The Smell of Apples*, 1995. Mark Behr's novel *The Smell of Apples* describes eleven-year-old Marnus Erasmus's loss of faith in the midst of a dark betrayal by his father, a general in the South African Defense Force. This passage illustrates the mentality of many members of the white minority under apartheid.

■ Dad tells the General that the rest of the world is against South Africa because we have all the gold and diamonds and other minerals. . . . He says . . . at least we didn't kill off all our blacks like America did to the Red Indians and the Australians to the Aborigines. Dad says you can say a whole lot of things about the Afrikaners [white Dutch settlers], but no one can say we're dishonest. We don't hide our laws like the rest of the world.

Dad says one of the problems is that all the best blacks were taken away by the slave merchants. The blood that was left in Africa was the blood of the dumber blacks—that's why you won't find an educated black anywhere. Have you ever heard about a Bantu inventing something like a telephone or a wheel or an engine? No. Dad says it's because all the clever ones and the strong ones were shipped out of Africa to America. Now America has all the clever blacks and they think they can come and teach the Republic how to deal with ours. The rest of the world is stirring up our natives to make them think the Republic actually belongs to them. . . .

But America is just as stupid. With all their threats of not selling arms and ammunition to the Republic, they play right into the hands of the Communists. The other day, after twelve drunk blacks were killed by police at Western Deep Levels gold-mine, some countries said they were going to stop selling arms to South Africa. They . . . don't really understand the problems we face in this country. Dad says it doesn't matter that much what the rest of the world says, anyway.

ANALYZING THE EVIDENCE

1. According to Nelson Mandela in Source 1, what is wrong with South Africa? What needs to be done?
2. How do Mandela in Source 1 and Marnus, the boy in Mark Behr's novel, in Source 2 regard communism?
3. What do you think Behr wanted to convey in the passage in Source 2, which was written in the years after apartheid ended?
4. What kinds of symbolism do the posters in Sources 3 and 4 employ to motivate opposition to apartheid?

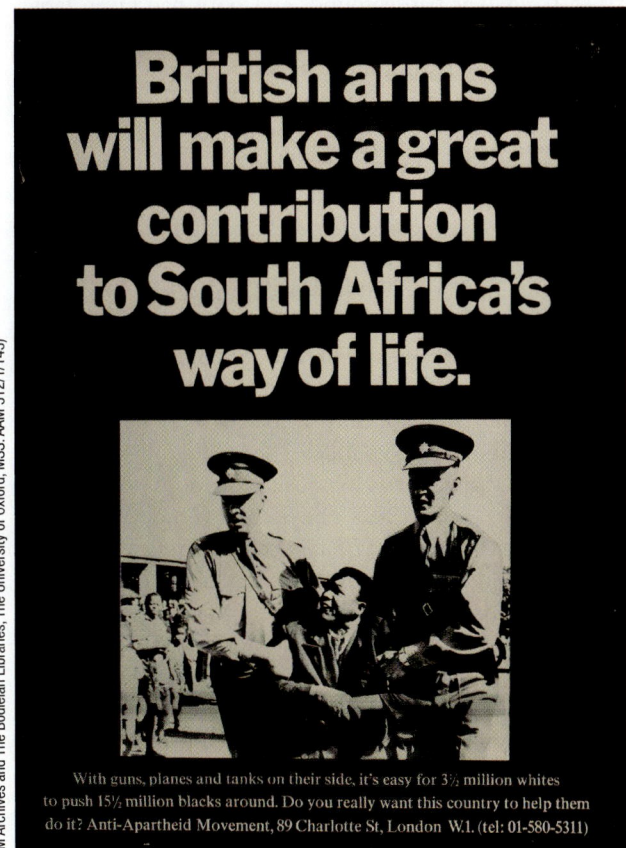

(AAM Archives and The Bodleian Libraries, The University of Oxford, MSS. AAM 512/1/143)

British arms will make a great contribution to South Africa's way of life.

With guns, planes and tanks on their side, it's easy for 3½ million whites to push 15½ million blacks around. Do you really want this country to help them do it? Anti-Apartheid Movement, 89 Charlotte St, London W.1. (tel: 01-580-5311)

3 **Poster from Britain's Anti-Apartheid Movement.** This poster was part of a campaign organized by Britain's Anti-Apartheid Movement, which began in the 1950s as an effort to persuade British consumers to boycott South African goods. Its agenda grew into calls for Britain to impose sanctions against the South African government.

(Pictures from History/CPA Media)

AFRICAN LIBERATION DAY May 20

12 noon
Malcolm X
Park
16th & Euclid N.W.
Wash. D.C.

· **Death to apartheid! Support the Zimbabwe Patriotic Front!**
· **Carter Vorster at it again, can't silence Biko nor the Wilmington Ten!**

4 **Poster announcing an anti-apartheid march in Washington, D.C., 1970s.** This poster for a 1970s protest links the anti-apartheid struggle to other movements for black liberation: it advocates for majority rule in Zimbabwe and for the release of the Wilmington Ten, a group of imprisoned activists who fought against racial discrimination in North Carolina.

PUTTING IT ALL TOGETHER

Using the sources above, along with what you have learned in class and in this chapter and Chapter 31, write a short essay that analyzes whether and how the anti-apartheid movement resembled other social or political movements.

Sources: (1) *I Am Prepared to Die: Nelson Mandela's Statement from the Dock at the Opening of the Defence Case in the Rivonia Trial*, April 20, 1964, nelsonmandela.org/content/page/speeches. Reprinted by permission of the Nelson Mandela Foundation; (2) Mark Behr, *The Smell of Apples* (New York: St. Martin's, 1995), pp. 66, 70.

Isolated politically, besieged by economic sanctions, and defeated on the battlefield, South African president Frederik W. de Klerk opened a dialogue with ANC leaders in 1989. He lifted the state of emergency imposed in 1985, legalized the ANC, and freed Mandela in February 1990. Mandela suspended the ANC's armed struggle and negotiated a 1991 agreement with de Klerk calling for universal suffrage and an end to apartheid legislation, which meant black-majority rule.

In May 1994 Mandela was elected president of South Africa by an overwhelming majority. Heading the new "government of national unity," which included de Klerk as vice president, Mandela along with the South African people set about building a multiracial democracy. The government established a Truth and Reconciliation Commission modeled on the commission impaneled in Chile to investigate abuses under Pinochet. The commission let black victims speak out, and it offered white perpetrators amnesty in return for fully confessing their crimes. Seeking to avoid white flight and to sustain the economy built through South Africa's industrialization, Mandela repudiated his Marxist beliefs and reassured domestic and foreign investors of his commitment to liberalization.

Political Change in Africa Since 1990

Democracy's rise in South Africa was part of a trend toward elected civilian rule that swept through sub-Saharan Africa after 1990. The end of the Cold War that followed the breakup of the Soviet Union in 1990 transformed Africa's relations with Russia and the United States. Both superpowers had treated Africa as a Cold War battleground, and both had given large-scale military and financial aid to their allies to undermine rivals. Communism's collapse in Europe brought an abrupt end to Communist aid to Russia's African clients. Since the world was no longer divided between allies of the United States and of the Soviet Union, U.S. support for pro-Western dictators, no matter how corrupt or repressive, declined as well. But the decrease in support for dictators left a power vacuum in which ethnic conflicts intensified, with often-disastrous results. For instance, in the early 1990s the United States cut off decades of support for the anticommunist General Mobutu Sese Seko (1930–1997), who seized power in 1965 in Zaire (the former Belgian Congo, renamed the Democratic Republic of the Congo in 1997) and looted the country. Opposition groups toppled the dying tyrant in 1997. The Second Congo War, a civil war that began in 1998 and continues, left more than 5 million dead over the next decade. Hundreds of thousands more have died in the years since, making it the world's deadliest conflict since World War II.

The agreement by national independence leaders across the continent to respect colonial borders prevented one kind of violence, but resulted in another. In countries whose national boundaries had been created by colonial powers irrespective of historic divisions, political parties were often based on ethnicity and kinship. The armed forces, too, were often dominated by a single ethnic group.

At times, ethnic strife boiled over into deep violence, such as the genocides of ethnic Hutus by Tutsis

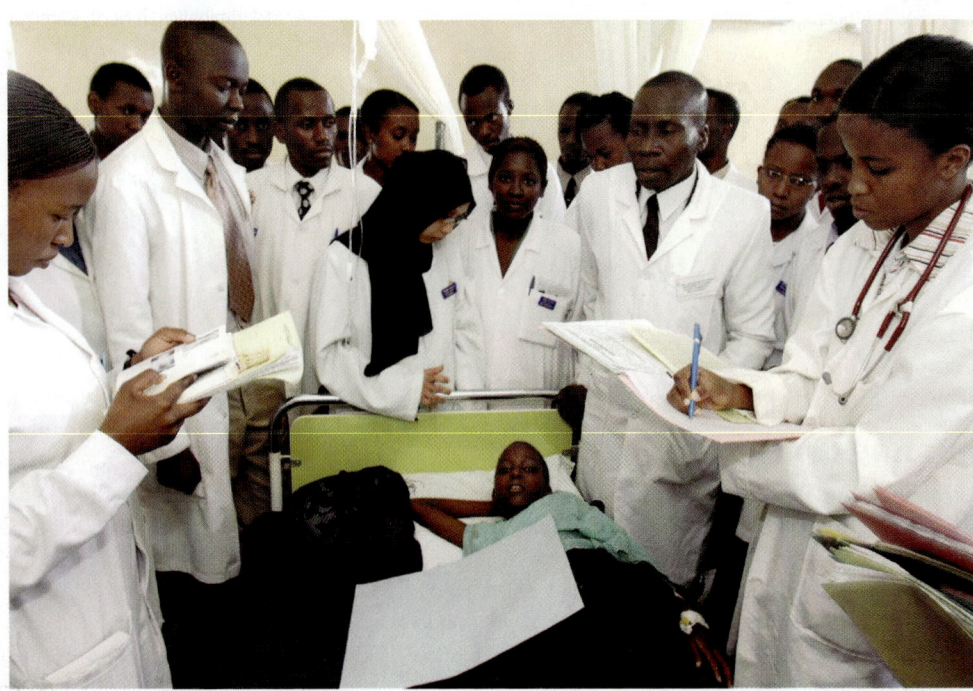

Medical Students in Kenya
Medical students make rounds at Moi University Hospital in Eldoret, Kenya. They are part of the growing professional classes in many African nations. (ullstein bild—CARO/Stefan Trappe/Granger, NYC—All rights reserved.)

in Burundi in 1972 and by Tutsis of Hutus in 1993 and 1994 in Rwanda, which left hundreds of thousands dead. In Kenya disputes about the legitimacy of the 2007 re-election of Mwai Kibaki left hundreds dead before the National Accord and Reconciliation Act in 2008 ended the violence. A test of the alternative to preserving national boundaries came amid efforts to ease tensions that had created famine and hardship in Sudan. In 2011, 98 percent of the electorate in southern Sudan voted to break away and form a new country, South Sudan. The early promise of peace after separation was challenged by increased ethnic and political violence in South Sudan.

Amid these conflicts, political and economic reform occurred in other African nations where years of mismanagement and repression had delegitimized one-party rule. Above all, the strength of the democratic opposition rested on a growing class of educated urban Africans. Postindependence governments expanded opportunities in education, especially higher education. In Cameroon, for example, the number of students graduating from the national university jumped from 213 in 1961 to 10,000 in 1982 and 41,000 in 1992.[3] The growing middle class of educated professionals chafed at the ostentatious privilege of tiny closed elites and pressed for political reforms that would democratize social and economic opportunities. Thus after 1990 sub-Saharan Africa accompanied the global trend toward liberalization and human rights.

Growth and Development in Asia

How have East and South Asian nations pursue economic development, and how have political regimes shaped those efforts?

China, Japan, and the countries that became known as the "Asian Tigers" (South Korea, Taiwan, Hong Kong, and Singapore) experienced fantastic economic growth in the last decades of the twentieth century. The Chinese Communist Party managed a transition in which it maintained tight political control amid liberalization and economic growth. Japan's economy stagnated in the 1990s and struggled to recover amid growing competition from its neighbors. In South Asia tensions between India and Pakistan persisted.

Japan's Economic Miracle and the Emergence of the "Asian Tigers"

Japan's postwar economic recovery, like Germany's, proceeded slowly at first. But during the Korean War, the Japanese economy took off and grew with spectacular speed. Between 1950 and 1970 Japan's economic growth averaged a breathtaking 10 percent a

year. By 1978 Japan had the second-largest economy in the world. In 1986 Japan's average per capita income exceeded that of the United States for the first time.

Japan's emergence as an economic superpower fascinated outsiders. Many Asians and Africans looked to Japan for the secrets of successful modernization, but some of Japan's Asian neighbors again feared Japanese exploitation. In the 1970s and 1980s some Americans and Europeans bitterly accused **"Japan, Inc."** of an unfair alliance between government and business and urged their own governments to retaliate.

In Japan's system of managed capitalism, the government protected its industry from foreign competition, decided which industries were important, and then made loans and encouraged mergers to create powerful firms in those industries. The government rewarded large corporations and encouraged them to develop extensive industrial and financial activities. Workers were hired for life, and employees' social lives revolved around the company. (Discrimination against women remained severe: their wages and job security were strikingly inferior to men's.) In the 1990s Japan's economy stagnated amid the bursting of a speculative bubble that crippled banks and led to record postwar unemployment as the country faced competition from industrializing neighbors in Asia. In the twenty-first century the return to growth remained elusive as Japan faced a decades-long crisis of deflation (a reduction of the value of goods and services that saps profits and increases debt burdens).

Japan's competition in Asia was intensified by the "Asian Tigers"—South Korea, Taiwan, Hong Kong, and Singapore—so named for their rapid economic development. In the early postwar years, South Korea and Taiwan were underdeveloped agrarian countries. They also had suffered from Japanese imperialism and from destructive civil wars with Communist foes.

Asian "Economic Tigers"

They pursued development through a similar series of reforms. First, land reform allowed small farmers to become competitive producers as well as consumers. Second, governments stimulated business through lending, import barriers, and control of labor. Third, nationalist leaders (Park Chung Hee in South Korea

---

"Japan, Inc." A nickname from the 1970s and 1980s used to describe what some considered the unfair relationship between Japan's business world and government.

and Jiang Jieshi in Taiwan) maintained stability at the expense of democracy. When Park was assassinated in 1979, South Korea faced an even more authoritarian regime until democracy was established at the end of the 1980s. By the late 1990s South Korea had one of the largest economies in the world, leading in shipbuilding and electronics.

In Singapore, Lee Kwan Yew (1923–2015), the prime minister who shepherded the island's independence from Britain in 1965 and held power until 1990, also pursued a modernization project that came at the cost of political dissent. This project made Singapore into an affluent banking and trade center linking markets in East Asia, the Middle East, Europe, and the United States.

In 1949, after Jiang Jieshi had fled to Taiwan with his Nationalist troops and around 2 million refugees, he re-established the Republic of China (ROC) in exile. Over the next fifty years Taiwan created one of the world's most industrialized economies, becoming a leader in electronic manufacturing and design. Mainland China continued to claim Taiwan, considering it part of "One China." Hong Kong, which was returned to Chinese control by Britain in 1997, became a Special Administrative Region (SAR), as did the former Portuguese colony Macau, under a "one country, two systems" formula of partial autonomy.

China's Economic Resurgence

Amid the Cultural Revolution of 1965–1969, Chairman Mao and the Red Guards mobilized the masses, shook up the Communist Party, and created greater social equality (see "The Communist Victory in China" in Chapter 31). But the Cultural Revolution also created chaos and a general crisis of confidence, especially in the cities. Intellectuals, technicians, and purged party officials launched a counterattack on the radicals and regained much of their influence by 1969. This shift opened the door to a limited but lasting reconciliation between China and the United States in 1972.

In the years following Mao's death in 1976, Chinese leader Deng Xiaoping (shee-ow-ping) (1904–1997) and his supporters initiated the "Four Modernizations": agriculture, industry, science and technology, and national defense. China's 800 million peasants experienced the greatest change from what Deng called China's "second revolution." Rigid collectivization had failed to provide the country with adequate food. Deng allowed peasants to farm in small family units rather than in large collectives and to "dare to be rich" by producing crops of their choice. Peasants responded enthusiastically, increasing food production by more than 50 percent by 1984.

The successful use of free markets in agriculture encouraged further experimentation. Foreign capitalists were allowed to open factories in southern China and to export their products around the world. Private enterprise was permitted in cities, where snack shops and other small businesses sprang up. China's Communist Party also drew on the business talent of "overseas" Chinese in Hong Kong and Taiwan who understood world markets and sought cheap labor. The Chinese economy grew rapidly between 1978 and 1987, and per capita income doubled in those years. Most large-scale industry remained state owned, however, and cultural change proceeded slowly.

Economic change was not accompanied by greater political openness. Pressures for democratization grew as Mao's health declined. After Mao's death, the People's Congress ratified a new constitution in 1978 that granted "Four Big Rights," which protected freedom of speech and political debate. This opening gave rise to popular political mobilization and debate, particularly in the form of the Democracy Wall Movement, in which citizens, first in Beijing and later in other cities, put up posters calling for political reforms. (See "Analyzing the Evidence: A Member of China's Red Guards on Democratic Reform," page 974.) The movement was suppressed in 1980. A new constitution enacted in 1982 removed references to the Four Big Rights, emphasizing economic development and reinforcing the political primacy of the Communist Party.

As the worldwide movement for political liberalization gained momentum, the government of China maintained restrictions on demonstrations and slowed economic reform. Inflation soared to more than 30 percent a year. The economic reversal, the continued lack of political freedom, and the conviction that Chinese society was becoming more corrupt led idealistic university students to spearhead demonstrations in 1989. (See "Analyzing the Evidence: Tiananmen Square," at right.)

More than a million people streamed into Beijing's central **Tiananmen Square** in support of the students' demands. The government declared martial law and ordered the army to clear the students. Masses of courageous citizens blocked the soldiers' entry into the city for two weeks, but in the early hours of June 4, 1989, tanks rolled into Tiananmen Square. At least seven hundred students died as a wave of repression, arrests, and executions descended on China. As communism fell in eastern Europe and the Soviet Union broke apart, China's rulers felt vindicated. They believed their action had preserved Communist power, prevented chaos, and demonstrated the limits of reform. People in China were not alone in pressing for democratization—popular protest met with repression in other Communist or military regimes, such as in Burma. (See "Global Viewpoints: Dissidents in Burma and China," page 977.)

Tiananmen Square The site of a Chinese student revolt in 1989 at which Communists imposed martial law and arrested, injured, or killed hundreds of students.

Tiananmen Square

The Tiananmen Square demonstrations of 1989 and their suppression by Chinese authorities are significant both for their impact on dissent in China and for the ways they reflected global patterns of protest. As in many countries, the protesters in Tiananmen Square were mainly students. They began gathering at Tiananmen Square in April 1989 for a series of demonstrations about different issues, all of which were ways of calling for greater political rights, such as freedom of speech and democratization.

The demonstrations occurred at Tiananmen Square both because it was a large and central public space in Beijing and because it was a location that was symbolically and politically important. Tiananmen Square was a historical site — the location of one of the gates to the Imperial City — and it was the stage of major political events such as Mao Zedong's public proclamation of the establishment of the People's Republic of China in 1949. The square was also the site of annual military parades and Mao's addresses to the Red Guards. Thus Tiananmen Square was a place where both state authority was projected and protests were performed.

(© Stuart Franklin/Magnum Photos)

In this photo taken on May 28, 1989, images and messages of the Chinese state compete with images created by protesters. The walls of the gate tower bear a portait of Mao, and the signs on each side read, "Long Live the People's Republic of China" and "Long Live the Great Unity of the World's Peoples." Before the walls, thousands of protesters gather, and at their center stands a 33-foot-tall statue, built by the students, named the *Goddess of Democracy*. Though it bears some resemblance to the U.S. Statue of Liberty, which draws on classical Greek imagery to express the idea of democracy, the *Goddess of Democracy* reflects the Socialist Realism style employed in the Soviet Union and China.

Unlike protests in eastern Europe and Latin America that resulted in liberalizing reforms, the Tiananmen Square protests were violently suppressed on June 3 and 4, 1989.

QUESTIONS FOR ANALYSIS

1. What competing political messages can you find in this image?
2. What do you think the statue symbolized for demonstrators in Tiananmen Square?
3. How does the backdrop of the fifteenth-century Imperial City gate relate to the messages of the state and of the protesters?

A Member of China's Red Guards on Democratic Reform

In the decades following the Cultural Revolution, China experienced repeated pressures for democratization such as the 1989 Tiananmen Square protests. The 1979 Democracy Wall Movement was one such effort that capitalized on a moment of Communist Party reform to push for political change. This account of the movement is by Fan Shen, who grew up in a military family during the Cultural Revolution and joined the Red Guards. He was sent to live in a peasant village at age fourteen and later worked in an aircraft factory, experiences that made him uneasy about the revolution. The Democracy Wall Movement began while he was a student at Lanzhou University in northwest China. After the movement was suppressed, Fan was posted to a teaching appointment in an industrial town, where, as everyone around him became ill from toxins in the water, he waited to become eligible for a passport to study in the United States.

■ The Democracy Wall Movement, which [the secret police] wanted me to spy on, started quietly in Beijing in 1979, like a hungry mosquito landing noiselessly on a content, unsuspecting pig. In January, to commemorate the late premier Zhou Enlai, . . . some people put out posters and wreaths on a stretch of wall in Xidan, a busy commercial district in Beijing. The brick wall, barely the length of a basketball court, attracted thousands of passers-by every day. The commemorative posters, however, had a political undertone from the beginning. The mourners, mostly young students and factory workers, cleverly played off of and expanded on the Communist Party's latest official policy—the "Four Modernizations"—to modernize industry, agriculture, the military, and science. The

posters suggested that China need[ed] modernization in a fifth area, democracy. The posters struck a chord in people's hearts. Within a few weeks the Democracy Wall became a nationwide movement. People began demanding free speech and free elections for student unions and trade unions.

Being fifteen hundred miles from the capital, Lanzhou University was slow to catch on to the democracy movement. But when it arrived, it exploded with a violent energy. To me, the spring of 1980 was almost a carbon copy of the spring of 1966 when the Cultural Revolution began. Hundreds of big letter posters appeared overnight on building walls, parades were held daily, and like the Red Guards, people soon separated into two opposing camps: the Official Election Committee headed by the Secretary of the Communist Party, and the Independent Student Election Committee headed by a lanky economics student, Song Pingtai. The latter's campaign headquarters was in a dormitory room, next to mine. Revolutions have a way of picking unlikely heroes. Few could have imagined that Song, a quiet and shy man, would be the hero who dared to run against a candidate picked by the Party.

When the Party consented to the demands of the Independent Student Committee to hold a debate before the election on campus—the first that anyone had experienced—the Democracy Movement became a euphoric festival. Perhaps because of my recent dealings with the secret police, I had a strong desire for political reform and I eagerly participated in Song's campaign. My roommates . . . also got involved. We wrote posters, printed handbills, and collected donations. The day before the debate, I spent the whole night writing a speech for Song. The next day, at the debate, our hero

---

China became politically Communist and economically capitalist. In 2001 China joined the World Trade Organization, completing its immersion in the liberal global economy. From 1978, when Deng Xiaoping began economic reforms, through 2012, the Chinese economy grew at an average annual rate of over 9 percent, and foreign trade at an average of 16 percent. Average per capita income in China doubled every ten years, and in March 2011 China replaced Japan as the world's second-largest economy, surpassed only by the United States. After 2012 China's economic growth slowed to near 7 percent—a high rate, but one that has strained the capacity of the government to pursue economic development and diminished Chinese imports. As China's economy became one of the

world's leading economic engines, its growth fueled global trade of commodities imported to China and manufactured goods exported around the world. In turn, the cooling of China's economy reduced demand for commodities, slowing growth from Asia to Africa and Latin America.

Development Versus Democracy in India and Pakistan

Jawaharlal Nehru's daughter, Indira Gandhi (no relation to Mohandas Gandhi) (1917–1984), became prime minister of India in 1966. She dominated Indian political life for a generation. In 1975 she subverted parliamentary democracy and proclaimed a state of emertrounced the Party candidate. Song won the election by a landslide, capturing seventy-eight percent of the student vote and becoming the first freely elected president of the Student Union.

A month later, he ran for the District People's Congress against another Party candidate, who was none other than [the university's party secretary]. The Party mobilized its members and campaigned hard. . . . But Song . . . again won handily. We were ecstatic. In May, we saw Song walk into the auditorium of the District People's Congress, and we could feel tremendous excitement and tension in the hall. All the gray heads of the Party delegates turned toward the door silently, as our man sauntered down the aisle in jeans and a blue jacket. "He is *The One*," we heard the gray heads say, and we knew what they meant. Song was the one who upset the tradition, the one not appointed by the Party, the one who was not one of them. There was anger among the roomful of tenured Party appointees. It was plain that to them the Democracy Movement had gone too far.

For five weeks, it was a wonderful spring. At the height of the euphoria, however, I had a nagging fear at the back of my mind that the Party would step in sooner or later and extinguish the flame of the free election because I knew how closely the secret police had been monitoring the democracy movement. But still I never expected the Party to put an end to the Democracy Movement so quickly and so brutally. Just three days after Song's triumphant march into the People's Congress, the police tore down all the democracy posters in the university and declared that the Independent Student Union was illegal and was banned. In Beijing and other cities, we soon heard, the police had arrested many activists of the movement.

"Another victory for the Democratic Dictatorship!" declared the headline of an editorial in the *People's Daily* a few days later. "The so-called Democracy Movement is actually an 'anti-revolutionary movement' aimed at under-mining the socialist dictatorship, and it has been mercilessly crushed." In just a few days, as all signs of the democracy movement disappeared, [the party secretary at the university] . . . resurfaced victoriously on campus and ordered a special two-week workshop for all students, to clear our minds of any thoughts of democracy.

"No one should doubt the Party's resolve," he said firmly to us on the first day of the workshop. "You young people often forget who brought liberation and freedom to China. You must remember that our freedom is socialist freedom, our democracy is socialist democracy, and they must be under the guidance of the Party. You must never forget that on top of democracy there is the Party. The Party hears the people and decides what's best for them. This is what the Great Leader [Mao] called democratic dictatorship. The Party will forgive most of you for what you have done as long as you confess your mistakes. But those who led the charge against the Party will be remembered and dealt with."

. . . All the leaders of the democracy movement were punished upon graduation two years later and were sent to the most remote regions. Song himself was sent to the Xinjiang Uighur Autonomous Region (China's Siberia), and none of us heard anything from him again.

QUESTIONS FOR ANALYSIS

1. What spaces did people take advantage of to challenge the Communist Party during the Democracy Wall Movement?
2. Why did Fan Shen see the protest movement as important despite the fact that it was suppressed?

Source: Fan Shen, *Gang of One: Memoirs of a Red Guard* (Lincoln: University of Nebraska Press, 2004), pp. 199–201. Reprinted by permission of the University of Nebraska Press. Copyright © 2004 by Fan Shen.

gency. Gandhi applied her expanded powers across a broad range of areas, including combating corruption, quelling labor unrest, and jailing political opponents. She also initiated a mass sterilization campaign to reduce population growth. More than 7 million men were forcibly sterilized in 1976. Many believed that Gandhi's emergency measures marked the end of liberal democracy, but in 1977 Gandhi called for free elections. She suffered a spectacular electoral defeat. Her successors fell to fighting among themselves, and in 1980 she returned to power in an equally stunning electoral victory.

Separatist ethnic nationalism plagued Indira Gandhi's last years in office. India remained a patchwork of religions, languages, and peoples, always threatening to further divide the country along ethnic or religious lines. Most notable were the 15 million Sikhs of the Punjab in northern India (see Map 31.2), with their own religion, distinctive culture, and aspirations for greater autonomy for the Punjab. By 1984 some Sikh radicals were fighting for independence. Gandhi cracked down and was assassinated by Sikhs in retaliation. Violence followed as Hindu mobs slaughtered over a thousand Sikhs throughout India.

One of Indira Gandhi's sons, Rajiv Gandhi, was elected prime minister in 1984. Rajiv Gandhi departed from his mother's and the Congress Party's socialism and prepared the way for Finance Minister Manmohan Singh to introduce market reforms, capitalist development, and Western technology and investment from

1991 onward. These reforms were successful, and since the 1990s India's economy has experienced rapid growth.

Though the Congress Party held power in India almost continuously after 1947, in the 1990s Hindu nationalists increasingly challenged the party's grip on power. These nationalists argued that India was based, above all, on Hindu culture and religion and that these values had been undermined by the Western secularism of the Congress Party and the influence of India's Muslims. The Hindu nationalist party, known as the BJP, gained power in 1998. The new government immediately tested nuclear devices, asserting its vision of a militant Hindu nationalism. Promising to accelerate economic growth, BJP candidate Narendra Modi became prime minister after a sweeping electoral victory in 2014.

When Pakistan announced that it had developed nuclear weapons in 1998, relations between Pakistan and India worsened. In 2001 the two nuclear powers seemed poised for conflict until intense diplomatic pressure brought them back from the brink of nuclear war. In 2005 both countries agreed to open business and trade relations and to try to negotiate a peaceful solution to the Kashmir dispute (see "Independence in India, Pakistan, and Bangladesh" in Chapter 31). Tensions again increased in 2008 when a Pakistan-based terrorist organization carried out a widely televised shooting and bombing attack across Mumbai, India's largest city, killing 164 and wounding over 300.

In the decades following the separation of Bangladesh, Pakistan alternated between civilian and military rule. General Muhammad Zia-ul-Haq, who ruled from 1977 to 1988, drew Pakistan into a close alliance with the United States that netted military and economic assistance. Relations with the United States chilled as Pakistan pursued its nuclear weapons program. In Afghanistan, west of Pakistan, Soviet military occupation lasted from 1979 to 1989. Civil war followed the Soviet withdrawal, and in 1996 a fundamentalist Muslim group, the Taliban, seized power. The Taliban's leadership allowed the terrorist organization al-Qaeda to base its operations in Afghanistan. It was from Afghanistan that al-Qaeda conducted acts of terrorism like the attack on the U.S. World Trade Center and the Pentagon in 2001. Following that attack, the United States invaded Afghanistan, driving the Taliban from power.

When the United States invaded Afghanistan in 2001, Pakistani dictator General Pervez Musharraf (b. 1943) renewed the alliance with the United States, and Pakistan received billions of dollars in U.S. military aid. But U.S. combat against the Taliban and al-Qaeda drove militants into regions of northwest Pakistan, where they undermined the government's already tenuous control. Cooperation between Pakistan and the United States in the war was strained when U.S. Special Forces killed al-Qaeda leader Osama bin Laden on May 1, 2011. He had been hiding for years in a compound several hundred yards away from a major Pakistani military academy outside of the capital, Islamabad.

In 2007 Musharraf attempted to reshape the country's Supreme Court by replacing the chief justice with one of his close allies, bringing about calls for his impeachment. Benazir Bhutto (1953–2007), who became the first female elected head of a Muslim state when she was elected prime minister in 1988, returned from exile to challenge Musharraf's increasingly repressive military rule. She was assassinated while campaigning. After being defeated at the polls in 2008, Musharraf resigned and went into exile in London.

The Election of Benazir Bhutto
Pakistan's Benazir Bhutto became the first female prime minister of a Muslim nation in 1988. (Chip HIRES/Getty Images)

Dissidents in Burma and China

Aung San Suu Kyi spent a total of fifteen years under house arrest between 1989 and 2010 for her opposition to the military junta that ruled Burma. Suu Kyi was arrested while campaigning for a peaceful transition to a democratic civilian government. In the first excerpt, from her 1991 acceptance speech for the Sakharov Prize for Freedom of Thought awarded by the European Parliament, she discusses resistance to the Burmese dictatorship. Liu Xiaobo was a professor of literature lecturing at Columbia University in New York when students began protesting in Beijing's Tiananmen Square in 1989. He returned to China to join the demonstrations and became a vocal critic of China's human rights policies, for which he faced repeated arrests. In 2009 he was sentenced to prison, where he remained until his death in 2017. Both dissidents received the Nobel Peace Prize for their efforts, but the Chinese government did not allow Liu to accept his award in 2010. Liu sent a letter that was read at the ceremony, from which the second excerpt is drawn.

Aung San Suu Kyi, "Freedom from Fear"

■ Fearlessness may be a gift but perhaps more precious is the courage acquired through endeavour, courage that comes from cultivating the habit of refusing to let fear dictate one's actions, courage that could be described as "grace under pressure"—grace which is renewed repeatedly in the face of harsh, unremitting pressure.

Within a system which denies the existence of basic human rights, fear tends to be the order of the day. Fear of imprisonment, fear of torture, fear of death, fear of losing friends, family, property or means of livelihood, fear of poverty, fear of isolation, fear of failure. . . . It is not easy for a people conditioned by fear under the iron rule of the principle that might is right to free themselves from the enervating miasma of fear. Yet even under the most crushing state machinery courage rises up again and again, for fear is not the natural state of civilized man.

The wellspring of courage and endurance in the face of unbridled power is generally a firm belief in the sanctity of ethical principles combined with a historical sense that despite all setbacks the condition of man is set on an ultimate course for both spiritual and material advancement. . . . Concepts such as truth, justice and compassion cannot be dismissed as trite when these are often the only bulwarks which stand against ruthless power.

Liu Xiaobo, "Final Statement"

■ I still want to tell the regime that deprives me of my freedom, I stand by the belief I expressed twenty years ago in my "June Second Hunger Strike Declaration"—I have no enemies, and no hatred. None of the police who have monitored, arrested and interrogated me, the prosecutors who prosecuted me, or the judges who sentence me, are my enemies. While I'm unable to accept your surveillance, arrest, prosecution or sentencing, I respect your professions and personalities. . . .

I firmly believe that China's political progress will never stop, and I'm full of optimistic expectations of freedom coming to China in the future, because no force can block the human desire for freedom. China will eventually become a country of the rule of law in which human rights are supreme. I'm also looking forward to such progress being reflected in the trial of this case, and look forward to the full court's just verdict—one that can stand the test of history. . . .

I look forward to my country being a land of free expression, where all citizens' speeches are treated the same; here, different values, ideas, beliefs, political views . . . both compete with each other and coexist peacefully; here, . . . political views different from those in power will be fully respected and protected; . . . I hope to be the last victim of China's endless literary inquisition, and that after this no one else will ever be jailed for their speech.

Freedom of expression is the basis of human rights, the source of humanity and the mother of truth. To block freedom of speech is to trample on human rights, to strangle humanity and to suppress the truth.

QUESTIONS FOR ANALYSIS

1. How do Suu Kyi and Liu frame their appeals as just?
2. What does freedom mean to Suu Kyi? To Liu?

Sources: Aung San Suu Kyi, *Freedom from Fear and Other Writings*, ed. Michael Aris (New York: Penguin, 2010), pp. 180–185; "Text of Chinese Dissident's 'Final Statement,'" *The Lede* (blog), *New York Times*, December 10, 2010, http://thelede.blogs.nytimes.com/2010/12/10/text-of-chinese-dissidents-final-statement/. Used by permission of David Kelly.

The End of the Cold War

How did decolonization and the end of the Cold War change Europe?

In the late 1960s and early 1970s the United States and the Soviet Union pursued a relaxation of Cold War tensions that became known as **détente** (day-TAHNT). But détente stalled when Brezhnev's Soviet Union invaded Afghanistan to save an unpopular Marxist regime.

The United States reacted with alarm to the spread of Soviet influence. Ronald Reagan (U.S. pres. 1981–1989) sought to halt the spread of Soviet influence, much like predecessors John F. Kennedy and Harry Truman had. But as Reagan and conservative allies in Europe rekindled the Cold War, the Soviet Union began reforms that culminated in the release of control over eastern Europe and the dismantling of the Soviet Union and its Communist state.

The Limits of Reform in the Soviet Union and Eastern Europe

After their 1968 intervention in Czechoslovakia, Soviet leaders worked to restore order and stability. Free expression and open protest disappeared throughout their satellite nations.

A rising standard of living helped ensure stability as well. Beneath this appearance of stability, however, the Soviet Union underwent a social revolution. The urban population expanded rapidly. The number of highly trained professionals increased fourfold between 1960 and 1985. The education that created expertise helped foster the growth of Soviet public opinion about questions ranging from pollution to urban transportation.

When Mikhail Gorbachev (b. 1931) became premier in 1985, he set out to reform the Soviet system with policies he called democratic socialism. The first set of reforms was intended to transform and restructure the economy. **Perestroika** permitted freer prices, more autonomy for state enterprises, and the establishment of some profit-seeking private cooperatives. A more far-reaching campaign of openness, or **glasnost**,

introduced in 1985, allowed significant new space for public debate by increasing transparency and allowing a more open media.

Democratization under Gorbachev led to the first free elections in the Soviet Union since 1917. Gorbachev and the party remained in control, but an independent minority was elected in 1989 to a revitalized Congress of People's Deputies. Democratization encouraged demands for greater autonomy from non-Russian minorities, especially in the Baltic region and in the Caucasus.

Finally, Gorbachev brought "new political thinking" to foreign affairs. He withdrew Soviet troops from Afghanistan in 1989 and sought to reduce Cold War tensions. Gorbachev pledged to respect the political choices of eastern Europe's peoples. Soon after, a wave of peaceful revolutions swept across eastern Europe, overturning Communist regimes.

Poland led the way. In August 1980 strikes grew into a working-class revolt. Led by Lech Wałęsa (lehk vah-LEHN-suh) (b. 1943), workers organized the independent trade union **Solidarity**. Communist leaders responded by imposing martial law in December 1981 and arresting Solidarity's leaders. By 1988 labor unrest and inflation had brought Poland to the brink of economic collapse, pressuring Poland's Communist Party leaders into legalizing Solidarity and allowing free elections in 1989 for some seats in the Polish parliament. Solidarity won every contested seat. A month later Solidarity member Tadeusz Mazowiecki (mah-zoh-VYEHT-skee) (1927–2013) was sworn in as the first noncommunist prime minister in eastern Europe in a generation.

Czechoslovakia and Romania reflected different paths to reform: Czechoslovakia's Velvet Revolution led to the peaceful ouster of Communist leaders amid massive street protests led by students and intellectuals. (See "Individuals in Society: Václav Havel," at right.)

But in Romania the revolution was violent. Communist dictator Nicolae Ceaușescu (chow-SHEHS-koo) (1918–1989) unleashed his security forces on protesters, sparking an armed uprising. After Ceaușescu's forces were defeated, he and his wife were captured and executed by a military court.

Amid the transformation of eastern Europe, Germany reunified. Reunification began with the millions of East Germans who flooded across their country's borders to reach West Germany (see Map 31.1). As neighboring countries liberalized, East Germany's leaders gave in to public pressure and opened the Berlin Wall in November 1989, before being swept aside. An "Alliance for Germany" won general elections and negotiated an economic union with West Germany.

West German chancellor Helmut Kohl reassured American, Soviet, and European leaders that a reunified Germany would have peaceful intentions. Within the year, East and West Germany merged into a single nation under West Germany's constitution and laws.

---

détente The progressive relaxation of Cold War tensions between the United States and the Soviet Union in the late 1960s and early 1970s.

perestroika Economic restructuring and reform implemented by Soviet premier Mikhail Gorbachev that permitted an easing of government price controls on some goods, more independence for state enterprises, and the establishment of profit-seeking private cooperatives.

glasnost Soviet premier Mikhail Gorbachev's popular campaign for government transparency and more open media.

Solidarity Led by Lech Wałęsa, an independent Polish trade union organized in 1980 that worked for the rights of workers and political reform.

INDIVIDUALS IN SOCIETY

Václav Havel

ON THE NIGHT OF NOVEMBER 24, 1989, the revolution in Czechoslovakia reached its climax. Three hundred thousand people had poured into Prague's historic Wenceslas Square to continue the massive protests that had erupted a week earlier after the police savagely beat student demonstrators. Now all eyes were focused on a high balcony. There an elderly man with a gentle smile and a middle-aged intellectual wearing jeans and a sports jacket stood arm in arm and acknowledged the cheers of the crowd. "Dubček-Havel," the people roared. "Dubček-Havel!" Alexander Dubček, who represented the failed promise of reform communism in the 1960s (see "The World in 1968" in Chapter 31), was symbolically passing the torch to Václav Havel, who embodied the uncompromising opposition to communism that was sweeping the country. That very evening, the hard-line Communist government resigned, and soon Havel was the unanimous choice to head a new democratic Czechoslovakia. Who was this man to whom the nation turned in 1989?

Born in 1936 into a prosperous, cultured, upper-middle-class family, the young Havel was denied admission to the university because of his class origins. Loving literature and philosophy, he gravitated to the theater, became a stagehand, and emerged in the 1960s as a leading playwright. His plays were set in vague settings, developed existential themes, and poked fun at the absurdities of life and the pretensions of communism. In his private life, Havel thrived on good talk, Prague's lively bar scene, and officially forbidden rock 'n' roll.

In 1968 the Soviets rolled into Czechoslovakia, and Havel watched in horror as a tank commander opened fire on a crowd of peaceful protesters in a small town. "That week," he recorded, "was an experience I shall never forget."* The free-spirited artist threw himself into the intellectual opposition to communism and became its leading figure for the next twenty years. The costs of defiance were enormous. Purged and blacklisted, Havel lifted barrels in a brewery and wrote bitter satires that could not be staged. In 1977 he and

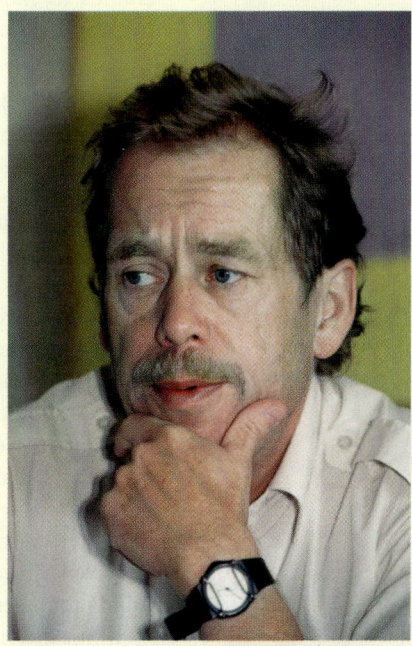

Václav Havel, playwright, dissident leader, and the first postcommunist president of the Czech Republic. (Pascal George/AFP/Getty Images)

a few other dissidents publicly protested Czechoslovakian violations of human rights, and in 1989 this Charter '77 group became the inspiration for Civic Forum, the democratic coalition that toppled communism. Havel spent five years in prison and was constantly harassed by the police.

Havel's thoughts and actions focused on truth, decency, and moral regeneration. In 1975, in a famous open letter to Czechoslovakia's Communist boss, Havel wrote that the people were indeed quiet, but only because they were "driven by fear. . . . Everyone has something to lose and so everyone has reason to be afraid." Havel saw lies, hypocrisy, and apathy undermining and poisoning all human relations in his country: "Order has been established— at the price of a paralysis of the spirit, a deadening of the heart, and a spiritual and moral crisis in society."†

Yet Havel saw a way out of the Communist quagmire. He argued that a profound but peaceful revolution in human values was possible. Such a revolution could lead to the moral reconstruction of Czech and Slovak society, where, in his words, "values like trust, openness, responsibility, solidarity and love" might again flourish and nurture the human spirit. Havel was a voice of hope and humanity who inspired his compatriots with a lofty vision of a moral postcommunist society. As president of his country from 1989 to 2003, Havel continued to speak eloquently on the great questions of our time.

QUESTIONS FOR ANALYSIS

1. Why did Havel oppose Communist rule? How did his goals differ from those of Dubček and other advocates of reform communism?
2. Havel has been called a "moralist in politics." Is this a good description of him? Why or why not?

*Quoted in M. Simmons, *The Reluctant President: A Political Life of Václav Havel* (London: Methuen, 1991), p. 91.

†Quoted ibid., p. 110.

Fall of the Berlin Wall A man stands atop the partially destroyed Berlin Wall flashing the *V* for victory sign as he and thousands of other Berliners celebrate the opening of the Berlin Wall in November 1989. Within a year the wall was torn down, communism collapsed, and the Cold War ended. (Lionel Cironneau/AP Photo/AP Images)

Many people in eastern Europe faced unexpected hardships in the process of liberalization as economies underwent difficult transformations and the state infrastructure of social welfare crumbled. But the greatest postcommunist tragedy was in Yugoslavia, whose federation of republics and regions had been held together under Josip Tito's Communist rule. After Tito's death in 1980, rising territorial and ethnic tensions were intensified by economic decline.

The revolutions of 1989 accelerated the breakup of Yugoslavia. Serbian president Slobodan Milošević (SLOH-buh-dayn muh-LOH-suh-vihch) (1941–2006) attempted to grab land from other republics to create a "greater Serbia." His ambitions led to civil wars that between 1991 and 2001 engulfed Kosovo, Slovenia, Croatia, and Bosnia-Herzegovina (Map 32.2). In 1999 Serbian aggression prompted NATO air strikes, led by

the United States, against the Serbian capital of Belgrade as well as against Serbian military forces until Milošević relented. Milošević was voted out of office in 2000. The new Serbian government extradited him to a United Nations war crimes tribunal in the Netherlands to stand trial for crimes against humanity as peace was restored to the former Yugoslav republics.

Recasting Russia Without Communism

In February 1990 the Soviet Communist Party was defeated in local elections throughout the country, eroding Gorbachev's power and strengthening his rival, Boris Yeltsin (1931–2007), the former mayor of Moscow. In May 1990, as leader of the Russian parliament, Yeltsin announced that Russia would declare its independence from the Soviet Union. In August 1991 Gorbachev faced an attempted coup by Communist hardliners who wanted to preserve a Communist Soviet Union. Instead their coup attempt hastened the end of the Soviet Union. Yeltsin emerged as a popular hero for his dramatic resistance: at one point, he climbed atop a tank deployed by the conspirators to deliver a rousing speech calling for a general strike in resistance to the coup.

In the aftermath of the attempted takeover, an anticommunist revolution swept the Russian Federation. The Communist Party was outlawed and its property confiscated. Yeltsin and his liberal allies declared Russia independent and withdrew from the Soviet Union. All the other Soviet republics followed suit. Gorbachev agreed to their independence, and the Soviet Union ceased to exist on December 25, 1991 (Map 32.3). The newly independent post-Soviet republics faced challenges, including the need to quickly build new political systems and the urgency of economic reforms meant to open socialist economies to free-market principles. Liberal reforms doomed much of Russia's industry, and its economy depended increasingly on oil and natural gas exports. Despite its weakened economy, Russia retained the world's second-largest nuclear arsenal, as well as a powerful vote (and veto) in the United Nations Security Council.

As Yeltsin presided over newly independent Russia, he opted for breakneck liberalization. This shock therapy, which followed methods similar to radical free-market policies in Chile and other parts of Latin America, freed prices on most goods and launched a rapid privatization of industry. Prices soared and production collapsed. State industrial monopolies became private monopolies that cut production and raised prices in order to maximize profits. The quality of public services and health care declined to the point that the average male life expectancy dropped from sixty-nine years in 1991 to fifty-nine years in 2007. In 2003 Russia's per capita income was lower than at any time since 1978.

MAP 32.2 The Breakup of Yugoslavia Yugoslavia had the most ethnically diverse population in eastern Europe. The Republic of Croatia had substantial Serbian and Muslim minorities, and Bosnia-Herzegovina had large Muslim, Serbian, and Croatian populations, none of which had a majority. In June 1991 Serbia's brutal effort to seize territory and unite all Serbs in a single state brought a tragic civil war to the region.

The election of Yeltsin's handpicked successor, President Vladimir Putin (b. 1952), in 2000 ushered in a new era of "managed democracy." Putin's stress on public order and economic reform was popular, even as he became progressively more authoritarian. Significant restrictions were placed on media freedoms, regional elections were abolished, and the distinction between judicial and executive authority collapsed. Putin consolidated the power and authority of the state around himself and his closest advisers, closing off the development of democratic pluralism and an independent legal system in Russia.

Putin's illiberal tendencies were also evident in his brutal military campaign against Chechnya (CHEHCH-nyuh), a tiny republic of 1 million Muslims in southern Russia (see Map 32.3, inset) that in 1991 declared its independence. Up to two hundred thousand Chechen civilians are estimated to have been killed between 1994 and 2011. Many more became refugees. Chechen resistance to Russian domination continued, often in the form of attacks such as a sui-

cide bombing at Moscow's airport in 2011 that killed scores of travelers.

In the aftermath of the dissolution of the Soviet Union, political and ethnic divisions threatened peace and stability among the post-Soviet republics. In Ukraine, in 2014 pro-Western protesters toppled a president who refused to sign agreements with the European Union. In the aftermath of the uprising, Russian forces occupied the Ukrainian province of Crimea along the Black Sea and backed secessionist movements in ethnically Russian regions of Ukraine. Russia's seizure of Crimea undermined the terms under which the Soviet Union had dissolved into separate republics, provoking unease among other new states such as the Baltic republics.

Integration and Reform in Europe

Germany and France continued to lead the push for European unity, building on integration efforts in the 1940s and 1950s established through NATO and the

MAP 32.3 Russia and the Successor States After the attempt in August 1991 to depose Gorbachev failed, an anticommunist revolution swept the Soviet Union. Led by Russia and Boris Yeltsin, the republics that formed the Soviet Union declared their sovereignty and independence. Eleven of the fifteen republics then formed a loose confederation called the Commonwealth of Independent States, but the integrated economy of the Soviet Union dissolved into separate national economies, each with its own goals and policies.

Common Market (see "Postwar Challenges in Western Europe and the United States" in Chapter 31). French president François Mitterrand (1916–1996) and German chancellor Helmut Kohl (b. 1930) pursued the economic integration of European Community members, and in 1993 the European Community rechristened itself the **European Union (EU)**. The European Union, a political and economic body, allowed for the free movement of people and goods among twelve member countries; created a common currency, the euro, introduced in 2002; and formed a European Parliament that established regulations and pooled infrastructure and education investments.

The creation of the European Union resolved diverse challenges for different parts of Europe. It created a logic for a unified Germany integrated with Europe. For eastern Europe it provided a blueprint for reforming economies and institutions in countries transitioning away from Soviet models. For western Europe it created an alternative path after the loss of colonies in Africa and Asia. For five centuries overseas empires had not only provided the engine for economic development at home but also shaped international relations as well as intellectual currents ranging from abolitionism to scientific racism and even Marxism. Empires had provided raw materials and markets that produced industrialization. For different reasons but for the first time since before the French Revolution, almost all of Europe now followed the same general political model.

European Union (EU) An economic and political alliance of twelve European nations formed in 1993 that has since grown to include twenty-eight European nations.

The European Union
- Founding members, 1951
- New members, 1973
- New members, 1981
- New members, 1986
- German reunification, 1990
- New members, 1995
- New members, 2004
- New members, 2007
- New members, 2013
- Candidate countries, 2017
- € Eurozone countries, 2017

* The United Kingdom voted in June 2016 to leave the E.U.

MAP 32.4 The European Union, 2017 No longer divided by ideological competition and the Cold War, much of today's Europe banded together in a European Union that has become strained by economic and migration pressures.

European leaders embraced a neoliberal, free-market vision of capitalism. The most radical economic changes had been implemented in the 1980s by Margaret Thatcher (1925–2013) in Britain, who drew inspiration from Pinochet's Chile. Other governments also introduced austerity measures to slow the growth of public spending and the welfare state. Many individuals suffered under the impact of these reductions in public spending and social welfare. Harder times meant that more women entered or remained in the workforce after they married.

The success of the euro encouraged the EU to accelerate plans for an ambitious enlargement to the east. On May 1, 2004, the EU started admitting eastern European countries and by 2009 had adopted a common constitution. In 2017 the European Union had twenty-eight member states, including most of eastern Europe, and a population of nearly 500 million. As it grew, the EU faced questions about the limits of its expansion and the meaning of European unity and

identity. If the EU expanded to include eastern Europe and some former Soviet republics, how could Turkey, a secular nation with a Muslim majority, be denied its long-standing request for membership? Turkey had been a member of NATO since 1952 and had labored to meet membership requirements (Map 32.4).

This debate deepened as the economic crisis that began in 2008 tested and frayed the European Union. Countries that had adopted the euro currency had to meet stringent fiscal standards and imposed deep budget cuts. The resulting reductions in health care and social benefits hit ordinary citizens hard. National governments could no longer expand their own monetary supplies to promote recovery, and governments were forced to slash budgets to meet debt obligations. At the same time, the EU struggled to find a unified response to the growing numbers of refugees crossing the Mediterranean from North Africa and the Middle East as they fled conflict zones and poverty. In western Europe, tensions also emerged over the movement of peoples from poorer eastern European member nations to wealthier countries like France and the United Kingdom.

Austerity brought ruinous economic conditions that crippled Greece, prompting its near-departure from the Eurozone in 2015, while the economies of Portugal, Spain, and Italy struggled. The consequences of liberalization in Europe resembled the consequences elsewhere: economic growth was greater, but economic hardship and dislocation were deeper. The costs of liberalization to European unity were felt again as voters in the United Kingdom chose in 2016 to leave the European Union after a campaign fueled by anxieties about immigration. The British voters' decision, popularly called Brexit, was the first vote of its kind and, together with the Greek economic crisis, cast doubts about the stability and future of the European Union.

Chapter Summary

In 1976 most of the world was governed by undemocratic regimes. These regimes came in many different types: some were controlled by Communist parties and others by right-wing military officers loyal to the United States. There were dictatorships ruled by nationalist leaders, by strongmen who unseated independence leaders, and by members of families that owned much of a nation's resources. Some of these dictators created an illusion of governing democratically, but they restricted opposition or required one-party rule.

Some dictatorships created the space to engage in utopian projects to remake nations. Even when such dictatorships succeeded in their goals, they did so at enormous costs, measured in debt and inflation, famine and malnutrition, the tattering of public institutions, and the reliance on repression to maintain order.

By the mid-1980s dictatorships around the world had begun to fall, and democratic transitions followed. During the 1980s most of Latin America returned to democracy, and in 1989 the fall of the Berlin Wall culminated a wave of political and economic change in the Soviet Union and eastern Europe. The end of the Cold War division of Europe accelerated a process of integration and unification that had its roots in reconstruction after the Second World War and the process of decolonization that dismantled European empires. Alongside political transitions, a wave of economic liberalization, often promoted by the United States, swept the world. Liberalization resulted in increased trade and economic activity, but it also created growing gaps between rich and poor.

Amid these changes, East Asia came to play a growing role in the world economy. The rapid economic growth of Japan and the industrialization of South Korea were accompanied by an economic liberalization without political liberalization in China. In the 1970s Japan became the second-largest national economy by GDP in the world after the United States. By 2010 China had surpassed Japan amid projections that it would soon emerge as the world's largest national economy.

NOTES

1. *Jornal do Brasil*, March 14, 1976, quoted in Roberto Jorge Ramalho Cavalcanti, "O presidente Ernesto Geisel e o estabelecimento do retorno à democracia ao Brasil pós Regime Militar de 1964," *Governo e Política*, November 7, 2010, http://www.webartigos.com/artigos/artigo-o-presidente-ernesto-geisel-e-o-estabelecimento-do-retorno-a-democracia-ao-brasil-pos-regime-militar-de-1964/51497/.
2. CIA Director Richard Helms, notes on Nixon's plan for Chile, September 15, 1970, accessed October 14, 2012, http://www2.gwu.edu/~nsarchiv/NSAEBB/NSAEBB8/docs/doc26.pdf.
3. D. Birmingham and P. Martin, eds., *History of Central Africa: The Contemporary Years Since 1960* (London: Routledge, 1998), p. 59.

CONNECTIONS

The experiences of people living under authoritarian regimes varied greatly. Many supported the regimes from which they drew privileges or found a reassuring sense of order. Others avoided political questions and stayed out of trouble. But even they were affected by authoritarianism: censorship and propaganda meant that official pronouncements lacked credibility, so rumors, some true and others wild, became their basic currency of exchange.

Many, however, resisted the regimes. For some, a closed political system meant the only tools available were armed resistance. Guerrilla movements against authoritarian regimes were common, though the imbalance in their resources meant they mostly met with violent ends at the hands of security forces. Another form of resistance proved more effective: nonviolent, and ostensibly nonpolitical, resistance was harder for regimes to repress. Mothers asking for the whereabouts of missing children or quilting the scenes of their grief in Argentina and Chile, or workers organizing an independent union in Poland, found ways to challenge their regimes.

The most successful resistance was often opposition that was not explicitly ideological, such as the defense of human rights, or the establishment of the rule of law that would restrict a regime's arbitrary power. These pressures had a similar effect when applied to right-wing or socialist dictatorships alike: they were liberalizing. As dictatorships in Latin America, East Asia, and eastern Europe moved toward multiparty democracy, and as the Soviet bloc disintegrated, those countries shared a historical moment in which liberal economic and political reforms swept the world.

CHAPTER 32 ## Review and Explore

Identify Key Terms

Identify and explain the significance of each item below.

Organization of the Petroleum Exporting Countries (OPEC) (p. 956)

petrodollars (p. 956)

neoliberalism (p. 957)

Washington Consensus (p. 957)

intifada (p. 959)

junta (p. 963)

apartheid (p. 967)

African National Congress (ANC) (p. 967)

"Japan, Inc." (p. 971)

Tiananmen Square (p. 972)

détente (p. 978)

perestroika (p. 978)

glasnost (p. 978)

Solidarity (p. 978)

European Union (EU) (p. 982)

Review the Main Ideas

Answer the focus questions from each section of the chapter.

1. What were the short-term and long-term consequences of the OPEC oil embargo? (p. 956)

2. How did war and revolution reshape the Middle East? (p. 959)

3. What effect did the Cold War and debt crisis have on Latin America? (p. 962)

4. How did white-minority rule end in southern Africa? (p. 966)

5. How have East and South Asian nations pursued economic development, and how have political regimes shaped those efforts? (p. 971)

6. How did decolonization and the end of the Cold War change Europe? (p. 978)

Make Comparisons and Connections

Analyze the larger developments and continuities within and across chapters.

1. How did transitions to democracy and free markets around the world draw on earlier ideologies (Chapters 22, 24, 29)?

2. How did the impact of oil shocks resemble previous economic crises?

3. What similarities do you see among social movements that advocated for democracy and for majority rule around the world?

4. What historical factors shaped the formation of the European Union? How have recent events challenged European unity?

TIMELINE

GLOBAL		**1983–1991** Transitions to democracy in the Soviet Union, eastern Europe, Latin America, South America
AFRICA	◆ **1975** Independence from Portugal of Angola and Mozambique ends European colonial rule in Africa	◆ **1980** Segregationist white-minority government in Rhodesia replaced by majority rule; country renamed Zimbabwe
MIDDLE EAST	← **1973** Yom Kippur War / Ramadan War triggers OPEC oil embargo	**1980–1988** Iran-Iraq War ◆ **1987** Palestinian intifada
	◆ **1979** Islamic revolution in Iran leads to second oil shock	
ASIA	◆ **1978** Deng Xiaoping initiates economic reforms in China	**1989** ◆ Tiananmen Square protests in China
AMERICAS		◆ **1982** Falklands (or Malvinas) War leads to collapse of Argentina's military junta
		◆ **1982** Mexico defaults on loan payments, triggering debt crisis
		1988 ◆ The "NO" vote wins the Chilean plebiscite ousting dictator Pinochet
EUROPE		◆ **1985** Glasnost leads to greater freedom of speech and expression in the Soviet Union

1975	1985

Suggested Resources

BOOKS

Beck, Roger B. *The History of South Africa.* 2d ed. 2013. Introduction to South African history with emphasis on the twentieth century.

Buchenau, Jurgen. *Mexican Mosaic: A Brief History of Mexico.* 2012. A concise but rich look at modern Mexico.

Dávila, Jerry. *Dictatorship in South America.* 2013. Examines the experiences with dictatorship, development, and democracy in Argentina, Brazil, and Chile.

Dobbs, Michael. *Down with Big Brother: The Fall of the Soviet Empire.* 1997. A superb account by a journalist who covered eastern Europe.

Guha, Ramachandra. *India After Gandhi: The History of the World's Largest Democracy.* 2007. In-depth study of the last sixty years of Indian history and development.

Judt, Tony. *Postwar: A History of Europe Since 1945.* 2006. A broad and insightful reading of reconstruction, the Cold War, and unification.

Kapuscinski, Ryszard. *Another Day of Life.* 2001. An account by a renowned Polish journalist of the South African invasion of Angola and the Cuban intervention.

Kingston, Jeffrey. *Japan's Quiet Transformation: Social Change and Civil Society in the 21st Century.* 2004. A leading scholar considers Japan's economic problems in the 1990s and their effects on Japanese politics and society.

Lampe, J. *Yugoslavia as History: Twice There Was a Country,* 2d ed. 2000. Judiciously and insightfully considers the history and violent collapse of Yugoslavia.

Mahbubani, Kishore. *The New Asian Hemisphere: The Irresistible Shift of Global Power to the East.* 2008. A history and analysis of the rise of Asia in world politics and economics by one of Asia's leading intellectuals.

McCann, Bryan. *The Throes of Democracy: Brazil Since 1989.* 2008. A rich overview of the Brazilian experience of redemocratization.

Nepstad, Sharon Erickson. *Nonviolent Revolutions: Civil Resistance in the Late 20th Century.* 2011. A comparative study of nonviolent political movements and their effect on political transitions.

◆ **1997** First civilian-to-civilian transfer of political power in Nigeria

1990–1991 Persian Gulf War

2003–2011 Second Persian Gulf War

2007 ➔
Hamas seizes control of Gaza Strip from Palestinian Authority

2009–2014 ➔
Popular uprisings and protests across the Middle East

◆ **1991** Congress Party in India embraces
Western capitalist reforms

1991–2001 Civil war in Yugoslavia

◆ **1993** Formation of the European Union

1995

2005

Wapshott, Nicholas. *Ronald Reagan and Margaret Thatcher: A Political Marriage*. 2007. Particularly good analysis of Reagan and Thatcher's policies of economic conservatism and anticommunism in the 1980s.

DOCUMENTARIES

The Tank Man (PBS, 2006). A *Frontline* episode that examines the 1989 Tiananmen Square protest and the Chinese government's suppression of it, with a focus on the man alone facing down a tank.

Tokyo Olympiad (Kon Ichikawa, 1965). This documentary about the 1964 Toyko Olympics reflects Japan's re-emergence in the decades following the Second World War, occupation, and reconstruction.

When We Were Kings (Leon Gast, 1996). Covers the 1974 "Rumble in the Jungle" boxing match in Zaire between Muhammad Ali and George Foreman, focusing on the dynamics of dictator Mobutu Sese Seko's rule and expressions of Pan-African connections.

FEATURE FILMS AND TELEVISION

The Americans (FX, 2013–2018). This TV series about two undercover Soviet agents in 1980s Washington captures the tensions of the rekindled Cold War.

The Official Story (Luis Puenzo, 1985). A film about children taken as infants by the Argentine military dictatorship that "disappeared" their parents.

24 City (Jia Zhang-Ke, 2008). A Chinese docudrama about the economic and social transitions that occur as a state aircraft factory is converted into luxury apartments. The film depicts interviews of generations of migrants drawn to work at the factory.

WEBSITES

Forward to Freedom: The History of the British Anti-Apartheid Movement, 1959–1994. The British Anti-Apartheid Movement organization maintains a retrospective website that includes interviews with participants in the movement, as well as documents and images. **www.aamarchives.org**

The National Security Archive. The National Security Archive at George Washington University has an incomparable online collection of declassified U.S. national security and foreign policy documents, including records that show secret U.S. support for dictatorships and their human rights violations in Latin America. **nsarchive.gwu.edu**

33

The Contemporary World in Historical Perspective

The approaches to the history of world societies in the preceding chapters give us critical thinking skills to help interpret the contemporary world. Through this lens, we can understand contemporary events and debates as rooted in history and also see those events as subjects of study that we can analyze using the same tools we employ for interpreting the past.

Since the end of the Cold War, many nations around the world have undergone transitions from dictatorship to democracy, and a growing number of nations have pursued free trade. These new experiences have been shaped by past struggles, and they have intensified global connections, aided by revolutions in communications and information technology. Amid these changes, stubborn regional and political conflicts remain in many parts of the world, and the experiences of poverty and marginalization continue to be widespread. But this is also a world in which, as in the past, humans have had the ability to shape, adapt, and transform the problems they confront.

Masterfile/Royalty-Free

The Digital Revolution

People throughout the world have embraced the ease and convenience of mobile phone technology, which has increased dramatically since the introduction of the first cellular phones in 1985.

CHAPTER PREVIEW

THE END OF HISTORY?
Does the contemporary world reflect the "end of history"?

GLOBAL CIRCULATION AND EXCHANGE
How have migration and the circulation of capital and technology continued to shape the world?

SOCIAL MOVEMENTS
What challenges did social reformers address at the turn of the twenty-first century?

SCIENCE AND TECHNOLOGY: CHANGES AND CHALLENGES
How have science and technology kept pace with population change?

The End of History?

Does the contemporary world reflect the "end of history"?

In 1989, as the Berlin Wall fell and the Soviet system disintegrated, a historian wrote a provocative article called "The End of History?" in which he argued that the collapse of the Soviet system meant the triumph of liberalism as a political and economic philosophy. Amid the transitions to democracy from Russia and eastern Europe to Latin America, political leaders embraced liberalism as the ideology of government and of economics. This was the "triumph of the West, of the Western *idea* . . . in the total exhaustion of viable systematic alternatives to Western liberalism."[1] Was liberalism the ultimate stage of human political and economic development?

By the beginning of the twenty-first century, liberalism had certainly emerged as the world's dominant political and economic philosophy. But there have been limits to liberalism's reach and effectiveness. For instance, economic liberalism has tended to increase social inequality and the disparity of wealth between nations and regions. As a result, liberalism has been met by a growing range of social activism aimed at reducing social inequality; gender, ethnic, and racial marginalization; and the environmental costs of economic development.

The tension between liberalism and activism is one example of the kinds of contradictory and competing pressures that shape the contemporary world. For instance, the earth's growing population has increased demands for food production, prompting a revolution in agricultural sciences. Although new technologies have helped meet the world's demand for food, the diversion of water resources and the expansion of farming at the expense of forests remind us that new technologies often bring unintended costs. Similarly, the end of the Cold War has been met not with peace but with regional conflicts around the world. And the intensification of communications, increase in travel, and spread of technology have been met with conservative, often religious reactions in different regions of the world. Some of the most intense reactions have come from movements in the Middle East and Africa whose actions have a global impact.

Complexity and Violence in a Multipolar World

The end of the Cold War led to the emergence of new regional relationships. Increasingly assertive **middle powers**, countries with significant economic influence either in relation to their neighbors or in broader trade networks, competed for regional leadership. Mexico, both highly industrialized and economically integrated with the United States, emerged as the leader of the Spanish-speaking Americas. Brazil, a rapidly industrializing country with 200 million people and vast territory and resources, emerged as the dominant nation-state in South America. France and Germany re-emerged as central economic powers in Europe. Nigeria and South Africa became the leading powers in sub-Saharan Africa. Turkey, Egypt, and Israel were also regional powers in the Middle East, and Iran increasingly projected its influence over neighbors like Iraq. China, India, and Japan all became leading regional powers, and several other Asian countries—notably South Korea, Indonesia, and Pakistan—were determined to join them.

While the end of the Cold War reduced superpower pressures that intensified regional conflicts, other factors continued to feed conflicts that killed over a million people and dispersed hundreds of thousands of refugees. Since 2000, new conflicts have caused millions more deaths and new currents of refugees, particularly in Syria, Sierra Leone, Liberia, the Democratic Republic of the Congo, Mali, Afghanistan, and Iraq. Rivalries between ethnic groups often lie at the heart of these wars.

An Expanding Atomic Age

After the bombing of Hiroshima and Nagasaki in 1945 (see "The War in the Pacific" in Chapter 30), the United States briefly held a monopoly on atomic weapons. Since then, a growing number of nations have developed nuclear arms.

The Cold War arms race resulted in intense competition for the development of increasingly powerful atomic weapons, and it also meant massive spending in the United States, the Soviet Union, and Europe on other military technologies. While the superpowers and their closest allies sought to restrict access to nuclear weapons, they also sold huge numbers of conventional arms to other nations.

Amid the Cold War arms race, atomic tests brought fear that radiation would enter the food chain and cause leukemia, bone cancer, and genetic damage. Concerned scientists called for a ban on atomic bomb testing. In 1963 the United States, Great Britain, and the Soviet Union reached an agreement, eventually joined by more than 150 countries, to ban nuclear tests in the atmosphere. In 1970 more than sixty countries signed the Treaty on the Non-Proliferation of Nuclear Weapons. The treaty slowed but did not stop the spread of nuclear weapons.

The nuclear arms race between the Soviet Union and the United States was so intense that after the

middle powers Countries with significant economic influence that became increasingly assertive regional leaders after the Cold War.

1960s both sides sought ways of slowing it and negotiated shared limits to their nuclear arsenals. But other nations pursued nuclear weapons to bolster their defense and their regional influence. French and Chinese leaders disregarded the test ban and by 1968 had developed their own nuclear weapons, although they later signed the nonproliferation treaty. India developed its atomic capability partly out of fear of China, but India's nuclear test in 1974 in turn frightened Pakistan, which pursued its own nuclear weapons. In 1998 both India and Pakistan tested nuclear devices within weeks of each other. Other nations discreetly pursued nuclear arms without publicly stating that they possessed them.

In the 1950s Israel began developing nuclear weapons, and it is generally believed to have had an arsenal of nuclear weapons since the 1970s, though Israel has never publicly confirmed this. Israel's apparent nuclear superiority was threatening to Arab states that for decades had tried to vanquish Israel. When Iraq attempted, with help from France, to develop nuclear capability in the 1980s, Israel responded by attacking and destroying the Iraqi nuclear reactor in 1981.

The risks associated with the proliferation of nuclear weapons helped mobilize the international community and contributed to positive developments through the 1980s and 1990s. Between 1983 and 2003 Argentina, Romania, Brazil, South Africa, and Libya all agreed to abandon their nuclear weapons programs. Several of the former Soviet republics that possessed nuclear arsenals, including Ukraine, Belarus (bay-luh-ROOS), and Kazakhstan (KA-zak-stan), returned their nuclear weapons to Russia. International agencies monitored exports of nuclear material, technology, and missiles that could carry atomic bombs. These measures encouraged confidence in global cooperation and in the nonproliferation treaty, eventually signed by 190 countries.

Despite these efforts, nuclear proliferation has continued. In 2003 the United States accused Iran of seeking to build nuclear weapons, and for many years diplomatic efforts, sanctions, and other punitive measures by France, Germany, Britain, China, the United States, and Russia failed to induce Iran to limit its nuclear program. However, the sanctions isolated Iran and undermined its economy, and in 2015 Iran signed an agreement freezing development of its nuclear program. There is also the threat that enriched nuclear materials will fall into the hands of terrorist organizations or that countries possessing nuclear weapons technology will share it with other nations.

In the new century long-standing tensions between North Korea and the United States, which had never signed a peace treaty to end the 1950–1953 Korean War, intensified over North Korea's pursuit of nuclear weapons and ballistic missile technology that would

Limiting Iran's Nuclear Energy Program Following sanctions from the United States, France, Germany, Great Britain, and Russia, Iran agreed to freeze its nuclear energy program. Here International Atomic Energy Agency inspectors and Iranian technicians gather to cut connections in uranium enrichment equipment in Iran's Natanz nuclear facility in 2014. (Kazem Ghane/ IRNA/AP Photo/AP Images)

allow it to launch atomic weapons at South Korea and Japan. As each side accused the other of failing to live up to its agreements, North Korea tested its first nuclear device in 2006. After 2009, North Korean authorities pursued the development of long-range ballistic missiles capable of delivering a bomb, engaging in nuclear brinksmanship not seen since the Cold War.

Al-Qaeda and Afghanistan

In the Middle East and Central Asia, conflicts that had involved the superpowers continued beyond the Cold War. The 1979 Soviet invasion of Afghanistan, as well as the Iranian revolution, which was followed by the Iran-Iraq War, led to enduring political upheaval that continued to draw the United States into violent conflicts in the twenty-first century.

In Afghanistan rebel groups supported by the United States fought the Soviet armed forces occupying the country and forced a humiliating Soviet withdrawal in 1989. In 1996, after years of civil war, a puritanical Islamic movement called the Taliban filled the military and political vacuum left by the Soviet Union. The Taliban pursued a radical religious transformation of Afghan society, in particular by imposing harsh restrictions on women. The Taliban government provided safe haven in Afghanistan for a terrorist organization called al-Qaeda (al-KIGH-duh), which included militants who had fought in Afghanistan against the

New York, September 11, 2001 Pedestrians race for safety as the World Trade Center towers collapse after being hit by jet airliners. (Amy Sanetta/AP Photo/AP Images)

Soviet occupation. In the 1990s, led by Osama bin Laden (1957–2011), al-Qaeda attacked U.S. diplomatic and military targets in Africa and the Middle East.

On September 11, 2001, al-Qaeda militants hijacked four passenger planes in the United States. They flew two of them into the World Trade Center buildings in New York City and a third into the Pentagon in Washington, D.C. A fourth, believed to be targeting the White House or the U.S. Capitol, crashed into a field in rural Pennsylvania. These terrorist attacks killed almost three thousand people. Though the U.S. government had repeatedly attacked al-Qaeda in the 1990s, it had failed to destroy it. Now the U.S. government demanded that the Taliban government in Afghanistan surrender the al-Qaeda leadership it hosted. When the Taliban refused, the United States formed a military coalition including NATO members as well as Russia, Pakistan, and rebel groups in Afghanistan. The coalition mounted an invasion, deposed the Taliban, and pursued al-Qaeda.

After the U.S.-led coalition deposed the Taliban in 2001 and installed a new government in Afghanistan, it faced a protracted guerrilla war against Taliban forces that controlled rural areas. The Taliban drew upon Afghanistan's long experience in resisting foreign military incursions such as the Soviet and earlier British invasions. The conflict in Afghanistan spread to Pakistan, where some members of al-Qaeda found refuge, and acts of terrorism increased around the world in the years following the invasion of Afghanistan.

Through years of war, the United States and allied governments devastated al-Qaeda's leadership, but local groups acting in conflicts in the Middle East and Africa continued to act under al-Qaeda's name. These actions included bombings in 2004 and 2005 that killed 191 in Madrid and 56 in London, as well as wounding thousands. A suicide bomber who may have had links to al-Qaeda has also been blamed for the 2007 assassination of Pakistani presidential candidate Benazir Bhutto. In 2011 U.S. intelligence services identified bin Laden's hideout in Pakistan in a compound located near the country's main military academy in Abbottabad. In a night raid, U.S. forces killed bin Laden.

In the decade following the conclusion of the Persian Gulf War (1990–1991), Iraq faced international economic sanctions along with constant political and military pressure from the United States to surrender its chemical and biological weapons stockpiles. After 2001, amid the U.S. invasion of Afghanistan, U.S. president George W. Bush accused Iraq of rebuilding its nuclear, chemical, and biological weapons programs. To build domestic support for an invasion, the U.S. government also falsely implied that there were connections between Iraq and al-Qaeda. In 2002 UN inspectors determined that Iraq's chemical and biological weapons had been destroyed. France, Russia, China, Germany, and a majority of the smaller states argued for continued weapons monitoring, and France threatened to veto any resolution authorizing an invasion of Iraq. Rather than risk this veto, the United States and Britain claimed that earlier Security Council resolutions provided sufficient authorization and invaded Iraq in 2003.

A coalition of U.S.-led forces defeated the Iraqi military, and in the power vacuum that ensued, armed groups representing all three main factions in Iraq—Sunni Muslims, Shi'ite Muslims, and Kurds—carried out daily attacks on Iraqi military and police, government officials, religious leaders, and civilians. Estimates of Iraqi deaths since the beginning of the war in 2003 and the U.S. withdrawal in 2011 ranged from 100,000 to over 1 million. Though the U.S. military

Iraq, ca. 2010

occupation ended in 2011, the violence continued. Ironically, though the connection between al-Qaeda and the government of Saddam Hussein implied by President Bush did not exist, the violent environment of postwar Iraq became a place where militant groups that identified with al-Qaeda proliferated.

The most powerful of these groups called itself the Islamic State (commonly known as ISIS). ISIS took advantage of the political vacuum created by the U.S. invasion of Iraq and the Syrian civil war to establish a radical Islamic regime that spanned regions of the two countries and controlled several major cities. ISIS emerged as an ideological and militant heir to al-Qaeda. It used a sophisticated Internet footprint to recruit disaffected youth around the world to join its ranks, prompting terrorist attacks in 2015 and 2016 by individuals claiming to act in ISIS's name in the United States, France, Turkey, and Bangladesh.

Global Circulation and Exchange

How have migration and the circulation of capital and technology continued to shape the world?

Much of the history in this textbook is driven by the circulation of peoples over great distances. Migration continues to be one of the great engines of history, though its experience exposes one of the major contradictions in the way liberalization has been conducted: governments have pressed for the free circulation of goods and capital, but have sought to limit the movement of people across borders.

Migration

National immigration policies vary considerably. In Europe the process of integration has meant that European Union member countries permit the free movement of citizens from other EU nations. But in many other cases, restrictions on migration have increased even as barriers to trade and investment have fallen.

The border between the United States and Mexico reflects many of the challenges of contemporary migrations. Since long before a border existed between the United States and Mexico, migrants have circulated throughout North America, but as the United States conquered land that had belonged to Mexico in the nineteenth century (see "Mexico and the United States" in Chapter 27), it restricted the movement of migrants northward across the border. At the beginning of the twenty-first century the U.S. government began building a wall at its border with Mexico, fur-

ther restricting the circulation of people even as the United States and Mexico implemented a free-trade agreement that made it easier for goods and capital to cross the border.

In the 2016 U.S. presidential election, the border between the United States and Mexico became a symbolic flash point of anxieties over two basic elements of globalization and liberalization: the movement of peoples and the free circulation of goods and capital. Real estate developer Donald Trump rode resentments over trade and migration into the presidency in a U.S. expression of the nationalist sentiments that provoked the British vote to exit the European Union and the rise of nationalist parties in continental Europe. The patterns of migration and the votes against migration that resulted in Brexit and Trump's election reflected the unevenness in wealth distribution both globally and within nations.

Behind the politics of immigration lies a more complex reality: circuits of migration—the patterns by which peoples move between one region of the world and another—are shaped by many forces. Historical connections, such as the spaces shared by indigenous and Latino peoples on both sides of the U.S.-Mexico border, are one such force. A second is the intensification of trade, which reshapes national economies and the connections between them. A third is the history of U.S. military intervention: countries that are the sites of conflict spurred by or involving the United States are reshaped in ways that often create migrant and refugee circuits connected to the United States. The experience of immigration following U.S. military intervention in Central America, the Caribbean, and Southeast Asia forms a pattern into which future immigration from the Middle East may well fit.

Since the 1960s millions of people, first from South Korea and then Vietnam, Cambodia, and Laos, countries that had experienced great upheavals in conflicts involving the United States, found legal refuge in the United States. (See "Individuals in Society: Sieng, a Mnong Refugee in an American High School," page 994.) Immigrants to the United States most commonly come from regions transformed by U.S. foreign policy or economic activity; new immigrants frequently encounter discrimination, and efforts are made to restrict the entry of future immigrants.

In many cases, restrictions on immigration have increased in countries where national economic growth has slowed. For instance, as Japanese industry boomed in the 1980s, the country welcomed descendants of Japanese emigrants who had settled in South America in the first half of the century. Because these migrants were culturally and linguistically different from natives, Japanese citizens considered them *dekasegi*, or "temporary guest workers," who had no right to citizenship despite their ancestry.

Sieng, a Mnong Refugee in an American High School

IN 2008, AT A LARGE URBAN HIGH SCHOOL IN THE U.S. South, Sieng, a seventeen-year-old Mnong refugee, recited the Pledge of Allegiance in his JROTC class. His aspiration to join the U.S. Marine Corps was an act of belonging that bridged both his life in the United States and his sense of his family and its history.

The Mnong are among a diverse group of ethnic minorities, known broadly as Montagnards, whose communities stretch across the central highlands of Vietnam. They are also a religious minority in Vietnam—many had converted to Christianity. During the Vietnam War, many Mnong provided military service alongside the United States, particularly with the U.S. Army Special Forces. After the war ended in 1975, the Mnong faced persecution, and over time many fled the country, joining the current of refugees who resettled in camps in Thailand, Malaysia, the Philippines, and later Cambodia. Sieng's family left Vietnam when he was a child in the late 1990s. He recalled his journey:

> We had a hard time in Vietnam, so we had to leave. We didn't have no choice because we had no food, and no land. And [the Vietnamese government] wanted my dad and took my grandpa. So we left in the night and went through the jungle. We walked and walked and got lost. So me and my dad tried to find the way and we found a house. Some people let us sleep there and also gave us food. Then we got to a [refugee] camp in Cambodia and stayed there for a year. I didn't have school in Vietnam, and I didn't have school at the camp. Then we came here.

Arriving in the United States at the age of sixteen, Sieng was not literate in Mnong, Vietnamese, or English, the language of his new school. Sieng aspired to become a Marine so he could help other refugees and his family. He explained, "A man needs to take care of the family too, and that's what I want to do. The Marines will help me take care of my family."

For Sieng, being a refugee instilled a sense of pride, a sense of what he and his family had overcome in coming to the United States, and a sense of what he desired for the future. As the oldest male child, Sieng was, in his words, "second in command" in the home while his father worked the third shift at a shipping facility. In the United States Sieng was an ethnic minority and a refugee with limited English skills. He was misunderstood. A classmate in a

Mnong students and their teaching assistant at a high school in Wisconsin recite the Pledge of Allegiance. (Morry Gash/AP Photo/AP Images)

world history class asked him where he was from in Mexico, and the question made him indignant:

> I am a *refugee*, not an immigrant! I am *Mnong*, not Vietnamese! But people call me Spanish. Some kids once asked me to say something in Spanish. . . . And Mexican students think I'm Chinese. They say, *"Hey Chino! Hey Chino!"* I get mad when they do this because I am more like American. My grandpa worked with Americans [in the war].

In a diverse school, amid other immigrants and ethnic minorities, Sieng found comfort in his identity as a refugee, reflecting on his family's past, its connection to the United States, and his role facilitating its journey, as he confronted a new environment, struggling to be understood.

QUESTIONS FOR ANALYSIS

1. What aspects of Sieng's experience reflect broader patterns of migration?
2. How does Sieng's experience as a refugee shape his identity?
3. What role does JROTC play in Sieng's sense of belonging?

Source: Liv T. Dávila, "Performing Allegiance: An Adolescent Refugee's Construction of Patriotism in JROTC," *Educational Studies* 39.5 (2014). Reprinted by permission of Taylor & Francis LLC (http://www.tandfonline.com).

Brazilians in Japan Over two hundred thousand descendants of Japanese migrants to Brazil and Peru now live in Japan as temporary workers, particularly in auto parts manufacturing. Here Brazilians of Japanese descent attend a church service in the Japanese city of Tsu. (Sean Sprague/Alamy Stock Photo)

As manufacturing and economic growth stagnated in the 1990s, this circuit of migration to Japan dwindled. Though pursuit of economic opportunity and flight from persecution are the major factors that drive international migration, other factors shape the creation of migratory circuits. A migratory circuit is a deep connection created between two regions through an initial experience of migration that results in a greater circulation of people. Migrants usually become ethnic, religious, or linguistic minorities in the countries where they settle, and they commonly face discrimination. Sometimes this discrimination is expressed in violence and oppression, such as that experienced by contemporary Zimbabwean workers in South Africa.

In 2015 the European Union became the setting of a new migration crisis as over 1 million refugees fled armed conflicts and poverty in Africa and the Middle East.[2] The largest contingent was refugees from Syria's civil war. The refugees faced a succession of challenges ranging from perilous crossings of the Mediterranean, in which thousands perished, to the hostility of peoples and governments, particularly in eastern Europe, where countries like Hungary had once welcomed East Germans fleeing communism but now blocked the transit of refugees. Countries began erecting fences and border controls to limit the flow of refugees, and British voters elected to exit the EU, threatening the principle of free movement that had been a pillar of the EU.

Urbanization

Cities in Africa, Asia, and Latin America expanded at an astonishing pace after 1945. Many doubled or even tripled in size in a single decade (Table 33.1). In 1950 there were only eight **megacities** (5 million or more inhabitants), and only two were in developing countries. Of the fifty-nine megacities anticipated to exist by 2017 forty-eight will be outside North America and Europe.

What caused this urban explosion? First, the overall population growth in the developing nations was critical. Urban residents gained substantially from a medical revolution that provided improved health care but only gradually began to reduce the size of their families. Second, more than half of all urban growth came from rural migration. Manufacturing jobs in the developing nations were concentrated in cities. In 1980 half of all the industrial jobs in Mexico were located in Mexico City. Even when industrial jobs have been scarce, migrants have streamed to cities, seeking any type of employment. As large landowners found it more profitable to produce export crops, their increasingly mechanized operations reduced the need for agricultural laborers. Ethnic or political unrest in the countryside can also send migrants into cities.

megacities Cities with populations of 5 million people or more.

TABLE 33.1 Urban Population as a Percentage of Total Population in the World and in Eight Major Areas, 1925–2025

AREA	1925	1950	1975	2000	2025 (EST.)
World Total	21%	28%	39%	50%	63%
North America	54	64	77	86	93
Europe	48	55	67	79	88
Soviet Union	18	39	61	76	87
East Asia	10	15	30	46	63
Latin America	25	41	60	74	85
Africa	8	13	24	37	54

Note: Little more than one-fifth of the world's population was urban in 1925. In 2000 the total urban proportion in the world was about 50 percent. According to United Nations experts, the proportion should reach two-thirds by about 2025. The most rapid urban growth will occur in Africa and Asia, where the move to cities is still in its early stages.

Most of the growing numbers of urban poor earned precarious livings in a **bazaar economy** made up of petty traders and unskilled labor. In the bazaar economy, which echoed early preindustrial markets, regular salaried jobs were rare and highly prized, and a complex world of tiny, unregulated businesses and service occupations predominated. Peddlers and pushcart operators hawked their wares, and sweatshops and home-based workers manufactured cheap goods for popular consumption. These workers typically lacked job security, unemployment insurance, and pensions.

After 1945 large-scale urban migration profoundly affected traditional family patterns in developing countries, just as it had during the Industrial Revolution.

Particularly in Africa and Asia, the great majority of migrants to cities were young men seeking temporary or seasonal work. For rural women, the consequences of male out-migration to cities were mixed. Asian and African women found themselves heads of households, faced with added burdens in managing the farm and sustaining families. African and Asian village women became unprecedentedly self-reliant and began to assert greater rights.

In Latin America migration patterns differed: whole families generally migrated, often to squatter settlements. These families frequently belonged to the class of landless laborers, which was generally larger in Latin America than in Africa and Asia. Migration was also

The Bazaar Economy
These merchant women selling vegetables in Pisac, Peru, form part of an informal economy.
(© Juergen Ritterbach/Vario Images RM/age-fotostock)

Per capita GDP

World average: $9,099

| Over $40,000 |
| $20,000–$40,000 |
| $9,099–$19,999 |
| $3,000–$9,098 |
| Under $3,000 |

☐ One square represents $20 billion in GDP

The top fifty countries are named; the GDP of the top twelve is listed.

MAPPING THE PAST

MAP 33.1 The Global Distribution of Wealth, ca. 2010 This size-comparison map, arranged according to global wealth distribution, vividly illustrates the gap in wealth between the Northern and Southern Hemispheres. The two small island nations of Japan and the United Kingdom have more wealth than all the nations of the Southern Hemisphere combined, although wealth creation in India and Brazil has advanced significantly. The wealthiest countries are also the most highly urbanized. As market capitalism expands in China, Vietnam, and other Asian countries and in Latin America and Africa, the relative-size ratios on the map will continue to change and evolve. Tiny Iceland, whose GDP is less than $20 billion, nevertheless has one of the highest per capita GDPs in the world.

ANALYZING THE MAP Which three countries are the wealthiest? Where are the poorest countries concentrated?

CONNECTIONS How were the two small nations of Japan and the United Kingdom able to acquire such enormous wealth?

more likely to be permanent. Another difference was that single women were as likely as single men to move to the cities, in part because women were in high demand as domestic servants. Some women also left to escape male-dominated villages where they faced narrow social and economic opportunities.

In cities the concentration of wealth in few hands has resulted in unequal consumption, education, and employment. The gap between rich and poor around the world can be measured both between the city and the countryside, and within cities (Map 33.1). Wealthy city dwellers in developing countries often had more in common with each other than with the poorer urban and rural people in their own country. As a result, the elites have often favored globalization that connects them with wealthier nations.

bazaar economy An economy with few salaried jobs and an abundance of tiny, unregulated businesses such as peddlers and pushcart operators.

Multinational Corporations

A striking feature of global interdependence beginning in the early 1950s was the rapid emergence of **multinational corporations**, or multinationals, which are business firms that operate in a number of different countries and tend to adopt a global rather than a national perspective. Their rise was partly due to the revival of capitalism after the Second World War, increasingly free international economic relations, and the worldwide drive for rapid industrialization. Multinationals treated the world as one big market, coordinating complex activities across political boundaries and escaping political controls and national policies.

The impact of multinational corporations, especially on less industrialized countries, has been mixed. The presence of multinationals helped spread the products and values of consumer society to elites in the developing world. Critics considered this part of the process of neocolonialism, whereby local elites abandoned their nation's interests and contributed to continued foreign domination. (See "Analyzing the Evidence: A Brazilian Band on Globalization," at right.)

Multinational corporations are among the main beneficiaries of economic liberalism: growing openness of national markets and growing economic integration allow corporations to move goods, capital, and technology more fluidly and more intensely. But the growing interconnectedness of world markets comes with costs. In particular, it has meant increased economic volatility, as exemplified by the banking crisis that swept the United States and Europe in 2008 and plunged countries into deep and long recessions.

Multinational Companies in China Shoppers at a Sam's Club in the outskirts of Beijing reflect the globalization of consumption. Global commodity chains, multinational corporations, and converging consumer tastes, particularly among the middle class, create increasingly similar experiences across the world. (David G. McIntyre/EPA/Newscom)

Social Movements

What challenges did social reformers address at the turn of the twenty-first century?

Just as nineteenth-century social reformers embraced the cause of ending slavery, modern social reformers have sought to end global inequality, racism, and sexism and to expand human rights. Social movements played a critical role in the victory of the democratic movements in Latin America and Europe and the end of the apartheid system in South Africa.

As movements for human rights and social reform gained ground in the 1960s and 1970s, activists increasingly looked beyond national borders to form alliances. Movements for women's rights, nuclear disarmament, environmental protection, and addressing climate change all became both local and global efforts. For example, the global anti-apartheid movement kept pressure on nations to apply economic and political sanctions on the white-minority regime in South Africa. But at the same time, the anti-apartheid movement served as a means to address local problems. For instance, in Brazil anti-apartheid activism helped draw attention to the country's own racial inequalities, while in the United States anti-apartheid activism on college campuses helped students organize movements concerned with other issues such as gender equality.

The 1977 Nestlé boycott exemplified the kinds of success such movements could achieve as well as their limitations. Critics charged that the Swiss company's marketing of powdered baby formula in poor countries or regions with little access to clean water posed a risk to children. Activists called on consumers around the world to boycott Nestlé products.

At first, Nestlé dismissed the boycott and sought to discredit the movement. The president of the company's Brazilian division declared that "the US Nestlé Co has advised me that their research indicates that this [boycott] is actually an indirect attack on the free world's economic system."[3] Condemnation of Nestlé mounted.

multinational corporations Business firms that operate in a number of different countries and tend to adopt a global rather than a national perspective.

A Brazilian Band on Globalization

The rock group Mundo Livre S/A was formed in 1984 in the northeastern Brazilian city Recife, in the region first settled by the Portuguese to cultivate sugarcane with slave labor. Mundo Livre S/A, whose name translates to "Free World, Inc.," sings about globalization from the perspective of those who live at its periphery, in poorer cities of developing countries.

"Forerunners (Resisting the Global Mugging)," 2000

The computers of the mega-corporations work *full time*
Day after day
Their senior executives circulate
In a world of fanaticism and devotion,
Venerating the omnipresent god *Naiq* [Nike]
Even when they should be off,
They never stop researching,
Investigating the streets
Searching for new clues.
For decades they have been buying and suborning
The congressmen, democrats, modernizers, liberals
Sponsoring presidential elections,
Financing plans of governance,
Arming, arranging new global consortiums
That quickly assume control
Of immense and strategic state patrimonies
Ultimately conquering small, medium,
And large emerging markets on all continents
(Those, those things that we used to call countries).

No, no, we are not only talking
About macroeconomics or geopolitics.
We are talking about multi-tutions:
Institutions, parties, values and concepts
(Religions, in the end)
That cancel each other out
Or vulgarly recycle themselves
With each turn of the earth
Of mutant souls and minds
Of the abject BMD beings—
—Bearers of Moral Deficiency.
But exhibiting their resplendent
Digital cell phones, palm-tops,
Bullet-proof windshields and *Naiq* hats,
They are merely the pathetic villains of our story.

To understand the heroes,
We have to change scenes.
Visualize a metropolitan area
In a decadent market,
Cradle to a true army
Of maladjusted forerunners
Alleys of hunger . . . Night sticks . . . Shotguns . . .
In that hostile environment,
The password for survival
Consists of a balanced response
To a recurring conflict
On the one hand,
The questionable and laughable resistance
From the hallowed traditions
And on the other,
The dangerous seductiveness of the antennas.

But a forerunner
Doesn't eat out of anyone's hands
We don't pray at the primer of the *Naiqmen*
Our fuel is music
Not the contaminated kind
Which the housewives compete for
On the shelves of special offers
Of the great incorporated magazines
Just because they heard it a million times
In the *Naiqspace*—sacred temples of *Saint Naiq*
Which will never be struck by cruise missiles
Straying from their targets

We feel from a distance
The smell of incorporated dilution
We are always in the margins
And we have the power to absorb
Only the beats that don't get beaten . . .

QUESTIONS FOR ANALYSIS

1. What response to globalization does the song suggest?
2. What is the "laughable resistance / From the hallowed traditions"? What does the band mean by "the dangerous seductiveness of the antennas"?

Source: Lyrics for the song "Batedores" from the album *Por Pouco* by Mundo Livre S/A. © Fred Zero Quatro, Mundo Livre S/A. Used by permission. Translated by Jerry Dávila.

In a 1978 hearing, U.S. senator Ted Kennedy asked a Nestlé executive: "Can a product which requires clean water, good sanitation, adequate family income and a literate parent to follow printed instructions be properly and safely used in areas where water is contaminated, sewage runs in the streets, poverty is severe and illiteracy is high?"[4]

In 1981 the UN World Health Organization responded to the campaign by developing a set of voluntary standards regulating the marketing of infant formula in countries where access to clean water was precarious. Nestlé agreed to follow the standards. The movement succeeded, but its success raised questions: multinational corporations operated beyond the reach of single governments and often operated in regions with weak regulatory or investigatory structures. As a result, it was hard to hold them accountable when their conduct was unethical. At the same time, social movements and nongovernmental organizations also acted outside the realm of public accountability.

Environmentalism

The modern environmental movement began with concerns about chemical waste, rapid consumption of energy and food supplies, global deforestation, and threats to wildlife. By the 1970s citizens had begun joining together in nongovernmental organizations to pursue preservation or restoration of the natural environment.

The environmental movement is actually several different movements, each with its own agenda. (See "Analyzing the Evidence: Protest Against Genetically Modified Foods," at right.) American biologist and writer Rachel Carson was an early proponent of the environmental health movement. In *Silent Spring* (1962), she warned of the dangers of pesticides and pollution:

> Along with the possibility of the extinction of mankind by nuclear war, the central problem of our age has therefore become the contamination of man's total environment with such substances of incredible potential for harm—substances that accumulate in the tissues of plants and animals and even penetrate the germ cells to shatter or alter the very material of heredity upon which the shape of the future depends.[5]

Carson and others were concerned about the harmful effects of chemicals, radiation, pollution, waste, and urban development on the environment and on human health. Environmentalists like Carson acted out of concern that all living things were connected and that damage to one part of an ecological system could have consequences across that ecosystem.

Environmentalists today are especially concerned about **global warming**, the increase of global temperatures over time caused by the buildup of carbon in the atmosphere that captures heat. As a result of global warming, average temperatures have increased worldwide in recent decades, a trend that most scientists expect will intensify without curbs on carbon emissions. The decade from 2000 to 2010 was the warmest in recorded history, and the decade beginning in 2010 is projected to be even warmer. Scientists believe that man-made climate change began with the Industrial Revolution in the eighteenth century. The subsequent release of hydrocarbons produced through the burning of fossil fuels—coal, oil, natural gas—has caused a greenhouse effect that traps these gases and heats up the earth's atmosphere. Paradoxically, industrialization and increased consumption in the developing world meant diminished global inequalities but intensified global carbon emissions.

Scientists predict that the effects of global warming over the next century will include a catastrophic rise in sea levels that threatens to put many coastal cities and islands underwater; ecosystem changes that may threaten many species; destruction of the earth's ozone layer, which shields the planet from harmful solar radiation; and a decline in agricultural production.

Global Warming In the twenty-first century development pressures meet growing concern about climate change.

(Joel Pett Editorial Cartoon used with the permission of Joel Pett and the Cartoonist Group)

global warming The consensus view of an overwhelming majority of the world's scientists that hydrocarbons produced through the burning of fossil fuels have caused a greenhouse effect that has increased global temperatures over time.

Protest Against Genetically Modified Foods

The Chilean demonstrators in this photo are protesting the introduction of genetically modified crops. The banner reads, "I do not want transgenic crops in Chile: Movement for Food Sovereignty." Worldwide, people oppose genetically modified (GMO) crops for a variety of reasons. Some opponents fear that GMO foods present unforeseen health risks. Other opponents believe that the proliferation of genetically modified crops could damage biodiversity by reducing the variety of strains that are planted; they are also concerned that gene transfer from GMOs, particularly through pollination, could be damaging to other plant species, as well as to other organisms such as bees. Some opponents also note that GMOs can undermine small farmers who cannot afford the patented seeds of multinational companies such as Monsanto, placing them at a disadvantage relative to large landowners and threatening their land tenure.

(Eliseo Fernandez/Reuters/Newscom)

The protesters in this image are members of a movement for food sovereignty that advocates for the production of crops from locally sourced seeds. Some are dressed as bees or clowns, and in the foreground a marcher dressed as the grim reaper bears a sign that reads, "Mon$anto patents your life."

QUESTIONS FOR ANALYSIS

1. What do the costumes suggest about the protesters' views about the effects of genetically modified foods?
2. Examine the concerns of these protesters in the context of the promises of the green revolution. What are some of the advantages and disadvantages of the scientific engineering of food crops?

International concerns over global warming resulted in a 1997 agreement, the Kyoto Protocol, which amended the United Nations Framework Convention on Climate Change. Countries that ratify the Kyoto Protocol agree to reduce their emissions of carbon dioxide and five other greenhouse gases. As of April 2014, 191 countries had ratified it. The most notable exception was the United States. The United Nations and environmental activists have continued to pursue an international environmental accord that can bring all nations into a shared effort to combat climate change. The U.S. government agreed to the voluntary limits on greenhouse gas emissions called for in the 2015 Paris Climate Agreement, which would be achieved by changing regulations in areas such as electicity production.

Lesbian, Gay, and Transgender Rights

In the United States and western Europe the growing focus on liberal individual freedoms since the 1960s has opened social space for same-sex unions and affinities, which had long been suppressed by religious and cultural strictures. By the early 1970s a global gay rights movement championed the human rights of people who are lesbian, gay, or transgender. The movement intensified in the 1980s as it became clear that governments neglected medical research and treatment for people sick with AIDS, which they dismissed as a "gay disease." The organization ACT UP's advocacy campaign for AIDS research created a powerful symbol using the words "Silence = Death" beneath a pink triangle to represent the AIDS crisis. A journalist who wrote about AIDS in the 1980s described his reaction to the ACT UP symbol:

When I first saw the [ACT UP] poster, I didn't really know what it was. . . . I recognized the triangle as the symbol of homosexual victimization by the Nazis, but this triangle pointed up. Did it suggest supremacy? And the phrase itself, with its diabolical math, lodged in my imagination. Did it suggest conspiracy? Because of the word "death" I supposed it was about AIDS; had I noticed the tiny type at the bottom, which for a time included the instruction "Turn anger, fear, grief into action," perhaps I would have been sure.[6]

By the 1990s gay rights activists had broadened their efforts to challenge discrimination in employment, education, and public life. In 1995 Canada became the first country to allow same-sex marriage. In the ensuing years many European countries followed suit. But the legalization of same-sex marriage was not only a Western achievement: by 2013 Argentina, South Africa, Ecuador, and Uruguay had legalized same-sex marriage, while many other nations provided legal protections for families that stopped shy of marriage. Argentina led the way in legal support for transgender people and made sexual reassignment surgery a legal right in 2012. In 2014 the U.S. Supreme Court invalidated state laws and constitutional amendments barring same-sex marriage.

The movement toward recognition of same-sex marriage reflects the connection between liberalization and human rights: beyond dignifying discriminated groups, marriage rights give same-sex families legal equality to manage property rights and financial activities, such as the ability to inherit a home or jointly purchase insurance. Human rights successes in Latin America or Europe have widened the disparity in the experiences of people who are lesbian, gay, or transgender in many other regions of the world, where religious strictures against same-sex relationships can include imprisonment or death.

Equal Marriage in Argentina José Maria Di Bella, right, and his partner, Alex Freyre, celebrate Latin America's first same-sex marriage, which occurred in Tierra del Fuego, Argentina, in 2009. (Roger Bacon/Reuters/Alamy Stock Photo)

Women's Right to Equality

The 1995 United Nations Fourth World Conference on Women, held in Beijing, China, called on the world community to take action in twelve areas of critical concern to women: poverty, access to education and training, access to health care, violence against women, women and war, economic inequality with men, political inequality with men, creation of institutions for women's advancement, lack of respect for women's rights, stereotyping of women, gender inequalities and the environment, and violation of girl children's rights.[7] These are concerns that all women share, although degrees of inequality vary greatly from one country to another.

The **feminization of poverty**, the disproportionate number of women living in extreme poverty, applies to even the wealthiest countries, where two out of every three poor adults are women. There are many causes for this phenomenon. Because women are primarily responsible for child care in many cultures, they have less time and opportunity for work. Male labor migration increases the number of households headed by women and thus the number of families living in poverty. Job restrictions, discrimination, and limited access to education reduce women's employment options, except in the "informal economy" of domestic service, prostitution, and street vending. Birthrates are higher among poor women, particularly among adolescents, who make up many of the estimated 585,000 women who die every year during pregnancy and childbirth. The poorest women usually suffer most from government policies, usually legislated by men, that restrict their access to reproductive health care and family planning.

Women have made gains in the workplace, making up 38 percent of the nonfarm-sector global workforce in the early 2000s, as compared to 35 percent in 1990. But segregated labor markets remain the rule, with higher-paying jobs reserved for men. In the farm sector, women produce more than half of all the food and up to 80 percent of subsistence crops grown in Africa. Because this is informal labor and often unpaid, these women laborers are denied access to loans, and many cannot own the land they farm. (See "Global Viewpoints: Women Activists in Chiapas, Mexico," page 1004.)

Beyond the labor market, women also began in the 1960s to experience more control over pregnancy and childbirth decisions, particularly following the introduction of the birth control pill in the early 1960s. In the early twenty-first century more than half of the world's couples practiced some form of birth control, up from one in eight just forty years earlier. Birth control and abortion were most accepted in North America, Protestant regions in Europe, the Soviet Union, and East Asia.

United Nations Fourth World Conference on Women International Women's Day, March 8, and the UN Conferences on Women have served as platforms for framing the rights of women as a basic component of human rights. Here Hillary Rodham Clinton addresses the Fourth World Conference on Women in Beijing in 1995. (Granger, NYC— All rights reserved.)

Social class continues to be a major divider of women's opportunities. Over the course of the twentieth century women from more affluent backgrounds experienced far greater gains in access to education, employment, and political representation than women in poverty did. In the aftermath of decolonization and state formation, women emerged as heads of state in Bangladesh, India, Israel, and Pakistan. A wave of democratic political transitions in the 1980s yielded women heads of state in the Philippines and Nicaragua. In the years following democratic transitions, the same occurred in Panama, Chile, Argentina, Brazil, Indonesia, and Liberia.

Children: The Right to Childhood

In 1989 the United Nations General Assembly adopted the Convention on the Rights of the Child, which spelled out a number of rights that are due every child. These include civil and human rights and economic, social, and cultural rights. The convention addresses the reality that globally a billion children live in poverty—one in every two children in the world—and that children make up half the world's refugees. It also focuses on the problems of child labor and exploitation, sexual violence and sex trafficking, police abuse of street children, HIV/AIDS orphans, lack of access to education, and lack of access to adequate health

feminization of poverty The issue that those living in extreme poverty are disproportionately women.

Women Activists in Chiapas, Mexico

In 1994 peasants and activists in the southern Mexican state of Chiapas staged a revolt against landowners, government authorities, and paramilitary groups who were taking their land. They called their movement the Zapatista Army for National Liberation, named after Emiliano Zapata, leader of a peasant army in the Mexican Revolution. Though the activists armed themselves for defense, they did not wage war. Instead they employed tools such as early Internet activism to demonstrate to the world the abuses their communities faced. These Zapatista women relate the struggles through which they built their political awareness.

María

■ Life on the plantation was very hard because there was never any rest from work. There was a man who was the overseer, who forced people to work all the time. . . . We had to give a third of all the firewood we cut to the plantation owner. Another service was to clean the patio. All these "services" were not paid, of course. We had to provide them in exchange for the little piece of land where we planted our corn. . . .

As a child my life was learning to make tortillas, cook the cornmeal and wash clothes. My mother liked to work in the fields with my father, so she would leave very early to go to the fields. When I was about 13 years old, I was in charge of the household. My siblings were boys, so I had to do everything—wash everybody's clothes, prepare the food and clean the house.

. . . We continued renting land at the plantation. My father grew potatoes, corn and beans on that land. . . . But after a few years, we were asked to plant grass [for the owner's cattle], and the owner put cattle on the grassland. We couldn't work the land after that. . . . We lost it. We lost our corn there.

Guadalupe

■ I'm about 50 years old, I think. My husband is about 80. He's much older than I am. I married when I was 14 years old. I had no father and my mother didn't want me to be alone, so she married me to this man. He was already very old. He doesn't work any more. I work. I built my own house. I work in the fields. . . . In my house I do everything. I carry the corn. I carry the wood for the fire. . . . I built my own house. It's my own. I owe it to my work, not to the government. . . .

Now, in my community . . . we can't go out to work. We can't go to our cornfields. Paz y Justicia [paramilitary] men are looking for people out on the roads. They have weapons and they kill people. . . . They killed all the cows my son had, and they ate the meat. They took my horses, too. I had seven good horses to carry wood and to carry the corn. They killed all my pigs. They even killed my dog with a machete.

Now the government says they don't have money to pay us back for our horses and for our cows. Why did they allow Paz y Justicia to do this to us in the first place? . . .

I'm really angry now! We've been at this sit-in for two months waiting in front of the government building.

Isabel

■ I went to work as a maid. I was only nine years old. I cleaned the house and took care of the children, and I lived in their house. There was a school nearby, so I asked my employers if I could go there to study, and they said yes. . . .

I was very lucky that I worked with these people. Many indigenous women who come from the countryside don't have it so good. A lot of them are mistreated. . . . There's a lot of racism and discrimination here in San Cristóbal, and the indigenous women are constantly humiliated. . . .

In 1992, [we] . . . formed an indigenous women's street theater group, and we began performing in village plazas, in the streets, in schools and in auditoriums. . . . [W]e started preparing our first play, *La mujer desesperada* (The Desperate Woman). This is a tragedy about domestic violence and violence in general. We performed this play in San Cristóbal on March 8, 1993, on International Women's Day.

QUESTIONS FOR ANALYSIS

1. What are the sources of insecurity in these women's lives?
2. How do these women respond to the pressures they face?
3. How do these accounts reflect themes of poverty, migration, and women's inequalities in the contemporary world?

Source: Teresa Ortiz, *Never Again a World Without Us: Voices of Mayan Women in Chiapas, Mexico* (Washington, D.C.: EPICA, 2001), pp. 38–40, 82–85, 153–154. Used by permission of the author.

care. The convention has been ratified by more countries than any other human rights treaty—196 countries as of 2017. The only United Nations member nation that has not ratified it is the United States.

As the twenty-first century began, nearly a billion people—mostly women denied equitable access to education—were illiterate. Increasing economic globalization has put pressure on all governments to improve literacy rates and educational opportunities; the result has been reduced gender inequalities in education. While the percentage of illiterate adults in 2010 who were women was 64 percent, the percentage of girls among illiterate children was 60 percent, with the greatest gains in literacy occurring in South Asia and the Middle East.

In the 1990s Mexico pioneered a new approach to combating poverty that has been implemented in a growing number of countries. Conditional cash transfer, or CCT, provides a stipend to families who meet certain goals, such as keeping their children in school. This approach addresses poverty directly, while enlisting families to work toward its long-term solution by increasing education levels, which will broaden opportunities for new generations. Mexico's Oportunidades (Opportunities) CCT was followed by Brazil's Bolsa Família (Family Scholarship) and by similar projects in many other countries in Latin America. Versions of the program have been introduced across Asia and the Middle East, including in Bangladesh, where a CCT program promotes the education of girls.

Science and Technology: Changes and Challenges

How have science and technology kept pace with population change?

Since 1950 the world's population has increased from 2.5 billion people to over 7 billion. This population growth has been matched by increasing demand for food and has placed growing strains on natural resources. Advances in agriculture and medicine have helped offset this challenge, while technological innovations in areas such as transportation and communications have increased the complexity of interactions among the world's growing population.

Intensified Agriculture and the Green Revolution

As the world's population grew in the second half of the twentieth century, food production strained to keep pace, prompting a greater emphasis on rural development and agricultural sciences. Before 1939 the countries of Asia, Africa, and Latin America had collectively produced more grain than they consumed. After 1945,

as their populations soared, they began importing food from countries like the United States. Although crops might fail in poor countries, starvation seemed a thing of the past.

Then, in 1966 and 1967, a devastating famine struck India. That close brush with mass starvation created widespread alarm that population growth was outpacing food production. The American scientist Paul Ehrlich envisioned a grim future in his 1968 bestseller *The Population Bomb*, which warned of a population crisis:

> The battle to feed all of humanity is over. In the 1970s the world will undergo famines—hundreds of millions of people are going to starve to death in spite of any crash programs embarked upon now.[8]

Ehrlich was not the first scientist to make such dire predictions, and like Thomas Malthus before him (see "Industry and Population" in Chapter 23), he failed to understand the adaptability of farmers and the ability of agricultural technology to keep pace with population growth.

Plant scientists continued to develop new genetically engineered and hybridized seeds to suit particular growing conditions. The first breakthrough came in Mexico in the 1950s when an American-led team developed new strains of wheat that enabled farmers to double their yields, though the plants required greater amounts of fertilizer and water for irrigation. Mexican wheat production soared. A similar innovation in Asia introduced a new "miracle rice" that allowed farmers to plant two to four crops a year rather than one. Thus began the transformation of agriculture in some poor countries—the so-called **green revolution**.

As they applied green revolution technologies, many Asian countries experienced rapid increases in grain production. Farmers in India increased production more than 60 percent in fifteen years. China followed with its own highly successful version of the green revolution.

The green revolution offered new hope to industrializing nations, though its benefits often flowed to large landowners and export farms that could afford the necessary investments in irrigation and fertilizer. Experiences in China and other Asian countries showed, however, that even peasant families with tiny farms could gain substantially. Indeed, the green revolution's greatest successes occurred in Asian countries with broad-based peasant ownership of land. However, few of the poorest villagers benefited from the technological revolution in equipment because they rarely owned land or had enough capital to invest in new agricultural technology to increase their yields. This helps explain why in Latin America, where 3 to 4 percent of

green revolution Beginning in the 1950s, the increase in food production stemming from the introduction of high-yielding wheat, hybrid seeds, and other advancements.

the rural population owned 60 to 80 percent of the land, the green revolution spread slowly beyond Mexico, where land had been redistributed after the 1910 revolution.

The Medical Revolution

The medical revolution began in the late nineteenth century with the development of the germ theory of disease (see "Urban Development" in Chapter 24) and continued rapidly after World War II. Scientists discovered vaccines for many of the most deadly diseases. The Salk polio vaccine, developed in 1952, was followed by the first oral polio vaccine (1962) and vaccines for measles (1964), mumps (1967), rubella (1970), chicken pox (1974), hepatitis B (1981), and human papilloma virus (2006). According to the UN World Health Organization, medical advances reduced deaths from smallpox, cholera, and plague by more than 95 percent worldwide between 1951 and 1966.

Following independence, Asian and African countries increased the small numbers of hospitals, doctors, and nurses they had inherited from colonial regimes. In addition, local people were successfully trained as paramedics to staff rural outpatient clinics that offered medical treatment, health education, and prenatal and postnatal care. Many paramedics were women, who traditionally addressed health problems that involved childbirth and infancy.

Medical advances significantly lowered death rates and lengthened life expectancies worldwide. Children became increasingly likely to survive their early years, although infant and juvenile mortality remained far higher in poor countries than in rich ones. By 1980 the average inhabitant of the developing countries could expect to live about fifty-four years, although life expectancy at birth varied from forty to sixty-four years depending on the country. In industrialized countries, life expectancy at birth averaged seventy-one years.

The medical benefits of scientific advances have been limited by unequal access to health care, which is more readily available to the wealthy than to the poor. Between 1980 and 2000 the number of children under the age of five dying annually of diarrhea dropped by 60 percent through the global distribution of a cheap sugar-salt solution mixed in water. Still, over 1.5 million children worldwide continue to die each year from diarrhea, primarily in poorer nations. Deaths worldwide from HIV/AIDS, malaria, and tuberculosis are concentrated in the world's poorest regions, while tuberculosis remains the leading killer of women worldwide.

Tuberculosis (TB) claims millions of lives every year, even though it is a curable disease. Malaria kills a million people a year worldwide, 90 percent of them in Africa. In 2007 the Population Division of the United Nations calculated that 36 million persons globally were infected with HIV, the virus that causes AIDS, and that AIDS was the world's fourth-leading cause of death. About 90 percent of all persons who die from AIDS and 86 percent of those currently infected with HIV live in sub-Saharan Africa (Map 33.2). In Africa HIV/AIDS is most commonly spread through heterosexual sex. Widespread disease and poverty are also significant factors in that Africans already suffering from other illnesses such as malaria or tuberculosis are less resistant to HIV and have less access to health care for treatment.

Another factor contributing to the spread of AIDS in Africa is political instability—particularly in the corridor running from Uganda to South Africa. This region was the scene of conflicts that resulted in massive numbers of refugees and a breakdown in health-care services. The people living in this area in the countries of Uganda, Rwanda, Burundi, Zaire/Congo, Angola, Zimbabwe, Mozambique, and South Africa have been decimated by HIV/AIDS. South Africa has the largest number of HIV/AIDS cases in the world. In 2010 around 10 percent of the South African population, about 5.6 million people, was living with HIV/AIDS. Since 2001 relatively inexpensive HIV/AIDS drugs that are widely available in the West have been dispensed freely to many of those infected in Africa and Asia, but the availability of these drugs has generally failed to keep up with the need.

Climate change has emerged as a growing factor in the spread of disease as the habitats for organisms that carry diseases—such as mosquitoes—expand. Changes in rainfall also play a role because areas that experience increasing rain have more standing water where mosquito larvae can incubate. Paradoxically, areas beset by drought also experience an intensification of mosquito-borne disease because in dry periods people tend to store water, which then becomes a breeding ground for mosquitoes. In Africa, Asia, the Pacific, and the Americas, these factors have accelerated the intensification of mosquito-borne diseases such as malaria, dengue, chikungunya, and, most recently, Zika. (See "Thinking Like a Historian: The Relationships Between Mosquitoes, People, and Epidemics," page 1008.)

A Digital Revolution

The invention of moving pictures, the telephone, and other communications technologies between 1875 and 1900 prepared the way for a twentieth-century era of mass communications. In parallel, new information-processing technologies began with the development of adding and calculating machines and culminated in the development of the first computers during the Second World War. As computing and communications technologies converged, they created the "information age." The global availability and affordability of radios and television sets in the 1950s introduced

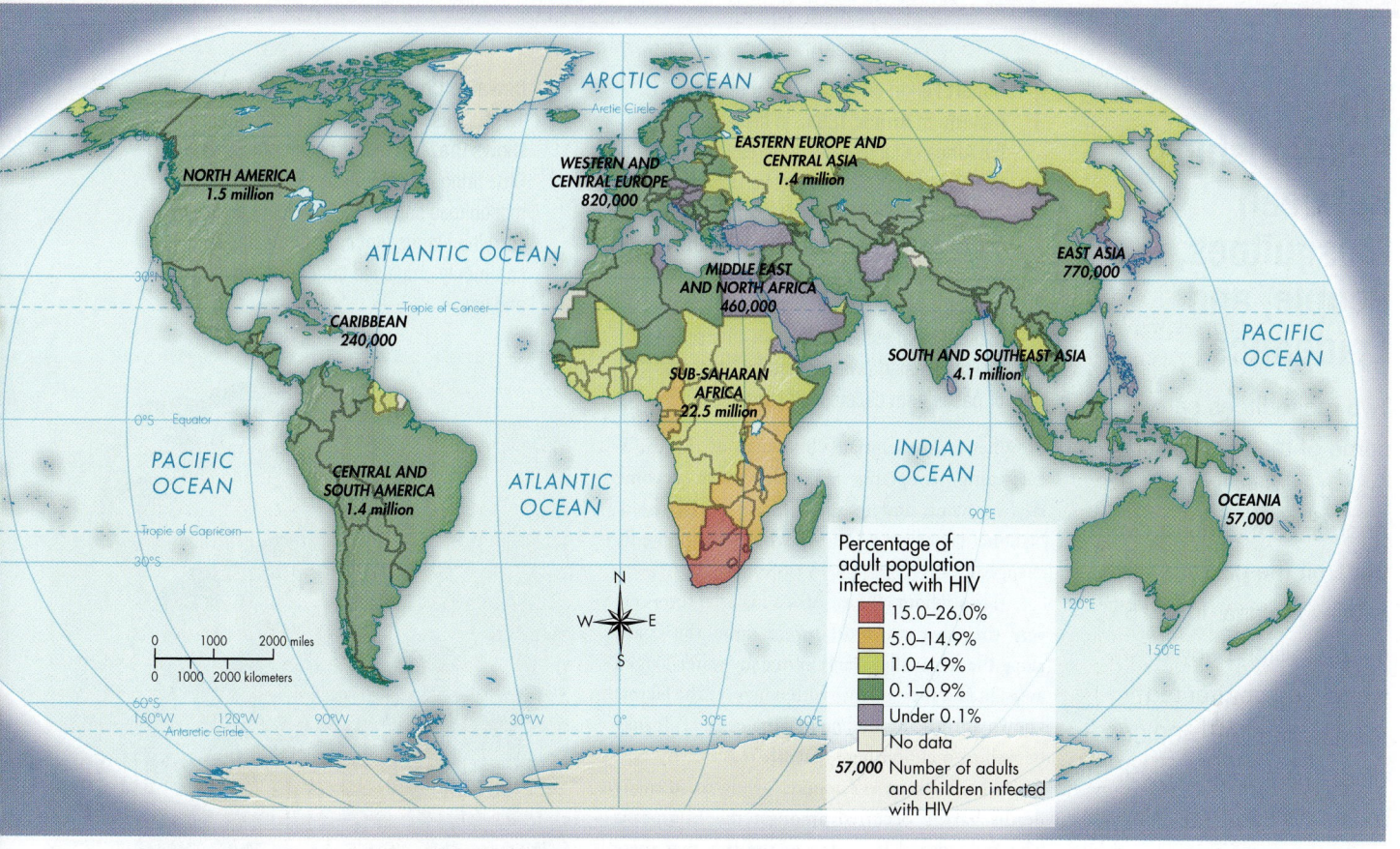

MAP 33.2 People Living with HIV/AIDS Worldwide, ca. 2010 As this map illustrates, Africa has been hit the hardest by the HIV/AIDS epidemic. It currently has 70 percent of the world's cases of HIV infection. AIDS researchers expect that in the coming decade, however, Russia and South and East Asia will overtake and then far surpass Africa in the number of infected people. (Source: Data from World Health Organization.)

a second communications revolution that followed the nineteenth-century first revolution (telegraph, telephone, and improvements in the circulation of newspapers and mail). The transistor radio penetrated the most isolated hamlets of the world. Governments embraced radio broadcasting as a means to project their power, disseminate propaganda, and broaden education. Though initially less common, television use expanded into nearly every country during the 1960s and 1970s, even if there was only one television in a village.

Governments recognized the power of the visual image to promote their ideologies or leaders, and a state television network became a source of national pride. In countries like Brazil, television transmission towers that rose up in the 1960s became monuments to modernity and development. Around the world, governments controlled the introduction of color television to symbolize progress. The Argentine military junta introduced color broadcasting to the nation for the 1978 soccer World Cup, transmitting games that took place within earshot of the detention centers where it waged its "dirty war." Television became a powerful

disseminator of culture: U.S. television programming reached around the world. Mexican television programs dominated Spanish-speaking regions. Brazilian soap operas gained loyal followers from the Soviet Union to Angola.

The third, and perhaps greatest, communications revolution began with the first personal computers in 1976, followed by the introduction of cell phones in 1985. The rapid diffusion of computing and cellular technology has allowed nations in the developing world to bypass traditional telephone lines, installation, and other obstacles. Smartphones have become the most common instruments for connecting to the Internet, allowing people in poorer and rural regions of the world to communicate and access information digitally without a computer or physical network.

Broader Internet access has made global access to information and communications seemingly infinite. Meanwhile, authoritarian governments have realized that the Internet and social media platforms like Facebook and Twitter pose a threat to their power and control. The governments of China and North Korea, for example, restrict information that travels in and out of

The Relationships Between Mosquitoes, People, and Epidemics

Two mosquitoes carry some of the world's most feared diseases. The *Anopheles* mosquito can transmit the parasite that causes malaria. In 2015 over 2 million people worldwide contracted malaria and over 400,000 died. The *Aedes aegypti* mosquito can transmit the viruses that cause Zika, dengue, chikungunya, and yellow fever. In 2016, as Zika spread through Latin America, it was linked to complications among pregnant women that in some cases led to microcephaly (reduced head size) in their children. These diseases thrive in urban environments because of the proximity between people and mosquitoes.

1 **Robert Felkin on race, character, and malaria in Africa, 1893.** In his lectures to the African Ethnological Congress at the 1893 Chicago World's Fair, Robert Felkin, a British doctor, drew a link between climate, disease, and character to support the European colonization of Africa. At the time he spoke, the link between malaria and mosquitoes had not been established. Like others, Felkin believed malaria was spread by "miasmas," or gases from decomposing matter.

When . . . the climate, like that of Africa, is enervating, emigrants from the north become lazy, indolent, and to some extent emasculated. National character is, on the whole, undoubtedly changed. . . .

Throughout all East Africa malarial fevers are very rife; they are most severe upon the coast, along the river valleys, and in marshy water-logged areas; in fact they are met with wherever the factors known as those producing malaria exist. . . . It may be well to mention here that the reason why East Africa has such an evil repute, owing to so many deaths having occurred amongst the Europeans who have visited it, is due to the fact that these explorers and missionaries have been compelled to make a long stay on the coast before proceeding inland, and have there become saturated, as it were, with the malarial poison. Were these conditions rectified, and were it possible for the whites to proceed rapidly to the interior, there is no doubt that their general health would be far better, and it is for this reason that for the last ten years I have so strongly advocated the construction of short railways to carry travellers rapidly across the malarious belt on the coast.

2 **Oswaldo Cruz directs his fire at the plague, 1911.** This image from a French magazine shows Brazilian public health official Oswaldo Cruz firing his cannon-like syringes at mosquitoes carrying yellow fever and rats carrying plague. Antimosquito campaigns commonly employed images of the military and war.

(*Chanteclair Journal*, October, 1911)

ANALYZING THE EVIDENCE

1. Why do you think military imagery is used to represent efforts to limit the diseases, as reflected in Sources 2 and 5?
2. How do race and ethnicity figure into the representations of the diseases in Sources 1, 2, 3, and 5?
3. What explanations for the spread of the diseases does Source 4 offer?
4. What does "man-made malaria" mean in Source 5?

3 **Shimomura Hachigoro on malaria control in Japanese-occupied Taiwan, 1935.** In Taiwan, held by Japan between 1895 and 1945, colonial officials perceived the persistence of malaria as rooted in the beliefs and practices of the population, an attitude shared with European colonial powers in Asia and Africa. Health technician Shimomura Hachigoro summarized the Japanese government's assessment.

■ In the anti-malaria districts, we had published pamphlets, hung posters, held exhibitions and given speeches in order to offer hygienic knowledge to the [Taiwanese] people, but they paid no attention to these things and forgot them immediately.... People are lacking of knowledge. Some even don't believe the fact that malaria is transmitted by mosquito.... But we believe that while mobilizing people to carry out anti-malaria work, the knowledge can be *infused* [emphasis in the original] into ignorant people through their hands, feet, eyes and ears.

4 **Donald G. McNeil, Jr., on the spread of Zika, 2016.** As with malaria and yellow fever in the past, the perception of a disease and of the peoples susceptible to it is socially constructed. A *New York Times* article by Donald G. McNeil, Jr., suggests a diminishing boundary between the United States and what have been perceived as "tropical" diseases.

■ Tropical diseases—some of them never before seen in the United States—are marching northward as climate change lets mosquitoes and ticks expand their ranges. But that does not mean that epidemics will break out, scientists say. Whether a few cases explode into a full-fledged outbreak depends on a set of factors far more complex than the weather. The list of scary bug-borne illnesses seems to get longer every year: Lyme, West Nile, Chagas, dengue, chikungunya—and now Zika, the first case of which turned up in Puerto Rico last week....

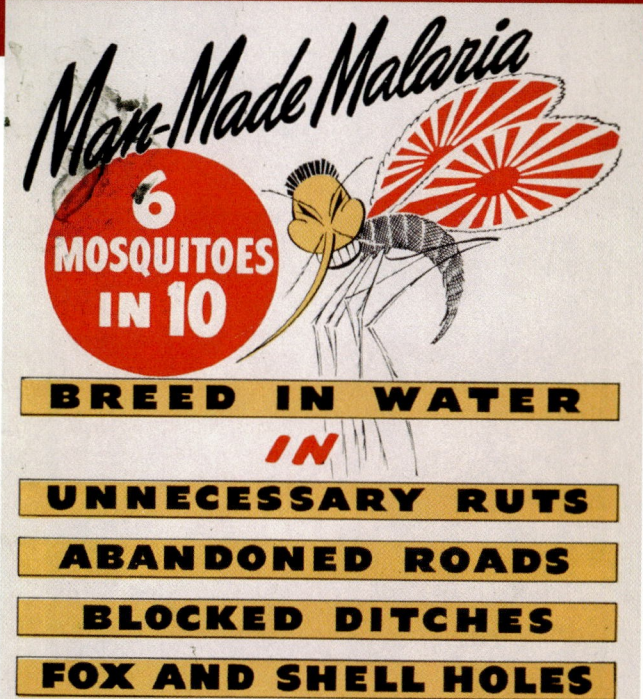

(United States National Library of Medicine, Image ID A025979/United States Navy Department Bureau of Medicine and Surgery, Government Printing Office, 1945)

5 **U.S. Navy, Second World War malaria campaign, 1945.** The U.S. armed forces waged education campaigns to prevent the spread of malaria among soldiers deployed in the Pacific during World War II. This poster created by the U.S. Navy equates mosquitoes with the enemy, giving the mosquito caricatured Japanese features and placing the Japanese flag on its wings. The image also has the effect of dehumanizing the Japanese by equating them with insects and disease.

In this hemisphere, chikungunya was first seen in late 2013 on the island of St. Martin. It started on the island's French-speaking half and jumped to other Francophone islands and to French Guiana.... Zika arrived on Easter Island in 2014. Although the island is Chilean territory, its original population was Polynesian. Zika has been island-hopping in the South Pacific since 2007. Easter Island holds an annual festival that attracts Polynesians, who may have brought Zika with them. The virus probably reached Brazil by a different route, via the influx of tourists during the 2014 World Cup, or paddlers from French Polynesia who participated in a canoe race in Rio de Janeiro.

PUTTING IT ALL TOGETHER

Using the sources above, along with what you have learned in this chapter, write a short essay discussing the ways in which studying the history of perceptions of mosquito-borne diseases and their control helps us understand the broader historical themes discussed in this book.

Sources: (1) R. W. Felkin, *On the Geographical Distribution of Tropical Diseases in Africa* (Edinburgh: William F. Clay, 1895), pp. 5, 25; (3) Quoted in Lu Shiyung, "The Theory and Practice of Malariology in Colonial Taiwan," in Ka-che Yip, ed., *Disease, Colonialism, and the State: Malaria in Modern East Asian History* (Hong Kong: Hong Kong University Press, 2009), p. 41; (4) Donald G. McNeil, Jr., "Newly Opening Door to Tropical Diseases," *New York Times*, January 5, 2016, © 2016 *The New York Times*. All rights reserved. Used by permission and protected by the Copyright Laws of the United States. The printing, copying, redistribution, or retransmission of this Content without express written permission is prohibited. www.nytimes.com.

Smartphones Expand Access to Information The rapid spread of cellular communication networks has made smartphone use the leading way in which people around the world access information and communicate. In this 2015 photo, a migrant mother uses her cell phone to map her route at the border between Serbia and Hungary. (© Balint Porneczi/Signatures/Redux)

also exists between the wealthy and poor, as well as between urban and rural areas within countries. As the Internet becomes more integral to business, education, and government, communities with no or limited access face growing disadvantages.

Chapter Summary

The end of the Cold War confrontation between superpowers has resulted in a world in which regional tensions endure and sometimes become international conflicts. Consequently, in a way similar to its actions in the Cold War era, the United States after 1990 continued to be involved in military conflicts far from home in regions ranging from the Balkans to Libya, Iraq, and Afghanistan. These conflicts have also spurred arms races that have led to the emergence of new nuclear powers in South Asia and East Asia.

The transitions to economic and political liberalism in the former Soviet bloc and in Latin America were particularly dramatic expressions of the rise of liberalism worldwide, which included the economic and political integration of Europe and the emergence of China as an economic superpower. Growing interconnectedness of world markets has meant increased economic volatility, such as the global financial market crisis of 2008. Cycles of economic growth and crisis, as well as contradictory experiences of integration and regional conflict, are tensions of the modern world rooted in historical experiences.

their countries over the Internet, while the governments of the United States and other nations have invested heavily in monitoring that information. Even as expanding means of communication through cell phones, computers, and their networks have made censorship more difficult to enforce, they have made it even harder to keep information or communications private.

The intensity of innovation in communications and information technology created new multinational giants. The success of these technology companies and the proliferation of computer, smartphone, and Internet use are remarkable changes, but they also deepen socioeconomic inequalities between countries and within countries. For instance, when Windows XP was released in 2001, a Nigerian cocoa laborer would have had to save his or her entire year's earnings to buy the Home Edition.[9] The unevenness of both the production and consumption of computer technology has resulted in a **digital divide**, meaning the gap in access to Internet, computer, and telecommunications resources. This gap is the greatest between nations like the United States, western European countries, and Japan and nations in Africa and South and Southeast Asia. The digital divide

NOTES

1. Francis Fukuyama, "The End of History?" *The National Interest,* Summer 1989, p. 3.
2. United Nations High Commisssioner for Human Rights (UN Refugee Agency), "Europe Situation," updated January 24, 2017, http://www.unhcr.org/europe-emergency.html.
3. Quoted in Judith Richter, *Holding Corporations Accountable: Corporate Conduct, International Codes, and Citizen Action* (London: Zed Books, 2002), p. 55.
4. Quoted in Simon Robinson, "Nestlé Baby Milk Substitute and International Marketing: A Case History," in *Case Histories in Business Ethics,* ed. Chris Megone and Simon Robinson (New York: Routledge, 2002), p. 141.
5. Rachel Carson, *Silent Spring* (1962; repr., New York: Houghton Mifflin, 1994), pp. 1–3, 7–8.
6. Jesse Green, "When Political Art Mattered," *New York Times,* December 7, 2003, http://www.nytimes.com/learning/teachers /featured_articles/20031208monday.html.
7. United Nations, "Critical Areas of Concern," *Report of the Fourth World Conference on Women* (New York: United Nations Department for Policy Coordination and Sustainable Development, 1995), ch. 1, annex II, ch. 3, pp. 41–44, http://www.un.org/esa/gopher-data/conf/fwcw/off/a--20.en. See also Population Reference Bureau, *Women of Our World 2005* (Washington, D.C.: Population Reference Bureau, 2005) for the latest data and ten-year follow-up to the Beijing meeting.
8. Paul Ehrlich, *The Population Bomb* (New York: Ballantine, 1968), p. 11.
9. James Gockowski and S. Oduwole, *Labor Practices in the Cocoa Sector of Southwest Nigeria with a Focus on the Role of Children* (Ibadan, Nigeria: International Institute of Tropical Agriculture, 2003), p. 23.

digital divide The gap between levels of access to computing, Internet, and telecommunications between rich and poor regions and populations.

CONNECTIONS

The present shapes the ways we ask questions about the past. Understanding of the past also shapes our questions about the present and the future. Our history of world societies shows that the forces that shape the world we live in have deep roots: Globalization reaches back for centuries. Current armed conflicts are based on historic tensions often rooted in ethnic differences or legacies of colonialism. The gaps between rich and poor countries, and between the rich and poor within countries, have sometimes been diminished by advances in science and technology or by reforms in social policy. But science, technology, and public policy also deepen those inequalities, as uneven industrialization and the digital divide reflect.

Our relationship with the past is one of continuity and change. The study of history allows us to frame questions about complex, competing, and often-contradictory experiences. Asking these questions sharpens our focus on not only the past but also the present. We are shaped by history. But we also make it.

CHAPTER 33 Review and Explore

Identify Key Terms

Identify and explain the significance of each item below.

middle powers (p. 990)

megacities (p. 995)

bazaar economy (p. 996)

multinational corporations (p. 998)

global warming (p. 1000)

feminization of poverty (p. 1003)

green revolution (p. 1005)

digital divide (p. 1010)

Review the Main Ideas

Answer the focus questions from each section of the chapter.

1. Does the contemporary world reflect the "end of history"? (p. 990)

2. How have migration and the circulation of capital and technology continued to shape the world? (p. 993)

3. What challenges did social reformers address at the turn of the twenty-first century? (p. 998)

4. How have science and technology kept pace with population change? (p. 1005)

Make Comparisons and Connections

Analyze the larger developments and continuities within and across chapters.

1. Why hasn't the end of the Cold War been followed by an easing of regional conflicts?

2. How do socioeconomic inequalities in the twenty-first-century world resemble the gaps between rich and poor in earlier eras?

3. How do contemporary technological and scientific developments reflect historical change and continuity?

TIMELINE

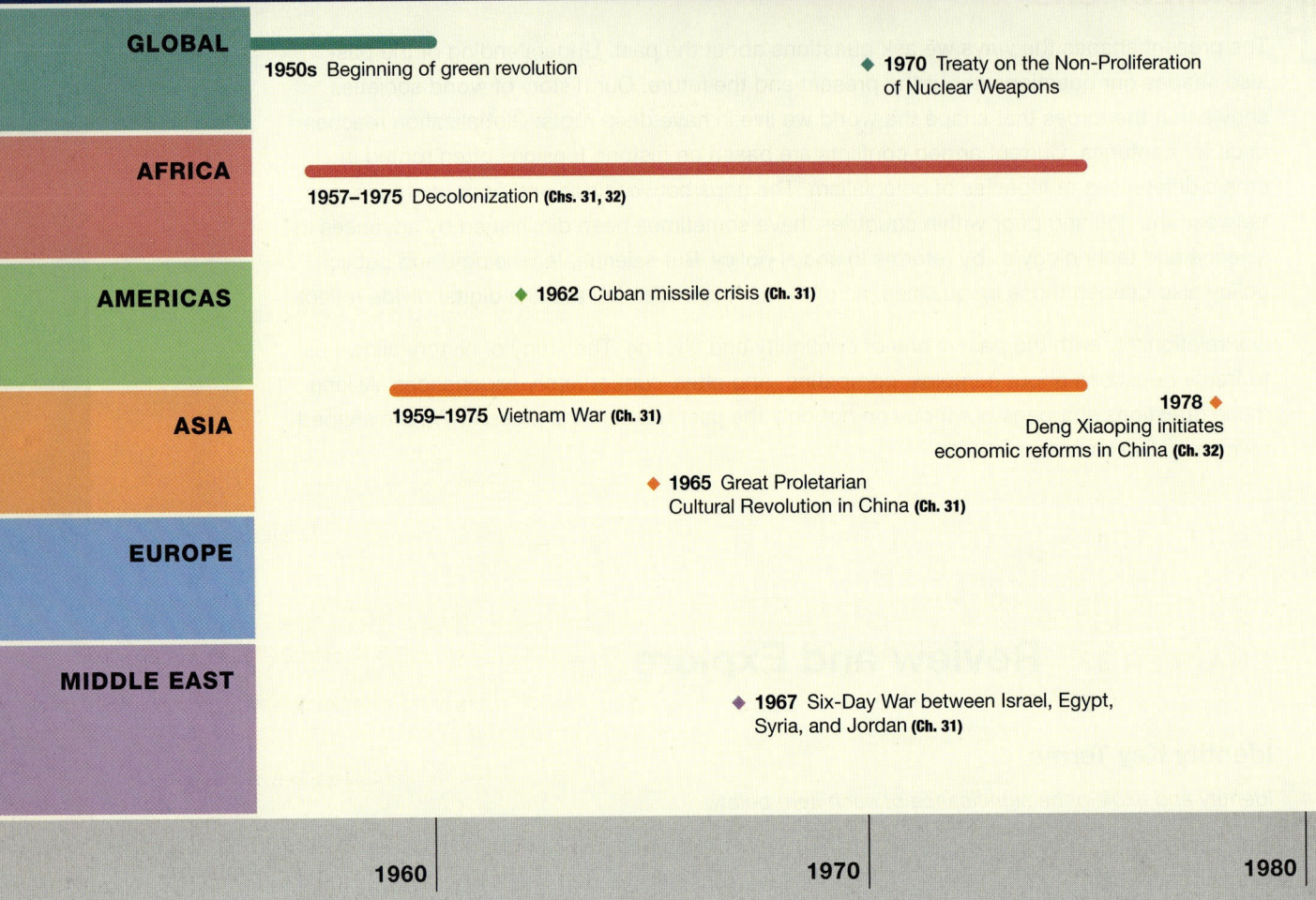

GLOBAL

1950s Beginning of green revolution

◆ 1970 Treaty on the Non-Proliferation of Nuclear Weapons

AFRICA

1957–1975 Decolonization (Chs. 31, 32)

AMERICAS

◆ 1962 Cuban missile crisis (Ch. 31)

ASIA

1959–1975 Vietnam War (Ch. 31)

1978 ◆
Deng Xiaoping initiates economic reforms in China (Ch. 32)

◆ 1965 Great Proletarian Cultural Revolution in China (Ch. 31)

EUROPE

MIDDLE EAST

◆ 1967 Six-Day War between Israel, Egypt, Syria, and Jordan (Ch. 31)

1960   1970   1980

Suggested Resources

BOOKS

Abrahamson, Mark. *Global Cities.* 2004. Explores the global historical patterns of urbanization.

Gareis, Sven Bernhard, and Johannes Varwick. *The United Nations: An Introduction.* 2005. An overview of the United Nations.

Gore, Al. *An Inconvenient Truth: The Planetary Emergency of Global Warming and What We Can Do About It.* 2006. Reasoned discussion of the greatest threat to the planet in the twenty-first century, for which Gore won the Nobel Peace Prize.

Hawkesworth, Mary. *Political Worlds of Women: Activism, Advocacy, and Governance in the Twenty-First Century.* 2012. A survey of global women's social movements amid persistent challenges of political exclusion and economic inequality.

Jones, Geoffrey. *Multinationals and Global Capitalism: From the Nineteenth to the Twenty-First Century.* 2005. A historical overview of the development of multinational corporations and a global capitalist economy.

Law, Randall D. *Terrorism: A History,* 2d ed. 2016. Explores the history of violent political actions, with a focus on ethnic, nationalist, and religious violence.

O'Neill, Bard E. *Insurgency and Terrorism: From Revolution to Apocalypse,* 2d ed. 2005. An excellent introduction to the nature of modern war.

O'Neill, John Terence, and Nicholas Rees. *United Nations Peacekeeping in the Post–Cold War Era.* 2005. Discusses the problems associated with United Nations peacekeeping efforts.

Pécoud, Antoine, and Paul de Guchteneire, eds. *Migration Without Borders: Essays on the Free Movement of People.* 2007. Regional perspectives on contemporary migration.

Piketty, Thomas. *Capital in the Twenty-First Century.* 2014. A fresh look at the history of social inequality and the accumulation of wealth.

Sasson, Tehila. "Milking the Third World? Humanitarianism, Capitalism, and the Moral Economy of the Nestlé Boycott." *American Historical Review* 121.4 (October 2016). Explores the role of human rights activism in relation to multinational corporations.

2000–2010 Warmest decade in recorded history

1997 Kyoto Protocol on global warming

1994 Nelson Mandela elected president of South Africa (Ch. 32)

1994 North American Free Trade Agreement (Ch. 32)

1994 Zapatista Army for National Liberation insurrection in Chiapas, Mexico

2001 Al-Qaeda attacks on World Trade Center and U.S. Pentagon

1993 Formation of the European Union (Ch. 32)

2016 → British "Brexit" vote to leave European Union

1989–1991 Fall of communism in the Soviet Union and eastern Europe (Ch. 32)

2003–2011 Second Persian Gulf War (Ch. 32)

1987 Palestinian intifada (Ch. 32)

2001 U.S. invasion and occupation of Afghanistan

2011 Civil war in Syria begins (Ch. 32)

| 1990 | 2000 | 2010 |

Seel, Peter B. *Digital Universe: The Global Telecommunication Revolution.* 2012. Discusses the historical trajectory of information and communications technology.

Shah, Sonia. *Pandemic: Tracking Contagions, from Cholera to Ebola and Beyond.* 2016. Examines patterns of global epidemics, both old and new.

DOCUMENTARIES

Children of Syria (PBS, 2016). A PBS *Frontline* documentary tracing the story of four refugee children from Syria who found a new home in Germany.

Last Train Home (Lixin Fan, 2009). Explores the experience of China's more than 100 million migrant workers, focusing on the tensions between rural agrarian and urban industrial settings.

The Salt of the Earth (Juliano Ribeiro Salgado and Wim Wenders, 2014). Unpacks the work of Brazilian photographer Sebastião Salgado, whose images capture peoples in motion, often fleeing the hardships of war. The documentary explores the question of healing amid conflict.

FEATURE FILMS

Dheepan (Jacques Audiard, 2015). Focuses on the experience of Sri Lankan refugees in a housing project in Paris's suburbs. Fleeing war, they find new conflicts fueled by the drug trade.

Sin Nombre (Cary Joji Fukunaga, 2009). Depicts the journey of two young Hondurans traveling through Mexico to reach the United States.

WEBSITES

Country Resources. Maintained by the Migration Policy Institute, this site presents country-by-country information on currents of international migration. **www.migrationpolicy.org/programs/migration -information-source/country-resources**

Europe's Migration Crisis. Resources maintained by the U.S. Council on Foreign Relations that offer a broad view on migration policy and pressures in Europe. **www.cfr.org/refugees-and-the-displaced/europes -migration-crisis/p32874**

Syrian Refugees: A Snapshot of the Crisis—in the Middle East and Europe. Resources and information on the Syrian refugee crisis in Europe, maintained by the Migration Policy Center of the European University Institute. **syrianrefugees.eu**

GLOSSARY

absolutism A political system common to early modern Europe in which monarchs claimed exclusive power to make and enforce laws, without checks by other institutions; this system was limited in practice by the need to maintain legitimacy and compromise with elites. (Ch. 18)

African National Congress (ANC) The main black nationalist organization in South Africa, led by Nelson Mandela. (Ch. 32)

Afrikaners Descendants of the Dutch settlers in the Cape Colony in southern Africa. (Ch. 25)

age-grade systems Among the societies of Senegambia, groups of teenage males and females whom the society initiated into adulthood at the same time. (Ch. 20)

alternate residence system Arrangement in which Japanese lords were required to live in Edo every other year and left their wives and sons there as hostages to the Tokugawa Shogunate. (Ch. 21)

anarcho-syndicalism A version of anarchism that advocated placing power in the hands of workers' unions. (Ch. 27)

Antifederalists Opponents of the American Constitution who felt it diminished individual rights and accorded too much power to the federal government at the expense of the states. (Ch. 22)

apartheid The system of racial segregation and discrimination that was supported by the Afrikaner government in South Africa. (Ch. 32)

Arab socialism A modernizing, secular, and nationalist project of nation building in the Middle East aimed at economic development and the development of a strong military. (Ch. 31)

Aztec Empire An alliance between the Mexica people and their conquered allies, with its capital in Tenochtitlan (now Mexico City), that rose in size and power in the fifteenth century and possessed a sophisticated society and culture, with advanced mathematics, astronomy, and engineering. (Ch. 16)

Balfour Declaration A 1917 statement by British foreign secretary Arthur Balfour that supported the idea of a Jewish homeland in Palestine. (Ch. 29)

banners Units of the Manchu army, composed of soldiers, their families, and slaves. (Ch. 21)

bazaar economy An economy with few salaried jobs and an abundance of tiny, unregulated businesses such as peddlers and pushcart operators. (Ch. 33)

Berlin Conference A meeting of European leaders held in 1884–1885 to lay down basic rules for imperialist competition in sub-Saharan Africa. (Ch. 25)

Bill of Rights of 1689 A bill passed by Parliament and accepted by William and Mary that limited the powers of British monarchs and affirmed those of Parliament. (Ch. 18)

Black Legend The notion that the Spanish were uniquely brutal and cruel in their conquest and settlement of the Americas, an idea propagated by rival European powers. (Ch. 16)

Black Shirts A private army under Mussolini in Italy that destroyed Socialist newspapers, union halls, and local Socialist Party headquarters, eventually pushing Socialists out of the city governments of northern Italy. (Ch. 30)

blitzkrieg "Lightning war" using planes, tanks, and trucks, first used by Hitler to crush Poland in four weeks. (Ch. 30)

Bolsheviks The "majority group"; this was Lenin's camp of the Russian party of Marxist socialism. (Ch. 28)

bourgeoisie The well-educated, prosperous, middle-class groups. (Ch. 24)

Boxers A Chinese secret society that blamed the country's ills on foreigners, especially missionaries, and rose in rebellion in 1900. (Ch. 26)

bride wealth In early modern Southeast Asia, a sum of money the groom paid the bride or her family at the time of marriage. This practice contrasted with the dowry in China, India, and Europe, which the husband controlled. (Ch. 16)

captaincies A system established by the Portuguese in Brazil in the 1530s, whereby hereditary grants of land were given to nobles and loyal officials who bore the costs of settling and administering their territories. (Ch. 16)

caravel A small, maneuverable, three-masted sailing ship that gave the Portuguese a distinct advantage in exploration and trade. (Ch. 16)

caudillismo Government by figures who rule through personal charisma and the support of armed followers in Latin America. (Ch. 27)

chattel An item of personal property; a term used in reference to enslaved people that conveys the idea that they are subhuman, like animals, and therefore may be treated like animals. (Ch. 20)

Circum-Caribbean The region encompassing the Antilles as well as the lands that bound the Caribbean Sea in Central America and northern South America. (Ch. 27)

civil service examinations A highly competitive series of written tests held at the prefecture, province, and capital levels in China to select men to become officials. (Ch. 21)

class-consciousness An individual's sense of class differentiation, a term introduced by Karl Marx. (Ch. 23)

cocoa holdups Mass protests in Africa's Gold Coast in the 1930s by producers of cocoa who refused to sell their beans to British firms and instead sold them directly to European and American chocolate manufacturers. (Ch. 31)

Cold War The post–World War II conflict between the United States and the Soviet Union. (Ch. 31)

collectivization Stalin's forcible consolidation, beginning in 1929, of individual peasant farms in the Soviet Union into large, state-controlled enterprises. (Ch. 30)

Columbian exchange The exchange of animals, plants, and diseases between the Old and the New Worlds. (Ch. 16)

Combination Acts English laws passed in 1799 that outlawed unions and strikes, favoring capitalist business owners over skilled artisans. Bitterly resented and widely disregarded by many craft guilds, the acts were repealed by Parliament in 1824. (Ch. 23)

Common Market The European Economic Community created in 1957. (Ch. 31)

concubine A woman who is a recognized spouse but of lower status than a wife. (Ch. 17)

Congress of Vienna A meeting of the Quadruple Alliance (Russia, Prussia, Austria, Great Britain) and France held in 1814–1815 to fashion a general peace settlement after the defeat of Napoleonic France. (Ch. 24)

conquistador Spanish for "conqueror"; a Spanish soldier-explorer, such as Hernán Cortés or Francisco Pizarro, who sought to conquer the New World for the Spanish crown. (Ch. 16)

conservatism A political philosophy that stressed retaining traditional values and institutions, including hereditary monarchy and a strong landowning aristocracy. (Ch. 24)

constitutionalism A form of government in which power is limited by law and balanced between the authority and power of the government, on the one hand, and the rights and liberties of the subject or citizen, on the other; it includes constitutional monarchies and republics. (Ch. 18)

Continental System A blockade imposed by Napoleon in which no ship coming from Britain or its colonies was permitted to dock at any port controlled by the French. (Ch. 22)

Copernican hypothesis The idea that the sun, not the earth, was the center of the universe. (Ch. 19)

Coptic Christianity Orthodox form of Christianity from Egypt practiced in Ethiopia. (Ch. 20)

Cossacks Free groups and outlaw armies living on the borders of Russian territory from the fourteenth century onward. In the mid-sixteenth century they formed an alliance with the Russian state. (Ch. 18)

cottage industry Manufacturing with hand tools in peasant cottages and work sheds, a form of economic activity that became important in eighteenth-century Europe. (Ch. 19)

cowrie shells Imported from the Maldives, they served as the medium of exchange in West Africa. (Ch. 20)

Creoles People of European descent born in the Americas. (Ch. 22)

Crystal Palace The location of the Great Exhibition in 1851 in London, an architectural masterpiece made entirely of glass and iron. (Ch. 23)

daimyo Regional lords in Japan, many of whom were self-made men. (Ch. 21)

Dawes Plan The product of the 1924 World War I reparations commission, accepted by Germany, France, and Britain, that reduced Germany's yearly reparations, made payment dependent on German economic prosperity, and granted Germany large loans from the United States to promote recovery. (Ch. 28)

Declaration of Independence The 1776 document in which the American colonies declared independence from Great Britain and recast traditional English rights as universal human rights. (Ch. 22)

deism Belief in a distant, noninterventionist deity, shared by many Enlightenment thinkers. (Ch. 19)

dependency theory The belief, formulated in Latin America in the mid-twentieth century, that development in some areas of the world locks other nations into underdevelopment. (Ch. 31)

détente The progressive relaxation of Cold War tensions between the United States and the Soviet Union in the late 1960s and early 1970s. (Ch. 32)

devshirme A process whereby the sultan's agents swept the provinces for Christian youths to be trained as soldiers or civil servants. (Ch. 17)

digital divide The gap between levels of access to computing, Internet, and telecommunications between rich and poor regions and populations. (Ch. 33)

divine right of kings The belief propagated by absolutist monarchs in Europe that they derived their power from God and were only answerable to him. (Ch. 18)

Dreyfus affair A divisive case in which Alfred Dreyfus, a Jewish captain in the French army, was falsely accused and convicted of treason. The Catholic Church sided with the anti-Semites against Dreyfus; after Dreyfus was declared innocent, the French government severed all ties between the state and the church. (Ch. 24)

economic liberalism The theory, associated with Adam Smith, that the pursuit of individual self-interest in a competitive market would lead to rising prosperity and greater social equality, rendering government intervention unnecessary and undesirable. (Ch. 19)

empiricism A theory of inductive reasoning that calls for acquiring evidence through observation and experimentation rather than reason and speculation. (Ch. 19)

Enabling Act An act pushed through the Reichstag by the Nazis in 1933 that gave Hitler absolute dictatorial power for four years. (Ch. 30)

enclosure The controversial process of fencing off common land to create privately owned fields that increased agricultural production at the cost of reducing poor farmers' access to land. (Ch. 19)

encomienda system A system whereby the Spanish crown granted the conquerors the right to forcibly employ groups of indigenous people as laborers and to demand tribute payments from them in exchange for providing food, shelter, and instruction in the Christian faith. (Ch. 16)

enlightened absolutism Term coined by historians to describe the rule of eighteenth-century monarchs who, without renouncing their own absolute authority, took up the call to reform their governments in accordance with the rational and humane principles of the Enlightenment. (Ch. 19)

Enlightenment An intellectual and cultural movement in late-seventeenth- and eighteenth-century Europe and the wide world that used rational and critical thinking to debate issues such as political sovereignty, religious tolerance, gender roles, and racial difference. (Ch. 19)

Estates General Traditional representative body of the three estates of France that met in 1789 in response to imminent state bankruptcy. (Ch. 22)

European Union (EU) An economic and political alliance of twelve European nations formed in 1993 that has since grown to include twenty-eight European nations. (Ch. 32)

Europe first policy The military strategy, set forth by Churchill and adopted by Roosevelt, that called for the defeat of Hitler in Europe before the United States launched an all-out strike against Japan in the Pacific. (Ch. 30)

evolution The idea, developed by Charles Darwin, that all life had gradually evolved from a common origin through a process of natural selection. (Ch. 24)

existentialism The name given to a highly diverse and even contradictory philosophy that stresses the meaninglessness of existence and the search for moral values in a world of terror and uncertainty. (Ch. 28)

extraterritoriality The legal principle that exempts individuals from local law, applicable in China because of the agreements reached after China's loss in the Opium War. (Ch. 26)

Factory Act of 1833 English law that led to a sharp decline in the employment of children by limiting the hours that children over age nine could work and banning employment of children younger than nine. (Ch. 23)

fascism A movement characterized by extreme, often expansionist nationalism, anti-socialism, a dynamic and violent leader, and glorification of war and the military. (Ch. 30)

feminization of poverty The issue that those living in extreme poverty are disproportionately women. (Ch. 33)

five-year plan Launched by Stalin in 1928 and termed the "revolution from above," its goal was to modernize the Soviet Union and generate a Communist society with new attitudes, new loyalties, and a new socialist humanity. (Ch. 30)

free womb laws Laws passed across the nineteenth-century Americas that instituted a gradual form of abolition through which children born to slaves gained their freedom. (Ch. 27)

functionalism The principle that buildings, like industrial products, should serve the purpose for which they were made as well as possible. (Ch. 28)

general will A concept associated with Rousseau, referring to the common interests of all the people, who have displaced the monarch as the holder of sovereign power. (Ch. 19)

germ theory The idea that disease is caused by the spread of living organisms that can be controlled. (Ch. 24)

Girondists A moderate group that fought for control of the French National Convention in 1793. (Ch. 22)

glasnost Soviet premier Mikhail Gorbachev's popular campaign for government transparency and more open media. (Ch. 32)

global warming The consensus view of an overwhelming majority of the world's scientists that hydrocarbons produced through the burning of fossil fuels have caused a greenhouse effect that has increased global temperatures over time. (Ch. 33)

Grand Empire The empire over which Napoleon and his allies ruled, encompassing virtually all of Europe except Great Britain. (Ch. 22)

Great Leap Forward Mao Zedong's acceleration of Chinese development in which industrial growth was to be based on small-scale backyard workshops run by peasants living in gigantic self-contained communes. (Ch. 31)

great migration The mass movement of people from Europe in the nineteenth century; one reason that the West's impact on the world was so powerful and complex. (Ch. 25)

Great Mutiny / Great Revolt The terms used by the British and the Indians, respectively, to describe the last armed resistance to British rule in India, which occurred in 1857. (Ch. 26)

Great Proletarian Cultural Revolution A movement launched in 1965 by Mao Zedong that attempted to recapture the revolutionary fervor of his guerrilla struggle. (Ch. 31)

great white walls Discriminatory laws passed by Americans and Australians to keep Asians from settling in their countries in the 1880s. (Ch. 25)

green revolution Beginning in the 1950s, the increase in food production stemming from the introduction of high-yielding wheat, hybrid seeds, and other advancements. (Ch. 33)

gunboat diplomacy The imposition of treaties and agreements under threat of military violence, such as the opening of Japan to trade after Commodore Perry's demands. (Ch. 26)

Haskalah A Jewish Enlightenment movement led by Prussian philosopher Moses Mendelssohn. (Ch. 19)

Holocaust The attempted systematic extermination of all European Jews and other "undesirables" by the Nazi state during World War II. (Ch. 30)

id, ego, superego Freudian terms for the primitive, irrational unconscious (id), the rationalizing conscious that mediates what a person can do (ego), and the ingrained moral values that specify what a person should do (superego). (Ch. 28)

import substitution industrialization (ISI) The use of trade barriers to keep certain foreign products out of one's country so that domestic industry can emerge and produce the same goods. (Ch. 31)

Inca Empire The vast and sophisticated Peruvian empire centered at the capital city of Cuzco that was at its peak in the fifteenth century but weakened by civil war at the time of the Spanish arrival. (Ch. 16)

indentured laborers Laborers who agreed to a term of employment, specified in a contract. (Ch. 26)

Indian Civil Service The bureaucracy that administered the government of India. Entry into its elite ranks was through examinations that Indians were eligible to take, but these tests were offered only in England. (Ch. 26)

Indian National Congress A political association formed in 1885 that worked for Indian self-government. (Ch. 26)

Industrial Revolution A term first coined in the 1830s to describe the burst of major inventions and economic expansion that took place in certain industries, such as cotton textiles and iron, between 1780 and 1850. (Ch. 23)

intifada Beginning in 1987, a prolonged campaign of civil disobedience by Palestinian youth against Israeli soldiers; the Arabic word *intifada* means "shaking off." (Ch. 32)

iron law of wages Theory proposed by English economist David Ricardo suggesting that the pressure of population growth prevents wages from rising above the subsistence level. (Ch. 23)

Jacobin club A political club during the French Revolution to which many of the deputies of the Legislative Assembly belonged. (Ch. 22)

janissaries Turkish for "recruits"; they formed the elite army corps. (Ch. 17)

"Japan, Inc." A nickname from the 1970s and 1980s used to describe what some considered the unfair relationship between Japan's business world and government. (Ch. 32)

Java War The 1825–1830 war between the Dutch government and the Javanese, fought over the extension of Dutch control of the island. (Ch. 26)

Jesuits Members of the Society of Jesus, founded by Ignatius Loyola in 1540, whose goal was the spread of the Roman Catholic faith through schools and missionary activity. (Ch. 18)

jihad Religious war waged by Muslim scholars and religious leaders against both animist rulers and Islamic states that they deemed corrupt. (Ch. 25)

junta A government headed by a council of commanders of the branches of the armed forces. (Ch. 32)

kibbutz A Jewish collective farm, first established by Zionists in Palestine, on which each member shared equally in the work, rewards, and defense. (Ch. 29)

laissez faire A doctrine of economic liberalism advocating unrestricted private enterprise and no government interference in the economy. (Ch. 24)

Lateran Agreement A 1929 agreement in which Mussolini in Italy recognized the Vatican as an independent state and agreed to give the church heavy financial support in return for the pope's public support. (Ch. 30)

latifundios Vast landed estates in Latin America. (Ch. 27)

law of inertia A law formulated by Galileo stating that motion, not rest, is the natural state of an object and that an object continues in motion forever unless stopped by some external force. (Ch. 19)

law of universal gravitation Newton's law that all objects are attracted to one another and that the force of attraction is proportional to the object's quantity of matter and inversely proportional to the square of the distance between them. (Ch. 19)

League of Nations A permanent international organization established during the 1919 Paris Peace Conference to protect member states from aggression and avert future wars. (Ch. 28)

Lerdo Law An 1856 Mexican law that barred corporate landholdings. (Ch. 27)

liberalism A philosophy whose principal ideas were equality and liberty; liberals demanded representative government and equality before the law as well as such individual freedoms as freedom of the press, freedom of speech, freedom of assembly, and freedom from arbitrary arrest. (Ch. 24)

liberation theology A movement within the Catholic Church to support the poor in situations of exploitation that emerged with particular force in Latin America in the 1960s. (Ch. 31)

Long March The 6,000-mile retreat of the Chinese Communist army in 1934 to a remote region on the northwestern border of China, during which tens of thousands lost their lives. (Ch. 29)

Lucknow Pact A 1916 alliance between the Hindus leading the Indian National Congress Party and the Muslim League. (Ch. 29)

Luddites Group of handicraft workers who attacked factories in northern England in 1811 and after, smashing the new machines that they believed were putting them out of work. (Ch. 23)

Majlis The national assembly established by the despotic shah of Iran in 1906. (Ch. 29)

manifest destiny The doctrine that the United States should absorb the territory spanning from the original Atlantic states to the Pacific Ocean. (Ch. 27)

March Revolution The first phase of the Russian Revolution of 1917, in which unplanned uprisings led to the abdication of the tsar and the establishment of a provisional democratic government that was then overthrown in November by Lenin and the Bolsheviks. (Ch. 28)

Marshall Plan A 1948 American plan for providing economic aid to Europe to help it rebuild after World War II. (Ch. 31)

May Fourth Movement A Chinese nationalist movement against foreign imperialists and warlord rule; it began as a 1919 student protest against the decision of the Paris Peace Conference to leave the Shandong Peninsula in the hands of Japan. (Ch. 29)

megacities Cities with populations of 5 million people or more. (Ch. 33)

Meiji Restoration The 1867 ousting of the Tokugawa Shogunate that "restored" the power of the Japanese emperors. (Ch. 26)

Mein Kampf Adolf Hitler's autobiography, published in 1925, which also contains Hitler's political ideology. (Ch. 28)

mercantilism A system of economic regulations aimed at increasing the power of the state derived from the belief that a nation's international power was based on its wealth, specifically its supply of gold and silver. (Ch. 18)

Middle Passage Enslaved Africans' horrific voyage across the Atlantic to the Americas, under appalling and often deadly conditions. (Ch. 20)

middle powers Countries with significant economic influence that became increasingly assertive regional leaders after the Cold War. (Ch. 33)

migration chain The movement of peoples in which one strong individual blazes the way and others follow. (Ch. 25)

militarism The glorification of the military as the supreme ideal of the state with all other interests subordinate to it. (Ch. 28)

Mines Act of 1842 English law prohibiting underground work for all women and girls as well as for boys under ten. (Ch. 23)

Ming Dynasty The Chinese dynasty in power from 1368 to 1644; it marked a period of vibrant urban culture. (Ch. 21)

modernism A variety of cultural movements at the end of the nineteenth century and beginning of the twentieth that rebelled against traditional forms and conventions of the past. (Ch. 28)

modernization The changes that enable a country to compete effectively with the leading countries at a given time. (Ch. 24)

modernization theory The belief, held in countries such as the United States in the mid-twentieth century, that all countries evolved in a linear progression from traditional to mature. (Ch. 31)

Monroe Doctrine An 1823 proclamation that established a U.S. sphere of influence over the Americas by opposing European imperialism on the continent. (Ch. 27)

moral economy The early modern European view that community needs predominated over competition and profit and that necessary goods should thus be sold at a fair price. (Ch. 18)

Mountain Led by Robespierre, the French National Convention's radical faction, which led the Convention in 1793. (Ch. 22)

Mughal A term used to refer to the Muslim empire of India, which was the largest, wealthiest, and most populous of the Islamic empires of the early modern world. (Ch. 17)

multinational corporations Business firms that operate in a number of different countries and tend to adopt a global rather than a national perspective. (Ch. 33)

Muslim League Political party founded in 1906 in colonial India that advocated for a separate Muslim homeland after independence. (Ch. 31)

Napoleonic Code French civil code promulgated in 1804 that reasserted the 1789 principles of the equality of all male citizens before the law and the absolute security of wealth and private property. (Ch. 22)

National Assembly French representative assembly formed in 1789 by the delegates of the third estate and some members of the clergy, the second estate. (Ch. 22)

nationalism The idea that each people had its own spirit and its own cultural unity, which manifested itself especially in a common language and history and could serve as the basis for an independent political state. (Ch. 24)

National Liberation Front The anticolonial movement in Algeria, which began a war against the French in 1954 and won independence in 1962. (Ch. 31)

NATO The North Atlantic Treaty Organization, an anti-Soviet military alliance of Western nations, formed in 1949. (Ch. 31)

Navigation Acts Mid-seventeenth-century English mercantilist laws that greatly restricted other countries' rights to trade with England and its colonies. (Ch. 18)

Nazism A movement born of extreme nationalism and racism and dominated by Adolf Hitler from 1933 until the end of World War II in 1945. (Ch. 30)

neocolonialism The establishment of political and economic influence over regions after they have ceased to be formal colonies. (Ch. 27)

neoliberalism A return beginning in the 1980s to policies intended to promote free markets and the free circulation of capital across national borders. (Ch. 32)

New Culture Movement An intellectual revolution beginning in 1916 that attacked traditional Chinese, particularly Confucian, culture and promoted Western ideas of science, democracy, and individualism. (Ch. 29)

New Deal Franklin Delano Roosevelt's plan to reform capitalism in the United States through forceful government intervention in the economy. (Ch. 30)

New Economic Policy (NEP) Lenin's 1921 policy re-establishing limited economic freedom in the Soviet Union in an attempt to rebuild agriculture and industry in the face of economic disintegration. (Ch. 30)

New Imperialism The late-nineteenth-century drive by European countries to create vast political empires abroad. (Ch. 25)

New Order Hitler's program, based on the guiding principle of racial imperialism, which gave preferential treatment to the Nordic peoples above "inferior" Latin peoples and, at the bottom, "subhuman" Slavs and Jews. (Ch. 30)

Nguyen Dynasty The last Vietnamese ruling house, which lasted from 1802 to 1945. (Ch. 26)

1911 Revolution The uprising that brought China's monarchy to an end. (Ch. 26)

Nō theater A type of Japanese theater performed on a bare stage by one or two actors wearing brilliant brocade robes, one actor wearing a mask. The performers conveyed emotions and ideas as much through gestures, stances, and dress as through words. (Ch. 21)

oba The title of the king of Benin. (Ch. 20)

October Manifesto The result of a great general strike in Russia in October 1905, it granted full civil rights and promised a popularly elected Duma (parliament) with real legislative power. (Ch. 24)

oligarchs In Latin America, the small number of individuals and families that had monopolized political power and economic resources since the colonial era. (Ch. 27)

Opium War The 1839–1842 war between the British and the Chinese over limitations on trade and the importation of opium into China. (Ch. 26)

Organization of the Petroleum Exporting Countries (OPEC) A cartel formed in 1960 by oil-exporting countries designed to coordinate oil production and raise prices, giving those countries greater capacity for economic development and greater leverage in world affairs. (Ch. 32)

Ottomans Ruling house of the Turkish empire that lasted from 1299 to 1922. (Ch. 17)

Palestine Liberation Organization (PLO) Created in 1964, a loose union of Palestinian refugee groups opposed to Israel and united in the goal of establishing a Palestinian state. (Ch. 31)

palm oil A West African tropical product often used to make soap; the British encouraged its cultivation as an alternative to the slave trade. (Ch. 25)

Pan-Africanists People who, through a movement beginning in 1919, sought black solidarity and envisioned a vast self-governing union of all African peoples. (Ch. 31)

peninsulares A term for natives of Spain and Portugal. (Ch. 22)

perestroika Economic restructuring and reform implemented by Soviet premier Mikhail Gorbachev that permitted an easing of government price controls on some goods, more independence for state enterprises, and the establishment of profit-seeking private cooperatives. (Ch. 32)

Permanent Mandates Commission A commission created by the League of Nations to oversee the developed nations' fulfillment of their international responsibility toward their mandates. (Ch. 29)

petrodollars The global recirculation by international banks of profits from the higher price of oil following the 1973 OPEC oil embargo. (Ch. 32)

Petrograd Soviet A counter-government to the 1917 Russian provisional government, this organization was a huge, fluctuating mass meeting of two to three thousand workers, soldiers, and socialist intellectuals. (Ch. 28)

philosophes A group of French intellectuals who proclaimed that they were bringing the light of knowledge to their fellow humans. (Ch. 19)

Plan de Ayala Document written by Zapatistas during the Mexican Revolution that demanded the government return all land, forests, and waters taken from rural communities. (Ch. 27)

Popular Front A party formed in 1936 in France that encouraged unions and launched a far-reaching New Deal–inspired program of social reform. (Ch. 30)

Porfiriato The regime of Porfirio Díaz, who presided in Mexico from 1876 to 1880 and again from 1884 to 1911. (Ch. 27)

proletariat The Marxist term for the working class of modern industrialized society. (Ch. 24)

protectorate An autonomous state or territory partly controlled and protected by a stronger outside power. (Ch. 25)

Protestant Reformation A religious reform movement that began in the early sixteenth century and split the Western Christian Church. (Ch. 18)

Ptolemy's *Geography* A second-century work translated into Latin around 1410 that synthesized the classical knowledge of geography and introduced latitude and longitude markings. (Ch. 16)

public sphere An idealized intellectual space that emerged in Europe during the Enlightenment. Here, the public came together to discuss important social, economic, and political issues. (Ch. 19)

Puritans Members of a sixteenth- and seventeenth-century reform movement within the Church of England that advocated purifying it of Roman Catholic elements, such as bishops, elaborate ceremonials, and wedding rings. (Ch. 18)

Qing Dynasty The dynasty founded by the Manchus that ruled China from 1644 to 1911. (Ch. 21)

Qizilbash Nomadic Turkish Sufis who supplied the early Safavid state with military troops in exchange for grazing rights. (Ch. 17)

quinine An agent that proved effective in controlling attacks of malaria, which had previously decimated Europeans in the tropics. (Ch. 25)

Reign of Terror The period from 1793 to 1794, during which Robespierre's Committee of Public Safety tried and executed thousands suspected of political crimes and a new revolutionary culture was imposed. (Ch. 22)

republicanism A form of government in which there is no monarch and power rests in the hands of the people as exercised through elected representatives. (Ch. 18)

revisionism An effort by various socialists to update Marxist doctrines to reflect the realities of the time. (Ch. 24)

Rocket The name given to George Stephenson's effective locomotive that was first tested in 1829 on the Liverpool and Manchester Railway and reached a maximum speed of 35 miles per hour. (Ch. 23)

Romanticism A movement in art, literature, and music characterized by a belief in emotional exuberance, unrestrained imagination, and spontaneity in both art and personal life. (Ch. 24)

Roosevelt Corollary A corollary to the Monroe Doctrine stating that the United States would correct what it saw as "chronic wrongdoing" in neighboring countries. (Ch. 27)

Russo-Japanese War The 1904–1905 war between Russia and Japan fought over imperial influence and territory in northeast China (Manchuria). (Ch. 26)

Safavid The dynasty that ruled all of Persia and other regions from 1501 to 1722; its state religion was Shi'ism. (Ch. 17)

salons Regular social gatherings held by talented and rich Parisian women in their homes, where philosophes and their followers met to discuss literature, science, and philosophy. (Ch. 19)

sans-culottes The laboring poor of Paris, so called because the men wore trousers instead of the knee breeches of the wealthy; the term came to refer to the militant radicals of the city. (Ch. 22)

satyagraha Loosely translated as "soul force," which Gandhi believed was the means of striving for truth and social justice through love, suffering, and conversion of the oppressor. (Ch. 29)

sensationalism An idea, espoused by John Locke, that all human ideas and thoughts are produced as a result of sensory impressions. (Ch. 19)

separate spheres A gender division of labor with the wife at home as mother and homemaker and the husband as wage earner. (Ch. 23)

sepoys The native Indian troops who were trained as infantrymen. (Ch. 17)

shah Persian word for "king." (Ch. 17)

shore trading A process for trading goods in which European ships sent boats ashore or invited African dealers to bring traders and slaves out to the ships. (Ch. 20)

Social Darwinism The application of the theory of biological evolution to human affairs, it sees the human race as driven to ever-greater specialization and progress by an unending economic struggle that determines the survival of the fittest. (Ch. 24)

socialism A radical political doctrine that opposed individualism and that advocated cooperation and a sense of community; key ideas were economic planning, greater economic equality, and state regulation of property. (Ch. 24)

Sokoto caliphate Founded in 1809 by Uthman dan Fodio, this African state was based on Islamic history and law. (Ch. 25)

Solidarity Led by Lech Wałęsa, an independent Polish trade union organized in 1980 that worked for the rights of workers and political reform. (Ch. 32)

sorting A collection or batch of British goods that would be traded for a slave or for a quantity of gold, ivory, or dyewood. (Ch. 20)

sovereignty Authority of states that possess a monopoly over the instruments of justice and the use of force within clearly defined boundaries and in which private armies present no threat to central control; seventeenth-century European states made important advances toward sovereignty. (Ch. 18)

spinning jenny A simple, inexpensive, hand-power spinning machine created by James Hargreaves about 1765. (Ch. 23)

steam engines A breakthrough invention by Thomas Savery in 1698 and Thomas Newcomen in 1705 that burned coal to produce steam, which was then used to operate a pump; the early models were superseded by James Watt's more efficient steam engine, patented in 1769. (Ch. 23)

sultan An Arabic word used by the Ottomans to describe a supreme political and military ruler. (Ch. 17)

Swahili Meaning "People of the Coast," the term used for the people living along the East African coast and on nearby islands. (Ch. 20)

Sykes-Picot Agreement The 1916 secret agreement between Britain and France that divided up the Arab lands of Lebanon, Syria, southern Turkey, Palestine, Jordan, and Iraq. (Ch. 29)

Taghaza A settlement in the western Sahara, the site of the main salt-mining center. (Ch. 20)

Taiping Rebellion A massive rebellion by believers in the religious teachings of Hong Xiuquan, begun in 1851 and not suppressed until 1864. (Ch. 26)

Tanzimat A set of radical reforms designed to remake the Ottoman Empire on a western European model. (Ch. 25)

tariff protection A government's way of supporting and aiding its own economy by laying high taxes on imported goods from other countries, as when the French responded to the flood of cheaper British goods in their country by imposing high tariffs on some imported products. (Ch. 23)

Thermidorian reaction A reaction in 1794 to the violence of the Reign of Terror, resulting in the execution of Robespierre and the loosening of economic controls. (Ch. 22)

Thirty Years' War A large-scale conflict extending from 1618 to 1648 that pitted Protestants against Catholics in central Europe, but also involved dynastic interests, notably of Spain and France. (Ch. 18)

Tiananmen Square The site of a Chinese student revolt in 1989 at which Communists imposed martial law and arrested, injured, or killed hundreds of students. (Ch. 32)

Tokugawa Shogunate The Japanese government in Edo founded by Tokugawa Ieyasu. It lasted from 1603 to 1867. (Ch. 21)

totalitarianism A radical dictatorship that exercises complete political power and control over all aspects of society and seeks to mobilize the masses for action. (Ch. 30)

total war Practiced by countries fighting in World War I, a war in which the government plans and controls all aspects of economic and social life in order to make the greatest possible military effort. (Ch. 28)

Treaty of Guadalupe Hidalgo The 1848 treaty between the United States and Mexico in which Mexico ceded large tracts of land to the United States. (Ch. 27)

Treaty of Lausanne The 1923 treaty that ended the Turkish war and recognized the territorial integrity of a truly independent Turkey. (Ch. 29)

Treaty of Paris The 1763 peace treaty that ended the Seven Years' War, according vast French territories in North America and India to Britain and Louisiana to Spain. (Ch. 22)

Treaty of Tordesillas The 1494 agreement giving Spain everything west of an imaginary line drawn down the Atlantic and giving Portugal everything to the east. (Ch. 16)

Treaty of Versailles The 1919 peace settlement that ended World War I; it declared Germany responsible for the war, limited Germany's army to one hundred thousand men, and forced Germany to pay huge reparations. (Ch. 28)

trench warfare Fighting behind rows of trenches, mines, and barbed wire; used in World War I with a staggering cost in lives and minimal gains in territory. (Ch. 28)

Triple Entente The alliance of Great Britain, France, and Russia in the First World War. (Ch. 28)

Truman Doctrine The 1945 American policy of preventing the spread of Communist rule. (Ch. 31)

Tuareg Major branch of the nomadic Berber peoples who controlled the north-south trans-Saharan trade in salt. (Ch. 20)

ulama Religious scholars who interpret the Qur'an and the Sunna, the deeds and sayings of Muhammad. (Ch. 17)

Valladolid debate A debate organized by Spanish king Charles I in 1550 in the city of Valladolid that pitted defenders of Spanish conquest and forcible conversion against critics of these practices. (Ch. 16)

viceroyalties The name for the four administrative units of Spanish possessions in the Americas: New Spain, Peru, New Granada, and La Plata. (Ch. 16)

viziers Chief assistants to caliphs. (Ch. 17)

War Communism The application of the total-war concept to a civil conflict; the Bolsheviks seized grain from peasants, introduced rationing, nationalized all banks and industry, and required everyone to work. (Ch. 28)

Washington Consensus Policies restricting public spending, lowering import barriers, privatizing state enterprises, and deregulating markets in response to the 1980s debt crisis in Latin America. (Ch. 32)

water frame A spinning machine created by Richard Arkwright that had a capacity of several hundred spindles and used waterpower; it therefore required a larger and more specialized mill—a factory. (Ch. 23)

white man's burden The idea that Europeans could and should civilize more primitive nonwhite peoples and that imperialism would eventually provide nonwhites with modern achievements and higher standards of living. (Ch. 25)

Young Turks Fervent patriots who seized power in the revolution of 1908, forcing the conservative sultan to implement reforms; they helped pave the way for the birth of modern secular Turkey. (Ch. 25)

zaibatsu Giant conglomerate firms established in Japan beginning in the Meiji period and lasting until the end of World War II. (Ch. 29)

Zionism The movement toward Jewish political nationhood started by Theodor Herzl. (Ch. 24)

	Africa	The Americas
10,000 B.C.E.	*Homo sapiens* evolve, ca. 200,000 years ago Farming begins in Nile River Valley, ca. 9000 Domestication of cattle; plow agriculture, ca. 7000 Unification of Egypt, 3100–2660	Possible migration into Americas begins, ca. 20,000–30,000 years ago Farming begins, ca. 10,000 Earliest mound building in North America, ca. 5500 Maize domesticated in Mexico, ca. 3000
2500 B.C.E.	Egypt's Old Kingdom, 2660–2180 Egypt's Middle Kingdom, 2080–1640 Migration of Hyksos, 1800–1600	First cities in Peru, ca. 2500 Textiles become important part of Peruvian culture, ca. 2500 Farmers in southwestern North America grow maize, ca. 2000
1500 B.C.E.	Egypt's New Kingdom, ca. 1570–1070 Ironworking spreads throughout Africa, ca. 1500 B.C.E.–300 C.E. Akhenaton institutes monotheistic worship of Aton, ca. 1351–1334	Olmec civilization in Mexico, ca. 1500–300 Earliest cities in the Andes built by Chavín people, ca. 1200
1000 B.C.E.	Political fragmentation of Egypt; rise of small kingdoms, ca. 1100–653 Bantu migrations across central and southern Africa, ca. 1000 B.C.E.–1500 C.E. Persians conquer Egypt, 525	Olmec center at San Lorenzo destroyed; power passes to La Venta, ca. 900
500 B.C.E.	Ptolemy conquers Egypt, 323	
250 B.C.E.	Scipio Africanus defeats Hannibal at Zama, 202 Meroë becomes iron-smelting center, ca. 100	Hopewell culture flourishes in North America, ca. 200 B.C.E.–600 C.E.

Asia and Oceania	Europe	Middle East
Farming begins in Yellow River Valley, ca. 9000 Domestication of cattle; plow agriculture begins, ca. 7000	Farming spreads to Greece, ca. 6500 Smelting of copper in Balkans, ca. 5500 Farming spreads to Britain, ca. 4000	Farming begins; domestication of goats and sheep in the Fertile Crescent, ca. 9000 Invention of pottery wheel in Mesopotamia, ca. 5000 First writing in Sumer; city-states emerge, ca. 3500
Harappan civilization in India, ca. 2800–1800	Minoan culture emerges, ca. 2000 Arrival of Greeks in peninsular Greece; founding of Mycenaean kingdom, ca. 1650	Bronze Age begins in Mesopotamia, ca. 2500 Establishment of Akkadian empire, ca. 2300 Hammurabi's law code, ca. 1755
Shang Dynasty; first writing in China, ca. 1500–1050 Vedic Age: Aryans dominate in north India; caste system develops; *Rig Veda*, ca. 1500–500	Mycenaeans conquer Minoan Crete, ca. 1450 Fall of Minoan and Mycenaean cultures, ca. 1100 Greek Dark Age, ca. 1100–800	Hittites expand empire in Mesopotamia, ca. 1600 Moses leads Hebrews out of Egypt, ca. 1300–1200 United Hebrew kingdom, ca. 1025–925
Early Zhou Dynasty, ca. 1050–400 *Upanishads*, foundation of Brahmanic religion, 750–500 Life of Confucius, 551–479 Persians conquer parts of India, 513 Founding of Buddhism and Jainism, ca. 500	Evolution of the polis, ca. 800–500 Rise of Sparta and Athens, 700–500 Roman Republic founded, 509	Assyrian Empire, ca. 900–612 Spread of Zoroastrianism, ca. 600–500 Babylonian captivity of Hebrews, 587–538 Cyrus the Great founds Persian Empire, 550
Warring States Period; golden age of Chinese philosophy, 403–221 Brahmanic religion develops into Hinduism, ca. 400 B.C.E.–200 C.E. Zhuangzi and development of Daoism, 369–286 Alexander the Great invades India, 326 Seleucus establishes Seleucid Empire, 323 Mauryan Empire, ca. 322–185 Reign of Ashoka; Buddhism spreads in Central Asia, 269–232	Flowering of Greek art and philosophy, 500–400 Persian wars, 499–479 Peloponnesian War, 431–404 Roman expansion, 390–146 Conquests of Alexander the Great, 336–324 Punic Wars; destruction of Carthage, 264–146	Persian Empire falls to Alexander the Great, 330 Alexander the Great dies in Babylon, 323
Qin Dynasty unifies China; construction of Great Wall, ca. 230–208 Han Dynasty, 206 B.C.E.–220 C.E. Han government controls Silk Road across Central Asia, 114 Chinese armies conquer Nam Viet, 111 *Bhagavad Gita*, ca. 100 B.C.E.–100 C.E.	Late Roman Republic, 133–27 Julius Caesar killed, 44 Octavian seizes power, rules imperial Rome as Augustus, 27 B.C.E.–14 C.E.	

	Africa	The Americas
1 C.E.	Expansion of Bantu-speaking peoples into eastern and southern Africa, ca. 100	Moche civilization flourishes in Peru, ca. 100–800
200 C.E.	Height of Aksum (Ethiopia) control of Red Sea trade, ca. 250–600	
300	Christianity comes to Ethiopia from Egypt, 328 Aksum accepts Christianity, ca. 350	Hohokam use irrigation to enhance farming in southwestern North America, ca. 300 Classical era in Mesoamerica and North America; Maya and other groups develop large advanced states, 300–900 Peak of Teotihuacan civilization in Mexico, ca. 300–650
500	Political and commercial ascendancy of Aksum, ca. 500–700 Christian missionaries convert Nubian rulers, ca. 600 Islam introduced to Africa, 639–642 Muslim conquest of Alexandria, Egypt, 641 Height of trans-Saharan and Mediterranean slave trade, ca. 650–1500	Peak of Maya civilization, ca. 600–900 Teotihuacan destroyed, 650
700	Expansion of Islam into Ethiopia weakens state, 700–800 Berbers control trans-Saharan trade, ca. 700–900 Islam spreads across Sahara, 800–900 Kingdom of Ghana, ca. 900–1100	Period of crop failure, disease, and war in Mesoamerica; collapse of Maya civilization, 800–1000 Toltec hegemony, ca. 980–1000
1000	Islam penetrates sub-Saharan Africa, ca. 1000–1100 Great Zimbabwe built, flourishes, ca. 1000–1450	Inca civilization in South America, ca. 1000–1500 Peak of Cahokia culture in North America, ca. 1150 Toltec state collapses, 1174
1200	Kingdom of Mali, ca. 1200–1450 Mongols conquer Baghdad; fall of Abbasid Dynasty, 1258	Cahokia's decline begins after earthquake, ca. 1200

Asia and Oceania	Europe	Middle East
Maritime trade between Chinese and Roman ports begins, ca. 100 Roman attacks on Parthian empire, ca. 100–200 Chinese invent paper, 105	Roman Empire at greatest extent, 96–192	Life of Jesus, ca. 3 B.C.E.–29 C.E.
Buddhism gains popularity in China, Japan, and Korea, ca. 200–600 Age of Division in China, 220–589 Fall of the Parthian empire; rise of the Sassanid, ca. 226	Reign of Diocletian: reforms Roman Empire; divides into western and eastern halves, 284–305	Sassanid Dynasty in Persia, 226–651
Three Kingdoms Period in Korea, 313–668 China divides into northern and southern regimes, 316 Gupta Empire unites northern India, ca. 320–480 Huns invade India, ca. 450	Reign of Constantine: legalizes Christianity; founds Constantinople, 306–337 Christianity official state religion of Roman Empire, 380 Germanic raids on western Europe, 400s Clovis rules Gauls, ca. 481–511	
Sui Dynasty restores order in China, 581–618 Prince Shōtoku introduces Chinese-style government in Japan, 604 Tang Dynasty in China; cultural flowering, 618–907 Korea unified, 668	Reign of Justinian; Code and *Digest*, 527–565 *Rule of Saint Benedict*, 529	Life of Muhammad, ca. 570–632 Publication of the Qur'an, 651 Umayyad Dynasty; expansion of Islam, 661–750
Creation of Japan's first capital at Nara, 710 Islam reaches India, 711 Heian era in Japan, 794–1185 Khmer Empire of Cambodia founded, 802 Koryŏ Dynasty in Korea, 935–1392 North Vietnam gains independence from China, 939 Song Dynasty in China; invention of movable type, 960–1279	Muslims defeat Visigothic kingdom in Spain, 711 Christian reconquest of Spain from Muslims, 722–1492 Carolingians defeat Muslims at Poitiers, 732 Viking, Magyar invasions, ca. 800–950 Treaty of Verdun divides Carolingian Empire, 843	Abbasid caliphate; Islamic capital moved to Baghdad, 750–1258 Height of Muslim learning and creativity, ca. 800–1300
Construction of Angkor Wat, ca. 1100–1150 Muslim conquests lead to decline of Buddhism in India, ca. 1100–1200 China divided into Song and Jin empires, 1127 Kamakura Shogunate in Japan, 1185–1333	Latin, Greek churches split, 1054 Norman Conquest of England, 1066 Crusades, 1095–1270 Growth of trade and towns, ca. 1100–1400	Seljuk Turks take Baghdad, 1055
Easter Island's most prosperous period, ca. 1200–1400 Turkish sultanate at Delhi, 1206–1526 Peak of Khmer Empire, 1219 Mongols' Yuan Dynasty in China, 1234–1368 Mongols invade Japan, 1274, 1281 Marco Polo travels in China, ca. 1275–1292 Mongol conquest of Song China, 1276	Magna Carta, 1215 Life of Thomas Aquinas; *Summa Theologica*, 1225–1274 Mongol raids into eastern Europe; Mongols gain control of Kieven Russia, 1237–1241	Mongols conquer Baghdad, 1258 Ottoman Empire, 1299–1922

	Africa	The Americas
1300	Height of Swahili city-states in East Africa, ca. 1300–1500 Mansa Musa rules Mali, ca. 1312–1337 Ibn Battuta's travels, 1325–1354	Construction of Aztec city Tenochtitlan begins, ca. 1325
1400	Songhai Empire, ca. 1464–1591 Arrival of Portuguese in Benin, 1485 Da Gama reaches East Africa; Swahili coast enters period of economic decline, 1498	Height of Inca Empire, 1438–1532 Reign of Moctezuma I; height of Aztec culture, 1440–1469 Inca city of Machu Picchu built, 1450 Columbus reaches Americas, 1492
1500	Portugal dominates East Africa, ca. 1500–1600 Era of transatlantic slave trade, ca. 1500–1900 Muslim occupation of Christian Ethiopia, 1531–1543 Height of Kanem-Bornu, 1571–1603	Portuguese reach Brazil, 1500 Atlantic slave trade begins, 1518 Cortés arrives in Mexico, 1519 Aztec Empire falls, 1521 Pizarro conquers Inca Empire, 1533 First English colony in North America founded at Roanoke, 1585
1600	Dutch West India Company founded; starts to bring slave coast of West Africa under its control, 1621 Jesuit missionaries expelled from Ethiopia, 1633 Dutch East India Company settles Cape Town, 1652 Importation of slaves into Cape Colony begins, 1658	British settle Jamestown, 1607 Champlain founds first permanent French settlement at Quebec, 1608 Caribbean islands colonized by French, English, Dutch, 1612–1697 English seize New Amsterdam from Dutch, 1664
1700	Major famine in West Africa, 1738–1756	Silver production quadruples in Mexico and Peru, ca. 1700–1800 Colonial dependence on Spanish goods, ca. 1700–1800
1750	Peak of transatlantic slave trade, 1780–1820 Olaudah Equiano publishes autobiography, 1789 British seize Cape Town, 1795 Napoleon's army invades Egypt, 1798	Seven Years' War, 1756–1763 Quebec Act, 1774 American Revolution, 1775–1783 Comuneros Revolt in New Granada, 1781 Haitian Revolution, 1791–1804

Asia and Oceania	Europe	Middle East
Ashikaga Shogunate, 1338–1573 Mongols defeated in China, 1368 Ming Dynasty in China, 1368–1644 Timur conquers the Delhi sultanate, 1398	Hundred Years' War, ca. 1337–1453 Black Death arrives in Europe, 1347 Italian Renaissance, ca. 1350–1520 Great Schism, 1378–1417	
Maritime trade and piracy connects East Asia and Southeast Asia with Europe, ca. 1400–1800 Zheng He's maritime expeditions to India, Middle East, Africa, 1405–1433 Reign of Sultan Mehmet II, 1451–1481	Development of movable type in Germany, ca. 1450 Age of Discovery, ca. 1450–1650 Ottomans capture Constantinople; end of Byzantine Empire, 1453 Unification of Spain; Jews expelled, 1492	Ottoman Empire conquers Byzantine Empire under rule of Sultan Mehmet II, 1451–1481
Increased availability of books in China, 1500–1600 Babur defeats Delhi sultanate; founds Mughal Empire, 1526 Japan unified under Toyotomi Hideyoshi, 1537–1590 First Christian missionaries land in Japan, 1549 Akbar expands Mughal Empire, 1556–1605 Spain founds port city of Manila in the Philippines, 1571	Scientific Revolution, ca. 1500–1700 Michelangelo paints Sistine Chapel, 1508–1512 Luther's Ninety-five Theses, 1517 English Reformation begins, 1527 Council of Trent, 1545–1563 Peace of Augsburg ends religious wars in Germany, 1555 Netherlands declares independence from Spain, 1581	Safavid Empire in Persia, 1501–1722 Peak of Ottoman power; cultural flowering under Suleiman, 1520–1566 Battle of Lepanto, 1571 Height of Safavid Empire under Shah Abbas, 1587–1629
Tokogawa Shogunate in Japan, 1603–1867 Japan closes its borders, 1639 Manchus establish Qing Dynasty in China, 1644–1911 Height of Edo urban culture in Japan, ca. 1650–1800 Dutch expel Portuguese in East Indies; gain control of spice trade, ca. 1660 French arrive in India, ca. 1670	Thirty Years' War, 1618–1648 English Civil War, 1642–1649 Habsburgs expel Ottomans from Hungary, 1683–1718 Revocation of Edict of Nantes, 1685 Glorious Revolution in England, 1688–1689 The Enlightenment, ca. 1690–1789	Shah Abbas captures much of Armenia from the Ottomans, 1603
Christian missionary work forbidden in China, 1715 Persian invaders loot Delhi, 1739 French and British fight for control of India, 1740–1763	Growth of book publishing, ca. 1700–1789 War of the Spanish Succession, 1701–1713 Peace of Utrecht, 1713	Afghans seize Isfahan from Persians, 1722
Treaty of Paris gives French colonies in India to Britain, 1763 Cook claims land in Australia for Britain, 1770 East India Company Act, 1784 First British convict-settlers arrive in Australia, 1788	Watt produces first steam engine, 1769 Industrial Revolution in Great Britain, ca. 1780–1850 French Revolution, 1789–1799 Romantic movement in literature and the arts, ca. 1790s–1840s National Convention declares France a republic, 1792	Ottoman ruler Selim III introduces reforms, 1789–1807

	Africa	The Americas
1800	Muhammad Ali modernizes Egypt, 1805–1848 Slave trade abolished in British Empire, 1807	Latin American wars of independence, 1810–1825 Brazil wins independence, 1822 Political instability in most Latin American countries, 1825–1870 Mexican-American War, 1846–1848

1850	Suez Canal opens, 1869
	Western and central Sudan unite under Islam, 1880
	European "scramble for Africa"; decline of slave trade,
	    1880–1914
	Battle of Omdurman, 1898
	South African War, 1899–1902
		U.S. Civil War, 1861–1865
		Dominion of Canada formed, 1867
		Latin American neocolonialism, ca. 1870–1929
		Díaz controls Mexico, 1876–1911
		Immigration from Europe and Asia to the
		    Americas, 1880–1914
		Spanish-American War, 1898

1900	Union of South Africa formed, 1910 Native Land Act in South Africa, 1913 Du Bois organizes first Pan-African congress, 1919	Mexican Revolution, 1910 Panama Canal opens, 1914 Mexico adopts constitution, 1917
1920	Cultural nationalism in Africa, 1920s Gold Coast farmers organize cocoa holdups, 1930–1931	U.S. consumer revolution, 1920s Stock market crash in U.S.; Great Depression begins, 1929 Flowering of Mexican culture, 1930s New Deal begins in U.S., 1933
1940	Decolonization in Africa, 1946–1964 Apartheid system in South Africa, 1948–1991	"Mexican miracle," 1940s–1970s Surprise attack by Japan on Pearl Harbor, 1941 United Nations established, 1945

1950	Egypt declared a republic; Nasser named premier, 1954
	French-British Suez invasion, 1956
	Morocco, Tunisia, Sudan, and Ghana gain independence,
	    1956–1957
	France offers commonwealth status to its territories; only
	    Guinea chooses independence, 1958
	Belgian Congo gains independence; violence follows, 1959
		Cuban Revolution, 1953–1959
		Military rule ends in Venezuela, 1958
		Castro takes power in Cuba, 1959

Asia and Oceania	Europe	Middle East
British found Singapore, 1819 Java War, 1825–1830 Opium War, 1839–1842 Treaty of Nanjing; Manchus surrender Hong Kong to British, 1842	Napoleonic Europe, 1804–1814 Congress of Vienna, 1814–1815 European economic penetration of non-Western countries, ca. 1816–1880 Greece wins independence, 1830 Revolutions in France, Austria, and Prussia, 1848	Ottoman Empire launches Tanzimat reforms, 1839
Taiping Rebellion, 1851–1864 Perry opens Japan to trade; Japan begins to industrialize, 1853 Great Mutiny/Revolt in India, 1857 Meiji Restoration in Japan, 1867 Indian National Congress, 1885 French Indochina formed, 1887 Sino-Japanese War, 1894–1895 U.S. gains Philippines, 1898	Unification of Italy, 1859–1870 Freeing of Russian serfs, 1861 Unification of Germany, 1866–1871 Massive industrialization surge in Russia, 1890–1900	Crimean War, 1853–1856 Ottoman state declares partial bankruptcy; European creditors take over, 1875
Boxer Uprising in China, 1900 Commonwealth of Australia, 1901 Russo-Japanese War, 1904–1905 Muslim League formed, 1906 Korea becomes province of Japan, 1910 Chinese Revolution; fall of Qing Dynasty, 1911 Chinese republic, 1912–1949 Amritsar Massacre in India, 1919	Revolution in Russia, 1905 World War I, 1914–1918 Bolshevik Revolution and civil war in Russia, 1917–1922 Treaty of Versailles, 1919	Young Turks seize power in Ottoman Empire, 1908 Turkish massacre of Armenians, 1915–1917 Sykes-Picot Agreement divides Ottoman Empire, 1916 Balfour Declaration establishes Jewish homeland in Palestine, 1917
Gandhi launches nonviolent campaign against British rule in India, 1920 Jiang Jieshi unites China, 1928 Japan invades Manchuria, 1931 Mao Zedong's Long March, 1934 Sino-Japanese War, 1937–1945 Japan conquers Southeast Asia, 1939–1942	Mussolini seizes power in Italy, 1922 Stalin takes power in U.S.S.R., 1927 Great Depression, 1929–1939 Hitler gains power in Germany, 1933 Civil war in Spain, 1936–1939 World War II, 1939–1945	Large numbers of European Jews immigrate to Palestine, 1920s–1930s Turkish republic recognized; Kemal begins to modernize and secularize, 1923 Reza Shah leads Iran, 1925–1941 Iraq gains independence, 1932
Japan announces "Asia for Asians"; signs alliance with Germany and Italy, 1940 U.S. drops atomic bombs on Hiroshima and Nagasaki, 1945 Chinese civil war; Communists win, 1945–1949 Philippines gain independence, 1946 Independence and separation of India and Pakistan, 1947	Marshall Plan, 1948 NATO formed, 1949 Soviet Union and Communist China sign 30-year alliance, 1949	Arabs and Jews at war in Palestine; Israel created, 1948
Japan begins long period of rapid economic growth, 1950 Korean War, 1950–1953 Vietnamese nationalists defeat French, 1954 Mao announces Great Leap Forward in China, 1958	Death of Stalin, 1953 Warsaw Pact, 1955 Revolution in Hungary, 1956 Common Market formed, 1957	Turkey joins NATO, 1953 Suez crisis, 1956

	Africa	The Americas
1960	Mali and Nigeria gain independence, 1960 Biafra declares independence from Nigeria, 1967	U.S. Alliance for Progress promotes development and reform in Latin America, 1961 Cuban missile crisis, 1962 U.S. Civil Rights Act, 1964 Military dictatorship in Brazil, 1964–1985 Military takeovers lead to brutal dictatorships in Argentina, 1966, 1976
1970	Growth of Islamic fundamentalism, 1970s to present	U.S. Watergate scandal, 1972 Nixon visits China; reconciliation between U.S. and China, 1972 Military coup in Chile, 1973 Revolution in Nicaragua, 1979
1980	Blacks win long civil war with white settlers in Zimbabwe, 1980 AIDS epidemic, 1980s to present South African government opens talks with African National Congress, 1989	Democratic wave gains momentum throughout Latin America, 1980s Nationalization of Mexico's banking system, 1982 Argentina restores civilian rule, 1983 Brazilians elect first civilian government in twenty years, 1985
1990	Nelson Mandela freed in South Africa, 1990 Rwandan genocide, 1994 Second Congo War, 1998 to present	Canada, Mexico, and U.S. form free-trade area (NAFTA), 1994 Haiti establishes democratic government, 1994 Socialist "Bolivarian revolution" in Venezuela, 1999
2000	Civil war and genocide in Darfur, 2003 to present Mugabe increases violence against opponents after losing Zimbabwean election, 2008	Terrorist attack on U.S., 2001 Economic, social, and political crisis in Argentina, 2001 Formation of the Union of South American Nations, 2008 Raúl Castro succeeds his ailing brother Fidel as president of Cuba, 2008
2010	Populist uprisings and protests break out in Tunisia, Egypt, and elsewhere in North Africa, 2010–2011 South Sudan becomes an independent nation, 2011 Nelson Mandela dies, 2013	Catastrophic earthquake in Haiti, 2010 U.S. withdraws combat troops from Iraq, 2011 U.S. begins troop drawdown in Afghanistan, 2011 Jorge Mario Bergoglio from Argentina elected as Pope Francis, 2013 Protests lead to the impeachment of Brazilian president Dilma Rousseff, 2016

Asia and Oceania	Europe	Middle East
Vietnam War, 1959–1975 Sino-Soviet split becomes apparent, 1960 Great Proletarian Cultural Revolution launched in China, 1965	Building of Berlin Wall, 1961 Student revolution in France, 1968 Soviet invasion of Czechoslovakia, 1968	OPEC founded, 1960 Arab-Israeli Six-Day War, 1967
Bangladesh breaks away from Pakistan, 1971 Communist victory in Vietnam War, 1975 China pursues modernization, 1976 to present	Helsinki Accord on human rights, 1975 Soviet invasion of Afghanistan, 1979	Revival of Islamic fundamentalism, 1970s to present Arab-Israeli Yom Kippur War, 1973 OPEC oil embargo, 1973 Civil war in Lebanon, 1975–1990 Camp David Accords, 1978 Islamic revolution in Iran, 1979
Japanese foreign investment surge, 1980–1992 Sikh nationalism in India, 1984 to present China crushes democracy movement, 1989	Soviet reform under Gorbachev, 1985–1991 Communism falls in eastern Europe, 1989–1990	Iran-Iraq War, 1980–1988 Palestinians start the intifada, 1987
Collapse of Japanese stock market, 1990–1992 Economic growth and political repression in China, 1990 to present Congress Party in India embraces Western capitalist reforms, 1991 Kyoto Protocol on global warming, 1997 Hong Kong returns to Chinese rule, 1997	Conservative economic policies, 1990s End of Soviet Union, 1991 Civil war in Yugoslavia, 1991–2001 Maastricht Treaty creates single currency, 1992 Creation of European Union, 1993	Persian Gulf War, 1990–1991 Israel and Palestinians sign peace agreement, 1993 Assassination of Israeli prime minister Yitzak Rabin, 1995
China joins World Trade Organization, 2001 India and Pakistan come close to all-out war, 2001 North Korea withdraws from 1970 Nuclear Non-Proliferation Treaty, 2003 Tsunami in Southeast Asia, 2004 Terrorist attack in Mumbai, India, 2008	Resurgence of Russian economy under Putin, 2000–2008 Euro note enters circulation, 2002 Madrid train bombing, 2004 London subway and bus bombing, 2005	Israel begins construction of West Bank barrier, 2003 Wars in Afghanistan and Iraq, 2001 to present Hamas establishes Palestinian Authority government, 2007
Massive earthquake in Japan, 2011 Al-Qaeda leader Osama bin Laden killed in Pakistan, 2011 Typhoon Haiyan kills thousands in the Philippines, 2013	European financial crisis intensifies, 2010 France legalizes same-sex marriage, 2013 Russia annexes Crimea region in Ukraine, 2014 British voters elect for Britain to leave the EU, 2016	Populist uprisings and protests across the Middle East, 2010–2011 Civil war in Syria begins; refugee crisis intensifies, 2011 Egyptian president Mohamed Morsi ousted following protests, 2013 International accord suspends Iranian nuclear program, 2015

THE CONTEMPORARY WORLD

CANADA

UNITED STATES

Alaska (U.S.)

Greenland (Den.)

ICELAND

ATLANTIC OCEAN

Azores (Port.)

Bermuda (U.K.)

MEXICO

Hawaii (U.S.)

BAHAMAS
DOMINICAN REPUBLIC
HAITI
CUBA
JAMAICA
BELIZE
GUATEMALA
EL SALVADOR
HONDURAS
NICARAGUA
COSTA RICA
PANAMA

Puerto Rico (U.S.)
ST. KITTS AND NEVIS
ANTIGUA AND BARBUDA
Guadeloupe (Fr.)
DOMINICA
Martinique (Fr.)
ST. VINCENT AND THE GRENADINES
ST. LUCIA
BARBADOS
GRENADA
TRINIDAD AND TOBAGO

VENEZUELA
COLOMBIA
GUYANA
SURINAME
French Guiana (Fr.)

MORO
Canary Is. (Sp.)
Western Sahara (Mor.)

MAURITAN

CAPE VERDE
SENEGAL
GAMBIA
GUINEA-BISSAU
GUINEA
BURKINA FASO
SIERRA LEONE
LIBERIA
CÔTE D'IVOIRE
GHANA

MA

PACIFIC OCEAN

Equator

Galápagos Is. (Ec.)

ECUADOR

PERU

BRAZIL

SAMOA

TONGA

Easter I. (Chile)

BOLIVIA

PARAGUAY

CHILE

URUGUAY

ARGENTINA

ATLANTIC OCEAN

Falkland Is. (U.K.)

N
W E
S

0   1,500   3,000 miles
0   1,500   3,000 kilometers

ARCTIC OCEAN

NORWAY
SWEDEN
FINLAND
ESTONIA
LATVIA
LITHUANIA
DEN.
NETH.
BEL.
GERMANY
LUX.
POLAND
BELARUS
AUS.
SLA.
CZ.
UKRAINE
SWITZ.
SLN.
HUNG.
MOLDOVA
ITALY
CR.
B.H.
ROMANIA
MO.
SE.
BULGARIA
M.B.
MAC.
GEORGIA
TUNISIA
GRECE
MALTA
ARMENIA
AZERBAIJAN
CYPRUS
SYRIA
LEBANON
ISRAEL
IRAQ
West Bank
Gaza Strip
JORDAN
KUWAIT

RUSSIAN FEDERATION

KAZAKHSTAN
UZBEKISTAN
KYRGYZSTAN
TURKMENISTAN
TAJIKISTAN
AFGHANISTAN
IRAN
PAKISTAN

MONGOLIA

CHINA

N. KOREA
S. KOREA
JAPAN

PACIFIC OCEAN

GERIA
LIBYA
EGYPT
SAUDI ARABIA
QATAR
UNITED ARAB
EMIRATES
BAHRAIN
OMAN
YEMEN

NIGER
CHAD
SUDAN
ERITREA
DJIBOUTI

NEPAL
BHUTAN
BANGLADESH
INDIA
MYANMAR
(BURMA)
LAOS
THAILAND
VIETNAM
CAMBODIA

Taiwan

Mariana Is.
(U.S.)
Guam
(U.S.)
MARSHALL
IS.

NIGERIA
BENIN
TOGO
CAMEROON
EQ.
GUINEA
GABON
CONGO
CENTRAL
AFRICAN REP.
SOUTH
SUDAN
ETHIOPIA
SOMALIA
UGANDA
RWANDA
KENYA
DEM. REP. OF
THE CONGO
BURUNDI
TANZANIA

MALDIVES

SRI
LANKA

BRUNEI
MALAYSIA
SINGAPORE

PHILIPPINES

PALAU

FEDERATED STATES
OF MICRONESIA

NAURU
KIRIBATI

SÃO
TOMÉ
& PRÍNCIPE
ANGOLA
ZAMBIA
MALAWI
ZIMBABWE
NAMIBIA
BOTSWANA
MADAGASCAR
COMOROS
SEYCHELLES

INDIAN OCEAN

INDONESIA
TIMOR
LESTE

PAPUA
NEW
GUINEA

SOLOMON
IS.

TUVALU

VANUATU
FIJI

MAURITIUS

New Caledonia
(Fr.)

AUSTRALIA

SOUTH
AFRICA
MOZAMBIQUE
SWAZILAND
LESOTHO

NEW
ZEALAND

Tasmania
(Aust.)

ABBREVIATIONS	
ALB.	ALBANIA
AUS.	AUSTRIA
BEL.	BELGIUM
B.H.	BOSNIA AND HERZEGOVINA
CR.	CROATIA
CZ.	CZECH REPUBLIC
DEN.	DENMARK
HUNG.	HUNGARY
KO.	KOSOVO
LUX.	LUXEMBOURG
MAC.	MACEDONIA
MO.	MONTENEGRO
NETH.	NETHERLANDS
SE.	SERBIA
SLK.	SLOVAKIA
SLN.	SLOVENIA
SWITZ.	SWITZERLAND

ANTARCTICA

20°E   40°E   60°E   80°E   100°E   120°E   140°E   160°E

NORTH AMERICA

R O C K Y   M T S.

APPALACHIAN MTS.

Mississippi R.

ATLANTIC OCEAN

Gulf of Mexico

Tropic of Cancer

Caribbean Sea

PACIFIC OCEAN

Equator

A N D E S   M T S.

Amazon R.

SOUTH AMERICA

Tropic of Capricorn

ATLANTIC OCEAN

Arctic Circle

Antarctic Circle

N
W   E
S

| 0 | 1,000 | 2,000 | 3,000 miles |
| 0 | 1,000 | 2,000 | 3,000 kilometers |

160°W   140°W   120°W   100°W   80°W   60°W   40°W   20°W

EUROPE

ALPS

Mediterranean Sea

URAL MTS.

Volga R.

Ob R.

ASIA

GOBI

Yellow R.
(Huang He)

HIMALAYA MTS.

Ganges R.

Yangzi R.

SAHARA

ARABIAN
DESERT

AFRICA

Nile R.

Arabian
Sea

Bay of
Bengal

South
China
Sea

PACIFIC OCEAN

Congo R.

INDIAN OCEAN

Zambezi R.

KALAHARI
DESERT

AUSTRALIA

Arctic Circle

Tropic of Cancer

Equator

Tropic of Capricorn

Antarctic Circle

20°E 40°E 60°E 80°E 100°E 120°E 140°E 160°E

80°N

60°N

40°N

20°N

0°

20°S

40°S

60°S

80°S

Vegetation zones

- Tundra
- Northern forest
- Temperate forest
- Temperate grassland
- Desert and dry shrub
- Mediterranean shrub
- Mountain grassland
- Tropical grassland and savanna
- Tropical forest
- Permanent ice cover

ABOUT THE AUTHORS

Merry E. Wiesner-Hanks (Ph.D., University of Wisconsin–Madison) taught first at Augustana College in Illinois and since 1985 at the University of Wisconsin–Milwaukee, where she is currently UWM Distinguished Professor in the department of history. She is the Senior Editor of the *Sixteenth Century Journal*, one of the editors of the *Journal of Global History*, and the author or editor of more than thirty books, including *A Concise History of the World*. From 2017 to 2019 she is serving as the president of the World History Association.

Patricia Buckley Ebrey (Ph.D., Columbia University), professor of history at the University of Washington in Seattle, specializes in China. She has published numerous journal articles and *The Cambridge Illustrated History of China*, as well as several monographs. In 2010 she won the Shimada Prize for outstanding work of East Asian Art History for *Accumulating Culture: The Collections of Emperor Huizong*.

Roger B. Beck (Ph.D., Indiana University) is Distinguished Professor of African and twentieth-century world history at Eastern Illinois University. His publications include *The History of South Africa*; a translation of P. J. van der Merwe's *The Migrant Farmer in the History of the Cape Colony, 1657–1842*; and more than a hundred articles, book chapters, and reviews. He is a former treasurer and Executive Council member of the World History Association.

Jerry Dávila (Ph.D., Brown University) is Jorge Paulo Lemann Professor of Brazilian History at the University of Illinois. He is the author of *Dictatorship in South America*; *Hotel Trópico: Brazil and the Challenge of African Decolonization*, winner of the Latin Studies Association Brazil Section Book Prize; and *Diploma of Whiteness: Race and Social Policy in Brazil, 1917–1945*. He has served as president of the Conference on Latin American History.

Clare Haru Crowston (Ph.D., Cornell University) teaches at the University of Illinois, where she is currently professor of history and department chair. She is the author of *Credit, Fashion, Sex: Economies of Regard in Old Regime France* and *Fabricating Women: The Seamstresses of Old Regime France, 1675–1791*, which won the Berkshire and Hagley Prizes. She edited two special issues of the *Journal of Women's History*, has published numerous journal articles and reviews, and is a past president of the Society for French Historical Studies.

John P. McKay (Ph.D., University of California, Berkeley) is professor emeritus at the University of Illinois. He has written or edited numerous works, including the Herbert Baxter Adams Prize–winning book *Pioneers for Profit: Foreign Entrepreneurship and Russian Industrialization, 1885–1913*.